CHAMBERS

POCKET
THESAURUS

CHAMBERS

CHAMBERS
An imprint of Chambers Harrap Publishers Ltd
7 Hopetoun Crescent
Edinburgh, EH7 4AY

Reprinted 2004

A CIP catalogue record for this book is available from the British Library.

ISBN 0-550-10043-1

Designed and typeset by Chambers Harrap Publishers Ltd, Edinburgh
Printed and bound in Great Britain by Mackays of Chatham Ltd

Contents

Contributors

Editor
Martin Manser

Project Manager
Ian Brookes

Publishing Manager
Patrick White

Assistant Editor
Alice Grandison

Prepress
David Reid

Preface

A thesaurus is a book that contains lists of synonyms – that is, words that have a similar meaning to another word. A thesaurus allows you to look up a common word and find a range of words that have the same or nearly the same meaning. *Chambers Pocket Thesaurus* is one of a series of thesauruses drawn from the extensive *Chambers Dictionary* database. It lists over 220,000 synonyms, allowing you to find a suitable word for every occasion.

Looking up a word in this thesaurus may help you to find a more exact term for an essay or report, a livelier phrase for a speech, or a simpler expression for a letter. This will enable you to say what you have to say using the full range of words available to you. Moreover, browsing through a thesaurus also offers you a fascinating insight into the richness and variety of the English language.

But this book offers much more than lists of alternative words. It also contains lists of antonyms – words that have an opposite meaning. This allows you the further option of describing things in terms of their opposites. Thus you can describe something that is dull not only as 'boring', but also as 'not interesting'.

Another feature of this thesaurus is the inclusion of over 350 panels containing related words. For example, look up the word 'dance' and you will find not only a number of alternative words (*ball, hop, knees-up*…) but also a list of various types of dance (*waltz, quickstep, foxtrot*…). This feature complements the lists of synonyms and makes the thesaurus even more useful as resource for solving puzzles and word games. A full list of these panels can be found at the end of the book.

A thesaurus is not the same as a dictionary. Synonyms listed in a thesaurus are not necessarily precise definitions of the word under which they are found, and there may be subtle distinctions between the words. For this reason it always advisable to use a thesaurus in conjunction with a dictionary. *Chambers Pocket Thesaurus* has been designed as a companion volume for *Chambers Pocket Dictionary*. Taken together, these books form a helpful and reliable guide to the language.

How to use the Thesaurus

Chambers Pocket Thesaurus has been designed to allow you to find the information you are looking for quickly and easily. The entries are arranged in alphabetical order, so you can go straight to the word you are looking for without having to search in an index.

The lists of synonyms are arranged according to shades of meaning and in order from the most common to the least frequently used or the most specialized term. So the closer a word is to the start of the synonym list, the more likely it is that you will be able to use it as an exact substitute for the word you have looked up.

Some synonyms are followed by a label which indicates that the word is restricted in use to certain occasions. Thus some words are only appropriate in informal contexts and should not be used in business correspondence or formal writing. Similarly, formal or technical words might not be appropriate for more general use. Some labels also indicate that a word is restricted to a certain variety of English, such as American or Australian English.

If the word you want can be used in a number of different senses, you will find these senses are clearly distinguished. Each sense is numbered and introduced either by a phrase in italics giving an example of the word in use, or by a 'key' synonym in capital letters. These features mean that it is easy for you to work out which sense of the word you are interested in.

Antonyms or opposite words are introduced by the symbol ▰. Where there is more than one part of speech in an entry, the antonyms are listed after the part of speech to which they apply. Where there are several senses of a word, the antonyms are numbered to indicate to which senses they apply.

Some entries include additional information, such as synonyms for related idioms and phrasal verbs (introduced by the symbol ♦) or panels of related words. The diagram on the facing page shows how these features appear in the text.

Headwords are shown in bold letters.

board *n* **1** *a wooden board:* sheet, panel, slab, plank, beam, timber, slat. **2** COMMITTEE, council, panel, jury, commission, directorate, directors, trustees, advisers. **3** MEALS, food, provisions, rations.
➤ *v* get on, embark, mount, enter, catch.

Different meanings are shown in numbered sections, introduced either by a phrase in italics showing the word in use or by a key synonym in capitals.

boast *v* brag, crow, swank (*infml*), claim, exaggerate, talk big (*infml*), bluster, trumpet, vaunt, strut, swagger, show off, exhibit, possess.
🖬 belittle, deprecate.
➤ *n* brag, swank (*infml*), claim, vaunt, pride, joy, gem, treasure.

Parts of speech are shown by traditional abbreviations. A change within an entry is signalled by an arrow.

boastful *adj* proud, conceited, vain, swollen-headed, big-headed (*infml*), puffed up, bragging, crowing, swanky (*infml*), cocky, swaggering.
🖬 modest, self-effacing, humble.

boats and ships

Synonyms are listed with the most commonly used ones before less frequent and more specialized terms.

Types of boat or ship include: canoe, dinghy, lifeboat, rowing-boat, kayak, coracle, skiff, punt, sampan, dhow, gondola, pedalo, catamaran, trimaran, yacht; cabin-cruiser, motor-boat, motor-launch, speedboat, trawler, barge, narrow boat, houseboat, dredger, junk, smack, lugger; hovercraft, hydrofoil; clipper, cutter, ketch, packet, brig, schooner, square-rigger, galleon; ferry, paddle-steamer, tug, freighter, liner, container-ship, tanker; warship, battleship, destroyer, submarine, U-boat, frigate, aircraft-carrier, cruiser, dreadnought, corvette, minesweeper, man-of-war.

Lists of related words are shown in panels after some entries.

bob *v* bounce, hop, skip, spring, jump, leap, twitch, jerk, jolt, shake, quiver, wobble, oscillate, nod, bow, curtsy.
♦ **bob up** appear, emerge, arrive, show up (*infml*), materialize, rise, surface, pop up, spring up, crop up, arise.

Idioms and phrasal verbs are grouped alphabetically at the end of some entries. These are indicated by the symbol ♦.

bode *v* predict, foretell, prophesy, indicate, signify, intimate, herald, threaten, warn, augur (*fml*), forebode (*fml*), foreshadow (*fml*), foreshow (*fml*), forewarn (*fml*).

Labels in italics indicate when synonyms are restricted to certain areas of language.

bodily *adj* physical, corporeal, carnal, fleshly, real, actual, tangible, substantial, concrete, material.
🖬 spiritual.
➤ *adv* altogether, en masse, collectively, as a whole, completely, fully, wholly, entirely, totally, in toto.
🖬 piecemeal.

Antonyms are introduced by the symbol 🖬.

Abbreviations used in the Thesaurus

adj	adjective
adv	adverb
Austr	Australian
conj	conjunction
fml	formal
infml	informal
interj	interjection
n	noun
prep	preposition
pron	pronoun
®	trademark
Scot	Scottish
sl	slang
US	American English
v	verb

Aa

abandon *v* **1** DESERT, leave, forsake, jilt, ditch (*sl*), leave in the lurch (*infml*), maroon, strand, leave behind, scrap. **2** *abandon ship*: vacate, evacuate, withdraw from, quit. **3** RENOUNCE, resign, give up, forgo, relinquish, surrender, yield, waive, drop.

☒ 1 support, maintain, keep. **3** continue.

abandoned *adj* **1** DESERTED, unoccupied, derelict, neglected, forsaken, forlorn, desolate. **2** DISSOLUTE, wild, uninhibited, wanton, wicked.

☒ 1 kept, occupied. **2** restrained.

abandonment *n* **1** DESERTION, leaving, forsaking, jilting, neglect, scrapping. **2** RENUNCIATION, resignation, giving up, relinquishment, surrender, yielding, waiver, dropping, discontinuation.

abase *v* humble, humiliate, debase (*fml*), demean (*fml*), mortify (*fml*), belittle (*fml*), malign (*fml*), disparage (*fml*).

☒ elevate, honour, raise.

abashed *adj* **1** ASHAMED, shamefaced, embarrassed, mortified, humiliated, humbled. **2** CONFUSED, bewildered, nonplussed, confounded, perturbed, discomposed, disconcerted, taken aback, dumbfounded, floored (*infml*), dismayed.

☒ 2 composed, at ease.

abate *v* **1** DECREASE, reduce, lessen, diminish, decline, sink, dwindle, taper off, fall off. **2** MODERATE, ease, relieve, alleviate, mitigate, remit, pacify, quell, subside, let up (*infml*), weaken, wane, slacken, slow, fade.

☒ 1 increase. **2** strengthen.

abbey *n* monastery, priory, friary, seminary, convent, nunnery, cloister.

abbreviate *v* shorten, cut, trim, clip, truncate, curtail, abridge, summarize, précis, abstract, digest, condense, compress, reduce, lessen, shrink, contract.

☒ extend, lengthen, expand, amplify.

abbreviation *n* shortening, clipping, curtailment, abridgement, summarization, summary, synopsis, résumé, précis, abstract, digest, compression, reduction, contraction.

☒ extension, expansion, amplification.

abdicate *v* **1** *the king abdicated*: resign, resign from the throne, stand down, give up, give up the throne, retire, relinquish/renounce the throne, quit (*infml*). **2** *abdicate responsibility*: abandon, give up, reject, refuse to accept any longer, surrender, disown, renounce (*fml*), relinquish (*fml*), cede (*fml*), yield (*fml*), forego (*fml*), abnegate (*fml*), repudiate (*fml*), shirk (*infml*), quit (*infml*), turn one's back on (*infml*), wash one's hands of (*infml*).

abdication *n* **1** *the abdication of the king*: resignation, retirement, standing-down, giving up of the throne, renunciation/relinquishment of the throne (*fml*). **2** *abdication of responsibilities*: abandonment, rejection, refusal, surrender, giving-up, disowning, renunciation (*fml*), relinquishment (*fml*), abnegation (*fml*), repudiation (*fml*).

abdomen *n* belly, guts, stomach, tummy (*infml*), paunch, midriff.

abdominal *adj* ventral, intestinal, visceral, gastric.

abduct *v* carry off, run away with, run off with (*infml*), make off with, spirit away, seduce, kidnap, snatch, seize, appropriate.

aberrant *adj* deviant, deviating, divergent, different, irregular, anomalous, odd, peculiar, eccentric, rogue, defective, corrupt, incongruous (*fml*), atypical (*fml*), freakish (*infml*), quirky (*infml*).

☒ regular, normal, typical.

aberration *n* deviation, straying, wandering, divergence, irregularity, nonconformity, anomaly, oddity, peculiarity, eccentricity, lapse, defect, quirk (*infml*), freak (*infml*).

☒ conformity.

abhor *v* hate, detest, loathe, abominate, shudder at, recoil from, shrink from, spurn, despise.

☒ love, adore.

abhorrence *n* hate, hatred, aversion, loathing, abomination, horror, repugnance, revulsion, disgust, distaste.

☒ love, adoration.

abhorrent *adj* detestable, loathsome, abominable, execrable, heinous, obnoxious, odious, hated, hateful, horrible, horrid, offensive, repugnant, repellent, repulsive, revolting, nauseating, disgusting, distasteful.
Ea delightful, attractive.

abide *v* **1** BEAR, stand, endure, tolerate, put up with, stomach, accept. **2** REMAIN, last, endure, continue, persist.
♦ **abide by 1** *abide by the rules*: obey, observe, follow, comply with, adhere to, conform to, submit to, go along with, agree to. **2** FULFIL, discharge, carry out, stand by, hold to, keep to.

abiding *adj* lasting, enduring, constant, continual, continuous, long-lasting, long-term, long-running, lifelong, persistent, unchanging, unchangeable, eternal, everlasting, immortal, unending, chronic, permanent, stable, firm, durable, immutable (*fml*).
Ea short-lived, short-term, ephemeral (*fml*), transient (*fml*).

ability *n* **1** CAPABILITY, capacity, faculty, facility, potentiality, power. **2** SKILL, dexterity, deftness, adeptness, competence, proficiency, qualification, aptitude, talent, gift, endowment, knack, flair, touch, expertise, know-how (*infml*), genius, forte, strength.
Ea **1** inability. **2** incompetence, weakness.

abject *adj* **1** CONTEMPTIBLE, worthless, low, mean, ignoble, dishonourable, deplorable, despicable, vile, sordid, debased, degenerate, submissive, servile, grovelling, slavish. **2** MISERABLE, wretched, forlorn, hopeless, pitiable, pathetic, outcast, degraded.
Ea **1** proud, exalted.

ablaze *adj* **1** BLAZING, flaming, burning, on fire, ignited, lighted, alight, illuminated, luminous, glowing, aglow, radiant, flashing, gleaming, sparkling, brilliant. **2** IMPASSIONED, passionate, fervent, ardent, fiery, enthusiastic, excited, exhilarated, stimulated, aroused, angry, furious, raging, incensed, frenzied.

able *adj* capable, fit, fitted, dexterous, adroit, deft, adept, competent, proficient, qualified, practised, experienced, skilled, accomplished, clever, expert, masterly, skilful, ingenious, talented, gifted, strong, powerful, effective, efficient, adequate.

Ea unable, incapable, incompetent, ineffective.

able-bodied *adj* fit, healthy, sound, strong, robust, hardy, tough, vigorous, powerful, hale, hearty, lusty, sturdy, strapping, stout, stalwart, staunch.
Ea infirm, delicate.

abnegation *n* abstinence, self-denial, surrender, self-sacrifice, giving-up, temperance, renunciation (*fml*), relinquishment (*fml*), forbearance (*fml*), repudiation (*fml*), eschewal (*fml*).

abnormal *adj* odd, strange, singular, peculiar, curious, queer, weird, eccentric, paranormal, unnatural, uncanny, extraordinary, exceptional, unusual, uncommon, unexpected, irregular, anomalous, aberrant, erratic, wayward, deviant, divergent, different.
Ea normal, regular, typical.

abnormality *n* oddity, peculiarity, singularity, eccentricity, strangeness, bizarreness, unnaturalness, unusualness, irregularity, exception, anomaly, deformity, flaw, aberration, deviation, divergence, difference.
Ea normality, regularity.

abode *n* home, dwelling, dwelling-place, lodgings, habitation, habitat, residence (*fml*), domicile (*fml*), pad (*infml*).

abolish *v* do away with, annul, nullify, invalidate, quash, repeal, rescind, revoke, cancel, obliterate, blot out, suppress, destroy, eliminate, eradicate, get rid of (*infml*), stamp out, end, put an end to, terminate, subvert, overthrow, overturn.
Ea create, retain, authorize, continue.

abolition *n* annulment, nullification, invalidation, quashing, repeal, abrogation, cancellation, obliteration, suppression, eradication, extinction, end, ending, termination, subversion, overturning, dissolution.
Ea creation, retention, continuance.

abominable *adj* loathsome, detestable, hateful, horrid, horrible, abhorrent, execrable, odious, repugnant, repulsive, repellent, disgusting, revolting, obnoxious, nauseating, foul, vile, heinous, atrocious, appalling, terrible, reprehensible, contemptible, despicable, wretched.
Ea delightful, pleasant, desirable.

abominate *v* hate, loathe, detest, abhor, execrate, despise, condemn.
Ea love, adore.

abomination n hate, hatred, aversion, loathing, abhorrence, repugnance, revulsion, disgust, distaste, hostility, offence, outrage, disgrace, anathema, horror, evil, curse, plague, torment, bête noire.
Ea adoration, delight.

aboriginal adj native, indigenous, original, earliest, first, primal, primeval, primitive, ancient, local, autochthonous (fml).

abort v miscarry, terminate, end, stop, arrest, halt, check, frustrate, thwart, nullify, call off, fail.
Ea continue.

abortion n miscarriage, termination, frustration, failure, misadventure.
Ea continuation, success.

abortive adj failed, unsuccessful, fruitless, unproductive, barren, sterile, vain, idle, futile, useless, ineffective, unavailing.
Ea successful, fruitful.

abound v be plentiful, proliferate, flourish, thrive, swell, increase, superabound, swarm, teem, run riot, overflow.

about prep 1 REGARDING, concerning, relating to, referring to, connected with, concerned with, as regards, with regard to, with respect to, with reference to. 2 CLOSE TO, near, nearby, beside, adjacent to. 3 ROUND, around, surrounding, encircling, encompassing, throughout, all over.
➤ adv 1 about twenty: around, approximately, roughly, in the region of, more or less, almost, nearly, approaching, nearing. 2 run about: to and fro, here and there, from place to place.
◆ about to on the point of, on the verge of, all but, ready to, intending to, preparing to.

above prep over, higher than, on top of, superior to, in excess of, exceeding, surpassing, beyond, before, prior to.
Ea below, under.
➤ adv overhead, aloft, on high, earlier.
Ea below, underneath.
➤ adj above-mentioned, above-stated, foregoing, preceding, previous, earlier, prior.

above-board adj honest, legitimate, straight, on the level, fair, fair and square, square, true, open, frank, candid, guileless, straightforward, forthright, truthful, veracious, trustworthy, honourable, reputable, upright.
Ea dishonest, shady (infml), underhand.

abrade v rub, graze, scratch, scrape, scour, grate, grind, chafe, erode, wear away/down.

abrasion n graze, scratch, scratching, scraping, scrape, scouring, grating, grinding, abrading, chafing, chafe, friction, rubbing, erosion, wearing away, wearing down.

abrasive adj scratching, scraping, grating, rough, harsh, chafing, frictional, galling, irritating, annoying, sharp, biting, caustic, hurtful, nasty, unpleasant.
Ea smooth, pleasant.

abreast adj acquainted, informed, knowledgeable, in the picture, au courant, up to date, in touch, au fait, conversant, familiar.
Ea unaware, out of touch.

abridge v shorten, cut (down), prune, curtail, abbreviate, contract, reduce, decrease, lessen, summarize, précis, abstract, digest, condense, compress, concentrate.
Ea expand, amplify, pad out.

abridgement n 1 SHORTENING, cutting, reduction, decrease, diminishing, concentration, contraction, restriction, limitation. 2 SUMMARY, synopsis, résumé, outline, précis, abstract, digest, epitome.
Ea 1 expansion, padding.

abroad adv 1 OVERSEAS, in foreign parts, out of the country, far and wide, widely, extensively. 2 AT LARGE, around, about, circulating, current.
Ea 1 at home.

abrupt adj 1 abrupt departure: sudden, unexpected, unforeseen, surprising, quick, rapid, swift, hasty, hurried, precipitate. 2 SHEER, precipitous, steep, sharp. 3 BRUSQUE, curt, terse, short, brisk, snappy, gruff, rude, uncivil, impolite, blunt, direct.
Ea 1 gradual, slow, leisurely. 3 expansive, ceremonious, polite.

abscond v run away, run off, make off, decamp, flee, fly, escape, bolt, quit, clear out (infml), disappear, take French leave.

absence n 1 NON-ATTENDANCE, non-appearance, truancy, absenteeism, non-existence. 2 LACK, need, want, deficiency, dearth, scarcity, unavailability, default, omission, vacancy.

▣ **1** presence, attendance, appearance. **2** existence.

absent *adj* **1** MISSING, not present, away, out, unavailable, gone, lacking, truant. **2** INATTENTIVE, daydreaming, dreamy, faraway, elsewhere, absent-minded, vacant, vague, distracted, preoccupied, unaware, oblivious, unheeding.
▣ **1** present. **2** alert, aware.

absent-minded *adj* forgetful, scatterbrained, absent, abstracted, withdrawn, faraway, distracted, preoccupied, absorbed, engrossed, pensive, musing, dreaming, dreamy, inattentive, unaware, oblivious, unconscious, heedless, unheeding, unthinking, impractical.
▣ attentive, practical, matter-of-fact.

absolute *adj* **1** UTTER, total, complete, entire, full, thorough, exhaustive, supreme, consummate, definitive, conclusive, final, categorical, definite, unequivocal, unquestionable, decided, decisive, positive, sure, certain, genuine, pure, perfect, sheer, unmixed, unqualified, downright, out-and-out, outright. **2** OMNIPOTENT, totalitarian, autocratic, tyrannical, despotic, dictatorial, sovereign, unlimited, unrestricted.

absolutely *adv* utterly, totally, dead, completely, entirely, fully, wholly, thoroughly, exhaustively, perfectly, supremely, unconditionally, conclusively, finally, categorically, definitely, positively, unequivocally, unambiguously, unquestionably, decidedly, decisively, surely, certainly, infallibly, genuinely, truly, purely, exactly, precisely.

absolution *n* forgiveness, pardon, deliverance, freedom, liberation, release, mercy, redemption, acquittal, amnesty, emancipation, exoneration (*fml*), remission (*fml*), vindication (*fml*), discharge (*fml*), purgation (*fml*), shrift (*fml*).

absolve *v* excuse, clear, forgive, pardon, deliver, free, set free, liberate, release, loose, have mercy on, show mercy towards, emancipate, exonerate (*fml*), vindicate (*fml*), justify (*fml*), acquit (*fml*), discharge (*fml*), remit (*fml*), let off (*infml*).

absorb *v* **1** TAKE IN, ingest, drink in, imbibe, suck up, soak up, consume, devour, engulf, digest, assimilate, understand, receive, hold, retain. **2** ENGROSS, involve, fascinate, enthral, monopolize, preoccupy, occupy, fill (up).
▣ **1** exude.

absorbed *adj* engrossed, involved, fascinated, interested, enthralled, captivated, preoccupied, occupied, taken up with, riveted.

absorbent *adj* receptive, porous, permeable, pervious, soaking, blotting, retentive, absorptive (*fml*), assimilative (*fml*), sorbefacient (*fml*), resorbent (*fml*).
▣ water-repellent, waterproof.

absorbing *adj* interesting, amusing, entertaining, diverting, engrossing, preoccupying, intriguing, fascinating, captivating, enthralling, spellbinding, gripping, riveting, compulsive, unputdownable (*infml*).
▣ boring, off-putting.

absorption *n* **1** *the absorption of liquid/heat*: taking-in, drawing-in, soaking-up, assimilation, osmosis (*fml*), ingestion (*fml*), consumption (*fml*), devouring (*infml*). **2** ENGROSSING, involvement, captivating, riveting, engagement, holding, preoccupation, occupation, attentiveness, concentration, intentness, monopoly.

abstain *v* refrain, decline, refuse, reject, resist, forbear, shun, avoid, keep from, stop, cease, desist, give up, renounce, forgo, go without, deny oneself.
▣ indulge.

abstemious *adj* abstinent, self-denying, self-disciplined, disciplined, sober, temperate, moderate, sparing, frugal, austere, ascetic, restrained.
▣ intemperate, gluttonous, luxurious.

abstention *n* not voting, refusal to vote, declining to vote.

abstinence *n* abstaining, abstention, abstemiousness, self-denial, non-indulgence, avoidance, forbearance, refraining, refusal, restraint, self-restraint, self-control, self-discipline, sobriety, teetotalism, temperance, moderation, frugality, asceticism.
▣ indulgence, self-indulgence.

abstract *adj* non-concrete, conceptual, intellectual, hypothetical, theoretical, unpractical, unrealistic, general, generalized, indefinite, metaphysical, philosophical, academic, complex, abstruse, deep, profound, subtle.
▣ concrete, real, actual.
➤ *n* synopsis, outline, summary,

recapitulation, résumé, précis, epitome, digest, abridgement, compression.
➤ *v* **1** SUMMARIZE, outline, précis, digest, condense, compress, abridge, abbreviate, shorten. **2** EXTRACT, remove, withdraw, isolate, detach, dissociate, separate.
F₃ **1** expand. **2** insert.

abstracted *adj* preoccupied, absent-minded, distracted, forgetful, scatterbrained, absent, withdrawn, absorbed, engrossed, pensive, musing, dreaming, dreamy, bemused, wool-gathering, inattentive, unaware, oblivious, unconscious, heedless, unheeding, unthinking, impractical, scatty (*infml*).
F₃ attentive, alert, on the ball (*infml*).

abstraction *n* **1** IDEA, notion, concept, thought, conception, theory, hypothesis, theorem, formula, generalization, generality. **2** INATTENTION, dream, dreaminess, absent-mindedness, distraction, pensiveness, preoccupation, absorption. **3** EXTRACTION, withdrawal, isolation, separation.

abstruse *adj* obscure, difficult to understand, deep, profound, complex, mysterious, cryptic, unfathomable, incomprehensible, perplexing, puzzling, arcane (*fml*), esoteric (*fml*), inscrutable (*fml*), enigmatic (*fml*), recondite (*fml*).
F₃ simple, obvious.

absurd *adj* ridiculous, ludicrous, preposterous, fantastic, incongruous, illogical, paradoxical, implausible, untenable, unreasonable, irrational, nonsensical, meaningless, senseless, foolish, silly, stupid, idiotic, crazy, farcical, comical, funny, humorous, laughable, risible, derisory, daft (*infml*).
F₃ logical, rational, sensible.

absurdity *n* ridiculousness, ludicrousness, illogicality, unreasonableness, meaninglessness, senselessness, foolishness, folly, silliness, fatuousness, idiocy, stupidity, craziness, inanity, paradox, humour, farce, charade, travesty, joke, nonsense, rubbish, incongruity (*fml*), irrationality (*fml*), implausibility (*fml*), daftness (*infml*), twaddle (*infml*), gibberish (*infml*), drivel (*infml*), claptrap (*infml*), balderdash (*infml*).
F₃ reasonableness, logicality, rationality, (good) sense.

abundance *n* plenty, fullness, great

supply, wealth, generosity, richness, riches, lavishness, overflow, land of milk and honey, glut, extravagance, excess, bonanza, fortune, amplitude (*fml*), bounty (*fml*), plethora (*fml*), copiousness (*fml*), profusion (*fml*), exuberance (*fml*), luxuriance (*fml*), plenitude (*fml*), opulence (*fml*), affluence (*fml*), bags (*infml*), heaps (*infml*), masses (*infml*), piles (*infml*), loads (*infml*), stacks (*infml*), lashings (*infml*), oodles (*infml*), lots (*infml*), scads (*US infml*).
F₃ shortage, scarcity, dearth (*fml*), paucity (*fml*).

abundant *adj* plentiful, in plenty, full, filled, well-supplied, ample, generous, bountiful, rich, copious, profuse, lavish, exuberant, teeming, overflowing.
F₃ scarce, sparse.

abuse *v* **1** MISUSE, misapply, exploit, take advantage of, oppress, wrong, ill-treat, maltreat, hurt, injure, molest, damage, spoil, harm. **2** INSULT, swear at, defame, libel, slander, smear, disparage, malign, revile, scold, upbraid.
F₃ **1** cherish, care for. **2** compliment, praise.
➤ *n* **1** MISUSE, misapplication, exploitation, imposition, oppression, wrong, ill-treatment, maltreatment, hurt, injury, molestation, damage, spoiling, harm. **2** INSULTS, swearing, cursing, offence, defamation, libel, slander, disparagement, reproach, scolding, upbraiding, tirade.
F₃ **1** care, attention. **2** compliment, praise.

abusive *adj* insulting, offensive, rude, scathing, hurtful, injurious, cruel, destructive, defamatory, libellous, slanderous, derogatory, disparaging, pejorative, vilifying, maligning, reviling, censorious, reproachful, scolding, upbraiding.
F₃ complimentary, polite.

abysmal *adj* dismal, shocking, disgraceful, dreadful, appalling, awful, complete, utter.

abyss *n* gulf, chasm, crevasse, fissure, gorge, canyon, crater, pit, depth, void.

academic *adj* **1** SCHOLARLY, erudite, learned, well-read, studious, bookish, scholastic, pedagogical, educational, instructional, literary, highbrow. **2** THEORETICAL, hypothetical, conjectural, speculative, notional, abstract, impractical.
➤ *n* professor, don, master, fellow, lecturer,

tutor, student, scholar, man of letters, pedant.

accelerate *v* **1** *the car/driver accelerated*: quicken, speed, speed up, drive faster, go faster, pick up/gather speed, gain momentum, open up (*infml*), put one's foot down (*infml*), step on it/the gas/the juice (*infml*), put on a spurt (*infml*). **2** *accelerate a process*: speed up, hurry, step up, stimulate, facilitate, advance, further, promote, spur on, forward, hasten (*fml*), expedite (*fml*), precipitate (*fml*).
ez 1, 2 decelerate, slow down, delay.

acceleration *n* **1** *the acceleration of a car*: speeding-up, rate of increase, momentum. **2** *acceleration of a process*: speeding-up, stepping-up, stimulation, promotion, forwarding, advancement (*fml*), furtherance (*fml*), hastening (*fml*), expedition (*fml*).
ez 1, 2 deceleration, slowing-down, delay.

accent *n* pronunciation, enunciation, articulation, brogue, twang (*infml*), tone, pitch, intonation, inflection, accentuation, stress, emphasis, intensity, force, cadence, rhythm, beat, pulse, pulsation.

accentuate *v* accent, stress, emphasize, underline, highlight, intensify, strengthen, deepen.
ez play down, weaken.

accept *v* **1** *accept a gift*: take, receive, obtain, acquire, gain, secure. **2** ACKNOWLEDGE, recognize, admit, allow, approve, agree to, consent to, take on, adopt. **3** TOLERATE, put up with, stand, bear, abide, face up to, yield to.
ez 1 refuse, turn down. **2** reject.

acceptable *adj* satisfactory, tolerable, moderate, passable, adequate, all right, OK (*infml*), so-so (*infml*), unexceptionable, admissible, suitable, conventional, correct, desirable, pleasant, gratifying, welcome.
ez unacceptable, unsatisfactory, unwelcome.

acceptance *n* **1** TAKING, accepting, receipt, obtaining, getting, acquiring, gaining, securing. **2** ACKNOWLEDGEMENT, recognition, admission, concession, affirmation, concurrence, agreement, assent, consent, permission, ratification, approval, stamp of approval, OK (*infml*), adoption, undertaking, belief, credence.
ez 1 refusal. **2** rejection, dissent.

accepted *adj* authorized, approved, ratified, sanctioned, agreed,

acknowledged, recognized, admitted, confirmed, acceptable, correct, conventional, unorthodox, traditional, customary, time-honoured, established, received, universal, regular, standard, normal, usual, common.
ez unconventional, unorthodox, controversial.

access *n* admission, admittance, entry, entering, entrance, gateway, door, key, approach, passage, road, path, course.
ez exit, outlet.

accessible *adj* **1** REACHABLE, get-at-able (*infml*), attainable, achievable, possible, obtainable, available, on hand, ready, handy, convenient, near, nearby. **2** FRIENDLY, affable, approachable, sociable, informal.
ez 1 inaccessible, remote. **2** unapproachable.

accession *n* **1** *accession to the throne*: inheritance, assumption (*fml*), attaining (*fml*), succession (*fml*). **2** *accessions to the library*: addition, acquisition, increase, possession, purchase, gift.

accessory *n* **1** EXTRA, supplement, addition, appendage, attachment, extension, component, fitting, accompaniment, decoration, adornment, frill, trimming. **2** ACCOMPLICE, partner, associate, colleague, confederate, assistant, helper, help, aid.

accident *n* **1** CHANCE, hazard, fortuity, luck, fortune, fate, serendipity, contingency, fluke. **2** MISFORTUNE, mischance, misadventure, mishap, casualty, blow, calamity, disaster. **3** *road accident*: collision, crash, shunt (*sl*), prang (*sl*), pile-up.

accidental *adj* unintentional, unintended, inadvertent, unplanned, uncalculated, unexpected, unforeseen, unlooked-for, chance, fortuitous (*infml*), flukey (*infml*), uncertain, haphazard, random, casual, incidental.
ez intentional, deliberate, calculated, premeditated.

accidentally *adv* unintentionally, inadvertently, unexpectedly, by chance, by accident, by mistake, unwittingly, haphazardly, randomly, incidentally, fortuitously (*fml*), adventitiously (*fml*), serendipitously (*fml*).
ez intentionally, deliberately.

acclaim *v* praise, commend, extol, exalt,

honour, hail, salute, welcome, applaud, clap, cheer, celebrate.
➢ n acclamation, praise, commendation, homage, tribute, eulogy, exaltation, honour, welcome, approbation (fml), approval, applause, ovation, clapping, cheers, cheering, shouting, celebration.
🔁 criticism, disapproval.

acclamation n praise, commendation, homage, tribute, exaltation, honour, welcome, approval, congratulations, applause, ovation, clapping, cheering, bravos, shouting, celebration, enthusiasm, approbation (fml), eulogy (fml), felicitations (fml).
🔁 criticism, disapproval, condemnation.

acclimatize v adjust, adapt, accustom, get used to, find one's way around, accommodate, familiarize, attune, conform, habituate (fml), acculturate (fml), inure (fml), naturalize (fml), find/get one's bearings (infml), find one's feet (infml).

accolade n award, honour, tribute, praise.

accommodate v 1 LODGE, board, put up, house, shelter. 2 OBLIGE, help, assist, aid, serve, provide, supply, comply, conform. 3 ADAPT, accustom, acclimatize, adjust, modify, fit, harmonize, reconcile, settle, compose.

accommodating adj obliging, indulgent, helpful, co-operative, willing, kind, considerate, unselfish, sympathetic, friendly, hospitable.
🔁 disobliging, selfish.

accommodation

Types of accommodation include: flat, apartment, bedsit, bedsitter, digs (infml), lodgings, hostel, halls of residence, rooms, residence, dwelling, shelter, pad (infml), squat (infml); bed and breakfast, board, guest house, hotel, youth hostel, villa, timeshare, motel, inn, pension, boarding-house; barracks, billet, married quarters. see also **house**; **room**.

accompaniment n 1 a musical accompaniment: support, background, backing, backup. 2 wine as an accompaniment to food: complement, accessory, supplement, addition, concomitant (fml), adjunct (fml), coexistence (fml).

accompany v 1 accompany someone on holiday: escort, attend, go (along) with, associate with, come (along) with, partner,

chaperone, usher, conduct, follow, consort (fml), convoy (fml), squire (fml), hang around with (infml). 2 a book accompanied by a study guide: complement, supplement, belong to, go with, coexist (fml), coincide (fml). 3 accompany someone on the guitar: play with, provide backing/support for.

accomplice n assistant, helper, abettor, mate, henchman, conspirator, collaborator, ally, confederate, partner, associate, colleague, participator, accessory.

accomplish v achieve, attain, do, perform, carry out, execute, fulfil, discharge, finish, complete, conclude, consummate, realize, effect, bring about, engineer, produce, obtain.

accomplished adj skilled, professional, practised, proficient, gifted, talented, skilful, adroit, adept, expert, masterly, consummate, polished, cultivated.
🔁 unskilled, inexpert, incapable.

accomplishment n 1 the accomplishment of a task: achievement, attainment, doing, performance, carrying out, execution, fulfilment, discharge, finishing, completion, conclusion, consummation, perfection, realization, fruition, production. 2 SKILL, art, aptitude, faculty, ability, capability, proficiency, gift, talent, forte. 3 EXPLOIT, feat, deed, stroke, triumph.

accord v 1 AGREE, concur, harmonize, match, conform, correspond, suit. 2 GIVE, tender, grant, allow, bestow, endow, confer.
🔁 1 disagree. 2 deny.
➢ n accordance, agreement, assent, unanimity, concert, unity, correspondence, conformity, harmony, sympathy.
🔁 conflict, discord, disharmony.

accordance n agreement, conformity, consonance.
◆ **in accordance with** in agreement with, consistent with, in keeping with, obedient to, in conformity with, in line with, in proportion to, in relation to, after, in the light of, in the manner of, commensurate with (fml), in concert with (fml), in consonance with (fml).

accordingly adv in accordance, in accord with, correspondingly, so, as a result, consequently, in consequence, therefore, thus, hence, appropriately, properly, suitably.

according to prep 1 according to this

book: as said/claimed/stated by, on the report of. **2** *play according to the rules*: in accordance with, in keeping with, obedient to, in conformity with, in line with, consistent with, after, in the light of, in the manner of, after the manner of, as per. **3** *be paid according to experience*: in proportion to, in relation to, depending on, as per, commensurate with (*fml*).

accost *v* approach, confront, buttonhole, waylay, stop, halt, detain, importune, solicit.

account *n* **1** *an account of what happened*: narrative, story, tale, chronicle, history, memoir, record, statement, report, communiqué, write-up, version, portrayal, sketch, description, presentation, explanation. **2** LEDGER, book, books, register, inventory, statement, invoice, bill, tab, charge, reckoning, computation, tally, score, balance.
♦ **account for** explain, elucidate, illuminate, clear up, rationalize, justify, vindicate, answer for, put paid to, destroy, kill.

accountability *n* responsibility, answerability, liability, amenability, reporting, obligation.

accountable *adj* answerable, responsible, liable, amenable, obliged, bound.

accredited *adj* recognized, official, authorized, qualified, endorsed, appointed, approved, certified, licensed, commissioned, certificated (*fml*).

accrue *v* accumulate, increase, mount (up), be added, build up, collect, amass, augment (*fml*).

accumulate *v* gather, assemble, collect, amass, aggregate, cumulate, accrue, grow, increase, multiply, build up, pile up, hoard, stockpile, stash (*infml*), store.
■ disseminate.

accumulation *n* gathering, assembly, collection, growth, increase, build-up, conglomeration, mass, heap, pile, stack, stock, store, reserve, hoard, stockpile.

accuracy *n* correctness, precision, exactness, authenticity, truth, veracity, closeness, faithfulness, fidelity, carefulness.
■ inaccuracy.

accurate *adj* correct, right, unerring, precise, exact, well-directed, spot-on (*infml*), faultless, perfect, word-perfect,

sound, authentic, factual, nice, true, truthful, veracious, just, proper, close, faithful, well-judged, careful, rigorous, scrupulous, meticulous, strict, minute.
■ inaccurate, wrong, imprecise, inexact.

accursed *adj* damned, wretched, hateful, despicable, abominable, condemned, doomed, bewitched, execrable (*fml*), anathematized (*fml*), bedevilled (*fml*).
■ blessed.

accusation *n* charge, allegation, imputation, indictment, denunciation, impeachment, recrimination, complaint, incrimination.

accuse *v* charge, indict, impugn, denounce, arraign, impeach, cite, allege, attribute, impute, blame, censure, recriminate, incriminate, criminate, inform against.

accustom *v* familiarize, adjust, adapt, accommodate, get used to, get familiar with, get acquainted with, conform, habituate (*fml*), inure (*fml*), attune (*fml*).

accustomed *adj* used, in the habit of, given to, confirmed, seasoned, hardened, inured, disciplined, trained, adapted, acclimatized, acquainted, familiar, wonted, habitual, routine, regular, normal, usual, ordinary, everyday, conventional, customary, traditional, established, fixed, prevailing, general.
■ unaccustomed, unusual.

ace *n* champion, expert, genius, master, maestro, winner, virtuoso, dab hand (*infml*), hotshot (*infml*), whizz (*infml*).
➤ *adj* brilliant, excellent, first-class, superb, outstanding, great, perfect.

ache *v* **1** HURT, be sore, pain, suffer, agonize, throb, pound, twinge, smart, sting. **2** YEARN, long, pine, hanker, desire, crave, hunger, thirst, itch.
➤ *n* **1** PAIN, hurt, soreness, suffering, anguish, agony, throb, throbbing, pounding, pang, twinge, smarting, stinging. **2** YEARNING, longing, craving, itch.

achieve *v* accomplish, attain, reach, get, obtain, acquire, procure, gain, earn, win, succeed, manage, do, perform, carry out, execute, fulfil, finish, complete, consummate, effect, bring about, realize, produce.
■ miss, fail.

achievement *n* **1** *the achievement of our aims*: accomplishment, attainment, acquirement, performance, execution, fulfilment, completion, success, realization, fruition. **2** ACT, deed, exploit, feat, effort.

acid *adj* **1** *an acid taste*: acidic, sour, bitter, tart, vinegary, sharp, pungent, acerbic, caustic, corrosive, acetic (*fml*), acetous (*fml*), acidulous (*fml*). **2** *an acid remark*: bitter, unkind, critical, sarcastic, stinging, biting, cutting, incisive, harsh, morose, hurtful, acerbic (*fml*), astringent (*fml*), mordant (*fml*), trenchant (*fml*), vitriolic (*fml*).
Ea 1 alkaline. **2** kind, complimentary.

Types of acid include: acetic, acrylic, amino, aqua fortis, aqua regia, ascorbic, benzoic, boric, carbolic, chloric, citric, DNA (deoxyribonucleic acid), fatty, folic, formic, hydrochloric, hydrocyanic, lactic, malic, nitric, nitrohydrochloric, nitrous, palmitic, pectic, phenol, phosphoric, prussic, RNA (ribonucleic acid), salicylic, spirits of salt, stearic, sulphuric, tannic, tartaric, uric. *see also* **amino acid**.

acknowledge *v* **1** *acknowledge an error*: admit, confess, own up to, declare, recognize, accept, grant, allow, concede. **2** GREET, address, notice, recognize. **3** *acknowledge a letter*: answer, reply to, respond to, confirm.
Ea 1 deny. **2** ignore.

acknowledged *adj* recognized, accepted, approved, accredited, declared, professed, attested, avowed, confirmed.

acknowledgement *n* **1** ADMISSION, confession, declaration, profession, recognition, acceptance. **2** GREETING, salutation, notice, recognition. **3** ANSWER, reply, response, reaction, affirmation. **4** GRATITUDE, thanks, appreciation, tribute.

acme *n* high point, height, peak, pinnacle, climax, culmination, crown, optimum, summit, apex (*fml*), zenith (*fml*), apogee (*fml*).
Ea low point, nadir (*fml*).

acquaint *v* accustom, familiarize, tell, notify, advise, inform, brief, enlighten, divulge, disclose, reveal, announce.

acquaintance *n* **1** AWARENESS, knowledge, understanding, experience, familiarity, intimacy, relationship, association, fellowship, companionship. **2** FRIEND, companion, colleague, associate, contact.

acquainted *adj* **1** FRIENDLY, on friendly terms, on good terms. **2** FAMILIAR, well-versed, knowledgeable, aware, abreast, au fait, conversant (*fml*), cognizant (*fml*), apprised (*fml*), in the know (*infml*).
Ea 2 unfamiliar, unaware, ignorant.

acquiesce *v* consent, submit, agree, accept, allow, approve, defer, concur (*fml*), accede (*fml*), give in (*infml*).
Ea disagree, object, resist.

acquiescent *adj* consenting, agreeable, agreeing, accepting, approving, amenable, obedient, submissive, yielding, deferential, servile, acceding (*fml*), concurrent (*fml*), compliant (*fml*), complaisant (*fml*).

acquire *v* buy, purchase, procure, appropriate, obtain, get, cop (*sl*), receive, collect, pick up, gather, net, gain, secure, earn, win, achieve, attain, realize.
Ea relinquish, forfeit.

acquisition *n* purchase, buy (*infml*), procurement, appropriation, gain, securing, achievement, attainment, accession, takeover, property, possession.

acquisitive *adj* greedy, covetous, grasping, avaricious (*fml*), avid (*fml*), predatory (*fml*), rapacious (*fml*), voracious (*fml*).

acquit *v* absolve, clear, reprieve, let off, exonerate, exculpate, excuse, vindicate, free, liberate, deliver, relieve, release, dismiss, discharge, settle, satisfy, repay.
Ea convict.

acquittal *n* absolution, clearance, reprieve, exoneration, exculpation, excusing, vindication, freeing, liberation, deliverance, relief, release, dismissal, discharge.
Ea conviction.

acrid *adj* pungent, sharp, stinging, acid, burning, caustic, acerbic, biting, cutting, incisive, trenchant, sarcastic, sardonic, bitter, acrimonious, virulent, harsh, vitriolic, nasty, malicious, venomous.

acrimonious *adj* bitter, biting, cutting, trenchant, sharp, virulent, severe, spiteful, censorious, abusive, ill-tempered.
Ea peaceable, kindly.

acrimony *n* bitterness, rancour, resentment, ill-will, petulance, gall, ill temper, irascibility, trenchancy, sarcasm, astringency, acerbity, harshness, virulence.

act *n* **1** DEED, action, undertaking, enterprise, operation, manoeuvre, move, step, doing, execution, accomplishment,

achievement, exploit, feat, stroke. **2** *put on an act*: pretence, make-believe, sham, fake, feigning, dissimulation, affectation, show, front. **3** LAW, statute, ordinance, edict, decree, resolution, measure, bill. **4** TURN, item, routine, sketch, performance, gig (*sl*).
➤ *v* **1** *act in a certain way; act fast*: behave, be, move, do, take action, take steps, take measures, be active, be busy, go about, react, conduct oneself (*fml*), acquit oneself (*fml*), exert oneself (*fml*), comport oneself (*fml*). **2** TAKE EFFECT, have an effect, work, operate, function, be efficacious (*fml*). **3** *the gear acts as a brake*: work, function, serve, operate, do, do the job of. **4** *act upset*: pretend, fake, put on, feign (*fml*), affect (*fml*), assume (*fml*), simulate (*fml*), dissemble (*fml*), dissimulate (*fml*), sham (*infml*). **5** *act in a play*: perform, go on the stage, play, portray, represent, mime, characterize, enact, mimic, imitate, impersonate.

◆ **act on 1** CARRY OUT, fulfil, comply with, conform to, obey, follow, heed, take. **2** AFFECT, influence, alter, modify, change, transform.

◆ **act up** not work, misbehave, behave badly, cause trouble, give bother, play up (*infml*), mess about (*infml*), muck around (*infml*).

acting *adj* temporary, provisional, interim, stopgap, supply, stand-by, substitute, reserve.
➤ *n* theatre, stagecraft, artistry, performing, performance, play-acting, melodrama, dramatics, theatricals, portrayal, characterization, impersonation, imitating.

action *n* **1** ACT, move, deed, exploit, feat, accomplishment, achievement, performance, effort, endeavour, enterprise, undertaking, proceeding, process, activity, liveliness, spirit, energy, vigour, power, force, exercise, exertion, work, functioning, operation, mechanism, movement, motion. **2** *killed in action*: warfare, battle, conflict, combat, fight, fray, engagement, skirmish, clash. **3** LITIGATION, lawsuit, suit, case, prosecution.

activate *v* start, initiate, trigger, set off, fire, switch on, set in motion, mobilize, propel, move, stir, rouse, arouse, stimulate, motivate, prompt, animate, energize, impel, excite, galvanize.
▣ deactivate, stop, arrest.

active *adj* **1** BUSY, occupied, on the go (*infml*), industrious, diligent, hard-working, forceful, spirited, vital, forward, enterprising, enthusiastic, devoted, engaged, involved, committed, militant, activist. **2** AGILE, nimble, sprightly, light-footed, quick, alert, animated, lively, energetic, vigorous. **3** IN OPERATION, functioning, working, running.
▣ **1** passive. **2** inert, dormant. **3** inactive.

activity *n* **1** LIVELINESS, life, activeness, action, motion, movement, commotion, bustle, hustle, industry, labour, exertion, exercise. **2** OCCUPATION, job, work, act, deed, project, scheme, task, venture, enterprise, endeavour, undertaking, pursuit, hobby, pastime, interest.

actor *n* actress, play-actor, comedian, tragedian, ham, player, performer, artist, impersonator, mime.

actual *adj* **1** REAL, existent, substantial, tangible, material, physical, concrete, positive, definite, absolute, certain, unquestionable, indisputable, confirmed, verified, factual, truthful, true, genuine, legitimate, bona fide, authentic, realistic. **2** CURRENT, present, present-day, prevailing, live, living.
▣ **1** theoretical, apparent, imaginary.

actually *adv* **1** *Did you actually see him fall?*: in fact, as a matter of fact, as it happens, in truth, in reality, really, truly, indeed, absolutely, de facto (*fml*). **2** *she took her degree eventually and actually got a first class*: even, though it may seem strange, surprisingly, as it happens.

actuate *v* move, stir, stimulate, activate, motivate, instigate, prompt, rouse, arouse, kindle, start, start working, set off, set going, trigger (off), switch/turn on, set in motion.

acumen *n* astuteness, shrewdness, sharpness, keenness, quickness, penetration, insight, intuition, discrimination, discernment, judgement, perception, sense, wit, wisdom, intelligence, cleverness, ingenuity.

acute *adj* **1** SEVERE, intense, extreme, violent, dangerous, serious, grave, urgent, crucial, vital, decisive, sharp, cutting, poignant, distressing. **2** *an acute mind*: sharp, keen, incisive, penetrating, astute, shrewd, judicious, discerning, observant, perceptive.
▣ **1** mild, slight.

acutely *adv* very, intensely, extremely,

strongly, seriously, gravely, sharply, keenly.

adage n maxim, saying, axiom, proverb, byword, precept, saw, aphorism (fml), apophthegm (fml).

adamant adj hard, resolute, determined, set, firm, insistent, rigid, stiff, inflexible, unbending, unrelenting, intransigent, unyielding, stubborn, uncompromising, tough, fixed, immovable, unshakable.
☛ hesitant, flexible, yielding.

adapt v alter, change, qualify, modify, adjust, convert, remodel, customize, fit, tailor, fashion, shape, harmonize, match, suit, conform, comply, prepare, familiarize, acclimatize.

adaptable adj alterable, changeable, variable, modifiable, adjustable, convertible, conformable, versatile, plastic, malleable, flexible, compliant, amenable, easy-going.
☛ inflexible, refractory.

adaptation n alteration, change, shift, transformation, modification, adjustment, accommodation, conversion, remodelling, reworking, reshaping, refitting, revision, variation, version.

add v append, annex, affix, attach, tack on, join, combine, supplement, augment.
☛ take away, remove.
♦ **add up 1** ADD, sum up, tot up, total, tally, count (up), reckon, compute. **2** AMOUNT, come to, constitute, include. **3** it doesn't add up: be consistent, hang together, make sense, mean, signify, indicate.
☛ subtract.

addendum n appendix, addition, postscript, supplement, codicil (fml), adjunct (fml), appendage (fml), augmentation (fml), attachment (fml), endorsement (fml).

addict n **1** ENTHUSIAST, fan, buff (infml), fiend, freak, devotee, follower, adherent. **2** DRUG-ADDICT, user (infml), dope-fiend (infml), junkie (infml), tripper (sl), mainliner (sl).

addicted adj dependent, hooked, obsessed, absorbed, devoted, dedicated, fond, inclined, disposed, accustomed.

addiction n dependence, craving, habit, monkey (sl), obsession.

addition n **1** ADDING, annexation, accession, extension, enlargement, increasing, increase, gain. **2** ADJUNCT, supplement, additive, addendum,

appendix, appendage, accessory, attachment, extra, increment. **3** SUMMING-UP, totting-up, totalling, counting, reckoning, inclusion.
☛ **1** removal. **3** subtraction.
♦ **in addition** additionally, too, also, as well, besides, moreover, further, furthermore, over and above.

additional adj added, extra, supplementary, spare, more, further, increased, other, new, fresh.

address n **1** RESIDENCE, dwelling, abode, house, home, lodging, direction, inscription, whereabouts, location, situation, place. **2** SPEECH, talk, lecture, sermon, discourse, dissertation.
➤ v lecture, speak to, talk to, greet, salute, hail, invoke, accost, approach, buttonhole.

adduce v cite, mention, allude to, refer to, put forward, point out, present, proffer (fml).

adept adj skilled, accomplished, expert, masterly, experienced, versed, practised, polished, proficient, able, adroit, deft, nimble.
☛ bungling, incompetent, inept.
➤ n master, expert, genius, maestro, dab hand (infml), hot stuff (infml), nobody's fool (infml), wizard (infml).
☛ bungler, incompetent.

adequacy n sufficiency, suitability, fitness, ability, competence, capability, serviceability, acceptability, satisfactoriness, reasonableness, passability, tolerability, tolerableness, fairness, indifference, mediocrity, commensurateness (fml), requisiteness (fml).
☛ inadequacy, insufficiency.

adequate adj enough, sufficient, commensurate (fml), requisite, suitable, fit, able, competent, capable, serviceable, acceptable, satisfactory, passable, tolerable, fair, respectable, presentable.
☛ inadequate, insufficient.

adhere v **1** STICK, glue, paste, cement, fix, fasten, attach, join, link, combine, coalesce, cohere, hold, cling, cleave to. **2** adhere to the agreement: observe, follow, abide by, comply with, fulfil, obey, keep, heed, respect, stand by.

adherent n supporter, upholder, advocate, partisan, follower, disciple, satellite, henchman, hanger-on, votary, devotee, admirer, fan, enthusiast, freak, nut.

adhesion *n* adherence, adhesiveness, bond, attachment, grip, cohesion.

adhesive *adj* sticky, tacky, self-adhesive, gummed, gummy, gluey, adherent, adhering, sticking, clinging, holding, attaching, cohesive.
➤ *n* glue, gum, paste, cement.

adjacent *adj* adjoining, abutting, touching, contiguous, bordering, alongside, beside, juxtaposed, next-door, neighbouring, next, closest, nearest, close, near.
🔁 remote, distant.

adjoin *v* abut (*fml*), touch, meet, border, verge, neighbour, interconnect, link, connect, join, combine, unite, couple, attach, annex, add.

adjoining *adj* adjacent, touching, bordering, near, neighbouring, next, next door, verging, interconnecting, linking, connecting, joining, combining, uniting, contiguous (*fml*), impinging (*fml*), abutting (*fml*), juxtaposed (*fml*), conjoining (*fml*).

adjourn *v* interrupt, suspend, discontinue, break off, delay, stay, defer, postpone, put off, recess, retire.
🔁 assemble, convene.

adjournment *n* interruption, suspension, discontinuation, break, pause, recess, delay, stay, deferment, deferral, postponement, putting off, dissolution.

adjudicate *v* judge, arbitrate, umpire, referee, settle, determine, decide, pronounce.

adjust *v* 1 MODIFY, change, adapt, alter, convert, dispose, shape, remodel, fit, accommodate, suit, measure, rectify, regulate, balance, temper, tune, fine-tune, fix, set, arrange, compose, settle, square. 2 ACCUSTOM, habituate, acclimatize, reconcile, harmonize, conform.
🔁 1 disarrange, upset.

adjustable *adj* adaptable, modifiable, convertible, flexible, movable.
🔁 fixed, immovable.

adjustment *n* 1 MODIFICATION, change, adaptation, alteration, conversion, remodelling, shaping, fitting, accommodation, rectification, regulation, tuning, fixing, setting, arranging, arrangement, ordering, settlement. 2 HABITUATION, orientation, acclimatization, naturalization, reconciliation, harmonization, conforming.

ad-lib *v* improvise, extemporize, make up, invent.
➤ *adj* impromptu, improvised, extempore, extemporaneous, off-the-cuff, unprepared, unpremeditated, unrehearsed, spontaneous, made up.
🔁 prepared.
➤ *adv* impromptu, extempore, extemporaneously, off the cuff, off the top of one's head, spontaneously, impulsively.

administer *v* 1 *administer an organization*: govern, rule, lead, head, preside over, officiate, manage, run, organize, direct, conduct, control, regulate, superintend, supervise, oversee. 2 GIVE, provide, supply, distribute, dole out, dispense, measure out, mete out, execute, impose, apply.

administration *n* 1 ADMINISTERING, governing, ruling, leadership, management, execution, running, organization, direction, control, superintendence, supervision, overseeing. 2 GOVERNING BODY, regime, government, ministry, leadership, directorship, management, executive, term of office.

administrative *adj* governmental, legislative, authoritative, directorial, managerial, management, executive, organizational, regulatory, supervisory.

administrator *n* manager, organizer, director, controller, superintendent, supervisor, overseer, governor, ruler, leader, president, chairman, chief executive, executive, managing director, head, chief, custodian (*fml*), guardian (*fml*), trustee (*fml*), boss (*infml*).

admirable *adj* praiseworthy, commendable, laudable, creditable, deserving, worthy, respected, fine, excellent, superior, wonderful, exquisite, choice, rare, valuable.
🔁 contemptible, despicable, deplorable.

admiration *n* esteem, regard, respect, reverence, veneration, worship, idolism, adoration, affection, approval, praise, appreciation, pleasure, delight, wonder, astonishment, amazement, surprise.
🔁 contempt.

admire *v* esteem, respect, revere, venerate, worship, idolize, adore, approve, praise, laud, applaud, appreciate, value.
🔁 despise, censure.

admirer *n* follower, disciple, adherent, supporter, fan, enthusiast, devotee,

worshipper, idolizer, suitor, boyfriend, girlfriend, sweetheart, lover.
Ea critic, opponent.

admissible *adj* acceptable, tolerable, tolerated, passable, allowable, permissible, allowed, permitted, lawful, legitimate, justifiable.
Ea inadmissible, illegitimate.

admission *n* confession, granting, acknowledgement, recognition, acceptance, allowance, concession, affirmation, declaration, profession, disclosure, divulgence, revelation, exposé.
Ea denial.

admit *v* 1 CONFESS, own (up), grant, acknowledge, recognize, accept, allow, concede, agree, affirm, declare, profess, disclose, divulge, reveal. 2 LET IN, allow to enter, give access, accept, receive, take in, introduce, initiate.
Ea 1 deny. 2 shut out, exclude.

admittance *n* admitting, admission, letting in, access, entrance, entry, acceptance, reception, introduction, initiation.
Ea exclusion.

admonish *v* scold, rebuke, reprimand, discipline, correct, reprove, warn, upbraid, chide, censure, exhort, counsel, berate (*fml*), tell off (*infml*).

admonition *n* rebuke, reprimand, reproof, scolding, correction, warning, censure, exhortation, counsel, berating (*fml*), reprehension (*fml*), telling-off (*infml*).

adolescence *n* teens, puberty, youth, minority, boyhood, girlhood, development, immaturity, youthfulness, boyishness, girlishness.

adolescent *adj* teenage, young, youthful, juvenile, puerile, boyish, girlish, immature, growing, developing.
➤ *n* teenager, youth, juvenile, minor.

adopt *v* 1 *adopt children*: take in, take as one's own, foster. 2 TAKE UP, take on, accept, assume, follow, choose, select, nominate, support, maintain, back, endorse, ratify, approve, appropriate (*fml*), embrace (*fml*), espouse (*fml*).
Ea 1 disown. 2 reject.

adoption *n* 1 *the adoption of children*: taking as one's own, taking-in, (long-term) fostering. 2 *the adoption of a suggestion*: taking-on, acceptance, taking-up, choice, selection, support, backing, endorsement,

ratification, approval, appropriation (*fml*), approbation (*fml*), embracement (*fml*), embracing (*fml*), espousal (*fml*).

adorable *adj* lovable, dear, darling, precious, appealing, sweet, winsome, charming, enchanting, captivating, winning, delightful, pleasing, attractive, fetching.
Ea hateful, abominable.

adore *v* love, cherish, dote on, admire, esteem, honour, revere, venerate, worship, idolize, exalt, glorify.
Ea hate, abhor.

adorn *v* decorate, deck, bedeck, ornament, crown, trim, garnish, gild, enhance, embellish, doll up, enrich, grace.

adornment *n* 1 *bodily adornment*: beautification, decorating, ornamentation, ornateness, enrichment, embellishment, garniture. 2 *gold adornments*: accessory, ornament, decoration, jewellery, frill, trappings, trimmings, garnish, flounce, frippery, garnishry (*fml*), gilding (*fml*).

adrift *adj* 1 *the boat had been cut adrift*: at sea, drifting, off course, anchorless. 2 *feel adrift and lonely*: aimless, rootless, directionless, goalless, insecure, unsettled.
Ea 1 anchored 2 stable.

adroit *adj* skilful, adept, able, clever, expert, masterful, proficient, deft, dexterous.
Ea clumsy, inept, maladroit.

adulation *n* flattery, idolization, personality cult, hero worship, praise, sycophancy, bootlicking, fawning, blandishment (*fml*).

adult *adj* grown-up, of age, full-grown, fully grown, developed, mature, ripe, ripened.
Ea immature.

adulterate *v* contaminate, pollute, taint, corrupt, defile, debase, dilute, water down, weaken, devalue, deteriorate.
Ea purify.

advance *v* 1 PROCEED, go forward, move on, go ahead, progress, prosper, flourish, thrive, improve. 2 ACCELERATE, speed, hasten, send forward. 3 FURTHER, promote, upgrade, foster, support, assist, benefit, facilitate, increase, grow. 4 *advance an idea*: present, submit, suggest, allege, cite, bring forward, offer, provide, supply, furnish. 5 *advance a sum of money*: lend, loan, pay beforehand, pay, give.
Ea 1 retreat. 2 retard. 3 impede.

➤ *n* **1** PROGRESS, forward movement, onward movement, headway, step, advancement, furtherance, breakthrough, development, growth, increase, improvement, amelioration. **2** DEPOSIT, down payment, prepayment, credit, loan.
Ea 1 retreat, recession.
◆ **in advance** beforehand, previously, early, earlier, sooner, ahead, in front, in the lead, in the forefront.
Ea later, behind.

advanced *adj* leading, foremost, ahead, forward, precocious, progressive, forward-looking, avant-garde, ultra-modern, sophisticated, complex, higher.
Ea backward, retarded, elementary.

advancement *n* furtherance, promotion, preferment, betterment, improvement, development, growth, rise, gain, advance, progress, headway.
Ea demotion, retardation.

advantage *n* **1** ASSET, blessing, benefit, good, welfare, interest, service, help, aid, assistance, use, avail, convenience, usefulness, utility, profit, gain, start. **2** LEAD, edge, upper hand, superiority, precedence, pre-eminence, sway.
Ea 1 disadvantage, drawback, hindrance.

advantageous *adj* beneficial, favourable, opportune, convenient, helpful, useful, worthwhile, valuable, profitable, gainful, remunerative, rewarding.
Ea disadvantageous, adverse, damaging.

advent *n* coming, appearance, approach, arrival, entrance, introduction, occurrence, onset, dawn, birth, beginning, accession (*fml*), inception (*fml*).

adventure *n* exploit, venture, undertaking, enterprise, risk, hazard, chance, speculation, experience, incident, occurrence.

adventurer *n* opportunist, hero, heroine, traveller, venturer, voyager, wanderer.

adventurous *adj* daring, intrepid, bold, audacious, headstrong, impetuous, reckless, rash, risky, venturesome, enterprising.
Ea cautious, chary, prudent.

adversary *n* enemy, opponent, antagonist, assailant, attacker, competitor, contestant, foe, opposer, rival.
Ea ally, supporter, friend.

adverse *adj* hostile, antagonistic, opposing, opposite, counter, contrary,

conflicting, counter-productive, negative, disadvantageous, unfavourable, inauspicious, unfortunate, unlucky, inopportune, detrimental, harmful, noxious, injurious, hurtful, unfriendly, uncongenial.
Ea advantageous, favourable.

adversity *n* misfortune, ill fortune, bad luck, ill luck, reverse, hardship, hard times, misery, wretchedness, affliction, suffering, distress, sorrow, woe, trouble, trial, tribulation, calamity, disaster, catastrophe.
Ea prosperity.

advertise *v* publicize, promote, push, plug (*infml*), praise, hype (*sl*), trumpet, blazon, herald, announce, declare, proclaim, broadcast, publish, display, make known, inform, notify.

advertisement *n* advert (*infml*), ad (*infml*), commercial, publicity, promotion, plug (*infml*), hype (*sl*), display, blurb, announcement, notice, poster, bill, placard, leaflet, handbill, circular, handout, propaganda.

advice *n* **1** WARNING, caution, do's and don'ts, injunction, instruction, counsel, help, guidance, direction, suggestion, recommendation, opinion, view. **2** NOTIFICATION, notice, memorandum, communication, information, intelligence.

advisability *n* desirability, suitability, appropriateness, aptness, wisdom, judiciousness, prudence, soundness, expediency (*fml*).
Ea inadvisability, folly.

advisable *adj* suggested, recommended, sensible, wise, prudent, judicious, sound, profitable, beneficial, desirable, suitable, appropriate, apt, fitting, fit, proper, correct.
Ea inadvisable, foolish.

advise *v* **1** COUNSEL, guide, warn, forewarn, caution, instruct, teach, tutor, suggest, recommend, commend, urge. **2** NOTIFY, inform, tell, acquaint, make known, report.

adviser *n* counsellor, consultant, authority, guide, teacher, tutor, instructor, coach, helper, aide, right-hand man, mentor, confidant(e), counsel, lawyer.

advisory *adj* advising, consultative, consulting, counselling, helping, recommending, consultatory (*fml*).

advocate *v* defend, champion, campaign for, press for, argue for, plead for, justify, urge, encourage, advise, recommend, propose, promote, endorse, support, uphold, patronize, adopt, subscribe to, favour, countenance.

🔁 impugn, disparage, deprecate.

➤ *n* defender, supporter, upholder, champion, campaigner, pleader, vindicator, proponent, promoter, speaker, spokesperson.

🔁 opponent, critic.

aegis *n* support, backing, auspices, guardianship, patronage, sponsorship, wing, advocacy, championship, favour.

aeroplane *see* aircraft.

affability *n* friendliness, amiability, approachability, openness, geniality, good humour, good nature, mildness, benevolence, kindliness, graciousness, obligingness, courtesy, amicability, congeniality, cordiality, warmth, sociability, pleasantness.

🔁 unfriendliness, reserve, reticence, coolness.

affable *adj* friendly, amiable, approachable, open, expansive, genial, good-humoured, good-natured, mild, benevolent, kindly, gracious, obliging, courteous, amicable, congenial, cordial, warm, sociable, pleasant, agreeable.

🔁 unfriendly, reserved, reticent, cool.

affair *n* **1** BUSINESS, transaction, operation, proceeding, undertaking, activity, project, responsibility, interest, concern, matter, question, issue, subject, topic, circumstance, happening, occurrence, incident, episode, event. **2** *have an affair*: relationship, liaison, intrigue, love affair, romance, amour.

affect *v* **1** CONCERN, regard, involve, relate to, apply to, bear upon, impinge upon, act on, change, transform, alter, modify, influence, sway, prevail over, attack, strike, impress, interest, stir, move, touch, upset, disturb, perturb, trouble, overcome. **2** ADOPT, assume, put on, feign, simulate, imitate, fake, counterfeit, sham, pretend, profess, aspire to.

affectation *n* airs, pretentiousness, mannerism, pose, act, show, appearance, façade, pretence, sham, simulation, imitation, artificiality, insincerity.

🔁 artlessness, ingenuousness.

affected *adj* assumed, put-on, feigned, simulated, artificial, fake, counterfeit, sham, phoney (*infml*), contrived, studied, precious, mannered, pretentious, pompous, stiff, unnatural, insincere,

🔁 genuine, natural.

affection *n* fondness, attachment, devotion, love, tenderness, care, warmth, feeling, kindness, friendliness, goodwill, favour, liking, partiality, inclination, penchant, passion, desire.

🔁 dislike, antipathy.

affectionate *adj* fond, attached, devoted, doting, loving, tender, caring, warm, warm-hearted, kind, friendly, amiable, cordial.

🔁 cold, undemonstrative.

affiliate *v* join, associate, ally, amalgamate, unite, annex, combine, connect, incorporate, join, merge, syndicate, band together, confederate (*fml*), conjoin (*fml*).

affiliation *n* connection, relationship, link, tie, bond, alliance, union, amalgamation, association, coalition, combination, confederation (*fml*), federation, incorporation, membership, joining, league, merger.

affinity *n* **1** RAPPORT, attraction, compatibility, fondness, liking, good terms, bond, partiality, predisposition (*fml*), propensity (*fml*), chemistry (*infml*). **2** RESEMBLANCE, similarity, likeness, correspondence, analogy, comparability, similitude (*fml*).

🔁 **1** hatred. **2** dissimilarity.

affirm *v* confirm, corroborate, endorse, ratify, certify, witness, testify, swear, maintain, state, assert, declare, pronounce.

🔁 refute, deny.

affirmation *n* assertion, statement, declaration, attestation, certification, confirmation, corroboration, endorsement, ratification, oath, pronouncement, testimony, witness, asseveration (*fml*), averment (*fml*), avouchment (*fml*), avowal (*fml*).

affirmative *adj* agreeing, concurring, approving, assenting, positive, confirming, corroborative, emphatic.

🔁 negative, dissenting.

affix *v* stick, glue, paste, pin on, tack, attach, add, annex, append, bind, connect, fasten, join, tag, adjoin (*fml*).

🔁 detach.

afflict *v* strike, visit, trouble, burden, oppress, distress, grieve, pain, hurt, wound, harm, try, harass, beset, plague, torment, torture.

🔁 comfort, solace.

affliction n distress, grief, sorrow, misery, depression, suffering, pain, torment, disease, illness, sickness, plague, curse, cross, ordeal, trial, tribulation, trouble, hardship, adversity, misfortune, calamity, disaster.
comfort, consolation, solace, blessing.

affluence n wealthiness, wealth, riches, fortune, substance, property, prosperity, opulence, abundance, profusion, plenty.
poverty.

affluent adj wealthy, rich, moneyed, loaded (sl), flush (infml), well-off, prosperous, well-to-do, opulent, comfortable.
poor, impoverished.

afford v 1 HAVE ENOUGH FOR, spare, allow, manage, sustain, bear. 2 PROVIDE, supply, furnish, give, grant, offer, impart, produce, yield, generate.

affront v offend, insult, abuse, snub, slight, provoke, displease, irritate, annoy, anger, vex, incense, outrage.
compliment, appease.
➤ n offence, insult, slur, rudeness, discourtesy, disrespect, indignity, snub, slight, wrong, injury, abuse, provocation, vexation, outrage.
compliment.

afoot adj about, around, circulating, current, going about, in the air, in the wind, brewing, abroad (fml), in the pipeline (infml).

afraid adj frightened, scared, alarmed, terrified, fearful, timorous, daunted, intimidated, faint-hearted, cowardly, reluctant, apprehensive, anxious, nervous, timid, distrustful, suspicious.
unafraid, brave, bold, confident.

afresh adv anew, again, once again, once more, newly, over again.

after prep following, subsequent to, in consequence of, as a result of, behind, below.
before.

aftermath n after-effects, effects, results, outcome, consequences, end, repercussions, upshot, wake.

again adv once more, once again, another time, over again, afresh, anew, encore.

against prep 1 against the wall: abutting, adjacent to, close up to, touching, in contact with, on. 2 OPPOSITE TO, facing, fronting, in the face of, confronting, opposing, versus, opposed to, in

opposition to, hostile to, resisting, in defiance of, in contrast to.
2 for, pro.

age n 1 ERA, epoch, day, days, generation, date, time, period, duration, span, years, aeon. 2 OLD AGE, maturity, elderliness, seniority, dotage, senility, decline.
2 youth.
➤ v grow old, mature, ripen, mellow, season, decline, deteriorate, degenerate.

aged adj old, elderly, advanced (in years), ageing, geriatric, grey, hoary, patriarchal, superannuated, senescent (fml), getting on (infml), past it (infml), over the hill (infml), having seen better days (infml), no spring chicken (infml), not as young as one was (infml), with one foot in the grave (infml), ancient (infml).
young, youthful.

agency n 1 recruitment agency: bureau, office, department, organization, business, work. 2 MEANS, medium, instrumentality, power, force, influence, effect, intervention, action, activity, operation, mechanism, workings.

agenda n list, plan, programme, schedule, calendar, diary, timetable, to-do list, scheme of work, menu.

agent n 1 SUBSTITUTE, deputy, delegate, envoy, emissary, representative, rep (infml), broker, middleman, go-between, intermediary, negotiator, mover, doer, performer, operator, operative, functionary, worker. 2 INSTRUMENT, vehicle, channel, means, agency, cause, force.

aggravate v 1 aggravate a problem: exacerbate, worsen, inflame, increase, intensify, heighten, magnify, exaggerate. 2 (infml) ANNOY, irritate, vex, irk, exasperate, incense, provoke, tease, pester, harass.
1 improve, alleviate. 2 appease, mollify.

aggravation (infml) n annoyance, exasperation, irritation, provocation, teasing, vexation, irksomeness, hassle (infml), thorn in the flesh (infml).

aggregate n total, sum, amount, whole, totality, entirety, generality, combination, collection, accumulation.
➤ adj cumulative, accumulated, collected, combined, united, added, total, complete, composite, mixed, collective.
individual, particular.

aggression n 1 ANTAGONISM, provocation, offence, injury, attack, offensive, assault, onslaught, raid, incursion, invasion, intrusion. **2** AGGRESSIVENESS, militancy, belligerence, combativeness, hostility.

☒ **1** peace, resistance. **2** passivity, gentleness.

aggressive *adj* argumentative, quarrelsome, contentious, belligerent, hostile, offensive, provocative, intrusive, invasive, bold, assertive, pushy, go-ahead, forceful, vigorous, zealous, ruthless, destructive.

☒ peaceable, friendly, submissive, timid.

aggressor *n* invader, attacker, assailant, assaulter, intruder, offender, provoker.

☒ victim.

aggrieved *adj* wronged, offended, hurt, injured, insulted, maltreated, ill-used, resentful, pained, distressed, saddened, unhappy, upset, annoyed.

☒ pleased.

aghast *adj* shocked, appalled, horrified, horror-struck, thunderstruck, stunned, stupefied, amazed, astonished, astounded, startled, confounded, dismayed.

agile *adj* active, lively, nimble, spry, sprightly, mobile, flexible, limber, lithe, fleet, quick, swift, brisk, prompt, sharp, acute, alert, quick-witted, clever, adroit, deft.

☒ clumsy, stiff.

agitate *v* **1** ROUSE, arouse, stir up, excite, stimulate, incite, inflame, ferment, work up, worry, trouble, upset, alarm, disturb, unsettle, disquiet, discompose, fluster, ruffle, flurry, unnerve, confuse, distract, disconcert. **2** SHAKE, rattle, rock, stir, beat, churn, toss, convulse.

☒ **1** calm, tranquillize.

agitated *adj* worried, troubled, upset, disturbed, anxious, unsettled, flustered, ruffled, distraught, unnerved, disconcerted, nervous, in a lather (*infml*).

☒ calm, composed.

agitator *n* troublemaker, rabble-rouser, revolutionary, stirrer (*sl*), inciter, instigator.

agog *adj* eager, excited, curious, enthralled, enthusiastic, impatient, in suspense, keen, avid, on the edge of one's seat (*infml*), on tenterhooks (*infml*).

☒ incurious.

agonize *v* worry, labour, strain, strive, struggle, trouble, wrestle.

agony *n* anguish, torment, torture, pain, spasm, throes, suffering, affliction,

tribulation, distress, woe, misery, wretchedness.

agree *v* **1** CONCUR, see eye to eye, get on, settle, accord, match, suit, fit, tally, correspond, conform. **2** CONSENT, allow, permit, assent, accede, grant, admit, concede, yield, comply.

☒ **1** disagree, differ, conflict. **2** refuse.

agreeable *adj* pleasant, congenial, likable, attractive, delightful, enjoyable, gratifying, satisfying, palatable, acceptable, proper, appropriate, suitable, fitting, in accord, consistent.

☒ disagreeable, nasty, distasteful.

agreement *n* **1** SETTLEMENT, compact, covenant, treaty, pact, contract, deal, bargain, arrangement, understanding. **2** *be in agreement*: concurrence, accord, concord, unanimity, union, harmony, sympathy, affinity, compatibility, similarity, correspondence, consistency, conformity, compliance, adherence, acceptance.

☒ **2** disagreement.

agricultural *adj* agronomic, agrarian, farming, farmed, cultivated, rural, pastoral, bucolic.

Types of agricultural implement and machinery include: axe, chainsaw, clover broadcaster, fertilizer distributor, field sprinkler, fork, hayfork, pitchfork, hoe, potato planter, rake, hayrake, reaping hook, saw, scythe, shovel, sickle, spade, wheelbarrow, whetstone; all-terrain vehicle (ATV), baler, bale wrapper, cultivator, drill, corn drill, seed drill, fertilizer spreader, fork-lift truck, front end loader, harrow, combination seed-harrow, disc harrow, harvester, combine harvester, hedgecutter, irrigator, milking machine, mower, flail mower, muckspreader, potato planter, plough, reversible plough, wheel plough, power lift, rotary hoe, Rotovator®, scarifier, slurry tanker, sprayer, tedder, tractor, trailer.

---

agriculture *n* agronomics, farming, husbandry, cultivation, culture, tillage.

aground *adj*, *adv* ashore, beached, foundered, grounded, high and dry, marooned, stranded, stuck, wrecked, on the rocks.

☒ afloat.

ahead *adv* forward, onward, leading, at the head, in front, in the lead, winning, at an advantage, advanced, superior, to the fore, in the forefront, in advance, before, earlier on.

aid *v* help, assist, succour, rally round, relieve, support, subsidize, sustain, second, serve, oblige, accommodate, favour, promote, boost, encourage, expedite, facilitate, ease.

ᴇ₃ hinder, impede, obstruct.

➤ *n* help, assistance, prop, support, relief, benefit, subsidy, donation, contribution, funding, grant, sponsorship, patronage, favour, encouragement, service.

ᴇ₃ hindrance, impediment, obstruction.

aide *n* adviser, assistant, right-hand person, right-hand man, supporter, adjutant, advocate, aide-de-camp, attaché, confidant, disciple, follower.

ailing *adj* unwell, ill, sick, poorly, indisposed, out of sorts (*infml*), under the weather (*infml*), off-colour, suffering, languishing, sickly, diseased, invalid, infirm, unsound, frail, weak, feeble, failing.

ᴇ₃ healthy, thriving, flourishing.

ailment *n* illness, sickness, complaint, malady, disease, infection, disorder, affliction, infirmity, disability, weakness.

aim *v* **1** POINT, direct, take aim, level, train, sight, zero in on (*infml*), target. **2** *aim to achieve*: aspire, want, wish, seek, resolve, purpose, intend, propose, mean, plan, design, strive, try, attempt, endeavour.
➤ *n* aspiration, ambition, hope, dream, desire, wish, plan, design, scheme, purpose, motive, end, intention, object, objective, target, mark, goal, direction, course.

aimless *adj* pointless, purposeless, unmotivated, irresolute, directionless, rambling, undirected, unguided, stray, chance, random, haphazard, erratic, unpredictable, wayward.

ᴇ₃ purposeful, positive, determined.

air *n* **1** ATMOSPHERE, oxygen, sky, heavens, breath, puff, waft, draught, breeze, wind, blast. **2** APPEARANCE, look, aspect, aura, bearing, demeanour, manner, character, effect, impression, feeling.
➤ *v* **1** *air a room*: ventilate, aerate, freshen. **2** *air an opinion*: utter, voice, express, give vent to, make known, communicate, tell, declare, reveal, disclose, divulge, expose, make public, broadcast, publish, circulate, disseminate, exhibit, display, parade, publicize.

aircraft

> Types of aircraft include: aeroplane, plane, jet, jumbo, Concorde, airbus, helicopter, monoplane, two-seater, air-ambulance, freighter, sea-plane, glider, hang-glider, microlight, hot-air balloon; fighter, spitfire, bomber, kite (*infml*), jump-jet, dive-bomber, chopper (*sl*), spy plane, delta-wing, swing-wing, troop-carrier, airship, turbojet, VTOL (vertical take-off and landing), warplane, zeppelin.

airing *n* **1** *give clothes an airing*: ventilation, aeration, freshening. **2** *the airing of opinions*: expression, making known, communication, declaration, statement, revelation, disclosure, divulgence, exposure, uttering, voicing, broadcast, publication, circulation, dissemination (*fml*).

airless *adj* unventilated, stuffy, musty, stale, suffocating, stifling, sultry, muggy, close, heavy, oppressive.

ᴇ₃ airy, fresh.

airs *n* arrogance, artificiality, haughtiness, posing, pretensions, pretentiousness, superciliousness, affectation (*fml*), affectedness (*fml*), hauteur (*fml*), pomposity (*fml*), swank (*infml*).

airy *adj* **1** ROOMY, spacious, open, well-ventilated, draughty, breezy, blowy, windy, gusty. **2** CHEERFUL, happy, light-hearted, high-spirited, lively, nonchalant, offhand.

ᴇ₃ **1** airless, stuffy, close, heavy, oppressive.

aisle *n* gangway, corridor, passage, passageway, alleyway, walkway, path, lane.

alarm *v* frighten, scare, startle, put the wind up (*infml*), terrify, panic, unnerve, daunt, dismay, distress, agitate.

ᴇ₃ reassure, calm, soothe.

➤ *n* **1** FRIGHT, scare, fear, terror, panic, horror, shock, consternation, dismay, distress, anxiety, nervousness, apprehension, trepidation, uneasiness. **2** DANGER SIGNAL, alert, warning, distress signal, siren, bell, alarm-bell.

ᴇ₃ **1** calmness, composure.

alarming *adj* frightening, scary, startling, terrifying, unnerving, daunting, ominous, threatening, dismaying, disturbing, distressing, shocking, dreadful.

ᴇ₃ reassuring.

alcohol *n* drink, booze (*sl*), liquor, spirits, hard stuff (*sl*), intoxicant.

alcoholic *adj* intoxicating, brewed,

fermented, distilled, strong, hard.
➤ n drunk, drunkard, inebriate, hard
drinker, dipsomaniac, wino (sl), alkie (sl).

alcove n niche, nook, recess, bay, corner,
cubby-hole, compartment, cubicle, booth,
carrel.

alert adj attentive, wide-awake, watchful,
vigilant, on the lookout, sharp-eyed,
observant, perceptive, sharp-witted, on
the ball (infml), active, lively, spirited,
quick, brisk, agile, nimble, ready, prepared,
careful, heedful, circumspect, wary.
🗷 slow, listless, unprepared.
➤ v warn, forewarn, notify, inform, tip off,
signal, alarm.

alias n pseudonym, false name, assumed
name, nom de guerre, nom de plume, pen
name, stage name, nickname, sobriquet.
➤ prep also known as, also called,
otherwise, formerly.

alibi n defence, justification, story,
explanation, excuse, pretext, reason.

alien adj strange, unfamiliar, outlandish,
incongruous, foreign, exotic,
extraterrestial, extraneous, remote,
estranged, separated, opposed, contrary,
conflicting, antagonistic, incompatible.
🗷 akin.
➤ n foreigner, immigrant, newcomer,
stranger, outsider.
🗷 native.

alienation n antagonization,
estrangement, turning away, indifference,
remoteness, rupture, separation, isolation,
severance, divorce, disunion, diversion,
disaffection (fml).
🗷 endearment.

alight¹ v descend, get down, dismount, get
off, disembark, land, touch down, come
down, come to rest, settle, light, perch.
🗷 ascend, board.

alight² adj lighted, lit, ignited, on fire,
burning, blazing, ablaze, flaming, fiery, lit
up, illuminated, bright, radiant, shining,
brilliant.
🗷 dark.

align v 1 STRAIGHTEN, range, line up, make
parallel, even (up), adjust, regulate,
regularize, order, co-ordinate. 2 ALLY, side,
sympathize, associate, affiliate, join, co-
operate, agree.

alike adj similar, resembling, comparable,
akin, analogous, corresponding,
equivalent, equal, the same, identical,
duplicate, parallel, even, uniform.

🗷 dissimilar, unlike, different.
➤ adv similarly, analogously,
correspondingly, equally, in common.

alive adj 1 LIVING, having life, live,
animate, breathing, existent, in existence,
extant (fml), (still) going strong (infml), in
the land of the living (infml). 2 LIVELY,
animated, spirited, awake, alert, active,
brisk, energetic, full of life, vigorous,
zestful, vivacious, vibrant, vital. 3 alive with
tourists: full of, teeming with, abounding in,
overflowing with, crawling with (infml),
swarming with (infml). 4 alive to the danger:
aware of, heedful of, alert to, sensitive to,
cognizant of (fml).
🗷 1 dead, extinct. 2 lifeless, apathetic. 4
unaware of, blind to, deaf to.

all adj 1 EACH, every, each and every, every
single, every one of, the whole of, every bit
of. 2 COMPLETE, entire, full, total, utter,
outright, perfect, greatest.
🗷 1 no, none.
➤ n everything, sum, total, aggregate, total
amount, whole amount, whole, entirety,
utmost, comprehensiveness, universality.
🗷 nothing, none.
➤ adv completely, entirely, wholly, fully,
totally, utterly, altogether, wholesale.

allay v alleviate, relieve, soothe, ease,
smooth, calm, tranquillize, quiet, quell,
pacify, mollify, soften, blunt, lessen,
reduce, diminish, check, moderate.
🗷 exacerbate, intensify.

allegation n accusation, charge, claim,
profession, assertion, affirmation,
declaration, statement, testimony, plea.

allege v assert, affirm, declare, state,
attest, maintain, insist, hold, contend,
claim, profess, plead.

alleged adj supposed, reputed, putative,
inferred, so-called, professed, declared,
stated, claimed, described, designated,
doubtful, dubious, suspect, suspicious.

allegiance n loyalty, fidelity, faithfulness,
constancy, duty, obligation, obedience,
devotion, support, adherence, friendship.
🗷 disloyalty, enmity.

allegorical adj figurative, representative,
symbolic, metaphorical, symbolizing,
typical, parabolic (fml), emblematic (fml).

allegory n analogy, comparison,
metaphor, symbol, parable, story, fable,
myth, legend, tale, symbolism, emblem
(fml), apologue (fml).

allergic adj sensitive, hypersensitive,

susceptible, affected, incompatible, averse, disinclined, opposed, hostile, antagonistic.
◼ tolerant.

alleviate *v* relieve, soothe, ease, palliate, mitigate, soften, cushion, dull, deaden, allay, abate, lessen, reduce, diminish, check, moderate, temper, subdue.
◼ aggravate.

alley *n* alleyway, back street, lane, street, road, mall, passage, passageway, pathway, close, gate, walk.

alliance *n* confederation, federation, association, affiliation, coalition, league, bloc, cartel, conglomerate, consortium, syndicate, guild, union, partnership, marriage, agreement, compact, bond, pact, treaty, combination, connection.
◼ separation, divorce, estrangement, enmity, hostility.

allied *adj* associated, connected, linked, bound, combined, in league, joined, joint, kindred, related, affiliated, amalgamated, coupled, unified, united, married, wed, hand in glove (*infml*), in cahoots (*infml*).
◼ estranged.

allocate *v* assign, designate, budget, allow, earmark, set aside, allot, apportion, share out, distribute, dispense, mete.

allocation *n* allotment, lot, apportionment, measure, share, portion, stint, ration, quota, budget, allowance, grant.

allot *v* divide, ration, apportion, share out, distribute, dispense, mete, dole out, allocate, assign, designate, budget, allow, grant, earmark, set aside.

allotment *n* division, partition, allocation, apportionment, measure, percentage, lot, portion, share, stint, ration, quota, allowance, grant.

all-out *adj* complete, full, total, undivided, comprehensive, exhaustive, thorough, intensive, thoroughgoing, wholesale, vigorous, powerful, full-scale, no-holds-barred, maximum, utmost, unlimited, unrestrained, resolute, determined.
◼ perfunctory, half-hearted.

allow *v* **1** PERMIT, let, enable, authorize, sanction, approve, tolerate, put up with, endure, suffer. **2** ADMIT, confess, own, acknowledge, concede, grant. **3** *allow two hours for the journey*: allot, allocate, assign, apportion, afford, give, provide.
◼ 1 forbid, prevent. **2** deny.

◆ allow for take into account, make provision for, make allowances for, provide for, foresee, plan for, arrange for, bear in mind, keep in mind, consider, include.
◼ discount.

allowable *adj* permissible, acceptable, admissible, justifiable, all right, appropriate, approved, legal, legitimate, lawful, sanctionable (*fml*), legit (*infml*).
◼ unacceptable.

allowance *n* **1** ALLOTMENT, lot, amount, allocation, portion, share, ration, quota. **2** REBATE, reduction, deduction, discount, concession, subsidy, weighting. **3** PAYMENT, remittance, pocket money, grant, maintenance, stipend, pension, annuity.

alloy *n* blend, compound, composite, amalgam, combination, mixture, fusion, coalescence.

all right *adj* **1** SATISFACTORY, passable, unobjectionable, acceptable, allowable, adequate, fair, average, OK (*infml*). **2** *are you all right?*: well, healthy, unhurt, uninjured, unharmed, unimpaired, whole, sound, safe, secure.
◼ 1 unacceptable, inadequate.
➢ *adv* satisfactorily, well enough, passably, unobjectionably, acceptably, suitably, appropriately, adequately, reasonably, OK (*infml*).
◼ unsatisfactorily, unacceptably.

allude *v* mention, refer, remark, speak of, hint, imply, infer, insinuate, intimate, suggest, touch on/upon, adumbrate (*fml*).

allure *v* lure, entice, seduce, lead on, tempt, coax, cajole, persuade, win over, disarm, charm, enchant, attract, interest, fascinate, captivate, entrance, beguile.
◼ repel.
➢ *n* lure, enticement, seduction, temptation, appeal, attraction, magnetism, fascination, glamour, captivation, charm, enchantment.

alluring *adj* attractive, fascinating, intriguing, interesting, captivating, winning, enchanting, engaging, enticing, arousing, beguiling, bewitching, fetching, seductive, sensuous, sexy, desirable, tempting, come-hither (*infml*).
◼ repellent, unattractive.

allusion *n* mention, reference, citation, quotation, remark, observation, suggestion, hint, intimation, implication, insinuation.

ally n confederate, associate, leaguer, consort, partner, sidekick, colleague, co-worker, collaborator, helper, helpmate, accomplice, accessory, friend.
☒ antagonist, enemy.
➤ v confederate, affiliate, league, associate, collaborate, join forces, band together, team up, fraternize, side, join, connect, link, marry, unite, unify, amalgamate, combine.
☒ estrange, separate.

almighty adj 1 OMNIPOTENT, all-powerful, supreme, absolute, great, invincible. 2 ENORMOUS, severe, intense, overwhelming, overpowering, terrible, awful, desperate.
☒ 1 impotent, weak.

almost adv nearly, well-nigh, practically, virtually, just about, as good as, all but, close to, not far from, approaching, nearing, not quite, about, approximately.

alone adj only, sole, single, unique, ...
isolated, apart, by oneself, by itself, on one's own, lonely, lonesome, deserted, abandoned, forsaken, forlorn, desolate, unaccompanied, unescorted, unattended, solo, single-handed, unaided, unassisted, mere.
☒ together, accompanied, escorted.

aloof adj distant, remote, offish, standoffish, haughty, supercilious, unapproachable, inaccessible, detached, forbidding, cool, chilly, cold, sympathetic, unresponsive, indifferent, uninterested, reserved, unforthcoming, unfriendly, unsociable, formal.
☒ sociable, friendly, concerned.

aloud adv out loud, audibly, intelligibly, clearly, plainly, distinctly, loudly, resoundingly, sonorously, noisily, vociferously.
☒ silently.

alphabets and writing systems

Alphabets and writing systems **include:** Byzantine, Chalcidian alphabet, cuneiform, Cyrillic, devanagari, estrangelo, finger-alphabet, futhark, Glagol, Glossic, Greek, Gurmukhi, hieroglyphs, hiragana, ideograph, initial teaching alphabet (i.t.a.), International Phonetic Alphabet (IPA), kana, kanji, katakana, Kufic, linear A, linear B, logograph, nagari, naskhi, ogam, pictograph, romaji, Roman, runic, syllabary.

already adv 1 *I've read the book already*: before now, beforehand, just now, previously, heretofore (*fml*), hitherto (*fml*). 2 *he can already count*: even now, even then, so soon (as this), so early, by now, by that time, by then, by this time.

also adv too, as well, and, plus, along with, including, as well as, additionally, in addition, besides, further, furthermore, moreover.

alter v change, vary, diversify, modify, qualify, shift, transpose, adjust, adapt, convert, turn, transmute, transform, reform, reshape, remodel, recast, revise, amend, emend.
☒ fix.

alteration n change, variation, variance, difference, diversification, shift, transposition, modification, adjustment, adaptation, conversion, transformation, transfiguration, metamorphosis, reformation, reshaping, remodelling, ...
☒ fixity.

alternate v interchange, reciprocate, rotate, take turns, follow one another, replace each other, substitute, change, alter, vary, oscillate, fluctuate, intersperse.
➤ adj alternating, every other, every second, interchanging, reciprocal, rotating, alternative.

alternative n option, choice, selection, preference, other, recourse, substitute, back-up.
➤ adj substitute, second, another, other, different, unorthodox, unconventional, fringe, alternate.

although conj though, even though, despite/in spite of the fact that, while, even if, even supposing, granted that, albeit (*fml*), notwithstanding (*fml*).

altitude n height, elevation, loftiness, tallness, stature.
☒ depth.

altogether adv totally, completely, entirely, wholly, fully, utterly, absolutely, quite, perfectly, thoroughly, in all, all told, in toto, all in all, as a whole, on the whole, generally, in general.

altruistic adj unselfish, self-sacrificing, disinterested, public-spirited, philanthropic, charitable, humanitarian, benevolent, generous, considerate, humane.
☒ selfish.

always *adv* every time, consistently, invariably, without exception, unfailingly, regularly, repeatedly, continually, constantly, perpetually, unceasingly, eternally, endlessly, evermore, forever, ever.
🆎 never.

amalgamate *v* merge, blend, mingle, commingle, intermix, homogenize, incorporate, alloy, integrate, compound, fuse, coalesce, synthesize, combine, unite, unify, ally.
🆎 separate.

amalgamation *n* merger, blend, incorporation, integration, joining, compound, fusion, coalescence, synthesis, combination, unity, union, unification, alliance, admixture (*fml*), commingling (*fml*), homogenization (*fml*).
🆎 separation.

amass *v* accumulate, accrue, assemble, collect, gather, heap (up), hoard, pile (up), store (up), gain, acquire, agglomerate (*fml*), agglutinate (*fml*), aggregate (*fml*), foregather (*fml*), garner (*fml*).

amateur *n* non-professional, layman, ham (*infml*), dilettante, dabbler, enthusiast, fancier, buff (*infml*).
🆎 professional.
➤ *adj* non-professional, lay, unpaid, unqualified, untrained, amateurish, inexpert, unprofessional.
🆎 professional.

amateurish *adj* non-professional, lay, unpaid, unqualified, untrained, unskilful, inexpert, unprofessional, clumsy, crude, inept.
🆎 professional, expert, skilled.

amaze *v* surprise, startle, astonish, astound, stun, stupefy, daze, stagger, floor (*infml*), dumbfound, flabbergast (*infml*), shock, dismay, disconcert, confound, bewilder.

amazement *n* surprise, astonishment, shock, dismay, confusion, perplexity, bewilderment, admiration, wonderment, wonder, marvel.

ambassador *n* emissary, envoy, legate, diplomat, consul, plenipotentiary, deputy, representative, agent, minister, apostle.

ambiguity *n* double meaning, double entendre, equivocality, equivocation, enigma, puzzle, confusion, obscurity, unclearness, vagueness, woolliness,

dubiousness, doubt, doubtfulness, uncertainty.
🆎 clarity.

ambiguous *adj* double-meaning, equivocal, multivocal, double-edged, back-handed, cryptic, enigmatic, puzzling, confusing, obscure, unclear, vague, indefinite, woolly, confused, dubious, doubtful, uncertain, inconclusive, indeterminate.
🆎 clear, definite.

ambition *n* **1** ASPIRATION, aim, goal, target, objective, intent, purpose, design, object, ideal, dream, hope, wish, desire, yearning, longing, hankering, craving, hunger. **2** *a woman of ambition*: enterprise, drive, push, thrust, striving, eagerness, commitment, zeal.
🆎 **2** apathy, diffidence.

ambitious *adj* **1** ASPIRING, hopeful, desirous, intent, purposeful, pushy, bold, assertive, go-ahead, enterprising, driving, energetic, enthusiastic, eager, keen, striving, industrious, zealous. **2** FORMIDABLE, hard, difficult, arduous, strenuous, demanding, challenging, exacting, impressive, grandiose, elaborate.
🆎 **1** lazy, unassuming. **2** modest, uninspiring.

ambivalence *n* contradiction, conflict, clash, opposition, inconsistency, confusion, fluctuation, wavering, hesitation, irresoluteness, uncertainty, doubt, inconclusiveness, vacillation (*fml*).
🆎 certainty.

ambivalent *adj* contradictory, conflicting, clashing, warring, opposed, inconsistent, mixed, confused, fluctuating, vacillating (*fml*), wavering, hesitant, irresolute, undecided, unresolved, unsettled, uncertain, unsure, doubtful, debatable, inconclusive.

amble *v* walk, saunter, toddle (*infml*), stroll, promenade, wander, drift, meander, ramble.
🆎 stride, march.

ambush *n* waylaying, surprise attack, trap, snare, cover, hiding-place.
➤ *v* lie in wait, waylay, surprise, trap, ensnare.

ameliorate *v* alleviate, improve, better, amend, benefit, ease, elevate, enhance, mend, mitigate, promote, relieve.
🆎 exacerbate, worsen.

amenable *adj* accommodating, flexible,

open, agreeable, persuadable, compliant, tractable, submissive, responsive, susceptible, liable, responsible.
Ea intractable.

amend *v* revise, correct, rectify, emend, fix, repair, mend, remedy, redress, reform, change, alter, adjust, modify, qualify, enhance, improve, ameliorate, better.
Ea impair, worsen.

amendment *n* revision, correction, corrigendum, rectification, emendation, repair, remedy, reform, change, alteration, adjustment, modification, qualification, clarification, addendum, addition, adjunct, improvement.
Ea impairment, deterioration.

amends *n* atonement, expiation, requital, satisfaction, recompense, compensation, indemnification, indemnity, reparation, redress, restoration, restitution.

amenity *n* facility, advantage, convenience, service, utility, resource.

amiable *adj* affable, friendly, approachable, genial, cheerful, good-tempered, good-natured, kind, obliging, charming, engaging, likable, pleasant, agreeable, congenial, companionable, sociable.
Ea unfriendly, curt, hostile.

amicable *adj* friendly, cordial, good-natured, civil, harmonious, civilized, peaceful.
Ea hostile.

amid *prep* amidst, midst, in the midst of, in the thick of, among, amongst, in the middle of, surrounded by.

amino acid

Amino acids include: alanine, arginine, asparagine, aspartic acid, cysteine, glutamic acid, glutamine, glycine, histidine, isoleucine, leucine, lysine, methionine, phenylalanine, proline, serine, threonine, trytophan, tyrosine, valine.

amiss *adj* wrong, awry, defective, false, faulty, improper, out of order, inaccurate, inappropriate, incorrect, unsuitable, untoward, imperfect, out of kilter, wonky (*infml*).
Ea right, well.

ammunition *n* missiles, bullets, shells, rockets, projectiles, cartridges, slugs, grenades, bombs, shot, mine, gunpowder.

amnesty *n* pardon, forgiveness,

absolution, mercy, lenience, indulgence, reprieve, remission, dispensation, immunity, oblivion.

amok *adv* berserk, crazy, in a frenzy, frenzied, insanely, like a lunatic, madly, wildly, uncontrollably, violently.

among *prep* amongst, between, in the middle of, surrounded by, amid, amidst, midst, in the midst of, in the thick of, with, together with.

amorous *adj* passionate, loving, affectionate, tender, fond, erotic, impassioned, in love, lovesick, lustful, amatory (*fml*), randy (*infml*).
Ea cold, indifferent.

amorphous *adj* formless, nebulous, shapeless, featureless, indeterminate, indistinct, irregular, undefined, unformed, unshapen, unstructured, vague, inchoate (*fml*).
Ea definite, distinctive, shapely.

amount *n* quantity, number, sum, total, sum total, whole, entirety, aggregate, lot, quota, supply, volume, mass, bulk, measure, magnitude, extent, expanse.
◆ **amount to** add up to, total, aggregate, come to, make, equal, mean, be tantamount to, be equivalent to, approximate to, become, grow.

amphibian

Amphibians include: frog, bullfrog, tree frog, toad, horned toad, midwife toad, natterjack, newt, eft, salamander, mud puppy, axolotl.

ample *adj* large, big, extensive, expansive, broad, wide, full, voluminous, roomy, spacious, commodious, great, considerable, substantial, handsome, generous, bountiful, munificent, liberal, lavish, copious, abundant, plentiful, plenty, unrestricted, profuse, rich.
Ea insufficient, inadequate, meagre.

amplify *v* enlarge, magnify, expand, dilate, fill out, bulk out, add to, supplement, augment, increase, extend, lengthen, widen, broaden, develop, elaborate, enhance, boost, intensify, strengthen, deepen, heighten, raise.
Ea reduce, decrease, abridge.

amputate *v* cut off, remove, sever, dissever, separate, dock, lop, curtail, truncate.

amuse *v* entertain, divert, regale, make

laugh, tickle (*infml*), crease (*infml*), slay (*infml*), cheer (up), gladden, enliven, please, charm, delight, enthral, engross, absorb, interest, occupy, recreate, relax.
Ea bore, displease.

amusement *n* entertainment, diversion, distraction, fun, enjoyment, pleasure, delight, merriment, mirth, hilarity, laughter, joke, prank, game, sport, recreation, hobby, pastime, interest.
Ea boredom, monotony.

amusing *adj* funny, humorous, hilarious, comical, laughable, ludicrous, droll, witty, facetious, jocular, jolly, enjoyable, pleasant, charming, delightful, entertaining, interesting.
Ea dull, boring.

anaemic *adj* bloodless, ashen, chalky, livid, pasty, pallid, sallow, whey-faced, pale, wan, colourless, insipid, weak, feeble, ineffectual, enervated, frail, infirm, sickly.
Ea ruddy, sanguine, full-blooded.

anaesthetic *n* painkiller, sedative, analgesic, anodyne, narcotic, opiate, palliative, soporific, epidural, stupefacient, stupefactive, premedication, local anaesthetic, general anaesthetic.

anaesthetize *v* desensitize, numb, deaden, dull, drug, dope, stupefy.

analogous *adj* comparable, similar, like, resembling, matching, kindred, parallel, corresponding, equivalent, relative, correlative, agreeing.
Ea disparate.

analogy *n* comparison, simile, metaphor, likeness, resemblance, similarity, parallel, correspondence, equivalence, relation, correlation, agreement.

analyse *v* break down, separate, divide, take apart, dissect, anatomize, reduce, resolve, sift, investigate, study, examine, scrutinize, review, interpret, test, judge, evaluate, estimate, consider.

analysis *n* breakdown, separation, division, dissection, reduction, resolution, sifting, investigation, enquiry, study, examination, scrutiny, review, exposition, explication, explanation, interpretation, test, judgement, opinion, evaluation, estimation, reasoning.
Ea synthesis.

analytical *adj* analytic, dissecting, detailed, in-depth, searching, critical, questioning, enquiring, inquisitive, investigative, diagnostic, systematic,

methodical, logical, rational, interpretative, explanatory, expository, studious.

anarchic *adj* lawless, ungoverned, anarchistic, libertarian, nihilist, revolutionary, rebellious, mutinous, riotous, chaotic, disordered, confused, disorganized.
Ea submissive, orderly.

anarchist *n* revolutionary, rebel, insurgent, libertarian, nihilist, terrorist.

anarchy *n* lawlessness, unrule, misrule, anarchism, revolution, rebellion, insurrection, mutiny, riot, pandemonium, chaos, disorder, confusion.
Ea rule, control, order.

anathema *n* aversion, abhorrence, abomination, object of loathing, bête noire, bugbear, bane, curse, proscription, taboo.

anatomy

> Anatomical terms include: aural, biceps, bone, cardiac, cartilage, cerebral, dental, diaphragm, dorsal, duodenal, elbow, epidermis, epiglottis, Fallopian tubes, foreskin, funny bone, gastric, genitalia, gingival, gristle, groin, gullet, hamstring, helix, hepatic, hock, intercostal, jugular, lachrymal, ligament, lumbar, mammary, membral, muscle, nasal, neural, ocular, oesophagus, optical, pectoral, pedal, pulmonary, renal, spine, tendon, triceps, umbilicus, uterus, uvula, voice-box, vulva, windpipe, wisdom tooth, womb. *see also* **bone**.

ancestor *n* forebear, forefather, progenitor, predecessor, forerunner, precursor, antecedent.
Ea descendant.

ancestral *adj* familial, parental, genealogical, lineal, hereditary, genetic.

ancestry *n* ancestors, forebears, forefathers, progenitors, parentage, family, lineage, line, descent, blood, race, stock, roots, pedigree, genealogy, extraction, derivation, origin, heritage, heredity.

anchor *v* moor, berth, tie up, make fast, fasten, attach, affix, fix.

> Types of anchor include: car, double fluked, grapnel, kedge, killick, mushroom, navy, sea, stocked, stockless, yachtsman.

ancient *adj* **1** OLD, aged, time-worn, age-old, antique, antediluvian, prehistoric, fossilized, primeval, immemorial. **2**

OLD-FASHIONED, out-of-date, antiquated, archaic, obsolete, bygone, early, original. **E3 1** recent, contemporary. **2** modern, up-to-date.

ancillary *adj* auxiliary, supporting, helping, accessory, contributory, extra, secondary, subordinate, additional, subsidiary, supplementary, adjuvant (*fml*), adminicular (*fml*).

and *conj* also, too, together (with), besides, as well (as), in addition (to), plus, including, furthermore, moreover, by the way, then, what's more (*infml*).

anecdote *n* story, tale, yarn, sketch, reminiscence.

anew *adv* afresh, again, once again, once more.

angel *n* **1** *angel of God*: archangel, cherub, seraph, divine messenger, principality. **2** DARLING, treasure, saint, paragon, ideal. **E3 1** devil, fiend.

The nine orders of angels are: seraph, cherub, throne, domination/dominion, virtue, power, principality, archangel, angel.

angelic *adj* cherubic, seraphic, celestial, heavenly, divine, holy, pious, saintly, pure, innocent, unworldly, virtuous, lovely, beautiful, adorable.
E3 devilish, fiendish.

anger *n* annoyance, irritation, antagonism, displeasure, irritability, temper, pique, vexation, ire, rage, fury, wrath, exasperation, outrage, indignation, gall, bitterness, rancour, resentment.
E3 forgiveness, forbearance.
➤ *v* annoy, irritate, aggravate (*infml*), wind up (*infml*), vex, irk, rile, miff (*infml*), needle, nettle, bother, ruffle, provoke, antagonize, offend, affront, gall, madden, enrage, incense, infuriate, exasperate, outrage.
E3 please, appease, calm.

angle *n* **1** CORNER, nook, bend, flexure, hook, crook, elbow, knee, crotch, edge, point. **2** ASPECT, outlook, facet, side, approach, direction, position, standpoint, viewpoint, point of view, slant, perspective.

angry *adj* annoyed, cross, irritated, aggravated (*infml*), displeased, uptight (*infml*), irate, mad (*infml*), enraged, incensed, infuriated, furious, raging, passionate, heated, hot, exasperated, outraged, indignant, bitter, resentful.
E3 content, happy, calm.

Informal ways of expressing becoming angry and losing one's temper include: blow up, blow a fuse, blow a gasket, blow one's cool, blow one's stack, blow one's top, boil over, burst a blood vessel, do one's nut, explode, flip one's lid, fly into a rage, fly off the handle, go mad, go off the deep end, go up the wall, hit the ceiling, hit the roof, lose one's cool, lose one's patience, lose one's rag, raise Cain, raise hell, see red, throw a tantrum, throw a wobbly, foam at the mouth, get all steamed up, go ape (*US*), go ballistic, lose one's marbles.

anguish *n* agony, anxiety, desolation, distress, suffering, torment, torture, grief, heartache, heartbreak, misery, pain, pang, rack, sorrow, tribulation, woe, wretchedness.
E3 happiness, solace.

anguished *adj* afflicted, tormented, stressed, distressed, harrowed, miserable, stricken, suffering, tortured, wretched, sick (*infml*), gutted (*sl*).

angular *adj* bony, thin, gaunt, gawky, lank, lanky, lean, rawboned, scrawny, skinny, spare.

animal *n* creature, mammal, beast, brute, barbarian, savage, monster, cur, pig, swine.

Animals include: cat, dog, hamster, gerbil, mouse, rat, rabbit, hare, fox, badger, beaver, mole, otter, weasel, ferret, ermine, mink, hedgehog, squirrel, horse, pig, cow, bull, goat, sheep; monkey, lemur, gibbon, ape, chimpanzee, orang-utan, baboon, gorilla; seal, sea lion, dolphin, walrus, whale; lion, tiger, cheetah, puma, panther, cougar, jaguar, ocelot, leopard; aardvark, armadillo, wolf, wolverine, hyena, mongoose, skunk, racoon, wombat, platypus, koala, polecat; deer, antelope, gazelle, eland, impala, reindeer, elk, caribou, moose, wallaby, kangaroo, bison, buffalo, gnu, camel, zebra, llama, panda, giant panda, grizzly bear, polar bear, giraffe, hippopotamus, rhinoceros, elephant. *see also* **amphibian**; **bird**; **butterflies and moths**; **cat**; **cattle**; **dog**; **fish**; **horse**; **insect**; **invertebrate**; **mammal**; **marsupial**; **mollusc**; **monkey**; **reptile**; **rodent**. *see also* **collective nouns**; **sound**[1].

➤ *adj* bestial, brutish, inhuman, savage, wild, instinctive, bodily, physical, carnal, fleshly, sensual.

animate *adj* alive, living, live, breathing, conscious.
🔁 inanimate.

animated *adj* lively, spirited, buoyant, vibrant, ebullient, vivacious, alive, vital, quick, brisk, vigorous, energetic, active, passionate, impassioned, vehement, ardent, fervent, glowing, radiant, excited, enthusiastic, eager.
🔁 lethargic, sluggish, inert.

animation *n* liveliness, spirit, action, activity, ebullience, passion, elation, energy, enthusiasm, excitement, exhilaration, fervour, high spirits, life, radiance, sparkle, sprightliness, verve, vibrancy, vigour, vitality, zeal, zest, pep (*infml*), zing (*infml*).
🔁 dullness, inertia.

animosity *n* ill feeling, ill-will, acrimony, bitterness, rancour, resentment, spite, malice, malignity, malevolence, hate, hatred, loathing, antagonism, hostility, enmity, feud.
🔁 goodwill.

annals *n* archives, chronicles, records, registers, history, journals, memoirs, reports.

annex *v* **1** ADD, append, affix, attach, fasten, adjoin, join, connect, unite, incorporate. **2** ACQUIRE, appropriate, seize, usurp, occupy, conquer, take over.

annexation *n* seizure, appropriation, acquisition, usurping, occupation, conquest, takeover, arrogation (*fml*).

annexe *n* wing, extension, attachment, addition, supplement, expansion.

annihilate *v* eliminate, eradicate, obliterate, erase, wipe out, liquidate (*infml*), murder, assassinate, exterminate, extinguish, raze, destroy, abolish.

anniversary

Names of wedding anniversaries include: 1st cotton, 2nd paper, 3rd leather, 4th flowers/fruit, 5th wood, 6th iron/sugar, 7th copper/wool, 8th bronze/pottery, 9th pottery/willow, 10th tin, 11th steel, 12th silk/linen, 13th lace, 14th ivory, 15th crystal, 20th china, 25th silver, 30th pearl, 35th coral, 40th ruby, 45th sapphire, 50th gold, 55th emerald, 60th diamond, 70th platinum.

annotate *v* note, gloss, comment, explain, interpret, elucidate, marginalize (*fml*), explicate (*fml*).

annotation *n* note, footnote, gloss, comment, commentary, exegesis, explanation, elucidation.

announce *v* declare, proclaim, report, state, reveal, disclose, divulge, make known, notify, intimate, promulgate, propound, publish, broadcast, advertise, publicize, blazon.
🔁 suppress.

announcement *n* declaration, proclamation, report, statement, communiqué, dispatch, bulletin, notification, intimation, revelation, disclosure, divulgence, publication, broadcast, advertisement.

announcer *n* broadcaster, newscaster, newsreader, commentator, compère, master of ceremonies, MC, town crier, herald, messenger.

annoy *v* irritate, rile, aggravate (*infml*), displease, anger, vex, irk, madden, exasperate, tease, provoke, ruffle, trouble, disturb, bother, pester, plague, harass, molest.
🔁 please, gratify, comfort.

annoyance *n* **1** NUISANCE, pest, disturbance, bother, trouble, bore, bind (*sl*), pain (*infml*), headache (*infml*), tease, provocation. **2** *express one's annoyance*: irritation, aggravation (*infml*), displeasure, anger, vexation, exasperation, harassment.
🔁 **2** pleasure.

annoyed *adj* irritated, cross, displeased, angry, vexed, piqued, exasperated, provoked, harassed.
🔁 pleased.

annoying *adj* irritating, aggravating (*infml*), vexatious, irksome, troublesome, bothersome, tiresome, trying, maddening, exasperating, galling, offensive, teasing, provoking, harassing.
🔁 pleasing, welcome.

annual *n* yearbook, almanac, calendar, register.
➤ *adj* yearly.

annul *v* nullify, invalidate, void, rescind, abrogate, suspend, cancel, abolish, quash, repeal, revoke, countermand, negate, retract, recall, reverse.
🔁 enact, restore.

anodyne *adj* bland, inoffensive, neutral, deadening.

anoint *v* **1** OIL, grease, lubricate, embrocate, rub, smear, daub. **2** BLESS, consecrate, sanctify, dedicate.

anomalous *adj* abnormal, atypical, exceptional, irregular, inconsistent, incongruous, deviant, freakish, eccentric, peculiar, odd, unusual, singular, rare.
Ea normal, regular, ordinary.

anomaly *n* abnormality, exception, irregularity, inconsistency, incongruity, aberration, deviation, divergence, departure, freak, misfit, eccentricity, peculiarity, oddity, rarity.

anonymous *adj* unnamed, nameless, unsigned, unacknowledged, unspecified, unidentified, unknown, incognito, faceless, impersonal, nondescript, unexceptional.
Ea named, signed, identifiable, distinctive.

answer *n* 1 REPLY, acknowledgement, response, reaction, rejoinder, retort, riposte, comeback, retaliation, rebuttal, vindication, defence, plea. 2 SOLUTION, explanation.
➤ *v* 1 REPLY, acknowledge, respond, react, retort, retaliate, refute, solve. 2 *answer one's needs*: fulfil, fill, meet, satisfy, match up to, correspond, correlate, conform, agree, fit, suit, serve, pass.
◆ **answer back** talk back, retort, riposte, retaliate, contradict, disagree, argue, dispute, rebut.
◆ **answer for 1** *answer for her loyalty*: vouch for, be responsible for, be liable for, speak for. 2 *answer for the crimes*: pay for, be punished for.

answerable *adj* liable, responsible, accountable, chargeable, blameworthy, to blame.

antagonism *n* hostility, opposition, rivalry, antipathy, ill feeling, ill-will, animosity, friction, discord, dissension, contention, conflict.
Ea rapport, sympathy, agreement.

antagonist *n* opponent, adversary, enemy, foe, rival, competitor, contestant, contender.
Ea ally, supporter.

antagonistic *adj* conflicting, opposed, adverse, at variance, incompatible, hostile, belligerent, contentious, unfriendly, ill-disposed, averse.
Ea sympathetic, friendly.

antagonize *v* alienate, estrange, disaffect, repel, embitter, offend, insult, provoke, annoy, irritate, anger, incense.
Ea disarm.

antecedent *n* 1 *antecedents of the aeroplane*: precursor, forerunner, precedent. 2 *with Welsh antecedents*: ancestors, forebears, forefathers, extraction, genealogy.

anthem *n* hymn, song, chorale, psalm, canticle, chant.

anthology *n* selection, collection, compilation, compendium, digest, treasury, miscellany.

anticipate *v* 1 FORESTALL, pre-empt, intercept, prevent, obviate, preclude. 2 EXPECT, foresee, predict, forecast, look for, await, look forward to, hope for, bank on, count upon.

anticipation *n* 1 *in anticipation of the shortage*: expectation, preparation, prediction. 2 *eager anticipation*: excitement, expectancy, hope, bated breath (*infml*).

anticlimax *n* bathos, comedown, let-down, disappointment, fiasco.

antics *n* foolery, tomfoolery, silliness, buffoonery, clowning, frolics, capers, skylarking, playfulness, mischief, tricks, monkey-tricks, pranks, stunts, doings.

antidote *n* remedy, cure, counter-agent, antitoxin, neutralizer, countermeasure, corrective.

antipathy *n* aversion, dislike, hate, hatred, loathing, abhorrence, distaste, disgust, repulsion, antagonism, animosity, ill-will, bad blood, enmity, hostility, opposition, incompatibility.
Ea sympathy, affection, rapport.

antiquated *adj* obsolete, old-fashioned, outdated, outmoded, out-of-date, dated, bygone, anachronistic, ancient, antediluvian, archaic, démodé, fossilized, outworn, passé, on the way out (*infml*), old hat (*infml*).
Ea forward-looking, modern.

antique *adj* antiquarian, ancient, old, veteran, vintage, quaint, antiquated, old-fashioned, outdated, archaic, obsolete.
➤ *n* antiquity, relic, bygone, period piece, heirloom, curio, museum piece, curiosity, rarity.

antiquity *n* ancient times, time immemorial, distant past, olden days, age, old age, oldness, agedness.
Ea modernity, novelty.

antiseptic *adj* disinfectant, medicated, aseptic, germ-free, clean, pure,

unpolluted, uncontaminated, sterile, sterilized, sanitized, sanitary, hygienic.
➢ *n* disinfectant, germicide, bactericide, purifier, cleanser.

antisocial *adj* asocial, unacceptable, disruptive, disorderly, rebellious, belligerent, antagonistic, hostile, unfriendly, unsociable, uncommunicative, reserved, retiring, withdrawn, alienated, unapproachable.
⊟ sociable, gregarious.

antithesis *n* **1** OPPOSITE, converse, reverse, opposite extreme. **2** OPPOSITION, contrast, contradiction, reversal.

anxiety *n* worry, concern, care, distress, nervousness, apprehension, dread, foreboding, misgiving, uneasiness, restlessness, fretfulness, impatience, suspense, tension, stress.
⊟ calm, composure, serenity.

anxious *adj* worried, concerned, nervous, apprehensive, afraid, fearful, uneasy, restless, fretful, impatient, in suspense, on tenterhooks, tense, taut, distressed, disturbed, troubled, tormented, tortured.
⊟ calm, composed.

apart *adv* **1** SEPARATELY, independently, individually, singly, alone, on one's own, by oneself, privately, aside, to one side, away, afar, distant, aloof, excluded, isolated, cut off, separated: divorced, separate, distinct. **2** *tear apart*: to pieces, to bits, into parts, in pieces, in bits, piecemeal.
⊟ **1** connected. **2** together.

apathetic *adj* uninterested, uninvolved, indifferent, cool, unemotional, emotionless, impassive, unmoved, unconcerned, cold, unfeeling, numb, unresponsive, passive, listless, unambitious.
⊟ enthusiastic, involved, concerned, feeling, responsive.

apathy *n* uninterestedness, indifference, coolness, impassivity, unconcern, coldness, insensibility, passivity, listlessness, lethargy, sluggishness, torpor, inertia.
⊟ enthusiasm, interest, concern.

ape *v* copy, imitate, echo, mirror, parrot, mimic, take off, caricature, parody, mock, counterfeit, affect.
➢ *n* monkey, chimpanzee, gibbon, gorilla, baboon, orang-utan.

aperture *n* gap, hole, opening, passage, perforation, breach, chink, cleft, crack,

eye, fissure, rent, slit, slot, space, vent, mouth, interstice (*fml*), orifice (*fml*).

apex *n* top, high point, peak, pinnacle, point, summit, tip, climax, consummation, crest, crown, crowning point, culmination, height, acme (*fml*), apogee (*fml*), vertex (*fml*), zenith (*fml*).
⊟ nadir.

aphorism *n* maxim, adage, axiom, dictum, maxim, precept, proverb, saw, saying, witticism, apophthegm (*fml*), epigram (*fml*), gnome (*fml*).

aphrodisiac *n* love potion, stimulant
➢ *adj* stimulant, erogenous, erotic.

aplomb *n* composure, calmness, equanimity, poise, balance, coolness, confidence, assurance, self-assurance, audacity.
⊟ discomposure.

apocryphal *adj* unauthenticated, unverified, unsubstantiated, unsupported, questionable, spurious, equivocal, doubtful, dubious, fabricated, concocted, fictitious, imaginary, legendary, mythical.
⊟ authentic, true.

apologetic *adj* sorry, repentant, penitent, contrite, remorseful, conscience-stricken, regretful, rueful.
⊟ unrepentant, impenitent, defiant.

apologize *v* say one is sorry, say sorry, regret, be apologetic, ask forgiveness, ask pardon, beg someone's pardon, acknowledge, confess, explain, justify, plead, swallow one's pride (*infml*), eat one's words (*infml*), eat humble pie (*infml*).

apology *n* acknowledgement, confession, excuse, explanation, justification, vindication, defence, plea.
⊟ defiance.

apostle *n* **1** *Jesus Christ's apostles*: disciple, messenger, evangelist, preacher, missionary, reformer, proselytizer. **2** *apostles of a united Europe*: advocate, champion, supporter, crusader, pioneer, proponent.

appal *v* horrify, shock, outrage, disgust, dismay, disconcert, daunt, intimidate, unnerve, alarm, scare, frighten, terrify.
⊟ reassure, encourage.

appalling *adj* horrifying, horrific, harrowing, shocking, outrageous, atrocious, disgusting, awful, dreadful, frightful, terrible, dire, grim, hideous, ghastly, horrible, horrid, loathsome, daunting, intimidating, unnerving,

alarming, frightening, terrifying.
☒ reassuring, encouraging.

apparatus *n* machine, appliance, gadget, device, contraption, equipment, gear, tackle, outfit, tools, implements, utensils, materials, machinery, system, mechanism, means.

apparent *adj* seeming, outward, visible, evident, noticeable, perceptible, plain, clear, distinct, marked, unmistakable, obvious, manifest, patent, open, declared.
☒ hidden, obscure.

apparently *adv* seemingly, ostensibly, outwardly, superficially, plainly, clearly, obviously, manifestly, patently.

apparition *n* ghost, spectre, phantom, spirit, chimera, vision, manifestation, materialization, presence.

appeal *n* 1 REQUEST, application, petition, suit, solicitation, plea, entreaty, supplication, prayer, invocation. 2 ATTRACTION, allure, interest, fascination, enchantment, charm, attractiveness, winsomeness, beauty, charisma, magnetism.
➤ *v* 1 *appeal for help*: ask, request, call, apply, address, petition, sue, solicit, plead, beg, beseech, implore, entreat, supplicate, pray, invoke, call upon. 2 ATTRACT, draw, allure, lure, tempt, entice, invite, interest, engage, fascinate, charm, please.

appear *v* 1 ARRIVE, enter, turn up, attend, materialize, develop, show (up), come into sight, come into view, loom, rise, surface, arise, occur, crop up, come to light, come out, emerge, issue, be published. 2 SEEM, look, turn out. 3 *appear in a show*: act, perform, play, take part.
☒ 1 disappear, vanish.

appearance *n* 1 APPEARING, arrival, advent, coming, rise, emergence, début, introduction. 2 LOOK, expression, face, aspect, air, bearing, demeanour, manner, looks, figure, form, semblance, show, front, guise, illusion, impression, image.
☒ 1 disappearance.

Expressions used when talking about someone's appearance include: a sight for sore eyes, as ugly as sin, beauty is in the eye of the beholder, beauty is only skin deep, cut a dash, done up like a dog's dinner, dressed up to the nines, easy on the eye, like something the cat brought in, look like a million dollars, look like nothing on earth, look the part, look one's best, mutton dressed as lamb, no oil painting, not a hair out of place, not much to look at, pretty as a picture.

appease *v* placate, pacify, reconcile, satisfy, mitigate, make peace with, conciliate, propitiate.
☒ aggravate.

appendix *n* addition, appendage, adjunct, addendum, supplement, epilogue, codicil, postscript, rider.

appetite *n* hunger, stomach, relish, zest, taste, propensity, inclination, liking, desire, longing, yearning, craving, eagerness, passion, zeal.
☒ distaste.

appetizing *adj* mouthwatering, tempting, inviting, appealing, palatable, tasty, delicious, scrumptious (*infml*), succulent, piquant, savoury.
☒ disgusting, distasteful.

applaud *v* clap, cheer, acclaim, compliment, congratulate, approve, commend, praise, laud, eulogize, extol.
☒ criticize, censure.

applause *n* ovation, clapping, cheering, cheers, acclaim, acclamation, accolade, congratulation, approval, commendation, praise.
☒ criticism, censure.

appliance *n* machine, device, contrivance, contraption, gadget, tool, implement, instrument, apparatus, mechanism.

applicable *adj* relevant, pertinent, apposite, apt, appropriate, fitting, suited, useful, suitable, fit, proper, valid, legitimate.
☒ inapplicable, inappropriate.

applicant *n* candidate, interviewee, contestant, competitor, aspirant, suitor, petitioner, inquirer.

application *n* 1 REQUEST, appeal, petition, suit, claim, inquiry. 2 RELEVANCE, pertinence, function, purpose, use, value. 3 DILIGENCE, industry, assiduity, effort, commitment, dedication, perseverance, keenness, attentiveness.

apply *v* 1 REQUEST, ask for, requisition, put in for, appeal, petition, solicit, sue, claim, inquire. 2 *apply oneself to a task*: address, buckle down, settle down, commit, devote, dedicate, give, direct, concentrate, study, persevere. **3** USE, exercise, utilize, employ, bring into play, engage, harness, ply, wield, administer, execute, implement, assign, direct, bring to bear, practise, resort to. **4** REFER, relate, be relevant, pertain, fit, suit. **5** *apply ointment*: put on, spread on, lay on, cover with, paint, anoint, smear, rub.

appoint *v* **1** NAME, nominate, elect, install, choose, select, engage, employ, take on, commission, delegate, assign, allot, designate, command, direct, charge, detail. **2** DECIDE, determine, arrange, settle, fix, set, establish, ordain, decree, destine.
✏ **1** reject, dismiss, discharge.

appointment *n* **1** ARRANGEMENT, engagement, date, meeting, rendezvous, interview, consultation. **2** JOB, position, situation, post, office, place. **3** NAMING, nomination, election, choosing, choice, selection, commissioning, delegation.

apportion *v* assign, allocate, allot, distribute, divide, dispense, deal (out), hand out, grant, measure out, mete (out), ration (out), share (out), dole out (*infml*).

apposite *adj* relevant, applicable, appropriate, apt, germane, suitable, suited, to the point, to the purpose, pertinent (*fml*), apropos (*fml*), befitting (*fml*).
✏ inapposite.

appraisal *n* valuation, rating, survey, inspection, review, examination, once-over (*infml*), evaluation, assessment, estimate, estimation, judgement, reckoning, opinion, appreciation.

appreciable *adj* noticeable, significant, considerable, substantial, definite, perceptible, discernible, recognizable.
✏ insignificant, imperceptible, negligible.

appreciate *v* **1** ENJOY, relish, savour, prize, treasure, value, cherish, admire, respect, regard, esteem, like, welcome, take kindly to. **2** *appreciate in value*: grow, increase, rise, mount, inflate, gain, strengthen, improve, enhance. **3** UNDERSTAND, comprehend, perceive, realize, recognize, acknowledge, sympathize with, know.
✏ **1** despise. **2** depreciate. **3** overlook.

appreciation *n* **1** ENJOYMENT, relish, admiration, respect, regard, esteem, gratitude, gratefulness, thankfulness, indebtedness, obligation, liking, sensitivity, responsiveness, valuation, assessment, estimation, judgement. **2** GROWTH, increase, rise, inflation, gain, improvement, enhancement. **3** UNDERSTANDING,

comprehension, perception, awareness, realization, recognition, acknowledgement, sympathy, knowledge.
✏ **1** ingratitude. **2** depreciation.

appreciative *adj* **1** GRATEFUL, thankful, obliged, indebted, pleased. **2** ADMIRING, encouraging, enthusiastic, respectful, sensitive, responsive, perceptive, knowledgeable, conscious, mindful.
✏ **1** ungrateful.

apprehend *v* **1** CATCH, arrest, capture, detain, seize, bust (*infml*), nick (*infml*), collar (*infml*), grab (*infml*), nab (*infml*), run in (*infml*). **2** UNDERSTAND, comprehend, grasp, believe, conceive, perceive, realize, recognize, see, twig (*infml*).

apprehension *n* dread, foreboding, misgiving, qualm, uneasiness, anxiety, worry, concern, disquiet, alarm, fear, doubt, suspicion, mistrust.

apprehensive *adj* nervous, anxious, worried, concerned, uneasy, doubtful, suspicious, mistrustful, distrustful, alarmed, afraid.
✏ assured, confident.

apprentice *n* trainee, probationer, student, pupil, learner, novice, beginner, starter, recruit, newcomer.
✏ expert.

approach *v* **1** ADVANCE, move towards, draw near, near, gain on, catch up, reach, meet. **2** APPLY TO, appeal to, sound out. **3** BEGIN, commence, set about, undertake, introduce, mention. **4** RESEMBLE, be like, compare with, approximate, come close.
➤ *n* **1** *the approach of winter*: advance, coming, advent, arrival. **2** ACCESS, road, avenue, way, passage, entrance, doorway, threshold. **3** APPLICATION, appeal, overture, proposition, proposal. **4** ATTITUDE, manner, style, technique, procedure, method, means.

approachable *adj* **1** FRIENDLY, easy to get on/along with, sociable, congenial, warm, affable, agreeable, open, informal. **2** ACCESSIBLE, attainable, reachable, get-at-able (*infml*).
✏ **1** aloof, unapproachable. **2** inaccessible, remote.

appropriate *adj* applicable, relevant, pertinent, to the point, well-chosen, apt, fitting, meet (*fml*), suitable, fit, befitting, becoming, proper, right, correct, spot-on (*infml*), well-timed, timely, seasonable, opportune.

◼ inappropriate, irrelevant, unsuitable.
➤ *v* **1** SEIZE, take, expropriate, commandeer, requisition, confiscate, impound, assume, usurp. **2** STEAL, pocket, filch, pilfer, purloin, embezzle, misappropriate.

approval *n* **1** ADMIRATION, esteem, regard, respect, good opinion, liking, appreciation, approbation, favour, recommendation, praise, commendation, acclaim, acclamation, honour, applause. **2** AGREEMENT, concurrence, assent, consent, permission, leave, sanction, authorization, licence, mandate, go-ahead, green light (*infml*), blessing, OK (*infml*), certification, ratification, validation, confirmation, support.
◼ **1** disapproval, condemnation.

approve *v* **1** ADMIRE, esteem, regard, like, appreciate, favour, recommend, praise, commend, acclaim, applaud. **2** *approve a proposal*: agree to, assent to, consent to, accede to, allow, permit, pass, sanction, authorize, mandate, bless, countenance, OK (*infml*), ratify, rubber-stamp (*infml*), validate, endorse, support, uphold, second, back, accept, adopt, confirm.
◼ **1** disapprove, condemn.

approximate *adj* estimated, guessed, rough, inexact, loose, close, near, like, similar, relative.
◼ exact.
➤ *v* approach, border on, verge on, be tantamount to, resemble.

approximately *adv* roughly, around, about, circa, more or less, loosely, approaching, close to, nearly, just about.

approximation *n* **1** ESTIMATE, rough calculation, rough idea, guess, conjecture, guesstimate (*infml*), ballpark figure (*infml*). **2** *an approximation to a dress*: semblance, likeness, resemblance, correspondence.

apt *adj* **1** RELEVANT, applicable, apposite, appropriate, fitting, suitable, fit, seemly, proper, correct, accurate, spot-on (*infml*), timely, seasonable. **2** CLEVER, gifted, talented, skilful, expert, intelligent, quick, sharp. **3** LIABLE, prone, given, disposed, likely, ready.
◼ **1** inapt. **2** stupid.

aptitude *n* ability, capability, capacity, faculty, gift, talent, flair, facility, proficiency, cleverness, intelligence, quickness, bent, inclination, leaning, disposition, tendency.
◼ inaptitude.

arable *adj* cultivable, ploughable, tillable, fertile, productive, fruitful, fecund (*fml*).

arachnid *see* insect.

arbiter *n* **1** ADJUDICATOR, judge, referee, umpire. **2** *an arbiter of style*: authority, expert, pundit, master, controller.

arbitrary *adj* **1** RANDOM, chance, capricious, inconsistent, discretionary, subjective, instinctive, unreasoned, illogical, irrational, unreasonable. **2** DESPOTIC, tyrannical, dictatorial, autocratic, absolute, imperious, magisterial, domineering, overbearing, high-handed, dogmatic.
◼ **1** reasoned, rational, circumspect.

arbitrate *v* judge, adjudicate, referee, umpire, mediate, settle, decide, determine.

arbitration *n* judgement, adjudication, intervention, mediation, negotiation, settlement, decision, determination.

arbitrator *n* judge, adjudicator, arbiter, referee, umpire, moderator, mediator, negotiator, intermediary, go-between.

arc *n* curve, curved line, bend, arch, bow, curvature, semicircle.

arcade *n* gallery, cloister, colonnade, covered way, mall, piazza, portico, precinct, shopping mall, shopping precinct, loggia (*fml*).

arch *n* archway, bridge, span, dome, vault, concave, bend, curve, curvature, bow, arc, semicircle.
➤ *v* bend, curve, bow, arc, vault, camber.

Types of arch include: basket handle, convex, corbel, equilateral, four-centre, Gothic, horseshoe, keel, lancet, Norman, ogee, parabolic, round, segmental, shouldered, skew, stilted, tented, trefoil, Tudor.

archaeology

Archaeological terms include: agger, amphitheatre, amphora, artefact, barrow, beaker, blade, bogman, bowl, bracteate, burin, cairn, cartouche, cave art/rock art, cist, cromlech, cup, dolmen, earthwork, eolith, flake, flask, flint, handaxe, henge, hieroglyph, hill fort, hoard, hypocaust, incised decoration, jar, jug, kitchen-midden, kurgan, ley lines, loom weight, lynchet, megalith, microlith, mosaic, mound, mummy, neolith, obelisk, palmette, palstave, papyrus, rock shelter, sondage, spindle, stele, stone circle, tell, tumulus, urn, vallum, whorl.

archaic *adj* antiquated, old-fashioned, outmoded, old hat (*infml*), passé, outdated, out-of-date, obsolete, old, ancient, antique, quaint, primitive.
🔳 modern, recent.

archetype *n* pattern, model, standard, form, type, prototype, original, precursor, classic, paradigm, ideal.

architect *n* designer, planner, master builder, prime mover, originator, founder, instigator, creator, author, inventor, engineer, maker, constructor, shaper.

architecture and building

Architectural and building terms include: alcove, annexe, architrave, baluster, barge-board, baroque, bas relief, capstone, casement window, classical, coping stone, Corinthian, corner-stone, cornice, coving, dado, decorated, dogtooth, dome, Doric, dormer, double-glazing, drawbridge, dry-stone, duplex, Early English, eaves, Edwardian, elevation, Elizabethan, façade, fanlight, fascia, festoon, fillet, finial, flamboyant, Flemish bond, fletton, fluting, French window, frieze, frontispiece, gable, gargoyle, gatehouse, Georgian, Gothic, groin, groundplan, half-timbered, Ionic, jamb, lintel, mullion, Norman, pagoda, pantile, parapet, pinnacle, plinth, Queen-Anne, rafters, Regency, reveal, ridge, rococo, Romanesque, roof, rotunda, roughcast, sacristy, scroll, soffit, stucco, terrazzo, Tudor, Tuscan, wainscot, weathering. *see also* **wall**.

archives *n* records, annals, chronicles, memorials, papers, documents, deeds, ledgers, registers, roll.

arctic *adj* **1** *the Arctic Ocean*: polar, far north. **2** *arctic weather*: freezing, freezing cold, bitterly cold, frozen, glacial, subzero.
🔳 **1** Antarctic.

ardent *adj* fervent, fiery, warm, passionate, impassioned, fierce, vehement, intense, spirited, enthusiastic, eager, keen, dedicated, devoted, zealous.
🔳 apathetic, unenthusiastic.

arduous *adj* hard, difficult, tough, rigorous, severe, harsh, formidable, strenuous, tiring, taxing, fatiguing, exhausting, backbreaking, punishing, gruelling, uphill, laborious, onerous.
🔳 easy.

area *n* locality, neighbourhood, environment, environs, patch, terrain, district, region, zone, sector, department, province, domain, realm, territory, sphere, field, range, scope, compass, size, extent, expanse, width, breadth, stretch, tract, part, portion, section.

arena *n* **1** STADIUM, field, ground, bowl, ring, area, amphitheatre, coliseum, hippodrome. **2** *the political arena*: sphere, scene, domain, world, realm, department, province, battlefield, battleground, area of conflict.

argue *v* **1** QUARREL, squabble, bicker, row, wrangle, haggle, remonstrate, join issue, fight, feud, fall out, disagree, dispute, question, debate, discuss. **2** REASON, assert, contend, hold, maintain, claim, plead, exhibit, display, show, manifest, demonstrate, indicate, denote, prove, evidence, suggest, imply.

argument *n* **1** QUARREL, squabble, row, wrangle, controversy, debate, discussion, dispute, disagreement, clash, conflict, fight, feud. **2** REASONING, reason, logic, assertion, contention, claim, demonstration, defence, case, synopsis, summary, theme.

argumentative *adj* quarrelsome, contentious, polemical, opinionated, belligerent, perverse, contrary.
🔳 complaisant.

arid *adj* **1** *arid landscape*: dry, parched, waterless, desiccated, torrid, barren, infertile, unproductive, desert, waste. **2** DULL, uninteresting, boring, monotonous, tedious, dry, sterile, dreary, colourless, lifeless, spiritless, uninspired.
🔳 **1** fertile. **2** lively.

arise *v* **1** ORIGINATE, begin, start, commence, derive, stem, spring, proceed, flow, emerge, issue, appear, come to light, crop up, occur, happen, result, ensue, follow. **2** RISE, get up, stand up, go up, ascend, climb, mount, lift, soar, tower.

aristocracy *n* upper class, gentry, nobility, peerage, ruling class, gentility, elite.
🔳 common people.

aristocrat *n* noble, patrician, nobleman, noblewoman, peer, peeress, lord, lady.
🔳 commoner.

aristocratic *adj* upper-class, highborn, well-born, noble, patrician, blue-blooded, titled, lordly, courtly, gentle, thoroughbred, elite.
🔳 plebeian, vulgar.

arm[1] *n* limb, upper limb, appendage, bough, branch, projection, extension, offshoot, section, division, detachment, department.

arm² *v* provide, supply, furnish, issue, equip, rig, outfit, ammunition, prime, prepare, forearm, gird, steel, brace, reinforce, strengthen, fortify, protect.

armed services

> Units in the armed services include: task-force, militia, garrison; *air force*: wing, squadron, flight; *army*: patrol, troop, corps, platoon, squad, battery, company, brigade, battalion, regiment; *marines*: Royal Marines, commandos; *navy*: fleet, flotilla, squadron, convoy. *see also* **rank¹**.

armour *n* protective covering, panoply, mail, chain mail, iron-cladding.

> Pieces of armour include: beaver, besageur, brassard, breastplate, casque, chamfron, coudière, coutère, cubitière, cuirass, cuish, cuissard, cuissart, cuisse, épaulière, flanchard, gauntlet, genouillère, gorget, greave, habergeon, haubergeon, helmet, jambeau, knee piece, morion, neck guard, pallette, panache, pauldron, pavais, pavis, pavise, poitrel, poleyn, rear brace, rerebrace, sabaton, sabbaton, skull, solleret, suit of armour, taces, tasse, tasset, throat piece, vambrace, ventail, visor.

armoured *adj* armour-plated, steel-plated, iron-clad, reinforced, protected, bullet-proof, bomb-proof.

armoury *n* arsenal, ordnance depot, ammunition dump, magazine, depot, repository, stock, stockpile.

arms *n* **1** WEAPONS, weaponry, firearms, guns, artillery, instruments of war, armaments, ordnance, munitions, ammunition. **2** COAT-OF-ARMS, armorial bearings, insignia, heraldic device, escutcheon, shield, crest, heraldry, blazonry.

army *n* armed force, military, militia, land forces, soldiers, troops, legions, cohorts, multitude, throng, host, horde.

aroma *n* smell, odour, scent, perfume, fragrance, bouquet, savour.

aromatic *adj* perfumed, fragrant, sweet-smelling, balmy, redolent, savoury, spicy, pungent.

around *prep* **1** SURROUNDING, round, encircling, encompassing, enclosing, on all sides of, on every side of. **2** *around a dozen*: approximately, roughly, about, circa, more or less.

➢ *adv* **1** EVERYWHERE, all over, in all directions, on all sides, about, here and there, to and fro. **2** CLOSE, close by, near, nearby, at hand.

arouse *v* rouse, startle, wake up, waken, awaken, instigate, summon up, call forth, spark, kindle, inflame, whet, sharpen, quicken, animate, excite, prompt, provoke, stimulate, galvanize, goad, spur, incite, agitate, stir up, whip up.

☒ calm, lull, quieten.

arrange *v* **1** ORDER, tidy, range, array, marshal, dispose, distribute, position, set out, lay out, align, group, class, classify, categorize, sort (out), sift, file, systematize, methodize, regulate, adjust. **2** ORGANIZE, co-ordinate, prepare, fix, plan, project, design, devise, contrive, determine, settle. **3** *arrange music*: adapt, set, score, orchestrate, instrument, harmonize.

☒ **1** untidy, disorganize, muddle.

arrangement *n* **1** ORDER, array, display, disposition, layout, line-up, grouping, classification, structure, system, method, set-up, organization, preparation, planning, plan, scheme, design, schedule. **2** AGREEMENT, settlement, contract, terms, compromise. **3** ADAPTATION, version, interpretation, setting, score, orchestration, instrumentation, harmonization.

array *n* ARRANGEMENT, display, show, exhibition, exposition, assortment, collection, assemblage, muster, order, formation, line-up, parade.

➢ *v* **1** ARRANGE, order, range, dispose, group, line up, align, draw up, marshal, assemble, muster, parade, display, show, exhibit. **2** CLOTHE, dress, robe, deck, adorn, decorate.

arrest *v* **1** *arrest a criminal*: capture, catch, seize, nick (*infml*), run in, apprehend, detain. **2** STOP, stem, check, restrain, inhibit, halt, interrupt, stall, delay, slow, retard, block, obstruct, impede, hinder.

arresting *adj* striking, amazing, surprising, stunning, extraordinary, impressive, remarkable, engaging, notable, noteworthy, conspicuous, noticeable, outstanding

☒ inconspicuous, unremarkable.

arrival *n* appearance, entrance, advent, coming, approach, occurrence.

☒ departure.

arrive *v* reach, get to, appear, materialize, turn up, show up (*infml*), roll up (*infml*), enter, come, occur, happen.
ᴇᴀ depart, leave.

arrogance *n* pride, conceit, boasting, haughtiness, vanity, superciliousness, disdain, scorn, contempt, superiority, egotism, condescension, lordliness, pomposity, high-handedness, imperiousness, self-importance, snobbishness, presumption, insolence, hubris (*fml*), nerve (*infml*).
ᴇᴀ humility, unassumingness, bashfulness.

arrogant *adj* haughty, supercilious, disdainful, scornful, contemptuous, superior, condescending, patronizing, high and mighty, lordly, overbearing, high-handed, imperious, self-important, presumptuous, assuming, insolent, proud, conceited, boastful.
ᴇᴀ humble, unassuming, bashful.

arrow *n* **1** *shoot with an arrow*: shaft, bolt, dart, flight. **2** *follow the arrows*: marker, indicator, pointer.

arsenal *n* armoury, ordnance depot, ammunition dump, magazine, (arms) depot, repository, stock, stockpile, garderobe.

art *n* **1** FINE ART, painting, sculpture, drawing, artwork, craft, artistry, draughtsmanship, craftsmanship. **2** SKILL, knack, technique, method, aptitude, facility, dexterity, finesse, ingenuity, mastery, expertise, profession, trade. **3** ARTFULNESS, cunning, craftiness, slyness, guile, deceit, trickery, astuteness, shrewdness.

Schools of art include: abstract, action painting, Aestheticism, Art Deco, Art Nouveau, Barbizon, Baroque, Bohemian, Byzantine, classical revival, classicism, Conceptual Art, Constructivism, Cubism, Dadaism, Etruscan art, Expressionism, Fauvism, Florentine, folk art, Futurism, Gothic, Hellenistic, Impressionism, junk art, Mannerism, medieval art, Minimal Art, Modernism, the Nabis, Naturalism, Neoclassicism, Neoexpressionism, Neoimpressionism, Neo-Plasticism, Op Art, plastic art, Pop Art, Postimpressionism, Post-Modernism, Purism, quattrocento, Realism, renaissance, Rococo, Romanesque, Romanticism, Suprematism, Surrealism, Symbolism, Venetian, Vorticism. *see also* **painting**; **picture**; **sculpture**.

Arts and crafts include: painting, oil painting, watercolour, fresco, portraiture, architecture, drawing, sketching, caricature, illustration; graphics, film, video; sculpture, modelling, woodcarving, woodcraft, marquetry, metalwork, enamelling, cloisonné, engraving, etching, pottery, ceramics, mosaic, jewellery, stained glass, photography, lithography, calligraphy, collage, origami, spinning, weaving, batik, silk-screen printing, needlework, tapestry, embroidery, patchwork, crochet, knitting. *see also* **embroidery**.

artful *adj* cunning, crafty, sly, foxy, wily, tricky, scheming, designing, deceitful, devious, subtle, sharp, shrewd, smart, clever, masterly, ingenious, resourceful, skilful, dexterous.
ᴇᴀ artless, naïve, ingenuous.

article *n* **1** *article in a magazine*: feature, report, story, account, piece, review, commentary, composition, essay, paper. **2** ITEM, thing, object, commodity, unit, part, constituent, piece, portion, division.

articulate *adj* distinct, well-spoken, clear, lucid, intelligible, comprehensible, understandable, coherent, fluent, vocal, expressive, meaningful.
ᴇᴀ inarticulate, incoherent.
➤ *v* say, utter, speak, talk, express, voice, vocalize, verbalize, state, pronounce, enunciate, breathe.

articulation *n* saying, utterance, speaking, talking, expression, voicing, vocalization, verbalization, pronunciation, enunciation, diction, delivery.

artifice *n* **1** TRICK, device, dodge, ruse, scheme, stratagem, strategy, subterfuge, tactic, wile, contrivance. **2** DECEIT, trickery, artfulness, deception, fraud, guile, craft, craftiness, cunning, slyness, subtlety, chicanery, cleverness.

artificial *adj* false, fake, bogus, counterfeit, spurious, phoney (*infml*), pseudo, specious, sham, insincere, assumed, affected, mannered, forced, contrived, made-up, feigned, pretended, simulated, imitation, mock, synthetic, plastic, man-made, manufactured, non-natural, unnatural.
ᴇᴀ genuine, true, real, natural.

artisan *n* craftsman, craftswoman, artificer, journeyman, expert, skilled worker, mechanic, technician.

artist

Types of artist include: architect, graphic designer, designer, draughtsman, draughtswoman, illustrator, cartoonist, photographer, printer, engraver, goldsmith, silversmith, blacksmith, carpenter, potter, weaver, sculptor, painter; craftsman, craftswoman, master.

artiste *n* performer, entertainer, variety artist, vaudevillian, comic, comedian, comedienne, player, trouper, actor, actress.

artistic *adj* aesthetic, ornamental, decorative, beautiful, exquisite, elegant, stylish, graceful, harmonious, sensitive, tasteful, refined, cultured, cultivated, skilled, talented, creative, imaginative, gifted.
Ea inelegant, tasteless.

artistry *n* craftsmanship, workmanship, skill, craft, talent, flair, brilliance, genius, finesse, style, mastery, expertise, proficiency, accomplishment, deftness, touch, sensitivity, creativity.
Ea ineptitude.

artless *adj* simple, natural, unpretentious, genuine, guileless, honest, ingenuous, sincere, straightforward, open, plain, pure, childlike, innocent, naïve, direct, frank, candid, true, trusting, unsophisticated, unwary, unworldly.
Ea artful, cunning.

as *conj, prep* **1** WHILE, when. **2** SUCH AS, for example, for instance, like, in the manner of. **3** BECAUSE, since, seeing that, considering that, inasmuch as, being.
◆ **as for** with reference to, as regards, with regard to, on the subject of, in connection with, in relation to, with relation to, with respect to.

ascend *v* rise, take off, lift off, go up, move up, slope upwards, climb, scale, mount, tower, float up, fly up, soar.
Ea descend, go down.

ascent *n* **1** ASCENDING, ascension, climb, climbing, scaling, escalation, rise, rising, mounting. **2** SLOPE, gradient, incline, ramp, hill, elevation. **3** *ascent to power*: rise, advance, progress.
Ea **1** descent.

ascertain *v* find out, learn, discover, determine, fix, establish, settle, locate, detect, identify, verify, confirm, make certain.

ascetic *adj* self-denying, self-disciplined, austere, abstemious, abstinent, self-controlled, stern, strict, severe, rigorous, harsh, plain, puritanical, Spartan.
➤ *n* hermit, recluse, solitary, anchorite, abstainer, celibate, monk, nun, puritan, fakir, dervish, yogi.

ascribe *v* attribute, credit, accredit, put down, assign, impute, charge, chalk up to.

ashamed *adj* sorry, apologetic, remorseful, contrite, guilty, conscience-stricken, sheepish, embarrassed, blushing, red-faced, mortified, humiliated, abashed, humbled, crestfallen, distressed, discomposed, confused, reluctant, hesitant, shy, self-conscious, bashful, modest, prudish.
Ea shameless, proud, defiant.

aside *adv* apart, on one side, in reserve, away, out of the way, separately, in isolation, alone, privately, secretly.
➤ *n* digression, parenthesis, departure, soliloquy, stage whisper, whisper.

ask *v* **1** REQUEST, appeal, petition, sue, plead, beg, entreat, implore, clamour, beseech, pray, supplicate, crave, demand, order, bid, require, seek, solicit, invite, summon. **2** INQUIRE, query, question, interrogate, quiz, press.

askance *adv* suspiciously, disapprovingly, contemptuously, scornfully, disdainfully, distrustfully, doubtfully, dubiously, mistrustfully, sceptically, indirectly, sideways, obliquely.

askew *adv, adj* crooked, lopsided, sideways, oblique, at an oblique angle, off-centre, out of line, asymmetric, crookedly, skew (*infml*), skew-whiff (*infml*).
Ea straight, level.

asleep *adj* sleeping, napping, snoozing, fast asleep, sound asleep, dormant, resting, inactive, inert, unconscious, numb, dozing.

aspect *n* angle, direction, elevation, side, facet, feature, face, expression, countenance, appearance, look, air, manner, bearing, attitude, condition, situation, position, standpoint, point of view, view, outlook, prospect, scene.

aspiration *n* aim, intent, purpose, endeavour, object, objective, goal, ambition, hope, dream, ideal, wish, desire, yearning, longing, craving, hankering.

aspire *v* aim, intend, purpose, seek,

pursue, hope, dream, wish, desire, yearn, long, crave, hanker.

aspiring *adj* would-be, aspirant, striving, endeavouring, ambitious, enterprising, keen, eager, hopeful, optimistic, wishful, longing.

assassin *n* murderer, killer, slayer, cut-throat, executioner, hatchet man (*infml*), gunman, hit man (*sl*), liquidator (*infml*).

assassinate *v* murder, kill, slay, dispatch, hit (*sl*), eliminate (*infml*), liquidate (*infml*).

assault *n* 1 ATTACK, offensive, onslaught, blitz, strike, raid, invasion, incursion, storm, storming, charge. 2 *charged with assault*: battery, grievous bodily harm, GBH (*infml*), mugging (*sl*), rape, abuse.
➤ *v* attack, charge, invade, strike, hit, set upon, fall on, beat up (*infml*), mug (*sl*), rape, molest, abuse.

assemble *v* 1 GATHER, congregate, muster, rally, convene, meet, join up, flock, group, collect, accumulate, amass, bring together, round up, marshal, mobilize. 2 CONSTRUCT, build, put together, piece together, compose, make, fabricate, manufacture.
🖅 1 scatter, disperse. 2 dismantle.

assembly *n* 1 GATHERING, rally, meeting, convention, conference, convocation, congress, council, group, body, company, congregation, flock, crowd, multitude, throng, collection, assemblage. 2 CONSTRUCTION, building, fabrication, manufacture.

assent *v* agree, approve, accept, allow, consent, grant, permit, sanction, submit, subscribe, yield, accede (*fml*), acquiesce (*fml*), comply (*fml*), concede (*fml*), concur (*fml*).
🖅 disagree.
➤ *n* agreement, approval, acceptance, capitulation, concession, consent, permission, sanction, submission, accord (*fml*), acquiescence (*fml*), compliance (*fml*), concurrence (*fml*), approbation (*fml*).

assert *v* affirm, attest, swear, testify to, allege, claim, contend, maintain, insist, stress, protest, defend, vindicate, uphold, promote, declare, profess, state, pronounce, lay down, advance.
🖅 deny, refute.

assertion *n* affirmation, attestation, word, allegation, claim, contention, insistence, vindication, declaration, profession, statement, pronouncement.
🖅 denial.

assertive *adj* bold, confident, self-assured, forward, pushy, insistent, emphatic, forceful, firm, decided, strong-willed, dogmatic, opinionated, presumptuous, assuming, overbearing, domineering, aggressive.
🖅 timid, diffident.

assess *v* gauge, estimate, evaluate, appraise, review, judge, consider, weigh, size up, compute, determine, fix, value, rate, tax, levy, impose, demand.

assessment *n* gauging, estimation, estimate, evaluation, appraisal, review, judgement, opinion, consideration, calculation, determination, valuation, rating, taxation.

asset *n* strength, resource, virtue, plus (*infml*), benefit, advantage, blessing, boon, help, aid.
🖅 liability.

assets *n* estate, property, possessions, goods, holdings, securities, money, wealth, capital, funds, reserves, resources, means.

assiduous *adj* industrious, diligent, hard-working, conscientious, constant, dedicated, devoted, attentive, persevering, persistent, steady, studious, unflagging, indefatigable, untiring.
🖅 negligent.

assign *v* 1 ALLOCATE, apportion, grant, give, dispense, distribute, allot, consign, delegate, name, nominate, designate, appoint, choose, select, determine, set, fix, specify, stipulate. 2 ATTRIBUTE, accredit, ascribe, put down.

assignation *n* secret meeting, appointment, arrangement, date, engagement, rendezvous.

assignment *n* commission, errand, task, project, job, position, post, duty, responsibility, charge, appointment, delegation, designation, nomination, selection, allocation, consignment, grant, distribution.

assimilate *v* 1 ABSORB, take in, pick up, incorporate, learn. 2 INTEGRATE, absorb, blend, mix, mingle, unite, accustom, adapt, adjust, acclimatize, accommodate.
🖅 1, 2 reject.

assist *v* help, aid, abet, rally round, co-operate, collaborate, back, second, support, reinforce, sustain, relieve, benefit,

serve, enable, facilitate, expedite, boost, further, advance.
⊟ hinder, thwart.

assistance *n* help, aid, succour, co-operation, collaboration, backing, support, reinforcement, relief, benefit, service, boost, furtherance.
⊟ hindrance, resistance.

assistant *n* helper, helpmate, aide, right-hand man, auxiliary, ancillary, subordinate, backer, second, supporter, accomplice, accessory, abettor, collaborator, colleague, partner, ally, confederate, associate.

associate *v* 1 AFFILIATE, confederate, ally, league, join, amalgamate, combine, unite, link, connect, correlate, relate, couple, pair, yoke. 2 *associate with bad company*: socialize, mingle, mix, fraternize, consort, hang around (*infml*).
➤ *n* partner, ally, confederate, affiliate, collaborator, co-worker, mate, colleague, peer, compeer, fellow, comrade, companion, friend, sidekick (*infml*), assistant, follower.

association *n* 1 ORGANIZATION, corporation, company, partnership, league, alliance, coalition, confederation, confederacy, federation, affiliation, consortium, cartel, syndicate, union, society, club, fraternity, fellowship, clique, group, band. 2 BOND, tie, connection, correlation, relation, relationship, involvement, intimacy, friendship, companionship, familiarity.

assorted *adj* miscellaneous, mixed, varied, different, differing, heterogeneous, diverse, sundry, various, several, manifold.

assortment *n* miscellany, medley, pot-pourri, jumble, mixture, variety, diversity, collection, selection, choice, arrangement, grouping.

assuage *v* 1 *assuage grief/pain*: relieve, ease, lessen, reduce, soften, allay, alleviate, calm, lighten, lower, lull, mitigate, moderate, soothe, mollify, pacify, palliate. 2 *assuage one's thirst*: alleviate, quench, satisfy, appease, slake (*fml*).
⊟ 1 exacerbate, worsen.

assume *v* 1 PRESUME, surmise, accept, take for granted, expect, understand, deduce, infer, guess, postulate, suppose, think, believe, imagine, fancy. 2 AFFECT, take on, feign, counterfeit, simulate, put on, pretend. 3 *assume command*:

undertake, adopt, embrace, seize, arrogate, commandeer, appropriate, usurp, take over.

assumed *adj* false, bogus, counterfeit, fake, phoney (*infml*), sham, affected, feigned, simulated, pretended, made-up, fictitious, hypothetical.
⊟ true, real, actual.

assumption *n* presumption, surmise, inference, supposition, guess, conjecture, theory, hypothesis, premise, postulate, idea, notion, belief, fancy.

assurance *n* 1 ASSERTION, declaration, affirmation, guarantee, pledge, promise, vow, word, oath. 2 CONFIDENCE, self-confidence, aplomb, boldness, audacity, courage, nerve, conviction, sureness, certainty.
⊟ 2 shyness, doubt, uncertainty.

assure *v* affirm, guarantee, warrant, pledge, promise, vow, swear, tell, convince, persuade, encourage, hearten, reassure, soothe, comfort, boost, strengthen, secure, ensure, confirm.

assured *adj* 1 SURE, certain, indisputable, irrefutable, confirmed, positive, definite, settled, fixed, guaranteed, secure. 2 SELF-ASSURED, confident, self-confident, self-possessed, bold, audacious, assertive.
⊟ 1 uncertain. 2 shy.

astonish *v* surprise, startle, amaze, astound, stun, stupefy, daze, stagger, floor (*infml*), dumbfound, flabbergast (*infml*), shock, confound, bewilder.

astonishing *adj* surprising, startling, amazing, astounding, stunning, breathtaking, impressive, striking, startling, staggering, shocking, bewildering, mind-boggling (*infml*).

astonishment *n* surprise, amazement, shock, dismay, consternation, confusion, bewilderment, wonder.

astound *v* surprise, startle, amaze, astonish, stun, take one's breath away, stupefy, overwhelm, shock, bewilder, knock for six (*infml*), bowl over (*infml*).

astounding *adj* surprising, startling, amazing, astonishing, stunning, breathtaking, stupefying, overwhelming, staggering, shocking, bewildering.

astray *adv* adrift, off course, lost, amiss, wrong, off the rails (*infml*), awry, off the mark.

astronaut *n* spaceman, spacewoman,

space traveller, cosmonaut.

astute *adj* shrewd, prudent, sagacious, wise, canny, knowing, intelligent, sharp, penetrating, keen, perceptive, discerning, subtle, clever, crafty, cunning, sly, wily.
 stupid, slow.

asylum *n* haven, sanctuary, refuge, shelter, retreat, safety.

asymmetric *adj* unsymmetrical, unbalanced, uneven, crooked, awry, unequal, disproportionate, irregular.
 symmetrical.

atheism *n* unbelief, non-belief, disbelief, scepticism, irreligion, ungodliness, godlessness, impiety, infidelity, paganism, heathenism, freethinking, rationalism.

atheist *n* unbeliever, non-believer, disbeliever, sceptic, infidel, pagan, heathen, freethinker.

athlete *n* sportsman, sportswoman, runner, gymnast, competitor, contestant, contender.

athletic *adj* fit, energetic, vigorous, active, sporty, muscular, sinewy, brawny, strapping, robust, sturdy, strong, powerful, well-knit, well-proportioned, wiry.
 puny.

athletics *n* sports, games, races, track events, field events, exercises, gymnastics.

atmosphere *n* **1** AIR, sky, aerospace, heavens, ether. **2** AMBIENCE, environment, surroundings, aura, feel, feeling, mood, spirit, tone, tenor, character, quality, flavour.

> **The different layers of the atmosphere are:** troposphere, stratosphere, mesosphere, thermosphere, ionosphere, exosphere.

atom *n* molecule, particle, bit, morsel, crumb, grain, spot, speck, mite, shred, scrap, hint, trace, scintilla, jot, iota, whit.

> **Subatomic particles include:** photon, electron, positron, neutrino, anti-neutrino, muon, pion, kaon, proton, anti-proton, neutron, anti-neutron, lambda particle, sigma particle, omega particle, psi particle.

atone *v* make amends, pay for, remedy, indemnify, reconcile, repent, compensate, recompense, make up for, make right, make good, offset, redeem, redress, appease, propitiate, expiate.

atonement *n* amends, reparation, repayment, reimbursement, requital, restitution, restoration, satisfaction, compensation, indemnity, payment, penance, recompense, redress, appeasement, propitiation, expiation, eye for an eye (*infml*).

atrocious *adj* shocking, appalling, abominable, dreadful, terrible, horrible, hideous, ghastly, heinous, grievous, savage, vicious, monstrous, fiendish, ruthless.
 admirable, fine.

atrocity *n* outrage, abomination, enormity, horror, monstrosity, savagery, barbarity, brutality, cruelty, viciousness, evil, villainy, wickedness, vileness, heinousness, hideousness, atrociousness.

attach *v* **1** *attach a label*: affix, stick, adhere, fasten, fix, secure, tie, bind, weld, join, unite, connect, link, couple, add, annex. **2** ASCRIBE, attribute, impute, assign, put, place, associate, relate to, belong.
 1 detach, unfasten.

attached *adj* **1** *very attached to her family*: affectionate, fond, loving, tender, liking, friendly, devoted. **2** *Is she attached?*: married, engaged, spoken for, in a relationship, involved with someone, going steady (*infml*).
 1 unloving. **2** single, unattached, on one's own.

attachment *n* **1** ACCESSORY, fitting, fixture, extension, appendage, extra, supplement, addition, adjunct, codicil. **2** FONDNESS, affection, tenderness, love, liking, partiality, loyalty, devotion, friendship, affinity, attraction, bond, tie, link.

attack *n* **1** OFFENSIVE, blitz, bombardment, invasion, incursion, foray, raid, strike, charge, rush, onslaught, assault, battery, aggression, criticism, censure, abuse. **2** SEIZURE, fit, convulsion, paroxysm, spasm, stroke.
> *v* **1** invade, raid, strike, storm, charge, assail, assault, set upon, fall on, lay into, do over (*sl*). **2** CRITICIZE, censure, blame, denounce, revile, malign, abuse.
 1 defend, protect.

attacker *n* assailant, mugger (*sl*), aggressor, invader, raider, critic, detractor, reviler, abuser, persecutor.
 defender, supporter.

attain *v* accomplish, achieve, fulfil,

complete, effect, realize, earn, reach, touch, arrive at, grasp, get, acquire, obtain, procure, secure, gain, win, net.

attainable *adj* achievable, feasible, viable, manageable, obtainable, possible, potential, practicable, probable, reachable, realistic, within reach, at hand, accessible, imaginable, conceivable, doable (*infml*).

🖃 unattainable.

attainment *n* accomplishment, achievement, feat, fulfilment, completion, consummation, realization, success, ability, capability, competence, proficiency, skill, art, talent, gift, aptitude, facility, mastery.

attempt *n* try, endeavour, shot (*infml*), go (*infml*), stab (*infml*), bash (*infml*), push, effort, struggle, bid, undertaking, venture, trial, experiment.
➤ *v* try, endeavour, have a go (*infml*), aspire, seek, strive, undertake, tackle, venture, experiment.

attend *v* **1** *attend a meeting*: be present, go to, frequent, visit. **2** ESCORT, chaperon, accompany, usher, follow, guard, look after, take care of, care for, nurse, tend, minister to, help, serve, wait on. **3** PAY ATTENTION, listen, hear, heed, mind, mark, note, notice, observe.
♦ **attend to** deal with, see to, take care of, look after, manage, direct, control, oversee, supervise.

attendance *n* presence, appearance, turnout, audience, house, crowd, gate.

attendant *n* aide, helper, assistant, auxiliary, steward, waiter, servant, page, retainer, guide, marshal, usher, escort, companion, follower, guard, custodian.
➤ *adj* accompanying, attached, associated, related, incidental, resultant, consequent, subsequent.

attention *n* alertness, vigilance, concentration, heed, notice, observation, regard, mindfulness, awareness, recognition, thought, contemplation, consideration, concern, care, treatment, service.

🖃 inattention, disregard, carelessness.

attentive *adj* **1** ALERT, awake, vigilant, watchful, observant, concentrating, heedful, mindful, careful, conscientious. **2** CONSIDERATE, thoughtful, kind, obliging, accommodating, polite, courteous, devoted.

🖃 **1** inattentive, heedless. **2** inconsiderate.

attest *v* prove, confirm, corroborate, demonstrate, show, display, manifest, endorse, certify, affirm, assert, certify, declare, demonstrate, vouch for, bear witness to, verify, adjure (*fml*), aver (*fml*), asseverate (*fml*), evince (*fml*), evidence (*fml*).

attitude *n* **1** OPINION, feeling, disposition, mood, aspect, manner, position, point of view, view, outlook, perspective, approach, way of thinking, mentality, mindset, world-view, Weltanschauung. **2** POSTURE, bearing, pose, stance, stand, deportment (*fml*), carriage (*fml*).

attract *v* pull, draw, lure, allure, entice, seduce, tempt, invite, induce, incline, appeal to, interest, engage, fascinate, enchant, charm, bewitch, captivate, excite.
🖃 repel, disgust.

attraction *n* pull, draw, magnetism, lure, allure, bait, enticement, inducement, seduction, temptation, invitation, appeal, interest, fascination, enchantment, charm, captivation.
🖃 repulsion.

attractive *adj* pretty, fair, fetching, good-looking, handsome, beautiful, gorgeous, stunning, glamorous, lovely, pleasant, pleasing, agreeable, appealing, winsome, winning, enticing, seductive, tempting, inviting, interesting, engaging, fascinating, charming, captivating, magnetic.
🖃 unattractive, repellent.

attribute *v* ascribe, accredit, credit, impute, assign, put down, blame, charge, refer, apply.
➤ *n* property, quality, virtue, point, aspect, facet, feature, trait, characteristic, idiosyncrasy, peculiarity, quirk, note, mark, sign, symbol.

attrition *n* **1** FRICTION, abrasion, rubbing, scraping, chafing, erosion, detrition (*fml*). **2** *a war of attrition*: wearing-away, wearing-down, grinding, harassment, attenuation (*fml*).

attuned *adj* acclimatized, assimilated, accustomed, familiarized, adapted, adjusted, regulated, co-ordinated, harmonized, set, tuned.

auburn *adj* red, chestnut, tawny, russet, copper, Titian.

audacious *adj* adventurous, daring, enterprising, courageous, rash, reckless, risky, assuming, assured, unabashed, bold,

brave, fearless, intrepid, dauntless, valiant, plucky, disrespectful, impertinent, forward, presumptuous, impudent, insolent, cheeky, pert, brazen, rude, shameless.
🖪 cautious, reserved, timid.

audible *adj* clear, distinct, recognizable, perceptible, discernible, detectable, appreciable.
🖪 inaudible, silent, unclear.

audience *n* spectators, onlookers, house, auditorium, listeners, viewers, crowd, turnout, gathering, assembly, congregation, fans, devotees, regulars, following, public.

audit *n* examination, inspection, check, verification, investigation, scrutiny, analysis, review, statement, balancing.

augment *v* add to, amplify, boost, enlarge, build up, put on, expand, extend, grow, increase, make greater, magnify, multiply, raise, inflate, enhance, heighten, intensify, reinforce, strengthen, swell.
🖪 decrease.

augur *v* bode, forebode, herald, presage, portend, prophesy, predict, promise, signify.

aura *n* air, ambience, atmosphere, mood, quality, emanation, feel, feeling, hint, suggestion, vibrations, vibes (*infml*).

auspices *n* aegis, authority, patronage, sponsorship, backing, support, protection, charge, care, supervision, control, influence, guidance.

auspicious *adj* favourable, propitious, encouraging, cheerful, bright, rosy, promising, hopeful, optimistic, fortunate, lucky, opportune, happy, prosperous.
🖪 inauspicious, ominous.

austere *adj* 1 STARK, bleak, plain, simple, unadorned, grim, forbidding. 2 SEVERE, stern, strict, cold, formal, rigid, rigorous, exacting, hard, harsh, spartan, grave, serious, solemn, sober, abstemious, self-denying, restrained, economical, frugal, ascetic, self-disciplined, puritanical, chaste.
🖪 1 ornate, elaborate. 2 genial.

austerity *n* plainness, simplicity, severity, coldness, formality, hardness, harshness, solemnity, abstemiousness, abstinence, economy, asceticism, puritanism.
🖪 elaborateness, materialism.

authentic *adj* genuine, true, real, actual, certain, bona fide, legitimate, honest,

valid, original, pure, factual, accurate, true-to-life, faithful, reliable, trustworthy.
🖪 false, fake, counterfeit, spurious.

authenticate *v* guarantee, warrant, vouch for, attest, authorize, accredit, validate, certify, endorse, confirm, verify, corroborate.

authenticity *n* genuineness, certainty, authoritativeness, validity, truth, veracity, truthfulness, honesty, accuracy, correctness, faithfulness, fidelity, reliability, dependability, trustworthiness.
🖪 spuriousness, invalidity.

author *n* 1 WRITER, novelist, dramatist, playwright, composer, pen, penman, penwoman. 2 CREATOR, founder, originator, initiator, parent, prime mover, mover, inventor, designer, architect, planner, maker, producer.

authoritarian *adj* strict, disciplinarian, severe, harsh, rigid, inflexible, unyielding, dogmatic, doctrinaire, absolute, autocratic, dictatorial, despotic, tyrannical, oppressive, domineering, imperious.
🖪 liberal.

authoritative *adj* scholarly, learned, official, authorized, legitimate, valid, approved, sanctioned, accepted, definitive, decisive, authentic, factual, true, truthful, accurate, faithful, convincing, sound, reliable, dependable, trustworthy.
🖪 unofficial, unreliable.

authority *n* 1 SOVEREIGNTY, supremacy, rule, sway, control, dominion, influence, power, force, government, administration, officialdom. 2 AUTHORIZATION, permission, sanction, permit, warrant, licence, credentials, right, prerogative. 3 *an authority on antiques*: expert, pundit, connoisseur, specialist, professional, master, scholar.

authorization *n* authority, permission, consent, sanction, approval, mandate, validation, ratification, confirmation, licence, entitlement, empowering, commission, warranty, permit, leave, credentials, accreditation (*fml*), OK (*infml*), go-ahead (*infml*), green light (*infml*).

authorize *v* legalize, validate, ratify, confirm, license, entitle, accredit, empower, enable, commission, warrant, permit, allow, consent to, sanction, approve, give the go-ahead (*infml*).

autocracy *n* absolutism, totalitarianism, dictatorship, despotism, tyranny, authoritarianism, fascism.
Ea democracy.

autocrat *n* absolutist, totalitarian, dictator, despot, tyrant, authoritarian, (little) Hitler (*infml*), fascist.

autocratic *adj* absolute, all-powerful, totalitarian, despotic, tyrannical, authoritarian, dictatorial, domineering, overbearing, imperious.
Ea democratic, liberal.

automatic *adj* **1** AUTOMATED, self-activating, mechanical, mechanized, programmed, self-regulating, computerized, push-button, robotic, self-propelling, unmanned. **2** SPONTANEOUS, reflex, involuntary, unwilled, unconscious, unthinking, natural, instinctive, routine, necessary, certain, inevitable, unavoidable, inescapable.

autonomy *n* self-government, self-rule, home rule, sovereignty, independence, self-determination, freedom, free will.
Ea subjection, compulsion.

auxiliary *adj* ancillary, assistant, subsidiary, accessory, secondary, supporting, supportive, helping, assisting, aiding, extra, supplementary, spare, reserve, back-up, emergency, substitute.

available *adj* free, vacant, to hand, within reach, at hand, accessible, handy, convenient, on hand, ready, on tap, obtainable.
Ea unavailable.

avalanche *n* landslide, landslip, cascade, torrent, deluge, flood, inundation, barrage.

avant-garde *adj* innovative, innovatory, pioneering, experimental, unconventional, far-out (*sl*), way-out (*sl*), progressive, advanced, forward-looking, enterprising, inventive.
Ea conservative.

avarice *n* covetousness, rapacity, acquisitiveness, greed, greediness, meanness.
Ea generosity, liberality.

avaricious *adj* covetous, grasping, rapacious, acquisitive, greedy, mercenary, mean, miserly.
Ea generous.

avenge *v* take revenge for, take vengeance for, punish, requite, repay, retaliate.

average *n* mean, mid-point, norm, standard, rule, par, medium, run.
Ea extreme, exception.
➤ *adj* mean, medial, median, middle, intermediate, medium, moderate, satisfactory, fair, mediocre, middling, indifferent, so-so (*infml*), passable, tolerable, undistinguished, run-of-the-mill, ordinary, everyday, common, usual, normal, regular, standard, typical, unexceptional.
Ea extreme, exceptional, remarkable.

averse *adj* reluctant, unwilling, loth, disinclined, ill-disposed, hostile, opposed, antagonistic, unfavourable.
Ea willing, keen, sympathetic.

aversion *n* dislike, hate, hatred, loathing, detestation, abhorrence, abomination, horror, phobia, reluctance, unwillingness, disinclination, distaste, disgust, revulsion, repugnance, repulsion, hostility, opposition, antagonism.
Ea liking, sympathy, desire.

avert *v* turn away, deflect, turn aside, parry, fend off, ward off, stave off, forestall, frustrate, prevent, obviate, avoid, evade.

aviation *n* aeronautics, flying, flight, aircraft industry.

Aviation terms include: aeronautics, aeroplane, aerospace, aileron, aircraft, airfield, air hostess, airline, air-miss, airplane (*US*), airport, airship, airspace, air steward, airstrip, air-traffic control, airway, altitude, automatic pilot, biplane, black box, captain, chocks away (*infml*), cockpit, console, control tower, crash-dive, crash-landing, dive, drag, fixed-wing, flap, flight, flight crew, flight deck, flight recorder, fly-by, fly-by-wire, fly-past, fuselage, George (*sl*), glider, ground-control, ground-speed, hangar, helicopter, hop, hot-air balloon, jet, jet engine, jet propulsion, jetstream, joystick, jumbo jet, landing, landing-gear, landing-strip, lift-off, loop-the-loop, Mach number, maiden flight, mid-air collision, monoplane, night-flying, nose dive, overshoot, parachute, pilot, plane, pressurized cabin, prang (*sl*), propeller, rotor blade, rudder, runway, solo flight, sonic boom, sound barrier, spoiler, supersonic, swing-wing, take-off, taxi, test flight, test pilot, thrust, touchdown, undercarriage, undershoot, vapour trail, vertical take-off and landing (VTOL), windsock, wingspan. *see also* **aircraft**.

avid *adj* eager, earnest, keen, enthusiastic, fanatical, devoted, dedicated, zealous, ardent, fervent, intense, passionate, insatiable, ravenous, hungry, thirsty, greedy, grasping, covetous.
Ea indifferent.

avoid *v* evade, elude, sidestep, dodge, shirk, duck (*infml*), escape, get out of, bypass, circumvent, balk, prevent, avert, shun, abstain from, refrain from, steer clear of.

avoidable *adj* escapable, preventable.
Ea inevitable.

avowed *adj* sworn, declared, professed, self-proclaimed, self-confessed, confessed, admitted, acknowledged, open, overt.

await *v* wait for, expect, hope for, look forward to, look for, be in store for, lie in wait.

awake *v* awaken, waken, wake, wake up, rouse, arouse.
➤ *adj* wakeful, wide-awake, aroused, alert, vigilant, watchful, observant, attentive, conscious, aware, sensitive, alive.

awakening *n* awaking, wakening, waking, rousing, arousal, stimulation, animating, enlivening, activation, revival, birth.

award *v* give, present, distribute, dispense, bestow, confer, accord, endow, gift, grant, allot, apportion, assign, allow, determine.
➤ *n* prize, trophy, decoration, medal, presentation, dispensation, bestowal, conferral, endowment, gift, grant, allotment, allowance, adjudication, judgement, decision, order.

aware *adj* conscious, alive to, sensitive, appreciative, sentient, familiar, conversant, acquainted, informed, enlightened, au courant, knowing, knowledgeable, cognizant, mindful, heedful, attentive, observant, sharp, alert, on the ball (*infml*), shrewd, sensible.
Ea unaware, oblivious, insensitive.

awe *n* wonder, veneration, reverence, respect, admiration, amazement, astonishment, fear, terror, dread, apprehension.
Ea contempt.

awe-inspiring *adj* wonderful, sublime, magnificent, stupendous, overwhelming, breathtaking, stupefying, stunning, astonishing, amazing, impressive, imposing, majestic, solemn, moving, awesome, formidable, daunting, intimidating, fearsome.
Ea contemptible, tame.

awful *adj* terrible, dreadful, fearful, frightful, ghastly, unpleasant, nasty, horrible, hideous, ugly, gruesome, dire, abysmal, atrocious, horrific, shocking, appalling, alarming, spine-chilling.
Ea wonderful, excellent.

awkward *adj* 1 CLUMSY, gauche, inept, inexpert, unskilful, bungling, ham-fisted, unco-ordinated, ungainly, graceless, ungraceful, inelegant, cumbersome, unwieldy, inconvenient, difficult, fiddly, delicate, troublesome, perplexing. 2 *feeling awkward in their presence*: uncomfortable, ill at ease, embarrassed. 3 OBSTINATE, stubborn, unco-operative, irritable, touchy, prickly, rude, unpleasant.
Ea 1 graceful, elegant, convenient, handy. 2 comfortable, relaxed. 3 amenable, pleasant.

awry *adv, adj* 1 *clothing left awry*: askew, asymmetrical, cock-eyed, crooked, misaligned, oblique, off-centre, skew-whiff, twisted, uneven, wonky (*infml*). 2 *plans gone awry*: wrong, amiss.
Ea 1 straight, symmetrical.

axe *n* hatchet, chopper, cleaver, tomahawk, battle-axe.
➤ *v* 1 CUT (DOWN), fell, hew, chop, cleave, split. 2 CANCEL, terminate, discontinue, remove, withdraw, eliminate, get rid of, throw out, dismiss, discharge, sack (*infml*), fire (*infml*).

axiom *n* principle, fundamental, truth, truism, precept, dictum, byword, maxim, adage, aphorism.

axiomatic *adj* manifest, assumed, certain, given, granted, self-evident, understood, unquestioned, presupposed, fundamental, accepted, proverbial, indubitable (*fml*), aphoristic (*fml*).

axis *n* centre-line, vertical, horizontal, pivot, hinge.

axle *n* shaft, spindle, rod, pin, pivot.

Bb

babble *v* **1** CHATTER, gabble, jabber, cackle, prate, mutter, mumble, murmur. **2** *the stream babbled*: burble, gurgle.
➤ *n* chatter, gabble, clamour, hubbub, gibberish, burble, murmur.

baby *n* babe, infant, suckling, child, tiny, toddler.
➤ *adj* miniature, small-scale, mini (*infml*), midget, small, little, tiny, minute, diminutive.

babyish *adj* childish, juvenile, puerile, infantile, silly, foolish, soft (*infml*), sissy (*infml*), baby, young, immature, naïve.
ᴇᴀ mature, precocious.

back *n* rear, stern, end, tail, tail end, hind part, hindquarters, posterior, backside, reverse.
ᴇᴀ front, face.
➤ *v* **1** GO BACKWARDS, reverse, recede, regress, backtrack, retreat, retire, withdraw, back away, recoil. **2** SUPPORT, sustain, assist, side with, champion, advocate, encourage, promote, boost, favour, sanction, countenance, endorse, second, countersign, sponsor, finance, subsidize, underwrite.
ᴇᴀ **1** advance, approach. **2** discourage, weaken.
➤ *adj* rear, end, tail, posterior, hind, hindmost, reverse.
ᴇᴀ front.
◆ **back down** concede, yield, give in, surrender, submit, retreat, withdraw, back-pedal.
◆ **back out** abandon, give up, chicken out (*infml*), withdraw, pull out (*infml*), resign, recant, go back on, cancel.
◆ **back up** confirm, corroborate, substantiate, endorse, second, champion, support, reinforce, bolster, assist, aid.
ᴇᴀ let down.

backbiting *n* criticism, slander, libel, defamation, abuse, disparagement, gossip, malice, scandalmongering, spite, spitefulness, aspersion (*fml*), denigration (*fml*), revilement (*fml*), vilification (*fml*), bitchiness (*infml*), cattiness (*infml*), slagging-off (*infml*), mud-slinging (*infml*).
ᴇᴀ praise.

backbone *n* **1** SPINE, spinal column, vertebrae, vertebral column, mainstay, support, core, foundation, basis, character. **2** COURAGE, mettle, pluck, nerve, grit, determination, resolve, tenacity, steadfastness, toughness, stamina, strength, power.
ᴇᴀ **2** spinelessness, weakness.

backbreaking *adj* arduous, exhausting, gruelling, strenuous, hard, heavy, crushing, killing, laborious, punishing.
ᴇᴀ easy.

backer *n* advocate, benefactor, promoter, second, seconder, sponsor, subscriber, supporter, underwriter, champion, patron, well-wisher.

backfire *v* recoil, rebound, rebol, boomerang, miscarry, fail, flop.

background *n* **1** SETTING, surroundings, environment, context, circumstances. **2** HISTORY, record, credentials, experience, grounding, preparation, education, upbringing, breeding, culture, tradition.

backhanded *adj* ambiguous, double-edged, two-edged, indirect, oblique, dubious, equivocal, ironic, sarcastic, sardonic.
ᴇᴀ sincere, wholehearted.

backing *n* support, accompaniment, aid, assistance, helpers, championing, advocacy, encouragement, moral support, favour, sanction, promotion, endorsement, seconding, patronage, sponsorship, finance, funds, grant, subsidy.

backlash *n* reaction, response, repercussion, reprisal, retaliation, recoil, kickback, backfire, boomerang.

backlog *n* accumulation, stock, supply, resources, reserve, reserves, excess.

backsliding *n* lapse, relapse, apostasy, defection, desertion, defaulting.

backward *adj* **1** *a backward step*: retrograde, retrogressive, regressive. **2** SHY, bashful, reluctant, unwilling, hesitant, hesitating, wavering, slow, behind, behindhand, late, immature, under-developed, retarded, subnormal, stupid.
ᴇᴀ **1** forward. **2** precocious.

backwoods n back of beyond, bush, outback, middle of nowhere (*infml*), sticks (*infml*).

bacteria n germs, bugs (*infml*), viruses, microbes, micro-organisms, bacilli.

bad adj 1 UNPLEASANT, disagreeable, nasty, undesirable, unfortunate, distressing, adverse, detrimental, harmful, damaging, injurious, serious, grave, severe, harsh. 2 EVIL, wicked, sinful, criminal, corrupt, immoral, vile. 3 *bad workmanship*: poor, inferior, substandard, imperfect, faulty, defective, deficient, unsatisfactory, useless. 4 ROTTEN, mouldy, decayed, spoilt, putrid, rancid, sour, off, tainted, contaminated. 5 *a bad child*: naughty, mischievous, ill-behaved, disobedient.
Ea 1 good, pleasant, mild, slight. 2 virtuous. 3 skilled. 4 fresh. 5 well-behaved.

badge n identification, emblem, device, insignia, sign, mark, token, stamp, brand, trademark, logo.

badger v pester, plague, torment, harass, bait, bully, chivvy, goad, harry, hound, nag, importune (*fml*), hassle (*infml*).

badly adv 1 GREATLY, extremely, exceedingly, intensely, deeply, acutely, bitterly, painfully, seriously, desperately, severely, critically, crucially. 2 WICKEDLY, criminally, immorally, shamefully, unfairly. 3 WRONG, wrongly, incorrectly, improperly, defectively, faultily, imperfectly, inadequately, unsatisfactorily, poorly, incompetently, negligently, carelessly. 4 UNFAVOURABLY, adversely, unfortunately, unsuccessfully.
Ea 3 well.

bad-tempered adj irritable, cross, crotchety, crabbed, crabby, snappy, grumpy, querulous, petulant, fractious, stroppy (*infml*).
Ea good-tempered, genial, equable.

baffle v puzzle, perplex, mystify, bemuse, bewilder, confuse, confound, bamboozle (*infml*), flummox (*infml*), daze, upset, disconcert, foil, thwart, frustrate, hinder, check, defeat, stump (*infml*).
Ea enlighten, help.

bag v 1 CATCH, capture, trap, land, kill, shoot. 2 OBTAIN, acquire, get, gain, corner, take, grab, appropriate, commandeer, reserve.
➣ n container, sack, case, suitcase, grip, carrier, hold-all, handbag,
shoulder-bag, satchel, rucksack, haversack, pack.

baggage n luggage, suitcases, bags, belongings, things, equipment, gear, paraphernalia, impedimenta (*fml*).

baggy adj loose, slack, roomy, ill-fitting, billowing, bulging, floppy, sagging, droopy.
Ea tight, firm.

bail n security, surety, pledge, bond, guarantee, warranty.
♦ **bail out** help, aid, assist, relieve, rescue, finance.

bait n lure, incentive, inducement, bribe, temptation, enticement, allurement, attraction.
Ea disincentive.
➣ v tease, provoke, goad, irritate, annoy, irk, needle (*infml*), harass, persecute, torment.

balance v 1 STEADY, poise, stabilize, level, square, equalize, equate, match, counterbalance, counteract, neutralize, offset, adjust. 2 COMPARE, consider, weigh, estimate.
Ea 1 unbalance, overbalance.
➣ n 1 EQUILIBRIUM, steadiness, stability, evenness, symmetry, equality, parity, equity, equivalence, correspondence. 2 COMPOSURE, self-possession, poise, equanimity. 3 REMAINDER, rest, residue, surplus, difference.
Ea 1 imbalance, instability.

balanced adj 1 *a balanced report*: objective, fair, impartial, unbiased, unprejudiced, equitable. 2 *a balanced diet*: well-rounded, healthy, complete. 3 *a balanced person*: calm, self-possessed, assured, level-headed, cool-headed, equitable, even-handed, sensible.
Ea 1 prejudiced, biased.

balcony n terrace, veranda, gallery, upper circle, gods.

bald adj 1 BALD-HEADED, hairless, smooth, uncovered. 2 BARE, naked, unadorned, plain, simple, severe, stark, barren, treeless. 3 *a bald statement*: forthright, direct, straight, outright, downright, straightforward.
Ea 1 hairy, hirsute. 2 adorned.

balderdash n rubbish, nonsense, drivel, gibberish, trash, tripe, twaddle, bunk (*infml*), bunkum (*infml*), claptrap (*infml*), piffle (*infml*), bilge (*infml*), poppycock (*infml*), hot air (*infml*), cobblers (*infml*), rot (*infml*), tommyrot (*infml*).

bale n bundle, truss, pack, package, parcel.

bale out v withdraw, retreat, quit, back out, cop out (sl), escape.

balk, baulk v 1 FLINCH, recoil, shrink, jib, boggle, hesitate, refuse, resist, dodge, evade, shirk. 2 THWART, frustrate, foil, forestall, disconcert, baffle, hinder, obstruct, check, stall, bar, prevent, defeat, counteract.

ball¹ n sphere, globe, orb, globule, drop, conglomeration, pellet, pill, shot, bullet, slug (infml).

ball² n dance, dinner-dance, party, soirée, masquerade, carnival, assembly.

ballad n poem, song, folk-song, shanty, carol, ditty.

ballet

Terms used in ballet include: à pointe, arabesque, attitude, ballerina, prima ballerina, ballon, barre, battement, batterie, battu, bourrée, capriole, chassé, choreography, ciseaux, company, corps de ballet, coryphée, divertissement, écarté, élévation, entrechat, fish dive, five positions, fouetté, fouetté en tournant, glissade, jeté, grand jeté, leotard, pas de deux, pas de seul, pirouette, plié, pointes, sur les pointes, port de bras, principal male dancer, régisseur, répétiteur, ballet shoe, point shoe, splits, stulchak, tutu.

balloon v bag, belly, billow, blow up, bulge, dilate, enlarge, expand, inflate, puff out, swell, rocket, soar, distend (fml).

ballot n poll, polling, vote, voting, election, referendum, plebiscite.

balm n soothing balm for the skin/a troubled spirit: cream, lotion, salve, sedative, unguent, balsam, bromide, calmative, curative, embrocation, emollient, lenitive, ointment, palliative, restorative, anodyne, comfort, consolation.
Ea irritant, vexation.

balmy adj warm, summery, gentle, mild, pleasant, soft, temperate, clement, soothing.
Ea inclement.

ban v forbid, prohibit, disallow, proscribe, bar, exclude, ostracize, outlaw, banish, suppress, restrict.
Ea allow, permit, authorize.
➤ n prohibition, embargo, veto, boycott, stoppage, restriction, suppression, censorship, outlawry, proscription, condemnation, denunciation, curse, taboo.
Ea permission, dispensation.

banal adj trite, commonplace, ordinary, everyday, humdrum, boring, unimaginative, hackneyed, clichéd, stock, stereotyped, corny (infml), stale, threadbare, tired, empty.
Ea original, fresh, imaginative.

band¹ n strip, belt, ribbon, tape, bandage, binding, tie, ligature, bond, strap, cord, chain.

band² n 1 TROOP, gang, crew, group, herd, flock, party, body, association, company, society, club, clique. 2 the band played on: group, orchestra, ensemble.
➤ v group, gather, join, unite, ally, collaborate, consolidate, amalgamate, merge, affiliate, federate.
Ea disband, disperse.

bandage n dressing, plaster, compress, ligature, tourniquet, swathe, swaddle.
➤ v bind, dress, cover, swathe, swaddle.

bandit n robber, thief, brigand, marauder, outlaw, highwayman, pirate, buccaneer, hijacker, cowboy, gunman, desperado, gangster.

bandy¹ v exchange, swap, trade, barter, interchange, reciprocate, pass, toss, throw.

bandy² adj bandy-legged, bow-legged, curved, bowed, bent, crooked.

bane n ruin, adversity, destruction, scourge, affliction, torment, trial, trouble, vexation, woe, annoyance, bête noire, blight, burden, calamity, curse, disaster, distress, downfall, evil, irritation, misery, misfortune, nuisance, ordeal, plague, pest, pestilence.
Ea blessing.

bang n 1 BLOW, hit, knock, bump, crash, collision, smack, punch, thump, wallop (infml), stroke, whack (infml). 2 a loud bang: explosion, detonation, pop, boom, clap, peal, clang, clash, thud, thump, slam, noise, report, shot.
➤ v 1 STRIKE, hit, bash, knock, bump, rap, drum, hammer, pound, thump, stamp. 2 EXPLODE, burst, detonate, boom, echo, resound, crash, slam, clatter, clang, peal, thunder.
➤ adv straight, directly, headlong, right, precisely, slap, smack, hard, noisily, suddenly, abruptly.

banish v expel, eject, evict, deport,

transport, exile, outlaw, ban, bar, debar, exclude, shut out, ostracize, excommunicate, dismiss, oust, dislodge, remove, get rid of, discard, dispel, eliminate, eradicate.

🖅 recall, welcome.

banishment *n* expulsion, eviction, deportation, expatriation, transportation, exile, outlawry, ostracism, excommunication.

🖅 return, recall, welcome.

bank¹ *n* accumulation, fund, pool, reservoir, depository, repository, treasury, savings, reserve, store, stock, stockpile, hoard, cache.

➤ *v* deposit, save, keep, store, accumulate, stockpile.

🖅 spend.

bank² *n* heap, pile, mass, mound, earthwork, ridge, rampart, embankment, side, slope, tilt, edge, shore.

➤ *v* **1** HEAP, pile, stack, mass, amass, accumulate, mound, drift. **2** SLOPE, incline, pitch, slant, tilt, tip.

bank³ *n* array, panel, bench, group, tier, rank, line, row, series, succession, sequence, train.

bankrupt *adj* insolvent, in liquidation, ruined, failed, beggared, destitute, impoverished, broke (*infml*), spent, exhausted, depleted, lacking.

🖅 solvent, wealthy.

➤ *n* insolvent, debtor, pauper.

bankruptcy *n* insolvency, (financial) ruin, liquidation, disaster, exhaustion, failure, indebtedness, lack, penury (*fml*), beggary (*fml*), ruination (*fml*).

🖅 solvency, wealth.

banner *n* flag, standard, colours, ensign, pennant, streamer.

banquet *n* feast, dinner, meal, repast (*fml*), treat.

banter *n* joking, jesting, pleasantry, badinage, repartee, word play, chaff, chaffing, kidding (*infml*), ribbing (*sl*), derision, mockery, ridicule.

baptism *n* christening, dedication, beginning, initiation, introduction, debut, launch, launching, immersion, sprinkling, purification.

baptize *v* christen, name, call, term, style, title, introduce, initiate, enrol, recruit, immerse, sprinkle, purify, cleanse.

bar *n* **1** PUBLIC HOUSE, pub (*infml*), inn,

tavern, saloon, lounge, counter. **2** SLAB, block, lump, chunk, wedge, ingot, nugget. **3** ROD, stick, shaft, pole, stake, stanchion, batten, cross-piece, rail, railing, paling, barricade. **4** OBSTACLE, impediment, hindrance, obstruction, barrier, stop, check, deterrent.

➤ *v* **1** EXCLUDE, debar, ban, forbid, prohibit, prevent, preclude, hinder, obstruct, restrain. **2** *bar the door*: barricade, lock, bolt, latch, fasten, secure.

barb *n* **1** *the barb on a fish hook*: arrow, point, spike, needle, thorn, prickle, bristle, fluke. **2** *critical barbs at leaders*: gibe, insult, affront, sneer, rebuff, sarcasm, scorn, dig (*infml*).

barbarian *n* savage, brute, ruffian, hooligan, vandal, lout, oaf, boor, philistine, ignoramus, illiterate.

barbaric *adj* barbarous, primitive, wild, savage, fierce, ferocious, cruel, inhuman, brutal, brutish, uncivilized, uncouth, vulgar, coarse, crude, rude.

🖅 humane, civilized, gracious.

barbarity *n* barbarousness, wildness, savagery, ferocity, viciousness, cruelty, inhumanity, brutality, brutishness, rudeness.

🖅 civilization, humanity, civility.

barbarous *adj* **1** *barbarous behaviour*: wild, savage, fierce, ferocious, vicious, cruel, inhuman, barbarian, barbaric, brutal, brutish, bestial, murderous, ruthless, heartless. **2** *barbarous by modern standards*: primitive, ignorant, uncivilized, unrefined, unsophisticated, uncultured, unlettered, vulgar, rough, rude, crude.

🖅 **2** civilized, cultured, educated.

barbed *adj* **1** PRICKLY, spiny, thorny, spiked, pronged, hooked, jagged, toothed, pointed. **2** *a barbed remark*: cutting, caustic, acid, hurtful, unkind, nasty, snide, hostile, critical.

bare *adj* **1** NAKED, nude, unclothed, undressed, stripped, denuded, uncovered, exposed. **2** PLAIN, simple, unadorned, unfurnished, empty, barren, bald, stark, basic, essential.

🖅 **1** clothed. **2** decorated, detailed.

barefaced *adj* brazen, shameless, blatant, bold, brash, flagrant, glaring, arrant, impudent, insolent, unabashed, undisguised, unconcealed, audacious, naked, obvious, manifest, open, palpable, patent, transparent, bald.

barely *adv* hardly, scarcely, only just, just, almost.

bargain *n* **1** DEAL, transaction, contract, treaty, pact, pledge, promise, agreement, understanding, arrangement, negotiation. **2** DISCOUNT, reduction, snip, giveaway, special offer.
➤ *v* negotiate, haggle, deal, trade, traffic, barter, buy, sell, transact, contract, covenant, promise, agree.
♦ **bargain for** expect, anticipate, plan for, include, reckon on, look for, foresee, imagine, contemplate, consider.

barge *v* bump, hit, collide, impinge, shove, elbow, push (in), muscle in, butt in, interrupt, gatecrash, intrude, interfere.
➤ *n* canal-boat, flatboat, narrow-boat, houseboat, lighter.

bark *n* yap, woof, yelp, snap, snarl, growl, bay, howl.
➤ *v* yap, woof, yelp, snap, snarl, growl, bay, howl.

baroque *adj* elaborate, ornate, rococo, florid, flamboyant, exuberant, vigorous, bold, convoluted, overdecorated, overwrought, extravagant, fanciful, fantastic, grotesque.
🔙 plain, simple.

barracks *n* garrison, camp, encampment, guardhouse, quarters, billet, lodging, accommodation.

barrage *n* bombardment, shelling, gunfire, cannonade, broadside, volley, salvo, burst, assault, attack, onset, onslaught, deluge, torrent, stream, storm, hail, rain, shower, mass, profusion.

barrel *n* cask, keg, tun, butt, water-butt.

barren *adj* **1** ARID, dry, desert, desolate, waste, empty, flat, dull, uninteresting, uninspiring, uninformative, uninstructive, unrewarding, unproductive, profitless, unfruitful, fruitless, pointless, useless, boring. **2** INFERTILE, sterile, childless, unprolific, unbearing.
🔙 **1** productive, fruitful, useful. **2** fertile.

barricade *n* blockade, obstruction, barrier, fence, stockade, bulwark, rampart, protection.
➤ *v* block, obstruct, bar, fortify, defend, protect.

barrier *n* **1** WALL, fence, railing, barricade, blockade, boom, rampart, fortification, ditch, frontier, boundary, bar, check. **2** *a barrier to success*: obstacle, hurdle, stumbling-block, impediment,
obstruction, hindrance, handicap, limitation, restriction, drawback, difficulty.

bartender *n* barman, barmaid, barkeeper, publican.

barter *v* exchange, swap, trade, traffic, deal, negotiate, bargain, haggle.

base¹ *n* **1** *the base of the statue*: bottom, foot, pedestal, plinth, stand, rest, support, foundation, bed, groundwork. **2** BASIS, fundamental, essential, principal, key, heart, core, essence, root, origin, source. **3** HEADQUARTERS, centre, post, station, camp, settlement, home, starting point.
➤ *v* establish, found, ground, locate, station, build, construct, derive, depend, hinge.

base² *adj* abject, contemptible, despicable, wicked, corrupt, immoral, evil, vile, reprobate, vulgar, shameful, sordid, depraved, unprincipled, disgraceful, disreputable, wretched, worthless, ignominious, infamous, scandalous, low, lowly, low-minded, mean, miserable, pitiful, poor, valueless.

baseless *adj* groundless, unfounded, unsupported, unsubstantiated, unauthenticated, unconfirmed, unjustified, uncalled-for, gratuitous.
🔙 justifiable.

bashful *adj* shy, retiring, backward, reticent, reserved, unforthcoming, hesitant, shrinking, nervous, timid, coy, diffident, modest, inhibited, self-conscious, embarrassed, blushing, abashed, shamefaced, sheepish.
🔙 bold, confident, aggressive.

basic *adj* fundamental, elementary, primary, root, underlying, key, central, inherent, intrinsic, essential, indispensable, vital, necessary, important.
🔙 inessential, peripheral.

basically *adv* fundamentally, at bottom, at heart, inherently, intrinsically, essentially, principally, primarily.

basics *n* fundamentals, rudiments, principles, essentials, necessaries, practicalities, brass tacks (*infml*), grass roots, bedrock, rock bottom, core, facts.

basin *n* bowl, dish, sink, crater, cavity, hollow, depression, dip.

basis *n* base, bottom, footing, support, foundation, ground, groundwork, fundamental, premise, principle, essential, heart, core, thrust.

bask *v* sunbathe, lie, lounge, relax, laze, wallow, revel, delight in, enjoy, relish, savour.

basket *n* hamper, creel, pannier, punnet, bassinet.

bass *adj* deep, low, low-toned, grave, resonant.

bastion *n* stronghold, citadel, fortress, defence, bulwark, mainstay, support, prop, pillar, rock.

batch *n* lot, consignment, parcel, pack, bunch, set, assortment, collection, assemblage, group, contingent, amount, quantity.

bath *n* wash, scrub, soak, shower, douche, tub, Jacuzzi®.
➤ *v* bathe, wash, clean, soak, shower.

bathe *v* swim, wet, moisten, immerse, wash, cleanse, rinse, soak, steep, flood, cover, suffuse.
➤ *n* swim, dip, paddle, wash, rinse, soak.

battalion *n* army, force, brigade, regiment, squadron, company, platoon, division, contingent, legion, horde, multitude, throng, host, mass, herd.

batten *n* strip, bar, board.
➤ *v* barricade, board up, clamp down, fasten, fix, nail down, secure, tighten.

batter *v* beat, pound, pummel, buffet, smash, dash, pelt, lash, thrash, wallop (*infml*), abuse, maltreat, ill-treat, manhandle, maul, assault, hurt, injure, bruise, disfigure, mangle, distress, crush, demolish, destroy, ruin, shatter.

battered *adj* beaten, abused, ill-treated, injured, bruised, weather-beaten, dilapidated, tumbledown, ramshackle, crumbling, damaged, crushed.

battery *n* **1** *a battery of tests/cameras*: sequence, series, set, cycle, succession. **2** *assault and battery*: attack, beating, grievous bodily harm, force, striking, thrashing, violence, mugging (*infml*). **3** *the military battery*: artillery, cannon, cannonry, emplacements, guns.

battle *n* war, warfare, hostilities, action, conflict, strife, combat, fight, engagement, encounter, attack, fray, skirmish, clash, struggle, contest, campaign, crusade, row, disagreement, dispute, debate, controversy.
➤ *v* fight, combat, war, feud, contend, struggle, strive, campaign, crusade, agitate, clamour, contest, argue, dispute.

battle-cry *n* war cry, war song, slogan, motto, watchword, catchword.

battlefield *n* battleground, field of battle, front, front line, war/combat zone, theatre of operations, arena.

bauble *n* knick-knack, trinket, toy, plaything, trifle, ornament, bagatelle, bibelot, flamfew, gewgaw, gimcrack, kickshaw, tinsel.

baulk *see* **balk**.

bawdy *adj* lewd, blue, pornographic, coarse, dirty, rude, vulgar, erotic, obscene, gross, improper, indecent, indecorous, indelicate, lecherous, lascivious, licentious, lustful, ribald, risqué, smutty, suggestive, prurient (*fml*), salacious (*fml*). ☒ chaste, clean.

bawl *v* **1** *the baby bawled*: cry, weep, sob, blubber, wail, snivel, squall. **2** *bawl loudly at someone*: yell, shout, cry (out), bellow, howl, roar, call (out), scream, screech, vociferate (*fml*), holler (*infml*).
♦ **bawl out** scold, rebuke, reprimand, yell at.

bay¹ *n* gulf, bight, arm, inlet, cove.

bay² *n* recess, alcove, niche, nook, opening, compartment, cubicle, booth, stall, carrel.

bay³ *v* howl, roar, bellow, bell, bawl, cry, holler (*infml*), bark.

bazaar *n* market, marketplace, mart, exchange, sale, fair, fête, bring-and-buy.

be *v* **1** EXIST, breathe, live, inhabit, reside, dwell. **2** STAY, remain, abide, last, endure, persist, continue, survive, stand, prevail, obtain. **3** HAPPEN, occur, arise, come about, take place, come to pass, befall, develop.

beach *n* sand, sands, shingle, shore, strand, seashore, seaside, water's edge, coast, seaboard.

beacon *n* signal, fire, watch fire, bonfire, light, beam, lighthouse, flare, rocket, sign.

bead *n* drop, droplet, drip, globule, glob (*infml*), blob, dot, bubble, pearl, jewel, pellet.

beaker *n* glass, tumbler, jar, cup, mug, tankard.

beam *n* **1** *a beam of light*: ray, shaft, gleam, glint, glimmer, glow. **2** PLANK, board, timber, rafter, joist, girder, spar, boom, bar, support.
➤ *v* **1** EMIT, broadcast, transmit, radiate, shine, glare, glitter, glow, glimmer. **2** SMILE, grin.

bean

Varieties of bean and pulse include:
adzuki bean, alfalfa, beansprout, black-eyed pea, broad bean, butter bean, carob bean, chick pea, chilli bean, dal, dwarf runner bean, fava bean, French bean, garbanzo pea, green bean, haricot bean, kidney bean, legume, lentil, lima bean (*US*), locust bean, mange tout, marrowfat pea, mung bean, navy bean (*US*), okra, pea, pinto bean (*US*), red kidney bean, runner bean, scarlet runner (*US*), snap bean, soya bean, split pea, string bean, sugar bean, tonka bean, wax bean (*US*).

bear *v* 1 CARRY, convey, transport, move, take, bring. 2 HOLD, support, shoulder, uphold, sustain, maintain, harbour, cherish. 3 *bear children*: give birth to, breed, propagate, beget, engender, produce, generate, develop, yield, bring forth, give up. 4 TOLERATE, stand, put up with, endure, abide, suffer, permit, allow, admit.
◆ **bear on** refer to, relate to, affect, concern, involve.
◆ **bear out** confirm, endorse, support, uphold, prove, demonstrate, corroborate, substantiate, vindicate, justify.
◆ **bear up** persevere, soldier on, carry on, suffer, endure, survive, withstand.
◆ **bear with** tolerate, put up with, endure, suffer, forbear, be patient with, make allowances for.

bearable *adj* tolerable, endurable, sufferable, supportable, sustainable, acceptable, manageable.
🖙 unbearable, intolerable.

bearded *adj* unshaven, bristly, whiskered, tufted, hairy, hirsute, shaggy, bushy.
🖙 beardless, clean-shaven, smooth.

bearer *n* carrier, conveyor, porter, courier, messenger, runner, holder, possessor.

bearing *n* 1 *have no bearing on the matter*: relevance, significance, connection, relation, reference. 2 DEMEANOUR, manner, mien, air, aspect, attitude, behaviour, comportment, poise, deportment, carriage, posture.

bearings *n* orientation, position, situation, location, whereabouts, course, track, way, direction, aim.

beast *n* animal, creature, brute, monster, savage, barbarian, pig, swine, devil, fiend.

beat *v* 1 WHIP, flog, lash, tan (*infml*), cane, strap, thrash, lay into, hit, punch, strike, swipe, knock, bang, wham, bash, pound, hammer, batter, buffet, pelt, bruise. 2 PULSATE, pulse, throb, thump, race, palpitate, flutter, vibrate, quiver, tremble, shake, quake. 3 DEFEAT, trounce, best, worst, hammer (*infml*), slaughter (*sl*), conquer, overcome, overwhelm, vanquish, subdue, surpass, excel, outdo, outstrip, outrun.
➤ *n* 1 PULSATION, pulse, stroke, throb, thump, palpitation, flutter. 2 RHYTHM, time, tempo, metre, measure, rhyme, stress, accent. 3 *a policeman's beat*: round, rounds, territory, circuit, course, journey, way, path, route.
◆ **beat up** (*infml*) attack, assault, knock about, knock around, batter, do over (*infml*).

beaten *adj* 1 HAMMERED, stamped, forged, wrought, worked, formed, shaped, fashioned. 2 WHISKED, whipped, mixed, blended, frothy, foamy.

beating *n* 1 CORPORAL PUNISHMENT, chastisement, whipping, flogging, caning, thrashing. 2 DEFEAT, conquest, rout, ruin, downfall.

beautiful *adj* attractive, fair, pretty, lovely, good-looking, handsome, gorgeous, radiant, ravishing, stunning (*infml*), pleasing, appealing, alluring, charming, delightful, fine, exquisite.
🖙 ugly, plain, hideous.

beautify *v* embellish, enhance, improve, grace, gild, garnish, decorate, ornament, deck, bedeck, adorn, array, glamorize, titivate (*infml*), tart up (*sl*).
🖙 disfigure, spoil.

beauty *n* attractiveness, fairness, prettiness, loveliness, (good) looks, handsomeness, glamour, appeal, allure, charm, grace, elegance, symmetry, excellence.
🖙 ugliness, repulsiveness.

beaver away *v* work hard, work at, put a lot of effort in, persist, persevere, slog (*infml*), plug away (*infml*), slave away (*infml*).

because *conj* as, for, since, owing to, on account of, by reason of, thanks to.

beckon *v* summon, motion, gesture, signal, nod, wave, gesticulate, call, invite, attract, pull, draw, lure, allure, entice, tempt, coax.

become *v* 1 *become old-fashioned*: turn, grow, get, change into, develop into. 2 SUIT, befit, flatter, enhance, grace, embellish, ornament, set off, harmonize.

becoming *adj* **1** *a hat in a more becoming style*: attractive, charming, flattering, graceful, elegant, tasteful, fetching, pretty, comely. **2** *becoming behaviour*: APPROPRIATE, suitable, fit, fitting, befitting, consistent, congruous, compatible.

■ **1, 2** unbecoming.

bed *n* **1** divan, couch, bunk, berth, cot, mattress, pallet, sack (*sl*). **2** LAYER, stratum, substratum, matrix, base, bottom, foundation, groundwork, watercourse, channel. **3** *bed of flowers*: garden, border, patch, plot.

> Kinds of bed include: berth, box bed, bunk bed, camp-bed, cot, cradle, crib, day bed, divan bed, double bed, foldaway bed, folding bed, four-poster, hammock, mattress, pallet, palliasse, Put-u-up®, put-you-up, single bed, sleigh bed, sofa bed, trucklebed, trundlebed, twin bed, water-bed, Z-bed.

bedclothes *n* bedding, bed-linen, sheets, pillowcases, pillowslips, covers, blankets, bedspreads, coverlets, quilts, eiderdowns, pillows.

bedevil *v* afflict, torment, confound, frustrate, harass, irk, pester, plague, tease, annoy, besiege, torture, trouble, distress, vex, fret, worry, irritate.

bedlam *n* chaos, pandemonium, madhouse, commotion, confusion, furore, clamour, hubbub, hullabaloo, noise, tumult, turmoil, uproar, babel, anarchy.

■ calm.

bedraggled *adj* untidy, unkempt, dishevelled, disordered, scruffy, slovenly, messy, dirty, muddy, muddied, soiled, wet, sodden, drenched.

■ neat, tidy, clean.

bedridden *adj* confined to bed, incapacitated, laid up (*infml*), flat on one's back (*infml*).

bedrock *n* foundation, support, basis, base, bottom, footing, reason(s), rationale, fundamentals, basics, essentials, fundamental point, starting-point, premise, first principles, essence, heart.

before *adv* ahead, in front, in advance, sooner, earlier, formerly, previously.

■ after, later.

beforehand *adv* in advance, preliminarily, already, before, previously, earlier, sooner.

befriend *v* help, aid, assist, succour, back, support, stand by, uphold, sustain, comfort, encourage, welcome, favour, benefit, take under one's wing, make friends with, get to know.

■ neglect, oppose.

beg *v* request, require, desire, crave, beseech, plead, entreat, implore, pray, supplicate, petition, solicit, cadge, scrounge, sponge.

beggar *n* mendicant, supplicant, pauper, down-and-out, tramp, vagrant, cadger, scrounger, sponger.

begin *v* start, commence, set about, embark on, set in motion, activate, originate, initiate, introduce, found, institute, instigate, arise, spring, emerge, appear.

■ end, finish, cease.

beginner *n* novice, tiro, starter, learner, trainee, apprentice, student, freshman, fresher, recruit, cub, tenderfoot, fledgling.

■ veteran, old hand, expert.

beginning *n* start, commencement, onset, outset, opening, preface, prelude, introduction, initiation, establishment, inauguration, inception, starting point, birth, dawn, origin, source, fountainhead, root, seed, emergence, rise.

■ end, finish.

begrudge *v* resent, grudge, mind, object to, envy, covet, stint.

■ allow.

beguile *v* **1** CHARM, enchant, bewitch, captivate, amuse, entertain, divert, distract, occupy, engross. **2** DECEIVE, fool, hoodwink, dupe, trick, cheat, delude, mislead.

behalf *n* sake, account, good, interest, benefit, advantage, profit, name, authority, side, support.

behave *v* act, react, respond, work, function, run, operate, perform, conduct oneself, acquit oneself, comport oneself (*fml*).

behaviour *n* conduct, comportment (*fml*), manner, manners, actions, doings, dealings, ways, habits, action, reaction, response, functioning, operation, performance.

behead *v* decapitate, execute, guillotine.

behind *prep* **1** FOLLOWING, after, later than, causing, responsible for, instigating, initiating. **2** SUPPORTING, backing, for.

➤ *adv* after, following, next, subsequently, behindhand, late, overdue, in arrears, in debt.

➤ *n* rump, rear, posterior (*infml*), buttocks, seat, bottom, backside (*infml*), bum (*sl*), butt (*US infml*), tail (*infml*).

beholden *adj* indebted, obligated, obliged, under obligation, bound, grateful, owing, thankful.

beige *adj* buff, fawn, mushroom, camel, sandy, khaki, coffee, neutral.

being *n* 1 EXISTENCE, actuality, reality, life, animation, essence, substance, nature, soul, spirit. 2 CREATURE, animal, beast, human being, mortal, person, individual, thing, entity.

belated *adj* late, tardy, overdue, delayed, behindhand, unpunctual.
🠆 punctual, timely.

belch *v* burp (*infml*), hiccup, emit, discharge, disgorge, spew.
➤ *n* burp (*infml*), hiccup.

beleaguered *adj* harassed, pestered, badgered, bothered, worried, vexed, plagued, persecuted, surrounded, beset, besieged.

belie *v* 1 *the statistics belie the theory*: disprove, contradict, deny, refute, negate, run counter to, gainsay (*fml*), confute (*fml*). 2 *her looks belie her age*: conceal, disguise, misrepresent, falsify, mislead, deceive.

belief *n* 1 CONVICTION, persuasion, credit, trust, reliance, confidence, assurance, certainty, sureness, presumption, expectation, feeling, intuition, impression, notion, theory, view, opinion, judgement. 2 IDEOLOGY, faith, creed, doctrine, dogma, tenet, principle.
🠆 1 disbelief.

believable *adj* credible, imaginable, conceivable, acceptable, plausible, possible, likely, probable, authoritative, reliable, trustworthy.
🠆 unbelievable, incredible, unconvincing.

believe *v* accept, wear (*infml*), swallow (*infml*), credit, trust, count on, depend on, rely on, swear by, hold, maintain, postulate, assume, presume, gather, speculate, conjecture, guess, imagine, think, consider, reckon, suppose, deem, judge.
🠆 disbelieve, doubt.

believer *n* convert, proselyte, disciple, follower, adherent, devotee, zealot, supporter, upholder.
🠆 unbeliever, sceptic.

belittle *v* minimize, play down, dismiss, underrate, undervalue, underestimate, lessen, diminish, detract from, deprecate, decry, disparage, run down, deride, scorn, ridicule.
🠆 exaggerate, praise.

belligerent *adj* aggressive, militant, argumentative, quarrelsome, contentious, combative, pugnacious, violent, bullying, antagonistic, warring, warlike, bellicose.
🠆 peaceable.

bellow *v* roar, yell, shout, bawl, cry, scream, shriek, howl, clamour.

belong *v* fit, go with, be part of, attach to, link up with, tie up with, be connected with, relate to.

belongings *n* possessions, property, chattels, goods, effects, things, stuff (*infml*), gear (*infml*), paraphernalia.

beloved *adj* loved, adored, cherished, treasured, prized, precious, pet, favourite, dearest, dear, darling, admired, revered.

below *adv* beneath, under, underneath, down, lower, lower down.
🠆 above.
➤ *prep* 1 UNDER, underneath, beneath. 2 INFERIOR TO, lesser than, subordinate to, subject to.
🠆 above.

belt *n* 1 SASH, girdle, waistband, girth, strap. 2 STRIP, band, swathe, stretch, tract, area, region, district, zone, layer.

bemoan *v* lament, mourn, bewail, deplore, grieve for, regret, rue, sigh for, sorrow over, weep for.
🠆 gloat.

bemused *adj* confused, muddled, bewildered, puzzled, perplexed, dazed, befuddled, stupefied.
🠆 clear-headed, clear, lucid.

bench *n* 1 SEAT, form, settle, pew, ledge, counter, table, stall, workbench, worktable. 2 COURT, courtroom, tribunal, judiciary, judicature, judge, magistrate.

benchmark *n* criterion, example, level, model, norm, pattern, reference, reference-point, point of reference, guideline(s), standard, scale, touchstone, yardstick.

bend *v* curve, turn, deflect, swerve, veer, diverge, twist, contort, flex, shape, mould, buckle, bow, incline, lean, stoop, crouch.
🠆 straighten.
➤ *n* curvature, curve, arc, bow, loop, hook,

crook, elbow, angle, corner, turn, twist, zigzag.

beneath *adv* below, under, underneath, lower, lower down.

➢ *prep* **1** UNDER, underneath, below, lower than. **2** UNWORTHY OF, unbefitting.

benediction *n* blessing, prayer, thanksgiving, consecration, favour, grace, invocation.

⇄ anathema, curse.

benefactor *n* philanthropist, patron, sponsor, angel (*infml*), backer, supporter, promoter, donor, contributor, subscriber, provider, helper, friend, well-wisher.

⇄ opponent, persecutor.

beneficial *adj* advantageous, favourable, useful, helpful, profitable, rewarding, valuable, improving, edifying, wholesome.

⇄ harmful, detrimental, useless.

beneficiary *n* payee, receiver, recipient, inheritor, legatee, heir, heiress, successor.

benefit *n* advantage, good, welfare, interest, favour, help, aid, assistance, service, use, avail, gain, profit, asset, blessing.

⇄ disadvantage, harm, damage.

➢ *v* help, aid, assist, serve, avail, advantage, profit, improve, enhance, better, further, advance, promote.

⇄ hinder, harm, undermine.

benevolent *adj* philanthropic, humanitarian, charitable, generous, liberal, munificent, altruistic, benign, humane, kind, kindly, well-disposed, compassionate, caring, considerate.

⇄ mean, selfish, malevolent.

benign *adj* **1** BENEVOLENT, good, gracious, gentle, kind, obliging, friendly, amiable, genial, sympathetic. **2** *a benign tumour*: curable, harmless. **3** FAVOURABLE, propitious, beneficial, temperate, mild, warm, refreshing, restorative, wholesome.

⇄ **1** hostile. **2** malignant. **3** harmful, unpleasant.

bent *adj* **1** ANGLED, curved, bowed, arched, folded, doubled, twisted, hunched, stooped. **2** (*infml*) DISHONEST, crooked (*infml*), illegal, criminal, corrupt, untrustworthy.

⇄ **1** straight, upright. **2** honest.

➢ *n* tendency, inclination, leaning, preference, ability, capacity, faculty, aptitude, facility, gift, talent, knack, flair, forte.

♦ **bent on** determined, resolved, set, fixed, inclined, disposed.

bequeath *v* will, leave, bestow, gift, endow, grant, settle, hand down, pass on, impart, transmit, assign, entrust, commit.

bequest *n* legacy, inheritance, heritage, trust, bestowal, endowment, gift, donation, estate, devisal, settlement.

bereavement *n* loss, deprivation, dispossession, death.

bereft *adj* deprived, robbed, stripped, destitute, devoid, lacking, wanting, minus.

berserk *adj* mad, crazy, demented, insane, deranged, frantic, frenzied, wild, raging, furious, violent, rabid, raving.

⇄ sane, calm.

berth *n* **1** BED, bunk, hammock, billet. **2** MOORING, anchorage, quay, wharf, dock, harbour, port.

beseech *v* beg, call on, entreat, implore, ask, petition, plead, pray, solicit, appeal to, supplicate, crave, desire, adjure (*fml*), importune (*fml*), exhort (*fml*).

beset *v* assail, attack, harass, entangle, worry, pester, plague, torment, bedevil, hem in, surround, hassle (*infml*).

besetting *adj* compulsive, habitual, persistent, dominant, inveterate, irresistible, uncontrollable, obsessive, prevalent, constant, recurring, troublesome, harassing.

beside *prep* alongside, abreast of, next to, adjacent, abutting, bordering, neighbouring, next door to, close to, near, overlooking.

besides *adv* also, as well, too, in addition, additionally, further, furthermore, moreover.

➢ *prep* apart from, other than, in addition to, over and above.

besiege *v* **1** LAY SIEGE TO, blockade, surround, encircle, confine. **2** TROUBLE, bother, importune, assail, beset, beleaguer, harass, pester, badger, nag, hound, plague.

besotted *adj* infatuated, doting, obsessed, smitten, hypnotized, spellbound, intoxicated.

⇄ indifferent, disenchanted.

best *adj* optimum, optimal, first, foremost, leading, unequalled, unsurpassed, matchless, incomparable, supreme, greatest, highest, largest, finest, excellent, outstanding, superlative, first-rate, first-class, perfect.

⇄ worst.

➤ *adv* greatly, extremely, exceptionally, excellently, superlatively.

Ea worst.

➤ *n* finest, cream, prime, elite, top, first, pick, choice, favourite.

Ea worst.

bestow *v* award, present, grant, confer, endow, bequeath, commit, entrust, impart, transmit, allot, apportion, accord, give, donate, lavish.

Ea withhold, deprive.

bet *n* wager, flutter (*infml*), gamble, speculation, risk, venture, stake, ante, bid, pledge.

➤ *v* wager, gamble, punt, speculate, risk, hazard, chance, venture, lay, stake, bid, pledge.

betray *v* **1** *betray a friend*: inform on, shop (*sl*), sell (out), double-cross, desert, abandon, forsake. **2** DISCLOSE, give away, tell, divulge, expose, reveal, show, manifest.

Ea ⬛⬛⬛ ⬛⬛ ⬛⬛⬛ ⬛⬛⬛⬛⬛⬛ **&** ⬛⬛⬛⬛⬛⬛ ⬛⬛⬛⬛

betrayal *n* treachery, treason, sell-out, disloyalty, unfaithfulness, double-dealing, duplicity, deception, trickery, falseness.

Ea loyalty, protection.

betrayer *n* traitor, Judas, informer, grass (*sl*), supergrass (*sl*), double-crosser, deceiver, conspirator, renegade, apostate.

Ea protector, supporter.

better *adj* **1** SUPERIOR, bigger, larger, longer, greater, worthier, finer, surpassing, preferable. **2** IMPROVING, progressing, on the mend, recovering, fitter, healthier, stronger, recovered, restored.

Ea 1 inferior. **2** worse.

➤ *v* **1** IMPROVE, ameliorate, enhance, raise, further, promote, forward, reform, mend, correct. **2** SURPASS, top, beat, outdo, outstrip, overtake.

Ea 1 worsen, deteriorate.

between *prep* mid, amid, amidst, among, amongst.

beverage *n* drink, draught, liquor, liquid, refreshment.

bevy *n* gathering, band, company, troupe, group, flock, gaggle, pack, bunch, crowd, throng.

bewail *v* grieve over, sorrow over, lament, bemoan, cry over, moan, mourn, regret, repent, rue, sigh over, deplore, keen.

Ea gloat, glory, vaunt.

beware *v* watch out, look out, mind, take

heed, steer clear of, avoid, shun, guard against.

bewilder *v* confuse, muddle, disconcert, confound, bamboozle (*infml*), baffle, puzzle, perplex, mystify, daze, stupefy, disorient.

bewildered *adj* confused, muddled, uncertain, disoriented, nonplussed, bamboozled (*infml*), baffled, puzzled, perplexed, mystified, bemused, surprised, stunned.

Ea unperturbed, collected.

bewitch *v* charm, enchant, allure, beguile, spellbind, possess, captivate, enrapture, obsess, fascinate, entrance, hypnotize.

beyond *prep* past, further than, apart from, away from, remote from, out of range of, out of reach of, above, over, superior to.

bias *n* slant, angle, distortion, bent, leaning, inclination, tendency, propensity, partiality, favouritism, prejudice, one-sidedness, unfairness, bigotry, intolerance.

Ea impartiality, fairness.

biased *adj* slanted, angled, distorted, warped, twisted, loaded, weighted, influenced, swayed, partial, predisposed, prejudiced, one-sided, unfair, bigoted, blinkered, jaundiced.

Ea impartial, fair.

Bible *n* **1** *study the Christian Bible*: Scriptures, holy Scriptures, Holy Bible, holy writ, Old Testament, New Testament, Apocrypha, writings, canon, revelation, Pentateuch, law, prophets, Gospels, epistles, letters, good book (*infml*). **2** *the gardener's bible*; *the cyclist's bible*: manual, handbook, authority, reference book, encyclopedia, dictionary, lexicon, guidebook, directory, companion, textbook, primer.

The books of the Bible are: *the Old Testament*: Genesis, Exodus, Leviticus, Numbers, Deuteronomy, Joshua, Judges, Ruth, 1 Samuel, 2 Samuel, 1 Kings, 2 Kings, 1 Chronicles, 2 Chronicles, Ezra, Nehemiah, Esther, Job, Psalms, Proverbs, Ecclesiastes, Song of Solomon (Song of Songs), Isaiah, Jeremiah, Lamentations, Ezekiel, Daniel, Hosea, Joel, Amos, Obadiah, Jonah, Micah, Nahum, Habakkuk, Zephaniah, Haggai, Zechariah, Malachi; *the New Testament*: Matthew, Mark, Luke, John, Acts of the Apostles, Romans, 1 Corinthians, 2

Corinthians, Galatians, Ephesians, Philippians, Colossians, 1 Thessalonians, 2 Thessalonians, 1 Timothy, 2 Timothy, Titus, Philemon, Hebrews, James, 1 Peter, 2 Peter, 1 John, 2 John, 3 John, Jude, Revelation; *the Apocrypha*: 1 Esdras, 2 Esdras, Tobit, Judith, Additions to Esther, Wisdom of Solomon, Ecclesiasticus, Baruch, Letter of Jeremiah, Prayer of Azariah, Song of the Three Young Men, History of Susanna, Bel and the Dragon, Prayer of Manasseh, 1 Maccabees, 2 Maccabees.

bicker *v* squabble, row, quarrel, wrangle, argue, scrap, spar, fight, clash, disagree, dispute.
☒ agree.

bicycle *n* cycle, bike (*infml*), two-wheeler, push-bike, racer, mountain-bike, tandem, penny-farthing.

Parts of a bicycle include: bell, brake, brake block, brake cable, brake caliper, brake lever, brake shoe, cable braking system, carrier, centre-pull brake cable, chain, chain guide, chain guard, chain link, chain stays, chain transmission, chain wheel, coaster brake, crank, crank lever, crankset, crossbar, derailleur gear, diamond frame, down tube, drum brake, dynamo, footrest, fork, frame, freewheel unit, gear, gear cable, gearwheel, handgrip, handlebars, handlebar stem, hub, hub gear, inner tube, kickstand, lamp, lamp bracket, mudguard, fender (*US*), pannier, pedal, prop stand, pulley, pump, reflector, rim brake, rim tape, rod braking system, roller chain, saddle, saddle spring, seat pillar, seat stays, seat tube, side-pull brake cable, speedometer, spokes, spoke nipples, sprocket (wheel), stabilizer, steering head, steering tube, stirrup guide, toe clip, tool bag, tyre, tire (*US*), tyre valve, Presta® valve, Schrader® valve, Woods® valve; wheel bearing, wheel lock, wheel nut, wheel rim, wheel spindle.

bid *v* **1** ASK, request, desire, instruct, direct, command, enjoin, require, charge, call, summon, invite, solicit. **2** *he bid more than the painting was worth*: offer, proffer, tender, submit, propose.
➤ *n* **1** OFFER, tender, sum, amount, price, advance, submission, proposal. **2** ATTEMPT, effort, try, go (*infml*), endeavour, venture.

big *adj* **1** LARGE, great, sizable, considerable, substantial, huge, enormous, immense, massive, colossal, gigantic, mammoth, burly, bulky, extensive, spacious, vast, voluminous. **2** IMPORTANT, significant, momentous, serious, main, principal, eminent, prominent, influential. **3** *that's big of you*: generous, magnanimous, gracious, unselfish.
☒ **1** small, little. **2** insignificant, unknown.

bigot *n* chauvinist, sectarian, racist, sexist, dogmatist, fanatic, zealot.
☒ liberal, humanitarian.

bigoted *adj* prejudiced, biased, intolerant, illiberal, narrow-minded, narrow, blinkered, closed, dogmatic, opinionated, obstinate.
☒ tolerant, liberal, broad-minded, enlightened.

bigotry *n* prejudice, discrimination, bias, injustice, unfairness, intolerance, narrow-mindedness, chauvinism, jingoism, sectarianism, racism, racialism, sexism, dogmatism, fanaticism.
☒ tolerance.

bile *n* anger, bitterness, bad temper, short temper, ill-humour, irascibility, irritability, testiness, peevishness, rancour, choler, gall, spleen.

bilious *adj* **1** IRRITABLE, choleric, cross, grumpy, crotchety, testy, grouchy, peevish. **2** SICK, queasy, nauseated, sickly, out of sorts (*infml*).

bill¹ *n* **1** INVOICE, statement, account, charges, reckoning, tally, score. **2** CIRCULAR, leaflet, handout, bulletin, handbill, broadsheet, advertisement, notice, poster, placard, playbill, programme. **3** *parliamentary bill*: proposal, measure, legislation.
➤ *v* invoice, charge, debit.

bill² *n* beak, mandible, neb, nib, rostrum.

billet *n* **1** ACCOMMODATION, quarters, barracks, lodging, housing, berth. **2** EMPLOYMENT, post, occupation.

billow *v* swell, expand, bulge, puff out, fill out, balloon, rise, heave, surge, roll, undulate.

bind *v* **1** FASTEN, tie, attach, fasten, secure, clamp, stick, lash, truss, rope, strap, fetter, tether, shackle, chain, bandage, cover, dress, wrap, tape. **2** OBLIGE, force, compel, constrain, impel, require, necessitate, restrict, confine, restrain, hamper, yoke. **3** UNITE, join, tie, unify, bond, stand together, pull together, close ranks.

➤ *n* bore, difficulty, inconvenience, irritation, dilemma, embarrassment, hole, impasse, nuisance, predicament, quandary, drag (*infml*), spot (*infml*), tight spot (*infml*).

binding *adj* obligatory, compulsory, mandatory, necessary, requisite, permanent, conclusive, irrevocable, unalterable, indissoluble, unbreakable, strict.

➤ *n* border, edging, trimming, tape, bandage, covering, wrapping.

biography *n* life story, life, history, autobiography, memoirs, recollections, curriculum vitae, account, record.

biology

Biological terms include: bacteriology, biochemistry, biology, bionics, botany, cybernetics, cytology, Darwinism, neo-Darwinism, ecology, embryology, endocrinology, evolution, Haeckel's law, genetics, Mendelism, Lamarckism, marine biology, natural history, palaeontology, pathology, physiology, systematics, taxonomy, zoology; amino acid, anatomy, animal behaviour, animal kingdom, bacillus, bacteria, biologist, botanist, cell, chromosome, class, coccus, conservation, corpuscle, cultivar, cytoplasm, deoxyribonucleic acid (DNA), diffusion, ecosystem, ectoplasm, embryo, endoplasmic reticulum (ER), enzyme, evolution, excretion, extinction, flora and fauna, food chain, fossil, gene, genetic engineering, genetic fingerprinting, population genetics, germ, Golgi apparatus, hereditary factor, homeostasis, living world, meiosis, membrane, metabolism, micro-organism, microbe, mitosis, molecule, mutation, natural selection, nuclear membrane, nucleus, nutrition, order, organism, osmosis, parasitism, photosynthesis, pollution, protein, protoplasm, reproduction, respiration, reticulum, ribonucleic acid (RNA), ribosome, secretion, survival of the fittest, symbiosis, virus.

bird

Birds include: sparrow, thrush, starling, blackbird, bluetit, chaffinch, greenfinch, bullfinch, dunnock, robin, wagtail, swallow, tit, wren, martin, swift, crow, magpie, dove, pigeon, skylark, nightingale, linnet, warbler, jay, jackdaw, rook, raven, cuckoo, woodpecker, yellowhammer; duck, mallard, eider, teal, swan, goose, heron, stork, flamingo, pelican, kingfisher, moorhen, coot, lapwing, peewit, plover, curlew, snipe, avocet, seagull, guillemot, tern, petrel, crane, bittern, petrel, albatross, gannet, cormorant, auk, puffin, dipper; eagle, owl, hawk, sparrowhawk, falcon, kestrel, osprey, buzzard, vulture, condor; emu, ostrich, kiwi, peacock, penguin; chicken, grouse, partridge, pheasant, quail, turkey; canary, budgerigar, budgie (*infml*), cockatiel, cockatoo, lovebird, parakeet, parrot, macaw, toucan, myna bird, mockingbird, kookaburra, bird of paradise.

birth *n* **1** CHILDBIRTH, parturition, confinement, delivery, nativity. **2** *of noble birth*: ancestry, family, parentage, descent, line, lineage, genealogy, pedigree, blood, stock, race, extraction, background, breeding. **3** BEGINNING, rise, emergence, origin, source, derivation.

birthplace *n* place of origin, native town, native country, fatherland, mother country, roots, provenance, source, fount.

bisect *v* halve, divide, separate, split, intersect, cross, fork, bifurcate.

bisexual *adj* androgynous, hermaphrodite, AC/DC (*infml*), bi (*infml*), swinging both ways (*infml*).
🖙 heterosexual, homosexual.

bit *n* fragment, part, segment, piece, slice, crumb, morsel, scrap, atom, mite, whit, jot, iota, grain, speck.
◆ **bit by bit** gradually, little by little, step by step, piecemeal.
🖙 wholesale.

bitchy *adj* catty, snide, nasty, mean, spiteful, malicious, vindictive, backbiting, venomous, cruel, vicious.
🖙 kind.

bite *v* **1** CHEW, masticate, munch, gnaw, nibble, champ, crunch, crush. **2** *the dog bit her hand*: nip, pierce, wound, tear, rend. **3** SMART, sting, tingle. **4** GRIP, hold, seize, pinch, take effect.

➤ *n* **1** NIP, wound, sting, smarting, pinch. **2** *a bite to eat*: snack, refreshment, mouthful, morsel, taste. **3** PUNGENCY, piquancy, kick (*infml*), punch.

biting *adj* **1** COLD, freezing, bitter, harsh, severe. **2** CUTTING, incisive, piercing, penetrating, raw, stinging, sharp, tart,

caustic, scathing, cynical, hurtful.
F3 1 mild. **2** bland.

bitter *adj* **1** ACID, tart, sharp, sour,
vinegary, unsweetened, pungent, tangy,
acrid (*fml*), astringent (*fml*), acerbic (*fml*). **2**
RESENTFUL, embittered, begrudging,
indignant, aggrieved, angry, sour, morose,
jaundiced, cynical, sullen, hostile, spiteful,
vindictive, venomous, scathing, caustic,
acrimonious (*fml*), acerbic (*fml*),
rancorous (*fml*), malevolent (*fml*), vitriolic
(*fml*), vituperative (*fml*), virulent (*fml*), with
a chip on one's shoulder (*infml*). **3** INTENSE,
severe, harsh, fierce, cruel, savage,
merciless, painful, sad, unhappy,
disappointing, tragic, distressing,
harrowing, heartbreaking, heart-rending. **4**
bitter winds: stinging, biting, sharp,
freezing, freezing cold, arctic, raw, harsh,
piercing, penetrating.
F3 1 sweet. **2** contented. **3** mild, happy. **4**
warm.

bitterness *n* **1** ACIDITY, tartness,
sharpness, sourness, vinegar, pungency,
tanginess. **2** RESENTMENT, embitterment,
grudge, indignation, anger, sourness,
moroseness, jaundice, cynicism,
sullenness, hostility, spite, vindictiveness,
venom, acrimony (*fml*), acerbicity (*fml*),
rancour (*fml*), malevolence (*fml*), virulence
(*fml*). **3** INTENSITY, severity, harshness,
ferocity, cruelty, pain, painfulness,
sadness, unhappiness, disappointment,
tragedy, distress, heartbreaking, heart-
rending. **4** *the bitterness of the winter*:
sharpness, coldness, rawness, harshness,
penetration, bite.

bizarre *adj* strange, odd, queer, curious,
weird, peculiar, eccentric, way-out (*infml*),
outlandish, ludicrous, ridiculous, fantastic,
extravagant, grotesque, freakish,
abnormal, deviant, unusual, extraordinary.
F3 normal, ordinary.

blab *v* blurt out, tell, reveal, disclose,
divulge, let slip, gossip, tattle, squeal
(*infml*), leak (*infml*).
F3 hide, hush up.

black *adj* **1** JET-BLACK, coal-black, jet,
ebony, sable, inky, sooty, dusky, swarthy. **2**
DARK, unlit, moonless, starless, overcast,
dingy, gloomy, sombre, funereal. **3** FILTHY,
dirty, soiled, grimy, grubby.
F3 1 white. **2** bright. **3** clean.
➤ *v* boycott, blacklist, ban, bar, taboo.
◆ **black out 1** FAINT, pass out, collapse,
flake out (*infml*). **2** DARKEN, eclipse, cover

up, conceal, suppress, withhold, censor,
gag.

blacken *v* **1** DARKEN, dirty, soil, smudge,
cloud. **2** DEFAME, malign, slander, libel,
vilify, revile, denigrate, detract, smear,
besmirch, sully, stain, tarnish, taint, defile,
discredit, dishonour.
F3 2 praise, enhance.

blacklist *v* debar, disallow, exclude, ban,
outlaw, bar, boycott, expel, ostracize,
reject, shut out, repudiate, snub, taboo,
veto, preclude (*fml*), proscribe (*fml*).
F3 accept, allow.

blackmail *n* extortion, chantage, hush
money (*infml*), intimidation, protection,
pay-off, ransom.
➤ *v* extort, bleed, milk, squeeze, hold to
ransom, threaten, lean on (*infml*), force,
compel, coerce, demand.

blackout *n* **1** *a news blackout*: suppression,
censorship, cover-up (*infml*),
concealment, secrecy. **2** FAINT, coma,
unconsciousness, oblivion. **3** power
failure, power cut.

blade *n* edge, knife, dagger, sword, scalpel,
razor, vane.

blame *n* censure, criticism, stick (*sl*),
reprimand, reproof, reproach,
recrimination, condemnation, accusation,
charge, rap (*sl*), incrimination, guilt,
culpability, fault, responsibility,
accountability, liability, onus.
➤ *v* accuse, charge, tax, reprimand, chide,
reprove, upbraid, reprehend, admonish,
rebuke, reproach, censure, criticize, find
fault with, disapprove, condemn.
F3 exonerate, vindicate.

blameless *adj* innocent, guiltless, clear,
faultless, perfect, unblemished, stainless,
virtuous, sinless, upright, above reproach,
irreproachable, unblamable,
unimpeachable.
F3 guilty, blameworthy.

blameworthy *adj* at fault, guilty,
discreditable, disreputable, shameful,
unworthy, indefensible, inexcusable,
reprehensible, reproachable, culpable
(*fml*), flagitious (*fml*).
F3 blameless.

blanch *v* blench, whiten, pale, fade,
bleach.
F3 colour, blush, redden.

bland *adj* boring, monotonous, humdrum,
tedious, dull, uninspiring, uninteresting,
unexciting, nondescript, characterless,

flat, insipid, tasteless, weak, mild, smooth, soft, gentle, non-irritant.

Ea lively, stimulating, sharp.

blandishments *n* flattery, compliments, enticements, fawning, inducements, ingratiation, blarney, cajolery, coaxing, persuasiveness, sycophancy, wheedling, inveiglement (*fml*), soft soap (*infml*), sweet talk (*infml*).

blank *adj* 1 *a blank page*: empty, unfilled, void, clear, bare, unmarked, plain, clean, white. 2 EXPRESSIONLESS, deadpan, poker-faced, impassive, apathetic, glazed, vacant, uncomprehending.
➤ *n* space, gap, break, void, emptiness, vacancy, vacuity, nothingness, vacuum.

blanket *n* covering, coating, coat, layer, film, carpet, rug, cloak, mantle, cover, sheet, envelope, wrapper, wrapping.
➤ *v* cover, coat, eclipse, hide, conceal, mask, cloak, surround, muffle, deaden, obscure, cloud.

blare *v* trumpet, clamour, roar, blast, boom, resound, ring, peal, clang, hoot, toot, honk.

blasé *adj* nonchalant, offhand, unimpressed, unmoved, unexcited, jaded, weary, bored, uninterested, uninspired, apathetic, indifferent, cool, unconcerned.
Ea excited, enthusiastic.

blaspheme *v* profane, desecrate, swear, curse, imprecate, damn, execrate, revile, abuse.

blasphemous *adj* profane, impious, sacrilegious, imprecatory, godless, ungodly, irreligious, irreverent.

blasphemy *n* profanity, curse, expletive, imprecation, cursing, swearing, execration, impiety, irreverence, sacrilege, desecration, violation, outrage.

blast *n* 1 EXPLOSION, detonation, bang, crash, clap, crack, volley, burst, outburst, discharge. 2 *a blast of cold air*: draught, gust, gale, squall, storm, tempest. 3 SOUND, blow, blare, roar, boom, peal, hoot, wail, scream, shriek.
➤ *v* 1 EXPLODE, blow up, burst, shatter, destroy, demolish, ruin, assail, attack. 2 SOUND, blare, roar, boom, peal, hoot, wail, scream, shriek. 3 CRITICIZE, reprimand, rebuke, tell off, reprove, upbraid, berate (*fml*).
◆ **blast off** take off, lift off, be launched.

blatant *adj* flagrant, brazen, barefaced, arrant, open, overt, undisguised,

ostentatious, glaring, conspicuous, obtrusive, prominent, pronounced, obvious, sheer, outright, unmitigated.

blaze *n* fire, flames, conflagration, bonfire, flare-up, explosion, blast, burst, outburst, radiance, brilliance, glare, flash, gleam, glitter, glow, light, flame.
➤ *v* burn, flame, flare (up), erupt, explode, burst, fire, flash, gleam, glare, beam, shine, glow.

bleach *v* whiten, blanch, decolorize, fade, pale, lighten.

bleak *adj* 1 GLOOMY, sombre, leaden, grim, dreary, dismal, depressing, joyless, cheerless, comfortless, hopeless, discouraging, disheartening. 2 COLD, chilly, raw, weather-beaten, unsheltered, windy, windswept, exposed, open, barren, bare, empty, desolate, gaunt.
Ea 1 bright, cheerful.

bleary *adj* bleary-eyed, blurred, blurry, cloudy, dim, tired, watery, rheumy.

bleed *v* HAEMORRHAGE, gush, spurt, flow, run, exude, weep, ooze, seep, trickle. 2 DRAIN, suck dry, exhaust, squeeze, milk, sap, reduce, deplete.

blemish *n* flaw, imperfection, defect, fault, deformity, disfigurement, birthmark, naevus, spot, mark, speck, smudge, blotch, blot, stain, taint, disgrace, dishonour.
➤ *v* flaw, deface, disfigure, spoil, mar, damage, impair, spot, mark, blot, blotch, stain, sully, taint, tarnish.

blend *v* 1 MERGE, amalgamate, coalesce, compound, synthesize, fuse, unite, combine, mix, mingle. 2 HARMONIZE, complement, fit, match.
Ea 1 separate.
➤ *n* compound, composite, alloy, amalgam, amalgamation, synthesis, fusion, combination, union, mix, mixture, concoction.

bless *v* 1 ANOINT, sanctify, consecrate, hallow, dedicate, ordain. 2 PRAISE, extol, magnify, glorify, exalt, thank. 3 APPROVE, countenance, favour, grace, bestow, endow, provide.
Ea 1 curse. 2 condemn.

blessed *adj* 1 HOLY, sacred, hallowed, sanctified, revered, adored, divine. 2 HAPPY, contented, glad, joyful, joyous, lucky, fortunate, prosperous, favoured, endowed.
Ea 1 cursed.

blessing n 1 CONSECRATION, dedication, benediction, grace, thanksgiving, invocation. 2 BENEFIT, advantage, favour, godsend, windfall, gift, gain, profit, help, service. 3 *give a proposal one's blessing*: approval, concurrence, backing, support, authority, sanction, consent, permission, leave.
🔁 2 curse, blight. 3 condemnation.

blight n curse, bane, evil, scourge, affliction, disease, cancer, canker, fungus, mildew, rot, decay, pollution, contamination, corruption, infestation.
🔁 blessing, boon.
➤ v spoil, mar, injure, undermine, ruin, wreck, crush, shatter, destroy, annihilate, blast, wither, shrivel, frustrate, disappoint.
🔁 bless.

blind adj 1 SIGHTLESS, unsighted, unseeing, eyeless, purblind, partially sighted. 2 IMPETUOUS, impulsive, hasty, rash, reckless, wild, mad, indiscriminate, careless, heedless, mindless, unthinking, unreasoning, irrational. 3 *blind to their needs*: ignorant, oblivious, unaware, unconscious, unobservant, inattentive, neglectful, indifferent, insensitive, thoughtless, inconsiderate. 4 CLOSED, obstructed, hidden, concealed, obscured.
🔁 1 sighted. 2 careful, cautious. 3 aware, sensitive.
➤ n screen, cover, cloak, mask, camouflage, masquerade, front, façade, distraction, smokescreen, cover-up (*infml*).

Ways of describing sight impairment include: amaurotic, astigmatic, having cataracts, colour-blind, far-sighted, glaucomatous, half-blind, hemeralopic, hypermetropic, long-sighted, myopic, near-sighted, night-blind, nyctalopic, partially-sighted, presbyopic, purblind, sand-blind, short-sighted, snow-blind, stone-blind, trachomatous, visually handicapped, visually impaired, blind as a bat (*infml*).

blink v 1 *his eyes blinked*: wink, nictate (*fml*), nictitate (*fml*). 2 *the light blinked*: flash, flicker, twinkle, shine, gleam, glimmer, glitter, sparkle, scintillate.

bliss n blissfulness, ecstasy, euphoria, rapture, joy, happiness, gladness, blessedness, paradise, heaven.
🔁 misery, hell, damnation.

blissful adj ecstatic, euphoric, elated, enraptured, rapturous, delighted,

enchanted, joyful, joyous, happy.
🔁 miserable, wretched.

blister n sore, swelling, cyst, boil, abscess, ulcer, pustule, pimple, carbuncle.

blithe adj casual, unthinking, thoughtless, careless, heedless, uncaring, unconcerned, carefree, untroubled, cheerful, cheery, light-hearted.
🔁 morose, thoughtful, serious.

blitz n 1 *the blitz during the war*: bombardment, attack, offensive, raid, strike, campaign, onslaught, blitzkrieg. 2 *have a blitz on the garden*: effort, all-out effort, attack, exertion, attempt, endeavour, campaign.

blizzard n snowstorm, squall, storm, tempest.

bloated adj swollen, puffy, blown up, inflated, distended, dilated, expanded, enlarged, turgid, bombastic.
🔁 thin, shrunken, shrivelled.

blob n drop, droplet, globule, glob (*infml*), bead, pearl, bubble, dab, spot, gob, lump, mass, ball, pellet, pill.

bloc n alliance, group, league, coalition, federation, union, ring, syndicate, entente, axis, cabal, cartel, clique, faction.

block n 1 *a block of stone*: piece, lump, mass, chunk, hunk, square, cube, brick, bar. 2 OBSTACLE, barrier, bar, jam, blockage, stoppage, resistance, obstruction, impediment, hindrance, let, delay.
➤ v choke, clog, plug, stop up, dam up, close, bar, obstruct, impede, hinder, stonewall, stop, check, arrest, halt, thwart, scotch, deter.

blockade n barrier, barricade, siege, obstruction, restriction, stoppage, closure.

blockage n blocking, obstruction, stoppage, occlusion, block, clot, jam, log-jam, congestion, hindrance, impediment.

blond, blonde adj fair, flaxen, golden, fair-haired, golden-haired, light-coloured, bleached.

blood n extraction, birth, descent, lineage, family, kindred, relations, ancestry, descendants, kinship, relationship.

bloodcurdling adj horrifying, chilling, spine-chilling, hair-raising, terrifying, frightening, scary, dreadful, fearful, horrible, horrid, horrendous.

bloodless adj 1 *a bloodless coup*: peaceful, non-violent, strife-free, unwarlike. **2** *her bloodless face*: ASHEN, anaemic, colourless, pale, pallid, pasty, sallow, sickly, wan, chalky, cold, drained, feeble, insipid, languid, lifeless, listless, unfeeling, unemotional, passionless, spiritless, torpid.

F3 1 bloody, violent. **2** bloody, ruddy, vigorous.

bloodshed *n* killing, murder, slaughter, massacre, blood-bath, butchery, carnage, gore, bloodletting.

bloodthirsty *adj* murderous, homicidal, warlike, savage, barbaric, barbarous, brutal, ferocious, vicious, cruel, inhuman, ruthless.

bloody *adj* bleeding, bloodstained, gory, sanguinary, murderous, savage, brutal, ferocious, fierce, cruel.

bloom *n* **1** BLOSSOM, flower, bud. **2** PRIME, heyday, perfection, blush, flush, glow, rosiness, beauty, radiance, lustre, health, vigour, freshness.

➤ *v* bud, sprout, grow, wax, develop, mature, blossom, flower, blow, open.

F3 fade, wither.

blossom *n* bloom, flower, bud.

➤ *v* develop, mature, bloom, flower, blow, flourish, thrive, prosper, succeed.

F3 fade, wither.

blot *n* spot, stain, smudge, blotch, smear, mark, speck, blemish, flaw, fault, defect, taint, disgrace.

➤ *v* spot, mark, stain, smudge, blur, sully, taint, tarnish, spoil, mar, disfigure, disgrace.

◆ **blot out** obliterate, cancel, delete, erase, expunge, darken, obscure, shadow, eclipse.

blotch *n* patch, splodge, splotch, splash, smudge, blot, spot, mark, stain, blemish.

blotchy *adj* spotty, spotted, patchy, uneven, smeary, blemished, reddened, inflamed.

blow¹ *v* **1** BREATHE, exhale, pant, puff, waft, fan, flutter, float, flow, stream, rush, whirl, whisk, sweep, fling, buffet, drive, blast. **2** *blow a horn*: play, sound, pipe, trumpet, toot, blare.

➤ *n* puff, draught, flurry, gust, blast, wind, gale, squall, tempest.

◆ **blow over** die down, subside, end, finish, cease, pass, vanish, disappear, dissipate, fizzle out, peter out.

◆ **blow up 1** EXPLODE, go off, detonate, burst, blast, bomb. **2** LOSE ONE'S TEMPER, blow one's top (*infml*), erupt, hit the roof

(*infml*), rage, go mad (*infml*). **3** INFLATE, pump up, swell, fill (out), puff up, bloat, distend, dilate, expand, enlarge, magnify, exaggerate, overstate.

blow² *n* **1** *a blow on the head*: concussion, box, cuff, clip, clout, swipe, biff (*infml*), bash, slap, smack, whack (*infml*), wallop (*infml*), belt (*infml*), buffet, bang, clap, knock, rap, stroke, thump, punch. **2** MISFORTUNE, affliction, reverse, setback, comedown, disappointment, upset, jolt, shock, bombshell, calamity, catastrophe, disaster.

blow-out *n* **1** PUNCTURE, flat tyre, burst tyre, flat (*infml*). **2** PARTY, celebration, feast, binge (*infml*), bash (*infml*), knees-up (*infml*), rave (*infml*), rave-up (*infml*), beanfeast (*infml*).

blowy *adj* breezy, windy, fresh, blustery, gusty, squally, stormy.

bludgeon *v* **1** BEAT, strike, club, batter, cosh (*sl*), cudgel. **2** FORCE, coerce, bulldoze, badger, hector, harass, browbeat, bully, terrorize, intimidate.

blue *adj* **1** AZURE, sapphire, cobalt, ultramarine, navy, indigo, aquamarine, turquoise, cyan. **2** DEPRESSED, low, down in the dumps (*infml*), dejected, downcast, dispirited, down-hearted, despondent, gloomy, glum, dismal, sad, unhappy, miserable, melancholy, morose, fed up (*infml*). **3** *a blue joke*: obscene, offensive, indecent, improper, coarse, vulgar, lewd, dirty, pornographic, bawdy, smutty, near the bone, near the knuckle, risqué.

F3 2 cheerful, happy. **3** decent, clean.

blueprint *n* archetype, prototype, model, pattern, design, outline, draft, sketch, pilot, guide, plan, scheme, project.

blues *n* depression, despondency, gloom, gloominess, moodiness, glumness, melancholy, miseries, dejection, doldrums, dumps (*infml*).

F3 euphoria.

bluff¹ *v* lie, pretend, feign, sham, fake, deceive, delude, mislead, hoodwink, blind, bamboozle (*infml*), fool.

➤ *n* lie, idle boast, bravado, humbug, pretence, show, sham, fake, fraud, trick, subterfuge, deceit, deception.

bluff² *adj* blunt, candid, direct, downright, open, outspoken, plain-spoken, straightforward, frank, genial, good-natured, hearty, affable.

F3 diplomatic, refined.

➤ *n* cliff, crag, escarpment, peak, precipice, promontory, foreland, bank, brow, headland, height, ridge, scarp, escarp.

blunder *n* mistake, error, solecism, howler (*infml*), bloomer (*infml*), clanger (*infml*), inaccuracy, slip, boob (*infml*), indiscretion, gaffe, faux pas, slip-up (*infml*), oversight, fault, cock-up (*sl*).

➤ *v* stumble, flounder, bumble, err, slip up (*infml*), miscalculate, misjudge, bungle, botch, fluff (*infml*), mismanage, cock up (*sl*).

blunt *adj* 1 UNSHARPENED, dull, worn, pointless, rounded, stubbed. 2 FRANK, candid, direct, forthright, unceremonious, explicit, plain-spoken, honest, downright, outspoken, tactless, insensitive, rude, impolite, uncivil, brusque, curt, abrupt.
🔄 1 sharp, pointed. 2 subtle, tactful.
➤ *v* dull, take the edge off, dampen, soften, deaden, numb, anaesthetize, alleviate, allay, abate, weaken.
🔄 sharpen, intensify.

blur *v* smear, smudge, mist, fog, befog, cloud, becloud, blear, dim, darken, obscure, mask, conceal, soften.
➤ *n* smear, smudge, blotch, haze, mist, fog, cloudiness, fuzziness, indistinctness, muddle, confusion, dimness, obscurity.

blurred *adj* out of focus, fuzzy, unclear, indistinct, vague, ill-defined, faint, hazy, misty, foggy, cloudy, bleary, dim, obscure, confused.
🔄 clear, distinct.

blurt out *v* exclaim, cry, gush, spout, utter, tell, reveal, disclose, divulge, blab (*infml*), let out, leak, let slip, spill the beans (*infml*).
🔄 bottle up, hush up.

blush *v* flush, redden, colour, glow.
🔄 blanch.
➤ *n* flush, reddening, rosiness, ruddiness, colour, glow.

blushing *adj* flushed, red, rosy, glowing, confused, embarrassed, ashamed, modest.
🔄 pale, white, composed.

bluster *v* boast, brag, crow, talk big (*infml*), swagger, strut, vaunt, show off, rant, roar, storm, bully, hector.
➤ *n* boasting, crowing, bravado, bluff, swagger.

blustery *adj* windy, gusty, squally, stormy, tempestuous, violent, wild, boisterous.
🔄 calm.

board *n* 1 *a wooden board*: sheet, panel, slab, plank, beam, timber, slat. 2 COMMITTEE, council, panel, jury, commission, directorate, directors, trustees, advisers. 3 MEALS, food, provisions, rations.
➤ *v* get on, embark, mount, enter, catch.

boast *v* brag, crow, swank (*infml*), claim, exaggerate, talk big (*infml*), bluster, trumpet, vaunt, strut, swagger, show off, exhibit, possess.
🔄 belittle, deprecate.
➤ *n* brag, swank (*infml*), claim, vaunt, pride, joy, gem, treasure.

boastful *adj* proud, conceited, vain, swollen-headed, big-headed (*infml*), puffed up, bragging, crowing, swanky (*infml*), cocky, swaggering.
🔄 modest, self-effacing, humble.

boats and ships

Types of boat or ship include: canoe, dinghy, lifeboat, rowing-boat, kayak, coracle, skiff, punt, sampan, dhow, gondola, pedalo, catamaran, trimaran, yacht; cabin-cruiser, motor-boat, motor-launch, speedboat, trawler, barge, narrow boat, houseboat, dredger, junk, smack, lugger; hovercraft, hydrofoil; clipper, cutter, ketch, packet, brig, schooner, square-rigger, galleon; ferry, paddle-steamer, tug, freighter, liner, container-ship, tanker; warship, battleship, destroyer, submarine, U-boat, frigate, aircraft-carrier, cruiser, dreadnought, corvette, minesweeper, man-of-war.

bob *v* bounce, hop, skip, spring, jump, leap, twitch, jerk, jolt, shake, quiver, wobble, oscillate, nod, bow, curtsy.
♦ **bob up** appear, emerge, arrive, show up (*infml*), materialize, rise, surface, pop up, spring up, crop up, arise.

bode *v* predict, foretell, prophesy, indicate, signify, intimate, herald, threaten, warn, augur (*fml*), forebode (*fml*), foreshadow (*fml*), foreshow (*fml*), forewarn (*fml*).

bodily *adj* physical, corporeal, carnal, fleshly, real, actual, tangible, substantial, concrete, material.
🔄 spiritual.
➤ *adv* altogether, en masse, collectively, as a whole, completely, fully, wholly, entirely, totally, in toto.
🔄 piecemeal.

body *n* 1 ANATOMY, physique, build, figure,

trunk, torso. **2** CORPSE, cadaver, carcase, stiff (*sl*). **3** COMPANY, association, society, corporation, confederation, bloc, cartel, syndicate, congress, collection, group, band, crowd, throng, multitude, mob, mass. **4** CONSISTENCY, density, solidity, firmness, bulk, mass, substance, essence, fullness, richness.

bodyguard *n* guard, protector, minder (*infml*).

boffin *n* scientist, engineer, designer, planner, inventor, mastermind, genius, brain, intellect, intellectual, thinker, egghead (*infml*), wizard (*infml*), backroom-boy (*infml*).

bog *n* marsh, swamp, fen, mire, quagmire, quag, slough, morass, quicksands, marshland, swampland, wetlands.
♦ **bog down** encumber, hinder, impede, overwhelm, deluge, sink, stick, slow down, slow up, delay, retard, halt, stall.

boggle *v* astound, startle, amaze, surprise, overwhelm, stagger, alarm, confuse, bowl over (*infml*), flabbergast (*infml*).

bogus *adj* false, fake, counterfeit, forged, fraudulent, phoney (*infml*), spurious, sham, pseudo, artificial, imitation, dummy.
🖼 genuine, true, real, valid.

bohemian *adj* artistic, arty (*infml*), unconventional, unorthodox, nonconformist, alternative, eccentric, offbeat, way-out (*sl*), bizarre, exotic.
🖼 bourgeois, conventional, orthodox.
➤ *n* beatnik, hippie, drop-out, nonconformist.
🖼 bourgeois, conformist.

boil[1] *v* **1** SIMMER, stew, seethe, brew, gurgle, bubble, fizz, effervesce, froth, foam, steam. **2** *boil with anger*: erupt, explode, rage, rave, storm, fulminate, fume.
♦ **boil down** reduce, concentrate, distil, condense, digest, abstract, summarize, abridge.

boil[2] *n* pustule, abscess, gumboil, ulcer, tumour, pimple, carbuncle, blister, inflammation.

boiling *adj* **1** *boiling water*: turbulent, gurgling, bubbling, steaming. **2** HOT, baking, roasting, scorching, blistering. **3** ANGRY, indignant, incensed, infuriated, enraged, furious, fuming, flaming.

boisterous *adj* exuberant, rumbustious (*infml*), rollicking, bouncy, turbulent, tumultuous, loud, noisy, clamorous, rowdy,

rough, disorderly, riotous, wild, unrestrained, unruly, obstreperous.
🖼 quiet, calm, restrained.

bold *adj* **1** FEARLESS, dauntless, daring, audacious, brave, courageous, valiant, heroic, gallant, intrepid, adventurous, venturesome, enterprising, plucky, spirited, confident, outgoing. **2** EYE-CATCHING, striking, conspicuous, prominent, strong, pronounced, bright, vivid, colourful, loud, flashy, showy, flamboyant. **3** BRAZEN, brash, forward, shameless, unabashed, cheeky (*infml*), impudent, insolent.
🖼 **1** cautious, timid, shy. **2** faint, restrained.

bolster *v* boost, aid, assist, help, maintain, prop, reinforce, strengthen, supplement, support, brace, buoy up, buttress, firm up, shore up, stay, stiffen, revitalize, invigorate, augment (*fml*).
🖼 undermine.
➤ *n* pillow, support, cushion.

bolt *n* bar, rod, shaft, pin, peg, rivet, fastener, latch, catch, lock.
➤ *v* **1** FASTEN, secure, bar, latch, lock. **2** ABSCOND, escape, flee, fly, run, sprint, rush, dash, hurtle. **3** *bolt one's food*: gulp, wolf, gobble, gorge, devour, cram, stuff.

bomb *n* atom bomb, petrol bomb, shell, bombshell, explosive, charge, grenade, mine, torpedo, rocket, missile, projectile.
➤ *v* bombard, shell, torpedo, attack, blow up, destroy.

bombard *v* attack, assault, assail, pelt, pound, strafe, blast, bomb, shell, blitz, besiege, hound, harass, pester.

bombardment *n* attack, assault, air-raid, bombing, shelling, blitz, barrage, cannonade, fusillade, salvo, fire, flak.

bombastic *adj* grandiloquent, magniloquent, grandiose, pompous, high-flown, inflated, bloated, windy, wordy, verbose.

bona fide *adj* genuine, real, valid, true, actual, authentic, lawful, legal, legitimate, kosher, honest, the real McCoy (*infml*).
🖼 bogus.

bonanza *n* windfall, sudden wealth, godsend, stroke of luck, blessing, boon.

bond *n* **1** CONNECTION, relation, link, tie, union, affiliation, attachment, affinity. **2**

CONTRACT, covenant, agreement, pledge, promise, word, obligation. **3** FETTER, shackle, manacle, chain, cord, band, binding.

➤ *v* connect, fasten, bind, unite, fuse, glue, gum, paste, stick, seal.

bondage *n* imprisonment, incarceration, captivity, confinement, restraint, slavery, enslavement, serfdom, servitude, subservience, subjection, subjugation, yoke.

🔁 freedom, independence.

bone

Human bones include: clavicle, coccyx, collar-bone, femur, fibula, hip-bone, humerus, ilium, ischium, mandible, maxilla, metacarpal, metatarsal, patella, pelvic girdle, pelvis, pubis, radius, rib, scapula, shoulder-blade, skull, sternum, stirrup-bone, temporal, thigh-bone, tibia, ulna, vertebra.

bonus *n* advantage, benefit, plus (*infml*), extra, perk (*infml*), perquisite, commission, dividend, premium, prize, reward, honorarium, tip, gratuity, gift, handout.

🔁 disadvantage, disincentive.

bony *adj* thin, lean, angular, lanky, gawky, gangling, skinny, scrawny, emaciated, rawboned, gaunt, drawn.

🔁 fat, plump.

book *n* volume, tome, publication, work, booklet, tract.

Types of book include: hardback, paperback, bestseller; fiction, novel, story, thriller, romantic novel; children's book, primer, picture-book, annual; reference book, encyclopedia, dictionary, lexicon, thesaurus, concordance, anthology, compendium, omnibus, atlas, guidebook, gazetteer, directory, anthology, pocket companion, handbook, manual, cookbook, yearbook, almanac, catalogue; notebook, exercise book, textbook, scrapbook, album, sketchbook, diary, jotter, pad, ledger; libretto, manuscript, hymn-book, hymnal, prayer-book, psalter, missal, lectionary. *see also* **literature**.

➤ *v* reserve, bag (*infml*), engage, charter, procure, order, arrange, organize, schedule, programme.

🔁 cancel.

◆ **book in** register, enrol, check in, record one's arrival.

bookbinding

Terms used in bookbinding include: adhesive binding, all edges gilt (aeg), backboard, backbone, back cornering, back lining, binder's board (*US*), binder's brass, binder's die (*US*), binding, blind blocking, blocking, boards, bolts, book block, buckram, case, casebound, casing-in, cloth-lined board, comb-binding, drawn-on, dust cover, embossing, endpaper, flyleaf, fore edge, front board, full bound, gather, half bound, hardback, head, headband, headcap, hinge, jacket, laminating, library binding, limp, lining, Linson®, loose-leaf, mechanical binding, millboard, morocco, notch binding, open-flat, paperback, pasteboard, perfect binding, quarter bound, raised band, ring binding, rounding and backing, saddle-stitch, sewing, shoulder, side-stitch, signature, smashing, soft-cover, spine, spiral binding, square back, stab-stitch, stamping (*US*), strawboard, tail, tailband, thermoplastic binding, thread sewing, unsewn binding, varnishing, whole bound, wire binding, wire stitching, wiro binding, yapp.

boom *v* **1** BANG, crash, roar, thunder, roll, rumble, resound, reverberate, blast, explode. **2** FLOURISH, thrive, prosper, succeed, develop, grow, increase, gain, expand, swell, escalate, intensify, strengthen, explode.

🔁 **2** fail, collapse, slump.

➤ *n* **1** BANG, clap, crash, roar, thunder, rumble, reverberation, blast, explosion, burst. **2** INCREASE, growth, expansion, gain, upsurge, jump, spurt, boost, upturn, improvement, advance, escalation, explosion.

🔁 **2** failure, collapse, slump, recession, depression.

boomerang *v* rebound, bounce back, spring back, recoil, ricochet, backfire.

boon *n* blessing, advantage, benefit, godsend, windfall, favour, kindness, gift, present, grant, gratuity.

🔁 disadvantage, blight.

boorish *adj* uncouth, oafish, loutish, ill-mannered, rude, coarse, crude, vulgar, unrefined, uncivilized, uneducated, ignorant.

🔁 polite, refined, cultured.

boost *n* improvement, enhancement, expansion, increase, rise, jump,

increment, addition, supplement, booster, lift, hoist, heave, push, thrust, help, advancement, promotion, praise, encouragement, fillip, ego-trip (*sl*).
🆎 setback, blow.
➢ *v* raise, elevate, improve, enhance, develop, enlarge, expand, amplify, increase, augment, heighten, lift, hoist, jack up, heave, push, thrust, help, aid, assist, advance, further, promote, advertise, plug (*infml*), praise, inspire, encourage, foster, support, sustain, bolster, supplement.
🆎 hinder, undermine.

boot *n* gumboot, wellington, welly (*infml*), galosh, overshoe, walking-boot, riding-boot, top-boot.
➢ *v* kick, shove.
◆ **boot out** dismiss, eject, expel, lay off, suspend, shed, give notice, make redundant, kick out (*infml*), fire (*infml*), sack (*infml*), give someone their cards (*infml*), give the heave (*infml*).

booth *n* kiosk, stall, stand, hut, box, compartment, cubicle, carrel.

booty *n* loot, plunder, pillage, spoils, swag (*sl*), haul, gains, takings, pickings, winnings.

border *n* **1** BOUNDARY, frontier, bound, bounds, confine, confines, limit, demarcation, borderline, margin, fringe, periphery, surround, perimeter, circumference, edge, rim, brim, verge, brink. **2** TRIMMING, frill, valance, skirt, hem, frieze.
◆ **border on 1** ADJOIN, abut, touch, impinge, join, connect, communicate with. **2** RESEMBLE, approximate, approach, verge on.

borderline *adj* marginal, problematic, indefinite, doubtful, uncertain, indecisive, indeterminate, ambivalent, iffy (*infml*).
🆎 certain, definite, clear-cut.

bore¹ *v* drill, mine, pierce, perforate, penetrate, sink, burrow, tunnel, undermine, sap.

bore² *v* tire, weary, fatigue, jade, trouble, bother, worry, irritate, annoy, vex, irk.
🆎 interest, excite.
➢ *n* (*infml*) nuisance, bother, bind (*infml*), drag (*infml*), pain (*infml*), headache (*infml*).
🆎 pleasure, delight.

bored *adj* uninterested, unexcited, tired, wearied, exhausted, ennuied (*fml*), ennuyé (*fml*), bored to tears (*infml*), bored stiff (*infml*), bored out of one's mind (*infml*), cheesed off (*infml*), fed up (*infml*), turned off (*infml*), sick and tired (*infml*), in a rut (*infml*), brassed off (*infml*), browned off (*infml*).
🆎 interested, excited.

boredom *n* tedium, tediousness, monotony, humdrum, dullness, sameness, flatness, apathy, listlessness, weariness, world-weariness, frustration, ennui (*fml*), malaise (*fml*).
🆎 interest, excitement.

boring *adj* tedious, monotonous, routine, repetitious, uninteresting, unexciting, uneventful, dull, dreary, humdrum, commonplace, trite, unimaginative, uninspired, dry, stale, flat, insipid.
🆎 interesting, exciting, stimulating, original.

borrow *v* steal, pilfer, filch, lift, plagiarize, crib, copy, imitate, mimic, echo, take, draw, derive, obtain, adopt, use, scrounge, cadge, sponge, appropriate, usurp.
🆎 lend.

bosom *n* **1** BUST, breasts, chest, breast. **2** HEART, core, centre, midst, protection, shelter, sanctuary.

boss *n* employer, governor, master, owner, captain, head, chief, leader, supremo, administrator, executive, director, manager, foreman, gaffer, superintendent, overseer, supervisor.
◆ **boss around** order around, order about, domineer, tyrannize, bully, bulldoze, browbeat, push around, dominate.

bossy *adj* authoritarian, autocratic, tyrannical, despotic, dictatorial, domineering, overbearing, oppressive, lordly, high-handed, imperious, insistent, assertive, demanding, exacting.
🆎 unassertive.

botch *v* bungle, mess (up), make a mess of, blunder, mar, mismanage, ruin, spoil, patch, foul up (*infml*), fluff (*infml*), muff (*infml*), make a hash of (*infml*), make a bad job of (*infml*), goof (*infml*), louse up (*sl*), screw up (*sl*), cock up (*sl*), balls up (*sl*).
🆎 accomplish, succeed.
➢ *n* blunder, bungle, failure, muddle, mess, miscarriage, farce (*infml*), shambles (*infml*), hash (*infml*), cock-up (*sl*), balls-up (*sl*).
🆎 success.

bother *v* disturb, inconvenience, harass,

hassle (*infml*), pester, plague, nag, annoy, irritate, irk, molest, trouble, worry, concern, alarm, dismay, distress, upset, vex.
➤ *n* inconvenience, trouble, problem, difficulty, hassle (*infml*), fuss, bustle, flurry, nuisance, pest, annoyance, irritation, aggravation (*infml*), vexation, worry, strain.

bothersome *adj* troublesome, annoying, irksome, irritating, infuriating, vexatious, vexing, inconvenient, distressing, exasperating, laborious, boring, tedious, tiresome, wearisome, aggravating (*infml*).

bottle *n* phial, flask, carafe, decanter, flagon, demijohn.
♦ **bottle up** hide, conceal, restrain, curb, hold back, suppress, inhibit, restrict, enclose, contain.
🔁 unbosom, unburden.

bottleneck *n* hold-up, traffic jam, snarl-up, congestion, clogging, blockage, obstruction, block, obstacle.

bottom *n* 1 UNDERSIDE, underneath, sole, base, foot, plinth, pedestal, support, foundation, substructure, ground, floor, bed, depths, nadir. 2 RUMP, rear, behind, posterior (*infml*), buttocks, seat, backside (*infml*), bum (*sl*), butt (*US infml*), tail (*infml*).
🔁 1 top.

bottomless *adj* deep, profound, fathomless, unfathomed, unplumbed, immeasurable, measureless, infinite, boundless, limitless, unlimited, inexhaustible.
🔁 shallow, limited.

bounce *v* spring, jump, leap, bound, bob, ricochet, rebound, recoil.
➤ *n* 1 SPRING, bound, springiness, elasticity, give, resilience, rebound, recoil. 2 EBULLIENCE, exuberance, vitality, vivacity, energy, vigour, go (*infml*), zip (*infml*), animation, liveliness.

bound¹ *adj* 1 FASTENED, secured, fixed, tied (up), chained, held, restricted, bandaged. 2 LIABLE, committed, duty-bound, obliged, required, forced, compelled, constrained, destined, fated, doomed, sure, certain.

bound² *v* jump, leap, vault, hurdle, spring, bounce, bob, hop, skip, frisk, gambol, frolic, caper, prance.
➤ *n* jump, leap, vault, spring, bounce, bob, hop, skip, gambol, frolic, caper, dance, prance.

boundary *n* border, frontier, barrier, line, borderline, demarcation, bounds,

confines, limits, margin, fringe, verge, brink, edge, perimeter, extremity, termination.

boundless *adj* unbounded, limitless, unlimited, unconfined, countless, untold, incalculable, vast, immense, measureless, immeasurable, infinite, endless, unending, interminable, inexhaustible, unflagging, indefatigable.
🔁 limited, restricted.

bounds *n* confines, limits, borders, marches, margins, fringes, periphery, circumference, edges, extremities.

bountiful *adj* abundant, plentiful, exuberant, profuse, ample, prolific, overflowing, ungrudging, unstinting, boundless, copious, generous, lavish, liberal, open-handed, princely, magnanimous (*fml*), munificent (*fml*), bounteous (*fml*), plenteous (*fml*), luxuriant (*fml*).
🔁 meagre, mean, sparse.

bounty *n* 1 GENEROSITY, liberality, munificence, largesse, almsgiving, charity, philanthropy, beneficence, kindness. 2 REWARD, recompense, premium, bonus, gratuity, gift, present, donation, grant, allowance.

bouquet *n* 1 *bouquet of flowers*: bunch, posy, nosegay, spray, corsage, buttonhole, wreath, garland. 2 AROMA, smell, odour, scent, perfume, fragrance.

bourgeois *adj* middle-class, materialistic, conservative, traditional, conformist, conventional, hide-bound, unadventurous, dull, humdrum, banal, commonplace, trite, unoriginal, unimaginative.
🔁 bohemian, unconventional, original.

bout *n* 1 FIGHT, battle, engagement, encounter, struggle, set-to, match, contest, competition, round, heat. 2 PERIOD, spell, time, stint, turn, go (*infml*), term, stretch, run, course, session, spree, attack, fit.

bow¹ *v* 1 *bow one's head*: incline, bend, nod, bob, curtsy, genuflect (*fml*), kowtow, salaam, stoop. 2 YIELD, give in, consent, surrender, capitulate, submit, acquiesce, concede, accept, comply, defer. 3 SUBDUE, overpower, conquer, vanquish, crush, subjugate.
➤ *n* inclination, bending, nod, bob, curtsy, genuflexion (*fml*), kowtow, salaam, obeisance (*fml*), salutation, acknowledgement.

◆ **bow out** withdraw, pull out, desert, abandon, defect, back out, chicken out (*infml*), retire, resign, quit, stand down, step down, give up.

bow² *n* front, beak, head, prow, stem, rostrum.

◨ stern.

bowdlerize *v* censor, cut, edit, excise, expunge, expurgate, purge, clean up, purify, modify, blue-pencil.

bowels *n* **1** INTESTINES, viscera, entrails, guts, insides, innards (*infml*). **2** DEPTHS, interior, inside, middle, centre, core, heart.

bowl¹ *n* receptacle, container, vessel, dish, basin, sink.

bowl² *v* throw, hurl, fling, pitch, roll, spin, whirl, rotate, revolve.

◆ **bowl over** surprise, amaze, astound, astonish, stagger, stun, dumbfound, flabbergast (*infml*), floor (*infml*).

box¹ *n* container, receptacle, case, crate, carton, packet, pack, package, present, chest, coffin, trunk, coffer.

➤ *v* case, encase, package, pack, wrap.

◆ **box in** enclose, surround, circumscribe, cordon off, hem in, corner, trap, confine, restrict, imprison, cage, coop up, contain.

box² *v* fight, spar, punch, hit, strike, slap, buffet, cuff, clout, sock (*sl*), wallop (*infml*), whack (*infml*).

boxer *n* fighter, prizefighter, sparring partner, pugilist (*fml*).

> Weight divisions in professional boxing: heavyweight, cruiserweight/junior-heavyweight, light-heavyweight, super-middleweight, middleweight, light-middleweight/junior-middleweight, welterweight, light-welterweight/junior-welterweight, lightweight, junior-lightweight/superfeatherweight, featherweight, super-bantamweight/junior-featherweight, bantamweight, super-flyweight/junior-bantamweight, flyweight, light-flyweight/junior-flyweight, mini-flyweight/straw-weight/minimum weight.

boxing *n* pugilism (*fml*), prizefighting, fisticuffs, sparring.

boy *n* son, lad, youngster, kid (*infml*), nipper (*infml*), stripling, youth, fellow.

boycott *v* refuse, reject, embargo, black, ban, prohibit, disallow, bar, exclude, blacklist, outlaw, ostracize, cold-shoulder, ignore, spurn.

◨ encourage, support.

boyfriend *n* young man, man, fellow (*infml*), bloke (*infml*), admirer, date, sweetheart, lover, fiancé, partner, common-law husband.

boyish *adj* youthful, childlike, adolescent, childish, immature, innocent, juvenile, puerile, tomboy, unfeminine, unmaidenly, young, green (*infml*).

brace¹ *n* support, stay, strap, prop, clamp, fastener, vice, beam, strut, reinforcement, truss, buttress, shoring, stanchion (*fml*).

➤ *v* strengthen, reinforce, bolster, buttress, prop (up), shore (up), support, hold up, steady, secure, tighten, fasten, tie, strap, bind, bandage, fortify (*fml*).

brace² *n* pair, couple, twosome, duo.

bracing *adj* fresh, crisp, refreshing, reviving, strengthening, fortifying, tonic, rousing, stimulating, exhilarating, invigorating, enlivening, energizing, brisk, energetic, vigorous.

◨ weakening, debilitating.

brackish *adj* bitter, briny, saline, salt, saltish, salty.

◨ fresh, clean, clear.

brag *v* bluster, boast, show off, swagger, vaunt, blow one's own trumpet (*infml*), blow one's own horn (*US infml*), crow (*infml*), talk big (*infml*), lay it on thick/with a trowel (*infml*).

◨ be modest, deprecate (*fml*), run down (*infml*).

braid *v* plait, interweave, interlace, intertwine, weave, lace, twine, entwine, ravel, twist, wind.

◨ undo, unravel.

brain *n* **1** CEREBRUM, grey matter, head, mind, intellect, nous, brains (*infml*), intelligence, wit, reason, sense, common sense, shrewdness, understanding. **2** MASTERMIND, intellectual, highbrow, egghead (*infml*), scholar, expert, boffin, genius, prodigy.

◨ **2** simpleton.

> Parts of the brain include: brainstem, cerebellum, cerebral cortex (grey matter), cerebrum, corpus callosum, forebrain, frontal lobe, hindbrain, hypothalamus, medulla oblongata, mesencephalon, midbrain, occipital lobe, optic thalamus, parietal lobe, pineal body, pituitary gland, pons, spinal cord, temporal lobe, thalamus.

brainwashing n indoctrination, conditioning, pressurizing, grilling, re-education, intellectual suicide, mind-bending, persuasion.

brainy (infml) adj intellectual, intelligent, clever, smart, bright, brilliant.
ⓔ dull.

brake n check, curb, rein, restraint, control, restriction, constraint, drag.
➤ v slow, decelerate, retard, drag, slacken, moderate, check, halt, stop, pull up.
ⓔ accelerate.

branch n 1 BOUGH, limb, sprig, shoot, offshoot, arm, wing, prong. 2 a different branch of the company: department, office, part, section, division, subsection, subdivision.
♦ **branch out** diversify, vary, develop, expand, enlarge, extend, broaden out, increase, multiply, proliferate, ramify.

brand n make, brand-name, tradename, trademark, logo, mark, symbol, sign, emblem, label, stamp, hallmark, grade, quality, class, kind, type, sort, line, variety, species.
➤ v mark, stamp, label, type, stigmatize, burn, scar, stain, taint, disgrace, discredit, denounce, censure.

brandish v wave, flourish, shake, raise, swing, wield, flash, flaunt, exhibit, display, parade.

brash adj 1 BRAZEN, forward, impertinent, impudent, insolent, rude, cocky, assured, bold, audacious. 2 RECKLESS, rash, impetuous, impulsive, hasty, precipitate, foolhardy, incautious, indiscreet.
ⓔ 1 reserved. 2 cautious.

bravado n swagger, boasting, bragging, bluster, bombast, talk, boast, vaunting, showing off, parade, show, pretence.
ⓔ modesty, restraint.

brave adj courageous, plucky, unafraid, fearless, dauntless, undaunted, bold, audacious, daring, intrepid, stalwart, hardy, stoical, resolute, stout-hearted, valiant, gallant, heroic, indomitable.
ⓔ cowardly, afraid, timid.
➤ v face, confront, defy, challenge, dare, stand up to, face up to, suffer, endure, bear, withstand.
ⓔ capitulate.

bravery n courage, pluck, guts (infml), fearlessness, dauntlessness, boldness, audacity, daring, intrepidity, stalwartness, hardiness, fortitude, resolution, stout-

heartedness, valiance, valour, gallantry, heroism, indomitability, grit, mettle, spirit.
ⓔ cowardice, faint-heartedness, timidity.

brawl n fight, punch-up (infml), scrap, scuffle, dust-up (infml), mêlée, free-for-all, fray, affray, broil, fracas, rumpus, disorder, row, argument, quarrel, squabble, altercation, dispute, clash.
➤ v fight, scrap, scuffle, wrestle, tussle, row, argue, quarrel, squabble, wrangle, dispute.

brawn n strength, might, muscle, muscles, bulk, bulkiness, muscularity, power, robustness, sinews, beef (infml), beefiness (infml).

brawny adj muscular, sinewy, athletic, well-built, burly, beefy, hefty, solid, bulky, hulking, massive, strapping, strong, powerful, vigorous, sturdy, robust, hardy.
ⓔ slight, frail.

bray v neigh, whinny, heehaw, blare, hoot, roar, screech, trumpet, bell, bellow.

brazen adj blatant, flagrant, brash, brassy, bold, forward, saucy, pert, barefaced, impudent, insolent, defiant, shameless, unashamed, unabashed, immodest.
ⓔ shy, shamefaced, modest.

breach n 1 a breach of the rules: violation, contravention, infringement, trespass, disobedience, offence, transgression, lapse, disruption. 2 QUARREL, disagreement, dissension, difference, variance, schism, rift, rupture, split, division, separation, parting, estrangement, alienation, disaffection, dissociation. 3 BREAK, crack, rift, rupture, fissure, cleft, crevice, opening, aperture, gap, space, hole, chasm.
➤ v 1 breach an agreement: violate, break, contravene, infringe. 2 breach the sea wall: rupture, break (open), open up, burst through, split.

bread n 1 bread and jam: crusts, roll, loaf, bap, plait, cob, sandwich, nan, chapati, paratha, pitta, matzo, croissant, baguette, brioche, bagel, French stick, pumpernickel. 2 our daily bread: food, provisions, diet, fare, nourishment, necessities, sustenance (fml), subsistence (fml). 3 earn one's daily bread: cash, money, funds.

breadth n width, broadness, wideness, latitude, thickness, size, magnitude, measure, scale, range, reach, scope, compass, span, sweep, extent, expanse, spread, comprehensiveness, extensiveness, vastness.

break v **1** FRACTURE, crack, snap, split, sever, separate, divide, rend, smash, disintegrate, splinter, shiver, shatter, ruin, destroy, demolish. **2** *break the law*: violate, contravene, infringe, breach, disobey, flout. **3** PAUSE, halt, stop, discontinue, interrupt, suspend, rest. **4** SUBDUE, tame, weaken, enfeeble, impair, undermine, demoralize. **5** *break the news*: tell, inform, impart, divulge, disclose, reveal, announce. **6** *break a record*: exceed, beat, better, excel, surpass, outdo, outstrip. ⊞ **1** mend. **2** keep, observe, abide by. **4** strengthen.
➤ n **1** FRACTURE, crack, split, rift, rupture, schism, separation, tear, gash, fissure, cleft, crevice, opening, gap, hole, breach. **2** INTERVAL, intermission, interlude, interruption, pause, halt, lull, let-up (*infml*), respite, rest, breather (*infml*), time out, holiday. **3** OPPORTUNITY, chance, advantage, fortune, luck.
◆ **break away** separate, split, part company, detach, secede, leave, depart, quit, run away, escape, flee, fly.
◆ **break down 1** *the van broke down*: fail, stop, pack up (*infml*), conk out (*sl*), seize up, give way, collapse, crack up (*infml*). **2** ANALYSE, dissect, separate, itemize, detail.
◆ **break in 1** INTERRUPT, butt in, interpose, interject, intervene, intrude, encroach, impinge. **2** BURGLE, rob, raid, invade.
◆ **break off 1** DETACH, snap off, sever, separate, part, divide, disconnect. **2** PAUSE, interrupt, suspend, discontinue, halt, stop, cease, end, finish, terminate.
◆ **break out 1** START, begin, commence, arise, emerge, happen, occur, erupt, flare up, burst out. **2** ESCAPE, abscond, bolt, flee.
◆ **break up 1** DISMANTLE, take apart, demolish, destroy, disintegrate, splinter, sever, divide, split, part, separate, divorce. **2** DISBAND, disperse, dissolve, adjourn, suspend, stop, finish, terminate.

breakable *adj* brittle, fragile, delicate, flimsy, insubstantial, frail. ⊞ unbreakable, durable, sturdy.

breakdown n **1** FAILURE, collapse, disintegration, malfunction, interruption, stoppage. **2** ANALYSIS, dissection, itemization, classification, categorization.

breaker n wave, roller, billow, white horses.

break-in n burglary, house-breaking, robbery, raid, invastion, intrusion, trespass.

breakthrough n discovery, find, finding, invention, innovation, advance, progress, headway, step, leap, development, improvement.

break-up n divorce, separation, parting, split, rift, finish, termination, dissolution, dispersal, disintegration, crumbling.

breakwater n groyne, mole, jetty, pier, quay, wharf, dock.

breast n **1** *beat one's breast in sorrow*: bosom, bust, chest, front, heart, thorax. **2** *a woman's breasts*: bust, nipple, teat, cleavage, boob (*sl*), bristol (*sl*), knocker (*sl*), tit (*sl*).

breath n **1** AIR, breathing, respiration, inhalation, exhalation, sigh, gasp, pant, gulp. **2** BREEZE, puff, waft, gust. **3** AROMA, smell, odour, whiff. **4** HINT, suggestion, suspicion, undertone, whisper, murmur.

breathe v **1** RESPIRE, inhale, exhale, expire, sigh, gasp, pant, puff. **2** SAY, utter, express, voice, articulate, murmur, whisper, impart, tell. **3** INSTIL, imbue, infuse, inject, inspire.

breathless *adj* **1** SHORT-WINDED, out of breath, panting, puffing, puffed (out), exhausted, winded, gasping, wheezing, choking. **2** *breathless anticipation*: expectant, impatient, eager, agog, excited, feverish, anxious.

breathtaking *adj* awe-inspiring, impressive, magnificent, overwhelming, amazing, astonishing, stunning, exciting, thrilling, stirring, moving.

breed v **1** REPRODUCE, procreate, multiply, propagate, hatch, bear, bring forth, rear, raise, bring up, educate, train, instruct. **2** PRODUCE, create, originate, arouse, cause, occasion, engender, generate, make, foster, nurture, nourish, cultivate, develop.
➤ n species, strain, variety, family, ilk, sort, kind, type, stamp, stock, race, progeny, line, lineage, pedigree.

breeding n **1** REPRODUCTION, procreation, nurture, development, rearing, raising, upbringing, education, training, background, ancestry, lineage, stock. **2** MANNERS, politeness, civility, gentility, urbanity, refinement, culture, polish. ⊞ **2** vulgarity.

breeze n wind, gust, flurry, waft, puff, breath, draught, air.

➤ *v* glide, sail, hurry, sweep, trip, wander, flit (*infml*), sally (*infml*).

breezy *adj* 1 WINDY, blowing, fresh, airy, gusty, blustery, squally. 2 ANIMATED, lively, vivacious, jaunty, buoyant, blithe, debonair, carefree, cheerful, easy-going (*infml*), casual, informal, light, bright, exhilarating.
🔁 1 still. 2 staid, serious.

brevity *n* briefness, shortness, terseness, conciseness, succinctness, pithiness, crispness, incisiveness, abruptness, curtness, impermanence, ephemerality, transience, transitoriness.
🔁 verbosity, permanence, longevity.

brew *v* 1 INFUSE, stew, boil, seethe, ferment, prepare, soak, steep, mix, cook. 2 PLOT, scheme, plan, project, devise, contrive, concoct, hatch, excite, foment, build up, gather, develop.
➤ *n* infusion, drink, beverage, liquor, potion, broth, gruel, stew, mixture, blend, concoction, preparation, fermentation, distillation.

bribe *n* incentive, inducement, allurement, enticement, back-hander (*infml*), kickback, payola, refresher (*infml*), sweetener (*infml*), hush money (*infml*), protection money.
➤ *v* corrupt, suborn, buy off, reward.

bribery *n* corruption, graft (*sl*), palm-greasing, inducement, lubrication.

bric-à-brac *n* knick-knacks, ornaments, curios, antiques, trinkets, baubles.

bridal *adj* wedding, nuptial, marriage, matrimonial, marital, conjugal.

bride *n* honeymooner, newly-wed, wife, spouse, marriage partner, war bride, GI bride.

bridegroom *n* honeymooner, newly-wed, husband, spouse, marriage partner, groom.

bridge *n* 1 *a bridge over the river*: arch, span, causeway, link. 2 *act as a bridge between the different factions*: link, connection, bond, tie.
➤ *v* span, cross, traverse, fill, link, connect, couple, join, unite, bind.

Types of bridge include: suspension bridge, arch bridge, cantilever bridge, flying bridge, flyover, overpass, footbridge, railway bridge, viaduct, aqueduct, humpback bridge, toll bridge, pontoon bridge, Bailey bridge, rope bridge, drawbridge, swing bridge.

bridle *v* check, curb, restrain, control, govern, master, subdue, moderate, repress, contain.
➤ *n* check, halter, control, curb, restraint.

brief *adj* 1 SHORT, terse, succinct, concise, pithy, crisp, compressed, thumbnail, laconic, abrupt, sharp, brusque, blunt, curt, surly. 2 SHORT-LIVED, momentary, ephemeral, transient, fleeting, passing, transitory, temporary, limited, cursory, hasty, quick, swift, fast.
🔁 1 long. 2 lengthy.
➤ *n* 1 ORDERS, instructions, directions, remit, mandate, directive, advice, briefing, data, information. 2 OUTLINE, summary, précis, dossier, case, defence, argument.
➤ *v* instruct, direct, explain, guide, advise, prepare, prime, inform, fill in (*infml*), gen up (*sl*).

briefing *n* meeting, conference, preparation, priming, filling-in (*infml*), gen (*sl*), low-down (*sl*), information, advice, guidance, directions, instructions, orders.

briefly *adv* 1 *speak briefly*: concisely, succinctly, cursorily, precisely, quickly, summarily, tersely, to the point. 2 *briefly, the answer is no*: in brief, in a word, in a few words, in a nutshell (*infml*).
🔁 1 at length, fully.

brigade *n* group, band, body, company, unit, corps, crew, force, party, squad, team, troop, contingent.

brigand *n* bandit, robber, desperado, gangster, outlaw, marauder, plunderer, ruffian, highwayman, freebooter.

bright *adj* 1 LUMINOUS, illuminated, radiant, shining, beaming, flashing, gleaming, glistening, glittering, sparkling, twinkling, shimmering, glowing, brilliant, resplendent, glorious, splendid, dazzling, glaring, blazing, intense, vivid. 2 HAPPY, cheerful, glad, joyful, merry, jolly, lively, vivacious. 3 *the future looks bright*: promising, propitious, auspicious, favourable, rosy, optimistic, hopeful, encouraging. 4 CLEVER, brainy (*infml*), smart, intelligent, quick-witted, quick, sharp, acute, keen, astute, perceptive. 5 CLEAR, transparent, translucent, lucid. 6 *a bright day*: fine, sunny, cloudless, unclouded.
🔁 1 dull. 2 sad. 3 depressing. 4 stupid. 5 muddy. 6 dark.

brighten *v* 1 LIGHT UP, illuminate, lighten, clear up. 2 POLISH, burnish, rub up, shine,

gleam, glow. **3** CHEER UP, gladden, hearten, encourage, enliven, perk up.
F3 1 darken. **2** dull, tarnish.

brilliance n **1** TALENT, virtuosity, genius, greatness, distinction, excellence, aptitude, cleverness. **2** RADIANCE, brightness, sparkle, dazzle, intensity, vividness, gloss, lustre, sheen, glamour, glory, magnificence, splendour.

brilliant adj **1** a brilliant pianist: gifted, talented, accomplished, expert, skilful, masterly, exceptional, outstanding, superb, illustrious, famous, celebrated. **2** SPARKLING, glittering, scintillating, dazzling, glaring, blazing, intense, vivid, bright, shining, glossy, showy, glorious, magnificent, splendid. **3** CLEVER, brainy (infml), intelligent, quick, astute.
F3 1 undistinguished. **2** dull. **3** stupid.

brim n rim, perimeter, circumference, lip, edge, margin, border, brink, verge, top, limit.

bring v **1** CARRY, bear, convey, transport, fetch, take, deliver, escort, accompany, usher, guide, conduct, lead. **2** CAUSE, produce, engender, create, prompt, provoke, force, attract, draw.
◆ **bring about** cause, occasion, create, produce, generate, effect, accomplish, achieve, fulfil, realize, manage, engineer, manoeuvre, manipulate.
◆ **bring down 1** bring down the government: OVERTHROW, unseat, oust, defeat, destroy, vanquish (fml), topple (infml), knock down (infml), shoot down (infml). **2** bring down blood pressure/unemployment: REDUCE, lower, cause to fall/drop.
◆ **bring forward** advance, put forward, make earlier.
F3 postpone, put back.
◆ **bring in** earn, net, gross, produce, yield, fetch, return, accrue, realize.
◆ **bring off** achieve, accomplish, fulfil, execute, discharge, perform, succeed, win.
◆ **bring on** cause, occasion, induce, lead to, give rise to, generate, inspire, prompt, provoke, precipitate, expedite, accelerate, advance.
F3 inhibit.
◆ **bring out 1** EMPHASIZE, stress, highlight, enhance, draw out. **2** PUBLISH, print, issue, launch, introduce.
◆ **bring round 1** REVIVE, resuscitate, bring to, rouse, awaken. **2** PERSUADE, convince, win over, convert, coax, cajole.

◆ **bring up 1** REAR, raise, foster, nurture, educate, teach, train, form. **2** bring up a subject: introduce, broach, mention, submit, propose. **3** VOMIT, regurgitate, throw up (infml).

brink n verge, threshold, edge, margin, fringe, border, boundary, limit, extremity, lip, rim, brim, bank.

brisk adj **1** ENERGETIC, vigorous, quick, snappy, lively, spirited, active, busy, bustling, agile, nimble, alert. **2** INVIGORATING, exhilarating, stimulating, bracing, refreshing, fresh, crisp.
F3 1 lazy, sluggish.

bristle n **1** shave off bristles: hair, whisker, stubble. **2** bristles on an animal's back: spine, prickle, barb, quill, thorn, awn.
➤ v **1** bristling with anger: seethe (with), draw oneself up, bridle at, be incensed at. **2** bristling with police: teem with, swarm with, abound in (fml), be thick with (infml), hum with (infml).

bristly adj hairy, whiskered, bearded, unshaven, stubbly, rough, spiny, prickly, spiky, thorny.
F3 clean-shaven, smooth.

brittle adj breakable, fragile, delicate, frail, crisp, crumbly, crumbling, friable, shattery, shivery.
F3 durable, resilient.

broach v introduce, raise, mention, propose, suggest, hint at.

broad adj **1** broad avenues/valleys: WIDE, large, vast, roomy, spacious, ample, extensive, widespread, capacious (fml). **2** WIDE-RANGING, far-reaching, encyclopedic, extensive, all-embracing, inclusive, comprehensive, general, sweeping, universal, unlimited, catholic (fml), eclectic (fml), compendious (fml). **3** the broad meaning of the term: general, vague, not detailed. **4** WIDESPREAD, extensive, general. **5** a broad hint: obvious, clear, plain, undisguised, unconcealed.
F3 1 narrow. **2** limited, restricted. **3** narrow, detailed, specific, precise. **4** limited. **5** veiled, disguised.

broadcast v **1** TRANSMIT, air, show, beam, relay, televise, cable. **2** broadcast the decision widely: make known, report, announce, publicize, advertise, publish, circulate, spread, scatter, promulgate (fml), disseminate (fml).
➤ n transmission, programme, show, access television, community

broadcasting, simulcast, simultaneous transmission, television première, teletext, satellite programme.

broaden v widen, thicken, swell, spread, enlarge, expand, extend, stretch, increase, augment, develop, open up, branch out, diversify.

broad-minded adj liberal, tolerant, permissive, enlightened, freethinking, open-minded, receptive, unbiased, unprejudiced.

Ea narrow-minded, intolerant, biased.

broadside n 1 fire a broadside at a ship: attack, assault, volley, battering, cannonade, blast, bombardment, counterblast. 2 verbal broadsides: criticism, denunciation, philippic (fml), diatribe (fml), fulmination (fml), harangue (fml), invective (fml), brickbat (infml), stick (infml).

brochure n leaflet, booklet, pamphlet, prospectus, broadsheet, handbill, circular, handout, folder.

broil v grill, cook, fry, barbecue, roast.

broke (infml) adj insolvent, penniless, bankrupt, bust, ruined, impoverished, destitute.

Ea solvent, rich, affluent.

broken adj 1 FRACTURED, burst, ruptured, severed, separated, faulty, defective, out of order, shattered, destroyed, demolished. 2 DISJOINTED, disconnected, fragmentary, discontinuous, interrupted, intermittent, spasmodic, erratic, hesitating, stammering, halting, imperfect. 3 a broken man: beaten, defeated, crushed, demoralized, down, weak, feeble, exhausted, tamed, subdued, oppressed.

Ea 1 mended. 2 fluent.

broken-down adj dilapidated, worn-out, ruined, collapsed, decayed, inoperative, out of order.

broken-hearted adj heartbroken, inconsolable, devastated, grief-stricken, desolate, despairing, miserable, wretched, mournful, sorrowful, sad, unhappy, dejected, despondent, crestfallen, disappointed.

broker n agent, middleman, dealer, factor, handler, intermediary, negotiator, stockbroker, jobber, stockjobber.

brooch n badge, pin, clip, clasp.

brood v ponder, ruminate, meditate, muse, mull over, go over, rehearse, dwell

on, agonize, fret, mope.

➤ n clutch, chicks, hatch, litter, young, offspring, issue, progeny, children, family.

brook n stream, rivulet, beck, burn, watercourse, channel.

brothel n bordello, bawdy-house, house of ill fame, house of ill repute, red light, whorehouse, bagnio, knocking-shop (sl), cathouse (US sl).

brother n 1 brothers and sisters: sibling, blood-brother, relation, relative. 2 brothers in the struggle against injustice: comrade, friend, mate, partner, colleague, associate, fellow, companion, chum (infml), mate (infml), pal (infml). 3 brothers in a monastery: monk, friar.

brotherhood n 1 feelings of brotherhood: fellowship, comradeship, friendship, friendliness cameraderie. 2 a brotherhood of monks: fraternity, association, society, league, confederation, confederacy, alliance, union, guild, fellowship, community, clique.

brotherly adj fraternal, loyal, affectionate, amicable, caring, sympathetic, friendly, kind, loving, benevolent, philanthropic.

Ea callous, unbrotherly.

brow n 1 sweat on one's brow: forehead, temples. 2 the brow of the hill: summit, ridge, top, tip, peak, verge, brink, cliff.

browbeat v bully, coerce, dragoon, bulldoze, awe, cow, intimidate, threaten, tyrannize, domineer, overbear, oppress, hound.

Ea coax.

brown adj mahogany, chocolate, coffee, hazel, bay, chestnut, umber, sepia, tan, tawny, russet, rust, rusty, brunette, dark, dusky, sunburnt, tanned, bronzed, browned, toasted.

browse v 1 LEAF THROUGH, flick through, dip into, skim, survey, scan, peruse. 2 GRAZE, pasture, feed, eat, nibble.

bruise v 1 bruise your leg: discolour, blacken, mark, blemish, injure, wound. 2 bruise someone's feelings: hurt, injure, insult, offend, grieve, upset, crush. 3 bruise fruit: damage, mark, spoil, blemish, crush.

➤ n contusion, discoloration, black eye, shiner (sl), mark, blemish, injury.

brunt n burden, thrust, (main) force, impact, impetus, pressure, (full) weight, shock, strain.

brush¹ *n* broom, sweeper, besom.
➤ *v* **1** CLEAN, sweep, flick, burnish, polish, shine. **2** TOUCH, contact, graze, kiss, stroke, rub, scrape.
◆ **brush aside** dismiss, pooh-pooh, belittle, disregard, ignore, flout, override.
◆ **brush off** disregard, ignore, slight, snub, cold-shoulder, rebuff, dismiss, spurn, reject, repulse, disown, repudiate (*fml*).
◆ **brush up 1** REVISE, relearn, improve, polish up, study, read up, swot (*infml*). **2** REFRESH, freshen up, clean, tidy.

brush² *n* scrub, thicket, bushes, shrubs, brushwood, undergrowth, ground cover.

brush³ *n* confrontation, encounter, clash, conflict, fight, scrap, skirmish, set-to, tussle, dust-up (*infml*), fracas.

brush-off *n* discouragement, dismissal, rebuff, refusal, rejection, repulse, slight, snub, repudiation (*fml*), cold shoulder (*infml*), kiss-off (*US sl*).
◼ encouragement.

brusque *adj* abrupt, sharp, short, terse, curt, gruff, surly, discourteous, impolite, uncivil, blunt, tactless, undiplomatic.
◼ courteous, polite, tactful.

brutal *adj* animal, bestial, beastly, brutish, inhuman, savage, bloodthirsty, vicious, ferocious, cruel, inhumane, remorseless, pitiless, merciless, ruthless, callous, insensitive, unfeeling, heartless, harsh, gruff, rough, coarse, crude, rude, uncivilized, barbarous.
◼ kindly, humane, civilized.

brutality *n* savagery, bloodthirstiness, viciousness, ferocity, cruelty, inhumanity, violence, atrocity, ruthlessness, callousness, roughness, coarseness, barbarism, barbarity.
◼ gentleness, kindness.

brute *n* animal, beast, swine, creature, monster, ogre, devil, fiend, savage, sadist, bully, lout.

bubble *n* blister, vesicle, globule, ball, drop, droplet, bead.
➤ *v* effervesce, fizz, sparkle, froth, foam, seethe, boil, burble, gurgle.

bubbly *adj* **1** EFFERVESCENT, fizzy, sparkling, carbonated, frothy, foaming, sudsy. **2** LIVELY, bouncy, happy, merry, elated, excited.
◼ **1** flat, still. **2** lethargic.

buccaneer *n* pirate, corsair, filibuster, freebooter, privateer, sea-robber, sea-rover, sea-wolf.

bucket *n* pail, can, bail, scuttle, vessel.

buckle *n* clasp, clip, catch, fastener.
➤ *v* **1** *buckle one's belt*: fasten, clasp, catch, hook, hitch, connect, close, secure. **2** BEND, warp, twist, distort, bulge, cave in, fold, wrinkle, crumple, collapse.

buck up *v* **1** *buck someone up*: cheer (up), encourage, improve, rally, stimulate, take heart, hearten, enliven, inspirit (*fml*), perk up (*infml*). **2** *Buck up or we'll be late!*: hurry (up), hasten (*fml*), get a move on (*infml*), get one's skates on (*infml*), step on it (*infml*).
◼ **1** discourage. **2** slow down.

bucolic *adj* pastoral, rural, agrarian, agricultural, country, countrified, rustic (*fml*).
◼ industrial, urban.

bud *n* shoot, sprout, germ, embryo.
➤ *v* shoot, sprout, burgeon, develop, grow.
◼ wither, waste away.

budding *adj* potential, promising, embryonic, burgeoning, developing, growing, flowering.

budge *v* move, stir, shift, remove, dislodge, push, roll, slide, propel, sway, influence, persuade, convince, change, bend, yield, give (way).

budget *n* finances, funds, resources, means, allowance, allotment, allocation, estimate.
➤ *v* plan, estimate, alow, allot, allocate, apportion, ration.

buff¹ *adj* yellowish-brown, straw, sandy, fawn, khaki.
➤ *v* polish, burnish, shine, smooth, rub, brush.

buff² (*infml*) *n* expert, connoisseur, enthusiast, fan, admirer, devotee, addict, fiend, freak.

buffer *n* shock-absorber, bumper, fender, pad, cushion, pillow, intermediary, screen, shield.

buffet¹ *n* snack-bar, counter, café, cafeteria.

buffet² *v* batter, hit, strike, knock, bang, bump, push, shove, pound, pummel, beat, thump, box, cuff, clout, slap.
➤ *n* blow, knock, bang, bump, jar, jolt, push, shove, thump, box, cuff, clout, slap, smack.

buffoon *n* clown, comedian, comic, fool, harlequin, jester, joker, wag, droll.

bug *n* **1** INSECT, flea, creepy-crawly (*infml*). **2** *a stomach bug*: virus, bacterium, germ,

microbe, micro-organism, infection, disease. **3** *a bug in a computer program*: fault, defect, flaw, blemish, imperfection, failing, error, gremlin (*infml*). **4** *bitten by the decorating bug*: craze, fad, obsession. **5** *put a bug in a room*: hidden microphone, listening device, wire-tap (*infml*), phone-tap (*infml*).
➤ *v* **1** ANNOY, irritate, vex, irk, bother, disturb, harass, needle (*infml*), wind up (*infml*). **2** *bug an office*: tap, listen in (on/to), eavesdrop (on) (*fml*), wire-tap (*infml*), phone-tap (*infml*).

bugbear *n* anathema, bane, bête noire, pet hate, dread, fiend, horror, nightmare.

build *v* **1** ERECT, raise, construct, fabricate, make, form, constitute, assemble, knock together, develop, enlarge, extend, increase, augment, escalate, intensify. **2** BASE, found, establish, institute, inaugurate, initiate, begin.
🔁 **1** destroy, demolish, knock down, lessen.
➤ *n* physique, figure, body, form, shape, size, frame, structure.
◆ **build up** strengthen, reinforce, fortify, extend, expand, develop, amplify, increase, escalate, intensify, heighten, boost, improve, enhance, publicize, advertise, promote, plug (*infml*), hype (*sl*).
🔁 weaken, lessen.

building *n* edifice, dwelling, erection, construction, fabrication, structure, architecture.

Types of building include: house, bungalow, cottage, block of flats, cabin, farmhouse, villa, mansion, chateau, castle, palace; church, chapel, cathedral, abbey, monastery, temple, pagoda, mosque, synagogue; shop, store, garage, factory, warehouse, silo, office block, tower block, skyscraper, theatre, cinema, gymnasium, sports hall, restaurant, café, hotel, pub (*infml*), public house, inn, school, college, museum, library, hospital, prison, power station, observatory; barracks, fort, fortress, monument, mausoleum; shed, barn, outhouse, stable, mill, lighthouse, pier, pavilion, boat-house, beach-hut, summerhouse, gazebo, dovecote, windmill. *see also* **architecture and building**; **house**; **shop**.

Types of building material include: aluminium, ashlar, asphalt, bitumen, breeze block, brick, building block, cast iron, cement, chipboard, clay, concrete, reinforced concrete, fixings, flagstone, girder, glass, glass fibre, gravel, granite, grout, gypsum, hardboard, hard core, insulation, foam insulation, loose fill insulation, lagging, lintel, lumber (*US*), marble, mortar, paving stone, paviour, plaster, plasterboard, plastic, plywood, sand, sandstone, shingle, slate, stainless steel, steel, steel beam, stone, tarmac, thatch, tile, floor tile, roof tile, timber, wattle and daub, wood.

build-up *n* **1** ENLARGEMENT, expansion, development, increase, gain, growth, escalation, publicity, promotion, plug (*infml*), hype (*sl*). **2** ACCUMULATION, mass, load, heap, stack, store, stockpile.
🔁 **1** reduction, decrease.

built-in *adj* **1** FITTED, integral, in-built, included. **2** *built-in safeguards*: inherent, included, incorporated, implicit, in-built, inseparable, integral, intrinsic, essential, fundamental, necessary.

bulbous *adj* rounded, swollen, swelling, bulging, convex, bloated, distended (*fml*).

bulbs and corms

Plants grown from bulbs and corms include: acidanthera, allium, amaryllis, anemone, bluebell (endymion), chincherinchee, chionodoxa, crocosmia, crocus, autumn crocus (colchicum), cyclamen, daffodil, crown imperial (fritillaria), galtonia, garlic, gladiolus, grape hyacinth (muscari), hyacinth, iris, ixia, jonquil, lily, montbretia, narcissus, nerine, ranunculus, scilla, snowdrop (galanthus), sparaxis, tulip, winter aconite.

bulge *n* **1** SWELLING, bump, lump, hump, distension, protuberance, projection. **2** RISE, increase, surge, upsurge, intensification.
➤ *v* swell, puff out, bulb, hump, dilate, expand, enlarge, distend, protrude, project.

bulk *n* size, magnitude, dimensions, extent, amplitude, bigness, largeness, immensity, volume, mass, weight, substance, body, preponderance, majority, most.

bulky *adj* substantial, big, large, huge, enormous, immense, mammoth, massive, colossal, hulking, hefty, heavy, weighty, unmanageable, unwieldy, awkward, cumbersome.
🔁 insubstantial, small, handy.

bulldoze v 1 *bulldoze buildings*: clear, flatten, level, raze, knock down. 2 FORCE, push (through), intimidate, browbeat, bully, coerce (*fml*), steamroller (*infml*).

bullet n shot, pellet, ball, slug (*infml*), missile, projectile.

bulletin n report, newsflash, dispatch, communiqué, statement, announcement, notification, communication, message.

bully n persecutor, tormentor, browbeater, intimidator, bully-boy, heavy (*sl*), ruffian, tough.
➤ v persecute, torment, terrorize, bulldoze, coerce (*fml*), browbeat, bullyrag, intimidate, cow, tyrannize, domineer, overbear, oppress, push around.

bulwark n bastion, buttress, defence, guard, safeguard, security, support, mainstay, outwork, buffer, embankment, fortification, partition, rampart, redoubt (*fml*).

bump v 1 HIT, strike, knock, bang, crash, collide (with). 2 JOLT, jerk, jar, jostle, rattle, shake, bounce.
➤ n 1 BLOW, hit, knock, bang, thump, thud, smash, crash, collision, impact, jolt, jar, shock. 2 LUMP, swelling, bulge, hump, protuberance.
♦ **bump into** meet, encounter, run into, chance upon, come across.
♦ **bump off** (*infml*) kill, murder, assassinate, eliminate (*sl*), liquidate (*sl*), do in (*sl*), top (*sl*).

bumper adj plentiful, abundant, large, great, enormous, massive, excellent, exceptional.
🔁 small.

bumpkin n country bumpkin, country yokel, boor, clodhopper, rustic, oaf, peasant, provincial, hillbilly (*infml*), hick (*infml*), hayseed (*infml*).

bumptious adj self-important, pompous, officious, overbearing, pushy, assertive, over-confident, presumptuous, forward, impudent, arrogant, cocky, conceited, swaggering, boastful, full of oneself, egotistic.
🔁 humble, modest.

bumpy adj jerky, jolting, bouncy, choppy, rough, lumpy, knobbly, knobby, uneven, irregular.
🔁 smooth, even.

bunch n 1 BUNDLE, sheaf, tuft, clump, cluster, batch, lot, heap, pile, stack, mass, number, quantity, collection, assortment. 2 *bunch of flowers*: bouquet, posy, spray. 3 GANG, band, troop, crew, team, party, gathering, flock, swarm, crowd, mob, multitude.
➤ v group, bundle, cluster, collect, assemble, congregate, gather, flock, herd, crowd, mass, pack, huddle.
🔁 disperse, scatter, spread out.

bundle n bunch, sheaf, roll, bale, truss, parcel, package, packet, carton, box, bag, pack, batch, consignment, group, set, collection, assortment, quantity, mass, accumulation, pile, stack, heap.
➤ v pack, wrap, bale, truss, bind, tie, fasten.

bungle v mismanage, cock up (*sl*), screw up (*sl*), foul up (*infml*), mess up (*infml*), ruin, spoil, mar, botch, fudge, blunder.

buoy n float, marker, signal, beacon.
♦ **buoy up** support, sustain, raise, lift, boost, encourage, cheer, hearten.
🔁 depress, discourage.

buoyant adj 1 *in buoyant mood*: light-hearted, carefree, bright, cheerful, happy, joyful, lively, animated, bouncy. 2 FLOATABLE, floating, afloat, light, weightless.
🔁 1 depressed, despairing. 2 heavy.

burden n cargo, load, weight, dead-weight, encumbrance, millstone, onus, responsibility, obligation, duty, strain, stress, worry, anxiety, care, trouble, trial, affliction, sorrow.
➤ v load, weigh down, encumber, handicap, bother, worry, tax, strain, overload, lie heavy on, oppress, overwhelm.
🔁 unburden, relieve.

bureau n service, agency, office, branch, department, division, counter, desk.

bureaucracy n administration, government, ministry, civil service, the authorities, the system, officialdom, red tape, regulations.

burglar n housebreaker, robber, thief, pilferer, trespasser.

burglary n housebreaking, break-in, robbery, theft, stealing, trespass.

burial n burying, interment, entombment, funeral, obsequies.

burlesque n caricature, mock, mockery, parody, ridicule, satire, travesty, take-off (*infml*), send-up (*infml*), spoof (*infml*), mickey-taking (*infml*).
➤ adj comic, derisive, farcical, mocking,

parodying, satirical, caricatural (*fml*).
ᴇᴀ serious.

burly *adj* big, well-built, hulking, hefty, heavy, stocky, sturdy, brawny, beefy, muscular, athletic, strapping, strong, powerful.
ᴇᴀ small, puny, thin, slim.

burn *v* 1 FLAME, blaze, flare, flash, glow, flicker, smoulder, smoke, fume, simmer, seethe. 2 IGNITE, light, kindle, incinerate, cremate, consume, corrode. 3 SCALD, scorch, parch, shrivel, singe, char, toast, brand, sear, smart, sting, bite, hurt, tingle.

burning *adj* 1 ABLAZE, aflame, afire, fiery, flaming, blazing, flashing, gleaming, glowing, smouldering, alight, lit, illuminated. 2 HOT, scalding, scorching, searing, piercing, acute, smarting, stinging, prickling, tingling, biting, caustic, pungent. 3 *burning desire*: ardent, fervent, eager, earnest, intense, vehement, passionate, impassioned, frantic, frenzied, consuming. 4 *burning issue*: urgent, pressing, important, significant, crucial, essential, vital.
ᴇᴀ 2 cold. 3 apathetic. 4 unimportant.

burnish *v* polish (up), brighten, buff, glaze, shine.

burrow *n* warren, hole, earth, set, den, lair, retreat, shelter, tunnel.
➤ *v* tunnel, dig, delve, excavate, mine, undermine.

burst *v* 1 *the tyre burst*: puncture, rupture, tear, split, crack, break (open), fragment, shatter, shiver, disintegrate. 2 *the dam burst*: gush, spout, rush, erupt. 3 *burst into a room*: rush, run, hurry, race, dart, break in on, barge (*infml*), push one's way (*infml*). 4 *the bomb burst*: explode, blow up.
➤ *n* 1 PUNCTURE, blow-out (*infml*), rupture, split, crack, break, breach, explosion, blast, bang, eruption. 2 DISCHARGE, gush, spurt, surge, rush, spate, torrent, outpouring, outburst, outbreak, fit.
♦ **burst out** 1 *burst out crying*: begin, start, commence (*fml*). 2 *"That's what I've been trying to tell you," she burst out*: exclaim, cry (out), call out, utter, blurt out (*infml*).

bury *v* 1 *bury the dead*: inter, entomb, lay to rest, shroud. 2 SINK, submerge, immerse, plant, implant, embed, conceal, hide, cover, enshroud, engulf, enclose, engross, occupy, engage, absorb.
ᴇᴀ 1 disinter, exhume. 2 uncover.

bush *n* 1 SHRUB, hedge, thicket. 2 SCRUB, brush, scrubland, backwoods, wilds.

bushy *adj* shaggy, thick, bristling, bristly, fluffy, fuzzy, luxuriant, spreading, stiff, unruly, rough, wiry.
ᴇᴀ thin, neat, tidy, trim, well-kept.

busily *adv* actively, diligently, assiduously, earnestly, energetically, hard, industriously, purposefully, briskly, speedily, strenuously.

business *n* 1 TRADE, commerce, industry, manufacturing, dealings, transactions, bargaining, trading, buying, selling. 2 COMPANY, firm, corporation, establishment, organization, concern, enterprise, venture. 3 JOB, occupation, work, employment, trade, profession, line, calling, career, vocation, duty, task, responsibility. 4 AFFAIR, matter, issue, subject, topic, question, problem, point.

businesslike *adj* professional, efficient, thorough, systematic, methodical, organized, orderly, well-ordered, practical, matter-of-fact, precise, correct, formal, impersonal.
ᴇᴀ inefficient, disorganized.

businessman, businesswoman *n* entrepreneur, industrialist, trader, merchant, tycoon, magnate, capitalist, financier, employer, executive.

bust *n* 1 SCULPTURE, head, torso, statue. 2 BOSOM, breasts, chest, breast.

bustle *v* dash, rush, scamper, scurry, hurry, hasten, scramble, fuss.
➤ *n* activity, stir, commotion, tumult, agitation, excitement, fuss, ado, flurry, hurry, haste.

busy *adj* 1 *be busy at the moment*: occupied, engaged, otherwise engaged, employed, unavailable, working, having a previous engagement/prior appointment, tied up (*infml*), hard at it (*infml*), busy as a bee (*infml*). 2 *a very busy day*: active, lively, energetic, strenuous, tiring, full, crowded, swarming, vibrant, teeming, bustling, hectic, frantic, eventful. 3 *busy preparing for the meeting*: occupied, involved, engrossed, working. 4 *a busy person*: active, having a lot to do, energetic, lively, diligent, industrious, assiduous, restless, tireless, sedulous (*fml*), on the go (*infml*), having a lot on (*infml*), having one's hands full (*infml*), fully stretched (*infml*), rushed off one's feet (*infml*), under pressure (*infml*), snowed under (*infml*), up to one's eyes in something (*infml*).

1 free, available. **2** quiet, leisured, empty. **3** unoccupied. **4** lazy, idle, at a loose end (*infml*).

➤ *v* occupy, engage, employ, engross, absorb, immerse, interest, concern, bother.

busybody *n* meddler, nosey parker (*infml*), intruder, pry, gossip, eavesdropper, snoop, snooper, troublemaker.

butt¹ *n* stub, end, tip, tail, base, foot, shaft, stock, handle, haft.

butt² *n* target, mark, object, subject, victim, laughing-stock, dupe.

butt³ *v, n* hit, bump, knock, buffet, push, shove, ram, thrust, punch, jab, prod, poke.
♦ **butt in** interrupt, cut in, interpose, intrude, meddle, interfere.

butterflies and moths

Types of butterfly include: red admiral, white admiral, apollo, cabbage white, chalkhill blue, common blue, brimstone, meadow brown, Camberwell beauty, clouded yellow, comma, large copper, small copper, fritillary, Duke of Burgundy fritillary, heath fritillary, gatekeeper, grayling, hairstreak, purple hairstreak, white letter hairstreak, hermit, monarch, orange-tip, painted lady, peacock, purple emperor, ringlet, grizzled skipper, swallowtail, tortoiseshell.

Types of moth include: brown-tail, buff-tip, burnet, six-spot, carpet, cinnabar, clothes, emperor, garden tiger, gypsy, death's head hawkmoth, privet hawkmoth, Kentish glory, lackey, lappet, leopard, lobster, magpie, oak hook-tip, pale tussock, peach blossom, peppered, puss, red underwing, silkworm, silver-Y, swallowtail, turnip, wax, winter.

buttocks *n* rump, hindquarters, rear, posterior (*infml*), seat, bottom, behind, backside (*infml*), arse (*sl*).

buttonhole *v* accost, waylay, catch, grab, nab, detain, importune.

buttress *n* support, prop, shore, stay, brace, pier, strut, stanchion, mainstay, reinforcement.

➤ *v* support, prop up, shore up, hold up,

brace, strengthen, reinforce, bolster up, sustain.

■ undermine, weaken.

buxom *adj* plump, ample, bosomy, busty, chesty, well-endowed, well-rounded, voluptuous (*fml*), comely (*fml*), busty (*infml*).

■ petite, slim, small.

buy *v* purchase, invest in (*infml*), pay for, procure, acquire, obtain, get.

■ sell.

➤ *n* purchase, acquisition, bargain, deal.

buyer *n* purchaser, shopper, consumer, customer, vendee, emptor.

■ seller, vendor.

buzz *v* **1** *bees buzzing round*: hum, whirr, drone, murmur, bombilate (*fml*), bombinate (*fml*), susurrate (*fml*). **2** *buzz with excitement*: hum, throb, pulse, bustle, race.

➤ *n* **1** *the buzz of bees*: hum, whirr, buzzing, drone, murmur, purr, tinnitus (*technical*), bombilation (*fml*), bombination (*fml*), susurration (*fml*), susurrus (*fml*). **2** *give someone a buzz*: ring, (phone) call. **3** *the latest buzz*: rumour, gossip, scandal, latest, hearsay. **4** THRILL, excitement, stimulation, kick(s) (*infml*), high (*infml*).

by *prep* near, next to, beside, along, over, through, via, past.

➤ *adv* near, close, handy, at hand, past, beyond, away, aside.

bygone *adj* past, ancient, departed, forgotten, former, previous, lost, olden, one-time, antiquated, erstwhile (*fml*).

■ modern, recent, future, forthcoming.

bypass *v* avoid, dodge, sidestep, skirt, circumvent, ignore, neglect, omit.

➤ *n* ring road, detour, diversion.

by-product *n* consequence, result, side-effect, fallout (*infml*), repercussion, after-effect.

bystander *n* spectator, onlooker, looker-on, watcher, observer, witness, eyewitness, passer-by.

byword *n* **1** *a byword for efficiency*: SLOGAN, catchword, dictum, maxim, motto. **2** PROVERB, saw, saying, precept, adage, aphorism (*fml*).

Cc

cab *n* **1** *hire a cab*: taxi, taxicab, minicab, hackney carriage. **2** *the cab in a lorry*: compartment, driver's compartment, cabin, quarters.

cabin *n* **1** BERTH, quarters, compartment, room. **2** HUT, shack, shanty, lodge, chalet, cottage, shed, shelter.

cabinet *n* cupboard, closet, dresser, case, locker.

cable *n* line, rope, cord, chain, wire, flex, lead.

cackle *v* laugh loudly, laugh unpleasantly, chortle, chuckle, crow, giggle, snigger, titter.

cadge *v* scrounge, sponge, beg, hitch.

café *n* coffee shop, tea shop, tea room, coffee bar, cafeteria, snackbar, bistro, brasserie, restaurant.

cage *v* encage, coop up, shut up, confine, restrain, fence in, imprison, impound, incarcerate, lock up.
■ release, let out, free.
➤ *n* aviary, coop, hutch, enclosure, pen, pound, corral.

cagey *adj* careful, chary, cautious, discreet, guarded, non-committal, secretive, shrewd, wary, wily, circumspect (*fml*), playing one's cards close to one's chest (*infml*).
■ frank, indiscreet, open.

cajole *v* coax, persuade, wheedle, flatter, sweet-talk (*infml*), butter up (*infml*), tempt, lure, seduce, entice, beguile, mislead, dupe.
■ bully, force, compel.

cake *v* coat, cover, encrust, dry, harden, solidify, consolidate, coagulate, congeal, thicken.
➤ *n* **1** *tea and cakes*: gâteau, fancy, madeleine, bun, pie, flan. **2** LUMP, mass, bar, slab, block, loaf.

calamitous *adj* disastrous, catastrophic, ruinous, devastating, deadly, fatal, dire, ghastly, dreadful, tragic, woeful, grievous.
■ good, fortunate, happy.

calamity *n* disaster, catastrophe, mishap, misadventure, mischance, misfortune, adversity, reverse, trial, tribulation, affliction, distress, tragedy, ruin, downfall.
■ blessing, godsend.

calculate *v* compute, work out, count, enumerate, reckon, figure, determine, weigh, rate, value, estimate, gauge, judge, consider, plan, intend, aim.

calculated *adj* considered, deliberate, intended, intentional, planned, purposeful, wilful, premeditated, purposed (*fml*).
■ unintended, unplanned.

calculating *adj* crafty, cunning, sly, devious, scheming, designing, contriving, sharp, shrewd.
■ artless, naïve.

calculation *n* sum, computation, answer, result, reckoning, figuring, estimate, forecast, judgement, planning, deliberation.

calendar *see* Chinese calendar; Jewish calendar.

calibre *n* **1** DIAMETER, bore, gauge, size, measure. **2** *candidates of the right calibre*: talent, gifts, strength, worth, merit, quality, character, ability, capacity, faculty, stature, distinction.

call *v* **1** NAME, christen, baptize, title, entitle, dub, style, term, label, designate. **2** SHOUT, yell, exclaim, cry. **3** SUMMON, invite, bid, convene, assemble. **4** TELEPHONE, phone, ring (up), contact.
➤ *n* **1** CRY, exclamation, shout, yell, scream. **2** VISIT, ring, summons, invitation. **3** *there's no call for it*: demand, need, occasion, cause, excuse, justification, reason, grounds, right. **4** APPEAL, request, plea, order, command, claim, announcement, signal.
◆ **call for 1** DEMAND, require, need, necessitate, involve, entail, occasion, suggest. **2** FETCH, collect, pick up.
◆ **call off** cancel, drop, abandon, discontinue, break off, withdraw.
◆ **call on 1** *call on a friend*: pay someone a (short) visit, visit, look in on, go and see. **2** *call on the government to resign*: appeal, appeal to, ask, bid, demand, urge, request, plead, press for, request (*fml*), summon (*fml*), supplicate (*fml*), entreat (*fml*).

calling *n* mission, vocation, career, profession, occupation, job, trade, business, line, work, employment, field, province, pursuit.

callous *adj* heartless, hard-hearted, cold, indifferent, uncaring, unsympathetic, unfeeling, insensitive, hardened, thick-skinned.
F3 kind, caring, sympathetic, sensitive.

callow *adj* inexperienced, immature, naïve, innocent, guileless, juvenile, puerile, raw, fledgling, uninitiated, unsophisticated, unfledged, untried, jejune (*fml*), green (*infml*).
F3 experienced.

calm *adj* 1 COMPOSED, self-possessed, collected, cool, dispassionate, unemotional, impassive, unmoved, placid, sedate, imperturbable, unflappable, unexcitable, laid back (*sl*), relaxed, unexcited, unruffled, unflustered, unperturbed, undisturbed, untroubled, unapprehensive. 2 *calm waters*: smooth, still, windless, unclouded, mild, tranquil, serene, peaceful, quiet, uneventful, restful.
F3 1 excitable, worried, anxious. 2 rough, wild, stormy.
➤ *v* compose, soothe, relax, sedate, tranquillize, hush, quieten, placate, pacify.
F3 excite, worry.
➤ *n* calmness, stillness, tranquillity, serenity, peacefulness, peace, quiet, hush, repose.
F3 storminess, restlessness.

camera

Types of camera include: automatic, bellows, binocular, box Brownie®, camcorder, camera obscura, cine, cinematographic, compact, daguerreotype, digital, disc, disposable, film, Instamatic®, large-format, miniature, subminiature, panoramic, plate, dry-plate, half-plate, quarter-plate, wet-plate, instant-and-press, Polaroid®, press, reflex, folding reflex, single-lens reflex (SLR), twin-lens reflex (TLR), security, sliding box, sound, still, stereo, Super 8®, TV, video. *see also* **photographic**.

Parts of a camera include: accessory shoe, AF lenses, aperture, aperture setting control, autofocus (AF), autofocus sensor, automatic focusing system, battery chamber, blind, cable release, card door, card on/off key, card window, compact lens, compound lens, data panel/display, diaphragm, exposure meter, exposure mode button, film advance/transport, film gate, film holder, fisheye lens, flash contact, flash setting, focal plane shutter, focus control/setting, focusing hood, focusing ring, frame counter, function adjustment button, function selector key, iris diaphragm, leaf shutter, lens, lens cap, lens release, light control, long-focus lens, magazine, medium focal-length lens, meter cell, mirror, mirror lens, mirror shutter, object lens, pentaprism, program card, program reset button, rangefinder window, reflex viewer, registration pin, release button, rewind handle/crank, shutter, shutter release, shutter speed control, shutter/film speed indicator, spool, spool knob, take-up reel/spool, telephoto lens, viewfinder eyepiece, viewfinder, viewing lens, wide-angle lens, zoom lens.

camouflage *n* disguise, guise, masquerade, mask, cloak, screen, blind, front, cover, concealment, deception.
➤ *v* disguise, mask, cloak, veil, screen, cover, conceal, hide, obscure.
F3 uncover, reveal.

camp¹ *n* 1 *a Scout camp*: campsite, camping-site, camping-ground, encampment, tents, bivouac. 2 *the union camp*: side, faction, group, party, section, set, crowd, caucus, clique.
➤ *v* pitch tents, set up camp, sleep outdoors, rough it (*infml*).

camp² *adj* affected, artificial, campy, exaggerated, mannered, ostentatious, posturing, theatrical, effeminate, queer, homosexual, over the top (*infml*), poncy (*infml*).

campaign *n* crusade, movement, promotion, drive, push, offensive, attack, battle, expedition, operation.
➤ *v* crusade, promote, push, advocate, fight, battle.

canal *n* 1 *the Grand Union Canal*: waterway, watercourse, channel, zanja. 2 *the alimentary canal*: tube, channel, passage.

cancel *v* call off, abort, abandon, drop, abolish, annul, quash, rescind, revoke, repeal, countermand, delete, erase, obliterate, eliminate, offset, compensate, redeem, neutralize, nullify.

cancellation *n* calling-off, abandoning, abandonment, abolition, dropping, stopping, deletion, elimination, neutralization, quashing, repeal, annulment, revocation, invalidation, nullifying, shelving (*infml*), scrubbing (*infml*).

cancer *n* 1 EVIL, blight, canker, pestilence, sickness, corruption, rot. 2 TUMOUR, growth, malignancy, carcinoma.

candid *adj* frank, open, truthful, honest, sincere, forthright, straightforward, ingenuous, guileless, simple, plain, clear, unequivocal, blunt, outspoken.
  ✗ guarded, evasive, devious.

candidate *n* applicant, aspirant, contender, contestant, competitor, entrant, runner, possibility, nominee, claimant, pretender, suitor.

candour *n* frankness, openness, truthfulness, honesty, plain-dealing, sincerity, straightforwardness, directness, ingenuousness, guilelessness, naïvety, artlessness, simplicity, plainness, bluntness, unequivocalness, outspokenness.
  ✗ evasiveness, deviousness.

cannon *n* gun, mortar, field gun, howitzer, artillery, battery, ordnance, big gun (*infml*).

canny *adj* shrewd, acute, sharp, astute, careful, cautious, prudent, clever, knowing, skilful, sly, subtle, wise, worldly-wise, artful, pawky, circumspect (*fml*), perspicacious (*fml*), judicious (*fml*), no flies on someone (*infml*).
  ✗ foolish, imprudent.

canon *n* 1 *a cathedral canon*: prebendary, clergyman, vicar, priest, minister, reverend. 2 *the canons of literary taste*: principle, rule, regulation, statute, criterion, standard, precept, dictate, yardstick.

canonical hours

Names of canonical hours include:
compline, lauds, matins, none, prime, sext, terce, vespers.

canopy *n* awning, covering, shade, shelter, sunshade, umbrella.

cantankerous *adj* irritable, irascible, grumpy, grouchy, crusty, crotchety, crabbed, crabby, testy, bad-tempered, ill-humoured, cross, peevish, difficult, perverse, contrary, quarrelsome.
  ✗ good-natured, easy-going (*infml*).

canter *n*, *v* amble, trot, jog, jogtrot, lope, gallop, run.

canvass *v* 1 ELECTIONEER, agitate, campaign, solicit, ask for, seek, poll. 2

EXAMINE, inspect, scrutinize, study, scan, investigate, analyse, sift, discuss, debate.
  ➤ *n* poll, survey, examination, scrutiny, investigation, inquiry.

canyon *n* gorge, ravine, gully, valley.

cap *v* exceed, surpass, transcend, better, beat, outdo, outstrip, eclipse, complete, finish, crown, top, cover.
  ➤ *n* 1 HAT, skullcap, beret, tam-o'-shanter. 2 LID, top, cover.

capability *n* ability, capacity, faculty, power, potential, means, facility, competence, qualification, skill, proficiency, talent.
  ✗ inability, incompetence.

capable *adj* able, competent, efficient, qualified, experienced, accomplished, skilful, proficient, gifted, talented, masterly, clever, intelligent, fitted, suited, apt, liable, disposed.
  ✗ incapable, incompetent, useless.

capacity *n* 1 VOLUME, space, room, size, dimensions, magnitude, extent, compass, range, scope. 2 CAPABILITY, ability, faculty, power, potential, competence, efficiency, skill, gift, talent, genius, cleverness, intelligence, aptitude, readiness. 3 *in her capacity as president*: role, function, position, office, post, appointment, job.

cape¹ *n* headland, head, promontory, point, ness, peninsula.

cape² *n* cloak, shawl, wrap, robe, poncho, coat.

capital *n* funds, finance, principal, money, cash, savings, investment(s), wealth, means, wherewithal, resources, assets, property, stock.

capitalize on *v* profit from, take advantage of, exploit, cash in on.

capitulate *v* surrender, throw in the towel, yield, give in, relent, submit, succumb.
  ✗ fight on.

caprice *n* whim, fad, fancy, impulse, whimsy, fantasy, notion, quirk, vagary, vapour, fickleness, fitfulness, inconstancy.

capricious *adj* changeable, inconstant, mercurial, erratic, fickle, uncertain, unpredictable, variable, wayward, fitful, fanciful, whimsical, freakish, impulsive, odd, queer, quirky.
  ✗ sensible, steady.

capsize *v* overturn, turn over, turn turtle, invert, keel over, upset.

capsule *n* pill, tablet, lozenge, receptacle, shell, sheath, pod, module.

captain *n* commander, master, skipper, pilot, head, chief, leader, boss, officer.

captivate *v* charm, enchant, bewitch, beguile, fascinate, enthral, hypnotize, mesmerize, lure, allure, seduce, win, attract, enamour, infatuate, enrapture, dazzle.
⊟ repel, disgust, appal.

captive *n* prisoner, hostage, slave, detainee, internee, convict.
➤ *adj* imprisoned, caged, confined, restricted, secure, locked up, enchained, enslaved, ensnared.
⊟ free.

captivity *n* custody, detention, imprisonment, incarceration, internment, confinement, restraint, bondage, duress, slavery, servitude.
⊟ freedom.

capture *v* catch, trap, snare, take, seize, arrest, apprehend, imprison, secure.
➤ *n* catching, trapping, taking, seizure, arrest, imprisonment.

car *n* automobile, motor car, motor, vehicle.

> Types of car include: saloon, hatchback, fastback, estate, sports car, cabriolet, convertible, limousine, limo (*infml*), wheels (*sl*), banger (*infml*), Mini, bubble-car, coupé, station wagon, shooting brake, veteran car, vintage car, Beetle (*infml*), four-wheel drive, Jeep®, buggy, Land Rover, Range Rover, panda car, patrol car, taxi, cab. *see also* **motor vehicle**.

carafe *n* bottle, decanter, flagon, flask, jug, pitcher.

carcase *n* body, corpse, cadaver, remains, relics, skeleton, shell, structure, framework, hulk.

cardinal *adj* chief, main, principal, fundamental, greatest, highest, important, key, leading, paramount, pre-eminent, primary, prime, central, essential, first, foremost, capital.

care *n* **1** CAREFULNESS, caution, forethought, watchfulness, pains, meticulousness, accuracy, prudence (*fml*), vigilance (*fml*), circumspection (*fml*). **2** *children need care*: looking-after, concern, attention, tending, minding, watching-over, heed, regard, consideration, interest, protection. **3** *in their care*: keeping, safekeeping, custody, guardianship, protection, ward, charge, responsibility, control, supervision, tutelage. **4** WORRY, anxiety, stress, strain, pressure, responsibility, burden, concern, trouble, distress, affliction, fear, disquiet, tribulation (*fml*), vexation (*fml*), hang-up (*infml*).
⊟ **1** carelessness. **2** carelessness, thoughtlessness, inattention, neglect.
➤ *v* worry, mind, bother, be concerned, be interested, give a damn (*infml*).
⊟ neglect, ignore, be indifferent.
♦ care for 1 LOOK AFTER, take care of, nurse, tend, mind, watch over, protect, provide for, minister to, attend, maintain. **2** BE FOND OF, feel affection for, love, be in love with, be keen on, be close to, enjoy, delight in, cherish. **3** *Would you care for a cup of tea?*: like, want, desire.

career *n* vocation, calling, life-work, occupation, pursuit, profession, trade, job, employment, livelihood.
➤ *v* rush, dash, tear, hurtle, race, run, gallop, speed, shoot, bolt.

carefree *adj* unworried, untroubled, unconcerned, blithe, breezy, happy-go-lucky, cheery, light-hearted, cheerful, happy, easy-going (*infml*), laid back (*infml*).
⊟ worried, anxious, despondent.

careful *adj* **1** CAUTIOUS, prudent, circumspect, judicious, wary, chary, vigilant, watchful, alert, attentive, mindful. **2** METICULOUS, painstaking, conscientious, scrupulous, thorough, detailed, punctilious, particular, accurate, precise, thoughtful.
⊟ **1** careless, inattentive, thoughtless, reckless. **2** careless.

careless *adj* **1** UNTHINKING, thoughtless, inconsiderate, uncaring, unconcerned, heedless, unmindful, forgetful, remiss, negligent, irresponsible, unguarded. **2** *careless work*: inaccurate, messy, untidy, disorderly, sloppy, neglectful, slipshod, slapdash, hasty, cursory, offhand, casual.
⊟ **1** thoughtful, prudent. **2** careful, accurate, meticulous.

caress *v* stroke, pet, fondle, cuddle, hug, embrace, kiss, touch, rub.
➤ *n* stroke, pat, fondle, cuddle, hug, embrace, kiss.

caretaker *n* janitor, porter, watchman, keeper, custodian, curator, warden, superintendent.

cargo *n* freight, load, pay-load, lading, tonnage, shipment, consignment, contents, goods, merchandise, baggage.

caricature *n* cartoon, parody, lampoon, burlesque, satire, send-up, take-off, imitation, representation, distortion, travesty.
➤ *v* parody, mock, ridicule, satirize, send up, take off, mimic, distort, exaggerate.

carnage *n* bloodshed, blood-bath, butchery, slaughter, killing, murder, massacre, holocaust.

carnal *adj* sensual, sexual, erotic, fleshly, physical, human, natural, animal, bodily, impure, lascivious, lecherous, lewd, licentious, lustful, corporeal (*fml*), libidinous (*fml*).
🔁 chaste, pure, spiritual.

carnival *n* festival, fiesta, gala, jamboree, fête, fair, holiday, jubilee, celebration, merrymaking, revelry.

carp *v* complain, criticize, censure, reproach, find faults, nag, quibble, ultracrepidate (*fml*), knock (*infml*), nit-pick (*infml*).
🔁 praise, compliment.

carpenter *n* woodworker, joiner, cabinet-maker.

carriage *n* **1** COACH, wagon, car, vehicle. **2** DEPORTMENT, posture, bearing, air, manner, mien, demeanour, behaviour, conduct. **3** CARRYING, conveyance, transport, transportation, delivery, postage.

carry *v* **1** BRING, convey, transport, haul, move, transfer, relay, release, conduct, take, fetch. **2** BEAR, shoulder, support, underpin, maintain, uphold, sustain, suffer, stand.
◆ **carry on 1** CONTINUE, proceed, last, endure, maintain, keep on, persist, persevere. **2** *carry on a business*: operate, run, manage, administer.
🔁 **1** stop, finish.
◆ **carry out** do, perform, undertake, discharge, conduct, execute, implement, fulfil, accomplish, achieve, realize, bring off.

cart *n* barrow, handcart, wheel-barrow, wagon, truck.
➤ *v* move, convey, transport, haul, lug (*infml*), hump (*infml*), bear, carry.

carton *n* box, packet, pack, case, container, package, parcel.

cartoon *n* comic strip, animation, sketch, drawing, caricature, parody.

cartridge *n* cassette, canister, cylinder, tube, container, case, capsule, shell, magazine, round, charge.

carve *v* cut, slice, hack, hew, chisel, chip, sculpt, sculpture, shape, form, fashion, mould, etch, engrave, incise, indent.

cascade *n* rush, gush, outpouring, flood, deluge, torrent, avalanche, cataract, waterfall, falls, fountain, shower.
🔁 trickle.
➤ *v* rush, gush, surge, flood, overflow, spill, tumble, fall, descend, shower, pour, plunge, pitch.

case[1] *n* container, receptacle, holder, suitcase, trunk, crate, box, carton, casket, chest, cabinet, showcase, casing, cartridge, shell, capsule, sheath, cover, jacket, wrapper.

case[2] *n* **1** CIRCUMSTANCES, context, state, condition, position, situation, contingency, occurrence, occasion, event, specimen, example, instance, illustration, point. **2** LAWSUIT, suit, trial, proceedings, action, process, cause, argument, dispute.

cash *n* money, hard money, ready money, bank-notes, notes, coins, change, legal tender, currency, hard currency, bullion, funds, resources, wherewithal.
➤ *v* encash, exchange, realize, liquidate.

cashier[1] *n* clerk, bank clerk, teller, treasurer, bursar, purser, banker, accountant, financial controller.

cashier[2] *v* discharge, dismiss, drum out, expel, break, discard, throw out, get rid of, sack (*infml*), give someone the boot (*infml*), unfrock (*infml*).

cask *n* barrel, tun, hogshead, firkin, vat, tub, butt.

cast *v* **1** THROW, hurl, lob, pitch, fling, toss, sling, shy, launch, impel, drive, direct, project, shed, emit, diffuse, spread, scatter. **2** MOULD, shape, form, model, found.
➤ *n* **1** COMPANY, troupe, actors, players, performers, characters, dramatis personae. **2** CASTING, mould, shape, form.
◆ **cast down** depress, discourage, dishearten, deject, sadden, crush, desolate.
🔁 cheer up, encourage.

caste *n* class, social class, social standing, order, group, position, rank, station, status, grade, lineage, background, degree, estate, stratum, race.

castle *n* stronghold, fortress, citadel, keep, tower, château, palace, mansion, stately home, country house.

Parts of a castle include: approach, bailey, barbican, bartizan, bastion, battlements, brattice, buttress, chapel, corbel, courtyard, crenel, crenellation, curtain wall, ditch, donjon, drawbridge, dungeon, embrasure, enclosure wall, fosse, gatehouse, inner wall, keep, merlon, moat, motte, mound, outer bailey, parapet, portcullis, postern, rampart, scarp, stockade, tower, lookout tower, turret, ward, watchtower.

castrate *v* emasculate, geld, neuter, unman, unsex.

casual *adj* **1** *a casual meeting*: chance, fortuitous, accidental, unintentional, unpremeditated, unexpected, unforeseen, irregular, random, occasional, incidental, superficial, cursory. **2** NONCHALANT, blasé, lackadaisical, negligent, couldn't-care-less (*infml*), apathetic, indifferent, unconcerned, informal, offhand, relaxed, laid back (*infml*).
Fa 1 deliberate, planned. **2** formal.

casualty *n* injury, loss, death, fatality, victim, sufferer, injured person, wounded, dead person.

cat

Breeds of cat include: Abyssinian, American shorthair, Balinese, Birman, Bombay, British shorthair, British longhair, Burmese, Carthusian, chinchilla, Cornish rex, Cymric, Devon rex, domestic tabby, Egyptian Mau, Exotic shorthair, Foreign Blue, Foreign spotted shorthair, Foreign White, Havana, Himalayan, Japanese Bobtail, Korat, Maine Coon, Manx, Norwegian Forest, Persian, rag-doll, rex, Russian Blue, Scottish Fold, Siamese, silver tabby, Singapura, Somali, Tiffany, Tonkinese, Tortoiseshell, Turkish Angora, Turkish Van.

catalogue *n* list, inventory, roll, register, roster, schedule, record, table, index, directory, gazetteer, brochure, prospectus.
➤ *v* list, register, record, index, classify, alphabetize, file.

catapult *v* hurl, fling, throw, pitch, toss, sling, launch, propel, shoot, fire.

cataract *n* waterfall, falls, rapids, force, cascade, downpour, torrent, deluge.

catastrophe *n* disaster, calamity, cataclysm, debacle, fiasco, failure, ruin, devastation, tragedy, blow, reverse, mischance, misfortune, adversity, affliction, trouble, upheaval.

catcall *n* jeer, boo, gibe, hiss, whistle, barracking, raspberry (*infml*).

catch *v* **1** *catch a ball*: hold, grab, take, seize, grasp, snatch, grip, clutch. **2** *catch an animal/a prisoner*: capture, trap, entrap, hunt down, snare, ensnare, hook, net, seize, lay hold of, arrest, apprehend, corner, round up, recapture, nab (*infml*), collar (*infml*), nick (*infml*). **3** HEAR, make out, perceive, recognize, understand, follow, take in, fathom, grasp, comprehend, get the hang of (*infml*), twig (*infml*). **4** SURPRISE, catch red-handed/in the act, expose, unmask, startle, find (out), discover, detect, discern. **5** *catch a cold*: get, develop, go down with, pick up, become infected with, become ill with, contract (*fml*), succumb to (*fml*). **6** *catch someone's attention*: attract, draw, win, entice, incite.
Fa 1 drop. **2** release, free. **3** miss.
➤ *n* **1** FASTENER, clip, hook, clasp, hasp, latch, lock, bolt. **2** DISADVANTAGE, drawback, snag, hitch, obstacle, problem, difficulty, fly in the ointment (*infml*).
◆ **catch on 1** *the new style is catching on quickly*: become popular, become fashionable, become all the rage (*infml*). **2** *catch on to what she said*: understand, follow, take in, fathom, grasp, comprehend.
◆ **catch up** draw level, gain on, overtake.

catching *adj* infectious, contagious, communicable, transmittable.

catchword *n* catch-phrase, slogan, motto, watchword, byword, password.

catchy *adj* memorable, haunting, popular, melodic, tuneful, attractive, captivating.
Fa dull, boring.

categorical *adj* absolute, total, utter, unqualified, unreserved, unconditional, downright, positive, definite, emphatic, unequivocal, clear, explicit, express, direct.
Fa tentative, qualified, vague.

categorize *v* class, classify, group, sort, grade, rank, order, list.

category *n* class, classification, group, grouping, sort, type, section, division, department, chapter, head, heading, grade, rank, order, list.

cater *v* provision, victual, provide, supply, furnish, serve, indulge, pander.

catholic *adj* broad, wide, wide-ranging, universal, global, general, comprehensive, inclusive, all-inclusive, all-embracing, liberal, tolerant, broad-minded.
Ea narrow, limited, narrow-minded.

cattle *n* cows, bulls, oxen, livestock, stock, beasts.

> **Breeds of cattle include:** Aberdeen Angus, Africander, Alderney, Ankole, Ayrshire, Blonde d'Aquitaine, Brahman, Brown Swiss, cattabu, cattalo, Charolais, Chillingham, Devon, dexter, Durham, Friesian, Galloway, Guernsey, Hereford, Highland, Holstein, Jersey, Latvian, Limousin, Longhorn, Luing, Red Poll, Romagnola, Santa Gertrudis, Shetland, Shorthorn, Simmenthaler, Teeswater, Ukrainian, Welsh Black.

catty *adj* bitchy, malicious, spiteful, venomous, vicious, mean, ill-natured, malevolent, back-biting, rancorous (*fml*).
Ea kind, pleasant.

caucus *n* assembly, meeting, session, convention, gathering, conclave, get-together, parley, set, clique.

cause *n* 1 SOURCE, origin, beginning, root, basis, spring, originator, creator, producer, maker, agent, agency. 2 REASON, motive, grounds, motivation, stimulus, incentive, inducement, impulse. 3 *a worthy cause*: object, purpose, end, ideal, belief, conviction, movement, undertaking, enterprise.
Ea 1 effect, result, consequence.
> *v* begin, give rise to, lead to, result in, occasion, bring about, effect, produce, generate, create, precipitate, motivate, stimulate, provoke, incite, induce, force, compel.
Ea stop, prevent.

caustic *adj* corrosive, acid, burning, stinging, biting, cutting, mordant, trenchant, keen, pungent, bitter, acrimonious, sarcastic, scathing, virulent, severe.
Ea soothing, mild.

caution *n* 1 CARE, carefulness, prudence, vigilance, watchfulness, alertness, heed, discretion, forethought, deliberation, wariness. 2 WARNING, caveat, injunction, admonition, advice, counsel.
Ea 1 carelessness, recklessness.
> *v* warn, admonish, advise, urge.

cautious *adj* careful, prudent, circumspect, judicious, vigilant, watchful, alert, heedful, discreet, tactful, chary, wary, cagey (*infml*), guarded, tentative, softly-softly, unadventurous.
Ea incautious, imprudent, heedless, reckless.

cavalcade *n* procession, parade, march-past, troop, array, retinue, train.

cavalier *n* horseman, equestrian, knight, gentleman, gallant, escort, partner.
> *adj* supercilious, condescending, lordly, haughty, lofty, arrogant, swaggering, insolent, scornful, disdainful, curt, offhand, free-and-easy.

cavalry *n* horsemen, equestrians, horse soldiers, cavalrymen, troopers, dragoons, hussars, lancers.

cave *n* cavern, grotto, hole, pothole, hollow, cavity.
◆ **cave in** collapse, subside, give way, yield, fall, slip.

caveat *n* caution, warning, alarm.

cavern *n* cave, cavity, den, grotto, hollow, pothole, vault, tunnel, dugout, underground chamber.

cavernous *adj* hollow, concave, gaping, yawning, echoing, resonant, deep, sunken.

cavity *n* hole, gap, dent, hollow, crater, pit, well, sinus, ventricle.

cavort *v* caper, frolic, gambol, prance, skip, dance, frisk, sport, romp.

cease *v* stop, desist, refrain, pack in (*sl*), halt, call a halt, break off, discontinue, finish, end, conclude, terminate, fail, die.
Ea begin, start, commence.

ceaseless *adj* endless, unending, never-ending, eternal, everlasting, continuous, non-stop, incessant, interminable, constant, perpetual, continual, persistent, untiring, unremitting.
Ea occasional, irregular.

cede *v* surrender, give up, resign, abdicate, renounce, abandon, yield, relinquish, convey, transfer, hand over, grant, allow, concede.

celebrate *v* commemorate, remember, observe, keep, rejoice, toast, drink to, honour, exalt, glorify, praise, extol, eulogize, commend, bless, solemnize.

celebrated *adj* famous, well-known, famed, renowned, illustrious, glorious, eminent, distinguished, notable, prominent, outstanding, popular, acclaimed, exalted, revered.

unknown, obscure, forgotten.

celebration n commemoration, remembrance, observance, anniversary, jubilee, festival, gala, merrymaking, jollification, revelry, festivity, party, rave-up (*infml*).

> Celebrations include: anniversary, banquet, baptism, bar mitzvah, birthday, centenary, christening, coming-of-age, commemoration, feast, fête, festival, gala, graduation, harvest festival, homecoming, Independence Day, jubilee, marriage, May Day, name-day, party, reception, remembrance, retirement, reunion, saint's day, thanksgiving, tribute, wedding. *see also* **anniversary**; **party**.

celebrity n personage, dignitary, VIP (*infml*), luminary, worthy, personality, name, big name, star, superstar.
■ nobody, nonentity.

celestial *adj* heavenly, divine, godlike, spiritual, angelic, seraphic, elysian, empyrean, ethereal, paradisaic, eternal, immortal, sublime, supernatural, transcendental, astral, starry.
■ earthly, mundane.

celibacy n singleness, bachelorhood, spinsterhood, virginity, chastity, purity, abstinence, continence.

cell n dungeon, prison, room, cubicle, chamber, compartment, cavity, unit.

cellar n basement, crypt, vault, storeroom, wine cellar.

cement v stick, bond, weld, solder, join, unite, bind, combine.
> n plaster, mortar, concrete.

cemetery n burial-ground, graveyard, churchyard.

censor v cut, edit, blue-pencil, bowdlerize, expurgate.

censorious *adj* condemnatory, disapproving, disparaging, fault-finding, carping, cavilling, critical, hypercritical, severe.
■ complimentary, approving.

censure n condemnation, blame, disapproval, criticism, admonishment, admonition, reprehension, reproof, reproach, rebuke, reprimand, telling-off (*infml*).
■ praise, compliments, approval.
> v condemn, denounce, blame, criticize, castigate, admonish, reprehend, reprove,

upbraid, reproach, rebuke, reprimand, scold, tell off (*infml*).
■ praise, compliment, approve.

central *adj* middle, mid, inner, interior, focal, main, chief, key, principal, primary, fundamental, vital, essential, important.
■ peripheral, minor, secondary.

centralize v concentrate, converge, bring/gather together, incorporate, rationalize, focus, streamline, amalgamate, compact, condense, unify.
■ decentralize.

centre n middle, mid-point, bull's-eye, heart, core, nucleus, pivot, hub, focus, crux.
■ edge, periphery, outskirts.
> v focus, concentrate, converge, gravitate, revolve, pivot, hinge.

ceremonial *adj* formal, official, stately, solemn, ritual, ritualistic.
■ informal, casual.
> n ceremony, formality, protocol, solemnity, ritual, rite.

ceremonious *adj* stately, dignified, grand, solemn, ritual, civil, polite, courteous, deferential, courtly, formal, stiff, starchy, exact, precise, punctilious.
■ unceremonious, informal, relaxed.

ceremony n 1 *wedding ceremony*: service, rite, commemoration, observance, celebration, function, parade. 2 ETIQUETTE, protocol, decorum, propriety, formality, form, niceties, ceremonial, ritual, pomp, show.

certain *adj* 1 SURE, positive, assured, confident, convinced, undoubted, indubitable, unquestionable, incontrovertible, undeniable, irrefutable, plain, conclusive, absolute, convincing, true. 2 INEVITABLE, unavoidable, bound, destined, fated. 3 SPECIFIC, special, particular, individual, precise, express, fixed, established, settled, decided, definite. 4 DEPENDABLE, reliable, trustworthy, constant, steady, stable.
■ 1 uncertain, unsure, hesitant, doubtful. 2 unlikely. 4 unreliable.

certainly *adv* of course, naturally, definitely, for sure, undoubtedly, doubtlessly.

certainty n sureness, positiveness, assurance, confidence, conviction, faith, trust, truth, validity, fact, reality, inevitability.
■ uncertainty, doubt, hesitation.

certificate n document, award, diploma, qualification, credentials, testimonial, guarantee, endorsement, warrant, licence, authorization, pass, voucher.

certify v declare, attest, aver, assure, guarantee, endorse, corroborate, confirm, vouch, testify, witness, verify, authenticate, validate, authorize, license.

chafe v 1 *chafe someone's skin*: rub, grate, irritate, rasp, scrape, inflame, scratch, wear, abrade (*fml*), excoriate (*fml*). 2 *chafing at the rules*: anger, annoy, enrage, exasperate, incense, provoke, inflame, vex, peeve (*infml*), get on someone's nerves (*infml*), get on someone's wick (*infml*).

chaff n husks, shells, pods, cases.

chagrin n annoyance, exasperation, indignation, disappointment, displeasure, irritation, vexation, disquiet, dissatisfaction, embarrassment, mortification, humiliation, shame, fretfulness, discomfiture (*fml*), discomposure (*fml*).
¤ delight, pleasure.
➤ v annoy, exasperate, disappoint, displease, irritate, vex, irk, disquiet, dissatisfy, embarrass, humiliate, mortify, peeve (*infml*).

chain n 1 FETTER, manacle, restraint, bond, link, coupling, union. 2 *chain of events*: sequence, succession, progression, string, train, series, set.
➤ v tether, fasten, secure, bind, restrain, confine, fetter, shackle, manacle, handcuff, enslave.
¤ release, free.

chairman, chairwoman n chairperson, chair, president, convenor, organizer, director, master of ceremonies, MC, toastmaster, speaker.

chalk up v achieve, attain, gain, log, score, tally, register, record, accumulate, ascribe, attribute, charge, credit, put down.

challenge v 1 DARE, defy, throw down the gauntlet, confront, brave, accost, provoke, test, tax, try. 2 DISPUTE, question, query, protest, object to.
➤ n dare, defiance, confrontation, provocation, test, trial, hurdle, obstacle, question, ultimatum.

chamber n 1 HALL, assembly room, auditorium, meeting-place. 2 ROOM, apartment, compartment, bedroom, boudoir. 3 *the chambers of the heart*: cavity, ventricle, compartment. 4 *the upper chamber of parliament*: assembly, legislature, parliament, council, house.

champion n winner, victor, conqueror, hero, guardian, protector, defender, vindicator, patron, backer, supporter, upholder, advocate.
➤ v defend, stand up for, back, support, maintain, uphold, espouse, advocate, promote.

chance n 1 ACCIDENT, fortuity, coincidence, fluke (*infml*), luck, fortune, providence, fate, destiny, risk, gamble, speculation, possibility, prospect, probability, likelihood, odds. 2 *a second chance*: opportunity, opening, occasion, time.
¤ 1 certainty.
➤ v 1 RISK, hazard, gamble, wager, stake, try, venture. 2 HAPPEN, occur.
➤ adj fortuitous, casual, accidental, inadvertent, unintentional, unintended, unforeseen, unlooked-for, random, haphazard, incidental.
¤ deliberate, intentional, foreseen, certain.

change v 1 *water changes into ice; prices keep changing*: make/become different, alter, vary, convert, turn, go, become, move, develop, modify, reorganize, reform, restructure, remodel, revise, renew, amend, adapt, customize, adjust, transform, evolve, transfer, move, shift, fluctuate, vacillate, be in a state of flux, mutate (*fml*), transmutate (*fml*), metamorphose (*fml*), transfigure (*fml*). 2 *change one thing for another*: substitute, replace, alternate, interchange, rotate, transpose, exchange, swap, trade, switch, barter, chop and change (*infml*). 3 *change buses*: transfer, connect, make a connection.
➤ n 1 *a change in the weather*: difference, alteration, variation, conversion, modification, reorganization, shake-up,

transition, trend, movement, diversion, novelty, innovation, variety, revolution, upheaval, development, reform, restructuring, remodelling, reconstruction, revision, renewal, amendment, adaptation, customization, adjustment, transformation, evolution, transfer, move, shift, fluctuation, vacillation, state of flux, reversal, about-turn, about-face, volte-face, turnabout, ebb and flow, mutation (*fml*), transmutation (*fml*), metamorphosis (*fml*), transfiguration (*fml*), vicissitude (*fml*), U-turn (*infml*). **2** *a change of government*: exchange, transposition, interchange, substitution, substitute, replacement, alternation, rotation, swap, trade, switch, barter. **3** *Have you got any change?*: coins, cash, silver, coppers.

changeable *adj* variable, mutable, fluid, kaleidoscopic, shifting, mobile, unsettled, uncertain, unpredictable, unreliable, erratic, irregular, inconstant, fickle, capricious, volatile, unstable, unsteady, wavering, vacillating.
🔁 constant, reliable.

channel *n* **1** DUCT, conduit, main, groove, furrow, trough, gutter, canal, flume, watercourse, waterway, strait, sound. **2** *channel of communication*: route, course, path, avenue, way, means, medium, approach, passage.
➤ *v* direct, guide, conduct, convey, send, transmit, force.

chant *n* plainsong, psalm, song, melody, chorus, refrain, slogan, war cry.
➤ *v* recite, intone, sing, chorus.

chaos *n* disorder, confusion, disorganization, anarchy, lawlessness, tumult, pandemonium, bedlam.
🔁 order.

chaotic *adj* disordered, confused, disorganized, topsy-turvy, deranged, anarchic, lawless, riotous, tumultuous, unruly, uncontrolled.
🔁 ordered, organized.

chap (*infml*) *n* fellow, bloke (*infml*), guy (*infml*), man, boy, person, individual, character, sort, type.

chaperone, chaperon *n* companion, escort, duenna.
➤ *v* escort, accompany, attend, guard, protect, safeguard, shepherd, take care of, look after, mind, watch over.

chapter *n* part, section, division, clause, topic, episode, period, phase, stage.

char *v* burn, cauterize, scorch, sear, singe, carbonize, brown.

character *n* **1** PERSONALITY, nature, disposition, temperament, temper, constitution, make-up, individuality, peculiarity, feature, attributes, quality, type, stamp, calibre, reputation, status, position, trait. **2** LETTER, figure, symbol, sign, mark, type, cipher, rune, hieroglyph, ideograph. **3** INDIVIDUAL, person, sort, type, role, part.

characteristic *adj* distinctive, distinguishing, individual, idiosyncratic, peculiar, specific, special, typical, representative, symbolic, symptomatic.
🔁 uncharacteristic, untypical.
➤ *n* peculiarity, idiosyncrasy, mannerism, feature, trait, attribute, property, quality, hallmark, mark, symptom.

characterize *v* typify, mark, stamp, brand, identify, distinguish, indicate, represent, portray.

charge *v* **1** *charge a high price*: ask, demand, levy, exact, debit. **2** ACCUSE, indict, impeach, incriminate, blame. **3** ATTACK, assail, storm, rush.
➤ *n* **1** PRICE, cost, fee, rate, amount, expense, expenditure, outlay, payment. **2** ACCUSATION, indictment, allegation, imputation. **3** ATTACK, assault, onslaught, sortie, rush. **4** *in your charge*: custody, keeping, care, safekeeping, guardianship, ward, trust, responsibility, duty.
♦ **in charge of** responsible for, managing, leading, controlling, directing, supervising, overseeing, heading up, looking after, taking care of.

charitable *adj* philanthropic, humanitarian, benevolent, benign, kind, compassionate, sympathetic, understanding, considerate, generous, magnanimous, liberal, tolerant, broad-minded, lenient, forgiving, indulgent, gracious.
🔁 uncharitable, inconsiderate, unforgiving.

charity *n* **1** GENEROSITY, bountifulness, alms-giving, beneficence, philanthropy, unselfishness, altruism, benevolence, benignness, kindness, goodness, humanity, compassion, tender-heartedness, love, affection, clemency, indulgence. **2** ALMS, gift, handout, aid, relief, assistance.
🔁 **1** selfishness, malice.

charlatan *n* impostor, cheat, fake, fraud, confidence trickster, pretender, bogus caller/official, quack, sham, swindler, mountebank, phoney (*infml*), con man (*infml*).

charm *v* please, delight, enrapture, captivate, fascinate, beguile, enchant, bewitch, mesmerize, attract, allure, cajole, win, enamour.
Ea repel.
➤ *n* **1** ATTRACTION, allure, magnetism, appeal, desirability, fascination, enchantment, spell, sorcery, magic. **2** *lucky charm*: trinket, talisman, amulet, fetish, idol.

charming *adj* pleasing, delightful, pleasant, lovely, captivating, enchanting, attractive, fetching, appealing, sweet, winsome, seductive, winning, irresistible.
Ea ugly, unattractive, repulsive.

chart *n* diagram, table, graph, map, plan, blueprint.
➤ *v* map, map out, sketch, draw, draft, outline, delineate, mark, plot, place.

charter *n* right, privilege, prerogative, authorization, permit, licence, franchise, concession, contract, indenture, deed, bond, document.
➤ *v* hire, rent, lease, commission, engage, employ, authorize, sanction, license.

chase *v* pursue, follow, hunt, track, drive, expel, rush, hurry.

chasm *n* gap, opening, gulf, abyss, void, hollow, cavity, crater, breach, rift, split, cleft, fissure, crevasse, canyon, gorge, ravine.

chassis *n* framework, bodywork, frame, fuselage, skeleton, structure, substructure, undercarriage.

chaste *adj* pure, virginal, unsullied, undefiled, immaculate, abstinent, continent, celibate, virtuous, moral, innocent, wholesome, modest, decent, plain, simple, austere.
Ea corrupt, lewd, vulgar, indecorous.

chasten *v* humble, humiliate, tame, subdue, repress, curb, moderate, soften, discipline, punish, correct, chastise, castigate, reprove.

chastise *v* punish, discipline, correct, beat, flog, whip, lash, scourge, smack, spank, castigate, reprove, admonish, scold, upbraid, berate, censure.

chat *n* talk, conversation, natter (*infml*), gossip, chinwag (*infml*), tête-à-tête, heart-to-heart.
➤ *v* talk, crack, natter (*infml*), gossip, chatter, rabbit (on) (*infml*).

chatter *v, n* prattle, babble, chat, natter (*infml*), gossip, tattle.

chatty *adj* talkative, gossipy, newsy, friendly, informal, colloquial, familiar.
Ea quiet.

cheap *adj* **1** INEXPENSIVE, reasonable, dirt-cheap, bargain, reduced, cut-price, knock-down, budget, economy, economical. **2** TAWDRY, tatty, cheapo (*sl*), shoddy, inferior, second-rate, worthless, vulgar, common, poor, paltry, mean, contemptible, despicable, low.
Ea 1 expensive, costly. **2** superior, noble, admirable.

cheapen *v* devalue, degrade, lower, demean, depreciate, belittle, disparage, denigrate, downgrade.

cheat *v* defraud, swindle, diddle, short-change, do (*infml*), rip off (*sl*), fleece, con (*infml*), double-cross, mislead, deceive, dupe, fool, trick, hoodwink, bamboozle (*infml*), beguile.
➤ *n* cheater, dodger, fraud, swindler, shark (*infml*), con man (*infml*), extortioner, double-crosser, impostor, charlatan, deceiver, trickster, rogue.

check *v* **1** EXAMINE, inspect, scrutinize, give the once-over (*infml*), investigate, probe, test, monitor, study, research, compare, cross-check, confirm, verify. **2** *check an impulse*: curb, bridle, restrain, control, limit, repress, inhibit, damp, thwart, hinder, impede, obstruct, bar, retard, delay, stop, arrest, halt.
➤ *n* **1** EXAMINATION, inspection, scrutiny, once-over (*infml*), check-up, investigation, audit, test, research. **2** CURB, restraint, control, limitation, constraint, inhibition, damper, blow, disappointment, reverse, setback, frustration, hindrance, impediment, obstruction, stoppage.
◆ **check in** register, book in, enrol, record one's arrival
◆ **check out 1** *check out of a hotel*: leave, pay the bill, settle up. **2** *check out the procedure*: examine, investigate, test, study, look into, recce (*infml*).
◆ **check up** investigate, inspect, evaluate, assess, analyse, probe, inquire into, ascertain, make sure, confirm, verify.

cheek (*infml*) *n* impertinence, impudence,

insolence, disrespect, effrontery, brazenness, temerity, audacity, nerve (*infml*), gall.

cheeky (*infml*) *adj* impertinent, impudent, insolent, disrespectful, forward, brazen, pert, saucy (*infml*), audacious.
ea respectful, polite.

cheer *v* 1 ACCLAIM, hail, clap, applaud. 2 COMFORT, console, brighten, gladden, warm, uplift, elate, exhilarate, encourage, hearten.
ea 1 boo, jeer. 2 dishearten.
➢ *n* acclamation, hurrah, bravo, applause, ovation.
♦ **cheer up** encourage, hearten, take heart, rally, buck up (*infml*), perk up (*infml*).

cheerful *adj* happy, glad, contented, joyful, joyous, blithe, carefree, light-hearted, cheery, good-humoured, sunny, optimistic, enthusiastic, hearty, genial, jovial, jolly, merry, lively, animated, bright, chirpy, breezy, jaunty, buoyant, sparkling.
ea sad, dejected, depressed.

cheerless *adj* gloomy, dismal, dreary, dull, depressing, dejected, despondent, austere, barren, desolate, forlorn, grim, bleak, cold, sad, unhappy, sombre, sorrowful, comfortless, joyless, lonely, melancholy, miserable, mournful, dank, dark, dingy, drab, sullen, sunless, winterly, uninviting.
ea bright, cheerful.

cheery *adj* happy, glad, contented, joyful, carefree, light-hearted, cheerful, optimistic, enthusiastic, hearty, genial, jovial, jolly, gay, merry, lively, animated, exuberant, bright, smiling, laughing, spirited, in good spirits, chirpy, breezy, jaunty, buoyant, sparkling.
ea downcast, sad.

cheese

Varieties of cheese include: Amsterdam, Bel Paese, Bleu d'Auvergne, Blue Cheshire, Blue Vinny, Boursin, Brie, Caboc, Caerphilly, Camembert, Carré, Cheddar, Cheshire, Churnton, cottage cheese, cream cheese, Crowdie, curd cheese, Danish blue, Derby, Dolcelatte, Dorset Blue, Double Gloucester, Dunlop, Edam, Emmental, Emmentaler, ewe-cheese, Feta, fromage frais, Gloucester, Gorgonzola, Gouda, Gruyère, Huntsman, Jarlsberg, Killarney, Lancashire, Leicester, Limburg(er), Lymeswold, mascarpone, mouse-trap, mozzarella, Neufchâtel, Orkney, Parmesan, Petit Suisse, Pont-l'Évêque, Port Salut, processed cheese, quark, Red Leicester, Red Windsor, ricotta, Roquefort, sage Derby, Saint-Paulin, Stilton, stracchino, Vacherin, vegetarian cheese, Wensleydale.

chemical elements

The chemical elements (with their symbols) are: actinium (Ac), aluminium (Al), americium (Am), antimony (Sb), argon (Ar), arsenic (As), astatine (At), barium (Ba), berkelium (Bk), beryllium (Be), bismuth (Bi), boron (B), bromine (Br), cadmium (Cd), caesium (Cs), calcium (Ca), californium (Cf), carbon (C), cerium (Ce), chlorine (Cl), chromium (Cr), cobalt (Co), copper (Cu), curium (Cm), dysprosium (Dy), einsteinium (Es), erbium (Er), europium (Eu), fermium (Fm), fluorine (F), francium (Fr), gadolinium (Gd), gallium (Ga), germanium (Ge), gold (Au), hafnium (Hf), hahnium (Ha), helium (He), holmium (Ho), hydrogen (H), indium (In), iodine (I), iridium (Ir), iron (Fe), krypton (Kr), lanthanum (La), lawrencium (Lr), lead (Pb), lithium (Li), lutetium (Lu), magnesium (Mg), manganese (Mn), mendelevium (Md), mercury (Hg), molybdenum (Mo), neodymium (Nd), neon (Ne), neptunium (Np), nickel (Ni), niobium (Nb), nitrogen (N), nobelium (No), osmium (Os), oxygen (O), palladium (Pd), phosphorus (P), platinum (Pt), plutonium (Pu), polonium (Po), potassium (K), praseodymium (Pr), promethium (Pm), protactinium (Pa), radium (Ra), radon (Rn), rhenium (Re), rhodium (Rh), rubidium (Rb), ruthenium (Ru), rutherfordium (Rf), samarium (Sm), scandium (Sc), selenium (Se), silicon (Si), silver (Ag), sodium (Na), strontium (Sr), sulphur (S), tantalum (Ta), technetium (Tc), tellurium (Te), terbium (Tb), thallium (Tl), thorium (Th), thulium (Tm), tin (Sn), titanium (Ti), tungsten (W), uranium (U), vanadium (V), xenon (Xe), ytterbium (Yb), yttrium (Y), zinc (Zn), zirconium (Zr).

chemistry

Terms used in chemistry include: analytical chemistry, biochemistry, inorganic chemistry, organic chemistry, physical chemistry; acid, alkali, analysis, atom, atomic number, atomic structure, subatomic particles, base, bond, buffer, catalysis, catalyst, chain reaction, chemical bond, chemical compound, chemical element, chemical equation, chemical reaction, chemist, chlorination, combustion, compound, corrosion, covalent bond, crystal, cycle, decomposition, diffusion, dissociation, distillation, electrochemical cell, electrode, electron, electrolysis, emulsion, fermentation, fixation, formula, free radical, gas, halogen, hydrolysis, immiscible, indicator, inert gas, ion, ionic bond, isomer, isotope, lipid, liquid, litmus paper, litmus test, mass, matter, metallic bond, mixture, mole, molecule, neutron, noble gas, nucleus, oxidation, periodic table, pH, polymer, proton, radioactivity, reaction, reduction, respiration, salt, solids, solution, solvent, substance, suspension, symbol, synthesis, valency, zwitterion. *see also* **acid**; **chemical elements**; **gas**; **minerals**.

chequered *adj* varied, mixed, diverse, with good and bad times/parts, with ups and downs, with sad and happy times/parts, with its fair share of rough and tumble.

cherish *v* foster, care for, look after, nurse, nurture, nourish, sustain, support, harbour, shelter, entertain, hold dear, value, prize, treasure.

chest *n* **1** *a man with a hairy chest*: breast, sternum (*technical*), thorax (*technical*). **2** *a treasure chest*: trunk, crate, box, case, casket, coffer, strongbox.

chew *v* masticate, gnaw, munch, champ, crunch, grind.

chide *v* scold, tell off, blame, criticize, censure, lecture, rebuke, reprehend, reprimand, reproach, reprove, admonish (*fml*), berate (*fml*), upbraid (*fml*).
Ea praise.

chief *adj* leading, foremost, uppermost, highest, supreme, grand, arch, premier, principal, main, key, central, prime, prevailing, predominant, pre-eminent, outstanding, vital, essential, primary, major.
Ea minor, unimportant.
➢ *n* ruler, chieftain, lord, master, supremo, head, principal, leader, commander, captain, governor, boss, director, manager, superintendent, superior, ringleader.

chiefly *adv* mainly, mostly, for the most part, predominantly, principally, primarily, essentially, especially, generally, usually.

child *n* youngster, kid (*infml*), nipper (*infml*), brat (*infml*), baby, infant, toddler,

tot (*infml*), minor, juvenile, offspring, issue, progeny, descendant.

childbirth *n* labour, delivery, confinement, child-bearing, lying-in, pregnancy, maternity, parturition (*fml*), travail (*fml*), accouchement (*fml*), puerperium (*fml*).

childhood *n* babyhood, infancy, boyhood, girlhood, schooldays, youth, adolescence, minority, immaturity.

childish *adj* babyish, boyish, girlish, infantile, puerile, juvenile, immature, silly, foolish, frivolous.
Ea mature, sensible.

childlike *adj* innocent, naïve, ingenuous, artless, guileless, credulous, trusting, trustful, simple, natural.

chill *v* **1** COOL, refrigerate, freeze, ice. **2** FRIGHTEN, terrify, dismay, dishearten, discourage, depress, dampen.
Ea 1 warm, heat.
➢ *n* coolness, cold, coldness, frigidity, rawness, bite, nip, crispness.
Ea warmth.

chilly *adj* **1** *chilly weather*: cold, fresh, brisk, crisp, nippy (*infml*), wintry. **2** *a chilly response*: cool, frigid, unsympathetic, unwelcoming, aloof, stony, unfriendly, hostile.
Ea 1 warm. **2** friendly.

chime *v* sound, strike, toll, ring, peal, clang, dong, jingle, tinkle.

china *adj* porcelain, ceramic, pottery, earthenware, terracotta.

Chinese calendar

The animals representing the years in which people are born: rat, buffalo, tiger, rabbit (or hare), dragon, snake, horse, goat (or sheep), monkey, rooster, dog, pig.

chink *n* crack, rift, cleft, fissure, crevice, slot, opening, aperture, gap, space.

chip *n* **1** NOTCH, nick, scratch, dent, flaw. **2** FRAGMENT, scrap, wafer, sliver, flake, shaving, paring.
➢ *v* chisel, whittle, nick, notch, gash, damage.
◆ **chip in 1** CONTRIBUTE, make a donation, donate, club together, have a collection, pay, subscribe, have a whip-round (*infml*). **2** *chip in when someone is talking*: interrupt, interpose (*fml*), chime in (*infml*), butt in (*infml*), cut in (*infml*).

chirp *v*, *n* chirrup, tweet, cheep, peep,

twitter, warble, sing, pipe, whistle.

chivalrous *adj* gentlemanly, polite, courteous, gallant, heroic, valiant, brave, courageous, bold, noble, honourable.
ख़ ungallant, cowardly.

chivalry *n* gentlemanliness, politeness, courtesy, gallantry, bravery, courage, boldness.

choice *n* option, alternative, selection, variety, pick, preference, say, decision, dilemma, election, discrimination, choosing, opting.
➤ *adj* best, superior, prime, plum, excellent, fine, exquisite, exclusive, select, hand-picked, special, prize, valuable, precious.
ख़ inferior, poor.

choke *v* 1 THROTTLE, strangle, asphyxiate, suffocate, stifle, smother, suppress. 2 OBSTRUCT, constrict, congest, clog, block, dam, bar, close, stop. 3 COUGH, gag, retch.

choose *v* pick, select, single out, designate, predestine, opt for, plump for, vote for, settle on, fix on, adopt, elect, prefer, wish, desire, see fit.

choosy (*infml*) *adj* selective, discriminating, picky (*infml*), fussy, particular, finicky, fastidious, exacting.
ख़ undemanding.

chop *v* cut, hack, hew, lop, sever, truncate, cleave, divide, split, slash.
◆ **chop up** cut (up), slice (up), divide, cube, dice, mince.

choppy *adj* rough, turbulent, tempestuous, stormy, squally, ruffled, wavy, uneven, broken.
ख़ calm, still.

chore *n* task, job, errand, duty, burden.

chorus *n* 1 REFRAIN, burden, response, call, shout. 2 CHOIR, choristers, singers, vocalists, ensemble.

christen *v* baptize, name, call, dub, title, style, term, designate, inaugurate, use.

Christmas *n* Xmas, Noel, Yule, Yuletide.

chronic *adj* 1 INCURABLE, deep-seated, recurring, incessant, persistent, inveterate, confirmed, habitual, ingrained, deep-rooted. 2 (*infml*) *a chronic film*: awful, terrible, dreadful, appalling, atrocious.
ख़ 1 acute, temporary.

chronicle *n* account, record, register, annals, archives, diary, calendar, history, journal, narrative, story, saga, epic.
➤ *v* recount, narrate, relate, report, tell,

write down, set down, record, put on record, register, enter, list.

chronological *adj* historical, consecutive, sequential, progressive, ordered.

chubby *adj* plump, podgy, fleshy, flabby, stout, portly, rotund, round, tubby, paunchy.
ख़ slim, skinny.

chuck *v* 1 THROW, cast, toss, fling, heave, hurl, jettison, pitch, shy, sling. 2 *chuck a habit/your boyfriend*: give up, abandon, reject, discard, get rid of, jilt, forsake (*fml*), quit (*infml*), dump (*infml*), pack in (*infml*), give the brush-off (*infml*), give the elbow (*infml*).

chuckle *v* laugh, giggle, titter, snigger, chortle, snort, crow.

chunk *n* lump, hunk, mass, wodge (*infml*), wedge, block, slab, piece, portion.

church *n* 1 *go to church*: place of worship, chapel, house of God, Lord's house, house of prayer, cathedral, minster, abbey, tabernacle, meeting-house, bethel, kirk, chantry, shrine. 2 *the Methodist Church*: denomination, tradition, grouping, sect, cult. 3 CONGREGATION, assembly, fellowship, community, people of God, body of Christ, bride of Christ.

Parts of a church or cathedral include:
aisle, almonry, altar, ambulatory, apse, arcade, arch, belfry, bell screen, bell tower, chancel, chapel, choir, clerestory, cloister, confessional, credence, crossing, crypt, fenestella, font, frontal, gallery, keystone, lectern, narthex, nave, parvis, pew, pinnacle, piscina, porch, portal, predella, presbytery, pulpit, reredos, ringing chamber, rood, rood screen, sacristy, sanctuary, sedile, shrine, slype, spire, squint, stall, steeple, stoup, tomb, tower, transept, triforium, vault, vestry.

Names of church services include:
baptism, christening, Christingle, communion, Holy Communion, confirmation, dedication, Eucharist, evening service, evensong, funeral, Lord's Supper, marriage, Mass, High Mass, Midnight Mass, nuptial Mass, Requiem Mass, Holy Matrimony, memorial service, morning prayers, morning service. *see also* **canonical hours**; **worship**.

churlish *adj* bad-tempered, ill-tempered, harsh, impolite, morose, rough, brusque,

rude, sullen, surly, uncivil, unmannerly, ill-mannered, ill-bred, discourteous, unneighbourly, unsociable, loutish, boorish, oafish, crabbed (*infml*).
ᴇ polite, urbane.

churn *v* **1** *my stomach is churning*: heave, turn, vomit, be sick, retch, throw up (*infml*), puke (*infml*). **2** *churn up mud*: move about violently, agitate, beat, swirl, toss, writhe, convulse, boil, foam, froth, seethe.
♦ **churn out** turn out, produce in great quantities, pump out, throw together, knock up.

chute *n* channel, incline, slide, slope, ramp, runway, shaft, funnel, gutter, trough.

cigarette *n* cigar, menthol, filter-tip, king-size, high-tar, low-tar, roll-up, roll-your-own, smoke, whiff, cig (*infml*), ciggy (*infml*), fag (*infml*), fag end (*infml*), dog end (*infml*), gasper (*infml*), joint (*infml*), spliff (*infml*), cancer-stick (*sl*), coffin-nail (*sl*).

cinema *n* **1** films, pictures, movies (*infml*), flicks (*sl*), big screen. **2** picture-house, picture-palace, fleapit (*infml*).

cipher *n* **1** CODE, secret system, coded message, cryptogram, cryptograph. **2** NONENTITY, nobody, yes-man.

circle *n* **1** RING, hoop, loop, round, disc, sphere, globe, orb, cycle, turn, revolution, circuit, orbit, circumference, perimeter, coil, spiral. **2** *circle of friends*: group, band, company, crowd, set, clique, coterie, club, society, fellowship, fraternity.
➤ *v* **1** RING, loop, encircle, surround, gird, encompass, enclose, hem in, circumscribe, circumnavigate. **2** ROTATE, revolve, pivot, gyrate, whirl, turn, coil, wind.

> Types of circle include: annulus, ball, band, belt, circuit, circumference, coil, cordon, coronet, crown, curl, cycle, disc, discus, ellipse, girdle, globe, halo, hoop, lap, loop, orb, orbit, oval, perimeter, plate, revolution, ring, rotation, round, saucer, sphere, spiral, turn, tyre, wheel, wreath.

circuit *n* lap, orbit, revolution, tour, journey, course, route, track, round, beat, district, area, region, circumference, boundary, bounds, limit, range, compass, ambit.

circuitous *adj* roundabout, periphrastic, indirect, oblique, devious, tortuous, winding, meandering, rambling, labyrinthine.
ᴇ direct, straight.

circular *adj* round, annular, ring-shaped, hoop-shaped, disc-shaped.
➤ *n* handbill, leaflet, pamphlet, notice, announcement, advertisement, letter.

circulate *v* **1** *circulate information*: spread, diffuse, broadcast, publicize, publish, issue, propagate, pass round, distribute. **2** GO ROUND, rotate, revolve, gyrate, whirl, swirl, flow.

circulation *n* **1** BLOOD-FLOW, flow, motion, rotation, circling. **2** SPREAD, transmission, publication, dissemination, distribution.

circumference *n* circuit, perimeter, rim, edge, outline, boundary, border, bounds, limits, extremity, margin, verge, fringe, periphery.

circumstances *n* details, particulars, facts, items, elements, factors, conditions, state, state of affairs, situation, position, status, lifestyle, means, resources.

circumstantial *adj* conjectural, presumed, deduced, contingent, hearsay, incidental, indirect, provisional, inferential, evidential (*fml*), presumptive (*fml*).

cistern *n* tank, reservoir, sink, basin, vat.

citadel *n* fortress, stronghold, bastion, castle, keep, tower, fortification, acropolis.

citation *n* **1** AWARD, commendation, honour. **2** QUOTATION, quote, cutting, excerpt, illustration, mention, passage, reference, source.

cite *v* quote, adduce, name, specify, enumerate, mention, refer to, advance, bring up.

citizen *n* city-dweller, townsman, townswoman, inhabitant, denizen, resident, householder, taxpayer, subject.

city *n* metropolis, town, municipality, conurbation.

civic *adj* city, urban, municipal, borough, community, local, public, communal.

civil *adj* **1** POLITE, courteous, well-mannered, well-bred, courtly, refined, civilized, polished, urbane, affable, complaisant, obliging, accommodating. **2** *civil affairs*: domestic, home, national, internal, interior, state, municipal, civic.
ᴇ **1** uncivil, discourteous, rude. **2** international, military.

civility *n* politeness, courteousness, courtesy, breeding, refinement, urbanity, graciousness, affability, amenity.
ᴇ discourtesy, rudeness.

civilization n progress, advancement, development, education, enlightenment, cultivation, culture, refinement, sophistication, urbanity.
Ea barbarity, primitiveness.

civilize v tame, humanize, educate, enlighten, cultivate, refine, polish, sophisticate, improve, perfect.

civilized adj advanced, developed, educated, enlightened, cultured, refined, sophisticated, urbane, polite, sociable.
Ea uncivilized, barbarous, primitive.

claim v 1 ALLEGE, pretend, profess, state, affirm, assert, maintain, contend, hold, insist. 2 claim a refund: ask, request, require, need, demand, exact, take, collect.
➤ n 1 ALLEGATION, pretension, affirmation, assertion, contention, insistence. 2 APPLICATION, petition, request, requirement, demand, call, right, privilege.

clairvoyant adj psychic, prophetic, visionary, telepathic, extra-sensory.
➤ n psychic, fortune-teller, prophet, prophetess, visionary, seer, soothsayer, augur, oracle, diviner, telepath.

clamber v scramble, claw, climb, scrabble, shin, scale, mount, ascend.

clammy adj damp, moist, sweaty, sweating, sticky, slimy, dank, muggy, heavy, close.

clamorous adj noisy, blaring, vociferous, deafening, lusty, riotous, tumultuous, uproarious, vehement, insistent.
Ea quiet, silent.

clamour v demand, ask for noisily, call for, press for, claim, insist, urge.
➤ n noise, uproar, commotion, shouting, din, racket, blare, agitation, hubbub, outcry, complaints, vociferation (fml).
Ea quietness, silence.

clamp n vice, grip, press, brace, bracket, fastener.
➤ v fasten, secure, fix, clinch, grip, brace.

clan n tribe, family, house, race, society, brotherhood, fraternity, confraternity, sect, faction, group, band, set, clique, coterie.

clandestine adj secret, surreptitious, undercover, underhand, concealed, hidden, covert, fraudulent, sly, sneaky, stealthy, underground, closet, furtive, private, backroom (infml), behind-door (infml), cloak-and-dagger (infml), under-the-counter (infml).
Ea open.

clang v, n clash, jangle, clank, clink, clunk, clatter, peal, bong, chime, resound, ring, toll.

clap v 1 APPLAUD, acclaim, cheer. 2 SLAP, smack, pat, wallop (infml), whack (infml), bang.

clarification n explanation, simplification, interpretation, exposition, definition, gloss, illumination, elucidation.

clarify v 1 EXPLAIN, throw light on, illuminate, elucidate, gloss, define, simplify, resolve, clear up. 2 REFINE, purify, filter, clear.
Ea 1 obscure, confuse. 2 cloud.

clarity n clearness, transparency, lucidity, simplicity, intelligibility, comprehensibility, explicitness, unambiguousness, obviousness, definition, precision.
Ea obscurity, vagueness, imprecision.

clash v 1 CRASH, bang, clank, clang, jangle, clatter, rattle, jar. 2 CONFLICT, disagree, quarrel, wrangle, grapple, fight, feud, war.
➤ n 1 CRASH, bang, jangle, clatter, noise. 2 a clash with the police: confrontation, showdown, conflict, disagreement, fight, brush.

clasp n 1 FASTENER, buckle, clip, pin, hasp, hook, catch. 2 HOLD, grip, grasp, embrace, hug.
➤ v 1 HOLD, grip, grasp, clutch, embrace, enfold, hug, squeeze, press. 2 FASTEN, connect, attach, grapple, hook, clip, pin.

class n 1 CATEGORY, classification, group, set, section, division, department, sphere, grouping, order, league, rank, status, caste, quality, grade, type, genre, sort, kind, species, genus, style. 2 a French class: lesson, lecture, seminar, tutorial, course.

Social classes/groups include:
aristocracy, nobility, gentry, landed gentry, gentlefolk, elite, nob (sl), high society, top drawer (infml), upper class, Sloane Ranger (sl), ruling class, jet set, middle class, lower class, working class, bourgeoisie, proletariat, hoi-polloi, commoner, serf, plebeian, pleb (infml). see also **nobility**.

➤ v categorize, classify, group, sort, rank, grade, rate, designate, brand.

classic adj typical, characteristic, standard, regular, usual, traditional, time-honoured, established, archetypal, model, exemplary, ideal, best, finest, first-rate, consummate, definitive, masterly, excellent, ageless, immortal,

undying, lasting, enduring, abiding.
Ea unrepresentative, second-rate.
➤ *n* standard, model, prototype, exemplar, masterwork, masterpiece, pièce de résistance.

classical *adj* elegant, refined, pure, traditional, excellent, well-proportioned, symmetrical, harmonious, restrained.
Ea modern, inferior.

classification *n* categorization, taxonomy, sorting, grading, arrangement, systematization, codification, tabulation, cataloguing.

classify *v* categorize, class, group, pigeonhole, sort, grade, rank, arrange, dispose, distribute, systematize, codify, tabulate, file, catalogue.

clause *n* article, item, part, section, subsection, paragraph, heading, chapter, passage, condition, proviso, provision, specification, point.

claw *n* talon, nail, pincer, nipper, gripper.
➤ *v* scratch, scrabble, scrape, graze, tear, rip, lacerate, maul, mangle.

clean *adj* **1** WASHED, laundered, sterile, aseptic, antiseptic, hygienic, sanitary, sterilized, sterile, cleansed, laundered, decontaminated, purified, pure, unadulterated, fresh, unpolluted, uncontaminated, immaculate, spotless, unspotted, unstained, unsoiled, unsullied, perfect, speckless, spick and span, faultless, flawless, unblemished, clean as a new pin (*infml*). **2** *a clean life*: innocent, guiltless, virtuous, pure, good, upright, moral, honest, honourable, righteous, reputable, upstanding, respectable, decent, chaste, squeaky-clean (*infml*). **3** *a clean sheet of paper*: blank, new, fresh, unmarked, unused. **4** *a clean game*: fair, just, according to the rules, even-handed, proper, above board (*infml*). **5** *clean lines*: simple, well-defined, clean-cut, smooth, regular, straight, neat, tidy.
Ea 1 dirty, polluted. **2** dishonourable, indecent. **4** dirty, rough. **5** ragged.
➤ *adv* completely, straight, directly, entirely, fully, totally, quite.

Ways to clean include: bath, bathe, bleach, brush, buff, cleanse, clear, comb, decontaminate, deodorize, disinfect, distil, dry-clean, dust, filter, floss, flush, freshen, freshen up, fumigate, groom, Hoover®, launder, mop, muck out, pasteurize, pick, polish, purge, purify, refine, rinse, rub,

sandblast, sanitize, scour, scrape, scrub, shampoo, shine, shower, soak, soap, sponge, spring-clean, spruce, spruce up, steep, sterilize, swab, sweep, swill, tidy, vacuum, valet, wash, wipe.

cleaner *n* char, charlady, charwoman, daily.

cleanse *v* **1** *cleanse a wound*: disinfect, sterilize, clean, bathe, wash, rinse, deterge (*fml*). **2** *cleansed from sin/cleanse your soul*: absolve, purify, purge, make free from, clear, lustrate (*fml*).
Ea 1 dirty. **2** defile.

cleanser *n* soap, soap powder, detergent, cleaner, solvent, scourer, scouring powder, purifier, disinfectant.

clear *adj* **1** PLAIN, distinct, comprehensible, intelligible, coherent, lucid, explicit, precise, unambiguous, well-defined, apparent, evident, patent, obvious, manifest, conspicuous, unmistakable, unquestionable, explicit, sure, unequivocal, incontrovertible, beyond question, crystal-clear, beyond doubt, certain, positive, definite, convinced. **2** *clear thinking*: sharp, keen, perceptive, penetrating, quick, sensible, reasonable, logical. **3** *clear water*: transparent, limpid, crystalline, glassy, translucent, see-through, clean, unclouded, colourless, pellucid (*fml*), diaphanous (*fml*). **4** *a clear day*: cloudless, unclouded, fine, fair, bright, sunny, light, luminous, undimmed. **5** UNOBSTRUCTED, unblocked, open, free, empty, unhindered, unimpeded. **6** *a clear conscience*: guiltless, innocent, blameless, in the clear, having no qualms (*fml*), having/feeling no compunction (*fml*). **7** AUDIBLE, perceptible, pronounced, distinct, recognizable, clear as a bell (*infml*).
Ea 1 unclear, vague, ambiguous, confusing, unsure. **2** muddled. **3** opaque, cloudy. **4** dull, cloudy, rainy, misty. **5** blocked. **6** guilty. **7** inaudible, indistinct, faint.
➤ *v* **1** *clear the dishes/room*: remove, take away, empty, unload, vacate, evacuate, move, shift, get rid of, rid, free, clean, fine, filter, tidy, wipe, erase, cleanse, refine, filter. **2** UNBLOCK, unclog, unstop, decongest, free, rid, extricate, disentangle, loosen. **3** *clear a fence*: jump (over), vault, leap over, go over. **4** ACQUIT, exonerate, absolve, pardon, vindicate, excuse, justify, free, liberate, release, let go, exculpate (*fml*). **5**

cleared for publication: permit, give permission, allow, authorize, approve, pass, sanction, give the green light (*infml*), give the go-ahead (*infml*). **6** *clear £100*: earn, take home, net, make a profit, make, gain, bring (in).

Ea 1 dirty. **2** block. **4** condemn. **5** prohibit.

◆ **clear out 1** *been told to clear out*: get out, leave, go away, depart, withdraw, beat it (*infml*), clear off (*infml*), push off (*infml*), shove off (*infml*), hop it (*infml*). **2** *clear out a cupboard*: tidy (up), empty, sort (out), throw out.

◆ **clear up 1** EXPLAIN, clarify, elucidate, unravel, solve, resolve, answer, straighten (out), sort out, iron out, crack (*infml*). **2** TIDY, order, sort, rearrange, put in order, straighten (up). **3** *the weather cleared up*: clear, become fine, become sunny, stop raining, brighten (up), improve.

clearance *n* **1** AUTHORIZATION, sanction, endorsement, permission, consent, leave, OK (*infml*), go-ahead, green light (*infml*). **2** SPACE, gap, headroom, margin, allowance.

clear-cut *adj* definite, explicit, well-defined, clear, precise, specific, straightforward, unambiguous, unequivocal, distinct, trenchant, plain, cut and dried (*infml*).

Ea ambiguous, vague.

clearing *n* space, gap, opening, glade, dell.

clearly *adv* obviously, without doubt, undoubtedly, undeniably, evidently, incontestably, incontrovertibly, indisputably, unmistakably, manifestly, plainly, patently, distinctly, openly, markedly.

cleave¹ *v* *cleave the tree in two*: split, divide, separate, sever, cut, slice, chop, crack, disunite, halve, hew, open, part, pierce, rend, dissever (*fml*), sunder (*fml*).

Ea join, unite.

cleave² *v* *cleave to your marriage partner*: adhere, cling, cohere, hold, stick, remain, attach, unite.

clergy *n* clergymen, churchmen, clerics, the church, the cloth, ministry, priesthood.

clergyman *n* churchman, cleric, ecclesiastic, divine, man of God, minister, priest, reverend, father, vicar, pastor, padre, parson, rector, canon, dean, deacon, chaplain, curate, presbyter, rabbi.

clerical *adj* **1** OFFICE, secretarial, white-collar, official, administrative. **2**

ECCLESIASTIC(AL), pastoral, ministerial, priestly, episcopal, canonical, sacerdotal.

> **Types of clerical vestment include:** alb, amice, biretta, cassock, chasuble, chimer, clerical collar, dog-collar (*infml*), cope, cotta, cowl, dalmatic, ephod, frock, Geneva bands, Geneva gown, habit, hood, maniple, mantle, mitre, mozzetta, pallium, rochet, scapular, scarf, skullcap, soutane, stole, surplice, tallith, tippet, tunicle, wimple, yarmulka.

clerk *n* account-keeper, record-keeper, assistant, official, administrative officer, administrator, notary, receptionist, secretary, typist, stenographer, shop-assistant, writer, copyist, protocolist, pen-pusher (*infml*).

clever *adj* intelligent, brainy (*infml*), bright, smart, witty, gifted, expert, knowledgeable, adroit, apt, able, capable, quick, quick-witted, sharp, keen, shrewd, knowing, discerning, cunning, ingenious, inventive, resourceful, sensible, rational.

Ea foolish, stupid, senseless, ignorant.

cliché *n* platitude, commonplace, banality, truism, bromide, chestnut, stereotype.

click *v* **1** *the machine clicked*: clack, clink, snap, snick, snip, tick, beat. **2** *it suddenly clicked*: (begin to) understand, make sense, fall into place, twig (*infml*), cotton on (*infml*).

➤ *n* beat, clack, clink, snap, snick, snip, tick.

client *n* customer, patron, regular, buyer, shopper, consumer, user, patient, applicant.

clientèle *n* business, clients, customers, following, market, patronage, patrons, regulars, trade, buyers, purchasers, shoppers, consumers, users.

cliff *n* bluff, face, rock-face, scar, scarp, escarpment, crag, overhang, precipice.

climate *n* weather, temperature, setting, milieu, environment, ambience, atmosphere, feeling, mood, temper, disposition, tendency, trend.

climax *n* culmination, height, high point, highlight, acme, zenith, peak, summit, top, head.

Ea nadir.

climb *v* **1** *climb the stairs*: go up, ascend, scale, shin up, clamber, mount, surmount. **2** *climb into the car*: move, stir, shift, clamber, scramble. **3** *unemployment is*

climbing: increase, go up, rise, soar, shoot up, top.
 ♦ **climb down** retract, back down, admit that one is wrong, concede, retreat, eat one's words (*infml*).

clinch *v* settle, secure, seal, close, conclude, decide, determine, confirm, verify, land (*infml*).

cling *v* clasp, clutch, grasp, grip, stick, adhere, cleave, fasten, embrace, hug.

clinic *n* medical centre, health centre, hospital, infirmary, doctor's, outpatients' department.

clinical *adj* 1 *clinical trials of the drug*: medical, hospital, patient. 2 *a clinical design*: simple, plain, austere, stark, basic, unadorned. 3 *a clinical attitude*: impersonal, analytic, business-like, cold, emotionless, unemotional, unfeeling, detached, disinterested, dispassionate, uninvolved, impassive, objective, scientific.
 ⊟ 2 decorated, ornamented. 3 warm, biased, subjective.

clip¹ *v* trim, snip, cut, prune, pare, shear, crop, dock, poll, truncate, curtail, shorten, abbreviate.

clip² *v* pin, staple, fasten, attach, fix, hold.

clipping *n* cutting, snippet, quotation, citation, passage, section, excerpt, extract, clip.

clique *n* circle, set, coterie, group, bunch, pack, gang, crowd, faction, clan.

cloak *n* cape, mantle, robe, wrap, coat, cover, shield, mask, front, pretext.
 ➤ *v* cover, veil, mask, screen, hide, conceal, obscure, disguise, camouflage.

clocks and watches

Types of clock or watch include: alarm-clock, digital clock, mantel clock, bracket clock, carriage clock, cuckoo-clock, longcase clock, grandfather clock, grandmother clock, speaking clock, Tim (*infml*); wrist-watch, fob-watch, repeating watch, chronograph, pendant watch, ring-watch, stop-watch; chronometer, sundial.

clog *v* block, choke, stop up, bung up, dam, congest, jam, obstruct, impede, hinder, hamper, burden.
 ⊟ unblock.

cloistered *adj* sheltered, secluded, confined, restricted, enclosed, shielded, withdrawn, insulated, protected, isolated,

reclusive (*fml*), sequestered (*fml*), cloistral (*fml*), hermitic (*fml*).
 ⊟ open.

close¹ *v* 1 SHUT, fasten, secure, lock, bar, obstruct, block, clog, plug, cork, stop up, fill, seal, fuse, join, unite. 2 END, finish, complete, conclude, terminate, wind up, stop, cease.
 ⊟ 1 open, separate. 2 start.
 ➤ *n* end, finish, completion, conclusion, culmination, ending, finale, dénouement, termination, cessation, stop, pause.

close² *adj* 1 NEAR, nearby, at hand, neighbouring, adjacent, adjoining, impending, imminent. 2 INTIMATE, dear, familiar, attached, devoted, loving. 3 OPPRESSIVE, heavy, muggy, humid, sultry, sweltering, airless, stifling, suffocating, stuffy, unventilated. 4 MISERLY, mean, parsimonious, tight (*infml*), stingy, niggardly. 5 SECRETIVE, uncommunicative, taciturn, private, secret, confidential. 6 *a close translation*: exact, precise, accurate, strict, literal, faithful. 7 *pay close attention*: fixed, concentrated, intense, keen. 8 DENSE, solid, packed, cramped.
 ⊟ 1 far, distant. 2 cool, unfriendly. 3 fresh, airy. 4 generous. 5 open. 6 rough.

clot *n* lump, mass, thrombus, thrombosis, clotting, coagulation.
 ➤ *v* coalesce, curdle, coagulate, congeal, thicken, solidify, set, gel.

cloth *n* 1 FABRIC, material, stuff, textile. 2 RAG, face-cloth, flannel, dish-cloth, floorcloth, duster, towel.

clothe *v* dress, put on, robe, attire, deck, outfit, rig, vest, invest, drape, cover.
 ⊟ undress, strip, disrobe.

clothes *n* clothing, garments, wear, attire, garb, gear (*infml*), togs (*infml*), outfit, get-up (*infml*), dress, costume, wardrobe.

Clothes include: suit, trouser suit, dress suit, catsuit, jumpsuit, tracksuit, shell suit, wet suit; dress, frock, evening-dress, shirtwaister, caftan, kimono, sari; skirt, mini skirt, dirndl, pencil-skirt, pinafore-skirt, divided-skirt, culottes, kilt, sarong; cardigan, jumper, jersey, sweater, polo-neck, turtle-neck, guernsey, pullover, twin-set, shirt, dress-shirt, sweat-shirt, tee-shirt, T-shirt, waistcoat, blouse, smock, tabard, tunic; trousers, jeans, Levis®, denims, slacks, cords, flannels, drainpipes, bell-bottoms, dungarees, leggings, pedal-pushers, breeches, plus-fours, jodhpurs, Bermuda shorts, hot pants, shorts; bra, brassière, body stocking, camisole, liberty bodice, corset, girdle, garter, suspender belt, suspenders, shift, slip, petticoat, teddy, basque, briefs, pants, panties, French knickers, camiknickers, pantihose, tights, stockings; underpants, boxer-shorts, Y-fronts, vest, string vest, singlet; swimsuit, bathing-costume, bikini, swimming costume, swimming trunks, leotard, salopette; nightdress, nightie (*infml*), pyjamas, bed-jacket, bedsocks, dressing-gown, housecoat, negligee; scarf, glove, mitten, muffler, earmuffs, leg-warmers, sock, tie, bow-tie, cravat, stole, shawl, belt, braces, cummerbund, veil, yashmak. *see also* **clerical**; **coat**; **footwear**; **hat**.

cloud *n* vapour, haze, mist, fog, gloom, darkness, obscurity.
➢ *v* mist, fog, blur, dull, dim, darken, shade, shadow, overshadow, eclipse, veil, shroud, obscure, muddle, confuse, obfuscate.
🔁 clear.

Types of cloud include: cirrus, cirrostratus, cirrocumulus, altocumulus, altostratus, cumulus, stratocumulus, nimbostratus, fractostratus, fractocumulus, cumulonimbus, stratus.

cloudy *adj* 1 *a cloudy sky*: overcast, dull, dark, murky, gloomy, sombre, grey, leaden, heavy, lowering, dim, sunless, hazy, misty, foggy. 2 *a cloudy liquid*: opaque, milky, muddy. 3 *cloudy issues*: indistinct, obscure, nebulous, hazy, misty, foggy, blurred, blurry, confused, muddled.
🔁 1 bright, sunny, cloudless. 2 clear. 3 clear, distinct, plain.

clown *n* buffoon, comic, comedian, joker, jester, fool, harlequin, pierrot.

club *n* 1 ASSOCIATION, society, company, league, guild, order, union, fraternity, group, set, circle, clique. 2 BAT, stick, mace, bludgeon, truncheon, cosh (*sl*), cudgel.
➢ *v* hit, strike, beat, bash, clout, clobber (*sl*), bludgeon, cosh (*sl*), batter, pummel.

clue *n* hint, tip, suggestion, idea, notion, lead, tip-off, pointer, sign, indication, evidence, trace, suspicion, inkling, intimation.

clump *n* cluster, bundle, bunch, mass, tuft, thicket.
➢ *v* tramp, clomp, stamp, stomp, plod, lumber, thump, thud.

clumsy *adj* bungling, ham-fisted,

unhandy, unskilful, inept, bumbling, blundering, lumbering, gauche, ungainly, gawky (*infml*), unco-ordinated, awkward, ungraceful, uncouth, rough, crude, ill-made, shapeless, unwieldy, heavy, bulky, cumbersome.
🔁 careful, graceful, elegant.

cluster *n* bunch, clump, batch, group, knot, mass, crowd, gathering, collection, assembly.
➢ *v* bunch, group, gather, collect, assemble, flock.

clutch *v* hold, clasp, grip, hang on to, grasp, seize, snatch, grab, catch, grapple, embrace.
➢ *n* 1 *in someone's clutches*: control, grasp, grip, power, sway, dominion, possession, hands, keeping, custody, embrace, mercy, claws, jaws. 2 *a clutch of eggs*: set, setting, group, hatching, incubation.

clutter *n* litter, mess, jumble, untidiness, disorder, disarray, muddle, confusion.
➢ *n* litter, encumber, fill, cover, strew, scatter.

coach *n* trainer, instructor, tutor, teacher.
➢ *v* train, drill, instruct, teach, tutor, cram, prepare.

coagulate *v* clot, curdle, congeal, thicken, solidify, gel.
🔁 melt.

coalesce *v* amalgamate, join (together), blend, mix, unite, combine, consolidate, cohere, fuse, incorporate, integrate, merge, affiliate, commingle (*fml*), commix (*fml*).

coalition *n* merger, amalgamation, combination, integration, fusion, alliance, league, bloc, compact, federation, confederation, confederacy, association, affiliation, union.

coarse *adj* 1 ROUGH, unpolished, unfinished, uneven, lumpy, unpurified, unrefined, unprocessed. 2 *coarse humour*: bawdy, ribald, earthy, smutty, vulgar, crude, offensive, foul-mouthed, boorish, loutish, rude, impolite, indelicate, improper, indecent, immodest.
🔁 1 smooth, fine. 2 refined, sophisticated, polite.

coast *n* coastline, seaboard, shore, beach, seaside.
➢ *v* free-wheel, glide, slide, sail, cruise, drift.

coat *n* 1 FUR, hair, fleece, pelt, hide, skin. 2 LAYER, coating, covering.

Types of coat include: overcoat, greatcoat, car-coat, duffel coat, Afghan, blanket, frock-coat, tail-coat, jacket, bomber jacket, dinner-jacket, donkey-jacket, hacking-jacket, reefer, pea-jacket, shooting-jacket, safari jacket, Eton jacket, matinee jacket, tuxedo, blazer, raincoat, trench-coat, mackintosh, mac (*infml*), Burberry, parka, anorak, cagoul, windcheater, jerkin, blouson, cape, cloak, poncho.

➤ *v* cover, paint, spread, smear, plaster.

coating *n* covering, layer, dusting, wash, coat, blanket, sheet, membrane, film, glaze, varnish, finish, veneer, lamination, overlay.

coax *v* persuade, cajole, wheedle, sweet-talk (*infml*), soft-soap, flatter, beguile, allure, entice, tempt.

cock-eyed *adj* **1** CROOKED, lopsided, askew, asymmetrical, awry, skew-whiff. **2** SENSELESS, absurd, crazy, ludicrous, nonsensical, preposterous, daft (*infml*), barmy (*infml*).
2 sensible, sober.

cocky *adj* arrogant, bumptious, self-important, conceited, vain, swollen-headed, egotistical, swaggering, brash, cocksure, self-assured, self-confident, overconfident.
humble, modest, shy.

code *n* **1** ETHICS, rules, regulations, principles, system, custom, convention, etiquette, manners. **2** *written in code*: cipher, secret language.

coerce *v* force, drive, compel, constrain, pressurize, bully, intimidate, browbeat, bludgeon, bulldoze, dragoon, press-gang.

coercion *n* force, duress, compulsion, constraint, pressure, bullying, intimidation, threats, browbeating.

coffer *n* casket, case, box, chest, trunk, strongbox, treasury, repository.

cogent *adj* convincing, compelling, conclusive, potent, powerful, strong, forceful, forcible, influential, weighty, irresistible, persuasive, unanswerable, effective, urgent.
weak, ineffective, unsound.

cognition *n* perception, awareness, knowledge, apprehension, discernment, insight, comprehension, understanding, intelligence, reasoning.

cohere *v* **1** STICK, adhere, cling, fuse, unite, bind, combine, coalesce, consolidate. **2** *the*

argument does not cohere: agree, square, correspond, harmonize, hold, hang together.
1 separate.

coherent *adj* articulate, intelligible, comprehensible, meaningful, lucid, consistent, logical, reasoned, rational, sensible, orderly, systematic, organized.
incoherent, unintelligible, meaningless.

coil *v* wind, spiral, convolute, curl, loop, twist, writhe, snake, wreathe, twine, entwine.

➤ *n* roll, curl, loop, ring, convolution, spiral, corkscrew, helix, twist.

coin *v* invent, make up, think up, conceive, devise, formulate, originate, create, fabricate, produce, mint, forge.

➤ *n* piece, bit, money, cash, change, small change, loose change, silver, copper.

Types of coin include: angel, bezant, bob (*infml*), copper, crown, dandiprat, denarius, dime, doubloon, ducat, farthing, florin, groat, guilder, guinea, half-crown, half guinea, halfpenny, half sovereign, ha'penny, krugerrand, louis d'or, moidore, napoleon, nickel, noble, obol, penny, pound, quid (*infml*), rap, real, sesterce, shilling, sixpence, solidus, sou, sovereign, spade guinea, stater, tanner (*infml*), thaler, threepenny bit.

coincide *v* coexist, synchronize, agree, concur, correspond, square, tally, accord, harmonize, match.

coincidence *n* **1** CHANCE, accident, eventuality, fluke (*infml*), luck, fortuity. **2** COEXISTENCE, conjunction, concurrence, correspondence, correlation.

coincidental *adj* **1** CHANCE, accidental, casual, unintentional, unplanned, flukey (*infml*), lucky, fortuitous. **2** COINCIDENT, coexistent, concurrent, simultaneous, synchronous.
1 deliberate, planned.

cold *adj* **1** UNHEATED, cool, chilled, chilly, chill, shivery, nippy, parky (*infml*), raw, biting, bitter, wintry, frosty, icy, glacial, freezing, frozen, arctic, polar. **2** UNSYMPATHETIC, unmoved, unfeeling, stony, frigid, unfriendly, distant, aloof, standoffish, reserved, undemonstrative, unresponsive, indifferent, lukewarm.
1 hot, warm. **2** friendly, responsive.
➤ *n* coldness, chill, chilliness, coolness, frigidity, iciness.
warmth.

cold-blooded *adj* cruel, inhuman, brutal, savage, barbaric, barbarous, merciless, pitiless, callous, unfeeling, heartless.

🇪 compassionate, merciful.

cold-hearted *adj* unfeeling, unkind, uncaring, insensitive, unsympathetic, uncompassionate, callous, stony-hearted, cold, heartless, indifferent, detached, flinty, inhuman.

🇪 warm-hearted.

collaborate *v* conspire, collude, work together, co-operate, join forces, team up, participate.

collaboration *n* conspiring, collusion, association, alliance, partnership, teamwork, co-operation.

collaborator *n* co-worker, associate, partner, team-mate, colleague, assistant, accomplice, traitor, turncoat.

collapse *v* 1 *collapse with exhaustion*: faint, pass out, crumple. 2 FALL, sink, founder, fail, fold (*infml*), fall apart, disintegrate, crumble, subside, cave in.
➤ *n* failure, breakdown, flop, debacle, downfall, ruin, disintegration, subsidence, cave-in, faint, exhaustion.

collar *n* neckband, ring, dog-collar, gorget, ruff, bertha, rebato, ruche.
➤ *v* stop, grab, capture, catch, seize, arrest, apprehend, nab (*infml*), nick (*infml*).

colleague *n* workmate, co-worker, team-mate, partner, collaborator, ally, associate, confederate, confrère, comrade, companion, aide, helper, assistant, auxiliary.

collect *v* gather, assemble, congregate, convene, muster, rally, converge, cluster, aggregate, accumulate, amass, heap, hoard, stockpile, save, acquire, obtain, secure.

🇪 disperse, scatter.

collected *adj* composed, self-possessed, placid, serene, calm, unruffled, unperturbed, imperturbable, cool.

🇪 anxious, worried, agitated.

collection *n* 1 GATHERING, assembly, convocation, congregation, crowd, group, cluster, accumulation, conglomeration, mass, heap, pile, hoard, stockpile, store. 2 SET, assemblage, assortment, job-lot, anthology, compilation.

collective *adj* united, combined, concerted, co-operative, joint, common, shared, corporate, democratic, composite, aggregate, cumulative.

🇪 individual.

collective nouns

Collective nouns (by animal) include:
shrewdness of *apes*, cete of *badgers*, sloth of *bears*, swarm of *bees*, obstinacy of *buffaloes*, clowder of *cats*, drove of *cattle*, brood of *chickens*, bask of *crocodiles*, murder of *crows*, herd of *deer*, pack of *dogs*, school of *dolphins*, dole of *doves*, team of *ducks*, parade of *elephants*, busyness of *ferrets*, charm of *finches*, shoal of *fish*, skulk of *foxes*, army of *frogs*, gaggle/skein of *geese*, tribe of *goats*, husk of *hares*, cast of *hawks*, brood of *hens*, bloat of *hippopotamuses*, string of *horses*, pack of *hounds*, troop of *kangaroos*, kindle of *kittens*, exaltation of *larks*, leap of *leopards*, pride of *lions*, swarm of *locusts*, tittering of *magpies*, troop of *monkeys*, watch of *nightingales*, family of *otters*, parliament of *owls*, pandemonium of *parrots*, covey of *partridges*, muster of *peacocks*, rookery of *penguins*, nye of *pheasants*, litter of *pigs*, school of *porpoises*, bury of *rabbits*, colony of *rats*, unkindness of *ravens*, crash of *rhinoceroses*, building of *rooks*, pod of *seals*, flock of *sheep*, murmuration of *starlings*, ambush of *tigers*, rafter of *turkeys*, turn of *turtles*, descent of *woodpeckers*, gam of *whales*, rout of *wolves*, zeal of *zebras*.

collectors and enthusiasts

Names of collectors and enthusiasts include: zoophile (*animals*), antiquary (*antiques*), tegestologist (*beer mats*), campanologist (*bell-ringing*), ornithologist (*birds*), bibliophile (*books*), audiophile (*broadcast and recorded sound*), lepidopterist (*butterflies*), cartophilist (*cigarette cards*), numismatist (*coins/medals*), conservationist (*countryside*), environmentalist (*the environment*), xenophile (*foreigners*), gourmet (*good food*), gastronome (*good-living*), discophile (*gramophone records*), chirographist (*hand-writing*), hippophile (*horses*), entomologist (*insects*), phillumenist (*matches/matchboxes*), monarchist (*the monarchy*), deltiologist (*postcards*), arachnologist (*spiders/arachnids*), philatelist (*stamps*), arctophile (*teddy bears*), etymologist (*words*).

college *n* educational institution, educational establishment, university, polytechnic, poly, institute, college of further education, technical college, adult education centre, academy, school, seminary.

collide v crash, bump, smash, clash, conflict, confront, meet.

collision n impact, crash, bump, smash, accident, pile-up, clash, conflict, confrontation, opposition.

colloquial adj conversational, informal, familiar, everyday, vernacular, idiomatic. ◰ formal.

collude v conspire, plot, connive, collaborate, scheme, machinate, intrigue.

collusion n complicity, deceit, conspiracy, plot, connivance, collaboration, league, scheme, scheming, intrigue, artifice, machination (fml), cahoots (infml).

colonist n colonial, settler, immigrant, emigrant, pioneer.

colonize v settle, occupy, people, populate.

colonnade n arcade, cloisters, portico, covered walk, stoa, columniation (fml), peristyle (fml).

colony n settlement, outpost, dependency, dominion, possession, territory, province.

colossal adj huge, enormous, immense, vast, massive, gigantic, mammoth, monstrous, monumental. ◰ tiny, minute.

colour n 1 HUE, shade, tinge, tone, tincture, tint, dye, paint, wash, pigment, pigmentation, coloration, complexion. 2 VIVIDNESS, brilliance, rosiness, ruddiness, glow, liveliness, animation. 3 a nation's colours: flag, standard, banner, emblem, ensign, insignia, badge.

The range of colours includes: red, crimson, scarlet, vermilion, cherry, cerise, magenta, maroon, burgundy, ruby, orange, tangerine, apricot, coral, salmon, peach, amber, brown, chestnut, mahogany, bronze, auburn, rust, copper, cinnamon, chocolate, tan, sepia, taupe, beige, fawn, yellow, lemon, canary, ochre, saffron, topaz, gold, chartreuse, green, eau de nil, emerald, jade, bottle, avocado, sage, khaki, turquoise, aquamarine, cobalt, blue, sapphire, gentian, indigo, navy, violet, purple, mauve, plum, lavender, lilac, pink, rose, magnolia, cream, ecru, milky, white, grey, silver, charcoal, ebony, jet, black.

➤ v 1 PAINT, crayon, dye, tint, stain, tinge. 2 BLUSH, flush, redden. 3 colour one's judgement: affect, bias, prejudice, distort, pervert, exaggerate, falsify.

colourful adj 1 MULTICOLOURED, kaleidoscopic, variegated, parti-coloured, vivid, bright, brilliant, rich, intense. 2 a colourful description: vivid, graphic, picturesque, lively, stimulating, exciting, interesting.
◰ 1 colourless, drab.

colourless adj 1 TRANSPARENT, neutral, bleached, washed out, faded, pale, ashen, sickly, anaemic. 2 INSIPID, lacklustre, dull, dreary, drab, plain, characterless, unmemorable, uninteresting, tame.
◰ 1 colourful. 2 bright, exciting.

column n 1 PILLAR, post, shaft, upright, support, obelisk. 2 LIST, line, row, rank, file, procession, queue, string.

coma n unconsciousness, hypnosis, insensibility, lethargy, oblivion, stupor, torpor, trance, drowsiness, somnolence (fml).

comatose adj unconscious, out, out cold, in a coma, insensible, lethargic, drowsy, sleepy, sluggish, stupefied, stunned, dazed, torpid, somnolent (fml).
◰ conscious.

comb v 1 comb one's hair: groom, neaten, tidy, untangle. 2 SEARCH, hunt, scour, sweep, sift, screen, rake, rummage, ransack.

combat n war, warfare, hostilities, action, battle, fight, skirmish, struggle, conflict, clash, encounter, engagement, contest, bout, duel.
➤ v fight, battle, strive, struggle, contend, contest, oppose, resist, withstand, defy.

combatant n fighter, warrior, soldier, serviceman, servicewoman, enemy, opponent, adversary, antagonist, belligerent, contender.

combination n 1 BLEND, mix, mixture, composite, amalgam, synthesis, compound. 2 MERGER, amalgamation, unification, alliance, coalition, association, federation, confederation, confederacy, combine, consortium, syndicate, union, integration, fusion, coalescence, connection.

combine v merge, amalgamate, unify, blend, mix, integrate, incorporate, synthesize, compound, fuse, bond, bind, join, connect, link, marry, unite, pool, associate, co-operate.

◨ divide, separate, detach.

come v 1 *they came to me*: advance, move towards, travel towards, move forward, approach, near, draw near. **2** *come to the river/party*: reach, attain, arrive, enter, get here, appear, put in an appearance, attend, materialize, turn up (*infml*), show up (*infml*), surface (*infml*), burst in (*infml*), barge in (*infml*). **3** *come to power*: reach, attain, achieve, gain, secure, pass into. **4** *the time for action has come*: arrive, occur, take place, happen, come about, present itself, come to pass, transpire. **5** *she comes from Belgium*: originate, be, be a native of, be ... by birth, have as one's home, hail, have as its source/origin. **6** *his arrogance comes from his insecurity*: result from, be caused by, follow, issue, develop, arise, stem, evolve. **7** *it may come to war*: pass into, become, turn, evolve into, develop into, enter, go as far as. **8** *the idea came to me*: think of, remember, strike, occur to, come to the mind of, dawn on.

◨ 1 go. **2** depart, leave. **3** fall from. **8** forget.

♦ **come about** happen, occur, come to pass, transpire, result, arise.

♦ **come across** find, discover, chance upon, happen upon, bump into, meet, encounter, notice.

♦ **come along** arrive, happen, develop, improve, progress, rally, mend, recover, recuperate.

♦ **come apart** disintegrate, fall to bits, break, separate, split, tear.

♦ **come between** separate, part, divide, split up, disunite, estrange, alienate.

♦ **come by** acquire, get, get hold of, obtain, secure, come into someone's possession, fall into someone's hands, procure (*fml*).

♦ **come clean** acknowledge, admit, confess, own up, reveal, tell all, make a clean breast of something (*infml*), spill the beans (*infml*).

♦ **come down** descend, fall, reduce, decline, deteriorate, worsen, degenerate.

♦ **come down on** blame, criticize, rebuke, reprimand, find fault with, chide, reprove, upbraid, reprehend, admonish, berate (*fml*), slate (*infml*), tear into (*infml*).

♦ **come down to** mean, be tantamount to, be equivalent to, correspond to, amount to, boil down to.

♦ **come down with** catch, fall ill with, get, develop, go down with, pick up, become

infected with, become ill with, contract (*fml*), succumb to (*fml*).

♦ **come forward** offer (oneself), offer one's services, volunteer, step forward.

♦ **come in** enter, appear, show up (*infml*), arrive, finish.

♦ **come in for** receive, get, suffer, endure, bear, undergo, experience, be subjected to.

♦ **come into** inherit, be left, have bequeathed to one, acquire, receive.

♦ **come off** happen, occur, take place, succeed.

♦ **come on** begin, appear, advance, proceed, progress, develop, improve, thrive, succeed.

♦ **come out 1** *the magazine comes out monthly*: be published, appear, be produced, become available, become known. **2** *everything came out all right in the end*: result, end (up), finish, conclude, terminate. **3** *gay people coming out*: come out of the closet, declare oneself to be, declare openly, admit, be outed by someone.

♦ **come out with** say, state, affirm, declare, exclaim, disclose, divulge.

♦ **come round 1** *come round from the anaesthetic*: recover, wake, awake. **2** YIELD, relent, concede, allow, grant, accede.

♦ **come through** endure, withstand, survive, prevail, triumph, succeed, accomplish, achieve.

♦ **come to 1** *come to after the operation*: recover, recover/regain consciousness, wake, awake. **2** *come to a total*: add up to, total, aggregate, amount to, make, equal, run to.

♦ **come up** rise, arise, happen, occur, crop up.

♦ **come up to** reach, meet, match up to, measure up to, live up to, make the grade, compare with, approach, bear comparison with.

♦ **come up with** suggest, put forward, propose, offer, present, think of, dream up, conceive, advance, produce, submit.

comeback n return, reappearance, resurgence, revival, recovery.

comedian n comic, clown, humorist, wit, joker, wag.

comedown n anticlimax, let-down, disappointment, deflation, blow, reverse, decline, descent, demotion, humiliation, degradation.

comedy n farce, slapstick, clowning,

hilarity, drollery, humour, wit, joking, jesting, facetiousness.

comfort _v_ ease, soothe, relieve, alleviate, assuage, console, cheer, gladden, reassure, hearten, encourage, invigorate, strengthen, enliven, refresh.
➤ _n_ **1** CONSOLATION, compensation, cheer, reassurance, encouragement, alleviation, relief, help, aid, support. **2** EASE, relaxation, luxury, snugness, cosiness, wellbeing, satisfaction, contentment, enjoyment.
Fa 1 distress. **2** discomfort.

comfortable _adj_ **1** SNUG, cosy, comfy (_infml_), relaxing, restful, easy, convenient, pleasant, agreeable, enjoyable, delightful. **2** AT EASE, relaxed, contented, happy. **3** AFFLUENT, well-off, well-to-do, prosperous.
Fa 1 uncomfortable, unpleasant. **2** uneasy, nervous. **3** poor.

comic _adj_ funny, hilarious, side-splitting, comical, droll, humorous, witty, amusing, entertaining, diverting, joking, facetious, light, farcical, ridiculous, ludicrous, absurd, laughable, priceless (_infml_), rich (_infml_).
Fa tragic, serious.
➤ _n_ comedian, gagster (_infml_), joker, jester, clown, buffoon, humorist, wit, wag.

coming _adj_ next, forthcoming, impending, imminent, due, approaching, near, future, aspiring, rising, up-and-coming.
➤ _n_ advent, approach, arrival, accession.

command _v_ **1** ORDER, bid, charge, enjoin, direct, instruct, require, demand, compel. **2** LEAD, head, rule, reign, govern, control, dominate, manage, supervise.
➤ _n_ **1** COMMANDMENT, decree, edict, precept, mandate, order, bidding, charge, injunction, directive, direction, instruction, requirement. **2** _be in command_: power, authority, leadership, control, domination, dominion, rule, sway, government, management.

commandeer _v_ seize, take possession of, confiscate, impound, hijack, usurp, appropriate (_fml_), requisition (_fml_), expropriate (_fml_), arrogate (_fml_), sequester (_fml_), sequestrate (_fml_).

commander _n_ leader, head, chief, boss, commander-in-chief, general, admiral, captain, commanding officer, officer.

commanding _adj_ **1** _in a commanding lead_: powerful, strong, superior, advantageous, dominant, dominating, controlling, directing. **2** _a commanding personality_: authoritative, forceful, powerful, assertive, confident, autocratic, peremptory (_fml_). **3** _the castle's commanding position_: dominating, imposing, impressive, lofty.

commemorate _v_ celebrate, solemnize, remember, memorialize, mark, honour, salute, immortalize, observe, keep.

commemoration _n_ celebration, observance, remembrance, tribute, honouring, ceremony.

commemorative _adj_ memorial, celebratory, remembering, marking, honouring, saluting, dedicatory, in memory of, in memoriam, in remembrance of, in honour of, as a tribute to, in recognition of.

commence _v_ begin, start, embark on, originate, initiate, inaugurate, open, launch.
Fa finish, end, cease.

commend _v_ **1** PRAISE, compliment, acclaim, extol, applaud, approve, recommend. **2** COMMIT, entrust, confide, consign, deliver, yield.
Fa 1 criticize, censure.

commendable _adj_ admirable, excellent, noble, praiseworthy, worthy, creditable, exemplary, deserving, estimable, laudable (_fml_), meritorious (_fml_).
Fa blameworthy, poor.

commendation _n_ praise, acclaim, acclamation, accolade, applause, high/good opinion, good word, approval, credit, recognition, encouragement, recommendation, special mention, approbation (_fml_).
Fa blame, criticism.

commensurate _adj_ proportionate, equivalent, corresponding, comparable, in proportion to, according to, corresponding to, consistent with, appropriate to, compatible with, acceptable, adequate, sufficient, due, fitting.

comment _v_ say, mention, interpose, interject, remark, observe, note, annotate, interpret, explain, elucidate, criticize.
➤ _n_ statement, remark, observation, note, annotation, footnote, marginal note, explanation, elucidation, illustration, exposition, commentary, criticism.

commentary _n_ narration, voice-over, analysis, description, review, critique, explanation, notes, treatise.

commentator *n* sportscaster, broadcaster, reporter, narrator, commenter, critic, annotator, interpreter.

commerce *n* trade, traffic, business, dealings, relations, dealing, trafficking, exchange, marketing, merchandising.

commercial *adj* trade, trading, business, sales, profit-making, profitable, sellable, saleable, popular, monetary, financial, mercenary, venal.

commiserate *v* express/offer sympathy, send/offer condolences, sympathize, comfort, understand, console, show consideration.

commission *n* **1** ASSIGNMENT, mission, errand, task, job, duty, function, appointment, employment, mandate, warrant, authority, charge, trust. **2** COMMITTEE, board, delegation, deputation, representative. **3** *commission on a sale*: percentage, cut (*infml*), rake-off (*infml*), allowance, fee.
➤ *v* nominate, select, appoint, engage, employ, authorize, empower, delegate, depute, send, order, request, ask for.

commit *v* **1** *commit a crime*: do, perform, execute, enact, perpetrate. **2** ENTRUST, confide, commend, consign, deliver, hand over, give, deposit. **3** BIND, obligate, pledge, engage, involve.
♦ **commit oneself** decide, undertake, promise, pledge, bind oneself.

commitment *n* undertaking, guarantee, assurance, promise, word, pledge, vow, engagement, involvement, dedication, devotion, adherence, loyalty, tie, obligation, duty, responsibility, liability.
ES vacillation, wavering.

committee *n* council, board, panel, jury, commission, advisory group, think-tank, working party, task force.

common *adj* **1** FAMILIAR, customary, habitual, usual, daily, everyday, routine, regular, frequent, widespread, prevalent, general, universal, standard, average, ordinary, plain, simple, workaday, run-of-the-mill, undistinguished, unexceptional, conventional, accepted, popular, commonplace. **2** VULGAR, coarse, unrefined, crude, inferior, low, ill-bred, loutish, plebeian. **3** COMMUNAL, public, shared, mutual, joint, collective.
ES **1** uncommon, unusual, rare, noteworthy. **2** tasteful, refined.

commonplace *adj* ordinary, everyday, common, humdrum, pedestrian, banal, trite, widespread, frequent, hackneyed, stock, stale, obvious, worn out, boring, uninteresting, threadbare.
ES memorable, exceptional.

common sense *n* good sense, sense, sensibleness, level-headedness, sanity, soundness, reason, pragmatism, hard-headedness, realism, experience, discernment, wisdom, shrewdness, astuteness, judgement, native intelligence, practicality, prudence (*fml*), judiciousness (*fml*), gumption (*infml*), nous (*infml*), savvy (*infml*).
ES folly, stupidity.

commonsense *adj* commonsensical, matter-of-fact, sensible, level-headed, sane, sound, reasonable, practical, down-to-earth, pragmatic, hard-headed, realistic, shrewd, astute, prudent, judicious.
ES foolish, unreasonable, unrealistic.

commonwealth

> **Members of the Commonwealth are:**
> Antigua and Barbuda, Australia, the Bahamas, Bangladesh, Barbados, Belize, Botswana, Brunei, Canada, Cyprus, Dominica, the Gambia, Ghana, Grenada, Guyana, India, Jamaica, Kenya, Kiribati, Lesotho, Malawi, Malaysia, the Maldives, Malta, Mauritius, Namibia, Nauru, New Zealand, Nigeria, Pakistan, Papua New Guinea, St Christopher and Nevis, St Lucia, St Vincent and the Grenadines, Seychelles, Sierra Leone, Singapore, Solomon Islands, South Africa, Sri Lanka, Swaziland, Tanzania, Tonga, Trinidad and Tobago, Tuvalu, Uganda, United Kingdom, Vanuatu, Western Samoa, Zambia, Zimbabwe.

commotion *n* agitation, hurly-burly, turmoil, tumult, excitement, ferment, fuss, bustle, ado, to-do (*infml*), uproar, furore, ballyhoo (*infml*), hullabaloo (*infml*), racket, hubbub, rumpus, fracas, disturbance, bust-up (*infml*), disorder, riot.

communal *adj* public, community, shared, joint, collective, general, common.
ES private, personal.

commune *n* collective, co-operative, kibbutz, community, fellowship, colony, settlement.
➤ *v* converse, discourse, communicate, make contact.

communicate v 1 ANNOUNCE, declare, proclaim, report, reveal, disclose, divulge, impart, inform, acquaint, intimate, notify, publish, disseminate, spread, diffuse, transmit, convey. 2 TALK, converse, commune, correspond, write, phone, telephone, contact.

communication n information, intelligence, intimation, disclosure, contact, connection, transmission, dissemination.

> **Forms of communication include:**
> media, mass media, broadcasting, radio, wireless, television, TV, cable TV, satellite, subscription TV, pay TV, pay-per-view, video, video-on-demand, teletext; telecommunications, data communication, information technology (IT); the Internet, the net, World Wide Web; newspaper, press, news, newsflash, magazine, journal, advertising, publicity, poster, leaflet, pamphlet, brochure, catalogue; post, dispatch, correspondence, letter, postcard, aerogram, e-mail, telegram, Telemessage®, cable, wire (*infml*), chain letter, junk mail, mailshot; conversation, word, message, dialogue, speech, gossip, grapevine (*infml*); notice, bulletin, announcement, communiqué, circular, memo, note, report, statement, press release; telephone, intercom, answering machine, walkie-talkie, bleeper, tannoy, telex, teleprinter, facsimile, fax, computer, word processor, typewriter, dictaphone, megaphone, loud-hailer; radar, Morse code, semaphore, Braille, sign language. *see also* **telephone**.

communicative *adj* talkative, voluble, expansive, informative, chatty, sociable, friendly, forthcoming, outgoing, extrovert, unreserved, free, open, frank, candid.
◢ quiet, reserved, reticent, secretive.

communion n 1 *communion with nature*: sharing thoughts, sharing feelings, communing, closeness, sympathy, empathy, togetherness, unity, harmony, fellowship, participation, rapport, affinity, accord (*fml*), concord (*fml*), intercourse (*fml*). 2 *Holy Communion*: Lord's Supper, Eucharist, Mass, Sacrament.

communiqué n announcement, bulletin, (official) communication, dispatch, message, report, statement, newsflash.

communism n collectivism, sovietism,

revisionism, socialism, totalitarianism, Bolshevism, Leninism, Marxism, Stalinism, Trotskyism, Maoism, Titoism.

community n district, locality, population, people, populace, public, residents, nation, state, colony, commune, kibbutz, society, association, fellowship, brotherhood, fraternity.

commute v 1 REDUCE, decrease, shorten, curtail, lighten, soften, mitigate, remit, adjust, modify, alter, change, exchange, alternate. 2 *commute by train*: travel, journey.

commuter n traveller, passenger, straphanger (*infml*), suburbanite (*infml*).

compact[1] *adj* small, neat, short, brief, terse, succinct, concise, pithy, condensed, pocket, little, compressed, pressed together, close, dense, impenetrable, solid, firm.
◢ large, rambling, diffuse.
➤ v compress, press down, press together, condense, consolidate, pack down, cram, flatten, ram, squeeze, tamp.

compact[2] n agreement, alliance, pact, treaty, arrangement, transaction, deal, settlement, bargain, understanding, bond, indenture, concordat, contract, covenant, entente.

companion n fellow, comrade, friend, buddy (*infml*), crony (*infml*), intimate, confidant(e), ally, confederate, colleague, associate, partner, mate, consort, escort, chaperon(e), attendant, aide, assistant, accomplice, follower.

companionship n fellowship, comradeship, camaraderie, esprit de corps, support, friendship, company, togetherness, conviviality, sympathy, rapport.

company n 1 *a manufacturing company*: firm, business, concern, association, corporation, establishment, house, partnership, syndicate, cartel, consortium. 2 TROUPE, group, band, ensemble, set, circle, crowd, throng, body, troop, crew, party, assembly, gathering, community, society. 3 GUESTS, visitors, callers, society, companionship, fellowship, support, attendance, presence.

comparable *adj* similar, alike, related, akin, cognate, corresponding, analogous, equivalent, tantamount, proportionate, commensurate, parallel, equal.
◢ dissimilar, unlike, unequal.

compare v liken, equate, contrast, juxtapose, balance, weigh, correlate, resemble, match, equal, parallel.

comparison n juxtaposition, analogy, parallel, correlation, relationship, likeness, resemblance, similarity, comparability, contrast, distinction.

compartment n section, division, subdivision, category, pigeonhole, cubbyhole, niche, alcove, bay, area, stall, booth, cubicle, locker, carrel, cell, chamber, berth, carriage.

compass n limit(s), range, scope, stretch, space, extent, sphere, area, reach, field, realm(s), boundary, bounds, circle, circuit, circumference, enclosure, round, scale, zone.

compassion n kindness, tenderness, fellow-feeling, humanity, mercy, pity, sympathy, commiseration, condolence, sorrow, concern, care.
F3 cruelty, indifference.

compassionate adj kind-hearted, kindly, tender-hearted, tender, caring, warm-hearted, benevolent, humanitarian, humane, merciful, clement, lenient, pitying, sympathetic, understanding, supportive.
F3 cruel, indifferent.

compatible adj harmonious, consistent, congruous, matching, consonant, accordant, suitable, reconcilable, adaptable, conformable, sympathetic, like-minded, well-matched, similar.
F3 incompatible, antagonistic, contradictory.

compatriot n fellow citizen, fellow national, countryman, fellow countryman, countrywoman, fellow countrywoman.

compel v force, make, constrain, oblige, necessitate, drive, urge, impel, coerce, pressurize, hustle, browbeat, bully, strongarm, bulldoze, press-gang, dragoon.

compelling adj forceful, coercive, imperative, urgent, pressing, irresistible, overriding, powerful, cogent, persuasive, convincing, conclusive, incontrovertible, irrefutable, gripping, enthralling, spellbinding, mesmeric, compulsive.
F3 weak, unconvincing, boring.

compensate v balance, counterbalance, cancel, neutralize, counteract, offset, redress, satisfy, requite, repay, refund, reimburse, indemnify, recompense, reward, remunerate, atone, redeem, make good, restore.

compensation n amends, redress, satisfaction, requital, repayment, refund, reimbursement, indemnification, indemnity, damages, reparation, recompense, reward, payment, remuneration, return, restoration, restitution, consolation, comfort.

compete v vie, contest, fight, battle, struggle, strive, oppose, challenge, rival, emulate, contend, participate, take part.

competent adj capable, able, adept, efficient, trained, qualified, well-qualified, skilled, experienced, proficient, expert, masterly, equal, fit, suitable, appropriate, satisfactory, adequate, sufficient.
F3 incompetent, incapable, unable, inefficient.

competition n **1** CONTEST, championship, tournament, cup, event, race, match, game, quiz. **2** RIVALRY, opposition, challenge, contention, conflict, struggle, strife, competitiveness, combativeness. **3** COMPETITORS, rivals, opponents, challengers, field.

competitive adj combative, contentious, antagonistic, aggressive, pushy, ambitious, keen, cut-throat.

competitor n contestant, contender, entrant, candidate, challenger, opponent, adversary, antagonist, rival, emulator, competition, opposition.

compilation n composition, collection, accumulation, collation, anthology, selection, organization, arrangement, thesaurus, treasury, album, compendium, miscellany, omnibus, potpourri, corpus, opus, work, assemblage (fml).

compile v compose, put together, collect, gather, garner, cull, accumulate, amass, assemble, marshal, organize, arrange.

complacent adj smug, self-satisfied, gloating, triumphant, proud, self-righteous, unconcerned, serene, self-assured, pleased, gratified, contented, satisfied.
F3 diffident, concerned, discontented.

complain v protest, grumble, grouse, gripe, beef, carp, fuss, lament, bemoan, bewail, moan, whine, groan, growl.

complaint n **1** PROTEST, objection, grumble, grouse, gripe, beef, moan, grievance, dissatisfaction, annoyance, fault-finding, criticism, censure, accusation, charge. **2** *a chest complaint*: ailment, illness, sickness, disease, malady, malaise, indisposition, affliction, disorder, trouble, upset.

complement *n* **1** *wine as a complement to the dinner*: companion, counterpart, addition, accessory, completion, consummation (*fml*). **2** *the ship's complement*: allowance, quota, total, totality, aggregate, sum, capacity, entirety.

➤ *v* go well with, go well together, combine well with, match, set off, contrast, round off, complete, crown.

complementary *adj* reciprocal, interdependent, correlative, interrelated, corresponding, matching, twin, fellow, companion.

🖪 contradictory, incompatible.

complete *adj* **1** UTTER, total, absolute, downright, out-and-out, thorough, perfect. **2** FINISHED, ended, concluded, over, done, accomplished, achieved. **3** UNABRIDGED, unabbreviated, unedited, unexpurgated, integral, whole, entire, full, undivided, intact.

🖪 **1** partial. **2** incomplete. **3** abridged.

➤ *v* finish, end, close, conclude, wind up, terminate, finalize, settle, clinch, perform, discharge, execute, fulfil, realize, accomplish, achieve, consummate, crown, perfect.

completely *adv* totally, utterly, wholly, fully, in full, absolutely, perfectly, quite, thoroughly, through and through, altogether, entirely, solidly, in every respect, lock stock and barrel (*infml*), from first to last (*infml*), root and branch (*infml*), every inch (*infml*), heart and soul (*infml*), hook line and sinker (*infml*).

completion *n* finish, end, close, conclusion, termination, finalization, settlement, discharge, fulfilment, realization, accomplishment, achievement, attainment, fruition, culmination, consummation, perfection.

complex *adj* complicated, intricate, elaborate, involved, convoluted, circuitous, tortuous, devious, mixed, varied, diverse, multiple, composite, compound, ramified.

🖪 simple, easy.

➤ *n* **1** NETWORK, structure, system, scheme, organization, establishment, institute, development. **2** FIXATION,

obsession, preoccupation, hang-up (*infml*), phobia.

complexion *n* **1** skin, colour, colouring, pigmentation. **2** look, appearance, aspect, light, character, nature, type, kind.

compliance *n* obedience, submissiveness, submission, agreement, assent, conformability, deference, passivity, yielding, acquiescence (*fml*), complaisance (*fml*), concurrence (*fml*).

🖪 defiance, disobedience.

complicate *v* compound, elaborate, involve, muddle, mix up, confuse, tangle, entangle.

🖪 simplify.

complicated *adj* complex, intricate, elaborate, involved, convoluted, tortuous, difficult, problematic, puzzling, perplexing.

🖪 simple, easy.

complication *n* difficulty, drawback, snag, obstacle, problem, ramification, repercussion, complexity, intricacy, elaboration, convolution, tangle, web, confusion, mixture.

complicity *n* collusion, collaboration, connivance, involvement, agreement, approval, knowledge, concurrence (*fml*).

🖪 ignorance, innocence.

compliment *n* **1** *pay someone a compliment*: flattery, flattering remark, admiration, favour, approval, congratulations, tribute, honour, accolade, bouquet, commendation, praise, eulogy (*fml*), homage (*fml*), felicitation (*fml*), laudation (*fml*). **2** *sends his compliments*: greetings, regards, best wishes, congratulations, remembrances, respects, salutation (*fml*).

🖪 **1** insult, criticism.

➤ *v* flatter, admire, commend, praise, extol, congratulate, applaud, salute.

🖪 insult, condemn.

complimentary *adj* **1** FLATTERING, admiring, favourable, approving, appreciative, congratulatory, commendatory, eulogistic. **2** *complimentary ticket*: free, gratis, honorary, courtesy.

🖪 **1** insulting, unflattering, critical.

comply *v* agree, consent, assent, accede, yield, submit, defer, respect, observe, obey, fall in, conform, follow, perform, discharge, fulfil, satisfy, meet, oblige, accommodate.

🖪 defy, disobey.

component n part, constituent, ingredient, element, factor, item, unit, piece, bit, spare part.

compose v 1 CONSTITUTE, make up, form. 2 CREATE, invent, devise, write, arrange, produce, make, form, fashion, build, construct, frame. 3 CALM, soothe, quiet, still, settle, tranquillize, quell, pacify, control, regulate.

composed adj calm, tranquil, serene, relaxed, unworried, unruffled, level-headed, cool, collected, self-possessed, confident, imperturbable, unflappable, placid.
☒ agitated, worried, troubled.

composite adj compound, conglomerate, complex, blended, combined, fused, mixed, patchwork, synthesized, heterogeneous (fml), agglutinate (fml).
☒ homogeneous, uniform.
➤ n compound, conglomerate, blend, combination, alloy, amalgam, fusion, mixture, synthesis, pastiche, patchwork, agglutination (fml).

composition n 1 MAKING, production, formation, creation, invention, design, formulation, writing, compilation, proportion. 2 CONSTITUTION, make-up, combination, mixture, form, structure, configuration, layout, arrangement, organization, harmony, consonance, balance, symmetry. 3 a musical composition: work, opus, piece, study, exercise.

compost n fertilizer, humus, mulch, manure, peat, dressing.

composure n calm, tranquillity, serenity, ease, coolness, self-possession, confidence, assurance, self-assurance, aplomb, poise, dignity, imperturbability, placidity, equanimity, dispassion, impassivity.
☒ agitation, nervousness, discomposure.

compound v 1 COMBINE, amalgamate, unite, fuse, coalesce, synthesize, alloy, blend, mix, mingle, intermingle. 2 WORSEN, exacerbate, aggravate, complicate, intensify, heighten, magnify, increase, augment.
➤ n alloy, blend, mixture, medley, composite, amalgam, synthesis, fusion, composition, amalgamation, combination.
➤ adj composite, mixed, multiple, complex, complicated, intricate.

comprehend v 1 UNDERSTAND, conceive, see, grasp, fathom, penetrate, tumble to (infml), realize, appreciate, know, apprehend, perceive, discern, take in, assimilate. 2 INCLUDE, comprise, encompass, embrace, cover.
☒ 1 misunderstand.

comprehensible adj understandable, intelligible, coherent, explicit, clear, lucid, plain, simple, straightforward.
☒ incomprehensible, obscure.

comprehension n understanding, conception, grasp, realization, appreciation, knowledge, apprehension, perception, discernment, judgement, sense, intelligence.
☒ incomprehension, unawareness.

comprehensive adj thorough, exhaustive, full, complete, encyclopedic, compendious, broad, wide, extensive, sweeping, general, blanket, inclusive, all-inclusive, all-embracing, across-the-board.
☒ partial, incomplete, selective.

compress v press, squeeze, crush, squash, flatten, jam, wedge, cram, stuff, compact, concentrate, condense, contract, telescope, shorten, abbreviate, summarize.
☒ expand, diffuse.

comprise v consist of, include, contain, incorporate, embody, involve, encompass, embrace, cover.

compromise v 1 NEGOTIATE, bargain, arbitrate, settle, agree, concede, make concessions, meet halfway, adapt, adjust. 2 compromise one's principles: weaken, undermine, expose, endanger, imperil, jeopardize, risk, prejudice. 3 DISHONOUR, discredit, embarrass, involve, implicate.
➤ n bargain, trade-off, settlement, agreement, concession, give and take, co-operation, accommodation, adjustment.
☒ disagreement, intransigence.

compulsive adj 1 IRRESISTIBLE, overwhelming, overpowering, uncontrollable, compelling, driving, urgent. 2 a compulsive gambler: obsessive, hardened, incorrigible, irredeemable, incurable, hopeless.

compulsory adj obligatory, mandatory, imperative, forced, required, requisite, set, stipulated, binding, contractual.
☒ optional, voluntary, discretionary.

compute v calculate, count (up), sum,

tally, add up, total, enumerate, reckon, estimate, assess, evaluate, figure, measure, rate.

computer *n* personal computer, PC, mainframe, processor, word-processor, data processor, calculator, adding machine.

Computing terms include: mainframe, microcomputer, minicomputer, PC (personal computer), Applemac®; hardware, CPU (central processing unit), disk drive, joystick, keyboard, lap-top, light pen, microprocessor, modem, monitor, mouse, mouse mat, notebook computer, printer, bubblejet printer, daisywheel printer, dot-matrix printer, ink-jet printer, laser printer, screen, VDU (visual display unit), software, program, Windows®, WordPerfect®, Wordstar®; disk, magnetic disk, floppy disk, hard disk, optical disk, magnetic tape; programming language, BASIC, COBOL, FORTRAN; memory, backing storage, external memory, immediate access memory, internal memory, RAM (Random Access Memory), ROM (Read Only Memory), CD-ROM (Compact Disc Read Only Memory); access, ASCII, backup, bit, boot, buffer, byte, kilobyte, megabyte, character, chip, silicon chip, computer game, computer graphics, computer literate, computer simulation, computer terminal, cursor, data, databank, database, default, desktop publishing (DTP), digitizer, directory, DOS (disk operating system), electronic mail, E-mail, format, function, grammar checker, graphics, hacking, interface, macro, menu, MSDOS (Microsoft® disk operating system), network, peripheral, pixel, scrolling, spellchecker, spreadsheet, template, toggle, toolbar, user-friendly, user interface, video game, virtual reality, virus, window, word-processing, work station, WYSIWYG (what you see is what you get). *see also* **Internet**.

comrade *n* fellow, companion, friend, intimate, confidant(e), ally, confederate, colleague, associate, partner, consort, escort, chaperon(e), attendant, aide, assistant, accomplice, follower, mate (*infml*), pal (*infml*), buddy (*infml*), crony (*infml*), sidekick (*infml*).

con (*infml*) *v* trick, hoax, dupe, deceive, mislead, inveigle, hoodwink, bamboozle (*infml*), cheat, double-cross, swindle, defraud, rip off (*sl*), rook.

➤ *n* confidence trick, trick, bluff, deception, swindle, fraud.

concave *adj* hollow, hollowed, cupped, scooped, excavated, sunken, depressed.
ᴇᴀ convex.

conceal *v* hide, obscure, disguise, camouflage, mask, screen, veil, cloak, cover, bury, submerge, smother, suppress, keep dark, keep quiet, hush up (*infml*).
ᴇᴀ reveal, disclose, uncover.

concede *v* **1** ADMIT, confess, acknowledge, recognize, own, grant, allow, accept. **2** YIELD, give up, surrender, relinquish, forfeit, sacrifice.
ᴇᴀ 1 deny.

conceit *n* conceitedness, vanity, boastfulness, swagger, egotism, self-love, self-importance, cockiness, self-satisfaction, complacency, pride, arrogance.
ᴇᴀ modesty, diffidence.

conceited *adj* vain, boastful, swollen-headed, bigheaded (*infml*), egotistical, self-important, cocky, self-satisfied, complacent, smug, proud, arrogant, stuck-up (*infml*), toffee-nosed (*infml*).
ᴇᴀ modest, self-effacing, diffident, humble.

conceivable *adj* imaginable, credible, believable, thinkable, tenable, possible, likely, probable.
ᴇᴀ inconceivable, unimaginable.

conceive *v* **1** IMAGINE, envisage, visualize, see, grasp, understand, comprehend, realize, appreciate, believe, think, suppose. **2** INVENT, design, devise, formulate, create, originate, form, produce, develop.

concentrate *v* **1** FOCUS, converge, centre, cluster, crowd, congregate, gather, collect, accumulate. **2** APPLY ONESELF, think, pay attention, attend. **3** CONDENSE, evaporate, reduce, thicken, intensify.
ᴇᴀ 1 disperse. **3** dilute.

concentrated *adj* **1** *concentrated liquid*: condensed, evaporated, reduced, thickened, dense, rich, strong, undiluted. **2** INTENSE, intensive, all-out, concerted, hard, deep.
ᴇᴀ 1 diluted. **2** half-hearted.

concentration *n* **1** CONVERGENCE, centralization, cluster, crowd, grouping, collection, accumulation, agglomeration, conglomeration. **2** ATTENTION, heed, absorption, application, single-mindedness, intensity. **3** COMPRESSION, reduction, consolidation, denseness, thickness.

🔁 **1** dispersal. **2** distraction. **3** dilution.

concept *n* idea, notion, plan, theory, hyphothesis, thought, abstraction, conception, conceptualization, visualization, image, picture, impression.

conception *n* **1** CONCEPT, idea, notion, thought. **2** KNOWLEDGE, understanding, appreciation, perception, visualization, image, picture, impression, inkling, clue. **3** INVENTION, design, birth, beginning, origin, outset, initiation, inauguration, formation. **4** *from conception to birth*: impregnation, insemination, fertilization.

concern *v* **1** UPSET, distress, trouble, disturb, bother, worry. **2** RELATE TO, refer to, regard, involve, interest, affect, touch.
➤ *n* **1** *a cause for concern*: anxiety, worry, unease, disquiet, care, sorrow, distress. **2** REGARD, consideration, attention, heed, thought. **3** *it's not my concern*: duty, responsibility, charge, job, task, field, business, affair, matter, problem, interest, involvement. **4** COMPANY, firm, business, corporation, establishment, enterprise, organization.

🔁 **1** joy. **2** indifference.

concerned *adj* **1** ANXIOUS, worried, uneasy, apprehensive, upset, unhappy, distressed, troubled, disturbed, bothered, attentive, caring. **2** CONNECTED, related, involved, implicated, interested, affected.

🔁 **1** unconcerned, indifferent, apathetic.

concerning *prep* about, regarding, with regard to, as regards, respecting, with reference to, relating to, in the matter of.

concert *n* **1** *a musical concert*: performance, entertainment, presentation, production, show, recital, appearance, engagement, rendering, rendition, gig, jam session, prom, soirée. **2** *work in concert with others*: agreement, harmony, unanimity, union, unison, accord (*fml*), concord (*fml*), concordance (*fml*), consonance (*fml*).

🔁 **2** disunity.

concerted *adj* combined, united, joint, collective, shared, collaborative, co-ordinated, organized, prearranged, planned.

🔁 separate, unco-ordinated, disorganized.

concession *n* compromise, adjustment, grant, allowance, exception, privilege,

favour, indulgence, permit, admission, acknowledgement.

conciliate *v* reconcile, pacify, placate, appease, restore harmony to, satisfy, soften, soothe, disarm, disembitter, mollify, propitiate.

🔁 antagonize.

conciliatory *adj* reconciliatory, peacemaking, peaceable, appeasing, disarming, mollifying, pacific, assuaging, irenic (*fml*), placatory (*fml*).

🔁 antagonistic.

concise *adj* short, brief, terse, succinct, pithy, compendious, compact, compressed, condensed, abridged, abbreviated, summary, synoptic.

🔁 diffuse, wordy.

conclave *n* assembly, (secret) meeting, council, conference, session cabinet, cabal, powwow (*infml*), parley (*infml*).

conclude *v* **1** INFER, deduce, assume, surmise, suppose, reckon, judge. **2** END, close, finish, complete, consummate, cease, terminate, culminate. **3** SETTLE, resolve, decide, establish, determine, clinch.

🔁 **2** start, commence.

conclusion *n* **1** INFERENCE, deduction, assumption, opinion, conviction, judgement, verdict, decision, resolution, settlement, result, consequence, outcome, upshot, answer, solution. **2** END, close, finish, completion, consummation, termination, culmination, finale.

conclusive *adj* final, ultimate, definitive, decisive, clear, convincing, definite, undeniable, irrefutable, indisputable, incontrovertible, unarguable, unanswerable, clinching.

🔁 inconclusive, questionable.

concoct *v* fabricate, invent, devise, contrive, formulate, plan, plot, hatch, brew, prepare, develop.

concoction *n* brew, potion, preparation, mixture, blend, compound, creation, contrivance.

concrete *adj* real, actual, factual, solid, physical, material, substantial, tangible, touchable, perceptible, visible, firm, definite, specific, explicit.

🔁 abstract, vague.

concubine *n* mistress, kept woman, paramour, lover, courtesan.

concurrent *adj* simultaneous,

synchronous, contemporaneous, coinciding, coincident, concomitant, coexisting, coexistent.

condemn v disapprove, reprehend, reprove, upbraid, reproach, castigate, blame, disparage, revile, denounce, censure, slam (*infml*), slate (*infml*), damn, doom, convict.
🖃 praise, approve.

condemnation n disapproval, reproof, reproach, castigation, blame, disparagement, denunciation, censure, thumbs-down (*infml*), damnation, conviction, sentence, judgement.
🖃 praise, approval.

condensation n 1 *condensation of liquid*: distillation, liquefaction, precipitation, concentration, evaporation, reduction, consolidation. 2 ABRIDGEMENT, précis, synopsis, digest, contraction, compression, curtailment.

condense v 1 *condense a book*: shorten, curtail, abbreviate, abridge, précis, summarize, encapsulate, contract, compress, compact. 2 DISTIL, precipitate, concentrate, evaporate, reduce, thicken, solidify, coagulate.
🖃 1 expand. 2 dilute.

condensed adj 1 *a condensed book*: shortened, cut (down), curtailed, abridged, abbreviated, summarized, abstracted, reduced, contracted, compact, concise. 2 *condensed liquid*: concentrated, evaporated, reduced, thickened, compressed, clotted, coagulated, dense, rich, strong, undiluted.
🖃 1 expanded. 2 diluted.

condescend v deign, see fit, stoop, bend, lower oneself, patronize, talk down.

condescending adj patronizing, disdainful, supercilious, snooty, snobbish, haughty, lofty, superior, lordly, imperious.
🖃 gracious, humble.

condition n 1 CASE, state, circumstances, position, situation, predicament, plight. 2 REQUIREMENT, obligation, prerequisite, terms, stipulation, proviso, qualification, limitation, restriction, rule. 3 *a heart condition*: disorder, defect, weakness, infirmity, problem, complaint, disease. 4 *out of condition*: fitness, health, state, shape, form, fettle, nick (*sl*).
➤ v indoctrinate, brainwash, influence, mould, educate, train, groom, equip, prepare, prime, accustom, season,

temper, adapt, adjust, tune.

conditional adj provisional, qualified, limited, restricted, tied, relative, dependent, contingent.
🖃 unconditional, absolute.

conditions n surroundings, environment, milieu, setting, atmosphere, background, context, circumstances, situation, state.

condom n sheath, French letter (*sl*), johnnie (*sl*), rubber (*sl*), protective.

condone v forgive, pardon, excuse, overlook, ignore, disregard, tolerate, brook, allow.
🖃 condemn, censure.

conducive adj leading, tending, contributory, productive, advantageous, beneficial, favourable, helpful, encouraging.
🖃 detrimental, adverse, unfavourable.

conduct n 1 *good conduct*: behaviour, comportment, actions, ways, manners, bearing, attitude. 2 ADMINISTRATION, management, direction, running, organization, operation, control, supervision, leadership, guidance.
➤ v 1 ADMINISTER, manage, run, organize, orchestrate, chair, control, handle, regulate. 2 ACCOMPANY, escort, usher, lead, guide, direct, pilot, steer. 3 *conduct heat*: convey, carry, bear, transmit. 4 *conduct oneself*: behave, acquit, comport, act.

confederacy n union, federation, alliance, coalition, confederation, league, partnership, compact (*fml*).

confederate n accomplice, ally, assistant, associate, colleague, friend, partner, supporter, collaborator, abettor, accessory, conspirator.
➤ adj federate, federal, allied, associated, combined, united.

confer v 1 DISCUSS, debate, deliberate, consult, talk, converse. 2 BESTOW, award, present, give, grant, accord, impart, lend.

conference n meeting, convention, congress, convocation, symposium, forum, discussion, debate, consultation.

confess v admit, confide, own (up), come clean (*infml*), grant, concede, acknowledge, recognize, affirm, assert, profess, declare, disclose, divulge, expose.
🖃 deny, conceal.

confession n admission, acknowledgement, affirmation, assertion, profession, declaration, disclosure,

divulgence, revelation, unburdening.
ᴇᴀ denial, concealment.

confidant, confidante n friend, close friend, bosom friend, intimate, companion, crony (infml), pal (infml), mate (infml).

confide v confess, admit, reveal, disclose, divulge, whisper, breathe, tell, impart, unburden.
ᴇᴀ hide, suppress.

confidence n certainty, faith, credence, trust, reliance, dependence, assurance, composure, calmness, self-possession, self-confidence, self-reliance, self-assurance, boldness, courage.
ᴇᴀ distrust, diffidence.

confident adj sure, certain, positive, convinced, assured, composed, self-possessed, cool, self-confident, self-reliant, self-assured, unselfconscious, bold, fearless, dauntless, unabashed.
ᴇᴀ doubtful, diffident.

confidential adj secret, top secret, classified, restricted, hush-hush (infml), off-the-record, private, personal, intimate, privy.

confidentially adv privately, in privacy, in private, in confidence, in secret, personally, between ourselves, entre nous, behind closed doors, on the quiet, within these four walls, in camera (fml), between you and me (infml), between you me and the gatepost/bedpost (infml).
ᴇᴀ openly.

configuration n arrangement, composition, figure, form, outline, shape, contour, cast, conformation (fml), disposition (fml).

confine v enclose, circumscribe, bound, limit, restrict, cramp, constrain, imprison, incarcerate, intern, cage, shut up, immure, bind, shackle, trammel, restrain, repress, inhibit.
ᴇᴀ free.

confined adj restricted, limited, narrow, constrained, controlled, enclosed, housebound, circumscribed (fml).
ᴇᴀ free, unrestricted.

confinement n 1 IMPRISONMENT, incarceration, internment, custody, detention, house arrest. 2 CHILDBIRTH, birth, labour, delivery.
ᴇᴀ 1 freedom, liberty.

confines n limits, bounds, border, boundary, frontier, circumference, perimeter, edge.

confirm v 1 ENDORSE, back, support, reinforce, strengthen, fortify, validate, authenticate, corroborate, substantiate, verify, prove, evidence. 2 ESTABLISH, fix, settle, clinch, ratify, sanction, approve.
ᴇᴀ 1 refute, deny.

confirmation n ratification, sanction, approval, assent, acceptance, agreement, endorsement, backing, support, validation, authentication, corroboration, substantiation, verification, proof, evidence, testimony.
ᴇᴀ denial.

confirmed adj inveterate, entrenched, dyed-in-the-wool, rooted, established, long-established, long-standing, habitual, chronic, seasoned, hardened, incorrigible, incurable.

confiscate v seize, appropriate, expropriate, remove, take away, impound, sequester, commandeer.
ᴇᴀ return, restore.

conflict n 1 DIFFERENCE, variance, discord, contention, disagreement, dissension, dispute, opposition, antagonism, hostility, friction, strife, unrest, confrontation. 2 BATTLE, war, warfare, combat, fight, contest, engagement, skirmish, set-to, fracas, brawl, quarrel, feud, encounter, clash.
ᴇᴀ 1 agreement, harmony, concord.
➤ v differ, clash, collide, disagree, contradict, oppose, contest, fight, combat, battle, war, strive, struggle, contend.
ᴇᴀ agree, harmonize.

conform v agree, accord, harmonize, match, correspond, tally, square, adapt, adjust, accommodate, comply, obey, follow.
ᴇᴀ differ, conflict, rebel.

conformist n conventionalist, traditionalist, yes-man (infml), stick-in-the-mud (infml), rubber-stamp (infml).
ᴇᴀ bohemian, nonconformist.

conformity n conventionality, orthodoxy, traditionalism, compliance, observance, allegiance, affinity, agreement, consonance, harmony, correspondence, congruity, likeness, similarity, resemblance.
ᴇᴀ nonconformity, rebellion, difference.

confound v 1 CONFUSE, bewilder, baffle, perplex, mystify, bamboozle (infml), nonplus, surprise, amaze, astonish, astound, flabbergast (infml), dumbfound, stupefy. **2** *confound their plans*: thwart, upset, defeat, overwhelm, overthrow, destroy, demolish, ruin.

confront *v* face, meet, encounter, accost, address, oppose, challenge, defy, brave, beard.
Ea evade.

confrontation *n* encounter, clash, collision, showdown, conflict, disagreement, fight, battle, quarrel, set-to, engagement, contest.

confuse *v* **1** PUZZLE, baffle, perplex, mystify, confound, bewilder, disorient, disconcert, fluster, discompose, upset, embarrass, mortify. **2** MUDDLE, mix up, mistake, jumble, disarrange, disorder, tangle, entangle, involve, mingle.
Ea 1 enlighten, clarify.

confused *adj* **1** MUDDLED, jumbled, disarranged, disordered, untidy, disorderly, higgledy-piggledy (*infml*), chaotic, disorganized. **2** PUZZLED, baffled, perplexed, flummoxed (*infml*), nonplussed, bewildered, disorientated.
Ea 1 orderly.

confusion *n* **1** DISORDER, disarray, untidiness, mess, clutter, jumble, muddle, mix-up, disorganization, chaos, turmoil, commotion, upheaval. **2** MISUNDERSTANDING, puzzlement, perplexity, mystification, bewilderment.
Ea 1 order. **2** clarity.

congeal *v* clot, curdle, coalesce, coagulate, thicken, stiffen, harden, solidify, set, gel, freeze.
Ea dissolve, melt.

congenial *adj* agreeable, pleasant, pleasing, relaxing, delightful, favourable, friendly, companionable, genial, sympathetic, homely, compatible, complaisant, cosy, like-minded, suitable, well-suited.
Ea disagreeable, unpleasant.

congenital *adj* **1** *a congenital disease*: hereditary, inborn, inbred, inherited, innate, inherent, constitutional, natural. **2** *a congenital liar*: inveterate, entrenched, habitual, chronic, seasoned, hardened, incorrigible, incurable, complete, thorough, utter, inured (*fml*).

congested *adj* clogged, blocked, jammed, packed, stuffed, crammed, full, crowded, overcrowded, overflowing, teeming.
Ea clear.

congestion *n* clogging, blockage, overcrowding, jam, traffic jam, snarl-up, gridlock, bottleneck.

conglomerate *n* corporation, multinational, merger, cartel, trust, consortium, company, firm, business, business organization, concern, association, partnership, establishment.

conglomeration *n* mass, agglomeration, aggregation, accumulation, collection, assemblage, composite, medley, hotchpotch.

congratulate *v* praise, felicitate, compliment, wish well.
Ea commiserate.

congratulations *n* compliments, good wishes, best wishes, greetings, felicitations (*fml*), pat on the back (*infml*), bouquet(s) (*infml*).
Ea commiserations, condolences.

congregate *v* gather, assemble, collect, muster, rally, rendezvous, meet, convene, converge, flock, crowd, throng, mass, accumulate, cluster, clump, conglomerate.
Ea disperse.

congregation *n* assembly, crowd, throng, multitude, host, flock, parishioners, parish, laity, fellowship.

congress *n* assembly, conference, convention, council, legislature, meeting, gathering, forum, parliament, synod, diet, conclave (*fml*), convocation (*fml*).

conical *adj* cone-shaped, pyramidal, tapering, tapered, pointed.

conjecture *v* speculate, theorize, hypothesize, guess, estimate, reckon, suppose, surmise, assume, infer, imagine, suspect.
➤ *n* speculation, theory, hypothesis, notion, guesswork, guess, estimate, supposition, surmise, assumption, presumption, conclusion, inference, extrapolation, projection.

conjure *v* summon, invoke, rouse, raise, bewitch, charm, fascinate, compel.
♦ **conjure up** evoke, create, produce, excite, awaken, recollect, recall.

conjurer *n* magician, illusionist, miracle-worker, sorcerer, wizard, prestidigitator (*fml*), thaumaturge (*fml*).

connect *v* join, link, unite, couple, combine, fasten, affix, attach, relate, associate, ally.
Ea disconnect, cut off, detach.

connected *adj* joined, linked, united, coupled, combined, related, akin, associated, affiliated, allied.
disconnected, unconnected.

connection *n* junction, coupling, fastening, attachment, bond, tie, link, association, alliance, relation, relationship, interrelation, contact, communication, correlation, correspondence, relevance.
disconnection.

connive *v* 1 *connive with someone to commit an offence*: collude, conspire, intrigue, plot, scheme, complot (*fml*), cabal (*fml*), coact (*fml*). 2 *connive at wrongdoing*: overlook, ignore, disregard, condone, tolerate, brook, let go, let pass, pass over, gloss over, allow, wink at, turn a blind eye to (*infml*).

connoisseur *n* authority, specialist, expert, judge, devotee, buff (*infml*), gourmet, epicure.

connotation *n* implication, suggestion, hint, nuance, undertone, overtone, colouring, association.

conquer *v* 1 DEFEAT, beat, overthrow, vanquish, rout, overrun, best, worst, get the better of, overcome, surmount, win, succeed, triumph, prevail, overpower, master, crush, subdue, quell, subjugate, humble. 2 SEIZE, take, annex, occupy, possess, acquire, obtain.
1 surrender, yield, give in.

conqueror *n* victor, winner, champion, champ (*infml*), hero, vanquisher, master, lord.

conquest *n* victory, triumph, defeat, overthrow, coup, rout, mastery, subjugation, subjection, invasion, occupation, capture, appropriation, annexation, acquisition.

conscience *n* principles, standards, morals, ethics, sense of right, sense of right and wrong, moral sense, moral code, still small voice, voice within, scruples, qualms.

conscience-stricken *adj* ashamed, sorry, contrite, guilt-ridden, guilty, penitent, regretful, remorseful, repentant, disturbed, troubled.
unashamed, unrepentant.

conscientious *adj* diligent, hard-working, scrupulous, painstaking, thorough, meticulous, punctilious, particular, careful, attentive, responsible, upright, honest, faithful, dutiful.

careless, irresponsible, unreliable.

conscious *adj* 1 AWAKE, alive, responsive, sentient, sensible, rational, reasoning, alert. 2 AWARE, self-conscious, heedful, mindful, knowing, deliberate, intentional, calculated, premeditated, studied, wilful, voluntary.
1 unconscious. **2** unaware.

consciousness *n* awareness, sentience, sensibility, knowledge, intuition, realization, recognition.
unconsciousness.

consecrate *v* sanctify, hallow, bless, dedicate, devote, ordain, venerate, revere, exalt.

consecutive *adj* sequential, successive, continuous, unbroken, uninterrupted, following, succeeding, running.
discontinuous.

consensus *n* agreement, consent, harmony, majority view, unanimity, unity, concord (*fml*), concurrence (*fml*).
disagreement.

consent *v* agree, concur, accede, assent, approve, permit, allow, grant, admit, concede, acquiesce, yield, comply.
refuse, decline, oppose.
➤ *n* agreement, concurrence, assent, approval, permission, go-ahead, green light (*infml*), sanction, concession, acquiescence, compliance.
disagreement, refusal, opposition.

consequence *n* 1 RESULT, outcome, issue, end, upshot, effect, side effect, repercussion. 2 *of no consequence*: importance, significance, concern, value, weight, note, eminence, distinction.
1 cause. **2** unimportance, insignificance.

consequent *adj* resultant, resulting, ensuing, subsequent, following, successive, sequential.

consequently *adv* as a result, therefore, with the result that, so that, accordingly, consequentially, necessarily, subsequently, then, ergo (*fml*), hence (*fml*), thus (*fml*).

conservation *n* keeping, safekeeping, custody, saving, economy, husbandry, maintenance, upkeep, preservation, protection, safeguarding, ecology, environmentalism.
destruction.

conservative *adj* Tory, right-wing, hidebound, die-hard, reactionary, establishmentarian, unprogressive, conventional, traditional, moderate, middle-of-the-road, cautious, guarded, sober.

▪ left-wing, radical, innovative.

➤ n Tory, right-winger, die-hard, stick-in-the-mud, reactionary, traditionalist, moderate.

▪ left-winger, radical.

conservatory n greenhouse, glasshouse, hothouse.

conserve v keep, save, store up, hoard, maintain, preserve, protect, guard, safeguard.

▪ use, waste, squander.

consider v **1** PONDER, deliberate, reflect, contemplate, meditate, muse, mull over, chew over, examine, study, weigh, respect, remember, take into account. **2** *consider it an honour*: regard, deem, think, believe, judge, rate, count.

considerable adj great, large, big, sizable, substantial, tidy (*infml*), ample, plentiful, abundant, lavish, marked, noticeable, perceptible, appreciable, reasonable, tolerable, respectable, important, significant, noteworthy, distinguished, influential.

▪ small, slight, insignificant, unremarkable.

considerably adv significantly, substantially, greatly, markedly, much, noticeably, remarkably, appreciably, abundantly.

▪ slightly.

considerate adj kind, thoughtful, caring, attentive, obliging, helpful, charitable, unselfish, altruistic, gracious, sensitive, tactful, discreet.

▪ inconsiderate, thoughtless, selfish.

consideration n **1** THOUGHT, deliberation, reflection, contemplation, meditation, examination, analysis, scrutiny, review, attention, notice, regard. **2** KINDNESS, thoughtfulness, care, attention, regard, respect.

▪ **1** disregard. **2** thoughtlessness.

considering prep taking into account/consideration, bearing in mind, making allowances for, in view of, in the light of.

➤ adv all things considered, all in all.

consign v entrust, commit, devote, hand over, transfer, deliver, convey, ship, banish, relegate.

consignment n cargo, shipment, load, batch, delivery, goods.

consist v **1** *a jury consists of twelve people*:

comprise, be composed of, be made up of, contain, include, incorporate, embody, be formed of, embrace, involve, amount to. **2** *the poem's beauty consists in its simplicity*: inhere, lie, reside, be contained, have as its main feature.

consistency n **1** *of the consistency of porridge*: viscosity, thickness, density, firmness. **2** STEADINESS, regularity, evenness, uniformity, sameness, identity, constancy, steadfastness. **3** AGREEMENT, accordance, correspondence, congruity, compatibility, harmony.

▪ **3** inconsistency.

consistent adj **1** STEADY, stable, regular, uniform, unchanging, undeviating, constant, persistent, unfailing, dependable. **2** AGREEING, accordant, consonant, congruous, compatible, harmonious, logical.

▪ **1** irregular, erratic. **2** inconsistent.

console v comfort, cheer, hearten, encourage, relieve, soothe, calm.

▪ upset, agitate.

consolidate v **1** *consolidate power/support*: reinforce, strengthen, make strong(er), secure, make (more) secure, stabilize, make (more) stable, cement, fortify (*fml*). **2** *consolidate businesses*: unite, join, combine, amalgamate, merge, unify, fuse.

consort n partner, companion, associate, escort, spouse, husband, wife.

➤ v associate, spend time, keep company, fraternize, mingle, mix.

conspicuous adj apparent, visible, noticeable, marked, clear, obvious, evident, patent, manifest, prominent, striking, blatant, flagrant, glaring, ostentatious, showy, flashy, garish.

▪ inconspicuous, concealed, hidden.

conspiracy n plot, scheme, intrigue, machination, fix (*infml*), frame-up (*infml*), collusion, league, treason.

conspirator n conspirer, plotter, schemer, intriguer, traitor.

conspire v plot, scheme, intrigue, manoeuvre, connive, collude, hatch, devise.

constancy n **1** STABILITY, steadiness, permanence, firmness, regularity, uniformity, resolution, perseverance, tenacity. **2** LOYALTY, faithfulness, fidelity, devotion.

▪ **1** change, irregularity. **2** fickleness.

constant *adj* **1** CONTINUOUS, unbroken, never-ending, non-stop, endless, interminable, ceaseless, incessant, eternal, everlasting, perpetual, continual, unremitting, relentless, persistent, resolute, persevering, unflagging, unwavering, stable, steady, unchanging, unvarying, changeless, immutable, invariable, unalterable, fixed, permanent, firm, even, regular, uniform. **2** *a constant friend*: loyal, faithful, staunch, steadfast, dependable, trustworthy, true, devoted.
☒ 1 variable, irregular, fitful, occasional. **2** disloyal, fickle.

constantly *adv* always, continually, all the time, forever, permanently, continuously, endlessly, non-stop, everlastingly, incessantly, interminably, invariably, perpetually, relentlessly, ad nauseam, ceaselessly (*fml*).
☒ occasionally.

constellation

> The constellations (with common English names) are: Andromeda, Antlia (Air Pump), Apus (Bird of Paradise), Aquarius (Water Bearer), Aquila (Eagle), Ara (Altar), Aries (Ram), Auriga (Charioteer), Boötes (Herdsman), Caelum (Chisel), Camelopardalis (Giraffe), Cancer (Crab), Canes Venatici (Hunting Dogs), Canis Major (Great Dog), Canis Minor (Little Dog), Capricornus (Sea Goat), Carina (Keel), Cassiopeia, Centaurus (Centaur), Cepheus, Cetus (Whale), Chamaeleon (Chameleon), Circinus (Compasses), Columba (Dove), Coma Berenices (Berenice's Hair), Corona Australis (Southern Crown), Corona Borealis (Northern Crown), Corvus (Crow), Crater (Cup), Crux (Southern Cross), Cygnus (Swan), Delphinus (Dolphin), Dorado (Swordfish), Draco (Dragon), Equuleus (Little Horse), Eridanus (River Eridanus), Fornax (Furnace), Gemini (Twins), Grus (Crane), Hercules, Horologium (Clock), Hydra (Sea Serpent), Hydrus (Water Snake), Indus (Indian), Lacerta (Lizard), Leo (Lion), Leo Minor (Little Lion), Lepus (Hare), Libra (Scales), Lupus (Wolf), Lynx, Lyra (Harp), Mensa (Table), Microscopium (Microscope), Monoceros (Unicorn), Musca (Fly), Norma (Level), Octans (Octant), Ophiuchus (Serpent Bearer), Orion, Pavo (Peacock), Pegasus (Winged Horse), Perseus, Phoenix, Pictor (Easel), Pisces (Fishes), Piscis Austrinus (Southern Fish), Puppis (Ship's Stern), Pyxis (Mariner's Compass), Reticulum (Net), Sagitta (Arrow), Sagittarius (Archer), Scorpius (Scorpion), Sculptor, Scutum (Shield), Serpens (Serpent), Sextans (Sextant), Taurus (Bull), Telescopium (Telescope), Triangulum (Triangle), Triangulum Australe (Southern Triangle), Tucana (Toucan), Ursa Major (Great Bear), Ursa Minor (Little Bear), Vela (Sails), Virgo (Virgin), Volans (Flying Fish), Vulpecula (Fox). *see also* **star**.

consternation *n* alarm, dismay, anxiety, fear, distress, dread, horror, fright, shock, terror, panic, awe, bewilderment, disquietude (*fml*), perturbation (*fml*), trepidation (*fml*).
☒ composure.

constituent *adj* component, integral, essential, basic, intrinsic, inherent.
➤ *n* ingredient, element, factor, principle, component, part, bit, section, unit.
☒ whole.

constitute *v* **1** *six counties constitute the province*: comprise, make up, form, compose. **2** *his remarks constitute a challenge to the leadership*: be, represent, mean, form, make, be equivalent to, amount to, add up to, be tantamount to, be regarded as. **3** *constitute a committee*: form, create, establish, set up, found, institute, appoint, authorize, commission, charter, empower.

constitution *n* **1** *a country's constitution*: laws, rules, statutes, basic principles, code, charter, codified law, bill of rights. **2** COMPOSITION, make-up, structure, organization, formation, configuration (*fml*). **3** HEALTH, condition, physique, physical condition, make-up, disposition, temperament, character, nature.

constitutional *adj* statutory, by law, according to the law, legal, legitimate, lawful, legislative, governmental, authorized, vested, codified, ratified.
➤ *n* walk, stroll, saunter, amble, promenade, turn, airing.

constrain *v* **1** FORCE, compel, oblige, necessitate, drive, impel, urge. **2** limit, confine, constrict, restrain, check, curb, bind.

constrained *adj* uneasy, embarrassed, inhibited, reticent, reserved, guarded, stiff, forced, unnatural.
☒ relaxed, free.

constraint n 1 FORCE, duress, compulsion, coercion, pressure, necessity, deterrent. 2 RESTRICTION, limitation, hindrance, restraint, check, curb, damper.

constrict v squeeze, compress, pinch, cramp, narrow, tighten, contract, shrink, choke, strangle, inhibit, limit, restrict.
☒ expand.

construct v build, erect, raise, elevate, make, manufacture, fabricate, assemble, put together, compose, form, shape, fashion, model, design, engineer, create, found, establish, formulate.
☒ demolish, destroy.

construction n building, edifice, erection, structure, fabric, form, shape, figure, model, manufacture, fabrication, assembly, composition, constitution, formation, creation.
☒ destruction.

constructive adj practical, productive, positive, helpful, useful, valuable, beneficial, advantageous.
☒ destructive, negative, unhelpful.

consult v refer to, ask, question, interrogate, confer, discuss, debate, deliberate.

consultant n adviser, expert, authority, specialist.

consultation n discussion, deliberation, dialogue, conference, meeting, hearing, interview, examination, appointment, session.

consume v 1 EAT, drink, swallow, devour, gobble. 2 USE, absorb, spend, expend, deplete, drain, exhaust, use up, dissipate, squander, waste. 3 DESTROY, demolish, annihilate, devastate, ravage.

consumer n user, end-user, customer, buyer, purchaser, shopper.

consuming adj dominating, compelling, absorbing, preoccupying, devouring, engrossing, gripping, obsessive, immoderate, monopolizing, overwhelming, tormenting.

consummate adj absolute, complete, total, utter, perfect, supreme, superior, ultimate, superb, transcendent, unqualified, skilled, accomplished, gifted, practised, proficient, distinguished, matchless, polished.
☒ imperfect.
➤ v perfect, accomplish, fulfil, realize, complete, perform, achieve, crown, cap, end, finish, conclude, terminate (fml),

execute (fml), effectuate (fml).

consumption n use, utilization, spending, expenditure, depletion, exhaustion, waste.

contact n touch, impact, juxtaposition, contiguity, communication, meeting, junction, union, connection, association.
➤ v approach, apply to, reach, get hold of, get in touch with, telephone, phone, ring, call, notify.

contagious adj infectious, catching, communicable, transmissible, spreading, epidemic.

contain v 1 INCLUDE, comprise, incorporate, embody, involve, embrace, enclose, hold, accommodate, seat. 2 contain one's feelings: repress, stifle, restrain, control, check, curb, limit.
☒ 1 exclude.

container n receptacle, vessel, holder, repository (fml).

Types of container include: bag, barrel, basin, basket, bath, beaker, bin, bottle, bowl, box, bucket, can, canister, carton, case, cask, casket, cauldron, chest, churn, cistern, crate, crock, cup, cylinder, dish, drum, dustbin, glass, hamper, jar, jug, keg, kettle, locker, mug, pack, packet, pail, pan, pannier, pitcher, pot, punnet, purse, sack, suitcase, tank, tea caddy, tea chest, teapot, tin, trough, trunk, tub, tube, tumbler, tureen, urn, vase, vat, waste bin, waste-paper basket, water-butt, well.

contaminate v infect, pollute, adulterate, taint, soil, sully, defile, corrupt, deprave, debase, stain, tarnish.
☒ purify.

contemplate v 1 MEDITATE, reflect on, ponder, mull over, deliberate, consider, regard, view, survey, observe, study, examine, inspect, scrutinize. 2 EXPECT, foresee, envisage, plan, design, propose, intend, mean.

contemplative adj thoughtful, reflective, meditative, introspective, musing, pensive, rapt, intent, deep in thought, cerebral (fml), ruminative (fml).
☒ impulsive, thoughtless.

contemporary adj 1 MODERN, current, present, present-day, recent, latest, up-to-date, fashionable, up-to-the-minute, ultra-modern. 2 CONTEMPORANEOUS, coexistent, concurrent, synchronous, simultaneous.

Ea 1 out-of-date, old-fashioned.

contempt *n* scorn, disdain, condescension, derision, ridicule, mockery, disrespect, dishonour, disregard, neglect, dislike, loathing, detestation.
Ea admiration, regard.

contemptible *adj* despicable, shameful, ignominious, low, mean, vile, detestable, loathsome, abject, wretched, pitiful, paltry, worthless.
Ea admirable, honourable.

contemptuous *adj* scornful, disdainful, sneering, supercilious, condescending, arrogant, haughty, high and mighty, cynical, derisive, insulting, disrespectful, insolent.
Ea humble, respectful.

contend *v* **1** MAINTAIN, hold, argue, allege, assert, declare, affirm. **2** COMPETE, vie, contest, dispute, clash, wrestle, grapple, struggle, strive, cope.

content *v* satisfy, humour, indulge, gratify, please, delight, appease, pacify, placate.
Ea displease.
➤ *n* **1** SUBSTANCE, matter, essence, gist, meaning, significance, text, subject matter, ideas, contents, load, burden. **2** CAPACITY, volume, size, measure.
➤ *adj* satisfied, fulfilled, contented, untroubled, pleased, happy, willing.
Ea dissatisfied, troubled.

contented *adj* happy, glad, pleased, cheerful, comfortable, relaxed, content, satisfied.
Ea discontented, unhappy, annoyed.

contention *n* **1** *it is my contention that ...*: belief, opinion, persuasion, feeling, intuition, impression, notion, theory, view, viewpoint, point of view, thesis, conviction, claim, judgement, stand, position, assertion, argument. **2** *a matter of contention*: disagreement, argument, controversy, dispute, debate, discord, dissension, enmity, feuding, hostility, strife, struggle, rivalry, wrangling.

contentious *adj* **1** *a contentious issue*: controversial, polemical, disputed, doubtful, questionable, debatable, disputable. **2** *a contentious person*: argumentative, antagonistic, quarrelsome, hostile, perverse, querulous, bickering, captious, pugnacious (*fml*).
Ea 1 uncontroversial. **2** co-operative, peaceable.

contentment *n* contentedness,

happiness, gladness, pleasure, gratification, comfort, ease, complacency, peace, peacefulness, serenity, equanimity, content, satisfaction, fulfilment.
Ea unhappiness, discontent, dissatisfaction.

contents *n* **1** *the contents of the package*: constituents, parts, elements, ingredients, content, load, items. **2** CHAPTERS, divisions, subjects, topics, themes.

contest *n* competition, game, match, tournament, encounter, fight, battle, set-to, combat, conflict, struggle, dispute, debate, controversy.
➤ *v* **1** DISPUTE, debate, question, doubt, challenge, oppose, argue against, litigate, deny, refute. **2** COMPETE, vie, contend, strive, fight.
Ea 1 accept.

contestant *n* competitor, contender, player, participant, entrant, candidate, aspirant, rival, opponent.

context *n* background, setting, surroundings, framework, frame of reference, situation, position, circumstances, conditions.

continent *n* mainland, terra firma.

The continents of the world are: Africa, Antarctica, Asia, Australia, Europe, North America, South America.

contingency *n*
eventuality, possibility, accident, randomness, arbitrariness, chance, chance event, emergency, event, happening, incident, uncertainty, fortuity (*fml*), juncture (*fml*).

contingent *n* body, company, deputation, delegation, detachment, section, group, set, batch, quota, complement.

continual *adj* constant, perpetual, incessant, interminable, eternal, everlasting, regular, frequent, recurrent, repeated.
Ea occasional, intermittent, temporary.

continuation *n* resumption, maintenance, prolongation, extension, development, furtherance, addition, supplement.
Ea cessation, termination.

continue *v* resume, recommence, carry on, go on, proceed, persevere, stick at, persist, last, endure, survive, remain, abide, stay, rest, pursue, sustain, maintain,

lengthen, prolong, extend, project.
🔁 discontinue, stop.

continuity n flow, progression, succession, sequence, linkage, interrelationship, connection, cohesion.
🔁 discontinuity.

continuous adj unbroken, uninterrupted, consecutive, non-stop, endless, ceaseless, unending, unceasing, constant, unremitting, prolonged, extended, continued, lasting.
🔁 discontinuous, broken, sporadic.

contort v twist, distort, warp, wrench, disfigure, deform, misshape, convolute, gnarl, knot, writhe, squirm, wriggle.

contour n outline, silhouette, shape, form, figure, curve, relief, profile, character, aspect.

contraband n banned/black-market goods, smuggling, forbidden/illegal traffic, bootlegging, prohibited/unlawful goods, proscribed goods (fml), hot goods (infml).

contraceptive

Contraceptives and other forms of birth control include: barrier contraceptive, barrier method, cervical cap, coil, coitus interruptus, condom, contraceptive ring, contraceptive sponge, diaphragm, Dutch cap, female condom, Femidom®, French letter (sl), injectable contraceptive, intrauterine device (IUD), johnnie (sl), loop, minipill, morning-after pill, oral contraceptive, pill, prophylactic, protective, rhythm method, rubber (sl), sheath, spermicide, vaginal ring, withdrawal method.

contract v 1 SHRINK, lessen, diminish, reduce, shorten, curtail, abbreviate, abridge, condense, compress, constrict, narrow, tighten, tense, shrivel, wrinkle. 2 contract pneumonia: catch, get, go down with, develop. 3 PLEDGE, promise, undertake, agree, stipulate, arrange, negotiate, bargain.
🔁 1 expand, enlarge, lengthen.
➤ n bond, commitment, engagement, covenant, treaty, convention, pact, compact, agreement, transaction, deal, bargain, settlement, arrangement, understanding.

contraction n 1 'Don't' is a contraction of 'do not': abbreviation, shortening, shortened form, abridgement. 2 the contraction of muscles: constriction, compression, narrowing, tightening,

tensing, drawing-in, shrivelling, shrinkage, lessening, reduction, curtailment, astringency (technical).
🔁 2 expansion, growth.

contradict v deny, disaffirm, confute, challenge, oppose, impugn, dispute, counter, negate, gainsay.
🔁 agree, confirm, corroborate.

contradictory adj contrary, opposite, paradoxical, conflicting, discrepant, inconsistent, incompatible, antagonistic, irreconcilable, opposed, repugnant.
🔁 consistent.

contraption n contrivance, device, gadget, apparatus, rig, machine, mechanism.

contrary adj 1 OPPOSITE, counter, reverse, conflicting, antagonistic, opposed, adverse, hostile. 2 PERVERSE, awkward, disobliging, difficult, wayward, obstinate, intractable, cantankerous, stroppy (infml).
🔁 1 like. 2 obliging.
➤ n opposite, converse, reverse.

contrast n difference, dissimilarity, disparity, divergence, distinction, differentiation, comparison, foil, antithesis, opposition.
🔁 similarity.
➤ v compare, differentiate, distinguish, discriminate, differ, oppose, clash, conflict.

contravene v infringe, violate, break, breach, disobey, defy, flout, transgress.
🔁 uphold, observe, obey.

contribute v donate, subscribe, chip in (infml), add, give, bestow, provide, supply, furnish, help, lead, conduce.
🔁 withhold.

contribution n donation, subscription, gift, gratuity, handout, grant, offering, input, addition.

contributor n 1 DONOR, subscriber, giver, patron, benefactor, sponsor, backer, supporter. 2 WRITER, journalist, reporter, correspondent, freelance.

contrite adj sorry, regretful, remorseful, repentant, penitent, conscience-stricken, chastened, humble, ashamed.

contrivance n 1 INVENTION, device, contraption, gadget, implement, appliance, machine, mechanism, apparatus, equipment, gear. 2 STRATAGEM, ploy, trick, dodge, ruse, expedient, plan, design, project, scheme, plot, intrigue, machination.

contrive v 1 *somehow contrived to blame me*: manage, succeed, arrange, bring about, create, design, devise, find a way. 2 *contrive a meeting between them*: engineer, manoeuvre, orchestrate, stage-manage, plan, plot, scheme, fabricate, create, devise, invent, concoct, construct, set up (*infml*), wangle (*infml*).

contrived adj unnatural, artificial, false, forced, strained, laboured, mannered, elaborate, overdone.
Ea natural, genuine.

control v 1 LEAD, govern, rule, command, direct, manage, oversee, supervise, superintend, run, operate. 2 *control the temperature*: regulate, adjust, monitor, verify. 3 *control one's temper*: restrain, check, curb, subdue, repress, hold back, contain.
➤ n 1 POWER, charge, authority, command, mastery, government, rule, direction, management, oversight, supervision, superintendence, discipline, guidance. 2 RESTRAINT, check, curb, repression. 3 INSTRUMENT, dial, switch, button, knob, lever.

controversial adj contentious, polemical, disputed, doubtful, questionable, debatable, disputable.

controversy n debate, discussion, war of words, polemic, dispute, disagreement, argument, quarrel, squabble, wrangle, strife, contention, dissension.
Ea accord, agreement.

convalescence n recuperation, getting better, improvement, recovery, rehabilitation, restoration.

convene v 1 *convene a meeting*: call (together), rally, summon. 2 *the court convened*: assemble, meet, gather, collect, congregate, muster, convoke (*fml*).

convenience n 1 ACCESSIBILITY, availability, handiness, usefulness, use, utility, serviceability, service, benefit, advantage, help, suitability, fitness. 2 *all modern conveniences*: facility, amenity, appliance.
Ea 1 inconvenience.

convenient adj nearby, at hand, accessible, available, handy, useful, commodious, beneficial, helpful, labour-saving, adapted, fitted, suited, suitable, fit, appropriate, opportune, timely, well-timed.
Ea inconvenient, awkward.

convention n 1 CUSTOM, tradition, practice, usage, protocol, etiquette, formality, matter of form, code. 2 ASSEMBLY, congress, conference, meeting, council, delegates, representatives.

conventional adj traditional, orthodox, formal, correct, proper, prevalent, prevailing, accepted, received, expected, unoriginal, ritual, routine, usual, customary, regular, standard, normal, ordinary, straight, stereotyped, hidebound, pedestrian, commonplace, common, run-of-the-mill.
Ea unconventional, unusual, exotic.

converge v focus, concentrate, approach, merge, coincide, meet, join, combine, gather.
Ea diverge, disperse.

convergence n concentration, approach, merging, confluence, blending, meeting, coincidence, junction, intersection, union.
Ea divergence, separation.

conversant with prep familiar with, acquainted with, experienced in, informed about, knowledgeable about, practised in, proficient in, skilled in, versed in, au fait with, apprised of (*fml*).
Ea ignorant of.

conversation n talk, chat, gossip, discussion, discourse, dialogue, exchange, communication.

converse¹ v talk, discuss, confer, communicate, chat, gossip, chatter, commune (*fml*), discourse (*fml*).

converse² n opposite, reverse, contrary, obverse, antithesis (*fml*), other way round (*infml*), other side of the coin (*infml*).
➤ adj opposite, opposing, reverse, counter, contrary, reversed, transposed, obverse, antithetical (*fml*).

conversion n 1 *a loft conversion*: alteration, change, transformation, turning, adaptation, modification, remodelling, reshaping, reconstruction, reorganization, customization, adjustment, metamorphosis (*fml*), mutation (*fml*), transmutation (*fml*). 2 *conversion of pounds into francs*: change, exchange, substitution, switch. 3 *conversion to Judaism*: persuasion, conviction, reformation, regeneration, rebirth, proselytization, preaching.

convert v 1 ALTER, change, turn, transform, adapt, modify, remodel, restyle, revise, reorganize. 2 WIN OVER, convince, persuade, reform, proselytize.

convex *adj* rounded, bulging, protuberant.
■ concave.

convey *v* carry, bear, bring, fetch, move, transport, send, forward, deliver, transfer, conduct, guide, transmit, communicate, impart, tell, relate, reveal.

conveyance *n* **1** VEHICLE, car, bus, coach, bicycle, motorcycle, lorry, truck, van, wagon, carriage. **2** *the conveyance of bicycles*: transport, transportation, movement, transfer, transference. **3** *the conveyance of property*: transfer, transference, granting, transmission, consignment, delivery, bequeathal, ceding.

convict *v* condemn, sentence, imprison.
➤ *n* criminal, felon, culprit, prisoner.

conviction *n* assurance, confidence, fervour, earnestness, certainty, firmness, persuasion, view, opinion, belief, faith, creed, tenet, principle.

convince *v* assure, persuade, sway, win over, bring round, reassure, satisfy.

convincing *adj* persuasive, cogent, powerful, telling, impressive, credible, plausible, likely, probable, conclusive, incontrovertible.
■ unconvincing, improbable.

convoluted *adj* twisting, winding, meandering, tortuous, involved, complicated, complex, tangled.
■ straight, straightforward.

convoy *n* fleet, escort, guard, protection, attendance, train.

convulsion *n* **1** FIT, seizure, paroxysm, spasm, cramp, contraction, tic, tremor. **2** ERUPTION, outburst, furore, disturbance, commotion, tumult, agitation, turbulence, upheaval.

convulsive *adj* jerky, spasmodic, fitful, sporadic, uncontrolled, violent.

cook *v* prepare, heat, warm, put on, put together, improvise, undercook, underdo, overcook, overdo, burn, rustle up (*infml*).

Ways of cooking include: bake, barbecue, boil, braise, broil, brown, casserole, coddle, curry, deep-fry, fricassee, fry, grill, microwave, oven-roast, parboil, poach, pot-roast, roast, sauté, scramble, simmer, spit-roast, steam, stew, stir-fry, toast.

Terms used in cookery include: bake, blind, bind, blend, bone, brown, caramelize, carve, chill, chop, cream, crumble, cure, defrost, deglaze, devil, drizzle, dust, fillet, flash fry, fold in, freeze, glaze, grate, grind, ice, joint, jug, knead, knock back, liquidize, marinate, mash, mince, mix, mull, peel, peppered, pickle, plate (up), potted, prep (*infml*), preserve, prove, purée, reduce, re-heat, rest, rise, sear, sieve, sift, skim, smoke, souse, stir, strain, stuff, sweat, thicken, truss, whisk. *see also* **kitchen utensils**.

Terms used in French cookery include: à la crème, à la Grècque, au gratin, au poivre, Bolognese, brûlée, cacciatore, chasseur, cordon bleu, coulis, en cocotte, en croute, farci, frappé, galette, gougère, haute cuisine, Lyonnaise, mornay, Niçoise, nouvelle cuisine, Provençal, roux, sur le plat.

Terms used in Indian cookery include: akhni, aloo, balti, bargar, bhajee or bhaji, bhindi or bindi, bhoona or bhuna, dhal, dhansak, dopiaza, dum, gosht, kalia, karahi, kofta, korma, madras, masala, Moglai, paneer, tandoori, tikka, vindaloo.

♦ **cook up** concoct, prepare, brew, invent, fabricate, contrive, devise, plan, plot, scheme.

cool *adj* **1** CHILLY, fresh, breezy, nippy, cold, chilled, iced, refreshing. **2** CALM, unruffled, unexcited, composed, self-possessed, level-headed, unemotional, quiet, relaxed, laid-back (*infml*). **3** *a cool reception*: unfriendly, unwelcoming, cold, frigid, lukewarm, half-hearted, unenthusiastic, apathetic, uninterested, unresponsive, uncommunicative, reserved, distant, aloof, standoffish.
■ **1** warm, hot. **2** excited, angry. **3** friendly, welcoming.
➤ *v* **1** CHILL, refrigerate, ice, freeze, fan. **2** MODERATE, lessen, temper, dampen, quiet, abate, calm, allay, assuage.
■ **1** warm, heat. **2** excite.
➤ *n* coolness, calmness, collectedness, composure, poise, self-possession, self-discipline, self-control, control, temper.

co-operate *v* collaborate, work together, play ball (*infml*), help, assist, aid, contribute, participate, combine, unite, conspire.

co-operation *n* helpfulness, assistance,

participation, collaboration, teamwork, unity, co-ordination, give-and-take.
🔁 opposition, rivalry, competition.

co-operative *adj* **1** HELPFUL, supportive, obliging, accommodating, willing. **2** COLLECTIVE, joint, shared, combined, united, concerted, co-ordinated.
🔁 **1** unco-operative, rebellious.

co-ordinate *v* organize, arrange, systematize, tabulate, integrate, mesh, synchronize, harmonize, match, correlate, regulate.

cope *v* manage, carry on, survive, get by, make do.
♦ **cope with** deal with, encounter, contend with, struggle with, grapple with, wrestle with, handle, manage, weather.

copious *adj* abundant, plentiful, inexhaustible, overflowing, profuse, rich, lavish, bountiful, liberal, full, ample, generous, extensive, great, huge.
🔁 scarce, meagre.

copy *n* duplicate, carbon copy, photocopy, Photostat®, Xerox®, facsimile, reproduction, print, tracing, transcript, transcription, replica, model, pattern, archetype, representation, image, likeness, counterfeit, forgery, fake, imitation, borrowing, plagiarism, crib.
🔁 original.
➤ *v* duplicate, photocopy, reproduce, print, trace, transcribe, forge, counterfeit, simulate, imitate, impersonate, mimic, ape, parrot, repeat, echo, mirror, follow, emulate, borrow, plagiarize, crib.

cord *n* string, twine, rope, line, cable, flex, connection, link, bond, tie.

cordial *adj* friendly, amicable, affable, affectionate, agreeable, cheerful, genial, sociable, pleasant, heartfelt, warm, warm-hearted, welcoming, wholehearted, earnest, hearty, stimulating, invigorating.
🔁 hostile, aloof, cool.

cordiality *n* friendliness, affability, affection, agreeableness, cheerfulness, geniality, sociability, heartiness, warmth, welcome, wholeheartedness, earnest, sincerity.
🔁 coolness, hostility.

cordon *n* line, ring, barrier, chain, fence.
♦ **cordon off** close off, fence off, isolate, separate, encircle, enclose, surround.

core *n* kernel, nucleus, heart, centre, middle, nub, crux, essence, gist, nitty-gritty (*infml*).
🔁 surface, exterior.

corm *see* **bulbs and corms**.

corner *n* **1** *round the corner*: angle, joint, crook, bend, turning. **2** NOOK, cranny, niche, recess, cavity, hole, hideout, hideaway, retreat.

corny *adj* banal, commonplace, hackneyed, stale, overused, stereotyped, trite, clichéd, sentimental, dull, feeble, maudlin, mawkish, platitudinous.
🔁 new, original.

corporate *adj* combined, collective, concerted, joint, communal, merged, pooled, shared, united, allied, amalgamated, collaborative.

corporation *n* council, authorities, association, society, organization, company, firm, combine, conglomerate.

corps *n* band, body, detachment, unit, squad, team, division, brigade, company, contingent, crew, regiment, squadron.

corpse *n* body, stiff (*sl*), carcase, skeleton, remains.

correct *v* **1** *correct an error*: rectify, put right, right, emend, remedy, cure, debug, redress, adjust, regulate, improve, amend. **2** PUNISH, discipline, reprimand, reprove, reform.
➤ *adj* **1** *the correct answer*: right, accurate, precise, exact, strict, true, truthful, word-perfect, faultless, flawless. **2** PROPER, acceptable, OK (*infml*), standard, regular, just, appropriate, fitting.
🔁 **1** incorrect, wrong, inaccurate.

correction *n* rectification, emendation, adjustment, alteration, modification, amendment, improvement.

corrective *adj* **1** *corrective measures*: remedial, curative, medicinal, palliative, restorative, therapeutic. **2** DISCIPLINARY, penal, punitive, reformatory, rehabilitative.

correlate *v* associate, compare, connect, show a connection/relationship, co-ordinate, correspond, agree, equate, interact, parallel, relate, link, tie in.

correlation *n* association, connection, relationship, correspondence, equivalence, interaction, interchange, interdependence, interrelationship, link, reciprocity.

correspond *v* **1** MATCH, fit, answer, conform, tally, square, agree, concur, coincide, correlate, accord, harmonize, dovetail, complement. **2** COMMUNICATE, write.

correspondence n 1 COMMUNICATION, writing, letters, post, mail. 2 CONFORMITY, agreement, concurrence, coincidence, correlation, relation, analogy, comparison, comparability, similarity, resemblance, congruity, equivalence, harmony, match. ▣ 2 divergence, incongruity.

correspondent n journalist, reporter, contributor, writer.

corresponding adj matching, complementary, reciprocal, interrelated, analogous, equivalent, similar, identical.

corridor n aisle, passageway, passage, hallway, hall, lobby.

corroborate v confirm, prove, bear out, support, endorse, ratify, substantiate, validate, authenticate, document, underpin, sustain. ▣ contradict.

corrode v erode, wear away, eat away, consume, waste, rust, oxidize, tarnish, impair, deteriorate, crumble, disintegrate.

corrosive adj corroding, acid, caustic, cutting, abrasive, erosive, wearing, consuming, wasting.

corrugated adj ridged, fluted, grooved, channelled, furrowed, wrinkled, crinkled, rumpled, creased.

corrupt adj rotten, unscrupulous, unprincipled, unethical, immoral, fraudulent, shady (infml), dishonest, bent (infml), crooked (infml), untrustworthy, depraved, degenerate, dissolute. ▣ ethical, virtuous, upright, honest, trustworthy. ➤ v contaminate, pollute, adulterate, taint, defile, debase, pervert, deprave, lead astray, lure, bribe, suborn. ▣ purify.

corruption n unscrupulousness, immorality, impurity, depravity, degeneration, degradation, perversion, distortion, dishonesty, crookedness (infml), fraud, shadiness (infml), bribery, extortion, vice, wickedness, iniquity, evil. ▣ honesty, virtue.

cosmetic adj superficial, surface. ▣ essential.

cosmetics n make-up, greasepaint.

Cosmetics include: blusher, cleanser, eyebrow pencil, eyelash dye, eyeliner, eye shadow, face cream, face mask, face pack, face powder, false eyelashes, foundation, greasepaint, kohl pencil, lip gloss, lip liner, lipstick, loose powder, maquillage, mascara, moisturizer, nail polish, nail varnish, pancake make-up, pressed powder, rouge, toner, war paint (infml).

cosmic adj 1 cosmic forces: worldwide, universal, in/from space, infinite, limitless, measureless. 2 changes of cosmic proportion: immense, vast, huge, grandiose, infinite, limitless, immeasurable, measureless.

cosmopolitan adj worldly, worldly-wise, well-travelled, sophisticated, urbane, international, universal. ▣ insular, parochial, rustic.

cosset v coddle, mollycoddle, baby, pamper, indulge, spoil, pet, fondle, cuddle, cherish.

cost n 1 EXPENSE, outlay, payment, expenditure, charge, price, selling price, asking price, rate, fee, quotation, amount, figure, value, valuation, worth, disbursement (fml), damage (infml). 2 cover costs: budget, expenses, expenditure, spending, outgoings, outlay, overheads. 3 the cost to her health: harm, injury, hurt, loss, suffering, deprivation, detriment, sacrifice, penalty, price. ➤ v 1 it costs £500: pay, charge, be priced at, ask for, sell for, retail at, buy for, be valued at, be worth, fetch, go for, come to, amount to, set back (infml), knock back (infml). 2 cost a job: price, estimate, cost out, quote, value, calculate, work out. 3 cost him his life: cause the loss/sacrifice of, cause harm/injury, deprive, harm, injure, hurt, be a high price to pay.

costly adj 1 EXPENSIVE, dear, pricey (infml), exorbitant, excessive, lavish, rich, splendid, valuable, precious, priceless. 2 HARMFUL, damaging, disastrous, catastrophic, loss-making. ▣ 1 cheap, inexpensive.

costume n outfit, uniform, livery, robes, vestments, dress, clothing, get-up (infml), fancy dress.

cosy adj snug, comfortable, comfy (infml), warm, sheltered, secure, homely, intimate. ▣ uncomfortable, cold.

cottage n lodge, chalet, bungalow, hut, cabin, shack.

couch n sofa, settee, chesterfield, chaise-longue, ottoman, divan, bed.

cough v clear one's throat, bark, hack, hawk, hem.

➤ *n* bark, hack, hawking, hem, clearing one's throat, frog in one's throat (*infml*).

♦ **cough up** pay up, pay, pay out, give, fork out (*infml*), shell out (*infml*), stump up (*infml*).

council *n* committee, panel, board, cabinet, ministry, parliament, congress, assembly, convention, conference.

counsel *n* **1** ADVICE, suggestion, recommendation, guidance, direction, information, consultation, deliberation, consideration, forethought. **2** *counsel for the defence*: lawyer, advocate, solicitor, attorney, barrister.

➤ *v* advise, warn, caution, suggest, recommend, advocate, urge, exhort, guide, direct, instruct.

count *v* **1** NUMBER, enumerate, list, include, reckon, calculate, compute, tell, check, add, total, tot up, score. **2** MATTER, signify, qualify. **3** *count oneself lucky*: consider, regard, deem, judge, think, reckon, hold.

➤ *n* numbering, enumeration, poll, reckoning, calculation, computation, sum, total, tally.

♦ **count on** depend on, rely on, bank on, reckon on, expect, believe, trust.

countenance *n* face, expression, appearance, features, look, mien (*fml*), physiognomy (*fml*), visage (*fml*).

➤ *v* tolerate, agree, allow, approve, brook, stand for, put up with, back, condone, endorse, endure, sanction.

counter *adv* against, in opposition, conversely.

➤ *adj* contrary, opposite, opposing, conflicting, contradictory, contrasting, opposed, against, adverse.

➤ *v* parry, resist, offset, answer, respond, retaliate, retort, return, meet.

counteract *v* neutralize, counterbalance, offset, countervail, act against, oppose, resist, hinder, check, thwart, frustrate, foil, defeat, undo, negate, annul, invalidate.
Ea support, assist.

counterbalance *v* balance, compensate for, make up for, equalize, neutralize, offset, undo, counterpoise (*fml*).

counterfeit *v* fake, forge, fabricate, copy, imitate, impersonate, pretend, feign, simulate, sham.

➤ *adj* fake, false, phoney (*infml*), forged, copied, fraudulent, bogus, pseudo, sham, spurious, imitation, artificial,

simulated, feigned, pretended.
Ea genuine, authentic, real.

➤ *n* fake, forgery, copy, reproduction, imitation, fraud, sham.

counterpart *n* equivalent, opposite number, complement, supplement, match, fellow, mate, twin, duplicate, copy.

countless *adj* innumerable, myriad, numberless, unnumbered, untold, incalculable, infinite, endless, immeasurable, measureless, limitless.
Ea finite, limited.

country *n* **1** STATE, nation, people, kingdom, realm, principality. **2** COUNTRYSIDE, green belt, farmland, provinces, sticks (*infml*), backwoods, wilds. **3** TERRAIN, land, territory, region, area, district.
Ea 2 town, city.

➤ *adj* rural, provincial, agrarian, agricultural, pastoral, rustic, bucolic, landed.
Ea urban.

countryman, countrywoman *n* **1** *fellow countrywomen*: compatriot, fellow citizen, fellow national. **2** *local countrymen's skills*: farmer, yokel, boor, clodhopper, rustic, peasant, provincial, backwoodsman, bushwhacker, bumpkin (*infml*), hillbilly (*infml*), hick (*infml*), hayseed (*infml*).

countryside *n* landscape, scenery, country, green belt, farmland, outdoors.

county *n* shire, province, region, area, district.

coup *n* **1** *a military coup*: coup d'état, overthrow, revolution, (military) takeover, uprising, palace revolution, putsch, rebellion, revolt. **2** *a big coup for the company*: feat, masterstroke, stroke, accomplishment, deed, exploit, stunt, action, manoeuvre, tour de force.

couple *n* pair, brace, twosome, duo.
➤ *v* pair, match, marry, wed, unite, join, link, connect, fasten, hitch, clasp, buckle, yoke.

coupon *n* voucher, token, slip, check, ticket, certificate.

courage *n* bravery, pluck, guts (*infml*), fearlessness, dauntlessness, heroism, gallantry, valour, boldness, audacity, nerve, daring, resolution, fortitude, spirit, mettle.
Ea cowardice, fear.

courageous *adj* brave, plucky, fearless, dauntless, indomitable, heroic, gallant, valiant, lion-hearted, hardy, bold, audacious, daring, intrepid, resolute. ☒ cowardly, afraid.

courier n **1** *the courier delivered the parcels*: messenger, carrier, dispatch rider, runner, bearer, emissary, envoy, representative, herald, legate, nuncio, estafette, pursuivant. **2** *a guided tour by the courier*: guide, travel guide, tour guide, escort, company representative.

course n **1** CURRICULUM, syllabus, classes, lessons, lectures, studies. **2** FLOW, movement, advance, progress, development, furtherance, order, sequence, series, succession, progression. **3** DURATION, time, period, term, passage. **4** DIRECTION, way, path, track, road, route, channel, trail, line, circuit, orbit, trajectory, flight path. **5** *course of action*: plan, schedule, programme, policy, procedure, method, mode.
➤ v **1** *tears coursing down her cheeks*: flow, run, move, pour, gush, stream, surge, dash. **2** *coursing hares*: chase, hunt, pursue, run after, follow, track, race.
♦ **in due course** in time, in due time, sooner or later, in the course of time, finally, eventually, to be sure.
♦ **of course** naturally, certainly, surely, by all means, definitely, without a doubt, no doubt, undoubtedly, doubtlessly, needless to say, indubitably (*fml*).

court n **1** LAW-COURT, bench, bar, tribunal, trial, session. **2** COURTYARD, yard, quadrangle, square, cloister, forecourt, enclosure. **3** ENTOURAGE, attendants, retinue, suite, train, cortège.

> **Types of court include:** Admiralty Division, assizes, Central Criminal Court, Chancery Division, children's court, circuit court, civil court, coroner's court, county court, court-martial, court of appeals, court of claims, Court of Common Pleas, Court of Exchequer, court of justice, Court of Protection, Court of Session, criminal court, crown court, district court, divorce court, European Court of Justice, family court, federal court, High Court, High Court of Justiciary, House of Lords, industrial tribunal, International Court of Justice, juvenile court, Lord Chancellor's Court, magistrates' court, municipal court, Old Bailey, police court, Privy Council, sheriff court, small claims court, Supreme Court.

➤ v **1** *court a young lady*: woo, pursue,

chase, go out, go with, date (*infml*), go steady (*infml*). **2** *court support/publicity*: cultivate, try to win, solicit, flatter, pander to, attract, prompt, provoke, incite, seek, invite.

courteous *adj* polite, civil, respectful, well-mannered, well-bred, ladylike, gentlemanly, gracious, obliging, considerate, attentive, gallant, courtly, urbane, debonair, refined, polished. ☒ discourteous, impolite, rude.

courtesy n politeness, civility, respect, manners, breeding, graciousness, consideration, attention, gallantry, urbanity. ☒ discourtesy, rudeness.

courtier n noble, nobleman, lord, lady, steward, page, attendant, follower, flatterer, sycophant, toady.

courtyard n yard, quadrangle, quad (*infml*), area, enclosure, court.

cove n bay, bight, inlet, estuary, firth, fiord, creek.

covenant n arrangement, promise, contract, bond, commitment, deed, engagement, pact, pledge, treaty, trust, convention, stipulation, undertaking, indenture (*fml*), compact (*fml*), concordat (*fml*).
➤ v agree, contract, promise, stipulate, undertake, engage, pledge.

cover v **1** HIDE, put/place over, conceal, bury, obscure, shroud, veil, wreathe, screen, mask, disguise, camouflage. **2** *covered with mud*: be over, coat, spread, daub, plaster, cake, encase, wrap, envelop, blanket, swaddle, clothe, dress, overlay, attire (*fml*), accoutre (*fml*). **3** SHELTER, put/place over, protect, shield, guard, safeguard, defend. **4** *cover a topic*: deal with, treat, consider, examine, investigate, give details of, review, survey, report, describe, encompass, embrace, incorporate, embody, involve, include, contain, comprise, take in. **5** *cover 25 miles*: travel (over), cross, go, go across, journey, do, traverse (*fml*). **6** *cover for a colleague*: stand in for, deputize, relieve, replace, take over from, be a replacement/substitute for. **7** *the estate covers some 500 acres*: extend over, stretch, continue, measure. **8** *£50 to cover expenses*: pay for, be enough for, recompense, make up for. **9** *the insurance will cover it*: protect, insure, provide for, indemnify (*fml*).

▣ 1 uncover. **2** strip. **3** expose. **4** exclude.
➤ *n* **1** SHELTER, refuge, protection, shield, guard, defence, concealment, hiding-place, sanctuary, refuge, disguise, camouflage. **2** COVERING, coating, top, lid, cup, jacket, wrapper, binding, case, envelope, package, coat, layer, film, skin, carpet, mantle, clothing, dress, bedclothes, blankets, duvet, bedspread, canopy. **3** *as a cover for illegal activity*: cover-up, concealment, screen, smokescreen, veil, mask, front, façade, pretence, conspiracy, complicity, whitewash (*infml*). **4** *insurance cover*: protection, insurance, compensation, assurance, indemnity (*fml*), indemnification (*fml*).
◆ **cover up** conceal, hide, suppress, keep secret, keep dark, repress, gloss over, dissemble (*fml*), whitewash (*infml*), hush up (*infml*).
▣ disclose, reveal.

covering *n* layer, coat, coating, blanket, film, veneer, skin, crust, shell, casing, housing, wrapping, clothing, protection, mask, overlay, cover, top, shelter, roof.

cover-up (*infml*) *n* concealment, whitewash, smokescreen, front, façade, pretence, conspiracy, complicity.

covet *v* envy, begrudge, crave, long for, yearn for, hanker for, want, desire, fancy (*infml*), lust after.

covetous *adj* yearning, craving, wanting, longing, hankering, hungering, thirsting, acquisitive, grasping, greedy, insatiable, jealous, envious, desirous (*fml*), avaricious (*fml*), rapacious (*fml*).
▣ generous, temperate.

coward *n* craven, faint-heart, chicken (*infml*), scaredy-cat, yellow-belly (*sl*), wimp (*infml*), renegade, deserter.
▣ hero.

cowardice *n* cowardliness, faint-heartedness, timorousness, spinelessness.
▣ courage, valour.

cowardly *adj* faint-hearted, craven, fearful, timorous, scared, unheroic, chicken-hearted, chicken-livered, chicken (*infml*), yellow-bellied (*sl*), yellow (*sl*), spineless, weak, weak-kneed, soft.
▣ brave, courageous, bold.

cower *v* crouch, grovel, skulk, shrink, flinch, cringe, quail, tremble, shake, shiver.

coy *adj* modest, demure, prudish, diffident, shy, bashful, timid, shrinking, backward,
retiring, self-effacing, reserved, evasive, arch, flirtatious, coquettish, skittish, kittenish.
▣ bold, forward.

crabbed, crabby *adj* bad-tempered, cross, ill-tempered, irritable, morose, snappish, cantankerous, petulant, perverse, acrid, acrimonious, awkward, difficult, harsh, tough, sour, captious, churlish, fretful, snappy, surly, tart, testy, crotchety (*infml*), grouchy (*infml*), prickly (*infml*).
▣ calm, placid.

crack *v* **1** SPLIT, burst, fracture, break, snap, shatter, splinter, chip. **2** EXPLODE, burst, pop, crackle, snap, crash, clap, slap, whack (*infml*). **3** *crack a code*: decipher, work out, solve.
➤ *n* **1** BREAK, fracture, split, rift, gap, crevice, fissure, chink, line, flaw, chip. **2** EXPLOSION, burst, pop, snap, crash, clap, blow, smack, slap, whack (*infml*). **3** JOKE, quip, witticism, gag (*infml*), wisecrack, gibe, dig.
➤ *adj* (*infml*) first-class, first-rate, top-notch (*infml*), excellent, superior, choice, hand-picked.
◆ **crack down on** clamp down on, end, stop, put a stop to, crush, suppress, check, repress, act against.
◆ **crack up** go mad, go to pieces, break down, collapse.

crackdown *n* clampdown, crushing, end, check, stop, repression, suppression.

cradle *n* **1** COT, crib, bed. **2** SOURCE, origin, spring, wellspring, fount, fountain-head, birthplace, beginning.
➤ *v* hold, support, rock, lull, nurse, nurture, tend.

craft *n* **1** SKILL, expertise, mastery, talent, knack, ability, aptitude, dexterity, cleverness, art, handicraft, handiwork. **2** TRADE, business, calling, vocation, job, occupation, work, employment. **3** VESSEL, boat, ship, aircraft, spacecraft, spaceship.

crafts *see* art.

craftsman, craftswoman *n* artisan, technician, master, maker, wright, smith.

craftsmanship *n* artistry, workmanship, technique, dexterity, expertise, mastery.

crafty *adj* sly, cunning, artful, wily, devious, subtle, scheming, calculating, designing, deceitful, fraudulent, sharp, shrewd, astute, canny.
▣ artless, naïve.

crag *n* bluff, cliff, escarpment, scarp, ridge, peak, pinnacle, rock, tor.

cram *v* stuff, jam, ram, force, press, squeeze, crush, compress, pack, crowd, overfill, glut, gorge.

cramp¹ *v* hinder, hamper, obstruct, impede, inhibit, handicap, thwart, frustrate, check, restrict, confine, shackle, tie.

cramp² *n* pain, ache, twinge, pang, contraction, convulsion, spasm, crick, stitch, pins and needles, stiffness.

cramped *adj* narrow, tight, uncomfortable, restricted, confined, crowded, packed, squashed, squeezed, overcrowded, jam-packed, congested.
🔁 spacious.

crank *n* eccentric, character, madman, idiot, freak (*infml*), weirdo (*infml*), oddball (*infml*), nutter (*infml*), crackpot (*infml*), loony (*infml*).

crash *n* **1** *car crash*: accident, collision, bump, smash, pile-up, smash-up (*infml*), wreck. **2** BANG, clash, clatter, clang, thud, thump, boom, thunder, racket, din. **3** *stock-market crash*: collapse, failure, ruin, downfall, bankruptcy, depression.
➤ *v* **1** COLLIDE, hit, knock, bump, bang. **2** BREAK, fracture, smash, dash, shatter, splinter, shiver, fragment, disintegrate. **3** FALL, topple, pitch, plunge, collapse, fail, fold (up), go under, go bust (*infml*).

crass *adj* stupid, indelicate, insensitive, tactless, unrefined, unsophisticated, blundering, rude, crude, coarse, dense, oafish.
🔁 refined, sensitive.

crate *n* container, box, case, tea-chest, packing-box, packing-case.

crave *v* hunger for, thirst for, long for, yearn for, pine for, hanker after, fancy (*infml*), desire, want, need, require.
🔁 dislike.

craving *n* appetite, hunger, thirst, longing, yearning, hankering, lust, desire, urge.
🔁 dislike, distaste.

crawl *v* **1** CREEP, inch, edge, slither, wriggle. **2** GROVEL, cringe, toady, fawn, flatter, suck up (*sl*).

craze *n* fad, novelty, fashion, vogue, mode, trend, rage (*infml*), thing (*infml*), obsession, preoccupation, mania, frenzy, passion, infatuation, enthusiasm.

crazy *adj* **1** MAD, insane, lunatic, unbalanced, deranged, demented, crazed, potty (*infml*), barmy (*infml*), daft (*infml*), silly, foolish, idiotic, senseless, unwise, imprudent, nonsensical, absurd, ludicrous, ridiculous, preposterous, outrageous, half-baked, impracticable, irresponsible, wild, berserk. **2** (*infml*) *crazy about golf*: enthusiastic, fanatical, zealous, ardent, passionate, infatuated, enamoured, smitten, mad, wild.
🔁 **1** sane, sensible. **2** indifferent.

creak *v* squeak, groan, grate, scrape, rasp, scratch, grind, squeal, screech.

cream *n* **1** PASTE, emulsion, oil, lotion, ointment, salve, cosmetic. **2** BEST, pick, elite, prime.

creamy *adj* **1** CREAM-COLOURED, off-white, yellowish-white. **2** MILKY, buttery, oily, smooth, velvety, rich, thick.

crease *v* fold, pleat, wrinkle, pucker, crumple, rumple, crinkle, crimp, corrugate, ridge.
➤ *n* fold, line, pleat, tuck, wrinkle, pucker, ruck, crinkle, corrugation, ridge, groove.

create *v* invent, coin, formulate, compose, design, devise, concoct, hatch, originate, initiate, found, establish, set up, institute, cause, occasion, produce, generate, engender, make, form, appoint, install, invest, ordain.
🔁 destroy.

creation *n* **1** MAKING, formation, constitution, invention, concoction, origination, foundation, establishment, institution, production, generation, procreation, conception, birth. **2** INVENTION, brainchild, concept, product, handiwork, chef d'oeuvre, achievement.
🔁 **1** destruction.

creative *adj* artistic, inventive, original, imaginative, inspired, visionary, talented, gifted, clever, ingenious, resourceful, fertile, productive.
🔁 unimaginative.

creativity *n* artistry, inventiveness, originality, imagination, imaginativeness, inspiration, vision, talent, gift, cleverness, ingenuity, resourcefulness, fertility, productiveness.
🔁 unimaginativeness.

creator *n* maker, inventor, designer, architect, author, originator, initiator.

creature *n* animal, beast, bird, fish, organism, being, mortal, individual, person, man, woman, body, soul.

credentials n diploma, certificate, reference, testimonial, recommendation, accreditation, authorization, warrant, licence, permit, passport, identity card, papers, documents, deed, title.

credibility n integrity, reliability, trustworthiness, plausibility, probability.
🔁 implausibility.

credible adj believable, imaginable, conceivable, thinkable, tenable, plausible, likely, probable, possible, reasonable, persuasive, convincing, sincere, honest, trustworthy, reliable, dependable.
🔁 incredible, unbelievable, implausible, unreliable.

credit n **1** get the credit for his success: acknowledgement, recognition, thanks, approval, commendation, praise, acclaim, tribute, laudation (fml). **2** your loyalty does you credit: glory, fame, prestige, distinction, honour, reputation, asset, boast, pride, esteem, estimation, feather in one's cap (infml), pride and joy (infml). **3** give someone credit for their ability: belief, trust, faith, credence, confidence. **4** be in credit: money in one's bank account, the black (infml).
🔁 **1** blame, discredit, shame. **4** overdraft, insolvency, the red (infml).
➤ v **1** credited with the invention: attribute, ascribe, put down, assign, charge, accredit (fml), impute (fml). **2** the reports are difficult to credit: believe, accept, subscribe to, trust, have faith, rely on, swallow (infml), fall for (infml), buy (infml).
🔁 **2** disbelieve.
◆ **on credit** on account, by instalments, by deferred payment, on hire purchase, on tick (infml), on the slate (infml), on the tab (infml), on the never-never (infml).

creditable adj honourable, reputable, respectable, estimable, admirable, commendable, praiseworthy, good, excellent, exemplary, worthy, deserving.
🔁 shameful, blameworthy.

credulous adj naïve, gullible, wide-eyed, trusting, unsuspecting, uncritical.
🔁 sceptical, suspicious.

creed n belief, faith, persuasion, credo, catechism, doctrine, principles, tenets, articles, canon, dogma.

creek n inlet, estuary, cove, bay, bight.

creep v inch, edge, tiptoe, steal, sneak, slink, crawl, slither, worm, wriggle, squirm, grovel, writhe.

creepy adj eerie, spooky, sinister, threatening, frightening, scary, terrifying, hair-raising, nightmarish, macabre, gruesome, horrible, unpleasant, disturbing.

crescent-shaped adj bow-shaped, sickle-shaped, falcate (fml), lunate (fml).

crest n **1** the crest of the hill: ridge, crown, top, peak, summit, pinnacle, apex, head. **2** TUFT, tassel, plume, comb, mane. **3** INSIGNIA, device, symbol, emblem, badge.

crestfallen adj disappointed, downhearted, dejected, sad, depressed, despondent, discouraged, disheartened, dispirited, downcast, disconsolate (fml), cheesed off (infml), in the doldrums (infml), down in the dumps (infml).
🔁 elated.

crevice n crack, fissure, split, rift, cleft, slit, chink, cranny, gap, hole, opening, break.

crew n team, party, squad, troop, corps, company, gang, band, bunch, crowd, mob, set, lot.

crime n law-breaking, lawlessness, delinquency, offence, felony, misdemeanour, misdeed, wrongdoing, misconduct, transgression, violation, sin, iniquity, vice, villainy, wickedness, atrocity, outrage.

Crimes include: theft, robbery, burglary, larceny, pilfering, mugging, poaching; assault, rape, grievous bodily harm, GBH (infml), battery, manslaughter, homicide, murder, assassination; fraud, bribery, corruption, embezzlement, extortion, blackmail; arson, treason, terrorism, hijack, piracy, kidnapping, sabotage, vandalism, hooliganism, drug-smuggling, forgery, counterfeiting, perjury, joy-riding, drink-driving, drunk and disorderly.

criminal n law-breaker, crook, felon, delinquent, offender, wrongdoer, miscreant, culprit, convict, prisoner.
➤ adj illegal, unlawful, illicit, lawless, wrong, culpable, indictable, crooked (infml), bent (infml), dishonest, corrupt, wicked, scandalous, deplorable.
🔁 legal, lawful, honest, upright.

cringe v shrink, recoil, shy, start, flinch, wince, quail, tremble, quiver, cower, crouch, bend, bow, stoop, grovel, crawl, creep.

cripple v lame, paralyse, disable, handicap, injure, maim, mutilate, damage, impair, spoil, ruin, destroy, sabotage, incapacitate, weaken, debilitate.

crippled *adj* lame, paralysed, disabled, handicapped, incapacitated.

crisis *n* emergency, extremity, crunch (*infml*), catastrophe, disaster, calamity, dilemma, quandary, predicament, difficulty, trouble, problem.

crisp *adj* **1** *a crisp biscuit*: crispy, crunchy, brittle, crumbly, firm, hard. **2** BRACING, invigorating, refreshing, fresh, brisk. **3** TERSE, pithy, snappy, brief, short, clear, incisive.
⊟ 1 soggy, limp, flabby. **2** muggy. **3** wordy, vague.

criterion *n* standard, norm, touchstone, benchmark, yardstick, measure, gauge, rule, principle, canon, test.

critic *n* reviewer, commentator, analyst, pundit, authority, expert, judge, censor, carper, fault-finder, attacker, knocker (*infml*).

critical *adj* **1** *at the critical moment*: crucial, vital, essential, all-important, momentous, decisive, urgent, pressing, serious, grave, dangerous, perilous. **2** ANALYTICAL, diagnostic, penetrating, probing, discerning, perceptive. **3** DISPARAGING, uncomplimentary, derogatory, disapproving, censorious, carping, fault-finding, cavilling, nit-picking (*infml*).
⊟ 1 unimportant. **3** complimentary, appreciative.

criticism *n* **1** CONDEMNATION, disapproval, disparagement, fault-finding, censure, blame, brickbat, flak (*infml*). **2** REVIEW, critique, assessment, evaluation, appraisal, judgement, analysis, commentary, appreciation.
⊟ 1 praise, commendation.

criticize *v* **1** CONDEMN, slate (*infml*), slam (*infml*), knock (*infml*), disparage, carp, find fault, censure, blame. **2** REVIEW, assess, evaluate, appraise, judge, analyse.
⊟ 1 praise, commend.

critique *n* review, essay, assessment, evaluation, appraisal, judgement, analysis, commentary, write-up, appreciation, explanation, interpretation, exposition (*fml*), explication (*fml*).

croak *v* rasp, squawk, caw, wheeze, speak harshly, gasp, grunt.

crockery *n* dishes, tableware, china, porcelain, earthenware, stoneware, pottery.

Items of crockery include: cup, saucer, coffee cup, mug, beaker, plate, side plate, dinner plate, bowl, cereal bowl, soup bowl, salad-bowl, sugar bowl, jug, milk-jug, basin, pot, teapot, coffee pot, percolator, cafetière, cakestand, meat dish, butter-dish, tureen, gravy boat, cruet, tea set, dinner service.

---

crook *n* criminal, thief, robber, swindler, cheat, shark (*infml*), rogue, villain.

crooked *adj* **1** ASKEW, skew-whiff (*infml*), awry, lopsided, asymmetric, irregular, uneven, off-centre, tilted, slanting, bent, angled, hooked, curved, bowed, warped, distorted, misshapen, deformed, twisted, tortuous, winding, zigzag. **2** (*infml*) ILLEGAL, unlawful, illicit, criminal, nefarious, dishonest, deceitful, bent (*infml*), corrupt, fraudulent, shady (*infml*), shifty, underhand, treacherous, unscrupulous, unprincipled, unethical.
⊟ 1 straight. **2** honest.

crop *n* growth, yield, produce, fruits, harvest, vintage, gathering.
➤ *v* cut, snip, clip, shear, trim, pare, prune, lop, shorten, curtail.
◆ crop up arise, emerge, occur, happen.

cross *adj* **1** IRRITABLE, annoyed, angry, vexed, shirty (*infml*), bad-tempered, ill-tempered, crotchety, grumpy, grouchy, irascible, crabby, short, snappy, snappish, surly, sullen, fractious, fretful, impatient. **2** TRANSVERSE, crosswise, oblique, diagonal, intersecting, opposite, reciprocal.
⊟ 1 placid, pleasant.
➤ *v* **1** *cross the river*: go across, traverse, ford, bridge, span. **2** INTERSECT, meet, criss-cross, lace, intertwine. **3** CROSSBREED, interbreed, mongrelize, hybridize, cross-fertilize, cross-pollinate, blend, mix. **4** THWART, frustrate, foil, hinder, impede, obstruct, block, oppose.
➤ *n* **1** BURDEN, load, affliction, misfortune, trouble, worry, trial, tribulation, grief, misery, woe. **2** CROSSBREED, hybrid, mongrel, blend, mixture, amalgam, combination. **3** CRUCIFIX.

Types of cross include: ankh, Avelian, botoné, Calvary, capital, cardinal, Celtic, Constantinian, Cornish, crosslet, crucifix, encolpion, fleury, fylfot, Geneva, Greek, Jerusalem, Latin, Lorraine, Maltese, moline, papal, patriarchal, potent, quadrate, rood, Russian, saltire, St Andrew's, St Anthony's, St George's, St Peter's, swastika, tau, Y-cross.

cross-examine *v* interrogate, question, cross-question, quiz, examine, grill (*infml*), pump (*infml*), give someone the third degree (*infml*).

crouch *v* squat, kneel, stoop, bend, bow, hunch, duck, cower, cringe.

crowd *n* **1** THRONG, multitude, host, mob, masses, populace, people, public, riff-raff, rabble, horde, swarm, flock, herd, pack, press, crush, squash, assembly, company, group, bunch, lot, set, circle, clique. **2** SPECTATORS, gate, attendance, audience.
➤ *v* gather, congregate, muster, huddle, mass, throng, swarm, flock, surge, stream, push, shove, elbow, jostle, press, squeeze, bundle, pile, pack, congest, cram, compress.

crowded *adj* full, filled, packed, jammed, jam-packed, congested, cramped, overcrowded, overpopulated, busy, teeming, swarming, overflowing.
🖪 empty, deserted.

crown *n* **1** CORONET, diadem, tiara, circlet, wreath, garland. **2** PRIZE, trophy, reward, honour, laurels. **3** SOVEREIGN, monarch, king, queen, ruler, sovereignty, monarchy, royalty. **4** TOP, tip, apex, crest, summit, pinnacle, peak, acme.
➤ *v* **1** ENTHRONE, anoint, adorn, festoon, honour, dignify, reward. **2** TOP, cap, complete, fulfil, consummate, perfect.

crowning *adj* culminating, final, perfect, supreme, top, ultimate, unmatched, unsurpassed, paramount, sovereign, climactic (*fml*), consummate (*fml*).
➤ *n* coronation, enthronement, installation, investiture, incoronation (*fml*).

crucial *adj* urgent, pressing, vital, essential, key, pivotal, central, important, momentous, decisive, critical, trying, testing, searching.
🖪 unimportant, trivial.

crucify *v* **1** *Christ was crucified*: kill on the cross, execute, put to death on a cross. **2** *crucified by the critics*: criticize, mock, ridicule, persecute, torment, punish, torture, rack, slam (*infml*), slate (*infml*), tear to pieces (*infml*).

crude *adj* **1** RAW, unprocessed, unrefined, rough, unfinished, unpolished, natural, primitive. **2** VULGAR, coarse, rude, indecent, obscene, gross, dirty, lewd.
🖪 **1** refined, finished. **2** polite, decent.

cruel *adj* fierce, ferocious, vicious, savage, barbarous, bloodthirsty, murderous, cold-blooded, sadistic, brutal, inhuman, inhumane, unkind, malevolent, spiteful, callous, heartless, unfeeling, merciless, pitiless, flinty, hard-hearted, stony-hearted, implacable, ruthless, remorseless, relentless, unrelenting, inexorable, grim, hellish, atrocious, bitter, harsh, severe, cutting, painful, excruciating.
🖪 kind, compassionate, merciful.

cruelty *n* ferocity, viciousness, savagery, barbarity, bloodthirstiness, murderousness, violence, sadism, brutality, bestiality, inhumanity, spite, venom, callousness, heartlessness, hard-heartedness, mercilessness, ruthlessness, tyranny, harshness, severity.
🖪 kindness, compassion, mercy.

cruise *n* holiday, voyage, sail, journey, trip.
➤ *v* **1** *cruising round the Mediterranean*: sail, travel, journey. **2** *cruising along comfortably*: sail, coast, drift, freewheel, glide, slide, taxi.

crumb *n* piece, scrap, morsel, bit, titbit, particle, grain, atom, flake, speck, iota, jot, mite, shred, sliver, snippet, soupçon.

crumble *v* fragment, break up, decompose, disintegrate, decay, degenerate, deteriorate, collapse, crush, pound, grind, powder, pulverize.

crumple *v* crush, wrinkle, pucker, crinkle, rumple, crease, fold, collapse.

crunch *v* munch, chomp, champ, masticate, grind, crush.

crusade *n* campaign, drive, push, movement, cause, undertaking, expedition, holy war, jihad.

crush *v* **1** SQUASH, compress, squeeze, press, pulp, break, smash, pound, pulverize, grind, crumble, crush, wrinkle. **2** *the rebels were crushed*: conquer, vanquish, demolish, devastate, overpower, overwhelm, overcome, quash, quell, subdue, put down, humiliate, shame, abash.

crust *n* surface, exterior, outside, covering, coat, coating, layer, film, skin, rind, shell, scab, incrustation, caking, concretion.

crux *n* nub, heart, core, essence.

cry *v* **1** WEEP, sob, blubber, wail, bawl, whimper, snivel. **2** SHOUT, call, exclaim, roar, bellow, yell, scream, shriek, screech.
➤ *n* **1** WEEP, sob, blubber, wail, bawl, whimper, snivel. **2** SHOUT, call, plea, exclamation, roar, bellow, yell, scream, shriek.

♦ **cry off** cancel, withdraw, excuse oneself, back out, decide against, change one's mind.

♦ **cry out for** need, call for, demand, want, require, necessitate (*fml*).

crypt *n* tomb, vault, burial chamber, catacomb, mausoleum, undercroft.

cryptic *adj* enigmatic, ambiguous, equivocal, puzzling, perplexing, mysterious, strange, bizarre, secret, hidden, veiled, obscure, abstruse, esoteric, dark, occult.
F3 straightforward, clear, obvious.

cuddle *v* hug, embrace, clasp, hold, nurse, nestle, snuggle, pet, fondle, caress.

cuddly *adj* cuddlesome, lovable, huggable, plump, soft, warm, cosy.

cue *n* signal, sign, nod, hint, suggestion, reminder, prompt, incentive, stimulus.

cuff *v* hit, thump, box, clip, knock, biff (*infml*), buffet, slap, smack, strike, clout, clobber (*sl*), belt (*infml*), beat, whack (*infml*).

culminate *v* climax, end (up), terminate, close, conclude, finish, consummate.
F3 start, begin.

culmination *n* climax, height, peak, pinnacle, summit, top, crown, perfection, consummation, finale, conclusion, completion.
F3 start, beginning.

culpable *adj* to blame, wrong, in the wrong, at fault, responsible, guilty, liable, offending, answerable, blamable, blameworthy, censurable, reprehensible.
F3 blameless, innocent.

culprit *n* guilty party, offender, wrongdoer, miscreant, law-breaker, criminal, felon, delinquent.

cult *n* 1 SECT, denomination, school, movement, party, faction. 2 CRAZE, fad, fashion, vogue, trend.

cultivate *v* 1 FARM, till, work, plough, grow, sow, plant, tend, harvest. 2 FOSTER, nurture, cherish, help, aid, support, encourage, promote, further, work on, develop, train, prepare, polish, refine, improve, enrich.
F3 2 neglect.

cultivated *adj* refined, cultured, civilized, sophisticated, polished, genteel, urbane, advanced, enlightened, educated, well-read, well-informed, scholarly, highbrow, discerning, discriminating.

cultural *adj* artistic, aesthetic, liberal, civilizing, humanizing, enlightening, educational, edifying, improving, enriching, elevating.

culture *n* 1 CIVILIZATION, society, lifestyle, way of life, customs, mores, the arts. 2 CULTIVATION, taste, education, enlightenment, breeding, gentility, refinement, politeness, urbanity.

cultured *adj* cultivated, civilized, advanced, enlightened, educated, well-read, well-informed, scholarly, highbrow, well-bred, refined, polished, genteel, urbane.
F3 uncultured, uneducated, ignorant.

cumbersome *adj* awkward, inconvenient, bulky, unwieldy, unmanageable, burdensome, onerous, heavy, weighty.
F3 convenient, manageable.

cumulative *adj* increasing, growing, mounting, multiplying, enlarging, collective, snowballing (*infml*).

cunning *adj* crafty, sly, artful, wily, tricky, devious, subtle, deceitful, guileful, sharp, shrewd, astute, canny, knowing, deep, imaginative, ingenious, skilful, deft, dexterous.
F3 naïve, ingenuous, gullible.
➤ *n* craftiness, slyness, artfulness, trickery, deviousness, subtlety, deceitfulness, guile, sharpness, shrewdness, astuteness, ingenuity, cleverness, adroitness.

cup *n* mug, tankard, beaker, goblet, chalice, trophy.

cupboard *n* cabinet, locker, closet, wardrobe.

curb *v* restrain, constrain, restrict, contain, control, check, moderate, bridle, muzzle, suppress, subdue, repress, inhibit, hinder, impede, hamper, retard.
F3 encourage, foster.

curdle *v* coagulate, congeal, clot, thicken, turn, sour, ferment.

cure *v* 1 HEAL, remedy, correct, restore, repair, mend, relieve, ease, alleviate, help. 2 PRESERVE, dry, smoke, salt, pickle, kipper.
➤ *n* remedy, antidote, panacea, medicine, specific, corrective, restorative, healing, treatment, therapy, alleviation, recovery.

curiosity *n* 1 INQUISITIVENESS, nosiness, prying, snooping, interest. 2 CURIO, objet d'art, antique, bygone, novelty, trinket, knick-knack. 3 ODDITY, rarity, freak, phenomenon, spectacle.

curious *adj* 1 INQUISITIVE, nosey, prying, meddlesome, questioning, inquiring, interested. 2 ODD, queer, funny (*infml*), strange, peculiar, bizarre, mysterious, puzzling, extraordinary, unusual, rare, unique, novel, exotic, unconventional, unorthodox, quaint.
🆎 1 uninterested, indifferent. 2 ordinary, usual, normal.

curl *v* crimp, frizz, wave, ripple, bend, curve, meander, loop, turn, twist, wind, wreathe, twine, coil, spiral, corkscrew, scroll.
🆎 uncurl.
➤ *n* wave, kink, swirl, twist, ringlet, coil, spiral, whorl.

curly *adj* wavy, kinky, curling, spiralled, corkscrew, curled, crimped, permed, frizzy, fuzzy.
🆎 straight.

currency *n* 1 MONEY, legal tender, coinage, coins, notes, bills. 2 ACCEPTANCE, publicity, popularity, vogue, circulation, prevalence, exposure.

Currencies of the world include: baht (Thailand), bolivar (Venezuela), cent (US, Canada, Australia, NZ, S Africa, etc), centavo (Portugal, Brazil, Mexico, etc), centime (France, Belgium, Algeria, etc), dinar (Iraq, Jordan, etc), dirham (Morocco), dollar (US, Canada, Australia, NZ, etc), dong (Vietnam), drachma (Greece), escudo (Portugal), euro (certain countries of the European Union), fils (Iraq, Jordan, etc), guilder (Netherlands), franc (France, Belgium, Switzerland, etc), karbovanets (Ukraine), koruna (Czech Republic, Slovakia), krona (Sweden), króna (Iceland), krone (Denmark, Norway), kyat (Myanmar), lek (Albania), leu (Romania), lev (Bulgaria), lira (Italy), mark (Germany), pence (UK), peseta (Spain), peso (Mexico, Chile, etc), pfennig (Germany), piastre (Egypt, Syria, etc), pound (UK, Egypt, etc), punt (Ireland), rand (S Africa), real (Brazil), rial (Iran), riyal (Saudi Arabia), rouble (Russia), rupee (India, Pakistan, etc), schilling (Austria), shekel (Israel), shilling (Kenya, Uganda, etc), som (Uzbekistan), sterling (UK), sucre (Ecuador), tolar (Slovenia), won (N Korea, S Korea), yen (Japan), yuan (China), zloty (Poland).

---

current *adj* present, on-going, existing, contemporary, present-day, modern, fashionable, up-to-date, up-to-the-minute, trendy (*infml*), popular, widespread, prevalent, common, general, prevailing, reigning, accepted.
🆎 obsolete, old-fashioned.
➤ *n* draught, stream, jet, flow, drift, tide, course, trend, tendency, undercurrent, mood, feeling.

curriculum *n* syllabus, core curriculum, national curriculum, subjects, course of studies, discipline, course, course of study, module, educational programme, timetable.

curse *n* 1 SWEAR-WORD, oath, expletive, obscenity, profanity, blasphemy. 2 JINX, anathema, bane, evil, plague, scourge, affliction, trouble, torment, ordeal, calamity, disaster.
🆎 2 blessing, advantage.
➤ *v* 1 SWEAR, blaspheme, damn, condemn, denounce, fulminate. 2 BLIGHT, plague, scourge, afflict, trouble, torment.
🆎 2 bless.

cursed *adj* damned, detestable, abominable, confounded, infernal, hateful, loathsome, odious, vile, fiendish, annoying, unpleasant, pernicious, infamous, blasted (*infml*), blooming (*infml*), flipping (*infml*), dashed (*infml*), dratted (*infml*).

cursory *adj* brief, slight, summary, superficial, desultory, quick, rapid, fleeting, hasty, hurried, offhand, dismissive, passing, perfunctory, careless, casual, slapdash.
🆎 painstaking, thorough.

curt *adj* abrupt, blunt, rude, sharp, brusque, gruff, laconic, offhand, short, short-spoken, tart, terse, snappish, unceremonious, uncivil, ungracious, brief, pithy, concise, succinct, summary.
🆎 voluble.

curtail *v* shorten, truncate, cut, trim, abridge, abbreviate, lessen, decrease, reduce, restrict.
🆎 lengthen, extend, prolong.

curtain *n* blind, screen, backdrop, hanging, drapery, tapestry.

curve *v* bend, arch, arc, bow, bulge, hook, crook, turn, wind, twist, spiral, coil.
➤ *n* bend, turn, arc, trajectory, loop, camber, curvature.

curved *adj* bent, arched, bowed, rounded, humped, convex, concave, crooked, twisted, sweeping, sinuous, serpentine.
🆎 straight.

cushion n pad, buffer, shock absorber, bolster, pillow, headrest, hassock.
➤ v soften, deaden, dampen, absorb, muffle, stifle, suppress, lessen, mitigate, protect, bolster, buttress, support.

custody n 1 KEEPING, possession, charge, care, safekeeping, protection, preservation, custodianship, trusteeship, guardianship, supervision. 2 DETENTION, confinement, imprisonment, incarceration.

custom n 1 national customs: tradition, usage, use, habit, routine, procedure, practice, policy, way, manner, style, form, fashion, way of behaving, convention, etiquette, ethos, formality, observance, ritual, rite, institution. 2 take my custom elsewhere: business, trade, patronage (fml).

customary adj traditional, conventional, accepted, established, habitual, routine, regular, usual, normal, ordinary, everyday, familiar, common, general, popular, fashionable, prevailing.
🔄 unusual, rare.

customer n client, patron, regular, punter (infml), consumer, shopper, buyer, purchaser, prospect.

cut v 1 cut the paper/your finger; cut a hole: slit, pierce, slice, sever, chop, hack, hew, carve, split, dock, lop, prune, excise. 2 cut meat: dissect, divide, carve, slice, chop (up), dice, mince, shred, grate, cleave (fml). 3 cut hair/grass: shorten, trim, clip, crop, snip, shear, mow, shave, pare, prune, dock. 4 cut glass: engrave, incise, chisel, score. 5 cut someone's throat: stab, wound, nick, slash, lacerate. 6 cut costs: reduce, decrease, lower, diminish, curtail, curb, prune, slash (infml), axe (infml). 7 cut a story/broadcast: shorten, make shorter, curtail, abbreviate, abridge, condense, précis, summarize, edit, delete, omit, excise (fml), expurgate (fml). 8 IGNORE, spurn, avoid, pretend not to see/notice, snub, slight, rebuff, insult, scorn, cut dead (infml), cold-shoulder (infml), look right through (infml), send to Coventry (infml).
➤ n 1 INCISION, wound, nick, gash, slit, slash, rip, laceration, notch, score. 2 go for a cut at the barber's: trim, clip, crop, shave. 3 spending cuts: reduction, decrease, lowering, cutback, saving, economy, lessening, retrenchment (fml). 4 a cut of meat: section, slice, piece, bit, part. 5 a power cut: failure, fault, breakdown, breaking-down, cutting-out, malfunctioning (fml). 6 SHARE, allocation, proportion, portion, quota, ration, slice (infml), slice of the cake (infml), whack (infml). 7 the cut of a garment: shape, style, fashion, form, profile.

◆ **cut back** check, crop, curb, curtail, decrease, economize, lessen, lop, lower, prune, reduce, trim, scale down, retrench (fml), slash (infml), downsize (infml).
◆ **cut down** 1 cut down a tree: fell, hew, lop, level, raze. 2 REDUCE, decrease, lower, lessen, diminish.
◆ **cut in** interrupt, butt in, interject, interpose, intervene, intrude.
◆ **cut off** 1 SEVER, amputate, separate, isolate, disconnect, block, obstruct, intercept. 2 STOP, end, halt, suspend, discontinue, disown, disinherit.
◆ **cut out** excise, extract, remove, delete, eliminate, exclude, debar, stop, cease.
◆ **cut up** chop, dice, mince, dissect, divide, carve, slice, slash.

cutback n cut, saving, economy, retrenchment, reduction, decrease, lowering, lessening.

cutlery

Items of cutlery include: knife, butter-knife, carving-knife, fish knife, steak knife, cheese knife, breadknife, vegetable knife, fork, fish fork, carving fork, spoon, dessert-spoon, tablespoon, teaspoon, soup-spoon, caddy spoon, salt spoon, apostle spoon, ladle, salad servers, fish slice, cake server, sugar tongs, chopsticks, canteen of cutlery.

cut-price adj reduced, sale, discount, bargain, cheap, low-priced.

cutter

Types of cutter include: axe, billhook, blade, chisel, chopper, clippers, guillotine, hedgetrimmer, knife, flick knife, penknife, pocket knife, Stanley knife®, Swiss army knife, lopper, machete, mower, lawnmower, plane, razor, saw, chainsaw, fretsaw, hacksaw, jigsaw, scalpel, scissors, scythe, secateurs, shears, pinking shears, sickle, Strimmer®, sword.

cut-throat adj ruthless, pitiless, relentless, fierce, highly/fiercely competitive, keen, keenly contested, cruel, brutal, dog-eat-dog (infml).

cutting adj sharp, keen, pointed, trenchant, incisive, penetrating, piercing, wounding, stinging, biting, mordant,

caustic, acid, scathing, sarcastic, malicious, bitter, raw, chill.
➤ *n* clipping, extract, piece.

cycle *n* circle, round, rotation, revolution, series, sequence, phase, period, era, age, epoch, aeon.

cylinder *n* column, barrel, drum, reel, bobbin, spool, spindle.

cynic *n* sceptic, doubter, pessimist, killjoy, spoilsport (*infml*), scoffer, knocker (*infml*).

cynical *adj* sceptical, doubtful, distrustful, pessimistic, negative, scornful, derisive, contemptuous, sneering, scoffing, mocking, sarcastic, sardonic, ironic.

cynicism *n* scepticism, doubt, disbelief, distrust, pessimism, scorn, sarcasm, irony.

Dd

dab v pat, tap, daub, swab, wipe.
➤ n **1** BIT, dollop (*infml*), drop, speck, spot, trace, smear, smudge, fleck. **2** TOUCH, pat, stroke, tap.
◆ **dab hand** expert, past master, wizard, ace, adept.

dabble v **1** TRIFLE, tinker, toy, dally, potter. **2** PADDLE, moisten, wet, sprinkle, splash.

dabbler n amateur, dilettante, trifler.
🔁 professional, expert.

daft adj **1** FOOLISH, crazy, silly, stupid, absurd, dotty (*infml*), idiotic, inane. **2** INSANE, mad, lunatic, simple, crazy, mental. **3** (*infml*) INFATUATED.
🔁 **1** sensible. **2** sane.

dagger n bayonet, poniard, stiletto, knife, blade, skean, dirk, skean-dhu, kris, kukri, jambiya, misericord, yatagan.

daily adj **1** REGULAR, routine, everyday, customary, common, commonplace, ordinary. **2** EVERYDAY, diurnal (*fml*).

dainty adj **1** DELICATE, elegant, exquisite, refined, fine, graceful, neat, charming, delectable. **2** FASTIDIOUS, fussy, particular, scrupulous, nice (*fml*).
🔁 **1** gross, clumsy.

dally v **1** DAWDLE, linger, loiter, delay, procrastinate (*fml*), tarry (*fml*). **2** *dally with an idea*: toy, play, flirt, trifle, frivol.
🔁 **1** hasten, hurry.

dam n barrier, barrage, embankment, blockage, obstruction, hindrance.
➤ v block, confine, restrict, check, barricade, staunch, stem, obstruct.

damage n **1** *extensive damage after the fire*: harm, injury, hurt, destruction, ruin, devastation, havoc, loss, abuse, suffering, mischief, mutilation, impairment, detriment, defacement, vandalism. **2** *pay damages*: compensation, fine, indemnity, reimbursement, reparation, restitution, satisfaction.
🔁 **1** repair.
➤ v harm, injure, hurt, spoil, ruin, impair, mar, wreck, deface, mutilate, weaken, tamper with, play havoc with, incapacitate.
🔁 mend, repair, fix.

damaging adj harmful, hurtful, injurious, unfavourable, bad, detrimental, disadvantageous, pernicious, prejudicial, ruinous, deleterious (*fml*).
🔁 favourable, helpful.

dame n **1** *Dame Edith Evans*: lady, noblewoman, baroness, dowager, peeress, aristocrat. **2** (*US sl*) WOMAN, female, broad.

damn v **1** CURSE, swear, blast, imprecate, blaspheme. **2** ABUSE, revile, denounce, criticize, censure, slate (*infml*), denunciate, execrate, castigate, slam (*infml*). **3** CONDEMN, doom, sentence.
🔁 **1** bless.

damnation n condemnation, doom, denunciation, perdition, excommunication, anathema.

damp n dampness, moisture, clamminess, dankness, humidity, wet, dew, drizzle, fog, mist, vapour.
🔁 dryness.
➤ adj moist, wet, clammy, dank, humid, dewy, muggy, drizzly, misty, soggy.
🔁 dry, arid.

dampen v **1** MOISTEN, wet, spray. **2** DISCOURAGE, dishearten, deter, dash, dull, deaden, restrain, check, depress, dismay, reduce, lessen, moderate, decrease, diminish, muffle, stifle, smother.
🔁 **1** dry. **2** encourage.

dance n ball, hop (*infml*), knees-up (*infml*), social, shindig (*infml*).

Dances include: waltz, quickstep, foxtrot, tango, polka, one-step, military two-step, valeta, Lancers, rumba, samba, mambo, bossanova, beguine, fandango, flamenco, mazurka, bolero, paso doble, can-can; rock 'n' roll, jive, twist, stomp, bop, jitterbug, mashed potato; black bottom, Charleston, cha-cha, turkey-trot; Circassian circle, Paul Jones, jig, reel, quadrille, Highland fling, morris-dance, clog dance, hoe-down, hokey-cokey, Lambeth Walk, conga, belly-dance; galliard, gavotte, minuet.

Types of dancing include: ballet, tap, ballroom, old-time, disco, folk, country, Irish, Highland, Latin-American, flamenco, clog-dancing, morris dancing, limbo-dancing, break-dancing, robotics. *see also* **ballet**.

Dance functions include: disco, dance, social, tea dance, barn dance, ball, fancy dress ball, charity ball, hunt ball, hop (*infml*), knees-up (*infml*), shindig (*infml*), rave (*infml*), prom (*US*), ceilidh.

danger n 1 *in danger of falling*: insecurity, endangerment, jeopardy, precariousness, liability, vulnerability. 2 *the dangers of smoking*: risk, threat, peril, hazard, menace.
■ 1 safety, security. 2 safety.

dangerous adj unsafe, insecure, risky, threatening, breakneck, hairy (*infml*), hazardous, perilous, precarious, reckless, treacherous, vulnerable, menacing, exposed, alarming, critical, severe, serious, grave, daring, nasty.
■ safe, secure, harmless.

dangle v 1 HANG, droop, swing, sway, flap, trail. 2 TEMPT, entice, flaunt, flourish, lure, tantalize.

dank adj damp, moist, clammy, dewy, slimy, soggy.
■ dry.

dapper adj trim, well-dressed, well-turned-out, well-groomed, chic, dainty, neat, smart, spruce, stylish, nimble, active, brisk, spry, natty (*infml*).
■ dishevelled, dowdy, scruffy, shabby, sloppy.

dappled adj speckled, mottled, spotted, stippled, dotted, flecked, freckled, variegated, bespeckled, piebald, checkered.

dare v 1 RISK, venture, brave, hazard, adventure, endanger, stake, gamble. 2 CHALLENGE, goad, provoke, taunt. 3 DEFY, presume.
➤ n challenge, provocation, taunt, gauntlet.

daredevil n adventurer, desperado, madcap.
■ coward.

daring adj bold, adventurous, intrepid, fearless, brave, plucky, audacious, dauntless, reckless, rash, impulsive, valiant.
■ cautious, timid, afraid.

➤ n boldness, fearlessness, courage, bravery, nerve, audacity, guts (*infml*), intrepidity, defiance, pluck, rashness, spirit, grit, gall, prowess.
■ caution, timidity, cowardice.

dark adj 1 *a dark room*: unlit, overcast, black, dim, unilluminated, shadowy, murky, cloudy, dusky, dingy. 2 *a dark manner*: gloomy, grim, cheerless, dismal, bleak, forbidding, sombre, sinister, mournful, ominous, menacing, drab. 3 *dark secrets*: hidden, mysterious, obscure, secret, unintelligible, enigmatic, cryptic, abstruse.
■ 1 light. 2 bright, cheerful. 3 comprehensible.
➤ n 1 DARKNESS, dimness, night, night-time, nightfall, gloom, dusk, twilight, murkiness. 2 CONCEALMENT, secrecy, obscurity.
■ 1 light. 2 openness.

darken v 1 DIM, obscure, blacken, cloud (over), shadow, overshadow, eclipse. 2 DEPRESS, sadden.
■ 1 lighten. 2 brighten.

darling n beloved, dear, dearest, favourite, sweetheart, love, pet.
➤ adj dear, beloved, adored, cherished, precious, treasured.

dart v 1 DASH, bound, sprint, flit, flash, fly, rush, run, race, spring, tear. 2 THROW, hurl, fling, shoot, sling, launch, propel, send.
➤ n bolt, arrow, barb, shaft.

dash v 1 RUSH, dart, hurry, race, sprint, run, bolt, tear. 2 FLING, throw, crash, hurl. 3 DISCOURAGE, disappoint, dampen, confound, blight, ruin, destroy, spoil, frustrate, smash, shatter.
➤ n 1 DROP, pinch, touch, flavour, soupçon, suggestion, hint, bit, little. 2 SPRINT, dart, bolt, rush, spurt, race, run.

dashing adj 1 LIVELY, vigorous, spirited, gallant, daring, bold, plucky, exuberant. 2 SMART, stylish, elegant, debonair, showy, flamboyant.
■ 1 lethargic. 2 dowdy.

data n information, documents, facts, input, statistics, figures, details, materials.

date n 1 TIME, age, period, era, stage, epoch. 2 APPOINTMENT, engagement, assignation, meeting, rendezvous. 3 ESCORT, steady (*infml*), partner, friend.
◆ **out-of-date** adj old-fashioned, unfashionable, outdated, obsolete, dated, outmoded, antiquated, passé.

fashionable, modern.

◆ **up-to-date** *adj* fashionable, modern, current, contemporary.
old-fashioned, dated.

dated *adj* old-fashioned, obsolete, outdated, outmoded, out-of-date, passé, superseded, unfashionable, obsolescent, antiquated, archaic, old hat (*infml*).
fashionable, up-to-the-minute.

daub *v* smear, plaster, coat, paint, cover, smirch, smudge, spatter, splatter, stain, sully.
➤ *n* smear, splash, splodge, splotch, spot, stain, blot, blotch.

daunt *v* 1 DISCOURAGE, dishearten, put off, dispirit, deter. 2 INTIMIDATE, overawe, unnerve, alarm, dismay, frighten, scare.
1 encourage.

dauntless *adj* fearless, undaunted, resolute, brave, courageous, bold, intrepid, daring, plucky, valiant.
discouraged, disheartened.

dawdle *v* delay, loiter, lag, hang about, dally, trail, potter, dilly-dally (*infml*).
hurry.

dawn *n* 1 SUNRISE, daybreak, morning, daylight. 2 BEGINNING, start, emergence, onset, origin, birth, advent.
1 dusk. 2 end.
➤ *v* 1 BREAK, brighten, lighten, gleam, glimmer. 2 BEGIN, appear, emerge, open, develop, originate, rise.

day *n* 1 DAYTIME, daylight. 2 AGE, period, time, date, era, generation, epoch.
1 night.

◆ **day after day** regularly, continually, endlessly, persistently, monotonously, perpetually, relentlessly.

◆ **day by day** gradually, progressively, slowly but surely, steadily.

daydream *n* fantasy, imagining, reverie, castles in the air, pipe dream, vision, musing, wish, dream, figment.
➤ *v* fantasize, imagine, muse, fancy, dream.

daze *v* 1 STUN, stupefy, shock. 2 DAZZLE, bewilder, blind, confuse, baffle, dumbfound, amaze, surprise, startle, perplex, astonish, flabbergast (*infml*), astound, stagger.
➤ *n* bewilderment, confusion, stupor, trance, shock, distraction.

dazed *adj* 1 STUNNED, stupefied, shocked, numbed, paralysed, unconscious, out (*infml*). 2 DAZZLED, bewildered, confused,

baffled, dumbfounded, speechless, amazed, surprised, shocked, stunned, startled, perplexed, astonished, astounded, staggered, taken aback, flabbergasted (*infml*).

dazzle *v* 1 DAZE, blind, confuse, blur. 2 SPARKLE, fascinate, impress, overwhelm, awe, overawe, scintillate, bedazzle, amaze, astonish, bewitch, stupefy.
➤ *n* sparkle, brilliance, magnificence, splendour, scintillation, glitter, glare.

dead *adj* 1 LIFELESS, deceased, inanimate, defunct, departed, late, gone. 2 UNRESPONSIVE, apathetic, dull, indifferent, insensitive, numb, cold, frigid, lukewarm, torpid. 3 EXHAUSTED, tired, worn out, dead-beat (*infml*). 4 EXACT, absolute, perfect, unqualified, utter, outright, complete, entire, total, downright.
1 alive. 2 lively. 3 refreshed.

deaden *v* reduce, blunt, muffle, lessen, quieten, suppress, weaken, numb, diminish, stifle, alleviate, anaesthetize, desensitize, smother, check, abate, allay, dampen, hush, mute, paralyse.
heighten.

deadlock *n* standstill, stalemate, impasse, halt.

deadly *adj* 1 *deadly poison*: lethal, fatal, dangerous, venomous, destructive, pernicious, malignant, murderous, mortal. 2 *a deadly lecture*: dull, boring, uninteresting, tedious, monotonous. 3 *deadly aim*: unerring, effective, true.
1 harmless. 2 exciting.

deaf *adj* 1 HARD OF HEARING, stone-deaf. 2 UNCONCERNED, indifferent, unmoved, oblivious, heedless, unmindful.
2 aware, conscious.

deafening *adj* piercing, ear-splitting, booming, resounding, thunderous, ringing, roaring.
quiet.

deal *v* 1 DISTRIBUTE, give out, share, dole out, divide, allot, dispense, assign, mete out, apportion (*fml*), bestow (*fml*). 2 TRADE, do business, buy and sell, negotiate, traffic, export, bargain, handle, treat, operate, market, stock. 3 *deal a blow*: deliver, administer, direct, mete, inflict.
➤ *n* 1 QUANTITY, amount, extent, degree, portion, share. 2 AGREEMENT, contract, understanding, pact, transaction, bargain, buy. 3 ROUND, hand, distribution.

◆ **deal with** attend to, concern, see to,

manage, handle, cope with, treat, consider, oversee.

dealer n trader, merchant, wholesaler, marketer, merchandiser.

dealings n business, commerce, trade, operations, traffic, trafficking, transactions, negotiations, relations, intercourse (fml), truck (infml).

dear adj 1 LOVED, beloved, treasured, valued, cherished, precious, favourite, esteemed, intimate, close, darling, familiar. 2 EXPENSIVE, high-priced, costly, overpriced, pric(e)y (infml).
Ea 1 disliked, hated. 2 cheap.
➤ n beloved, loved one, precious, darling, treasure.

dearly adv 1 he loves her dearly: fondly, affectionately, lovingly, devotedly, tenderly. 2 I wish it dearly: greatly, extremely, profoundly.

dearth n scarcity, shortage, insufficiency, inadequacy, deficiency, lack, want, absence, scantiness, sparsity, need, paucity, poverty, famine.
Ea excess, abundance.

death n 1 DECEASE, end, finish, loss, demise, departure, fatality, cessation, passing, expiration, dissolution. 2 DESTRUCTION, ruin, undoing, annihilation, downfall, extermination, extinction, obliteration, eradication.
Ea 1 life, birth.

deathly adj 1 ASHEN, grim, haggard, pale, pallid, ghastly, wan. 2 FATAL, deadly, mortal, intense.

debacle n fiasco, catastrophe, failure, collapse, defeat, devastation, disaster, downfall, havoc, cataclysm, overthrow, reversal, rout, turmoil, disintegration, ruin, ruination, stampede, farce.

debase v 1 DEGRADE, demean, devalue, disgrace, dishonour, shame, humble, humiliate, lower, reduce, abase, defile. 2 CONTAMINATE, pollute, corrupt, adulterate, taint.
Ea 1 elevate. 2 purify.

debatable adj questionable, uncertain, disputable, contestable, controversial, arguable, open to question, doubtful, contentious, undecided, unsettled, problematical, dubious, moot.
Ea unquestionable, certain, incontrovertible.

debate v 1 DISPUTE, argue, discuss, contend, wrangle. 2 CONSIDER, deliberate,

ponder, reflect, meditate on, mull over, weigh.
➤ n discussion, argument, controversy, disputation, deliberation, consideration, contention, dispute, reflection, polemic.

debauchery n depravity, intemperance, overindulgence, dissipation, licentiousness, dissoluteness, excess, decadence, wantonness, lewdness, carousal, orgy, revel, lust, riot.
Ea restraint, temperance.

debilitate v weaken, enervate, undermine, sap, incapacitate, wear out, exhaust, impair.
Ea strengthen, invigorate, energize.

debonair adj suave, refined, urbane, well-bred, smooth, dashing, elegant, affable, breezy, buoyant, charming, courteous, cheerful, jaunty, light-hearted.

debris n remains, ruins, rubbish, waste, wreck, wreckage, litter, fragments, rubble, trash, pieces, bits, sweepings, drift.

debt n indebtedness, obligation, debit, arrears, due, liability, duty, bill, commitment, claim, score.
Ea credit, asset.

debtor n borrower, bankrupt, insolvent, defaulter, mortgagor.
Ea creditor.

debunk v expose, deflate, show up, ridicule, mock, explode, lampoon.

debut n introduction, launching, beginning, entrance, presentation, inauguration, première, appearance, initiation.

decadent adj 1 CORRUPT, debased, debauched, depraved, dissolute, immoral, degenerate, degraded, self-indulgent. 2 DECAYING, declining.
Ea 1 moral.

decapitate v behead, execute, guillotine, unhead.

decay v 1 ROT, go bad, putrefy, decompose, spoil, perish, mortify. 2 DECLINE, deteriorate, disintegrate, corrode, crumble, waste away, degenerate, wear away, dwindle, shrivel, wither, sink.
Ea 2 flourish, grow.
➤ n 1 ROT, decomposition, rotting, perishing. 2 DECLINE, deterioration, disintegration, degeneration, collapse, decadence, wasting, failing, withering, fading.

decease n death, dying, demise,

departure, passing, dissolution.

deceased adj dead, departed, former, late, lost, defunct, expired, gone, finished, extinct.

➤ n dead, departed.

deceit n deception, pretence, cheating, misrepresentation, fraud, duplicity, trickery, fraudulence, double-dealing, underhandedness, fake, guile, sham, subterfuge, swindle, treachery, hypocrisy, artifice, ruse, cunning, slyness, craftiness, stratagem, wile, imposition, feint, shift, abuse.

🔼 honesty, openness, frankness.

deceitful adj dishonest, deceptive, deceiving, false, insincere, untrustworthy, double-dealing, fraudulent, two-faced (infml), treacherous, duplicitous, guileful, tricky (infml), underhand, sneaky, counterfeit, crafty, hypocritical, designing, illusory, knavish.

🔼 honest, open.

deceive v mislead, delude, cheat, betray, fool, take in (infml), trick, dissemble, hoax, con (infml), have on (infml), take for a ride (infml), double-cross (infml), dupe, kid (infml), swindle, impose upon, bamboozle (infml), two-time (infml), lead on, outwit, hoodwink, beguile, ensnare, camouflage, abuse, befool, gull.

decency n propriety, courtesy, modesty, decorum, respectability, civility, correctness, fitness, etiquette, helpfulness.

🔼 impropriety, discourtesy.

decent adj 1 RESPECTABLE, proper, fitting, decorous, chaste, seemly, suitable, modest, appropriate, presentable, pure, fit, becoming, befitting, nice. 2 KIND, obliging, courteous, helpful, generous, polite, gracious. 3 ADEQUATE, acceptable, satisfactory, reasonable, sufficient, tolerable, competent.

🔼 1 indecent. 2 disobliging.

deception n deceit, pretence, trick, cheat, fraud, imposture, lie, dissembling, deceptiveness, insincerity, con (infml), sham, subterfuge, artifice, hypocrisy, bluff, treachery, hoax, fraudulence, duplicity, ruse, snare, stratagem, leg-pull (infml), illusion, wile, guile, craftiness, cunning.

🔼 openness, honesty.

deceptive adj dishonest, false, fraudulent, misleading, unreliable, illusive, fake, illusory, spurious, mock, fallacious, ambiguous, specious.

🔼 genuine, artless, open.

decide v choose, determine, resolve, reach a decision, settle, elect, opt, judge, adjudicate, conclude, fix, purpose, decree.

decided adj 1 DEFINITE, certain, undeniable, indisputable, absolute, clear-cut, undisputed, unmistakable, unquestionable, positive, unambiguous, categorical, distinct, emphatic. 2 RESOLUTE, decisive, determined, firm, unhesitating, deliberate, forthright.

🔼 1 inconclusive. 2 irresolute.

decidedly adv very, absolutely, certainly, downright, positively, quite, unquestionably, unequivocally, unmistakably, clearly, definitely, distinctly, obviously, decisively.

decipher v decode, unscramble, crack, construe, interpret, make out (infml), figure out (infml), understand, transliterate.

🔼 encode.

decision n 1 RESULT, conclusion, outcome, verdict, finding, settlement, judgement, arbitration, ruling. 2 DETERMINATION, decisiveness, firmness, resolve, purpose.

decisive adj 1 CONCLUSIVE, definite, definitive, absolute, final. 2 DETERMINED, resolute, decided, positive, firm, forceful, forthright, strong-minded. 3 SIGNIFICANT, critical, crucial, influential, momentous, fateful.

🔼 1 inconclusive. 2 indecisive. 3 insignificant.

deck v decorate, ornament, adorn, beautify, embellish, trim, garnish, garland, festoon, grace, enrich, prettify, trick out, array (fml), bedeck (fml), tart up (infml), rig (infml), tog (infml).

declaration n 1 AFFIRMATION, acknowledgement, assertion, statement, testimony, attestation, disclosure, profession, revelation. 2 ANNOUNCEMENT, notification, pronouncement, proclamation, edict, manifesto, promulgation.

declare v 1 AFFIRM, assert, claim, profess, maintain, state, attest, certify, confess, confirm, disclose, reveal, show, aver, swear, testify, witness, validate. 2 ANNOUNCE, proclaim, pronounce, decree, broadcast.

decline v 1 REFUSE, reject, deny, forgo, avoid, balk. 2 DIMINISH, decrease, dwindle, lessen, fall, sink, wane. 3 DECAY,

deteriorate, worsen, degenerate. **4**
DESCEND, sink, slope, dip, slant.
⊟ 3 improve. **4** rise.
➤ n **1** DETERIORATION, dwindling,
lessening, decay, degeneration,
weakening, worsening, failing, downturn,
diminution, falling-off, recession, slump,
abatement. **2** DESCENT, dip, declivity,
declination, hill, slope, incline, divergence,
deviation.
⊟ 1 improvement. **2** rise.

decode v decipher, interpret, unscramble,
translate, transliterate, uncipher.
⊟ encode.

decompose v disintegrate, rot, decay,
putrefy, break down, break up, crumble,
spoil, dissolve, separate, fester.

décor n decoration, furnishings, colour
scheme, ornamentation, scenery.

decorate v **1** ORNAMENT, adorn, beautify,
embellish, trim, deck, tart up (sl), grace,
enrich, prettify, trick out. **2** RENOVATE, do up
(infml), paint, paper, colour, refurbish. **3**
HONOUR, crown, cite, garland, bemedal.

decoration n **1** ORNAMENT, adornment,
ornamentation, trimming, embellishment,
beautification, garnish, flourish,
enrichment, elaboration, frill, scroll,
bauble. **2** AWARD, medal, order, badge,
garland, crown, colours, ribbon, laurel,
star, emblem.

decorative adj ornamental, fancy,
adorning, beautifying, embellishing, non-
functional, pretty, ornate, enhancing.
⊟ plain.

decorous adj polite, refined, correct,
courtly, decent, dignified, proper, well-
behaved, appropriate, suitable, becoming,
befitting, comely, comme il faut, fit,
mannerly, modest, sedate, staid, seemly
(fml).
⊟ indecorous.

decorum n propriety, seemliness,
etiquette, good manners, respectability,
protocol, behaviour, decency, dignity,
deportment, restraint, politeness,
modesty, grace, breeding.
⊟ impropriety, indecorum, bad manners.

decoy n lure, trap, enticement,
inducement, ensnarement, pretence,
attraction, bait.
➤ v bait, lure, entrap, entice, ensnare,
allure, tempt, deceive, attract, seduce,
lead, draw.

decrease v lessen, lower, diminish,

dwindle, decline, fall off, reduce, subside,
abate, cut down, contract, drop, ease,
shrink, taper, wane, slim, slacken, peter
out, curtail.
⊟ increase.
➤ n lessening, reduction, decline, falling-
off, dwindling, loss, diminution,
abatement, cutback, contraction,
downturn, ebb, shrinkage, subsidence,
step-down.
⊟ increase.

decree n order, command, law, ordinance,
regulation, ruling, statute, act, enactment,
edict, proclamation, mandate, precept,
interlocution.
➤ v order, command, rule, lay down,
dictate, decide, determine, ordain,
prescribe, proclaim, pronounce, enact.

decrepit adj dilapidated, run-down,
rickety, broken-down, worn-out, tumbledown.

dedicate v **1** DEVOTE, commit, assign, give
over to, pledge, present, offer, sacrifice,
surrender. **2** CONSECRATE, bless, sanctify,
set apart, hallow. **3** dedicate a book:
inscribe, address.

dedicated adj **1** a dedicated teacher:
devoted, committed, enthusiastic, single-
minded, wholehearted, single-hearted,
zealous, given over to, purposeful, hard-
working, industrious, diligent. **2**
CUSTOMIZED, custom-built, bespoke.
⊟ 1 uncommitted, apathetic.

dedication n **1** COMMITMENT, devotion,
single-mindedness, wholeheartedness,
allegiance, attachment, adherence,
faithfulness, loyalty, self-sacrifice. **2**
CONSECRATION, hallowing, presentation. **3**
INSCRIPTION, address.
⊟ 1 apathy.

deduce v derive, infer, gather, conclude,
reason, surmise, understand, draw, glean.

deduct v subtract, take away, remove,
reduce by, decrease by, knock off (infml),
withdraw.
⊟ add.

deduction n **1** INFERENCE, reasoning,
finding, conclusion, corollary, assumption,
result. **2** SUBTRACTION, reduction,
decrease, diminution, abatement,
withdrawal, discount, allowance.
⊟ 2 addition, increase.

deed n **1** ACTION, act, achievement,
performance, exploit, feat, fact, truth,
reality. **2** DOCUMENT, contract, record,

title, transaction, indenture (*fml*).

deem *v* judge, believe, suppose, think, conceive, consider, estimate, hold, imagine, account, reckon, regard, adjudge (*fml*), esteem (*fml*).

deep *adj* **1** PROFOUND, bottomless, unplumbed, fathomless, yawning, immersed. **2** OBSCURE, mysterious, difficult, recondite, abstruse, esoteric. **3** WISE, perceptive, discerning, profound, learned, astute. **4** INTENSE, serious, earnest, extreme. **5** LOW, bass, resonant, booming.
☒ 1 shallow, open. **2** clear, plain, open. **3** superficial. **4** light. **5** high.

deepen *v* **1** INTENSIFY, grow, increase, strengthen, reinforce, magnify. **2** HOLLOW, scoop out.

deeply *adv* intensely, seriously, earnestly, extremely, completely, thoroughly, profoundly, very much, severely, passionately, fervently, ardently, movingly, strongly, vigorously, acutely, distressingly, feelingly, gravely, mournfully, sadly, to the quick.
☒ slightly.

deep-seated *adj* ingrained, entrenched, deep-rooted, fixed, confirmed, deep, settled.
☒ eradicable, temporary.

deface *v* damage, spoil, disfigure, blemish, impair, mutilate, mar, sully, tarnish, vandalize, deform, obliterate, injure, destroy.
☒ repair.

defamation (*fml*) *n* vilification (*fml*), aspersion (*fml*), slander, libel, disparagement, slur, smear, innuendo, scandal.
☒ commendation, praise.

defamatory (*fml*) *adj* vilifying (*fml*), slanderous, libellous, denigrating (*fml*), disparaging, pejorative, insulting, injurious, derogatory.
☒ complimentary, appreciative.

defame *v* slander, libel, discredit, disgrace, dishonour, besmirch, disparage, libel, malign, blacken, smear, speak evil of, stigmatize, cast aspersions (*fml*), denigrate (*fml*), calumniate (*fml*), traduce (*fml*), vilify (*fml*), vituperate (*fml*), run down (*infml*), drag through the mud (*infml*), sling/throw mud at (*infml*).
☒ compliment, praise.

default *n* failure, absence, neglect, non-

payment, omission, deficiency, lapse, fault, want, lack, defect.
➤ *v* fail, evade, defraud, neglect, dodge, swindle, backslide.

defaulter *n* non-payer, offender.

defeat *v* **1** CONQUER, beat, overpower, subdue, overthrow, worst, repel, subjugate, overwhelm, rout, ruin, thump (*infml*), quell, vanquish (*fml*). **2** FRUSTRATE, confound, balk, get the better of, disappoint, foil, thwart, baffle, checkmate.
➤ *n* **1** CONQUEST, beating, overthrow, rout, subjugation, vanquishment (*fml*). **2** FRUSTRATION, failure, setback, reverse, disappointment, checkmate.

defeatist *n* pessimist, quitter, prophet of doom.
☒ optimist.
➤ *adj* pessimistic, resigned, fatalistic, despondent, helpless, hopeless, despairing, gloomy.
☒ optimistic.

defect *n* imperfection, fault, flaw, deficiency, failing, mistake, inadequacy, blemish, error, bug (*infml*), shortcoming, want, weakness, frailty, lack, spot, absence, taint.
➤ *v* desert, break faith, rebel, apostatize (*fml*), revolt, renegue.

defection *n* desertion, abandonment, disloyalty, backsliding, rebellion, revolt, mutiny, betrayal, treason, apostasy (*fml*), dereliction (*fml*), perfidy (*fml*).

defective *adj* faulty, imperfect, out of order, flawed, deficient, broken, abnormal.
☒ in order, operative.

defence *n* **1** PROTECTION, resistance, security, fortification, cover, safeguard, shelter, guard, shield, deterrence, barricade, bastion, immunity, bulwark, rampart, buttress. **2** JUSTIFICATION, explanation, excuse, argument, exoneration, plea, vindication, apologia (*fml*), pleading, alibi, case.
☒ 1 attack, assault. **2** accusation.

defenceless *adj* unprotected, undefended, unarmed, unguarded, vulnerable, exposed, helpless, powerless.
☒ protected, guarded.

defend *v* **1** PROTECT, guard, safeguard, shelter, fortify, secure, shield, screen, cover, contest. **2** SUPPORT, stand up for, stand by, uphold, endorse, vindicate, champion, argue for, speak up for, justify, plead.
☒ 1 attack. **2** accuse.

defendant *n* accused, offender, prisoner, respondent.

defender *n* 1 PROTECTOR, guard, bodyguard. 2 SUPPORTER, advocate, vindicator, champion, patron, sponsor, counsel.

🗲 1 attacker. 2 accuser.

defensible *adj* justifiable, tenable, arguable, permissible, plausible, valid, maintainable, safe, secure, unassailable, impregnable, pardonable, vindicable.

🗲 indefensible, insecure.

defensive *adj* 1 PROTECTIVE, defending, safeguarding, wary, opposing, cautious, watchful. 2 SELF-JUSTIFYING, apologetic.

defer[1] *v* delay, postpone, put off, adjourn, hold over, shelve, suspend, procrastinate, prorogue (*fml*), protract, waive.

defer[2] *v* yield, give way, comply, submit, accede, capitulate, respect, bow.

deference *n* 1 SUBMISSION, submissiveness, compliance, acquiescence, obedience, yielding. 2 RESPECT, regard, honour, esteem, reverence, courtesy, civility, politeness, consideration.

🗲 1 resistance. 2 contempt.

deferential *adj* respectful, reverent, reverential, courteous, civil, dutiful, polite, attentive, considerate, thoughtful, ingratiating, complaisant (*fml*), obsequious (*fml*).

🗲 arrogant, immodest.

deferment *n* delay, postponement, putting-off, adjournment, holding-over, shelving, suspension, stay, moratorium, waiving, procrastination (*fml*).

defiance *n* opposition, confrontation, resistance, challenge, disobedience, rebelliousness, contempt, insubordination, disregard, insolence.

🗲 compliance, acquiescence, submissiveness.

defiant *adj* challenging, resistant, antagonistic, aggressive, rebellious, insubordinate, disobedient, intransigent, bold, contumacious (*fml*), insolent, obstinate, unco-operative, provocative.

🗲 compliant, acquiescent, submissive.

deficiency *n* 1 SHORTAGE, lack, inadequacy, scarcity, insufficiency, dearth, want, scantiness, absence, deficit. 2 IMPERFECTION, shortcoming, weakness, fault, defect, flaw, failing, frailty.

🗲 1 excess, surfeit. 2 perfection.

deficient *adj* 1 INADEQUATE, insufficient, scarce, short, lacking, wanting, meagre, scanty, skimpy, incomplete. 2 IMPERFECT, impaired, flawed, faulty, defective, unsatisfactory, inferior, weak.

🗲 1 excessive. 2 perfect.

deficit *n* shortage, shortfall, deficiency, loss, arrears, lack, default.

🗲 excess.

defile *v* pollute, violate, contaminate, degrade, dishonour, desecrate, debase, soil, stain, sully, tarnish, taint, profane, corrupt, disgrace.

define *v define the boundaries*: bound, limit, delimit, demarcate, mark out. 2 *define the meaning*: explain, characterize, describe, interpret, expound, determine, designate, specify, spell out, detail.

definite *adj* 1 CERTAIN, settled, sure, positive, fixed, decided, determined, assured, guaranteed. 2 CLEAR, clear-cut, exact, precise, specific, explicit, particular, obvious, marked.

🗲 1 indefinite. 2 vague.

definitely *adv* positively, surely, unquestionably, absolutely, certainly, categorically, undeniably, clearly, doubtless, unmistakably, plainly, obviously, Indeed, easily.

definition *n* 1 DELINEATION, demarcation, delimitation. 2 EXPLANATION, description, interpretation, exposition, clarification, elucidation, determination. 3 DISTINCTNESS, clarity, precision, clearness, focus, contrast, sharpness.

definitive *adj* decisive, conclusive, final, authoritative, standard, correct, ultimate, reliable, exhaustive, perfect, exact, absolute, complete.

🗲 interim.

deflate *v* 1 FLATTEN, puncture, collapse, exhaust, squash, empty, contract, void, shrink, squeeze. 2 DEBUNK, humiliate, put down (*infml*), dash, dispirit, humble, mortify, disconcert. 3 DECREASE, devalue, reduce, lessen, lower, diminish, depreciate, depress.

🗲 1 inflate. 2 boost. 3 increase.

deflect *v* deviate, diverge, turn (aside), swerve, veer, sidetrack, twist, avert, wind, glance off, bend, ricochet.

deflection *n* deviation, divergence, turning, turning-aside, swerve, veer, changing course, sidetracking, drift, twisting, glancing-off, bend, ricochet, aberration (*fml*), refraction (*fml*).

deform *v* distort, contort, disfigure, warp, mar, pervert, ruin, spoil, twist.

deformed *adj* distorted, misshapen, contorted, disfigured, crippled, crooked, bent, twisted, warped, buckled, defaced, mangled, maimed, marred, ruined, mutilated, perverted, corrupted.

deformity *n* distortion, misshapenness, malformation, disfigurement, abnormality, irregularity, misproportion, defect, ugliness, monstrosity, corruption.

defraud *v* cheat, swindle, dupe, fleece, sting (*infml*), rip off (*infml*), do (*infml*), diddle (*infml*), rob, trick, con (*infml*), rook, deceive, delude, embezzle, beguile.

deft *adj* adept, handy, dexterous, nimble, skilful, adroit, agile, expert, nifty, proficient, able, neat, clever.
■ clumsy, awkward.

defunct *adj* 1 DEAD, deceased, departed, gone, expired, extinct. 2 OBSOLETE, invalid, inoperative, expired.
■ 1 alive, live. 2 operative.

defy *v* 1 *defy the authorities*: challenge, confront, resist, dare, brave, face, repel, spurn, beard, flout, withstand, disregard, scorn, despise, defeat, provoke, thwart. 2 *her writings defy categorization*: elude, frustrate, baffle, foil.
■ 1 obey. 2 permit.

degenerate *adj* dissolute, debauched, depraved, degraded, debased, base, low, decadent, corrupt, fallen, immoral, mean, degenerated, perverted, deteriorated.
■ moral, upright.
➤ *v* decline, deteriorate, sink, decay, rot, slip, worsen, regress, fall off, lapse, decrease.
■ improve.

degeneration *n* decline, deterioration, debasement, decay, failure, slip, worsening, falling-off, sinking, drop, slide, lapse, atrophy, decrease, regression (*fml*).
■ improvement.

degradation *n* 1 DETERIORATION, degeneration, decline, downgrading, demotion. 2 ABASEMENT, humiliation, mortification, dishonour, disgrace, shame, ignominy, decadence.
■ 1 virtue. 2 enhancement.

degrade *v* 1 DISHONOUR, disgrace, debase, abase, shame, humiliate, humble, discredit, demean, lower, weaken, impair,

deteriorate, cheapen, adulterate, corrupt. 2 DEMOTE, depose, downgrade, deprive, cashier.
■ 1 exalt. 2 promote.

degrading *adj* humiliating, dishonourable, disgraceful, debasing, base, shameful, contemptible, discrediting, mortifying, demeaning, belittling, cheapening, ignoble, undignified, unworthy.
■ enhancing.

degree *n* 1 GRADE, class, rank, order, position, standing, status. 2 EXTENT, measure, range, stage, step, level, intensity, standard. 3 LEVEL, limit, unit, mark.

deify *v* exalt, elevate, worship, glorify, idolize, extol, venerate, immortalize, ennoble, idealize.

deign *v* condescend, stoop, lower oneself, consent, demean oneself.

deity *n* god, goddess, divinity, godhead, idol, demigod, demigoddess, power, immortal.

dejected *adj* downcast, despondent, depressed, downhearted, disheartened, down, low, melancholy, disconsolate, sad, miserable, cast down, gloomy, glum, crestfallen, dismal, wretched, doleful, morose, spiritless.
■ cheerful, high-spirited, happy.

dejection *n* despondency, depression, downheartedness, discouragement, low spirits, despair, melancholy, sadness, sorrow, unhappiness, misery, gloom, gloominess, wretchedness, dolefulness, moroseness, dispiritedness, disconsolation (*fml*), blues (*infml*), dumps (*infml*).
■ happiness, high spirits.

delay *v* 1 OBSTRUCT, hinder, impede, hold up, check, hold back, set back, stop, halt, detain. 2 DEFER, put off, postpone, procrastinate, suspend, shelve, hold over, stall. 3 DAWDLE, linger, lag, loiter, dilly-dally (*infml*), tarry.
■ 1 accelerate. 2 bring forward. 3 hurry.
➤ *n* 1 OBSTRUCTION, hindrance, impediment, hold-up, check, setback, stay, stoppage. 2 DEFERMENT, postponement, procrastination, suspension. 3 DAWDLING, lingering, tarrying. 4 INTERRUPTION, lull, interval, wait.
■ 1 hastening. 3 hurry. 4 continuation.

delegate *n* representative, agent, envoy, messenger, deputy, ambassador, commissioner.

➤ *v* authorize, appoint, depute, charge, commission, assign, empower, entrust, devolve, consign, designate, nominate, name, hand over.

delegation *n* 1 DEPUTATION, commission, legation, mission, contingent, embassy. 2 AUTHORIZATION, commissioning, assignment.

delete *v* erase, remove, cross out, cancel, rub out, strike (out), obliterate, edit (out), blot out, efface.
✗ add, insert.

deliberate *v* consider, ponder, reflect, think, cogitate, meditate, mull over, debate, discuss, weigh, consult.
➤ *adj* 1 INTENTIONAL, planned, calculated, prearranged, premeditated, willed, conscious, designed, considered, advised. 2 CAREFUL, unhurried, thoughtful, methodical, cautious, circumspect, studied, prudent, slow, ponderous, measured, heedful.
✗ 1 unintentional, accidental. 2 hasty.

deliberately *adv* 1 INTENTIONALLY, on purpose, consciously, pointedly, calculatingly, by design, in cold blood, knowingly, wittingly, wilfully, with malice aforethought. 2 CAREFULLY, unhurriedly, thoughtfully, methodically, cautiously, prudently, slowly, ponderously, steadily, circumspectly (*fml*).
✗ 1 unintentionally, by accident, accidentally, by mistake. 2 hastily.

deliberation *n* 1 CONSIDERATION, reflection, thought, calculation, forethought, meditation, rumination, study, debate, discussion, consultation, speculation. 2 CARE, carefulness, caution, circumspection, prudence.

delicacy *n* 1 DAINTINESS, fineness, elegance, exquisiteness, lightness, precision. 2 REFINEMENT, sensitivity, subtlety, finesse, discrimination, tact, niceness. 3 TITBIT, dainty, taste, sweetmeat, savoury, relish.
✗ 1 coarseness, roughness. 2 tactlessness.

delicate *adj* 1 FINE, fragile, dainty, exquisite, flimsy, elegant, graceful. 2 FRAIL, weak, ailing, faint. 3 SENSITIVE, scrupulous, discriminating, careful, accurate, precise. 4 SUBTLE, muted, pastel, soft.
✗ 1 coarse, clumsy. 2 healthy.

delicious *adj* 1 ENJOYABLE, pleasant, agreeable, delightful. 2 APPETIZING,

palatable, tasty, delectable, scrumptious (*infml*), mouth-watering, succulent, savoury.
✗ 1 unpleasant. 2 unpalatable.

delight *n* bliss, happiness, joy, pleasure, ecstasy, enjoyment, gladness, rapture, transport, gratification, jubilation.
✗ disgust, displeasure.
➤ *v* please, charm, gratify, enchant, tickle, thrill, ravish.
✗ displease, dismay.
◆ **delight in** enjoy, relish, like, love, savour, appreciate, revel in, take pride in, glory in.
✗ dislike, hate.

delighted *adj* charmed, elated, happy, pleased, enchanted, captivated, ecstatic, thrilled, overjoyed, jubilant, joyous.
✗ disappointed, dismayed.

delightful *adj* charming, enchanting, captivating, enjoyable, pleasant, thrilling, agreeable, pleasurable, engaging, attractive, pleasing, gratifying, entertaining, fascinating.
✗ nasty, unpleasant.

delinquency *n* crime, offence, wrong-doing, misbehaviour, misconduct, law-breaking, misdemeanour, criminality.

delinquent *n* offender, criminal, wrong-doer, law-breaker, hooligan, culprit, miscreant (*fml*).

delirious *adj* demented, raving, incoherent, beside oneself, deranged, frenzied, light-headed, wild, mad, frantic, insane, crazy, ecstatic.
✗ sane.

delirium *n* 1 *feverish delirium*: derangement, raving, incoherence, irrationality, fever, frenzy, passion, wildness, madness, insanity, lunacy, craziness, hallucination, hysteria, jimjams (*infml*). 2 *the delirium of first love*: ecstasy, euphoria, joy, elation, excitement, jubilation, wildness, passion.
✗ 1 sanity.

deliver *v* 1 *deliver a parcel*: convey, bring, send, give, carry, supply. 2 SURRENDER, hand over, relinquish, yield, transfer, grant, entrust, commit. 3 UTTER, speak, proclaim, pronounce. 4 ADMINISTER, inflict, direct. 5 SET FREE, liberate, release, emancipate.

delivery *n* 1 CONVEYANCE, consignment, dispatch, transmission, transfer, surrender. 2 ARTICULATION, enunciation, speech, utterance, intonation, elocution. 3 CHILDBIRTH, labour, confinement.

delude v deceive, mislead, beguile, dupe, take in, trick, hoodwink, hoax, cheat, misinform.

deluge n flood, inundation, downpour, torrent, spate, rush.
➤ v flood, inundate, drench, drown, overwhelm, soak, swamp, engulf, submerge.

delusion n illusion, hallucination, fancy, misconception, misapprehension, deception, misbelief, fallacy.

delve v burrow, rummage, search, dig into, hunt in/through, poke, ransack, root, probe, examine, explore, investigate, go/look into, research.

demagogue n agitator, orator, firebrand, haranguer, rabble-rouser, tub-thumper.

demand v 1 ASK, request, call for, insist on, solicit, claim, exact, inquire, question, interrogate. 2 NECESSITATE, need, require, involve.
➤ n 1 REQUEST, question, claim, order, inquiry, desire, interrogation. 2 NEED, necessity, call.

demanding adj hard, difficult, challenging, exacting, taxing, tough, exhausting, wearing, back-breaking, insistent, pressing, urgent, trying.
Ea easy, undemanding, easy-going.

demarcation n boundary, bound, differentiation, distinction, division, separation, enclosure, limit, line, margin, determination, establishment, fixing, marking off/out, delimitation, definition.

demean v lower, humble, degrade, humiliate, debase, abase, descend, stoop, condescend.
Ea exalt, enhance.

demeanour n bearing, manner, deportment, conduct, behaviour, air.

demented adj mad, insane, lunatic, out of one's mind, crazy, loony (sl), deranged, unbalanced, frenzied.
Ea sane.

demise n 1 DEATH, decease, end, passing, departure, termination, expiration. 2 DOWNFALL, fall, collapse, failure, ruin. 3 TRANSFER, conveyance, inheritance, transmission, alienation.

democracy n self-government, commonwealth, autonomy, republic.

democratic adj self-governing, representative, egalitarian, autonomous, popular, populist, republican.

demolish v 1 DESTROY, dismantle, knock down, pull down, flatten, bulldoze, raze, tear down, level. 2 RUIN, defeat, destroy, annihilate, wreck, overturn, overthrow, crush, devastate.
Ea 1 build up.

demolition n destruction, dismantling, levelling, razing.

demon n 1 DEVIL, fiend, evil spirit, fallen angel, imp. 2 VILLAIN, devil, rogue, monster.

demonstrable adj verifiable, provable, arguable, attestable, self-evident, obvious, evident, certain, clear, positive.
Ea unverifiable.

demonstrate v 1 SHOW, display, prove, establish, exhibit, substantiate, manifest, testify to, indicate. 2 EXPLAIN, illustrate, describe, teach. 3 PROTEST, march, parade, rally, picket, sit in.

demonstration n 1 DISPLAY, exhibition, manifestation, proof, confirmation, affirmation, substantiation, validation, evidence, testimony, expression. 2 EXPLANATION, illustration, description, exposition, presentation, test, trial. 3 PROTEST, march, demo (infml), rally, picket, sit-in, parade.

demonstrative adj affectionate, expressive, expansive, emotional, open, loving.
Ea reserved, cold, restrained.

demoralize v 1 DISCOURAGE, dishearten, dispirit, undermine, depress, deject, crush, lower, disconcert. 2 CORRUPT, deprave, debase.
Ea 1 encourage. 2 improve.

demote v downgrade, degrade, relegate, reduce, cashier.
Ea promote, upgrade.

demur v disagree, dissent, object, take exception, refuse, protest, dispute, balk, scruple, doubt, hesitate.

demure adj modest, reserved, reticent, prim, coy, shy, retiring, prissy, grave, prudish, sober, strait-laced, staid.
Ea wanton, forward.

den n lair, hide-out, hole, retreat, study, hideaway, shelter, sanctuary, haunt.

denial n 1 CONTRADICTION, negation, dissent, repudiation, disavowal, disclaimer, dismissal, renunciation. 2 REFUSAL, rebuff, rejection, prohibition, veto.

denigrate v disparage, run down, slander, revile, defame, malign, vilify, decry, besmirch, impugn, belittle, abuse, assail, criticize.

■ praise, acclaim.

denomination n 1 CLASSIFICATION, category, class, kind, sort. 2 RELIGION, persuasion, sect, belief, faith, creed, communion, school.

denote v indicate, stand for, signify, represent, symbolize, mean, express, designate, typify, mark, show, imply.

dénouement n climax, culmination, conclusion, outcome, upshot, pay-off (*infml*), finale, resolution, finish, solution, close.

denounce v condemn, censure, accuse, revile, decry, attack, inform against, betray, impugn, vilify, fulminate.

■ acclaim, praise.

dense adj 1 COMPACT, thick, compressed, condensed, close, close-knit, heavy, solid, opaque, impenetrable, packed, crowded. 2 STUPID, thick (*infml*), crass, dull, slow, slow-witted.

■ 1 thin, sparse. 2 quick-witted, clever.

density n body, mass, bulk, closeness, compactness, consistency, denseness, solidity, solidness, thickness, tightness, impenetrability.

■ sparseness.

dent n hollow, depression, dip, concavity, indentation, crater, dimple, dint, pit.
➢ v depress, gouge, push in, indent.

denude v strip, divest, expose, uncover, bare, deforest.

■ cover, clothe.

denunciation n condemnation, denouncement, censure, accusation, incrimination, invective, criticism.

■ praise.

deny v 1 *deny God's existence*: contradict, oppose, refute, disagree with, disaffirm, disprove. 2 *deny one's parentage*: disown, disclaim, renounce, repudiate, recant. 3 *deny their human rights*: refuse, turn down, forbid, reject, withhold, rebuff, veto.

■ 1 admit. 3 allow.

deodorant n anti-perspirant, deodorizer, air-freshener, disinfectant, fumigant, fumigator.

depart v 1 GO, leave, withdraw, exit, make off, quit, decamp, take one's leave, absent oneself, set off, remove, retreat, migrate, escape, disappear, retire, vanish. 2 DEVIATE, digress, differ, diverge, swerve, veer.

■ 1 arrive, return. 2 keep to.

departed adj dead, deceased, gone, late, expired.

department n 1 DIVISION, branch, subdivision, section, sector, office, station, unit, region, district. 2 SPHERE, realm, province, domain, field, area, concern, responsibility, speciality, line.

departure n 1 EXIT, going, leave-taking, removal, withdrawal, retirement, exodus. 2 DEVIATION, digression, divergence, variation, innovation, branching (out), difference, change, shift, veering.

■ 1 arrival, return.

dependable adj reliable, trustworthy, steady, trusty, responsible, faithful, unfailing, sure, honest, conscientious, certain.

■ unreliable, fickle.

dependant n child, minor, relative, charge, protégé, ward, client, hanger-on, henchman, minion, subordinate, parasite.

dependence n 1 RELIANCE, confidence, faith, trust, need, expectation. 2 SUBORDINATION, attachment, subservience, helplessness, addiction.

■ 2 independence.

dependent adj 1 RELIANT, helpless, weak, immature, subject, subordinate, vulnerable. 2 CONTINGENT, conditional, determined by, relative.

■ 1 independent.

depend on v 1 RELY UPON, count on, bank on (*infml*), calculate on, reckon on (*infml*), build upon, trust in, lean on, expect. 2 HINGE ON, rest on, revolve around, be contingent upon, hang on.

depict v portray, illustrate, delineate, sketch, outline, draw, picture, paint, trace, describe, characterize, detail.

deplete v empty, drain, exhaust, evacuate, use up, expend, run down, reduce, lessen, decrease.

deplorable adj 1 GRIEVOUS, lamentable, pitiable, regrettable, unfortunate, wretched, distressing, sad, miserable, heartbreaking, melancholy, disastrous, dire, appalling. 2 REPREHENSIBLE, disgraceful, scandalous, shameful, dishonourable, disreputable.

■ 1 excellent. 2 commendable.

deplore v **1** GRIEVE FOR, lament, mourn, regret, bemoan, rue. **2** CENSURE, condemn, denounce, deprecate.
🔁 **2** extol.

deploy v dispose, arrange, position, station, use, utilize, distribute.

deport v expel, banish, exile, extradite, transport, expatriate, oust, ostracize.

deportation n expulsion, banishment, exile, extradition, repatriation, transportation, ousting, ostracism.

deportment n manner, air, appearance, aspect, bearing, behaviour, carriage, conduct, pose, posture, stance, etiquette, comportment (fml), demeanour (fml), mien (fml).

depose v demote, dethrone, downgrade, dismiss, unseat, topple, disestablish, displace, oust.

deposit v **1** LAY, drop, place, put, settle, dump (infml), park, precipitate, sit, locate. **2** SAVE, store, hoard, bank, amass, consign, entrust, lodge, file.
➤ n **1** SEDIMENT, accumulation, dregs, precipitate, lees, silt. **2** SECURITY, stake, down payment, pledge, retainer, instalment, part payment, money.

depot n **1** military depot: storehouse, store, warehouse, depository, repository, arsenal. **2** bus depot: station, garage, terminus.

deprave v corrupt, debauch, debase, degrade, pervert, subvert, infect, demoralize, seduce.
🔁 improve, reform.

depraved adj corrupt, debauched, degenerate, perverted, debased, dissolute, immoral, base, shameless, licentious, wicked, sinful, vile, evil.
🔁 moral, upright.

depravity n corruption, debauchery, degeneracy, perversion, debasement, reprobacy, dissoluteness, immorality, baseness, wickedness, sinfulness, vileness, evil, iniquity, vice, turpitude (fml).
🔁 uprightness.

deprecate (fml) v deplore, condemn, censure, disapprove of, object to, protest at, reject.
🔁 approve, commend.

depreciate v **1** DEVALUE, deflate, downgrade, decrease, reduce, lower, drop, fall, lessen, decline, slump. **2** DISPARAGE, belittle, undervalue, underestimate, underrate, slight.
🔁 **1** appreciate. **2** overrate.

depreciation n **1** DEVALUATION, deflation, depression, slump, fall. **2** DISPARAGEMENT, belittlement, underestimation.

depress v **1** DEJECT, sadden, dishearten, discourage, oppress, upset, daunt, burden, overburden. **2** WEAKEN, undermine, sap, tire, drain, exhaust, weary, impair, reduce, lessen, press, lower, level. **3** DEVALUE, bring down, lower.
🔁 **1** cheer. **2** fortify. **3** increase, raise.

depressed adj **1** DEJECTED, low-spirited, melancholy, dispirited, sad, unhappy, low, down, downcast, disheartened, fed up (infml), miserable, moody, cast down, discouraged, glum, downhearted, distressed, despondent, morose, crestfallen, pessimistic. **2** POOR, disadvantaged, deprived, destitute. **3** SUNKEN, recessed, concave, hollow, indented, dented.
🔁 **1** cheerful. **2** affluent. **3** convex, protuberant.

depressing adj dejecting, dismal, bleak, gloomy, saddening, cheerless, dreary, disheartening, sad, melancholy, sombre, grey, black, daunting, discouraging, heartbreaking, distressing, hopeless.
🔁 cheerful, encouraging.

depression n **1** DEJECTION, despair, despondency, melancholy, low spirits, sadness, gloominess, doldrums, blues (infml), glumness, dumps (infml), hopelessness. **2** RECESSION, slump, stagnation, hard times, decline, inactivity. **3** INDENTATION, hollow, dip, concavity, dent, dimple, valley, pit, sink, dint, bowl, cavity, basin, impression, dish, excavation.
🔁 **1** cheerfulness. **2** prosperity, boom. **3** convexity, protuberance.

deprivation n **1** deprivation of sleep: denial, withdrawal, withholding, removal, lack, dispossession. **2** deprivation in inner cities: hardship, poverty, want, need, disadvantage, destitution (fml), privation (fml), penury (fml).

deprive v **1** DISPOSSESS, strip, divest, denude, bereave, expropriate, rob. **2** DENY, withhold, refuse.
🔁 **1** endow. **2** provide.

deprived adj poor, needy, underprivileged, disadvantaged, impoverished, destitute, lacking, bereft.
🔁 prosperous.

depth n **1** DEEPNESS, profoundness, extent, measure, drop, profundity (fml). **2** INTENSITY, strength, thoroughness, seriousness, severity, gravity, earnestness, passion, vigour, fervour. **3** WISDOM, insight, discernment, perception, penetration, awareness, intuition, astuteness, cleverness, shrewdness, acumen, profundity (fml). **4** the depths of their knowledge: extent, extensiveness, scope, amount, profundity (fml). **5** depth of colour: intensity, strength, richness, vividness, brilliance, warmth, glow, darkness. **6** the depths of the sea: remotest area, bed, floor, bottom, abyss, deep, gulf, middle, midst.
Ea 1 shallowness. **6** surface.
♦ **in depth** comprehensively, thoroughly, exhaustively, extensively, in detail.
Ea superficially, broadly.

deputation n commission, delegation, embassy, mission, representatives, legation.

deputize v **1** REPRESENT, stand in for, substitute, replace, understudy, double. **2** DELEGATE, commission.

deputy n representative, agent, delegate, proxy, substitute, second-in-command, ambassador, commissioner, lieutenant, surrogate, subordinate, assistant, locum.

deranged adj disordered, demented, crazy, mad, lunatic, insane, unbalanced, disturbed, confused, frantic, delirious, distraught, berserk.
Ea sane, calm.

derelict adj abandoned, neglected, deserted, forsaken, desolate, discarded, dilapidated, ruined.

dereliction n **1** DILAPIDATION, abandonment, neglect, desertion, forsaking, desolation, ruin(s), disrepair. **2** dereliction of duty: abdication, abandonment, desertion, evasion, failure, faithlessness, forsaking, betrayal, neglect, negligence, relinquishment, remissness, renunciation, apostasy (fml), renegation (fml).
Ea 2 devotion, faithfulness, fulfilment.

deride v ridicule, mock, scoff, scorn, jeer, sneer, satirize, knock (infml), gibe, disparage, insult, belittle, disdain, taunt.
Ea respect, praise.

derision n ridicule, mockery, scorn, contempt, scoffing, satire, sneering, disrespect, insult, disparagement, disdain.
Ea respect, praise.

derisive adj mocking, scornful, contemptuous, disrespectful, irreverent, jeering, disdainful, taunting.
Ea respectful, flattering.

derisory adj laughable, ludicrous, absurd, ridiculous, contemptible, insulting, outrageous, preposterous, tiny, paltry, risible (fml).

derivation n source, origin, root, beginning, etymology, extraction, foundation, genealogy, ancestry, basis, descent, deduction, inference.

derivative adj unoriginal, acquired, copied, borrowed, derived, imitative, obtained, second-hand, secondary, plagiarized, cribbed (infml), hackneyed, trite.
➤ n derivation, offshoot, by-product, development, branch, outgrowth, spin-off, product, descendant.

derive v **1** GAIN, obtain, get, draw, extract, receive, procure, acquire, borrow. **2** ORIGINATE, arise, spring, flow, emanate, descend, proceed, stem, issue, follow, develop. **3** INFER, deduce, trace, gather, glean.

derogatory adj insulting, pejorative, offensive, disparaging, depreciative, critical, defamatory, injurious.
Ea flattering.

descend v **1** DROP, go down, fall, plummet, plunge, tumble, swoop, sink, arrive, alight, dismount, dip, slope, subside. **2** DEGENERATE, deteriorate. **3** CONDESCEND, deign, stoop. **4** ORIGINATE, proceed, spring, stem.
Ea 1 ascend, rise.

descendants n offspring, children, issue, progeny, successors, lineage, line, seed (fml).

descent n **1** FALL, drop, plunge, dip, decline, incline, slope. **2** COMEDOWN, debasement, degradation. **3** ANCESTRY, parentage, heredity, family tree, genealogy, lineage, extraction, origin.
Ea 1 ascent, rise.

describe v portray, depict, delineate, illustrate, characterize, specify, draw, define, detail, explain, express, tell, narrate, outline, relate, recount, present, report, sketch, mark out, trace.

description n **1** PORTRAYAL, representation, characterization, account, delineation, depiction, sketch, presentation, report, outline, explanation, exposition, narration. **2** SORT, type, kind, variety, specification, order.

descriptive *adj* illustrative, explanatory, expressive, detailed, graphic, colourful, pictorial, vivid.

desecrate *v* defile, violate, pervert, pollute, profane, contaminate, debase, dishallow, dishonour, insult, abuse, blaspheme, vandalize, violate.

desert¹ *n* wasteland, wilderness, wilds, void.

➤ *adj* bare, barren, waste, wild, uninhabited, uncultivated, dry, arid, infertile, desolate, sterile, solitary.

Deserts of the world, with locations, include: Sahara, N Africa; Arabian, SW Asia; Gobi, Mongolia and NE China; Patagonian, Argentina; Great Basin, SW USA; Chihuahuan, Mexico; Great Sandy, NW Australia; Nubian, Sudan; Great Victoria, SW Australia; Thar, India/Pakistan; Sonoran, SW USA; Kara Kum, Turkmenistan; Kyzyl-Kum, Kazakhstan; Takla Makan, N China; Kalahari, SW Africa.

desert² *v* abandon, forsake, leave, maroon, strand, decamp, defect, give up, renounce, relinquish, jilt, abscond, quit.
■ stand by, support.

desert³ *n* **1** DUE, right, reward, deserts, return, retribution, come-uppance (*infml*), payment, recompense, remuneration. **2** WORTH, merit, virtue.

deserted *adj* abandoned, forsaken, empty, derelict, desolate, godforsaken, neglected, underpopulated, stranded, isolated, bereft, vacant, betrayed, lonely, solitary, unoccupied.
■ populous.

deserter *n* runaway, absconder, escapee, truant, renegade, defector, rat (*infml*), traitor, fugitive, betrayer, apostate, backslider, delinquent.

deserve *v* earn, be worthy of, merit, be entitled to, warrant, justify, win, rate, incur.

deserved *adj* due, earned, merited, justifiable, warranted, right, rightful, well-earned, suitable, proper, fitting, fair, just, appropriate, apt, legitimate, apposite, meet (*fml*).
■ gratuitous, undeserved.

deserving *adj* worthy, estimable, exemplary, praiseworthy, admirable, commendable, laudable, righteous.

■ undeserving, unworthy.

design *n* **1** BLUEPRINT, draft, pattern, plan, prototype, sketch, drawing, outline, model, guide. **2** STYLE, shape, form, figure, structure, organization, arrangement, composition, construction, motif. **3** AIM, intention, goal, purpose, plan, end, object, objective, scheme, plot, project, meaning, target, undertaking.

➤ *v* **1** PLAN, plot, intend, devise, purpose, aim, scheme, shape, project, propose, tailor, mean. **2** SKETCH, draft, outline, draw (up). **3** INVENT, originate, conceive, create, think up, develop, construct, fashion, form, model, fabricate, make.

designate *v* **1** *designated as a listed building*: call, name, title, entitle, term, dub, style, describe, christen. **2** *designated to be chairman*: choose, appoint, nominate, select, elect, assign, specify, define, stipulate, earmark, set aside, show, denote, indicate.

designation *n* **1** NAME, title, label, epithet, nickname. **2** INDICATION, specification, description, definition, classification, category. **3** NOMINATION, appointment, selection.

designer *n* deviser, originator, maker, stylist, inventor, creator, contriver, fashioner, architect, author.

designing *adj* artful, crafty, scheming, conspiring, devious, intriguing, plotting, tricky, wily, sly, deceitful, cunning, guileful, underhand, sharp, shrewd.
■ artless, naïve.

desirable *adj* **1** ADVANTAGEOUS, profitable, worthwhile, advisable, appropriate, expedient, beneficial, preferable, sensible, eligible, good, pleasing. **2** ATTRACTIVE, alluring, sexy (*infml*), seductive, fetching, tempting.
■ **1** undesirable. **2** unattractive.

desire *v* **1** ASK, request, petition, solicit. **2** WANT, wish for, covet, long for, need, crave, hunger for, yearn for, fancy (*infml*), hanker after.

➤ *n* **1** WANT, longing, wish, need, yearning, craving, hankering, appetite, aspiration. **2** LUST, passion, concupiscence (*fml*), ardour. **3** REQUEST, petition, appeal, supplication.

desirous *adj* ready, willing, ambitious, aspiring, avid, burning, craving, itching, eager, enthusiastic, hopeful, hoping, keen, longing, anxious, wishing, yearning.
■ reluctant, unenthusiastic.

desist v stop, cease, leave off, refrain, discontinue, end, break off, give up, halt, abstain, suspend, pause, peter out, remit, forbear (*fml*).
E3 continue, resume.

desk n bureau, lectern, reading-desk, davenport, écritoire, secretaire, writing-table, ambo.

desolate adj 1 DESERTED, uninhabited, abandoned, unfrequented, barren, bare, arid, bleak, gloomy, dismal, dreary, lonely, god-forsaken, forsaken, waste, depressing. 2 FORLORN, bereft, depressed, dejected, forsaken, despondent, distressed, melancholy, miserable, lonely, gloomy, disheartened, dismal, downcast, solitary, wretched.
E3 1 populous. 2 cheerful.
➤ v devastate, lay waste, destroy, despoil, spoil, wreck, denude, depopulate, ruin, waste, ravage, plunder, pillage.

desolation n 1 DESTRUCTION, ruin, devastation, ravages. 2 DEJECTION, despair, despondency, gloom, misery, sadness, melancholy, sorrow, unhappiness, anguish, grief, distress, wretchedness. 3 BARRENNESS, bleakness, emptiness, forlornness, loneliness, isolation, solitude, wildness.

despair v lose heart, lose hope, give up, give in, collapse, surrender.
E3 hope.
➤ n despondency, gloom, hopelessness, desperation, anguish, inconsolableness, melancholy, misery, wretchedness.
E3 cheerfulness, resilience.

despairing adj despondent, distraught, inconsolable, desolate, desperate, heart-broken, suicidal, grief-stricken, hopeless, disheartened, dejected, miserable, wretched, sorrowful, dismayed, downcast.
E3 cheerful, hopeful.

despatch see **dispatch**.

desperado n bandit, criminal, brigand, gangster, hoodlum (*infml*), outlaw, ruffian, thug, cut-throat, law-breaker.

desperate adj 1 HOPELESS, inconsolable, wretched, despondent, abandoned. 2 RECKLESS, rash, impetuous, audacious, daring, dangerous, do-or-die, foolhardy, risky, hazardous, hasty, precipitate, wild, violent, frantic, frenzied, determined. 3 CRITICAL, acute, serious, severe, extreme, urgent.
E3 1 hopeful. 2 cautious.

desperately adv dangerously, critically, gravely, hopelessly, seriously, severely, badly, dreadfully, fearfully, frightfully.

desperation n 1 DESPAIR, despondency, anguish, hopelessness, misery, agony, distress, pain, sorrow, trouble, worry, anxiety. 2 RECKLESSNESS, rashness, frenzy, madness, hastiness.

despicable adj contemptible, vile, worthless, detestable, disgusting, mean, wretched, disgraceful, disreputable, shameful, reprobate.
E3 admirable, noble.

despise v scorn, deride, look down on, disdain, condemn, spurn, undervalue, slight, revile, deplore, dislike, detest, loathe.
E3 admire.

despite prep in spite of, notwithstanding, regardless of, in the face of, undeterred by, against, defying.

despondent adj depressed, dejected, disheartened, downcast, down, low, gloomy, glum, discouraged, miserable, melancholy, sad, sorrowful, doleful, despairing, heart-broken, inconsolable, mournful, wretched.
E3 cheerful, heartened, hopeful.

despot n autocrat, tyrant, dictator, oppressor, absolutist, boss.

despotic adj autocratic, tyrannical, imperious, oppressive, dictatorial, authoritarian, domineering, absolute, overbearing, arbitrary, arrogant.
E3 democratic, egalitarian, liberal, tolerant.

despotism n autocracy, totalitarianism, tyranny, dictatorship, absolutism, oppression, repression.
E3 democracy, egalitarianism, liberalism, tolerance.

destination n 1 GOAL, aim, objective, object, purpose, target, end, intention, aspiration, design, ambition. 2 JOURNEY'S END, terminus, station, stop.

destined adj 1 FATED, doomed, inevitable, predetermined, ordained, certain, foreordained, meant, unavoidable, inescapable, intended, designed, appointed. 2 BOUND, directed, en route, headed, heading, scheduled, assigned, booked.

destiny n fate, doom, fortune, karma, lot (*fml*), portion (*fml*), predestiny, kismet.

destitute *adj* **1** LACKING, needy, wanting, devoid of, bereft, innocent of, deprived, deficient, depleted. **2** POOR, penniless, poverty-stricken, impoverished, down and out (*infml*), distressed, bankrupt.
ea 2 prosperous, rich.

destitution *n* poverty, pennilessness, impoverishment, distress, bankruptcy, beggary, starvation, straits, impecuniousness (*fml*), indigence (*fml*), penury (*fml*).
ea prosperity, wealth.

destroy *v* **1** DEMOLISH, ruin, shatter, wreck, devastate, smash, break, crush, overthrow, sabotage, undo, dismantle, thwart, undermine, waste, gut, level, ravage, raze, torpedo, unshape. **2** KILL, annihilate, eliminate, extinguish, eradicate, dispatch, slay (*fml*), nullify.
ea 1 build up. **2** create.

destruction *n* **1** RUIN, devastation, shattering, crushing, wreckage, demolition, defeat, downfall, overthrow, ruination, desolation, undoing, wastage, havoc, ravagement. **2** ANNIHILATION, extermination, eradication, elimination, extinction, slaughter, massacre, end, liquidation, nullification.
ea 2 creation.

destructive *adj* **1** *destructive storms*: devastating, damaging, catastrophic, disastrous, deadly, harmful, fatal, disruptive, lethal, ruinous, detrimental, hurtful, malignant, mischievous, nullifying, slaughterous. **2** *destructive criticism*: adverse, hostile, negative, discouraging, disparaging, contrary, undermining, subversive, vicious.
ea 1 creative. **2** constructive.

desultory *adj* random, erratic, aimless, disorderly, haphazard, irregular, spasmodic, inconsistent, undirected, unco-ordinated, unsystematic, unmethodical, fitful, disconnected, loose, capricious.
ea systematic, methodical.

detach *v* separate, disconnect, unfasten, disjoin, cut off, disengage, remove, undo, uncouple, sever, dissociate, isolate, loosen, free, unfix, unhitch, segregate, divide, disentangle, estrange.
ea attach.

detached *adj* **1** SEPARATE, disconnected, dissociated, severed, free, loose, divided, discrete. **2** ALOOF, dispassionate,

impersonal, neutral, impartial, independent, disinterested, objective.
ea 1 connected. **2** involved.

detachment *n* **1** ALOOFNESS, remoteness, coolness, unconcern, indifference, impassivity, disinterestedness, neutrality, impartiality, objectivity, fairness. **2** SEPARATION, disconnection, disunion, disengagement. **3** SQUAD, unit, force, corps, brigade, patrol, task force.

detail *n* particular, item, factor, element, aspect, component, feature, point, specific, ingredient, attribute, count, respect, technicality, complication, intricacy, triviality, fact, thoroughness, elaboration, meticulousness, refinement, nicety.
➤ *v* **1** LIST, enumerate, itemize, specify, catalogue, recount, relate. **2** ASSIGN, appoint, charge, delegate, commission.

detailed *adj* comprehensive, exhaustive, full, blow-by-blow (*infml*), thorough, minute, exact, specific, particular, itemized, intricate, elaborate, complex, complicated, meticulous, descriptive.
ea cursory, general.

detain *v* **1** DELAY, hold (up), hinder, impede, check, retard, slow, stay, stop. **2** CONFINE, arrest, intern, hold, restrain, keep.
ea 2 release.

detect *v* **1** NOTICE, ascertain, note, observe, perceive, recognize, discern, distinguish, identify, sight, spot, spy. **2** UNCOVER, catch, discover, disclose, expose, find, track down, unmask, reveal.

detection *n* **1** NOTICING, ascertaining, note, observation, perception, recognition, discernment, distinguishing, identification, sighting. **2** UNCOVERING, discovery, disclosure, exposé, exposure, tracking-down, smelling-out, sniffing-out, unearthing, unmasking, revelation.

detective *n* investigator, private eye (*infml*), sleuth (*infml*), sleuth-hound (*infml*), operative (*US*).

detention *n* **1** DETAINMENT, custody, confinement, imprisonment, restraint, incarceration, constraint, quarantine. **2** DELAY, hindrance, holding back.
ea 1 release.

deter *v* discourage, put off, inhibit, intimidate, dissuade, daunt, turn off (*infml*), check, caution, warn, restrain,

hinder, frighten, disincline, prevent, prohibit, stop.
◼ encourage.

detergent n cleaner, cleanser, soap, washing powder, washing-up liquid, abstergent (fml).

deteriorate v **1** WORSEN, decline, degenerate, depreciate, go downhill (infml), fail, fall off, lapse, slide, relapse, slip. **2** DECAY, disintegrate, decompose, weaken, fade.
◼ **1** improve. **2** progress.

deterioration n worsening, decline, degeneration, drop, failure, falling-off, downturn, lapse, slide, relapse, slipping, waning, ebb, atrophy, corrosion, debasement, degradation, disintegration, retrogression (fml), exacerbation (fml), pejoration (fml).
◼ improvement.

determination n **1** RESOLUTENESS, tenacity, firmness, will-power, perseverance, persistence, purpose, backbone, guts (infml), grit (infml), steadfastness, single-mindedness, will, insistence, conviction, dedication, drive, fortitude. **2** DECISION, judgement, settlement, resolution, conclusion.
◼ **1** irresolution.

Informal expressions showing determination include: mean business, stick to one's guns, go to great lengths, go all out, go to extremes, go the whole hog, go for it, move heaven and earth, stop at nothing, do one's utmost, give one's all, leave no stone unturned, pull out all the stops, put one's heart and soul into, strain every nerve, be hell-bent, get stuck into.

determine v **1** DECIDE, settle, resolve, make up one's mind, choose, conclude, fix on, elect, clinch, finish. **2** DISCOVER, establish, find out, ascertain, identify, check, detect, verify. **3** AFFECT, influence, govern, control, dictate, direct, guide, regulate, ordain.

determined adj resolute, firm, purposeful, strong-willed, single-minded, persevering, persistent, strong-minded, steadfast, tenacious, dogged, insistent, intent, fixed, convinced, decided, unflinching.
◼ irresolute, wavering.

deterrent n hindrance, impediment, obstacle, repellent, check, bar,

discouragement, obstruction, curb, restraint, difficulty.
◼ incentive, encouragement.

detest v hate, abhor, loathe, abominate, execrate (fml), dislike, recoil from, deplore, despise.
◼ adore, love.

detestable adj hateful, loathsome, abhorrent, abominable, repellent, obnoxious, execrable (fml), despicable, revolting, repulsive, repugnant, offensive, vile, disgusting, accursed (fml), heinous, shocking, sordid.
◼ adorable, admirable.

detonate v blow up, discharge, blast, explode, ignite, kindle, set off, let off, spark off, fulminate (fml).

detour n deviation, diversion, indirect route, circuitous route, roundabout route, digression, byroad, byway, bypath, bypass.

detract (from) v diminish, subtract from, take away from, reduce, lessen, lower, devaluate, depreciate, belittle, disparage.
◼ add to, enhance, praise.

detractor n backbiter, belittler, defamer, slanderer, muck-raker, reviler, scandalmonger, enemy, denigrator (fml), disparager (fml), traducer (fml), vilifier (fml).
◼ flatterer, supporter, defender.

detriment n damage, harm, hurt, disadvantage, loss, ill, injury, disservice, evil, mischief, prejudice.
◼ advantage, benefit.

detrimental adj damaging, harmful, hurtful, adverse, disadvantageous, injurious, prejudicial, mischievous, destructive.
◼ advantageous, favourable, beneficial.

devastate v **1** DESTROY, desolate, lay waste, demolish, spoil, despoil, wreck, ruin, ravage, waste, ransack, plunder, level, raze, pillage, sack. **2** DISCONCERT, overwhelm, take aback, confound, shatter (infml), floor (infml), nonplus, discomfit.

devastating adj **1** devastating storms: destructive, disastrous. **2** a devastating argument: effective, incisive, overwhelming, stunning.

devastation n destruction, desolation, havoc, ruin, wreckage, ravages, demolition, annihilation, pillage, plunder, spoliation.

develop v **1** ADVANCE, evolve, expand,

progress, foster, flourish, mature, prosper, branch out. **2** ELABORATE, amplify, argument, enhance, unfold. **3** ACQUIRE, contract, begin, generate, create, invent. **4** RESULT, come about, grow, ensue, arise, follow, happen.

development *n* **1** GROWTH, evolution, advance, blossoming, elaboration, furtherance, progress, unfolding, expansion, extension, spread, increase, improvement, maturity, promotion, refinement, issue. **2** OCCURRENCE, happening, event, change, outcome, situation, result, phenomenon.

deviant *adj* divergent, aberrant, anomalous, abnormal, irregular, variant, bizarre, eccentric, quirky, freakish, perverse, perverted, twisted, wayward, bent (*infml*), kinky (*infml*), oddball (*infml*), with a screw loose (*infml*), with bats in the belfry (*infml*).
✇ normal.
➢ *n* freak, oddity, misfit, dropout, odd sort, pervert, oddball (*infml*), kook (*infml*), crank (*infml*), weirdo (*infml*), geek (*sl*), goof (*sl*).
✇ straight.

deviate *v* diverge, veer, turn (aside), digress, swerve, vary, differ, depart, stray, yaw, wander, err, go astray, go off the rails (*infml*), drift, part.

deviation *n* divergence, aberration, departure, abnormality, irregularity, variance, variation, digression, eccentricity, anomaly, deflection, alteration, disparity, discrepancy, detour, fluctuation, change, quirk, shift, freak.
✇ conformity, regularity.

device *n* **1** TOOL, implement, appliance, gadget, contrivance, contraption (*infml*), apparatus, utensil, instrument, machine. **2** SCHEME, ruse, strategy, plan, plot, gambit, manoeuvre, wile, trick, dodge (*infml*), machination. **3** EMBLEM, symbol, motif, logo (*infml*), design, insignia, crest, badge, shield.

devil *n* **1** DEMON, Satan, fiend, evil spirit, arch-fiend, Lucifer, imp, Evil One, Prince of Darkness, Adversary, Beelzebub, Mephistopheles, Old Nick (*infml*), Old Harry (*infml*). **2** BRUTE, rogue, monster, ogre.

devilish *adj* diabolical, diabolic, fiendish, satanic, demonic, hellish, damnable, evil, infernal, wicked, vile, atrocious, dreadful, outrageous, shocking, disastrous,

excruciating, accursed, execrable (*fml*).

devious *adj* **1** UNDERHAND, deceitful, dishonest, disingenuous, double-dealing, scheming, tricky (*infml*), insidious, insincere, calculating, cunning, evasive, wily, sly, slippery (*infml*), surreptitious, treacherous, misleading. **2** INDIRECT, circuitous, rambling, roundabout, wandering, winding, tortuous, erratic.
✇ straightforward.

devise *v* invent, contrive, plan, plot, design, conceive, arrange, formulate, imagine, scheme, construct, concoct, forge, frame, project, shape, form.

devoid *adj* lacking, wanting, without, free, bereft, destitute, deficient, deprived, barren, empty, vacant, void.
✇ endowed.

devolution *n* decentralization, delegation of power, distribution, transference of power, dispersal.
✇ centralization.

devolve *v* hand down, delegate, transfer, consign, convey, deliver, depute, entrust, commission, fall to, rest with.

devote *v* dedicate, consecrate, commit, give oneself, set apart, set aside, reserve, apply, allocate, allot, sacrifice, enshrine, assign, appropriate, surrender, pledge.

devoted *adj* dedicated, ardent, committed, loyal, faithful, devout, loving, staunch, steadfast, true, constant, fond, unswerving, tireless, concerned, attentive, caring.
✇ indifferent, disloyal.

devotee *n* enthusiast, fan (*infml*), fanatic, addict, aficionado, follower, supporter, zealot, adherent, admirer, disciple, buff (*infml*), freak (*infml*), merchant (*infml*), fiend (*infml*), hound.

devotion *n* **1** DEDICATION, commitment, consecration, ardour, loyalty, allegiance, adherence, zeal, support, love, passion, fervour, fondness, attachment, adoration, affection, faithfulness, reverence, steadfastness, regard, earnestness. **2** DEVOUTNESS, piety, godliness, faith, holiness, spirituality. **3** PRAYER, worship.
✇ **1** inconstancy. **2** irreverence.

devour *v* **1** EAT, consume, guzzle, gulp, gorge, gobble, bolt, wolf down, swallow, stuff (*infml*), cram, polish off (*infml*), gormandize, feast on, relish, revel in. **2** DESTROY, consume, absorb, engulf, ravage, dispatch.

devout *adj* 1 SINCERE, earnest, devoted, fervent, genuine, staunch, steadfast, ardent, passionate, serious, wholehearted, constant, faithful, intense, heartfelt, zealous, unswerving, deep, profound. 2 PIOUS, godly, religious, reverent, prayerful, saintly, holy, orthodox.
Ea 1 insincere. 2 irreligious.

dexterity *n* deftness, adeptness, address, adroitness, agility, handiness, nimbleness, proficiency, mastery, readiness, skilfulness, ability, skill, expertise, aptitude, art, artistry, expertness, facility, knack, finesse, legerdemain, sleight, ingenuity, effortlessness.
Ea clumsiness, awkwardness, ineptitude.

dexterous *adj* deft, adroit, agile, able, nimble, proficient, skilful, clever, expert, nifty, nippy, handy, facile, nimble-fingered, neat-handed.
Ea clumsy, inept, awkward.

diabolical *adj* devilish, fiendish, demonic, hellish, damnable, evil, infernal, wicked, vile, dreadful, outrageous, shocking, disastrous, excruciating, atrocious.

diagnose *v* identify, determine, recognize, pinpoint, distinguish, analyse, explain, isolate, interpret, investigate.

diagnosis *n* identification, verdict, explanation, conclusion, answer, interpretation, analysis, opinion, investigation, examination, scrutiny.

diagonal *adj* oblique, slanting, cross, crosswise, sloping, crooked, angled, cornerways.

diagonally *adv* obliquely, crossways, crosswise, at an angle, cornerwise, on the cross, on the slant, slantwise, aslant, on the bias.

diagram *n* plan, sketch, chart, drawing, figure, representation, schema, illustration, outline, graph, picture, layout, table.

dial *n* circle, disc, face, clock, control.
➤ *v* phone, ring, call (up).

dialect *n* idiom, language, regionalism, patois, provincialism, vernacular, argot, jargon, accent, lingo (*infml*), speech, diction.

dialectic *adj* dialectical, logical, rational, argumentative, analytical, rationalistic, logistic, polemical, inductive, deductive.
➤ *n* dialectics, logic, reasoning, rationale,

disputation, analysis, debate, argumentation, contention, discussion, polemics, induction, deduction.

dialogue *n* 1 CONVERSATION, interchange, discourse, communication, talk, exchange, discussion, converse, debate, conference. 2 LINES, script.

diametric *adj* diametrical, opposed, opposite, contrary, counter, contrasting, antithetical.

diametrically *adv* directly, completely, absolutely, utterly, antithetically (*fml*).

diarrhoea *n* looseness of the bowels, gippy tummy, holiday tummy, Montezuma's revenge, dysentery, the runs (*infml*), the trots (*infml*), Spanish tummy (*infml*), Delhi belly (*infml*), Aztec two-step (*sl*).
Ea constipation.

diary *n* journal, day-book, logbook, chronicle, year-book, appointment book, engagement book.

diatribe *n* tirade, invective, abuse, harangue, attack, onslaught, denunciation, criticism, insult, reviling, upbraiding.
Ea praise, eulogy.

dicey (*infml*) *adj* risky, chancy, unpredictable, tricky, problematic, dangerous, difficult, iffy (*infml*), dubious, hairy (*infml*).
Ea certain.

dictate *v* 1 SAY, speak, utter, announce, pronounce, transmit. 2 COMMAND, order, direct, decree, instruct, rule.
➤ *n* command, decree, precept, principle, rule, direction, injunction, edict, order, ruling, statute, requirement, ordinance, law, bidding, mandate, ultimatum, word.

dictator *n* despot, autocrat, tyrant, supremo (*infml*), Big Brother (*infml*).

dictatorial *adj* tyrannical, despotic, totalitarian, authoritarian, autocratic, oppressive, imperious, domineering, bossy (*infml*), absolute, repressive, overbearing, arbitrary, dogmatic.
Ea democratic, egalitarian, liberal.

dictatorship *n* tyranny, despotism, totalitarianism, authoritarianism, autocracy, absolute rule, fascism, police state, reign of terror, Hitlerism.
Ea democracy, egalitarianism.

diction *n* speech, articulation, language, elocution, enunciation, intonation, pronunciation, inflection, fluency, delivery, expression, phrasing.

dictionary *n* lexicon, glossary, thesaurus, vocabulary, wordbook, encyclopaedia, concordance.

dictum *n* pronouncement, ruling, maxim, decree, dictate, edict, fiat (*fml*), precept, axiom, command, order, utterance.

didactic *adj* instructive, educational, educative, pedagogic, prescriptive, pedantic, moralizing, moral.

die *v* 1 DECEASE, perish, pass away, expire, depart, breathe one's last, peg out (*infml*), snuff it (*sl*), bite the dust (*infml*), kick the bucket (*sl*). 2 DWINDLE, fade, ebb, sink, wane, wilt, wither, peter out, decline, decay, finish, lapse, end, disappear, vanish, subside. 3 LONG FOR, pine for, yearn, desire.
Ea 1 live.
♦ **die away** fade, become weak, become faint, disappear.
♦ **die down** decrease, subside, decline, quieten, stop.
♦ **die out** become rarer/less common, disappear, vanish, peter out (*infml*).

die-hard *n* reactionary, intransigent, hardliner, blimp (*infml*), ultra-conservative, old fogey (*infml*), stick-in-the-mud (*infml*), rightist, fanatic.

diet *n* 1 FOOD, nutrition, provisions, sustenance, rations, foodstuffs, subsistence. 2 FAST, abstinence, regimen.
➢ *v* lose weight, slim, fast, reduce, abstain, weight-watch (*infml*).

differ *v* 1 VARY, diverge, deviate, depart from, contradict, contrast. 2 DISAGREE, argue, conflict, oppose, dispute, dissent, be at odds with, clash, quarrel, fall out, debate, contend, take issue.
Ea 1 conform. 2 agree.

difference *n* 1 DISSIMILARITY, unlikeness, discrepancy, divergence, diversity, variation, variety, distinctness, distinction, deviation, differentiation, contrast, disparity, singularity, exception. 2 DISAGREEMENT, clash, dispute, conflict, contention, controversy. 3 REMAINDER, rest.
Ea 1 conformity. 2 agreement.

different *adj* 1 DISSIMILAR, unlike, contrasting, divergent, inconsistent, deviating, at odds, clashing, opposed. 2 VARIED, various, diverse, miscellaneous, assorted, disparate, many, numerous, several, sundry, other. 3 UNUSUAL,

unconventional, unique, distinct, distinctive, extraordinary, individual, original, special, strange, separate, peculiar, rare, bizarre, anomalous.
Ea 1 similar. 2 same. 3 conventional.

differentiate *v* distinguish, tell apart, discriminate, contrast, separate, mark off, individualize, particularize.

differentiation *n* distinction, distinguishing, discrimination, contrast, separation, demarcation, individualization, particularization, modification.
Ea assimilation, association, confusion, connection.

difficult *adj* 1 HARD, laborious, demanding, arduous, strenuous, tough, wearisome, uphill, formidable. 2 COMPLEX, complicated, intricate, involved, abstruse, obscure, dark, knotty, thorny, problematical, perplexing, abstract, baffling, intractable. 3 UNMANAGEABLE, perverse, troublesome, trying, unco-operative, tiresome, stubborn, obstinate, intractable.
Ea 1 easy. 2 straightforward. 3 manageable.

difficulty *n* 1 HARDSHIP, trouble, labour, arduousness, painfulness, trial, tribulation, awkwardness. 2 PROBLEM, predicament, dilemma, quandary, perplexity, embarrassment, plight, distress, fix (*infml*), mess (*infml*), jam (*infml*), spot (*infml*), hiccup (*infml*), hang-up. 3 OBSTACLE, hindrance, hurdle, impediment, objection, opposition, block, complication, pitfall, protest, stumbling-block.
Ea 1 ease.
♦ **in difficulties** having problems, in trouble, up against it (*infml*), stumped (*infml*), at the end of one's tether (*infml*), out of one's depth (*infml*), not knowing which way to turn (*infml*), in the soup (*infml*), in a fix/mess/jam/hole (*infml*), in dire straits (*infml*), in a scrape (*infml*), in hot/deep water (*infml*), in a tight spot (*infml*).

diffidence *n* unassertiveness, modesty, shyness, self-consciousness, self-effacement, timidity, insecurity, reserve, bashfulness, humility, inhibition, meekness, self-distrust, self-doubt, hesitancy, reluctance, backwardness.
Ea confidence.

diffident *adj* unassertive, modest, shy, timid, self-conscious, self-effacing, insecure, bashful, abashed, meek, reserved, withdrawn, tentative, shrinking, inhibited, hesitant, reluctant, unsure, shamefaced.

☒ assertive, confident.

diffuse *adj* **1** *diffuse outbreaks of rain*: scattered, unconcentrated, diffused, dispersed, disconnected. **2** *a diffuse prose style*: verbose, imprecise, wordy, rambling, long-winded, waffling (*infml*), vague, discursive.

☒ **1** concentrated. **2** succinct.

➤ *v* spread, scatter, disperse, distribute, propagate, dispense, disseminate, circulate, dissipate.

☒ concentrate.

dig *v* **1** EXCAVATE, penetrate, burrow, mine, quarry, scoop, tunnel, till, gouge, delve, pierce. **2** POKE, prod. **3** INVESTIGATE, probe, go into, research, search.

➤ *n* gibe, jeer, sneer, taunt, crack, insinuation, insult, wisecrack.

☒ compliment.

◆ dig up discover, unearth, uncover, disinter, expose, extricate, exhume, find, retrieve, track down.

☒ bury, obscure.

digest *v* **1** ABSORB, assimilate, incorporate, process, dissolve. **2** TAKE IN, absorb, understand, assimilate, grasp, study, consider, contemplate, meditate, ponder. **3** SHORTEN, summarize, condense, compress, reduce.

➤ *n* summary, abridgement, abstract, précis, synopsis, résumé, reduction, abbreviation, compression, compendium.

digestion *n* absorption, assimilation, breaking-down, transformation, ingestion (*fml*), eupepsia (*fml*).

digestive system

> Parts of the human digestive system include: alimentary canal, anus, bile, buccal cavity, colon, digestive enzymes, duodenum, gall bladder, gastric juices, ileum, intestine, large intestine, small intestine, jejunum, liver, mouth, oesophagus (gullet), pancreas, pancreatic juice, rectum, salivary glands, stomach.

dignified *adj* stately, solemn, imposing, majestic, noble, august, lordly, lofty, exalted, formal, distinguished, grave, impressive, reserved, honourable.

☒ undignified, lowly.

dignitary *n* worthy, notable, VIP (*infml*), high-up, personage, bigwig (*infml*).

dignity *n* stateliness, propriety, solemnity, decorum, courtliness, grandeur, loftiness, majesty, honour, eminence, importance, nobility, self-respect, self-esteem, standing, poise, respectability, greatness, status, pride.

digress *v* diverge, deviate, stray, wander, go off at a tangent, drift, depart, ramble.

digression *n* divergence, deviation, straying, wandering, aside, departure, diversion, footnote, parenthesis, excursus (*fml*).

dilapidated *adj* ramshackle, shabby, broken-down, neglected, tumble-down, uncared-for, rickety, decrepit, crumbling, run-down, worn-out, ruined, decayed, decaying.

dilate *v* distend, enlarge, expand, spread, broaden, widen, increase, extend, stretch, swell.

☒ contract.

dilatory *adj* delaying, procrastinating, slow, tardy, tarrying, sluggish, lingering, lackadaisical, slack.

☒ prompt.

dilemma *n* quandary, conflict, predicament, problem, catch-22 (*infml*), difficulty, puzzle, embarrassment, perplexity, plight.

dilettante *n* dabbler, amateur, trifler, potterer, aesthete (*fml*).

☒ professional.

diligence *n* assiduity, assiduousness, industry, conscientiousness, attention, care, thoroughness, dedication, attentiveness, application, constancy, earnestness, intentness, laboriousness, perseverance.

☒ laziness.

diligent *adj* assiduous, industrious, hard-working, conscientious, painstaking, busy, attentive, tireless, careful, meticulous, persevering, persistent, studious.

☒ negligent, lazy.

dilly-dally *v* dally, dawdle, delay, falter, hesitate, hover, linger, loiter, dither, potter, vacillate, waver, take one's time, procrastinate (*fml*), tarry (*fml*), shilly-shally (*infml*).

dilute *v* adulterate, water down, thin (out), attenuate, weaken, diffuse, diminish, decrease, lessen, reduce, temper, mitigate.

☒ concentrate.

dim *adj* **1** DARK, dull, dusky, cloudy,

shadowy, gloomy, sombre, dingy, lack-lustre, feeble, imperfect. **2** INDISTINCT, blurred, hazy, ill-defined, obscure, misty, unclear, foggy, fuzzy, vague, faint, weak. **3** STUPID, dense, obtuse, thick (*infml*), doltish.

Ea 1 bright. **2** distinct. **3** bright, intelligent.
➤ *v* darken, dull, obscure, cloud, blur, fade, tarnish, shade.
Ea brighten, illuminate.

dimension(s) *n* extent, measurement, measure, size, scope, magnitude, largeness, capacity, mass, scale, range, bulk, importance, greatness.

diminish *v* **1** DECREASE, lessen, reduce, lower, contract, decline, dwindle, shrink, recede, taper off, wane, weaken, abate, fade, sink, subside, ebb, slacken, cut. **2** BELITTLE, disparage, deprecate, devalue.
Ea 1 increase. **2** exaggerate.

diminution *n* reduction, lessening, contraction, decline, ebb, decrease, cut, cutback, curtailment, deduction, decay, subsidence, weakening, shortening, shrinkage, abatement (*fml*), retrenchment (*fml*).
Ea enlargement, increase, growth.

diminutive *adj* undersized, small, tiny, little, miniature, minute, infinitesimal, wee, petite, midget, mini (*infml*), teeny (*infml*), teeny-weeny (*infml*), Lilliputian, dinky (*infml*), pint-size(d) (*infml*), pocket(-sized), pygmy.
Ea big, large, oversized.

din *n* noise, row, racket, clash, clatter, clamour, pandemonium, uproar, commotion, crash, hullabaloo (*infml*), hubbub, outcry, shout, babble.
Ea quiet, calm.

dine *v* eat, feast, sup, lunch, banquet, feed.

dingy *adj* dark, drab, grimy, murky, faded, dull, dim, shabby, soiled, discoloured, dirty, dreary, gloomy, seedy, sombre, obscure, run-down, colourless, dusky, worn.
Ea bright, clean.

dinner *n* meal, supper, tea (*infml*), banquet, feast, spread, repast (*fml*).

dinosaur

Dinosaurs include: Ornithischia, Saurischia; Allosaurus, Ankylosaurus, Apatosaurus, Barosaurus, Brachiosaurus, Brontosaurus, Camptosaurus, Coelophysis, Compsognathus, Corythosaurus, Deinonychus, Diplodocus, Heterodontosaurus, Iguanodon, Ophiacodon, Ornithomimus, Pachycephalosaurus, Parasaurolophus, Plateosaurus, Stegosaurus, Styracosaurus, Triceratops, Tyrannosaurus.

dip *v* **1** PLUNGE, immerse, submerge, duck, dunk, bathe, douse, sink. **2** DESCEND, decline, drop, fall, subside, slump, sink, lower.
➤ *n* **1** HOLLOW, basin, decline, hole, concavity, incline, depression, fall, slope, slump, lowering. **2** BATHE, immersion, plunge, soaking, ducking, swim, drenching, infusion, dive.
◆ **dip into 1** *dip into a book*: look at, leaf through, look through, run through, flick through, thumb through, skim, browse. **2** *dip into your savings*: spend, draw on, use.

diplomacy *n* **1** TACT, tactfulness, finesse, delicacy, discretion, savoir-faire, subtlety, skill, craft. **2** STATECRAFT, statesmanship, politics, negotiation, manoeuvring.

diplomat *n* go-between, mediator, negotiator, ambassador, envoy, conciliator, peacemaker, moderator, politician.

diplomatic *adj* tactful, politic, discreet, judicious, subtle, sensitive, prudent, discreet.
Ea tactless.

dire *adj* **1** DISASTROUS, dreadful, awful, appalling, calamitous, catastrophic. **2** DESPERATE, urgent, grave, drastic, crucial, extreme, alarming, ominous.

direct *v* **1** CONTROL, manage, run, administer, organize, lead, govern, regulate, superintend, supervise. **2** INSTRUCT, command, order, charge. **3** GUIDE, lead, conduct, point. **4** AIM, point, focus, turn.
➤ *adj* **1** STRAIGHT, undeviating, through, uninterrupted. **2** STRAIGHTFORWARD, outspoken, blunt, frank, unequivocal, sincere, candid, honest, explicit. **3** IMMEDIATE, first-hand, face-to-face, personal.
Ea 1 circuitous. **2** equivocal. **3** indirect.

direction *n* **1** CONTROL, administration, management, government, supervision, guidance, leadership. **2** ROUTE, way, line, road.

directions *n* instructions, guidelines, orders, briefing, guidance, recommendations, indication, plan.

directive *n* command, instruction, order,

regulation, ruling, imperative, dictate, decree, charge, mandate, injunction, ordinance, edict, fiat, notice.

directly *adv* 1 IMMEDIATELY, instantly, promptly, right away, speedily, forthwith, instantaneously, quickly, soon, presently, straightaway, straight. 2 FRANKLY, bluntly, candidly, honestly.

director *n* manager, head, boss, chief, controller, executive, principal, governor, leader, organizer, supervisor, administrator, producer, conductor.

dirge *n* elegy, lament, funeral song, requiem, dead-march, coronach, threnody, monody.

dirt *n* 1 EARTH, soil, clay, dust, mud. 2 FILTH, grime, muck, mire, excrement, stain, smudge, slime, tarnish. 3 INDECENCY, impurity, obscenity, pornography.

dirty *adj* 1 FILTHY, grimy, grubby, mucky, soiled, unwashed, foul, messy, muddy, polluted, unsanitary, dull, mingy, scruffy, shabby, sullied, clouded, dark. 2 INDECENT, obscene, filthy, smutty, sordid, salacious, vulgar, pornographic, corrupt.
🔁 1 clean. 2 decent.
➤ *v* pollute, soil, stain, foul, mess up, defile, smear, smirch, spoil, smudge, sully, muddy, blacken.
🔁 clean, cleanse.

disability *n* handicap, impairment, disablement, disorder, inability, incapacity, infirmity, defect, unfitness, disqualification, affliction, ailment, complaint, weakness.

disable *v* cripple, lame, incapacitate, damage, handicap, impair, debilitate, disqualify, weaken, immobilize, invalidate, paralyse, prostrate.

disabled *adj* handicapped, incapacitated, impaired, infirm, crippled, lame, immobilized, maimed, weak, weakened, paralysed, wrecked.
🔁 able, able-bodied.

disadvantage *n* 1 HARM, damage, detriment, hurt, injury, loss, prejudice. 2 DRAWBACK, snag, hindrance, handicap, impediment, inconvenience, flaw, nuisance, weakness, trouble.
🔁 2 advantage, benefit.

disadvantaged *adj* deprived, underprivileged, poor, handicapped, impoverished, struggling.
🔁 privileged.

disadvantageous *adj* harmful, detrimental, inopportune, unfavourable, prejudicial, adverse, damaging, hurtful, injurious, inconvenient, ill-timed.
🔁 advantageous, auspicious.

disaffected *adj* disloyal, hostile, estranged, alienated, antagonistic, rebellious, dissatisfied, disgruntled, discontented.
🔁 loyal.

disaffection *n* disloyalty, hostility, alienation, discontentment, resentment, ill-will, dissatisfaction, animosity, coolness, unfriendliness, antagonism, disharmony, discord, disagreement, aversion, dislike.
🔁 loyalty, contentment.

disagree *v* 1 DISSENT, oppose, quarrel, argue, bicker, fall out (*infml*), wrangle, fight, squabble, contend, dispute, contest, object. 2 CONFLICT, clash, diverge, contradict, counter, differ, deviate, depart, run counter to, vary.
🔁 1 agree. 2 correspond.

disagreeable *adj* 1 *a disagreeable old man*: bad-tempered, ill-humoured, difficult, peevish, rude, surly, churlish, irritable, contrary, cross, brusque. 2 *a disagreeable taste*: disgusting, offensive, repulsive, repellent, obnoxious, unsavoury, objectionable, nasty.
🔁 1 amiable, pleasant. 2 agreeable.

disagreement *n* 1 DISPUTE, argument, conflict, altercation (*fml*), quarrel, clash, dissent, falling-out, contention, strife, misunderstanding, squabble, tiff (*infml*), wrangle. 2 DIFFERENCE, variance, unlikeness, disparity, discrepancy, deviation, discord, dissimilarity, incompatibility, divergence, diversity, incongruity.
🔁 1 agreement, harmony. 2 similarity.

> Ways of expressing disagreement include: a bone of contention, a difference of opinion, agree to disagree, agree to differ, argue the toss, be at loggerheads with, be at odds with, beg to differ, I don't agree, not see eye to eye, not true!, on the contrary, put the opposite view/case, take issue with.

disappear *v* 1 VANISH, wane, recede, fade, evaporate, dissolve, ebb. 2 GO, depart, withdraw, retire, flee, fly, escape,

scarper (*infml*), hide. **3** END, expire, perish, pass.
≋ 1 appear. **3** emerge.

disappearance *n* vanishing, fading, evaporation, departure, loss, going, passing, melting, desertion, flight.
≋ appearance, manifestation.

disappoint *v* fail, dissatisfy, let down, disillusion, dash, dismay, disenchant, sadden, thwart, vex, frustrate, foil, dishearten, disgruntle, disconcert, hamper, hinder, deceive, defeat, delude.
≋ satisfy, please, delight.

disappointed *adj* let down, frustrated, thwarted, disillusioned, dissatisfied, miffed (*infml*), upset, discouraged, disgruntled, disheartened, distressed, down-hearted, saddened, despondent, depressed.
≋ pleased, satisfied.

disappointing *adj* unsatisfactory, inferior, inadequate, insufficient, unworthy, pathetic, sad, sorry, unhappy, discouraging, disconcerting, depressing, disagreeable, anticlimactic, not all it's cracked up to be (*infml*), underwhelming (*infml*).
≋ encouraging, pleasant, satisfactory.

disappointment *n* **1** FRUSTRATION, dissatisfaction, failure, disenchantment, disillusionment, displeasure, discouragement, distress, regret. **2** FAILURE, let-down, setback, comedown, blow, misfortune, fiasco, disaster, calamity, washout (*infml*), damp squib (*infml*), swiz (*infml*), swizzle (*infml*).
≋ 1 pleasure, satisfaction, delight. **2** success.

disapproval *n* censure, disapprobation (*fml*), condemnation, criticism, displeasure, reproach, objection, dissatisfaction, denunciation, dislike.
≋ approbation (*fml*), approval.

disapprove *v* censure, condemn, blame, take exception to, object to, deplore, denounce, disparage, dislike, reject, spurn.
≋ approve of.

disarm *v* **1** DISABLE, unarm, demilitarize, demobilize, deactivate, disband. **2** APPEASE, conciliate, win, mollify, persuade.
≋ 1 arm.

disarmament *n* demilitarization, demobilization, deactivation, laying-down of arms/weapons, arms control/limitation/reduction.

disarming *adj* charming, winning, persuasive, conciliatory, irresistible, likable, mollifying.

disarray *n* disorder, confusion, chaos, mess, muddle, shambles (*infml*), disorganization, clutter, untidiness, unruliness, jumble, indiscipline, tangle, upset.
≋ order.

disaster *n* calamity, catastrophe, misfortune, reverse, tragedy, blow, accident, act of God, cataclysm, debacle, mishap, failure, flop (*infml*), fiasco, ruin, stroke, trouble, mischance, ruination.
≋ success, triumph.

disastrous *adj* calamitous, catastrophic, cataclysmic, devastating, ruinous, tragic, unfortunate, dreadful, dire, terrible, destructive, ill-fated, fatal, miserable.
≋ successful, auspicious.

disband *v* disperse, break up, scatter, dismiss, demobilize, part company, separate, dissolve.
≋ assemble, muster.

disbelief *n* unbelief, incredulity, doubt, scepticism, suspicion, distrust, mistrust, rejection.
≋ belief.

Informal expressions of disbelief include: a good one!; a likely story!; come, come!; come off it!; do me a favour!; don't give me that!; don't make me laugh!; don't tell me!; do you mean to say?; excuses, excuses!; fancy that!; get along (with you)!; get away (with you)!; go on!; go on with you!; good heavens!; good Lord!; goodness gracious me!; goodness me!; heavens above!; I ask you!; I bet!; I don't think!; I'll eat my hat!; I've heard that one before!; if you believe that, you'd believe anything!; just fancy!; make me laugh!; my (giddy) aunt!; my foot!; my goodness!; my hat!; no kidding!; oh, yeah!; promises, promises!; pull the other one, it's got bells on!; says who?; says you!; sez who?; sez you!; stone me!; stone the crows!; strike a light!; strike me dead!; strike me pink!; stuff and nonsense!; tell it to the marines!; tell me another!; that's a tall story!; that's news to me!; that's rich!; the devil you do!; the hell you will!; what a load of cobblers!; you can't be serious!; you don't say!; you'll be lucky!; you must be joking!; you must be kidding!; you're kidding!; you're pulling my leg!; you what!

disbelieve v discount, discredit, repudiate, reject, mistrust, suspect.
🔁 believe, trust.

disc n 1 CIRCLE, face, plate, ring. 2 RECORD, album, LP, CD. 3 DISK, diskette, hard disk, floppy disk, CD-ROM.

discard v reject, abandon, dispose of, get rid of, jettison, dispense with, cast aside, ditch (*infml*), dump (*infml*), drop, scrap, shed, remove, relinquish.
🔁 retain, adopt.

discern v 1 PERCEIVE, make out, observe, detect, recognize, see, ascertain, notice, determine, discover, descry. 2 DISCRIMINATE, distinguish, differentiate, judge.

discernible adj perceptible, noticeable, detectable, appreciable, distinct, observable, recognizable, visible, apparent, clear, obvious, plain, patent, manifest, discoverable.
🔁 imperceptible.

discerning adj discriminating, perceptive, astute, clear-sighted, sensitive, shrewd, wise, sharp, subtle, sagacious, penetrating, acute, piercing, critical, eagle-eyed.
🔁 dull, obtuse.

discharge v 1 LIBERATE, free, pardon, release, clear, absolve, exonerate, acquit, relieve, dismiss. 2 EXECUTE, carry out, perform, fulfil, dispense. 3 FIRE, shoot, let off, detonate, explode. 4 EMIT, sack (*infml*), remove, fire (*infml*), expel, oust, eject.
🔁 1 detain. 2 neglect. 4 appoint.
➤ n 1 LIBERATION, release, acquittal, exoneration. 2 EMISSION, secretion, ejection. 3 EXECUTION, accomplishment, fulfilment.
🔁 1 confinement, detention. 2 absorption. 3 neglect.

disciple n follower, convert, proselyte, adherent, believer, devotee, supporter, learner, pupil, student.

disciplinarian n authoritarian, taskmaster, autocrat, stickler, despot, tyrant.

discipline n 1 TRAINING, exercise, drill, practice. 2 PUNISHMENT, chastisement, correction. 3 STRICTNESS, restraint, regulation, self-control, orderliness.
🔁 3 indiscipline.
➤ v 1 TRAIN, instruct, drill, educate, exercise, break in. 2 CHECK, control,

correct, restrain, govern. 3 PUNISH, chastise, chasten, penalize, reprimand, castigate.

disclaim v deny, disown, repudiate, abandon, renounce, reject, abjure (*fml*).
🔁 accept, confess.

disclose v 1 DIVULGE, make known, reveal, tell, confess, let slip, relate, publish, communicate, impart, leak (*infml*). 2 EXPOSE, reveal, uncover, lay bare, unveil, discover.
🔁 conceal.

disclosure n divulgence, exposure, exposé, revelation, uncovering, publication, leak (*infml*), discovery, admission, acknowledgement, announcement, declaration.

discoloration n blemish, stain, spot, streak, mark, patch, blot, blotch, splotch.

discolour v disfigure, fade, stain, soil, mark, mar, rust, streak, tarnish, tinge, weather.

discomfort n ache, pain, uneasiness, malaise, trouble, distress, disquiet, hardship, vexation, irritation, annoyance.
🔁 comfort, ease.

disconcerting adj disturbing, confusing, upsetting, unnerving, alarming, bewildering, off-putting (*infml*), distracting, embarrassing, awkward, baffling, perplexing, dismaying, bothersome.

disconnect v cut off, disengage, uncouple, sever, separate, detach, unplug, unhook, part, divide.
🔁 attach, connect.

disconnected adj confused, incoherent, rambling, unco-ordinated, unintelligible, loose, irrational, disjointed, illogical, jumbled.
🔁 coherent, connected.

disconsolate adj desolate, dejected, dispirited, sad, melancholy, unhappy, wretched, miserable, gloomy, forlorn, inconsolable, crushed, heavy-hearted, hopeless.
🔁 cheerful, joyful.

discontent n uneasiness, dissatisfaction, disquiet, restlessness, fretfulness, unrest, impatience, vexation, regret.
🔁 content.

discontented adj dissatisfied, fed up (*infml*), disgruntled, unhappy, browned off (*infml*), cheesed off (*infml*), disaffected,

miserable, exasperated, complaining.
☒ contented, satisfied.

discontinue v stop, end, finish, cease, break off, terminate, halt, drop, suspend, abandon, cancel, interrupt.
☒ continue.

discord n 1 DISSENSION, disagreement, discordance, clashing, disunity, incompatibility, conflict, difference, dispute, contention, friction, division, opposition, strife, split, wrangling. 2 DISSONANCE, disharmony, cacophony (*fml*), jangle, jarring, harshness.
☒ 1 concord, agreement. 2 harmony.

discordant adj 1 DISAGREEING, conflicting, at odds, clashing, contradictory, incongruous, incompatible, inconsistent. 2 DISSONANT, cacophonous (*fml*), grating, jangling, jarring, harsh.
☒ 1 harmonious. 2 harmonious.

discount¹ v 1 DISREGARD, ignore, overlook, disbelieve, gloss over. 2 REDUCE, deduct, mark down, knock off (*infml*).

discount² n reduction, rebate, allowance, cut, concession, deduction, mark-down.

discourage v 1 DISHEARTEN, dampen, dispirit, depress, demoralize, dismay, unnerve, deject, disappoint. 2 DETER, dissuade, hinder, put off, restrain, prevent.
☒ 1 hearten. 2 encourage.

discouraged adj disheartened, let-down, deflated, dispirited, depressed, demoralized, dejected, dismayed, downcast, glum, pessimistic, daunted, dashed, crestfallen.
☒ encouraged, heartened.

discouragement n 1 DOWNHEARTEDNESS, despondency, pessimism, dismay, depression, dejection, despair, disappointment. 2 DETERRENT, damper, setback, impediment, obstacle, opposition, hindrance, restraint, rebuff.
☒ 1 encouragement. 2 incentive.

discouraging adj disheartening, dispiriting, depressing, disappointing, demoralizing, off-putting, unfavourable, dampening, daunting, inauspicious (*fml*), unpropitious (*fml*).
☒ encouraging, heartening.

discourse n 1 CONVERSATION, dialogue, chat, communication, talk, converse, discussion. 2 SPEECH, address, oration (*fml*), lecture, sermon, essay, treatise, dissertation, homily.

➢ v converse, talk, discuss, debate, confer, lecture.

discourteous adj rude, bad-mannered, ill-mannered, impolite, boorish, disrespectful, ill-bred, uncivil, unceremonious, insolent, offhand, curt, brusque, abrupt.
☒ courteous, polite.

discover v 1 FIND, uncover, unearth, dig up, disclose, reveal, light on, locate. 2 ASCERTAIN, determine, realize, notice, recognize, perceive, see, find out, spot, discern, learn, detect. 3 ORIGINATE, invent, pioneer.
☒ 1 miss. 2 conceal, cover (up).

discoverer n explorer, finder, founder, pioneer, initiator, inventor, originator, author, deviser, creator.

discovery n 1 BREAKTHROUGH, find, origination, introduction, innovation, invention, exploration. 2 DISCLOSURE, detection, revelation, location.

discredit v 1 DISBELIEVE, distrust, doubt, question, mistrust, challenge. 2 DISPARAGE, dishonour, degrade, defame, disgrace, slander, slur, smear, reproach, vilify.
☒ 1 believe. 2 honour.
➢ n 1 DISBELIEF, distrust, doubt, mistrust, scepticism, suspicion. 2 DISHONOUR, disrepute, censure, aspersion, disgrace, blame, shame, reproach, slur, smear, scandal.
☒ 1 belief. 2 credit.

discreditable adj dishonourable, disreputable, disgraceful, reprehensible, scandalous, blameworthy, shameful, infamous, degrading, improper.
☒ creditable.

discreet adj tactful, careful, diplomatic, politic, prudent, cautious, delicate, judicious, reserved, wary, sensible.
☒ tactless, indiscreet.

discrepancy n difference, disparity, variance, variation, inconsistency, dissimilarity, discordance, divergence, disagreement, conflict, inequality.

discretion n 1 TACT, diplomacy, judiciousness, caution, prudence, wisdom, circumspection, discernment, judgement, care, carefulness, consideration, wariness. 2 CHOICE, freedom, preference, will, wish.
☒ 1 indiscretion.

discretionary *adj* optional, voluntary, elective, open.

 fixed, mandatory, compulsory, automatic.

discriminate *v* distinguish, differentiate, discern, tell apart, make a distinction, segregate, separate.

 confuse, confound.

♦ **discriminate (against)** be prejudiced, be biased, victimize.

discriminating *adj* discerning, fastidious, selective, critical, perceptive, particular, tasteful, astute, sensitive, cultivated.

discrimination *n* **1** BIAS, prejudice, intolerance, unfairness, bigotry, favouritism, inequity, racism, sexism. **2** DISCERNMENT, judgement, acumen, perception, acuteness, insight, penetration, subtlety, keenness, refinement, taste.

discriminatory *adj* biased, prejudiced, favouring, inequitable, prejudicial, unfair, unjust, discriminative, partial, partisan, preferential, loaded, weighted, one-sided.

 fair, impartial, unbiased.

discursive *adj* rambling, digressing, wandering, long-winded, meandering, wide-ranging, circuitous.

 terse.

discuss *v* debate, talk about, confer, argue, consider, deliberate, converse, consult, examine.

discussion *n* debate, conference, argument, conversation, dialogue, exchange, consultation, discourse, deliberation, consideration, analysis, review, examination, scrutiny, seminar, symposium.

disdain *n* scorn, contempt, arrogance, haughtiness, derision, sneering, dislike, snobbishness.

 admiration, respect.

disdainful *adj* scornful, contemptuous, derisive, haughty, aloof, arrogant, supercilious, sneering, superior, proud, insolent.

 respectful.

disease *n* illness, sickness, ill-health, infirmity, complaint, disorder, ailment, indisposition, malady, condition, affliction, infection, epidemic.

 health.

Diseases and disorders include:
Addison's disease, AIDS, alopecia, Alzheimer's disease, anaemia, angina, anorexia nervosa, anthrax, arthritis, asbestosis, asthma, athlete's foot, autism, Bell's palsy, beriberi, Black Death, botulism, Bright's disease, bronchitis, brucellosis, bubonic plague, bulimia, cancer, cerebral palsy, chickenpox, cholera, cirrhosis, coeliac disease, common cold, consumption, croup, cystic fibrosis, diabetes, diphtheria, dropsy, dysentery, eclampsia, emphysema, encephalitis, endometriosis, enteritis, farmer's lung, flu (*infml*), foot-and-mouth disease, gangrene, German measles, gingivitis, glandular fever, glaucoma, gonorrhoea, haemophilia, hepatitis, herpes, Hodgkin's disease, Huntington's chorea, hydrophobia, impetigo, influenza, Lassa fever, Legionnaire's Disease, leprosy, leukaemia, lockjaw, malaria, mastoiditis, measles, meningitis, motor neurone disease, multiple sclerosis (MS), mumps, muscular dystrophy, myalgic encephalomyelitis (ME), nephritis, osteomyelitis, osteoporosis, Paget's disease, Parkinson's disease, peritonitis, pneumonia, poliomyelitis, psittacosis, psoriasis, pyorrhoea, rabies, rheumatic fever, rheumatoid arthritis, rickets, ringworm, rubella, scabies, scarlet fever, schistosomiasis, schizophrenia, scurvy, septicaemia, shingles, silicosis, smallpox, syphilis, tapeworm, tetanus, thrombosis, thrush, tinnitus, tuberculosis (TB), typhoid, typhus, vertigo, whooping cough, yellow fever.

---

diseased *adj* sick, ill, unhealthy, ailing, unsound, contaminated, infected.

 healthy.

disembark *v* land, arrive, alight, debark.

 embark.

disembodied *adj* bodiless, incorporeal (*fml*), ghostly, phantom, spiritual, immaterial, intangible.

disengage *v* disconnect, detach, loosen, free, extricate, undo, release, liberate, separate, disentangle, untie, withdraw.

 connect, engage.

disentangle *v* **1** LOOSE, free, extricate, disconnect, untangle, disengage, detach, unravel, separate, unfold. **2** RESOLVE, clarify, simplify.

 1 entangle.

disfigure *v* deface, blemish, mutilate,

scar, mar, deform, distort, damage, spoil.
ea adorn, embellish.

disfigurement *n* blemish, defacement, defect, deformity, mutilation, scar, spot, blotch, stain, disgrace, impairment, injury, distortion, uglification.
ea adornment.

disgorge *v* discharge, empty, eject, expel, vomit, spew, spout, belch, regurgitate, relinquish, renounce, surrender, throw up (*infml*).

disgrace *n* shame, ignominy, disrepute, dishonour, disfavour, humiliation, defamation, discredit, scandal, reproach, slur, stain.
ea honour, esteem.
➤ *v* shame, dishonour, abase, defame, humiliate, disfavour, stain, discredit, reproach, slur, sully, taint, stigmatize.
ea honour, respect.

disgraced *adj* discredited, shamed, dishonoured, humiliated, degraded, branded, stigmatized, in the doghouse (*infml*).
ea honoured, respected.

disgraceful *adj* shameful, dishonourable, disreputable, ignominious, scandalous, shocking, unworthy, dreadful, appalling.
ea honourable, respectable.

disgruntled *adj* discontented, dissatisfied, displeased, annoyed, exasperated, grumpy, irritated, peeved, peevish, resentful, sulky, sullen, testy, vexed, put out, petulant, fed up (*infml*), hacked off (*infml*), cheesed off (*infml*), browned off (*infml*), brassed off (*infml*).
ea pleased, satisfied.

disguise *v* 1 CONCEAL, cover, camouflage, mask, hide, dress up, cloak, screen, veil, shroud. 2 FALSIFY, deceive, dissemble, misrepresent, fake, fudge.
ea 1 reveal, expose.
➤ *n* concealment, camouflage, cloak, cover, costume, mask, front, façade, masquerade, deception, pretence, travesty, screen, veil.

disguised *adj* camouflaged, cloaked, veiled, hidden, made-up, masked, incognito, undercover, unrecognizable, fake, false, covert (*fml*), feigned (*fml*).

disgust *v* offend, displease, nauseate, revolt, sicken, repel, outrage, put off.
ea delight, please.
➤ *n* revulsion, repulsion, repugnance, distaste, aversion, abhorrence, nausea, loathing, detestation, hatred.

disgusted *adj* repelled, repulsed, revolted, offended, appalled, outraged.
ea attracted, delighted.

disgusting *adj* repugnant, repellent, revolting, offensive, sickening, nauseating, odious, foul, unappetizing, unpleasant, vile, obscene, abominable, detestable, objectionable, nasty.
ea delightful, pleasant.

dish *n* plate, bowl, platter, food, recipe.
◆ **dish out** distribute, give out, hand out, dole out, allocate, mete out, inflict.
◆ **dish up** serve, present, ladle, spoon, dispense, scoop.

dishearten *v* discourage, dispirit, dampen, cast down, depress, dismay, dash, disappoint, deject, daunt, crush, deter.
ea encourage, hearten.

dishevelled *adj* tousled, unkempt, uncombed, untidy, bedraggled, messy, ruffled, slovenly, disordered.
ea neat, tidy.

dishonest *adj* untruthful, fraudulent, deceitful, false, lying, deceptive, double-dealing, cheating, crooked (*infml*), treacherous, unprincipled, swindling, shady (*infml*), corrupt, disreputable.
ea honest, trustworthy, scrupulous.

dishonesty *n* deceit, falsehood, falsity, fraudulence, fraud, criminality, insincerity, treachery, cheating, crookedness (*infml*), corruption, unscrupulousness, trickery.
ea honesty, truthfulness.

Expressions used when talking about dishonesty or dishonest behaviour: a bad apple, a bad egg, a fast talker, a pack of lies, a slippery customer, a snake in the grass, a tall story, a tissue of lies, be economical with the truth, be up to no good, catch someone red-handed, catch someone with their hand in the till, cook the books, daylight robbery, duck and dive, fall off the back of a lorry, feed someone a line, funny business, get a five-finger discount (*Austr*) [= shoplift something], have light fingers, have the shirt off someone's back, lie through/in one's teeth, lift anything that isn't nailed down, on the fiddle, on the sly, pull a fast one, pull the wool over someone's eyes, put one over on someone, rob someone blind, sell someone a bill of goods (*US*), sell someone a pup, sharp practice, smell fishy, spin a yarn, take someone for a ride, under false pretences, under the counter, under the table.

dishonour v disgrace, shame, humiliate, debase, defile, degrade, defame, discredit, demean, debauch.
Ea honour.
➤ n disgrace, abasement, humiliation, shame, degradation, discredit, disrepute, indignity, ignominy, reproach, slight, slur, scandal, insult, disfavour, outrage, aspersion, abuse, discourtesy.
Ea honour.

dishonourable adj disreputable, unprincipled, unscrupulous, untrustworthy, unethical, unworthy, corrupt, discreditable, treacherous, scandalous, shameful, shameless, disgraceful, contemptible, despicable, infamous, ignoble, ignominious (fml), perfidious (fml), shady (infml).
Ea honourable.

disillusioned adj disenchanted, disabused, undeceived, disappointed.

disincentive n deterrent, barrier, constraint, damper, determent, discouragement, dissuasion, hindrance, impediment, obstacle, repellent, restriction, turn-off.
Ea encouragement, incentive.

disinclined adj averse, reluctant, resistant, indisposed, loath, opposed, hesitant.
Ea inclined, willing.

disinfect v sterilize, fumigate, sanitize, decontaminate, cleanse, purify, purge, clean.
Ea contaminate, infect.

disinfectant n sterilizer, antiseptic, sanitizer.

disingenuous adj insincere, deceitful, dishonest, devious, designing, guileful, wily, sly, crafty, artful, cunning, two-faced, shifty (infml), insidious, uncandid.
Ea artless, frank, ingenuous, naïve, duplicitous (fml), feigned (fml).

disinherit v cut off, renounce, reject, abandon, dispossess, impoverish, repudiate, cut someone out of one's will, cut off without a penny (infml), turn one's back on (infml).

disintegrate v break up, decompose, fall apart, crumble, rot, moulder, separate, splinter.

disinterest n disinterestedness, impartiality, neutrality, detachment, unbiasedness, dispassionateness, fairness.

disinterested adj unbiased, neutral, impartial, unprejudiced, dispassionate, detached, uninvolved, open-minded, equitable, even-handed, unselfish.
Ea biased, concerned.

disjointed adj 1 DISCONNECTED, dislocated, divided, separated, disunited, displaced, broken, fitful, split, disarticulated. 2 INCOHERENT, aimless, confused, disordered, loose, unconnected, bitty, rambling, spasmodic.
Ea 2 coherent.

dislike n aversion, hatred, repugnance, hostility, distaste, disinclination, disapproval, disapprobation, displeasure, animosity, antagonism, enmity, detestation, disgust, loathing.
Ea liking, predilection.
➤ v hate, detest, object to, loathe, abhor, abominate, disapprove, shun, despise, scorn.
Ea like, favour.

dislocate v disjoint, displace, misplace, disengage, put out (infml), disorder, shift, disconnect, disrupt, disunite.

dislocation n disruption, disturbance, disarray, disorder, disorganization.
Ea order.

dislodge v displace, eject, remove, oust, extricate, shift, move, uproot.

disloyal adj treacherous, faithless, false, traitorous, two-faced (infml), unfaithful, apostate, unpatriotic.
Ea loyal, trustworthy.

dismal adj dreary, gloomy, depressing, bleak, cheerless, dull, drab, low-spirited, melancholy, sad, sombre, lugubrious, forlorn, despondent, dark, sorrowful, long-faced (infml), hopeless, discouraging.
Ea cheerful, bright.

dismantle v demolish, take apart, disassemble, strip.
Ea assemble, put together.

dismay v alarm, daunt, frighten, unnerve, unsettle, scare, put off, dispirit, distress, disconcert, dishearten, discourage, disillusion, depress, horrify, disappoint.
Ea encourage, hearten.
➤ n consternation, alarm, distress, apprehension, agitation, dread, fear, trepidation, fright, horror, terror, discouragement, disappointment.
Ea boldness, encouragement.

dismember v disjoint, amputate, dissect, dislocate, divide, mutilate, sever.
Ea assemble, join.

dismiss v 1 *the class was dismissed*:
discharge, free, let go, release, send
away, remove, drop, discard, banish. 2
dismiss employees: sack (*infml*), make
redundant, lay off, fire (*infml*), relegate. 3
dismiss it from your mind: discount,
disregard, reject, repudiate, set aside,
shelve, spurn.
ea 1 retain. 2 appoint. 3 accept.

dismissal n notice, redundancy, laying-
off, discharge, removal, expulsion,
marching-orders, papers (*infml*), sacking
(*infml*), firing (*infml*), sack (*infml*), push
(*infml*), boot (*infml*), elbow (*infml*).
ea appointment, hiring.

disobedience n unruliness,
waywardness, defiance, rebellion,
wilfulness, contrariness, indiscipline,
mutiny, revolt, insubordination (*fml*),
recalcitrance (*fml*).
ea obedience.

disobey v contravene, infringe, violate,
transgress, flout, disregard, defy, ignore,
resist, rebel.
ea obey.

disorder n 1 CONFUSION, chaos, muddle,
disarray, mess, untidiness, shambles
(*infml*), clutter, disorganization, jumble. 2
DISTURBANCE, tumult, riot, confusion,
commotion, uproar, fracas, brawl, fight,
clamour, quarrel. 3 ILLNESS, complaint,
disease, sickness, disability, ailment,
malady, affliction.
ea 1 neatness, order. 2 law and order, peace.
➤ v disturb, mess up, disarrange, mix up,
muddle, upset, disorganize, confuse,
confound, clutter, jumble, discompose,
scatter, unsettle.
ea arrange, organize.

disorderly adj 1 DISORGANIZED,
confused, chaotic, irregular, messy, untidy.
2 UNRULY, undisciplined, unmanageable,
obstreperous, rowdy, turbulent, rebellious,
lawless.
ea 1 neat, tidy. 2 well-behaved.

disorganize v disorder, disrupt, disturb,
disarrange, muddle, upset, confuse,
discompose, jumble, play havoc with,
unsettle, break up, destroy.
ea organize.

disorganized adj 1 CONFUSED,
disordered, haphazard, jumbled, muddled,
chaotic, unsorted, unsystematized, topsy-
turvy, shambolic (*infml*). 2
UNMETHODICAL, unorganized,

unstructured, unsystematic, careless,
muddled, untogether (*infml*).
ea 1 organized, tidy. 2 organized,
methodical.

disown v repudiate, renounce, disclaim,
deny, cast off, disallow, reject, abandon.
ea accept, acknowledge.

disparage v belittle, criticize, defame,
slander, decry, degrade, detract from,
disdain, discredit, dishonour, malign,
ridicule, scorn, run down, minimize,
dismiss, underestimate, underrate,
undervalue, denigrate (*fml*), deprecate
(*fml*), vilify (*fml*), traduce (*fml*), cast
aspersions on (*fml*).
ea praise.

disparaging adj derisive, derogatory,
mocking, scornful, critical, insulting, snide
(*infml*).
ea flattering, praising.

dispassionate adj detached, objective,
impartial, neutral, disinterested,
impersonal, fair, cool, calm, composed.
ea biased, emotional.

dispatch, despatch v 1 SEND, express,
transmit, forward, consign, expedite,
accelerate. 2 DISPOSE OF, finish, perform,
discharge, conclude. 3 KILL, murder,
execute.
ea 1 receive.
➤ n 1 COMMUNICATION, message, report,
bulletin, communiqué, news, letter,
account. 2 PROMPTNESS, speed, alacrity,
expedition, celerity, haste, rapidity,
swiftness.
ea 2 slowness.

dispel v banish, drive away, chase away,
get rid of, rid, dismiss, disperse, allay,
eliminate, expel, rout, scatter, melt away,
dissipate (*fml*), disseminate (*fml*).

dispensable adj unnecessary,
disposable, expendable, inessential, non-
essential, replaceable, superfluous,
needless, gratuitous, useless.
ea indispensable, essential.

dispensation n 1 PERMISSION,
exemption, exception, release, remission,
relief, reprieve, immunity, licence. 2 ISSUE,
distribution, allocation, allotment,
apportionment, handing-out, sharing-out,
endowment (*fml*), bestowal (*fml*). 3
AUTHORITY, order, system, organization,
arrangement, plan, scheme, direction,
administration, discharge, application,
economy (*fml*).

dispense v 1 DISTRIBUTE, give out, apportion, allot, allocate, assign, share, mete out. 2 ADMINISTER, apply, implement, enforce, discharge, execute, operate.
♦ **dispense with** dispose of, get rid of, abolish, discard, omit, disregard, cancel, forgo, ignore, waive.

disperse v scatter, dispel, spread, distribute, diffuse, dissolve, break up, dismiss, separate.
Fa gather.

displace v 1 DISLODGE, move, shift, misplace, disturb, dislocate. 2 DEPOSE, oust, remove, replace, dismiss, discharge, supplant, eject, evict, succeed, supersede.

display v 1 SHOW, present, demonstrate, exhibit. 2 BETRAY, disclose, reveal, show, expose. 3 SHOW OFF, flourish, parade, flaunt.
Fa 1 conceal. 2 disguise.
➤ n show, exhibition, demonstration, presentation, parade, spectacle, revelation.

displease v offend, annoy, irritate, anger, upset, put out (infml), infuriate, exasperate, incense.
Fa please.

displeasure n offence, annoyance, disapproval, irritation, resentment, disfavour, anger, indignation, wrath.
Fa pleasure.

disposable adj throwaway, expendable, non-returnable, biodegradable.

disposal n 1 ARRANGEMENT, grouping, order. 2 CONTROL, direction, command. 3 REMOVAL, riddance, discarding, jettisoning.

disposed adj liable, inclined, predisposed, prone, likely, apt, minded, subject, ready, willing.
Fa disinclined.

dispose of v 1 DEAL WITH, decide, settle. 2 GET RID OF, discard, scrap, destroy, dump (infml), jettison.
Fa 2 keep.

disposition n character, nature, temperament, inclination, make-up, bent, leaning, predisposition, constitution, habit, spirit, tendency, proneness.

disproportionate adj unequal, uneven, incommensurate, excessive, unreasonable.
Fa balanced.

disprove v refute, rebut, confute,

discredit, invalidate, contradict, expose.
Fa confirm, prove.

dispute v argue, debate, question, contend, challenge, discuss, doubt, contest, contradict, deny, quarrel, clash, wrangle, squabble.
Fa agree.
➤ n argument, debate, disagreement, controversy, conflict, contention, quarrel, wrangle, feud, strife, squabble.
Fa agreement, settlement.

disqualified adj eliminated, ineligible, struck off, debarred (fml), precluded (fml), disentitled (fml).
Fa accepted, eligible, qualified.

disqualify v 1 INCAPACITATE, disable, invalidate. 2 DEBAR (fml), preclude (fml), rule out, disentitle (fml), eliminate, prohibit.
Fa 2 qualify, accept.

disquiet n anxiety, worry, concern, nervousness, uneasiness, restlessness, alarm, distress, fretfulness, fear, disturbance, trouble.
Fa calm, reassurance.

disregard v 1 IGNORE, overlook, discount, neglect, pass over, disobey, make light of, turn a blind eye to (infml), brush aside. 2 SLIGHT, snub, despise, disdain, disparage.
Fa 1 heed, pay attention to. 2 respect.
➤ n neglect, negligence, inattention, oversight, indifference, disrespect, contempt, disdain, brush-off (infml).
Fa attention, heed.

disrepair n dilapidation, deterioration, decay, collapse, ruin, shabbiness.
Fa good repair.

disreputable adj 1 DISGRACEFUL, discreditable, dishonourable, unrespectable, notorious, scandalous, shameful, shady, base, contemptible, low, mean, shocking. 2 SCRUFFY, shabby, seedy, unkempt.
Fa 1 respectable. 2 smart.

disrepute n disgrace, dishonour, shame, disfavour, discredit, disreputation, infamy, disesteem (fml), ignominy (fml), obloquy (fml).
Fa honour.

disrespect n impoliteness, disregard, discourtesy, incivility, irreverence, rudeness, dishonour, contempt, scorn, insolence, impertinence, impudence, cheek.

respect, politeness, civility, consideration.

disrespectful *adj* rude, discourteous, impertinent, impolite, impudent, insolent, uncivil, unmannerly, cheeky, insulting, irreverent, contemptuous.
polite, respectful.

disrupt *v* disturb, disorganize, confuse, interrupt, break up, unsettle, intrude, upset.

disruption *n* disorder, confusion, disorganization, turmoil, disarray, disorderliness, disturbance, interference, interruption, stoppage, upheaval, upset.

disruptive *adj* troublesome, unruly, undisciplined, obstreperous, disorderly, boisterous, noisy, turbulent, distracting, disturbing, unsettling, upsetting.
well-behaved, manageable.

dissatisfaction *n* discontent, displeasure, dislike, discomfort, disappointment, frustration, annoyance, irritation, exasperation, regret, resentment.
satisfaction.

dissatisfied *adj* discontented, displeased, disgruntled, disappointed, disillusioned, disenchanted, frustrated, angry, annoyed, irritated, exasperated, unfulfilled, unhappy, unsatisfied, fed up (*infml*), cheesed off (*infml*), brassed off (*infml*), browned off (*infml*).
fulfilled, satisfied.

dissect *v* 1 DISMEMBER, anatomize. 2 ANALYSE, investigate, scrutinize, examine, inspect, pore over.

disseminate *v* circulate, distribute, spread, broadcast, scatter, sow, diffuse, disperse, publish, publicize, propagate, proclaim, promulgate (*fml*).

dissension *n* disagreement, discord, dissent, dispute, contention, conflict, strife, friction, quarrel.
agreement.

dissent *v* disagree, differ, protest, object, refuse, quibble.
assent.
➤ *n* disagreement, difference, dissension, discord, resistance, opposition, objection.
agreement, conformity.

disservice *n* disfavour, injury, wrong, bad turn, harm, unkindness, injustice.
favour.

dissident *adj* disagreeing, differing,

dissenting, discordant, nonconformist, heterodox (*fml*).
acquiescent, orthodox.
➤ *n* dissenter, protestor, noncomformist, rebel, agitator, revolutionary, schismatic, recusant.
assenter.

dissimilar *adj* unlike, different, divergent, disparate, unrelated, incompatible, mismatched, diverse, various, heterogeneous.
similar, like.

dissipate *v* 1 *he dissipated his inheritance*: spend, waste, squander, expend, consume, deplete, fritter away, burn up. 2 *the clouds dissipated*: disperse, vanish, disappear, dispel, diffuse, evaporate, dissolve.
1 accumulate. 2 appear.

dissipated *adj* dissolute, debauched, abandoned, self-indulgent, rakish, wasted, corrupt, wild, depraved, degenerate, profligate (*fml*), licentious (*fml*).
conserved, virtuous, upright.

dissociate *v* separate, detach, break off, disunite, disengage, disconnect, cut off, disband, divorce, disrupt, isolate, segregate.
associate, join.

dissolute *adj* dissipated, debauched, degenerate, depraved, wanton, abandoned, corrupt, immoral, licentious, lewd, wild.
restrained, virtuous.

dissolution *n* 1 DISINTEGRATION, decomposition, separation, resolution, division. 2 ENDING, termination, conclusion, finish, discontinuation, divorce, dismissal, dispersal, destruction, overthrow. 3 EVAPORATION, disappearance.

dissolve *v* 1 EVAPORATE, disintegrate, liquefy, melt. 2 DECOMPOSE, disintegrate, disperse, break up, disappear, crumble. 3 END, terminate, separate, sever, divorce.

dissuade *v* deter, discourage, put off, disincline.
persuade.

distance *n* 1 SPACE, interval, gap, extent, range, reach, length, width. 2 ALOOFNESS, reserve, coolness, coldness, remoteness.
1 closeness. 2 approachability.

distant *adj* 1 FAR, faraway, far-flung, out-of-the-way, remote, outlying, abroad, dispersed. 2 ALOOF, cool, reserved,

stand-offish (*infml*), formal, cold, restrained, stiff.
🔄 1 close. 2 approachable.

distaste *n* dislike, aversion, repugnance, disgust, revulsion, loathing, abhorrence.
🔄 liking.

distasteful *adj* disagreeable, offensive, unpleasant, objectionable, repulsive, obnoxious, repugnant, unsavoury, loathsome, abhorrent.
🔄 pleasing.

distil *v* vaporize, evaporate, condense, extract, press out, draw out, derive, express, drip, trickle, leak, flow, purify, refine, sublimate (*fml*).

distillation *n* extract, extraction, evaporation, condensation, essence, spirit.

distinct *adj* 1 SEPARATE, different, detached, individual, dissimilar. 2 CLEAR, plain, evident, obvious, apparent, marked, definite, noticeable, recognizable.
🔄 2 indistinct, vague.

distinction *n* 1 DIFFERENTIATION, discrimination, discernment, separation, difference, dissimilarity, contrast. 2 CHARACTERISTIC, peculiarity, individuality, feature, quality, mark. 3 RENOWN, fame, celebrity, prominence, eminence, importance, reputation, greatness, honour, prestige, repute, superiority, worth, merit, excellence, quality.
🔄 3 unimportance, obscurity.

distinctive *adj* characteristic, distinguishing, individual, peculiar, different, unique, singular, special, original, extraordinary, idiosyncratic.
🔄 ordinary, common.

distinguish *v* 1 DIFFERENTIATE, tell apart, discriminate, determine, categorize, characterize, classify. 2 DISCERN, perceive, identify, ascertain, make out, recognize, see, discriminate.

distinguishable *adj* recognizable, discernible, clear, plain, plainly seen, evident, noticeable, conspicuous, obvious, perceptible, appreciable, observable, manifest (*fml*).
🔄 indistinguishable.

distinguished *adj* famous, eminent, celebrated, well-known, acclaimed, illustrious, notable, noted, renowned, famed, honoured, outstanding, striking, marked, extraordinary, conspicuous.
🔄 insignificant, obscure, unimpressive.

distort *v* 1 DEFORM, contort, bend, misshape, disfigure, twist, warp. 2 FALSIFY, misrepresent, pervert, slant, colour, garble.

distortion *n* 1 DEFORMITY, twist, bend, buckle, contortion, crookedness, skew, slant, warp. 2 MISREPRESENTATION, falsification, perversion, bias, twisting, colouring, garbling.

distract *v* 1 DIVERT, sidetrack, deflect. 2 CONFUSE, disconcert, bewilder, confound, disturb, perplex, puzzle. 3 AMUSE, occupy, divert, engross.

distracted *adj* 1 DISTRAUGHT, agitated, anxious, overwrought, upset, distressed, grief-stricken, beside oneself, worked up, frantic, hysterical, raving, mad, wild, crazy. 2 *their attention was distracted*: abstracted, wandering, absent-minded, preoccupied, inattentive, dreaming, miles away (*infml*), not with it (*infml*).
🔄 1 calm, untroubled. 2 attentive.

distraction *n* 1 DISTURBANCE, interruption, diversion, interference, confusion, derangement (*fml*). 2 DIVERSION, amusement, entertainment, game, sport, hobby, pastime, recreation, divertissement.

distraught *adj* agitated, anxious, overwrought, upset, distressed, distracted, beside oneself, worked up, frantic, hysterical, raving, mad, wild, crazy.
🔄 calm, untroubled.

distress *n* 1 ANGUISH, grief, misery, sorrow, heartache, affliction, suffering, torment, wretchedness, sadness, worry, anxiety, desolation, pain, agony. 2 ADVERSITY, hardship, poverty, need, privation, destitution, misfortune, trouble, difficulties, trial.
🔄 1 content. 2 comfort, ease.
➤ *v* upset, afflict, grieve, disturb, trouble, sadden, worry, torment, harass, harrow, pain, agonize, bother.
🔄 comfort.

distribute *v* 1 DISPENSE, allocate, dole out, dish out, share, deal, divide, apportion. 2 DELIVER, hand out, spread, issue, circulate, diffuse, disperse, scatter.
🔄 2 collect.

distribution *n* 1 ALLOCATION, apportionment, division, sharing. 2 CIRCULATION, spreading, scattering, delivery, dissemination, supply, dealing,

handling. **3** ARRANGEMENT, grouping, classification, organization.
■ **2** collection.

district *n* region, area, quarter, neighbourhood, locality, sector, precinct, parish, locale, community, vicinity, ward.

distrust *v* mistrust, doubt, disbelieve, suspect, question.
■ trust.
➤ *n* mistrust, doubt, disbelief, suspicion, misgiving, wariness, scepticism, question, qualm.
■ trust.

disturb *v* **1** DISRUPT, interrupt, distract. **2** AGITATE, unsettle, upset, distress, worry, fluster, annoy, bother. **3** DISARRANGE, disorder, confuse, upset.
■ **2** reassure. **3** order.

disturbance *n* **1** DISRUPTION, agitation, interruption, intrusion, upheaval, upset, confusion, annoyance, bother, trouble, hindrance. **2** DISORDER, uproar, commotion, tumult, turmoil, fracas, fray, brawl, riot.
■ **1** peace. **2** order.

disturbed *adj* **1** *disturbed by the news*: anxious, apprehensive, bothered, concerned, troubled, worried, upset, confused, discomposed, uneasy, flustered. **2** *emotionally disturbed*: maladjusted, neurotic, unbalanced, psychotic, mentally ill, paranoid, upset, screwed-up (*infml*), hung-up (*infml*).
■ **1** calm.

disuse *n* neglect, desuetude (*fml*), abandonment, discontinuance, decay.
■ use.

ditch *n* trench, dyke, channel, gully, furrow, moat, drain, level, watercourse.

dither *v* hesitate, shilly-shally (*infml*), waver, vacillate.

dive *v* plunge, plummet, dip, submerge, jump, leap, nose-dive, fall, drop, swoop, descend, pitch.
➤ *n* **1** PLUNGE, lunge, header, jump, leap, nose-dive, swoop, dash, spring. **2** (*infml*) BAR, club, saloon.

diverge *v* **1** DIVIDE, branch, fork, separate, spread, split. **2** DEVIATE, digress, stray, wander. **3** DIFFER, vary, disagree, dissent, conflict.
■ **1** converge. **3** agree.

divergence *n* difference, disagreement, variation, clash, conflict, deviation, separation, parting, deflection, departure,

digression, branching-out, disparity (*fml*).
■ agreement.

diverse *adj* various, varied, varying, sundry, different, differing, assorted, dissimilar, miscellaneous, discrete, separate, several, distinct.
■ similar, identical.

diversify *v* vary, change, expand, branch out, spread out, alter, mix, assort.

diversion *n* **1** DEVIATION, detour. **2** AMUSEMENT, entertainment, distraction, pastime, recreation, relaxation, play, game. **3** ALTERATION, change.

diversity *n* variety, dissimilarity, difference, variance, assortment, range, medley.
■ similarity, likeness.

divert *v* **1** DEFLECT, redirect, reroute, side-track, avert, distract, switch. **2** AMUSE, entertain, occupy, distract, interest.

divest *v* deprive, strip, remove, dispossess, undress, unclothe, disrobe, denude (*fml*), despoil (*fml*).
■ clothe.

divide *v* **1** SPLIT, separate, part, cut, break up, detach, bisect, disconnect. **2** DISTRIBUTE, share, allocate, deal out, allot, apportion. **3** DISUNITE, separate, estrange, alienate. **4** CLASSIFY, group, sort, grade, segregate.
■ **1** join. **2** collect. **3** unite.

dividend *n* **1** *shareholders' dividends*: share, bonus, portion, surplus, gain, cut (*infml*), divvy (*infml*), whack (*infml*). **2** BENEFIT, bonus, extra, gain, plus.

divine *adj* **1** GODLIKE, superhuman, supernatural, celestial, heavenly, angelic, spiritual. **2** HOLY, sacred, sanctified, consecrated, transcendent, exalted, glorious, religious, supreme.
■ **1** human. **2** mundane.

divinity *n* god, goddess, deity, godliness, holiness, sanctity, godhead, spirit.

division *n* **1** SEPARATION, detaching, parting, cutting, disunion. **2** BREACH, rupture, split, schism, disunion, estrangement, disagreement, feud. **3** DISTRIBUTION, sharing, allotment, apportionment. **4** SECTION, sector, segment, part, department, category, class, compartment, branch.
■ **1** union. **2** unity. **3** collection. **4** whole.

divisive *adj* alienating, damaging, injurious, disruptive, troublesome,

troublemaking, inharmonious.
🆎 harmonious, unifying.

divorce n dissolution, annulment, break-up, split-up, rupture, separation, breach, disunion.

➢ v separate, part, annul, split up, sever, dissolve, divide, dissociate.
🆎 marry, unite.

divulge v disclose, reveal, communicate, tell, leak (*infml*), impart, confess, betray, uncover, let slip, expose, publish, proclaim.

dizzy adj **1** GIDDY, faint, light-headed, woozy (*infml*), shaky, reeling. **2** CONFUSED, bewildered, dazed, muddled.

do v **1** PERFORM, carry out, execute, accomplish, achieve, fulfil, implement, complete, discharge, undertake, work, put on, present, end, finish, put into practice, conclude (*fml*). **2** BEHAVE, act, conduct oneself, comport oneself (*fml*). **3** *do the tea*: prepare, get ready, fix, organize, arrange, deal with, look after, take care of, manage, be in charge of, be responsible for, produce, make, create, cause, proceed. **4** *Will this do?*: be enough, be adequate, be sufficient, be satisfactory, fit the bill, satisfy, serve, suffice (*fml*). **5** *What do you do?*: have a job, work as, be employed as, earn a living as. **6** *do something about a problem*: try to solve, deal with, work out, find the answer to, sort out, figure out, tackle, resolve (*fml*), crack (*infml*), get to the bottom of (*infml*). **7** *do French at school*: study, learn, master, read, work at/on, take, major in. **8** *do deliveries for you*: provide, supply, furnish, offer. **9** *do 150 kph*: travel at, go at, reach, achieve. **10** *do well/badly; How are you doing?*: get on, get along, come on, come along, fare, progress, develop, manage, make a good/bad job of. **11** CHEAT, defraud, swindle, trick, deceive, dupe, hoodwink, con (*infml*), rip off (*infml*), have (*infml*), fleece (*infml*), take for a ride (*infml*).

➢ n function, affair, event, gathering, party, celebration, soirée, occasion, bash (*infml*), knees-up (*infml*), rave-up (*infml*).

◆ **do away with 1** GET RID OF, discard, dispose of, abolish, remove, eliminate, discontinue (*fml*), nullify (*fml*), annul (*fml*). **2** KILL, murder, slaughter, slay, exterminate, assassinate, do in (*infml*), knock off (*infml*), bump off (*infml*).

◆ **do down** critcize, condemn, blame, censure, find fault with.

◆ **do in** kill, murder, slaughter, slay,

exterminate, assassinate, knock off (*infml*), bump off (*infml*).

◆ **do out of** prevent from having, deprive of, cheat out of, trick out of, swindle out of, con out of (*infml*), diddle out of (*infml*), fleece (*infml*).

◆ **dos and don'ts** rules, regulations, code, instructions, standards, customs, etiquette.

◆ **do up 1** FASTEN, tie, lace, button, zip up, pack. **2** RENOVATE, redecorate, decorate, restore, modernize, repair, recondition.

◆ **do without** go without, manage without, give up, dispense with, deny oneself, refrain, forgo (*fml*), abstain from (*fml*), relinquish (*fml*).

docile adj tractable, co-operative, manageable, submissive, obedient, amenable, controlled, obliging.
🆎 truculent, unco-operative.

dock¹ n harbour, wharf, quay, boat-yard, pier, waterfront, marina.
➢ v anchor, moor, drop anchor, land, berth, put in, tie up.

dock² v crop, clip, cut, shorten, curtail, deduct, reduce, lessen, withhold, decrease, subtract, diminish.

docket n certificate, ticket, label, receipt, tab, tag, bill, chit, chitty, counterfoil, tally, documentation, paperwork.
➢ v label, mark, tab, tag, ticket, register, catalogue, file, index.

doctor n physician, general practitioner, GP, medic (*infml*), medical officer, consultant, clinician.

Types of medical doctor include:
general practitioner, GP, family doctor, family practitioner, locum, hospital doctor, houseman, intern, resident, registrar, consultant, medical officer (MO), doc (*infml*), bones (*infml*), quack (*infml*), dentist, veterinary surgeon, vet (*infml*). *see also* **medical**.

➢ v **1** ALTER, tamper with, falsify, misrepresent, pervert, adulterate, change, disguise, dilute. **2** REPAIR, fix, patch up.

doctrinaire adj dogmatic, inflexible, rigid, insistent, opinionated, pedantic, biased, fanatical.
🆎 flexible.

doctrine n dogma, creed, belief, tenet, principle, teaching, precept, conviction, opinion, canon.

document n paper, certificate, deed,

record, report, form, instrument (*fml*).
➤ *v* **1** RECORD, report, chronicle, list, detail, cite. **2** SUPPORT, prove, corroborate, verify.

dodge *v* avoid, elude, evade, swerve, side-step, shirk, shift.
➤ *n* trick, ruse, ploy, wile, scheme, stratagem, machination, manoeuvre.

dog *n* hound, cur, mongrel, canine, puppy, pup, bitch, mutt (*infml*), pooch (*infml*).

Breeds of dog include: Afghan hound, alsatian, basset-hound, beagle, Border collie, borzoi, bull-mastiff, bulldog, bull-terrier, cairn terrier, chihuahua, chow, cocker spaniel, collie, corgi, dachshund, Dalmatian, Doberman pinscher, foxhound, fox-terrier, German Shepherd, golden retriever, Great Dane, greyhound, husky, Irish wolfhound, Jack Russell, King Charles spaniel, Labrador, lhasa apso, lurcher, Maltese, Old English sheepdog, Pekingese, pit bull terrier, pointer, poodle, pug, Rottweiler, saluki, sausage-dog (*infml*), schnauzer, Scottie (*infml*), Scottish terrier, Sealyham, setter, sheltie, shih tzu, springer spaniel, St Bernard, terrier, whippet, West Highland terrier, Westie (*infml*), wolf-hound, Yorkshire terrier.

➤ *v* pursue, follow, trail, track, tail, hound, shadow, plague, harry, haunt, trouble, worry.

dogged *adj* determined, resolute, persistent, persevering, intent, tenacious, firm, steadfast, staunch, single-minded, indefatigable, steady, unshakable, stubborn, obstinate, relentless, unyielding.
⊟ irresolute, apathetic.

dogma *n* doctrine, creed, belief, precept, principle, article (of faith), credo, tenet, conviction, teaching, opinion.

dogmatic *adj* opinionated, assertive, authoritative, positive, doctrinaire, dictatorial, doctrinal, categorical, emphatic, overbearing, arbitrary.

doldrums *n* depression, dejection, downheartedness, gloom, listlessness, low-spiritedness, apathy, boredom, tedium, dullness, inertia, stagnation, sluggishness, torpor, ennui (*fml*), lassitude (*fml*), malaise (*fml*), acedia (*fml*), blues (*infml*), dumps (*infml*).

dole out *v* distribute, allocate, hand out, dish out, apportion, allot, mete out, share, divide, deal, issue, ration, dispense, administer, assign.

dollop *n* lump, blob, clump, bunch, ball,

glob, gob, gobbet, helping, portion, serving.

domain *n* **1** DOMINION, kingdom, realm, territory, region, empire, lands, province. **2** FIELD, area, speciality, concern, department, sphere, discipline, jurisdiction.

domestic *adj* **1** HOME, family, household, home-loving, stay-at-home, homely, house-trained, tame, pet, private. **2** INTERNAL, indigenous, native.
➤ *n* servant, maid, charwoman, char, daily help, daily, au pair.

Types of domestic appliance include: washing machine, washer, washer/drier, tumble-drier, clothes airer, iron, steam iron, steam press, trouser press; dishwasher, vacuum cleaner, upright cleaner, cylinder cleaner, wet-and-dry cleaner, Hoover®, floor polisher, carpet sweeper, carpet shampooer; oven, Aga®, barbecue, cooker, Dutch oven, electric cooker, fan oven, gas stove, kitchen range, microwave oven, stove, hob, hotplate, grill, electric grill, griddle, rotisserie, spit, waffle iron, deep fryer, slow cooker, sandwich maker, toaster; food processor, mixer, blender, liquidizer, ice-cream maker, juicer, juice extractor, food slicer, electric knife, knife sharpener, kettle, tea/coffee maker, percolator, coffee mill, electric tin opener, timer, water filter; refrigerator, fridge (*infml*), icebox, fridge-freezer, freezer, deep-freeze; hostess-trolley, humidifier, ionizer, fire extinguisher.

domesticate *v* tame, house-train, break, train, accustom, familiarize.

domesticated *adj* tame, tamed, pet, house-trained, broken (in), domestic, home-loving, homely, house-proud, housewifely, naturalized.
⊟ feral, wild.

dominant *adj* **1** AUTHORITATIVE, controlling, governing, ruling, powerful, assertive, influential. **2** PRINCIPAL, main, outstanding, chief, important, predominant, primary, prominent, leading, pre-eminent, prevailing, prevalent, commanding.
⊟ **1** submissive. **2** subordinate.

dominate *v* **1** CONTROL, domineer, govern, rule, direct, monopolize, master, lead, overrule, prevail, overbear, tyrannize. **2** OVERSHADOW, eclipse, dwarf.

domineering *adj* overbearing,

authoritarian, imperious, autocratic, bossy (*infml*), dictatorial, despotic, masterful, high-handed, oppressive, tyrannical, arrogant.
E2 meek, servile.

dominion *n* 1 POWER, authority, domination, command, control, rule, sway, jurisdiction, government, lordship, mastery, supremacy, sovereignty. 2 DOMAIN, country, territory, province, colony, realm, kingdom, empire.

donate *v* give, contribute, present, bequeath, cough up (*infml*), fork out (*infml*), bestow (*fml*), confer (*fml*), subscribe.
E2 receive.

donation *n* gift, present, offering, grant, gratuity, largess(e), contribution, presentation, subscription, alms, benefaction (*fml*), bequest.

done *adj* 1 FINISHED, over, accomplished, completed, ended, concluded, settled, realized, executed. 2 CONVENTIONAL, acceptable, proper. 3 COOKED, ready.

donor *n* giver, donator, benefactor, contributor, philanthropist, provider, fairy godmother (*infml*).
E2 beneficiary.

doom *n* 1 FATE, fortune, destiny, portion, lot. 2 DESTRUCTION, catastrophe, downfall, ruin, death, death-knell. 3 CONDEMNATION, judgement, sentence, verdict.
➤ *v* condemn, damn, consign, judge, sentence, destine.

doomed *adj* condemned, damned, fated, ill-fated, ill-omened, cursed, destined, hopeless, luckless, ill-starred.

door *n* opening, entrance, entry, exit, doorway, portal, hatch.

dope (*infml*) *n* 1 NARCOTIC, drugs, marijuana, cannabis, opiate, hallucinogen. 2 FOOL, dolt, idiot, half-wit (*infml*), dimwit (*infml*), dunce, simpleton, clot (*infml*), blockhead. 3 INFORMATION, facts, low-down (*infml*), details.
➤ *v* drug, sedate, anaesthetize, stupefy, medicate, narcotize, inject, doctor.

dormant *adj* 1 INACTIVE, asleep, sleeping, inert, resting, slumbering, sluggish, torpid, hibernating, fallow, comatose. 2 LATENT, unrealized, potential, undeveloped, undisclosed.
E2 1 active, awake. 2 realized, developed.

dose *n* measure, dosage, amount, portion, quantity, draught, potion, prescription, shot.

➤ *v* medicate, administer, prescribe, dispense, treat.

dot *n* point, spot, speck, mark, fleck, circle, pin-point, atom, decimal point, full stop, iota, jot.
➤ *v* spot, sprinkle, stud, dab, punctuate.

dotage *n* old age, senility, second childhood, infirmity, weakness, feebleness, imbecility, decrepitude (*fml*).

dote on *v* adore, idolize, treasure, admire, indulge.

doting *adj* adoring, devoted, fond, loving, affectionate, tender, soft, indulgent.

double *adj* dual, twofold, twice, duplicate, twin, paired, doubled, coupled.
E2 single, half.
➤ *v* duplicate, enlarge, increase, repeat, multiply, fold, magnify.
➤ *n* twin, duplicate, copy, clone, replica, doppelgänger, lookalike, spitting image (*infml*), ringer (*infml*), image, counterpart, impersonator.
◆ **at the double** immediately, at once, quickly, without delay.

double-cross *v* cheat, swindle, defraud, trick, con (*infml*), hoodwink, betray, two-time (*infml*), mislead.

double-dealing *n* cheating, swindling, betrayal, treachery, defrauding, tricking, hoodwinking, misleading, two-facedness, duplicity (*fml*), perfidy (*fml*), mendacity (*fml*), two-timing (*infml*), crookedness (*infml*).

doubt *v* 1 DISTRUST, mistrust, query, question, suspect, fear. 2 BE UNCERTAIN, be dubious, hesitate, vacillate, waver.
E2 1 believe, trust.
➤ *n* 1 DISTRUST, suspicion, mistrust, scepticism, reservation, misgiving, incredulity, apprehension, hesitation. 2 UNCERTAINTY, difficulty, confusion, ambiguity, problem, indecision, perplexity, dilemma, quandary.
E2 1 trust, faith. 2 certainty, belief.

doubter *n* questioner, sceptic, disbeliever, unbeliever, agnostic, doubting Thomas, cynic, scoffer.
E2 believer.

doubtful *adj* 1 *doubtful about his future*: uncertain, unsure, undecided, suspicious, irresolute, wavering, hesitant, vacillating, tentative, sceptical. 2 *writing of doubtful origin*: dubious, questionable, unclear, ambiguous, vague, obscure, debatable.
E2 1 certain, decided. 2 definite, settled.

doubtless adv 1 CERTAINLY, without doubt, undoubtedly, unquestionably, indisputably, no doubt, clearly, surely, of course, truly, precisely. 2 PROBABLY, presumably, most likely, seemingly, supposedly.

dour adj 1 GLOOMY, dismal, forbidding, grim, morose, unfriendly, dreary, austere, sour, sullen. 2 HARD, inflexible, unyielding, rigid, severe, rigorous, strict, obstinate. ☒ 1 cheerful, bright. 2 easy-going.

douse, dowse v 1 SOAK, saturate, steep, submerge, immerse, immerge, dip, duck, drench, dunk, plunge. 2 EXTINGUISH, put out, blow out, smother, snuff.

dovetail v fit together, correspond, match, coincide, conform, agree, tally, harmonize, join, interlock, link, accord (fml).

dowdy adj unfashionable, ill-dressed, frumpish, drab, shabby, tatty (infml), frowsy, tacky (infml), dingy, old-fashioned, slovenly. ☒ fashionable, smart.

down prep, adv to a lower level/position, to the ground, to the floor, to the bottom. ☒ up.
➤ adj 1 SAD, depressed, unhappy, melancholy, miserable, downhearted, dejected, downcast, dispirited, wretched, low, blue (infml), down in the dumps (infml). 2 the computer is down: out of order, out of action, not working, crashed, inoperative (fml), bust (infml), conked out (sl). ☒ 1 happy. 2 operational.
➤ v 1 KNOCK DOWN, fell, floor, prostrate, throw, topple. 2 SWALLOW, drink, gulp, swig (infml), knock back (infml).
♦ **down and out** destitute, impoverished, penniless, derelict, ruined.
♦ **down with** get rid of, away with.

downcast adj dejected, depressed, despondent, sad, unhappy, miserable, down, low, disheartened, dispirited, blue (infml), fed up (infml), discouraged, disappointed, crestfallen, dismayed. ☒ cheerful, happy, elated.

downfall n fall, ruin, failure, collapse, destruction, disgrace, debacle, undoing, overthrow.

downgrade v 1 DEGRADE, demote, lower, humble. 2 DISPARAGE, denigrate, belittle, run down, decry. ☒ 1 upgrade, improve. 2 praise.

downhearted adj depressed, dejected, despondent, sad, downcast, discouraged, disheartened, low-spirited, unhappy, gloomy, glum, dismayed. ☒ cheerful, enthusiastic.

downpour n cloudburst, deluge, rainstorm, flood, inundation, torrent.

downright adj, adv absolute(ly), outright, plain(ly), utter(ly), clear(ly), complete(ly), out-and-out, frank(ly), explicit(ly).

down-to-earth adj commonsense, commonsensical, hard-headed, matter-of-fact, mundane, no-nonsense, plain-spoken, practical, realistic, sane, sensible, unsentimental, idealistic. ☒ fantastic, impractical.

down-trodden adj oppressed, subjugated, subservient, exploited, trampled on, abused, tyrannized, victimized, helpless.

downward adj descending, declining, downhill, sliding, slipping. ☒ upward.

dowse see **douse**.

doze v sleep, nod off, drop off, snooze (infml), kip (infml), zizz (sl).
➤ n nap, catnap, siesta, snooze (infml), forty winks (infml), kip (infml), shut-eye (infml), zizz (sl).

drab adj dull, dingy, dreary, dismal, gloomy, flat, grey, lacklustre, cheerless, sombre, shabby. ☒ bright, cheerful.

draft¹ v draw (up), outline, sketch, plan, design, formulate, compose.
➤ n outline, sketch, plan, delineation, abstract, rough, blueprint, protocol (fml).

draft² n bill of exchange, cheque, money order, letter of credit, postal order.

drag v 1 DRAW, pull, haul, lug, tug, trail, tow. 2 GO SLOWLY, creep, crawl, lag.
➤ n (infml) bore, annoyance, nuisance, pain (infml), bother.

drain v 1 EMPTY, remove, evacuate, draw off, strain, dry, milk, bleed. 2 DISCHARGE, trickle, flow out, leak, ooze. 3 EXHAUST, consume, sap, use up, deplete, drink up, swallow. ☒ 1 fill.
➤ n 1 CHANNEL, conduit, culvert, duct, outlet, trench, ditch, pipe, sewer. 2 DEPLETION, exhaustion, sap, strain.

drama n 1 PLAY, acting, theatre, show,

spectacle, stage-craft, scene, melodrama. **2** EXCITEMENT, crisis, turmoil.

dramatic *adj* **1** EXCITING, striking, stirring, thrilling, marked, significant, expressive, impressive. **2** HISTRIONIC, exaggerated, melodramatic, flamboyant.

dramatist *n* playwright, scriptwriter, play-writer, screen writer, comedian, dramaturge, dramaturgist, tragedian.

dramatize *v* **1** STAGE, put on, adapt. **2** ACT, play-act, exaggerate, overdo, overstate.

drape *v* cover, wrap, hang, fold, drop, suspend.

drastic *adj* extreme, radical, strong, forceful, severe, harsh, far-reaching, desperate, dire.
■ moderate, cautious.

draught *n* **1** PUFF, current, influx, flow. **2** DRINK, potion, quantity. **3** PULLING, traction.

draw *v* **1** *draw a picture*: sketch, portray, trace, pencil, paint, represent, map out, depict, design, chart, scribble, doodle, delineate (*fml*). **2** MOVE, go, proceed, progress, travel, come, approach, advance. **3** PULL, drag, haul, tow, tug, lug, trail. **4** *draw a knife; draw water from a well*: take out, pull out, bring out, produce, extract, remove, withdraw. **5** *draw a breath*: breathe in, inhale (*fml*), respire (*fml*). **6** *draw money from a bank*: take, get, receive, obtain, procure (*fml*). **7** ATTRACT, allure, lure, entice, bring in, influence, persuade, elicit, prompt. **8** *draw a conclusion*: conclude, deduce, infer, gather, come to, reason. **9** *draw lots*: pick, choose, select, decide on, go for, plump for (*infml*). **10** TIE, be equal, be even, be all square (*infml*).
■ **3** push. **7** repel.
➤ *n* **1** ATTRACTION, enticement, lure, allure, appeal, bait, interest, magnetism. **2** TIE, stalemate, dead heat.
◆ **draw back** recoil, wince, flinch, shrink, start back, withdraw, retract, retreat.
◆ **draw on** make use of, use, put to use, exploit, apply, employ, quarry, rely on, have recourse to, utilize (*fml*).
◆ **draw out** **1** *the train drew out of the station*: pull out, move out, set out, depart, leave, start. **2** EXTEND, prolong, lengthen, spin out, elongate, stretch, protract (*fml*). **3** *draw someone out*: encourage to talk, induce to talk/speak, put at ease, make feel less nervous.
■ **2** shorten.

◆ **draw up** **1** DRAFT, compose, formulate, prepare, frame, write out, put in writing. **2** PULL UP, stop, halt, run in.

drawback *n* disadvantage, snag, hitch, obstacle, impediment, hindrance, difficulty, flaw, fault, fly in the ointment (*infml*), catch, stumbling block, nuisance, trouble, defect, handicap, deficiency, imperfection.
■ advantage, benefit.

drawing *n* sketch, picture, outline, representation, delineation, portrayal, illustration, cartoon, graphic, portrait.

drawl *v* speak slowly, draw out one's vowels, drone, haw-haw, protract, twang.

drawn *adj* tired, fatigued, worn, haggard, gaunt, pinched, strained, stressed, taut, tense, fraught, harassed, sapped, washed out, hassled (*infml*).

dread *v* fear, shrink from, quail, cringe at, flinch, shy, shudder, tremble.
➤ *n* fear, apprehension, misgiving, trepidation, dismay, alarm, horror, terror, fright, disquiet, worry, quietly, qualm.
■ confidence, security.

dreadful *adj* awful, terrible, frightful, horrible, appalling, dire, shocking, ghastly, horrendous, tragic, grievous, hideous, tremendous.
■ wonderful, comforting.

dream *n* **1** VISION, illusion, reverie, trance, fantasy, daydream, nightmare, hallucination, delusion, imagination. **2** ASPIRATION, wish, hope, ambition, desire, pipe-dream, ideal, goal, design, speculation.
➤ *v* imagine, envisage, fancy, fantasize, daydream, hallucinate, conceive, visualize, conjure up, muse.
◆ **dream up** invent, devise, conceive, think up, imagine, concoct, hatch, create, spin, contrive.

dreamer *n* idealist, visionary, fantasizes, romancer, daydreamer, star-gazer, theorizer.
■ realist, pragmatist.

dreamy *adj* **1** FANTASTIC, unreal, imaginary, shadowy, vague, misty. **2** IMPRACTICAL, fanciful, daydreaming, romantic, visionary, faraway, absent, musing, pensive.
■ **1** real. **2** practical, down-to-earth.

dreary *adj* **1** *a dreary job*: boring, tedious, uneventful, dull, humdrum, routine, monotonous, wearisome, commonplace, colourless, lifeless. **2** *a dreary landscape*: gloomy, depressing, drab, dismal, bleak, sombre, sad, mournful.

Ea 1 interesting. **2** cheerful.

dregs *n* **1** SEDIMENT, deposit, residue, lees, grounds, scum, dross, trash, waste. **2** OUTCASTS, rabble, riff-raff, scum, down-and-outs.

drench *v* soak, saturate, steep, wet, douse, souse, immerse, inundate, duck, flood, imbue, drown.

dress *n* **1** FROCK, gown, robe. **2** CLOTHES, clothing, garment(s), outfit, costume, garb, get-up (*infml*), gear (*infml*), togs (*infml*).
➤ *v* **1** CLOTHE, put on, garb, rig, robe, wear, don, decorate, deck, garnish, trim, adorn, fit, drape. **2** ARRANGE, adjust, dispose, prepare, groom, straighten. **3** BANDAGE, tend, treat.

Ea 1 strip, undress.

♦ **dress down** rebuke, reprimand, reprove, scold, chide, berate (*fml*), upbraid (*fml*), carpet (*infml*), haul over the coals (*infml*), tear off a strip (*infml*), tell off (*infml*), give someone an earful (*infml*).

♦ **dress up** beautify, adorn, embellish, improve, deck, doll up, tart up (*infml*), gild, disguise.

dressing *n* **1** *a salad dressing*: sauce, condiment, relish, salad dressing, French dressing, Thousand Island dressing. **2** BANDAGE, plaster, Elastoplast®, gauze, lint, compress, poultice, tourniquet, pad, spica, ligature.

dribble *v* **1** TRICKLE, drip, leak, run, seep, drop, ooze. **2** DROOL, slaver, slobber, drivel.

drift *v* **1** WANDER, waft, stray, float, freewheel, coast. **2** GATHER, accumulate, pile up, drive.
➤ *n* **1** ACCUMULATION, mound, pile, bank, mass, heap. **2** TREND, tendency, course, direction, flow, movement, current, rush, sweep. **3** MEANING, intention, implication, gist, tenor, thrust, significance, aim, design, scope.

drill *v* **1** TEACH, train, instruct, coach, practise, school, rehearse, exercise, discipline. **2** BORE, pierce, penetrate, puncture, perforate.
➤ *n* **1** INSTRUCTION, training, practice, coaching, exercise, repetition, tuition, preparation, discipline. **2** BORER, awl, bit, gimlet.

drink *v* **1** IMBIBE, swallow, sip, drain, down, gulp, swig (*infml*), knock back (*infml*), sup,

quaff, absorb, guzzle, partake of (*fml*), swill. **2** GET DRUNK, booze (*infml*), tipple (*infml*), indulge, carouse, revel, tank up (*infml*).
➤ *n* **1** BEVERAGE, liquid, refreshment, draught, sip, swallow, swig (*infml*), gulp. **2** ALCOHOL, spirits, booze (*infml*), liquor, tipple (*infml*), tot, the bottle (*infml*), stiffener (*infml*).

Types of non-alcoholic drink include: Assam tea, Indian tea, Earl Grey, China tea, lapsang souchong, green tea, herbal tea, fruit tea, camomile tea, peppermint tea, rosehip tea, lemon tea, tisane, julep, mint-julep; coffee, café au lait, café filtre, café noir, cappuccino, espresso, Irish coffee, Turkish coffee; cocoa, hot chocolate, Horlicks®, Ovaltine®, milk, milk shake, float; fizzy drink, pop (*infml*), cherryade, Coca Cola®, Coke® (*infml*), cream soda, ginger beer, lemonade, limeade, Pepsi®, root beer, sarsaparilla, cordial, squash, barley water, Ribena®, fruit juice, mixer, bitter lemon, Canada Dry®, ginger ale, soda water, tonic water, mineral water, Perrier®, seltzer, Vichy water, Lucozade®, Wincarnis®, beef tea.

Alcoholic drinks include: ale, beer, cider, lager, shandy, stout, Guinness®; aquavit, Armagnac, bourbon, brandy, Calvados, Cognac, gin, gin-and-tonic, pink gin, sloe gin, rum, grog, rye, vodka, whisky, Scotch and soda, hot toddy; wine, red wine, vin rouge, vin rosé, white wine, vin blanc, Beaujolais, Beaune, Bordeaux, burgundy, claret, mulled wine, muscatel, Chianti, Graves, Rioja, Chablis, champagne, bubbly (*infml*), hock, Moselle, Riesling, Sauterne, mead, perry, vino (*infml*), plonk (*infml*); absinthe, advocaat, Benedictine, Chartreuse, black velvet, bloody Mary, Buck's fizz, Campari, cherry brandy, cocktail, Cointreau®, crème de menthe, daiquiri, eggnog, ginger wine, kirsch, Marsala, Martini®, ouzo, Pernod®, piña colada, port, punch, retsina, sake, sangria, schnapps, sherry, snowball, tequila, Tom Collins, vermouth. *see also* **wine**.

---

drip *v* drop, dribble, trickle, plop, perculate, drizzle, splash, sprinkle, weep.
➤ *n* **1** DROP, trickle, dribble, leak, bead, tear. **2** (*infml*) WEAKLING, wimp (*infml*), softy (*infml*), bore, wet (*infml*), ninny (*infml*).

drive *v* **1** DIRECT, control, manage, operate,

run, handle, motivate. **2** FORCE, compel, impel, coerce, constrain, press, push, urge, dragoon, gpad, guide, oblige. **3** STEER, motor, propel, ride, travel.

➤ *n* **1** ENERGY, enterprise, ambition, initiative, get-up-and-go (*infml*), vigour, motivation, determination. **2** CAMPAIGN, crusade, appeal, effort, action. **3** EXCURSION, outing, journey, ride, spin, trip, jaunt. **4** URGE, instinct, impulse, need, desire.

♦ **drive at** imply, allude to, intimate, mean, suggest, hint, get at, intend, refer to, signify, insinuate, indicate.

driving *adj* compelling, forceful, vigorous, dynamic, energetic, forthright, heavy, violent, sweeping.

drizzle *n* mist, mizzle, rain, spray, shower.
➤ *v* spit, spray, sprinkle, rain, spot, shower.

droll *adj* bizarre, odd, queer, eccentric, peculiar, comical, amusing, humorous, ridiculous, laughable, ludicrous, funny, clownish, zany, farcical, waggish, whimsical, witty, comic, diverting, entertaining, jocular.

drone *v* **1** HUM, buzz, purr, thrum, vibrate, whirr, drawl, chant, bombilate (*fml*), bombinate (*fml*). **2** *the lecturer droned on and on*: go on and on, speak interminably, talk monotonously, intone.
➤ *n* **1** HUM, buzz, purr, thrum, vibration, whirr, whirring, murmuring, chant. **2** LAZY PERSON, idler, loafer, slacker, dreamer, layabout, parasite, leech, hanger-on, lazybones (*infml*), sponger (*infml*), scrounger (*infml*).

drool *v* **1** DRIBBLE, slobber, slaver, salivate, drivel, water at the mouth. **2** *drool over the new baby*: dote, enthuse, gloat, gush, slobber over.

droop *v* **1** HANG DOWN, dangle, sag, bend, wilt, stoop, bow, fall down, sink, drop, slump. **2** LANGUISH, decline, flag, falter, slump, lose heart, wilt, wither, drop, faint, fall down, fade, slouch.
🔁 **1** straighten. **2** flourish, rise.

drop *n* **1** DROPLET, bead, lear, drip, bubble, globule, trickle. **2** DASH, pinch, spot, sip, trace, dab. **3** FALL, decline, falling-off, lowering, downturn, decrease, reduction, slump, plunge, deterioration. **4** DESCENT, precipice, slope, chasm, abyss.
➤ *v* **1** FALL, sink, decline, plunge, plummet, tumble, dive, descend, lower, droop, depress, diminish. **2** ABANDON,

forsake, desert, give up, relinquish, reject, jilt, leave, renounce, throw over, repudiate, cease, discontinue, quit.
🔁 **1** rise.

♦ **drop back** fall behind, lag (behind), fall back, retreat (*fml*).

♦ **drop in** call (round), call by, come over, come round, visit, come by, pop in (*infml*).

♦ **drop off 1** NOD OFF, doze, snooze (*infml*), have forty winks (*infml*). **2** DECLINE, fall off, decrease, dwindle, lessen, diminish, slacken. **3** DELIVER, set down, leave.
🔁 **1** wake up. **2** increase. **3** pick up.

♦ **drop out** back out, abandon, cry off, withdraw, forsake, leave, quit.

♦ **drop out of** back out of, withdraw from, leave, opt out, pull out, abandon, renounce (*fml*), renege (*fml*), cry off from (*infml*), quit (*infml*).

drought *n* dryness, aridity, parchedness, dehydration, desiccation, shortage, want.

drove *n* herd, horde, gathering, crowd, multitude, swarm, throng, flock, company, mob, press.

drown *v* **1** SUBMERGE, immerse, inundate, go under, flood, sink, deluge, engulf, drench. **2** OVERWHELM, overpower, overcome, swamp, wipe out, extinguish.

drowsy *adj* sleepy, tired, lethargic, nodding, dreamy, dozy, somnolent (*fml*).
🔁 alert, awake.

drudge *n* toiler, menial, dogsbody (*infml*), hack, servant, slave, factotum, worker, skivvy (*infml*), galley-slavy, lackey.
➤ *v* plod, toil, work, slave, plug away (*infml*), grind (*infml*), labour, beaver (*infml*).
🔁 idle, laze.

drudgery *n* labour, donkey-work (*infml*), hack-work, slog (*infml*), grind (*infml*), slavery, sweat, sweated labour, toil, skivvying, chore.

drug *n* medication, medicine, remedy, potion.

Types of drug include: anaesthetic, analgesic, antibiotic, antidepressant, antihistamine, barbiturate, narcotic, opiate, hallucinogenic, sedative, steroid, stimulant, tranquillizer; chloroform, aspirin, codeine, paracetamol, morphine, penicillin, diazepam, Valium®, cortisone, insulin, digitalis, laudanum, quinine, progesterone, oestrogen, cannabis, marijuana, smack (*sl*), LSD.

acid (*infml*), ecstasy, E (*sl*), heroin, opium, cocaine, crack (*infml*), dope (*infml*), amphetamine, downer (*sl*), speed (*sl*). *see also* **medicine**.

➤ *v* medicate, sedate, tranquillize, dope (*infml*), anaesthetize, dose, knock out (*infml*), stupefy, deaden, numb.

drum *v* beat, pulsate, tap, throb, thrum, tattoo, reverberate, rap.

◆ **drum up** obtain, round up, collect, gather, solicit, canvass, petition, attract.

drunk *adj* inebriated, intoxicated, under the influence, drunken, stoned (*sl*), legless (*sl*), paralytic (*infml*), sloshed (*infml*), merry (*infml*), tight (*infml*), tipsy (*infml*), tanked up (*infml*), tiddly (*infml*), plastered (*infml*), loaded (*infml*), lit up (*infml*), sozzled (*infml*), well-oiled (*infml*), canned (*sl*), blotto (*sl*).

🔁 sober, temperate, abstinent, teetotal.

drunkard *n* drunk, inebriate, alcoholic, dipsomaniac, boozer (*infml*), wino (*infml*), tippler (*infml*), soak (*infml*), lush (*infml*), sot (*infml*).

drunken *adj* **1** DRUNK, INEBRIATE (*fml*), intoxicated (*fml*), crapulent (*fml*), merry (*infml*), tight (*infml*), tipsy (*infml*), tiddly (*infml*), happy (*infml*), boozy (*sl*), stoned (*sl*), loaded (*sl*), lit up (*sl*), sloshed (*sl*), pissed (*sl*), bombed (*sl*). **2** *a drunken party*: debauched, dissipated, riotous, intemperate, bacchanalian.

🔁 **1** sober.

dry *adj* **1** ARID, parched, thirsty, dehydrated, desiccated, barren. **2** BORING, dull, dreary, tedious, monotonous. **3** *dry humour*: ironic, cynical, droll, deadpan, sarcastic, cutting.

🔁 **1** wet. **2** interesting.

➤ *v* dehydrate, parch, desiccate, drain, shrivel, wither.

🔁 soak.

dual *adj* double, twofold, duplicate, duplex, binary, combined, paired, twin, matched.

dubious *adj* **1** DOUBTFUL, uncertain, undecided, unsure, wavering, unsettled, suspicious, sceptical, hesitant. **2** QUESTIONABLE, debatable, unreliable, ambiguous, suspect, obscure, fishy (*infml*), shady (*infml*).

🔁 **1** certain. **2** trustworthy.

duck *v* **1** CROUCH, stoop, bob, bend. **2** AVOID, dodge, evade, shirk, sidestep. **3** DIP,

immerse, plunge, dunk, dive, submerge, douse, souse, wet, lower.

duct *n* pipe, tube, channel, conduit, passage, vessel, canal, funnel.

due *adj* **1** OWED, owing, payable, unpaid, outstanding, in arrears. **2** RIGHTFUL, fitting, appropriate, proper, merited, deserved, justified, suitable. **3** ADEQUATE, enough, sufficient, ample, plenty of. **4** EXPECTED, scheduled.

🔁 **1** paid. **3** inadequate.

➤ *adv* exactly, direct(ly), precisely, straight, dead (*infml*).

➤ *n* **1** *give him his due*: rights, (just) deserts, merits, prerogative, privilege, birthright, come-uppance (*infml*). **2** *pay dues*: charge(s), contribution, fee, membership fee, levy, subscription.

◆ **due to** owing to, as a result of, caused by, because of.

duel *n* affair of honour, combat, contest, fight, clash, competition, rivalry, encounter.

dull *adj* **1** BORING, uninteresting, unexciting, flat, dreary, monotonous, tedious, uneventful, humdrum, unimaginative, dismal, lifeless, plain, insipid, heavy. **2** DARK, gloomy, drab, murky, indistinct, grey, cloudy, lack-lustre, opaque, dim, overcast. **3** UNINTELLIGENT, dense, dim, dimwitted (*infml*), thick (*infml*), stupid, slow.

🔁 **1** interesting, exciting. **2** bright. **3** intelligent, clever.

➤ *v* **1** BLUNT, alleviate, mitigate, moderate, lessen, relieve, soften. **2** DEADEN, numb, paralyse. **3** DISCOURAGE, dampen, subdue, sadden. **4** DIM, obscure, fade.

duly *adv* accordingly, appropriately, correctly, fitly, fittingly, properly, rightfully, suitably, sure enough, deservedly, befittingly (*fml*), decorously (*fml*).

dumb *adj* silent, mute, soundless, speechless, tongue-tied, inarticulate, mum (*infml*).

dumbfounded *adj* astonished, amazed, astounded, overwhelmed, speechless, taken aback, thrown (*infml*), startled, overcome, confounded, flabbergasted (*infml*), staggered, confused, bowled over, dumb, floored (*infml*), paralysed.

dummy *n* **1** COPY, duplicate, imitation, counterfeit, substitute. **2** MODEL, lay-figure, mannequin, figure, form. **3** TEAT, pacifier.

➤ *adj* **1** ARTIFICIAL, fake, imitation, false,

bogus, mock, sham, phoney. **2** SIMULATED, practice, trial.

dump *v* **1** DEPOSIT, drop, offload, throw down, let fall, unload, empty out, discharge, park. **2** GET RID OF, scrap, throw away, dispose of, ditch, tip, jettison.
➤ *n* **1** RUBBISH-TIP, junk-yard, rubbish-heap, tip. **2** HOVEL, slum, shack, shanty, hole (*infml*), joint (*infml*), pigsty, mess.

dungeon *n* cell, prison, jail, gaol, cage, lock-up, keep, oubliette, vault.

dupe *n* victim, sucker (*infml*), fool, gull, mug (*infml*), push-over (*infml*), fall guy (*infml*), pawn, puppet, instrument, stooge (*infml*), simpleton.
➤ *v* deceive, delude, fool, trick, outwit, con (*infml*), cheat, hoax, swindle, rip off (*infml*), take in, hoodwink, defraud, bamboozle (*infml*).

duplicate *adj* identical, matching, twin, twofold, corresponding, matched.
➤ *n* copy, replica, reproduction, photocopy, carbon (copy), match, facsimile.
➤ *v* copy, reproduce, repeat, photocopy, double, clone, echo.

duplicity *n* deceit, deception, dishonesty, falsehood, fraud, guile, hypocrisy, double-dealing, treachery, betrayal, artifice, chicanery, dissimulation (*fml*), perfidy (*fml*).

durable *adj* lasting, enduring, long-lasting, abiding, hard-wearing, strong, sturdy, tough, unfading, substantial, sound, reliable, dependable, stable, resistant, persistent, constant, permanent, firm, fixed, fast.
🔳 perishable, weak, fragile.

duress *n* constraint, coercion, compulsion, pressure, restraint, threat, force.

dusk *n* twilight, sunset, nightfall, evening, sundown, gloaming, darkness, dark, gloom, shadows, shade.
🔳 dawn, brightness.

dust *n* powder, particles, dirt, earth, soil, ground, grit, grime.

dusty *adj* **1** DIRTY, grubby, filthy. **2** POWDERY, granular, crumbly, chalky, sandy.
🔳 **1** clean. **2** solid, hard.

dutiful *adj* obedient, respectful,

conscientious, devoted, filial, reverential, submissive.

duty *n* **1** OBLIGATION, responsibility, assignment, calling, charge, role, task, job, business, function, work, office, service. **2** OBEDIENCE, respect, loyalty. **3** TAX, toll, tariff, levy, customs, excise.
♦ **on duty** at work, engaged, busy.

dwarf *n* **1** PERSON OF RESTRICTED GROWTH, midget, pygmy, TomThumb, Lilliputian. **2** GNOME, goblin.
➤ *adj* miniature, small, tiny, pocket, mini (*infml*), diminutive, petite, Lilliputian, baby.
🔳 large.
➤ *v* **1** STUNT, retard, check. **2** OVERSHADOW, tower over, dominate.

dwell *v* live, inhabit, reside, stay, settle, populate, people, lodge, rest, abide (*fml*).
♦ **dwell on** brood on, think about, meditate on, turn over in one's mind, reflect on, mull over, harp on, linger over, elaborate, emphasize, ruminate on (*fml*).
🔳 pass over.

dwelling *n* home, house, establishment, residence, quarters, dwelling-house, lodge, lodging, cottage, hut, shanty, tent, abode (*fml*), domicile (*fml*), habitation (*fml*).

dwindle *v* diminish, decrease, decline, lessen, subside, ebb, fade, weaken, taper off, tail off, shrink, peter out, fall, wane, waste away, die out, wither, shrivel, disappear.
🔳 increase, grow.

dye *n* colour, colouring, stain, pigment, tint, tinge.
➤ *v* colour, tint, stain, pigment, tinge, imbue.

dying *adj* moribund, passing, final, going, mortal, not long for this world, perishing, failing, fading, vanishing.
🔳 reviving.

dynamic *adj* forceful, powerful, energetic, vigorous, go-ahead, high-powered, driving, self-starting, spirited, vital, lively, active.
🔳 inactive, apathetic.

dynasty *n* house, line, succession, dominion, regime, government, rule, empire, sovereignty.

Ee

each *adj* every, every single, every individual.

➤ *pron* each one, each in their own way, each and every one.

➤ *adv* apiece, individually, per capita, per head, per person, respectively, separately, singly.

eager *adj* **1** KEEN, enthusiastic, fervent, intent, earnest, zealous. **2** LONGING, yearning.

🖪 **1** unenthusiastic, indifferent.

ear *n* **1** ATTENTION, heed, notice, regard. **2** *an ear for language*: perception, sensitivity, discrimination, appreciation, hearing, skill, ability.

> Parts of the ear include: anvil (incus), auditory canal, auditory nerve, auricle, cochlea, concha, eardrum, eustachian tube, hammer (malleus), helix, labyrinth, lobe, oval window, pinna, round window, semicircular canal, stirrup (stapes), tragus, tympanum, vestibular nerve, vestibule.

early *adj* **1** *early symptoms*: forward, advanced, premature, untimely, undeveloped. **2** *early theatre*: primitive, ancient, primeval.

➤ *adv* ahead of time, in good time, beforehand, in advance, prematurely.

🖪 late.

earmark *v* set aside, put aside, designate, allocate, keep back, reserve, label, mark out, tag.

earn *v* **1** *earn a good salary*: receive, obtain, make, get, draw, bring in (*infml*), gain, realize, gross, reap. **2** *earn one's reputation*: deserve, merit, warrant, win, rate.

🖪 **1** spend, lose.

earnest *adj* **1** RESOLUTE, devoted, ardent, conscientious, intent, keen, fervent, firm, fixed, eager, enthusiastic, steady. **2** SERIOUS, sincere, solemn, grave, heartfelt.

🖪 **1** apathetic. **2** frivolous, flippant.

earnings *n* pay, income, salary, wages, profits, gain, proceeds, reward, receipts, return, revenue, remuneration, stipend.

🖪 expenditure, outgoings.

earth *n* **1** WORLD, planet, globe, sphere. **2** LAND, ground, soil, clay, loam, sod, humus.

earthenware *n* pottery, ceramics, crockery, pots.

earthly *adj* **1** *our earthly life*: material, physical, human, worldly, mortal, mundane, fleshly, secular, sensual, profane, temporal. **2** *no earthly explanation*: possible, likely, conceivable, slightest.

🖪 **1** spiritual, heavenly.

earthy *adj* crude, coarse, vulgar, bawdy, rough, raunchy (*infml*), down-to-earth, ribald, robust.

🖪 refined, modest.

ease *n* **1** FACILITY, effortlessness, skilfulness, deftness, dexterity, naturalness, cleverness. **2** COMFORT, contentment, peace, affluence, repose, leisure, relaxation, rest, quiet, happiness.

🖪 **1** difficulty. **2** discomfort.

➤ *v* **1** *ease the pain*: alleviate, moderate, lessen, lighten, relieve, mitigate, abate, relent, allay, assuage, relax, comfort, calm, soothe, facilitate, smooth. **2** *ease it into position*: inch, steer, slide, still.

🖪 **1** aggravate, intensify, worsen.

easily *adv* **1** EFFORTLESSLY, comfortably, readily, simply. **2** BY FAR, undoubtedly, indisputably, definitely, certainly, doubtlessly, clearly, far and away, undeniably, simply, surely, probably, well.

🖪 **1** laboriously.

easy *adj* **1** EFFORTLESS, simple, uncomplicated, undemanding, straightforward, manageable, cushy (*infml*). **2** RELAXED, carefree, easy-going, comfortable, informal, calm, natural, leisurely.

🖪 **1** difficult, demanding, exacting. **2** tense, uneasy.

easy-going *adj* relaxed, tolerant, laid-back (*infml*), amenable, happy-go-lucky (*infml*), carefree, calm, even-tempered, serene.

🖪 strict, intolerant, critical.

eat *v* **1** CONSUME, feed, swallow, devour, chew, scoff (*infml*), munch, dine.

2 CORRODE, erode, wear away, decay, rot, crumble, dissolve.

eatable *adj* edible, palatable, good, wholesome, digestible, comestible (*fml*), harmless.
🆎 inedible, unpalatable.

eavesdrop *v* listen in, spy, overhear, snoop (*infml*), tap (*infml*), bug (*infml*), monitor.

ebb *v* **1** *the tide ebbed*: fall, fall back, flow back, go out, recede, retrocede (*fml*). **2** *his confidence ebbed away*: decline, decrease, diminish, drop, dwindle, flag, weaken, deteriorate, decay, degenerate, fade away, shrink, sink, slacken, subside, recede, lessen, wane, abate (*fml*), peter out (*infml*).
🆎 **1** rise. **2** increase, rise.
➤ *n* **1** *at ebb tide*: low tide, low water, ebb tide, fall, going out, flowing-back, retreat. **2** *her health is at a low ebb*: decline, decrease, drop, decay, lagging, lessening, deterioration, degeneration, slackening, weakening, subsidence, wane, waning, dwindling,
🆎 **1** rise, flow. **2** increase.

ebullient *adj* exhilarated, effusive, enthusiastic, excited, exuberant, bright, buoyant, elated, gushing, vivacious, effervescent, breezy, irrepressible, zestful, chirpy (*infml*).
🆎 apathetic, dull, lifeless.

eccentric *adj* odd, peculiar, abnormal, unconventional, strange, quirky, weird, way-out (*infml*), queer, outlandish, idiosyncratic, bizarre, freakish, erratic, singular, dotty.
🆎 conventional, orthodox, normal.
➤ *n* nonconformist, oddball (*infml*), oddity, crank (*infml*), freak (*infml*), character (*infml*).

eccentricity *n* unconventionality, strangeness, peculiarity, nonconformity, abnormality, oddity, weirdness, idiosyncrasy, singularity, quirk, freakishness, aberration, anomaly, capriciousness.
🆎 conventionality, ordinariness.

ecclesiastical *adj* church, churchly, religious, clerical, priestly, divine, spiritual.

echo *v* **1** REVERBERATE, resound, repeat, reflect, reiterate, ring. **2** IMITATE, copy, reproduce, mirror, resemble, mimic.
➤ *n* **1** REVERBERATION, reiteration, repetition, reflection. **2** IMITATION, copy, reproduction, mirror image, image, parallel.

eclipse *v* **1** BLOT OUT, obscure, cloud, veil, darken, dim. **2** OUTDO, overshadow, outshine, surpass, transcend.
➤ *n* **1** OBSCURATION, overshadowing, darkening, shading, dimming. **2** DECLINE, failure, fall, loss.

economic *adj* **1** COMMERCIAL, business, industrial. **2** FINANCIAL, budgetary, fiscal, monetary. **3** PROFITABLE, profit-making, money-making, productive, cost-effective, viable.

economical *adj* **1** THRIFTY, careful, prudent, saving, sparing, frugal. **2** CHEAP, inexpensive, low-priced, reasonable, cost-effective, modest, efficient.
🆎 **1** wasteful. **2** expensive, uneconomical.

economize *v* save, cut back, tighten one's belt (*infml*), cut costs.
🆎 waste, squander.

economy *n* thrift, saving, restraint, prudence, frugality, parsimony, providence, husbandry.
🆎 extravagance.

ecstasy *n* delight, rapture, bliss, elation, joy, euphoria, frenzy, exaltation, fervour.
🆎 misery, torment.

ecstatic *adj* elated, blissful, joyful, rapturous, overjoyed, euphoric, delirious, frenzied, fervent.
🆎 downcast.

eddy *n* whirlpool, swirl, vortex, twist.
➤ *v* swirl, whirl.

edge *n* **1** BORDER, rim, boundary, limit, brim, threshold, brink, fringe, margin, outline, side, verge, line, perimeter, periphery, lip. **2** ADVANTAGE, superiority, force. **3** SHARPNESS, acuteness, keenness, incisiveness, pungency, zest.
➤ *v* creep, inch, ease, sidle.

edgy *adj* on edge, nervous, tense, anxious, ill at ease, keyed-up, touchy, irritable.
🆎 calm.

edible *adj* eatable, palatable, digestible, wholesome, good, harmless.
🆎 inedible.

edict *n* command, order, proclamation, law, decree, regulation, pronouncement, ruling, mandate, statute, injunction, manifesto.

edifice *n* building, construction, structure, erection.

edify *v* instruct, improve, enlighten, inform, guide, educate, nurture, teach.

edit *v* correct, emend, revise, rewrite,

reorder, rearrange, adapt, check, compile, rephrase, select, polish, annotate, censor.

edition *n* copy, volume, impression, printing, issue, version, number.

educate *v* teach, train, instruct, tutor, coach, school, inform, cultivate, edify, drill, improve, discipline, develop.

educated *adj* learned, taught, schooled, trained, knowledgeable, informed, instructed, lettered, cultured, civilized, tutored, refined, well-bred.
Ea uneducated, uncultured.

education *n* teaching, training, schooling, tuition, tutoring, coaching, guidance, instruction, cultivation, culture, scholarship, improvement, enlightenment, knowledge, nurture, development.

Educational establishments include:
kindergarten, nursery school, infant school, primary school, middle school, combined school, secondary school, secondary modern, upper school, high school, grammar school, grant-maintained school, preparatory school, public school, private school, boarding-school, college, sixth-form college, polytechnic, poly, city technical college, CTC, technical college, university, adult-education centre, academy, seminary, finishing school, business school, secretarial college, Sunday school, convent school, summer-school.

Educational terms include: adult education, assisted places scheme, A-level, baccalaureate, board of governors, break time, bursar, campus, catchment area, certificate, classroom, coeducation, common entrance, course, curriculum, degree, diploma, double-first, eleven-plus, enrolment, examination, exercise book, final exam, finals, further education, GCSE (General Certificate of Secondary Education), governor, graduation, half-term, head boy, head girl, head teacher, higher education, homework, intake, invigilator, lecture, literacy, matriculation, matron, mixed-ability teaching, modular course, national curriculum, NVQ (national vocational qualification), numeracy, O-level, opting out, parent governor, PTA (parent teacher association), playground, playtime, prefect, primary education, proctor, professor, pupil, quadrangle, qualification, refresher course, register, report, scholarship, school term, secondary education, special education,

statemented, streaming, student, student grant, student loan, study, subject, syllabus, teacher, teacher training, test paper, textbook, thesis, timetable, truancy, university entrance, work experience.

eerie *adj* weird, strange, uncanny, spooky (*infml*), creepy, frightening, scary, spine-chilling.

effect *n* **1** OUTCOME, result, conclusion, consequence, upshot, aftermath, issue.
2 POWER, force, impact, efficacy, impression, strength. **3** MEANING, significance, import.
➤ *v* cause, execute, create, achieve, accomplish, perform, produce, make, initiate, fulfil, complete.
♦ **in effect** in fact, actually, really, in reality, to all intents and purposes, for all practical purposes, essentially, effectively, virtually.
♦ **take effect** be effective, become operative, come into force, come into operation, be implemented, begin, work.

effective *adj* **1** EFFICIENT, efficacious, productive, adequate, capable, useful.
2 OPERATIVE, in force, functioning, current, active. **3** STRIKING, impressive, forceful, cogent, powerful, persuasive, convincing, telling.
Ea 1 ineffective, powerless.

effects *n* belongings, possessions, property, goods, gear (*infml*), movables, chattels (*fml*), things, trappings.

effeminate *adj* unmanly, womanly, womanish, feminine, sissy (*infml*), delicate.
Ea manly.

effervescent *adj* **1** BUBBLY, sparkling, fizzy, frothy, carbonated, foaming.
2 LIVELY, ebullient, vivacious, animated, buoyant, exhilarated, enthusiastic, exuberant, excited, vital.
Ea 1 flat. **2** dull.

efficiency *n* effectiveness, competence, proficiency, skill, expertise, skilfulness, capability, ability, productivity.
Ea inefficiency, incompetence.

efficient *adj* effective, competent, proficient, skilful, capable, able, productive, well-organized, businesslike, powerful, well-conducted.
Ea inefficient, incompetent.

effigy *n* figure, statue, carving, representation, likeness, picture, portrait, image, icon, idol, dummy, guy.

effort *n* **1** EXERTION, strain, application,

struggle, trouble, energy, toil, striving, pains, travail (*fml*). **2** ATTEMPT, try, go (*infml*), endeavour, shot, stab. **3** ACHIEVEMENT, accomplishment, feat, exploit, production, creation, deed, product, work.

> Expressions about effort include: be at pains, beaver away, blood, sweat and tears, break the back of something, bust a gut, can't be bothered, do one's bit, do one's utmost, fight tooth and nail, go all out, go out of one's way, go the extra mile, go to a lot of trouble, go to great lengths, go to the trouble of, have one's nose to the grindstone, huff and puff, knock one's pan in, make a point of doing something, make the effort, pull out all the stops, pull one's finger out, pull one's socks up, pull one's weight, put one's back into something, put one's shoulder to the wheel, stay the course, sweat blood over something, take a bit of doing, take the trouble to, use a bit of elbow grease, use a sledgehammer to crack a nut, work one's guts out.

effortless *adj* easy, simple, undemanding, facile, painless, smooth. **F3** difficult.

effrontery *n* audacity, impertinence, insolence, cheek (*infml*), impudence, temerity, boldness, brazenness, cheekiness, gall, nerve, presumption, disrespect, arrogance, brashness. **F3** respect, timidity.

effusive *adj* fulsome, gushing, unrestrained, expansive, ebullient, demonstrative, profuse, overflowing, enthusiastic, exuberant, extravagant, lavish, talkative, voluble. **F3** reserved, restrained.

egg on *v* encourage, incite, push, urge, drive, excite, stimulate, spur, prompt, coax, talk into, goad, prod, prick, exhort (*fml*). **F3** discourage.

egotism *n* egoism, egomania, self-centredness, self-importance, conceitedness, self-regard, self-love, self-conceit, narcissism, self-admiration, vanity, bigheadedness (*infml*). **F3** humility.

egotistic *adj* egoistic, egocentric, self-centred, self-important, conceited, vain, swollen-headed (*infml*), bigheaded (*infml*), boasting, bragging. **F3** humble.

ejaculate *v* **1** DISCHARGE, eject, spurt, emit. **2** EXCLAIM, call, blurt (out), cry, shout, yell, utter, scream.

eject *v* **1** EMIT, expel, discharge, spout, spew, evacuate, vomit. **2** OUST, evict, throw out, drive out, turn out, expel, remove, banish, deport, dismiss, exile, kick out, fire (*infml*), sack (*infml*).

ejection *n* eviction, expulsion, removal, banishment, dismissal, discharge, exile, deportation, ousting, firing (*infml*), sacking (*infml*), the boot (*infml*), the sack (*infml*).

eke out *v* **1** *eke out supplies*: make something stretch, stretch, spin out, fill out, husband, economize on, be economical with, add to, increase, supplement, go easy with (*infml*). **2** *eke out a living*: scrimp and save, scrape, scratch, get by, survive, live from hand to mouth (*infml*), feel the pinch (*infml*).

elaborate *adj* **1** *elaborate plans*: detailed, careful, thorough, exact, extensive, painstaking, precise, perfected, minute, laboured, studied. **2** *elaborate design*: intricate, complex, complicated, involved, ornamental, ornate, fancy, decorated, ostentatious, showy, fussy. **F3 2** simple, plain.
➤ *v* amplify, develop, enlarge, expand, flesh out, polish, improve, refine, devise, explain. **F3** précis, simplify.

elapse *v* pass, lapse, go by, slip away.

elastic *adj* **1** PLIABLE, flexible, stretchable, supple, resilient, yielding, springy, rubbery, pliant, plastic, bouncy, buoyant. **2** ADAPTABLE, accommodating, flexible, tolerant, adjustable. **F3 1** rigid. **2** inflexible.

elasticity *n* **1** PLIABILITY, flexibility, resilience, stretch, springiness, suppleness, give, plasticity, bounce, buoyancy. **2** ADAPTABILITY, flexibility, tolerance, adjustability. **F3 1** rigidity. **2** inflexibility.

elated *adj* exhilarated, excited, euphoric, ecstatic, exultant, jubilant, overjoyed, joyful. **F3** despondent, downcast.

elation *n* exhilaration, delight, transports of delight, euphoria, ecstasy, rapture, bliss, exultation, glee, high spirits, joy, joyfulness, jubilation, joyousness (*fml*). **F3** depression, despondency.

elbow *v* jostle, nudge, push, shove,

bump, crowd, knock, shoulder.

elder *adj* older, senior, first-born, ancient.
🔁 younger.

elderly *adj* aging, aged, old, hoary, senile.
🔁 young, youthful.

elect *v* choose, pick, opt for, select, vote
for, prefer, adopt, designate, appoint,
determine.
➤ *adj* choice, elite, chosen, designated,
designate, picked, prospective, selected, to
be, preferred, hand-picked.

election *n* choice, selection, voting,
ballot, poll, appointment, determination,
decision, preference.

elector *n* selector, voter, constituent.

electric *adj* electrifying, exciting,
stimulating, thrilling, charged, dynamic,
stirring, tense, rousing.
🔁 unexciting, flat.

electrical components

Types of electrical component and
device include: adaptor, ammeter,
armature, battery, bayonet fitting, cable,
ceiling rose, circuit breaker, conduit,
continuity tester, copper conductor, dimmer
switch, dry-cell battery, earthed plug,
electrical screwdriver, electricity meter,
extension lead, fluorescent tube, fuse,
fusebox, fuse carrier, high voltage tester,
insulating tape, lampholder, light bulb,
multimeter, neon lamp, socket, test lamp,
three-core cable, three-pin plug, transducer,
transformer, two-pin plug, universal test
meter, voltage doubler, wire strippers.

electricity

Electricity and electronic terms include:
alternating current (AC), alternator, amp,
ampere, amplifier, analogue signal, anode,
band-pass filter, battery, bioelectricity,
capacitance, capacitor, cathode, cathode-
ray tube, cell, commutator, condenser,
conductivity, coulomb, digital signal, diode,
direct current (DC), Dolby (system), dynamo,
eddy current, electrode, electrolyte,
electromagnet, electron tube, farad, Faraday
cage, Foucault current, frequency
modulation, galvanic, galvanometer,
generator, grid system, henry, impedance,
induced current, inductance, integrated
circuit, isoelectric, isoelectronic, logic gate,
loudspeaker, microchip, mutual induction,
ohm, optoelectronics, oscillator,
oscilloscope, piezoelectricity, polarity, power

station, reactance, resistance, resistor,
rheostat, semiconductor, siemens, silicon
chip, solenoid, solid state circuit, static
electricity, step-down transformer,
superconductivity, switch, thermionics,
thermistor, thyristor, transformer, transistor,
triode, truth table, turboalternator, tweeter,
valve, volt, voltage amplifier, voltaic, watt,
Wheatstone bridge, woofer.

electrify *v* thrill, excite, shock, invigorate,
animate, stimulate, stir, rouse, fire, jolt,
galvanize, amaze, astonish, astound,
stagger.
🔁 bore.

elegant *adj* stylish, chic, fashionable,
modish, smart, refined, polished, genteel,
smooth, tasteful, fine, exquisite, beautiful,
graceful, handsome, delicate, neat,
artistic.
🔁 inelegant, unrefined, unfashionable.

elegy *n* dirge, lament, requiem, plaint.

element *n* factor, component,
constituent, ingredient, member, part,
piece, fragment, feature, trace.
🔁 whole.

elementary *adj* basic, fundamental,
rudimentary, principal, primary, clear,
easy, introductory, straightforward,
uncomplicated, simple.
🔁 advanced.

elements *n* basics, fundamentals,
foundations, principles, rudiments,
essentials.

elevate *v* 1 LIFT, raise, hoist, heighten,
intensify, magnify. 2 EXALT, advance,
promote, aggrandize, upgrade. 3 UPLIFT,
rouse, boost, brighten.
🔁 1 lower. 2 downgrade.

elevated *adj* raised, lofty, exalted, high,
grand, noble, dignified, sublime.
🔁 base.

elevation *n* 1 RISE, promotion,
advancement, preferment,
aggrandizement. 2 EXALTATION, loftiness,
grandeur, eminence, nobility. 3 HEIGHT,
altitude, hill, rise.
🔁 1 demotion. 2 dip.

elicit *v* evoke, draw out, derive, extract,
obtain, exact, extort, cause.

eligible *adj* qualified, fit, appropriate,
suitable, acceptable, worthy, proper,
desirable.
🔁 ineligible.

eliminate *v* remove, get rid of, cut out,

take out, exclude, delete, dispense with, rub out, omit, reject, disregard, dispose of, drop, do away with, eradicate, expel, extinguish, stamp out, exterminate, knock out, kill, murder.
🔁 include, accept.

elite n best, elect, aristocracy, upper classes, nobility, gentry, crème de la crème, establishment, high society.
➤ adj choice, best, exclusive, selected, first-class, aristocratic, noble, upper-class.

elixir n cure-all, panacea, remedy, solution, mixture, concentrate, essence, extract, pith, potion, principle, quintessence, syrup, tincture.

elocution n delivery, articulation, diction, enunciation, pronunciation, oratory, rhetoric, speech, utterance.

elongated adj lengthened, extended, prolonged, protracted, stretched, long.

elope v run off, run away, decamp, bolt, abscond, do a bunk (infml), escape, steal away, leave, disappear.

eloquent adj articulate, fluent, well-expressed, glib, expressive, vocal, voluble, persuasive, moving, forceful, graceful, plausible, stirring, vivid.
🔁 inarticulate, tongue-tied.

elsewhere adv somewhere else, in/to another place, not here, absent, removed, abroad.
🔁 here, present.

elucidate v explain, clarify, clear up, interpret, spell out, illustrate, unfold.
🔁 confuse.

elude v 1 AVOID, escape, evade, dodge, shirk, duck (infml), flee. 2 PUZZLE, frustrate, baffle, confound, thwart, stump, foil.

elusive adj 1 INDEFINABLE, intangible, unanalysable, subtle, puzzling, baffling, transient, transitory. 2 EVASIVE, shifty, slippery, tricky.

emaciated adj thin, gaunt, lean, haggard, wasted, scrawny, skeletal, pinched, attenuated, meagre, lank.
🔁 plump, well-fed.

emanate v 1 ORIGINATE, proceed, arise, derive, issue, spring, stem, flow, come, emerge. 2 DISCHARGE, send out, emit, give out, give off, radiate.

emancipate v free, liberate, release, set free, enfranchise, deliver, discharge, loose,

unchain, unshackle, unfetter.
🔁 enslave.

emancipation n liberation, freedom, setting free, release, deliverance, liberty, discharge, enfranchisement, unbinding, unfettering, unchaining, manumission (fml).
🔁 enslavement.

embalm v preserve, mummify, store, lay out, enshrine, cherish, consecrate, conserve, treasure.

embankment n causeway, dam, rampart, levee, earthwork.

embargo n restriction, ban, prohibition, restraint, proscription, bar, barrier, interdiction (fml), impediment, check, hindrance, blockage, stoppage, seizure.

embark v board (ship), go aboard, take ship.
🔁 disembark.
◆ **embark on** begin, start, commence, set about, launch, undertake, enter, initiate, engage in.
🔁 complete, finish.

embarrass v disconcert, mortify, show up, discompose, fluster, humiliate, shame, distress.

embarrassed adj awkward, uncomfortable, self-conscious, upset, confused, distressed, disconcerted, ashamed, shamed, guilty, shown up, humiliated, mortified, abashed, discomfited (fml), sheepish (infml).
🔁 unembarrassed.

embarrassing adj awkward, uncomfortable, disconcerting, distressing, upsetting, sensitive, mortifying, humiliating, shameful, shaming, tricky, compromising, painful, discomfiting (fml), touchy (infml).

embarrassment n 1 DISCOMPOSURE, self-consciousness, chagrin, mortification, humiliation, shame, awkwardness, confusion, bashfulness. 2 DIFFICULTY, constraint, predicament, distress, discomfort.

embellish v adorn, ornament, decorate, deck, dress up, beautify, gild, garnish, festoon, elaborate, embroider, enrich, exaggerate, enhance, varnish, grace.
🔁 simplify, denude.

embellishment n adornment, ornament, ornamentation, decoration, elaboration, garnish, trimming, gilding, enrichment, enhancement, embroidery, exaggeration.

embezzle v appropriate, misappropriate, steal, pilfer, filch, pinch (*infml*).

embezzlement n appropriation, misappropriation, pilfering, fraud, stealing, theft, filching.

embittered adj bitter, disaffected, sour, disillusioned.

emblazon v 1 DECORATE, adorn, ornament, blazon, embellish, depict, colour, illuminate, paint. 2 PROCLAIM, publicize, publish, extol, praise, glorify, trumpet, laud (*fml*).

emblem n symbol, sign, token, representation, logo, insignia, device, crest, mark, badge, figure.

embodiment n incarnation, personification, exemplification, expression, epitome, example, incorporation, realization, representation, manifestation, concentration.

embody v 1 PERSONIFY, exemplify, represent, stand for, symbolize, incorporate, express, manifest. 2 INCLUDE, contain, integrate.

embrace v 1 HUG, clasp, cuddle, hold, grasp, squeeze. 2 INCLUDE, encompass, incorporate, contain, comprise, cover, involve. 3 ACCEPT, take up, welcome.
➤ n hug, cuddle, clasp, clinch (*infml*).

embroidery n fancywork, needlework, sewing, tapestry, tatting, needlepoint.

> Types of embroidery stitch include:
> backstitch, blanket, bullion, chain, chevron, cross, feather, fishbone, French knot, half-cross, herringbone, lazy-daisy, longstitch, long-and-short, moss, Oriental couching, Romanian couching, running, satin, stem, straight, Swiss darning, tent.

embroil v involve, implicate, entangle, enmesh, mix up, incriminate.

embryo n nucleus, germ, beginning, root.

embryonic adj undeveloped, rudimentary, immature, early, germinal, primary.
🖃 developed.

emerge v 1 ARISE, rise, surface, appear, develop, crop up (*infml*), transpire, turn up, materialize. 2 EMANATE, issue, proceed.
🖃 1 disappear.

emergence n appearance, rise, advent, coming, dawn, development, arrival, disclosure, issue.
🖃 disappearance.

emergency n crisis, danger, difficulty, exigency (*fml*), predicament, plight, pinch, strait, quandary.

emigrate v migrate, relocate, move, depart.

emigration n moving abroad, migration, removal, departure, exodus, journey, relocation, expatriation.

eminence n distinction, fame, pre-eminence, prominence, renown, reputation, greatness, importance, esteem, note, prestige, rank.

eminent adj distinguished, famous, prominent, illustrious, outstanding, notable, pre-eminent, prestigious, celebrated, renowned, noteworthy, conspicuous, esteemed, important, well-known, elevated, respected, great, high-ranking, grand, superior.
🖃 unknown, obscure, unimportant.

eminently adv highly, well, very, greatly, exceedingly, exceptionally, extremely, outstandingly, prominently, remarkably, notably, signally, strikingly, conspicuously, surpassingly, par excellence.

emissary n ambassador, agent, envoy, messenger, delegate, herald, courier, representative, scout, deputy, spy.

emission n discharge, issue, ejection, emanation, ejaculation, diffusion, transmission, exhalation, radiation, release, exudation, vent.

emit v discharge, issue, eject, emanate, exude, give out, give off, diffuse, radiate, release, shed, vent.
🖃 absorb.

emolument n pay, salary, wages, payment, remuneration, return, reward, allowance, benefit, earnings, fee, gain, profit(s), hire, honorarium, stipend, compensation, recompense.

emotion n feeling, passion, sensation, sentiment, ardour, fervour, warmth, reaction, vehemence, excitement.

emotional adj 1 FEELING, passionate, sensitive, responsive, ardent, tender, warm, roused, demonstrative, excitable, enthusiastic, fervent, impassioned, moved, sentimental, zealous, hot-blooded, heated, tempestuous, overcharged, temperamental, fiery. 2 EMOTIVE, moving, poignant, thrilling, touching, stirring, heart-warming, exciting, pathetic.
🖃 1 unemotional, cold, detached, calm.

emotive *adj* controversial, delicate, inflammatory, sensitive, awkward, touchy.

emphasis *n* stress, weight, significance, importance, priority, underscoring, accent, force, power, prominence, pre-eminence, attention, intensity, strength, urgency, positiveness, insistence, mark, moment.

emphasize *v* stress, accentuate, underline, highlight, accent, feature, dwell on, weight, point up, spotlight, play up, insist on, press home, intensify, strengthen, punctuate.
☒ play down, understate.

emphatic *adj* forceful, positive, insistent, certain, definite, decided, unequivocal, absolute, categorical, earnest, marked, pronounced, significant, strong, striking, vigorous, distinct, energetic, forcible, important, impressive, momentous, powerful, punctuated, telling, vivid, graphic, direct.
☒ tentative, hesitant, understated.

empire *n* 1 SUPREMACY, sovereignty, rule, authority, command, government, jurisdiction, control, power, sway.
2 DOMAIN, dominion, kingdom, realm, commonwealth, territory.

empirical *adj* practical, pragmatic, experimental, observed, experiential (*fml*).
☒ theoretical, conjectural, speculative.

employ *v* 1 ENGAGE, hire, take on, recruit, enlist, commission, retain, fill, occupy, take up. 2 USE, utilize, make use of, apply, bring to bear, ply, exercise.

employed *adj* working, in work, in employment, with a job, earning, hired, occupied, engaged, active, preoccupied, busy.
☒ unemployed, jobless.

employee *n* worker, member of staff, job-holder, hand, wage-earner.

employer *n* boss, proprietor, owner, manager, gaffer (*infml*), management, company, firm, business, establishment.

employment *n* 1 JOB, work, occupation, situation, business, calling, profession, line (*infml*), vocation, trade, pursuit, craft.
2 ENLISTMENT, employ, engagement, hire.
☒ 1 unemployment.

empower *v* authorize, warrant, enable, license, sanction, permit, entitle, commission, delegate, qualify.

emptiness *n* 1 VACUUM, vacantness, void, hollowness, hunger, bareness, barrenness, desolation. 2 FUTILITY, meaninglessness, worthlessness, aimlessness, ineffectiveness, unreality.
☒ 1 fullness.

empty *adj* 1 VACANT, void, unoccupied, uninhabited, unfilled, deserted, bare, hollow, desolate, blank, clear. 2 FUTILE, aimless, meaningless, senseless, trivial, vain, worthless, useless, insubstantial, ineffective, insincere. 3 VACUOUS, inane, expressionless, blank, vacant.
☒ 1 full. 2 meaningful.
➤ *v* drain, exhaust, discharge, clear, evacuate, vacate, pour out, unload, void, gut.
☒ fill.

empty-headed *adj* inane, silly, frivolous, scatter-brained (*infml*), feather-brained (*infml*).

emulate *v* match, copy, mimic, follow, imitate, echo, compete with, contend with, rival, vie with.

enable *v* equip, qualify, empower, authorize, sanction, warrant, allow, permit, prepare, fit, facilitate, license, commission, endue.
☒ prevent, inhibit, forbid.

enact *v* 1 DECREE, ordain, order, authorize, command, legislate, sanction, ratify, pass, establish. 2 ACT (OUT), perform, play, portray, represent, depict.
☒ 1 repeal, rescind.

enactment *n* 1 PASSING, authorization, approval, sanction, ratification, legislation, rule, bill, act, statute, law, order, decree, edict, command, commandment, ordinance, regulation. 2 PERFORMANCE, play, playing, performing, acting, portrayal, representation, staging.
☒ 1 repeal.

enamoured *adj* charmed, infatuated, in love with, enchanted, captivated, entranced, smitten, keen, taken, fascinated, fond.

encampment *n* camp, camping-ground, campsite, base, bivouac, quarters, tents.

encapsulate *v* sum up, summarize, typify, exemplify, epitomize, capture, include, contain, take in, represent, condense, digest, abridge, compress, précis.

enchant *v* 1 CAPTIVATE, charm, fascinate, enrapture, attract, allure, appeal, delight, thrill. 2 ENTRANCE, enthral, bewitch,

spellbind, hypnotize, mesmerize.
E3 1 repel.

enchanting *adj* charming, delightful,
attractive, fascinating, appealing, lovely,
pleasant, wonderful, alluring, bewitching,
captivating, endearing, entrancing,
irresistible, mesmerizing, ravishing,
winsome.
E3 boring, repellent.

enchantment *n* **1** DELIGHT, fascination,
charm, appeal, attractiveness, allure,
allurement, glamour, bliss, rapture,
ecstasy. **2** SPELL, magic, witchcraft,
wizardry, hypnotism, sorcery, incantation,
charm, mesmerism, conjuration (*fml*),
necromancy (*fml*).
E3 1 disenchantment.

enclose *v* encircle, encompass, surround,
fence, hedge, hem in, bound, encase,
embrace, envelop, confine, hold, shut in,
wrap, pen, cover, circumscribe,
incorporate, include, insert, contain,
comprehend.

enclosure *n* pen, pound, compound,
paddock, fold, stockade, sty, arena, corral,
court, ring, cloister.

encompass *v* **1** ENCIRCLE, circle, ring,
surround, gird, envelop, circumscribe, hem
in, enclose, hold. **2** INCLUDE, cover,
embrace, contain, comprise, admit,
incorporate, involve, embody,
comprehend.

encounter *v* **1** MEET, come across, run
into (*infml*), happen on, chance upon, run
across, confront, face, experience.
2 FIGHT, clash with, combat, cross swords
with (*infml*), engage, grapple with,
struggle, strive, contend.
➤ *n* **1** MEETING, brush, confrontation. **2**
CLASH, fight, combat, conflict, contest,
battle, set-to (*infml*), dispute, engagement,
action, skirmish, run-in, collision.

encourage *v* **1** HEARTEN, exhort,
stimulate, spur, reassure, rally, inspire,
incite, egg on (*infml*), buoy up, cheer, urge,
rouse, comfort, console. **2** PROMOTE,
advance, aid, boost, forward, further,
foster, support, help, strengthen.
E3 1 discourage, depress. **2** discourage.

encouragement *n* **1** REASSURANCE,
inspiration, cheer, exhortation, incitement,
pep talk (*infml*), urging, stimulation,
consolation, succour (*fml*). **2** PROMOTION,
help, aid, boost, shot in the arm (*infml*),
incentive, support, stimulus.

E3 1 discouragement, disapproval.

encouraging *adj* heartening, promising,
hopeful, reassuring, stimulating, uplifting,
auspicious, cheering, comforting, bright,
rosy, cheerful, satisfactory.
E3 discouraging.

encroach *v* intrude, invade, impinge,
trespass, infringe, usurp, overstep, make
inroads, muscle in (*infml*).

encroachment *n* intrusion, invasion,
trespassing, infringement, overstepping,
infiltration, incursion (*fml*).

encumber *v* burden, overload, weigh
down, saddle, oppress, handicap, hamper,
hinder, impede, slow down, obstruct,
inconvenience, prevent, retard, cramp.

encumbrance *n* burden, cumbrance,
load, cross, millstone, albatross, difficulty,
handicap, impediment, obstruction,
obstacle, inconvenience, hindrance,
liability.

end *n* **1** FINISH, conclusion, termination,
close, completion, cessation, culmination,
dénouement. **2** EXTREMITY, boundary,
edge, limit, tip. **3** REMAINDER, tip, butt, left-
over, remnant, stub, scrap, fragment.
4 AIM, object, objective, purpose,
intention, goal, point, reason, design. **5**
RESULT, outcome, consequence, upshot.
6 DEATH, demise, destruction,
extermination, downfall, doom, ruin,
dissolution.
E3 1 beginning, start. **6** birth.
➤ *v* **1** FINISH, close, cease, conclude, stop,
terminate, complete, culminate, wind up.
2 DESTROY, annihilate, exterminate,
extinguish, ruin, abolish, dissolve.
E3 1 begin, start.

endanger *v* imperil, hazard, jeopardize,
risk, expose, threaten, compromise.
E3 protect.

endearing *adj* lovable, charming,
appealing, attractive, winsome, delightful,
enchanting.

endearment *n* love, affection, fondness,
attachment, diminutive, pet-name, sweet
nothing.

endeavour *n* attempt, effort, go (*infml*),
try, shot (*infml*), stab (*infml*), undertaking,
enterprise, aim, venture.
➤ *v* attempt, try, strive, aim, aspire,
undertake, venture, struggle, labour, take
pains.

ending *n* end, close, finish, completion,
termination, conclusion, culmination,

climax, resolution, consummation, dénouement, finale, epilogue.

ea beginning, start.

endless adj **1** INFINITE, boundless, unlimited, measureless. **2** EVERLASTING, ceaseless, perpetual, constant, continual, continuous, undying, eternal, interminable, monotonous.

ea **1** finite, limited. **2** temporary.

endorse v **1** APPROVE, sanction, authorize, support, back, affirm, ratify, confirm, vouch for, advocate, warrant, recommend, subscribe to, sustain, adopt. **2** SIGN, countersign.

endorsement n **1** APPROVAL, sanction, authorization, support, backing, affirmation, ratification, confirmation, advocacy, warrant, recommendation, commendation, seal of approval, testimonial, OK (infml). **2** SIGNATURE, countersignature.

endow v bestow, bequeath, leave, will, give, donate, endue (fml), confer, grant, present, award, finance, fund, support, make over, furnish, provide, supply.

endowment n **1** BEQUEST, legacy, award, grant, fund, gift, provision, settlement, donation, bestowal, benefaction, dowry, income, revenue. **2** TALENT, attribute, faculty, gift, ability, quality, flair, genius, qualification.

endurance n fortitude, patience, staying power, stamina, resignation, stoicism, tenacity, perseverance, resolution, stability, persistence, strength, toleration.

endure v **1** endure hardship: bear, stand, put up with, tolerate, weather, brave, cope with, face, go through, experience, submit to, suffer, sustain, swallow, undergo, withstand, stick, stomach, allow, permit, support. **2** a peace that will endure for ever: last, abide (fml), remain, live, survive, stay, persist, hold, prevail.

enduring adj lasting, long-lasting, durable, permanent, perpetual, abiding, remaining, continuing, long-standing, stable, steady, firm, steadfast, persistent, persisting, chronic, prevailing, surviving, unfaltering, unwavering, eternal, immortal, imperishable.

ea changeable, fleeting, brief, ephemeral, momentary, passing.

enemy n adversary, opponent, foe (fml), rival, antagonist, the opposition, competitor, opposer, other side.

ea friend, ally.

energetic adj lively, vigorous, active, animated, dynamic, spirited, tireless, zestful, brisk, strong, forceful, potent, powerful, strenuous, high-powered.

ea lethargic, sluggish, inactive, idle.

energy n liveliness, vigour, activity, animation, drive, dynamism, get-up-and-go (infml), life, spirit, verve, vivacity, vitality, zest, zeal, ardour, fire, efficiency, force, forcefulness, zip (infml), strength, power, intensity, exertion, stamina.

ea lethargy, inertia, weakness.

enfold v **1** ENCLOSE, envelop, shroud, swathe, encircle, encompass, fold, enwrap, wrap (up). **2** EMBRACE, clasp, hug, hold.

enforce v impose, administer, implement, apply, execute, discharge, insist on, compel, oblige, urge, carry out, constrain, require, coerce, prosecute, reinforce.

enforcement n imposition, administration, implementation, application, execution, discharge, fulfilment, insistence, coercion, obligation, compulsion, constraint, pressure, prosecution, requirement.

enfranchise v give the right to vote to, give the vote to, free, liberate, release, emancipate (fml), manumit (fml), give suffrage to (fml).

ea disenfranchise.

enfranchisement n giving the right to vote, voting rights, freedom, freeing, liberating, liberation, release, emancipation (fml), manumission (fml), suffrage (fml)

ea disenfranchisement.

engage v **1** PARTICIPATE, take part, embark on, take up, practise, involve. **2** ATTRACT, allure, draw, captivate, charm, catch. **3** OCCUPY, engross, absorb, busy, tie up, grip. **4** EMPLOY, hire, appoint, take on, enlist, enrol, commission, recruit, contract. **5** INTERLOCK, mesh, interconnect, join, interact, attach. **6** FIGHT, battle with, attack, take on, encounter, assail, combat.

ea **2** repel. **4** dismiss, discharge. **5** disengage.

engaged adj **1** engaged in his work: occupied, busy, engrossed, immersed, absorbed, preoccupied, involved, employed. **2** engaged to be married: promised, betrothed (fml), pledged, spoken for, committed. **3** the phone is *engaged*: busy, tied up, unavailable.

engagement *n* **1** APPOINTMENT, meeting, date, arrangement, assignation, fixture, rendezvous. **2** PROMISE, pledge, betrothal (*fml*), commitment, obligation, assurance, vow, troth (*fml*). **3** FIGHT, battle, combat, conflict, action, encounter, confrontation, contest.

engaging *adj* charming, attractive, appealing, captivating, pleasing, delightful, winsome, lovable, likable, pleasant, fetching, fascinating, agreeable.
E3 repulsive, repellant.

engine *n* motor, machine, mechanism, appliance, contraption, apparatus, device, instrument, tool, locomotive, dynamo.

Types of engine include: diesel, donkey, fuel-injection, internal-combustion, jet, petrol, steam, turbine, turbojet, turboprop, V-engine.

Parts of an automotive engine and its ancillaries include: air filter, alternator, camshaft, camshaft cover, carburettor, choke, connecting rod, con-rod (*infml*), cooling fan, crankshaft, crankshaft pulley, cylinder block, cylinder head, drive belt, exhaust manifold, exhaust valve, fan belt, flywheel, fuel and ignition ECU (electronic control unit), fuel injector, gasket, ignition coil, ignition distributor, inlet manifold, inlet valve, oil filter, oil pump, oil seal, petrol pump, piston, piston ring, power-steering pump, push-rod, radiator, rocker arm, rocker cover, rotor arm, spark plug, starter motor, sump, tappet, thermostat, timing belt, timing pulley, turbocharger.

engineer *n* **1** MECHANIC, technician, engine driver. **2** DESIGNER, originator, planner, inventor, deviser, mastermind, architect.
➤ *v* plan, contrive, devise, manoeuvre, cause, manipulate, control, bring about, mastermind, originate, orchestrate, effect, plot, scheme, manage, create, rig.

engrave *v* **1** INSCRIBE, cut, carve, chisel, etch, chase. **2** *engraved on her mind*: imprint, impress, fix, stamp, lodge, ingrain.

engraving *n* print, impression, inscription, carving, etching, woodcut, plate, block, cutting, chiselling, mark.

engross *v* absorb, occupy, engage, grip, hold, preoccupy, rivet, fascinate, captivate, enthral, arrest, involve, intrigue.
E3 bore.

engrossed *adj* absorbed, occupied, taken up, preoccupied, gripped, engaged, caught up, enthralled, fascinated, captivated, immersed, intent, intrigued, rapt, riveted, mesmerized, wrapped, lost, fixated.
E3 bored, disinterested.

engulf *v* overwhelm, swamp, flood, deluge, drown, inundate, plunge, immerse, submerge, overrun, overtake, swallow up, devour, consume, bury, absorb, engross, envelop.

enhance *v* heighten, intensify, increase, improve, elevate, magnify, swell, exalt, raise, lift, boost, strengthen, reinforce, embellish.
E3 reduce, minimize.

enigma *n* mystery, riddle, puzzle, conundrum, problem, poser (*infml*), brain-teaser.

enigmatic *adj* mysterious, puzzling, cryptic, obscure, strange, perplexing.
E3 simple, straightforward.

enjoy *v* take pleasure in, delight in, appreciate, like, relish, revel in, rejoice in, savour.
E3 dislike, hate.
♦ **enjoy oneself** have a good time, have fun, make merry.

enjoyable *adj* pleasant, agreeable, delightful, pleasing, gratifying, entertaining, amusing, fun, delicious, good, satisfying.
E3 disagreeable.

enjoyment *n* **1** PLEASURE, delight, amusement, gratification, entertainment, relish, joy, fun, happiness, diversion, indulgence, recreation, zest, satisfaction. **2** POSSESSION, use, advantage, benefit.
E3 **1** displeasure.

Expressions of enjoyment include: a night on the town, bask in, carpe diem, enjoy it while you can, enter into the spirit of things, get into the swing of things, have a ball, have a field day, have a great time, have a whale of a time, have the time of one's life, hit the spot, in raptures about something, it's yummy!, kick off one's shoes, lap it up, let one's hair down, live for the day, live it up, make a night of it, make merry, make the most of it, mmm!, paint the town red, rave it up, seize the day, sow one's wild oats, take pleasure in, the life of Riley.

enlarge v increase, expand, augment, add to, grow, extend, magnify, inflate, swell, wax, stretch, multiply, develop, amplify, blow up, widen, broaden, lengthen, heighten, elaborate.
ᴇᴀ diminish, shrink.

enlargement n 1 *enlargement of the building/a gland*: increase, expansion, extension, magnification, inflation, swelling, stretching, multiplication, development, amplification, distension (*fml*), dilation (*fml*), augmentation (*fml*). 2 *a photographic enlargement*: blow-up, magnification.
ᴇᴀ 2 contraction, decrease, reduction.

enlighten v instruct, edify, educate, inform, illuminate, teach, counsel, apprise, advise.
ᴇᴀ confuse.

enlightened adj informed, aware, knowledgeable, educated, civilized, cultivated, refined, sophisticated, conversant, wise, reasonable, liberal, open-minded, literate.
ᴇᴀ ignorant, confused.

enlightenment n awareness, knowledge, teaching, understanding, education, instruction, wisdom, information, insight, comprehension, civilization, cultivation, refinement, learning, literacy, edification, sophistication, broad-mindedness, open-mindedness, erudition (*fml*), sapience (*fml*).
ᴇᴀ confusion, ignorance.

enlist v engage, enrol, register, sign up, recruit, conscript, employ, volunteer, join (up), gather, muster, secure, obtain, procure, enter.

enliven v excite, exhilarate, brighten, cheer (up), gladden, hearten, invigorate, rouse, wake up, liven (up), stimulate, revitalize, inspire, animate, buoy up, fire, kindle, quicken, spark, vivify (*fml*), pep up (*infml*), perk up (*infml*), give a lift to (*infml*).
ᴇᴀ subdue.

enmity n animosity, hostility, antagonism, discord, strife, feud, antipathy, acrimony, bitterness, hatred, aversion, ill-will, bad blood, rancour, malevolence, malice, venom.
ᴇᴀ friendship.

enormity n atrocity, outrage, iniquity, horror, evil, crime, abomination, monstrosity, wickedness, vileness,

depravity, atrociousness, viciousness.

enormous adj huge, immense, vast, gigantic, massive, colossal, gross, gargantuan, monstrous, mammoth, jumbo (*infml*), tremendous, prodigious.
ᴇᴀ small, tiny.

enough adj sufficient, adequate, ample, plenty, abundant.
➤ n sufficiency, adequacy, plenty, abundance.
➤ adv sufficiently, adequately, reasonably, tolerably, passably, moderately, fairly, satisfactorily, amply.

enquire *see* inquire.

enquiry *see* inquiry.

enrage v incense, infuriate, anger, madden, provoke, incite, inflame, exasperate, irritate, rile.
ᴇᴀ calm, placate.

enrich v 1 ENDOW, enhance, improve, refine, develop, cultivate, augment. 2 ADORN, ornament, beautify, embellish, decorate, grace.
ᴇᴀ 1 impoverish.

enrol v 1 REGISTER, enlist, sign on, sign up, join up, recruit, engage, admit. 2 RECORD, list, note, inscribe.

enrolment n registration, recruitment, enlistment, admission, acceptance.

ensemble n 1 WHOLE, total, entirety, sum, aggregate, set, collection. 2 OUTFIT, costume, get-up (*infml*), rig-out (*infml*). 3 GROUP, band, company, troupe, chorus.

enshrine v preserve, protect, guard, shield, treasure, cherish, immortalize, consecrate, dedicate, exalt, hallow, revere, sanctify, idolize, embalm, apotheosize (*fml*).

ensign n banner, standard, flag, colours, pennant, jack, badge.

enslave v subjugate, subject, dominate, bind, enchain, yoke.
ᴇᴀ free, emancipate.

ensue v follow, issue, proceed, succeed, result, arise, happen, turn out, befall, flow, derive, stem.
ᴇᴀ precede.

ensure v 1 CERTIFY, guarantee, warrant. 2 PROTECT, guard, safeguard, secure.

entail v involve, necessitate, occasion, require, demand, cause, give rise to, lead to, result in.

entangle v enmesh, ensnare, embroil, involve, implicate, snare, tangle, entrap,

trap, catch, mix up, knot, ravel, muddle.
 ☒ disentangle.

entanglement *n* 1 TANGLE, knot, mesh,
tie, trap, jumble, ensnarement,
entrapment, snare. 2 INVOLVEMENT,
complication, embarrassment, confusion,
muddle, snarl-up, difficulty, mess, mix-up,
predicament, liaison, affair.
 ☒ 1, 2 disentanglement.

enter *v* 1 COME IN, go in, arrive, insert,
introduce, board, penetrate. 2 RECORD,
log, note, register, take down, inscribe.
3 JOIN, embark upon, enrol, enlist, set
about, sign up, participate, commence,
start, begin.
 ☒ 1 depart. 2 delete.

enterprise *n* 1 UNDERTAKING, venture,
project, plan, effort, operation,
programme, endeavour. 2 INITIATIVE,
resourcefulness, drive, adventurousness,
boldness, get-up-and-go (*infml*), push,
energy, enthusiasm, spirit. 3 BUSINESS,
company, firm, establishment, concern.
 ☒ 2 apathy.

enterprising *adj* venturesome,
adventurous, bold, daring, go-ahead,
imaginative, resourceful, self-reliant,
enthusiastic, energetic, keen, ambitious,
aspiring, spirited, active.
 ☒ unenterprising, lethargic.

entertain *v* 1 AMUSE, divert, please,
delight, cheer. 2 RECEIVE, have guests,
accommodate, put up, treat. 3 HARBOUR,
countenance, contemplate, consider,
imagine, conceive.
 ☒ 1 bore. 3 reject.

entertainer

Entertainers include: acrobat, actor,
actress, busker, chat-show host, clown,
comedian, comic, conjuror, dancer, disc
jockey, DJ (*infml*), escapologist, game-show
host, hypnotist, ice-skater, impressionist,
jester, juggler, magician, mimic, mind-reader,
minstrel, musician, presenter, singer, song-
and-dance act, stand-up comic, stripper
(*infml*), striptease-artist, tight-rope walker,
trapeze-artist, ventriloquist; performer,
artiste. see also **musician**; **singer**.

entertaining *adj* amusing, diverting, fun,
delightful, interesting, pleasant, pleasing,
humorous, witty.
 ☒ boring.

entertainment *n* 1 AMUSEMENT,
diversion, recreation, enjoyment, play,
pastime, fun, sport, distraction, pleasure.
2 SHOW, spectacle, performance,
extravaganza.

Forms of entertainment include:
cinema, cartoon show, video, radio,
television, theatre, pantomime; dance, disco,
discothèque, concert, recital, musical, opera,
variety show, music hall, revue, karaoke,
cabaret, night-club, casino; magic-show,
puppet show, Punch-and-Judy show, circus,
gymkhana, waxworks, laser-light show, zoo,
rodeo, carnival, pageant, fête, festival,
firework party, barbecue. see also **theatrical**.

enthral *v* captivate, entrance, enchant,
fascinate, charm, beguile, thrill, intrigue,
hypnotize, mesmerize, engross.
 ☒ bore.

enthusiasm *n* zeal, ardour, fervour,
passion, keenness, eagerness,
vehemence, warmth, frenzy, excitement,
earnestness, relish, spirit, devotion, craze,
mania, rage.
 ☒ apathy.

enthusiast *n* devotee, zealot, admirer, fan
(*infml*), supporter, follower, buff (*infml*),
freak (*infml*), fanatic, fiend (*infml*), lover.

enthusiastic *adj* keen, ardent, eager,
fervent, vehement, passionate, warm,
wholehearted, zealous, vigorous, spirited,
earnest, devoted, avid, excited, exuberant.
 ☒ unenthusiastic, apathetic.

entice *v* tempt, lure, attract, seduce, lead
on, draw, coax, persuade, induce, sweet-
talk (*infml*).

entire *adj* complete, whole, total, full,
intact, perfect.
 ☒ incomplete, partial.

entirely *adv* completely, wholly, totally,
fully, utterly, unreservedly, absolutely, in
toto, thoroughly, altogether, perfectly,
solely, exclusively, every inch.
 ☒ partially.

entirety *n* totality, fullness, completeness,
wholeness, whole.

entitle *v* 1 AUTHORIZE, qualify, empower,
enable, allow, permit, license, warrant.
2 NAME, call, term, title, style, christen, dub,
label, designate.

entity *n* being, existence, thing, body,
creature, individual, organism, substance.

entourage *n* retinue, attendants,
company, companions, followers,
following, escort, staff, suite, court, train,

retainers, associates, cortège, coterie.

entrails *n* intestines, offal, viscera, bowels, internal organs, vital organs, giblets, umbles, guts (*infml*), innards (*infml*), insides (*infml*).

entrance¹ *n* **1** ACCESS, admission, admittance, entry, entrée. **2** ARRIVAL, appearance, debut, initiation, introduction, start. **3** OPENING, way in, door, doorway, gate.
🔁 **2** departure. **3** exit.

entrance² *v* charm, enchant, enrapture, captivate, bewitch, spellbind, fascinate, delight, ravish, transport, hypnotize, mesmerize.
🔁 repel.

entrant *n* **1** NOVICE, beginner, newcomer, initiate, convert, probationer.
2 COMPETITOR, candidate, contestant, contender, entry, participant, player.

entreat *v* beg, implore, plead with, beseech, crave, supplicate, pray, invoke, ask, petition, request, appeal to.

entreaty *n* appeal, plea, prayer, petition, supplication, suit, invocation, cry, solicitation, request.

entrench *v* establish, fix, embed, dig in, ensconce, install, lodge, root, ingrain, settle, seat, plant, anchor, set.
🔁 dislodge.

entrenched *adj* deep-rooted, deep-seated, rooted, well-established, firm, fixed, implanted, ingrained, inbred, set, inflexible, diehard, unshakable, dyed-in-the-wool, indelible, ineradicable, intransigent (*fml*), stick-in-the-mud (*infml*).

entrepreneur *n* business executive, businessman, businesswoman, financier, industrialist, middleman, promoter, agent, dealer, broker, contractor, magnate, tycoon, speculator, money-maker, manager, impresario.

entrust *v* trust, commit, confide, consign, authorize, charge, assign, turn over, commend, depute, invest, delegate, deliver.

entry *n* **1** ENTRANCE, appearance, admittance, admission, access, entrée, introduction. **2** OPENING, entrance, door, doorway, access, threshold, way in, passage, gate. **3** RECORD, item, minute, note, memorandum, statement, account. **4** ENTRANT, competitor, contestant, candidate, participant, player.
🔁 **2** exit.

entwine *v* wind, twist, intertwine, interlace, interlink, interweave, intwine, braid, knit, plait, twine, weave, wreathe, knot, ravel, entangle, embroil.
🔁 unravel.

enumerate *v* list, name, itemize, cite, detail, specify, count, number, relate, recount, spell out, tell, mention, calculate, quote, recite, reckon.

enunciate *v* **1** ARTICULATE, pronounce, vocalize, voice, express, say, speak, utter, sound. **2** STATE, declare, proclaim, announce, propound.

envelop *v* wrap, enfold, enwrap, encase, cover, swathe, shroud, engulf, enclose, encircle, encompass, surround, cloak, veil, blanket, conceal, obscure, hide.

envelope *n* wrapper, wrapping, cover, case, casing, sheath, covering, shell, skin, jacket, coating.

enviable *adj* desirable, privileged, favoured, blessed, fortunate, lucky, advantageous, sought-after, excellent, fine.
🔁 unenviable.

envious *adj* covetous, jealous, resentful, green (with envy), dissatisfied, grudging, jaundiced, green-eyed (*infml*).

environment *n* surroundings, conditions, circumstances, milieu, atmosphere, habitat, situation, element, medium, background, ambience, setting, context, territory, domain.

environmentalist *n* conservationist, ecologist, preservationist, Friend of the Earth, ecofreak (*infml*), econut (*infml*), ecowarrior (*infml*), tree-hugger (*infml*), green (*infml*).

environs *n* neighbourhood, surroundings, surrounding area, vicinity, outskirts, suburbs, district, locality, precincts, purlieus.

envisage *v* visualize, imagine, picture, envision, conceive of, preconceive, predict, anticipate, foresee, image, see, contemplate.

envoy *n* agent, representative, ambassador, diplomat, messenger, legate, emissary, minister, delegate, deputy, courier, intermediary.

envy *n* covetousness, jealousy, resentfulness, resentment, dissatisfaction, grudge, ill-will, malice, spite.
➤ *v* covet, resent, begrudge, grudge, crave.

ephemeral *adj* transient, short-lived, fleeting, brief, momentary, passing, short, temporary, transitory, impermanent, flitting, evanescent (*fml*), fugacious (*fml*).
🔁 enduring, lasting, perpetual.

epic *adj* heroic, grand, majestic, elevated, exalted, lofty, imposing, impressive, vast, ambitious, long, large, large-scale, great, colossal, huge, grandiloquent (*fml*), sublime (*fml*).
🔁 ordinary.
➤ *n* long story/poem, narrative, history, legend, saga, myth.

epicurean *adj* gourmet, gastronomic, gormandizing, sensual, voluptuous, luxurious, self-indulgent, gluttonous, luscious, lush, unrestrained, hedonistic, Sybaritic, libertine.

epidemic *adj* widespread, prevalent, rife, rampant, pandemic, sweeping, wide-ranging, prevailing.
➤ *n* plague, outbreak, spread, rash, upsurge, wave.

epigram *n* witticism, quip, bon mot, saying, proverb, maxim, aphorism, gnome.

epilogue *n* afterword, postscript, coda, conclusion.
🔁 foreword, prologue, preface.

episode *n* 1 INCIDENT, event, occurrence, happening, occasion, circumstance, experience, adventure, matter, business. 2 INSTALMENT, part, chapter, passage, section, scene.

epitome *n* 1 PERSONIFICATION, embodiment, representation, model, archetype, type, essence. 2 SUMMARY, abstract, abridgement, digest.

epitomize *v* 1 PERSONIFY, embody, represent, exemplify, encapsulate, illustrate, typify, symbolize, sum up. 2 ABRIDGE, shorten, summarize, abbreviate, abstract, précis, reduce, compress, condense, contract, curtail, cut.
🔁 2 elaborate, expand.

epoch *n* age, era, period, time, date.

equable *adj* 1 *an equable person*: even-tempered, placid, calm, serene, unexcitable, tranquil, unflappable, composed, level-headed, easy-going. 2 *an equable climate*: uniform, even, consistent, constant, regular, temperate, unvarying, steady, stable, smooth.
🔁 1 excitable. 2 variable.

equal *adj* 1 IDENTICAL, the same, alike, like, equivalent, corresponding, commensurate, comparable. 2 EVEN, uniform, regular, unvarying, balanced, matched. 3 COMPETENT, able, adequate, fit, capable, suitable.
🔁 1 different. 2 unequal. 3 unsuitable.
➤ *n* peer, counterpart, equivalent, coequal, match, parallel, twin, fellow.
➤ *v* match, parallel, correspond to, balance, square with, tally with, equalize, equate, rival, level, even.

equality *n* 1 UNIFORMITY, evenness, equivalence, correspondence, balance, parity, par, symmetry, proportion, identity, sameness, likeness. 2 IMPARTIALITY, fairness, justice, egalitarianism.
🔁 2 inequality.

equalize *v* level, even up, match, equal, equate, draw level, balance, square, standardize, compensate, smooth.

equate *v* compare, liken, match, pair, correspond to, correspond with, balance, parallel, equalize, offset, square, agree, tally, juxtapose.

equation *n* equality, correspondence, equivalence, balancing, agreement, parallel, pairing, comparison, match, likeness, juxtaposition.

equestrian *n* horseman, horsewoman, rider, courier, cavalryman, knight, cavalier, hussar, trooper, cowboy, cowgirl, rancher, herder, jockey.
➤ *adj* mounted, riding, horse-riding, equine (*fml*).

equilibrium *n* 1 BALANCE, poise, symmetry, evenness, stability. 2 EQUANIMITY, self-possession, composure, calmness, coolness, serenity.
🔁 1 imbalance.

equip *v* provide, fit out, supply, furnish, prepare, arm, fit up, kit out, stock, endow, rig, dress, array, deck out.

equipment *n* apparatus, gear, supplies, tackle, rig-out (*infml*), tools, material, furnishings, baggage, outfit, paraphernalia, stuff, things, accessories, furniture.

equitable *adj* even-handed, fair, proper, reasonable, right, rightful, due, fair-and-square, square, honest, ethical, impartial, just, unbiased, unprejudiced, legitimate, disinterested, dispassionate, objective.
🔁 inequitable, unfair.

equity *n* even-handedness, equitableness, fairness, fair play, fair-mindedness, reasonableness,

righteousness, uprightness, honesty, integrity, justice, justness, objectivity, impartiality, disinterestedness, rectitude (*fml*).
F3 inequity.

equivalence *n* identity, parity, correspondence, agreement, likeness, interchangeability, similarity, substitutability, correlation, parallel, conformity, sameness.
F3 unlikeness, dissimilarity.

equivalent *adj* equal, same, similar, substitutable, corresponding, alike, comparable, interchangeable, even, tantamount, twin.
F3 unlike, different.

equivocal *adj* ambiguous, uncertain, obscure, vague, evasive, oblique, misleading, dubious, confusing, indefinite.
F3 unequivocal, clear.

equivocate *v* prevaricate, evade, dodge, fence, beat about the bush (*infml*), hedge, mislead.

era *n* age, epoch, period, date, day, days, time, aeon, stage, century.

eradicate *v* eliminate, annihilate, get rid of, remove, root out, suppress, destroy, exterminate, extinguish, weed out, stamp out, abolish, erase, obliterate.

erase *v* obliterate, rub out, expunge (*fml*), delete, blot out, cancel, efface, get rid of, remove, eradicate.

erect *adj* upright, straight, vertical, upstanding, standing, raised, rigid, stiff.
➤ *v* build, construct, put up, establish, set up, elevate, assemble, found, form, institute, initiate, raise, rear, lift, mount, pitch, create.

erection *n* **1** BUILDING, construction, edifice, structure, assembly, establishment, manufacture, fabrication, creation, elevation, raising, pile (*infml*). **2** RIGIDITY, stiffness.

erode *v* wear away, eat away, wear down, corrode, abrade, consume, grind down, disintegrate, deteriorate, spoil.

erosion *n* wear, corrosion, abrasion, attrition, denudation, disintegration, deterioration, destruction, undermining.

erotic *adj* aphrodisiac, seductive, sexy, sensual, titillating, pornographic, lascivious, stimulating, suggestive, amorous, amatory, venereal, carnal, lustful, voluptuous.

err *v* **1** MAKE A MISTAKE, be wrong, miscalculate, mistake, misjudge, slip up, blunder, misunderstand. **2** DO WRONG, sin, misbehave, go astray, offend, transgress, deviate.

errand *n* commission, charge, mission, assignment, message, task, job, duty.

errant *adj* **1** WAYWARD, wrong, erring, stray, straying, deviant, offending, criminal, lawless, disobedient, sinful, sinning, loose, aberrant (*fml*). **2** ROAMING, rambling, roving, itinerant, journeying, wandering, nomadic, peripatetic (*fml*).

erratic *adj* changeable, variable, fitful, fluctuating, inconsistent, irregular, unstable, shifting, inconstant, unpredictable, unreliable, aberrant, abnormal, eccentric, desultory, meandering.
F3 steady, consistent, stable.

erroneous *adj* incorrect, wrong, mistaken, false, untrue, inaccurate, inexact, invalid, illogical, unfounded, faulty, flawed.
F3 correct, right.

error *n* mistake, inaccuracy, slip, slip-up, blunder, howler (*infml*), gaffe, faux pas, solecism, lapse, miscalculation, misunderstanding, misconception, misapprehension, misprint, oversight, omission, fallacy, flaw, fault, wrong.

erudite *adj* learned, scholarly, well-educated, knowledgeable, lettered, educated, well-read, literate, academic, cultured, wise, highbrow, profound.
F3 illiterate, ignorant.

erupt *v* break out, explode, belch, discharge, burst, gush, spew, spout, eject, expel, emit, flare up, vomit, break.

eruption *n* **1** OUTBURST, discharge, ejection, emission, explosion, flare-up. **2** RASH, outbreak, inflammation.

escalate *v* increase, intensify, grow, accelerate, rise, step up, heighten, raise, spiral, magnify, enlarge, expand, extend, mount, ascend, climb, amplify.
F3 decrease, diminish.

escapade *n* adventure, exploit, fling, prank, caper, romp, spree, lark (*infml*), antic, stunt, trick.

escape *v* **1** GET AWAY, break free, run away, bolt, abscond, flee, fly, decamp, break loose, break out, do a bunk (*infml*), flit, slip away, shake off, slip. **2** AVOID, evade, elude, dodge, skip, shun. **3** LEAK, seep, flow,

drain, gush, issue, discharge, ooze, trickle, pour forth, pass.
➤ *n* **1** GETAWAY, flight, bolt, flit, break-out, decampment, jail-break. **2** AVOIDANCE, evasion. **3** LEAK, seepage, leakage, outflow, gush, drain, discharge, emission, spurt, outpour, emanation. **4** ESCAPISM, diversion, distraction, recreation, relaxation, pastime, safety-valve.

escapist *n* dreamer, daydreamer, fantasizer, wishful thinker, non-realist, ostrich (*infml*).
🔁 realist.

eschew *v* avoid, give up, refrain from, abandon, keep clear of, repudiate, shun, spurn, disdain, abstain from, forgo (*fml*), forswear (*fml*), renounce (*fml*).
🔁 embrace.

escort *n* **1** COMPANION, chaperon(e), partner, attendant, aide, squire, guide, bodyguard, protector. **2** ENTOURAGE, company, retinue, suite, train, guard, convoy, cortège.
➤ *v* accompany, partner, chaperone, guide, lead, usher, conduct, guard, protect.

esoteric *adj* recondite, obscure, abstruse, cryptic, inscrutable, mysterious, mystic, mystical, occult, hidden, secret, confidential, private, inside.
🔁 well-known, familiar.

especially *adv* **1** CHIEFLY, mainly, principally, primarily, pre-eminently, above all. **2** PARTICULARLY, specially, markedly, notably, exceptionally, outstandingly, expressly, supremely, uniquely, unusually, strikingly, very.

espionage *n* counter-intelligence, infiltration, intelligence, investigation, probing, reconnaissance, spying, surveillance, intercepting, industrial espionage, undercover operations/work, fifth column, snooping (*infml*), bugging (*infml*), wiretapping (*infml*).

espouse *v* take up, adopt, embrace, support, advocate, back, choose, stand up for, defend, champion, patronize, maintain, opt for.

essay *n* composition, dissertation, paper, article, assignment, thesis, piece, commentary, critique, discourse, treatise, review, leader, tract.

essence *n* **1** NATURE, being, quintessence, substance, soul, spirit, core, centre, heart, meaning, quality, significance, life, entity, crux, kernel, marrow, pith, character,

characteristics, attributes, principle. **2** CONCENTRATE, extract, distillation, spirits.

essential *adj* **1** FUNDAMENTAL, basic, intrinsic, inherent, principal, main, key, characteristic, definitive, typical, constituent. **2** CRUCIAL, indispensable, necessary, vital, requisite, required, needed, important.
🔁 **1** incidental. **2** dispensable, inessential.
➤ *n* necessity, prerequisite, must, requisite, sine qua non (*fml*), requirement, basic, fundamental, necessary, principle.
🔁 inessential.

establish *v* **1** SET UP, found, start, form, institute, create, organize, inaugurate, introduce, install, plant, settle, secure, lodge, base. **2** PROVE, substantiate, demonstrate, authenticate, ratify, verify, validate, certify, confirm, affirm.
🔁 **1** uproot. **2** refute.

establishment *n* **1** FORMATION, setting up, founding, creation, foundation, installation, institution, inauguration. **2** BUSINESS, company, firm, institute, organization, concern, institution, enterprise. **3** RULING CLASS, the system, the authorities, the powers that be.

estate *n* **1** POSSESSIONS, effects, assets, belongings, holdings, property, goods, lands. **2** AREA, development, land, manor. **3** (*fml*) STATUS, standing, situation, position, class, place, condition, state, rank.

estimate *v* assess, reckon, evaluate, calculate, gauge, guess, value, conjecture, consider, judge, think, number, count, compute, believe.
➤ *n* reckoning, valuation, judgement, guess, approximation, assessment, estimation, evaluation, computation, opinion.

estimation *n* **1** JUDGEMENT, opinion, belief, consideration, estimate, view, evaluation, assessment, reckoning, conception, calculation, computation. **2** RESPECT, regard, appreciation, esteem, credit.

estranged *adj* divided, separate, alienated, disaffected, antagonized.
🔁 reconciled, united.

estuary *n* inlet, mouth, firth, fjord, creek, arm, sea-loch.

et cetera *adv* and so on, and so forth, and the like, and the rest, &c, and suchlike, et al, and what have you (*infml*), and/or whatever (*infml*).

etch *v* cut, carve, engrave, burn, furrow, dig, groove, impress, imprint, incise, ingrain, inscribe, bite, corrode, stamp.

etching *n* carving, cut, engraving, inscription, impression, imprint, print, sketch.

eternal *adj* 1 *eternal bliss*: unending, endless, ceaseless, everlasting, never-ending, infinite, limitless, immortal, undying, imperishable. 2 *eternal truths*: unchanging, timeless, enduring, lasting, perennial, abiding. 3 (*infml*) *eternal quarrelling*: constant, continuous, perpetual, incessant, interminable.
ea 1 ephemeral, temporary. 2 changeable.

eternity *n* 1 EVERLASTINGNESS, endlessness, everlasting, imperishability, infinity, timelessness, perpetuity, immutability, ages, age, aeon.
2 AFTERLIFE, hereafter, immortality, heaven, paradise, next world, world to come.

ethical *adj* moral, principled, just, right, proper, virtuous, honourable, fair, upright, righteous, seemly, honest, good, correct, commendable, fitting, noble, meet (*fml*).
ea unethical.

ethics *n* moral values, morality, principles, standards, code, moral philosophy, rules, beliefs, propriety, conscience, equity.

ethnic *adj* racial, native, indigenous, traditional, tribal, folk, cultural, national, aboriginal.

ethos *n* attitude, beliefs, standards, manners, ethics, morality, code, principles, spirit, tenor, rationale, character, disposition.

etiquette *n* code, formalities, standards, correctness, conventions, customs, protocol (*fml*), rules, manners, politeness, courtesy, civility, decorum, ceremony, decency.

eulogize *v* praise, acclaim, sing/sound the praises of, wax lyrical, applaud, approve, celebrate, exalt, extol, glorify, honour, magnify, commend, compliment, congratulate, laud (*fml*), panegyrize (*fml*), rave about (*infml*), hype (*infml*), plug (*infml*).
ea condemn.

eulogy *n* praise, tribute, acclaim, acclamation, accolade, commendation, exaltation, glorification, compliment,

applause, plaudit, encomium (*fml*), laud (*fml*), laudation (*fml*), laudatory (*fml*), paean (*fml*), panegyric (*fml*).
ea condemnation.

euphemism *n* evasion, polite term, substitution, genteelism, politeness, understatement.

euphoria *n* elation, ecstasy, bliss, rapture, high spirits, well-being, high (*infml*), exhilaration, exultation, joy, intoxication, jubilation, transport, glee, exaltation, enthusiasm, cheerfulness.
ea depression, despondency.

euthanasia *n* mercy killing, release, happy/merciful release, quietus.

evacuate *v* 1 LEAVE, depart, withdraw, quit, remove, retire from, clear (out) (*infml*), abandon, desert, forsake, vacate, decamp, relinquish. 2 EMPTY, eject, void, expel, discharge, eliminate, defecate, purge.

evacuation *n* 1 DEPARTURE, withdrawal, retreat, exodus, removal, quitting, desertion, abandonment, clearance, relinquishment, retirement, vacation.
2 EMPTYING, expulsion, ejection, discharge, elimination, defecation, urination.

evade *v* 1 *evade one's duties*: elude, avoid, escape, dodge, shirk, steer clear of, shun, sidestep, duck (*infml*), balk, skive (*infml*), fend off, chicken out (*infml*), cop out (*infml*). 2 *evade a question*: prevaricate, equivocate, fence, fudge, parry, quibble, hedge.
ea 1 confront, face.

evaluate *v* value, assess, appraise, estimate, reckon, calculate, gauge, judge, rate, size up, weigh, compute, rank.

evaluation *n* valuation, appraisal, assessment, estimation, estimate, judgement, reckoning, calculation, opinion, computation.

evangelical *adj* 1 *evangelical Christianity*: biblical, Bible-believing, scriptural, orthodox, fundamentalist, missionary, crusading, Bible-bashing (*infml*), Bible-thumping (*infml*), Bible-punching (*infml*). 2 ENTHUSIASTIC, zealous, campaigning, crusading, evangelistic, missionary, propagandizing, propagandist, proselytizing.

evaporate *v* 1 DISAPPEAR, dematerialize, vanish, melt (away), dissolve, disperse, dispel, dissipate, fade. 2 VAPORIZE, dry, dehydrate, exhale.

evaporation *n* vaporization, drying, dehydration, condensation, distillation, dematerialization, dissolution, fading, melting, vanishing, desiccation (*fml*).

evasion *n* avoidance, escape, dodge, equivocation, excuse, prevarication, put-off, trickery, subterfuge, shirking.
✷ frankness, directness.

evasive *adj* equivocating, indirect, prevaricating, devious, shifty (*infml*), unforthcoming, slippery (*infml*), misleading, deceitful, deceptive, cagey (*infml*), oblique, secretive, tricky, cunning.
✷ direct, frank.

eve *n* day before, verge, brink, edge, threshold.

even *adj* 1 LEVEL, flat, smooth, horizontal, flush, parallel, plane. 2 STEADY, unvarying, constant, regular, uniform. 3 EQUAL, balanced, matching, same, similar, like, symmetrical, fifty-fifty, level, side by side, neck and neck (*infml*). 4 EVEN-TEMPERED, calm, placid, serene, tranquil, composed, unruffled. 5 EVEN-HANDED, balanced, equitable, fair, impartial.
✷ 1 uneven. 3 unequal.
➤ *v* smooth, flatten, level, match, regularize, balance, equalize, align, square, stabilize, steady, straighten.
➤ *adv* 1 *even worse*: all the more, still, yet, more, to a greater extent/degree. 2 *even a child could do that*: surprisingly, unexpectedly, unusually, oddly, as well, also, too, still more, likewise. 3 *sad, even depressed*: more exactly, more precisely, indeed. 4 *not even write his own name*: hardly, scarcely, at all, so much as.
♦ **even so** however, but, all the same, despite that, in spite of that, however that may be, nevertheless, nonetheless, still, yet, notwithstanding that (*fml*).

even-handed *adj* fair, just, impartial, balanced, disinterested, dispassionate, equitable, neutral, unbiased, unprejudiced, reasonable, non-discriminatory, square, fair and square, without fear or favour.
✷ inequitable, discriminatory.

evening *n* nightfall, dusk, eve, eventide, twilight, sunset, sundown.

event *n* 1 HAPPENING, occurrence, incident, occasion, affair, circumstance, episode, eventuality, experience, matter, case, adventure, business, fact, possibility, milestone. 2 CONSEQUENCE, result,

outcome, conclusion, end, effect, issue, termination. 3 GAME, match, competition, contest, tournament, engagement.

even-tempered *adj* calm, level-headed, placid, stable, tranquil, serene, composed, cool, steady, peaceful, peaceable.
✷ excitable, erratic.

eventful *adj* busy, exciting, lively, active, full, interesting, remarkable, significant, memorable, momentous, notable, noteworthy, unforgettable.
✷ dull, ordinary.

eventual *adj* final, ultimate, resulting, concluding, ensuing, future, later, subsequent, prospective, projected, planned, impending.

eventuality *n* possibility, probability, likelihood, chance, contingency, event, happening, circumstance, case, outcome, crisis, emergency, mishap.

eventually *adv* finally, ultimately, at last, in the end, at length, subsequently, after all, sooner or later.

ever *adv* 1 ALWAYS, evermore, for ever, perpetually, constantly, at all times, continually, endlessly. 2 AT ANY TIME, in any case, in any circumstances, at all, on any account.
✷ 1 never.

everlasting *adj* eternal, undying, never-ending, endless, immortal, infinite, imperishable, constant, permanent, perpetual, indestructible, timeless.
✷ temporary, transient.

every *adj* 1 EACH, every single, every individual. 2 *make every effort*: all possible, as much as possible. 3 *have every confidence*: all, complete, total, full, entire.

everybody *n* everyone, one and all, each one, each person, every person, all and sundry, the whole world.

everyday *adj* ordinary, common, commonplace, day-to-day, familiar, run-of-the-mill, regular, plain, routine, usual, workaday, common-or-garden (*infml*), normal, customary, stock, accustomed, conventional, daily, habitual, monotonous, frequent, simple, informal.
✷ unusual, exceptional, special.

everyone *n* everybody, one and all, each one, all and sundry, the whole world.

everything *n* all, all things, each thing, the lot, the whole lot, the entirety, the sum, the total, lock, stock and barrel, the aggregate (*fml*), the whole caboodle (*infml*), the whole shooting-match (*infml*), the whole bag of tricks (*infml*).

everywhere *adv* all around, all over, throughout, far and near, far and wide, high and low, ubiquitous, left, right and centre (*infml*).

evict *v* expel, eject, dispossess, put out, turn out, turf out (*infml*), kick out (*infml*), force out, remove, cast out, chuck out (*infml*), oust, dislodge, expropriate.

eviction *n* expulsion, ejection, dispossession, removal, clearance, dislodgement, the boot (*infml*), the push (*infml*), the elbow (*infml*).

evidence *n* **1** PROOF, verification, confirmation, affirmation, grounds, substantiation, documentation, data. **2** TESTIMONY, declaration. **3** INDICATION, manifestation, suggestion, sign, mark, hint, demonstration, token.

evident *adj* clear, obvious, manifest, apparent, plain, patent, visible, conspicuous, noticeable, clear-cut, unmistakable, perceptible, distinct, discernible, tangible, incontestable, indisputable, incontrovertible.

evidently *adv* clearly, apparently, plainly, patently, manifestly, obviously, seemingly, undoubtedly, doubtless(ly), indisputably.

evil *adj* **1** WICKED, wrong, sinful, bad, immoral, vicious, vile, malevolent, iniquitous, cruel, base, corrupt, heinous, malicious, malignant, devilish, depraved, mischievous. **2** HARMFUL, pernicious, destructive, deadly, detrimental, hurtful, poisonous. **3** DISASTROUS, ruinous, calamitous, catastrophic, adverse, dire, inauspicious. **4** OFFENSIVE, noxious, foul. ➤ *n* **1** WICKEDNESS, wrong-doing, wrong, immorality, badness, sin, sinfulness, vice, viciousness, iniquity, depravity, baseness, corruption, malignity, mischief, heinousness. **2** ADVERSITY, affliction, calamity, disaster, misfortune, suffering, sorrow, ruin, catastrophe, blow, curse, distress, hurt, harm, ill, injury, misery, woe.

evoke *v* summon (up), call, elicit, invoke, arouse, stir, raise, stimulate, call forth, call up, conjure up, awaken, provoke, excite, recall.
🔳 suppress.

evolution *n* development, growth, progression, progress, expansion, increase, ripening, derivation, descent.

evolve *v* develop, grow, increase, mature, progress, unravel, expand, enlarge, emerge, descend, derive, result, elaborate.

exact *adj* **1** PRECISE, accurate, correct, faithful, literal, flawless, faultless, right, true, veracious, definite, explicit, detailed, specific, strict, unerring, close, factual, identical, express, word-perfect, blow-by-blow (*infml*). **2** CAREFUL, scrupulous, particular, rigorous, methodical, meticulous, orderly, painstaking.
🔳 **1** inexact, imprecise.
➤ *v* extort, extract, claim, insist on, wrest, wring, compel, demand, command, force, impose, require, squeeze, milk (*infml*).

exacting *adj* demanding, difficult, hard, laborious, arduous, rigorous, taxing, tough, harsh, painstaking, severe, strict, unsparing.
🔳 easy.

exactly *adv* **1** PRECISELY, accurately, literally, faithfully, correctly, specifically, rigorously, scrupulously, veraciously, verbatim, carefully, faultlessly, unerringly, strictly, to the letter, particularly, methodically, explicitly, expressly, dead (*infml*). **2** ABSOLUTELY, definitely, precisely, indeed, certainly, truly, quite, just, unequivocally.
🔳 **1** inaccurately, roughly.

exaggerate *v* overstate, overdo, magnify, overemphasize, emphasize, embellish, embroider, enlarge, amplify, oversell, pile it on (*infml*).
🔳 understate.

exaggeration *n* overstatement, overemphasis, emphasis, magnification, overestimation, excess, extravagance, embellishment, enlargement, pretentiousness, amplification, burlesque, caricature, parody, hyperbole (*fml*).
🔳 understatement.

exalt *v* **1** PRAISE, extol, glorify, magnify, acclaim, applaud, bless, honour, adore, revere, worship, reverence, eulogize, laud (*fml*), venerate (*fml*). **2** DELIGHT, elate, overjoy, transport, promote, raise, prefer, elevate, upgrade, enliven, excite, exhilarate, aggrandize (*fml*).

examination *n* **1** INSPECTION, enquiry, scrutiny, study, survey, search, analysis, exploration, investigation, probe, appraisal, observation, research, review, scan, once-over (*infml*), perusal, check, check-up, audit, critique. **2** TEST, exam, quiz, questioning, cross-examination, cross-questioning, trial, inquisition, interrogation, viva.

examine v 1 INSPECT, investigate, scrutinize, study, survey, analyse, explore, enquire, consider, probe, review, scan, check (out), ponder, pore over, sift, vet, weigh up, appraise, assay, audit, peruse, case (sl). 2 TEST, quiz, question, cross-examine, cross-question, interrogate, grill (infml), catechize (fml).

example n instance, case, case in point, illustration, exemplification, sample, specimen, model, pattern, ideal, archetype, prototype, standard, type, lesson, citation.

exasperate v infuriate, annoy, anger, incense, irritate, madden, provoke, get on someone's nerves, enrage, irk, rile, rankle, rouse, get to (infml), goad, vex.
🖃 appease, pacify.

excavate v dig (out), dig up, hollow, burrow, tunnel, delve, unearth, mine, quarry, disinter, gouge, scoop, exhume, uncover.

excavation n hole, hollow, pit, quarry, mine, dugout, dig, diggings, burrow, cavity, crater, trench, trough, shaft, ditch, cutting.

exceed v surpass, outdo, outstrip, beat, better, pass, overtake, top, outshine, eclipse, outreach, outrun, transcend, cap, overdo, overstep.

exceedingly adv very, very much, extremely, greatly, highly, unusually, exceptionally, especially, enormously, excessively, hugely, immensely, vastly, inordinately, unprecedentedly, superlatively, surpassingly, amazingly, astonishingly, extraordinarily.

excel v 1 SURPASS, outdo, beat, outclass, outperform, outrank, eclipse, better. 2 BE EXCELLENT, succeed, shine, stand out, predominate.

excellence n superiority, pre-eminence, distinction, merit, supremacy, quality, worth, fineness, eminence, goodness, greatness, virtue, perfection, purity.

excellent adj superior, first-class, first-rate, prime, superlative, unequalled, outstanding, surpassing, remarkable, distinguished, great, good, exemplary, select, superb, admirable, commendable, top-notch (infml), splendid, noteworthy, notable, fine, wonderful, worthy.
🖃 inferior, second-rate.

except prep excepting, but, apart from, other than, save, omitting, not counting, leaving out, excluding, except for, besides, bar, minus, less.
➢ v leave out, omit, bar, exclude, reject, rule out.

exception n oddity, anomaly, deviation, abnormality, irregularity, peculiarity, inconsistency, rarity, special case, quirk.

exceptional adj 1 ABNORMAL, unusual, anomalous, strange, odd, irregular, extraordinary, peculiar, special, rare, uncommon. 2 OUTSTANDING, remarkable, phenomenal, prodigious, notable, noteworthy, superior, unequalled, marvellous.
🖃 1 normal. 2 mediocre.

excerpt n extract, passage, portion, section, selection, quote, quotation, part, citation, scrap, fragment.

excess n 1 SURFEIT, overabundance, glut, plethora, superfluity, superabundance, surplus, overflow, overkill, remainder, left-over. 2 OVERINDULGENCE, dissipation, immoderateness, intemperance, extravagance, unrestraint, debauchery.
🖃 1 deficiency. 2 restraint.
➢ adj extra, surplus, spare, redundant, remaining, residual, left-over, additional, superfluous, supernumerary.
🖃 inadequate.

excessive adj immoderate, inordinate, extreme, undue, uncalled-for, disproportionate, unnecessary, unneeded, superfluous, unreasonable, exorbitant, extravagant, steep (infml).
🖃 insufficient.

exchange v barter, change, trade, swap, switch, replace, interchange, convert, commute, substitute, reciprocate, bargain, bandy.
➢ n 1 CONVERSATION, discussion, chat. 2 TRADE, commerce, dealing, market, traffic, barter, bargain. 3 INTERCHANGE, swap, switch, replacement, substitution, reciprocity.

excitable adj temperamental, volatile, passionate, emotional, highly-strung, fiery, hot-headed, hasty, nervous, hot-tempered, irascible, quick-tempered, sensitive, susceptible.
🖃 calm, stable.

excite v 1 MOVE, agitate, disturb, upset, touch, stir up, thrill, elate, turn on (infml), impress. 2 AROUSE, rouse, animate,

awaken, fire, inflame, kindle, motivate, stimulate, engender, inspire, instigate, incite, induce, ignite, galvanize, generate, provoke, sway, quicken, evoke.
F3 1 calm.

excited adj aroused, roused, stimulated, stirred, thrilled, elated, enthusiastic, eager, moved, high (infml), worked up, wrought-up, overwrought, restless, frantic, frenzied, wild.
F3 calm, apathetic.

excitement n 1 UNREST, ado, action, activity, commotion, fuss, tumult, flurry, furore, adventure. 2 DISCOMPOSURE, agitation, passion, thrill, animation, elation, enthusiasm, restlessness, kicks (infml), ferment, fever, eagerness, stimulation.
F3 1 calm. 2 apathy.

exciting adj stimulating, stirring, intoxicating, exhilarating, thrilling, rousing, moving, enthralling, electrifying, nail-biting (infml), cliff-hanging (infml), striking, sensational, provocative, inspiring, interesting.
F3 dull, unexciting.

exclaim v cry (out), declare, blurt (out), call, yell, shout, proclaim, utter.

exclamation n cry, call, yell, shout, expletive, interjection, ejaculation, outcry, utterance.

exclude v 1 BAN, bar, prohibit, disallow, veto, proscribe, forbid, blacklist. 2 OMIT, leave out, keep out, refuse, reject, ignore, shut out, rule out, ostracize, eliminate. 3 EXPEL, eject, evict, excommunicate.
F3 1 admit. 2 include.

exclusion n 1 OMISSION, rejection, elimination, ruling out, refusal, repudiation, preclusion (fml). 2 BAN, bar, prohibition, embargo, veto, boycott, interdict (fml), proscription (fml). 3 EJECTION, expulsion, eviction, removal, boycott, exception.
F3 1 inclusion. 2 allowance. 3 admittance.

exclusive adj 1 SOLE, single, unique, only, undivided, unshared, whole, total, peculiar. 2 RESTRICTED, limited, closed, private, narrow, restrictive, choice, select, discriminative, cliquey, chic, classy (infml), elegant, fashionable, posh (infml), snobbish.

excommunicate v ban, banish, eject, denounce, exclude, expel, remove, bar, blacklist, debar, outlaw, repudiate,

unchurch, anathematize (fml), proscribe (fml), execrate (fml).

excruciating adj agonizing, painful, severe, tormenting, unbearable, insufferable, acute, intolerable, intense, sharp, piercing, extreme, atrocious, racking, harrowing, savage, burning, bitter.

excursion n outing, trip, jaunt, expedition, day trip, journey, tour, airing, breather, junket (infml), ride, drive, walk, ramble.

excusable adj understandable, minor, slight, allowable, permissible, defensible, explainable, forgivable, pardonable, justifiable.
F3 blameworthy.

excuse v 1 FORGIVE, pardon, overlook, absolve, acquit, exonerate, tolerate, ignore, indulge. 2 RELEASE, free, discharge, liberate, let off, relieve, spare, exempt. 3 CONDONE, explain, mitigate, justify, vindicate, defend, apologize for.
F3 1 criticize. 2 punish.
➤ n justification, explanation, grounds, defence, plea, alibi, reason, apology, pretext, pretence, exoneration, evasion, cop-out (infml), shift, substitute.

execute v 1 PUT TO DEATH, kill, liquidate, hang, electrocute, shoot, guillotine, decapitate, behead. 2 CARRY OUT, perform, do, accomplish, achieve, fulfil, complete, discharge, effect, enact, deliver, enforce, finish, implement, administer, consummate, realize, dispatch, expedite, validate, serve, render, sign.

execution n 1 DEATH PENALTY, death sentence, capital punishment, putting to death, killing. 2 ACCOMPLISHMENT, operation, performance, completion, achievement, administration, effect, enactment, implementation, realization, discharge, dispatch, consummation, enforcement. 3 STYLE, technique, rendition, delivery, performance, manner, mode.

Means of execution include: beheading, burning, crucifixion, decapitation, electrocution, firing squad, garrotting, gassing, guillotining, hanging, lethal injection, lynching, shooting, stoning, stringing up (infml).

executive n 1 ADMINISTRATION, management, government, leadership, hierarchy. 2 ADMINISTRATOR, manager, organizer, leader, controller, director, governor, official.

➤ *adj* administrative, managerial, controlling, supervisory, regulating, decision-making, governing, organizing, directing, directorial, organizational, leading, guiding.

exemplary *adj* 1 MODEL, ideal, perfect, admirable, excellent, faultless, flawless, correct, good, commendable, praiseworthy, worthy, laudable, estimable, honourable. 2 CAUTIONARY, warning.
🗷 1 imperfect, unworthy.

exemplify *v* illustrate, demonstrate, show, instance, represent, typify, manifest, embody, epitomize, exhibit, depict, display.

exempt *v* excuse, release, relieve, let off, free, absolve, discharge, dismiss, liberate, spare.
➤ *adj* excused, not liable, immune, released, spared, absolved, discharged, excluded, free, liberated, clear.
🗷 liable.

exemption *n* exception, exclusion, immunity, privilege, indulgence, release, freedom, indemnity, discharge, absolution (*fml*), dispensation (*fml*), exoneration (*fml*).
🗷 liability.

exercise *v* 1 USE, utilize, employ, apply, exert, practise, wield, try, discharge. 2 TRAIN, drill, practise, work out (*infml*), keep fit. 3 WORRY, disturb, trouble, upset, burden, distress, vex, annoy, agitate, afflict.
➤ *n* 1 TRAINING, drill, practice, effort, exertion, task, lesson, work, discipline, activity, physical jerks (*infml*), work-out (*infml*), aerobics, labour. 2 USE, utilization, employment, application, implementation, practice, operation, discharge, assignment, fulfilment, accomplishment.

exert *v* use, utilize, employ, apply, exercise, bring to bear, wield, expend.
♦ **exert oneself** strive, struggle, strain, make every effort, take pains, toil, labour, work, sweat (*infml*), endeavour, apply oneself.

exertion *n* 1 EFFORT, industry, labour, toil, work, struggle, diligence, assiduousness, perseverance, pains, endeavour, attempt, strain, travail (*fml*), trial. 2 USE, utilization, employment, application, exercise, operation, action.
🗷 1 idleness, rest.

exhale *v* breathe (out), give off, blow, discharge, emit, expel, issue, respire, steam, evaporate, emanate (*fml*), expire (*fml*).
🗷 inhale.

exhaust *v* 1 CONSUME, empty, deplete, drain, sap, spend, waste, squander, dissipate, impoverish, use up, finish, dry, bankrupt. 2 TIRE (OUT), weary, fatigue, tax, strain, weaken, overwork, wear out.
🗷 1 renew. 2 refresh.
➤ *n* emission, exhalation, discharge, fumes.

exhausted *adj* 1 EMPTY, finished, depleted, spent, used up, drained, dry, worn out, void. 2 TIRED (OUT), dead tired, dead-beat (*infml*), all in (*infml*), done (in) (*infml*), fatigued, weak, washed-out, whacked (*infml*), knackered (*infml*), jaded.
🗷 1 fresh. 2 vigorous.

exhausting *adj* tiring, strenuous, taxing, gruelling, arduous, hard, laborious, backbreaking, draining, severe, testing, punishing, formidable, debilitating.
🗷 refreshing.

exhaustion *n* fatigue, tiredness, weariness, debility, feebleness, jet-lag.
🗷 freshness, liveliness.

exhaustive *adj* comprehensive, all-embracing, all-inclusive, far-reaching, complete, extensive, encyclopedic, full-scale, thorough, full, in-depth, intensive, detailed, definitive, all-out, sweeping.
🗷 incomplete, restricted.

exhibit *v* display, show, present, demonstrate, manifest, expose, parade, reveal, express, disclose, indicate, air, flaunt, offer.
🗷 conceal.
➤ *n* display, exhibition, show, illustration, model.

exhibition *n* display, show, demonstration, exhibit, presentation, manifestation, spectacle, exposition, expo (*infml*), showing, fair, performance, airing, representation, showcase.

exhilarate *v* thrill, excite, elate, animate, enliven, invigorate, vitalize, stimulate.
🗷 bore.

exhilaration *n* excitement, thrill, happiness, cheerfulness, gladness, delight, elation, joy, joyfulness, exaltation, glee, high spirits, liveliness, vivacity, zeal, enthusiasm, animation, ardour,

invigoration, revitalization, stimulation.
ᴇᴀ boredom, discouragement.

exile n 1 BANISHMENT, deportation,
expatriation, expulsion, ostracism,
transportation. 2 EXPATRIATE, refugee,
émigré, deportee, outcast.
➤ v banish, expel, deport, expatriate, drive
out, ostracize, oust.

exist v 1 BE, live, abide, continue, endure,
have one's being, breathe, prevail.
2 SUBSIST, survive. 3 BE PRESENT, occur,
happen, be available, remain.

existence n 1 BEING, life, reality, actuality,
continuance, continuation, endurance,
survival, breath, subsistence. 2 CREATION,
the world. 3 (fml) ENTITY, creature, thing.
ᴇᴀ 1 death, non-existence.

exit n 1 DEPARTURE, going, retreat,
withdrawal, leave-taking, retirement,
farewell, exodus. 2 DOOR, way out,
doorway, gate, vent.
ᴇᴀ 1 entrance, arrival. 2 entrance.
➤ v depart, leave, go, retire, withdraw, take
one's leave, retreat, issue.
ᴇᴀ arrive, enter.

exodus n departure, evacuation, mass
departure, mass evacuation, flight, fleeing,
escape, leaving, migration, retirement,
long march, retreat, withdrawal, exit,
hegira.

exonerate v 1 ABSOLVE, acquit, clear,
vindicate, exculpate (fml), justify, pardon,
discharge. 2 EXEMPT, excuse, spare, let off,
release, relieve.
ᴇᴀ 1 incriminate.

exorbitant adj excessive, unreasonable,
unwarranted, undue, inordinate,
immoderate, extravagant, extortionate,
enormous, preposterous.
ᴇᴀ reasonable, moderate.

exorcism n casting out, deliverance,
freeing, expulsion, purification, adjuration
(fml).

exorcize v cast out, drive out, free, expel,
purify, adjure (fml).

exotic adj 1 FOREIGN, alien, imported,
introduced. 2 UNUSUAL, striking, different,
unfamiliar, extraordinary, bizarre, curious,
strange, fascinating, colourful, peculiar,
outlandish.
ᴇᴀ 1 native. 2 ordinary.

expand v 1 STRETCH, swell, widen,
lengthen, thicken, magnify, multiply,
inflate, broaden, blow up, open out, fill out,
fatten. 2 INCREASE, grow, extend, enlarge,

develop, amplify, spread, branch out,
diversify, elaborate.
ᴇᴀ 1 contract.

expanse n extent, space, area, breadth,
range, stretch, sweep, field, plain, tract.

expansive adj 1 FRIENDLY, genial,
outgoing, open, affable, sociable, talkative,
warm, communicative, effusive.
2 EXTENSIVE, broad, comprehensive, wide-
ranging, all-embracing, thorough.
ᴇᴀ 1 reserved, cold. 2 restricted, narrow.

expatriate n emigrant, émigré, exile,
refugee, displaced person, ex-pat, outcast.
➤ v banish, exile, deport, extradite, drive
out, uproot, expel, oust, repatriate.
➤ adj banished, exiled, deported,
expelled, uprooted, emigrant, émigré.

expect v 1 expect the money soon:
anticipate, await, look forward to, hope for,
look for, bank on, bargain for, envisage,
predict, forecast, contemplate, project,
foresee. 2 expect you to comply: require,
want, wish, insist on, demand, rely on,
count on. 3 expect you're right: suppose,
surmise, assume, believe, think, presume,
imagine, reckon, guess (infml), trust.

expectant adj 1 AWAITING, anticipating,
hopeful, in suspense, ready, apprehensive,
anxious, watchful, eager, curious.
2 PREGNANT, expecting (infml), with child
(fml).

expectation n belief, anticipation,
assumption, presumption, surmise,
supposition, calculation, forecast,
projection, prediction, eagerness,
requirement, demand, insistence,
promise, want, wish, reliance, trust,
prospect, confidence, assurance,
suspense, optimism, possibility,
probability, outlook, conjecture (fml).

expecting adj pregnant, going to have a
baby, expectant, gravid (fml), with child
(fml), enceinte (fml), in the family way
(infml), in the club (infml).

expedient adj convenient, suitable,
appropriate, fitting, opportune, politic, in
one's own interest, profitable, useful,
beneficial, advantageous, advisable,
sensible, practical, pragmatic, tactical,
prudent (fml).
ᴇᴀ inexpedient.
➤ n stratagem, scheme, means, method,
tactic, ploy, manoeuvre, plan, trick, shift,
contrivance, device, stopgap, dodge
(infml)

expedite *v* speed up, accelerate, step up, quicken, hasten, hurry, further, facilitate, assist, promote, press, dispatch, discharge, hurry through, precipitate (*fml*).
🔄 delay.

expedition *n* 1 JOURNEY, excursion, trip, voyage, tour, exploration, trek, safari, hike, sail, ramble, raid, quest, pilgrimage, mission, crusade. 2 (*fml*) PROMPTNESS, speed, alacrity, haste.

expel *v* 1 DRIVE OUT, eject, evict, banish, throw out, ban, bar, oust, exile, expatriate. 2 DISCHARGE, evacuate, void, cast out.
🔄 1 welcome.

expend *v* 1 SPEND, pay, disburse (*fml*), fork out (*infml*). 2 CONSUME, use (up), dissipate, exhaust, employ.
🔄 1 save. 2 conserve.

expenditure *n* spending, expense, outlay, outgoings, disbursement (*fml*), payment, output.
🔄 income.

expense *n* spending, expenditure, disbursement (*fml*), outlay, payment, loss, cost, charge.

expensive *adj* dear, high-priced, costly, exorbitant, extortionate, steep (*infml*), extravagant, lavish.
🔄 cheap, inexpensive.

experience *n* 1 KNOWLEDGE, familiarity, know-how, involvement, participation, practice, understanding. 2 INCIDENT, event, episode, happening, encounter, occurrence, adventure.
🔄 1 inexperience.
➤ *v* undergo, go through, live through, suffer, feel, endure, encounter, face, meet, know, try, perceive, sustain.

experienced *adj* 1 PRACTISED, knowledgeable, familiar, capable, competent, well-versed, expert, accomplished, qualified, skilled, tried, trained, professional. 2 MATURE, seasoned, wise, veteran.
🔄 1 inexperienced, unskilled.

experiment *n* trial, test, investigation, experimentation, research, examination, trial run, venture, trial and error, attempt, procedure, proof.
➤ *v* try, test, investigate, examine, research, sample, verify.

experimental *adj* trial, test, exploratory, empirical (*fml*), tentative, provisional, speculative, pilot, preliminary, trial-and-error.

expert *n* specialist, connoisseur, authority, professional, pro (*infml*), dab hand (*infml*), maestro, virtuoso.
➤ *adj* proficient, adept, skilled, skilful, knowledgeable, experienced, able, practised, professional, masterly, specialist, qualified, virtuoso.
🔄 amateurish, novice.

expertise *n* expertness, proficiency, skill, skilfulness, know-how, knack (*infml*), knowledge, mastery, dexterity, virtuosity.
🔄 inexperience.

expire *v* end, cease, finish, stop, terminate, close, conclude, discontinue, run out, lapse, die, depart, decease, perish.
🔄 begin.

explain *v* 1 INTERPRET, clarify, describe, define, make clear, elucidate, simplify, resolve, solve, spell out, translate, unfold, unravel, untangle, illustrate, demonstrate, disclose, expound, teach. 2 JUSTIFY, excuse, account for, rationalize.
🔄 1 obscure, confound.

explanation *n* 1 INTERPRETATION, clarification, definition, elucidation, illustration, demonstration, account, description, exegesis (*fml*). 2 JUSTIFICATION, excuse, warrant, rationalization. 3 ANSWER, meaning, motive, reason, key, sense, significance.

explanatory *adj* descriptive, interpretive, explicative, demonstrative, expository (*fml*), justifying.

explicit *adj* 1 CLEAR, distinct, exact, categorical, absolute, certain, positive, precise, specific, unambiguous, express, definite, declared, detailed, stated. 2 OPEN, direct, frank, outspoken, straightforward, unreserved, plain.
🔄 1 implicit, unspoken, vague.

explode *v* 1 BLOW UP, burst, go off, set off, detonate, discharge, blast, erupt. 2 DISCREDIT, disprove, give the lie to, debunk, invalidate, refute, rebut, repudiate.
🔄 2 prove, confirm.

exploit *n* deed, feat, adventure, achievement, accomplishment, attainment, stunt.
➤ *v* 1 USE, utilize, capitalize on, profit by, turn to account, take advantage of, cash in on, make capital out of. 2 MISUSE, abuse, oppress, ill-treat, impose on, manipulate, rip off (*infml*), fleece (*infml*).

exploration *n* 1 INVESTIGATION,

examination, enquiry, research, scrutiny, study, inspection, analysis, probe. **2** EXPEDITION, survey, reconnaissance, search, trip, tour, voyage, travel, safari.

exploratory adj investigative, fact-finding, experimental, pilot, probing, searching, analytic, tentative, trial.

explore v **1** INVESTIGATE, examine, inspect, research, scrutinize, probe, analyse. **2** TRAVEL, tour, search, reconnoitre, prospect, scout, survey.

explosion n detonation, blast, burst, outburst, discharge, eruption, bang, outbreak, clap, crack, fit, report.

explosive adj unstable, volatile, sensitive, tense, fraught, charged, touchy, overwrought, dangerous, hazardous, perilous, stormy.
Ea stable, calm.

exponent n **1** ADVOCATE, promoter, supporter, upholder, defender, backer, adherent, spokesman, spokeswoman, spokesperson, champion, proponent (fml). **2** PRACTITIONER, adept, expert, master, specialist, player, performer.

export v trade, deal with, sell abroad/overseas, traffic in, transport.
➤ n exported product/commodity/goods, transfer, trade, foreign trade, international trade.

expose v **1** REVEAL, show, exhibit, display, disclose, uncover, bring to light, present, manifest, detect, divulge, unveil, unmask, denounce. **2** ENDANGER, jeopardize, imperil, risk, hazard.
Ea **1** conceal. **2** cover up.

exposed adj bare, open, revealed, laid bare, unprotected, vulnerable, exhibited, on display, on show, on view, shown, susceptible.
Ea covered, sheltered.

exposition n **1** EXPLANATION, description, analysis, unfolding, clarification, illumination, commentary, interpretation, account, illustration, critique, presentation, paper, study, thesis, monograph, discourse (fml), elucidation (fml), exegesis (fml), explication (fml). **2** EXHIBITION, show, fair, display, demonstration, expo (infml).

exposure n **1** REVELATION, uncovering, disclosure, exposé, showing, unmasking, unveiling, display, airing, exhibition, presentation, publicity, manifestation, discovery, divulgence. **2** FAMILIARITY,

experience, knowledge, contact. **3** JEOPARDY, danger, hazard, risk, vulnerability.

express v **1** ARTICULATE, verbalize, utter, voice, say, speak, state, communicate, pronounce, tell, assert, declare, put across, formulate, intimate, testify, convey. **2** SHOW, manifest, exhibit, disclose, divulge, reveal, indicate, denote, depict, embody. **3** SYMBOLIZE, stand for, represent, signify, designate.
➤ adj **1** SPECIFIC, explicit, exact, definite, clear, categorical, precise, distinct, clear-cut, certain, plain, manifest, particular, stated, unambiguous. **2** FAST, speedy, rapid, quick, high-speed, non-stop.
Ea **1** vague.

expression n **1** LOOK, air, aspect, countenance, appearance, mien (fml). **2** REPRESENTATION, manifestation, demonstration, indication, exhibition, embodiment, show, sign, symbol, style. **3** UTTERANCE, verbalization, communication, articulation, statement, assertion, announcement, declaration, pronouncement, speech. **4** TONE, intonation, delivery, diction, enunciation, modulation, wording. **5** PHRASE, term, turn of phrase, saying, set phrase, idiom.

expressionless adj dull, blank, dead-pan, impassive, straight-faced, poker-faced (infml), inscrutable, empty, vacuous, glassy.
Ea expressive.

expressive adj eloquent, meaningful, forceful, telling, revealing, informative, indicative, communicative, demonstrative, emphatic, moving, poignant, lively, striking, suggestive, significant, thoughtful, vivid, sympathetic.

expulsion n ejection, eviction, exile, banishment, removal, discharge, exclusion, dismissal.

exquisite adj **1** BEAUTIFUL, attractive, dainty, delicate, charming, elegant, delightful, lovely, pleasing. **2** PERFECT, flawless, fine, excellent, choice, precious, rare, outstanding. **3** REFINED, discriminating, meticulous, sensitive, impeccable. **4** INTENSE, keen, sharp, poignant.
Ea **1** ugly. **2** flawed. **3** unrefined.

extempore adv impromptu, ad lib, on the spur of the moment, spontaneously, off the cuff (infml), off the top of one's head (infml).

➤ *adj* impromptu, improvised, ad-lib, unscripted, spontaneous, unplanned, unrehearsed, unprepared, extemporaneous, off-the-cuff (*infml*).
🔼 planned.

extemporize *v* ad-lib, improvise, play it by ear, think on one's feet, make up.

extend *v* 1 SPREAD, stretch, reach, continue. 2 ENLARGE, increase, expand, develop, amplify, lengthen, widen, elongate, draw out, protract, prolong, spin out, unwind. 3 OFFER, give, grant, hold out, impart, present, bestow, confer.
🔼 2 contract, shorten. 3 withhold.

extended *adj* lengthy, long, lengthened, increased, enlarged, expanded, developed, amplified.

extension *n* 1 ENLARGEMENT, increase, stretching, broadening, widening, lengthening, expansion, elongation, development, enhancement, protraction, continuation. 2 ADDITION, supplement, appendix, annexe, addendum (*fml*). 3 DELAY, postponement.

extensive *adj* 1 BROAD, comprehensive, far-reaching, large-scale, thorough, widespread, universal, extended, all-inclusive, general, pervasive, prevalent. 2 LARGE, huge, roomy, spacious, vast, voluminous, long, lengthy, wide.
🔼 1 restricted, narrow. 2 small.

extent *n* 1 DIMENSION(S), amount, magnitude, expanse, size, area, bulk, degree, breadth, quantity, spread, stretch, volume, width, measure, duration, term, time. 2 LIMIT, bounds, lengths, range, reach, scope, compass, sphere, play, sweep.

extenuating *adj* mitigating, moderating, qualifying, justifying, palliative, diminishing, excusing, lessening, minimizing, modifying, softening.

exterior *n* outside, surface, covering, coating, face, façade, shell, skin, finish, externals, appearance.
🔼 inside, interior.
➤ *adj* outer, outside, outermost, surface, external, superficial, surrounding, outward, peripheral, extrinsic.
🔼 inside, interior.

exterminate *v* annihilate, eradicate, destroy, eliminate, massacre, abolish, wipe out.

external *adj* outer, surface, outside, exterior, superficial, outward, outermost, apparent, visible, extraneous,

extrinsic, extramural, independent.
🔼 internal.

extinct *adj* 1 DEFUNCT, dead, gone, obsolete, ended, exterminated, terminated, vanished, lost, abolished. 2 EXTINGUISHED, quenched, inactive, out.
🔼 1 living.

extinction *n* annihilation, extermination, death, eradication, obliteration, destruction, abolition, excision.

extinguish *v* 1 PUT OUT, blow out, snuff out, stifle, smother, douse, quench. 2 ANNIHILATE, exterminate, eliminate, destroy, kill, eradicate, erase, expunge, abolish, remove, end, suppress.

extol *v* praise, acclaim, exalt, magnify, glorify, sing the praises of, applaud, celebrate, commend, laud (*fml*), eulogize (*fml*), rhapsodize (*fml*).
🔼 blame, denigrate (*fml*).

extort *v* extract, wring, exact, coerce, force, milk (*infml*), blackmail, squeeze, bleed (*infml*), bully.

extortionate *adj* exorbitant, excessive, grasping, exacting, immoderate, rapacious, unreasonable, oppressive, blood-sucking (*infml*), rigorous, severe, hard, harsh, inordinate.

extra *adj* 1 ADDITIONAL, added, auxiliary, supplementary, new, more, further, ancillary, fresh, other. 2 EXCESS, spare, superfluous, supernumerary, surplus, unused, unneeded, leftover, reserve, redundant.
🔼 1 integral. 2 essential.
➤ *n* addition, supplement, extension, accessory, appendage, bonus, complement, adjunct, addendum (*fml*), attachment.
➤ *adv* especially, exceptionally, extraordinarily, particularly, unusually, remarkably, extremely.

extract *v* 1 REMOVE, take out, draw out, exact, uproot, withdraw. 2 DERIVE, draw, distil, obtain, get, gather, glean, wrest, wring, elicit. 3 CHOOSE, select, cull, abstract, cite, quote.
🔼 1 insert.
➤ *n* 1 DISTILLATION, essence, juice. 2 EXCERPT, passage, selection, clip, cutting, quotation, abstract, citation.

extradite *v* send back, send home, deport, repatriate, banish, expel, exile.

extraneous *adj* superfluous, supplementary, redundant, irrelevant, immaterial, inapplicable, inappropriate, inessential, inapt, incidental, tangential, needless, unnecessary, unneeded, non-essential, unessential, unrelated, unconnected, extra, additional, peripheral, exterior, external, extrinsic, alien, strange, foreign, inapposite (*fml*). **Fa** integral, essential.

extraordinary *adj* remarkable, unusual, exceptional, notable, noteworthy, outstanding, unique, special, strange, peculiar, rare, surprising, amazing, wonderful, unprecedented, marvellous, fantastic, significant, particular. **Fa** commonplace, ordinary.

extravagance *n* **1** OVERSPENDING, profligacy, squandering, waste. **2** EXCESS, immoderation, recklessness, profusion, outrageousness, folly. **Fa 1** thrift. **2** moderation.

extravagant *adj* **1** PROFLIGATE, prodigal, spendthrift, thriftless, wasteful, reckless. **2** IMMODERATE, flamboyant, preposterous, outrageous, ostentatious, pretentious, lavish, ornate, flashy (*infml*), fanciful, fantastic, wild. **3** OVERPRICED, exorbitant, expensive, excessive, costly. **Fa 1** thrifty. **2** moderate. **3** reasonable.

extreme *adj* **1** INTENSE, great, immoderate, inordinate, utmost, utter, out-and-out, maximum, acute, downright, extraordinary, exceptional, greatest, highest, unreasonable, remarkable. **2** FARTHEST, far-off, faraway, distant, endmost, outermost, remotest, uttermost, final, last, terminal, ultimate. **3** RADICAL, zealous, extremist, fanatical. **4** DRASTIC, dire, uncompromising, stern, strict, rigid, severe, harsh. **Fa 1** mild. **2** moderate. ➤ *n* extremity, limit, maximum, ultimate, utmost, excess, top, pinnacle, peak, height, end, climax, depth, edge, termination.

extremely *adv* exceedingly, excessively, very, really, exceptionally, extraordinarily, intensely, thoroughly, remarkably, utterly, greatly, highly, unusually, unreasonably, immoderately, uncommonly, inordinately, acutely, severely, decidedly, awfully (*infml*), terribly (*infml*), dreadfully (*infml*), frightfully (*infml*), terrifically (*infml*).

extremist *n* fanatic, hardliner, fundamentalist, militant, radical, zealot, diehard, ultra, terrorist. **Fa** moderate.

extremity *n* **1** EXTREME, limit, boundary, brink, verge, bound, border, apex, height, tip, top, edge, excess, end, acme, termination, peak, pinnacle, margin, terminal, terminus, ultimate, pole, maximum, minimum, frontier, depth. **2** CRISIS, danger, emergency, plight, hardship.

extricate *v* disentangle, clear, disengage, free, deliver, liberate, release, rescue, relieve, remove, withdraw. **Fa** involve.

extroverted *adj* outgoing, friendly, sociable, amicable, amiable, exuberant. **Fa** introverted.

exuberant *adj* **1** LIVELY, vivacious, spirited, zestful, high-spirited, effervescent, ebullient, enthusiastic, sparkling, excited, exhilarated, effusive, cheerful, fulsome. **2** PLENTIFUL, lavish, overflowing, plenteous. **Fa 1** apathetic. **2** scarce.

exude *v* **1** *exude confidence*: radiate, ooze, display, show, emanate, emit, exhibit, manifest (*fml*). **2** DISCHARGE, issue, flow out, bleed, excrete, leak, secrete, seep, perspire, sweat, trickle, weep, well.

exult *v* rejoice, revel, delight, glory, celebrate, relish, crow, gloat, triumph.

eye *n* **1** APPRECIATION, discrimination, discernment, perception, recognition. **2** VIEWPOINT, opinion, judgement, mind. **3** WATCH, observation, lookout.

Parts of the eye include: anterior chamber, aqueous humour, blind spot, choroid, ciliary body, cone, conjunctiva, cornea, eyelash, fovea, iris, lacrimal duct, lens, lower eyelid, ocular muscle, optic nerve, papilla, posterior chamber, pupil, retina, rod, sclera, suspension ligament, upper eyelid, vitreous humour.

➤ *v* look at, watch, regard, observe, stare at, gaze at, glance at, view, scrutinize, scan, examine, peruse, study, survey, inspect, contemplate.

eyesight *n* vision, sight, perception, observation, view.

eyesore *n* ugliness, blemish, monstrosity, blot on the landscape, disfigurement, horror, blight, atrocity, mess.

eyewitness *n* witness, observer, spectator, looker-on, onlooker, bystander, viewer, passer-by.

Ff

fable n allegory, parable, story, tale, yarn, myth, legend, fiction, fabrication, invention, lie, untruth, falsehood, tall story, old wives' tale.

fabric n 1 CLOTH, material, textile, stuff, web, texture. 2 STRUCTURE, framework, construction, make-up, constitution, organization, infrastructure, foundations.

> Fabrics include: alpaca, angora, astrakhan, barathea, bouclé, cashmere, chenille, duffel, felt, flannel, fleece, Harris tweed®, mohair, paisley, serge, sheepskin, Shetland wool, tweed, vicuña, wool, worsted; buckram, calico, cambric, candlewick, canvas, chambray, cheesecloth, chino, chintz, cord, corduroy, cotton, crepe, denim, drill, jean, flannelette, gaberdine, gingham, jersey, lawn, linen, lisle, madras, moleskin, muslin, needlecord, piqué, poplin, sateen, seersucker, terry towelling, ticking, Viyella®, webbing, winceyette; brocade, grosgrain, damask, Brussels lace, chiffon, georgette, gossamer, voile, organdie, organza, tulle, net, crêpe de Chine, silk, taffeta, shantung, velvet, velour; polycotton, polyester, rayon, nylon, Crimplene®, Terylene®, Lurex®, lamé; hessian, horsehair, chamois, kid, leather, leather-cloth, sharkskin, suede.

fabricate v 1 FAKE, falsify, forge, invent, make up, trump up, concoct. 2 MAKE, manufacture, construct, assemble, build, erect, form, shape, fashion, create, devise. **E3** 2 demolish, destroy.

fabrication n 1 FAKE, falsehood, forgery, invention, concoction, fable, fiction, figment, story, myth, untruth, cock-and-bull story (infml), fairy story (infml). 2 MANUFACTURE, assembly, building, construction, erection, production. **E3** 1 truth.

fabulous adj 1 WONDERFUL, marvellous, fantastic, superb, breathtaking, spectacular, phenomenal, amazing, astounding, unbelievable, incredible, inconceivable. 2 a fabulous beast: mythical, legendary, fabled, fantastic,

fictitious, invented, imaginary. **E3** 2 real.

façade n 1 FRONT, exterior, frontage, face. 2 SHOW, semblance, appearance, cover, cloak, veil, guise, mask, disguise, pretence, veneer.

face n 1 FEATURES, countenance, visage, physiognomy. 2 EXPRESSION, look, appearance, air. 3 pull a face: grimace, frown, scowl, pout. 4 EXTERIOR, outside, surface, cover, front, façade, aspect, side. ➤ v 1 BE OPPOSITE, give on to, front, overlook. 2 CONFRONT, face up to, deal with, cope with, tackle, brave, defy, oppose, encounter, meet, experience. 3 COVER, coat, dress, clad, overlay, veneer.
◆ **face to face** opposite, eye to eye, eyeball to eyeball, in confrontation.
◆ **face up to** accept, come to terms with, acknowledge, recognize, cope with, deal with, confront, meet head-on, stand up to.

facet n surface, plane, side, face, aspect, angle, point, feature, characteristic.

facetious adj flippant, frivolous, playful, jocular, jesting, tongue-in-cheek, funny, amusing, humorous, comical, witty. **E3** serious.

facile adj easy, simple, simplistic, ready, quick, hasty, glib, fluent, smooth, slick, plausible, shallow, superficial. **E3** complicated, profound.

facilitate v ease, help, assist, further, promote, forward, expedite, speed up.

facilities n amenities, services, conveniences, resources, prerequisites, equipment, mod cons (infml), means, opportunities.

facility n ease, effortlessness, readiness, quickness, fluency, proficiency, skill, skilfulness, talent, gift, knack, ability.

facsimile n copy, imitation, reproduction, repro, replica, carbon copy, carbon, duplicate, image, fax, photocopy, Photostat®, Xerox®, mimeograph, transcript, print.

fact n 1 facts and figures: information, datum, detail, particular, specific, point, item, circumstance, event, incident, occurrence, happening, act, deed, fait accompli. **2** REALITY, actuality, truth.

☒ **2** fiction.

♦ **in fact** actually, in actual fact, in point of fact, as a matter of fact, in reality, really, indeed.

faction *n* splinter group, ginger group, minority, division, section, contingent, party, camp, set, clique, coterie, cabal, junta, lobby, pressure group.

factor *n* cause, influence, circumstance, contingency, consideration, element, ingredient, component, part, point, aspect, fact, item, detail.

factory *n* works, plant, mill, shop floor, assembly line, manufactory.

factual *adj* true, historical, actual, real, genuine, authentic, correct, accurate, precise, exact, literal, faithful, close, detailed, unbiased, objective.

☒ false, fictitious, imaginary, fictional.

faculties *n* wits, senses, intelligence, reason, powers, capabilities.

faculty *n* ability, capability, capacity, power, facility, knack, gift, talent, skill, aptitude, bent.

fad *n* craze, rage (*infml*), mania, fashion, mode, vogue, trend, whim, fancy, affectation.

fade *v* **1** DISCOLOUR, bleach, blanch, blench, pale, whiten, dim, dull. **2** DECLINE, fall, diminish, dwindle, ebb, wane, disappear, vanish, flag, weaken, droop, wilt, wither, shrivel, perish, die.

fail *v* **1** GO WRONG, miscarry, misfire, flop, miss, flunk (*sl*), fall through, come to grief, collapse, fold (*infml*), go bankrupt, go bust, go under, founder, sink, decline, fall, weaken, dwindle, fade, wane, peter out, cease, die. **2** *fail to pay a bill*: omit, neglect, forget. **3** LET DOWN, disappoint, leave, desert, abandon, forsake.

☒ **1** succeed, prosper.

failing *n* weakness, foible, fault, defect, imperfection, flaw, blemish, drawback, deficiency, shortcoming, failure, lapse, error.

☒ strength, advantage.

failure *n* **1** MISCARRIAGE, flop, washout (*infml*), fiasco, disappointment, loss, defeat, downfall, decline, decay, deterioration, ruin, bankruptcy, crash, collapse, breakdown, stoppage. **2** OMISSION, slip-up (*infml*), neglect,

negligence, failing, shortcoming, deficiency.

☒ **1** success, prosperity.

faint *adj* **1** SLIGHT, weak, feeble, soft, low, hushed, muffled, subdued, faded, bleached, light, pale, dull, dim, hazy, indistinct, vague. **2** *I feel faint*: dizzy, giddy, woozy (*infml*), light-headed, weak, feeble, exhausted.

☒ **1** strong, clear.

➤ *v* black out, pass out, swoon, collapse, flake out (*infml*), keel over (*infml*), drop.

➤ *n* blackout, swoon, collapse, unconsciousness.

fair[1] *adj* **1** JUST, equitable, square, even-handed, dispassionate, impartial, objective, disinterested, unbiased, unprejudiced, right, proper, lawful, legitimate, honest, trustworthy, upright, honourable. **2** FAIR-HAIRED, fair-headed, blond(e), light. **3** *fair weather*: fine, dry, sunny, bright, clear, cloudless, unclouded. **4** AVERAGE, moderate, middling, not bad, all right, OK (*infml*), satisfactory, adequate, acceptable, tolerable, reasonable, passable, mediocre, so-so (*infml*).

☒ **1** unfair. **2** dark. **3** inclement, cloudy. **4** excellent, poor.

fair[2] *n* show, exhibition, exposition, expo (*infml*), market, bazaar, fête, festival, carnival, gala.

fairly *adv* **1** QUITE, rather, somewhat, reasonably, tolerably, moderately, adequately, pretty. **2** POSITIVELY, absolutely, impartially, really, fully, veritably. **3** JUSTLY, equitably, honestly, objectively, unbiasedly, properly, legally, lawfully.

☒ **3** unfairly.

fairness *n* justice, equitableness, equity, even-handedness, unbiasedness, impartiality, legitimacy, rightfulness, rightness, uprightness, disinterestedness, decency, legitimateness.

☒ unfairness.

fairy *n* elf, fay, pixie, imp, brownie, leprechaun, sprite, Robin Goodfellow, Puck, hob, hobgoblin, nymph, rusalka, peri, fée.

fairy tale *n* **1** FAIRY STORY, folk-tale, myth, romance, fiction, fantasy. **2** LIE, untruth, invention, fabrication, cock-and-bull story (*infml*), tall story (*infml*).

faith *n* **1** BELIEF, credit, trust, reliance, dependence, conviction, confidence, assurance. **2** RELIGION, denomination, persuasion, church, creed, dogma. **3** FAITHFULNESS, fidelity, loyalty, allegiance, honour, sincerity, honesty, truthfulness.

 ■ **1** mistrust. **3** unfaithfulness, treachery.

faithful *adj* **1** LOYAL, devoted, staunch, steadfast, constant, trusty, reliable, dependable, true. **2** *a faithful description*: accurate, precise, exact, strict, close, true, truthful.

 ■ **1** disloyal, treacherous. **2** inaccurate, vague.

fake *v* forge, fabricate, counterfeit, copy, imitate, simulate, feign, sham, pretend, put on, affect, assume.
 ➤ *n* forgery, copy, reproduction, replica, imitation, simulation, sham, hoax, fraud, phoney (*infml*), impostor, charlatan.
 ➤ *adj* forged, counterfeit, false, spurious, phoney (*infml*), pseudo, bogus, assumed, affected, sham, artificial, simulated, mock, imitation, reproduction.

 ■ genuine.

fall *v* **1** TUMBLE, stumble, trip, topple, keel over, collapse, slump, crash. **2** DESCEND, go down, drop, slope, incline, slide, sink, dive, plunge, plummet, nose-dive, pitch. **3** DECREASE, lessen, decline, diminish, dwindle, fall off, subside.

 ■ **2** rise. **3** increase.

 ➤ *n* **1** TUMBLE, descent, slope, incline, dive, plunge, decrease, reduction, lessening, drop, decline, dwindling, slump, crash.
 2 *the fall of Rome*: defeat, conquest, overthrow, downfall, collapse, surrender, capitulation.

 ◆ **fall apart** break, go to pieces, shatter, disintegrate, crumble, decompose, decay, rot.

 ◆ **fall asleep** drop off, doze off, nod off (*infml*).

 ◆ **fall back on** resort to, have recourse to, use, turn to, look to.

 ◆ **fall behind** lag, trail, drop back.

 ◆ **fall for 1** FALL IN LOVE WITH, be attached to, become infatuated with, desire, take to, fancy (*infml*), be crazy about (*infml*), have a crush on (*infml*), fall head over heels in love with (*infml*). **2** ACCEPT, be taken in by, be fooled by, be deceived by, swallow (*infml*), buy (*infml*).

 ◆ **fall in** cave in, come down, collapse, give way, subside, sink.

 ◆ **fall in with** agree with, assent to, go along with, accept, comply with, co-operate with.

 ◆ **fall off** decrease, lessen, drop, slump,

decline, deteriorate, worsen, slow, slacken.

 ◆ **fall out** quarrel, argue, squabble, bicker, fight, clash, disagree, differ.

 ■ agree.

 ◆ **fall through** come to nothing, fail, miscarry, founder, collapse.

 ■ come off, succeed.

fallacy *n* misconception, delusion, mistake, error, flaw, inconsistency, falsehood.

 ■ truth.

fallow *adj* uncultivated, unplanted, unsown, undeveloped, unused, idle, inactive, dormant, resting.

false *adj* **1** WRONG, incorrect, mistaken, erroneous, inaccurate, inexact, misleading, faulty, fallacious, invalid. **2** UNREAL, artificial, synthetic, imitation, simulated, mock, fake, counterfeit, forged, feigned, pretended, sham, bogus, assumed, fictitious. **3** *false friends*: disloyal, unfaithful, faithless, lying, deceitful, insincere, hypocritical, two-faced, double-dealing, treacherous, unreliable.

 ■ **1** true, right. **2** real, genuine. **3** faithful, reliable.

falsehood *n* untruth, lie, fib, story, fiction, fabrication, perjury, untruthfulness, deceit, deception, dishonesty.

 ■ truth, truthfulness.

falsify *v* alter, cook (*infml*), tamper with, doctor, distort, pervert, misrepresent, misstate, forge, counterfeit, fake.

falter *v* totter, stumble, stammer, stutter, hesitate, waver, vacillate, flinch, quail, shake, tremble, flag, fail.

fame *n* renown, celebrity, stardom, prominence, eminence, illustriousness, glory, honour, esteem, reputation, name.

familiar *adj* **1** EVERYDAY, routine, household, common, ordinary, well-known, recognizable. **2** INTIMATE, close, confidential, friendly, informal, free, free-and-easy, relaxed. **3** *familiar with the procedure*: aware, acquainted, abreast, knowledgeable, versed, conversant.

 ■ **1** unfamiliar, strange. **2** formal, reserved. **3** unfamiliar, ignorant.

familiarity *n* **1** INTIMACY, liberty, closeness, friendliness, sociability, openness, naturalness, informality.
 2 AWARENESS, acquaintance, experience, knowledge, understanding, grasp.

familiarize *v* accustom, acclimatize, school, train, coach, instruct, prime, brief.

family n 1 RELATIVES, relations, kin, kindred, kinsmen, people, folk (*infml*), ancestors, forebears, children, offspring, issue, progeny, descendants. 2 CLAN, tribe, race, dynasty, house, pedigree, ancestry, parentage, descent, line, lineage, extraction, blood, stock, birth. 3 CLASS, group, classification.

Members of a family include: ancestor, forebear, forefather, descendant, offspring, heir; husband, wife, spouse, parent, father, dad (*infml*), daddy (*infml*), old man (*infml*), mother, mum (*infml*), mummy (*infml*), mom (*US infml*), grandparent, grandfather, grandmother, granny (*infml*), nanny (*infml*), grandchild, son, daughter, brother, half-brother, sister, half-sister, sibling, uncle, aunt, nephew, niece, cousin, godfather, godmother, godchild, stepfather, stepmother, foster-parent, foster-child.

♦ **family tree** ancestry, pedigree, genealogy, line, lineage, extraction.

famine n starvation, hunger, destitution, want, scarcity, death.
🖭 plenty.

famished adj starved, starving, famishing, ravenous, hungry, undernourished, voracious.
🖭 sated.

famous adj well-known, famed, renowned, celebrated, noted, great, distinguished, illustrious, eminent, honoured, acclaimed, glorious, legendary, remarkable, notable, prominent, signal.
🖭 unheard-of, unknown, obscure.

fan[1] v 1 COOL, ventilate, air, air-condition, air-cool, blow, refresh. 2 INCREASE, provoke, stimulate, rouse, arouse, excite, agitate, stir up, work up, whip up.
➤ n extractor fan, ventilator, air-conditioner, blower, propeller, vane.

fan[2] n enthusiast, admirer, supporter, follower, adherent, devotee, lover, buff (*infml*), fiend, freak.

fanatic n zealot, devotee, enthusiast, addict, fiend, freak, maniac, visionary, bigot, extremist, militant, activist.

fanatical adj overenthusiastic, extreme, passionate, zealous, fervent, burning, mad, wild, frenzied, rabid, obsessive, single-minded, bigoted, visionary.
🖭 moderate, unenthusiastic.

fanaticism n extremism, monomania, single-mindedness, obsessiveness, madness, infatuation, bigotry, zeal, fervour, enthusiasm, dedication.
🖭 moderation.

fanciful adj imaginary, mythical, fabulous, fantastic, visionary, romantic, fairy-tale, airy-fairy, vaporous, whimsical, wild, extravagant, curious.
🖭 real, ordinary.

fancy v 1 LIKE, be attracted to, take a liking to, take to, go for, prefer, favour, desire, wish for, long for, yearn for. 2 THINK, conceive, imagine, dream of, picture, conjecture, believe, suppose, reckon, guess.
🖭 1 dislike.
➤ n 1 DESIRE, craving, hankering, urge, liking, fondness, inclination, preference. 2 NOTION, thought, impression, imagination, dream, fantasy.
🖭 1 dislike, aversion. 2 fact, reality.
➤ adj elaborate, ornate, decorated, ornamented, rococo, baroque, elegant, extravagant, fantastic, fanciful, far-fetched.
🖭 plain.

fantasize v imagine, daydream, dream, hallucinate, invent, romance, build castles in the air (*infml*), live in a dream (*infml*).

fantastic adj 1 WONDERFUL, marvellous, sensational, superb, excellent, first-rate, tremendous, terrific, great, incredible, unbelievable, overwhelming, enormous, extreme. 2 STRANGE, weird, odd, exotic, outlandish, fanciful, fabulous, imaginative, visionary.
🖭 1 ordinary. 2 real.

fantasy n dream, daydream, reverie, pipe-dream, nightmare, vision, hallucination, illusion, mirage, apparition, invention, fancy, flight of fancy, delusion, misconception, imagination, unreality.
🖭 reality.

far adv a long way, a good way, miles (*infml*), much, greatly, considerably, extremely, decidedly, incomparably.
🖭 near, close.
➤ adj distant, far-off, faraway, far-flung, outlying, remote, out-of-the-way, godforsaken, removed, far-removed, further, opposite, other.
🖭 nearby, close.

farce n 1 COMEDY, slapstick, buffoonery, satire, burlesque. 2 TRAVESTY, sham, parody, joke, mockery, ridiculousness, absurdity, nonsense.

farcical adj ridiculous, absurd, ludicrous,

preposterous, nonsensical, stupid, laughable, comic, silly, derisory, diverting. ☒ sensible.

fare n 1 *pay one's fare*: charge, cost, price, fee, passage. 2 FOOD, eatables (*infml*), provisions, rations, sustenance, meals, diet, menu, board, table.

far-fetched adj implausible, improbable, unlikely, dubious, incredible, unbelievable, fantastic, preposterous, crazy, unrealistic. ☒ plausible.

farm n ranch, farmstead, grange, homestead, station, land, holding, acreage, acres.

> Types of farm include: arable farm, cattle ranch, dairy farm, fish farm, mixed farm, organic farm, pig farm, sheep station, croft, smallholding, estate, plantation.

> v cultivate, till, work the land, plant, operate.

farmer n agriculturist, crofter, smallholder, husbandman, yeoman.

farming n agriculture, cultivation, husbandry, crofting.

far-reaching adj broad, extensive, widespread, sweeping, important, significant, momentous. ☒ insignificant.

fascinate v absorb, engross, intrigue, delight, charm, captivate, spellbind, enthral, rivet, transfix, hypnotize, mesmerize. ☒ bore, repel.

fascinated adj absorbed, engrossed, curious, intrigued, delighted, charmed, enticed, spellbound, enthralled, entranced, captivated, bewitched, beguiled, hypnotized, mesmerized, infatuated, smitten, hooked (*infml*). ☒ bored, uninterested.

fascinating adj intriguing, gripping, exciting, interesting, engaging, engrossing, irresistible, compelling, alluring, bewitching, captivating, enchanting, riveting, enticing, seductive, tempting, charming, absorbing, stimulating, delightful, mesmerizing. ☒ boring, uninteresting.

fascination n interest, attraction, lure, magnetism, pull, charm, enchantment, spell, sorcery, magic. ☒ boredom, repulsion.

fashion n 1 MANNER, way, method, mode,

style, shape, form, pattern, line, cut, look, appearance, type, sort, kind. 2 VOGUE, trend, mode, style, fad, craze, rage (*infml*), latest (*infml*), custom, convention. > v create, form, shape, mould, model, design, fit, tailor, alter, adjust, adapt, suit.

fashionable adj chic, smart, elegant, stylish, modish, à la mode, in vogue, trendy (*infml*), in, all the rage (*infml*), popular, prevailing, current, latest, up-to-the-minute, contemporary, modern, up-to-date. ☒ unfashionable.

fast[1] adj 1 QUICK, swift, rapid, brisk, accelerated, speedy, nippy (*infml*), hasty, hurried, flying. 2 FASTENED, secure, fixed, immovable, immobile, firm, tight. ☒ 1 slow, unhurried. 2 loose. > adv quickly, swiftly, rapidly, speedily, like a flash, like a shot, hastily, hurriedly, apace, presto. ☒ slowly, gradually.

fast[2] v go hungry, diet, starve, abstain. > n fasting, diet, starvation, abstinence. ☒ gluttony, self-indulgence.

fasten v fix, attach, clamp, grip, anchor, rivet, nail, seal, close, shut, lock, bolt, secure, tie, bind, chain, link, interlock, connect, join, unite, do up, button, lace, buckle. ☒ unfasten, untie.

fat adj plump, obese, tubby, stout, corpulent, portly, round, rotund, paunchy, pot-bellied, overweight, heavy, beefy, solid, chubby, podgy, fleshy, flabby, gross. ☒ thin, slim, poor. > n fatness, obesity, overweight, corpulence, paunch, pot (belly), blubber, flab (*infml*).

fatal adj deadly, lethal, mortal, killing, incurable, malignant, terminal, final, destructive, calamitous, catastrophic, disastrous. ☒ harmless.

fatality n death, mortality, loss, casualty, deadliness, lethality, disaster.

fate n destiny, providence, chance, future, fortune, horoscope, stars, lot, doom, end, outcome, ruin, destruction, death.

fated adj destined, predestined, preordained, foreordained, doomed, unavoidable, inevitable, inescapable, certain, sure. ☒ avoidable.

fateful adj crucial, critical, decisive,

important, momentous, significant, fatal,
lethal, disastrous.
▪ unimportant.

father n **1** PARENT, begetter, procreator,
progenitor, sire (fml), papa, dad (infml),
daddy (infml), old man (infml), patriarch,
elder, forefather, ancestor, forebear,
predecessor. **2** FOUNDER, creator,
originator, inventor, maker, architect,
author, patron, leader, prime mover. **3**
PRIEST, padre, abbé, curé.
➤ v beget, procreate, sire, produce.

fathom v **1** MEASURE, gauge, plumb,
sound, probe, penetrate. **2** UNDERSTAND,
comprehend, grasp, see, work out, get to
the bottom of, interpret.

fatigue n tiredness, weariness,
exhaustion, lethargy, listlessness,
lassitude, weakness, debility.
▪ energy.
➤ v tire, wear out, weary, exhaust, drain,
weaken, debilitate.

fatten v feed, nourish, build up, overfeed,
cram, stuff, bloat, swell, fill out, spread,
expand, thicken.

fatty adj fat, greasy, oily.

fault n **1** DEFECT, flaw, blemish,
imperfection, deficiency, shortcoming,
weakness, failing, foible, negligence,
omission, oversight. **2** ERROR, mistake,
blunder, slip-up (infml), slip, lapse,
misdeed, offence, wrong, sin. **3** it's your
fault: responsibility, accountability, liability,
culpability.
➤ v find fault with, pick holes in, criticize,
knock (infml), impugn, censure, blame,
call to account.
▪ praise.
◆ **at fault** (in the) wrong, blameworthy, to
blame, responsible, guilty, culpable.

faultless adj perfect, flawless,
unblemished, spotless, immaculate,
unsullied, pure, blameless, exemplary,
model, correct, accurate.
▪ faulty, imperfect, flawed.

faulty adj imperfect, defective, flawed,
blemished, damaged, impaired, out of
order, broken, wrong.
▪ faultless.

favour n **1** APPROVAL, esteem, support,
backing, sympathy, goodwill, patronage,
favouritism, preference, partiality. **2** he did
me a favour: kindness, service, good turn,
courtesy.
▪ **1** disapproval.

➤ v **1** PREFER, choose, opt for, like, approve,
support, back, advocate, champion.
2 HELP, assist, aid, benefit, promote,
encourage, pamper, spoil.
▪ **1** dislike. **2** mistreat.
◆ **in favour of** for, supporting, on the side
of.
▪ against.

favourable adj beneficial, advantageous,
helpful, fit, suitable, convenient, timely,
opportune, good, fair, promising,
auspicious, hopeful, positive,
encouraging, complimentary,
enthusiastic, friendly, amicable, well-
disposed, kind, sympathetic,
understanding, reassuring.
▪ unfavourable, unhelpful, negative.

favourite adj preferred, favoured, pet,
best-loved, dearest, beloved, esteemed,
chosen.
▪ hated.
➤ n preference, choice, pick, pet, blue-
eyed boy, teacher's pet, the apple of one's
eye, darling, idol.
▪ bête noire, pet hate.

favouritism n nepotism, preferential
treatment, preference, partiality, one-
sidedness, partisanship, bias, injustice.
▪ impartiality.

fawn¹ adj beige, buff, yellowish-brown,
sandy, sand-coloured, khaki.

fawn² v flatter, grovel, bow and scrape,
court, curry favour, dance attendance,
kowtow, pay court, ingratiate oneself,
toady, bootlick (infml), crawl (infml), creep
(infml), cringe (infml), smarm (infml), lick
someone's boots (infml), suck up to (infml),
butter up (infml), soft-soap (infml).

fear n **1** TERROR, dread, alarm, fright,
panic, fearfulness, agitation,
apprehension, foreboding, dismay,
distress, trembling, shaking, quivering,
phobia, aversion, terror, horror, nightmare,
bête noire, trepidation, consternation. **2**
ANXIETY, worry, concern, unease,
uneasiness, qualms, misgivings, disquiet,
suspicion, doubt. **3** AWE, reverence,
respect, wonder, honour, fear, fear of God,
terror, dread, veneration. **4** no fear of being
misunderstood: chance, risk, likelihood,
possibility, probability, prospect,
expectation, scope.
▪ **1** courage, bravery, confidence. **3**
contempt.
➤ v **1** BE AFRAID OF, be scared of, dread,

shudder at, shrink from, tremble, lose one's nerve, take fright at, have a horror of, have a phobia about, panic, have one's heart in one's mouth (*infml*), one's heart melts (*infml*), one's stomach turns (*infml*), get the wind up (*infml*), be in a cold sweat (*infml*), freak out (*infml*), lose one's bottle (*infml*). **2** WORRY, be anxious about, be uneasy about, be concerned about, have misgivings/qualms about, tremble for. **3** *fear God:* stand in awe of, revere, hold in reverence, reverence, wonder at, venerate (*fml*). **4** *I fear I can't help you:* be afraid, suspect, expect, foresee, anticipate.

fearful *adj* **1** FRIGHTENED, afraid, scared, alarmed, nervous, anxious, tense, uneasy, apprehensive, hesitant, nervy, panicky. **2** TERRIBLE, fearsome (*fml*), dreadful, awful, frightful, atrocious, shocking, appalling, monstrous, gruesome, hideous, ghastly, horrible.
⊟ 1 brave, courageous, fearless.
2 wonderful, delightful.

feasible *adj* practicable, practical, workable, achievable, attainable, realizable, viable, reasonable, possible, likely.
⊟ impossible.

feast *n* **1** BANQUET, dinner, spread, blow-out (*sl*), binge (*infml*), beano (*infml*), junket. **2** FESTIVAL, holiday, gala, fête, celebration, revels.
➤ *v* gorge, eat one's fill, wine and dine, treat, entertain.

feat *n* exploit, deed, act, accomplishment, achievement, attainment, performance.

feature *n* **1** ASPECT, facet, point, factor, attribute, quality, property, trait, lineament, characteristic, peculiarity, mark, hallmark, speciality, highlight. **2** *a magazine feature:* column, article, report, story, piece, item, comment.
➤ *v* **1** EMPHASIZE, highlight, spotlight, play up, promote, show, present. **2** APPEAR, figure, participate, act, perform, star.

federation *n* confederation, confederacy, alliance, league, amalgamation, association, coalition, combination, syndicate, union, copartnership, federacy.

fed up *adj* depressed, bored, discontented, annoyed, dismal, dissatisfied, gloomy, glum, tired, weary, having had enough, blue (*infml*), brassed off (*infml*), browned off (*infml*), cheesed off (*infml*), down (*infml*), sick and tired (*infml*),

hacked off (*infml*), having had it up to here (*infml*), at the end of one's tether (*infml*), pissed off (*sl*).
⊟ contented.

fee *n* charge, terms, bill, account, pay, remuneration, payment, retainer, subscription, reward, recompense, hire, toll.

feeble *adj* **1** WEAK, faint, exhausted, frail, delicate, puny, sickly, infirm, powerless, helpless. **2** INADEQUATE, lame, poor, thin, flimsy, ineffective, incompetent, indecisive.
⊟ 1 strong, powerful.

feed *v* nourish, cater for, provide for, supply, sustain, suckle, nurture, foster, strengthen, fuel, graze, pasture, eat, dine.
➤ *n* food, fodder, forage, pasture, silage.
◆ **feed on** eat, consume, devour, live on, exist on.

feel *v* **1** EXPERIENCE, go through, undergo, suffer, endure, enjoy. **2** TOUCH, finger, handle, manipulate, hold, stroke, caress, fondle, paw, fumble, grope. **3** *feel soft:* seem, appear. **4** THINK, believe, consider, reckon, judge. **5** SENSE, perceive, notice, observe, know.
➤ *n* texture, surface, finish, touch, knack, sense, impression, feeling, quality.
◆ **feel for** pity, sympathize (with), commiserate (with), be sorry for.
◆ **feel like** fancy, want, desire.

feeler *n* **1** ANTENNA, horn, tentacle, sense-organ. **2** *put out feelers:* advance, approach, overture(s), probe, trial balloon, ballon d'essai.

feeling *n* **1** SENSATION, perception, sense, instinct, hunch, suspicion, inkling, impression, idea, notion, opinion, view, point of view. **2** EMOTION, passion, intensity, warmth, compassion, sympathy, understanding, pity, concern, affection, fondness, sentiment, sentimentality, susceptibility, sensibility, sensitivity, appreciation. **3** AIR, aura, atmosphere, mood, quality.

fell *v* cut down, hew, knock down, strike down, floor, level, flatten, raze, demolish.

fellow *n* **1** PERSON, man, boy, chap (*infml*), bloke (*infml*), guy (*infml*), individual, character. **2** PEER, compeer, equal, partner, associate, colleague, co-worker, companion, comrade, friend, counterpart, match, mate, twin, double.

> *adj* co-, associate, associated, related, like, similar.

fellowship *n* 1 COMPANIONSHIP, camaraderie, communion, familiarity, intimacy. 2 ASSOCIATION, league, guild, society, club, fraternity, brotherhood, sisterhood, order.

female *adj* feminine, she-, girlish, womanly.
🔳 male.

> Female terms include: girl, lass, maiden, woman, lady, daughter, sister, girlfriend, fiancée, bride, wife, mother, aunt, niece, grandmother, matriarch, godmother, widow, dowager, dame, madam, mistress, virgin, spinster, old-maid, bird (*sl*), chick (*sl*), lesbian, bitch (*sl*), prostitute, whore, harlot; cow, heifer, bitch, doe, ewe, hen, mare, filly, nanny-goat, sow, tigress, vixen.

feminine *adj* 1 FEMALE, womanly, ladylike, graceful, gentle, tender. 2 EFFEMINATE, unmanly, womanish, girlish, sissy.
🔳 1 masculine. 2 manly.

feminism *n* women's movement, women's lib(eration), female emancipation, women's rights.

fence *n* barrier, railing, paling, wall, hedge, windbreak, guard, defence, barricade, stockade, rampart.
> *v* 1 SURROUND, encircle, bound, hedge, wall, enclose, pen, coop, confine, restrict, separate, protect, guard, defend, fortify. 2 PARRY, dodge, evade, hedge, equivocate, quibble, pussyfoot, stonewall.

fencing

> Fencing terms include: appel, attack, balestra, barrage, coquille, disengage, en garde, epee, feint, fleche, foible, foil, forte, hit, lunge, on guard, parry, counter-parry, pink, piste, plastron, remise, reprise, riposte, counter-riposte, sabre, tac-au-tac, thrust, touch, touche, volt.

fend for *v* look after, take care of, shift for, support, maintain, sustain, provide for.

fend off *v* ward off, beat off, parry, deflect, avert, resist, repel, repulse, hold at bay, keep off, shut out.

ferment *v* 1 BUBBLE, effervesce, froth, foam, boil, seethe, smoulder, fester, brew, rise. 2 ROUSE, stir up, excite, work up, agitate, foment, incite, provoke, inflame, heat.

> *n* unrest, agitation, turbulence, stir, excitement, turmoil, disruption, commotion, tumult, hubbub, uproar, furore, frenzy, fever, glow.
🔳 calm.

ferocious *adj* vicious, savage, fierce, wild, barbarous, barbaric, brutal, inhuman, cruel, sadistic, murderous, bloodthirsty, violent, merciless, pitiless, ruthless.
🔳 gentle, mild, tame.

ferocity *n* viciousness, savagery, fierceness, wildness, barbarity, brutality, inhumanity, cruelty, sadism, bloodthirstiness, violence, ruthlessness.
🔳 gentleness, mildness.

ferret *v* search, rummage, hunt, go through, scour, forage, rifle.
◆ **ferret out** discover, search out, find, hunt down, track down, trace, elicit, extract, unearth, dig up, nose out, root out, worm out, run to earth, suss out (*infml*).

ferry *n* ferry-boat, car ferry, ship, boat, vessel.
> *v* transport, ship, convey, carry, take, shuttle, taxi, drive, run, move, shift.

fertile *adj* 1 *fertile soil*: fruitful, productive, rich, abundant, fecund (*fml*), luxuriant (*fml*). 2 *a fertile imagination*: creative, resourceful, inventive, prolific, productive, imaginative, inspired, visionary. 3 *fertile animals*: generative, prolific, able to have children, potent, reproductive, virile, fecund (*fml*).
🔳 1 unfruitful, unproductive. 2 barren. 3 sterile, infertile, barren.

fertility *n* 1 FRUITFULNESS, productiveness, abundance, richness, luxuriance (*fml*), fecundity (*fml*). 2 *fertility tests*: generativeness, prolificness, potency, reproductiveness, virility.
🔳 1 aridity. 2 barrenness, sterility.

fertilize *v* 1 IMPREGNATE, inseminate, pollinate. 2 *fertilize land*: enrich, feed, dress, compost, manure, dung.

fertilizer *n* dressing, compost, manure, dung.

fervent *adj* ardent, earnest, eager, enthusiastic, wholehearted, excited, energetic, vigorous, fiery, spirited, intense, vehement, passionate, full-blooded, zealous, devout, heartfelt, impassioned, emotional, warm.
🔳 cool, indifferent, apathetic.

fervour *n* ardour, eagerness, enthusiasm, excitement, animation, energy, vigour,

spirit, verve, intensity, vehemence, passion, zeal, warmth.
🖪 apathy.

fester *v* ulcerate, gather, suppurate, discharge, putrefy, rot, decay, rankle, smoulder.

festival *n* celebration, commemoration, anniversary, jubilee, holiday, feast, gala, fête, carnival, fiesta, party, merrymaking, entertainment, festivities.

festive *adj* celebratory, festal, holiday, gala, carnival, happy, joyful, merry, hearty, cheery, jolly, jovial, cordial, convivial.
🖪 gloomy, sombre, sober.

festivity *n* celebration, jubilation, feasting, banqueting, fun, enjoyment, pleasure, entertainment, sport, amusement, merriment, merrymaking, revelry, jollity, joviality, conviviality.

festoon *v* adorn, deck, bedeck, garland, wreathe, drape, hang, swathe, decorate, garnish.

fetch *v* *fetch a bucket*: get, collect, bring, carry, transport, deliver, escort. **2** SELL FOR, go for, bring in, yield, realize, make, earn.

fetching *adj* attractive, pretty, sweet, cute, charming, enchanting, fascinating, captivating.
🖪 repellent.

fête *n* fair, bazaar, sale of work, garden party, gala, carnival, festival.
➤ *v* entertain, treat, regale, welcome, honour, lionize.

fetish *n* **1** FIXATION, obsession, mania, idée fixe, thing (*infml*). **2** CHARM, amulet, talisman, idol, image, cult object, ju-ju, totem.

feud *n* vendetta, quarrel, row, argument, disagreement, dispute, conflict, strife, discord, animosity, ill will, bitterness, enmity, hostility, antagonism, rivalry.
🖪 agreement, peace.

fever *n* **1** FEVERISHNESS, (high) temperature, delirium. **2** EXCITEMENT, agitation, turmoil, unrest, restlessness, heat, passion, ecstasy.

feverish *adj* **1** DELIRIOUS, hot, burning, flushed. **2** EXCITED, impatient, agitated, restless, nervous, overwrought, frenzied, frantic, hectic, hasty, hurried.
🖪 **1** cool. **2** calm.

few *adj* scarce, rare, uncommon, sporadic, infrequent, sparse, thin, scant, scanty,

meagre, inconsiderable, inadequate, insufficient, in short supply.
🖪 many.
➤ *pron* not many, hardly any, one or two, a couple, scattering, sprinkling, handful, some.
🖪 many.

fiasco *n* failure, catastrophe, calamity, collapse, debacle, disaster, ruin, rout, mess, cropper (*infml*), damp squib (*infml*), flop (*infml*), washout (*infml*).
🖪 success.

fib *n* lie, untruth, white lie, falsehood, story, tale, yarn, concoction, fantasy, fiction, invention, misrepresentation, evasion, prevarication, whopper (*infml*).
➤ *v* evade, fabricate, falsify, fantasize, invent, lie, prevaricate, sidestep, dissemble.

fibre *n* **1** FILAMENT, strand, thread, nerve, sinew, pile, texture. **2** *moral fibre*: character, calibre, backbone, strength, stamina, toughness, courage, resolution, determination.

fickle *adj* inconstant, disloyal, unfaithful, faithless, treacherous, unreliable, unpredictable, changeable, capricious, mercurial, irresolute, vacillating.
🖪 constant, steady, stable.

fiction *n* **1** FANTASY, fancy, imagination, figment, invention, fabrication, concoction, improvisation, story-telling. **2** NOVEL, romance, story, tale, yarn, fable, parable, legend, myth, lie.
🖪 **2** non-fiction, fact, truth.

fictional *adj* literary, invented, made-up, imaginary, make-believe, legendary, mythical, mythological, fabulous, non-existent, unreal.
🖪 factual, real.

fictitious *adj* false, untrue, invented, made-up, fabricated, apocryphal, imaginary, non-existent, bogus, counterfeit, spurious, assumed, supposed.
🖪 true, genuine.

fiddle *v* **1** *fiddling with her necklace*: play, tinker, toy, trifle, tamper, mess around, meddle, interfere, fidget. **2** CHEAT, swindle, diddle, cook the books (*infml*), juggle, manoeuvre, racketeer, graft (*sl*).
➤ *n* swindle, con (*infml*), rip-off (*sl*), fraud, racket, sharp practice, graft (*sl*).

fiddling *adj* trifling, petty, trivial, insignificant, negligible, paltry.
🖪 important, significant.

fidelity n 1 FAITHFULNESS, loyalty, allegiance, devotion, constancy, reliability. 2 ACCURACY, exactness, precision, closeness, adherence.
🖃 1 infidelity, inconstancy, treachery. 2 inaccuracy.

fidget v squirm, wriggle, shuffle, twitch, jerk, jump, fret, fuss, bustle, fiddle, mess about, play around.

fidgety adj restless, impatient, uneasy, nervous, agitated, jittery, jumpy, twitchy, on edge.
🖃 still.

field n 1 GRASSLAND, meadow, pasture, paddock, playing-field, ground, pitch, green, lawn. 2 RANGE, scope, bounds, limits, confines, territory, area, province, domain, sphere, environment, department, discipline, speciality, line, forte. 3 PARTICIPANTS, entrants, contestants, competitors, contenders, runners, candidates, applicants, opponents, opposition, competition.

fiend n 1 EVIL SPIRIT, demon, devil, monster. 2 *a health fiend*: enthusiast, fanatic, addict, devotee, freak (*infml*), nut (*infml*).

fiendish adj devilish, diabolical, infernal, wicked, malevolent, cunning, cruel, inhuman, savage, monstrous, unspeakable.

fierce adj ferocious, vicious, savage, cruel, brutal, merciless, aggressive, dangerous, murderous, frightening, menacing, threatening, stern, grim, relentless, raging, wild, passionate, intense, strong, powerful.
🖃 gentle, kind, calm.

fiercely adv ferociously, viciously, savagely, cruelly, brutally, wildly, mercilessly, murderously, ruthlessly, aggressively, dangerously, menacingly, threateningly, sternly, terribly, intensely, implacably, fanatically, bitterly, strongly, powerfully, passionately, relentlessly, violently, furiously, tempestuously, severely, keenly, tooth and nail (*infml*).
🖃 gently, kindly.

fiery adj 1 BURNING, afire, flaming, aflame, blazing, ablaze, red-hot, glowing, aglow, flushed, hot, torrid, sultry. 2 PASSIONATE, inflamed, ardent, fervent, impatient, excitable, impetuous, impulsive, hot-headed, fierce, violent, heated.
🖃 1 cold. 2 impassive.

fight v 1 WRESTLE, box, fence, joust, brawl, scrap, scuffle, tussle, skirmish, combat, battle, do battle, war, wage war, clash, cross swords, engage, grapple, struggle, strive, contend. 2 QUARREL, argue, dispute, squabble, bicker, wrangle. 3 OPPOSE, contest, campaign against, resist, withstand, defy, stand up to.
➢ n 1 BOUT, contest, duel, combat, action, battle, war, hostilities, brawl, scrap, scuffle, tussle, struggle, skirmish, set-to, clash, engagement, brush, encounter, conflict, fray, free-for-all, fracas, riot. 2 QUARREL, row, argument, dispute, dissension.
◆ **fight back** 1 RETALIATE, defend oneself, resist, put up a fight, retort, reply. 2 *fight back the tears*: hold back, restrain, curb, control, repress, bottle up, contain, suppress.
◆ **fight off** hold off, keep at bay, ward off, stave off, resist, repel, rebuff, beat off, rout, put to flight.

fighter n combatant, contestant, contender, disputant, boxer, wrestler, pugilist, prizefighter, soldier, trouper, mercenary, warrior, man-at-arms, swordsman, gladiator.

figurative adj metaphorical, symbolic, emblematic, representative, allegorical, parabolic, descriptive, pictorial.
🖃 literal.

figure n 1 NUMBER, numeral, digit, integer, sum, amount. 2 SHAPE, form, outline, silhouette, body, frame, build, physique. 3 *public figure*: dignitary, celebrity, personality, character, person. 4 DIAGRAM, illustration, picture, drawing, sketch, image, representation, symbol.
➢ v 1 RECKON, guess, estimate, judge, think, believe. 2 FEATURE, appear, crop up.
◆ **figure out** work out, calculate, compute, reckon, puzzle out, resolve, fathom, understand, see, make out, decipher.

figurehead n mouthpiece, front man, name, dummy, puppet.

filament n fibre, strand, thread, hair, whisker, wire, string, pile.

file[1] v rub (down), sand, abrade, scour, scrape, grate, rasp, hone, whet, shave, plane, smooth, polish.

file[2] n folder, dossier, portfolio, binder, case, record, documents, data, information.
➢ v record, register, note, enter, process, store, classify, categorize, pigeonhole, catalogue.

file³ *n* line, queue, column, row, procession, cortège, train, string, stream, trail.
➤ *v* march, troop, parade, stream, trail.

fill *v* **1** REPLENISH, stock, supply, furnish, satisfy, pack, crowd, cram, stuff, congest, block, clog, plug, bung, cork, stop, close, seal. **2** PERVADE, imbue, permeate, soak, impregnate. **3** *fill a post*: take up, hold, occupy, discharge, fulfil.
🔁 **1** empty, drain.
➤ *n* enough, abundance, ample, plenty, sufficiency, sufficient, all one wants, more than enough, all one can take.
◆ **fill in 1** *fill in a form*: complete, fill out, answer. **2** (*infml*) STAND IN, deputize, understudy, substitute, replace, represent, act for. **3** (*infml*) BRIEF, inform, advise, acquaint, bring up to date.

filling *n* contents, inside, stuffing, padding, wadding, filler.
➤ *adj* satisfying, nutritious, square, solid, substantial, heavy, large, big, generous, ample.
🔁 insubstantial.

film *n* **1** MOTION PICTURE, picture, movie (*infml*), video, feature film, short, documentary. **2** LAYER, covering, dusting, coat, coating, glaze, skin, membrane, tissue, sheet, veil, screen, cloud, mist, haze.
➤ *v* photograph, shoot, video, videotape.

Kinds of film include: action, adult, adventure, animated, art-house, avant-garde, biopic, B-movie, black comedy, blaxploitation, blockbuster, blue (*infml*), Bollywood, buddy, burlesque, Carry-on, cartoon, Charlie Chaplin, cinéma-vérité, classic, cliff-hanger, comedy, comedy thriller, courtroom drama, cowboy and Indian, crime, cult, detective, disaster, Disney, documentary, Ealing comedy, epic, erotic, escapist, ethnographic, exploitation, expressionist, family, fantasy, farce, film à clef, film noir, flashback, gangster, historical romance, Hitchcock, Hollywood, horror, James Bond, kitchen sink, love story, low-budget, medieval, melodrama, multiple-story, murder, murder mystery, musical, newsreel, new wave, nouvelle vague, period epic, police, police thriller, political, pornographic, psychological thriller, realist, remake, rites of passage, road movie, robbery, romantic, romantic comedy, satirical, science-fiction, screwball comedy, serial, sexploitation, short, silent, slasher, snuff, social comedy, social problem, space-age, space exploration, spaghetti western, spoof, spy, surrealist, tear-jerker (*infml*), thriller, tragedy, tragicomedy, travelogue, underground, war, western, whodunnit.

filter *v* strain, sieve, sift, screen, refine, purify, clarify, percolate, ooze, seep, leak, trickle, dribble.
➤ *n* strainer, sieve, sifter, colander, mesh, gauze, membrane.

filth *n* **1** DIRT, grime, muck, dung, excrement, faeces, sewage, refuse, rubbish, garbage, trash, slime, sludge, effluent, pollution, contamination, corruption, impurity, uncleanness, foulness, sordidness, squalor. **2** OBSCENITY, pornography, smut, indecency, vulgarity, coarseness.
🔁 **1** cleanness, cleanliness, purity.

filthy *adj* **1** DIRTY, soiled, unwashed, grimy, grubby, mucky, muddy, slimy, sooty, unclean, impure, foul, gross, sordid, squalid, vile, low, mean, base, contemptible, despicable. **2** OBSCENE, pornographic, smutty, bawdy, suggestive, indecent, offensive, foul-mouthed, vulgar, coarse, corrupt, depraved.
🔁 **1** clean, pure. **2** decent.

final *adj* last, latest, closing, concluding, finishing, end, ultimate, terminal, dying, last-minute, eventual, conclusive, definitive, decisive, definite, incontrovertible.
🔁 first, initial.

finale *n* climax, dénouement, culmination, crowning glory, end, conclusion, close, curtain, epilogue.

finalize *v* conclude, finish, complete, round off, resolve, settle, agree, decide, close, clinch, sew up (*infml*), wrap up (*infml*).

finally *adv* lastly, in conclusion, ultimately, eventually, at last, at length, in the end, conclusively, once and for all, for ever, irreversibly, irrevocably, definitely.

finance *n* **1** *corporate finance*: economics, money management, accounting, banking, investment, stock market, business, commerce, trade, money, funding, sponsorship, subsidy. **2** *the company's finances*: accounts, affairs, budget, bank account, income, revenue, liquidity, resources, funding, assets,

means, capital, wealth, money, cash, funds, wherewithal, savings.
➤ *v* pay for, fund, sponsor, back, support, underwrite, guarantee, subsidize, capitalize, float, set up.

Terms used in accounting and finance include: above the line, accounting period, accounts rendered, accounts payable, accounts receivable, accrual basis, allowable expense, annual accounts, annual report, appreciation, APR (Annual Percentage Rate), asset-stripping, audit, authorized capital, bad debt, balance sheet, below the line, benefit in kind, bookkeeping, break-even point, budgetary control, capital expenditure, capital gain, capitalization, cash flow, circulating capital, collateral, compound interest, consolidated accounts, cost accounting, cost-benefit analysis, creative accounting, credit control, creditor, current assets, current liabilities, debit, debt/equity ratio, debtor, deferred credit, deferred expenditure, deferred liability, deficit, depreciating asset, depreciation, direct costs, disinvestment, dividend, double-entry bookkeeping, earnings per share, equity, fiduciary loan, fictitious assets, financial year, first cost, fiscal year, fixed assets, fixed capital, fixed costs, fixtures and fittings, floating capital, frozen assets, funds flow statement, gearing, going concern, gross margin, gross profit, gross receipts, grossing up, historic cost, income, intangible assets, interim accounts, ledger, liability, liquid assets, liquidation, liquidity, loan capital, loss, net assets, net profit, nominal capital, overheads, outgoings, payroll, petty cash, poison pill, profit and loss account, rate of return, realization of assets, refinance, replacement cost, reserves, return on capital, revenue expenditure, ring fencing (funds), running costs, secured loan, simple interest, statutory income, statutory returns, takeover, hostile takeover, tangible assets, tax loss, taxable profits, total costs, trading account, trial balance, turnover, unit costs, variable costs, wasting asset, watering, white knight, windfall profit, write off.

financial *adj* monetary, money, pecuniary, economic, fiscal, budgetary, commercial.

financier *n* financialist, banker, stockbroker, money-maker, investor, speculator.

find *v* 1 DISCOVER, locate, track down,

trace, retrieve, recover, unearth, uncover, expose, reveal, come across, chance on, stumble on, meet, encounter, detect, recognize, notice, observe, perceive, realize, learn. 2 ATTAIN, achieve, win, reach, gain, obtain, get. 3 *find it difficult*: consider, think, judge, declare.
🔁 1 lose.
◆ **find out** 1 LEARN, ascertain, discover, detect, note, observe, perceive, realize. 2 UNMASK, expose, show up, uncover, reveal, disclose, catch, suss out (*sl*), rumble (*sl*), tumble to (*infml*).

finding *n* 1 FIND, discovery, breakthrough. 2 DECISION, conclusion, judgement, verdict, pronouncement, decree, recommendation, award.

fine¹ *adj* 1 EXCELLENT, outstanding, exceptional, superior, exquisite, splendid, magnificent, brilliant, beautiful, handsome, attractive, elegant, lovely, nice, good. 2 THIN, slender, sheer, gauzy, powdery, flimsy, fragile, delicate, dainty. 3 SATISFACTORY, acceptable, all right, OK (*infml*). 4 *fine weather*: bright, sunny, clear, cloudless, dry, fair.
🔁 1 mediocre. 2 thick, coarse. 4 cloudy.

fine² *n* penalty, punishment, forfeit, forfeiture, damages.
➤ *v* penalize, punish, amerce (*fml*), mulct (*fml*), sting (*infml*).

finery *n* decorations, frippery, best clothes, Sunday best, jewellery, ornaments, showiness, splendour, gaudery, trappings, glad rags (*infml*), best bib and tucker (*infml*).

finesse *n* skill, flair, expertise, deftness, adeptness, adroitness, cleverness, delicacy, diplomacy, tact, discretion, subtlety, savoir-faire, elegance, gracefulness, polish, neatness, refinement, sophistication, quickness, know-how (*infml*).
➤ *v* bluff, evade, manipulate, manoeuvre, trick.

finger *v* touch, handle, manipulate, feel, stroke, caress, fondle, paw, fiddle with, toy with, play about with, meddle with.

finicky *adj* 1 PARTICULAR, finickety, pernickety, fussy, choosy (*infml*), fastidious, meticulous, scrupulous, critical, hypercritical, nit-picking. 2 FIDDLY, intricate, tricky, difficult, delicate.
🔁 1 easy-going. 2 easy.

finish *v* 1 END, terminate, stop, cease,

complete, accomplish, achieve, fulfil, discharge, deal with, do, conclude, close, wind up, settle, round off, culminate, perfect. **2** DESTROY, ruin, exterminate, get rid of, annihilate, defeat, overcome, rout, overthrow. **3** USE (UP), consume, devour, eat, drink, exhaust, drain, empty.

Ea 1 begin, start.

➤ *n* **1** END, termination, completion, conclusion, close, ending, finale, culmination. **2** SURFACE, appearance, texture, grain, polish, shine, gloss, lustre, smoothness.

Ea 1 beginning, start, commencement.

finished *adj* **1** COMPLETED, complete, concluded, dealt with, over, at an end, over and done with (*infml*), through (*infml*), wrapped up (*infml*), sewn up (*infml*). **2** USELESS, defeated, ruined, doomed, drained, exhausted, empty, spent, undone, unwanted, unpopular, done for (*infml*), played out (*infml*), zonked (*infml*). **3** *a finished performance:* accomplished, proficient, professional, expert, polished, impeccable, faultless, flawless, perfect, masterly, consummate, refined, sophisticated, urbane, virtuoso.

Ea 1 unfinished, incomplete. **2** useful, productive. **3** incompetent, hopeless (*infml*).

finite *adj* limited, restricted, bounded, demarcated, terminable, definable, fixed, measurable, calculable, countable, numbered.

Ea infinite.

fire *n* **1** FLAMES, blaze, bonfire, conflagration, inferno, burning, combustion. **2** PASSION, feeling, excitement, enthusiasm, spirit, intensity, heat, radiance, sparkle.

➤ *v* **1** IGNITE, light, kindle, set fire to, set on fire, set alight. **2** *fire a missile:* shoot, launch, set off, let off, detonate, explode. **3** DISMISS, discharge, sack (*infml*), eject. **4** EXCITE, whet, enliven, galvanize, electrify, stir, arouse, rouse, stimulate, inspire, incite, spark off, trigger off.

♦ **on fire** burning, alight, ignited, flaming, in flames, aflame, blazing, ablaze, fiery.

fireworks *n* **1** PYROTECHNICS, explosions, illuminations, feux d'artifice. **2** UPROAR, trouble, outburst, frenzy, fit, rage, rows, storm, temper, sparks, hysterics.

firm[1] *adj* **1** *firm ground:* dense, compressed, compact, concentrated, set,

solid, hard, unyielding, stiff, rigid, inflexible. **2** FIXED, embedded, fast, tight, secure, fastened, anchored, immovable, motionless, stationary, steady, stable, sturdy, strong. **3** ADAMANT, unshakable, resolute, determined, dogged, unwavering, strict, constant, steadfast, staunch, dependable, true, sure, convinced, definite, settled, committed.

Ea 1 soft, flabby. **2** unsteady. **3** hesitant.

firm[2] *n* company, corporation, business, enterprise, concern, house, establishment, institution, organization, association, partnership, syndicate, conglomerate.

firmly *adv* securely, tightly, steadily, stably, sturdily, strongly, robustly, unshakably, unwaveringly, strictly, immovably, unalterably, unchangeably, unflinchingly, resolutely, inflexibly, decisively, definitely, determinedly, doggedly, enduringly, staunchly, steadfastly.

Ea hesitantly, uncertainly, unsoundly.

firmness *n* **1** STIFFNESS, hardness, rigidity, solidity, density, compactness, inflexibility, inelasticity, tautness, tension, fixity, immovability, tightness. **2** STRENGTH, strength of will, determination, resolution, resolve, dependability, reliability, staunchness, steadfastness, steadiness, willpower, constancy, conviction, changelessness, stability, strictness, resistance, sureness, doggedness.

Ea 1 softness. **2** uncertainty.

first *adj* **1** INITIAL, opening, introductory, preliminary, elementary, primary, basic, fundamental. **2** ORIGINAL, earliest, earlier, prior, primitive, primeval, oldest, eldest, senior. **3** CHIEF, main, key, cardinal, principal, head, leading, ruling, sovereign, highest, uppermost, paramount, prime, predominant, pre-eminent.

Ea 1 last, final.

➤ *adv* initially, to begin with, to start with, at the outset, beforehand, originally, in preference, rather, sooner.

♦ **first name** forename, Christian name, baptismal name, given name.

first-rate *adj* first-class, A1, second-to-none, matchless, peerless, top, top-notch (*infml*), top-flight, leading, supreme, superior, prime, excellent, outstanding, superlative, exceptional, splendid, superb, fine, admirable.

Ea inferior.

fish

> Types of fish include: bloater, brisling, cod, coley, Dover sole, haddock, hake, halibut, herring, jellied eel, kipper, mackerel, pilchard, plaice, rainbow trout, salmon, sardine, sole, sprat, trout, tuna, turbot, whitebait; bass, Bombay duck, bream, brill, carp, catfish, chub, conger eel, cuttlefish, dab, dace, dogfish, dory, eel, goldfish, guppy, marlin, minnow, monkfish, mullet, octopus, perch, pike, piranha, roach, shark, skate, snapper, squid, stickleback, stingray, sturgeon, swordfish, tench, whiting; clam, cockle, crab, crayfish, crawfish (US), kingprawn, lobster, mussel, oyster, prawn, scallop, shrimp, whelk. *see also* **shark**.

➤ *v* angle, trawl, delve, hunt, seek, invite, solicit.

◆ **fish out** produce, take out, extract, find, come up with, dredge up, haul up.

fishing *n* angling, trawling.

fishy *adj* 1 *a fishy taste*: fish-like, piscatorial, piscatory, piscine. 2 ODD, suspicious, questionable, shady, suspect, doubtful, dubious, implausible, improbable, funny, irregular, queer.
🠒 2 honest, legitimate.

fissure *n* crack, opening, cleft, fracture, breach, break, cranny, crevasse, crevice, rent, rift, rupture, chasm, hole, gap, gash, slit, split, chink, fault, cleavage (*fml*), interstice (*fml*), scissure (*fml*).

fit[1] *adj* 1 SUITABLE, appropriate, apt, fitting, correct, right, proper, ready, prepared, able, capable, competent, qualified, eligible, worthy. 2 HEALTHY, well, able-bodied, in good form, in good shape, sound, sturdy, strong, robust, hale and hearty.
🠒 1 unsuitable, unworthy. 2 unfit.
➤ *v* 1 MATCH, correspond, conform, follow, agree, concur, tally, suit, harmonize, go, belong, dovetail, interlock, join, meet, arrange, place, position, accommodate. 2 ALTER, modify, change, adjust, adapt, tailor, shape, fashion.
◆ **fit out** equip, rig out, kit out, outfit, provide, supply, furnish, prepare, arm.

fit[2] *n* seizure, convulsion, spasm, paroxysm, attack, outbreak, bout, spell, burst, surge, outburst, eruption, explosion.

fitful *adj* sporadic, intermittent, occasional, spasmodic, erratic, irregular, uneven, broken, disturbed.
🠒 steady, regular.

fitness *n* 1 SUITABILITY, qualifications, readiness, preparedness, eligibility, appropriateness, aptness, competence, adequacy, applicability, condition, pertinence (*fml*). 2 HEALTH, healthiness, strength, vigour, condition, shape, trim, good health, robustness, haleness.
🠒 1 unsuitability. 2 unfitness.

fitted *adj* 1 *fitted wardrobe*: built-in, permanent. 2 EQUIPPED, rigged out, provided, furnished, appointed, prepared, armed. 3 SUITED, right, suitable, fit, qualified.

fitting *adj* apt, appropriate, suitable, fit, correct, right, proper, seemly, meet (*fml*), desirable, deserved.
🠒 unsuitable, improper.
➤ *n* connection, attachment, accessory, part, component, piece, unit, fitment.

fittings *n* equipment, furnishings, furniture, fixtures, installations, fitments, accessories, extras.

fix *v* 1 FASTEN, secure, tie, bind, attach, join, connect, link, couple, anchor, pin, nail, rivet, stick, glue, cement, set, harden, solidify, stiffen, stabilize, plant, root, implant, embed, establish, install, place, locate, position. 2 *fix a date*: arrange, set, specify, define, agree on, decide, determine, settle, resolve, finalize. 3 MEND, repair, correct, rectify, adjust, restore.
🠒 1 move, shift. 3 damage.
➤ *n* (*infml*) dilemma, quandary, predicament, plight, difficulty, hole (*infml*), corner, spot (*infml*), mess, muddle.
◆ **fix up** arrange, organize, plan, lay on, provide, supply, furnish, equip, settle, sort out, produce, bring about.

fixation *n* preoccupation, obsession, mania, fetish, thing (*infml*), infatuation, compulsion, hang-up (*infml*), complex.

fixed *adj* decided, settled, established, definite, arranged, planned, set, firm, rigid, inflexible, steady, secure, fast, rooted, permanent.
🠒 variable.

fizz *v* effervesce, sparkle, bubble, froth, foam, fizzle, hiss, sizzle, sputter, spit.

fizzy *adj* effervescent, sparkling, aerated, carbonated, gassy, bubbly, bubbling, frothy, foaming.

flabbergasted (*infml*) *adj* amazed, confounded, astonished, astounded, staggered, dumbfounded, speechless, stunned, dazed, overcome, overwhelmed, bowled over.

flabby *adj* fleshy, soft, yielding, flaccid, limp, floppy, drooping, hanging, sagging, slack, loose, lax, weak, feeble.
🔁 firm, strong.

flag¹ *v* lessen, diminish, decline, fall (off), abate, subside, sink, slump, dwindle, peter out, fade, fail, weaken, slow, falter, tire, weary, wilt, droop, sag, flop, faint, die.
🔁 revive.

flag² *n* ensign, jack, pennant, colours, standard, banner, streamer.

> Types of flag include: banner, bunting, burgee, colours, cornet, gonfalon, jack, oriflamme, pennant, pilot flag, signal flag, standard, streamer, swallow tail.

> Names of flags include: Blue Ensign, Blue Peter, Crescent, Hammer and Sickle, Jolly Roger, Old Glory, Olympic Flag, Red Ensign, Rising Sun, Skull and Crossbones, Star Spangled Banner, Stars and Stripes, Tricolour, Union Jack, White Ensign, Yellow Jack.

➤ *v* 1 SIGNAL, wave, salute, motion. 2 MARK, indicate, label, tag, note.

flagging *adj* lessening, diminishing, declining, subsiding, sinking, dwindling, ebbing, waning, decreasing, fading, failing, weakening, slowing, faltering, sagging, tiring, drooping, wilting, abating.
🔁 returning, reviving.

flagrant *adj* scandalous, outrageous, glaring, disgraceful, dreadful, shameless, blatant, ostentatious, open, atrocious, enormous, heinous, infamous, notorious, bold, brazen, audacious, barefaced, conspicuous, unashamed, undisguised, overt, rank, gross, arrant.
🔁 covert, secret.

flail *v* thresh, thrash, beat, whip.

flair *n* skill, ability, aptitude, faculty, gift, talent, facility, knack, mastery, genius, feel, taste, discernment, acumen, style, elegance, stylishness, panache.
🔁 inability, ineptitude.

flake *n* scale, peeling, paring, shaving, sliver, wafer, chip, splinter.
➤ *v* scale, peel, chip, splinter.
◆ **flake out** collapse, pass out, faint, keel over, drop, fall asleep, relax completely.

flamboyant *adj* showy, ostentatious, flashy, gaudy, colourful, brilliant, dazzling,

striking, extravagant, rich, elaborate, ornate, florid.
🔁 modest, restrained.

flame *v* burn, flare, blaze, glare, flash, beam, shine, glow, radiate.
➤ *n* 1 FIRE, blaze, light, brightness, heat, warmth. 2 PASSION, ardour, fervour, enthusiasm, zeal, intensity, radiance.

flaming *adj* 1 *a flaming torch*: burning, alight, aflame, blazing, fiery, brilliant, scintillating, red-hot, glowing, smouldering. 2 INTENSE, vivid, aroused, impassioned, hot, raging, frenzied.

flammable *adj* inflammable, ignitable, combustible.
🔁 non-flammable, incombustible, flameproof, fire-resistant.

flank *n* side, edge, quarter, wing, loin, hip, thigh.
➤ *v* edge, fringe, skirt, line, border, bound, confine, wall, screen.

flap *v* flutter, vibrate, wave, agitate, shake, wag, swing, swish, thrash, beat.
➤ *n* 1 FOLD, fly, lapel, tab, lug, tag, tail, skirt, aileron. 2 (*infml*) PANIC, state (*infml*), fuss, commotion, fluster, agitation, flutter, dither, tizzy (*infml*).

flare *v* 1 FLAME, burn, blaze, glare, flash, flicker, burst, explode, erupt. 2 BROADEN, widen, flare out, spread out, splay.
➤ *n* 1 FLAME, blaze, glare, flash, flicker, burst. 2 BROADENING, widening, splay.
◆ **flare up** erupt, break out, explode, blow up.

flash *v* 1 BEAM, shine, light up, flare, blaze, glare, gleam, glint, flicker, twinkle, sparkle, glitter, shimmer. 2 *the train flashed past*: streak, fly, dart, race, dash.
➤ *n* beam, ray, shaft, spark, blaze, flare, burst, streak, gleam, glint, flicker, twinkle, sparkle, shimmer.

flashy *adj* showy, ostentatious, flamboyant, glamorous, bold, loud, garish, gaudy, jazzy, flash, tawdry, cheap, vulgar, tasteless.
🔁 plain, tasteful.

flat¹ *adj* 1 LEVEL, plane, even, smooth, uniform, unbroken, horizontal, outstretched, prostrate, prone, recumbent, reclining, low. 2 DULL, boring, monotonous, tedious, uninteresting, unexciting, stale, lifeless, dead, spiritless, lacklustre, vapid, insipid, weak, watery, empty, pointless. 3 *a flat refusal*: absolute, utter, total, unequivocal, categorical, positive, unconditional, unqualified, point-blank, direct, straight, explicit, plain, final. **4** *a flat tyre*: punctured, burst, deflated, collapsed.

≡ 1 bumpy, vertical. **2** exciting, full. **3** equivocal.

♦ flat out at top speed, at full speed, all out, for all one is worth.

flat² *n* apartment, penthouse, maisonette, tenement, flatlet, rooms, suite, bed-sit(ter).

flatly *adv* categorically, point-blank, positively, absolutely, completely, uncompromisingly, unconditionally, unhesitatingly.

flatness *n* **1** EVENNESS, levelness, smoothness, horizontality, uniformity. **2** DULLNESS, monotony, tedium, boredom, staleness, emptiness, tastelessness, insipidity, vapidity.

flatten *v* **1** SMOOTH, iron, press, roll, crush, squash, compress, level, even out. **2** KNOCK DOWN, prostrate, floor, fell, demolish, raze, overwhelm, subdue.

flatter *v* praise, compliment, sweet-talk (*infml*), adulate, fawn, butter up (*infml*), wheedle, humour, play up to, court, curry favour with.

≡ criticize.

flattering *adj* complimentary, kind, favourable, enhancing, gratifying, becoming, adulatory, ingratiating, fawning, fulsome, effusive, servile, smooth-spoken, smooth-tongued, honeyed, honey-tongued, sugared, sugary.

≡ candid, uncompromising, unflattering.

flattery *n* adulation, eulogy, sweet talk (*infml*), soft soap (*infml*), flannel (*infml*), blarney, cajolery, fawning, toadyism, sycophancy, ingratiation, servility.

≡ criticism.

flaunt *v* show off, display, parade, flourish, brandish, exhibit, boast, air, sport, vaunt, wield, dangle, flash.

flavour *n* **1** TASTE, tang, smack, savour, relish, zest, zing (*infml*), aroma, odour. **2** QUALITY, property, character, style, aspect, feeling, feel, atmosphere. **3** HINT, suggestion, touch, tinge, tone.

➢ *v* season, spice, ginger up, infuse, imbue.

flavouring *n* seasoning, zest, essence, extract, additive.

flaw *n* defect, imperfection, fault, blemish, spot, mark, speck, crack, crevice, fissure, cleft, split, rift, break, fracture, weakness,

shortcoming, failing, fallacy, lapse, slip, error, mistake.

flawed *adj* imperfect, defective, faulty, blemished, marked, damaged, spoilt, marred, cracked, chipped, broken, unsound, fallacious, erroneous.

≡ flawless, perfect.

flawless *adj* perfect, faultless, unblemished, spotless, immaculate, stainless, sound, intact, whole, unbroken, undamaged.

≡ flawed, imperfect.

fleck *v* dot, spot, mark, speckle, dapple, mottle, streak, sprinkle, dust.

➢ *n* dot, point, spot, mark, speck, speckle, streak.

flee *v* run away, bolt, fly, take flight, take off, make off, cut and run, escape, get away, decamp, abscond, leave, depart, withdraw, retreat, vanish, disappear.

≡ stay.

fleet *n* flotilla, armada, navy, task force, squadron.

fleeting *adj* short, brief, flying, short-lived, momentary, ephemeral, transient, transitory, passing, temporary.

≡ lasting, permanent.

flesh *n* body, tissue, fat, muscle, brawn, skin, meat, pulp, substance, matter, physicality.

flex *v* bend, bow, curve, angle, ply, double up, tighten, contract.

≡ straighten, extend.

➢ *n* cable, wire, lead, cord.

flexibility *n* **1** BENDABILITY, pliability, pliancy, elasticity, resilience, spring, springiness, suppleness, give, flexion. **2** ADAPTABILITY, agreeability, adjustability, amenability, complaisance (*fml*).

≡ 1, 2 inflexibility.

flexible *adj* **1** BENDABLE, bendy (*infml*), pliable, pliant, plastic, malleable, mouldable, elastic, stretchy, springy, yielding, supple, lithe, limber, double-jointed, mobile. **2** ADAPTABLE, adjustable, amenable, accommodating, variable, open.

≡ 1 inflexible, rigid.

flick *v* hit, strike, rap, tap, touch, dab, flip, jerk, whip, lash.

➢ *n* rap, tap, touch, dab, flip, jerk, click.

♦ flick through flip through, thumb through, leaf through, glance at, skim, scan.

flicker *v* flash, blink, wink, twinkle, sparkle, glimmer, shimmer, gutter, flutter, vibrate, quiver, waver.
➤ *n* flash, gleam, glint, twinkle, glimmer, spark, trace, drop, iota, atom, indication.

flight[1] *n* 1 FLYING, aviation, aeronautics, air transport, air travel. 2 JOURNEY, trip, voyage.

flight[2] *n* fleeing, escape, getaway, breakaway, exit, departure, exodus, retreat.

flimsy *adj* thin, fine, light, slight, insubstantial, ethereal, fragile, delicate, shaky, rickety, makeshift, weak, feeble, meagre, inadequate, shallow, superficial, trivial, poor, unconvincing, implausible.
Ea sturdy.

flinch *v* wince, start, cringe, cower, quail, tremble, shake, quake, shudder, shiver, shrink, recoil, draw back, balk, shy away, duck, shirk, withdraw, retreat, flee.

fling *v* throw, hurl, pitch, lob, toss, chuck (*infml*), cast, sling, catapult, launch, propel, send, let fly, heave, jerk.

flip *v* flick, spin, twirl, twist, turn, toss, throw, cast, pitch, jerk, flap.
➤ *n* flick, spin, twirl, twist, turn, toss, jerk, flap.

flippancy *n* facetiousness, light-heartedness, frivolity, superficiality, shallowness, thoughtlessness, disrespect, disrespectfulness, glibness, pertness, impertinence, irreverence, levity, cheek (*infml*), cheekiness (*infml*), sauciness (*infml*).
Ea earnestness, seriousness.

flippant *adj* facetious, light-hearted, frivolous, superficial, offhand, flip, glib, pert, saucy (*infml*), cheeky (*infml*), impudent, impertinent, rude, disrespectful, irreverent.
Ea serious, respectful.

flirt *v* chat up, make up to, lead on, philander, dally.
♦ **flirt with** consider, entertain, toy with, play with, trifle with, dabble in, try.

flit *v* dart, speed, flash, fly, wing, flutter, whisk, skim, slip, pass, bob, dance.

float *v* 1 GLIDE, sail, swim, bob, drift, waft, hover, hang. 2 LAUNCH, initiate, set up, promote.
Ea 1 sink.

floating *adj* 1 AFLOAT, buoyant, unsinkable, sailing, swimming, bobbing, drifting. 2 VARIABLE, fluctuating, movable, migratory, transitory, wandering, unattached, free, uncommitted.
Ea 1 sinking. 2 fixed.

flock *v* herd, swarm, troop, converge, mass, bunch, cluster, huddle, crowd, throng, group, gather, collect, congregate.
➤ *n* herd, pack, crowd, throng, multitude, mass, bunch, cluster, group, gathering, assembly, congregation.

flog *v* beat, whip, lash, flagellate, scourge, birch, cane, flay, drub, thrash, whack (*infml*), chastise, punish.

flogging *n* beating, whipping, lashing, flagellation, scourging, birching, caning, flaying, thrashing, hiding.

flood *v* 1 DELUGE, inundate, soak, drench, saturate, fill, overflow, immerse, submerge, engulf, swamp, overwhelm, drown. 2 FLOW, pour, stream, rush, surge, gush.
➤ *n* deluge, inundation, downpour, torrent, flow, tide, stream, rush, spate, outpouring, overflow, glut, excess, abundance, profusion.
Ea drought, trickle, dearth.

floor *n* 1 FLOORING, ground, base, basis. 2 *on the third floor*: storey, level, stage, landing, deck, tier.
➤ *v* (*infml*) defeat, overwhelm, beat, stump (*infml*), frustrate, confound, perplex, baffle, puzzle, bewilder, disconcert, throw.

flop *v* 1 DROOP, hang, dangle, sag, drop, fall, topple, tumble, slump, collapse. 2 FAIL, misfire, fall flat, founder, fold.
➤ *n* failure, non-starter, fiasco, debacle, washout (*infml*), disaster.

floppy *adj* droopy, hanging, dangling, sagging, limp, loose, baggy, soft, flabby.
Ea firm.

florid *adj* 1 FLOWERY, ornate, elaborate, fussy, overelaborate, baroque, rococo, flamboyant, grandiloquent. 2 *a florid complexion*: ruddy, red, purple.
Ea 1 plain, simple. 2 pale.

flotsam *n* jetsam, wreckage, debris, rubbish, junk, oddments.

flounder *v* wallow, struggle, grope, fumble, blunder, stagger, stumble, falter.

flourish *v* 1 THRIVE, grow, wax, increase, flower, blossom, bloom, develop, progress, get on, do well, prosper, succeed, boom. 2 BRANDISH, wave, shake, twirl, swing, display, wield, flaunt, parade, vaunt.
Ea 1 decline, languish, fail.

➤ *n* display, parade, show, gesture, wave, sweep, fanfare, ornament, decoration, panache, pizzazz (*infml*).

flourishing *adj* thriving, blooming, prosperous, successful, booming.

flout *v* defy, disobey, violate, break, disregard, spurn, reject, scorn, jeer at, scoff at, mock, ridicule.

◪ obey, respect, regard.

flow *v* 1 CIRCULATE, ooze, trickle, ripple, bubble, well, spurt, squirt, gush, spill, run, pour, cascade, rush, stream, teem, flood, overflow, surge, sweep, move, drift, slip, slide, glide, roll, swirl. 2 ORIGINATE, derive, arise, spring, emerge, issue, result, proceed, emanate.

➤ *n* course, flux, tide, current, drift, outpouring, stream, deluge, cascade, spurt, gush, flood, spate, abundance, plenty.

flower *n* 1 BLOOM, blossom, bud, floret. 2 BEST, cream, pick, choice, elite.

Flowers include: African violet, alyssum, anemone, aster, aubrietia, azalea, begonia, bluebell, busy lizzie (impatiens), calendula, candytuft, carnation, chrysanthemum, cornflower, cowslip, crocus, cyclamen, daffodil, dahlia, daisy, delphinium, forget-me-not, foxglove (digitalis), freesia, fuchsia, gardenia, geranium, gladioli, hollyhock, hyacinth, iris (flag), lily, lily-of-the-valley, lobelia, lupin, marigold, narcissus, nasturtium, nemesia, nicotiana, night-scented stock, orchid, pansy, petunia, pink (dianthus), phlox, poinsettia, polyanthus, poppy, primrose, primula, rose, salvia, snapdragon (antirrhinum), snowdrop, stock, sunflower, sweet pea, sweet william, tulip, verbena, viola, violet, wallflower, zinnia. *see also* **plant**; **shrub**; **wild flower**.

Parts of a flower include: anther, calyx, capitulum, carpel, corolla, corymb, dichasium, filament, gynoecium, monochasium, nectary, ovary, ovule, panicle, pedicel, petal, pistil, raceme, receptacle, sepal, spadix, spike, stalk, stamen, stigma, style, thalamus, torus, umbel.

➤ *v* bud, burgeon, bloom, blossom, open, come out.

flowery *adj* florid, ornate, elaborate, fancy, baroque, rhetorical.

◪ plain, simple.

flowing *adj* 1 *flowing rivers/traffic*: moving, oozing, seeping, bubbling, welling, gushing, pouring, rushing, cascading, streaming, surging, sweeping, overflowing. 2 FLUENT, effortless, easy, smooth, continuous, uninterrupted, unbroken. 3 *flowing hair*: hanging, hanging loose, hanging freely, falling, rolling.

fluctuate *v* vary, change, alter, shift, rise and fall, seesaw, ebb and flow, alternate, swing, sway, oscillate, vacillate, waver.

fluency *n* ease, eloquence, smoothness, articulateness, assurance, command, control, facility, readiness, glibness, slickness, volubility.

◪ incoherence.

fluent *adj* flowing, smooth, easy, effortless, articulate, eloquent, voluble, glib, ready.

◪ broken, inarticulate, tongue-tied.

fluff *n* down, nap, pile, fuzz, floss, lint, dust.

fluffy *adj* furry, fuzzy, downy, feathery, flaggy, woolly, hairy, shaggy, velvety, silky, soft.

fluid *adj* 1 LIQUID, liquefied, aqueous, watery, running, runny, melted, molten. 2 *a fluid situation*: variable, changeable, unstable, inconstant, shifting, mobile, adjustable, adaptable, flexible, open. 3 *fluid movements*: flowing, smooth, graceful.

◪ 1 solid. 2 stable.

➤ *n* liquid, solution, liquor, juice, gas, vapour.

fluke *n* stroke, stroke of luck, lucky break, accident, quirk, blessing, windfall, break, chance, coincidence, fortuity, serendipity, freak (*infml*).

flurry *n* 1 BURST, outbreak, spell, spurt, gust, blast, squall. 2 BUSTLE, hurry, fluster, fuss, to-do, commotion, tumult, whirl, disturbance, stir, flap (*infml*).

flush¹ *v* 1 BLUSH, go red, redden, crimson, colour, burn, glow, suffuse. 2 CLEANSE, wash, rinse, hose, swab, clear, empty, evacuate.

➤ *adj* 1 ABUNDANT, lavish, generous, full, overflowing, rich, wealthy, moneyed, prosperous, well-off, well-heeled, well-to-do. 2 LEVEL, even, smooth, flat, plane, square, true.

flush² *v* start, rouse, disturb, drive out, force out, expel, eject, run to earth, discover, uncover.

fluster *v* bother, upset, embarrass,

disturb, perturb, agitate, ruffle, discompose, confuse, confound, unnerve, disconcert, rattle (*infml*), put off, distract. **E3** calm.
➤ *n* flurry, bustle, commotion, disturbance, turmoil, state (*infml*), agitation, embarrassment, flap (*infml*), dither, tizzy (*infml*).
E3 calm.

fluted *adj* grooved, furrowed, channelled, corrugated, ribbed, ridged.

flutter *v* flap, wave, beat, bat, flicker, vibrate, palpitate, agitate, shake, tremble, quiver, shiver, ruffle, ripple, twitch, toss, waver, fluctuate.
➤ *n* flapping, beat, flicker, vibration, palpitation, tremble, tremor, quiver, shiver, shudder, twitch.

flux *n* fluctuation, instability, change, alteration, modification, fluidity, flow, movement, motion, transition, development.
E3 stability, rest.

fly *v* 1 TAKE OFF, rise, ascend, mount, soar, glide, float, hover, flit, flutter, wing. 2 *fly an aeroplane:* control, operate, pilot, guide, manoeuvre, steer. 3 *fly a flag:* show, wave, display, exhibit, present, reveal. 4 RACE, sprint, dash, tear, rush, go/pass quickly, slip by, hurry, speed, zoom, shoot, bolt, dart, career, jet, hasten (*fml*).
♦ **fly at** attack, go for, fall upon.

flying *adj* 1 *flying insects:* gliding, floating, hovering, flapping, fluttering, airborne, winged, winging, wind-borne, soaring, mobile. 2 *a flying visit:* brief, hurried, fleeting, rapid, fast, hasty, rushed, speedy.

foam *n* froth, lather, suds, head, bubbles, effervescence.
➤ *v* froth, lather, bubble, effervesce, fizz, boil, seethe.

fob off *v* foist, pass off, palm off (*infml*), get rid of, dump, unload, inflict, impose, deceive, put off.

focus *n* focal point, target, centre, heart, core, nucleus, kernel, crux, hub, axis, linchpin, pivot, hinge.
➤ *v* converge, meet, join, centre, concentrate, aim, direct, fix, spotlight, home in, zoom in, zero in (*infml*).

foe *n* enemy, adversary, antagonist, opponent, combatant, rival, ill-wisher.
E3 friend.

fog *n* 1 MIST, haze, cloud, gloom, murkiness, smog, pea-souper.

2 PERPLEXITY, puzzlement, confusion, bewilderment, daze, trance, vagueness, obscurity.
➤ *v* mist, steam up, cloud, dull, dim, darken, obscure, blur, confuse, muddle.

foggy *adj* misty, hazy, smoggy, cloudy, murky, dark, shadowy, dim, indistinct, obscure.
E3 clear.

foil¹ *v* defeat, outwit, frustrate, thwart, baffle, counter, nullify, stop, check, obstruct, block, circumvent, elude.
E3 abet.

foil² *n* setting, background, relief, contrast, complement, balance.

foist *v* force, impose, introduce, thrust, unload, pass off, get rid of, fob off, wish on, palm off (*infml*).

fold *v* 1 BEND, ply, double, overlap, tuck, pleat, crease, crumple, crimp, crinkle. 2 (*infml*) *the business folded:* fail, go bust, shut down, collapse, crash. 3 ENFOLD, embrace, hug, clasp, envelop, wrap (up), enclose, entwine, intertwine.
➤ *n* bend, turn, layer, ply, overlap, tuck, pleat, crease, knife-edge, line, wrinkle, furrow, corrugation.

folder *n* file, binder, folio, portfolio, envelope, holder.

folk *n* people, society, nation, race, tribe, clan, family, kin, kindred.
➤ *adj* ethnic, national, traditional, native, indigenous, tribal, ancestral.

follow *v* 1 *night follows day:* come after, succeed, come next, replace, supersede, supplant. 2 CHASE, pursue, go after, hunt, track, trail, shadow, tail, hound, catch. 3 ACCOMPANY, go (along) with, escort, attend. 4 RESULT, ensue, develop, emanate, arise. 5 OBEY, comply with, adhere to, heed, mind, observe, conform to, carry out, practise. 6 GRASP, understand, comprehend, fathom.
E3 1 precede. 3 abandon, desert. 5 disobey.
♦ **follow through** continue, pursue, see through, finish, complete, conclude, fulfil, implement.
♦ **follow up** investigate, check out, continue, pursue, reinforce, consolidate.

follower *n* attendant, retainer, helper, companion, sidekick (*infml*), apostle, disciple, pupil, imitator, emulator, adherent, hanger-on, believer, convert, backer, supporter, admirer, fan,

devotee, freak (*infml*), buff (*infml*).
🔁 leader, opponent.

following *adj* subsequent, next, succeeding, successive, resulting, ensuing, consequent, later.
🔁 previous.
➤ *n* followers, suite, retinue, entourage, circle, fans, supporters, support, backing, patronage, clientèle, audience, public.

folly *n* foolishness, stupidity, senselessness, rashness, recklessness, irresponsibility, indiscretion, craziness, madness, lunacy, insanity, idiocy, imbecility, silliness, absurdity, nonsense.
🔁 wisdom, prudence, sanity.

fond *adj* affectionate, warm, tender, caring, loving, adoring, devoted, doting, indulgent.
♦ **fond of** partial to, attached to, enamoured of, keen on, addicted to, hooked on.

fondle *v* caress, stroke, pat, pet, cuddle.

fondness *n* affection, devotion, kindness, tenderness, love, liking, fancy, attachment, enthusiasm, inclination, leaning, partiality, preference, weakness, soft spot, taste, susceptibility, penchant, predilection.
🔁 aversion, hate.

food *n* foodstuffs, comestibles, eatables (*infml*), provisions, stores, rations, eats (*infml*), grub (*sl*), nosh (*sl*), refreshment, sustenance, nourishment, nutrition, nutriment, subsistence, feed, fodder, diet, fare, cooking, cuisine, menu, board, table, larder.

| Kinds of food include: soup, broth, minestrone, bouillabaisse, borsch, cockaleekie, consommé, gazpacho, goulash, vichyssoise; chips, French fries, ratatouille, sauerkraut, bubble-and-squeak, nut cutlet, cauliflower cheese, chilladas, hummus, macaroni cheese; pasta, cannelloni, fettuccine, ravioli, spaghetti bolognese, tortellini, lasagne; fish and chips, fishcake, fish-finger, fisherman's pie, kedgeree, gefilte fish, kipper, pickled herring, scampi, calamari, prawn cocktail, caviar; meat, casserole, cassoulet, hotpot, shepherd's pie, cottage pie, chilli con carne, biriyani, chop suey, moussaka, paella, samosa, pizza, ragout, risotto, tandoori, vindaloo, Wiener schnitzel, smögåsbord, stroganoff, Scotch woodcock, welsh rarebit, faggot, haggis, sausage, frankfurter, hot dog, fritter, hamburger, McDonald's®, Big Mac®, Wimpy®, bacon, egg, omelette, quiche, tofu, Quorn®, |

Yorkshire pudding, toad-in-the-hole; ice cream, charlotte russe, egg custard, fruit salad, fruit cocktail, gateau, millefeuilles, pavlova, profiterole, Sachertorte, soufflé, summer pudding, Bakewell tart, trifle, yogurt, sundae, syllabub, queen of puddings, Christmas pudding, tapioca, rice pudding, roly-poly pudding, spotted dick, zabaglione; doughnut, Chelsea bun, Eccles cake, éclair, flapjack, fruitcake, Danish pastry, Genoa cake, Battenburg cake, Madeira cake, lardy cake, hot-cross-bun, ginger nut, gingerbread, shortbread, ginger snap, macaroon, Garibaldi biscuit; bread, French bread, French toast, pumpernickel, cottage loaf, croissant; gravy, fondue, salad cream, mayonnaise, French dressing; sauces: tartare, Worcestershire, bechamel, white, barbecue, tomato ketchup, hollandaise, Tabasco®, apple, mint, cranberry, horseradish, pesto. *see also* **cheese**; **fish**; **fruit**; **meat**; **nut**; **pasta**; **pastry**; **sugar**; **sweets**; **vegetable**.

fool *n* blockhead, fat-head, nincompoop (*infml*), ass (*infml*), chump (*infml*), ninny (*infml*), clot (*infml*), dope (*infml*), wally (*sl*), twit (*infml*), nitwit (*infml*), nit (*infml*), dunce, dimwit, simpleton, halfwit, idiot, imbecile, moron, dupe, sucker (*infml*), mug (*infml*), stooge, clown, buffoon, jester.
➤ *v* deceive, take in, delude, mislead, dupe, gull, hoodwink, put one over on, trick, hoax, con (*infml*), cheat, swindle, diddle (*infml*), string along (*infml*), have on (*infml*), kid (*infml*), tease, joke, jest.
♦ **fool about** lark about, horse around (*sl*), play about, mess about (*infml*), mess around (*infml*).

foolhardy *adj* rash, reckless, imprudent, ill-advised, irresponsible.
🔁 cautious, prudent.

foolish *adj* stupid, senseless, unwise, ill-advised, ill-considered, short-sighted, half-baked, daft (*infml*), crazy, mad, insane, idiotic, moronic, hair-brained, half-witted, simple-minded, simple, unintelligent, inept, inane, silly, absurd, ridiculous, ludicrous, nonsensical.
🔁 wise, prudent.

foolishness *n* stupidity, silliness, senselessness, absurdity, irresponsibility, weakness, craziness, madness, lunacy, nonsense, rubbish, folly, foolery, inanity, ineptitude, indiscretion, imprudence, incaution, unreason, unwisdom, bunkum (*infml*), claptrap (*infml*), baloney (*infml*), daftness (*infml*), hogwash (*infml*), rot (*infml*), piffle (*infml*), poppycock (*infml*), bunk (*infml*), claptrap (*infml*), bilge (*infml*), cobblers (*infml*), crap (*sl*), balls (*sl*), bullshit (*sl*).

foolproof *adj* idiot-proof, infallible, fail-safe, sure, certain, sure-fire (*infml*), guaranteed.
☒ unreliable.

footing *n* base, foundation, basis, ground, relations, relationship, terms, conditions, state, standing, status, grade, rank, position, balance, foothold, purchase.

footprint *n* footmark, track, trail, trace, vestige.

footstep *n* footmark, track, step, tread, footfall, plod, tramp, trudge.

footwear

> Types of footwear include: shoe, court-shoe, brogue, casual, lace-up (*infml*), slip-on (*infml*), slingback, sandal, espadrille, stiletto heel, platform heel, moccasin, Doc Martens®, slipper, flip-flop (*infml*), boot, bootee, wellington boot, welly (*infml*), galosh, gumboot, football boot, rugby boot, tennis shoe, plimsoll, pump, sneaker, trainer, ballet shoe, clog, sabot, snow-shoe, beetle-crushers (*sl*), brothel-creepers (*sl*).

forage *n* fodder, pasturage, feed, food, foodstuffs.
➤ *v* rummage, search, cast about, scour, hunt, scavenge, ransack, plunder, raid.

foray *n* raid, offensive, attack, assault, ravage, sortie, sally, swoop, invasion, inroad, incursion, reconnaissance.

forbearance *n* self-control, patience, moderation, endurance, leniency, mildness, restraint, temperance, tolerance, toleration, avoidance, clemency, long-suffering, resignation, refraining, sufferance, abstinence (*fml*).
☒ intolerance.

forbearing *adj* long-suffering, patient, moderate, lenient, self-controlled, restrained, tolerant, merciful, mild, easy, forgiving, indulgent, clement.
☒ intolerant, merciless.

forbid *v* prohibit, disallow, ban, proscribe, interdict, veto, refuse, deny, outlaw, debar, exclude, rule out, preclude, prevent, block, hinder, inhibit.
☒ allow, permit, approve.

forbidden *adj* prohibited, banned, proscribed, taboo, vetoed, outlawed, out of bounds.

forbidding *adj* stern, formidable, awesome, daunting, off-putting, uninviting, menacing, threatening, ominous, sinister, frightening.
☒ approachable, congenial.

force *n* 1 COMPULSION, impulse, influence, coercion, constraint, pressure, duress, violence, aggression. 2 POWER, might, strength, intensity, effort, energy, vigour, drive, dynamism, stress, emphasis.
3 ARMY, troop, body, corps, regiment, squadron, battalion, division, unit, detachment, patrol.
☒ 2 weakness.
➤ *v* 1 COMPEL, make, oblige, necessitate, urge, coerce, constrain, press, pressurize, lean on (*infml*), press-gang, bulldoze, drive, propel, push, thrust. 2 PRISE, wrench, wrest, extort, exact, wring.

forced *adj* unnatural, stiff, wooden, stilted, laboured, strained, false, artificial, contrived, feigned, affected, insincere.
☒ spontaneous, sincere.

forceful *adj* strong, mighty, powerful, potent, effective, compelling, convincing, persuasive, cogent, telling, weighty, urgent, emphatic, vehement, forcible, dynamic, energetic, vigorous.
☒ weak, feeble.

forcible *adj* 1 VIOLENT, aggressive, coercive, forced, by/using force. 2 POWERFUL, strong, compelling, compulsory, effective, impressive, telling, weighty, cogent, energetic, forceful, vehement, mighty, potent.
☒ 1, 2 feeble, weak.

forebear *n* ancestor, forefather, father, predecessor, forerunner, antecedent.
☒ descendant.

foreboding *n* misgiving, anxiety, worry, apprehension, dread, fear, omen, sign, token, premonition, warning, prediction, prognostication, intuition, feeling.

forecast *v* predict, prophesy, foretell, foresee, anticipate, expect, estimate, calculate.
➤ *n* prediction, prophecy, expectation, prognosis, outlook, projection, guess, guesstimate (*infml*).

forefather *n* ancestor, forebear, father, predecessor, forerunner, antecedent.
☒ descendant.

forefront *n* front, front line, firing line, van, vanguard, lead, fore, avant-garde.
✷ rear.

foregoing *adj* preceding, antecedent, above, previous, earlier, former, prior.
✷ following.

foreign *adj* alien, immigrant, imported, international, external, outside, overseas, exotic, faraway, distant, remote, strange, unfamiliar, unknown, uncharacteristic, incongruous, extraneous, borrowed.
✷ native, indigenous.

foreigner *n* alien, immigrant, incomer, stranger, newcomer, visitor.
✷ native.

foremost *adj* first, leading, front, chief, main, principal, primary, cardinal, paramount, central, highest, uppermost, supreme, prime, pre-eminent.

forerunner *n* predecessor, ancestor, antecedent, precursor, harbinger, herald, envoy, sign, token.
✷ successor, follower.

foresee *v* envisage, anticipate, expect, forecast, predict, prophesy, prognosticate, foretell, forebode, divine.

foreshadow *v* prefigure, presage, augur, predict, prophesy, signal, indicate, promise.

foresight *n* anticipation, planning, forethought, far-sightedness, vision, caution, prudence, circumspection, care, readiness, preparedness, provision, precaution.
✷ improvidence.

forestall *v* pre-empt, anticipate, preclude, obviate, avert, head off, ward off, parry, balk, frustrate, thwart, hinder, prevent.

foretaste *n* preview, trailer, sample, specimen, example, whiff, indication, warning, premonition.

foretell *v* prophesy, forecast, predict, prognosticate, augur, presage, signify, foreshadow, forewarn.

forethought *n* preparation, planning, forward planning, provision, precaution, anticipation, foresight, far-sightedness, circumspection, prudence, caution.
✷ improvidence, carelessness.

forever *adv* **1** ETERNALLY, always, ever, evermore, for all time, permanently, till the end of time, till kingdom come (*infml*), till the cows come home (*infml*), for good

(*infml*), until hell freezes over (*infml*). **2** CONTINUALLY, constantly, always, persistently, incessantly, perpetually, endlessly, interminably (*fml*), all the time (*infml*).

forewarn *v* alert, advise, caution, tip off, give advance warning to, apprise, admonish, dissuade, previse.

foreword *n* preface, introduction, prologue.
✷ appendix, postscript, epilogue.

forfeit *n* loss, surrender, confiscation, sequestration, penalty, fine, damages.
➤ *v* lose, give up, surrender, relinquish, sacrifice, forgo, renounce, abandon.

forge *v* **1** MAKE, mould, cast, shape, form, fashion, beat out, hammer out, work, create, invent. **2** *forge a document*: fake, counterfeit, falsify, copy, imitate, simulate, feign.

forgery *n* fake, counterfeit, copy, replica, reproduction, imitation, dud (*infml*), phoney (*infml*), sham, fraud.
✷ original.

forget *v* omit, fail, neglect, let slip, overlook, disregard, ignore, lose sight of, dismiss, think no more of, unlearn.
✷ remember, recall, recollect.

forgetful *adj* absent-minded, dreamy, inattentive, oblivious, negligent, lax, heedless.
✷ attentive, heedful.

forgive *v* pardon, absolve, excuse, exonerate, exculpate, acquit, remit, let off, overlook, condone.
✷ punish, censure.

forgiveness *n* pardon, absolution, exoneration, acquittal, remission, amnesty, mercy, clemency, leniency.
✷ punishment, censure, blame.

forgiving *adj* merciful, clement, lenient, tolerant, forbearing, indulgent, kind, humane, compassionate, soft-hearted, mild.
✷ merciless, censorious, harsh.

forgo *v* give up, yield, surrender, relinquish, sacrifice, forfeit, waive, renounce, abandon, resign, pass up, do without, abstain from, refrain from.
✷ claim, indulge in.

forgotten *adj* unremembered, unrecalled, blotted out, disregarded, ignored, neglected, obliterated, overlooked, omitted, out of mind, past recollection, past recall, gone, left behind, buried, bygone, past, lost, irrecoverable, irretrievable, unretrieved.

☒ remembered.

fork *v* split, divide, part, separate, diverge, branch (off).

♦ **fork out** pay (up), give, cough up (*infml*), shell out (*infml*), stump up (*infml*).

forlorn *adj* deserted, abandoned, forsaken, forgotten, bereft, friendless, lonely, lost, homeless, destitute, desolate, hopeless, unhappy, miserable, wretched, helpless, pathetic, pitiable.

☒ cheerful.

form *v* 1 SHAPE, mould, model, fashion, make, manufacture, produce, create, found, establish, build, construct, assemble, put together, arrange, organize. 2 COMPRISE, constitute, make up, compose. 3 APPEAR, take shape, materialize, crystallize, grow, develop.

➤ *n* 1 APPEARANCE, shape, mould, cast, cut, outline, silhouette, figure, build, frame, structure, format, model, pattern, design, arrangement, organization, system. 2 *a form of punishment*: type, kind, sort, order, species, variety, genre, style, manner, nature, character, description. 3 CLASS, year, grade, stream. 4 *on top form*: health, fitness, fettle, condition, spirits. 5 ETIQUETTE, protocol, custom, convention, ritual, behaviour, manners. 6 QUESTIONNAIRE, document, paper, sheet.

formal *adj* 1 OFFICIAL, ceremonial, stately, solemn, conventional, orthodox, correct, fixed, set, regular. 2 PRIM, starchy, stiff, strict, rigid, precise, exact, punctilious, ceremonious, stilted, reserved.

☒ 2 informal, casual.

formality *n* custom, convention, ceremony, ritual, procedure, matter of form, bureaucracy, red tape, protocol, etiquette, form, correctness, propriety, decorum, politeness.

☒ informality.

format *n* appearance, form, order, presentation, design, layout, pattern, plan, shape, structure, style, arrangement, make-up, look, type, construction, dimensions, configuration.

formation *n* 1 STRUCTURE, construction, composition, constitution, configuration, format, organization, arrangement, grouping, pattern, design, figure.

2 CREATION, generation, production, manufacture, appearance, development, establishment.

formative *adj* determining, controlling, influential, dominant, shaping, growing, guiding, moulding, developmental, impressionable, teachable, malleable, mouldable, pliant, susceptible, sensitive.

☒ destructive.

former *adj* past, ex-, one-time, sometime, late, departed, old, old-time, ancient, bygone, earlier, prior, previous, preceding, antecedent, foregoing, above.

☒ current, present, future, following.

formerly *adv* once, previously, earlier, before, at one time, lately.

☒ currently, now, later.

formidable *adj* daunting, challenging, intimidating, threatening, frightening, terrifying, terrific, frightful, fearful, great, huge, tremendous, prodigious, impressive, awesome, overwhelming, staggering.

formula *n* recipe, prescription, proposal, blueprint, code, wording, rubric, rule, principle, form, procedure, technique, method, way.

formulate *v* create, invent, originate, found, form, devise, work out, plan, design, draw up, frame, define, express, state, specify, detail, develop, evolve.

forsake *v* desert, abandon, jilt, throw over, discard, jettison, reject, disown, leave, quit, give up, surrender, relinquish, renounce, forgo.

forsaken *adj* abandoned, deserted, neglected, godforsaken, remote, isolated, desolate, forlorn, lonely, marooned, solitary, derelict, dreary, destitute, cast off, discarded, disowned, rejected, shunned, outcast, ignored, friendless, jilted (*infml*), left in the lurch (*infml*).

fort *n* fortress, castle, tower, citadel, stronghold, fortification, garrison, station, camp.

forte *n* strong point, strength, skill, speciality, gift, talent, aptitude, bent, métier.

☒ weak point, inadequacy.

forthcoming *adj* 1 *their forthcoming wedding*: impending, imminent, approaching, coming, future, prospective, projected, expected. 2 COMMUNICATIVE, talkative, chatty, conversational, sociable, informative, expansive, open, frank, direct.

☒ 2 reticent, reserved.

forthright *adj* direct, straightforward, blunt, frank, candid, plain, open, bold, outspoken.
🔁 devious, secretive.

fortification *n* defence, strengthening, reinforcement, protection, castle, citadel, fort, fortress, keep, stronghold, earthwork, rampart, bulwark, bastion, battlements, parapet, barricade, palisade, buttressing, embattlement, entrenchment, munition, outwork, redoubt, stockade.

fortify *v* 1 STRENGTHEN, reinforce, brace, shore up, buttress, garrison, defend, protect, secure. 2 INVIGORATE, sustain, support, boost, encourage, hearten, cheer, reassure.
🔁 1 weaken.

fortitude *n* courage, bravery, valour, grit, pluck, resolution, determination, perseverance, firmness, strength of mind, willpower, hardihood, endurance, stoicism.
🔁 cowardice, fear.

fortress *n* stronghold, castle, citadel, fortification, fastness, tower, keep, garrison, battlements.

fortuitous *adj* accidental, chance, random, arbitrary, casual, incidental, unforeseen, lucky, fortunate, providential.
🔁 intentional, planned.

fortunate *adj* lucky, providential, happy, felicitous, prosperous, successful, well-off, timely, well-timed, opportune, convenient, propitious, advantageous, favourable, auspicious.
🔁 unlucky, unfortunate, unhappy.

fortunately *adv* luckily, happily, conveniently, encouragingly, providentially.
🔁 unfortunately.

fortune *n* 1 WEALTH, riches, treasure, mint (*infml*), pile (*infml*), income, means, assets, estate, property, possessions, affluence, prosperity, success. 2 LUCK, chance, accident, providence, fate, destiny, doom, lot, portion, life, history, future.

forward *adj* 1 FIRST, head, front, fore, foremost, leading, onward, progressive, go-ahead, forward-looking, enterprising. 2 CONFIDENT, assertive, pushy, bold, audacious, brazen, brash, barefaced, cheeky (*infml*), impudent, impertinent, fresh (*sl*), familiar, presumptuous. 3 EARLY, advance, precocious, premature, advanced, well-advanced, well-developed.

🔁 1 backward, retrograde. 2 shy, modest. 3 late, retarded.
➤ *adv* forwards, ahead, on, onward, out, into view.
➤ *v* advance, promote, further, foster, encourage, support, back, favour, help, assist, aid, facilitate, accelerate, speed, hurry, hasten, expedite, dispatch, send (on), post, transport, ship.
🔁 impede, obstruct, hinder, slow.

foster *v* raise, rear, bring up, nurse, care for, take care of, nourish, feed, sustain, support, promote, advance, encourage, stimulate, cultivate, nurture, cherish, entertain, harbour.
🔁 neglect, discourage.

foul *adj* 1 DIRTY, filthy, unclean, tainted, polluted, contaminated, rank, fetid, stinking, smelly, putrid, rotten, nauseating, offensive, repulsive, revolting, disgusting, squalid. 2 *foul language*: obscene, lewd, smutty, indecent, coarse, vulgar, gross, blasphemous, abusive. 3 NASTY, disagreeable, wicked, vicious, vile, base, abhorrent, disgraceful, shameful. 4 *foul weather*: bad, unpleasant, rainy, wet, stormy, rough.
🔁 1 clean. 4 fine.
➤ *v* 1 DIRTY, soil, stain, sully, defile, taint, pollute, contaminate. 2 BLOCK, obstruct, clog, choke, foul up. 3 ENTANGLE, catch, snarl, twist, ensnare.
🔁 1 clean. 2 clear. 3 disentangle.

found *v* 1 START, originate, create, initiate, institute, inaugurate, set up, establish, endow, organize. 2 BASE, ground, bottom, rest, settle, fix, plant, raise, build, erect, construct.

foundation *n* 1 BASE, foot, bottom, ground, bedrock, substance, basis, footing. 2 SETTING UP, establishment, institution, inauguration, endowment, organization, groundwork.

founder[1] *n* originator, initiator, father, mother, benefactor, creator, author, architect, designer, inventor, maker, builder, constructor, organizer.

founder[2] *v* sink, go down, submerge, subside, collapse, break down, fall, come to grief, fail, misfire, miscarry, abort, fall through, come to nothing.

fountain *n* 1 SPRAY, jet, spout, spring, well, wellspring, reservoir, waterworks. 2 SOURCE, origin, fount, font, fountainhead, wellhead.

foyer *n* entrance hall, hall, reception, lobby, vestibule, antechamber, anteroom.

fracas *n* brawl, disturbance, fight, free-for-all, quarrel, riot, trouble, uproar, row, rumpus, scuffle, barney, affray, ruckus, ruction, rout, ruffle, shindy, melee, aggro (*infml*).

fraction *n* proportion, amount, ratio, subdivision, part, bit.

fractious *adj* awkward, quarrelsome, cross, irritable, touchy, bad-tempered, petulant, testy, unruly, captious, fretful, peevish, crabby (*infml*), crotchety (*infml*), grouchy (*infml*), grumpy (*infml*).
E3 complaisant, placid.

fracture *n* break, crack, fissure, cleft, rupture, split, rift, rent, schism, breach, gap, opening.
➤ *v* break, crack, rupture, split, splinter, chip.
E3 join.

fragile *adj* brittle, breakable, frail, delicate, flimsy, dainty, fine, slight, insubstantial, weak, feeble, infirm.
E3 robust, tough, durable.

fragment *n* piece, bit, part, portion, fraction, particle, crumb, morsel, scrap, remnant, shred, chip, splinter, shiver, sliver, shard.
➤ *v* break, shatter, splinter, shiver, crumble, disintegrate, come to pieces, come apart, break up, divide, split (up), disunite.
E3 hold together, join.

fragmentary *adj* bitty, piecemeal, scrappy, broken, disjointed, disconnected, separate, scattered, sketchy, partial, incomplete.
E3 whole, complete.

fragrance *n* perfume, scent, smell, odour, aroma, bouquet.

fragrant *adj* perfumed, scented, sweet-smelling, sweet, balmy, aromatic, odorous.
E3 unscented.

frail *adj* delicate, brittle, breakable, fragile, flimsy, insubstantial, slight, puny, weak, feeble, infirm, vulnerable.
E3 robust, tough, strong.

frailty *n* weakness, foible, failing, deficiency, shortcoming, fault, defect, flaw, blemish, imperfection, fallibility, susceptibility.
E3 strength, robustness, toughness.

frame *v* **1** COMPOSE, formulate, conceive, devise, contrive, concoct, cook up, plan, map out, sketch, draw up, draft, shape, form, model, fashion, mould, forge, assemble, put together, build, construct, fabricate, make. **2** SURROUND, enclose, box in, case, mount. **3** *I've been framed*: set up, fit up (*sl*), trap.
➤ *n* **1** STRUCTURE, fabric, framework, skeleton, carcase, shell, casing, chassis, construction, bodywork, body, build, form. **2** MOUNT, mounting, setting, surround, border, edge.
♦ **frame of mind** state of mind, mood, humour, temper, disposition, spirit, outlook, attitude.

framework *n* structure, fabric, bare bones, skeleton, shell, frame, outline, plan, foundation, groundwork.

franchise *n* concession, licence, charter, authorization, privilege, right, suffrage, liberty, freedom, immunity, exemption.

frank *adj* honest, truthful, sincere, candid, blunt, open, free, plain, direct, forthright, straight, straightforward, downright, outspoken.
E3 insincere, evasive.

frankly *adv* to be frank, to be honest, in truth, honestly, candidly, bluntly, openly, freely, plainly, directly, straight.
E3 insincerely, evasively.

frantic *adj* agitated, overwrought, fraught, desperate, beside oneself, furious, raging, mad, wild, raving, frenzied, berserk, hectic.
E3 calm, composed.

fraternity *n* comradeship, brotherhood, kinship, camaraderie, companionship, set, society, association, circle, club, company, guild, order, league, union, fellowship, clan.

fraternize *v* mix, mingle, socialize, consort, associate, affiliate, unite, sympathize.
E3 shun, ignore.

fraud *n* **1** DECEIT, deception, guile, cheating, swindling, double-dealing, sharp practice, fake, counterfeit, forgery, sham, hoax, trick. **2** (*infml*) CHARLATAN, impostor, pretender, phoney (*infml*), bluffer, hoaxer, cheat, swindler, double-dealer, con man (*infml*).

fraudulent *adj* dishonest, crooked (*infml*), criminal, deceitful, deceptive, false, bogus, phoney (*infml*), sham,

counterfeit, swindling, double-dealing.
☒ honest, genuine.

fray *n* brawl, scuffle, dust-up (*infml*), free-for-all, set-to, clash, conflict, fight, combat, battle, quarrel, row, rumpus, disturbance, riot.

frayed *adj* ragged, tattered, worn, threadbare, unravelled.

freak *n* 1 MONSTER, mutant, monstrosity, malformation, deformity, irregularity, anomaly, abnormality, aberration, oddity, curiosity, quirk, caprice, vagary, twist, turn. 2 ENTHUSIAST, fanatic, addict, devotee, fan, buff (*infml*), fiend (*infml*), nut (*infml*).
➤ *adj* abnormal, atypical, unusual, exceptional, odd, queer, bizarre, aberrant, capricious, erratic, unpredictable, unexpected, surprise, chance, fortuitous, flukey.
☒ normal, common.

free *adj* 1 AT LIBERTY, at large, loose, unattached, unrestrained, liberated, emancipated, independent, democratic, self-governing. 2 *free time*: spare, available, idle, unemployed, unoccupied, vacant, empty. 3 *free tickets*: gratis, without charge, free of charge, complimentary, on the house. 4 CLEAR, unobstructed, unimpeded, open. 5 GENEROUS, liberal, open-handed, lavish, charitable, hospitable.
☒ 1 imprisoned, confined, restricted. 2 busy, occupied.
➤ *v* release, let go, loose, turn loose, set free, untie, unbind, unchain, unleash, liberate, emancipate, rescue, deliver, save, ransom, disentangle, disengage, extricate, clear, rid, relieve, unburden, exempt, absolve, acquit.
☒ imprison, confine.
♦ **free of** lacking, devoid of, without, unaffected by, immune to, exempt from, safe from.

freedom *n* 1 LIBERTY, emancipation, deliverance, release, exemption, immunity, impunity. 2 INDEPENDENCE, autonomy, self-government, home rule. 3 RANGE, scope, play, leeway, latitude, licence, privilege, power, free rein, free hand, opportunity, informality.
☒ 1 captivity, confinement. 3 restriction.

freely *adv* 1 READILY, willingly, voluntarily, spontaneously, easily. 2 *give freely*: generously, liberally, lavishly, extravagantly, amply, abundantly. 3 *speak*

freely: frankly, candidly, unreservedly, openly, plainly.
☒ 2 grudgingly. 3 evasively, cautiously.

freeze *v* 1 ICE OVER, ice up, glaciate, congeal, solidify, harden, stiffen. 2 DEEP-FREEZE, ice, refrigerate, chill, cool. 3 STOP, suspend, fix, immobilize, hold.
➤ *n* 1 FROST, freeze-up. 2 STOPPAGE, halt, standstill, shutdown, suspension, interruption, postponement, stay, embargo, moratorium.

freezing *adj* icy, frosty, glacial, arctic, polar, Siberian, wintry, raw, bitter, biting, cutting, penetrating, numbing, cold, chilly.
☒ hot, warm.

freight *n* cargo, load, lading, pay-load, contents, goods, merchandise, consignment, shipment, transportation, conveyance, carriage, haulage.

frenzied *adj* frantic, frenetic, hectic, feverish, desperate, furious, wild, uncontrolled, mad, demented, hysterical.
☒ calm, composed.

frenzy *n* 1 TURMOIL, agitation, distraction, derangement, madness, lunacy, mania, hysteria, delirium, fever. 2 BURST, fit, spasm, paroxysm, convulsion, seizure, outburst, transport, passion, rage, fury.
☒ 1 calm, composure.

frequent *adj* 1 NUMEROUS, countless, incessant, constant, continual, persistent, repeated, recurring, regular. 2 COMMON, commonplace, everyday, familiar, usual, customary.
☒ 1 infrequent.
➤ *v* visit, patronize, attend, haunt, hang out at (*infml*), associate with, hang about with (*infml*), hang out with (*infml*).

frequently *adv* often, commonly, many times, much, many a time, over and over, repeatedly, persistently, continually, habitually, customarily, oftentimes, nine times out of ten (*infml*), more times than you've had hot dinners (*infml*).
☒ infrequently, seldom.

fresh *adj* 1 ADDITIONAL, supplementary, extra, more, further, other. 2 NEW, novel, innovative, original, different, unconventional, modern, up-to-date, recent, latest. 3 REFRESHING, bracing, invigorating, brisk, crisp, keen, cool, fair, bright, clear, pure. 4 *fresh fruit*: raw, natural, unprocessed, crude.
5 REFRESHED, revived, restored, renewed, rested, invigorated, energetic, vigorous,

lively, alert. **6** PERT, saucy (*infml*), cheeky (*infml*), disrespectful, impudent, insolent, bold, brazen, forward, familiar, presumptuous.
fa 2 old, hackneyed. **3** stale. **4** processed. **5** tired.

freshen *v* **1** AIR, ventilate, purify. **2** REFRESH, restore, revitalize, reinvigorate, liven, enliven, spruce up, tart up (*infml*).
fa 2 tire.

fret *v* **1** WORRY, agonize, brood, pine. **2** VEX, irritate, nettle, bother, trouble, torment.

fretful *adj* worried, anxious, unhappy, upset, distressed, disturbed, uneasy, fearful, tense, restless, troubled, edgy (*infml*), uptight (*infml*).
fa calm.

friction *n* **1** DISAGREEMENT, dissension, dispute, disharmony, conflict, antagonism, hostility, opposition, rivalry, animosity, ill feeling, bad blood, resentment. **2** RUBBING, chafing, irritation, abrasion, scraping, grating, rasping, erosion, wearing away, resistance.

friend *n* mate (*infml*), pal (*infml*), chum (*infml*), buddy (*infml*), crony (*infml*), intimate, confidant(e), bosom friend, soul mate, comrade, ally, partner, associate, companion, playmate, pen-friend, acquaintance, well-wisher, supporter.
fa enemy, opponent.

friendliness *n* affability, amiability, companionability, congeniality, conviviality, approachability, kindness, kindliness, warmth, neighbourliness, sociability, geniality, matiness (*infml*).
fa coldness, unsociableness.

friendly *adj* **1** AMIABLE, affable, genial, kind, kindly, neighbourly, helpful, sympathetic, fond, affectionate, familiar, intimate, close, matey (*infml*), pally (*infml*), chummy (*infml*), companionable, sociable, outgoing, approachable, receptive, comradely, amicable, peaceable, well-disposed, favourable. **2** *a friendly atmosphere*: convivial, congenial, cordial, welcoming, warm.
fa 1 hostile, unsociable. **2** cold.

friendship *n* closeness, intimacy, familiarity, affinity, rapport, attachment, affection, fondness, love, harmony, concord, goodwill, friendliness, alliance, fellowship, comradeship.
fa enmity, animosity.

fright *n* shock, scare, alarm, consternation, dismay, dread, apprehension, trepidation, fear, terror, horror, panic.

frighten *v* alarm, daunt, unnerve, dismay, intimidate, terrorize, scare, startle, scare stiff, terrify, petrify, horrify, appal, shock.
fa reassure, calm.

frightened *adj* afraid, dismayed, scared, terrified, unnerved, terrorized, terror-stricken, alarmed, cowed, frozen, petrified, scared stiff, startled, trembly, quivery, panicky, panic-stricken, scared out of one's wits (*infml*), scared to death (*infml*), having kittens (*infml*), shaking like a leaf (*infml*), with one's heart in one's mouth (*infml*).
fa calm, courageous.

frightening *adj* alarming, daunting, formidable, fearsome, scary, terrifying, hair-raising, bloodcurdling, spine-chilling, petrifying, traumatic.

frightful *adj* unpleasant, disagreeable, awful, dreadful, fearful, terrible, appalling, shocking, harrowing, unspeakable, dire, grim, ghastly, hideous, horrible, horrid, grisly, macabre, gruesome.
fa pleasant, agreeable.

frigid *adj* **1** UNFEELING, unresponsive, passionless, unloving, cool, aloof, passive, lifeless. **2** FROZEN, icy, frosty, glacial, arctic, cold, chill, chilly, wintry.
fa 1 responsive. **2** hot.

frill *n* **1** *a blouse with frills*: flounce, gathering, ruff, ruffle, trimming, tuck, valance, fold, fringe, furbelow, ruche, ruching, purfle, orphrey. **2** *the basic model without the frills*: trimmings, addition, extra, ornamentation, decoration, embellishment, fanciness, accessory, ostentation, superfluity, finery, frilliness, fandangle, frippery.

frilly *adj* ruffled, crimped, gathered, frilled, trimmed, lacy, fancy, ornate.
fa plain.

fringe *n* **1** MARGIN, periphery, outskirts, edge, perimeter, limits, borderline. **2** BORDER, edging, trimming, tassel, frill, valance.
➤ *adj* unconventional, unorthodox, unofficial, alternative, avant-garde.
fa conventional, mainstream.

frisk *v* jump, leap, skip, hop, bounce, caper, dance, gambol, frolic, romp, play, sport.

frisky *adj* lively, spirited, high-spirited,

frolicsome, playful, romping, rollicking, bouncy.

🆇 quiet.

fritter v waste, squander, dissipate, idle, misspend, blow (sl).

frivolity n fun, gaiety, flippancy, facetiousness, jest, light-heartedness, levity, triviality, superficiality, silliness, folly, nonsense.

🆇 seriousness.

frivolous adj trifling, trivial, unimportant, shallow, superficial, light, flippant, jocular, light-hearted, juvenile, puerile, foolish, silly, idle, vain, pointless.

🆇 serious, sensible.

frolic v gambol, caper, romp, play, lark around, rollick, make merry, frisk, prance, cavort, dance.

➤ n fun, amusement, sport, gaiety, jollity, merriment, revel, romp, prank, lark, caper, high jinks, antics.

front n 1 at the front: face, aspect, frontage, façade, outside, exterior, facing, cover, obverse, top, head, lead, vanguard, forefront, front line, foreground, forepart, bow. 2 PRETENCE, show, air, appearance, look, expression, manner, façade, cover, mask, disguise, pretext, cover-up.

🆇 1 back, rear.

➤ adj fore, leading, foremost, head, first.

🆇 back, rear, last.

◆ in front ahead, leading, first, in advance, before, preceding.

🆇 behind.

frontier n border, boundary, borderline, limit, edge, perimeter, confines, marches, bounds, verge.

frost n freeze, freeze-up, Jack Frost, hoar-frost, rime, coldness.

frosty adj 1 ICY, frozen, freezing, frigid, wintry, cold, chilly. 2 UNFRIENDLY, unwelcoming, cool, aloof, standoffish, stiff, discouraging.

🆇 warm.

froth n bubbles, effervescence, foam, lather, suds, head, scum.

➤ v foam, lather, ferment, fizz, effervesce, bubble.

frothy adj 1 BUBBLING, bubbly, foaming, foamy, yeasty, sudsy, spumescent (fml), spumous (fml), spumy (fml), fizzy (infml). 2 INSUBSTANTIAL, empty, trivial, frivolous, trifling, slight, vain.

🆇 1 flat. 2 substantial, significant.

frown v scowl, glower, lour, glare, grimace.

➤ n scowl, glower, dirty look (infml), glare, grimace.

◆ **frown on** disapprove of, object to, dislike, discourage.

🆇 approve of.

frozen adj iced, chilled, icy, icebound, ice-covered, arctic, ice-cold, frigid, freezing, numb, solidified, stiff, rigid, fixed.

🆇 warm.

frugal adj thrifty, penny-wise, parsimonious, careful, provident, saving, economical, sparing, meagre.

🆇 wasteful, generous.

fruit n 1 CROP, harvest, produce, fruitage. 2 BENEFIT, consequence, advantage, effect, outcome, reward, return, result, yield, product, profit.

Varieties of fruit include: apple, Bramley, Cox's Orange Pippin, Golden Delicious, Granny Smith, crab apple; pear, William, Conference; orange, Jaffa, mandarin, mineola, clementine, satsuma, tangerine, Cⁱⁱⁱⁱⁱ ⁱⁱⁱⁱⁱⁱⁱ, ⁱⁱⁱⁱⁱ ⁱⁱⁱ ⁱⁱⁱⁱⁱ ⁱ ⁱⁱⁱⁱⁱⁱ, cherry, sloe, damson, greengage, grape, gooseberry, goosegog (infml), rhubarb, tomato; banana, pineapple, olive, lemon, lime, ugli fruit, star fruit, lychee, date, fig, grapefruit, kiwi fruit, mango, avocado; melon, honeydew, cantaloupe, watermelon; strawberry, raspberry, blackberry, bilberry, loganberry, elderberry, blueberry, boysenberry, cranberry; redcurrant, blackcurrant.

---

fruitful adj 1 FERTILE, rich, teeming, plentiful, abundant, prolific, productive. 2 REWARDING, profitable, advantageous, beneficial, worthwhile, well-spent, useful, successful.

🆇 1 barren. 2 fruitless.

fruition n realization, fulfilment, attainment, achievement, completion, maturity, ripeness, consummation, perfection, success, enjoyment.

fruitless adj unsuccessful, abortive, useless, futile, pointless, vain, idle, hopeless, barren, sterile.

🆇 fruitful, successful, profitable.

frustrate v 1 THWART, foil, balk, baffle, block, check, spike, defeat, circumvent, forestall, counter, nullify, neutralize, inhibit. 2 DISAPPOINT, discourage, dishearten, depress.

🆇 1 further, promote. 2 encourage.

frustrated adj disappointed,

discontented, discouraged, dissatisfied, disheartened, embittered, resentful, angry, annoyed, thwarted, blighted, repressed.
Ea fulfilled, satisfied.

frustration n **1** DISAPPOINTMENT, discouragement, dissatisfaction, resentment, annoyance, anger, vexation, irritation. **2** THWARTING, foiling, balking, blocking, defeat, curbing, failure, non-fulfilment, obstruction, contravention, circumvention (fml).
Ea 1 fulfilment. **2** furthering, promoting.

fuel n **1** a tax on fuel: combustible, propellant, motive power. **2** PROVOCATION, incitement, encouragement, ammunition, material.

> **Fuels include:** gas, Calor gas®, propane, butane, methane, acetylene, electricity, coal, coke, anthracite, charcoal, oil, petrol, gasoline, diesel, derv, paraffin, kerosine, methylated spirit, wood, logs, peat, nuclear power.

> v incite, inflame, fire, encourage, fan, feed, nourish, sustain, stoke up.
Ea discourage, damp down.

fugitive n escapee, runaway, deserter, refugee.
> adj fleeting, transient, transitory, passing, short, brief, flying, temporary, ephemeral, elusive.
Ea permanent.

fulfil v complete, finish, conclude, consummate, perfect, realize, achieve, accomplish, perform, execute, discharge, implement, carry out, comply with, observe, keep, obey, conform to, satisfy, fill, answer.
Ea fail, break.

fulfilment n completion, perfection, consummation, realization, achievement, accomplishment, success, performance, execution, discharge, implementation, observance, satisfaction.
Ea failure.

full adj **1** FILLED, loaded, packed, crowded, crammed, stuffed, jammed. **2** ENTIRE, whole, intact, total, complete, unabridged, unexpurgated. **3** THOROUGH, comprehensive, exhaustive, all-inclusive, broad, vast, extensive, ample, generous, abundant, plentiful, copious, profuse. **4** a full sound: rich, resonant, loud, deep, clear, distinct. **5** at full speed: maximum, top, highest, greatest, utmost.

Ea 1 empty. **2** partial, incomplete. **3** superficial.

full-grown adj adult, grown-up, of age, mature, ripe, developed, full-blown, full-scale.
Ea young, undeveloped.

fullness n **1** THOROUGHNESS, comprehensiveness, vastness, extensiveness, abundance, plenty, profusion, ampleness, completeness, totality, richness, resonance, strength, loudness, wholeness, variety. **2** SATISFACTION, glut, fill, satedness.
Ea 1 incompleteness. **2** emptiness.

full-scale adj exhaustive, extensive, complete, sweeping, thorough, thoroughgoing, wide-ranging, comprehensive, all-out, in-depth, all-encompassing, intensive, major.
Ea partial.

fully adv completely, totally, utterly, wholly, entirely, thoroughly, altogether, quite, positively, without reserve, perfectly.
Ea partly.

fulsome adj extravagant, excessive, immoderate, overdone, gross, inordinate, insincere, adulatory, effusive, fawning, ingratiating, sycophantic, unctuous, sickening, nauseating, cloying, nauseous, offensive, saccharine, smarmy (infml), slimy (infml), buttery (infml), over the top (infml).
Ea sincere.

fumble v grope, feel, bungle, botch, mishandle, mismanage.

fume v **1** SMOKE, smoulder, boil, steam. **2** RAGE, storm, rant, rave, seethe.

fumes n exhaust, smoke, gas, vapour, haze, fog, smog, pollution.

fumigate v deodorize, disinfect, sterilize, purify, cleanse.

fun n enjoyment, pleasure, amusement, entertainment, diversion, distraction, recreation, play, sport, game, foolery, tomfoolery, horseplay, skylarking, romp, merrymaking, mirth, jollity, jocularity, joking, jesting.
♦ **make fun of** rag, jeer at, ridicule, laugh at, mock, taunt, tease, rib (sl).

function n **1** ROLE, part, office, duty, charge, responsibility, concern, job, task, occupation, business, activity, purpose, use. **2** RECEPTION, party, gathering, affair, do (infml), dinner, luncheon.

> *v* work, operate, run, go, serve, act, perform, behave.

functional *adj* working, operational, practical, useful, utilitarian, utility, plain, hard-wearing.
☒ useless, decorative.

fund *n* pool, kitty, treasury, repository, storehouse, store, reserve, stock, hoard, cache, stack, mine, well, source, supply.
> *v* finance, capitalize, endow, subsidize, underwrite, sponsor, back, support, promote, float.

fundamental *adj* basic, primary, first, rudimentary, elementary, underlying, integral, central, principal, cardinal, prime, main, key, essential, indispensable, vital, necessary, crucial, important.

fundamentally *adv* basically, essentially, in essence, at bottom, at heart, deep down, inherently, intrinsically, primarily.

fundamentals *n* basics, essentials, first principles, laws, rules, rudiments, facts, necessaries, practicalities, brass tacks (*infml*), nitty-gritty (*infml*), nuts and bolts (*infml*).

funds *n* money, finance, backing, capital, resources, savings, wealth, cash.

funeral *n* burial, interment, entombment, cremation, obsequies, wake.

fungus

Types of fungus include: black spot, blight, botritis, brown rot, candida, downy mildew, ergot, grey mould, mushroom, orange-peel fungus, penicillium, potato blight, powdery mildew, rust, scab, smut, sooty mould, toadstool, yeast, brewer's yeast. *see also* **mushrooms and toadstools**.

funnel *v* channel, direct, convey, move, transfer, pass, pour, siphon, filter.

funny *adj* 1 HUMOROUS, amusing, entertaining, comic, comical, hilarious, witty, facetious, droll, farcical, laughable, ridiculous, absurd, silly. 2 ODD, strange, peculiar, curious, queer, weird, unusual, remarkable, puzzling, perplexing, mysterious, suspicious, dubious.
☒ 1 serious, solemn, sad. 2 normal, ordinary, usual.

furious *adj* 1 ANGRY, mad (*infml*), up in arms (*infml*), livid, enraged, infuriated, incensed, raging, fuming, boiling.
2 VIOLENT, wild, fierce, intense, vigorous, frantic, boisterous, stormy, tempestuous.
☒ 1 calm, pleased.

furnish *v* equip, fit out, decorate, rig, stock, provide, supply, afford, grant, give, offer, present.
☒ divest.

furniture *n* equipment, appliances, furnishings, fittings, fitments, household goods, movables, possessions, effects, things.

Types of furniture include: table, dining-table, gateleg table, refectory table, lowboy, side-table, coffee-table, card table; chair, easy chair, armchair, rocking-chair, recliner, dining-chair, carver, kitchen chair, stool, swivel-chair, high-chair, suite, settee, sofa, couch, studio couch, chesterfield, pouffe, footstool, bean-bag; bed, four-poster, chaise-longue, daybed, bed-settee, divan, camp-bed, bunk, water-bed, cot, cradle; desk, bureau, secretaire, bookcase, cupboard, cabinet, china cabinet, Welsh dresser, sideboard, buffet, dumb-waiter; fireplace, overmantel, fender, firescreen, hallstand, umbrella-stand, mirror, magazine rack; wardrobe, armoire, dressing-table, vanity unit, washstand, chest-of-drawers, tallboy, chiffonier, commode, ottoman, chest, coffer, blanket box.

furrow *n* groove, channel, trench, hollow, rut, track, line, crease, wrinkle.
> *v* seam, flute, corrugate, groove, crease, wrinkle, draw together, knit.

further *adj* more, additional, supplementary, extra, fresh, new, other.
> *v* advance, forward, promote, champion, push, encourage, foster, help, aid, assist, ease, facilitate, speed, hasten, accelerate, expedite.
☒ stop, frustrate.
> *adv* moreover, furthermore, besides, in addition, additionally, also, as well, too, what's more (*infml*).

furthermore *adv* moreover, what's more (*infml*), in addition, further, besides, also, too, as well, additionally.

furthest *adj* farthest, furthermost, remotest, outermost, outmost, extreme, ultimate, utmost, uttermost.
☒ nearest.

furtive *adj* surreptitious, sly, stealthy, secretive, underhand, hidden, covert, secret.
☒ open.

fury n anger, rage, wrath, frenzy, madness, passion, vehemence, fierceness, ferocity, violence, wildness, turbulence, power.
▣ calm, peacefulness.

fusion n melting, smelting, welding, union, synthesis, blending, coalescence, amalgamation, integration, merger, federation.

fuss n bother, trouble, hassle (*infml*), palaver, to-do (*infml*), hoo-ha (*infml*), furore, squabble, row, commotion, stir, fluster, confusion, upset, worry, agitation, flap (*infml*), excitement, bustle, flurry, hurry.
▣ calm.
➤ v complain, grumble, fret, worry, flap (*infml*), take pains, bother, bustle, fidget.

fussy adj 1 PARTICULAR, fastidious, scrupulous, finicky, pernickety, difficult, hard to please, choosy (*infml*), discriminating. 2 FANCY, elaborate, ornate, cluttered.
▣ 1 casual, uncritical. 2 plain.

futile adj pointless, useless, worthless, vain, idle, wasted, fruitless, profitless, unavailing, unsuccessful, abortive, unprofitable, unproductive, barren, empty, hollow, forlorn.
▣ fruitful, profitable.

futility n pointlessness, uselessness, worthlessness, vanity, emptiness, hollowness, aimlessness.
▣ use, purpose.

future n hereafter, tomorrow, outlook, prospects, expectations.
▣ past.
➤ adj prospective, designate, to be, fated, destined, to come, forthcoming, in the offing, impending, coming, approaching, expected, planned, unborn, later, subsequent, eventual.
▣ past.

fuzzy adj 1 FRIZZY, fluffy, furry, woolly, fleecy, downy, velvety, napped. 2 BLURRED, unfocused, ill-defined, unclear, vague, faint, hazy, shadowy, woolly, muffled, distorted.
▣ 2 clear, distinct.

Gg

gabble v babble, chatter, jabber, prattle, spout, splutter, cackle, sputter, gaggle, gibber, rattle, blab, blabber, blether.
➤ n babble, chatter, blabber, cackling, prattle, twaddle, blethering, waffle, nonsense, drivel, gibberish.

gad about v gallivant, run around, travel, roam, wander, range, rove, flit about, ramble, stray, traipse, dot about.

gadget n tool, appliance, device, contrivance, contraption, thing, thingumajig (*infml*), invention, novelty, gimmick.

gag¹ v 1 SILENCE, muffle, muzzle, quiet, stifle, smother, block, plug, clog, put a gag on, throttle, suppress, restrain, curb, check, still. 2 RETCH, choke, heave, nearly vomit.

gag² n joke, jest, quip, wisecrack, one-liner, pun, witticism, crack (*infml*), funny (*infml*).

gaiety n happiness, glee, cheerfulness, joie de vivre, jollity, merriment, mirth, hilarity, fun, merrymaking, revelry, festivity, celebration, joviality, good humour, high spirits, light-heartedness, liveliness, brightness, brilliance, sparkle, colour, colourfulness, show, showiness.
ea sadness, drabness.

gaily adv happily, joyfully, merrily, blithely, brightly, brilliantly, colourfully, flamboyantly.
ea sadly, dully.

gain v 1 EARN, make, produce, gross, net, clear, profit, yield, bring in, reap, harvest, win, capture, secure, net, obtain, acquire, procure. 2 REACH, arrive at, come to, get to, attain, achieve, realize. 3 *gain speed*: increase, pick up, gather, collect, advance, progress, improve.
ea 1 lose. 3 lose.
➤ n earnings, proceeds, income, revenue, winnings, profit, return, yield, dividend, growth, increase, increment, rise, advance, progress, headway, improvement, advantage, benefit, attainment, achievement, acquisition.
ea loss.
◆ **gain on** close with, narrow the gap, approach, catch up, level with, overtake, outdistance, leave behind.

gainsay v deny, contradict, disagree with, dispute, oppose, challenge, contravene (*fml*), controvert (*fml*), disaffirm (*fml*).
ea agree.

gala n festivity, celebration, festival, carnival, jubilee, jamboree, fête, fair, pageant, procession.

gale n 1 WIND, squall, storm, hurricane, tornado, typhoon, cyclone. 2 BURST, outburst, outbreak, fit, eruption, explosion, blast.

gall¹ n 1 IMPERTINENCE, impudence, brazenness, insolence, presumption, presumptuousness, effrontery (*fml*), nerve (*infml*), neck (*infml*), cheek (*infml*), chutzpah (*infml*), sauciness (*infml*), brass (*infml*), brass neck (*infml*). 2 BITTERNESS, rancour, sourness, spite, animosity, hostility, enmity, antipathy, malice, venom, virulence, acrimony (*fml*), animus (*fml*), malevolence (*fml*).
ea 1 modesty, reserve. 2 friendliness.

gall² v annoy, irritate, irk, exasperate, vex, bother, get to, nettle, peeve, pester, provoke, plague, rile, rankle, ruffle, harass, nag, aggravate (*infml*).
ea please.

gallant adj chivalrous, gentlemanly, courteous, polite, gracious, courtly, noble, dashing, heroic, valiant, brave, courageous, fearless, dauntless, bold, daring.
ea ungentlemanly, cowardly.

gallery n art gallery, museum, arcade, passage, walk, balcony, circle, gods (*infml*), spectators.

gallivant v gad about, run around, travel, roam, wander, ramble, range, rove, stray, traipse, flit about, dot about.

gallop v bolt, run, sprint, race, career, fly, dash, tear, speed, zoom, shoot, dart, rush, hurry, hasten.
ea amble.

galvanize v electrify, shock, jolt, prod, spur, provoke, stimulate, stir, move, arouse, excite, fire, invigorate, vitalize.

gamble *v* bet, wager, have a flutter (*infml*), try one's luck, punt, play, game, stake, chance, take a chance, risk, hazard, venture, speculate, back.
➤ *n* bet, wager, flutter (*infml*), punt, lottery, chance, risk, venture, speculation.

gambler *n* better, punter.

gambol *v* caper, frolic, frisk, skip, jump, bound, hop, bounce.

game¹ *n* **1** RECREATION, play, sport, pastime, diversion, distraction, entertainment, amusement, fun, frolic, romp, joke, jest. **2** COMPETITION, contest, match, round, tournament, event, meeting. **3** GAME BIRDS, animals, meat, flesh, prey, quarry, bag, spoils.

Types of indoor game include: board game, backgammon, checkers (*US*), chess, Cluedo®, draughts, halma, ludo, mah-jong, Monopoly®, nine men's morris, Scrabble®, snakes and ladders, Trivial Pursuit®: card game, baccarat, beggar-my-neighbour, bezique, blackjack, brag, bridge, canasta, chemin de fer, crib, cribbage, faro, gin rummy, rummy, happy families, nap (*infml*), napoleon, newmarket, old maid, patience, Pelmanism, picquet, poker, draw poker, stud poker, pontoon, vingt-et-un, snap, solitaire, twenty-one, whist, partner whist, solo whist; bagatelle, pinball, billiards, pool, snooker, bowling, ten-pin bowling, bowls, darts, dice, craps, dominoes, roulette, shove ha'penny, table tennis, ping pong.

Types of children's game include: battleships, blind man's buff, charades, Chinese whispers, consequences, fivestones, forfeits, hangman, hide-and-seek, I-spy, jacks, jackstraws, musical chairs, noughts and crosses, pass the parcel, piggy-in-the-middle, pin the tail on the donkey, postman's knock, sardines, Simon says, spillikins, spin the bottle, tiddlywinks. *see also* **toy**.

Types of game (killed for sport) include: antelope, badger, bear, blackcock, boar, wild boar, caribou, deer, fallow deer, red deer, roe deer, duck, elk, fox, grouse, hazel grouse, wood grouse, hare, lion, moose, mountain lion, partridge, pheasant, quail, rabbit, snipe, squirrel, stag, tiger, waterfowl.

game² *adj* (*infml*) **1** *game for anything*: willing, inclined, ready, prepared, eager.

2 BOLD, daring, intrepid, brave, courageous, fearless, resolute, spirited.
F3 **1** unwilling. **2** cowardly.

gamut *n* scale, series, range, sweep, scope, compass, spectrum, field, area.

gang *n* group, band, ring, pack, herd, mob, crowd, circle, clique, coterie, set, lot, team, crew, squad, shift, party.

gangling *adj* lanky, gawky, gangly, skinny, spindly, bony, angular, raw-boned, loose-jointed, awkward, tall, ungainly, rangy, gauche.

gangster *n* mobster (*US infml*), desperado, hoodlum, ruffian, rough, tough, thug, heavy (*infml*), racketeer, bandit, brigand, robber, criminal, crook (*infml*).

gaol *see* **jail**.

gaoler *see* **jailer**.

gap *n* **1** SPACE, blank, void, hole, opening, crack, chink, crevice, cleft, breach, rift, divide, divergence, difference. **2** INTERRUPTION, break, recess, pause, lull, interlude, intermission, interval.

gape *v* **1** STARE, gaze, gawp (*infml*), goggle, gawk (*infml*). **2** OPEN, yawn, part, split, crack.

gaping *adj* open, yawning, broad, wide, vast, cavernous.
F3 tiny.

garage *n* lock-up, petrol station, service station.

garbage *n* **1** WASTE, rubbish, trash, refuse, remains, leftovers, scourings, scraps, slops, swill, filth, muck, debris, dross, junk, litter, bits and pieces, odds and ends, sweepings, detritus (*fml*). **2** NONSENSE, rubbish, gibberish, trash, tripe, twaddle, bunk (*infml*), bunkum (*infml*), claptrap (*infml*), piffle (*infml*), bilge (*infml*), poppycock (*infml*), hot air (*infml*), cobblers (*infml*), rot (*infml*), tommyrot (*infml*).

garble *v* confuse, muddle, jumble, scramble, mix up, twist, distort, pervert, slant, misrepresent, falsify.
F3 decipher.

garden *n* yard, backyard, plot, allotment, orchard, park.

garish *adj* gaudy, lurid, loud, glaring, flashy, showy, tawdry, vulgar, tasteless.
F3 quiet, tasteful.

garland *n* wreath, festoon, decoration, flowers, laurels, honours.
➤ *v* wreathe, festoon, deck, adorn, crown.

garments *n* clothes, clothing, wear, attire,

gear (*infml*), togs (*infml*), outfit, get-up (*infml*), dress, costume, uniform.

garnish *v* decorate, adorn, ornament, trim, embellish, enhance, grace, set off.
ea divest.
➤ *n* decoration, ornament, trimming, embellishment, enhancement, relish.

garrison *n* **1** ARMED FORCE, detachment, troops, unit, command. **2** FORT, fortress, fortification, stronghold, station, post, base, barracks, camp, encampment, casern, zareba.
➤ *v* **1** PROTECT, defend, guard. **2** OCCUPY, position, place, mount, station, assign, furnish, man, post.

garrulous *adj* talkative, chatty, windy, long-winded, verbose, wordy, gabby, gassy, glib, yabbering, gossiping, gushing, chattering, babbling, effusive, prattling, prating, mouthy, loquacious (*fml*), prolix (*fml*), voluble (*fml*).
ea taciturn, terse.

gas

Types of gas include: acetylene, ammonia, black damp, butane, carbon dioxide, carbon monoxide, chloroform, choke damp, CS gas, cyanogen, ether, ethylene, fire damp, helium, hydrogen sulphide, krypton, laughing gas, marsh gas, methane, mustard gas, natural gas, neon, nerve gas, niton, nitrous oxide, ozone, propane, radon, tear gas, town gas, xenon.

gash *v* cut, wound, slash, slit, incise, lacerate, tear, rend, split, score, gouge.
➤ *n* cut, wound, slash, slit, incision, laceration, tear, rent, split, score, gouge.

gasp *v* pant, puff, blow, breathe, wheeze, choke, gulp.
➤ *n* pant, puff, blow, breath, gulp, exclamation.

gate *n* barrier, door, doorway, gateway, opening, entrance, exit, access, passage.

gather *v* **1** CONGREGATE, convene, muster, rally, round up, assemble, collect, group, amass, accumulate, hoard, stockpile, heap, pile up, build. **2** INFER, deduce, conclude, surmise, assume, understand, learn, hear. **3** FOLD, pleat, tuck, pucker. **4** *gather flowers*: pick, pluck, cull, select, reap, harvest, glean.
ea 1 scatter, dissipate.

gathering *n* assembly, convocation, convention, meeting, round-up, rally, get-together, jamboree, party, group, company,

congregation, mass, crowd, throng, turnout.

gauche *adj* awkward, clumsy, shy, ungainly, inelegant, ungraceful, unpolished, gawky, graceless, uncultured, unsophisticated, ignorant, ill-bred, ill-mannered, insensitive, inept, farouche, tactless, maladroit (*fml*).
ea graceful, elegant, urbane.

gaudy *adj* bright, brilliant, glaring, garish, loud, flashy, showy, ostentatious, tinselly, glitzy (*infml*), tawdry, vulgar, tasteless.
ea drab, plain.

gauge *v* estimate, guess, judge, assess, evaluate, value, rate, reckon, figure, calculate, compute, count, measure, weigh, determine, ascertain.
➤ *n* **1** STANDARD, norm, criterion, benchmark, yardstick, rule, guideline, indicator, measure, meter, test, sample, example, model, pattern. **2** SIZE, magnitude, measure, capacity, bore, calibre, thickness, width, span, extent, scope, height, depth, degree.

gaunt *adj* **1** HAGGARD, hollow-eyed, angular, bony, thin, lean, lank, skinny, scraggy, scrawny, skeletal, emaciated, wasted. **2** BLEAK, stark, bare, desolate, forlorn, dismal, dreary, grim, harsh.
ea 1 plump.

gawky *adj* awkward, clumsy, maladroit, gauche, inept, oafish, ungainly, gangling, unco-ordinated, graceless.
ea graceful.

gay *adj* **1** HOMOSEXUAL, lesbian, bisexual, camp (*infml*), butch (*infml*), queer (*sl*), bent (*sl*), dikey (*sl*). **2** HAPPY, joyful, jolly, merry, cheerful, bright, blithe, sunny, carefree, debonair, fun-loving, pleasure-seeking, vivacious, lively, animated, exuberant, sprightly, playful, light-hearted, in good/high spirits. **3** *gay colours*: vivid, rich, bright, brilliant, sparkling, festive, colourful, gaudy, garish, flashy, showy, flamboyant.
ea 1 heterosexual, straight (*sl*). **2** sad, gloomy.
➤ *n* homosexual, lesbian, queer (*sl*), poof (*sl*), dike (*sl*), faggot (*sl*), fag (*sl*), fairy (*sl*), pansy (*sl*), queen (*sl*), homo (*sl*), nancy (*sl*), woofter (*sl*).
ea heterosexual, straight (*sl*).

gaze *v* stare, contemplate, regard, watch, view, look, gape, wonder.
➤ *n* stare, look.

gear n **1** EQUIPMENT, kit, outfit, tackle, apparatus, tools, instruments, accessories. **2** GEARWHEEL, cogwheel, cog, gearing, mechanism, machinery, works. **3** (*infml*) BELONGINGS, possessions, things, stuff, baggage, luggage, paraphernalia. **4** (*infml*) CLOTHES, clothing, garments, attire, dress, garb (*infml*), togs (*infml*), get-up (*infml*).

gel, jell v set, congeal, coagulate, crystallize, harden, thicken, solidify, materialize, come together, finalize, form, take shape.

gelatinous adj jelly-like, jellied, congealed, rubbery, glutinous, gummy, gluey, gooey (*infml*), sticky, viscous.

gem n gemstone, precious stone, stone, jewel, treasure, prize, masterpiece, pièce de résistance.

> **Gems and gemstones include:**
> diamond, white sapphire, zircon, cubic zirconia, marcasite, rhinestone, pearl, moonstone, onyx, opal, mother-of-pearl, amber, citrine, fire opal, topaz, agate, tiger's eye, jasper, morganite, ruby, garnet, rose quartz, beryl, cornelian, coral, amethyst, sapphire, turquoise, lapis lazuli, emerald, aquamarine, bloodstone, jade, peridot, tourmaline, jet.

genealogy n family tree, pedigree, lineage, ancestry, descent, derivation, extraction, family, line.

general adj **1** *a general statement*: broad, sweeping, blanket, all-inclusive, comprehensive, universal, global, total, across-the-board, widespread, prevalent, extensive, overall, panoramic. **2** VAGUE, ill-defined, indefinite, imprecise, inexact, approximate, loose, unspecific. **3** USUAL, regular, normal, typical, ordinary, everyday, customary, conventional, common, public. **1** particular, limited. **2** specific. **3** rare.

generality n **1** GENERALIZATION, sweeping statement, general statement, impreciseness, indefiniteness, inexactness, looseness, approximateness, vagueness. **2** COMMONNESS, extensiveness, popularity, prevalence, universality, comprehensiveness, breadth, catholicity, ecumenicity, miscellaneity. **1** detail, exactness, particular. **2** uncommonness.

generally adv usually, normally, as a rule, by and large, on the whole, mostly, mainly, chiefly, broadly, commonly, universally.

generate v produce, engender, whip up, arouse, cause, bring about, give rise to, create, originate, initiate, make, form, breed, propagate. **1** prevent.

generation n **1** AGE GROUP, age, era, epoch, period, time. **2** PRODUCTION, creation, origination, formation, genesis, procreation, reproduction, propagation, breeding.

generic adj **1** GENERAL, common, comprehensive, inclusive, universal, sweeping, wide, all-inclusive, blanket, all-encompassing, collective. **2** *generic drugs*: unbranded, non-trademarked, non-registered, non-proprietary. **1** particular. **2** branded, trademarked, registered, proprietary.

generosity n liberality, munificence, open-handedness, bounty, charity, magnanimity, philanthropy, kindness, big-heartedness, benevolence, goodness. **1** meanness, selfishness.

generous adj **1** LIBERAL, free, bountiful, open-handed, unstinting, unsparing, lavish. **2** MAGNANIMOUS, charitable, philanthropic, public-spirited, unselfish, kind, big-hearted, benevolent, good, high-minded, noble. **3** AMPLE, full, plentiful, abundant, copious, overflowing. **1** mean, miserly. **2** selfish. **3** meagre.

genesis n origin, beginning, birth, outset, root, source, start, foundation, founding, generation, initiation, engendering, formation, propagation, creation, dawn, commencement (*fml*), inception (*fml*). **1** end, finish.

genial adj affable, amiable, friendly, convivial, cordial, kindly, kind, warm-hearted, warm, hearty, jovial, jolly, cheerful, happy, good-natured, easy-going (*infml*), agreeable, pleasant.

genitals n sexual organs, reproductive organs, private parts, vulva, clitoris, labia majora/minora, vagina, womb, uterus, penis, scrotum, testicles, pudenda (*fml*), pudendum (*fml*), genitalia (*fml*), privates (*infml*).

genius n **1** VIRTUOSO, maestro, master, past master, expert, adept, egghead (*infml*), intellectual, mastermind, brain, intellect. **2** INTELLIGENCE, brightness, brilliance, ability, aptitude, gift, talent, flair, knack, bent, inclination, propensity, capacity, faculty.

genre *n* type, form, style, class, fashion, brand, group, kind, sort, variety, category, character, school, strain, genus (*fml*).

genteel *adj* respectable, refined, cultivated, polished, elegant, polite, stylish, fashionable, cultured, aristocratic, formal, civil, gentlemanly, graceful, mannerly, well-mannered, well-bred, courteous, courtly, ladylike, urbane.
Ea crude, rough, unpolished, vulgar.

gentle *adj* **1** KIND, kindly, amiable, tender, soft-hearted, compassionate, sympathetic, merciful, mild, placid, calm, tranquil. **2** *a gentle slope*: gradual, slow, easy, smooth, moderate, slight, light, imperceptible. **3** SOOTHING, peaceful, serene, quiet, soft, balmy.
Ea 1 unkind, rough, harsh, wild.

gentlemanly *adj* courteous, polite, refined, polished, urbane, well-bred, well-mannered, cultivated, civilized, civil, honourable, mannerly, gentlemanlike, noble, gallant, genteel, reputable, suave, obliging.
Ea impolite, rough.

gentry *n* nobility, nobles, upper class, aristocracy, elite, gentility.

genuine *adj* real, actual, natural, pure, original, authentic, veritable, true, bona fide, legitimate, honest, sincere, frank, candid, earnest.
Ea artificial, false, insincere.

geology

A scale into which the Earth's geological history can be subdivided: *Cenozoic*: Quaternary (2 million years ago to present: Holocene, Pleistocene), Tertiary (65 million years ago to 2 million years ago: Pliocene, Miocene, Oligocene, Eocene, Palaeocene); *Mesozoic*: Cretaceous (140 million years ago to 65 million years ago), Jurassic (210 million yeas ago to 140 million years ago), Triassic (250 million years ago to 210 million years ago); *Palaeozoic*: Permian (290 million years ago to 250 million years ago), Carboniferous (360 million years ago to 290 million years ago: Pennsylvanian, Mississippian), Devonian (410 million yeas ago to 360 million years ago), Silurian (440 million years ago to 410 million years ago), Ordovician (505 million years ago to 440 million years ago), Cambrian (580 million years ago to 505 million years ago); *Precambrian* (before 580 million years ago).

germ *n* **1** MICRO-ORGANISM, microbe, bacterium, bacillus, virus, bug (*infml*). **2** BEGINNING, start, origin, source, cause, spark, rudiment, nucleus, root, seed, embryo, bud, sprout.

germinate *v* bud, sprout, shoot, develop, grow, swell.

gestation *n* development, incubation, pregnancy, conception, evolution, ripening, planning, drafting, maturation (*fml*).

gesticulate *v* wave, signal, gesture, indicate, sign.

gesture *n* act, action, movement, motion, indication, sign, signal, wave, gesticulation.
➤ *v* indicate, sign, motion, beckon, point, signal, wave, gesticulate.

get *v* **1** OBTAIN, acquire, procure, come by, receive, earn, gain, win, secure, achieve, realize. **2** *it's getting dark*: become, turn, go, grow. **3** *get him to help*: persuade, coax, induce, urge, influence, sway. **4** MOVE, go, come, reach, arrive. **5** FETCH, collect, pick up, take, catch, capture, seize, grab. **6** CONTRACT, catch, pick up, develop, come down with.
Ea 1 lose. **4** leave.
♦ **get across** communicate, transmit, convey, impart, put across, bring home to.
♦ **get ahead** advance, progress, get on, go places (*infml*), thrive, flourish, prosper, succeed, make good, make it, get there (*infml*).
Ea fall behind, fail.
♦ **get along 1** COPE, manage, get by, survive, fare, progress, develop. **2** AGREE, harmonize, get on, hit it off.
♦ **get at 1** REACH, attain, find, discover. **2** (*infml*) BRIBE, suborn, corrupt, influence. **3** (*infml*) MEAN, intend, imply, insinuate, hint, suggest. **4** (*infml*) CRITICIZE, find fault with, pick on, attack, make fun of.
♦ **get away** escape, get out, break out, break away, run away, flee, depart, leave.
♦ **get back** recover, regain, recoup, repossess, retrieve.
♦ **get by** cope, get along, manage, survive, exist, fare, subsist (*fml*), make ends meet (*infml*), scrape through (*infml*), hang on (*infml*), keep ones' head above water (*infml*), keep the wolf from the door (*infml*), weather the storm (*infml*), see it through (*infml*).
♦ **get down 1** DEPRESS, sadden, dishearten,

dispirit. **2** DESCEND, dismount, disembark, alight, get off.
E3 1 encourage. **2** board.

◆ **get in** enter, penetrate, infiltrate, arrive, come, land, embark.

◆ **get off 1** *get off a train*: alight, disembark, dismount, descend. **2** REMOVE, detach, separate, shed, get down.
E3 1 get on. **2** put on.

◆ **get on 1** BOARD, embark, mount, ascend. **2** COPE, manage, fare, get along, make out, prosper, succeed. **3** CONTINUE, proceed, press on, advance, progress.
E3 1 get off.

◆ **get out 1** ESCAPE, flee, break out, extricate oneself, free oneself, leave, quit, vacate, evacuate, clear out, clear off (*infml*). **2** *she got out a pen*: take out, produce.

◆ **get out of** avoid, escape, evade, shirk, dodge (*infml*), skive (*infml*).

◆ **get over 1** RECOVER FROM, shake off, survive. **2** SURMOUNT, overcome, defeat, deal with. **3** COMMUNICATE, get across, convey, put over, impart, explain.

◆ **get round 1** CIRCUMVENT, bypass, evade, avoid. **2** PERSUADE, win over, talk round, coax, prevail upon.

◆ **get together** assemble, collect, gather, congregate, rally, meet, join, unite, collaborate.

◆ **get up** stand (up), arise, rise, ascend, climb, mount, scale.

getaway *n* escape, breakout, flight, start, absconding, decampment, break.

ghastly *adj* awful, dreadful, frightful, terrible, grim, gruesome, hideous, horrible, horrid, loathsome, repellent, shocking, appalling.
E3 delightful, attractive.

ghost *n* spectre, phantom, spook (*infml*), apparition, visitant, spirit, wraith, soul, shade, shadow.

ghostly *adj* eerie, spooky (*infml*), creepy, supernatural, unearthly, ghostlike, spectral, wraith-like, phantom, illusory.

giant *n* monster, titan, colossus, Goliath, Hercules.
➤ *adj* gigantic, colossal, titanic, mammoth, jumbo (*infml*), king-size, huge, enormous, immense, vast, large.

gibberish *n* nonsense, rubbish, drivel, jargon, twaddle, balderdash, prattle, yammer, gobbledygook (*infml*), mumbo-jumbo (*infml*), poppycock (*infml*),

tommyrot (*infml*), cobblers (*infml*), bunkum (*infml*).
E3 sense.

gibe, jibe *n* jeer, sneer, mockery, ridicule, taunt, derision, scoff, dig (*infml*), crack (*infml*), poke, quip.

giddy *adj* **1** DIZZY, faint, light-headed, unsteady, reeling, vertiginous. **2** SILLY, flighty, wild.

gift *n* **1** PRESENT, offering, donation, contribution, bounty, largess, gratuity, tip, bonus, freebie (*sl*), legacy, bequest, endowment. **2** TALENT, genius, flair, aptitude, bent, knack, power, faculty, attribute, ability, capability, capacity.

gifted *adj* talented, adept, skilful, expert, masterly, skilled, accomplished, able, capable, clever, intelligent, bright, brilliant.

gigantic *adj* huge, enormous, immense, vast, giant, colossal, titanic, mammoth, gargantuan, Brobdingnagian.
E3 tiny, Lilliputian.

giggle *v, n* titter, snigger, chuckle, chortle, laugh.

gilded *adj* gilt, gold, golden, gold-plated.

gimmick *n* attraction, ploy, stratagem, ruse, scheme, trick, stunt, dodge, device, contrivance, gadget.

gingerly *adv* tentatively, hesitantly, warily, cautiously, carefully, delicately.
E3 boldly, carelessly.

gipsy *see* **gypsy**.

girdle *n* belt, sash, band, waistband, corset.

girl *n* lass, young woman, girlfriend, sweetheart, daughter.

girlfriend *n* young lady, girl, lass, partner, date, sweetheart, lover, fiancée, mistress, old flame, cohabitee, live-in lover, common-law spouse, date, steady.

girlish *adj* youthful, childlike, adolescent, childish, immature, innocent, unmasculine.

girth *n* circumference, perimeter, measure, size, bulk, strap, band.

gist *n* pith, essence, marrow, substance, matter, meaning, significance, import, sense, idea, drift, direction, point, nub, core, quintessence.

give *v* **1** PRESENT, award, confer, offer, lend, donate, contribute, provide, supply, furnish, grant, bestow, endow, gift, make over, hand over, deliver, entrust, commit, devote. **2** *give news*: communicate, transmit, impart, utter, announce, declare, pronounce, publish, set forth. **3** CONCEDE, allow, admit, yield, give way, surrender. **4** *give trouble*: cause, occasion, make, produce, do, perform. **5** SINK, yield, bend, give way, break, collapse, fall.

ᴇᴀ **1** take, withhold. **5** withstand.

◆ **give away** betray, inform on, expose, uncover, divulge, let slip, disclose, reveal, leak, let out.

◆ **give in** surrender, capitulate, submit, yield, give way, concede, give up, quit.

ᴇᴀ hold out.

◆ **give off** emit, discharge, release, give out, send out, throw out, pour out, exhale, exude, produce.

◆ **give out 1** DISTRIBUTE, hand out, dole out, deal. **2** ANNOUNCE, declare, broadcast, publish, disseminate, communicate, transmit, impart, notify, advertise.

◆ **give up 1** STOP, cease, quit, resign, abandon, renounce, relinquish, waive. **2** SURRENDER, capitulate, give in.

ᴇᴀ **1** start. **2** hold out.

give-and-take *n* adaptability, compromise, negotiation, flexibility, goodwill, willingness, compliance.

given *adj* **1** *a given number*: specified, particular, definite. **2** INCLINED, disposed, likely, liable, prone.

glacial *adj* **1** FREEZING, frozen, biting, bitter, chill, chilly, cold, frosty, raw, wintry, stiff, frigid, icy, piercing, polar, arctic, Siberian, brumous (*fml*), gelid (*fml*). **2** UNFRIENDLY, antagonistic, cold, icy, hostile, inimical (*fml*).

ᴇᴀ **1, 2** warm.

glad *adj* **1** PLEASED, delighted, gratified, contented, happy, joyful, merry, cheerful, cheery, bright. **2** WILLING, eager, keen, ready, inclined, disposed.

ᴇᴀ **1** sad, unhappy. **2** unwilling, reluctant.

gladden *v* brighten, cheer, encourage, delight, please, hearten, gratify, rejoice, elate, enliven, exhilarate, raise the spirits of, buck up (*infml*).

ᴇᴀ sadden.

gladly *adv* happily, cheerfully, freely, willingly, readily, with good grace, with pleasure.

ᴇᴀ sadly, unwillingly, reluctantly.

glamorous *adj* smart, elegant, attractive, beautiful, gorgeous, enchanting,

captivating, alluring, appealing, fascinating, exciting, dazzling, glossy, colourful.

ᴇᴀ plain, drab, boring.

glamour *n* attraction, allure, appeal, fascination, charm, magic, beauty, elegance, glitter, prestige.

glance *v* peep, peek, glimpse, view, look, scan, skim, leaf, flip, thumb, dip, browse.

➤ *n* peep, peek, glimpse, look.

gland

Types of gland include: adrenal, apocrine, cortex, eccrine, endocrine, exocrine, holocrine, lachrymal, lymph, lymph node, mammary, medulla, merocrine, ovary, pancreas, parathyroid, parotid, pineal, pituitary, prostate, sebaceous, testicle, thymus, thyroid.

glare *v* **1** GLOWER, look daggers, frown, scowl, stare. **2** DAZZLE, blaze, flame, flare, shine, reflect.

➤ *n* **1** *her icy glare*: dirty look (*infml*), frown, scowl, stare, look. **2** BRIGHTNESS, brilliance, blaze, flame, dazzle, spotlight.

glaring *adj* blatant, flagrant, open, conspicuous, manifest, patent, obvious, outrageous, gross.

ᴇᴀ hidden, concealed, minor.

glassy *adj* **1** GLASSLIKE, smooth, slippery, icy, shiny, glossy, transparent, clear. **2** *a glassy stare*: expressionless, blank, empty, vacant, dazed, fixed, glazed, cold, lifeless, dull.

glaze *v* coat, enamel, gloss, varnish, lacquer, polish, burnish.

➤ *n* coat, coating, finish, enamel, varnish, lacquer, polish, shine, lustre, gloss.

gleam *n* glint, flash, beam, ray, flicker, glimmer, shimmer, sparkle, glitter, gloss, glow.

➤ *v* glint, flash, glance, flare, shine, glisten, glimmer, glitter, sparkle, shimmer, glow.

glee *n* delight, cheerfulness, pleasure, fun, joy, joyfulness, merriment, mirth, gladness, liveliness, exhilaration, exuberance, exultation, elation, hilarity, jocularity, jollity, joviality, gaiety, gratification, triumph, verve, joyousness (*fml*).

glib *adj* fluent, easy, facile, quick, ready, talkative, plausible, insincere, smooth, slick, suave, smooth-tongued.

ᴇᴀ tongue-tied, implausible.

glide *v* slide, slip, skate, skim, fly, float,

drift, sail, coast, roll, run, flow.

glimmer *v* glow, shimmer, glisten, glitter, sparkle, twinkle, wink, blink, flicker, gleam, shine.

➤ *n* 1 GLOW, shimmer, sparkle, twinkle, flicker, glint, gleam. 2 TRACE, hint, suggestion, grain.

glimpse *n* peep, peek, squint, glance, look, sight, sighting, view.

➤ *v* spy, espy, spot, catch sight of, sight, view.

glint *v* flash, gleam, shine, reflect, glitter, sparkle, twinkle, glimmer.

➤ *n* flash, gleam, shine, reflection, glitter, sparkle, twinkle, glimmer.

glisten *v* shine, gleam, glint, glitter, sparkle, twinkle, glimmer, shimmer.

glitter *v* sparkle, spangle, scintillate, twinkle, shimmer, glimmer, glisten, glint, gleam, flash, shine.

➤ *n* sparkle, coruscation, scintillation, twinkle, shimmer, glimmer, glint, gleam, flash, shine, lustre, sheen, brightness, radiance, brilliance, splendour, showiness, glamour, tinsel.

gloat *v* triumph, glory, exult, rejoice, revel in, relish, crow, boast, vaunt, rub it in (*infml*).

global *adj* universal, worldwide, international, general, all-encompassing, total, thorough, exhaustive, comprehensive, all-inclusive, encylopedic, wide-ranging.

🔼 parochial, limited.

globe *n* world, earth, planet, sphere, ball, orb, round.

gloom *n* 1 DEPRESSION, low spirits, despondency, dejection, sadness, unhappiness, glumness, melancholy, misery, desolation, despair. 2 DARK, darkness, shade, shadow, dusk, twilight, dimness, obscurity, cloud, cloudiness, dullness.

🔼 1 cheerfulness, happiness. 2 brightness.

gloomy *adj* 1 DEPRESSED, down, low, despondent, dejected, downcast, dispirited, down-hearted, sad, miserable, glum, morose, pessimistic, cheerless, dismal, depressing. 2 DARK, sombre, shadowy, dim, obscure, overcast, dull, dreary.

🔼 1 cheerful. 2 bright.

glorify *v* 1 *glorify God*: praise, worship, exalt, adore, honour, thank, bless, magnify, revere, extol, sanctify, laud (*fml*), venerate

(*fml*). 2 *glorify violence/war*: celebrate, praise, magnify, hail, lionize, idolize, elevate, enshrine, immortalize, romanticize, panegyrize, eulogize (*fml*).

🔼 1 denounce, vilify (*fml*).

glorious *adj* 1 ILLUSTRIOUS, eminent, distinguished, famous, renowned, noted, great, noble, splendid, magnificent, grand, majestic, triumphant. 2 FINE, bright, radiant, shining, brilliant, dazzling, beautiful, gorgeous, superb, excellent, wonderful, marvellous, delightful, heavenly.

🔼 1 unknown.

glory *n* 1 FAME, renown, celebrity, illustriousness, greatness, eminence, distinction, honour, prestige, kudos, triumph. 2 PRAISE, homage, tribute, worship, veneration, adoration, exaltation, blessing, thanksgiving, gratitude. 3 BRIGHTNESS, radiance, brilliance, beauty, splendour, resplendence, magnificence, grandeur, majesty, dignity.

gloss¹ *n* polish, varnish, lustre, sheen, shine, brightness, brilliance, show, appearance, semblance, surface, front, façade, veneer, window-dressing.

◆ **gloss over** conceal, hide, veil, mask, disguise, camouflage, cover up, whitewash, explain away.

gloss² *n* annotation, note, footnote, explanation, elucidation, interpretation, translation, definition, comment, commentary.

➤ *v* annotate, define, explain, elucidate, interpret, construe, translate, comment.

glossy *adj* shiny, sheeny, lustrous, sleek, silky, smooth, glassy, polished, burnished, glazed, enamelled, bright, shining, brilliant.

🔼 matt.

glow *n* 1 LIGHT, gleam, glimmer, radiance, luminosity, brightness, vividness, brilliance, splendour. 2 ARDOUR, fervour, intensity, warmth, passion, enthusiasm, excitement, burning, redness.

➤ *v* 1 SHINE, radiate, gleam, glimmer, burn, smoulder. 2 *their faces glowed*: flush, blush, colour, redden.

glower *v* glare, look daggers, frown, scowl.

➤ *n* glare, black look, dirty look (*infml*), frown, scowl, stare, look.

glowing *adj* 1 BRIGHT, luminous, vivid,

vibrant, rich, warm, flushed, red, flaming. **2** *a glowing review*: complimentary, enthusiastic, ecstatic, rhapsodic, rave (*infml*).

☒ **1** dull, colourless. **2** restrained.

glue *n* adhesive, gum, paste, size, cement. ➤ *v* stick, affix, gum, paste, seal, bond, cement, fix.

glum *adj* gloomy, unhappy, forlorn, sad, miserable, depressed, despondent, moody, dejected, morose, pessimistic, doleful, crestfallen, sour, sulky, sullen, surly, grumpy, gruff, ill-humoured, churlish, crabbed, down (*infml*), low (*infml*), down in the dumps (*infml*).

☒ ecstatic, happy.

glut *n* surplus, excess, superfluity, surfeit, overabundance, superabundance, saturation, overflow.

☒ scarcity, lack.

glutton *n* gourmand, gormandizer, guzzler, gorger, gobbler, pig.

☒ ascetic.

gluttonous *adj* greedy, gluttonish, voracious, ravenous, insatiable, gormandizing, gutsy (*infml*), hoggish (*infml*), piggish (*infml*).

☒ abstemious, ascetic.

gluttony *n* gourmandise, gourmandism, greed, greediness, voracity, insatiability, piggishness.

☒ abstinence, asceticism.

gnarled *adj* gnarly, knotted, knotty, twisted, contorted, distorted, rough, rugged, weather-beaten.

gnaw *v* **1** BITE, nibble, munch, chew, eat, devour, consume, erode, wear, haunt. **2** WORRY, niggle, fret, trouble, plague, nag, prey.

go *v* **1** MOVE, pass, advance, progress, proceed, make for, travel, journey, start, begin, depart, leave, take one's leave, retreat, withdraw, disappear, vanish. **2** OPERATE, function, work, run, act, perform. **3** EXTEND, spread, stretch, reach, span, continue, unfold. **4** *time goes quickly*: pass, elapse, lapse, roll on.

☒ **2** break down, fail.

➤ *n* (*infml*) **1** *have a go*: attempt, try, shot (*infml*), bash (*infml*), stab (*infml*), turn. **2** ENERGY, get-up-and-go (*infml*), vitality, life, spirit, dynamism, effort.

♦ **go about** approach, begin, set about, address, tackle, attend to, undertake, engage in, perform.

♦ **go ahead** begin, proceed, carry on, continue, advance, progress, move.

♦ **go along with** accept, agree with, obey, follow, support, abide by, comply with (*fml*), concur with (*fml*).

♦ **go away** depart, leave, clear off (*infml*), withdraw, retreat, disappear, vanish.

Informal expressions telling someone to go away include: away!, away with you!, be off!, beat it!, buzz off!, clear off!, clear out!, do me a favour!, get out of here!, get out!, get the hell out of here!, go and jump in the lake!, go fly a kite!, never darken my door again!, off with you!, off you go!, on your way!, out of my sight!, push off!, run along!, scarper!, scat!, scram!, shove off!, skeddadle!, take a running jump!, vamoose!

♦ **go back** return, revert, backslide, retreat.

♦ **go back on** renege on, default on, deny, break one's promise.

♦ **go by 1** PASS, elapse, flow. **2** *go by the rules*: observe, follow, comply with, heed.

♦ **go down** descend, sink, set, fall, drop, decrease, decline, deteriorate, degenerate, fail, founder, go under, collapse, fold (*infml*).

♦ **go for 1** (*infml*) CHOOSE, prefer, favour, like, admire, enjoy. **2** ATTACK, assail, set about, lunge at.

♦ **go in for** enter, take part in, participate in, engage in, take up, embrace, adopt, undertake, practise, pursue, follow.

♦ **go into** discuss, consider, review, examine, study, scrutinize, investigate, inquire into, check out, probe, delve into, analyse, dissect.

♦ **go off 1** DEPART, leave, quit, abscond, vanish, disappear. **2** EXPLODE, blow up, detonate. **3** *the milk has gone off*: deteriorate, turn, sour, go bad, rot.

♦ **go on 1** CONTINUE, carry on, proceed, persist, stay, endure, last. **2** CHATTER, rabbit (*infml*), witter (*infml*), ramble on. **3** HAPPEN, occur, take place.

♦ **go out** exit, depart, leave.

♦ **go over** examine, peruse, study, revise, scan, read, inspect, check, review, repeat, rehearse, list.

♦ **go through 1** SUFFER, undergo, experience, bear, tolerate, endure, withstand. **2** INVESTIGATE, check, examine, look, search, hunt, explore. **3** USE, consume, exhaust, spend, squander.

♦ **go together** match, harmonize, accord, fit.

♦ **go under 1** CLOSE DOWN, collapse, default, die, fail, go out of business, founder, go bankrupt, fold (*infml*), flop (*infml*), go to the wall (*infml*), go bust (*infml*). **2** SINK, go down, founder, submerge, succumb, drown.

♦ **go with 1** MATCH, harmonize, co-ordinate, blend, complement, suit, fit, correspond. **2** ACCOMPANY, escort, take, usher.
Ea 1 clash.

♦ **go without** abstain, forgo, do without, manage without, lack, want.

goad *v* prod, prick, spur, impel, push, drive, provoke, incite, instigate, arouse, stimulate, prompt, urge, nag, hound, harass, annoy, irritate, vex.

go-ahead *n* permission, authorization, clearance, green light (*infml*), sanction, assent, consent, OK (*infml*), agreement.
Ea ban, veto, embargo.
➤ *adj* enterprising, pioneering, progressive, ambitious, up-and-coming, dynamic, energetic.
Ea unenterprising, sluggish.

goal *n* target, mark, objective, aim, intention, object, purpose, end, ambition, aspiration.

gobble *v* bolt, guzzle, gorge, cram, stuff, devour, consume, put away (*infml*), swallow, gulp.

gobbledygook *n* jargon, journalese, computerese, psychobabble, buzz words, nonsense, rubbish, drivel, twaddle, balderdash, prattle.

go-between *n* intermediary, mediator, liaison, contact, middleman, broker, dealer, agent, messenger, medium.

God *n* Supreme Being, Creator, Providence, Lord, Almighty, Holy One, Jehovah, Yahweh, Allah, Brahma, Zeus.

god, goddess *n* deity, divinity, idol, spirit, power.

godforsaken *adj* remote, isolated, lonely, bleak, desolate, abandoned, deserted, forlorn, dismal, dreary, gloomy, miserable, wretched.

godless *adj* ungodly, atheistic, heathen, pagan, irreligious, unholy, impious, sacrilegious, profane, irreverent, bad, evil, wicked.
Ea godly, pious.

godly *adj* religious, holy, pious, devout, God-fearing, righteous, good, virtuous, pure, innocent.
Ea godless, impious.

godsend *n* blessing, boon, stroke of luck, windfall, miracle.
Ea blow, setback.

golden *adj* **1** GOLD, gilded, gilt, yellow, blond(e), fair, bright, shining, lustrous, resplendent. **2** PROSPEROUS, successful, glorious, excellent, happy, joyful, favourable, auspicious, promising, rosy.

golf club

Types of golf club include: driver, brassie, spoon, wood, iron, driving iron, midiron, midmashie, mashie iron, mashie, spade mashie, mashie niblick, pitching niblick, niblick, putter, pitching wedge, sand wedge.

good *adj* **1** ACCEPTABLE, satisfactory, pleasant, agreeable, nice, enjoyable, pleasing, commendable, excellent, great (*infml*), super (*infml*), first-class, first-rate, superior, advantageous, beneficial, favourable, auspicious, helpful, useful, worthwhile, profitable, appropriate, suitable, fitting. **2** *good at her job*: competent, proficient, skilled, expert, accomplished, professional, skilful, clever, talented, gifted, fit, able, capable, dependable, reliable. **3** KIND, considerate, gracious, benevolent, charitable, philanthropic. **4** VIRTUOUS, exemplary, moral, upright, honest, trustworthy, worthy, righteous. **5** WELL-BEHAVED, obedient, well-mannered. **6** THOROUGH, complete, whole, substantial, considerable.
Ea 1 bad, poor. **2** incompetent. **3** unkind, inconsiderate. **4** wicked, immoral. **5** naughty, disobedient.
➤ *n* **1** VIRTUE, morality, goodness, righteousness, right. **2** USE, purpose, avail, advantage, profit, gain, worth, merit, usefulness, service. **3** *for your own good*: welfare, wellbeing, interest, sake, behalf, benefit, convenience.

goodbye *n* farewell, adieu, au revoir, valediction, leave-taking, parting.

Some ways of saying goodbye and expressions used when leaving include: adios, bye, bye bye, cheerio, ciao, good afternoon, goodbye, good day, goodnight, have a nice day, see you later, see you later alligator, in a while crocodile, see you when I see you, seeya, ta ta, ta ta for now, take one's leave, ttfn, until later.

good-humoured *adj* cheerful, happy,

jovial, genial, affable, amiable, friendly, congenial, pleasant, good-tempered, approachable.
Ea ill-humoured.

good-looking *adj* attractive, handsome, beautiful, fair, pretty, personable, presentable.
Ea ugly, plain.

good-natured *adj* kind, kindly, kind-hearted, sympathetic, benevolent, helpful, neighbourly, gentle, good-tempered, approachable, friendly, tolerant, patient.
Ea ill-natured.

goodness *n* virtue, uprightness, rectitude, honesty, probity, kindness, compassion, graciousness, goodwill, benevolence, unselfishness, generosity, friendliness, helpfulness.
Ea badness, wickedness.

goods *n* **1** PROPERTY, chattels, effects, possessions, belongings, paraphernalia, stuff, things, gear (*infml*). **2** MERCHANDISE, wares, commodities, stock, freight.

goodwill *n* benevolence, kindness, generosity, favour, friendliness, friendship, zeal.
Ea ill-will.

gore *v* pierce, penetrate, stab, spear, stick, impale, wound.

gorge *n* canyon, ravine, gully, defile, chasm, abyss, cleft, fissure, gap, pass.
➤ *v* feed, guzzle, gobble, devour, bolt, wolf, gulp, swallow, cram, stuff, fill, sate, surfeit, glut, overeat.
Ea fast.

gorgeous *adj* magnificent, splendid, grand, glorious, superb, fine, rich, sumptuous, luxurious, brilliant, dazzling, showy, glamorous, attractive, beautiful, handsome, good-looking, delightful, pleasing, lovely, enjoyable, good.
Ea dull, plain.

gory *adj* bloody, sanguinary, bloodstained, blood-soaked, grisly, brutal, savage, murderous.

gospel *n* **1** LIFE OF CHRIST, teaching of Christ, message of Christ, good news, New Testament **2** TEACHING, doctrine, creed, credo, certainty, truth, fact, verity (*fml*).

gossip *n* **1** IDLE TALK, prattle, chitchat, tittle-tattle, rumour, hearsay, report, scandal. **2** GOSSIP-MONGER, scandalmonger, whisperer, prattler, babbler, chatterbox, nosey parker (*infml*), busybody, talebearer, tell-tale, tattler.
➤ *v* talk, chat, natter, chatter, gabble, prattle, tattle, tell tales, whisper, rumour, blether (*infml*).

gouge *v* chisel, cut, hack, incise, score, groove, scratch, claw, gash, slash, dig, scoop, hollow, extract.

gourmet *n* gastronome, epicure, epicurean, connoisseur, bon vivant, foodie (*infml*).

govern *v* **1** RULE, reign, direct, manage, superintend, supervise, oversee, preside, lead, head, command, influence, guide, conduct, steer, pilot. **2** *govern one's temper*: dominate, master, control, regulate, curb, check, restrain, contain, quell, subdue, tame, discipline.

government *n* **1** *blame the government*: administration, executive, ministry, Establishment, authorities, powers that be, state, régime. **2** RULE, sovereignty, sway, direction, management, superintendence, supervision, surveillance, command, charge, authority, guidance, conduct, domination, dominion, control, regulation, restraint.

> Government systems include:
> absolutism, autocracy, commonwealth, communism, democracy, despotism, dictatorship, empire, federation, hierocracy, junta, kingdom, monarchy, plutocracy, puppet government, republic, theocracy, triumvirate. *see also* **parliament**.

governor *n* ruler, commissioner, administrator, executive, director, manager, leader, head, chief, commander, superintendent, supervisor, overseer, controller, boss.

gown *n* robe, dress, frock, dressing-gown, habit, costume.

grab *v* seize, snatch, take, nab (*infml*), pluck, snap up, catch hold of, grasp, clutch, grip, catch, bag, capture, collar (*infml*), commandeer, appropriate, usurp, annex.

grace *n* **1** GRACEFULNESS, poise, beauty, attractiveness, loveliness, shapeliness, elegance, tastefulness, refinement, polish, breeding, manners, etiquette, decorum, decency, courtesy, charm. **2** KINDNESS, kindliness, compassion, consideration, goodness, virtue, generosity, charity, benevolence, goodwill, favour, forgiveness, indulgence, mercy, leniency, pardon, reprieve. **3** *say grace*: blessing, benediction, thanksgiving, prayer.

☒ **2** cruelty, harshness.

➤ *v* favour, honour, dignify, distinguish, embellish, enhance, set off, trim, garnish, decorate, ornament, adorn.

☒ spoil, detract from.

graceful *adj* easy, flowing, smooth, supple, agile, deft, natural, slender, fine, tasteful, elegant, beautiful, charming, suave.

☒ graceless, awkward, clumsy, ungainly.

gracious *adj* elegant, refined, polite, courteous, well-mannered, considerate, sweet, obliging, accommodating, kind, compassionate, kindly, benevolent, generous, magnanimous, charitable, hospitable, forgiving, indulgent, lenient, mild, clement, merciful.

☒ ungracious.

grade *n* rank, status, standing, station, place, position, level, stage, degree, step, rung, notch, mark, brand, quality, standard, condition, size, order, group, class, category.

➤ *v* sort, arrange, categorize, order, group, class, rate, size, rank, range, classify, evaluate, assess, value, mark, brand, label, pigeonhole, type.

gradient *n* slope, incline, hill, bank, rise, declivity.

gradual *adj* slow, leisurely, unhurried, easy, gentle, moderate, regular, even, measured, steady, continuous, progressive, step-by-step.

☒ sudden, precipitate.

gradually *adv* little by little, bit by bit, imperceptibly, inch by inch, step by step, progressively, by degrees, piecemeal, slowly, gently, cautiously, gingerly, moderately, evenly, steadily.

graduate *v* **1** *graduate from medical school*: pass, qualify. **2** CALIBRATE, mark off, measure out, proportion, grade, arrange, range, order, rank, sort, group, classify.

graft *n* implant, implantation, transplant, splice, bud, sprout, shoot, scion.

➤ *v* engraft, implant, insert, transplant, join, splice.

grain *n* **1** BIT, piece, fragment, scrap, morsel, crumb, granule, particle, molecule, atom, jot, iota, mite, speck, modicum, trace. **2** SEED, kernel, corn, cereals.

3 TEXTURE, fibre, weave, pattern, marking, surface.

grand *adj* **1** MAJESTIC, regal, stately, splendid, magnificent, glorious, superb, sublime, fine, excellent, outstanding, first-rate, impressive, imposing, striking, monumental, large, noble, lordly, lofty, pompous, pretentious, grandiose, ambitious. **2** SUPREME, pre-eminent, leading, head, chief, arch, highest, senior, great, illustrious.

☒ **1** humble, common, poor.

grandeur *n* majesty, stateliness, pomp, state, dignity, splendour, magnificence, nobility, greatness, illustriousness, importance.

☒ humbleness, lowliness, simplicity.

grandiose *adj* pompous, pretentious, high-flown, lofty, ambitious, extravagant, ostentatious, showy, flamboyant, grand, majestic, stately, magnificent, impressive, imposing, monumental.

☒ unpretentious.

grant *v* **1** GIVE, donate, present, award, confer, bestow, impart, transmit, dispense, apportion, assign, allot, allocate, provide, supply. **2** ADMIT, acknowledge, concede, allow, permit, consent to, agree to, accede to.

☒ **1** withhold. **2** deny.

➤ *n* allowance, subsidy, concession, award, bursary, scholarship, gift, donation, endowment, bequest, annuity, pension, honorarium.

granular *adj* grainy, granulated, gritty, sandy, lumpy, rough, crumbly, friable.

granule *n* piece, particle, grain, scrap, crumb, bead, speck, fragment, iota, jot, atom, molecule, pellet, seed.

graph *n* diagram, chart, table, grid.

graphic *adj* vivid, descriptive, expressive, striking, telling, lively, realistic, explicit, clear, lucid, specific, detailed, blow-by-blow, visual, pictorial, diagrammatic, illustrative.

☒ vague, impressionistic.

grapple *v* seize, grasp, snatch, grab, grip, clutch, clasp, hold, wrestle, tussle, struggle, contend, fight, combat, clash, engage, encounter, face, confront, tackle, deal with, cope with.

☒ release, avoid, evade.

grasp *v* **1** HOLD, clasp, clutch, grip, grapple, seize, snatch, grab, catch. **2** *grasp a concept*: understand, comprehend, get (*infml*), follow, see, realize.

➤ *n* **1** GRIP, clasp, hold, embrace,

clutches, possession, control, power.
2 UNDERSTANDING, comprehension, apprehension, mastery, familiarity, knowledge.

grasping *adj* avaricious, greedy, rapacious, acquisitive, mercenary, mean, selfish, miserly, close-fisted, tight-fisted, parsimonious.
🗲 generous.

grass *n* turf, lawn, green, grassland, field, meadow, pasture, prairie, pampas, savanna, steppe.

> Types of grass include: bamboo, barley, beard grass, bent, buckwheat, cane, cocksfoot, corn, couch grass, English ryegrass, esparto, fescue, Italian ryegrass, Kentucky bluegrass, kangaroo grass, knot grass, maize, marram grass, meadow foxtail, meadow grass, millet, oats, paddy, pampas grass, papyrus, rattan, reed, rice, rye, ryegrass, sorghum, squirrel-tail grass, sugar cane, switch grass, twitch grass, wheat, wild oat.

grate *v* **1** GRIND, shred, mince, pulverize, rub, rasp, scrape. **2** JAR, set one's teeth on edge, annoy, irritate, aggravate (*infml*), get on one's nerves, vex, irk, exasperate.

grateful *adj* thankful, appreciative, indebted, obliged, obligated, beholden.
🗲 ungrateful.

gratify *v* satisfy, fulfil, indulge, pander to, humour, favour, please, gladden, delight, thrill.
🗲 frustrate, thwart.

grating¹ *adj* harsh, rasping, scraping, squeaky, strident, discordant, jarring, annoying, irritating, unpleasant, disagreeable.
🗲 harmonious, pleasing.

grating² *n* grate, grill, grid, lattice, trellis.

gratitude *n* gratefulness, thankfulness, thanks, appreciation, acknowledgement, recognition, indebtedness, obligation.
🗲 ingratitude, ungratefulness.

gratuitous *adj* wanton, unnecessary, needless, superfluous, unwarranted, unjustified, groundless, undeserved, unprovoked, uncalled-for, unasked-for, unsolicited, voluntary, free, gratis, complimentary.
🗲 justified, provoked.

gratuity *n* tip, bonus, perk (*infml*), gift, present, donation, reward, recompense.

grave¹ *n* burial-place, tomb, vault, crypt, sepulchre, mausoleum, pit, barrow, tumulus, cairn.

grave² *adj* **1** *a grave mistake*: important, significant, weighty, momentous, serious, critical, vital, crucial, urgent, acute, severe, dangerous, hazardous. **2** SOLEMN, dignified, sober, sedate, serious, thoughtful, pensive, grim, long-faced, quiet, reserved, subdued, restrained.
🗲 **1** trivial, light, slight. **2** cheerful.

graveyard *n* cemetery, burial-ground, churchyard.

gravitate *v* fall, descend, drop, head for, move, precipitate, sink, incline, lean, tend, drift, be attached to, be drawn to, settle.

gravity *n* **1** IMPORTANCE, significance, seriousness, urgency, acuteness, severity, danger. **2** SOLEMNITY, dignity, sobriety, seriousness, thoughtfulness, sombreness, reserve, restraint. **3** GRAVITATION, attraction, pull, weight, heaviness.
🗲 **1** triviality. **2** levity.

graze¹ *v* crop, feed, fodder, pasture, browse, ruminate (*fml*).

graze² *v* **1** SCRATCH, scrape, skin, bruise, rub, chafe, abrade (*fml*). **2** BRUSH, skim, touch, kiss, shave, glance off.
➤ *n* scratch, scrape, abrasion.

grease *n* oil, lubrication, fat, lard, dripping, tallow.

greasy *adj* oily, fatty, lardy, buttery, smeary, slimy, slippery, smooth, waxy.

great *adj* **1** LARGE, big, huge, enormous, massive, colossal, gigantic, mammoth, immense, vast, impressive. **2** *with great care*: considerable, pronounced, extreme, excessive, inordinate. **3** FAMOUS, renowned, celebrated, illustrious, eminent, distinguished, prominent, noteworthy, notable, remarkable, outstanding, grand, glorious, fine.
4 IMPORTANT, significant, serious, major, principal, primary, main, chief, leading. **5** (*infml*) EXCELLENT, first-rate, superb, wonderful, marvellous, tremendous, terrific, fantastic, fabulous.
🗲 **1** small. **2** slight. **3** unknown. **4** unimportant, insignificant.

greatly *adv* much, considerably, enormously, highly, extremely, immensely, vastly, noticeably, significantly, remarkably, impressively, notably, substantially, markedly, mightily, tremendously, hugely, powerfully, exceedingly, abundantly.

greatness n fame, renown, illustriousness, eminence, heroism, distinction, note, significance, importance, weight, momentousness, seriousness, power, magnitude, intensity, excellence, glory, genius, grandeur.
◼ insignificance, pettiness, smallness.

greed n 1 HUNGER, ravenousness, gluttony, gourmandism, voracity, insatiability. 2 ACQUISITIVENESS, covetousness, desire, craving, longing, eagerness, avarice, selfishness.
◼ 1 abstemiousness, self-restraint.

greedy adj 1 HUNGRY, starving, ravenous, gluttonous, gormandizing, voracious, insatiable. 2 ACQUISITIVE, covetous, desirous, craving, eager, impatient, avaricious, grasping, selfish.
◼ 1 abstemious.

green adj 1 GRASSY, leafy, verdant, unripe, unseasoned, tender, fresh, budding, blooming, flourishing. 2 green with envy: envious, covetous, jealous, resentful. 3 IMMATURE, naïve, unsophisticated, ignorant, inexperienced, untrained, raw, new, recent, young. 4 ECOLOGICAL, environmental, eco-friendly, environmentally aware.
➤ n common, lawn, grass, turf.

greenhouse n glasshouse, hothouse, conservatory, pavilion, vinery, orangery.

greet v hail, salute, acknowledge, address, accost, meet, receive, welcome.
◼ ignore.

greeting n salutation, acknowledgement, wave, hallo, the time of day, address, reception, welcome.

greetings n regards, respects, compliments, salutations, best wishes, good wishes, love.

gregarious adj sociable, outgoing, extrovert, friendly, affable, social, convivial, cordial, warm.
◼ unsociable.

grey adj 1 NEUTRAL, colourless, pale, ashen, leaden, dull, cloudy, overcast, dim, dark, murky. 2 GLOOMY, dismal, cheerless, depressing, dreary, bleak.

grief n sorrow, sadness, unhappiness, depression, dejection, desolation, distress, misery, woe, heartbreak, mourning, bereavement, heartache, anguish, agony, pain, suffering, affliction, trouble, regret, remorse.
◼ happiness, delight.

grievance n complaint, moan (infml), grumble (infml), resentment, objection, protest, charge, wrong, injustice, injury, damage, trouble, affliction, hardship, trial, tribulation.

grieve v 1 SORROW, mope, lament, mourn, wail, cry, weep. 2 SADDEN, upset, dismay, distress, afflict, pain, hurt, wound.
◼ 1 rejoice. 2 please, gladden.

grievous adj 1 SEVERE, grave, tragic, appalling, distressing, dreadful, atrocious, burdensome, calamitous, devastating, damaging, shameful, harmful, outrageous, overwhelming, shocking, deplorable, intolerable, unbearable, monstrous, flagrant, glaring. 2 WOUNDING, injurious, hurtful, painful, damaging, sore.

grim adj 1 UNPLEASANT, horrible, horrid, ghastly, gruesome, grisly, sinister, frightening, fearsome, terrible, shocking. 2 STERN, severe, harsh, dour, forbidding, surly, sullen, morose, gloomy, depressing, unattractive.
◼ 1 pleasant. 2 attractive.

grimace n frown, scowl, pout, smirk, sneer, face.
➤ v make a face, pull a face, frown, scowl, pout, smirk, sneer.

grime n dirt, muck, filth, soot, dust.

grimy adj dirty, mucky, grubby, soiled, filthy, sooty, smutty, dusty, smudgy.
◼ clean.

grind v crush, pound, pulverize, powder, mill, grate, scrape, gnash, rut, abrade, sand, file, smooth, polish, sharpen, whet.

grip n hold, grasp, clasp, embrace, clutches, control, power.
➤ v 1 HOLD, grasp, clasp, clutch, seize, grab, catch. 2 FASCINATE, thrill, enthral, spellbind, mesmerize, hypnotize, rivet, engross, absorb, involve, engage, compel.

gripping adj fascinating, thrilling, enthralling, compelling, compulsive, exciting, suspenseful, spellbinding, entrancing, riveting, engrossing, absorbing, unputdownable (infml).

grisly adj gruesome, gory, grim, macabre, horrid, horrible, ghastly, awful, frightful, terrible, dreadful, abominable, appalling, shocking.
◼ delightful.

grit n gravel, pebbles, shingle, sand, dust.
➤ v clench, gnash, grate, grind.

groan n moan, sigh, cry, whine, wail,

lament, complaint, objection, protest, outcry.

▪ cheer.

➤ *v* moan, sigh, cry, whine, wail, lament, complain, object, protest.

▪ cheer.

groggy *adj* weak, dopey, unsteady, wobbly, shaky, staggering, stunned, dazed, confused, befuddled, bewildered, stupefied, punch-drunk, dizzy, faint, reeling, muzzy (*infml*), woozy (*infml*).

▪ healthy, strong, lucid.

groom *v* 1 SMARTEN, neaten, tidy (up), spruce up, prepare, put in order, arrange, adjust, fix, do, smooth. 2 CLEAN, brush, curry, preen, dress. 3 *groomed for her new post*: prepare, make ready, train, school, teach, educate, instruct, tutor, drill, coach, prime.

➤ *n* 1 BRIDEGROOM, honeymooner, newly-wed, husband, spouse, marriage partner. 2 STABLEBOY, stableman, stable lad/lass, stable hand.

groove *n* furrow, rut, track, slot, channel, gutter, trench, hollow, indentation, score.

▪ ridge.

grope *v* feel, fumble, scrabble, flounder, cast about, fish, search, probe.

gross *adj* 1 *gross misconduct*: serious, grievous, blatant, flagrant, glaring, obvious, plain, sheer, utter, outright, shameful, shocking. 2 OBSCENE, lewd, improper, indecent, offensive, rude, coarse, crude, vulgar, tasteless. 3 FAT, obese, overweight, big, large, huge, colossal, hulking, bulky, heavy. 4 *gross earnings*: inclusive, all-inclusive, total, aggregate, entire, complete, whole.

▪ 3 slight. 4 net.

grotesque *adj* bizarre, odd, weird, unnatural, freakish, monstrous, hideous, ugly, unsightly, misshapen, deformed, distorted, twisted, fantastic, fanciful, extravagant, absurd, surreal, macabre.

▪ normal, graceful.

ground *n* 1 BOTTOM, foundation, surface, land, terrain, dry land, terra firma, earth, soil, clay, loam, dirt, dust. 2 *football ground*: field, pitch, stadium, arena, park.

➤ *v* 1 BASE, found, establish, set, fix, settle. 2 PREPARE, introduce, initiate, familiarize with, acquaint with, inform, instruct, teach, train, drill, coach, tutor.

groundless *adj* baseless, unfounded, unsubstantiated, unsupported, empty, imaginary, false, unjustified, unwarranted, unprovoked, uncalled-for.

▪ well-founded, reasonable, justified.

grounds¹ *n* land, terrain, holding, estate, property, territory, domain, gardens, park, campus, surroundings, fields, acres.

grounds² *n* base, foundation, justification, excuse, vindication, reason, motive, inducement, cause, occasion, call, score, account, argument, principle, basis.

groundwork *n* basis, base, essentials, foundation, fundamentals, preparation, preliminaries, research, homework, cornerstone, footing, spadework, underpinnings.

group *n* band, gang, pack, team, crew, troop, squad, detachment, party, faction, set, circle, clique, club, society, association, organization, company, gathering, congregation, crowd, collection, bunch, clump, cluster, conglomeration, constellation, batch, lot, combination, formation, grouping, class, classification, category, genus, species.

➤ *v* 1 GATHER, collect, assemble, congregate, mass, cluster, clump, bunch. 2 *group them according to size*: sort, range, arrange, marshal, organize, order, class, classify, categorize, band, link, associate.

grouse *v* complain, grumble, moan, find fault, beef (*infml*), bellyache (*infml*), carp (*infml*), grouch (*infml*), gripe (*infml*), whine (*infml*), whinge (*infml*), bitch (*infml*).

▪ acquiesce.

➤ *n* complaint, groan, grumble, moan, objection, protest, grievance, bellyache (*infml*), gripe (*infml*), grouch (*infml*), whine (*infml*), whinge (*infml*).

grovel *v* crawl, creep, ingratiate oneself, toady, suck up (*sl*), flatter, fawn, cringe, cower, kowtow, defer, demean oneself.

grow *v* 1 INCREASE, rise, expand, enlarge, swell, spread, extend, stretch, develop, proliferate, mushroom. 2 ORIGINATE, arise, issue, spring, germinate, shoot, sprout, bud, flower, mature, develop, progress, thrive, flourish, prosper. 3 CULTIVATE, farm, produce, propagate, breed, raise. 4 *grow cold*: become, get, go, turn.

▪ 1 decrease, shrink.

growl *v* snarl, snap, yap, rumble, roar.

grown-up *adj* adult, mature, of age, full-grown, fully-fledged.

▪ young, immature.

➤ *n* adult, man, woman.
🔳 child.

growth *n* **1** INCREASE, rise, extension, enlargement, expansion, spread, proliferation, development, evolution, progress, advance, improvement, success, prosperity. **2** TUMOUR, lump, swelling, protuberance, outgrowth.
🔳 **1** decrease, decline, failure.

grub *v* dig, burrow, delve, probe, root, rummage, forage, ferret, hunt, search, scour, explore.
➤ *n* maggot, worm, larva, pupa, caterpillar, chrysalis.

grubby *adj* dirty, soiled, unwashed, mucky, grimy, filthy, squalid, seedy, scruffy.
🔳 clean.

grudge *n* resentment, bitterness, envy, jealousy, spite, malice, enmity, antagonism, hate, dislike, animosity, ill-will, hard feelings, grievance.
🔳 favour.
➤ *v* begrudge, resent, envy, covet, dislike, take exception to, object to, mind.

grudging *adj* reluctant, unwilling, hesitant, half-hearted, unenthusiastic, resentful, envious, jealous.

gruelling *adj* hard, difficult, taxing, demanding, tiring, exhausting, laborious, arduous, strenuous, backbreaking, harsh, severe, tough, punishing.
🔳 easy.

gruesome *adj* horrible, disgusting, repellent, repugnant, repulsive, hideous, grisly, macabre, grim, ghastly, awful, terrible, horrific, shocking, monstrous, abominable.
🔳 pleasant.

gruff *adj* **1** CURT, brusque, abrupt, blunt, rude, surly, sullen, grumpy, bad-tempered. **2** *a gruff voice*: rough, harsh, rasping, guttural, throaty, husky, hoarse.
🔳 **1** friendly, courteous.

grumble *v* complain, moan, whine, bleat, grouch, gripe, mutter, murmur, carp, find fault.

grumpy *adj* bad-tempered, ill-tempered, crotchety, crabbed, cantankerous, cross, irritable, surly, sullen, sulky, grouchy, discontented.
🔳 contented.

guarantee *n* warranty, insurance, assurance, promise, word of honour, pledge, oath, bond, security, collateral, surety, endorsement, testimonial.
➤ *v* assure, promise, pledge, swear, vouch for, answer for, warrant, certify, underwrite, endorse, secure, protect, insure, ensure, make sure, make certain.

guarantor *n* underwriter, guarantee, sponsor, supporter, backer, surety, warrantor, referee, voucher, bondsman, bailsman, covenantor, angel (*infml*).

guard *v* protect, safeguard, save, preserve, shield, screen, shelter, cover, defend, patrol, police, escort, supervise, oversee, watch, look out, mind, beware.
➤ *n* **1** PROTECTOR, defender, custodian, warder, escort, bodyguard, minder (*sl*), watchman, lookout, sentry, picket, patrol, security. **2** PROTECTION, safeguard, defence, wall, barrier, screen, shield, bumper, buffer, pad.

guarded *adj* cautious, wary, careful, watchful, discreet, non-committal, reticent, reserved, secretive, cagey (*infml*).
🔳 communicative, frank.

guardian *n* trustee, curator, custodian, keeper, warden, protector, preserver, defender, champion, guard, warder, escort, attendant.

guerrilla *n* freedomfighter, terrorist, irregular, resistance fighter, partisan, sniper.

guess *v* speculate, conjecture, predict, estimate, judge, reckon, work out, suppose, assume, surmise, think, believe, imagine, fancy, feel, suspect.
➤ *n* prediction, estimate, speculation, conjecture, supposition, assumption, belief, fancy, idea, notion, theory, hypothesis, opinion, feeling, suspicion, intuition.

guesswork *n* speculation, conjecture, estimation, reckoning, supposition, assumption, surmise, intuition.

guest *n* visitor, caller, boarder, lodger, resident, patron, regular.

guidance *n* leadership, direction, management, control, teaching, instruction, advice, counsel, counselling, help, instructions, directions, guidelines, indications, pointers, recommendations.

guide *v* **1** LEAD, conduct, direct, navigate, point, steer, pilot, manoeuvre, usher, escort, show, show the way, accompany, attend, hold someone's hand (*infml*). **2** CONTROL, govern, manage, direct, be in charge of, rule, preside over, oversee, supervise, superintend, command. **3**

ADVISE, counsel, give directions/ recommendations to, influence, educate, teach, instruct, train.
➤ *n* 1 LEADER, courier, navigator, pilot, helmsman, steersman, usher, escort, chaperon, attendant, companion, adviser, counsellor, mentor, guru, teacher, instructor. 2 MANUAL, handbook, guidebook, catalogue, directory.
3 GUIDELINE, example, model, standard, criterion, indication, pointer, signpost, sign, marker.

guideline *n* instruction, recommendation, suggestion, direction, advice, information, indication, rule, regulation, standard, criterion, measure, benchmark, yardstick, touchstone, framework, parameter, constraint, procedure, principle, terms.

guild *n* organization, association, alliance, federation, society, club, union, fellowship, league, order, company, chapel, brotherhood, lodge, fraternity, sorority, corporation, incorporation.

guile *n* deceit, deception, cunning, treachery, double-dealing, fraud, trickery, trickiness, wiliness, cleverness, slyness, craft, craftiness, deviousness, artfulness, artifice, ruse, gamesmanship, knavery, duplicity (*fml*).
🔳 artlessness, guilelessness.

guilt *n* 1 *he confessed his guilt*: culpability, responsibility, blame, disgrace, dishonour. 2 *a feeling of guilt*: guilty conscience, conscience, shame, self-condemnation, self-reproach, regret, remorse, contrition.
🔳 1 innocence, righteousness.
2 shamelessness.

guilty *adj* 1 CULPABLE, responsible, blamable, blameworthy, offending, wrong, sinful, wicked, criminal, convicted.
2 CONSCIENCE-STRICKEN, ashamed, shamefaced, sheepish, sorry, regretful, remorseful, contrite, penitent, repentant.
🔳 1 innocent, guiltless, blameless.
2 shameless.

gulf *n* bay, bight, basin, gap, opening, separation, rift, split, breach, cleft, chasm, gorge, abyss, void.

gullible *adj* credulous, suggestible, impressionable, trusting, unsuspecting, foolish, naïve, green, unsophisticated, innocent.
🔳 astute.

gully *n* channel, watercourse, gutter, ditch, ravine.

gulp *v* swallow, swig, swill, knock back (*infml*), bolt, wolf (*infml*), gobble, guzzle, devour, stuff.
🔳 sip, nibble.
➤ *n* swallow, swig, draught, mouthful.

gum *n* adhesive, glue, paste, cement.
➤ *v* stick, glue, paste, fix, cement, seal, clog.

gun *n* firearm, handgun, pistol, revolver, shooter (*sl*), shooting iron (*sl*), rifle, shotgun, bazooka, howitzer, cannon.

gunman *n* assassin, terrorist, thug, killer, murderer, bandit, gangster, sniper, shootist, bravo, desperado, gunslinger, hatchet man (*infml*), hit man (*infml*), mobster (*US infml*).

gurgle *v* bubble, babble, burble, murmur, ripple, lap, splash, crow.
➤ *n* babble, murmur, ripple.

guru *n* expert, authority, instructor, master, teacher, tutor, leader, mentor, luminary, guiding light, pundit, maharishi, Svengali, swami, sage.

gush *v* 1 FLOW, run, pour, stream, cascade, flood, rush, burst, spurt, spout, jet.
2 ENTHUSE, chatter, babble, jabber, go on (*infml*), drivel.
➤ *n* flow, outflow, stream, torrent, cascade, flood, tide, rush, burst, outburst, spurt, spout, jet.

gust *n* blast, burst, rush, flurry, blow, puff, breeze, wind, gale, squall.

gusto *n* zest, relish, appreciation, enjoyment, pleasure, delight, enthusiasm, exuberance, élan, verve, zeal.
🔳 distaste, apathy.

gut *v* 1 *gut fish*: disembowel, draw, clean (out). 2 STRIP, clear, empty, rifle, ransack, plunder, loot, sack, ravage.

guts *n* 1 INTESTINES, bowels, viscera, entrails, insides, innards (*infml*), belly, stomach. 2 (*infml*) COURAGE, bravery, pluck, grit, nerve, mettle.

gutsy *adj* bold, brave, courageous, determined, resolute, plucky, indomitable, mettlesome, passionate, spirited, staunch, gallant, game.
🔳 quiet, timid.

gutter *n* drain, sluice, ditch, trench, trough, channel, duct, conduit, passage, pipe, tube.

guttural *adj* rasping, throaty, croaking,

hoarse, harsh, gruff, rough, grating, gravelly, husky, deep, low, thick. ▪ dulcet.

guy (*infml*) *n* fellow, bloke (*infml*), chap (*infml*), man, boy, youth, person, individual.

guzzle *v* bolt, devour, gobble, gormandize, stuff, cram, gulp, swallow, swill, quaff, swig, wolf (*infml*), scoff (*infml*), polish off (*infml*), put away (*infml*), tuck into (*infml*), knock back (*infml*).

gypsy, gipsy *n* Romany, traveller, wanderer, nomad, tinker.

gyrate *v* turn, revolve, rotate, twirl, pirouette, spin, whirl, wheel, circle, spiral, swirl.

Hh

habit *n* custom, usage, practice, routine, rule, second nature, way, manner, mode, wont, inclination, tendency, bent, mannerism, quirk, addiction, dependence, fixation, obsession, weakness.

habitat *n* home, abode, domain, element, environment, surroundings, locality, territory, terrain.

habitation *n* **1** OCCUPANCY, occupation, quarters, residence, tenancy, housing, lodging, inhabitance, inhabitancy, inhabitation. **2** HOME, house, cottage, accommodation, flat, apartment, hut, quarters, living quarters, lodging, mansion, abode (*fml*), domicile (*fml*), dwelling (*fml*), dwelling-place (*fml*), residence (*fml*), digs (*infml*), pad (*infml*), joint (*infml*), roof over one's head (*infml*).

habitual *adj* **1** CUSTOMARY, traditional, wonted, routine, usual, ordinary, common, natural, normal, standard, regular, recurrent, fixed, established, familiar. **2** *habitual drinker*: confirmed, inveterate, hardened, addicted, dependent, persistent.
€ **1** occasional, infrequent.

hack¹ *v* cut, chop, hew, notch, gash, slash, lacerate, mutilate, mangle.

hack² *n* scribbler, journalist, drudge, slave.

hackneyed *adj* stale, overworked, tired, worn-out, time-worn, threadbare, unoriginal, corny (*infml*), clichéed, stereotyped, stock, banal, trite, commonplace, common, pedestrian, uninspired.
€ original, new, fresh.

hag *n* crone, witch, battle-axe (*infml*), shrew, termagant, vixen.

haggard *adj* drawn, gaunt, careworn, thin, wasted, shrunken, pinched, pale, wan, ghastly.
€ hale.

haggle *v* bargain, negotiate, barter, wrangle, squabble, bicker, quarrel, dispute.

hail¹ *n* barrage, bombardment, volley, torrent, shower, rain, storm.

➤ *v* pelt, bombard, shower, rain, batter, attack, assail.

hail² *v* greet, address, acknowledge, salute, wave, signal to, flag down, shout, call, acclaim, cheer, applaud, honour, welcome.

hair *n* locks, tresses, shock, mop, mane.

hairdresser *n* hairstylist, stylist, barber, coiffeur, coiffeuse.

hairless *adj* bald, bald-headed, shorn, tonsured, shaven, clean-shaven, beardless.
€ hairy, hirsute.

hair-raising *adj* frightening, scary, terrifying, horrifying, shocking, bloodcurdling, spine-chilling, eerie, alarming, startling, thrilling.

hairstyle *n* style, coiffure, hairdo (*infml*), cut, haircut, set, perm (*infml*).

Hairstyles include: Afro, backcombed, bangs, beehive, bob, bouffant, braid, bun, chignon, corn rows, cowlick, crewcut, crimped, crop, curled, dreadlocks, Eton crop, French plait, fringe, frizette, marcel wave, mohican, pageboy, perm, pigtail, plait, pompadour, ponytail, pouffe, quiff, ringlets, shingle, short back and sides, sideboards, sideburns, skinhead, tonsure, topknot, undercut; hair-piece, toupee, wig.

hairy *adj* hirsute, bearded, shaggy, bushy, fuzzy, furry, woolly.
€ bald, clean-shaven.

half *n* fifty per cent, bisection, hemisphere, semicircle, section, segment, portion, share, fraction.

➤ *adj* semi-, halved, divided, fractional, part, partial, incomplete, moderate, limited.
€ whole.

➤ *adv* partly, partially, incompletely, moderately, slightly.
€ completely.

half-baked *adj* impractical, stupid, ill-conceived, unplanned, undeveloped, ill-judged, short-sighted, silly, crazy, foolish, senseless, hair-brained, crackpot (*infml*).
€ sensible, thought out.

half-hearted *adj* lukewarm, cool, weak,

feeble, passive, apathetic, uninterested, indifferent, neutral.
🔁 wholehearted, enthusiastic.

halfway *adv* midway, in the middle, centrally.
➤ *adj* middle, central, equidistant, mid, midway, intermediate.

hall *n* hallway, corridor, passage, passageway, entrance-hall, foyer, vestibule, lobby, concert-hall, auditorium, chamber, assembly room.

hallmark *n* stamp, mark, trademark, brand-name, sign, indication, symbol, emblem, device, badge.

hallowed *adj* honoured, revered, sacred, sacrosanct, blessed, sanctified, consecrated, holy, dedicated, established, inviolable, age-old.

hallucinate *v* dream, imagine, see things, daydream, fantasize, freak out (*sl*), trip (*sl*).

hallucination *n* illusion, mirage, vision, apparition, dream, daydream, fantasy, figment, delusion, freak-out (*sl*), trip (*sl*).

halo *n* circle of light, crown, ring, corona, glory, nimbus, radiance, aura, aureole, aureola, gloria, gloriole, halation.

halt *v* stop, draw up, pull up, pause, wait, rest, break off, discontinue, cease, desist, quit, end, terminate, check, stem, curb, obstruct, impede.
🔁 start, continue.
➤ *n* stop, stoppage, arrest, interruption, break, pause, rest, standstill, end, close, termination.
🔁 start, continuation.

halting *adj* hesitant, stuttering, stammering, faltering, stumbling, broken, imperfect, laboured, awkward.
🔁 fluent.

halve *v* bisect, cut in half, split in two, divide, split, share, cut down, reduce, lessen.

hammer *v* hit, strike, beat, drum, bang, bash, pound, batter, knock, drive, shape, form, make.
➤ *n* mallet, gavel.
♦ **hammer out** settle, sort out, negotiate, thrash out, produce, bring about, accomplish, complete, finish.

hamper *v* hinder, impede, obstruct, slow down, hold up, frustrate, thwart, prevent, handicap, hamstring, shackle, cramp, restrict, curb, restrain.
🔁 aid, facilitate.

hand *n* **1** FIST, palm, paw (*infml*), mitt (*sl*). **2** *give me a hand*: help, aid, assistance, support, participation, part, influence. **3** WORKER, employee, operative, workman, labourer, farm-hand, hireling.
➤ *v* give, pass, offer, submit, present, yield, deliver, transmit, conduct, convey.
♦ **at hand** near, close, to hand, handy, accessible, available, ready, imminent.
♦ **hand down** bequeath, will, pass on, transfer, give, grant.
♦ **hand out** distribute, deal out, give out, share out, dish out (*infml*), mete out, dispense.
♦ **hand over** yield, relinquish, surrender, turn over, deliver, release, give, donate, present.
🔁 keep, retain.

handbook *n* manual, instruction book, guide, guidebook, companion.

handful *n* few, sprinkling, scattering, smattering.
🔁 a lot, many.

handicap *n* obstacle, block, barrier, impediment, stumbling-block, hindrance, drawback, disadvantage, restriction, limitation, penalty, disability, impairment, defect, shortcoming.
🔁 assistance, advantage.
➤ *v* impede, hinder, disadvantage, hold back, retard, hamper, burden, encumber, restrict, limit, disable.
🔁 help, assist.

handicraft *n* craft, art, craftwork, handwork, handiwork.

handiwork *n* work, doing, responsibility, achievement, product, result, design, invention, creation, production, skill, workmanship, craftsmanship, artisanship.

handle *n* grip, handgrip, knob, stock, shaft, hilt.
➤ *v* **1** TOUCH, finger, feel, fondle, pick up, hold, grasp. **2** *handle a situation*: tackle, treat, deal with, manage, cope with, control, supervise.

handling *n* management, conduct, approach, operation, running, treatment, direction, administration, discussion, transaction, manipulation.

handout *n* **1** CHARITY, alms, dole, largess(e), share, issue, free sample, freebie (*sl*). **2** LEAFLET, circular, bulletin, statement, press release, literature.

hand-picked *adj* choice, select,

selected, chosen, elect, elite, picked, screened, recherché.

hands n care, custody, possession, charge, authority, command, power, control, supervision.

handsome adj 1 GOOD-LOOKING, attractive, fair, personable, elegant. 2 GENEROUS, liberal, large, considerable, ample.
☒ 1 ugly, unattractive. 2 mean.

handwriting n writing, script, hand, fist (infml), penmanship, calligraphy.

handy adj 1 AVAILABLE, to hand, ready, at hand, near, accessible, convenient, practical, useful, helpful. 2 SKILFUL, proficient, expert, skilled, clever, practical.
☒ 1 inconvenient. 2 clumsy.

handyman n DIYer, odd-jobman, odd-jobber, Jack-of-all-trades, factotum.

hang v 1 SUSPEND, dangle, swing, drape, drop, flop, droop, sag, trail. 2 FASTEN, attach, fix, stick. 3 hang in the air float, drift, hover, linger, remain, cling.
◆ **hang about** hang around, linger, loiter, dawdle, waste time, associate with, frequent, haunt.
◆ **hang back** hold back, demur, hesitate, shy away, recoil.
◆ **hang on** 1 WAIT, hold on, remain, hold out, endure, continue, carry on, persevere, persist. 2 GRIP, grasp, hold fast. 3 DEPEND ON, hinge on, turn on.
☒ 1 give up.

hanger-on n follower, minion, lackey, toady, sycophant, parasite, sponger, dependant.

hangover n after-effects, katzenjammer, morning after, the morning after the night before, crapulence (fml).

hang-up n inhibition, difficulty, problem, obsession, preoccupation, thing (infml), block, mental block.

hanker for v hanker after, crave, hunger for, thirst for, want, wish for, desire, covet, yearn for, long for, pine for, itch for.

hankering n craving, hunger, thirst, wish, desire, yearning, longing, itch, urge.

haphazard adj random, chance, casual, arbitrary, hit-or-miss, unsystematic, disorganized, disorderly, careless, slapdash, slipshod.
☒ methodical, orderly.

happen v 1 OCCUR, take place, fall, arise, crop up, develop, present itself, turn up, go on, come about, come true, result, ensue, follow, turn out, appear, come into being, transpire (fml), supervene (fml), eventuate (fml), materialize (infml). 2 happen to do something: have the good/bad luck to, have the good/bad fortune to. 3 happen on something: find, discover, hit on, light on, stumble on, come across, chance on.

happening n occurrence, phenomenon, event, incident, episode, occasion, adventure, experience, accident, chance, circumstance, case, affair.

happiness n joy, joyfulness, gladness, cheerfulness, contentment, pleasure, delight, glee, elation, bliss, ecstasy, euphoria.
☒ unhappiness, sadness.

> **Ways of expressing happiness include:**
> couldn't be happier, floating on air, full of the joys of spring, happy as a sandboy, I'm/he's a happy chappie, in high spirits, in seventh heaven, joy unbounded, jump for joy, make someone's day, on cloud nine, on top of the world, over the moon, thrilled to bits, tickled pink, walking on air, weigh-hey!

happy adj 1 JOYFUL, jolly, merry, cheerful, glad, pleased, delighted, thrilled, elated, satisfied, content, contented. 2 a happy coincidence: lucky, fortunate, felicitous, favourable, appropriate, apt, fitting.
☒ 1 unhappy, sad, discontented. 2 unfortunate, inappropriate.

happy-go-lucky adj easy-going, carefree, casual, nonchalant, cheerful, devil-may-care, light-hearted, unconcerned, untroubled, unworried, reckless, irresponsible, heedless, improvident, blithe (fml), insouciant (fml).
☒ anxious, wary.

harangue n diatribe, tirade, lecture, speech, address.
➢ v lecture, preach, hold forth, spout, declaim, address.

harass v pester, badger, harry, plague, torment, persecute, exasperate, vex, annoy, irritate, bother, disturb, hassle (infml), trouble, worry, stress, tire, wear out, exhaust, fatigue.

harassed adj distraught, pressurized, pressured, stressed, under pressure, under stress, strained, distressed, troubled, worried, careworn, hounded, pestered, plagued, tormented, harried, vexed,

hassled (*infml*), stressed out (*infml*), uptight (*infml*).
🔁 carefree.

harassment *n* annoyance, nuisance, pestering, trouble, molestation, persecution, pressuring, torment, bother, distress, aggravation, badgering, bedevilment, irritation, vexation, hassle (*infml*).
🔁 assistance.

harbour *n* port, dock, quay, wharf, marina, mooring, anchorage, haven, shelter.
➤ *v* **1** HIDE, conceal, protect, shelter. **2** *harbour a feeling*: hold, retain, cling to, entertain, foster, nurse, nurture, cherish, believe, imagine.

hard *adj* **1** SOLID, firm, unyielding, tough, strong, dense, condensed, compressed, compact, compacted, impenetrable, resistant, stiff, rigid, inflexible, unpliable, hard as stone/iron/rock (*infml*). **2** COMPLICATED, difficult, complex, involved, intricate, knotty, baffling, puzzling, perplexing, bewildering. **3** STRENUOUS, difficult, arduous, onerous, laborious, tough, tiring, toilsome, exhausting, backbreaking, heavy, exacting, rigorous. **4** HARSH, severe, strict, callous, unfeeling, unsympathetic, cruel, cold-hearted, hard-hearted, stern, tyrannical, oppressive, pitiless, merciless, ruthless, implacable, unsparing, unyielding, unrelenting, distressing, painful, unpleasant, obdurate (*fml*), hard as flint (*infml*), standing no nonsense (*infml*), ruling with a rod of iron (*infml*). **5** *hard times*: tough, unpleasant, difficult, harsh, grim, severe, painful, distressing, uncomfortable, disagreeable, austere. **6** *a hard worker*: hard-working, industrious, diligent, assiduous, conscientious, zealous, enthusiastic, keen, busy, energetic. **7** *a hard push*: forceful, powerful, strong, intense, heavy, sharp, violent. **8** *a hard winter*: cold, severe, harsh, raw, bitter, freezing. **9** *hard evidence*: true, indisputable, undeniable, unquestionable, definite, actual, certain, real, verified. **10** *hard drugs*: addictive, harmful, habit-forming, narcotic, heavy, strong, potent.
🔁 **1** soft, yielding. **2** easy, simple. **4** kind, pleasant, compassionate, gentle. **5** easy, comfortable. **6** lazy, idle. **8** mild. **9** uncertain.
➤ *adv* **1** FORCEFULLY, powerfully, energetically, intensely, strongly, heavily,

sharply, violently, vigorously, with all one's might (*fml*). **2** *work hard*: diligently, industriously, assiduously, conscientiously, energetically, intensely, busily, enthusiastically, eagerly, keenly. **3** *look/think hard*: carefully, attentively, closely, intently, sharply, keenly. **4** *a hard-won victory*: with difficulty, arduously, strenuously, laboriously, after a struggle, vigorously. **5** *snowing hard*: intensely, severely, strongly, heavily, steadily.
🔁 **3** carelessly. **4** effortlessly. **5** lightly.

♦ **hard and fast** binding, fixed, definite, immutable, incontrovertible, inflexible, invariable, rigid, set, strict, stringent, unalterable, unchangeable, unchanging, uncompromising.
🔁 flexible.

♦ **hard up** poor, broke (*infml*), penniless, impoverished, in the red, bankrupt, bust, short, lacking.
🔁 rich.

harden *v* solidify, set, freeze, bake, stiffen, strengthen, reinforce, fortify, buttress, brace, steel, nerve, toughen, season, accustom, train.
🔁 soften, weaken.

hard-headed *adj* shrewd, astute, businesslike, level-headed, clear-thinking, sensible, realistic, pragmatic, practical, hard-boiled, tough, unsentimental.
🔁 unrealistic.

hard-hearted *adj* callous, unfeeling, cold, hard, stony, heartless, unsympathetic, cruel, inhuman, pitiless, merciless.
🔁 soft-hearted, kind, merciful.

hard-hitting *adj* condemnatory, critical, unsparing, no-holds-barred, vigorous, forceful, tough.
🔁 mild.

hardiness *n* robustness, toughness, resilience, resolution, boldness, courage, valour, ruggedness, sturdiness, intrepidity, fortitude (*fml*).
🔁 timidity.

hardline *adj* strict, tough, extreme, immoderate, inflexible, militant, uncompromising, unyielding, undeviating, intransigent (*fml*).
🔁 moderate, flexible.

hardly *adv* barely, scarcely, just, only just, not quite, not at all, by no means.

hard-pressed *adj* hard-pushed, hard put, harassed, harried, pushed, under

pressure, overburdened, overtaxed, up against it (*infml*), in a corner (*infml*), with one's back to the wall (*infml*).
≉ untroubled.

hardship *n* misfortune, adversity, trouble, difficulty, affliction, distress, suffering, trial, tribulation, want, need, privation, austerity, poverty, destitution, misery.
≉ ease, comfort, prosperity.

hard-wearing *adj* durable, lasting, strong, tough, sturdy, stout, rugged, resilient.
≉ delicate.

hard-working *adj* industrious, diligent, assiduous, conscientious, zealous, busy, energetic.
≉ idle, lazy.

hardy *adj* strong, tough, sturdy, robust, vigorous, fit, sound, healthy.
≉ weak, unhealthy.

hair-brained *adj* foolish, stupid, silly, wild, daft (*infml*), ill-conceived, careless, rash, reckless, inane, giddy, half-baked, crackpot (*infml*), scatty (*infml*), scatterbrained (*infml*).
≉ sensible.

hark back *v* remember, recall, recollect, go back, turn back, revert, regress (*fml*).

harm *n* damage, loss, injury, hurt, detriment, ill, misfortune, wrong, abuse.
≉ benefit.
➤ *v* damage, impair, blemish, spoil, mar, ruin, hurt, injure, wound, ill-treat, maltreat, abuse, misuse.
≉ benefit, improve.

harmful *adj* damaging, detrimental, pernicious, noxious, unhealthy, unwholesome, injurious, dangerous, hazardous, poisonous, toxic, destructive.
≉ harmless.

harmless *adj* safe, innocuous, non-toxic, inoffensive, gentle, innocent.
≉ harmful, dangerous, destructive.

harmonious *adj* 1 MELODIOUS, tuneful, musical, sweet-sounding. 2 MATCHING, co-ordinated, balanced, compatible, like-minded, agreeable, cordial, amicable, friendly, sympathetic.
≉ 1 discordant.

harmonize *v* match, co-ordinate, balance, fit in, suit, tone, blend, correspond, agree, reconcile, accommodate, adapt, arrange, compose.
≉ clash.

harmony *n* 1 TUNEFULNESS, tune, melody, euphony. 2 *live in harmony*: agreement, unanimity, accord (*fml*), concord, unity, compatibility, like-mindedness, peace, goodwill, rapport, sympathy, understanding, amicability, friendliness, co-operation, co-ordination, balance, symmetry, correspondence, conformity.
≉ 1 discord. 2 conflict.

harness *n* tackle, gear, equipment, reins, straps, tack.

> Parts of a horse's harness include:
> backband, bellyband, bit, blinders (*US*), blinkers, breeching, bridle, collar, crupper, girth, hackamore, halter, hames, headstall (*US*), martingale, noseband, reins, saddle, saddlepad, stirrup, throatlatch/throatlash (*US*), traces.

➤ *v* control, channel, use, utilize, exploit, make use of, employ, mobilize, apply.

harp on *v* keep talking about, dwell on, labour, press, reiterate, renew, repeat, nag, go on and on about (*infml*).

harrowing *adj* distressing, upsetting, heart-rending, disturbing, alarming, frightening, terrifying, nerve-racking, traumatic, agonizing, excruciating.

harry *v* badger, pester, nag, chivvy, harass, plague, torment, persecute, annoy, vex, worry, trouble, bother, hassle (*infml*), disturb, molest.

harsh *adj* 1 SEVERE, strict, draconian, unfeeling, cruel, hard, pitiless, austere, Spartan, bleak, grim, comfortless. 2 *a harsh sound*: rough, coarse, rasping, croaking, guttural, grating, jarring, discordant, strident, raucous, sharp, shrill, unpleasant. 3 BRIGHT, dazzling, glaring, gaudy, lurid.
≉ 1 lenient. 2 soft.

harvest *n* 1 HARVEST-TIME, ingathering, reaping, collection. 2 CROP, yield, return, produce, fruits, result, consequence.
➤ *v* reap, mow, pick, gather, collect, accumulate, amass.

hash *n* mess, botch, muddle, mix-up, jumble, confusion, hotchpotch, mishmash.

hassle *n* bother, inconvenience, nuisance, difficulty, trouble, problem, struggle, argument, disagreement, quarrel, squabble, trial, upset, fight, dispute, bickering, wrangle, altercation (*fml*), aggro (*infml*).
≉ agreement, peace.

➢ *v* bother, pester, trouble, annoy, badger, harass, hound, harry, chivvy, bug (*infml*).
🔛 assist, calm.

haste *n* hurry, rush, hustle, bustle, speed, velocity, rapidity, swiftness, quickness, briskness, urgency, rashness, recklessness, impetuosity.
🔛 slowness.

hasten *v* hurry, rush, make haste, run, sprint, dash, tear, race, fly, bolt, accelerate, speed (up), quicken, expedite, dispatch, precipitate, urge, press, advance, step up.
🔛 dawdle, delay.

hasty *adj* hurried, rushed, impatient, headlong, rash, reckless, heedless, thoughtless, impetuous, impulsive, hot-headed, fast, quick, rapid, swift, speedy, brisk, prompt, short, brief, cursory.
🔛 slow, careful, deliberate.

hat

Hats include: trilby, bowler, fedora, top-hat, Homburg, derby (*US*), pork-pie hat, flat-cap, beret, bonnet, Tam o'Shanter, tammy, deerstalker, hunting-cap, stovepipe hat, Stetson®, ten-gallon hat, boater, sunhat, panama, straw hat, picture-hat, pill-box, cloche, beanie (*US*), poke-bonnet, mob-cap, turban, fez, sombrero, sou'wester, glengarry, bearskin, busby, peaked cap, sailor-hat, baseball cap, balaclava, hood, snood, toque, helmet, mortar-board, skullcap, yarmulka, mitre, biretta.

hatch *v* **1** INCUBATE, brood, breed. **2** CONCOCT, formulate, originate, think up, dream up, conceive, devise, contrive, plot, scheme, design, plan, project.

hate *v* dislike, despise, detest, loathe, abhor, abominate, execrate.
🔛 like, love.
➢ *n* hatred, aversion, dislike, loathing, abhorrence, abomination.
🔛 liking, love.

hateful *adj* horrid, horrible, loathsome, detestable, abominable, offensive, disgusting, obnoxious, odious, revolting, repulsive, nasty, unpleasant, disagreeable, despicable, vile, contemptible, foul, evil, heinous, abhorrent (*fml*), execrable (*fml*), repellent (*fml*), repugnant (*fml*).
🔛 pleasing.

hatred *n* hate, aversion, dislike, detestation, loathing, repugnance, revulsion, abhorrence, abomination, execration, animosity, ill-will, antagonism,

hostility, enmity, antipathy.
🔛 liking, love.

haughty *adj* lofty, imperious, high and mighty, supercilious, cavalier, snooty (*infml*), contemptuous, disdainful, scornful, superior, snobbish, arrogant, proud, stuck-up (*infml*), conceited.
🔛 humble, modest.

haul *v* pull, heave, tug, draw, tow, drag, trail, move, transport, convey, carry, cart, lug, hump (*infml*).
🔛 push.
➢ *n* loot, booty, plunder, swag (*sl*), spoils, takings, gain, yield, find.

haunt *v* **1** FREQUENT, patronize, visit.
2 *memories haunted her*: plague, torment, trouble, disturb, recur, prey on, beset, obsess, possess.
➢ *n* resort, hangout (*infml*), stamping-ground, den, meeting-place, rendezvous.

haunted *adj* **1** POSSESSED, cursed, eerie, ghostly, jinxed, hag-ridden, spooky (*infml*).
2 TROUBLED, worried, plagued, tormented, obsessed, preoccupied.

haunting *adj* memorable, unforgettable, persistent, recurrent, evocative, nostalgic, poignant.
🔛 unmemorable.

have *v* **1** OWN, possess, get, obtain, gain, be given, acquire, secure, take, receive, accept, keep, hold, use, procure (*fml*). **2** FEEL, experience, enjoy, suffer, undergo, submit to, be subjected to, endure, tolerate, put up with, go through, find, meet, encounter. **3** CONTAIN, include, take in, embody, incorporate, consist of, comprise (*fml*), embrace (*fml*), comprehend (*fml*). **4** *have a party*: hold, arrange, organize, take part in, participate in. **5** *have to go now*: must, be forced, be compelled, be obliged, be required, ought, should. **6** *have someone do something*: cause, make, arrange, get, oblige, require, persuade, talk into, ask, tell, request, order, command, bid, force, compel, coerce, enjoin (*fml*), prevail upon (*fml*). **7** *have pity on someone*: show, demonstrate, display, exhibit, express, feel, manifest (*fml*). **8** *have food/drink*: eat, swallow, consume, take, drink, devour, down, gulp, guzzle, partake of (*fml*), put away (*infml*), tuck into (*infml*), knock back (*infml*). **9** *have a baby*: give birth to, bear, bring into the world, be delivered of. **10** *I won't have such behaviour*: tolerate, put up with, take, accept, allow, permit, stand,

abide, brook. **11** *you've been had*: deceive, dupe, fool, trick, cheat, swindle, take in, con (*infml*), diddle (*infml*).
F3 1 lack.
♦ **have done with** finish with, give up, stop, be through with, cease (*fml*), desist (*fml*), throw over (*infml*), wash one's hands of (*infml*).
♦ **have had it** be in trouble, have no hope, be defeated, be exhausted, be lost, have no chance of success, bite the dust (*infml*), come to a sticky end (*infml*).
♦ **have on 1** WEAR, be dressed in, be clothed in. **2** *What have you got on this week?*: have an engagement, have an appointment, have arranged, have planned. **3** TEASE, trick, play a joke on, kid (*infml*), rag (*infml*), pull someone's leg (*infml*).

haven *n* harbour, port, anchorage, shelter, refuge, sanctuary, asylum, retreat.

havoc *n* chaos, confusion, disorder, disruption, damage, destruction, ruin, wreck, rack and ruin, devastation, waste, desolation.

haywire (*infml*) *adj* wrong, tangled, out of control, crazy, mad, wild, chaotic, confused, disordered, disorganized, topsy-turvy.

hazard *n* risk, danger, peril, jeopardy, threat, death-trap, accident, chance.
F3 safety.
➤ *v* **1** RISK, endanger, jeopardize, expose. **2** CHANCE, gamble, stake, venture, suggest, speculate.

hazardous *adj* risky, dangerous, unsafe, perilous, precarious, insecure, chancy, difficult, tricky.
F3 safe, secure.

haze *n* mist, fog, cloud, steam, vapour, film, mistiness, smokiness, dimness, obscurity.

hazy *adj* misty, foggy, smoky, clouded, cloudy, milky, fuzzy, blurred, ill-defined, veiled, obscure, dim, faint, unclear, indistinct, vague, indefinite, uncertain.
F3 clear, bright, definite.

head *n* **1** SKULL, cranium, noddle (*infml*), nut (*infml*), conk (*infml*), bonce (*infml*). **2** MIND, brain, mentality, mental abilities, intellect, intelligence, wit(s), sense, understanding, wisdom, thought, reasoning, common sense, brains (*infml*), loaf (*infml*), noddle (*infml*), little grey cells (*infml*), grey matter (*infml*). **3** TOP, peak, summit, crown, crest, tip, apex, vertex,

height, climax. **4** FRONT, fore, forefront, vanguard, van, lead. **5** LEADER, chief, captain, commander, director, manager, managing director, superintendent, supervisor, principal, head teacher, headmaster, headmistress, ruler, controller, administrator, president, governor, chair, chairman, chairwoman, chairperson, boss (*infml*). **6** COMMAND, control(s), leadership, directorship, management, supervision, charge. **7** CRISIS, critical point, climax, emergency, catastrophe, calamity, dilemma, crunch (*infml*). **8** *the head of a river*: source, origin, fount, spring, rise, wellspring, wellhead. **9** *no head on the beer*: froth, foam, bubbles, fizz, suds, lather.
F3 1 foot, tail. **3** base, foot. **4** back. **5** subordinate.
➤ *adj* leading, front, foremost, first, chief, main, prime, principal, top, topmost, highest, supreme, premier, dominant, pre-eminent.
➤ *v* **1** *head the queue*: be at the front of, be first in, go first, lead. **2** LEAD, rule, govern, command, direct, be in charge of, be in control of, manage, run, superintend, oversee, supervise, administer, control, guide, steer.
♦ **go to one's head 1** MAKE DRUNK, intoxicate, inebriate, make dizzy, befuddle, make woozy (*infml*). **2** *success has gone to his head*: make arrogant, make conceited, make proud, make one full of oneself, puff up (*infml*).
♦ **head for** make for, go towards, direct towards, aim for, point to, turn for, steer for.
♦ **head off** forestall, intercept, intervene, interpose, deflect, divert, fend off, ward off, avert, prevent, stop.
♦ **head over heels** completely, utterly, uncontrollably, wholeheartedly, recklessly, thoroughly, intensely, wildly.
♦ **keep one's head** keep calm, stay calm and collected, keep control of oneself, keep/maintain one's composure, keep one's cool (*infml*).
♦ **lose one's head** panic, lose control of oneself, lose one's composure, lose one's cool (*infml*), flap (*infml*), go round like a headless chicken (*infml*).

headache *n* **1** *suffer from headaches*: migraine, neuralgia. **2** BOTHER, nuisance, trouble, inconvenience, problem, worry, pest, vexation, bane, hassle (*infml*).

heading *n* title, name, headline, rubric,

caption, section, division, category, class.

headland n promontory, cape, head, point, foreland.

headlong adj hasty, precipitate, impetuous, impulsive, rash, reckless, dangerous, breakneck, head-first.
➤ adv head first, hurriedly, hastily, precipitately, rashly, recklessly, heedlessly, thoughtlessly, wildly.

headquarters n HQ, base (camp), head office, nerve centre.

headstrong adj stubborn, obstinate, intractable, pigheaded, wilful, self-willed, perverse, contrary.
🖙 tractable, docile.

headway n advance, progress, way, improvement.

heady adj intoxicating, strong, stimulating, exhilarating, thrilling, exciting.

heal v cure, remedy, mend, restore, treat, soothe, salve, settle, reconcile, patch up.

health n fitness, constitution, form, shape, trim, fettle, condition, tone, state, healthiness, good condition, wellbeing, welfare, soundness, robustness, strength, vigour.
🖙 illness, infirmity.

healthy adj 1 WELL, fit, good, fine, in condition, in good shape, in fine fettle, sound, sturdy, robust, strong, vigorous, hale and hearty, blooming, flourishing, thriving. 2 healthy food: wholesome, nutritious, nourishing, bracing, invigorating, healthful.
🖙 1 ill, sick, infirm.

heap n pile, stack, mound, mountain, lot, mass, accumulation, collection, hoard, stockpile, store.
➤ v pile, stack, mound, bank, build, amass, accumulate, collect, gather, hoard, stockpile, store, load, burden, shower, lavish.

hear v 1 LISTEN, catch, pick up, overhear, eavesdrop, heed, pay attention. 2 LEARN, find out, discover, ascertain, understand, gather. 3 JUDGE, try, examine, investigate.

hearing n 1 EARSHOT, sound, range, reach, ear, perception. 2 TRIAL, inquiry, investigation, inquest, audition, interview, audience.

hearsay n rumour, word of mouth, talk, gossip, tittle-tattle, report, buzz (infml).

heart n 1 SOUL, mind, character, disposition, nature, temperament, feeling,

emotion, sentiment, love, tenderness, compassion, sympathy, pity. 2 lose heart: courage, bravery, boldness, spirit, resolution, determination. 3 CENTRE, middle, core, kernel, nucleus, nub, crux, essence.
🖙 2 cowardice. 3 periphery.
♦ by heart by rote, parrot-fashion, pat, off pat, word for word, verbatim.

> **Parts of the heart include:** aortic valve, ascending aorta, bicuspid valve, carotid artery, descending thoracic aorta, inferior vena cava, left atrium, left pulmonary artery, left pulmonary veins, left ventricle, mitral valve, myocardium, papillary muscle, pulmonary valve, right atrium, right pulmonary artery, right pulmonary veins, right ventricle, superior vena cava, tricuspid valve, ventricular septum.

heartache n sorrow, anxiety, worry, grief, despair, anguish, agony, heartbreak, pain, suffering, despondency, dejection, bitterness, distress, remorse, torment, torture, affliction (fml).

heartbreaking adj distressing, sad, tragic, harrowing, heart-rending, pitiful, agonizing, grievous, bitter, disappointing.
🖙 heartwarming, heartening.

heartbroken adj broken-hearted, desolate, sad, miserable, dejected, despondent, downcast, crestfallen, disappointed, dispirited, grieved, crushed.
🖙 delighted, elated.

hearten v comfort, console, reassure, cheer (up), buck up (infml), encourage, boost, inspire, stimulate, rouse, pep up (infml).
🖙 dishearten, depress, dismay.

heartfelt adj deep, profound, sincere, honest, genuine, earnest, ardent, fervent, wholehearted, warm.
🖙 insincere, false.

heartless adj unfeeling, uncaring, cold, hard, hard-hearted, callous, unkind, cruel, inhuman, brutal, pitiless, merciless.
🖙 kind, considerate, sympathetic, merciful.

heart-rending adj harrowing, heartbreaking, agonizing, pitiful, piteous, pathetic, tragic, sad, distressing, moving, affecting, poignant.

heartwarming adj pleasing, gratifying, satisfying, cheering, heartening,

encouraging, touching, moving, affecting.
■ heartbreaking.

hearty adj **1** ENTHUSIASTIC, wholehearted,
unreserved, heartfelt, sincere, genuine,
warm, friendly, cordial, jovial, cheerful,
ebullient, exuberant, boisterous,
energetic, vigorous. **2** a hearty breakfast:
large, sizable, substantial, filling, ample,
generous.
■ **1** half-hearted, cool, cold.

heat n **1** HOTNESS, warmth, sultriness,
closeness, high temperature, fever.
2 ARDOUR, fervour, fieriness, passion,
intensity, vehemence, fury, excitement,
impetuosity, earnestness, zeal.
■ **1** cold(ness). **2** coolness.
➤ v warm, boil, toast, cook, bake, roast,
reheat, warm up, inflame, excite, animate,
rouse, stimulate, flush, glow.
■ cool, chill.

heated adj angry, furious, raging,
passionate, fiery, stormy, tempestuous,
bitter, fierce, intense, vehement, violent,
frenzied.
■ calm.

heave v **1** PULL, haul, drag, tug, raise, lift,
hitch, hoist, lever, rise, surge. **2** THROW,
fling, hurl, cast, toss, chuck, let fly.
3 RETCH, vomit, throw up (infml), spew.

heaven n sky, firmament, next world,
hereafter, afterlife, paradise, utopia,
ecstasy, rapture, bliss, happiness, joy.
■ hell.

heavenly adj **1** BLISSFUL, wonderful,
glorious, beautiful, lovely, delightful, out of
this world. **2** CELESTIAL, unearthly,
supernatural, spiritual, divine, godlike,
angelic, immortal, sublime, blessed.
■ **1** hellish. **2** infernal.

heavy adj **1** WEIGHTY, hefty, ponderous,
burdensome, cumbersome, awkward,
massive, substantial, large, bulky, hulking,
solid, dense, thick, weighing a ton (infml),
heavy as lead (infml). **2** heavy work: hard,
difficult, tough, arduous, laborious,
strenuous, troublesome, demanding,
taxing, exacting, harsh, severe. **3** SERIOUS,
intense, grave, sombre, deep, profound,
dull, tedious, dry, uninteresting. **4** heavy
fighting; a heavy shower: severe, intense,
extreme, excessive, considerable, strong,
great, immoderate, inordinate. **5** a heavy
blow on the head: forceful, hard, powerful,
strong, intense, sharp, violent. **6** heavy
responsibilities: burdensome, onerous,

unbearable, intolerable, crushing, difficult,
weighty, exacting, irksome, oppressive,
taxing, troublesome, trying, wearisome. **7**
with a heavy heart: sad, miserable,
despondent, depressed, discouraged,
downcast, gloomy, crushed. **8** a heavy
meal: filling, substantial, solid, big, large,
stodgy, indigestible, starchy. **9** tables heavy
with food: laden, loaded, full, burdened,
weighed down, encumbered, groaning. **10**
the weather is heavy: sultry, humid,
oppressive, muggy, close, steamy, sticky. **11**
a heavy sky: dark, cloudy, overcast, dull,
grey, gloomy, leaden.
■ **1** light. **2** easy. **3** light. **4** light. **5**
gentle. **6** light. **8** light. **10** cool, fresh. **11**
bright.

heavy-handed adj clumsy, awkward,
unsubtle, tactless, insensitive, thoughtless,
oppressive, overbearing, domineering,
autocratic.

heckle v barrack, shout down, interrupt,
disrupt, jeer, taunt, pester, gibe, catcall,
bait.

hectic adj busy, frantic, frenetic, chaotic,
fast, feverish, excited, heated, furious,
wild.
■ leisurely.

hedge n hedgerow, screen, windbreak,
barrier, fence, dike, boundary.
➤ v **1** SURROUND, enclose, hem in, confine,
restrict, fortify, guard, shield, protect,
safeguard, cover. **2** STALL, temporize,
equivocate, dodge, sidestep, evade, duck.

hedonism n gratification, luxuriousness,
self-indulgence, sensualism, sensuality,
voluptuousness, pleasure-seeking,
epicureanism, epicurism, dolce vita,
sybaritism.
■ asceticism.

hedonist n pleasure-seeker, sensualist,
voluptuary, epicure, epicurean, bon vivant,
bon viveur, sybarite.
■ ascetic.

heed v listen, pay attention, mind, note,
regard, observe, follow, obey.
■ ignore, disregard.

heedless adj oblivious, unthinking,
careless, negligent, rash, reckless,
inattentive, unobservant, thoughtless,
unconcerned.
■ heedful, mindful, attentive.

hefty adj heavy, weighty, big, large, burly,
hulking, beefy, brawny, strong, powerful,
vigorous, robust, strapping, solid,

substantial, massive, colossal, bulky, unwieldy.
☞ slight, small.

height n 1 HIGHNESS, altitude, elevation, tallness, loftiness, stature. 2 TOP, summit, peak, pinnacle, apex, crest, crown, zenith, apogee, culmination, climax, extremity, maximum, limit, ceiling.
☞ 1 depth.

heighten v raise, elevate, increase, add to, magnify, intensify, strengthen, sharpen, improve, enhance.
☞ lower, decrease, diminish.

heinous adj evil, monstrous, atrocious, abominable, detestable, loathsome, contemptible, despicable, iniquitous, outrageous, shocking, flagrant, vicious, wicked, awful, hideous, villainous, revolting, hateful, odious, infamous, unspeakable, grave, abhorrent (fml), execrable (fml).

heir, heiress n beneficiary, co-heir, inheritor, inheritress, inheritrix, successor, scion, legatee (fml).

hell n 1 heaven and hell: underworld, Hades, inferno, lower regions, nether world, abyss. 2 SUFFERING, anguish, agony, torment, ordeal, nightmare, misery.
☞ 1 heaven.

hellish adj infernal, devilish, diabolical, fiendish, accursed, damnable, monstrous, abominable, atrocious, dreadful.
☞ heavenly.

helm n tiller, wheel, driving seat, reins, saddle, command, control, leadership, direction.

help v 1 AID, assist, lend a hand, serve, be of use, collaborate, co-operate, back, stand by, support. 2 IMPROVE, ameliorate, relieve, alleviate, mitigate, ease, facilitate.
☞ 1 hinder. 2 worsen.
➤ n aid, assistance, collaboration, co-operation, support, advice, guidance, service, use, utility, avail, benefit.
☞ hindrance.

helper n assistant, deputy, auxiliary, subsidiary, attendant, right-hand man, PA, mate, partner, associate, colleague, collaborator, accomplice, ally, supporter, second.

helpful adj 1 USEFUL, practical, constructive, worthwhile, valuable, beneficial, advantageous. 2 a helpful person: co-operative, obliging, neighbourly, friendly, caring, considerate,

kind, sympathetic, supportive.
☞ 1 useless, futile.

helping n serving, portion, share, ration, amount, plateful, piece, dollop (infml).

helpless adj weak, feeble, powerless, dependent, vulnerable, exposed, unprotected, defenceless, abandoned, friendless, destitute, forlorn, incapable, incompetent, infirm, disabled, paralysed.
☞ strong, independent, competent.

hem n edge, border, margin, fringe, trimming.
♦ **hem in** surround, enclose, box in, confine, restrict.

henchman n aide, associate, subordinate, supporter, attendant, follower, right-hand man/woman, minion, bodyguard, lackey, underling, heavy (infml), hit man (infml), hatchet man (infml), crony (infml), minder (infml), sidekick (infml).

henpecked adj dominated, subjugated, browbeaten, bullied, intimidated, meek, timid.
☞ dominant.

herald n messenger, courier, harbinger, forerunner, precursor, omen, token, signal, sign, indication.
➤ v announce, proclaim, broadcast, advertise, publicize, trumpet, pave the way, precede, usher in, show, indicate, promise.

heraldry

Heraldic terms include: shield, crest, mantling, helmet, supporters, field, charge, compartment, motto, dexter, centre, sinister, annulet, fleur-de-lis, martlet, mullet, rampant, passant, sejant, caboched, statant, displayed, couchant, dormant, urinant, volant, chevron, pile, pall, saltire, quarter, orle, bordure, gyronny, lozenge, impale, escutcheon, antelope, camelopard, cockatrice, eagle, griffin, lion, phoenix, unicorn, wivern, addorsed, bezant, blazon, canton, cinquefoil, quatrefoil, roundel, semé, tierced, undee, urdé.

herbs and spices

Herbs and spices include: angelica, anise, basil, bay, bergamot, borage, camomile, catmint, chervil, chives, comfrey, cumin, dill, fennel, garlic, hyssop, lavender, lemon balm, lovage, marjoram, mint, oregano, parsley, rosemary, sage, savory, sorrel, tarragon, thyme; allspice, caper, caraway seeds, cardamon, cayenne pepper, chilli, cinnamon, cloves, coriander, curry, ginger, mace, mustard, nutmeg, paprika, pepper, saffron, sesame, turmeric, vanilla.

herculean *adj* arduous, laborious, onerous, toilsome, demanding, strong, tough, exacting, difficult, enormous, powerful, exhausting, strenuous, tremendous, colossal, large, gigantic, massive, great, huge, mammoth, formidable, daunting, gruelling, heavy, hard.

herd *n* drove, flock, swarm, pack, press, crush, mass, horde, throng, multitude, crowd, mob, the masses, rabble.
➤ *v* **1** FLOCK, congregate, gather, collect, assemble, rally. **2** LEAD, guide, shepherd, round up, drive, force.

here *adv* **1** *come here*: in/to/at this place, present, around, in. **2** *I must finish here*: at this point, at this time, now, at this stage.
🔁 **1** there, away, absent, missing. **2** then.

hereafter *adv* from now on, from this time forward/onwards, hence, henceforth, henceforward, in the future, later, eventually.
➤ *n* afterlife, heaven, paradise, life after death, life to come, next world, elysian fields, happy hunting-ground.

hereditary *adj* inherited, bequeathed, handed down, family, ancestral, inborn, inbred, innate, natural, congenital, genetic.

heresy *n* heterodoxy, unorthodoxy, freethinking, apostasy, dissidence, schism, blasphemy.
🔁 orthodoxy.

heretic *n* freethinker, nonconformist, apostate, dissident, dissenter, revisionist, separatist, schismatic, sectarian, renegade.
🔁 conformist.

heretical *adj* heterodox, unorthodox, freethinking, rationalistic, schismatic, impious, irreverent, iconoclastic, blasphemous.
🔁 orthodox, conventional, conformist.

heritage *n* **1** INHERITANCE, legacy, bequest, endowment, lot, portion, share, birthright, due. **2** HISTORY, past, tradition, culture.

hermetic *adj* airtight, sealed, watertight, shut, hermetical.

hermit *n* recluse, solitary, monk, ascetic, anchorite.

hero *n* **1** *the hero of a play*: protagonist, leading male role/part, leading actor, male lead, lead. **2** *heroes in battle*: conqueror, victor, champion, man/person of courage, cavalier, lion, celebrity, goody (*infml*). **3** IDOL, star, superstar, pin-up, ideal, paragon, celebrity, god, heart-throb (*infml*).
🔁 **1** villain.

heroic *adj* brave, courageous, fearless, dauntless, undaunted, lion-hearted, stout-hearted, valiant, bold, daring, intrepid, adventurous, gallant, chivalrous, noble, selfless.
🔁 cowardly, timid.

heroine *n* **1** *the heroine of a play*: protagonist, leading female role/part, leading actress/lady, female lead, lead, diva, prima donna, prima ballerina. **2** *heroines in battle*: conqueror, victor, champion, woman/person of courage, cavalier, lion, celebrity, goody (*infml*). **3** IDOL, star, superstar, pin-up, ideal, paragon, celebrity, goddess.
🔁 **1** villain.

heroism *n* bravery, courage, valour, boldness, daring, intrepidity, gallantry, prowess, selflessness.
🔁 cowardice, timidity.

hesitant *adj* hesitating, reluctant, half-hearted, uncertain, unsure, indecisive, irresolute, vacillating, wavering, tentative, wary, shy, timid, halting, stammering, stuttering.
🔁 decisive, resolute, confident, fluent.

hesitate *v* pause, delay, wait, be reluctant, be unwilling, think twice, hold back, shrink from, scruple, boggle, demur, vacillate, waver, be uncertain, dither, shilly-shally, falter, stumble, halt, stammer, stutter.
🔁 decide.

hesitation *n* pause, delay, reluctance, unwillingness, hesitance, scruple(s), qualm(s), misgivings, doubt, second thoughts, vacillation, uncertainty, indecision, irresolution, faltering, stumbling, stammering, stuttering.
🔁 eagerness, assurance.

heterogeneous *adj* diverse, varied, miscellaneous, assorted, different, mixed, motley, diversified, divergent, catholic, opposed, unlike, unrelated, dissimilar, contrary, contrasted, discrepant, multiform (*fml*), disparate (*fml*), incongruous (*fml*).
🔁 homogeneous.

hew *v* cut, fell, axe, lop, chop, hack, sever, split, carve, sculpt, sculpture, fashion, model, form, shape, make.

heyday *n* peak, prime, flush, bloom, flowering, golden age, boom time.

hidden *adj* 1 *a hidden door*: concealed, covered, shrouded, veiled, disguised, camouflaged, unseen, secret. 2 OBSCURE, dark, occult, secret, covert, close, cryptic, mysterious, abstruse, mystical, latent, ulterior.
■ 1 showing, apparent. 2 obvious.

hide¹ *v* 1 CONCEAL, cover, cloak, shroud, veil, screen, mask, disguise, camouflage, obscure, shadow, eclipse, bury, stash (*infml*), secrete, withhold, keep dark, suppress. 2 TAKE COVER, shelter, lie low, go to ground, hole up (*infml*).
■ 1 reveal, show, display.

hide² *n* skin, pelt, fell, fur, leather.

hidebound *adj* set, rigid, entrenched, narrow-minded, strait-laced, conventional, ultra-conservative.
■ liberal, progressive.

hideous *adj* ugly, repulsive, grotesque, monstrous, horrid, ghastly, awful, dreadful, frightful, terrible, grim, gruesome, macabre, terrifying, shocking, appalling, disgusting, revolting, horrible.
■ beautiful, attractive.

hideout *n* retreat, hiding-place, hideaway, refuge, sanctuary, shelter, cloister, hermitage, haven, nest, den, lair, hole.

hiding¹ *n* beating, flogging, whipping, caning, spanking, thrashing, walloping (*infml*).

hiding² *n* concealment, cover, veiling, screening, disguise, camouflage.

hiding-place *n* hideaway, hideout, lair, den, hole, hide, cover, refuge, haven, sanctuary, retreat.

hierarchy *n* pecking order, ranking, grading, scale, series, ladder, echelons, strata.

high *adj* 1 TALL, lofty, elevated, soaring, towering. 2 GREAT, strong, powerful, forceful, vigorous, violent, intense, extreme. 3 IMPORTANT, influential, powerful, eminent, distinguished, notable, prominent, chief, top, principal, leading, senior, high-ranking, elevated, exalted. 4 *a higher form of life*: advanced, complex, elaborate, progressive, ultra-modern,

hi-tech. 5 *a high standard*: good, excellent, fine, outstanding, great, perfect, exemplary, commendable, noteworthy, first-class, first-rate, superior, superlative, surpassing, unequalled, unparalleled, select, choice, quality, de luxe, gilt-edged, tiptop, top-class, blue-chip, classy (*infml*). 6 *have a high opinion of someone*: favourable, good, positive, well-disposed, approving, complimentary, admiring, agreeable, appreciative. 7 *high moral principles*: noble, moral, ethical, lofty, virtuous, upright, admirable, honourable, worthy. 8 *a high price*: expensive, dear, costly, exorbitant, excessive, inflated, extortionate, steep (*infml*). 9 HIGH-PITCHED, soprano, treble, falsetto, sharp, shrill, tinny, piping, piercing, penetrating, acute. 10 *high on drugs*: intoxicated, inebriated, hallucinating, turned on (*infml*), having one's mind blown (*infml*), doped (*infml*), on a trip (*infml*), stoned (*infml*), freaked out (*infml*), spaced out (*infml*), wasted (*infml*), zonked (*infml*), wired (*US infml*), bombed (*sl*), loaded (*sl*), blitzed (*sl*), blasted (*sl*), out of it (*sl*). 11 *meat going high*: bad, off, rotting, smelling, decayed, putrid, rancid.
■ 1 low, short. 2 low, slight. 3 unimportant, lowly. 4 low. 5 low, poor, inferior. 6 low, poor, bad. 7 low. 8 cheap. 9 deep, low.
➢ *n* 1 *feeling on a high*: intoxication, inebriation, hallucination, trip (*infml*), turn-on (*infml*), freak-out (*infml*). 2 RECORD, height, summit, peak, top, zenith (*fml*).
■ 1, 2 low.

◆ **high and dry** abandoned, marooned, stranded, helpless, bereft, destitute, ditched (*infml*), dumped (*infml*).

◆ **high and mighty** arrogant, conceited, haughty, overbearing, self-important, snobbish, superior, proud, egotistic, condescending, patronizing, disdainful, cavalier, imperious, overweening, stuck-up (*infml*), swanky (*infml*).

high-born *adj* noble, aristocratic, blue-blooded, thoroughbred.
■ low-born.

highbrow *n* intellectual, egghead (*infml*), scholar, academic.
➢ *adj* intellectual, sophisticated, cultured, cultivated, academic, bookish, brainy (*infml*), deep, serious, classical.
■ low-brow.

high-class *adj* upper-class, posh (*infml*),

classy (*infml*), top-class, top-flight, high-quality, quality, de luxe, superior, excellent, first-rate, choice, select, exclusive.
🗚 ordinary, mediocre.

high-flown *adj* florid, extravagant, exaggerated, elaborate, flamboyant, ostentatious, pretentious, high-standing, grandiose, pompous, bombastic, turgid, artificial, stilted, affected, lofty, highfalutin, la-di-da (*infml*), supercilious.

high-handed *adj* overbearing, domineering, bossy (*infml*), imperious, dictatorial, autocratic, despotic, tyrannical, oppressive, arbitrary.

highlight *n* high point, high spot, peak, climax, best, cream.
➤ *v* underline, emphasize, stress, accentuate, play up, point up, spotlight, illuminate, show up, set off, focus on, feature.

highly *adv* very, greatly, considerably, decidedly, extremely, immensely, tremendously, exceptionally, extraordinarily, enthusiastically, warmly, well.

highly-strung *adj* sensitive, neurotic, nervy, jumpy, edgy, temperamental, excitable, restless, nervous, tense.
🗚 calm.

high-minded *adj* lofty, noble, moral, ethical, principled, idealistic, virtuous, upright, righteous, honourable, worthy.
🗚 immoral, unscrupulous.

high-powered *adj* powerful, forceful, driving, aggressive, dynamic, go-ahead, enterprising, energetic, vigorous.

high-spirited *adj* boisterous, bouncy, exuberant, effervescent, frolicsome, ebullient, sparkling, vibrant, vivacious, lively, energetic, spirited, dashing, bold, daring.
🗚 quiet, sedate.

hijack *v* commandeer, expropriate, skyjack, seize, take over.

hike *v* ramble, walk, trek, tramp, trudge, plod.
➤ *n* ramble, walk, trek, tramp, march.

hilarious *adj* funny, amusing, comical, side-splitting, hysterical (*infml*), uproarious, noisy, rollicking, merry, jolly, jovial.
🗚 serious, grave.

hilarity *n* mirth, laughter, fun, amusement, levity, frivolity, merriment,

jollity, conviviality, high spirits, boisterousness, exuberance, exhilaration.
🗚 seriousness, gravity.

hill *n* 1 HILLOCK, knoll, mound, prominence, eminence, elevation, foothill, down, fell, mountain, height. 2 *a steep hill*: slope, incline, gradient, ramp, rise, ascent, acclivity, drop, descent, declivity.

hilt *n* handle, grip, handgrip, shaft, haft, heft, helve.
♦ **to the hilt** completely, fully, as fully as possible, wholly, entirely, utterly, to the full, to the end, to the maximum extent, in every respect, all the way (*infml*), from first to last (*infml*), from beginning to end (*infml*).

hind *adj* rear, back, hinder, tail, after, posterior, caudal.
🗚 fore.

hinder *v* hamper, obstruct, impede, encumber, handicap, hamstring, hold up, delay, retard, slow down, hold back, check, curb, stop, prevent, frustrate, thwart, oppose.
🗚 help, aid, assist.

hindrance *n* obstruction, impediment, handicap, encumbrance, obstacle, stumbling-block, barrier, bar, check, restraint, restriction, limitation, difficulty, drag, snag, hitch, drawback, disadvantage, inconvenience, deterrent.
🗚 help, aid, assistance.

hinge *v* centre, turn, revolve, pivot, hang, depend, rest.

hint *n* 1 TIP, advice, suggestion, help, clue, inkling, suspicion, tip-off, reminder, indication, sign, pointer, mention, allusion, intimation, insinuation, implication, innuendo. 2 *a hint of garlic*: touch, trace, tinge, taste, dash, soupçon, speck.
➤ *v* suggest, prompt, tip off, indicate, imply, insinuate, intimate, allude, mention.

hire *v* rent, let, lease, charter, commission, book, reserve, employ, take on, sign up, engage, appoint, retain.
🗚 dismiss, fire.
➤ *n* rent, rental, fee, charge, cost, price.

hiss *v* 1 WHISTLE, shrill, whizz, sizzle.
2 JEER, mock, ridicule, deride, boo, hoot.

historian *n* chronicler, archivist, annalist, diarist, narrator, recorder, historiographer, chronologer.

historic *adj* momentous, consequential, important, significant, epoch-making, notable, remarkable, outstanding, extraordinary, celebrated, renowned, famed, famous.

◨ unimportant, insignificant, unknown.

historical *adj* real, actual, authentic, factual, documented, recorded, attested, verifiable.

◨ legendary, fictional.

history *n* **1** PAST, olden days, days of old, antiquity. **2** CHRONICLE, record, annals, archives, chronology, account, narrative, story, tale, saga, biography, life, autobiography, memoirs.

histrionics *n* overacting, theatricality, dramatics, performance, artificiality, insincerity, unnaturalness, sensationalism, staginess, tantrums, scene, affectation (*fml*), ranting and raving (*infml*).

hit *v* **1** STRIKE, knock, tap, smack, slap, thrash, bash, bat, thump, punch, beat, pound, batter, buffet, cuff, box, thrash, whack (*infml*), belt (*infml*), wallop (*infml*), clout (*infml*), biff (*infml*), sock (*infml*), clobber (*infml*), zap (*infml*). **2** BUMP, collide with, bang, crash into, smash into, run into, meet head-on, plough into, damage, harm. **3** AFFECT, have an effect on, upset, disturb, trouble, overwhelm, move, touch, perturb (*fml*), knock for six (*infml*). **4** *the thought hit me*: come to mind, come to, strike, occur to, be remembered, be thought of, dawn on.
➤ *n* **1** STROKE, shot, blow, knock, tap, slap, smack, buffet, thrashing, beating, punch, cuff, box, bash, bump, collision, impact, crash, smash, clout (*infml*), whack (*infml*), belt (*infml*), wallop (*infml*), clobbering (*infml*), biff (*infml*), sock (*infml*). **2** SUCCESS, triumph, winner (*infml*).

◨ **2** failure.

◆ **hit back** retaliate, reciprocate, counter-attack, strike back, criticize in return.

◆ **hit it off** get along with, get on (well) with, be/become friendly with, become friends, warm to, grow to like, relate well to each other, get on good terms with, become thick as thieves (*infml*).

◆ **hit on** realize, arrive at, guess, think of, chance on, stumble on, light on, uncover, discover, invent.

◆ **hit out** lash out, assail, attack, rail, strike out, denounce, condemn, criticize, denounce (*fml*), inveigh (*fml*), vilify (*fml*).

hitch *v* **1** FASTEN, attach, tie, harness, yoke, couple, connect, join, unite. **2** PULL, heave, yank (*infml*), tug, jerk, hoist, hike (up) (*infml*).

◨ **1** unhitch, unfasten.

➤ *n* delay, hold-up, trouble, problem, difficulty, mishap, setback, hiccup, drawback, snag, catch, impediment, hindrance.

hit-or-miss *adj* disorganized, haphazard, indiscriminate, undirected, unplanned, careless, offhand, casual, aimless, random, trial-and-error, perfunctory, lackadaisical, apathetic, cursory, uneven.

◨ directed, planned, organized.

hoard *n* collection, accumulation, mass, heap, pile, fund, reservoir, supply, reserve, store, stockpile, cache, treasure-trove, stash (*infml*).
➤ *v* collect, gather, amass, accumulate, save, put by, lay up, store, stash away (*infml*), stockpile, keep, treasure.

◨ use, spend, squander.

hoarse *adj* husky, croaky, throaty, guttural, gravelly, gruff, growling, rough, harsh, rasping, grating, raucous, discordant.

◨ clear, smooth.

hoary *adj* **1** WHITE-HAIRED, white, grey, grey-haired, silvery, grizzled, venerable, old, aged, ancient, antique, antiquated, canescent (*fml*), senescent (*fml*). **2** *that hoary old joke*: old, familiar, ancient, archaic, old-hat (*infml*).

hoax *n* trick, prank, practical joke, put-on, joke, leg-pull (*infml*), spoof, fake, fraud, deception, bluff, humbug, cheat, swindle, con (*infml*).
➤ *v* trick, deceive, take in, fool, dupe, gull, delude, have on (*infml*), pull someone's leg (*infml*), con (*infml*), swindle, take for a ride (*infml*), cheat, hoodwink, bamboozle (*infml*), bluff.

hobble *v* limp, stumble, falter, stagger, totter, dodder, shuffle.

hobby *n* pastime, diversion, recreation, relaxation, pursuit, sideline.

hoist *v* lift, elevate, raise, erect, jack up, winch up, heave, rear, uplift.
➤ *n* jack, winch, crane, tackle, lift, elevator.

hold *v* **1** GRIP, have in one's hand(s), grasp, clutch, clasp, seize, cling to, embrace, enfold, hug, have, own, possess, keep, retain. **2** *hold a meeting*: run, organize, conduct, carry on, continue, call, summon, convene, assemble, preside over. **3** *hold someone's attention*: keep, engage, occupy, maintain, catch, arrest, absorb, engross, fascinate, enthral, captivate, rivet, fill, monopolize. **4** CONSIDER, regard, judge, reckon, suppose, view, treat, think, believe, maintain, assume, presume, esteem (*fml*), deem (*fml*). **5** BEAR, support, hold up, keep up, sustain, carry, take, buttress, prop up, brace. **6** IMPRISON, detain, confine, impound, hold in custody, lock up, stop, arrest, check, curb, restrain, incarcerate (*fml*). **7** CLING, stick, adhere, stay, remain. **8** *the memories that they held dear*: cherish, treasure, value, prize, hold dear. **9** *the bus holds 53 passengers*: contain, accommodate, take, have a capacity of, comprise. **10** *hold office as prime minister*: occupy, fill, take up, continue, fulfil, have, hold down. **11** *the fine weather will hold*: continue, carry on, last, remain, stay, keep up. **12** *the invitation/theory still holds*: stay, apply, remain, remain valid/true, be in force/operation, hold up.

E3 1 drop. **5** collapse, fall, break. **6** release, free, liberate.

➢ *n* **1** GRIP, grasp, clasp, embrace. **2** INFLUENCE, power, sway, mastery, dominance, authority, control, leverage.

◆ **hold back 1** CONTROL, curb, check, restrain, suppress, stifle, retain, withhold, repress, inhibit. **2** HESITATE, delay, desist, refrain, shrink, refuse.

E3 1 release.

◆ **hold forth** speak, talk, lecture, discourse, orate, preach, declaim.

◆ **hold off 1** FEND OFF, ward off, stave off, keep off, repel, rebuff. **2** PUT OFF, postpone, defer, delay, wait.

◆ **hold out 1** OFFER, give, present, extend. **2** LAST, continue, persist, endure, persevere, stand fast, hang on.

E3 2 give in, yield.

◆ **hold over** defer, postpone, put off, delay, adjourn, suspend, shelve.

◆ **hold up 1** SUPPORT, sustain, brace, shore up, lift, raise. **2** DELAY, detain, retard, slow, hinder, impede.

◆ **hold with** agree with, go along with, approve of, countenance, support, subscribe to, accept.

holder *n* **1** *holders of British passports*: bearer, owner, possessor, proprietor, keeper, custodian, occupant, incumbent. **2** CONTAINER, receptacle, case, housing, cover, sheath, rest, stand.

holdings *n* investments, shares, stocks, securities, bonds, assets, resources, land, real estate, possessions, property, estate, tenure.

hold-up *n* **1** DELAY, wait, hitch, setback, snag, difficulty, trouble, obstruction, stoppage, (traffic) jam, bottleneck. **2** ROBBERY, heist (*sl*), stick-up (*sl*).

hole *n* aperture, opening, orifice, pore, puncture, perforation, eyelet, tear, split, vent, outlet, shaft, slot, gap, breach, break, crack, fissure, fault, defect, flaw, dent, dimple, depression, hollow, cavity, crater, pit, excavation, cavern, cave, chamber, pocket, niche, recess, burrow, nest, lair, retreat.

holiday *n* vacation, recess, leave, time off, day off, break, rest, half-term, bank-holiday, feast-day, festival, celebration, anniversary.

holier-than-thou *adj* self-righteous, sanctimonious, self-satisfied, complacent, self-approving, smug, priggish, pietistic, pious, religiose, unctuous (*fml*), goody-goody (*infml*).

E3 humble, modest, meek.

holiness *n* sacredness, sanctity, spirituality, divinity, piety, devoutness, godliness, saintliness, virtuousness, righteousness, purity.

E3 impiety.

hollow *adj* **1** CONCAVE, indented, depressed, sunken, deep, cavernous, empty, vacant, unfilled. **2** FALSE, artificial, deceptive, insincere, meaningless, empty, vain, futile, fruitless, worthless.

E3 1 solid. **2** real.

➢ *n* hole, pit, well, cavity, crater, excavation, cavern, cave, depression, concavity, basin, bowl, cup, dimple, dent, indentation, groove, channel, trough, valley.

➢ *v* dig, excavate, burrow, tunnel, scoop, gouge, channel, groove, furrow, pit, dent, indent.

holocaust *n* conflagration, flames, inferno, destruction, devastation, annihilation, extermination, extinction, massacre, carnage, mass murder, genocide, ethnic cleansing, sacrifice, slaughter, pogrom, hecatomb, immolation (*fml*).

holy *adj* **1** *holy ground*: sacred, hallowed, consecrated, sanctified, dedicated, blessed, venerated, revered, spiritual, divine, evangelical. **2** PIOUS, religious, devout, godly, God-fearing, saintly, virtuous, good, righteous, faithful, pure, perfect.

E3 1 unsanctified. **2** impious, irreligious.

homage *n* recognition,

acknowledgement, tribute, honour, praise, adulation, admiration, regard, esteem, respect, deference, reverence, adoration, awe, veneration, worship, devotion.

home n residence, domicile, dwelling-place, abode, base, house, pied-à-terre, hearth, fireside, birthplace, home town, home ground, territory, habitat, element.
➤ adj domestic, household, family, internal, local, national, inland.
🖪 foreign, international.
♦ **at home 1** COMFORTABLE, relaxed, at ease. **2** FAMILIAR, knowledgeable, experienced, skilled.

homeland n native land, native country, fatherland, motherland.

homeless adj itinerant, travelling, nomadic, wandering, vagrant, rootless, unsettled, displaced, dispossessed, evicted, exiled, outcast, abandoned, forsaken, destitute, down-and-out.
➤ n travellers, vagabonds, vagrants, tramps, down-and-outs, dossers (sl), squatters.

homely adj homelike, homey, comfortable, cosy, snug, relaxed, informal, friendly, intimate, familiar, everyday, ordinary, domestic, natural, plain, simple, modest, unassuming, unpretentious, unsophisticated, folksy, homespun.
🖪 grand, formal.

homicide n murder, manslaughter, assassination, killing, bloodshed.

homily n sermon, lecture, talk, speech, address, harangue, preaching, discourse (fml), oration (fml), spiel (infml).

homogeneous adj uniform, consistent, unvarying, identical, similar, alike, akin, kindred, analogous, comparable, harmonious, compatible.
🖪 different, heterogeneous.

homosexual n gay, queer (sl), poof (sl), lesbian, dike (sl).
🖪 heterosexual, straight (sl).
➤ adj gay, queer (sl), lesbian.

hone v sharpen, whet, point, edge, grind, file, polish.

honest adj **1** TRUTHFUL, sincere, frank, candid, blunt, outspoken, direct, straight, outright, forthright, straightforward, plain, simple, open, above-board, legitimate, legal, lawful, on the level (infml), fair, just, impartial, objective. **2** LAW-ABIDING, virtuous, upright, ethical, moral, high-minded, scrupulous, honourable,

reputable, respectable, reliable, trustworthy, true, genuine, real.
🖪 dishonest. **2** dishonourable.

honestly adv truly, really, truthfully, sincerely, frankly, directly, outright, plainly, openly, legitimately, legally, lawfully, on the level, fairly, justly, objectively, honourably, in good faith.
🖪 dishonestly, dishonourably.

honesty n **1** TRUTHFULNESS, sincerity, frankness, candour, bluntness, outspokenness, straightforwardness, plain-speaking, explicitness, openness, legitimacy, legality, equity, fairness, justness, objectivity, even-handedness. **2** VIRTUE, uprightness, honour, integrity, morality, scrupulousness, trustworthiness, genuineness, veracity.
🖪 **1** dishonesty.

honorary adj unpaid, unofficial, titular, nominal, in name only, honorific, formal.
🖪 paid.

honour n **1** REPUTATION, good name, repute, renown, distinction, esteem, regard, respect, credit, dignity, self-respect, pride, integrity, morality, decency, rectitude, probity. **2** AWARD, accolade, commendation, acknowledgement, recognition, tribute, privilege. **3** PRAISE, acclaim, homage, admiration, reverence, worship, adoration.
🖪 **1** dishonour, disgrace.
➤ v **1** PRAISE, acclaim, exalt, glorify, pay homage to, decorate, crown, celebrate, commemorate, remember, admire, esteem, respect, revere, worship, prize, value. **2** honour a promise: keep, observe, respect, fulfil, carry out, discharge, execute, perform.
🖪 **1** dishonour, disgrace.

honourable adj great, eminent, distinguished, renowned, respected, worthy, prestigious, trusty, reputable, respectable, virtuous, upright, upstanding, straight, honest, trustworthy, true, sincere, noble, high-minded, principled, moral, ethical, fair, just, right, proper, decent.
🖪 dishonourable, unworthy, dishonest.

hoodwink v deceive, dupe, fool, take in, delude, bamboozle (infml), have on (infml), mislead, hoax, trick, cheat, con (infml), rook, gull, swindle.

hook n crook, sickle, peg, barb, trap, snare, catch, fastener, clasp, hasp.
➤ v **1** BEND, crook, curve, curl. **2** CATCH,

capture, bag, grab, trap, snare, ensnare, entangle. **3** FASTEN, clasp, hitch, fix, secure.

hooligan *n* ruffian, rowdy, hoodlum, mobster, bovver boy (*sl*), thug, tough, lout, yob (*sl*), vandal, delinquent.

hoop *n* ring, circle, round, loop, wheel, band, girdle, circlet.

hoot *n*, *v* call, cry, shout, shriek, whoop, toot, beep, whistle, boo, jeer, laugh, howl.

hop *v* jump, leap, spring, bound, vault, skip, dance, prance, frisk, limp, hobble.
➤ *n* jump, leap, spring, bound, vault, bounce, step, skip, dance.

hope *n* hopefulness, optimism, ambition, aspiration, wish, desire, longing, dream, expectation, anticipation, prospect, promise, belief, confidence, assurance, conviction, faith.
◼ pessimism, despair.
➤ *v* aspire, wish, desire, long, expect, await, look forward, anticipate, contemplate, foresee, believe, trust, rely, reckon on, assume.
◼ despair.

hopeful *adj* **1** OPTIMISTIC, bullish (*infml*), confident, assured, expectant, sanguine, cheerful, buoyant. **2** *a hopeful sign*: encouraging, heartening, reassuring, favourable, auspicious, promising, rosy, bright.
◼ **1** pessimistic, despairing.
2 discouraging.

hopefully *adv* **1** *hopefully the weather will improve*: I hope, if all goes well, with luck, all being well, probably, conceivably, it is to be hoped that. **2** EXPECTANTLY, with hope, with anticipation, confidently, eagerly, optimistically, expectedly, sanguinely, bullishly (*infml*).

hopeless *adj* **1** PESSIMISTIC, defeatist, negative, despairing, demoralized, downhearted, dejected, despondent, forlorn, wretched. **2** UNATTAINABLE, unachievable, impracticable, impossible, vain, foolish, futile, useless, pointless, worthless, poor, helpless, lost, irremediable, irreparable, incurable.
◼ **1** hopeful, optimistic. **2** curable.

horde *n* band, gang, pack, herd, drove, flock, swarm, crowd, mob, throng, multitude, host.

horizon *n* skyline, vista, prospect, compass, range, scope, perspective.

horizontal *adj* level, flat, plane, smooth, levelled, on its side, supine (*fml*).

horrible *adj* unpleasant, disagreeable, nasty, unkind, horrid, disgusting, revolting, offensive, repulsive, hideous, grim, ghastly, awful, dreadful, frightful, fearful, terrible, abominable, shocking, appalling, horrific.
◼ pleasant, agreeable, lovely, attractive.

horrid *adj* **1** HORRIFIC, shocking, appalling, horrifying, terrifying, frightening, harrowing, bloodcurdling, hair-raising, terrible, dreadful, frightful, repulsive, revolting, abominable, grim, hideous, gruesome, ghastly, awful. **2** UNKIND, mean, nasty, awful, cruel, dreadful, obnoxious, hateful, beastly (*infml*).
◼ **1, 2** lovely, pleasant.

horrific *adj* horrifying, shocking, appalling, awful, dreadful, ghastly, gruesome, terrifying, frightening, scary, harrowing, bloodcurdling.

horrify *v* shock, outrage, scandalize, appal, disgust, sicken, dismay, alarm, startle, scare, frighten, terrify.
◼ please, delight.

horror *n* **1** *recoil in horror*: shock, outrage, disgust, revulsion, repugnance, abhorrence, loathing, dismay, consternation, alarm, fright, fear, terror, panic, dread, apprehension. **2** GHASTLINESS, awfulness, frightfulness, hideousness.
◼ **1** approval, delight.

horse *n* steed, mount, stallion, nag, mustang, mare, colt, filly, bay, sorrel, roan, hack, bronc(h)o, charger, cob, dobbin, hackney, centaur.

The parts of a horse are: back, breast, cannon, chestnut, crest of the neck, croup/crupper/rump, ear, elbow, eye, face, fetlock, forearm, forefoot, forehead, forelock, gaskin, haunch, head, hind leg, hip, hock, hoof, knee, loins, lower jaw, lower/under lip, mane, mouth, neck, nose, nostril, pastern, root/dock of the tail, shoulder, spur vein, stifle (joint), tail, throat, upper lip, withers.

Breeds of horse include: Akhal-Teké, Alter-Réal, American Quarter Horse, American Saddle Horse, American Trotter, Andalusian, Anglo-Arab, Anglo-Norman, Appaloosa, Arab, Ardennias, Auxois, Barb, Bavarian Warmblood, Boulonnais, Brabannçon, Breton, British Warmblood,

Brumby, Budyonny, Calabrese, Charollais
Halfbred, Cleveland Bay, Clydesdale, Comtois,
Criollo, Danubian, Døle Gudbrandsdal, Døle
Trotter, Don, Dutch Draught, East Bulgarian,
East Friesian, Einsiedler, Finnish,
Frederiksborg, Freiberger, French Saddle
Horse, French Trotter, Friesian, Furioso,
Gelderland, German Trotter, Groningen,
Hanoverian, Hispano, Holstein, Iomud, Irish
Draught, Irish Hunter, Italian Heavy Draught,
Jutland, Kabardin, Karabair, Karabakh,
Kladruber, Knabstrup, Kustanair, Latvian
Harness Horse, Limousin Halfbred,
Lipizzaner, Lithuanian Heavy Draught, Lokai,
Lusitano, Mangalarga, Maremmana,
Masuren, Mecklenburg, Metis Trotter, Morgan,
Muraköz, Murgese, Mustang, New Kirgiz,
Nonius, North Swedish, Oldenburg, Orlov
Trotter, Palomino, Paso Fino, Percheron,
Peruvian Stepping Horse, Pinto, Pinzgauer
Noriker, Plateau Persian, Poitevin, Rhineland
Heavy Draught, Russian Heavy Draught,
Salerno, Sardinian, Shagya Arab, Shire,
Suffolk Punch, Swedish Halfbred,
Tchenaran, Tennessee Walking Horse, Tersky,
Thoroughbred, Toric, Trait du Nord, Trakehner,
Vladimir Heavy Draught, Waler, Welsh Cob,
Württemberg.

Breeds of pony include: Connemara,
Dales, Dartmoor, Exmoor, Falabella, Fell,
Hackney, Highland, New Forest, Przewalski's
Horse, Shetland, Welsh Mountain Pony,
Welsh Pony.

horseman, horsewoman n
equestrian, rider, jockey, cavalryman,
hussar.

horseplay n clowning, buffoonery,
foolery, tomfoolery, skylarking, pranks,
capers, high jinks, fun and games, rough-
and-tumble.

hospitable adj friendly, sociable,
welcoming, receptive, cordial, amicable,
congenial, convivial, genial, kind,
gracious, generous, liberal.
🔁 inhospitable, unfriendly, hostile.

hospitality n friendliness, sociability,
welcome, accommodation, entertainment,
conviviality, warmth, cheer, generosity,
open-handedness.
🔁 unfriendliness.

host¹ n 1 COMPÈRE, master of ceremonies,
presenter, announcer, anchorman,
anchorwoman, linkman. 2 PUBLICAN,
innkeeper, landlord, proprietor.

➤ v present, introduce, compère.

host² n multitude, myriad, array, army,
horde, crowd, throng, swarm, pack,
band.

hostage n prisoner, captive, pawn, surety,
security, pledge.

hostel n youth hostel, residence,
dosshouse (sl), boarding-house, guest-
house, hotel, inn.

hostile adj belligerent, warlike, ill-
disposed, unsympathetic, unfriendly,
inhospitable, inimical, antagonistic,
opposed, adverse, unfavourable, contrary,
opposite.
🔁 friendly, welcoming, favourable.

hostilities n war, warfare, battle, fighting,
conflict, strife, bloodshed.

hostility n opposition, aggression,
belligerence, enmity, estrangement,
antagonism, animosity, ill-will, malice,
resentment, hate, hatred, dislike, aversion,
abhorrence.
🔁 friendliness, friendship.

hot adj 1 WARM, heated, fiery, burning,
scalding, scorching, blistering, red hot,
roasting, baking, boiling, piping, steaming,
sizzling, sweltering, parching, searing,
sultry, torrid, tropical. 2 SPICY, peppery,
piquant, sharp, pungent, strong, fiery. 3
FEVERISH, delirious, burning, flushed, red,
with a temperature. 4 his hot temper: fiery,
furious, angry, indignant, raging, boiling,
seething, fuming, livid, violent, heated,
inflamed, incensed, enraged. 5 hot
competition: fierce, intense, strong, furious,
keen, cut-throat. 6 not very hot on the idea:
keen, enthusiastic, eager, warm, earnest,
zealous, diligent, devoted. 7 hot news: recent, new, fresh, latest, up-to-date, exciting. 8 hot goods: illegally obtained/
imported, contraband, stolen, pilfered, ill-
gotten.
🔁 1 cold, cool, chilly. 2 mild, bland. 4 calm.
7 old, stale.

hot-blooded adj temperamental,
excitable, spirited, wild, rash, impulsive,
impetuous, high-spirited, heated, fervent,
fiery, bold, eager, ardent, passionate,
lustful, sensual, lusty, perfervid (fml),
precipitate (fml).
🔁 cool, dispassionate.

hotchpotch n mishmash, medley,
miscellany, collection, mix, mixture,
jumble, confusion, mess.

hotel n boarding-house, guest-house,

pension, motel, inn, public house, pub (*infml*), hostel.

hotheaded *adj* headstrong, impetuous, impulsive, hasty, rash, reckless, fiery, volatile, hot-tempered, quick-tempered. ⊟ cool, calm.

hothouse *n* greenhouse, glasshouse, conservatory, orangery, vinery.

hound *v* chase, pursue, hunt (down), drive, goad, prod, chivvy, nag, pester, badger, harry, harass, persecute.

house *n* 1 BUILDING, dwelling, residence, home. 2 DYNASTY, family, clan, tribe.

> Types of house include: semi-detached, semi (*infml*), detached, terraced, town-house, council house, cottage, thatched cottage, prefab (*infml*), pied-à-terre, bungalow, chalet bungalow; flat, bedsit, apartment, studio, maisonette, penthouse, granny flat, duplex (*US*), condominium (*US*); manor, hall, lodge, grange, villa, mansion, rectory, vicarage, parsonage, manse, croft, farmhouse, homestead, ranchhouse, chalet, log cabin, shack, shanty, hut, igloo, hacienda.

> *v* 1 LODGE, quarter, billet, board, accommodate, put up, take in, shelter, harbour. 2 HOLD, contain, protect, cover, sheathe, place, keep, store.

household *n* family, family circle, house, home, ménage, establishment, set-up.
> *adj* domestic, home, family, ordinary, plain, everyday, common, familiar, well-known, established.

householder *n* resident, tenant, occupier, occupant, owner, landlady, freeholder, leaseholder, proprietor, landlord, home-owner, head of the household.

housekeeping *n* home economics, domestic science, household management, running a home, domestic work/matters, homemaking, housewifery.

housing *n* 1 ACCOMMODATION, houses, homes, dwellings, habitation, shelter. 2 CASING, case, container, holder, covering, cover, sheath, protection.

hovel *n* shack, shanty, cabin, hut, shed, dump, hole (*infml*).

hover *v* 1 HANG, poise, float, drift, fly, flutter, flap. 2 *he hovered by the door*: pause, linger, hang about, hesitate, waver, fluctuate, seesaw.

however *conj* nevertheless, nonetheless, still, yet, even so, notwithstanding (*fml*), though, anyhow.

howl *n*, *v* wail, cry, shriek, scream, shout, yell, roar, bellow, bay, yelp, hoot, moan, groan.

hub *n* centre, middle, focus, focal point, axis, pivot, linchpin, nerve centre, core, heart.

hubbub *n* noise, racket, din, clamour, commotion, disturbance, riot, uproar, hullabaloo, rumpus, confusion, disorder, tumult, hurly-burly, chaos, pandemonium. ⊟ peace, quiet.

huddle *n* 1 CLUSTER, clump, knot, mass, crowd, muddle, jumble. 2 CONCLAVE, conference, meeting.
> *v* cluster, gravitate, converge, meet, gather, congregate, crowd, flock, throng, press, cuddle, snuggle, nestle, curl up, crouch, hunch.
⊟ disperse.

hue *n* colour, shade, tint, dye, tinge, nuance, tone, complexion, aspect, light.

hue and cry *n* furore, fuss, hullabaloo, outcry, rumpus, uproar, brouhaha, clamour, ado, chase, ruction (*infml*), to-do (*infml*).

huff *n* pique, sulks, mood, bad mood, anger, rage, passion.

hug *v* embrace, cuddle, squeeze, enfold, hold, clasp, clutch, grip, cling to, enclose.
> *n* embrace, cuddle, squeeze, clasp, hold, clinch.

huge *adj* immense, vast, enormous, massive, colossal, titanic, giant, gigantic, mammoth, monumental, tremendous, great, big, large, bulky, unwieldy. ⊟ tiny, minute.

hulk *n* 1 WRECK, shipwreck, remains, derelict, frame, hull, shell. 2 LOUT, lump, lubber, oaf, clod (*infml*).

hulking *adj* massive, heavy, unwieldy, bulky, awkward, ungainly. ⊟ small, delicate.

hull *n* body, frame, framework, structure, casing, covering.

hullabaloo *n* fuss, palaver, to-do (*infml*), outcry, furore, hue and cry, uproar, pandemonium, rumpus, disturbance, commotion, hubbub. ⊟ calm, peace.

hum *v* buzz, whirr, purr, drone, thrum, croon, sing, murmur, mumble, throb, pulse, vibrate.

➤ *n* buzz, whirr, purring, drone, murmur, mumble, throb, pulsation, vibration.

human *adj* **1** MORTAL, fallible, susceptible, reasonable, rational. **2** KIND, considerate, understanding, humane, compassionate.
ᴇᴀ 2 inhuman.
➤ *n* human being, mortal, homo sapiens, man, woman, child, person, individual, body, soul.

humane *adj* kind, compassionate, sympathetic, understanding, kind-hearted, good-natured, gentle, tender, loving, mild, lenient, merciful, forgiving, forbearing, kindly, benevolent, charitable, humanitarian, good.
ᴇᴀ inhumane, cruel.

humanitarian *adj* benevolent, charitable, philanthropic, public-spirited, compassionate, humane, altruistic, unselfish.
ᴇᴀ selfish, self-seeking.
➤ *n* philanthropist, benefactor, good Samaritan, do-gooder, altruist.
ᴇᴀ egoist, self-seeker.

humanity *n* **1** HUMAN RACE, humankind, mankind, womankind, mortality, people. **2** HUMANENESS, kindness, compassion, fellow-feeling, understanding, tenderness, benevolence, generosity, goodwill.
ᴇᴀ 2 inhumanity.

humanize *v* domesticate, tame, civilize, cultivate, educate, enlighten, edify, improve, better, polish, refine.

humble *adj* **1** MEEK, submissive, unassertive, self-effacing, polite, respectful, deferential, servile, subservient, sycophantic, obsequious. **2** LOWLY, low, mean, insignificant, unimportant, common, commonplace, ordinary, plain, simple, modest, unassuming, unpretentious, unostentatious.
ᴇᴀ 1 proud, assertive. **2** important, pretentious.
➤ *v* bring down, lower, bring low, abase, demean, sink, discredit, disgrace, shame, humiliate, mortify, chasten, crush, deflate, subdue.
ᴇᴀ exalt.

humbug *n* **1** DECEPTION, pretence, sham, found, swindle, trick, hoax, deceit, trickery. **2** NONSENSE, rubbish, baloney (*sl*), bunkum (*infml*), claptrap (*infml*), eye-wash (*infml*), bluff, cant, hypocrisy.

humdrum *adj* boring, tedious, monotonous, routine, dull, dreary, uninteresting, uneventful, ordinary, mundane, everyday, commonplace.
ᴇᴀ lively, unusual, exceptional.

humid *adj* damp, moist, dank, clammy, sticky, muggy, sultry, steamy.
ᴇᴀ dry.

humiliate *v* mortify, embarrass, confound, crush, break, deflate, chasten, shame, disgrace, discredit, degrade, demean, humble, bring low.
ᴇᴀ dignify, exalt.

humiliating *adj* humbling, mortifying, shaming, crushing, chastening, deflating, degrading, embarrassing, disgraceful, ignominious, inglorious, disgracing, snubbing, discomfiting (*fml*), humiliant (*fml*), humiliative (*fml*), humiliatory (*fml*).
ᴇᴀ gratifying, triumphant.

humiliation *n* mortification, embarrassment, shame, disgrace, dishonour, ignominy, abasement, deflation, put-down (*infml*), snub, rebuff, affront.
ᴇᴀ gratification, triumph.

humility *n* meekness, submissiveness, deference, self-abasement, servility, humbleness, lowliness, modesty, unpretentiousness.
ᴇᴀ pride, arrogance, assertiveness.

humorist *n* wit, satirist, comedian, comic, joker, wag, jester, clown.

humorous *adj* funny, amusing, comic, entertaining, witty, satirical, jocular, facetious, playful, waggish, droll, whimsical, comical, farcical, zany (*infml*), ludicrous, absurd, hilarious, side-splitting.
ᴇᴀ serious, humourless.

humour *n* **1** WIT, drollery, jokes, jesting, badinage, repartee, facetiousness, satire, comedy, farce, fun, amusement. **2** *in a bad humour*: mood, temper, frame of mind, spirits, disposition, temperament.
➤ *v* go along with, comply with, accommodate, gratify, indulge, pamper, spoil, favour, please, mollify, flatter.

humourless *adj* boring, tedious, dull, dry, solemn, serious, glum, morose.
ᴇᴀ humorous, witty.

hump *n* hunch, lump, knob, bump, projection, protuberance, bulge, swelling, mound, prominence.

hunch *n* premonition, presentiment, intuition, suspicion, feeling, impression, idea, guess.

➤ *v* hump, bend, curve, arch, stoop, crouch, squat, huddle, draw in, curl up.

hunger *n* **1** HUNGRINESS, emptiness, starvation, malnutrition, famine, appetite, ravenousness, voracity, greed, greediness. **2** *hunger for power*: desire, craving, longing, yearning, itch, thirst.
➤ *v* starve, want, wish, desire, crave, hanker, long, yearn, pine, ache, itch, thirst.

hungry *adj* **1** STARVING, underfed, undernourished, peckish (*infml*), empty, hollow, famished, ravenous, greedy. **2** *hungry for knowledge*: desirous, craving, longing, aching, thirsty, eager, avid.
🖛 **1** satisfied, full.

hunk *n* chunk, lump, piece, block, slab, wedge, mass, clod.

hunt *v* **1** CHASE, pursue, hound, dog, stalk, track, trail. **2** SEEK, look for, search, scour, rummage, forage, investigate.
➤ *n* chase, pursuit, search, quest, investigation.

hunter *n* huntsman, chaser, chasseur, woodman, woodsman, jäger, montero, venator, venerer.

hurdle *n* jump, fence, wall, hedge, barrier, barricade, obstacle, obstruction, stumbling-block, hindrance, impediment, handicap, problem, snag, difficulty, complication.

hurl *v* throw, toss, fling, sling, catapult, project, propel, fire, launch, send.

hurly-burly *n* bustle, hustle, commotion, confusion, trouble, disorder, disruption, unrest, pandemonium, uproar, chaos, furore, upheaval, tumult, turbulence, turmoil, frenzy, distraction, agitation, hubbub, brouhaha, bedlam, hassle (*infml*).

hurricane *n* gale, tornado, typhoon, cyclone, whirlwind, squall, storm, tempest.

hurried *adj* rushed, hectic, hasty, precipitate, speedy, quick, swift, rapid, passing, brief, short, cursory, superficial, shallow, careless, slapdash.
🖛 leisurely.

hurry *v* rush, dash, fly, get a move on (*infml*), hasten, quicken, speed up, hustle, push.
🖛 slow down, delay.
➤ *n* rush, haste, quickness, speed, urgency, hustle, bustle, flurry, commotion.
🖛 leisureliness, calm.

hurt *v* **1** *my leg hurts*: ache, pain, throb, sting. **2** INJURE, wound, maltreat, ill-treat,

bruise, cut, burn, torture, maim, disable. **3** DAMAGE, impair, harm, mar, spoil. **4** UPSET, sadden, grieve, distress, afflict, offend, annoy.
➤ *n* pain, soreness, discomfort, suffering, injury, wound, damage, harm, distress, sorrow.
➤ *adj* **1** INJURED, wounded, bruised, grazed, cut, scarred, maimed. **2** UPSET, sad, saddened, distressed, aggrieved, annoyed, offended, affronted.

hurtful *adj* **1** UPSETTING, wounding, vicious, cruel, mean, unkind, nasty, malicious, spiteful, catty, derogatory, scathing, cutting. **2** HARMFUL, damaging, injurious, pernicious, destructive.
🖛 **1** kind.

hurtle *v* dash, tear, race, fly, shoot, speed, rush, charge, plunge, dive, crash, rattle.

husband *n* spouse, partner, mate, better half, hubby (*infml*), groom, married man.

husbandry *n* **1** FARMING, agriculture, cultivation, tillage, land management, farm management, conservation, agribusiness (*fml*), agronomics (*fml*), agronomy (*fml*). **2** MANAGEMENT, saving, thrift, thriftiness, frugality, economy, good housekeeping.
🖛 **2** wastefulness, squandering.

hush *v* quieten, silence, still, settle, compose, calm, soothe, subdue.
🖛 disturb, rouse.
➤ *n* quietness, silence, peace, stillness, repose, calm, calmness, tranquillity, serenity.
🖛 noise, clamour.
➤ *interj* quiet, hold your tongue, shut up, not another word.
◆ **hush up** keep dark, suppress, conceal, cover up, stifle, gag.
🖛 publicize.

hush-hush *adj* secret, confidential, classified, restricted, under wraps (*infml*), top-secret.
🖛 open, public.

husk *n* covering, case, shell, pod, hull, rind, bran, chaff.

husky *adj* hoarse, croaky, croaking, low, throaty, guttural, gruff, rasping, rough, harsh.

hustle *v* hasten, rush, hurry, bustle, force, push, shove, thrust, bundle, elbow, jostle.

hut *n* cabin, shack, shanty, booth, shed, lean-to, shelter, den.

hybrid *n* cross, crossbreed, half-breed,

mongrel, composite, combination, mixture, amalgam, compound.
➤ *adj* crossbred, mongrel, composite, combined, mixed, heterogeneous, compound.
Ea pure-bred.

hygiene *n* sanitariness, sanitation, sterility, disinfection, cleanliness, purity, wholesomeness.
Ea insanitariness.

hygienic *adj* sanitary, sterile, aseptic, germ-free, disinfected, clean, pure, salubrious, healthy, wholesome.
Ea unhygienic, insanitary.

hymn *n* song of praise, song, chorus, spiritual, psalm, anthem, carol, chant, cantata, canticle, motet, doxology, introit, choral(e), offertory, paean, paraphrase.

hype *n* publicity, advertisement, advertising, promotion, puffing, ballyhoo, build-up, racket, fuss, plugging (*infml*), razzmatazz (*infml*).
➤ *v* promote, publicize, advertise, build up, plug (*infml*).

hyperbole *n* overstatement, exaggeration, magnification, extravagance.
Ea understatement.

hypnotic *adj* mesmerizing, soporific, sleep-inducing, spellbinding, fascinating, compelling, irresistible, magnetic.

hypnotism *n* hypnosis, mesmerism, suggestion.

hypnotize *v* mesmerize, spellbind, bewitch, enchant, entrance, fascinate, captivate, magnetize.

hypocrisy *n* insincerity, double-talk, double-dealing, falsity, deceit, deception, pretence.
Ea sincerity.

hypocrite *n* deceiver, fraud, impostor, pretender, mountebank, Pharisee, canter, charlatan, whited sepulchre, Holy Willie, dissembler (*fml*), phoney (*infml*), pseud (*infml*), pseudo (*infml*).

hypocritical *adj* insincere, two-faced, self-righteous, double-dealing, false, hollow, deceptive, spurious, deceitful, dissembling, pharisaic(al).
Ea sincere, genuine.

hypothesis *n* theory, thesis, premise, postulate, proposition, supposition, conjecture, speculation.

hypothetical *adj* theoretical, imaginary, supposed, assumed, proposed, conjectural, speculative.
Ea real, actual.

hysteria *n* agitation, frenzy, panic, hysterics, neurosis, mania, madness.
Ea calm, composure.

hysterical *adj* 1 FRANTIC, frenzied, berserk, uncontrollable, mad, raving, crazed, demented, overwrought, neurotic. 2 (*infml*) HILARIOUS, uproarious, side-splitting, priceless (*infml*), rich (*infml*).
Ea 1 calm, composed, self-possessed.

ice n frost, rime, icicle, glacier, iciness, frostiness, coldness, chill.
➤ v freeze, refrigerate, chill, cool, frost, glaze.

ice-cold adj frozen, iced, chilled, icy, frosty, icebound, arctic, bitterly cold, raw, polar, glacial, Siberian, frigid, freezing, numb, hard, frosted, solidified, stiff, frozen-stiff.
☒ warm, hot.

icon n idol, portrait, image, representation, symbol.

icy adj 1 ICE-COLD, arctic, polar, glacial, freezing, frozen, raw, bitter, biting, cold, chill, chilly. 2 icy roads: frosty, slippery, glassy, frozen, icebound, frostbound. 3 HOSTILE, cold, stony, cool, indifferent, aloof, distant, formal.
☒ 1 hot. 3 friendly, warm.

idea n 1 THOUGHT, concept, notion, theory, hypothesis, guess, conjecture, belief, opinion, view, viewpoint, judgement, conception, vision, image, impression, perception, interpretation, understanding, inkling, suspicion, clue. 2 a good idea: brainwave, suggestion, proposal, proposition, recommendation, plan, scheme, design. 3 AIM, intention, purpose, reason, point, object.

ideal n perfection, epitome, acme, paragon, exemplar, example, model, pattern, archetype, prototype, type, image, criterion, standard.
➤ adj 1 PERFECT, dream, utopian, best, optimum, optimal, supreme, highest, model, archetypal. 2 UNREAL, imaginary, theoretical, hypothetical, unattainable, impractical, idealistic.

idealist n perfectionist, romantic, visionary, dreamer, optimist.
☒ realist, pragmatist.

idealistic adj perfectionist, utopian, visionary, romantic, quixotic, starry-eyed, optimistic, unrealistic, impractical, impracticable.
☒ realistic, pragmatic.

idealize v utopianize, romanticize, glamorize, glorify, exalt, worship, idolize.
☒ caricature.

ideally adv perfectly, in a perfect world, in an ideal world, at best, in theory, theoretically, hypothetically.

identical adj same, self-same, indistinguishable, interchangeable, twin, duplicate, like, alike, corresponding, matching, equal, equivalent.
☒ different.

identification n 1 RECOGNITION, detection, diagnosis, naming, labelling, classification. 2 EMPATHY, association, involvement, rapport, relationship, sympathy, fellow-feeling. 3 IDENTITY CARD, documents, papers, credentials.

identify v recognize, know, pick out, single out, distinguish, perceive, make out, discern, notice, detect, diagnose, name, label, tag, specify, pinpoint, place, catalogue, classify.
◆ **identify with** empathize with, relate to, associate with, respond to, sympathize with, feel for.

identity n 1 INDIVIDUALITY, particularity, singularity, uniqueness, self, personality, character, existence. 2 SAMENESS, likeness.

ideology n philosophy, world-view, ideas, principles, tenets, doctrine(s), convictions, belief(s), faith, creed, dogma.

idiocy n folly, stupidity, silliness, senselessness, lunacy.
☒ wisdom, sanity.

idiom n phrase, expression, colloquialism, language, turn of phrase, phraseology, style, usage, jargon, vernacular.

idiomatic adj colloquial, everyday, vernacular, native, grammatical, correct, dialectal, dialectical, idiolectal.
☒ unidiomatic.

idiosyncrasy n characteristic, peculiarity, singularity, oddity, eccentricity, freak, quirk, habit, mannerism, trait, feature.

idiosyncratic adj personal, individual, characteristic, distinctive, peculiar, singular, odd, eccentric, quirky.
☒ general, common.

idiot *n* fool, imbecile, fat-head, dunce, dimwit, simpleton, halfwit, cretin, clown, ignoramus, thickhead (*infml*), numskull (*infml*), nincompoop (*infml*), ass (*infml*), chump (*infml*), ninny (*infml*), clot (*infml*), dope (*infml*), twit (*infml*), nitwit (*infml*), nit (*infml*), sucker (*infml*), mug (*infml*), twerp (*infml*), birdbrain (*infml*), jerk (*sl*), nerd (*sl*), wally (*sl*), dumbo (*sl*), pillock (*sl*), prat (*sl*), dork (*sl*), geek (*sl*), plonker (*sl*), prick (*sl*).

idiotic *adj* foolish, stupid, senseless, silly, absurd, ridiculous, ludicrous, nonsensical, unwise, ill-advised, ill-considered, short-sighted, half-baked, crazy, mad, insane, moronic, hare-brained, half-witted, simple-minded, simple, ignorant, unintelligent, inept, inane, pointless, unreasonable, fatuous (*fml*), risible (*fml*), injudicious (*fml*), thick-headed (*infml*), daft (*infml*), crack-brained (*infml*), dumb (*infml*), dotty (*infml*), potty (*infml*), batty (*infml*), barmy (*infml*), nutty (*infml*).
₣ sensible, sane.

idle *adj* **1** INACTIVE, inoperative, unused, unoccupied, unemployed, jobless, redundant. **2** LAZY, work-shy, indolent. **3** *idle talk*: empty, trivial, casual, futile, vain, pointless, unproductive.
₣ **1** active. **2** busy.
➢ *v* do nothing, laze, lounge, take it easy, kill time, potter, loiter, dawdle, fritter, waste, loaf, slack, skive (*infml*).
₣ work.

idol *n* icon, effigy, image, graven image, god, deity, fetish, favourite, darling, hero, heroine, pin-up.

idolatry *n* worshipping, admiration, reverence, adoration, adulation, deification, exaltation, glorification, hero-worship, idolizing, idolism, iconolatry, icon worship, paganism, heathenism, fetishism.
₣ vilification.

idolize *v* hero-worship, lionize, exalt, glorify, worship, venerate, revere, admire, adore, love, dote on.
₣ despise.

idyllic *adj* perfect, idealized, heavenly, delightful, charming, picturesque, pastoral, rustic, unspoiled, peaceful, happy.
₣ unpleasant.

if *conj* in the event of, in case of, on condition that, as/so long as, provided, providing, assuming (that), supposing (that).

ignite *v* set fire to, set alight, catch fire, flare up, burn, conflagrate, fire, kindle, touch off, spark off.
₣ quench.

ignoble *adj* low, mean, petty, base, vulgar, wretched, contemptible, despicable, vile, heinous, infamous, disgraceful, dishonourable, shameless.
₣ noble, worthy, honourable.

ignominious *adj* humiliating, mortifying, degrading, undignified, shameful, dishonourable, disreputable, disgraceful, despicable, scandalous.
₣ triumphant, honourable.

ignorance *n* unintelligence, illiteracy, unawareness, unconsciousness, oblivion, unfamiliarity, inexperience, innocence, naïvety.
₣ knowledge, wisdom.

ignorant *adj* uneducated, illiterate, unread, untaught, untrained, inexperienced, stupid, clueless (*infml*), uninitiated, unenlightened, uninformed, ill-informed, unwitting, unaware, unconscious, oblivious.
₣ educated, knowledgeable, clever, wise.

ignore *v* disregard, take no notice of, shut one's eyes to, overlook, pass over, neglect, omit, reject, snub, cold-shoulder.
₣ notice, observe.

ill *adj* **1** SICK, poorly, unwell, laid up, ailing, off-colour, seedy, queasy, diseased, unhealthy, infirm, frail, weak, feeble, bedridden, afflicted (*fml*), indisposed (*fml*), valetudinarian (*fml*), in a bad way (*infml*), dicky (*infml*), out of sorts (*infml*), under the weather (*infml*), run down (*infml*), rough (*infml*), groggy (*infml*), like death warmed up (*infml*). **2** *an ill omen*: bad, evil, damaging, harmful, unpleasant, injurious, destructive, ruinous, detrimental, adverse, unfavourable, unpromising, sinister, ominous, threatening, unlucky, unfortunate, difficult, harsh, severe, inauspicious (*fml*), unpropitious (*fml*), infelicitous (*fml*), deleterious (*fml*). **3** *ill feelings*: unkind, unfriendly, antagonistic, hostile, resentful, belligerent.
₣ **1** well, healthy. **2** good, favourable, fortunate. **3** kind, friendly.

ill-advised *adj* imprudent, injudicious, unwise, foolish, ill-considered, thoughtless, hasty, rash, short-sighted, misguided, inappropriate.
₣ wise, sensible, well-advised.

ill-bred *adj* bad-mannered, ill-mannered, discourteous, impolite, rude, coarse, indelicate.
☒ well-bred, polite.

ill-disposed *adj* unfriendly, unsympathetic, hostile, antagonistic, opposed, unco-operative, unwelcoming, against, averse (*fml*), inimical (*fml*), anti (*infml*).
☒ well-disposed.

illegal *adj* unlawful, illicit, criminal, wrong, forbidden, prohibited, banned, outlawed, unauthorized, under-the-counter, black-market, unconstitutional, wrongful.
☒ legal, lawful.

illegible *adj* unreadable, indecipherable, scrawled, obscure, faint, indistinct.
☒ legible.

illegitimate *adj* **1** *an illegitimate child*: natural, bastard, born out of wedlock (*fml*). **2** ILLEGAL, unlawful, illicit, unauthorized, unwarranted, improper, incorrect, inadmissible, spurious, invalid, unsound.
☒ **1** legitimate. **2** legal.

ill-fated *adj* doomed, ill-starred, ill-omened, unfortunate, unlucky, luckless, unhappy.
☒ lucky.

illicit *adj* illegal, unlawful, criminal, wrong, illegitimate, improper, forbidden, prohibited, unauthorized, unlicensed, black-market, contraband, ill-gotten, under-the-counter, furtive, clandestine.
☒ legal, permissible.

illiterate *adj* ignorant, uneducated, unschooled, unlearned, untaught, unlettered, untutored, uncultured.
☒ literate.

ill-natured *adj* spiteful, vindictive, nasty, perverse, mean, surly, sulky, sullen, unfriendly, unkind, unpleasant, vicious, bad-tempered, cross, disagreeable, malicious, malignant, churlish, malevolent (*fml*), petulant (*fml*), crabbed (*infml*).
☒ good-natured.

illness *n* disease, disorder, complaint, ailment, sickness, ill health, ill-being, indisposition, infirmity, disability, affliction.

illogical *adj* irrational, unreasonable, unscientific, invalid, unsound, faulty, fallacious, specious, sophistical, inconsistent, senseless, meaningless, absurd.
☒ logical.

ill-treat *v* maltreat, abuse, injure, harm, damage, neglect, mistreat, mishandle, misuse, wrong, oppress.

illuminate *v* **1** LIGHT, light up, brighten, decorate. **2** ENLIGHTEN, edify, instruct, elucidate, illustrate, explain, clarify, clear up.
☒ **1** darken. **2** mystify.

illumination *n* light, lights, lighting, beam, ray, brightness, radiance, decoration, ornamentation.
☒ darkness.

illusion *n* apparition, mirage, hallucination, figment, fantasy, fancy, delusion, misapprehension, misconception, error, fallacy.
☒ reality, truth.

illusory *adj* illusive, deceptive, misleading, apparent, seeming, deluding, delusive, unreal, unsubstantial, sham, false, fallacious, untrue, mistaken.
☒ real.

illustrate *n* draw, sketch, depict, picture, show, exhibit, demonstrate, exemplify, explain, interpret, clarify, elucidate, illuminate, decorate, ornament, adorn.

illustration *n* **1** PICTURE, plate, half-tone, photograph, drawing, sketch, figure, representation, decoration. **2** EXAMPLE, specimen, instance, case, analogy, demonstration, explanation, interpretation.

illustrious *adj* great, noble, eminent, distinguished, celebrated, famous, famed, renowned, noted, prominent, outstanding, remarkable, notable, brilliant, excellent, splendid, magnificent, glorious, exalted.
☒ ignoble, inglorious.

ill-will *n* hostility, antagonism, bad blood, enmity, unfriendliness, malevolence, malice, spite, animosity, ill-feeling, resentment, hard feelings, grudge, dislike, aversion, hatred.
☒ goodwill, friendship.

image *n* **1** IDEA, notion, concept, impression, perception.
2 REPRESENTATION, likeness, picture, portrait, icon, effigy, figure, statue, idol, replica, reflection.

imaginable *adj* conceivable, thinkable, believable, credible, plausible, likely, possible.
☒ unimaginable.

imaginary *adj* imagined, fanciful, illusory, hallucinatory, visionary, pretend,

make-believe, unreal, non-existent, fictional, fabulous, legendary, mythological, made-up, invented, fictitious, assumed, supposed, hypothetical.
≠ real.

imagination *n* imaginativeness, creativity, inventiveness, originality, inspiration, insight, ingenuity, resourcefulness, enterprise, wit, vision, mind's eye, fancy, illusion.
≠ unimaginativeness, reality.

imaginative *adj* creative, inventive, innovative, original, inspired, visionary, ingenious, clever, resourceful, enterprising, fanciful, fantastic, vivid.
≠ unimaginative.

imagine *v* **1** PICTURE, visualize, envisage, conceive, fancy, fantasize, pretend, make believe, conjure up, dream up, think up, invent, devise, create, plan, project. **2** *I imagine so*: think, believe, judge, suppose, guess, conjecture, assume, take it, gather.

imbalance *n* unevenness, inequality, disparity, disproportion, unfairness, partiality, bias.
≠ balance, parity.

imbecile *n* idiot, halfwit, simpleton, moron, cretin, fool, blockhead, bungler.

imbue *v* permeate, impregnate, pervade, suffuse, fill, saturate, steep, inculcate, instil, tinge, tint.

imitate *v* copy, emulate, follow, ape, mimic, impersonate, take off, caricature, parody, send up, spoof, mock, parrot, repeat, echo, mirror, duplicate, reproduce, simulate, counterfeit, forge.

imitation *n* **1** MIMICRY, impersonation, impression, take-off, caricature, parody, send-up, spoof, mockery, travesty. **2** COPY, duplicate, reproduction, replica, simulation, counterfeit, fake, forgery, sham, likeness, resemblance, reflection, dummy.
➢ *adj* artificial, synthetic, man-made, ersatz, fake, phoney (*infml*), mock, pseudo, reproduction, simulated, sham, dummy.
≠ genuine.

imitative *adj* copying, mimicking, parrot-like, unoriginal, derivative, plagiarized, second-hand, simulated, mock.

imitator *n* mimic, impersonator, impressionist, parrot, copycat (*infml*), copier, emulator, follower.

immaculate *adj* perfect, unblemished, flawless, faultless, impeccable, spotless, clean, spick and span, pure, unsullied, undefiled, untainted, stainless, blameless, innocent.
≠ blemished, stained, contaminated.

immaterial *adj* irrelevant, insignificant, unimportant, minor, trivial, trifling, inconsequential.
≠ relevant, important.

immature *adj* young, under-age, adolescent, juvenile, childish, puerile, infantile, babyish, raw, crude, callow, inexperienced, green, unripe, undeveloped.
≠ mature.

immeasurable *adj* vast, immense, infinite, limitless, unlimited, boundless, unbounded, endless, bottomless, inexhaustible, incalculable, inestimable.
≠ limited.

immediate *adj* **1** INSTANT, instantaneous, direct, prompt, swift, current, present, existing, urgent, pressing. **2** NEAREST, next, adjacent, near, close, recent.
≠ **1** delayed. **2** distant.

immediately *adv* now, straight away, right away, at once, instantly, directly, forthwith, without delay, promptly, unhesitatingly.
≠ eventually, never.

immense *adj* vast, great, huge, enormous, massive, giant, gigantic, tremendous, monumental.
≠ tiny, minute.

immensity *n* magnitude, bulk, expanse, vastness, greatness, hugeness, enormousness, massiveness.
≠ minuteness.

immerse *v* plunge, submerge, submerse, sink, duck, dip, douse, bathe.

immigrant *n* incomer, settler, newcomer, alien.
≠ emigrant.

imminent *adj* impending, forthcoming, in the offing, approaching, coming, near, close, looming, menacing, threatening, brewing, in the air.
≠ remote, far-off.

immobile *adj* stationary, motionless, unmoving, still, stock-still, static, immovable, rooted, fixed, frozen, rigid, stiff.
≠ mobile, moving.

immobilize v stop, halt, fix, freeze, transfix, paralyse, cripple, disable.
☒ mobilize.

immodest adj indecent, revealing, shameless, forward, improper, immoral, obscene, lewd, coarse, risqué.

immoral adj unethical, wrong, bad, sinful, evil, wicked, unscrupulous, unprincipled, dishonest, corrupt, depraved, degenerate, dissolute, lewd, indecent, pornographic, obscene, impure.
☒ moral, right, good.

immorality n wrong, wrongdoing, badness, sin, sinfulness, evil, wickedness, dishonesty, vileness, corruption, vice, depravity, dissoluteness, debauchery, impurity, lewdness, indecency, pornography, obscenity, licentiousness, iniquity (fml), profligacy (fml), turpitude (fml).
☒ morality.

immortal adj undying, imperishable, eternal, everlasting, perpetual, endless, ceaseless, lasting, enduring, abiding, timeless, ageless.
☒ mortal.

immortality n 1 ETERNAL LIFE, everlasting life, eternity, endlessness, deathlessness, incorruptibility, imperishability, indestructibility, timelessness, perpetuity. 2 FAME, glorification, gloriousness, glory, greatness, renown, celebrity, honour, distinction.
☒ 1 mortality.

immortalize v celebrate, commemorate, memorialize, perpetuate, enshrine.

immovable adj fixed, rooted, immobile, stuck, fast, secure, stable, constant, firm, set, determined, resolute, adamant, unshakable, obstinate, unyielding.
☒ movable.

immune adj invulnerable, unsusceptible, resistant, proof, protected, safe, exempt, free, clear.
☒ susceptible.

The immune system's components and responses include: antibody, antigen [= antibody generator], commensals, complement system, cytotoxic cells, histamine, immunoglobulins, interferon, leucocyte, lymphocyte, B-lymphocytes, T-cells, T-lymphocytes, killer T-cells, helper T-cells, memory T-cells, lysosome, lysozyme, phagocyte, plasma cells, receptor (binding) site; acquired immunity, artificially acquired immunity (immunization), naturally acquired immunity, passive immunity, cell-mediated immunity, cellular response, humoral immunity/response, adaptive immune system, innate immune system, non-specific immune response, specific immune response, autoimmune response, primary response, secondary response, inflammatory response, immunosurveillance, allergy, phagocyte action (adherence/ingestion/digestion), phagocytosis, sneeze reflex, tissue rejection.

immunity n resistance, protection, exemption, indemnity, impunity, exoneration, freedom, liberty, licence, franchise, privilege, right.
☒ susceptibility.

immunize v vaccinate, inoculate, inject, protect, safeguard.

imp n 1 SPRITE, demon, devil, goblin, hobgoblin, gnome, puck. 2 MISCHIEVOUS CHILD, rascal, rogue, scamp, brat, minx, troublemaker, mischief-maker, trickster, prankster, flibbertigibbet, gamin, urchin.

impact n 1 the impact of the reforms: effect, consequences, repercussions, impression, power, influence, significance, meaning. 2 COLLISION, crash, smash, bang, bump, blow, knock, contact, jolt, shock, brunt.
➤ v 1 COLLIDE, crash, hit, clash, crush, fix, strike, press together. 2 AFFECT, have an effect on, influence, apply to, impinge.

impair v damage, harm, injure, hinder, mar, spoil, worsen, undermine, weaken, reduce, lessen, diminish, blunt.
☒ improve, enhance.

impale v pierce, puncture, perforate, run through, spear, lance, spike, skewer, spit, stick, transfix.

impart v tell, relate, communicate, make known, disclose, divulge, reveal, convey, pass on, give, grant, confer, offer, contribute, lend.
☒ withhold.

impartial adj objective, dispassionate, detached, disinterested, neutral, non-partisan, unbiased, unprejudiced, open-minded, fair, just, equitable, even-handed, equal.
☒ biased, prejudiced.

impartiality n neutrality, non-partisanship, objectivity, unbiasedness,

fairness, justice, even-handedness, open-mindedness, detachment, disinterest, disinterestedness, dispassion, equality, equity.
ⓔ bias, prejudice, favouritism, discrimination.

impassable *adj* blocked, closed, obstructed, unnavigable, unpassable, pathless, trackless, impenetrable, insurmountable, insuperable, unassailable, invincible.
ⓔ passable.

impasse *n* deadlock, stalemate, dead end, cul-de-sac, blind alley, halt, standstill.

impassioned *adj* fervent, ardent, passionate, intense, inspired, stirring, spirited, rousing, emotional, enthusiastic, eager, excited, fervid, vigorous, forceful, violent, furious, fiery, vehement, animated, glowing, inflamed, blazing, heated.
ⓔ apathetic, mild.

impassive *adj* expressionless, calm, composed, unruffled, unconcerned, cool, unfeeling, unemotional, unmoved, imperturbable, unexcitable, stoical, indifferent, dispassionate.
ⓔ responsive, moved.

impatience *n* eagerness, keenness, restlessness, agitation, anxiety, nervousness, irritability, intolerance, shortness, brusqueness, haste, rashness.
ⓔ patience.

impatient *adj* eager, keen, restless, fidgety, fretful, edgy, irritable, snappy, hot-tempered, quick-tempered, intolerant, brusque, abrupt, impetuous, hasty, precipitate, headlong.
ⓔ patient.

impeach *v* accuse, charge, indict (*fml*), arraign (*fml*), denounce, impugn, disparage (*fml*), criticize, censure, blame.

impeachment *n* accusation, charge, arraignment (*fml*), indictment (*fml*), disparagement (*fml*).

impeccable *adj* perfect, faultless, precise, exact, flawless, unblemished, stainless, immaculate, pure, irreproachable, blameless, innocent.
ⓔ faulty, flawed, corrupt.

impede *v* hinder, hamper, obstruct, block, clog, slow, retard, hold up, delay, check, curb, restrain, thwart, disrupt, stop, bar.
ⓔ aid, promote, further.

impediment *n* hindrance, obstacle, obstruction, barrier, bar, block, stumbling-block, snag, difficulty, handicap, check, curb, restraint, restriction.
ⓔ aid.

impel *v* urge, force, oblige, compel, constrain, drive, propel, push, spur, goad, prompt, stimulate, excite, instigate, motivate, inspire, move.
ⓔ deter, dissuade.

impending *adj* imminent, forthcoming, approaching, coming, close, near, looming, menacing, threatening.
ⓔ remote.

impenetrable *adj* 1 *impenetrable jungle*: solid, thick, dense, impassable.
2 UNINTELLIGIBLE, incomprehensible, unfathomable, baffling, mysterious, cryptic, enigmatic, obscure, dark, inscrutable.
ⓔ 2 accessible, understandable.

imperative *adj* compulsory, obligatory, essential, vital, crucial, pressing, urgent.
ⓔ optional, unimportant.

imperceptible *adj* inappreciable, indiscernible, inaudible, faint, slight, negligible, infinitesimal, microscopic, minute, tiny, small, fine, subtle, gradual.
ⓔ perceptible.

imperfect *adj* faulty, flawed, defective, damaged, broken, chipped, deficient, incomplete.
ⓔ perfect.

imperfection *n* fault, flaw, defect, blemish, deficiency, shortcoming, weakness, failing.
ⓔ perfection.

imperial *adj* sovereign, supreme, royal, regal, majestic, grand, magnificent, great, noble.

imperil *v* endanger, jeopardize, risk, hazard, expose, compromise, threaten.

imperious *adj* overbearing, domineering, autocratic, despotic, tyrannical, dictatorial, high-handed, commanding, arrogant, haughty.
ⓔ humble.

imperishable *adj* enduring, permanent, incorruptible, indestructible, inextinguishable, undying, unfading, unforgettable, abiding, perpetual, perennial, eternal, everlasting, immortal, deathless.
ⓔ perishable.

impermeable *adj* impervious, impenetrable, impassable, sealed,

hermetic, non-porous, damp-proof, waterproof, proof, water-resistant, resistant, water-repellent.
🔁 permeable, porous.

impersonal *adj* formal, official, businesslike, bureaucratic, faceless, aloof, remote, distant, detached, neutral, objective, dispassionate, cold, frosty, glassy.
🔁 informal, friendly.

impersonate *v* imitate, mimic, take off, parody, caricature, mock, masquerade as, pose as, act, portray.

impertinence *n* rudeness, impoliteness, disrespect, insolence, impudence, cheek (*infml*), brass (*sl*), effrontery, nerve (*infml*), audacity, boldness, brazenness, forwardness, presumption.
🔁 politeness, respect.

impertinent *adj* rude, impolite, ill-mannered, discourteous, disrespectful, insolent, impudent, cheeky (*infml*), saucy (*infml*), pert, bold, brazen, forward, presumptuous, fresh.
🔁 polite, respectful.

imperturbable *adj* unexcitable, unflappable (*infml*), calm, tranquil, composed, collected, self-possessed, cool, unmoved, unruffled.

impervious *adj* 1 IMPERMEABLE, waterproof, damp-proof, watertight, hermetic, closed, sealed, impenetrable. 2 *impervious to criticism*: immune, invulnerable, untouched, unaffected, unmoved, resistant.
🔁 1 porous, pervious. 2 responsive, vulnerable.

impetuous *adj* impulsive, spontaneous, unplanned, unpremeditated, hasty, precipitate, rash, reckless, thoughtless, unthinking.
🔁 cautious, wary, circumspect.

impetus *n* impulse, momentum, force, energy, power, drive, boost, push, spur, stimulus, incentive, motivation.

impinge *v* hit, touch (on), affect, influence, encroach, infringe, intrude, trespass, invade.

implacable *adj* inexorable, relentless, remorseless, merciless, pitiless, cruel, ruthless, intransigent, inflexible.
🔁 compassionate.

implant *v* graft, engraft, embed, sow, plant, fix, root, insert, instil, inculcate.

implausible *adj* improbable, unlikely, far-fetched, dubious, suspect, unconvincing, weak, flimsy, thin, transparent.
🔁 plausible, likely, reasonable.

implement *n* tool, instrument, utensil, gadget, device, apparatus, appliance.
➤ *v* enforce, effect, bring about, carry out, execute, discharge, perform, do, fulfil, complete, accomplish, realize.

implementation *n* carrying out, performance, performing, fulfilling, fulfilment, accomplishment, completion, operation, action, enforcement, realization, discharge (*fml*), effecting (*fml*), execution (*fml*).

implicate *v* involve, embroil, entangle, incriminate, compromise, include, concern, connect, associate.
🔁 exonerate.

implication *n* 1 INFERENCE, insinuation, suggestion, meaning, significance, ramification, repercusssion.
2 involvement, entanglement, incrimination, connection, association.

implicit *adj* 1 IMPLIED, inferred, insinuated, indirect, unsaid, unspoken, tacit, understood. 2 *implicit belief*: unquestioning, utter, total, full, complete, absolute, unqualified, unreserved, wholehearted.
🔁 1 explicit. 2 half-hearted.

implicitly *adv* absolutely, totally, utterly, completely, unconditionally, unhesitatingly, unquestioningly, unreservedly, steadfastly, wholeheartedly, firmly.
🔁 explicitly.

imply *v* suggest, insinuate, hint, intimate, mean, signify, point to, indicate, involve, require.
🔁 state.

impolite *adj* rude, discourteous, bad-mannered, ill-mannered, ill-bred, disrespectful, insolent, rough, coarse, vulgar, abrupt.
🔁 polite, courteous.

import *n* 1 *exports and imports*: imported product/commodity/goods, foreign product/commodity/goods, foreign trade. 2 IMPORTANCE, consequence, significance, weight, substance. 3 CONTENT, sense, substance, nub, meaning, implication, intention, thrust, message, drift, essence, gist, purport (*fml*).
➤ *v* betoken, bring in, imply, indicate,

introduce, mean, purport, signify.

importance n momentousness, significance, consequence, substance, matter, concern, interest, usefulness, value, worth, weight, influence, mark, prominence, eminence, distinction, esteem, prestige, status, standing.
𝕰 unimportance.

important adj 1 MOMENTOUS, noteworthy, significant, meaningful, relevant, material, salient, urgent, vital, essential, key, primary, major, substantial, valuable, seminal, weighty, serious, grave, far-reaching. 2 LEADING, foremost, high-level, high-ranking, influential, powerful, pre-eminent, prominent, outstanding, eminent, noted.
𝕰 1 unimportant, insignificant, trivial.

importunate adj insistent, persistent, troublesome, impatient, tenacious, dogged, pressing, urgent, pertinacious (fml).

impose v 1 INTRODUCE, institute, enforce, promulgate, exact, levy, set, fix, put, place, lay, inflict, burden, encumber, saddle. 2 INTRUDE, butt in, encroach, trespass, obtrude, force oneself, presume, take liberties.

imposing adj impressive, striking, grand, stately, majestic, dignified.
𝕰 unimposing, modest.

imposition n 1 INTRODUCTION, infliction, exaction, levying. 2 INTRUSION, encroachment, liberty, burden, constraint, charge, duty, task, punishment.

impossibility n hopelessness, impracticability, unattainableness, unobtainableness, unacceptability, untenability, unviability, inability, inconceivability, preposterousness, absurdity, ludicrousness, ridiculousness.
𝕰 possibility.

impossible adj hopeless, impracticable, unworkable, unattainable, unachievable, unobtainable, insoluble, unreasonable, unacceptable, inconceivable, unthinkable, preposterous, absurd, ludicrous, ridiculous.
𝕰 possible.

impostor n fraud, fake, phoney (infml), quack, charlatan, impersonator, pretender, con man (infml), swindler, cheat, rogue.

impotent adj powerless, helpless, unable, incapable, ineffective, weak, feeble, incompetent, inadequate, inept, infirm,

frail, infirm, disabled, incapacitated, paralysed.
𝕰 potent, strong.

impoverished adj poor, needy, impecunious, poverty-stricken, destitute, bankrupt, ruined.
𝕰 rich.

impracticable adj unworkable, unfeasible, unattainable, unachievable, impossible, unviable, useless, unserviceable, inoperable.
𝕰 practicable.

impractical adj unrealistic, idealistic, romantic, starry-eyed, impracticable, unworkable, impossible, awkward, inconvenient.
𝕰 practical, realistic, sensible.

imprecise adj inexact, inaccurate, approximate, estimated, rough, loose, indefinite, vague, woolly, hazy, ill-defined, sloppy, ambiguous, equivocal.
𝕰 precise, exact.

impregnable adj impenetrable, unconquerable, invincible, unbeatable, unassailable, indestructible, fortified, strong, solid, secure, safe, invulnerable.
𝕰 vulnerable.

impregnate v 1 SOAK, steep, saturate, fill, permeate, pervade, suffuse, imbue. 2 INSEMINATE, fertilize.

impress v 1 I'm not impressed: strike, move, touch, affect, influence, stir, inspire, excite, grab (sl). 2 STAMP, imprint, mark, indent, instil, inculcate.

impression n 1 FEELING, awareness, consciousness, sense, illusion, idea, notion, opinion, belief, conviction, suspicion, hunch, memory, recollection. 2 STAMP, mark, print, dent, outline. 3 IMPERSONATION, imitation, take-off, parody, send-up. 4 make a good impression: effect, impact, influence.

impressionable adj naïve, gullible, susceptible, vulnerable, sensitive, responsive, open, receptive.

impressive adj striking, imposing, grand, powerful, effective, stirring, exciting, moving, touching.
𝕰 unimpressive, uninspiring.

imprint n print, mark, stamp, impression, sign, logo.
➤ v print, mark, brand, stamp, impress, engrave, etch.

imprison v jail, incarcerate, intern,

detain, send down (*infml*), put away (*infml*), lock up, cage, confine, shut in.
⊟ release, free.

imprisonment *n* incarceration, internment, detention, custody, confinement.
⊟ freedom, liberty.

improbability *n* uncertainty, doubt, doubtfulness, dubiousness, unlikelihood, unlikeliness, far-fetchedness, preposterousness, ridiculousness, implausibility, dubiety (*fml*).
⊟ probability.

improbable *adj* uncertain, questionable, doubtful, unlikely, dubious, implausible, unconvincing, far-fetched, preposterous, unbelievable, incredible.
⊟ probable, likely, convincing.

impromptu *adj* improvised, extempore, ad-lib, off the cuff, unscripted, unrehearsed, unprepared, spontaneous.
⊟ rehearsed.
➤ *adv* extempore, ad lib, off the cuff, off the top of one's head, spontaneously, on the spur of the moment.

improper *adj* wrong, incorrect, irregular, unsuitable, inappropriate, inopportune, incongruous (*fml*), out of place, indecent, rude, vulgar, unseemly (*fml*), unbecoming, shocking.
⊟ proper, appropriate, decent.

impropriety *n* mistake, lapse, slip, blunder, faux pas, gaffe, bad taste, vulgarity, gaucherie, immodesty, indecency, unsuitability, incongruity (*fml*), indecorousness (*fml*), indecorum (*fml*), solecism (*fml*), unseemliness (*fml*).
⊟ propriety (*fml*).

improve *v* better, ameliorate, enhance, polish, touch up, mend, rectify, correct, amend, reform, upgrade, increase, rise, pick up, develop, look up, advance, progress, get better, recover, recuperate, rally, perk up, mend one's ways, turn over a new leaf.
⊟ worsen, deteriorate, decline.

improvement *n* betterment, amelioration, enhancement, rectification, correction, amendment, reformation, increase, rise, upswing, gain, development, advance, progress, furtherance, recovery, rally.
⊟ deterioration, decline.

improvisation *n* ad-lib, ad-libbing, extemporizing, impromptu, invention,

spontaneity, makeshift, expedient, vamp.

improvise *v* 1 CONTRIVE, devise, concoct, invent, throw together, make do.
2 EXTEMPORIZE, ad-lib, play by ear, vamp.

imprudent *adj* unwise, ill-advised, foolish, short-sighted, rash, reckless, hasty, irresponsible, careless, heedless, impolitic, indiscreet.
⊟ prudent, wise, cautious.

impudence *n* impertinence, cheek (*infml*), effrontery, nerve (*infml*), face (*infml*), boldness, insolence, rudeness, presumption.
⊟ politeness.

impudent *adj* impertinent, cheeky (*infml*), saucy (*infml*), bold, forward, shameless, cocky, insolent, rude, presumptuous, fresh.
⊟ polite.

impulse *n* 1 URGE, wish, desire, inclination, whim, notion, instinct, feeling, passion. 2 IMPETUS, momentum, force, pressure, drive, thrust, push, incitement, stimulus, motive.

impulsive *adj* impetuous, rash, reckless, hasty, quick, spontaneous, automatic, instinctive, intuitive.
⊟ cautious, premeditated.

impunity *n* exemption, freedom, immunity, liberty, licence, dispensation, permission, security, amnesty, excusal.
⊟ liability.

impure *adj* 1 UNREFINED, adulterated, diluted, contaminated, polluted, tainted, infected, corrupt, debased, unclean, dirty, foul. 2 OBSCENE, indecent, immodest.
⊟ 1 pure. 2 chaste, decent.

impurity *n* adulteration, contamination, pollution, infection, corruption, dirtiness, contaminant, dirt, filth, foreign body, mark, spot.
⊟ purity.

impute *v* ascribe, assign, attribute, put down to, charge, credit, refer, accredit (*fml*).

inability *n* incapability, incapacity, powerlessness, impotence, inadequacy, weakness, handicap, disability.
⊟ ability.

inaccessible *adj* isolated, remote, unfrequented, unapproachable, unreachable, unget-at-able (*infml*), unattainable.
⊟ accessible.

inaccuracy n mistake, error, miscalculation, slip, blunder, fault, defect, imprecision, inexactness, unreliability.
F3 accuracy, precision.

inaccurate adj incorrect, wrong, erroneous, mistaken, faulty, flawed, defective, imprecise, inexact, loose, unreliable, unfaithful, untrue.
F3 accurate, correct.

inaction n inactivity, immobility, inertia, rest, idleness, lethargy, torpor, stagnation.
F3 action.

inactive adj immobile, inert, idle, unused, inoperative, dormant, passive, sedentary, lazy, lethargic, sluggish, torpid, sleepy.
F3 active, working, busy.

inadequacy n 1 INSUFFICIENCY, lack, shortage, dearth, want, deficiency, scantiness, meagreness, defectiveness, ineffectiveness, inability, incompetence. 2 the inadequacies of the system: fault, defect, imperfection, weakness, failing, shortcoming.
F3 1 adequacy.

inadequate adj 1 INSUFFICIENT, short, wanting, deficient, scanty, sparse, meagre, niggardly. 2 INCOMPETENT, incapable, unequal, unqualified, ineffective, faulty, defective, imperfect, unsatisfactory.
F3 1 adequate. 2 satisfactory.

inadmissible adj unacceptable, irrelevant, immaterial, inappropriate, disallowed, prohibited.
F3 admissible.

inadvertent adj accidental, chance, unintentional, unintended, unplanned, unpremeditated, careless.
F3 deliberate, conscious, careful.

inadvertently adv accidentally, by accident, by mistake, by chance, unintentionally, unthinkingly, unwittingly, unconsciously, involuntarily, carelessly, heedlessly, negligently, mistakenly, remissly, thoughtlessly.
F3 deliberately.

inadvisable adj unwise, imprudent, injudicious, foolish, silly, ill-advised, misguided, indiscreet.
F3 advisable, wise.

inane adj senseless, foolish, stupid, unintelligent, silly, idiotic, fatuous, frivolous, trifling, puerile, mindless, vapid, empty, vacuous, vain, worthless, futile.
F3 sensible.

inanimate adj lifeless, dead, defunct,

extinct, unconscious, inactive, inert, dormant, immobile, stagnant, spiritless, dull.
F3 animate, living, alive.

inappropriate adj unsuitable, inapt, ill-suited, ill-fitted, irrelevant, incongruous, out of place, untimely, ill-timed, tactless, improper, unseemly, unbecoming, unfitting.
F3 appropriate, suitable.

inarticulate adj incoherent, unintelligible, incomprehensible, unclear, indistinct, hesitant, faltering, halting, tongue-tied, speechless, dumb, mute.
F3 articulate.

inattention n carelessness, negligence, disregard, absent-mindedness, forgetfulness, daydreaming, preoccupation.

inattentive adj distracted, dreamy, daydreaming, preoccupied, absent-minded, unmindful, heedless, regardless, careless, negligent.
F3 attentive.

inaudible adj silent, noiseless, imperceptible, faint, indistinct, muffled, muted, low, mumbled.
F3 audible, loud.

inaugural adj opening, introductory, first, initial.

inaugurate v institute, originate, begin, commence (fml), start, set up, open, launch, introduce, usher in, initiate, induct, ordain, invest, install, commission, dedicate, consecrate.

inauguration n 1 INSTITUTION, setting up, starting, opening, launch, launching, initiation, commencement (fml). 2 INDUCTION, ordination, investiture, consecration, enthronement, installation, installing.

inauspicious adj unfavourable, bad, unlucky, unfortunate, unpromising, discouraging, threatening, ominous, black.
F3 auspicious, promising.

inborn adj innate, inherent, natural, native, congenital, inbred, hereditary, inherited, ingrained, instinctive, intuitive.
F3 learned.

inbred adj innate, inherent, natural, native, ingrained, constitutional, connate (fml), ingenerate (fml).
F3 learned.

incalculable adj countless, untold,

inestimable, limitless, unlimited, immense, vast.

☒ limited, restricted.

incantation n chant, charm, spell, abracadabra, formula, magic formula, invocation, mantra, mantram, rune, hex, conjuration (*fml*).

incapable *adj* unable, powerless, impotent, helpless, weak, feeble, unfit, unsuited, unqualified, incompetent, inept, inadequate, ineffective.

☒ capable.

incapacitate v disable, cripple, paralyse, immobilize, disqualify, put out of action, lay up, scupper (*infml*).

incapacity n incapability, inability, disability, powerlessness, impotence, ineffectiveness, weakness, feebleness, inadequacy, incompetency.

☒ capability.

incarnate *adj* human, in human form, embodied, made flesh, in the flesh, fleshly, personified, typified, corporeal (*fml*).

incarnation n personification, embodiment, manifestation, impersonation.

incautious *adj* careless, imprudent, injudicious, ill-judged, unthinking, thoughtless, inconsiderate, rash, reckless, hasty, impulsive.

☒ cautious, careful.

incendiary *adj* 1 *an incendiary bomb*: fire-raising, flammable, combustible, pyromaniac. 2 INCITING, inflammatory, provocative, stirring, seditious, subversive, dissentious, rabble-rousing, proceleusmatic (*fml*).

☒ 2 calming.

➤ n 1 AGITATOR, insurgent, revolutionary, rabble-rouser, demagogue, firebrand. 2 FIRE-RAISER, pyromaniac, arsonist, firebug, pétroleur, pétroleuse. 3 FIRE-BOMB, bomb, explosive, charge, grenade, mine, petrol bomb.

incense¹ n perfume, scent, aroma, balm, bouquet, fragrance, joss-stick.

incense² v anger, enrage, infuriate, madden, exasperate, irritate, rile, provoke, excite.

☒ calm.

incensed *adj* enraged, angry, fuming, furious, exasperated, mad, maddened, steamed up, indignant, infuriated, irate, ireful, wrathful, furibund (*fml*), in a paddy

(*infml*), on the warpath (*infml*), up in arms (*infml*).

☒ calm.

incentive n bait, lure, enticement, carrot (*infml*), sweetener (*sl*), reward, encouragement, inducement, reason, motive, impetus, spur, stimulus, motivation.

☒ disincentive, discouragement, deterrent.

incessant *adj* ceaseless, unceasing, endless, never-ending, interminable, continual, persistent, constant, perpetual, eternal, everlasting, continuous, unbroken, unremitting, non-stop.

☒ intermittent, sporadic, periodic, temporary.

incidence n frequency, commonness, prevalence, extent, range, amount, degree, rate, occurrence.

incident n 1 OCCURRENCE, happening, event, episode, adventure, affair, occasion, instance. 2 CONFRONTATION, clash, fight, skirmish, commotion, disturbance, scene, upset, mishap.

incidental *adj* accidental, chance, random, minor, non-essential, secondary, subordinate, subsidiary, ancillary, supplementary, accompanying, attendant, related, contributory.

☒ important, essential.

incidentally *adv* 1 BY THE WAY, in passing, secondarily, parenthetically, en passant, apropos, by the by (*infml*). 2 ACCIDENTALLY, by accident, coincidentally, unexpectedly, by chance, casually, digressively, fortuitously (*fml*).

incinerate v burn, cremate, reduce to ashes.

incise v cut, cut into, carve, chisel, engrave, sculpt, sculpture, etch, gash, slit, slash, nick, notch.

incision n cut, opening, slit, gash, notch.

incisive *adj* cutting, keen, sharp, acute, trenchant, piercing, penetrating, biting, caustic, acid, astute, perceptive.

☒ vague.

incite v prompt, instigate, rouse, foment, stir up, whip up, work up, excite, animate, provoke, stimulate, spur, goad, impel, drive, urge, encourage, egg on (*infml*).

☒ restrain.

incitement n prompting, instigation, agitation, provocation, spur, goad,

impetus, stimulus, motivation,
encouragement, inducement, incentive.
E3 discouragement.

inclement *adj* intemperate, harsh,
severe, stormy, tempestuous, rough.
E3 fine.

inclination *n* 1 LIKING, fondness, taste,
predilection, preference, partiality, bias,
tendency, trend, disposition, propensity,
leaning. 2 *an inclination of 45 degrees*:
angle, slope, gradient, incline, pitch, slant,
tilt, bend, bow, nod.
E3 1 disinclination, dislike.

incline *v* 1 DISPOSE, influence, persuade,
affect, bias, prejudice. 2 LEAN, slope, slant,
tilt, tip, bend, bow, tend, veer.
➤ *n* slope, gradient, ramp, hill, rise, ascent,
acclivity, dip, descent, declivity.

inclined *adj* liable, likely, given, apt,
disposed, of a mind, willing.

include *v* comprise, incorporate, embody,
comprehend, contain, enclose, embrace,
encompass, cover, subsume, take in, add,
allow for, take into account, involve, rope in.
E3 exclude, omit, eliminate.

including *prep* counting, inclusive of,
with, together with, included.
E3 excluding.

inclusion *n* incorporation, involvement,
addition, insertion.
E3 exclusion.

inclusive *adj* comprehensive, full, all-in,
all-inclusive, all-embracing, blanket,
across-the-board, general, catch-all,
overall, sweeping.
E3 exclusive, narrow.

incognito *adj* in disguise, disguised,
masked, veiled, unmarked, unidentified,
unrecognizable, unknown.
E3 undisguised.

incoherent *adj* unintelligible,
incomprehensible, inarticulate, rambling,
stammering, stuttering, unconnected,
disconnected, broken, garbled, scrambled,
confused, muddled, jumbled, disordered.
E3 coherent, intelligible.

income *n* revenue, returns, proceeds,
gains, profits, interest, takings, receipts,
earnings, pay, salary, wages, means.
E3 expenditure, expenses.

incoming *adj* arriving, entering,
approaching, coming, homeward,
returning, ensuing, succeeding, next, new.
E3 outgoing.

incomparable *adj* matchless,
unmatched, unequalled, unparalleled,
unrivalled, peerless, supreme, superlative,
superb, brilliant.
E3 ordinary, run-of-the-mill, poor.

incomparably *adv* by far, far and away,
beyond compare, immeasurably, infinitely,
easily, supremely, superbly, superlatively,
eminently, brilliantly.
E3 poorly, slightly.

incompatible *adj* irreconcilable,
contradictory, conflicting, at variance,
inconsistent, clashing, mismatched,
unsuited.
E3 compatible.

incompetent *adj* incapable, unable,
unfit, inefficient, inexpert, unskilful,
bungling, stupid, useless, ineffective.
E3 competent, able.

incomplete *adj* deficient, lacking, short,
unfinished, abridged, partial, part,
fragmentary, broken, imperfect, defective.
E3 complete, exhaustive.

incomprehensible *adj* unintelligible,
impenetrable, unfathomable, above one's
head, puzzling, perplexing, baffling,
mysterious, inscrutable, obscure, opaque.
E3 comprehensible, intelligible.

inconceivable *adj* unthinkable,
unimaginable, mind-boggling (*infml*),
staggering, unheard-of, unbelievable,
incredible, implausible.
E3 conceivable.

inconclusive *adj* unsettled, undecided,
open, uncertain, indecisive, ambiguous,
vague, unconvincing, unsatisfying.
E3 conclusive.

incongruity *n* inappropriateness,
unsuitability, inconsistency,
incompatibility, conflict, clash,
irreconcilability, contradiction,
discrepancy, inharmoniousness,
inaptness, disparity (*fml*).
E3 consistency, harmoniousness.

incongruous *adj* inappropriate,
unsuitable, out of place, out of
keeping, inconsistent, conflicting,
incompatible, irreconcilable,
contradictory, contrary.
E3 consistent, compatible.

inconsequential *adj* minor, trivial,
trifling, unimportant, insignificant,
immaterial.
E3 important.

inconsiderable *adj* small, slight,

negligible, trivial, petty, minor, unimportant, insignificant.
Ea considerable, large.

inconsiderate *adj* unkind, uncaring, unconcerned, selfish, self-centred, intolerant, insensitive, tactless, rude, thoughtless, unthinking, careless, heedless.
Ea considerate.

inconsistent *adj* 1 CONFLICTING, at variance, at odds, incompatible, contradictory, contrary, incongruous, discordant. 2 CHANGEABLE, variable, irregular, unpredictable, varying, unstable, unsteady, inconstant, fickle.
Ea 2 constant.

inconsolable *adj* heartbroken, brokenhearted, devastated, desolate, despairing, wretched.

inconspicuous *adj* hidden, concealed, camouflaged, plain, ordinary, unobtrusive, discreet, low-key, modest, unassuming, quiet, retiring, insignificant.
Ea conspicuous, noticeable, obtrusive.

incontinent *adj* uncontrollable, uncontrolled, ungovernable, ungoverned, unrestrained, unbridled, unchecked, loose, promiscuous, unchaste, dissipated, dissolute, debauched, lewd, licentious, lascivious, lecherous, lustful, wanton.
Ea continent.

incontrovertible *adj* indisputable, unquestionable, irrefutable, undeniable, certain, clear, self-evident.
Ea questionable, uncertain.

inconvenience *n* awkwardness, difficulty, annoyance, nuisance, hindrance, drawback, bother, trouble, fuss, upset, disturbance, disruption.
Ea convenience.
➤ *v* bother, disturb, disrupt, put out, trouble, upset, irk.
Ea convenience.

inconvenient *adj* awkward, ill-timed, untimely, inopportune, unsuitable, difficult, embarrassing, annoying, troublesome, unwieldy, unmanageable.
Ea convenient.

incorporate *v* include, embody, contain, subsume, take in, absorb, assimilate, integrate, combine, unite, merge, blend, mix, fuse, coalesce, consolidate.
Ea separate.

incorrect *adj* wrong, mistaken, erroneous, inaccurate, imprecise, inexact,

false, untrue, faulty, ungrammatical, improper, illegitimate, inappropriate, unsuitable.
Ea correct.

incorrigible *adj* irredeemable, incurable, inveterate, hardened, hopeless.

incorruptible *adj* honest, straight, upright, moral, honourable, trustworthy, unbribable, just.
Ea corruptible.

increase *v* raise, boost, add to, improve, enhance, advance, step up, intensify, strengthen, heighten, grow, develop, build up, wax, enlarge, extend, prolong, expand, spread, swell, magnify, multiply, proliferate, rise, mount, soar, escalate.
Ea decrease, reduce, decline.
➤ *n* rise, surge, upsurge, upturn, gain, boost, addition, increment, advance, step-up, intensification, growth, development, enlargement, extension, expansion, spread, proliferation, escalation.
Ea decrease, reduction, decline.

increasingly *adv* more and more, all the more, more so, to an increasing degree/ extent, progressively, cumulatively.

incredible *adj* unbelievable, improbable, implausible, far-fetched, preposterous, absurd, impossible, inconceivable, unthinkable, unimaginable, extraordinary, amazing, astonishing, astounding.
Ea credible, believable.

incredulity *n* unbelief, disbelief, scepticism, doubt, distrust, mistrust.
Ea credulity.

incredulous *adj* unbelieving, disbelieving, unconvinced, sceptical, doubting, distrustful, suspicious, dubious, doubtful, uncertain.
Ea credulous.

increment *n* increase, gain, addition, step-up, advancement, extension, supplement, growth, enlargement, expansion, accretion, accrual (*fml*), accrument (*fml*), addendum (*fml*), augmentation (*fml*).
Ea decrease.

incriminate *v* inculpate, implicate, involve, accuse, charge, impeach, indict, point the finger at, blame.
Ea exonerate.

incumbent *adj* binding, necessary, obligatory, compulsory, prescribed, up to, mandatory (*fml*).
➤ *n* office-holder, office-bearer, official,

officer, functionary, member.

incur v suffer, sustain, provoke, arouse, bring upon oneself, expose oneself to, meet with, run up, gain, earn.

incurable adj 1 an incurable disease: terminal, fatal, untreatable, inoperable, hopeless. 2 INCORRIGIBLE, inveterate, hardened, dyed-in-the-wool.
ɛ 1 curable.

indebted adj obliged, grateful, thankful.

indecency n immodesty, indecorum, impurity, obscenity, pornography, lewdness, vulgarity, coarseness, crudity, foulness, grossness.
ɛ decency, modesty.

indecent adj improper, immodest, impure, indelicate, offensive, obscene, pornographic, lewd, licentious, vulgar, coarse, crude, dirty, filthy, foul, gross, outrageous, shocking.
ɛ decent, modest.

indecipherable adj indistinguishable, unreadable, illegible, unintelligible, indistinct, unclear, tiny, crabbed, cramped.
ɛ readable.

indecision n indecisiveness, irresolution, vacillation, wavering, hesitation, hesitancy, ambivalence, uncertainty, doubt.
ɛ decisiveness, resolution.

indecisive adj undecided, irresolute, undetermined, vacillating, wavering, in two minds, hesitating, faltering, tentative, uncertain, unsure, doubtful, inconclusive, indefinite, indeterminate, unclear.
ɛ decisive.

indeed adv really, actually, in fact, certainly, positively, truly, undeniably, undoubtedly, to be sure.

indefensible adj unjustifiable, inexcusable, unforgivable, unpardonable, insupportable, untenable, wrong, faulty.
ɛ defensible, excusable.

indefinable adj indescribable, inexpressible, indistinct, unrealized, nameless, obscure, unclear, vague, subtle, dim, hazy, impalpable.
ɛ definable.

indefinite adj unknown, uncertain, unsettled, unresolved, undecided, undetermined, undefined, unspecified, unlimited, ill-defined, vague, indistinct, unclear, obscure, ambiguous, imprecise, inexact, loose, general.
ɛ definite, limited, clear.

indefinitely adv for ever, eternally, endlessly, continually, ad infinitum.

indelible adj lasting, enduring, permanent, fast, ineffaceable, ingrained, indestructible.
ɛ erasable.

indelicate adj rude, embarrassing, suggestive, immodest, improper, indecent, offensive, tasteless, in bad taste, unbecoming, vulgar, coarse, crude, gross, low, obscene, risqué, indecorous (fml), unseemly (fml), untoward (fml), blue (infml), off-colour (infml).
ɛ delicate.

indemnify v protect, secure, underwrite, guarantee, insure, endorse, exempt, free, reimburse, compensate, repair, repay, requite, satisfy, pay, remunerate.

indemnity n compensation, reimbursement, remuneration, reparation, insurance, guarantee, security, protection, immunity, amnesty.

indentation n notch, nick, cut, serration, dent, groove, furrow, depression, dip, hollow, pit, dimple.

independence n autonomy, self-government, self-determination, self-rule, home rule, sovereignty, freedom, liberty, individualism, separation.
ɛ dependence.

independent adj 1 AUTONOMOUS, self-governing, self-determining, sovereign, absolute, non-aligned, neutral, impartial, unbiased. 2 FREE, liberated, unconstrained, individualistic, unconventional, self-sufficient, self-supporting, self-reliant, unaided. 3 INDIVIDUAL, self-contained, separate, unconnected, unrelated.
ɛ 1 dependent.

independently adv alone, by oneself, on one's own, individually, separately, solo, unaided, autonomously, under one's own steam (infml), on one's tod (infml).
ɛ together.

indescribable adj indefinable, inexpressible, unutterable, unspeakable.
ɛ describable.

indestructible adj unbreakable, durable, tough, strong, lasting, enduring, abiding, permanent, eternal, everlasting, immortal, imperishable.
ɛ breakable, mortal.

indeterminate adj unspecified, unstated, undefined, unfixed, imprecise,

inexact, indefinite, vague, open-ended, undecided, undetermined, uncertain.
☒ known, specified, fixed.

index n 1 index of names: table, key, list, catalogue, directory, guide. 2 INDICATOR, pointer, needle, hand, sign, token, mark, indication, clue.

indicate v register, record, show, reveal, display, manifest, point to, designate, specify, point out, mark, signify, mean, denote, express, suggest, imply.

indication n mark, sign, manifestation, evidence, symptom, signal, warning, omen, intimation, suggestion, hint, clue, note, explanation.

indicative adj symptomatic, suggestive, demonstrative, characteristic, typical, significant, symbolic, denotative (fml), exhibitive (fml), indicatory (fml).

indicator n pointer, needle, marker, sign, symbol, token, signal, display, dial, gauge, meter, index, guide, signpost.

indict v charge, accuse, arraign, impeach, summon, summons, prosecute, incriminate.
☒ exonerate.

indictment n charge, accusation, impeachment, allegation, recrimination, summons, prosecution, incrimination, arraignment (fml), inculpation (fml).
☒ exoneration.

indifference n apathy, unconcern, coldness, coolness, inattention, disregard, negligence, neutrality, disinterestedness.
☒ interest, concern.

indifferent adj 1 UNINTERESTED, unenthusiastic, unexcited, apathetic, unconcerned, unmoved, uncaring, unsympathetic, cold, cool, distant, aloof, detached, uninvolved, neutral, disinterested. 2 MEDIOCRE, average, middling, passable, moderate, fair, ordinary.
☒ 1 interested, caring. 2 excellent.

indigenous adj native, aboriginal, original, local, home-grown.
☒ foreign.

indigestion n dyspepsia, dyspepsy, heartburn, cardialgia, acidity, pyrosis.

indignant adj annoyed, angry, irate, heated, fuming, livid, furious, incensed, infuriated, exasperated, outraged.
☒ pleased, delighted.

indignation n annoyance, anger, ire,

wrath, rage, fury, exasperation, outrage, scorn, contempt.
☒ pleasure, delight.

indignity n humiliation, abuse, insult, slight, snub, affront, contempt, mistreatment, offence, disgrace, outrage, reproach, dishonour, disrespect, incivility, injury, contumely (fml), obloquy (fml), opprobrium (fml), slap in the face (infml), kick in the teeth (infml), cold shoulder (infml), put-down (infml).
☒ honour.

indirect adj 1 ROUNDABOUT, circuitous, wandering, rambling, winding, meandering, zigzag, tortuous. 2 an indirect effect: secondary, incidental, unintended, subsidiary, ancillary.
☒ 1 direct. 2 primary.

indiscernible adj imperceptible, minuscule, minute, microscopic, tiny, undiscernible, undetectable, unapparent, indistinct, unclear, obscure, indistinguishable, invisible, hidden, impalpable.
☒ clear, apparent.

indiscreet adj tactless, undiplomatic, impolitic, injudicious, imprudent, unwise, foolish, rash, reckless, hasty, careless, heedless, unthinking.
☒ discreet, cautious.

indiscretion n mistake, error, slip, boob (infml), faux pas, gaffe, tactlessness, rashness, recklessness, foolishness, folly.

indiscriminate adj general, sweeping, wholesale, random, haphazard, hit-or-miss, aimless, unsystematic, unmethodical, mixed, motley, miscellaneous.
☒ selective, specific, precise.

indispensable adj vital, essential, basic, key, crucial, imperative, required, requisite, needed, necessary.
☒ dispensable, unnecessary.

indisposed adj ill, sick, unwell, poorly, ailing, laid up.
☒ well.

indisputable adj incontrovertible, unquestionable, irrefutable, undeniable, absolute, undisputed, definite, positive, certain, sure.
☒ doubtful.

indistinct adj unclear, ill-defined, blurred, fuzzy, misty, hazy, shadowy, obscure, dim, faint, muffled, confused, unintelligible, vague, woolly, ambiguous, indefinite.

🖛 distinct, clear.

indistinguishable *adj* identical, interchangeable, same, twin, alike, hard to make out the difference, cloned, tantamount, like as two peas in a pod (*infml*).

🖛 distinguishable, unalike, different, dissimilar.

individual *n* person, being, creature, party, body, soul, character, fellow.
➤ *adj* distinctive, characteristic, idiosyncratic, peculiar, singular, unique, exclusive, special, personal, own, proper, respective, several, separate, distinct, specific, personalized, particular, single.

🖛 collective, shared, general.

individualism *n* independence, originality, self-direction, freethinking, self-interest, self-reliance, free-thought, eccentricity, egocentricity, egoism, anarchism, libertarianism.

🖛 conventionality.

individuality *n* character, personality, distinctiveness, peculiarity, singularity, uniqueness, separateness, distinction.

🖛 sameness.

indoctrinate *v* brainwash, teach, instruct, school, ground, train, drill.

indoctrination *n* brainwashing, instruction, schooling, training, teaching, grounding, inculcation, drilling, instilling.

induce *v* 1 CAUSE, effect, bring about, occasion, give rise to, lead to, incite, instigate, prompt, provoke, produce, generate. 2 COAX, prevail upon, encourage, press, persuade, talk into, move, influence, draw, tempt.

🖛 2 discourage, deter.

inducement *n* lure, bait, attraction, enticement, encouragement, incentive, reward, spur, stimulus, motive, reason.

🖛 disincentive.

indulge *v* gratify, satisfy, humour, pander to, go along with, give in to, yield to, favour, pet, cosset, mollycoddle, pamper, spoil, treat, regale.

indulgence *n* extravagance, luxury, excess, immoderation, intemperance, favour, tolerance.

indulgent *adj* tolerant, easy-going (*infml*), lenient, permissive, generous, liberal, kind, fond, tender, understanding, patient.

🖛 strict, harsh.

industrialist *n* manufacturer, producer, magnate, tycoon, baron, captain of industry, capitalist, financier.

industrious *adj* busy, productive, hard-working, diligent, assiduous, conscientious, zealous, active, energetic, tireless, persistent, persevering.

🖛 lazy, idle.

industry *n* 1 *the steel industry*: business, trade, commerce, manufacturing, production. 2 INDUSTRIOUSNESS, diligence, application, effort, labour, toil, persistence, perseverance, determination.

inebriated *adj* drunk, intoxicated, tipsy, merry.

🖛 sober.

inedible *adj* uneatable, unpalatable, indigestible, harmful, noxious, poisonous, deadly.

🖛 edible.

ineffective *adj* useless, worthless, vain, idle, futile, unavailing, fruitless, unproductive, unsuccessful, powerless, impotent, ineffectual, inadequate, weak, feeble, inept, incompetent.

🖛 effective, effectual.

inefficient *adj* uneconomic, wasteful, money-wasting, time-wasting, incompetent, inexpert, unworkmanlike, slipshod, sloppy, careless, negligent.

🖛 efficient.

inelegant *adj* graceless, ungraceful, clumsy, awkward, laboured, ugly, unrefined, crude, unpolished, rough, unsophisticated, uncultivated, uncouth.

🖛 elegant.

ineligible *adj* disqualified, ruled out, unacceptable, undesirable, unworthy, unsuitable, unfit, unqualified, unequipped.

🖛 eligible.

inept *adj* awkward, clumsy, bungling, incompetent, unskilful, inexpert, foolish, stupid.

🖛 competent, skilful.

inequality *n* unequalness, difference, diversity, dissimilarity, disparity, unevenness, disproportion, bias, prejudice.

🖛 equality.

inert *adj* immobile, motionless, unmoving, still, inactive, inanimate, lifeless, dead, passive, unresponsive, apathetic, dormant, idle, lazy, lethargic, sluggish, torpid, sleepy.

🖛 lively, animated.

inertia *n* immobility, stillness, inactivity, passivity, unresponsiveness, apathy, idleness, laziness, lethargy, torpor.
🆎 activity, liveliness.

inescapable *adj* inevitable, unavoidable, destined, fated, certain, sure, irrevocable, unalterable.
🆎 escapable.

inestimable *adj* incalculable, measureless, infinite, immeasurable, invaluable, precious, priceless, unlimited, uncountable, unfathomable, incomputable, immense, vast, untold, prodigious (*fml*), mind-boggling (*infml*), worth a fortune (*infml*).
🆎 insignificant.

inevitable *adj* unavoidable, inescapable, necessary, definite, certain, sure, decreed, ordained, destined, fated, automatic, assured, fixed, unalterable, irrevocable, inexorable.
🆎 avoidable, uncertain, alterable.

inexcusable *adj* indefensible, unforgivable, unpardonable, intolerable, unacceptable, outrageous, shameful, blameworthy, reprehensible.
🆎 excusable, justifiable.

inexhaustible *adj* **1** *an inexhaustible supply*: unlimited, limitless, boundless, unbounded, infinite, endless, never-ending, abundant. **2** INDEFATIGABLE, tireless, untiring, unflagging, unwearied, unwearying.
🆎 **1** limited.

inexorable *adj* relentless, unrelenting, remorseless, unalterable, inevitable, unpreventable, unavertable, irresistible, irrevocable, inescapable, immovable, unyielding, unceasing, incessant, unstoppable, unfaltering, ordained, destined, fated, definite, certain, sure, ineluctable (*fml*).
🆎 avoidable, preventable.

inexpensive *adj* cheap, low-priced, reasonable, modest, bargain, budget, low-cost, economical.
🆎 expensive, dear.

inexperience *n* inexpertness, ignorance, unfamiliarity, strangeness, newness, rawness, naïveness, innocence.
🆎 experience.

inexperienced *adj* inexpert, untrained, unskilled, amateur, probationary, apprentice, unacquainted, unfamiliar, unaccustomed, new, fresh, raw, callow, young, immature, naïve, unsophisticated, innocent.
🆎 experienced, mature.

inexplicable *adj* unexplainable, unaccountable, strange, mystifying, puzzling, baffling, mysterious, enigmatic, unfathomable, incomprehensible, incredible, unbelievable, miraculous.
🆎 explicable.

inexpressive *adj* unexpressive, expressionless, deadpan, inscrutable, blank, vacant, empty, emotionless, impassive.
🆎 expressive.

inextricably *adv* inseparably, indissolubly, indivisibly, indistinguishably, intricately, irresolubly, irretrievably, irreversibly.

infallible *adj* accurate, unerring, unfailing, foolproof, fail-safe, sure-fire (*infml*), certain, sure, reliable, dependable, trustworthy, sound, perfect, faultless, impeccable.
🆎 fallible.

infamous *adj* notorious, ill-famed, disreputable, disgraceful, shameful, shocking, outrageous, scandalous, wicked, iniquitous.
🆎 illustrious, glorious.

infamy *n* notoriety, disrepute, disgrace, shame, dishonour, discredit, ignominy, wickedness.
🆎 glory.

infancy *n* **1** BABYHOOD, childhood, youth. **2** BEGINNING, start, commencement, inception, outset, birth, dawn, genesis, emergence, origins, early stages.
🆎 **1** adulthood.

infant *n* baby, toddler, tot (*infml*), child, babe (*fml*), babe in arms (*fml*).
🆎 adult.
➤ *adj* newborn, baby, young, youthful, juvenile, immature, growing, developing, rudimentary, early, initial, new.
🆎 adult, mature.

infantile *adj* babyish, childish, puerile, juvenile, young, youthful, adolescent, immature.
🆎 adult, mature.

infatuated *adj* besotted, obsessed, enamoured, smitten (*infml*), crazy (*infml*), spellbound, mesmerized, captivated, fascinated, enraptured, ravished.
🆎 indifferent, disenchanted.

infatuation *n* besottedness, obsession,

fixation, passion, crush (*sl*), love, fondness, fascination.
≠ indifference, disenchantment.

infect *v* contaminate, pollute, defile, taint, blight, poison, corrupt, pervert, influence, affect, touch, inspire.

infection *n* illness, disease, virus, epidemic, contagion, pestilence, contamination, pollution, defilement, taint, blight, poison, corruption, influence.

infectious *adj* contagious, communicable, transmissible, infective, catching, spreading, epidemic, virulent, deadly, contaminating, polluting, defiling, corrupting.

infer *v* derive, extrapolate, deduce, conclude, assume, presume, surmise, gather, understand.

inference *n* deduction, conclusion, corollary, consequence, assumption, presumption, surmise, conjecture, extrapolation, construction, interpretation, reading.

inferior *adj* 1 LOWER, lesser, minor, secondary, junior, subordinate, subsidiary, second-class, low, humble, menial. 2 *inferior work*: substandard, second-rate, mediocre, bad, poor, unsatisfactory, slipshod, shoddy.
≠ 1 superior. 2 excellent.
➤ *n* subordinate, junior, underling (*infml*), minion, vassal, menial.
≠ superior.

inferiority *n* 1 SUBORDINATION, subservience, humbleness, lowliness, meanness, insignificance. 2 MEDIOCRITY, imperfection, inadequacy, slovenliness, shoddiness.
≠ 1 superiority. 2 excellence.

infernal *adj* hellish, satanic, devilish, diabolical, fiendish, accursed, damned.
≠ heavenly.

infertile *adj* barren, sterile, childless, unproductive, unfruitful, arid, parched, dried-up.
≠ fertile, fruitful.

infest *v* swarm, teem, throng, flood, overrun, invade, infiltrate, penetrate, permeate, pervade, ravage.

infested *adj* swarming, teeming, crawling, bristling, beset, alive, pervaded, plagued, ravaged, ridden, overrun, overspread, infiltrated, permeated, vermined.

infidelity *n* adultery, unfaithfulness, faithlessness, disloyalty, duplicity, treachery, betrayal, cheating, falseness.
≠ fidelity, faithfulness.

infiltrate *v* penetrate, enter, creep into, insinuate, intrude, pervade, permeate, filter, percolate.

infinite *adj* limitless, unlimited, boundless, unbounded, endless, never-ending, inexhaustible, bottomless, innumerable, numberless, uncountable, countless, untold, incalculable, inestimable, immeasurable, unfathomable, vast, immense, enormous, huge, absolute, total.
≠ finite, limited.

infinitesimal *adj* tiny, minute, microscopic, minuscule, inconsiderable, insignificant, negligible, inappreciable, imperceptible.
≠ great, large, enormous.

infinity *n* eternity, perpetuity, limitlessness, boundlessness, endlessness, inexhaustibility, countlessness, immeasurableness, vastness, immensity.
≠ finiteness, limitation.

infirm *adj* weak, feeble, frail, ill, unwell, poorly, sickly, failing, faltering, unsteady, shaky, wobbly, doddery, lame.
≠ healthy, strong.

infirmity *n* weakness, feebleness, frailty, ailment, illness, ill health, disease, complaint, sickness, sickliness, disorder, failing, decrepitude, vulnerability, instability, dodderiness, debility (*fml*), malady (*fml*).
≠ health, strength.

inflame *v* anger, enrage, infuriate, incense, exasperate, madden, provoke, stimulate, excite, rouse, arouse, agitate, foment, kindle, ignite, fire, heat, fan, fuel, increase, intensify, worsen, aggravate.
≠ cool, quench.

inflamed *adj* sore, swollen, septic, infected, poisoned, red, hot, heated, fevered, feverish.

inflammable *adj* flammable, combustible, burnable.
≠ non-flammable, incombustible, flameproof.

inflammation *n* soreness, painfulness, tenderness, swelling, abscess, infection, redness, heat, rash, sore, irritation.

inflammatory *adj* 1 PROVOCATIVE,

incendiary, explosive, fiery, rabble-rousing, rabid, riotous, seditious, insurgent, intemperate, inciting, incitative, inflaming, instigative, anarchic, demagogic. **2** SORE, painful, tender, swollen, allergic, festering, septic, infected.
≠ 1 calming, pacific.

inflate *v* **1** *inflate a life jacket*: blow up, pump up, bloat, expand, dilate, enlarge, aerate, swell, puff out, distend (*fml*). **2** *inflated prices*: increase, raise, boost, step up, escalate, amplify, extend, intensify, augment (*fml*), hike up (*infml*), push up (*infml*). **3** *inflate the importance of something*: exaggerate, overstate, overrate, overestimate, boost, magnify, aggrandize (*fml*).
≠ 1 deflate. **2** decrease, lower. **3** understate, play down.

inflated *adj* **1** BLOWN UP, swollen, puffed out, dilated, bloated, ballooned, distended (*fml*), tumefied (*fml*), tumid (*fml*). **2** INCREASED, raised, escalated, extended, intensified. **3** EXAGGERATED, overblown, ostentatious, pompous, bombastic, grandiloquent (*fml*), magniloquent (*fml*), euphuistic (*fml*).
≠ 1 deflated.

inflation *n* expansion, increase, rise, escalation, hyperinflation.
≠ deflation.

inflexible *adj* rigid, stiff, hard, solid, set, fixed, fast, immovable, firm, strict, stringent, unbending, unyielding, adamant, resolute, relentless, implacable, uncompromising, stubborn, obstinate, intransigent, entrenched, dyed-in-the-wool.
≠ flexible, yielding, adaptable.

inflict *v* impose, enforce, perpetrate, wreak, administer, apply, deliver, deal, mete out, lay, burden, exact, levy.

influence *n* power, sway, rule, authority, domination, mastery, hold, control, direction, guidance, bias, prejudice, pull, pressure, effect, impact, weight, importance, prestige, standing.
➢ *v* dominate, control, manipulate, direct, guide, manoeuvre, change, alter, modify, affect, impress, move, stir, arouse, rouse, sway, persuade, induce, incite, instigate, prompt, motivate, dispose, incline, bias, prejudice, predispose.

influential *adj* dominant, controlling, leading, authoritative, charismatic, persuasive, convincing, compelling, inspiring, moving, powerful, potent, effective, telling, strong, weighty, momentous, important, significant, instrumental, guiding.
≠ ineffective, unimportant.

influx *n* inflow, inrush, invasion, arrival, stream, flow, rush, flood, inundation.

inform *v* tell, advise, notify, communicate, impart, leak, tip off, acquaint, fill in (*infml*), brief, instruct, enlighten, illuminate.
◆ **inform on** betray, incriminate, shop (*sl*), tell on (*infml*), squeal (*sl*), blab, grass (*sl*), denounce.

informal *adj* unofficial, unceremonious, casual, relaxed, easy, free, natural, simple, unpretentious, familiar, colloquial.
≠ formal, solemn.

informality *n* unceremoniousness, casualness, congeniality, ease, freedom, familiarity, naturalness, relaxation, simplicity, unpretentiousness, approachability, homeliness, cosiness.
≠ formality, ceremony.

information *n* facts, data, input, gen (*infml*), bumf (*sl*), intelligence, news, report, bulletin, communiqué, message, word, advice, notice, briefing, instruction, knowledge, dossier, database, databank, clues, evidence.

informative *adj* educational, instructive, edifying, enlightening, illuminating, revealing, forthcoming, communicative, chatty, gossipy, newsy, helpful, useful, constructive.
≠ uninformative.

informed *adj* **1** *we'll keep you informed*: familiar, conversant, acquainted, enlightened, briefed, primed, posted, up to date, abreast, au fait, in the know (*infml*). **2** *an informed opinion*: well-informed, authoritative, expert, versed, well-read, erudite, learned, knowledgeable, well-researched.
≠ 1 ignorant, unaware.

informer *n* informant, grass (*sl*), supergrass (*sl*), betrayer, traitor, Judas, tell-tale, sneak, spy, mole (*infml*).

infrequent *adj* exceptional, intermittent, occasional, rare, scanty, sparse, spasmodic, sporadic, uncommon, unusual, few and far between (*infml*), like gold dust (*infml*).
≠ frequent.

infringe *v* **1** BREAK, violate, contravene,

transgress, overstep, disobey, defy, flout, ignore. **2** INTRUDE, encroach, trespass, invade.

infringement n **1** *infringement of the rules*: breach, breaking, disobedience, violation, defiance, contravention, evasion, non-compliance, non-observance, infraction (*fml*), transgression (*fml*). **2** INTRUSION, encroachment, trespass, invasion.

infuriate v anger, vex, enrage, incense, exasperate, madden, provoke, rouse, annoy, irritate, rile, antagonize.
ea calm, pacify.

ingenious adj clever, shrewd, cunning, crafty, skilful, masterly, imaginative, creative, inventive, resourceful, original, innovative.
ea unimaginative.

ingenuity n ingeniousness, cleverness, shrewdness, astuteness, sharpness, skill, skilfulness, creativeness, adroitness, cunning, slyness, innovativeness, invention, inventiveness, deftness, originality, resourcefulness, genius, gift, faculty, flair, knack.
ea clumsiness, dullness.

ingenuous adj artless, guileless, innocent, honest, sincere, frank, open, plain, simple, unsophisticated, naïve, trusting.
ea artful, sly.

ingrained adj fixed, rooted, deep-rooted, deep-seated, entrenched, immovable, ineradicable, permanent, inbuilt, inborn, inbred.

ingratiate v curry favour, flatter, creep, crawl, grovel, fawn, get in with.

ingratitude n ungratefulness, thanklessness, unappreciativeness, ungraciousness.
ea gratitude, thankfulness.

ingredient n constituent, element, factor, component, part.

inhabit v live, dwell, reside, occupy, possess, colonize, settle, people, populate, stay.

inhabitant n resident, dweller, citizen, native, occupier, occupant, inmate, tenant, lodger.

inhabited adj lived-in, occupied, peopled, populated, settled, possessed, colonized, held, developed, tenanted, overrun.
ea uninhabited.

inhale v breathe in, draw in, draw, suck in, inspire, whiff, respire (*fml*).

inherent adj inborn, inbred, innate, inherited, hereditary, native, natural, inbuilt, built-in, intrinsic, ingrained, essential, fundamental, basic.

inherit v succeed to, accede to, assume, come into, be left, receive.

inheritance n legacy, bequest, heritage, birthright, heredity, descent, succession.

inheritor n heir, heiress, successor, beneficiary, recipient.

inhibit v discourage, repress, hold back, suppress, curb, check, restrain, hinder, impede, obstruct, interfere with, frustrate, thwart, prevent, stop, stanch, stem.
ea encourage, assist.

inhibited adj repressed, self-conscious, shy, reticent, withdrawn, reserved, guarded, subdued.
ea uninhibited, open, relaxed.

inhibition n repression, hang-up (*sl*), self-consciousness, shyness, reticence, reserve, restraint, curb, check, hindrance, impediment, obstruction, bar.
ea freedom.

inhuman adj barbaric, barbarous, animal, bestial, vicious, savage, sadistic, cold-blooded, brutal, cruel, inhumane.
ea human.

inhumane adj unkind, insensitive, callous, unfeeling, heartless, cold-hearted, hard-hearted, pitiless, ruthless, cruel, brutal, inhuman.
ea humane, kind, compassionate.

inimitable adj unique, incomparable, matchless, unmatched, unparalleled, unrivalled, unsurpassable, unsurpassed, unequalled, peerless, consummate, sublime, superlative, supreme, distinctive, exceptional, nonpareil, unexampled.

iniquity n wickedness, injustice, offence, misdeed, wrong, wrongdoing, evil, evil-doing, sin, sinfulness, enormity, baseness, vice, viciousness, infamy, abomination, crime, lawlessness, unrighteousness, ungodliness, heinousness (*fml*), transgression (*fml*).
ea virtue.

initial adj first, beginning, opening, introductory, inaugural, original, primary, early, formative.
ea final, last.

initially adv at first, at the beginning, to

begin with, to start with, originally, first, firstly, first of all.

☒ finally, in the end.

initiate v begin, start, commence, originate, pioneer, institute, set up, introduce, launch, open, inaugurate, instigate, activate, trigger, prompt, stimulate, cause.

initiation n admission, reception, entrance, entry, debut, introduction, enrolment, induction, investiture, installation, inauguration, inception.

initiative n 1 ENERGY, drive, dynamism, get-up-and-go (infml), ambition, enterprise, resourcefulness, inventiveness, originality, innovativeness. 2 SUGGESTION, recommendation, action, lead, first move, first step.

inject v 1 inject drugs: inoculate, vaccinate, shoot (sl). 2 INTRODUCE, insert, add, bring, infuse, instil.

injection n inoculation, vaccination, jab (infml), shot (infml), fix (sl), dose, insertion, introduction.

injunction n command, order, directive, ruling, mandate, direction, instruction, precept.

injure v hurt, harm, damage, impair, spoil, mar, ruin, disfigure, deface, mutilate, wound, cut, break, fracture, maim, disable, cripple, lame, ill-treat, maltreat, abuse, offend, wrong, upset, put out.

injury n wound, cut, lesion, fracture, trauma, hurt, mischief, ill, harm, damage, impairment, ruin, disfigurement, mutilation, ill-treatment, abuse, insult, offence, wrong, injustice.

injustice n unfairness, inequality, disparity, discrimination, oppression, bias, prejudice, one-sidedness, partisanship, partiality, favouritism, wrong, iniquity.

☒ justice, fairness.

inkling n suspicion, idea, notion, faintest (infml), glimmering, clue, hint, intimation, suggestion, allusion, indication, sign, pointer.

inlet n bay, cove, creek, fiord, opening, entrance, passage.

inn n public house, pub (infml), local (infml), tavern, hostelry, hotel.

innate adj inborn, inbred, inherent, intrinsic, native, natural, instinctive, intuitive.

☒ acquired, learnt.

inner adj internal, interior, inside, inward, innermost, central, middle, concealed, hidden, secret, private, personal, intimate, mental, psychological, spiritual, emotional.

☒ outer, outward.

innermost adj deepest, deep, central, inmost, intimate, personal, dearest, private, secret, confidential, closest, essential, hidden, buried, basic, esoteric (fml).

innocence n 1 GUILTLESSNESS, blamelessness, honesty, virtue, righteousness, purity, chastity, virginity, incorruptibility, harmlessness, innocuousness. 2 ARTLESSNESS, guilelessness, naïvety, inexperience, ignorance, naturalness, simplicity, unsophistication, unworldliness, credulity, gullibility, trustfulness.

☒ 1 guilt. 2 experience.

innocent adj 1 innocent of the crime: guiltless, blameless, irreproachable, unimpeachable, honest, upright, virtuous, righteous, sinless, faultless, impeccable, stainless, spotless, immaculate, unsullied, untainted, uncontaminated, pure, chaste, virginal, incorrupt, inoffensive, harmless, innocuous. 2 ARTLESS, guileless, ingenuous, naïve, green, inexperienced, fresh, natural, simple, unsophisticated, unworldly, childlike, credulous, gullible, trusting.

☒ 1 guilty. 2 experienced.

innocuous adj harmless, safe, inoffensive, unobjectionable, innocent.

☒ harmful.

innovation n newness, novelty, neologism, modernization, progress, reform, change, alteration, variation, departure.

innovative adj new, fresh, original, creative, imaginative, inventive, resourceful, enterprising, go-ahead, progressive, reforming, bold, daring, adventurous.

☒ conservative, unimaginative.

innuendo n insinuation, aspersion, slur, whisper, hint, intimation, suggestion, implication.

innumerable adj numberless, unnumbered, countless, uncountable, untold, incalculable, infinite, numerous, many.

inoculation n vaccination, injection,

immunization, protection, shot (*infml*), jab (*infml*).

inoffensive *adj* harmless, innocuous, innocent, peaceable, mild, unobtrusive, unassertive, quiet, retiring.
☒ offensive, harmful, provocative.

inordinate *adj* excessive, immoderate, unwarranted, undue, unreasonable, disproportionate, great.
☒ moderate, reasonable.

input *v* feed in, insert, key in, code, capture, process, store.
➤ *n* information, data, facts, figures, statistics, material, details, particulars, resources.
☒ output.

inquest *n* inquiry, investigation, examination, hearing, post-mortem, inspection.

inquire, enquire *v* ASK, question, quiz, query, investigate, look into, probe, examine, inspect, scrutinize, search, explore.

inquiry, enquiry *n* question, query, investigation, inquest, hearing, inquisition, examination, inspection, scrutiny, study, survey, poll, search, probe, exploration.

inquisition *n* interrogation, cross-examination, cross-questioning, examination, investigation, questioning, quizzing, inquiry, inquest, grilling (*infml*), third degree (*infml*), witch hunt (*infml*).

inquisitive *adj* curious, questioning, probing, searching, prying, peeping, snooping, nosey, interfering, meddlesome, intrusive.

inroad *n* advance, progress, encroachment, foray, impingement, incursion, intrusion, trespassing, invasion, irruption, onslaught, attack, assault, offensive, charge, raid, sally, sortie, trespass.

insane *adj* 1 MAD, crazy, mentally ill, lunatic, mental (*sl*), demented, deranged, unhinged, disturbed. 2 FOOLISH, stupid, senseless, impractical.
☒ 1 sane. 2 sensible.

insanity *n* madness, craziness, lunacy, mental illness, neurosis, psychosis, mania, dementia, derangement, folly, stupidity, senselessness, irresponsibility.
☒ sanity.

insatiable *adj* unquenchable, unsatisfiable, ravenous, voracious, immoderate, inordinate.

inscribe *v* engrave, etch, carve, cut, incise, imprint, impress, stamp, print, write, sign, autograph, dedicate.

inscription *n* engraving, epitaph, caption, legend, lettering, words, writing, signature, autograph, dedication.

inscrutable *adj* incomprehensible, unfathomable, impenetrable, deep, inexplicable, unexplainable, baffling, mysterious, enigmatic, cryptic, hidden.
☒ comprehensible, expressive.

insect

Insects include: fly, gnat, midge, mosquito, tsetse-fly, locust, dragonfly, cranefly, daddy longlegs (*infml*), horsefly, mayfly, butterfly, red admiral, cabbage-white, moth, tiger moth, bee, bumblebee, wasp, hornet, aphid, blackfly, greenfly, whitefly, froghopper, ladybird, water boatman, lacewing; beetle, cockroach, roach (*US*), earwig, stick insect, grasshopper, cricket, cicada, flea, louse, nit, leatherjacket, termite, glowworm, woodworm, weevil, woodlouse.

Arachnids include: spider, black widow, tarantula, scorpion, mite, tick.

Parts of an insect: abdomen, antenna, cercus, compound eye, forewing, head, hindwing, legs, mandible, mouthpart, ocellus, ovipositor, segment, spiracle, thorax.

insecure *adj* 1 ANXIOUS, worried, nervous, uncertain, unsure, afraid. 2 UNSAFE, dangerous, hazardous, perilous, precarious, unsteady, shaky, loose, unprotected, defenceless, exposed, vulnerable.
☒ 1 confident, self-assured. 2 secure, safe.

insecurity *n* 1 ANXIETY, worry, nervousness, uncertainty, unsureness, apprehension, fear, uneasiness, lack of confidence. 2 UNSAFETY, unsafeness, danger, hazard, peril, precariousness, unsteadiness, shakiness, instability, weakness, frailness, flimsiness, defencelessness, vulnerability.
☒ 1 confidence. 2 safety, security.

insensible *adj* numb, anaesthetized, dead, cold, insensitive, unresponsive, blind, deaf, unconscious, unaware, oblivious, unmindful.
☒ conscious.

insensitive *adj* hardened, tough, resistant, impenetrable, impervious, immune, unsusceptible, thick-skinned, unfeeling, impassive, indifferent, unaffected, unmoved, untouched, uncaring, unconcerned, callous, thoughtless, tactless, crass.
☎ sensitive.

inseparable *adj* indivisible, indissoluble, inextricable, close, intimate, bosom, devoted.
☎ separable.

insert *v* put, place, put in, stick in, push in, introduce, implant, embed, engraft, set, inset, let in, interleave, intercalate, interpolate (*fml*), interpose.
➤ *n* insertion, enclosure, inset, notice, advertisement, supplement, addition.

insertion *n* addition, entry, inclusion, insert, inset, introduction, implant, supplement, intrusion, interpolation (*fml*).

inside *n* interior, content, contents, middle, centre, heart, core.
☎ outside.
➤ *adv* within, indoors, internally, inwardly, secretly, privately.
☎ outside.
➤ *adj* interior, internal, inner, innermost, inward, secret, classified, confidential, private.

insides *n* entrails, guts, intestines, bowels, innards (*infml*), organs, viscera, belly, stomach.

insidious *adj* subtle, sly, crafty, cunning, wily, deceptive, devious, stealthy, surreptitious, furtive, sneaking, treacherous.
☎ direct, straightforward.

insight *n* awareness, knowledge, comprehension, understanding, grasp, apprehension, perception, intuition, sensitivity, discernment, judgement, acumen, penetration, observation, vision, wisdom, intelligence.

insignia *n* emblem, badge, regalia, crest, sign(s), ensign, medallion, ribbon, decoration, mark, hallmark(s), symbol, trademark, brand.

insignificant *adj* unimportant, irrelevant, meaningless, inconsequential, minor, trivial, trifling, petty, paltry, small, tiny, insubstantial, inconsiderable, negligible, non-essential.
☎ significant, important.

insincere *adj* hypocritical, two-faced,

double-dealing, lying, untruthful, dishonest, deceitful, devious, unfaithful, faithless, untrue, false, feigned, pretended, phoney (*infml*), hollow.
☎ sincere.

insinuate *v* imply, suggest, allude, hint, intimate, get at (*infml*), indicate.

insipid *adj* tasteless, flavourless, unsavoury, unappetizing, watery, weak, bland, wishy-washy (*infml*), colourless, drab, dull, monotonous, boring, uninteresting, tame, flat, lifeless, spiritless, characterless, trite, unimaginative, dry.
☎ tasty, spicy, piquant, appetizing.

insist *v* demand, require, urge, stress, emphasize, repeat, reiterate, dwell on, harp on, assert, maintain, claim, contend, hold, vow, swear, persist, stand firm.

insistence *n* demand, entreaty, exhortation (*fml*), urging, stress, emphasis, repetition, reiteration, assertion, claim, contention, persistence, determination, resolution, firmness.

insistent *adj* demanding, importunate, emphatic, forceful, pressing, urgent, dogged, tenacious, persistent, persevering, relentless, unrelenting, unremitting, incessant.

insolent *adj* rude, abusive, insulting, disrespectful, cheeky (*infml*), impertinent, impudent, saucy (*infml*), bold, forward, fresh, presumptuous, arrogant, defiant, insubordinate.
☎ polite, respectful.

insoluble *adj* unsolvable, unexplainable, inexplicable, incomprehensible, unfathomable, impenetrable, obscure, mystifying, puzzling, perplexing, baffling.
☎ explicable.

insolvency *n* bankruptcy, default, failure, liquidation, ruin, indebtedness, destitution, impoverishment, pennilessness, impecuniosity (*fml*).
☎ solvency.

insolvent *adj* bankrupt, bust, failed, ruined, broke (*infml*), penniless, destitute.
☎ solvent.

insomnia *n* sleeplessness, restlessness, wakefulness, insomnolence (*fml*).
☎ sleep.

inspect *v* check, vet, look over, examine, search, investigate, scrutinize, study, scan, survey, superintend, supervise, oversee, visit.

inspection n check, check-up, examination, scrutiny, scan, study, survey, review, search, investigation, supervision, visit.

inspector n supervisor, superintendent, overseer, surveyor, controller, scrutineer, checker, tester, examiner, investigator, reviewer, critic.

inspiration n 1 CREATIVITY, imagination, genius, muse, influence, encouragement, stimulation, motivation, spur, stimulus. 2 IDEA, brainwave, insight, illumination, revelation, awakening.

inspire v encourage, hearten, influence, impress, animate, enliven, quicken, galvanize, fire, kindle, stir, arouse, trigger, spark off, prompt, spur, motivate, provoke, stimulate, excite, exhilarate, thrill, enthral, enthuse, imbue, infuse.

inspired adj brilliant, impressive, superlative, wonderful, outstanding, exciting, dazzling, memorable, thrilling, enthralling, marvellous, exceptional, splendid, remarkable.
F3 dull, uninspired.

inspiring adj encouraging, heartening, uplifting, invigorating, stirring, rousing, stimulating, exciting, exhilarating, thrilling, enthralling, moving, affecting, memorable, impressive.
F3 uninspiring, dull.

instability n unsteadiness, shakiness, vacillation, wavering, irresolution, uncertainty, unpredictability, changeableness, variability, fluctuation, volatility, capriciousness, fickleness, inconstancy, unreliability, insecurity, unsafeness, unsoundness.
F3 stability.

install v 1 install a new phone system: fix, fit, lay, put (in), insert, place, position, locate, lodge, site, situate, station, plant, settle, establish, set up, introduce. 2 install her as president: institute, inaugurate, invest, induct, ordain, consecrate, instate.

installation n 1 FITTING, insertion, positioning, location, placing, siting. 2 EQUIPMENT, machinery, plant, system. 3 her installation as president: inauguration, investiture, instatement, induction, consecration, ordination. 4 a military installation: base, station, post, centre, site, settlement, establishment, headquarters.

instalment n 1 pay in instalments: payment, repayment, portion. 2 EPISODE, chapter, part, section, division.

instance n 1 several instances of bullying: case, example, illustration, exemplification, case in point, citation, occurrence, occasion, sample. 2 at his instance: request, urging, incitement, demand, initiative, insistence, entreaty, instigation, pressure, prompting, solicitation, behest (fml), exhortation (fml), importunity (fml).
➤ v mention, quote, refer to, specify, give, name, cite, point to, exemplify, adduce (fml).

instant n flash, twinkling, trice, moment, tick (infml), split second, second, minute, time, occasion.
➤ adj instantaneous, immediate, on-the-spot, direct, prompt, urgent, unhesitating, quick, fast, rapid, swift.
F3 slow.

instantaneous adj immediate, instant, direct, prompt, rapid, unhesitating, sudden, on-the-spot.
F3 eventual.

instantaneously adv at once, directly, forthwith, immediately, right away, instantly, on the spot, promptly, speedily, quickly, rapidly, straight away, there and then, unhesitatingly, without hesitation, without delay, pronto (infml), before you can say Jack Robinson (infml), in two shakes of a lamb's tail (infml).
F3 eventually.

instantly adv immediately, instantaneously, at once, right away, straight away, there and then, forthwith, now, on the spot, without delay, directly, pronto (infml).
F3 eventually.

instead adv alternatively, preferably, rather.
◆ **instead of** in place of, in lieu of, on behalf of, in preference to, rather than.

instigate v initiate, set on, start, begin, cause, generate, inspire, move, influence, encourage, urge, spur, prompt, provoke, stimulate, incite, stir up, whip up, foment, rouse, excite.

instil v infuse, imbue, insinuate, introduce, inject, implant, inculcate, impress, din into (infml).

instinct n intuition, sixth sense, gut reaction (infml), impulse, urge, feeling, hunch, flair, knack, gift, talent, feel, faculty, ability, aptitude, predisposition, tendency.

instinctive *adj* natural, native, inborn, innate, inherent, intuitive, impulsive, involuntary, automatic, mechanical, reflex, spontaneous, immediate, unthinking, unpremeditated, gut (*infml*), visceral.
🗷 conscious, voluntary, deliberate.

institute *v* originate, initiate, introduce, enact, begin, start, commence, create, establish, set up, organize, found, inaugurate, open, launch, appoint, install, invest, induct, ordain.
🗷 cancel, discontinue, abolish.
➢ *n* school, college, academy, conservatory, foundation, institution.

institution *n* 1 CUSTOM, tradition, usage, practice, ritual, convention, rule, law.
2 ORGANIZATION, association, society, guild, concern, corporation, foundation, establishment, institute, hospital, home.
3 INITIATION, introduction, enactment, inception, creation, establishment, formation, founding, foundation, installation.

institutional *adj* established, organized, establishment, accepted, customary, conventional, formal, methodical, orderly, systematic, orthodox, regimented, set, routine, uniform, ritualistic, bureaucratic, clinical, impersonal, cold, unwelcoming, dreary, dull, drab, forbidding, monotonous, cheerless.
🗷 individualistic, unconventional.

instruct *v* 1 TEACH, educate, tutor, coach, train, drill, ground, school, discipline.
2 ORDER, command, direct, mandate, tell, inform, notify, advise, counsel, guide.

instruction *n* 1 *follow the instructions*: direction, recommendation, advice, guidance, information, order, command, injunction, mandate, directive, ruling.
2 EDUCATION, schooling, lesson(s), tuition, teaching, training, coaching, drilling, grounding, preparation.

instructive *adj* informative, educational, edifying, enlightening, illuminating, helpful, useful.
🗷 unenlightening.

instructor *n* teacher, master, mistress, tutor, coach, trainer, demonstrator, exponent, adviser, mentor, guide, guru.

instrument *n* 1 TOOL, implement, utensil, appliance, gadget, contraption, device, contrivance, apparatus, mechanism.
2 AGENT, agency, vehicle, organ, medium, factor, channel, way, means.

instrumental *adj* active, involved, contributory, conducive, influential, useful, helpful, auxiliary, subsidiary.
🗷 obstructive, unhelpful.

insubordinate *adj* disobedient, rebellious, defiant, ungovernable, unruly, disorderly, undisciplined, rude, riotous, seditious, insurgent, mutinous, turbulent, impertinent, impudent, contumacious (*fml*), recalcitrant (*fml*), refractory (*fml*).
🗷 docile, obedient, compliant.

insubstantial *adj* 1 FLIMSY, frail, feeble, weak, tenuous, poor, slight, thin. 2 UNREAL, false, illusory, fanciful, imaginary, idle, vaporous, immaterial, incorporeal, moonshine, chimerical (*fml*), ephemeral (*fml*).
🗷 1 solid, strong. 2 real.

insufferable *adj* intolerable, unbearable, detestable, loathsome, dreadful, impossible.
🗷 pleasant, tolerable.

insufficiency *n* inadequacy, shortage, deficiency, lack, scarcity, dearth, want, need, poverty.
🗷 sufficiency, excess.

insufficient *adj* inadequate, short, deficient, lacking, sparse, scanty, scarce.
🗷 sufficient, excessive.

insular *adj* parochial, provincial, cut off, detached, isolated, remote, withdrawn, inward-looking, blinkered, closed, narrow-minded, narrow, limited, petty.

insulate *v* cushion, pad, lag, cocoon, protect, shield, shelter, isolate, separate, cut off.

insult *v* abuse, call names, disparage, revile, libel, slander, slight, snub, injure, affront, offend, outrage.
🗷 compliment, praise.
➢ *n* abuse, rudeness, insolence, defamation, libel, slander, slight, snub, affront, indignity, offence, outrage.
🗷 compliment, praise.

insuperable *adj* insurmountable, formidable, overwhelming, invincible, un-conquerable, unassailable, impassable.
🗷 surmountable.

insurance *n* cover, protection, safeguard, security, provision, assurance, indemnity, guarantee, warranty, policy, premium.

insure *v* cover, protect, assure, underwrite, indemnify, guarantee, warrant.

insurgent *n* rebel, revolter, revolutionary, rioter, insurrectionist, seditionist, mutineer, partisan, revolutionist, resister.
➤ *adj* rebellious, revolting, revolutionary, mutinous, riotous, seditious, disobedient, insubordinate, insurrectionary, partisan.

insurmountable *adj* insuperable, unconquerable, invincible, overwhelming, hopeless, impossible.
F3 surmountable.

insurrection *n* rising, uprising, insurgence, riot, rebellion, mutiny, revolt, revolution, coup, putsch.

intact *adj* unbroken, all in one piece, whole, complete, integral, entire, perfect, sound, undamaged, unhurt, uninjured.
F3 broken, incomplete, damaged.

intangible *adj* insubstantial, imponderable, elusive, fleeting, airy, shadowy, vague, indefinite, abstract, unreal, invisible.
F3 tangible, real.

integral *adj* 1 *an integral part*: intrinsic, constituent, elemental, basic, fundamental, necessary, essential, indispensable. 2 COMPLETE, entire, full, whole, undivided.
F3 1 extra, additional, unnecessary.

integrate *v* assimilate, merge, join, unite, combine, amalgamate, incorporate, coalesce, fuse, knit, mesh, mix, blend, harmonize.
F3 divide, separate.

integration *n* assimilation, merger, unity, unification, combination, amalgamation, consolidation, incorporation, fusion, blend, harmony, mix, desegregation.
F3 separation, segregation.

integrity *n* 1 HONESTY, uprightness, probity, incorruptibility, purity, morality, principle, honour, virtue, goodness, righteousness. 2 COMPLETENESS, wholeness, unity, coherence, cohesion.
F3 1 dishonesty. 2 incompleteness.

intellect *n* mind, brain(s) (*infml*), brainpower, intelligence, genius, reason, understanding, sense, wisdom, judgement.
F3 stupidity.

intellectual *adj* academic, scholarly, intelligent, studious, thoughtful, cerebral, mental, highbrow, cultural.
F3 low-brow.
➤ *n* thinker, academic, highbrow,

egghead, mastermind, genius.
F3 low-brow.

intelligence *n* 1 INTELLECT, reason, wit(s), brain(s) (*infml*), brainpower, cleverness, brightness, aptitude, quickness, alertness, discernment, perception, understanding, comprehension. 2 INFORMATION, facts, data, low-down (*sl*), knowledge, findings, news, report, warning, tip-off.
F3 1 stupidity, foolishness.

intelligent *adj* clever, bright, smart, brainy (*infml*), quick, alert, quick-witted, sharp, acute, knowing, knowledgeable, well-informed, thinking, rational, sensible.
F3 unintelligent, stupid, foolish.

intelligentsia *n* academics, intellectuals, cognoscenti, literati, highbrows, illuminati, brains (*infml*), eggheads (*infml*).

intelligible *adj* comprehensible, understandable, clear, plain, lucid, distinct, open, explicit, legible, decipherable, fathomable, penetrable.
F3 unintelligible.

intend *v* aim, have a mind, contemplate, mean, propose, plan, project, scheme, plot, design, purpose, resolve, determine, destine, mark out, earmark, set apart.

intense *adj* great, deep, profound, strong, powerful, forceful, fierce, harsh, severe, acute, sharp, keen, eager, earnest, ardent, fervent, fervid, passionate, vehement, energetic, violent, intensive, concentrated, heightened.
F3 moderate, mild, weak.

intensify *v* increase, step up, escalate, heighten, hot up (*infml*), fire, boost, fuel, aggravate, add to, strengthen, reinforce, sharpen, whet, quicken, deepen, concentrate, emphasize, enhance.
F3 reduce, weaken.

intensity *n* greatness, extremity, intenseness, depth, profundity, strength, power, vigour, potency, force, fierceness, severity, acuteness, keenness, eagerness, earnestness, ardour, enthusiasm, zeal, fanaticism, fervency, fervour, fire, emotion, passion, concentration, energy, vehemence, strain, tension.

intensive *adj* concentrated, thorough, exhaustive, comprehensive, detailed, in-depth, thoroughgoing, all-out, intense.
F3 superficial.

intent *adj* determined, resolved, resolute,

set, bent, concentrated, eager, earnest, committed, steadfast, fixed, alert, attentive, concentrating, preoccupied, engrossed, wrapped up, absorbed, occupied.

a absent-minded, distracted.

intention n aim, purpose, object, end, point, target, goal, objective, idea, plan, design, view, intent, meaning.

intentional adj designed, wilful, conscious, planned, deliberate, prearranged, premeditated, calculated, studied, intended, meant.

a unintentional, accidental.

intercede v mediate, arbitrate, intervene, plead, entreat, beseech, speak.

intercept v head off, ambush, interrupt, cut off, stop, arrest, catch, take, seize, check, block, obstruct, delay, frustrate, thwart.

interchange n 1 EXCHANGE, trading, barter, swap, alternation, reciprocation, interplay, crossfire, give-and-take (infml). 2 INTERSECTION, junction, crossroad(s), crossing.
➤ v exchange, swap, switch, alternate, reciprocate, replace, substitute, trade, barter, transpose, reverse.

interchangeable adj reciprocal, equivalent, similar, identical, the same, synonymous, standard.

a different.

intercourse n 1 sexual intercourse: sex, sexual relations, intimacy, intimate relations, love-making, copulation, carnal knowledge, the sex act, coition (fml), coitus (fml), sleeping with someone (infml), going to bed with someone (infml), it (infml), nookie (infml), fuck (taboo sl), screw (taboo sl), bonk (taboo sl), bang (taboo sl), shag (taboo sl). 2 ASSOCIATION, communication, communion, contact, connection, dealings, conversation, converse, correspondence, commerce, trade, intercommunication, congress, traffic.

interest n 1 have an interest in dance: curiosity, inquisitiveness, concern, care, attention, attentiveness, notice, regard, heed, charm, allure, appeal, attraction, fascination, involvement, engagement. 2 IMPORTANCE, significance, consequence, moment, consideration, magnitude, relevance, prominence, weight, value, note, urgency, priority, seriousness, gravity.

3 leisure interests: activity, pursuit, pastime, hobby, diversion, recreation, amusement. 4 ADVANTAGE, good, benefit, profit, gain. 5 business interests: share, stake, concern, business, claim, involvement, participation, portion, investment, stock, equity. 6 earn interest: dividend, return, profit, gain, receipts, revenue, proceeds, credits, bonus, premium, percentage.

a 1 boredom. 2 meaninglessness. 4 loss.
➤ v concern, involve, touch, move, attract, appeal to, divert, amuse, occupy, engage, absorb, engross, fascinate, intrigue.

a bore.

interested adj 1 ATTENTIVE, curious, absorbed, engrossed, fascinated, enthusiastic, keen, attracted. 2 CONCERNED, involved, affected.

a 1 uninterested, indifferent, apathetic. 2 disinterested, unaffected.

interesting adj attractive, appealing, entertaining, engaging, absorbing, engrossing, fascinating, intriguing, compelling, gripping, stimulating, thought-provoking, curious, unusual.

a uninteresting, boring, monotonous, tedious.

interfere v 1 INTRUDE, poke one's nose in, pry, butt in, interrupt, intervene, meddle, tamper. 2 HINDER, hamper, obstruct, block, impede, handicap, cramp, inhibit, conflict, clash.

a 2 assist.

interference n 1 INTRUSION, prying, interruption, intervention, meddling. 2 OBSTRUCTION, opposition, conflict, clashing.

a 2 assistance.

interim adj temporary, provisional, stopgap, makeshift, improvised, stand-in, acting, caretaker.
➤ n meantime, meanwhile, interval.

interior adj 1 INTERNAL, inside, inner, central, inward, mental, spiritual, private, secret, hidden. 2 HOME, domestic, inland, up-country, remote.

a 1 exterior, external.
➤ n inside, centre, middle, core, heart, depths.

a exterior, outside.

interjection n exclamation, ejaculation, cry, shout, call, interpolation.

interlude n interval, intermission, break, breathing-space, pause, rest, recess, stop, stoppage, respite, wait, delay, halt, spell, hiatus (*fml*), breather (*infml*), let-up (*infml*).

intermediary *n* mediator, go-between, middleman, broker, agent.

intermediate *adj* midway, halfway, in-between, middle, mid, median, mean, intermediary, intervening, transitional.
🖙 extreme.

interminable *adj* endless, never-ending, ceaseless, perpetual, limitless, unlimited, long, long-winded, long-drawn-out, dragging, wearisome.
🖙 limited, brief.

intermission *n* interval, entr'acte, interlude, break, recess, rest, respite, breather (*infml*), breathing-space, pause, lull, let-up (*infml*), remission, suspension, interruption, halt, stop, stoppage, cessation.

intermittent *adj* occasional, periodic, sporadic, spasmodic, fitful, erratic, irregular, broken.
🖙 continuous, constant.

intern *v* confine, detain, hold, hold in custody, jail, imprison.
🖙 free, release.

internal *adj* inside, inner, interior, inward, intimate, private, personal, domestic, in-house.
🖙 external.

international *adj* global, worldwide, intercontinental, cosmopolitan, universal, general.
🖙 national, local, parochial.

Internet

Internet terms include: ad click, address, ADSL (Asynchronous Digital Subscriber Line), alias, anonymous FTP, applet, attachment, backbone, backbone cabling, bandwidth, banner, BBS (Bulletin Board System), bookmark, bounced mail, bps (bits per second), broadband, browser, cable-free connection, chat, chatroom, connect time, cookie, country code, cybercafé, cyberspace, dialer, dial up connection, dedicated line, digital signing, DNS (Domain Name Server/System), domain name, dotcom, download, e-commerce, email *or* e-mail, emoticon, encryption, e-tailing, extranet, firewall, flame, FTP (File Transfer Protocol), gateway, heavy site, helper application, hit, home page, host, host name, HTML (HyperText Markup Language), HTTP *or* http (Hypertext Transfer Protocol),

hyperlink, hypertext, IMAP (Internet Message Access Protocol), intelligent agent, Internet access provider (IAP), Internet Protocol (IP), Internet Relay Chat (IRC), Internet service provider (ISP), intranet, ISDN (Integrated Services Digital Network), Java, JPEG (Joint Photographics Experts Group), junk mail, kill file, latency, link, mailbox, mailing list, mail server, Microsoft Internet Explorer®, MIME (Multipurpose Internet Mail Extensions), modem, moderated mailing lists/newsgroup, Netscape Navigator®, newsgroup, newsreader, NNTP (Network News Transfer Protocol), node, offline, online, online service, packet, plain text, plug-in, POP (Point of Presence), POP3 (Post Office Protocol), portal, postmaster, PPP (Point to Point Protocol), private commercial community, protocol, protocol name, search engine, server, set-top box, signature file, smiley, snail mail, spam, surf, TCP/IP (Transmission Control Protocol/ Internet Protocol), timeout, upload, URL (Uniform *or* Universal Resource Locator), Usenet, user name, viral email, WAN (wide area network), WAP (Wireless Application Protocol), Web cam, web page, World Wide Web (WWW *or* www).

interplay *n* exchange, interchange, interaction, reciprocation, give-and-take (*infml*).

interpose *v* insert, introduce, interject, interpolate, put in, thrust in, interrupt, intrude, interfere, come between, intervene, step in, mediate.

interpret *v* explain, expound, elucidate, clarify, throw light on, define, paraphrase, translate, render, decode, decipher, solve, make sense of, understand, construe, read, take.

interpretation *n* explanation, clarification, analysis, translation, rendering, version, performance, reading, understanding, sense, meaning.

interpreter *n* translator, linguist, commentator, annotator, hermeneutist (*fml*), elucidator (*fml*), exegete (*fml*), exponent (*fml*), expositor (*fml*).

interrogate *v* question, quiz, examine, cross-examine, grill (*infml*), give the third degree, pump, debrief.

interrogation *n* questioning, cross-questioning, examination, cross-examination, grilling (*infml*), third degree (*infml*), inquisition, inquiry, inquest.

interrogative *adj* questioning, quizzical, curious, inquisitive, probing, inquiring, interrogatory, inquisitional (*fml*), inquisitorial (*fml*), catechetical (*fml*), erotetic (*fml*).

interrupt *v* intrude, barge in (*infml*), butt in, interject, break in, heckle, disturb, disrupt, interfere, obstruct, check, hinder, hold up, stop, halt, suspend, discontinue, cut off, disconnect, punctuate, separate, divide, cut, break.

interruption *n* intrusion, interjection, disturbance, disruption, obstruction, impediment, obstacle, hitch, pause, break, halt, stop, stoppage, suspension, discontinuance, disconnection, separation, division.

intersect *v* cross, criss-cross, cut across, bisect, divide, meet, converge.

intersection *n* junction, interchange, crossroads, crossing.

intertwine *v* entwine, interweave, interlace, interlink, twist, twine, cross, weave.

interval *n* interlude, intermission, break, rest, pause, delay, wait, interim, meantime, meanwhile, gap, opening, space, distance, period, spell, time, season.

intervene *v* **1** STEP IN, mediate, arbitrate, interfere, interrupt, intrude. **2** OCCUR, happen, elapse, pass.

intervention *n* involvement, interference, intrusion, mediation, agency, intercession.

interview *n* audience, consultation, talk, dialogue, meeting, conference, press conference, oral examination, viva.
➤ *v* question, interrogate, examine, vet.

interviewer *n* examiner, questioner, investigator, reporter, correspondent, evaluator, appraiser, assessor, interrogator, inquisitor, interlocutor (*fml*), interrogant (*fml*).

intestines *n* bowels, guts, entrails, insides, innards (*infml*), offal, viscera, vitals.

intimacy *n* friendship, closeness, familiarity, confidence, confidentiality, privacy.
🔄 distance.

intimate¹ *v* hint, insinuate, imply, suggest, indicate, communicate, impart, tell, state, declare, announce.

intimate² *adj* friendly, informal, familiar, cosy, warm, affectionate, dear, bosom, close, near, confidential, secret, private, personal, internal, innermost, deep, penetrating, detailed, exhaustive.
🔄 unfriendly, cold, distant.
➤ *n* friend, bosom friend, confidant(e), associate.
🔄 stranger.

intimation *n* hint, inkling, insinuation, implication, suggestion, indication, announcement, communication, signal, declaration, notice, statement, reference, warning, reminder, allusion.

intimidate *v* daunt, cow, overawe, appal, dismay, alarm, scare, frighten, terrify, threaten, menace, terrorize, bully, browbeat, bulldoze, coerce, pressure, pressurize, lean on (*sl*).

intimidation *n* frightening, terrifying, menaces, threats, threatening, threatening behaviour, terrorization, terrorizing, domineering, tyrannization, bullying, browbeating, coercion, compulsion, pressure, fear, terror, arm-twisting (*infml*), screws (*infml*), frighteners (*infml*), big stick (*infml*).
🔄 persuasion.

intolerable *adj* unbearable, unendurable, insupportable, unacceptable, insufferable, impossible.
🔄 tolerable.

intolerant *adj* impatient, prejudiced, bigoted, narrow-minded, small-minded, opinionated, dogmatic, illiberal, uncharitable.
🔄 tolerant.

intonation *n* modulation, tone, accentuation, inflection.

intoxicated *adj* **1** DRUNK, drunken, inebriated, tipsy. **2** EXCITED, elated, exhilarated, thrilled.
🔄 **1** sober.

intoxicating *adj* **1** *intoxicating liquor*: alcoholic, strong. **2** EXCITING, stimulating, heady, exhilarating, thrilling.
🔄 **1** sobering.

intoxication *n* **1** DRUNKENNESS, inebriation, tipsiness. **2** EXCITEMENT, elation, exhilaration, euphoria.
🔄 **1** sobriety.

intrepid *adj* bold, daring, brave, courageous, plucky, valiant, lion-hearted, fearless, dauntless, undaunted, stout-hearted, stalwart, gallant, heroic.
🔄 cowardly, timid.

intricate *adj* elaborate, fancy, ornate, rococo, complicated, complex, sophisticated, involved, convoluted, tortuous, tangled, entangled, knotty, perplexing, difficult.
ẽ simple, plain, straightforward.

intrigue *n* **1** PLOT, scheme, conspiracy, collusion, machination, manoeuvre, stratagem, ruse, wile, trickery, double-dealing, sharp practice. **2** ROMANCE, liaison, affair, amour, intimacy.
➤ *v* **1** FASCINATE, rivet, puzzle, tantalize, attract, charm, captivate. **2** PLOT, scheme, conspire, connive, machinate, manoeuvre.
ẽ **1** bore.

intriguing *adj* fascinating, appealing, charming, absorbing, riveting, compelling, captivating, diverting, exciting, interesting, beguiling, attractive, tantalizing, titillating, puzzling.
ẽ boring, uninteresting, dull.

intrinsic *adj* basic, central, essential, fundamental, natural, underlying, built-in, in-built, inborn, inbred, interior, inherent, inward, native, indigenous, congenital, constitutional, elemental, genuine.
ẽ extrinsic.

introduce *v* **1** INSTITUTE, begin, start, commence, establish, found, inaugurate, launch, open, bring in, announce, present, acquaint, familiarize, initiate. **2** PUT FORWARD, advance, submit, offer, propose, suggest.
ẽ **1** end, conclude. **2** remove, take away.

introduction *n* **1** INSTITUTION, beginning, start, commencement, establishment, inauguration, launch, presentation, debut, initiation. **2** FOREWORD, preface, preamble, prologue, preliminaries, overture, prelude, lead-in, opening.
ẽ **1** removal, withdrawal. **2** appendix, conclusion.

introductory *adj* preliminary, preparatory, opening, inaugural, first, initial, early, elementary, basic.

introspective *adj* inward-looking, contemplative, meditative, pensive, thoughtful, brooding, introverted, self-centred, reserved, withdrawn.
ẽ outward-looking.

introverted *adj* introspective, inward-looking, self-centred, withdrawn, shy, reserved, quiet.
ẽ extroverted.

intrude *v* interrupt, butt in, meddle, interfere, violate, infringe, encroach, trespass.
ẽ withdraw, stand back.

intruder *n* trespasser, prowler, burglar, raider, invader, infiltrator, interloper, gatecrasher.

intrusion *n* interruption, interference, violation, infringement, encroachment, trespass, invasion, incursion.
ẽ withdrawal.

intrusive *adj* disturbing, interfering, irritating, annoying, troublesome, invasive, obtrusive, interrupting, trespassing, meddlesome, uncalled-for, unwanted, unwelcome, uninvited, forward, impertinent, officious, presumptuous, importunate (*fml*), nosey (*infml*), pushy (*infml*), snooping (*infml*), go-getting (*infml*).
ẽ unintrusive, welcome.

intuition *n* instinct, sixth sense, perception, discernment, insight, hunch, feeling, gut feeling (*infml*).
ẽ reasoning.

intuitive *adj* instinctive, spontaneous, involuntary, innate, untaught.
ẽ reasoned.

inundate *v* flood, deluge, swamp, engulf, submerge, immerse, drown, bury, overwhelm, overrun.

invade *v* enter, penetrate, infiltrate, burst in, descend on, attack, raid, seize, occupy, overrun, swarm over, infest, pervade, encroach, infringe, violate.
ẽ withdraw, evacuate.

invalid¹ *adj* sick, ill, poorly, ailing, sickly, weak, feeble, frail, infirm, disabled, bedridden.
ẽ healthy.
➤ *n* patient, convalescent.

invalid² *adj* **1** FALSE, fallacious, unsound, ill-founded, unfounded, baseless, illogical, irrational, unscientific, wrong, incorrect. **2** ILLEGAL, null, void, worthless.
ẽ **1** valid. **2** legal.

invalidate *v* annul, cancel, quash, void, veto, discredit, negate, undo, overrule, overthrow, undermine, weaken, abrogate (*fml*), nullify (*fml*), rescind (*fml*), revoke (*fml*), terminate (*fml*).
ẽ validate.

invaluable *adj* priceless, inestimable, incalculable, precious, valuable, useful.
ẽ worthless, cheap.

invariable *adj* fixed, set, unvarying, unchanging, unchangeable, permanent, constant, steady, unwavering, uniform, rigid, inflexible, habitual, regular.
🖙 variable.

invariably *adv* always, without exception, without fail, unfailingly, consistently, regularly, habitually.
🖙 never.

invasion *n* attack, offensive, onslaught, raid, incursion, foray, breach, penetration, infiltration, intrusion, encroachment, infringement, violation.
🖙 withdrawal, evacuation.

invent *v* conceive, think up, design, discover, create, originate, formulate, frame, devise, contrive, improvise, fabricate, make up, concoct, cook up, trump up, imagine, dream up.

invention *n* **1** *her latest invention*: design, creation, brainchild, discovery, development, device, gadget. **2** LIE, falsehood, deceit, fabrication, fiction, tall story, fantasy, figment. **3** INVENTIVENESS, imagination, creativity, innovation, originality, ingenuity, inspiration, genius.
🖙 **2** truth.

inventive *adj* imaginative, creative, innovative, original, ingenious, resourceful, fertile, inspired, gifted, clever.

inventor *n* designer, discoverer, creator, originator, author, architect, maker, scientist, engineer.

inverse *adj* inverted, upside down, transposed, reversed, opposite, contrary, reverse, converse.

invert *v* upturn, turn upside down, overturn, capsize, upset, transpose, reverse.
🖙 right.

invertebrate

Invertebrates include: *sponges*: calcareous, glass, horny; *jellyfish, corals and sea anemones*: Portuguese man-of-war, box jellyfish, sea wasp, dead-men's fingers, sea pansy, sea gooseberry, Venus's girdle; *echinoderms*: sea lily, feather star, starfish, crown-of-thorns, brittle star, sea urchin, sand dollar, sea cucumber; *worms*: annelid worm, arrow worm, blood fluke, bristle worm, earthworm, eelworm, flatworm, fluke, hookworm, leech, liver fluke, lugworm, peanut worm, pinworm, ragworm, ribbonworm, roundworm, sea mouse, tapeworm, threadworm; *crustaceans*: acorn barnacle, barnacle, brine shrimp, crayfish, daphnia, fairy shrimp, fiddler crab, fish louse, goose barnacle, hermit crab, krill, lobster, mantis shrimp, mussel shrimp, pill bug, prawn, sand hopper, seed shrimp, spider crab, spiny lobster, tadpole shrimp, water flea, whale louse, woodlouse; centipede, millipede, velvet worm. *see also* **butterflies and moths**; **insect**; **mollusc**.

invest *v* **1** SPEND, lay out, put in, sink.
2 PROVIDE, supply, endow, vest, empower, authorize, sanction.

investigate *v* inquire into, look into, consider, examine, study, inspect, scrutinize, analyse, go into, probe, explore, search, sift.

investigation *n* inquiry, inquest, hearing, examination, study, research, survey, review, inspection, scrutiny, analysis, probe, exploration, search.

investigator *n* examiner, researcher, detective, sleuth (*infml*), private detective, private eye (*infml*).

investiture *n* installation, induction, inauguration, investing, investment, ordination, coronation, enthronement, admission, instatement.

investment *n* asset, speculation, venture, stake, contribution, outlay, expenditure, transaction.

inveterate *adj* chronic, habitual, hardened, diehard, dyed-in-the-wool, entrenched, confirmed, established, hard-core, obstinate, incorrigible, incurable, irreformable, inured, addicted, long-standing.
🖙 impermanent.

invidious *adj* awkward, difficult, undesirable, unpleasant, objectionable, hateful, obnoxious, offensive, slighting, odious, discriminating, discriminatory, repugnant (*fml*).
🖙 desirable, pleasant.

invigorate *v* vitalize, energize, animate, enliven, liven up, quicken, strengthen, fortify, brace, stimulate, inspire, exhilarate, perk up, refresh, freshen, revitalize, rejuvenate.
🖙 tire, weary, dishearten.

invincible *adj* unbeatable, unconquerable, insuperable, unsurmountable, indomitable,

unassailable, impregnable, impenetrable, invulnerable, indestructible.
ᴇᴢ beatable.

invisible *adj* unseen, out of sight, hidden, concealed, disguised, inconspicuous, indiscernible, imperceptible, infinitesimal, microscopic, imaginary, non-existent.
ᴇᴢ visible.

invitation *n* request, solicitation, call, summons, temptation, enticement, allurement, come-on (*infml*), encouragement, inducement, provocation, incitement, challenge.

invite *v* ask, call, summon, welcome, encourage, lead, draw, attract, tempt, entice, allure, bring on, provoke, ask for, request, solicit, seek.

inviting *adj* welcoming, appealing, attractive, tempting, seductive, enticing, alluring, pleasing, delightful, captivating, fascinating, intriguing, tantalizing.
ᴇᴢ uninviting, unappealing.

invoke *v* call upon, conjure, appeal to, petition, solicit, implore, entreat, beg, beseech, supplicate, pray.

involuntary *adj* spontaneous, unconscious, automatic, mechanical, reflex, instinctive, conditioned, impulsive, unthinking, blind, uncontrolled, unintentional.
ᴇᴢ deliberate, intentional.

involve *v* 1 REQUIRE, necessitate, mean, imply, entail, include, incorporate, embrace, cover, take in, affect, concern. 2 IMPLICATE, incriminate, inculpate, draw in, mix up, embroil, associate. 3 ENGAGE, occupy, absorb, engross, preoccupy, hold, grip, rivet.
ᴇᴢ 1 exclude.

involved *adj* 1 CONCERNED, implicated, mixed up, caught up, in on (*sl*), participating. 2 *an involved explanation*: complicated, complex, intricate, elaborate, tangled, knotty, tortuous, confusing.
ᴇᴢ 1 uninvolved. 2 simple.

involvement *n* concern, interest, responsibility, association, connection, participation, implication, entanglement.

invulnerable *adj* safe, secure, unassailable, impenetrable, invincible, indestructible.
ᴇᴢ vulnerable.

inward *adj* incoming, entering, inside, interior, internal, inner, innermost, inmost, personal, private, secret, confidential.
ᴇᴢ outward, external.

inwardly *adv* inside, to oneself, within, at heart, in one's heart of hearts, deep down, deep inside one, privately, secretly.
ᴇᴢ externally, outwardly.

iota *n* scrap, bit, mite, jot, speck, trace, hint, grain, particle, atom.

irate *adj* annoyed, irritated, indignant, up in arms, angry, enraged, mad (*infml*), furious, infuriated, incensed, worked up, fuming, livid, exasperated.
ᴇᴢ calm, composed.

iron *adj* rigid, inflexible, adamant, determined, hard, steely, tough, strong.
ᴇᴢ pliable, weak.
➤ *v* press, smooth, flatten.
♦ **iron out** resolve, settle, sort out, straighten out, clear up, put right, reconcile, deal with, get rid of, eradicate, eliminate.

ironic *adj* ironical, sarcastic, sardonic, scornful, contemptuous, derisive, sneering, scoffing, mocking, satirical, wry, paradoxical.

irony *n* sarcasm, mockery, satire, paradox, contrariness, incongruity.

irrational *adj* unreasonable, unsound, illogical, absurd, crazy, wild, foolish, silly, senseless, unwise.
ᴇᴢ rational.

irreconcilable *adj* incompatible, opposed, conflicting, clashing, contradictory, inconsistent.
ᴇᴢ reconcilable.

irrefutable *adj* undeniable, incontrovertible, indisputable, incontestable, unquestionable, unanswerable, certain, sure.

irregular *adj* 1 ROUGH, bumpy, uneven, crooked. 2 VARIABLE, fluctuating, wavering, erratic, fitful, intermittent, sporadic, spasmodic, occasional, random, haphazard, disorderly, unsystematic. 3 ABNORMAL, unconventional, unorthodox, improper, unusual, exceptional, anomalous.
ᴇᴢ 1 smooth, level. 2 regular. 3 conventional.

irrelevant *adj* immaterial, beside the point, inapplicable, inappropriate, unrelated, unconnected, inconsequent, peripheral, tangential.
ᴇᴢ relevant.

irreparable *adj* irreversible, irreclaimable, irrecoverable, irremediable,

irretrievable, incurable, unrepairable.
🔁 recoverable, remediable.

irreplaceable *adj* indispensable, essential, vital, unique, priceless, peerless, matchless, unmatched.
🔁 replaceable.

irrepressible *adj* ebullient, bubbly, uninhibited, buoyant, resilient, boisterous, uncontrollable, ungovernable, unstoppable.

irreproachable *adj* irreprehensible, blameless, unimpeachable, faultless, impeccable, perfect, unblemished, immaculate, stainless, spotless, pure.
🔁 blameworthy, culpable.

irresistible *adj* overwhelming, overpowering, unavoidable, inevitable, inescapable, uncontrollable, potent, compelling, imperative, pressing, urgent, tempting, seductive, ravishing, enchanting, charming, fascinating.
🔁 resistible, avoidable.

irrespective of *conj* regardless of, disregarding, no matter, without considering, ignoring, not affecting, however, whatever, whichever, whoever, never mind, notwithstanding (*fml*).

irresponsible *adj* unreliable, untrustworthy, careless, negligent, thoughtless, heedless, ill-considered, rash, reckless, wild, carefree, light-hearted, immature.
🔁 responsible, cautious.

irreverent *adj* **1** IMPIOUS, godless, irreligious, profane, sacrilegious, blasphemous. **2** DISRESPECTFUL, discourteous, rude, impudent, impertinent, mocking, flippant.
🔁 **1** reverent. **2** respectful.

irreversible *adj* irrevocable, unalterable, final, permanent, lasting, irreparable, irremediable, irretrievable, incurable, hopeless.
🔁 reversible, remediable, curable.

irrevocable *adj* unalterable, unchangeable, changeless, invariable, immutable, final, fixed, settled, predetermined, irreversible, irretrievable.
🔁 alterable, flexible, reversible.

irrigate *v* water, flood, inundate, wet, moisten, dampen.

irritable *adj* cross, bad-tempered, ill-tempered, crotchety, crusty, cantankerous, crabby, testy, short-tempered, snappish, snappy, short, impatient, touchy, edgy, thin-skinned, hypersensitive, prickly, peevish, fretful, fractious.
🔁 good-tempered, cheerful.

irritate *v* **1** ANNOY, get on one's nerves, aggravate (*infml*), bother, harass, rouse, provoke, rile, anger, enrage, infuriate, incense, exasperate, peeve (*infml*), put out (*infml*). **2** INFLAME, chafe, rub, tickle, itch.
🔁 **1** please, gratify.

irritated *adj* annoyed, bothered, angry, cross, exasperated, irked, irritable, nettled, vexed, ruffled, roused, riled, edgy, impatient, uptight, harassed, flustered, discomposed, displeased, piqued, peeved (*infml*), put out (*infml*), ratty (*infml*), narked (*infml*), miffed (*infml*), in a huff (*infml*).
🔁 composed, gratified, pleased.

irritating *adj* **1** ANNOYING, infuriating, maddening, troublesome, bothersome, irksome, tiresome, grating, worrisome, vexatious, vexing, disturbing, upsetting, nagging, displeasing, galling, provoking, thorny, trying, aggravating (*infml*), pesky (*infml*). **2** ABRASIVE, rubbing, chafing, sore, ticklish, itchy.
🔁 **1** pleasant, pleasing.

irritation *n* displeasure, dissatisfaction, annoyance, aggravation (*infml*), provocation, anger, vexation, indignation, fury, exasperation, irritability, crossness, testiness, snappiness, impatience.
🔁 pleasure, satisfaction, delight.

island *n* isle, islet, atoll, archipelago, eyot, holm, cay, key, skerry.

The world's largest islands include:
Australia, Greenland, New Guinea, Borneo, Madagascar, Sumatra, Baffin (Canada), Honshu (Japan), Great Britain, Victoria (Canada).

---

isolate *v* set apart, sequester, seclude, keep apart, segregate, quarantine, insulate, cut off, detach, remove, disconnect, separate, divorce, alienate, shut out, ostracize, exclude.
🔁 assimilate, incorporate.

isolated *adj* **1** REMOTE, out-of-the-way, outlying, godforsaken, deserted, unfrequented, secluded, detached, cut off, lonely, solitary, single. **2** *an isolated occurrence*: unique, special, exceptional, atypical, unusual, freak, abnormal, anomalous.
🔁 **1** populous. **2** typical.

isolation *n* quarantine, solitude,

solitariness, loneliness, remoteness, seclusion, retirement, withdrawal, exile, segregation, insulation, separation, detachment, disconnection, dissociation, alienation.

issue n 1 MATTER, affair, concern, problem, point, subject, topic, question, debate, argument, dispute, controversy.
2 PUBLICATION, release, distribution, supply, delivery, circulation, promulgation, broadcast, announcement. **3** *last week's issue*: copy, number, instalment, edition, impression, printing.
➤ v **1** PUBLISH, release, distribute, supply, deliver, give out, deal out, circulate, promulgate, broadcast, announce, put out, emit, produce. **2** ORIGINATE, stem, spring, rise, emerge, burst forth, gush, flow, proceed, emanate, arise.

itch v tickle, irritate, tingle, prickle, crawl.
➤ n **1** ITCHINESS, tickle, irritation, prickling. **2** EAGERNESS, keenness, desire, longing, yearning, hankering, craving.

itching adj dying, longing, burning, hankering, aching, eager, greedy, impatient, inquisitive, avid, raring.

item n **1** OBJECT, article, thing, piece, component, ingredient, element, factor, point, detail, particular, aspect, feature, consideration, matter. **2** *an item in the local paper*: article, piece, report, account, notice, entry, paragraph.

itemize v list, record, specify, detail, document, instance, particularize, count, mention, overname, number, enumerate, tabulate, make an inventory.

itinerant adj travelling, peripatetic, roving, roaming, wandering, rambling, nomadic, migratory, rootless, unsettled.
🖪 stationary, settled.

itinerary n route, course, journey, tour, circuit, plan, programme, schedule.

Jj

jab *v* poke, prod, dig, nudge, stab, push, elbow, lunge, punch, tap, thrust.

jacket *n* casing, cover, covering, wrapping, wrap, wrapper, case, sheath, shell, skin, envelope, folder.

jackpot *n* prize, winnings, kitty, pool, pot, reward, award, big time (*infml*), bonanza.

jack up *v* **1** LIFT, raise, hoist, elevate. **2** *jack up prices*: increase, inflate, put up, push up, hike (up).

jaded *adj* fatigued, exhausted, dulled, played-out, tired, tired out, weary, spent, bored, fagged (*infml*).
🔃 fresh, refreshed.

jagged *adj* uneven, irregular, notched, indented, rough, serrated, saw-edged, toothed, ragged, pointed, ridged, craggy, barbed, broken.
🔃 even, smooth.

jail, gaol *n* prison, jailhouse, custody, lock-up, penitentiary, guardhouse, inside (*infml*), nick (*sl*), clink (*sl*).
➤ *v* imprison, incarcerate, lock up, put away, send down, confine, detain, intern, impound, immure.

jailer, gaoler *n* prison officer, warden, warder, guard, screw (*sl*), keeper, captor.

jam¹ *v* **1** CRAM, pack, wedge, squash, squeeze, press, crush, crowd, congest, ram, stuff, confine, force. **2** BLOCK, clog, obstruct, stall, stick.
➤ *n* **1** CRUSH, crowd, press, congestion, pack, mob, throng, bottleneck, traffic jam. **2** PREDICAMENT, trouble, quandary, plight, fix (*infml*).

jam² *n* conserve, preserve, jelly, spread, marmalade.

jamboree *n* celebration, party, rally, festivity, festival, carnival, jubilee, junket, fête, frolic, revelry, spree, carousal, merriment, field day, gathering, get-together, convention, shindig (*infml*).

jangle *v* clank, clash, jar, clatter, jingle, chime, rattle, vibrate.
➤ *n* clang, clash, rattle, jar, cacophony, dissonance, din, discord, racket, reverberation.
🔃 euphony.

janitor *n* caretaker, doorkeeper, doorman, custodian, concierge, porter.

jar¹ *n* pot, container, vessel, receptacle, crock, pitcher, urn, vase, flask, flagon, carafe, jug, mug.

jar² *v* **1** JOLT, agitate, rattle, shake, vibrate, jangle, rock, disturb, discompose.
2 ANNOY, irritate, grate, nettle (*infml*), offend, upset, irk. **3** BICKER, quarrel, clash, disagree.

jargon *n* **1** PARLANCE, cant, argot, vernacular, idiom. **2** NONSENSE, gobbledygook (*infml*), mumbo-jumbo (*infml*), gibberish.

jarring *adj* discordant, jangling, harsh, grating, irritating, cacophonous, rasping, strident, upsetting, disturbing, jolting.

jaundiced *adj* **1** BITTER, cynical, pessimistic, sceptical, distrustful, disbelieving, envious, jealous, hostile, jaded, suspicious, resentful. **2** DISTORTED, biased, prejudiced, preconceived.

jaunt *n* trip, outing, excursion, holiday, tour, ride, drive, spin, ramble, stroll.

jaunty *adj* sprightly, lively, perky, breezy, buoyant, high-spirited, self-confident, carefree, airy, cheeky, debonair, dapper, smart, showy, spruce.
🔃 depressed, dowdy.

jaw (*infml*) *v* chat, chatter, gossip, natter (*infml*), talk, rabbit (on) (*infml*), gabble, babble.
➤ *n* talk, gossip, chat, conversation, discussion, chinwag, natter (*infml*).

jazz

> Kinds of jazz include: acid jazz, Afro-Cuban, avant-garde, bebop, blues, boogie-woogie, bop, cool, Dixieland, free-form, fusion, hot jazz, jive, mainstream, modern, New Orleans, post-bop, ragtime, soul jazz, spiel, swing, third stream, trad, West Coast.

jazz up *v* liven up, enliven, smarten up, brighten up.

jealous *adj* **1** ENVIOUS, covetous, grudging, resentful, green (*infml*), green-eyed (*infml*). **2** SUSPICIOUS, wary, distrustful,

anxious, possessive, protective.
F3 1 contented, satisfied.

jealousy *n* **1** ENVY, covetousness, grudge, resentment, spite, ill-will. **2** SUSPICION, distrust, mistrust, possessiveness.

jeer *v* mock, scoff, taunt, jibe, ridicule, sneer, deride, make fun of, chaff, barrack, twit, knock (*infml*), heckle, banter.
➤ *n* mockery, derision, ridicule, taunt, jibe, sneer, scoff, abuse, catcall, dig (*infml*), hiss, hoot.

jell *see* **gel**.

jeopardize *v* endanger, imperil, risk, hazard, venture, gamble, chance, threaten, menace, expose, stake.
F3 protect, safeguard.

jeopardy *n* danger, peril, risk, hazard, endangerment, venture, vulnerability, precariousness, insecurity, exposure, liability.
F3 safety, security.

jerk *n* jolt, tug, twitch, jar, jog, yank, wrench, pull, pluck, lurch, throw, thrust, shrug.
➤ *v* jolt, tug, twitch, jog, yank, wrench, pull, jiggle, lurch, pluck, thrust, shrug, throw, bounce.

jerky *adj* fitful, twitchy, spasmodic, jumpy, jolting, convulsive, disconnected, bumpy, bouncy, shaky, rough, unco-ordinated, uncontrolled, incoherent.
F3 smooth.

jerry-built *adj* insubstantial, ramshackle, thrown together, quickly built, built on the cheap, rickety, unstable, cheap, shoddy, defective, faulty, flimsy, unsubstantial, slipshod, cheapjack.
F3 firm, stable, substantial.

jest *n* joke, quip, wisecrack (*infml*), witticism, crack (*infml*), banter, fooling, gag (*infml*), prank, kidding (*infml*), leg-pull (*infml*), trick, hoax.
➤ *v* joke, quip, fool, kid (*infml*), tease, mock, jeer.

jet¹ *n* gush, spurt, spout, spray, spring, sprinkler, sprayer, fountain, flow, stream, squirt.

jet² *adj* black, pitch-black, ebony, sable, sooty.

jettison *v* discard, scrap, throw away, get rid of, abandon, offload, unload, eject, expel, heave, ditch (*infml*), dump (*infml*), chuck (*infml*).
F3 load, take on.

jetty *n* breakwater, pier, dock, groyne, quay, wharf.

jewel *n* **1** GEM, precious stone, gemstone, ornament, rock (*sl*). **2** TREASURE, find, prize, rarity, paragon, pearl.

jewellery

Types of jewellery include: bangle, bracelet, charm bracelet, anklet, cufflink, tiepin, hatpin, brooch, cameo, earring, nose-ring, ring, signet-ring, solitaire ring, necklace, necklet, choker, pendant, locket, chain, beads, amulet, torque, tiara, coronet, diadem.

Jewish calendar

The Jewish calendar and its Gregorian equivalents: Tishri (September-October), Hesshvan (October-November), Kislev (November-December), Tevet (December-January), Shevat (January-February), Adar (February-March), Adar Sheni (leap years only), Nisan (March-April), Iyar (April-May), Sivan (May-June), Tammuz (June-July), Av (July-August), Elul (August-September).

jibe *see* **gibe**.

jig *v* jerk, prance, caper, hop, jump, twitch, skip, bounce, bob, wiggle, shake, wobble.

jilt *v* abandon, reject, desert, discard, brush off, ditch (*infml*), drop, spurn, betray.

jingle *v* clink, tinkle, ring, chime, chink, jangle, clatter, rattle.
➤ *n* **1** CLINK, tinkle, ringing, clang, rattle, clangour. **2** RHYME, verse, song, tune, ditty, doggerel, melody, poem, chant, chorus.

jingoism *n* chauvinism, flag-waving, patriotism, nationalism, imperialism, warmongering, insularity.

jinx (*infml*) *n* spell, curse, evil eye, hex, voodoo, hoodoo, black magic, gremlin (*infml*), charm, plague.
➤ *v* curse, bewitch, bedevil, doom, plague.

jitters *n* nerves, nervousness, tenseness, anxiety, fidgets, agitation, trembling, uneasiness, heebie-jeebies (*infml*), habdabs (*infml*), the creeps (*infml*), the shakes (*infml*), the shivers (*infml*), the willies (*infml*), jimjams (*infml*).

job *n* **1** *she has a good job*: work, employment, occupation, position, post, situation, profession, career, calling, vocation, trade, métier, capacity, business, livelihood. **2** *it's a difficult job*: task, chore, duty, responsibility, charge, commission,

mission, activity, affair, concern, proceeding, project, enterprise, office, pursuit, role, undertaking, venture, province, part, place, share, errand, function, contribution, stint, assignment, consignment.

jobless *adj* unemployed, out of work, laid off, on the dole, inactive, redundant.
≈ employed.

jockey *n* equestrian, horseman, horsewoman, rider.
➤ *v* manipulate, manoeuvre, engineer, negotiate, wheedle, cajole, coax, induce, ease, edge.

jocular *adj* joking, jesting, funny, jocose (*fml*), humorous, jovial, amusing, comical, entertaining, facetious, droll, whimsical, teasing, witty.
≈ serious.

jog *v* **1** JOLT, jar, bump, jostle, jerk, joggle, nudge, poke, shake, prod, bounce, push, rock. **2** PROMPT, remind, stir, arouse, activate, stimulate. **3** RUN, trot.
➤ *n* **1** JOLT, bump, jerk, nudge, shove, push, poke, prod, shake. **2** RUN, trot.

join *v* **1** UNITE, connect, combine, conjoin, attach, link, amalgamate, fasten, merge, marry, couple, yoke, tie, splice, knit, cement, add, adhere, annex. **2** ABUT, adjoin, border (on), verge on, touch, meet, coincide, march with. **3** ASSOCIATE, affiliate, accompany, ally, enlist, enrol, enter, sign up, team.
≈ **1** divide, separate. **3** leave.

joint *n* junction, connection, union, juncture, intersection, hinge, knot, articulation, seam.
➤ *adj* combined, common, communal, joined, shared, united, collective, amalgamated, mutual, co-operative, co-ordinated, consolidated, concerted.

joke *n* **1** JEST, quip, crack (*infml*), gag (*infml*), witticism, wisecrack (*infml*), one-liner (*infml*), pun, hoot, whimsy, yarn. **2** TRICK, jape, lark, prank, spoof, fun.
➤ *v* jest, quip, clown, fool, pun, wisecrack (*infml*), kid (*infml*), tease, banter, mock, laugh, frolic, gambol.

joker *n* comedian, comic, wit, humorist, jester, trickster, wag, clown, buffoon, kidder, droll, card (*infml*), character, sport.

jolly *adj* jovial, merry, cheerful, playful, hearty, happy, exuberant.
≈ sad.

jolt *v* **1** JAR, jerk, jog, bump, jostle, knock,

bounce, shake, push. **2** UPSET, startle, shock, surprise, stun, discompose, disconcert, disturb.
➤ *n* **1** JAR, jerk, jog, bump, blow, impact, lurch, shake. **2** SHOCK, surprise, reversal, setback, start.

jostle *v* push, shove, jog, bump, elbow, hustle, jolt, crowd, shoulder, joggle, shake, squeeze, throng.

jot down *v* write down, take down, note, list, record, scribble, register, enter.

journal *n* newspaper, periodical, magazine, paper, publication, review, weekly, monthly, register, chronicle, diary, gazette, daybook, log, record.

journalist *n* reporter, news-writer, hack, correspondent, editor, columnist, feature-writer, commentator, broadcaster, contributor.

journey *n* voyage, trip, travel, expedition, passage, trek, tour, ramble, outing, wanderings, safari, progress.
➤ *v* travel, voyage, go, trek, tour, roam, rove, proceed, wander, tramp, ramble, range, gallivant.

jovial *adj* jolly, cheery, merry, affable, cordial, genial.
≈ gloomy.

joy *n* happiness, gladness, delight, pleasure, bliss, ecstasy, elation, joyfulness, exultation, gratification, rapture.
≈ despair, grief.

joyful *adj* happy, pleased, delighted, glad, elated, ecstatic, triumphant.
≈ sorrowful.

jubilant *adj* joyful, rejoicing, overjoyed, delighted, elated, triumphant, exuberant, excited, euphoric, thrilled.

jubilation *n* euphoria, ecstasy, elation, triumph, excitement, exultation, jollification, joy, celebration, festivity, jamboree, jubilee.
≈ depression, lamentation.

jubilee *n* celebration, commemoration, anniversary, festival, festivity, gala, fête, carnival.

judge *n* **1** JUSTICE, Law Lord, magistrate, arbiter, adjudicator, arbitrator, mediator, moderator, referee, umpire, beak (*sl*). **2** CONNOISSEUR, authority, expert, evaluator, assessor, critic.
➤ *v* **1** ADJUDICATE, arbitrate, try, referee, umpire, decree, mediate, examine, sentence, review, rule, find. **2** ASCERTAIN,

determine, decide, assess, appraise,
evaluate, estimate, value, distinguish,
discern, reckon, believe, think, consider,
conclude, rate. **3** CONDEMN, criticize,
doom.

judgement *n* **1** VERDICT, sentence,
ruling, decree, conclusion, decision,
arbitration, finding, result, mediation,
order. **2** DISCERNMENT, discrimination,
understanding, wisdom, prudence,
common sense, sense, intelligence, taste,
shrewdness, penetration, enlightenment.
3 ASSESSMENT, evaluation, appraisal,
estimate, opinion, view, belief, diagnosis.
4 CONVICTION, damnation, punishment,
retribution, doom, fate, misfortune.

judicial *adj* legal, judiciary, magistral,
forensic, official, discriminating, critical,
impartial.

judicious *adj* wise, prudent, careful,
cautious, astute, discerning, informed,
shrewd, thoughtful, reasonable, sensible,
sound, well-judged, well-advised,
considered.
E3 injudicious.

jug *n* pitcher, carafe, ewer, flagon, urn, jar,
vessel, container.

juggle *v* alter, change, manipulate, falsify,
rearrange, rig, doctor (*infml*), cook (*infml*),
disguise.

juice *n* liquid, fluid, extract, essence, sap,
secretion, nectar, liquor.

juicy *adj* **1** SUCCULENT, moist, lush, watery.
2 (*infml*) INTERESTING, colourful,
sensational, racy, risqué, suggestive, lurid.
E3 1 dry.

jumble *v* disarrange, confuse,
disorganize, mix (up), muddle, shuffle,
tangle.
E3 order.
➤ *n* disorder, disarray, confusion, mess,
chaos, mix-up, muddle, clutter, mixture,
hotch-potch, mishmash (*infml*), medley.

jump *v* **1** LEAP, spring, bound, vault, clear,
bounce, skip, hop, prance, frolic, gambol.
2 START, flinch, jerk, recoil, jump out of
one's skin (*infml*), wince, quail. **3** OMIT,
leave out, miss, skip, pass over, bypass,
disregard, ignore, avoid, digress. **4** RISE,
increase, gain, appreciate, ascend,
escalate, mount, advance, surge, spiral.
➤ *n* **1** LEAP, spring, bound, vault, hop, skip,
bounce, prance, frisk, frolic, pounce.
2 START, jerk, jolt, jar, lurch, shock, spasm,
quiver, shiver, twitch. **3** BREAK, gap,

interruption, lapse, omission, interval,
breach, switch. **4** RISE, increase,
escalation, boost, advance, increment,
upsurge, upturn, mounting. **5** HURDLE,
fence, gate, hedge, barricade, obstacle.

jumper *n* sweater, jersey, pullover,
sweatshirt, woolly.

jumpy *adj* nervous, anxious, agitated,
apprehensive, jittery, tense, edgy, fidgety,
shaky.
E3 calm, composed.

junction *n* joint, join, joining, connection,
juncture, union, intersection, linking,
coupling, meeting-point, confluence.

juncture *n* point, period, stage, time,
occasion, minute, moment, crisis,
emergency, crux, predicament.

junior *adj* younger, minor, lesser, lower,
subordinate, secondary, subsidiary,
inferior.
E3 senior.

junk *n* rubbish, refuse, trash, debris,
garbage, waste, scrap, litter, clutter,
oddments, rummage, dregs, wreckage.

jurisdiction *n* power, authority, control,
influence, dominion, province,
sovereignty, command, domination, rule,
prerogative (*fml*), sway, orbit, bounds,
area, field, scope, range, reach, sphere,
zone.

just *adj* **1** *a just ruler*: fair, equitable,
impartial, unbiased, unprejudiced, fair-
minded, even-handed, objective,
righteous, upright, virtuous, honourable,
good, honest, irreproachable. **2** *a just
punishment*: deserved, merited, fitting,
well-deserved, appropriate, suitable, due,
proper, reasonable, rightful, lawful,
legitimate.
E3 1 unjust. **2** undeserved.
➤ *adv* **1** *he's just left*: a short time ago, a
moment ago, recently, lately. **2** *that's just
like him*: exactly, precisely, perfectly,
completely, absolutely, quite, bang on
(*infml*), spot on (*infml*), to aT (*infml*). **3** *she's
just a child*: only, merely, simply, purely,
nothing but, barely, hardly, scarcely.
♦ **just about** practically, almost, virtually,
nearly, as good as, all but, well-nigh, more
or less, to all intents and purposes.

justice *n* **1** FAIRNESS, equity, impartiality,
objectivity, equitableness, justness,
legitimacy, honesty, right, rightfulness,
rightness, justifiableness, reasonableness,
rectitude. **2** LEGALITY, law, penalty,

recompense, reparation, satisfaction.
3 JUDGE, Justice of the Peace, JP,
magistrate.
🔁 **1** injustice, unfairness.

justifiable *adj* defensible, excusable,
warranted, reasonable, justified, lawful,
legitimate, acceptable, explainable,
forgivable, pardonable, understandable,
valid, well-founded, right, proper,
explicable, fit, tenable.
🔁 unjustifiable.

justification *n* defence, plea, mitigation,
apology, explanation, excuse, vindication,
warrant, rationalization, reason, grounds.

justify *v* vindicate, exonerate, warrant,
substantiate, defend, acquit, absolve,

excuse, forgive, explain, pardon, validate,
uphold, sustain, support, maintain,
establish.

jut out *v* project, protrude, stick out,
overhang, extend.
🔁 recede.

juvenile *n* child, youth, minor, young
person, youngster, adolescent, teenager,
boy, girl, kid (*infml*), infant.
➤ *adj* young, youthful, immature, childish,
puerile, infantile, adolescent, babyish,
unsophisticated.
🔁 mature.

juxtaposition *n* contiguity, proximity,
nearness, closeness, contact, vicinity,
immediacy.

Kk

kaleidoscopic *adj* **1** MANY-COLOURED, multicoloured, variegated, many-splendoured, motley, polychromatic *(fml)*, polychrome *(fml)*. **2** EVER-CHANGING, changeable, fluctuating, manifold, fluid, multifarious *(fml)*.

Fa **1** dull, monochrome, monotonous.

karate

keel over *v* **1** OVERTURN, capsize, founder, collapse, upset. **2** FAINT, pass out, swoon, fall, drop, stagger, topple over.

keen *adj* **1** EAGER, avid, fervent, enthusiastic, earnest, devoted, diligent, industrious. **2** ASTUTE, shrewd, clever, perceptive, wise, discerning, quick, deep, sensitive. **3** SHARP, piercing, penetrating, incisive, acute, pointed, intense, pungent, trenchant.

Fa **1** apathetic. **2** superficial. **3** dull.

keep *v* **1** RETAIN, hold, preserve, hold on to, hang on to, store, stock, possess, amass, accumulate, collect, stack, conserve, deposit, heap, pile, place, maintain, furnish. **2** CARRY ON, keep on, continue, persist, remain. **3** LOOK AFTER, tend, care for, have charge of, have custody of, maintain, provide for, subsidize, support, sustain, be responsible for, foster, mind, protect, shelter, guard, defend, watch (over), shield, safeguard, feed, nurture, manage. **4** DETAIN, delay, retard, check, hinder, hold (up), impede, obstruct, prevent, block, curb, interfere with, restrain, limit, inhibit, deter, hamper, keep back, control, constrain, arrest, withhold. **5** OBSERVE, comply with, respect, obey, fulfil, adhere to, recognize, keep up, keep faith with, commemorate, celebrate, hold, maintain, perform, perpetuate, mark, honour.

➤ **1** SUBSISTENCE, board, livelihood, living, maintenance, support, upkeep, means, food, nourishment, nurture. **2** FORT, fortress, tower, castle, citadel, stronghold, dungeon.

♦ **keep at** persevere, stick at, be steadfast, continue, carry on, complete, endure, finish, last, maintain, remain, stay, persist, plug away at, toil, grind, drudge, labour, beaver away at, slog at *(infml)*.

Fa abandon, neglect.

♦ **keep back** **1** RESTRAIN, check, constrain, curb, impede, limit, prohibit, retard, stop, control, delay. **2** HOLD BACK, restrict, suppress, withhold, conceal, censor, hide, hush up, stifle, reserve, retain.

♦ **keep in** **1** REPRESS, keep back, inhibit, bottle up, conceal, stifle, suppress, hide, control, restrain, quell, stop up. **2** CONFINE, detain, shut in, coop up.

Fa **1** declare. **2** release.

♦ **keep on** continue, carry on, endure, persevere, persist, keep at it, last, remain, stay, stay the course, soldier on *(infml)*, hold on, retain, maintain.

♦ **keep up** keep pace, equal, contend, compete, vie, rival, match, emulate, continue, maintain, persevere, support, sustain, preserve.

keeper *n* guard, custodian, curator, caretaker, attendant, guardian, overseer, steward, warder, jailer, gaoler, warden, supervisor, minder *(infml)*, inspector, conservator *(fml)*, defender, governor, superintendent, surveyor.

keeping *n* **1** CUSTODY, guardianship, supervision, care, charge, safekeeping, retention, protection, maintenance, surveillance, trust, tutelage, ward, cure, patronage, auspices *(fml)*. **2** in *keeping with the architecture*: agreement, harmony, conformity, correspondence, consistency, balance, proportion, accord *(fml)*, congruity *(fml)*.

keepsake *n* memento, souvenir, remembrance, relic, reminder, token, pledge, emblem.

kernel *n* core, grain, seed, nucleus, heart, nub, essence, germ, marrow, substance, nitty-gritty *(infml)*, gist.

key *n* **1** CLUE, cue, indicator, pointer,

explanation, sign, answer, solution, interpretation, means, secret. **2** GUIDE, glossary, translation, legend, code, table, index.

➤ *adj* important, essential, vital, crucial, necessary, principal, decisive, central, chief, main, major, leading, basic, fundamental.

keynote *n* core, centre, heart, substance, theme, gist, essence, emphasis, accent, stress.

keystone *n* cornerstone, core, crux, base, basis, foundation, ground, linchpin, principle, root, mainspring, source, spring, motive.

kick *v* **1** BOOT, hit, strike, jolt. **2** (*infml*) GIVE UP, quit, stop, leave off, abandon, desist from, break.

➤ *n* **1** BLOW, recoil, jolt, striking. **2** (*infml*) STIMULATION, thrill, excitement.

◆ **kick off** begin, commence (*fml*), start, open, get under way, open the proceedings, set the ball rolling, introduce, inaugurate, initiate.

◆ **kick out** eject, evict, expel, oust, remove, chuck out (*infml*), discharge, dismiss, get rid of, sack (*infml*), throw out, reject.

kick-off *n* beginning, start, outset, opening, introduction, commencement (*fml*), inception (*fml*), word go (*infml*).

kid¹ *n* child, youngster, youth, juvenile, infant, girl, boy, teenager, lad, nipper (*infml*), tot (*infml*).

kid² *v* tease, joke, have on (*infml*), hoax, fool, pull someone's leg (*infml*), pretend, trick, delude, dupe, con (*infml*), jest, hoodwink, humbug, bamboozle.

kidnap *v* abduct, capture, seize, hold to ransom, snatch, hijack, steal.

kill *v* **1** SLAUGHTER, murder, slay, put to death, exterminate, assassinate, do to death, do in (*infml*), bump off (*infml*), finish off, massacre, smite (*fml*), execute, eliminate (*sl*), destroy, dispatch (*infml*), do away with, butcher, annihilate, liquidate (*sl*), knock off (*infml*), rub out (*sl*). **2** STIFLE, deaden, smother, quash, quell, suppress.

killer *n* murderer, assassin, executioner, destroyer, slaughterer, exterminator, butcher (*infml*), cut-throat, gunman, hatchet man (*infml*), hit man (*infml*).

killing *n* **1** SLAUGHTER, murder, massacre, homicide, assassination, execution, slaying, manslaughter, extermination, carnage, bloodshed, elimination, fatality,

liquidation. **2** (*infml*) GAIN, fortune, windfall, profit, lucky break, coup, clean-up (*infml*), success, stroke of luck, bonanza (*infml*), hit, big hit.

➤ *adj* (*infml*) **1** FUNNY, hilarious, comical, amusing, side-splitting (*infml*), ludicrous. **2** EXHAUSTING, hard, taxing, arduous.

kind *n* sort, type, class, category, set, variety, character, genus, genre, style, brand, family, breed, race, nature, persuasion, description, species, stamp, temperament, manner.

➤ *adj* benevolent, kind-hearted, kindly, good-hearted, good-natured, helpful, obliging, humane, generous, compassionate, charitable, amiable, friendly, congenial, soft-hearted, thoughtful, warm, warm-hearted, considerate, courteous, sympathetic, tender-hearted, understanding, lenient, mild, hospitable, gentle, indulgent, neighbourly, tactful, giving, good, loving, gracious.

◘ cruel, inconsiderate, unhelpful.

kindle *v* **1** IGNITE, light, set alight, set on fire. **2** INFLAME, fire, stir, thrill, stimulate, rouse, arouse, awaken, excite, fan, incite, inspire, induce, provoke.

kindly *adj* benevolent, kind, compassionate, charitable, good-natured, helpful, warm, generous, cordial, favourable, giving, indulgent, pleasant, sympathetic, tender, gentle, mild, patient, polite.

◘ cruel, uncharitable.

kindness *n* **1** BENEVOLENCE, kindliness, charity, magnanimity, compassion, generosity, hospitality, humanity, loving-kindness (*fml*), courtesy, friendliness, good will, goodness, grace, indulgence, tolerance, understanding, gentleness. **2** FAVOUR, good turn, assistance, help, service.

◘ **1** cruelty, inhumanity. **2** disservice.

kindred *n* relatives, relations, flesh and blood, family, people, folk, connections, clan, relationship, kinsfolk, lineage, consanguinity (*fml*).

➤ *adj* similar, common, related, matching, like, corresponding, affiliated, connected, allied, akin, cognate (*fml*).

king *n* monarch, ruler, sovereign, majesty, emperor, chief, chieftain, prince, supremo, leading light (*infml*).

kingdom *n* monarchy, sovereignty, reign,

realm, empire, dominion, commonwealth, nation, principality, state, country, domain, dynasty, province, sphere, territory, land, division.

kink n **1** CURL, twist, bend, dent, indentation, knot, loop, crimp, coil, tangle, wrinkle. **2** QUIRK, eccentricity, idiosyncracy, foible, perversion.

kinky adj **1** STRANGE, odd, unconventional, freakish, eccentric, outlandish, queer, quirky, idiosyncratic, peculiar, perverted, deviant, unnatural, warped, weird, bizarre, whimsical, degenerate, depraved, licentious, capricious (fml). **2** CURLED, coiled, twisted, crumpled, tangled, curly, wavy, wrinkled, crimped, frizzy.

kinship n **1** KIN, blood, relation. **2** AFFINITY, similarity, association, alliance, connection, correspondence, relationship, tie, community, conformity.

kiosk n booth, stall, stand, news-stand, bookstall, cabin, box, counter.

kiss v **1** CARESS, peck (infml), smooch (infml), neck (infml), snog (sl). **2** TOUCH, graze, glance, brush, lick, scrape, fan.
➤ n peck (infml), smack (infml), smacker (sl).

kit n equipment, gear, apparatus, supplies, tackle, provisions, outfit, implements, set, tools, trappings, rig, instruments, paraphernalia, utensils, effects, luggage, baggage.
♦ **kit out** equip, fit out, outfit, supply, fix up, furnish, prepare, arm, deck out, dress.

kitchen utensils

Kitchen utensils include: baster, blender, bottle opener, breadbin, breadboard, butter curler, butter dish, can-opener, cheese board, cheese slicer, chopping-board, colander, corer, corkscrew, cruet set, dough hook, egg separator, egg slicer, egg-timer, fish slice, flour dredger, food processor, fork, garlic press, grater, herb mill, ice-cream scoop, icing syringe, jelly mould, kitchen scales, knife block, lemon squeezer, liquidizer, mandolin, measuring jug, meat thermometer, mincer, mixing bowl, nutcracker, nutmeg grater, pasta maker, pastry board, pastry brush, pastry cutter, peeler, pepper mill, pie funnel, potato masher, pudding basin, punch bowl, rolling-pin, salad spinner, scissors, sharpening steel, shears, sieve, sifter, skewer, spatula, spice rack, stoner, storage jar, tea

caddy, tea infuser, tea strainer, toast rack, tongs, tureen, vegetable brush, whisk, wine cooler, wine rack, yoghurt maker, zester; knives: boning knife, bread knife, butter-knife, carving knife, cheese knife, cleaver, cocktail knife, cook's knife, fish knife, grapefruit knife, Kitchen Devils®, palette knife, paring knife, steak knife, table knife, vegetable knife; spoons: dessert spoon, draining spoon, ladle, measuring spoon, serving spoon, skimmer, straining spoon, tablespoon, teaspoon, wooden spoon.

Types of cooking utensil include:
baking sheet, bun tin, cake tin, flan tin, loaf tin, muffin tin, pie plate, quiche dish; bain-marie, brochette, casserole, cocotte, deep-fat fryer, egg coddler, egg poacher, fish kettle, fondue set, frying-pan, grill pan, milk pan, preserving pan, pressure cooker, ramekin, roasting pan, saucepan, skillet, slow cooker, soufflé dish, steamer, stockpot, terrine, vegetable steamer, wok.

knack n flair, faculty, facility, hang (infml), bent, skill, talent, genius, gift, trick, propensity, ability, expertise, skilfulness, forte, capacity, handiness, dexterity, quickness, turn.

knapsack n bag, pack, haversack, rucksack, backpack.

knead v manipulate, press, massage, work, ply, squeeze, shape, rub, form, mould, knuckle.

kneel v fall to one's knees, bow (down), get down on one's knees, stoop, bend, curtsy, revere, defer to, kowtow, genuflect (fml), make obeisance (fml).

knell n toll, ringing, chime, peal, knoll.

knickers n pants, panties, briefs, underwear, lingerie, bikini briefs, camiknickers, knickerbockers, Directoire knickers, bloomers, drawers (infml), smalls (infml).

knick-knack n trinket, trifle, bauble, gewgaw, gimcrack, bric-à-brac, plaything.

knife n blade, cutter, carver, dagger, pen-knife, pocket-knife, switchblade, jack-knife, flick-knife, machete.
➤ v cut, rip, slash, stab, pierce, wound.

knit v **1** JOIN, unite, secure, connect, tie, fasten, link, mend, interlace, intertwine. **2** KNOT, loop, crotchet, weave. **3** WRINKLE, furrow.

knob n **1** HANDLE, door-handle, switch. **2**

LUMP, ball, boss, protrusion, bump, projection, protuberance, nub. **3** KNOT, knurl, gnarl, swell, knub, swelling, tumour, tuber.

knock *v* hit, strike, rap, thump, pound, slap, smack.
➤ *n* blow, box, rap, thump, cuff, clip, pounding, hammering, slap, smack.
♦ **knock about 1** WANDER, travel, roam, rove, saunter, traipse, ramble, range.
2 ASSOCIATE, go around. **3** BEAT UP, batter, abuse, mistreat, hurt, hit, bash, damage, maltreat, manhandle, bruise, buffet.
♦ **knock down** demolish, destroy, fell, floor, level, wreck, raze, pound, batter, clout, smash, wallop.
♦ **knock off 1** (*infml*) FINISH, cease, stop, pack (it) in, clock off, clock out, terminate.
2 (*infml*) STEAL, rob, pilfer, pinch (*infml*), nick (*infml*), filch. **3** DEDUCT, take away.
4 (*sl*) KILL, murder, slay, assassinate, do away with, bump off (*infml*), do in (*infml*), waste (*sl*).

knockout (*infml*) *n* success, triumph, sensation, hit, smash (*infml*), smash-hit (*infml*), winner, stunner (*infml*).
Ea flop, loser.

knot *v* tie, secure, bind, entangle, tangle, knit, entwine, ravel, weave.
➤ *n* **1** TIE, bond, joint, fastening, loop, splice, hitch. **2** BUNCH, cluster, clump, group.

> Types of knot include: bend, Blackwall hitch, blood knot, bow, bowline, running bowline, carrick bend, clove hitch, common whipping, double-overhang, Englishman's tie (or knot), figure of eight, fisherman's bend, fisherman's knot, flat knot, granny knot, half hitch, highwayman's hitch, hitch, Hunter's bend, loop knot, overhand knot or thumb knot, reef knot or square knot, rolling hitch, round turn and two half hitches, seizing, sheepshank, sheet bend or common bend or swab hitch, slipknot, spade-end knot, surgeon's knot, tie, timber hitch, Turk's head, turle knot, wall knot, weaver's knot, Windsor knot.

know *v* **1** *know French*: understand, comprehend, apprehend, perceive, notice,

be aware, fathom, experience, realize, see, undergo. **2** *I know George*: be acquainted with, be familiar with, recognize, identify. **3** *know a good wine*: distinguish, discriminate, discern, differentiate, make out, tell.

know-how *n* expertise, knowledge, experience, proficiency, competence, gumption, savoir-faire, ability, capability, skill, ingenuity, dexterity, aptitude, adroitness, adeptness, talent, faculty, bent, flair, knack, savvy (*infml*).

knowing *adj* meaningful, expressive, perceptive, shrewd, significant, discerning, conscious, cunning, astute, aware.

knowingly *adv* intentionally, willingly, on purpose, purposely, consciously, studiedly, wilfully, wittingly, deliberately, designedly, by design, calculatedly.

knowledge *n* **1** LEARNING, scholarship, erudition, education, schooling, instruction, tuition, information, enlightenment, know-how.
2 ACQUAINTANCE, familiarity, awareness, cognizance, intimacy, consciousness.
3 UNDERSTANDING, comprehension, cognition, apprehension, recognition, judgement, discernment, ability, grasp, wisdom, intelligence.
Ea **1** ignorance. **2** unawareness.

knowledgeable *adj* **1** EDUCATED, scholarly, learned, well-informed, lettered, intelligent. **2** AWARE, acquainted, conscious, familiar, au fait, in the know (*infml*), conversant, experienced.
Ea **1** ignorant.

known *adj* acknowledged, recognized, well-known, noted, obvious, patent, plain, admitted, familiar, avowed, commonplace, published, confessed, celebrated, famous.

knuckle down *v* buckle down, start to work hard, begin to study.

knuckle under *v* submit, yield, give way, give in, succumb, surrender, capitulate, defer, buckle under, accede (*fml*), acquiesce (*fml*).

kowtow *v* defer, cringe, fawn, grovel, pander, suck up (*infml*), toady (*infml*), flatter, kneel.

Ll

label n **1** TAG, ticket, docket, mark, marker, sticker, trademark. **2** DESCRIPTION, categorization, identification, characterization, classification, badge, brand.
➤ v **1** TAG, mark, stamp. **2** DEFINE, describe, classify, categorize, characterize, identify, class, designate, brand, call, dub, name.

laboratory

Laboratory apparatus includes:
autoclave, beaker, bell jar, boiling tube, Buchner funnel, Bunsen burner, burette, centrifuge, clamp, condenser, conical flask, crucible, cylinder, desiccator, distillation apparatus, dropper, evaporating dish, filter flask, filter paper, flask, fume cupboard, funnel, glove box, Kipp's apparatus, Liebig condenser, measuring cylinder, microscope, mortar, pestle, Petri dish, pipette, retort, separating funnel, slide, spatula, stand, still, stirrer, stop clock, test tube, test tube rack, thermometer, top-pan balance, tripod, trough, U-tube, volumetric flask, Woulfe bottle.

laborious adj **1** HARD, arduous, difficult, strenuous, tough, backbreaking, wearisome, tiresome, uphill, onerous, heavy, toilsome. **2** HARD-WORKING, industrious, painstaking, indefatigable, diligent.
Ea **1** easy, effortless. **2** lazy.

labour n **1** WORK, task, job, chore, toil, effort, exertion, drudgery, grind (infml), slog (infml), sweat (infml). **2** WORKERS, employees, workforce, labourers. **3** CHILDBIRTH, birth, delivery, labour pains, contractions.
Ea **1** ease, leisure. **2** management.
➤ v **1** WORK, toil, drudge, slave, strive, endeavour, struggle, grind (infml), sweat (infml), plod, travail (fml). **2** TOSS, pitch, roll. **3** OVERDO, overemphasize, dwell on, elaborate, overstress, strain.
Ea **1** laze, idle, lounge.

laboured adj awkward, unnatural, forced, difficult, complicated, heavy, overdone, overwrought, stiff, stilted, strained, ponderous, studied, contrived, affected (fml).
Ea easy, natural.

labourer n manual worker, blue-collar worker, navvy, hand, worker, drudge, hireling.

labyrinth n maze, complexity, intricacy, complication, puzzle, riddle, windings, tangle, jungle.

lace n **1** NETTING, mesh-work, open-work, tatting, crochet. **2** STRING, cord, thong, tie, shoelace, bootlace.
➤ v **1** TIE, do up, fasten, thread, close, bind, attach, string, intertwine, interweave. **2** ADD TO, mix in, spike (infml), fortify.

lacerate v tear, rip, rend, cut, gash, slash, wound, claw, mangle, maim, torture, torment, distress, afflict.

lack n need, want, scarcity, shortage, insufficiency, dearth, deficiency, absence, scantiness, vacancy, void, privation, deprivation, destitution, emptiness.
Ea abundance, profusion.
➤ v need, want, require, miss.

lackadaisical adj apathetic, lazy, lethargic, inert, limp, spiritless, listless, indifferent, idle, dreamy, dull, lukewarm, half-hearted, abstracted, enervated (fml), indolent (fml), languorous (fml), languid (fml).
Ea active, dynamic, energetic, vigorous.

lacking adj needing, wanting, without, short of, missing, minus, inadequate, deficient, defective, flawed.

lacklustre adj drab, dull, flat, boring, leaden, lifeless, unimaginative, dim.
Ea brilliant, inspired.

laconic adj terse, succinct, pithy, concise, crisp, taciturn, short, curt, brief.
Ea verbose, wordy.

lad n boy, youth, youngster, kid (infml), schoolboy, chap, guy (infml), fellow.

laden adj loaded, charged, weighed down, burdened, oppressed, packed, stuffed, weighted, full, chock-full, fraught, encumbered, hampered, taxed, jammed.
Ea empty.

ladylike *adj* refined, well-bred, well-mannered, polite, courteous, proper, respectable, polished, modest, cultured, elegant, courtly, queenly, genteel, matronly, decorous (*fml*).

lag *v* dawdle, loiter, hang back, linger, straggle, trail, saunter, delay, shuffle, tarry, idle.
🔁 hurry, lead.

laid-back *adj* relaxed, at ease, casual, leisurely, easy-going (*infml*), unhurried, untroubled, unworried, calm, cool, passionless, free and easy, imperturbable (*fml*), unflappable (*infml*).
🔁 tense, uptight (*infml*).

lair

> Lairs and homes of creatures include:
> sett (*badger*); den (*bear*); lodge (*beaver*); hive (*bee*); nest (*bird*); byre (*cow*); eyrie (*eagle*); coop (*fowl*); earth (*fox*); form (*hare*); den (*lion*); fortress (*mole*); hole, nest (*mouse*); holt (*otter*); sty (*pig*); dovecote (*pigeon*); burrow, warren (*rabbit*); pen, fold (*sheep*); shell (*snail*); drey (*squirrel*); nest, vespiary (*wasp*).

lake *n* lagoon, reservoir, loch, mere, tarn.

lame *adj* **1** DISABLED, handicapped, crippled, limping, hobbling. **2** WEAK, feeble, flimsy, inadequate, unsatisfactory, poor.
🔁 **1** able-bodied. **2** convincing.

lament *v* mourn, bewail, bemoan, grieve, sorrow, weep, wail, complain, deplore, regret.
🔁 rejoice, celebrate.
➤ *n* lamentation, dirge, elegy, requiem, threnody (*fml*), complaint, moan, wail.

lamentable *adj* **1** DEPLORABLE, regrettable, mournful, distressing, tragic, unfortunate, sorrowful. **2** MEAGRE, low, inadequate, insufficient, mean, unsatisfactory, pitiful, miserable, poor, disappointing.

laminate *v* cover, layer, plate, stratify, veneer, coat, face, flake, separate, split, foliate (*fml*), exfoliate (*fml*).

lampoon *n* satire, skit, caricature, parody, send-up (*infml*), spoof, take-off (*infml*), burlesque.
➤ *v* satirize, caricature, parody, send up (*infml*), take off (*infml*), spoof, make fun of, ridicule, mock, burlesque.

land *n* **1** EARTH, ground, soil, terra firma.

2 PROPERTY, grounds, estate, real estate, country, countryside, farmland, tract.
3 COUNTRY, nation, region, territory, province.
➤ *v* **1** ALIGHT, disembark, dock, berth, touch down, come to rest, arrive, deposit, wind up, end up, drop, settle, turn up.
2 OBTAIN, secure, gain, get, acquire, net, capture, achieve, win.

landlord *n* owner, proprietor, host, publican, innkeeper, hotelier, restaurateur, hotel-keeper, freeholder.
🔁 tenant.

landmark *n* feature, monument, signpost, turning-point, watershed, milestone, beacon, cairn.

landscape *n* scene, scenery, view, panorama, outlook, vista, prospect, countryside, aspect.

landslide *n* landslip, earthfall, rock-fall, avalanche.
➤ *adj* overwhelming, decisive, emphatic, runaway.

language *n* **1** SPEECH, vocabulary, terminology, parlance. **2** TALK, conversation, discourse. **3** WORDING, style, phraseology, phrasing, expression, utterance, diction.

> Language terms include: brogue, dialect, idiom, patois, tongue, pidgin, creole, lingua franca, vernacular, argot, cant, jargon, doublespeak, gobbledygook, buzzword, journalese, lingo (*infml*), patter, slang, cockney rhyming slang; etymology, lexicography, linguistics, phonetics, semantics, syntax, usage, grammar, orthography, sociolinguistics.

> Languages of the world include: Aborigine, Afghan, Afrikaans, Arabic, Balinese, Bantu, Basque, Bengali, Burmese, Belorussian, Catalan, Celtic, Chinese, Cornish, Czech, Danish, Dutch, English, Esperanto, Estonian, Ethiopian, Farsi, Finnish, Flemish, French, Gaelic, German, Greek, Haitian, Hawaiian, Hebrew, Hindi, Hindustani, Hottentot, Hungarian, Icelandic, Indonesian, Inuit, Iranian, Iraqi, Irish, Italian, Japanese, Kurdish, Lapp, Latin, Latvian, Lithuanian, Magyar, Malay, Maltese, Mandarin, Manx, Maori, Nahuatl, Navajo, Norwegian, Persian, Polish, Portuguese, Punjabi, Quechua, Romanian, Romany, Russian, Sanskrit, Scots, Serbo-Croat, Siamese, Sinhalese, Slavonic,

Slovak, Slovenian, Somali, Spanish, Swahili, Swedish, Swiss, Tamil, Thai, Tibetan, Tupí, Turkish, Ukrainian, Urdu, Vietnamese, Volapük, Welsh, Yiddish, Zulu.

languish v 1 WILT, droop, fade, fail, flag, wither, waste away, weaken, sink, faint, decline, mope, waste, grieve, sorrow, sigh, sicken. 2 PINE, yearn, want, long, desire, hanker, hunger.
🔳 1 flourish.

lanky adj gaunt, gangling, scrawny, tall, thin, scraggy, weedy.
🔳 short, squat.

lap¹ v drink, sip, sup, lick.

lap² n circuit, round, orbit, tour, loop, course, circle, distance.
➤ v wrap, fold, envelop, enfold, swathe, surround, cover, swaddle, overlap.

lapse n 1 ERROR, slip, mistake, negligence, omission, oversight, fault, failing, indiscretion, aberration, backsliding, relapse. 2 FALL, descent, decline, drop, deterioration. 3 BREAK, gap, interval, lull, interruption, intermission, pause.
➤ v 1 DECLINE, fall, sink, drop, deteriorate, slide, slip, fail, worsen, degenerate, backslide. 2 EXPIRE, run out, end, stop, terminate.

large adj 1 BIG, huge, immense, massive, vast, sizable, great, giant, gigantic, bulky, enormous, king-sized, broad, considerable, monumental, substantial. 2 FULL, extensive, generous, liberal, roomy, plentiful, spacious, grand, sweeping, grandiose.
🔳 1 small, tiny.
◆ at large free, at liberty, on the loose, on the run, independent.

largely adv mainly, principally, chiefly, generally, primarily, predominantly, mostly, considerably, by and large, widely, extensively, greatly.

largesse n generosity, kindness, liberality, philanthropy, benefaction, open-handedness, bounty, donation, gift, present, aid, grant, handout, endowment, bequest, charity, allowance, alms, munificence (fml).
🔳 meanness.

lark n escapade, antic, fling, prank, romp, skylark (infml), revel, mischief, frolic, caper, game.

lascivious adj lecherous, lewd, licentious (fml), lustful, ribald, sensual, obscene,

pornographic, crude, vulgar, coarse, bawdy, wanton, dirty, indecent, offensive, suggestive, salacious, scurrilous, unchaste, libidinous (fml), prurient (fml), blue (infml), horny (infml), randy (infml), smutty (infml).

lash¹ n blow, whip, stroke, swipe, hit.
➤ v 1 WHIP, flog, beat, hit, thrash, strike, scourge. 2 ATTACK, criticize, lay into, scold.

lash² v tie, bind, fasten, secure, make fast, join, affix, rope, tether, strap.

lassitude n sluggishness, tiredness, weariness, lethargy, listlessness, drowsiness, apathy, dullness, exhaustion, fatigue, heaviness, enervation (fml), languor (fml), torpor (fml).
🔳 energy, vigour.

last¹ adj final, ultimate, closing, latest, rearmost, terminal, furthest, concluding, remotest, utmost, extreme, conclusive, definitive.
🔳 first, initial.
➤ adv finally, ultimately, behind, after.
🔳 first, firstly.
◆ at last eventually, finally, in the end, in due course, at length.

last² v continue, endure, remain, persist, keep (on), survive, hold out, carry on, wear, stay, hold on, stand up, abide (fml).
🔳 cease, stop, fade.

last-ditch adj final, desperate, frenzied, wild, last-chance, straining, struggling, frantic, heroic, all-out, eleventh-hour (infml), last-gasp (infml).

lasting adj enduring, unchanging, unceasing, unending, continuing, permanent, perpetual, lifelong, long-standing, long-term.
🔳 brief, fleeting, short-lived.

lastly adv finally, ultimately, in conclusion, in the end, to sum up.
🔳 firstly.

latch n fastening, catch, bar, bolt, lock, hook, hasp.

late adj 1 OVERDUE, behind, behind-hand, slow, unpunctual, delayed, last-minute. 2 FORMER, previous, departed, dead, deceased, past, preceding, old. 3 RECENT, up-to-date, current, fresh, new.
🔳 1 early, punctual.

lately adv recently, of late, latterly.

latent adj potential, dormant, undeveloped, unrealized, lurking, unexpressed, unseen, secret, concealed,

hidden, invisible, underlying, veiled.
☒ active, conspicuous.

later *adv* next, afterwards, subsequently, after, successively.
☒ earlier.

lateral *adj* sideways, side, oblique, sideward, edgeways, marginal, flanking.

latest *adj* modern, newest, most recent, ultimate, up-to-date, current, now, fashionable, in (*infml*), with it (*infml*), up-to-the-minute (*infml*).
☒ earliest.

lather *n* 1 FOAM, suds, soap-suds, froth, bubbles, soap, shampoo. 2 AGITATION, fluster, fuss, dither, state (*infml*), flutter, flap (*infml*), fever.
➤ *v* foam, froth, soap, shampoo, whip up.

latitude *n* 1 SCOPE, range, room, space, play, clearance, breadth, width, spread, sweep, reach, span, field, extent.
2 FREEDOM, liberty, licence, leeway, indulgence.

latter *adj* last-mentioned, last, later, closing, concluding, ensuing, succeeding, successive, second.
☒ former.

latterly *adv* lately, recently, most recently, of late, hitherto (*fml*).
☒ formerly.

lattice *n* lattice-work, openwork, fretwork, mesh, web, grate, grating, network, espalier, grid, grille, tracery, trellis, reticulation (*fml*).

laudable *adj* praiseworthy, commendable, estimable, of note, excellent, exemplary, worthy, admirable, creditable, sterling, meritorious (*fml*).
☒ damnable, execrable.

laugh *v* chuckle, giggle, guffaw, snigger, titter, chortle, split one's sides, fall about (*infml*), crease up (*infml*).
➤ *n* giggle, chuckle, snigger, titter, guffaw, chortle, lark, scream (*infml*), hoot (*infml*), joke.
◆ **laugh at** mock, ridicule, deride, jeer, make fun of, scoff at, scorn, taunt.
◆ **laugh off** dismiss, disregard, ignore, brush aside, belittle, shrug off, make little of, minimize.

laughable *adj* 1 FUNNY, amusing, comical, humorous, hilarious, droll, farcical, diverting. 2 RIDICULOUS, absurd, ludicrous, preposterous, nonsensical, derisory, derisive.
☒ 1 serious.

laughing-stock *n* figure of fun, butt, victim, target, fair game.

laughter *n* laughing, giggling, chuckling, chortling, guffawing, tittering, hilarity, amusement, merriment, mirth, glee, convulsions.

launch *v* 1 PROPEL, dispatch, discharge, send off, project, float, set in motion, throw, fire. 2 BEGIN, commence, start, embark on, establish, found, open, initiate, inaugurate, introduce, instigate.

laundry *n* 1 WASHING, (dirty) clothes, wash. 2 LAUNDERETTE, dry cleaner's, Laundromat® (*US*).

lavatory *n* toilet, loo (*infml*), WC, bathroom, cloakroom, washroom, water closet, public convenience, Ladies (*infml*), Gents (*infml*), bog (*sl*), urinal, powder-room.

lavish *adj* 1 ABUNDANT, lush, luxuriant, plentiful, profuse, unlimited, prolific. 2 GENEROUS, liberal, open-handed, extravagant, thriftless, prodigal, immoderate, intemperate, unstinting.
☒ 1 scant. 2 frugal, thrifty.

law *n* 1 RULE, act, decree, edict, order, statute, regulation, command, ordinance, charter, constitution, enactment. 2 PRINCIPLE, axiom, criterion, standard, precept, formula, code, canon. 3 JURISPRUDENCE, legislation, litigation.

law-abiding *adj* obedient, upright, orderly, lawful, honest, honourable, decent, good.
☒ lawless.

lawful *adj* legal, legitimate, permissible, legalized, authorized, allowable, warranted, valid, proper, rightful.
☒ illegal, unlawful, illicit.

lawless *adj* disorderly, rebellious, anarchic(al), unruly, riotous, mutinous, unrestrained, chaotic, wild, reckless.
☒ law-abiding.

lawsuit *n* litigation, suit, action, proceedings, case, prosecution, dispute, process, trial, argument, contest, cause.

lawyer *n* solicitor, barrister, advocate, attorney, counsel, QC.

lax *adj* 1 CASUAL, careless, easy-going (*infml*), slack, lenient, negligent, remiss (*fml*). 2 IMPRECISE, inexact, indefinite, loose.
☒ 1 strict. 2 exact.

lay¹ *v* 1 PUT, place, deposit, set down, settle,

lodge, plant, set, establish, leave.
2 ARRANGE, position, set out, locate, work out, devise, prepare, present, submit.
3 ATTRIBUTE, ascribe, assign, charge.
◆ **lay aside 1** PUT ASIDE, save, keep, store. **2** REJECT, set aside, put out of one's mind, abandon, discard, dismiss, shelve, postpone, put off, cast aside.
◆ **lay down 1** SURRENDER, yield, give up, give, discard, drop, relinquish (*fml*). **2** STIPULATE, assert, postulate, affirm, state, establish, formulate, prescribe, ordain.
◆ **lay in** store (up), stock up, amass, accumulate, hoard, stockpile, gather, collect, build up, glean.
◆ **lay into** (*infml*) attack, assail, pitch into, set about, tear into, let fly at.
◆ **lay off 1** DISMISS, discharge, make redundant, sack (*infml*), pay off, let go. **2** (*infml*) GIVE UP, drop, stop, quit, cease, desist, leave off, leave alone, let up.
◆ **lay on** provide, supply, cater, furnish, give, set up.
◆ **lay out 1** DISPLAY, set out, spread out, exhibit, arrange, plan, design. **2** (*infml*) KNOCK OUT, fell, flatten, demolish. **3** (*infml*) SPEND, pay, shell out (*infml*), fork out (*infml*), give, invest.
◆ **lay up** store up, hoard, accumulate, amass, keep, save, put away.

lay² *adj* **1** LAIC, secular. **2** AMATEUR, non-professional, non-specialist.
Ea 1 clergy. **2** expert.

layabout *n* good-for-nothing, ne'er-do-well, waster, idler, laggard, lounger, loafer (*infml*), shirker (*infml*), skiver (*infml*), lazybones (*infml*), lounge-lizard (*infml*).

layer *n* **1** COVER, coating, coat, covering, film, blanket, mantle, sheet, lamina. **2** STRATUM, seam, thickness, tier, bed, plate, row, ply.

layman *n* **1** LAYPERSON, parishioner. **2** AMATEUR, outsider.
Ea 1 clergyman. **2** expert.

lay-off *n* redundancy, discharge, dismissal, unemployment, sack (*infml*), sacking (*infml*), papers (*infml*), firing (*infml*), push (*infml*), boot (*infml*), elbow (*infml*).

layout *n* arrangement, design, outline, plan, sketch, draft, map.

laze *v* idle, loaf (*infml*), lounge, sit around, lie around, loll.

lazy *adj* idle, slothful, slack, work-shy, inactive, lethargic.
Ea industrious.

lead *v* **1** GUIDE, conduct, escort, steer, pilot, usher. **2** RULE, govern, head, preside over, direct, supervise. **3** INFLUENCE, persuade, incline. **4** SURPASS, outdo, excel, outstrip, transcend. **5** PASS, spend, live, undergo.
Ea 1 follow.
➤ *n* **1** PRIORITY, precedence, first place, start, van, vanguard, advantage, edge, margin. **2** LEADERSHIP, guidance, direction, example, model. **3** CLUE, hint, indication, guide, tip, suggestion. **4** TITLE ROLE, starring part, principal.
◆ **lead off** begin, commence, open, get going, start (off), inaugurate, initiate, kick off (*infml*), start the ball rolling.
◆ **lead on** entice, lure, seduce, tempt, draw on, beguile, persuade, string along, deceive, trick.
◆ **lead to** cause, result in, produce, bring about, bring on, contribute to, tend towards.
◆ **lead up to** prepare (the way) for, approach, introduce, make overtures, pave the way.

leaden *adj* **1** GREY, overcast, cloudy, gloomy, dingy, dismal, dreary, ashen, greyish, oppressive, sombre. **2** DULL, heavy, burdensome, onerous, laboured, lifeless, lacklustre, listless, spiritless, sluggish, humdrum, inert, stilted, languid (*fml*). **3** CUMBERSOME, wooden, stiff, heavy, laboured, plodding, lead.

leader *n* head, chief, director, ruler, principal, commander, captain, boss (*infml*), superior, chieftain, ringleader, guide, conductor.
Ea follower.

leadership *n* direction, control, command, management, authority, guidance, domination, pre-eminence, premiership, administration, sway, directorship.

leading *adj* main, principal, chief, primary, first, supreme, outstanding, foremost, dominant, ruling, superior, greatest, highest, governing, pre-eminent, number one.
Ea subordinate.

leaf *n* **1** *the leaves of a tree*: blade, bract, frond, pad, calyx, needle, sepal, leaflet, cotyledon (*fml*), foliole (*fml*). **2** PAGE, sheet, folio.

Leaf parts include: auxiliary bud, blade, chloroplasts, epidermis, leaf axil, leaf cells, margin, midrib, petiole, sheath, stipule, stomata, tip, vein.

Leaf shapes include: abruptly pinnate, acerose, ciliate, cordate, crenate, dentate, digitate, doubly dentate, elliptic, entire, falcate, hastate, lanceolate, linear, lobed, lyrate, obovate, orbicular, ovate, palmate, peltate, pinnate, pinnatifid, reniform, runcinate, sagittate, spathulate, subulate, ternate, trifoliate.

➤ *v* thumb (through), browse, flip, glance, skim.

leaflet *n* pamphlet, booklet, brochure, circular, handout.

league *n* 1 ASSOCIATION, confederation, alliance, union, federation, confederacy, coalition, combination, band, syndicate, guild, consortium, cartel, combine, partnership, fellowship, compact.
2 CATEGORY, class, level, group.
♦ **in league** allied, collaborating, conspiring.

leak *n* 1 CRACK, hole, opening, puncture, crevice, chink. 2 LEAKAGE, leaking, seepage, drip, oozing, percolation.
3 DISCLOSURE, divulgence.
➤ *v* 1 SEEP, drip, ooze, escape, spill, trickle, percolate, exude, discharge. 2 DIVULGE, disclose, reveal, let slip, make known, make public, tell, give away, pass on.

leaky *adj* leaking, holey, perforated, punctured, split, cracked, porous, permeable.

lean¹ *v* 1 SLANT, slope, bend, tilt, list, tend.
2 RECLINE, prop, rest. 3 INCLINE, favour, prefer.

lean² *adj* 1 THIN, skinny, bony, gaunt, lank, angular, slim, scraggy, scrawny, emaciated.
2 SCANTY, inadequate, bare, barren.
E3 1 fat.

leaning *n* tendency, inclination, propensity (*fml*), partiality, liking, bent, bias, disposition (*fml*), aptitude.

leap *v* 1 JUMP (OVER), bound, spring, vault, clear, skip, hop, bounce, caper, gambol.
2 SOAR, surge, increase, rocket, escalate, rise.
E3 2 drop, fall.
➤ *n* 1 JUMP, bound, spring, vault, hop, skip, caper. 2 INCREASE, upsurge, upswing, surge, rise, escalation.

learn *v* 1 GRASP, comprehend, understand, master, acquire, pick up, gather, assimilate, discern. 2 MEMORIZE, learn by heart.
3 DISCOVER, find out, ascertain, hear, detect, determine.

learned *adj* scholarly, erudite (*fml*), well-informed, well-read, cultured, academic, lettered, literate, intellectual, versed.
E3 uneducated, illiterate.

learner *n* novice, beginner, student, trainee, pupil, scholar, apprentice.

learning *n* scholarship, erudition (*fml*), education, schooling, knowledge, information, letters, study, wisdom, tuition, culture, edification, research.

lease *v* let, loan, rent, hire, sublet, charter.

leash *n* lead, tether, rein, cord, check, control, curb, restraint, discipline.

least *adj* smallest, lowest, minimum, fewest, slightest, poorest.
E3 most.

leave¹ *v* 1 DEPART, go, go away, set out, take off, decamp, exit, move, quit, retire, withdraw, disappear, do a bunk (*infml*).
2 ABANDON, desert, forsake, give up, drop, relinquish, renounce, pull out, surrender, desist, cease. 3 ASSIGN, commit, entrust, consign, bequeath, will, hand down, leave behind, give over, transmit.
E3 1 arrive. 3 receive.
♦ **leave off** stop, cease, discontinue, desist, abstain, refrain, lay off, quit, terminate, break off, end, halt, give over.
♦ **leave out** omit, exclude, overlook, ignore, except, disregard, pass over, count out, cut (out), eliminate, neglect, reject, cast aside, bar.

leave² *n* 1 PERMISSION, authorization, consent, allowance, sanction, concession, dispensation, indulgence, liberty, freedom.
2 HOLIDAY, time off, vacation, sabbatical, furlough.
E3 1 refusal, rejection.

lecherous *adj* lewd, womanizing, carnal, promiscuous, lustful, lascivious, degenerate, debauched, dissolute, dissipated, unchaste, wanton, salacious, libidinous (*fml*), licentious (*fml*), prurient (*fml*), randy (*infml*), raunchy (*infml*), horny (*infml*).

lechery *n* lewdness, womanizing, carnality, libertinism, debauchery, rakishness, lust, lustfulness, libidinousness, licentiousness (*fml*), salaciousness, sensuality, wantonness, lasciviousness, prurience (*fml*), randiness (*infml*), raunchiness (*infml*).

lecture *n* 1 DISCOURSE, address, lesson, speech, talk, instruction. 2 REPRIMAND, rebuke, reproof, scolding, harangue,

censure, chiding, telling-off (*infml*),
talking-to (*infml*), dressing-down (*infml*).
➤ *v* **1** TALK, teach, hold forth, speak,
expound, address. **2** REPRIMAND, reprove,
scold, admonish, harangue, chide,
censure, tell off (*infml*).

ledge *n* shelf, sill, mantle, ridge,
projection, step.

leech *n* hanger-on, parasite, sycophant,
toady, bloodsucker, freeloader, extortioner,
usurer, sponger (*infml*), scrounger (*infml*).

leer *v* eye, ogle, look lecherously at, stare,
wink, squint, gloat, goggle, grin, smirk,
sneer.
➤ *n* ogle, lecherous look, stare, wink,
squint, grin, smirk, sneer.

leeway *n* space, room, latitude, elbow-
room, play, scope.

left *adj* **1** LEFT-HAND, port, sinistral.
2 LEFT-WING, socialist, radical,
progressive, revolutionary, liberal,
communist, red (*infml*).
✏ **1** right. **2** right-wing.

left-overs *n* leavings, remainder, remains,
remnants, residue, surplus, scraps,
sweepings, refuse, dregs, excess.

leg *n* **1** LIMB, member, shank, pin (*infml*),
stump (*infml*). **2** SUPPORT, prop, upright,
brace. **3** STAGE, part, section, portion,
stretch, segment, lap.

legacy *n* bequest, endowment, gift,
heritage, heritance, inheritance, birthright,
estate, heirloom.

legal *adj* **1** LAWFUL, legitimate,
permissible, sanctioned, allowed,
authorized, allowable, legalized,
constitutional, valid, warranted, above-
board, proper, rightful. **2** JUDICIAL,
forensic. **3** judiciary.
✏ **1** illegal.

Legal terms include: *criminal law*:
acquittal, age of consent, alibi, arrest, bail,
caution, charge, confession, contempt of
court, dock, fine, guilty, indictment,
innocent, malice aforethought, pardon,
parole, plead guilty, plead not guilty, prisoner,
probation, remand, reprieve, sentence;
marriage and divorce: adultery, alimony,
annulment, bigamy, decree absolute, decree
nisi, divorce, maintenance, settlement;
people: accessory, accomplice, accused,
advocate, Attorney General, barrister, brief
(*infml*), clerk of the court, client,
commissioner for oaths, convict, coroner,

criminal, defendant, Director of Public
Prosecutions (DPP), executor, felon, judge,
jury, justice of the peace (JP), juvenile, Law
Lord, lawyer, Lord Advocate, Lord
Chancellor, Lord Chief Justice, liquidator,
magistrate, notary public, offender, plaintiff,
procurator fiscal, receiver, Queen's Counsel
(QC), sheriff, solicitor, witness, young
offender; *property or ownership*: asset,
conveyance, copyright, deed, easement,
endowment, estate, exchange of contracts,
fee simple, foreclosure, freehold, inheritance,
intestacy, lease, leasehold, legacy, local
search, mortgage, patent, tenancy, title,
trademark, will; *miscellaneous*: act of God,
Act of Parliament, adjournment, affidavit,
agreement, allegation, amnesty, appeal,
arbitration, bar, bench, Bill of Rights, brief, by-
law, charter, civil law, claim, codicil, common
law, constitution, contract, covenant,
courtcase, court martial, cross-examine,
custody, damages, defence, demand, equity,
eviction, evidence, extradition, grant,
hearing, hung jury, indemnity, injunction,
inquest, inquiry, judgment, judiciary, lawsuit,
legal aid, liability, mandate, misadventure,
miscarriage of justice, oath, party, penalty,
power of attorney, precedent, probate,
proceedings, proof, proxy, public inquiry,
repeal, sanction, settlement, statute,
subpoena, sue, summons, testimony, trial,
tribunal, verdict, waiver, ward of court,
warrant, will, writ. *see also* **court**; **crime**.

---

legality *n* lawfulness, legitimacy, validity,
rightness, rightfulness, soundness,
admissibleness, permissibility,
constitutionality.
✏ illegality.

legalize *v* legitimize, license, permit,
sanction, allow, authorize, warrant,
validate, approve.

legend *n* **1** MYTH, story, tale, folk-tale,
fable, fiction, narrative. **2** INSCRIPTION,
caption, key, motto.

legendary *adj* **1** MYTHICAL, fabulous,
story-book, fictitious, traditional.
2 FAMOUS, celebrated, renowned, well-
known, illustrious.

legible *adj* readable, intelligible,
decipherable, clear, distinct, neat.
✏ illegible.

legion *n* **1** *Roman legions*: army, battalion,
brigade, company, division, regiment, unit,
cohort, troop, force. **2** *legions of foreign
tourists*: host, number, multitude, myriad,

swarm, throng, drove, mass, horde.
➤ *adj* countless, numerous, myriad, numberless, innumerable, illimitable, multitudinous.

legislate *v* enact, ordain, authorize, codify, constitutionalize, prescribe, establish.

legislation *n* **1** LAW, statute, regulation, bill, act, charter, authorization, ruling, measure. **2** LAW-MAKING, enactment, codification.

legislative *adj* law-making, law-giving, judicial, parliamentary, congressional, senatorial.

legislator *n* law-maker, law-giver, member of parliament, parliamentarian.

legislature *n* assembly, chamber, house, parliament, congress, senate.

legitimate *adj* **1** LEGAL, lawful, authorized, statutory, rightful, proper, correct, real, acknowledged. **2** REASONABLE, sensible, admissible, acceptable, justifiable, warranted, well-founded, valid, true.
🔁 **1** illegal. **2** invalid.

legitimize *v* sanction, authorize, permit, allow, warrant, license, validate, charter, entitle, legalize, decriminalize, legitimate (*fml*).

leisure *n* relaxation, rest, spare time, time off, ease, freedom, liberty, recreation, retirement, holiday, vacation.
🔁 work.

leisurely *adj* unhurried, slow, relaxed, comfortable, easy, unhasty, tranquil, restful, gentle, carefree, laid-back (*infml*), lazy, loose.
🔁 rushed, hectic.

lend *v* **1** LOAN, advance. **2** give, grant, bestow, provide, furnish, confer, supply, impart, contribute.
🔁 **1** borrow.

length *n* **1** EXTENT, distance, measure, reach, piece, portion, section, segment. **2** DURATION, period, term, stretch, space, span.
♦ **at length 1** THOROUGHLY, in great detail, comprehensively, exhaustively. **2** EVENTUALLY, finally, in due course, at last.

lengthen *v* stretch, extend, elongate, draw out, prolong, protract, spin out, eke (out), pad out, increase, expand, continue.
🔁 reduce, shorten.

lengthy *adj* long, prolonged, protracted,

extended, lengthened, overlong, long-drawn-out, long-winded, rambling, diffuse, verbose, drawn-out, interminable.
🔁 brief, concise.

lenient *adj* tolerant, forbearing, sparing, indulgent, merciful, forgiving, soft-hearted, kind, mild, gentle, compassionate.
🔁 strict, severe.

leper *n* outcast, social outcast, undesirable, untouchable, pariah, lazar.

lesbian *n* gay, homosexual, sapphist, tribade, butch (*infml*), les (*infml*), lez (*infml*), lezzy (*infml*), queer (*infml*), dyke (*sl*).
➤ *adj* gay, homosexual, Sapphic, tribadic, butch (*infml*), dykey (*sl*).

lesion *n* injury, wound, abrasion, sore, scratch, scrape, bruise, cut, gash, laceration, impairment, hurt, trauma, contusion (*fml*).

less *n* fewer, smaller amount, not as/so much, not as/so many.
🔁 more
➤ *adv* to a lesser degree/extent, to a smaller extent, not as/so much.
🔁 more.

lessen *v* decrease, reduce, diminish, lower, ease, abate (*fml*), contract, die down, dwindle, lighten, slow down, weaken, shrink, abridge, de-escalate, erode, minimize, narrow, moderate, slack, flag, fail, deaden, impair.
🔁 grow, increase.

lesser *adj* lower, secondary, inferior, smaller, subordinate, slighter, minor.
🔁 greater.

lesson *n* **1** CLASS, period, instruction, lecture, tutorial, teaching, coaching. **2** ASSIGNMENT, exercise, homework, practice, task, drill. **3** EXAMPLE, model, warning, deterrent.

let *v* **1** PERMIT, allow, give leave, give permission, authorize, consent to, agree to, sanction, grant, OK, enable, tolerate. **2** LEASE, hire, rent.
🔁 **1** prohibit, forbid.
♦ **let alone** not to mention, not forgetting, never mind, apart from, also, as well as.
♦ **let in** admit, accept, receive, take in, include, incorporate, welcome.
🔁 prohibit, bar, forbid.
♦ **let off 1** EXCUSE, absolve, pardon, exempt, forgive, acquit, exonerate, spare, ignore, liberate, release. **2** DISCHARGE, detonate, fire, explode, emit.
🔁 **1** punish.

♦ **let on** disclose, reveal, let slip, make known, make public, tell, relate, give away, pass on, divulge (*fml*), impart (*fml*), blab (*infml*), squeal (*infml*), let the cat out of the bag (*infml*), spill the beans (*infml*).

♦ **let out 1** FREE, release, let go, discharge, leak (*infml*). **2** REVEAL, disclose, make known, utter, betray, let slip.
ɛ₃ 1 keep in.

♦ **let up** abate, subside, ease (up), moderate, slacken, diminish, decrease, stop, end, cease, halt.
ɛ₃ continue.

let-down *n* anticlimax, disappointment, disillusionment, set-back, betrayal, desertion, washout (*infml*).

lethal *adj* fatal, deadly, deathly, mortal, dangerous, poisonous, noxious, destructive, devastating.
ɛ₃ harmless, safe.

lethargic *adj* listless, sluggish, dull, lifeless, inert, slow, lazy, inactive, idle, slothful, apathetic, drowsy, heavy, sleepy, weary, debilitated (*fml*), enervated (*fml*), languid (*fml*), somnolent (*fml*), torpid (*fml*).
ɛ₃ lively.

lethargy *n* lassitude, listlessness, sluggishness, torpor, dullness, inertia, slowness, apathy, inaction, indifference, sleepiness, drowsiness, stupor.
ɛ₃ liveliness.

letter *n* **1** NOTE, message, line, missive, epistle (*fml*), dispatch, communication, chit, acknowledgement. **2** CHARACTER, symbol, sign, grapheme.

let-up *n* break, interval, lessening, pause, recess, remission, slackening, respite, lull, abatement (*fml*), cessation (*fml*), breather (*infml*).
ɛ₃ continuation.

level *adj* **1** FLAT, smooth, even, flush, horizontal, aligned, plane. **2** EQUAL, balanced, even, on a par, neck and neck, matching, uniform.
ɛ₃ 1 uneven. **2** unequal.
➤ *v* **1** DEMOLISH, destroy, devastate, flatten, knock down, raze, pull down, bulldoze, tear down, lay low. **2** EVEN OUT, flush, plane, smooth, equalize. **3** DIRECT, point.
➤ *n* **1** HEIGHT, elevation, altitude. **2** POSITION, rank, status, class, degree, grade, standard, standing, plane, echelon, layer, stratum, storey, stage, zone.

level-headed *adj* calm, balanced, even-tempered, sensible, steady, reasonable,

composed, cool, unflappable (*infml*), sane, self-possessed, dependable.

lever *n* bar, crowbar, jemmy, joy-stick, handle.
➤ *v* force, prise, pry, raise, dislodge, jemmy, shift, move, heave.

leverage *n* force, strength, power, advantage, authority, influence, rank, weight, purchase (*fml*), clout (*infml*), pull (*infml*).

levity *n* light-heartedness, frivolity, facetiousness, flippancy, irreverence, triviality, silliness.
ɛ₃ seriousness.

levy *v* tax, impose, exact, demand, charge.
➤ *n* tax, toll, subscription, contribution, duty, fee, tariff, collection.

lewd *adj* obscene, smutty (*infml*), indecent, bawdy, pornographic, salacious, licentious (*fml*), lascivious, impure, vulgar, unchaste, lustful.
ɛ₃ decent, chaste.

liability *n* **1** ACCOUNTABILITY, duty, obligation, responsibility, onus. **2** DEBT, arrears, indebtedness. **3** DRAWBACK, disadvantage, hindrance, impediment, drag (*infml*).

liable *adj* **1** INCLINED, likely, apt, disposed, prone, tending, susceptible.
2 RESPONSIBLE, answerable, accountable, amenable.

liaise *v* contact, communicate, intercommunicate, work together, co-operate, collaborate, exchange information, relate to, network, interface.

liaison *n* **1** CONTACT, connection, go-between, link. **2** LOVE AFFAIR, affair, romance, intrigue, amour, entanglement.

liar *n* falsifier, perjurer, deceiver, fibber (*infml*).

libel *n* defamation, slur, smear, slander, vilification (*fml*), aspersion, calumny.
➤ *v* defame, slur, smear, slander, vilify (*fml*), malign.

libellous *adj* defamatory, vilifying, slanderous, derogatory, maligning, injurious, scurrilous, untrue.

liberal *adj* **1** BROAD-MINDED, open-minded, tolerant, lenient. **2** PROGRESSIVE, reformist, moderate. **3** GENEROUS, ample, bountiful, lavish, plentiful, handsome.
ɛ₃ 1 narrow-minded. **2** conservative.
3 mean, miserly.

liberalism n progressivism, radicalism, freethinking, humanitarianism, libertarianism, latitudinarianism.
🖪 conservatism, narrow-mindedness.

liberate v free, emancipate, release, let loose, let go, let out, set free, deliver, unchain, discharge, rescue, ransom.
🖪 imprison, enslave.

liberation n freedom, freeing, liberating, liberty, emancipation, release, deliverance, loosing, unchaining, uncaging, unfettering, unshackling, unpenning, ransoming, enfranchisement, manumission (fml), redemption (fml).
🖪 enslavement, imprisonment, restriction.

liberator n rescuer, deliverer, freer, saviour, ransomer, redeemer, emancipator, manumitter (fml).
🖪 enslaver, jailer.

liberty n 1 FREEDOM, emancipation, release, independence, autonomy.
2 LICENCE, permission, sanction, right, authorization, dispensation, franchise.
3 FAMILIARITY, disrespect, overfamiliarity, presumption, impertinence, impudence.
🖪 1 imprisonment. 3 respect.
♦ **at liberty** free, unconstrained, unrestricted, not confined.

libido n sexual desire, sex drive, sexual appetite, sexual urge, erotic desire, passion, ardour, lust, eroticism, randiness (infml), the hots (infml).

licence n 1 PERMISSION, permit, leave, warrant, authorization, authority, certificate, charter, right, imprimatur, entitlement, privilege, dispensation, carte blanche, freedom, liberty, exemption, independence. 2 ABANDON, dissipation, excess, immoderation, indulgence, lawlessness, unruliness, anarchy, disorder, debauchery, dissoluteness, impropriety, irresponsibility.
🖪 1 prohibition, restriction. 2 decorum, moderation.

license v permit, allow, authorize, certify, warrant, entitle, empower, sanction, commission, accredit.
🖪 ban, prohibit.

licentious adj debauched, dissolute, profligate, lascivious, immoral, abandoned, lewd, promiscuous, libertine, impure, lax, lustful, disorderly, wanton, unchaste.
🖪 modest, chaste.

lick v tongue, touch, wash, lap, taste, dart, flick, flicker, play over, smear, brush.

lie[1] v perjure, misrepresent, fabricate, falsify, fib (infml), invent, equivocate, prevaricate, forswear oneself (fml).
➤ n falsehood, untruth, falsification, fabrication, invention, fiction, deceit, fib (infml), falsity, white lie, prevarication, whopper (infml).
🖪 truth.

lie[2] v be, exist, dwell, belong, extend, remain.
♦ **lie down** repose, rest, recline, stretch out, lounge, couch, laze.

life n 1 BEING, existence, animation, breath, viability, entity, soul. 2 DURATION, course, span, career. 3 LIVELINESS, vigour, vitality, vivacity, verve, zest, energy, élan, spirit, sparkle, activity.

lifeblood n essential part/factor, life-force, spirit, soul, core, centre, heart, inspiration.

lifeless adj 1 DEAD, deceased, defunct, cold, unconscious, inanimate, insensible, stiff. 2 LETHARGIC, listless, sluggish, dull, apathetic, passive, insipid, colourless, slow. 3 BARREN, bare, empty, desolate, arid.
🖪 1 alive. 2 lively.

lifelike adj realistic, true-to-life, real, true, vivid, natural, authentic, faithful, exact, graphic.
🖪 unrealistic, unnatural.

lifelong adj lifetime, long-lasting, long-standing, persistent, lasting, enduring, abiding, permanent, constant.
🖪 impermanent, temporary.

lifetime n duration, existence, life, lifespan, span, period, time, course, day(s), career.

lift v 1 she lifted the chair: raise, elevate, hoist, upraise. 2 he lifted their spirits: uplift, exalt, buoy up, boost. 3 the ban has been lifted: revoke, cancel, relax.
🖪 1 drop. 2 lower.
➤ n 1 ELEVATOR, escalator, hoist, paternoster. 2 give you a lift home: drive, hitch, ride, run, transport. 3 BOOST, fillip, encouragement, pick-me-up, uplift, spur, reassurance, shot in the arm (infml).
🖪 3 discouragement.

light[1] n 1 ILLUMINATION, brightness, brilliance, luminescence, radiance, glow, ray, shine, glare, gleam, glint, lustre, flash, blaze. 2 LAMP, lantern, lighter, match, torch, candle, bulb, beacon. **3** DAY, daybreak, daylight, daytime, dawn, sunrise. **4** ENLIGHTENMENT, explanation, elucidation, understanding.

◨ **1** darkness. **3** night.

> **Sources of light include:** *natural light*: aurora borealis, daylight, lightning, moonlight, starlight, sunlight; infrared, ultraviolet; *electric light*: Belisha beacon, brake light, chandelier, courtesy light, fairy light, flashgun, floodlight, fluorescent light, fog lamp, footlight, halogen light, headlamp, headlight, indicator light, laser, light bulb, light buoy, lighthouse, navigation light, neon light, night light, pedestrian light, range light, runway light, searchlight, sidelight, spotlight, standard lamp, streetlight, strip light, strobe light, sun-lamp, tail-light, torch, traffic light; *fire light*: bonfire, candle, candlelight, fire, firework, flame, flare, spark, taper, gaslight, hurricane lamp, lighter, match, oil lamp, pilot light.

➤ *v* **1** IGNITE, fire, set alight, set fire to, kindle. **2** ILLUMINATE, light up, lighten, brighten, animate, cheer, switch on, turn on, put on.

◨ **1** extinguish. **2** darken.

➤ *adj* **1** ILLUMINATED, bright, brilliant, luminous, glowing, shining, well-lit, sunny. **2** PALE, pastel, fair, blond, blonde, bleached, faded, faint.

◨ **1** dark. **2** black.

light² *adj* **1** WEIGHTLESS, insubstantial, delicate, airy, buoyant, flimsy, feathery, slight. **2** TRIVIAL, inconsiderable, trifling, inconsequential, worthless. **3** CHEERFUL, cheery, carefree, lively, merry, blithe. **4** ENTERTAINING, amusing, funny, humorous, frivolous, witty, pleasing.

◨ **1** heavy, weighty. **2** important, serious. **3** solemn. **4** serious.

lighten¹ *v* illuminate, illumine, brighten, light up, shine.

◨ darken.

lighten² *v* **1** EASE, lessen, unload, lift, relieve, reduce, mitigate, alleviate. **2** BRIGHTEN, cheer, encourage, hearten, inspirit, uplift, gladden, revive, elate, buoy up, inspire.

◨ **1** burden. **2** depress.

light-headed *adj* **1** FAINT, giddy, dizzy, woozy (*infml*), delirious. **2** FLIGHTY, scatter-brained (*infml*), foolish, frivolous, silly, superficial, shallow, feather-brained

(*infml*), flippant, vacuous, trifling.

◨ **2** level-headed, solemn.

light-hearted *adj* cheerful, joyful, jolly, happy-go-lucky, bright, carefree, untroubled, merry, sunny, glad, elated, jovial, playful.

◨ sad, unhappy, serious.

lightly *adv* **1** SLIGHTLY, gently, faintly, delicately, softly, thinly, sparingly, sparsely, slightingly. **2** EASILY, effortlessly, readily, airily, breezily, gaily, facilely, gingerly. **3** FRIVOLOUSLY, flippantly, carelessly, heedlessly, thoughtlessly. **4** LENIENTLY, mildly, easily.

◨ **1** heavily. **3** soberly.

lightness *n* **1** *lightness of the clothes*: weightlessness, slightness, airiness, buoyancy, crumbliness, porosity, porousness, sandiness, delicacy, delicateness, flimsiness, thinness. **2** *lightness of movement*: grace, gracefulness, agility, gentleness, litheness, nimbleness, mildness. **3** *lightness of spirit*: cheerfulness, cheeriness, light-heartedness, liveliness, gaiety, animation, blitheness (*fml*). **4** FICKLENESS, triviality, frivolity, levity.

◨ **1** heaviness, solidity. **2** clumsiness. **3** heaviness. **4** sadness, severity, sobriety.

likable *adj* lovable, pleasing, appealing, agreeable, charming, engaging, winsome, pleasant, amiable, congenial, attractive, sympathetic.

◨ unpleasant, disagreeable.

like¹ *adj* similar, resembling, alike, same, identical, equivalent, akin, corresponding, related, relating, parallel, allied, analogous, approximating.

◨ unlike, dissimilar.

like² *v* **1** ENJOY, delight in, care for, admire, appreciate, love, adore, hold dear, esteem, cherish, prize, relish, revel in, approve, take (kindly) to. **2** PREFER, choose, select, feel inclined, go for (*infml*), desire, want, wish.

◨ **1** dislike. **2** reject.

likelihood *n* likeliness, probability, possibility, chance, prospect, liability.

◨ improbability, unlikeliness.

likely *adj* **1** PROBABLE, possible, anticipated, expected, liable, prone, tending, predictable, odds-on (*infml*), inclined, foreseeable. **2** CREDIBLE, believable, plausible, feasible, reasonable. **3** PROMISING, hopeful, pleasing, appropriate, proper, suitable.

☛ 1 unlikely. **3** unsuitable.
➤ *adv* probably, presumably, like as not, in all probability, no doubt, doubtlessly.

like-minded *adj* agreeing, in agreement, of one mind, of the same mind, unanimous, in harmony, in rapport, compatible, harmonious, in accord (*fml*).
☛ disagreeing.

liken *v* compare, equate, match, parallel, relate, juxtapose, associate, set beside.

likeness *n* **1** SIMILARITY, resemblance, affinity, correspondence.
2 REPRESENTATION, image, copy, reproduction, replica, facsimile, effigy, picture, portrait, photograph, counterpart.
3 SEMBLANCE, guise, appearance, form.
☛ 1 dissimilarity, unlikeness.

likewise *adv* moreover, furthermore, in addition, similarly, also, further, besides, by the same token, too.

liking *n* fondness, love, affection, preference, partiality, affinity, predilection (*fml*), penchant, taste, attraction, appreciation, proneness, propensity (*fml*), inclination, tendency, bias, desire, weakness, fancy, soft spot (*infml*).
☛ dislike, aversion, hatred.

lilt *n* rise and fall, rhythm, sway, swing, song, measure, beat, cadence, air.

limb *n* arm, leg, member, appendage, branch, projection, offshoot, wing, fork, extension, part, spur, extremity, bough.

limber up *v* loosen up, warm up, work out, exercise, prepare.

limelight *n* fame, celebrity, spotlight, stardom, recognition, renown, attention, prominence, publicity, public eye.

limit *n* **1** BOUNDARY, bound, border, frontier, confines, edge, brink, threshold, verge, brim, end, perimeter, rim, compass, termination, ultimate, utmost, terminus, extent. **2** CHECK, curb, restraint, restriction, limitation, ceiling, maximum, cut-off point, saturation point, deadline.
➤ *v* check, curb, restrict, restrain, constrain, confine, demarcate, delimit, bound, hem in, ration, specify, hinder.

limitation *n* **1** CHECK, restriction, curb, control, constraint, restraint, delimitation, demarcation, block.
2 INADEQUACY, shortcoming, disadvantage, drawback, condition, qualification, reservation.
☛ 1 extension.

limited *adj* restricted, circumscribed, constrained, controlled, confined, checked, defined, finite, fixed, minimal, narrow, inadequate, insufficient.
☛ limitless.

limitless *adj* unlimited, unbounded, boundless, illimited, undefined, immeasurable, incalculable, infinite, countless, endless, never-ending, unending, inexhaustible, untold, vast.
☛ limited.

limp[1] *v* hobble, falter, stumble, hop, shuffle, shamble.

limp[2] *adj* **1** FLABBY, drooping, flaccid, floppy, loose, slack, relaxed, lax, soft, flexible, pliable, limber. **2** TIRED, weary, exhausted, spent, weak, worn out, lethargic, debilitated, enervated.
☛ 1 stiff. **2** vigorous.

line[1] *n* **1** STROKE, band, bar, stripe, mark, strip, rule, dash, strand, streak, underline, score, scratch. **2** ROW, rank, queue, file, column, sequence, series, procession, chain, trail. **3** LIMIT, boundary, border, borderline, edge, frontier, demarcation.
4 STRING, rope, cord, cable, thread, filament, wire. **5** PROFILE, contour, outline, silhouette, figure, formation, configuration. **6** CREASE, wrinkle, furrow, groove, corrugation. **7** COURSE, path, direction, track, route, axis. **8** APPROACH, avenue, course (of action), belief, ideology, policy, system, position, practice, procedure, method, scheme.
9 OCCUPATION, business, trade, profession, vocation, job, activity, interest, employment, department, calling, field, province, forte, area, pursuit, specialization, specialty, specialism, speciality. **10** ANCESTRY, family, descent, extraction, lineage, pedigree, stock, race, breed.
♦ line up 1 ALIGN, range, straighten, marshal, order, regiment, queue up, form ranks, fall in, array, assemble. **2** ORGANIZE, lay on, arrange, prepare, produce, procure, secure, obtain.

line[2] *v* encase, cover, fill, pad, stuff, reinforce.

lineage *n* ancestry, descent, extraction, genealogy, family, line, pedigree, race, stock, birth, breed, house, heredity, ancestors, forebears, descendants, offspring, succession.

lined *adj* **1** RULED, feint. **2** WRINKLED,

furrowed, creased, wizened, worn.
F3 1 unlined. **2** smooth.

line-up n array, arrangement, queue, row, selection, cast, team, bill.

linger v loiter, delay, dally, tarry, wait, remain, stay, hang on, lag, procrastinate, dawdle, dilly-dally (*infml*), idle, stop, endure, hold out, last, persist, survive.
F3 leave, rush.

lingerie n underclothes, underwear, underclothing, undergarments, panties, knickers, camiknickers, camisole, slip, half-slip, teddy, body stocking, panty girdle, brassiere, bra, suspender belt, unmentionables, inexpressibles, frillies (*infml*), undies (*infml*), smalls (*infml*).

lingering adj persistent, remaining, slow, dragging, long-drawn-out, prolonged, protracted (*fml*).
F3 quick.

lining n inlay, interfacing, padding, backing, encasement, stiffening.

link n **1** CONNECTION, bond, tie, association, joint, relationship, tie-up, union, knot, liaison, attachment, communication. **2** PART, piece, element, member, constituent, component, division.
➤ v connect, join, couple, tie, fasten, unite, bind, amalgamate, merge, associate, ally, bracket, identify, relate, yoke, attach, hook up, join forces, team up.
F3 separate, unfasten.

lionize v glorify, hero-worship, treat as a hero, honour, idolize, magnify, fête, exalt, celebrate, praise, sing the praises of, acclaim, adulate, aggrandize (*fml*), eulogize (*fml*), put on a pedestal (*infml*).
F3 vilify.

lip n edge, brim, border, brink, rim, margin, verge.

liquefy v dissolve, fuse, liquidize, melt, smelt, run, thaw, flux, fluidize.
F3 solidify.

liquid n liquor, fluid, juice, drink, sap, solution, lotion.
➤ adj fluid, flowing, liquefied, watery, wet, runny, melted, molten, thawed, clear, smooth.
F3 solid.

liquidate v **1** ANNIHILATE, terminate, do away with, dissolve, kill, murder, massacre, assassinate, destroy, dispatch, abolish, eliminate (*infml*), exterminate (*infml*), remove, finish off, rub out (*infml*). **2** PAY

(OFF), close down, clear, discharge, wind up, sell.

liquor n alcohol, intoxicant, strong drink, spirits, drink, hard stuff (*infml*), booze (*infml*).

list¹ n catalogue, roll, inventory, register, enumeration, schedule, index, listing, record, file, directory, table, tabulation, tally, series, syllabus, invoice.
➤ v enumerate, register, itemize, catalogue, index, tabulate, record, file, enrol, enter, note, bill, book, set down, write down.

list² v lean, incline, tilt, slope, heel (over), tip.

listen v hark, attend, pay attention, hear, heed (*fml*), hearken, hang on (someone's) words, prick up one's ears, take notice, lend an ear, eavesdrop, overhear, give ear.

listless adj sluggish, lethargic, languid (*fml*), torpid, enervated, spiritless, limp, lifeless, inert, inactive, impassive, indifferent, uninterested, vacant, apathetic, indolent, depressed, bored, heavy.
F3 energetic, enthusiastic.

litany n **1** PRAYER, petition, supplication, devotion, invocation (*fml*). **2** CATALOGUE, account, enumeration, list, repetition, recital, recitation.

literacy n ability to read, ability to write, proficiency, education, culture, cultivation, intelligence, knowledge, learning, scholarship, learnedness, articulacy, articulateness, erudition (*fml*).
F3 illiteracy.

literal adj **1** VERBATIM, word-for-word, strict, close, actual, precise, faithful, exact, accurate, factual, true, genuine, unexaggerated. **2** PROSAIC, unimaginative, uninspired, matter-of-fact, down-to-earth, humdrum.
F3 1 imprecise, loose. **2** imaginative.

literally adv **1** *many people in Africa are literally starving*: actually, really, truly, certainly. **2** *translate literally*: exactly, faithfully, to the letter, strictly, precisely, closely, plainly, word for word, verbatim.
F3 2 imprecisely, loosely.

literary adj educated, well-read, bookish, learned, erudite, scholarly, lettered, literate, cultured, cultivated, refined, formal.
F3 ignorant, illiterate.

literature n **1** WRITINGS, letters, paper(s).

2 INFORMATION, leaflet(s), pamphlet(s), circular(s), brochure(s), handout(s), bumf (*infml*).

Types of literature include: allegory, anti-novel, autobiography, belles-lettres (*fml*), biography, classic novel, criticism, drama, epic, epistle, essay, fiction, Gothic novel, lampoon, libretto, magnum opus, non-fiction, novel, novella, parody, pastiche, penny dreadful (*infml*), picaresque novel, poetry, polemic, postil, prose, roman novel, saga, satire, thesis, tragedy, treatise, triad, trilogy, verse. *see also* **poem**; **story**.

litigant *n* contender, contestant, disputant, claimant, complainant, litigator, plaintiff, party.

litigation *n* lawsuit, action, suit, case, prosecution, process, contention.

litter *n* **1** RUBBISH, debris, refuse, waste, mess, disorder, clutter, confusion, disarray, untidiness, junk (*infml*), muck, jumble, fragments, shreds. **2** OFFSPRING, young, progeny (*fml*), brood, family.
➤ *v* strew, scatter, mess up, disorder, clutter.
🔁 tidy.

little *adj* **1** SMALL, short, tiny, wee (*infml*), minute, teeny (*infml*), diminutive, miniature, infinitesimal, mini (*infml*), microscopic, petite, pint-size(d) (*infml*), slender. **2** SHORT-LIVED, brief, fleeting, passing, transient. **3** INSUFFICIENT, sparse, scant, meagre, paltry, skimpy. **4** INSIGNIFICANT, inconsiderable, negligible, trivial, petty, trifling, unimportant.
🔁 **1** big. **2** lengthy. **3** ample. **4** considerable.
➤ *adv* barely, hardly, scarcely, rarely, seldom, infrequently, not much.
🔁 frequently.
➤ *n* bit, dash, pinch, spot, trace, drop, dab, speck, touch, taste, particle, hint, fragment, modicum, trifle.
🔁 lot.

liturgy *n* service, office, form, formula, rite, usage, worship, ceremony, ritual, observance, sacrament, ordinance, celebration.

live¹ *v* **1** BE, exist, breathe, draw breath. **2** LAST, endure, continue, remain, persist, survive. **3** DWELL, inhabit, reside, lodge, abide. **4** PASS, spend, lead.
🔁 **1** die. **2** cease.

live² *adj* **1** ALIVE, living, existent. **2** LIVELY, vital, active, energetic, dynamic, alert, vigorous. **3** BURNING, glowing, blazing, ignited. **4** RELEVANT, current, topical, pertinent, controversial.
🔁 **1** dead. **2** apathetic.

livelihood *n* occupation, employment, job, living, means, income, maintenance, work, support, subsistence, sustenance.

lively *adj* **1** ANIMATED, alert, active, energetic, spirited, vivacious, vigorous, sprightly, spry, agile, nimble, quick, keen. **2** CHEERFUL, blithe, merry, frisky, perky (*infml*), breezy, chirpy (*infml*), frolicsome. **3** BUSY, bustling, brisk, crowded, eventful, exciting, buzzing. **4** VIVID, bright, colourful, stimulating, stirring, invigorating, racy, refreshing, sparkling.
🔁 **1** moribund, apathetic. **3** inactive.

liven (up) *v* enliven, vitalize, put life into, rouse, invigorate, animate, energize, brighten, stir (up), buck up (*infml*), pep up (*infml*), perk up (*infml*), hot up (*infml*).
🔁 dishearten.

livery *n* uniform, costume, regalia, dress, clothes, clothing, apparel (*fml*), attire, vestments, suit, garb, habit.

livid *adj* **1** LEADEN, black-and-blue, bruised, discoloured, greyish, purple. **2** PALE, pallid, ashen, blanched, bloodless, wan, waxy, pasty. **3** (*infml*) ANGRY, furious, infuriated, irate, outraged, enraged, raging, fuming, indignant, incensed, exasperated, mad (*infml*).
🔁 **3** calm.

living *adj* alive, breathing, existing, live, current, extant, operative, strong, vigorous, active, lively, vital, animated.
🔁 dead, sluggish.
➤ *n* **1** BEING, life, animation, existence. **2** LIVELIHOOD, maintenance, support, income, subsistence, sustenance, work, job, occupation, profession, benefice, way of life.

load *n* **1** BURDEN, onus, encumbrance, weight, pressure, oppression, millstone. **2** CARGO, consignment, shipment, goods, lading, freight.
➤ *v* **1** BURDEN, weigh down, encumber, overburden, oppress, trouble, weight, saddle with. **2** PACK, pile, heap, freight, fill, stack.

loaded *adj* burdened, charged, laden, full, weighted.

loaf¹ *n* **1** *a loaf of bread*. block, slab, brick,

mass, lump, cube, cake. **2** *use your loaf*:
common sense, sense, head, noddle (*sl*),
brains (*infml*), gumption (*infml*), nous
(*infml*).

loaf² *v* stand about, idle, laze, loiter, take it
easy (*infml*), hang around (*infml*), lounge
around (*infml*), mooch (*infml*).
Ea toil.

loafer *n* (*infml*) idler, layabout (*infml*),
shirker (*infml*), skiver (*infml*), sluggard,
wastrel, lounger, ne'er-do-well, lazybones
(*infml*).

loan *n* advance, credit, mortgage,
allowance.
➤ *v* lend, advance, credit, allow.

loath *adj* reluctant, unwilling, resisting,
disinclined, opposed, grudging, hesitant,
indisposed, against, averse (*fml*).
Ea willing.

loathe *v* hate, detest, abominate, abhor,
despise, dislike.
Ea adore, love.

loathing *n* hatred, detestation,
abhorrence, abomination, repugnance,
revulsion, repulsion, dislike, disgust,
aversion, horror.
Ea affection, love.

loathsome *adj* detestable, abhorrent,
odious, repulsive, abominable, hateful,
repugnant (*fml*), repellent, offensive,
horrible, disgusting, vile, revolting, nasty.

lob *v* throw, toss, hurl, pitch, fling, heave,
launch, lift, shy, loft, chuck (*infml*).

lobby *v* campaign for, press for, demand,
persuade, call for, urge, push for, influence,
solicit, pressure, promote.
➤ *n* **1** VESTIBULE, foyer, porch, anteroom,
hall, hallway, waiting-room, entrance hall,
corridor, passage. **2** PRESSURE GROUP,
campaign, ginger group.

local *adj* regional, provincial, community,
district, neighbourhood, parochial,
vernacular, small-town, limited, narrow,
restricted, parish-pump.
Ea national.
➤ *n* **1** INHABITANT, citizen, resident,
native. **2** (*infml*) PUB.

locale *n* place, position, scene, setting,
site, spot, venue, area, locality, location,
neighbourhood, environment, zone,
formal locus.

locality *n* neighbourhood, vicinity,
district, area, locale, region, position,
place, site, spot, scene, setting.

localize *v* **1** IDENTIFY, specify, zero in on,
narrow down, pinpoint, ascribe, assign. **2**
RESTRAIN, limit, restrict, confine, contain,
concentrate, delimit, delimitate,
circumscribe (*fml*).

locate *v* **1** FIND, discover, unearth, run to
earth (*infml*), track down, detect, lay one's
hands on (*infml*), pinpoint, identify. **2**
SITUATE, settle, fix, establish, place, put,
set, seat.

location *n* position, situation, place,
locus, whereabouts, venue, site, locale,
bearings, spot, point.

lock¹ *n* fastening, bolt, clasp, catch,
padlock, mortise lock, combination lock,
spring lock, Chubb® lock, Yale® lock.

> **Parts of a lock include:** barrel, bolt,
> cylinder, cylinder hole, dead bolt,
> escutcheon, face plate, hasp, key, key card,
> keyhole, keyway, knob, latch, latch bolt, latch
> follower, latch lever, mortise bolt, pin, push
> button, rose, sash, sash bolt, spindle, spindle
> hole, spring, strike plate, staple.

➤ *v* **1** FASTEN, secure, bolt, latch, seal, shut.
2 JOIN, unite, engage, link, mesh, entangle,
entwine, clench. **3** CLASP, hug, embrace,
grasp, encircle, enclose, clutch, grapple.
Ea 1, 2 unlock.
◆ **lock out** shut out, refuse admittance to,
keep out, exclude, bar, debar.
◆ **lock up** imprison, jail, confine, shut in,
shut up, incarcerate, secure, cage, pen,
detain, close up.
Ea free.

lock² *n* strand, tress, tuft, plait, ringlet,
curl.

locomotion *n* movement, motion,
moving, progress, progression, travel,
travelling, headway, action, walking.

lodge *n* hut, cabin, cottage, chalet, shelter,
retreat, den, gatehouse, house, hunting-
lodge, meeting-place, club, haunt.
➤ *v* **1** ACCOMMODATE, put up (*infml*),
quarter, board, billet, shelter. **2** LIVE, stay,
reside. **3** FIX, embed, implant, get stuck.
4 DEPOSIT, place, put, submit, register.

lodger *n* boarder, paying guest, resident,
tenant, roomer, inmate, guest.

lodgings *n* accommodation, digs (*infml*),
dwelling, quarters, billet, abode, boarding-
house, rooms, pad (*infml*), residence.

lofty *adj* **1** *lofty ideals*: noble, grand,
exalted, distinguished, illustrious,
majestic, sublime, stately, imposing,

dignified, imperial, renowned, esteemed (*fml*). **2** HIGH, tall, sky-high, elevated, raised, towering, soaring. **3** ARROGANT, proud, haughty, condescending, disdainful, patronizing, supercilious, superior, lordly, snooty, high and mighty (*infml*), toffee-nosed (*infml*).
◪ **2** low. **3** humble, lowly, modest.

log *n* **1** TIMBER, trunk, block, chunk. **2** RECORD, diary, journal, logbook, daybook, account, tally.
➤ *v* record, register, write up, note, book, chart, tally.

loggerheads *n*
◆ **at loggerheads** disagreeing, in conflict, at odds, in opposition, quarrelling, at daggers drawn (*infml*), at each other's throats (*infml*), like cat and dog (*infml*).

logic *n* reasoning, reason, sense, deduction, rationale, argumentation.

logical *adj* reasonable, rational, reasoned, coherent, consistent, valid, sound, well-founded, clear, sensible, deducible, methodical, well-organized.
◪ illogical, irrational.

logistics *n* organization, co-ordination, management, masterminding, orchestration, strategy, tactics, planning, plans, direction, engineering.

loiter *v* dawdle, hang about, idle, linger, dally, dilly-dally (*infml*), delay, mooch, lag, saunter.

lone *adj* single, sole, one, only, isolated, solitary, separate, separated, unattached, unaccompanied, unattended.
◪ accompanied.

loneliness *n* aloneness, isolation, lonesomeness, solitariness, solitude, seclusion, desolation.

lonely *adj* **1** ALONE, friendless, lonesome, solitary, abandoned, forsaken, companionless, unaccompanied, destitute. **2** ISOLATED, uninhabited, remote, out-of-the-way, unfrequented, secluded, abandoned, deserted, forsaken, desolate.
◪ **1** popular. **2** crowded, populous.

loner *n* individualist, recluse, solitary, hermit, lone wolf (*infml*).

long *adj* lengthy, extensive, extended, expanded, prolonged, protracted, stretched, spread out, sustained, expansive, far-reaching, long-drawn-out, interminable, slow.
◪ brief, short, fleeting, abbreviated.

◆ **long for** yearn for, crave, want, wish, desire, dream of, hanker for, pine, thirst for, lust after, covet, itch for, yen for (*infml*).

longing *n* craving, desire, yearning, hungering, hankering, yen, thirst, wish, urge, coveting, aspiration, ambition.

long-lasting *adj* permanent, imperishable, enduring, unchanging, unfading, continuing, abiding, long-standing, prolonged, protracted.
◪ short-lived, ephemeral, transient.

long-standing *adj* established, long-established, long-lived, long-lasting, enduring, abiding, time-honoured, traditional.

long-suffering *adj* uncomplaining, forbearing, forgiving, tolerant, easy-going, patient, stoical.

long-winded *adj* lengthy, overlong, prolonged, diffuse, verbose, wordy, voluble, long-drawn-out, discursive, repetitious, rambling, tedious.
◪ brief, terse.

look *v* **1** WATCH, see, observe, view, survey, regard, gaze, study, stare, examine, inspect, scrutinize, glance, contemplate, scan, peep, gawp (*infml*). **2** SEEM, appear, show, exhibit, display.
➤ *n* **1** VIEW, survey, inspection, examination, observation, sight, review, once-over (*infml*), glance, glimpse, gaze, peek. **2** APPEARANCE, aspect, manner, semblance, mien, expression, bearing, face, complexion.

◆ **look after** take care of, mind, care for, attend to, take charge of, tend, keep an eye on, watch over, protect, supervise, guard.
◪ neglect.

◆ **look down on** despise, scorn, sneer at, hold in contempt, disdain, look down one's nose at (*infml*), turn one's nose up at (*infml*).
◪ esteem, approve.

◆ **look forward to** anticipate, await, expect, hope for, long for, envisage, envision, count on, wait for, look for.

◆ **look into** investigate, probe, research, study, go into, examine, enquire about, explore, check out, inspect, scrutinize, look over, plumb, fathom.

◆ **look out** pay attention, watch out, beware, be careful, keep an eye out.

◆ **look over** inspect, examine, check, give a once-over (*infml*), cast an eye over, look through, scan, view.

♦ **look up** n 1 SEARCH FOR, research, hunt for, find, track down. **2** VISIT, call on, drop in on, look in on, pay a visit to, stop by, drop by. **3** IMPROVE, get better, pick up, progress, come on.

♦ **look up to** admire, esteem, respect, revere, honour, have a high opinion of.

look-alike n double, replica, twin, spitting image (infml), living image, clone, spit (infml), ringer (infml), doppelgänger.

look-out n 1 GUARD, sentry, watch, watchtower, watchman, sentinel, tower, post. **2** (infml) CONCERN, responsibility, worry, affair, business, problem.

loom v appear, emerge, take shape, menace, threaten, impend, hang over, dominate, tower, overhang, rise, soar, overshadow, overtop.

loop n hoop, ring, circle, noose, coil, eyelet, loophole, spiral, curve, curl, kink, twist, whorl, twirl, turn, bend.
➤ v coil, encircle, roll, bend, circle, curve round, turn, twist, spiral, connect, join, knot, fold, braid.

loophole n let-out, escape, evasion, excuse, pretext, plea, pretence.

loose adj 1 FREE, unfastened, untied, movable, unattached, insecure, wobbly. **2** SLACK, lax, baggy, hanging. **3** IMPRECISE, vague, inexact, ill-defined, indefinite, inaccurate, indistinct.
☒ 1 firm, secure. **2** tight. **3** precise.

loosen v 1 EASE, relax, loose, slacken, undo, unbind, untie, unfasten. **2** FREE, set free, release, let go, let out, deliver.
☒ 1 tighten.

loot n spoils, booty, plunder, haul, swag (infml), prize.
➤ v plunder, pillage, rob, sack, rifle, raid, maraud, ransack, ravage.

lop v chop, cut (off), dock, prune, sever, trim, clip, crop, hack, shorten, curtail, detach, remove, take off, reduce, truncate.

lop-sided adj asymmetrical, unbalanced, askew, off balance, uneven.
☒ balanced, symmetrical.

loquacious adj talkative, chatty, chattering, babbling, blathering, gossipy, wordy, garrulous, voluble (fml), gabby (infml), gassy (infml).
☒ succinct, taciturn, terse, reserved.

lord n 1 PEER, noble, earl, duke, count, baron. **2** MASTER, ruler, superior, overlord, leader, commander, governor, king.

♦ **lord it over** domineer, tyrannize, be overbearing, order around, queen it over, oppress, repress, pull rank, swagger, put on airs (fml), act big (infml), boss around (infml).

lordly adj 1 NOBLE, dignified, aristocratic. **2** PROUD, arrogant, disdainful, haughty, imperious, condescending, high-handed, domineering, overbearing.
☒ 1 low(ly). **2** humble.

lore n knowledge, wisdom, learning, erudition, scholarship, traditions, teaching, beliefs, sayings.

lose v 1 MISLAY, misplace, forget, miss, forfeit. **2** WASTE, squander, dissipate, use up, exhaust, expend, drain. **3** FAIL, fall short, suffer defeat.
☒ 1 gain. **2** make. **3** win.

loser n failure, also-ran, runner-up, flop (infml), no-hoper.
☒ winner.

loss n 1 MISLAYING, misplacement, missing, forfeiture, forgetting, dropping. **2** DEPRIVATION, disappearance, bereavement, dispossession, disadvantage, harm, hurt, impairment, undoing, waste, privation (fml). **3** losses in war: casualties, fatalities, death toll, dead, missing, wounded. **4** the business made a loss: deficit, debt, deficiency.
☒ 1 finding. **2** gain. **4** profit.

♦ **at a loss** puzzled, perplexed, bewildered, mystified, not knowing what to do/say.

lost adj 1 MISLAID, missing, vanished, disappeared, misplaced, astray. **2** CONFUSED, disoriented, bewildered, puzzled, baffled, perplexed, preoccupied. **3** WASTED, squandered, ruined, destroyed.
☒ 1 found.

lot n 1 COLLECTION, batch, assortment, quantity, group, set, crowd. **2** SHARE, portion, allowance, ration, quota, part, piece, parcel.

lotion n ointment, balm, cream, salve.

lottery n 1 DRAW, raffle, sweepstake. **2** SPECULATION, venture, risk, gamble.

loud adj 1 NOISY, deafening, booming, resounding, ear-piercing, ear-splitting, piercing, thundering, blaring, clamorous, vociferous. **2** GARISH, gaudy, glaring, flashy, brash, showy, ostentatious, tasteless.
☒ 1 quiet. **2** subdued.

lounge v relax, loll, idle, laze, waste time, kill time, lie about, take it easy,

sprawl, recline, lie back, slump.
➤ *n* sitting-room, living-room, drawing-room, day-room, parlour.

lovable *adj* adorable, endearing, winsome, captivating, charming, engaging, attractive, fetching, sweet, lovely, pleasing, delightful.
Ea detestable, hateful.

love *v* **1** *he loves his wife*: adore, cherish, dote on, treasure, hold dear, idolize, worship. **2** *I love macaroons*: like, take pleasure in, enjoy, delight in, appreciate, desire, fancy.
Ea detest, hate.
➤ *n* **1** FONDNESS, affection, adoration, attachment, care, regard, concern, liking, amorousness, ardour, intimacy, desire, devotion, adulation, passion, rapture, tenderness, warmth, inclination, infatuation, lust, delight, enjoyment, weakness, taste, friendship, brotherhood, sympathy, kindness, soft spot (*infml*). **2** *a love of power*: pleasure, enjoyment, delight, liking, appreciation, weakness, partiality, relish, soft spot (*infml*). **3** *come here, my love*: darling, beloved, dear, dear one, dearest, favourite, sweetheart, honey, angel, pet, treasure
Ea **1** hate, hatred, dislike. **2** detestation, loathing.
◆ make love have sex with, sleep with (*infml*), sleep together (*infml*), go to bed with (*infml*), have it off with (*sl*), get one's leg over (*sl*).

love affair *n* affair, romance, liaison, relationship, love, passion.

loveless *adj* cold, cold-hearted, hard, icy, insensitive, unresponsive, unloved, unloving, passionless, unfeeling, unfriendly, unappreciated, friendless, disliked, frigid, forsaken, unvalued, heartless, uncherished.
Ea passionate.

lovely *adj* beautiful, charming, delightful, attractive, enchanting, pleasing, pleasant, pretty, adorable, agreeable, enjoyable, sweet, winning, exquisite.
Ea ugly, hideous.

lover *n* **1** BELOVED, loved one, admirer, boyfriend, man friend, girlfriend, woman friend, sweetheart, partner, live-in partner, suitor, mistress, lady love, fiancé(e), other man, other woman, significant other, flame (*infml*), bit on the side (*infml*), vamp (*infml*), wolf (*infml*), bird (*infml*), date (*infml*), fella

(*infml*), toy boy (*infml*), heart-throb (*infml*). **2** ENTHUSIAST, devotee, admirer, fan, supporter, follower, fanatic, buff (*infml*), freak (*infml*), fiend (*infml*).

lovesick *adj* infatuated, desiring, longing, pining, yearning, languishing, lovelorn, unrequited in love.

loving *adj* amorous, affectionate, devoted, doting, fond, ardent, passionate, warm, warm-hearted, tender.

low *adj* **1** SHORT, small, squat, stunted, little, shallow, deep, depressed, sunken. **2** INADEQUATE, deficient, poor, sparse, meagre, paltry, scant, insignificant. **3** UNHAPPY, depressed, downcast, gloomy. **4** BASE, coarse, vulgar, mean, contemptible. **5** CHEAP, inexpensive, reasonable. **6** subdued, muted, soft.
Ea **1** high. **2** high. **3** cheerful. **4** honourable. **5** exorbitant. **6** loud.

lower *adj* inferior, lesser, subordinate, secondary, minor, second-class, low-level, lowly, junior.
Ea higher.
➤ *v* **1** DROP, depress, sink, descend, let down. **2** REDUCE, decrease, cut, lessen, diminish.
Ea **1** raise. **2** increase.

low-key *adj* muted, quiet, restrained, subdued, understated, easy-going, relaxed, subtle, slight, soft.
Ea showy, impressive.

lowly *adj* humble, low-born, obscure, poor, plebeian, plain, simple, modest, ordinary, inferior, meek, mild, mean, submissive, subordinate.
Ea lofty, noble.

low-spirited *adj* depressed, gloomy, heavy-hearted, low, down, down-hearted, despondent, fed up (*infml*), sad, unhappy, miserable, moody.
Ea high-spirited, cheerful.

loyal *adj* true, faithful, steadfast, staunch, devoted, trustworthy, sincere, patriotic.
Ea disloyal, treacherous.

loyalty *n* allegiance, faithfulness, fidelity, devotion, steadfastness, constancy, trustworthiness, reliability, patriotism.
Ea disloyalty, treachery.

lubricate *v* oil, grease, smear, wax, lard.

lucid *adj* **1** CLEAR, comprehensible, plain, explicit, distinct, intelligible, obvious, evident. **2** CLEAR-HEADED, sane, rational, reasonable, intelligible, sensible, sober, sound, of sound mind, compos mentis. **3**

SHINING, bright, brilliant, beaming, transparent, translucent, gleaming, radiant, glassy, luminous, resplendent, crystalline, pure, diaphanous (*fml*), effulgent (*fml*), limpid (*fml*), pellucid (*fml*). **Ea** 1 unclear. 2 unintelligible. 3 dark, murky.

luck *n* 1 CHANCE, fortune, accident, fate, fortuity (*fml*), fluke (*infml*), destiny. 2 GOOD FORTUNE, success, break (*infml*), godsend. **Ea** 1 design. 2 misfortune.

luckily *adv* fortunately, happily, providentially. **Ea** unfortunately.

lucky *adj* fortunate, in luck, promising, favoured, charmed, successful, prosperous, timely, opportune, expedient, providential, auspicious (*fml*), fortuitous (*fml*), propitious (*fml*), jammy (*infml*). **Ea** unlucky.

lucrative *adj* profitable, well-paid, remunerative, advantageous. **Ea** unprofitable.

ludicrous *adj* absurd, ridiculous, preposterous, nonsensical, laughable, farcical, silly, comical, funny, outlandish, crazy (*infml*). **Ea** serious.

lug *v* pull, drag, haul, carry, tow, heave, hump.

luggage

> Types of luggage include: case, suitcase, vanity-case, bag, holdall, portmanteau, valise, overnight-bag, kit-bag, flight bag, hand-luggage, travel bag, Gladstone bag, grip, rucksack, knapsack, haversack, backpack, briefcase, attaché case, portfolio, satchel, basket, hamper, trunk, chest, box.

lukewarm *adj* cool, half-hearted, apathetic, tepid, indifferent, unenthusiastic, uninterested, unresponsive, unconcerned.

lull *v* soothe, subdue, calm, hush, pacify, quieten down, quiet, quell, compose. **Ea** agitate.
> *n* calm, peace, quiet, tranquillity, stillness, let-up (*infml*), pause, hush, silence. **Ea** agitation.

lumber¹ *n* clutter, jumble, rubbish, bits and pieces, odds and ends, junk.

lumber² *v* clump, shamble, plod, shuffle, stump, trundle.

luminary *n* expert, authority, leader,

leading light, celebrity, VIP, dignitary, worthy, notable, personage, star, superstar, big name (*infml*), bigwig (*infml*).

luminous *adj* glowing, illuminated, lit, lighted, radiant, shining, fluorescent, brilliant, lustrous, bright.

lump *n* 1 MASS, cluster, clump, clod, ball, bunch, piece, chunk, cake, hunk, nugget, wedge. 2 SWELLING, growth, bulge, bump, protuberance, protrusion, tumour.
> *v* collect, mass, gather, cluster, combine, coalesce, group, consolidate, unite.

lunacy *n* madness, insanity, aberration, derangement, mania, craziness (*infml*), idiocy, imbecility, folly, absurdity, stupidity. **Ea** sanity.

lunatic *n* psychotic, psychopath, madman, maniac, loony (*infml*), nutcase (*infml*), nutter (*infml*), fruitcake (*infml*).
> *adj* mad, insane, deranged, psychotic, irrational, crazy (*infml*), bonkers (*infml*). **Ea** sane.

lunge *v* thrust, jab, stab, pounce, plunge, pitch into, charge, dart, dash, dive, poke, strike (at), fall upon, grab (at), hit (at), leap.
> *n* thrust, stab, pounce, charge, jab, pass, cut, spring.

lurch *v* roll, rock, pitch, sway, stagger, reel, list.

lure *v* tempt, entice, draw, attract, allure, seduce, ensnare, lead on.
> *n* temptation, enticement, attraction, bait, inducement.

lurid *adj* 1 SENSATIONAL, shocking, startling, graphic, exaggerated. 2 MACABRE, gruesome, gory, ghastly, grisly. 3 BRIGHTLY COLOURED, garish, glaring, loud, vivid.

lurk *v* skulk, prowl, lie in wait, crouch, lie low, hide, snoop.

luscious *adj* delicious, juicy, succulent, appetizing, mouth-watering, sweet, tasty, savoury, desirable.

lush *adj* 1 FLOURISHING, luxuriant, abundant, prolific, overgrown, green, verdant. 2 SUMPTUOUS, opulent, ornate, plush, rich.

lust *n* 1 SENSUALITY, libido, lechery, licentiousness (*fml*), lewdness. 2 CRAVING, desire, appetite, longing, passion, greed, covetousness.
♦ **lust after** desire, crave, yearn for, want, need, hunger for, thirst for.

lustful *adj* sensual, passionate, licentious,

lewd, lascivious, lecherous, carnal, unchaste, wanton, craving, hankering, salacious, libidinous (*fml*), horny (*infml*), randy (*infml*), raunchy (*infml*).

lustily *adv* loudly, hard, robustly, strongly, vigorously, forcefully, powerfully, stoutly, with all one's might, with might and main (*fml*).

◨ weakly, feebly.

lustre *n* 1 SHINE, gloss, sheen, gleam, glow, brilliance, brightness, radiance, sparkle, resplendence, burnish, glitter, glint. 2 GLORY, honour, prestige, illustriousness.

lusty *adj* robust, strong, sturdy, vigorous, hale, hearty, healthy, gutsy (*infml*), energetic, strapping, rugged, powerful.

luxuriant *adj* 1 ABUNDANT, prolific, lush, superabundant, sumptuous, profuse, plentiful, plenteous, overflowing, ample, lavish, teeming, thriving, rich, riotous, rank, copious, dense, productive, fertile, fecund (*fml*). 2 ELABORATE, extravagant, fancy, ornate, flamboyant, flowery, opulent, excessive, rococo, baroque, florid (*fml*).

◨ 1 barren, infertile.

luxurious *adj* sumptuous, opulent (*fml*),

lavish, de luxe, plush (*infml*), magnificent, splendid, expensive, costly, self-indulgent, pampered.

◨ austere, spartan.

luxury *n* sumptuousness, opulence (*fml*), hedonism, splendour, affluence, richness, magnificence, pleasure, indulgence, gratification, comfort, extravagance, satisfaction.

◨ austerity.

lying *adj* deceitful, dishonest, false, untruthful, double-dealing, two-faced (*infml*).

◨ honest, truthful.

➤ *n* dishonesty, untruthfulness, deceit, falsity, fibbing (*infml*), perjury, duplicity, fabrication, double-dealing.

◨ honesty, truthfulness.

lyric *adj* emotional, passionate, personal, subjective, direct, strong, poetic, musical.

lyrical *adj* 1 POETIC, musical, romantic. 2 ENTHUSIASTIC, emotional, rapturous, rhapsodic, ecstatic, effusive, passionate, carried away, expressive, impassioned, inspired.

lyrics *n* text, words, book, libretto.

Mm

macabre *adj* gruesome, grisly, grim, horrible, frightful, dreadful, ghostly, eerie.

Machiavellian *adj* devious, crafty, designing, scheming, shrewd, sly, cunning, wily, artful, astute, calculating, deceitful, double-dealing, guileful, underhand, opportunist, foxy, intriguing, unscrupulous.

machination *n* scheme, intrigue, plot, design, manoeuvre, conspiracy, tactic, wile, ruse, ploy, stratagem, trick, device, dodge (*infml*), cabal, artifice (*fml*), shenanigans (*infml*).

machine *n* **1** INSTRUMENT, device, contrivance, tool, mechanism, engine, apparatus, appliance. **2** AGENCY, organization, structure, system.

machinery *n* **1** INSTRUMENTS, mechanism, tools, apparatus, equipment, tackle, gear. **2** ORGANIZATION, channels, structure, system, procedure.

> Types of heavy machinery include: all-terrain fork lift, bulldozer, caterpillar tractor, combine harvester, concrete mixer, concrete pump, crane, crawler crane, crawler tractor, digger, dragline excavator, dredger, dumper, dump truck, dustcart, excavator, fertilizer spreader, fire appliance, fork-lift truck, gantry crane, grader, grapple, gritter, hydraulic bale loader, hydraulic shovel, JCB®, muck spreader, pick-up loader, pile-driver, platform hoist, riding mower, road roller, road-sweeping lorry, Rotovator®, silage harvester, snowplough, straw baler, threshing machine, tower crane, tracklayer, tractor, tractor-scraper, truck crane, wheel loader.

mad *adj* **1** INSANE, lunatic, unbalanced, psychotic, deranged, demented, out of one's mind, crazy (*infml*), of unsound mind, unstable, unhinged, crazed, nuts (*infml*), barmy (*infml*), bonkers (*infml*). **2** (*infml*) ANGRY, furious, enraged, infuriated, incensed. **3** IRRATIONAL, illogical, unreasonable, absurd, preposterous, foolish. **4** FANATICAL, enthusiastic, infatuated, ardent.

F3 **1** sane. **2** calm. **3** sensible. **4** apathetic.

madden *v* anger, enrage, infuriate, incense, exasperate, provoke, annoy, irritate.

F3 calm, pacify.

made-up *adj* **1** INVENTED, make-believe, unreal, untrue, false, fictional, imaginary, specious, fabricated, fairytale, mythical, trumped-up (*infml*). **2** WEARING MAKE-UP, painted, powdered, done up.

F3 **1** real, factual, true.

madly *adv* **1** INSANELY, dementedly, hysterically, wildly. **2** EXCITEDLY, frantically, furiously, recklessly, violently, energetically, rapidly, hastily, hurriedly. **3** *madly in love*: intensely, extremely, exceedingly, fervently, devotedly.

madman, madwoman *n* lunatic, psychotic, psychopath, maniac, loony (*infml*), nutcase (*infml*), fruitcake (*infml*).

madness *n* **1** INSANITY, lunacy, dementia, psychosis, mental instability, mania, derangement, distraction, delusion, craziness (*infml*). **2** FURY, rage, raving, frenzy, hysteria, anger, agitation, exasperation, wrath, ire. **3** FOLLY, craziness, irrationality, unreasonableness, insanity, stupidity, silliness, inanity, absurdity, nonsense, foolishness, foolhardiness, preposterousness, wildness, daftness (*infml*). **4** KEENNESS, enthusiasm, ardour, craze, abandon, zeal, wildness, unrestraint, uproar, riot, passion, excitement, fanaticism, infatuation, intoxication.

F3 **1** sanity. **2** calmness. **3** reasonableness.

> Some colloquial expressions used when talking about madness: crazy, nuts, nutty, nutty as a fruitcake, barmy, bonkers, batty, crackers, dippy, daffy, bananas, loony, loopy, off the wall, needing one's head examined, having bats in the belfry, barking (mad), doolally, have a few tiles missing, have a screw loose, have lost one's marbles, lose one's mind, mad as a hatter, mad as a March hare, not playing with a full deck, off one's chump, off one's head, off one's rocker, off one's trolley, out of one's mind, out to lunch, round the bend, round the twist, running on three wheels, stir-crazy.

maestro n expert, master, genius, prodigy, virtuoso, wizard (*infml*), ace (*infml*).

magazine n 1 JOURNAL, periodical, paper, weekly, monthly, quarterly. 2 ARSENAL, storehouse, ammunition dump, depot, ordnance.

magic n 1 SORCERY, enchantment, occultism, black art, witchcraft, spell. 2 CONJURING, illusion, sleight of hand, trickery. 3 CHARM, fascination, glamour, allure.
➤ *adj* charming, enchanting, bewitching, fascinating, spellbinding.

magician n sorcerer, miracle-worker, conjuror, enchanter, wizard, witch, warlock, spellbinder, wonder-worker.

magistrate n judge, justice, justice of the peace, JP, stipendiary, bailiff, tribune, aedile, beak (*infml*).

magnanimous adj generous, liberal, open-handed, benevolent, selfless, charitable, big-hearted, kind, noble, unselfish, ungrudging.
🗷 mean.

magnate n tycoon, captain of industry, industrialist, mogul, entrepreneur, plutocrat, baron, personage, notable.

magnetic adj attractive, alluring, fascinating, charming, mesmerizing, seductive, irresistible, entrancing, captivating, gripping, absorbing, charismatic.
🗷 repellent, repulsive.

magnetism n attraction, allure, fascination, charm, lure, appeal, drawing power, draw, pull, hypnotism, mesmerism, charisma, grip, magic, power, spell.

magnificent adj splendid, grand, imposing, impressive, glorious, gorgeous, brilliant, excellent, majestic, superb, sumptuous, noble, elegant, fine, rich.
🗷 modest, humble, poor.

magnify v enlarge, amplify, increase, expand, intensify, boost, enhance, greaten, heighten, deepen, build up, exaggerate, dramatize, overemphasize, overplay, overstate, overdo, blow up (*infml*).
🗷 belittle, play down.

magnitude n 1 SIZE, extent, measure, amount, expanse, dimensions, mass, proportions, quantity, volume, bulk, largeness, space, strength, amplitude. 2 IMPORTANCE, consequence, significance, weight, greatness, moment, intensity.

maiden n girl, virgin, lass, lassie, damsel (*fml*), miss.

mail n post, letters, correspondence, packages, parcels, delivery.
➤ *v* post, send, dispatch, forward.

maim v mutilate, wound, incapacitate, injure, disable, hurt, impair, cripple, lame.

main adj principal, chief, leading, first, foremost, predominant, pre-eminent, primary, prime, supreme, paramount, central, cardinal, outstanding, essential, critical, crucial, necessary, vital.
🗷 minor, unimportant, insignificant.
➤ *n* pipe, duct, conduit, channel, cable, line.

mainly adv primarily, principally, chiefly, in the main, mostly, on the whole, for the most part, generally, in general, especially, as a rule, above all, largely, overall.

mainstay n support, buttress, bulwark, linchpin, prop, pillar, backbone, foundation.

mainstream adj normal, average, central, general, typical, regular, standard, conventional, established, orthodox, received, accepted, mainline.
🗷 heterodox, peripheral, marginal.

maintain v 1 CARRY ON, continue, keep (up), sustain, retain. 2 CARE FOR, conserve, look after, take care of, preserve, support, finance, supply. 3 ASSERT, affirm, claim, contend, declare, hold, state, insist, believe, fight for.
🗷 2 neglect. 3 deny.

maintenance n 1 CONTINUATION, continuance, perpetuation. 2 CARE, conservation, preservation, support, repairs, protection, upkeep, running. 3 KEEP, subsistence, living, livelihood, allowance, alimony.
🗷 2 neglect.

majestic adj magnificent, grand, dignified, noble, royal, stately, splendid, imperial, impressive, exalted, imposing, regal, sublime, superb, lofty, monumental, pompous.
🗷 lowly, unimpressive, unimposing.

majesty n grandeur, glory, dignity, magnificence, nobility, royalty, resplendence, splendour, stateliness, pomp, exaltedness, impressiveness, loftiness.

major *adj* greater, chief, main, larger, bigger, higher, leading, outstanding, notable, supreme, uppermost, significant, crucial, important, key, keynote, great, senior, older, superior, pre-eminent, vital, weighty.
🔁 minor, unimportant, trivial.

majority *n* 1 BULK, mass, preponderance, most, greater part. 2 ADULTHOOD, maturity, manhood, womanhood, years of discretion.
🔁 1 minority.

make *v* 1 CREATE, manufacture, fabricate, construct, build, produce, put together, originate, compose, form, shape. 2 CAUSE, bring about, effect, accomplish, occasion, give rise to, generate, render, perform. 3 COERCE, force, oblige, constrain, compel, prevail upon, pressurize, press, require. 4 APPOINT, elect, designate, nominate, ordain, install. 5 EARN, gain, net, obtain, acquire. 6 CONSTITUTE, compose, comprise, add up to, amount to.
🔁 1 dismantle. 5 spend.
➤ *n* brand, sort, type, style, variety, manufacture, model, mark, kind, form, structure.

♦ **make away with** 1 STEAL, run off with, walk off with, snatch, seize, carry off, kidnap, pinch (*infml*), lift (*infml*), nick (*infml*), nab (*infml*), swipe (*infml*). 2 KILL, do away with, murder, slaughter, assassinate, do in (*infml*), knock off (*infml*), bump off (*infml*).

♦ **make believe** pretend, play, play-act, imagine, dream, enact, fantasize, act, feign (*fml*), make castles in the air (*infml*).

♦ **make do** cope, manage, survive, get along, get by, improvise, make out, muddle through, scrape by (*infml*), make the best of a bad job (*infml*), keep one's head above water (*infml*).

♦ **make for** 1 HEAD FOR, aim for, go towards, move towards. 2 PRODUCE, lead to, promote, contribute to, facilitate, favour, forward, further, be conducive to.

♦ **make off** run off, run away, depart, bolt, leave, fly, cut and run (*infml*), beat a hasty retreat (*infml*), clear off (*infml*).

♦ **make out** 1 DISCERN, perceive, decipher, distinguish, recognize, see, detect, discover, understand, work out, grasp, follow, fathom. 2 DRAW UP, complete, fill in, write out. 3 MAINTAIN, imply, claim, assert, describe, demonstrate, prove. 4 MANAGE, get on, progress, succeed, fare (*fml*).

♦ **make up** 1 CREATE, invent, devise, fabricate, construct, originate, formulate, dream up, compose. 2 COMPLETE, fill, supply, meet, supplement. 3 COMPRISE, constitute, compose, form. 4 BE RECONCILED, make peace, settle differences, bury the hatchet (*infml*), forgive and forget, call it quits (*infml*).

♦ **make up for** compensate for, make good, make amends for, redress, recompense, redeem, atone for.

make-believe *n* pretence, imagination, fantasy, unreality, play-acting, role-play, dream, charade.
🔁 reality.

maker *n* creator, manufacturer, constructor, builder, producer, director, architect, author.

makeshift *adj* temporary, improvised, rough and ready, provisional, substitute, stop-gap, expedient, make-do.
🔁 permanent.

make-up *n* 1 COSMETICS, paint, powder, maquillage, war paint (*infml*). 2 CONSTITUTION, nature, composition, character, construction, form, format, formation, arrangement, organization, style, structure, assembly.

making *n* 1 PRODUCTION, producing, creation, creating, manufacture, assembly, building, composition, construction, fabrication, modelling, moulding, forging. 2 POTENTIAL, qualities, potentiality, promise, capability, capacity, possibilities, beginnings, materials, ingredients. 3 EARNINGS, income, profits, proceeds, revenue, returns, takings.
🔁 1 dismantling.

♦ **in the making** budding, potential, promising, coming, developing, emergent, up and coming, nascent (*fml*), burgeoning (*fml*), incipient (*fml*).

maladjusted *adj* disturbed, unstable, confused, alienated, neurotic, estranged.
🔁 well-adjusted.

malaise *n* uneasiness, unease, discontent, depression, discomfort, disquiet, weariness, anxiety, anguish, doldrums, angst, illness, disease, sickness, weakness, lassitude (*fml*), melancholy (*fml*), indisposition (*fml*), enervation (*fml*).
🔁 happiness, well-being.

male *adj* masculine, manly, virile, boyish, he-.
🔁 female.

Male terms include: boy, lad, youth, man, gentleman, gent (*infml*), bachelor, chap (*infml*), bloke (*infml*), guy (*infml*), son, brother, boyfriend, beau, toy boy (*sl*), fiancé, bridegroom, husband, father, uncle, nephew, grandfather, patriarch, godfather, widower, sugar daddy (*sl*), hunk (*sl*), gigolo, homosexual, gay, rent boy, male chauvinist pig (MCP) (*sl*); bull, dog, buck, tup, cock, cockerel, stallion, billy-goat, boar, dog fox, stag, ram, tom cat, drake, gander.

malevolent *adj* malicious, malign, spiteful, vindictive, ill-natured, hostile, vicious, venomous, evil-minded.
E3 benevolent, kind.

malformation *n* irregularity, deformity, distortion, warp.

malformed *adj* misshapen, irregular, deformed, distorted, twisted, warped, crooked, bent.
E3 perfect.

malfunction *n* fault, defect, failure, breakdown.
➤ *v* break down, go wrong, fail.

malice *n* malevolence (*fml*), enmity, animosity, ill-will, hatred, hate, spite, vindictiveness, bitterness.
E3 love.

malicious *adj* malevolent (*fml*), ill-natured, malign, spiteful, venomous, vicious, vengeful, evil-minded, bitter, resentful.
E3 kind, friendly.

malign *adj* malignant, malevolent, bad, evil, harmful, hurtful, injurious, destructive, hostile.
E3 benign.
➤ *v* defame, slander, libel, disparage, abuse, run down (*infml*), harm, injure.
E3 praise.

malignant *adj* 1 MALEVOLENT (*fml*), malicious, spiteful, evil, hostile, vicious, venomous, destructive, harmful, hurtful, pernicious. 2 FATAL, deadly, incurable, dangerous, cancerous, uncontrollable, virulent.
E3 1 kind. 2 benign.

malleable *adj* 1 SUPPLE, plastic, pliable, pliant, flexible, soft, workable, ductile (*fml*). 2 IMPRESSIONABLE, manageable, receptive, flexible, susceptible, persuadable, pliant, pliable, adaptable, biddable, governable, compliant (*fml*), tractable (*fml*).

E3 1 rigid. 2 intractable (*fml*).

malpractice *n* misconduct, mismanagement, negligence, impropriety, dereliction of duty (*fml*), abuse, misdeed.

maltreat *v* ill-treat, mistreat, misuse, abuse, injure, harm, damage, hurt.
E3 care for.

mammal

Mammals include: aardvark, African black rhinoceros, African elephant, anteater, antelope, armadillo, baboon, Bactrian camel, badger, bat, bear, beaver, bushbaby, cat, chimpanzee, chipmunk, cow, deer, dog, dolphin, duck-billed platypus, dugong, echidna, flying lemur, fox, gerbil, gibbon, giraffe, goat, gorilla, guinea pig, hamster, hare, hedgehog, hippopotamus, horse, human being, hyena, Indian elephant, kangaroo, koala, lemming, leopard, lion, manatee, marmoset, marmot, marsupial mouse, mole, mouse, opossum, orang utan, otter, pig, porcupine, porpoise, rabbit, raccoon, rat, sea cow, seal, sea lion, sheep, shrew, sloth, squirrel, tamarin, tapir, tiger, vole, wallaby, walrus, weasel, whale, wolf, zebra. *see also* **cat**; **cattle**; **dog**; **horse**; **marsupial**; **monkey**; **rodent**.

mammoth *adj* enormous, huge, vast, colossal, gigantic, giant, massive, immense, monumental, mighty.
E3 tiny, minute.

man *n* 1 MALE, gentleman, fellow, bloke (*infml*), chap (*infml*), guy (*infml*). 2 HUMAN BEING, person, individual, adult, human. 3 HUMANITY, humankind, mankind, human race, people, Homo sapiens, mortals.
4 MANSERVANT, servant, worker, employee, hand, soldier, valet, houseman, houseboy.
➤ *v* staff, crew, take charge of, operate, occupy.

manacle *v* handcuff, shackle, restrain, fetter, chain, put in chains, bind, curb, check, hamper, inhibit.
E3 free, unshackle.

manage *v* 1 ACCOMPLISH, succeed, bring about, bring off, effect. 2 ADMINISTER, direct, run, command, govern, preside over, rule, superintend, supervise, oversee, conduct. 3 CONTROL, influence, deal with, handle, operate, manipulate, guide.
4 COPE, fare, survive, get by, get along, get on, make do.
E3 1 fail. 2 mismanage.

manageable *adj* tractable (*infml*), governable, controllable, amenable, submissive, docile.
⊟ unmanageable.

management *n* **1** ADMINISTRATION, direction, control, government, command, running, superintendence, supervision, charge, care, handling. **2** MANAGERS, directors, directorate, executive, executives, governors, board, bosses (*infml*), supervisors.
⊟ 1 mismanagement. **2** workers.

manager *n* director, executive, administrator, controller, superintendent, supervisor, overseer, governor, organizer, head, boss (*infml*).

mandate *n* order, command, decree, edict, injunction, charge, directive, warrant, authorization, authority, instruction, commission, sanction.

mandatory *adj* obligatory, compulsory, binding, required, necessary, requisite (*fml*), essential.
⊟ optional.

manfully *adv* bravely, courageously, valiantly, heroically, intrepidly, boldly, gallantly, pluckily, determinedly, hard, vigorously, strongly, powerfully, unflinchingly, desperately, resolutely, stalwartly, stoutly, steadfastly, nobly.
⊟ half-heartedly, timidly.

mangle *v* mutilate, disfigure, mar, maim, spoil, butcher, destroy, deform, wreck, twist, maul, distort, crush, cut, hack, tear, rend.

mangy *adj* seedy, shabby, scruffy, scabby, tatty (*infml*), shoddy, moth-eaten, dirty, mean.

manhandle *v* **1** *the porters manhandled the baggage*: haul, heave, hump, pull, push, shove, tug. **2** *the police manhandled the demonstrators*: maul, mistreat, maltreat, misuse, abuse, knock about (*infml*), rough up (*infml*).

manhood *n* **1** ADULTHOOD, maturity. **2** MASCULINITY, virility, manliness, manfulness, machismo (*infml*).

mania *n* **1** MADNESS, insanity, lunacy, psychosis, derangement, disorder, aberration, craziness (*infml*), frenzy. **2** PASSION, craze, rage, obsession, compulsion, enthusiasm, fad (*infml*), infatuation, fixation, craving, urge, fetish.

Manias (by name of disorder) include:
dipsomania (*alcohol*), bibliomania (*books*), ailuromania (*cats*), demomania (*crowds*), necromania (*dead bodies*), thanatomania (*death*), cynomania (*dogs*), narcomania (*drugs*), pyromania (*fire-raising*), anthomania (*flowers*), hippomania (*horses*), mythomania (*lying and exaggerating*), egomania (*oneself*), ablutomania (*personal cleanliness*), hedonomania (*pleasure*), megalomania (*power*), theomania (*religion*), nymphomania (*sex*), monomania (*single idea or thing*), kleptomania (*stealing*), tomomania (*surgery*), logomania (*talking*), ergomania (*work*). see also **phobia**.

maniac *n* **1** LUNATIC, madman, madwoman, psychotic, psychopath, loony (*infml*). **2** ENTHUSIAST, fan (*infml*), fanatic, fiend (*infml*), freak (*infml*).

manifest *adj* obvious, evident, clear, apparent, plain, open, patent, noticeable, conspicuous, unmistakable, visible, unconcealed.
⊟ unclear.
➤ *v* show, exhibit, display, demonstrate, reveal, set forth, expose, prove, illustrate, establish.
⊟ conceal.

manifestation *n* display, exhibition, demonstration, show, revelation, exposure, disclosure, appearance, expression, sign, indication.

manifesto *n* statement, declaration, policies, platform.

manifold *adj* (*fml*) many, numerous, varied, various, diverse, multiple, kaleidoscopic, abundant, copious.

manipulate *v* **1** HANDLE, control, wield, operate, use, manoeuvre, influence, engineer, guide, direct, steer, negotiate, work. **2** FALSIFY, rig, juggle with, doctor (*infml*), cook (*infml*), fiddle (*infml*).

mankind *n* humankind, humanity, human race, man, Homo sapiens, people.

manly *adj* masculine, male, virile, manful, macho (*infml*), robust.

man-made *adj* synthetic, manufactured, simulated, imitation, artificial.
⊟ natural.

manner *n* **1** WAY, method, means, fashion, style, procedure, process, form. **2** BEHAVIOUR, conduct, bearing, demeanour, air, appearance, look, character.

mannered *adj* artificial, posed, pretentious, stilted, precious, affected (*fml*), euphuistic (*fml*), pseudo (*infml*), put-on (*infml*).
⊟ natural.

mannerism *n* idiosyncrasy, peculiarity, characteristic, quirk, trait, feature, foible, habit.

manners *n* behaviour, conduct, demeanour, etiquette, politeness, bearing, courtesy, formalities, social graces, p's and q's.

manoeuvre *n* move, movement, operation, action, exercise, plan, ploy, plot, ruse, stratagem, machination, gambit, tactic, trick, scheme, dodge (*infml*).
➤ *v* 1 MOVE, manipulate, handle, guide, pilot, steer, navigate, jockey, direct, drive, exercise. 2 CONTRIVE, engineer, plot, scheme, wangle (*infml*), pull strings (*infml*), manipulate, manage, plan, devise, negotiate.

mansion *n* home, hall, house, manor, manor-house, castle, château, Schloss, villa, seat, abode (*fml*), dwelling (*fml*), habitation (*fml*), residence (*fml*).

mantle *n* cloak, cover, covering, cape, hood, blanket, shawl, veil, wrap, shroud, screen.

manual *n* handbook, guide, guidebook, instructions, Bible, vade mecum, directions.
➤ *adj* hand-operated, by hand, physical, human.

manufacture *v* 1 MAKE, produce, construct, build, fabricate, create, assemble, mass-produce, turn out, process, forge, form. 2 INVENT, make up, concoct, fabricate, think up.
➤ *n* production, making, construction, fabrication, mass-production, assembly, creation, formation.

manufacturer *n* maker, producer, industrialist, constructor, factory-owner, builder, creator.

manure *n* fertilizer, compost, muck, dung.

many *adj* numerous, countless, lots of (*infml*), manifold (*fml*), various, varied, sundry, diverse, umpteen (*infml*).
⊟ few.

map *n* chart, plan, street plan, atlas, graph, plot.

mar *v* spoil, impair, harm, hurt, damage, deface, disfigure, mutilate, injure, maim,

scar, detract from, mangle, ruin, wreck, tarnish.
⊟ enhance.

maraud *v* plunder, raid, ravage, ransack, loot, pillage, harry, forage, foray, sack, despoil (*fml*), spoliate (*fml*), depredate (*fml*).

marauder *n* bandit, brigand, robber, raider, plunderer, pillager, pirate, buccaneer, outlaw, ravager, predator.

march *v* walk, stride, parade, pace, file, tread, stalk.
➤ *n* 1 STEP, pace, stride. 2 WALK, trek, hike, footslog (*infml*). 3 PROCESSION, parade, demonstration, demo (*infml*). 4 ADVANCE, development, progress, evolution, passage.

margin *n* 1 BORDER, edge, boundary, bound, periphery, perimeter, rim, brink, limit, confine, verge, side, skirt.
2 ALLOWANCE, play, leeway, latitude, scope, room, space, surplus, extra.

marginal *adj* borderline, peripheral, negligible, minimal, insignificant, minor, slight, doubtful, low, small.
⊟ central, core.

marine *adj* sea, maritime, naval, nautical, seafaring, sea-going, ocean-going, salt-water.

mariner *n* sailor, seaman, seafarer, deckhand, navigator, tar (*infml*), sea-dog (*infml*), salt (*infml*).

marital *adj* conjugal (*fml*), matrimonial (*fml*), married, wedded, nuptial (*fml*), connubial (*fml*).

maritime *adj* marine, nautical, naval, seafaring, sea, seaside, oceanic, coastal.

mark *n* 1 SPOT, stain, blemish, patch, pimple, freckle, birthmark, blot, blotch, smudge, smear, dent, impression, trace, fingerprint(s), track(s), imprint, speck, notch, chip, cut, scar, scratch, bruise, score, line, nick, stigma (*fml*), zit (*infml*). 2 SIGN, indication, character, symbol, stamp, token, characteristic, feature, quality, attribute, symptom, clue, proof, hint, evidence, impression, print. 3 SCORE, grade, percentage, tick, assessment, evaluation, letter, number, symbol, emblem, brand, stamp, seal, badge, device, logo, trademark, motto, monogram. 4 *inflation reaching the 5% mark*: point, level, stage, norm, standard, criterion, gauge, scale, measure, yardstick. 5 TARGET, goal, aim, objective, object,

purpose, end, intention, bull's-eye.
➤ *v* **1** STAIN, blemish, blot, smudge,
discolour, dent, scar, scratch, bruise, dent,
chip, cut, score, nick. **2** BRAND, label,
stamp, tag, flag, characterize, identify,
distinguish. **3** EVALUATE, assess, correct,
grade, appraise (*fml*). **4** WRITE DOWN, note
(down), indicate, name, label, specify,
designate, jot down. **5** CHARACTERIZE,
identify, stamp, brand, typify, distinguish. **6**
mark an event/occasion: observe,
remember, celebrate, commemorate,
keep, honour, recognize. **7** *mark my words*:
listen, mind, note, spot, observe, regard,
see, notice, take note of, discern, pay
attention to, bear in mind, take to heart,
heed (*fml*), take heed of (*fml*).

marked *adj* **1** NOTICEABLE, obvious,
conspicuous, evident, pronounced,
distinct, decided, emphatic, considerable,
remarkable, apparent, glaring.
2 SUSPECTED, watched, doomed.
🇪 **1** unnoticeable, slight.

markedly *adv* noticeably, obviously,
conspicuously, prominently, signally,
evidently, clearly, distinctly, decidedly,
emphatically, considerably, remarkably,
glaringly, strikingly, blatantly, unmistakably.

market *n* mart, marketplace, bazaar, fair,
exchange, outlet.
➤ *v* sell, retail, hawk, peddle.
🇪 buy.

marketable *adj* in demand, sought after,
wanted, saleable, sellable, merchantable,
vendible (*fml*).
🇪 unsaleable.

marketing

Terms used in marketing include:
above-the-line advertising, account
executive (AE), ACORN [= A Classification
of Residential Neighbourhoods], adopter,
after-sales service, AIDA [= attention,
interest, desire, action], aided or prompted
recall, area sampling, articles of ostentation,
ASA [= Advertising Standards Authority],
attitude research, audience research, below-
the-line advertising, blanket coverage, blind
advertisement, BOGO(F)F [= buy one get
one (for) free], brand awareness, brand
image, brand leader, brand loyalty, buyers'
market, buying motives, call rate, campaign,
cannibalism, canvass, captive audience,
captive market, classified advertising, cluster
sampling, cold call, commando salesman,
commercial, comparative advertising,

competitive market, concentrated marketing,
concept testing, consumer panel, consumer
research, consumer sovereignty, co-
operative advertising, corner a market,
corporate identity, corporate image,
coverage, credibility gap, customer
orientation, customer profile, DAGMAR [=
Defining Advertising Goals for Measured
Advertising Results], dealer brand,
demarketing, early adopter, elasticity of
demand, face-to-face selling, family brand,
family life cycle, field selling, filter question,
flash pack, FMCGs [= fast moving consumer
goods], focus group survey, four p's [=
product, price, promotion and place], free
gift/sample, frequency, Gallup poll, gap
analysis, generic, geographical
concentration, Giffen good, gimmick, give-
away, group discussion, growth-share
matrix, cash cow, dog, star, problem children
or wildcats, halo effect, hard sell, harvesting
strategy, heavy user, heterogeneous
products, hierarchy of effects, hierarchy of
needs, high-involvement products, high-
pressure selling, hit rate, horizontal marketing,
homogeneous products, house-to-house,
impulse buying, incentive marketing,
industrial advertising, inertia selling,
institutional advertising, international
marketing, island display, jingle, journey
planning, key prospects, launch, leading
question, loss leader, low-involvement
products, low-pressure selling, loyalty card,
macro marketing, mailshot, market demand,
market leader, market orientation, market
penetration, market potential, market profile,
market research, market segmentation,
market share, marketing audit, marketing
board, marketing concept, marketing
intelligence, marketing mix, matched sample,
media buyer, media independent, media
planner, media research, merchandising,
micro marketing, missionary selling, mock-
up, motivation research, multi-brand strategy,
necessity good, Nielsen index, normal good,
observation, opportunity to see, opinion
leaders, outdoor advertising, own label,
paired comparisons, party selling, perceptual
map, perfect competition, personal selling,
personality promotion, piggy-back
promotion, predatory pricing, product
differentiation/orientation/positioning,
promotion, psychographic measurement,
pyramid selling, random sampling,
recognition, reference group, response rate,
retail audit, rolling launch, sales aid, sales

campaign, sales drive, saturation point, shout, skimming pricing, slogan, social marketing, socio-economic groups, solus position, static market, subliminal advertising, tachistoscope, target audience, Target Group Index, telephone selling, test marketing, unaided recall, undifferentiated marketing, unprompted response, up-market, USP [= unique selling proposition], vertical marketing, viral marketing, visualizer.

marksman, markswoman n crack shot, dead shot, sharpshooter, sniper, bersagliere.

maroon v abandon, cast away, desert, put ashore, strand, leave, isolate.

marriage n 1 MATRIMONY, wedlock, wedding, nuptials (fml). 2 UNION, alliance, merger, coupling, amalgamation, link, association, confederation.
⊟ 1 divorce. 2 separation.

married adj marital, wedded, united, wed, joined, husbandly, wifely, wived, yoked, conjugal (fml), connubial (fml), matrimonial (fml), nuptial (fml), spousal (fml), hitched (infml), spliced (infml).
⊟ divorced, single.

marrow n essence, heart, nub, kernel, core, soul, spirit, substance, quick, stuff, gist.

marry v 1 WED, join in matrimony, tie the knot (infml), get hitched (infml), get spliced (infml). 2 UNITE, ally, join, merge, match, link, knit.
⊟ 1 divorce. 2 separate.

marsh n marshland, bog, swamp, fen, morass, quagmire, slough.

marshal v 1 ARRANGE, dispose, order, line up, align, array, rank, organize, assemble, gather, muster, group, collect, draw up, deploy. 2 GUIDE, lead, escort, conduct, usher.

marshy adj boggy, fenny, fennish, swampy, quaggy, waterlogged, wet, muddy, squelchy, miry, slumpy, spongy.
⊟ solid, firm, dry.

marsupial

Marsupials include: bandicoot, cuscus, kangaroo, rat kangaroo, tree kangaroo, wallaroo, koala, marsupial anteater, marsupial mouse, marsupial mole, marsupial rat, opossum, pademelon, phalanger, Tasmanian Devil, Tasmanian wolf, wallaby, rock wallaby, wombat.

martial adj warlike, military, belligerent, soldierly, militant, heroic, brave.

martinet n disciplinarian, stickler, tyrant, taskmaster, taskmistress, formalist, slave-driver (infml).

martyr v put to death, make a martyr of, crucify, stone, persecute, torture, torment, burn at the stake, throw to the lions, put on the rack, give the works (infml), give the third degree (infml).

martyrdom n death, suffering, torture, torment, persecution, excruciation, ordeal, agony, anguish.

marvel n wonder, miracle, phenomenon, prodigy, spectacle, sensation, genius.
➤ v wonder, gape, gaze, be amazed at.

marvellous adj 1 WONDERFUL, excellent, splendid, superb, magnificent, terrific (infml), super, fantastic (infml).
2 EXTRAORDINARY, amazing, astonishing, astounding, miraculous, remarkable, surprising, unbelievable, incredible, glorious.
⊟ 1 terrible, awful. 2 ordinary, run-of-the-mill.

masculine adj 1 MALE, manlike, manly, mannish, virile, macho (infml).
2 VIGOROUS, strong, strapping, robust, powerful, muscular, red-blooded, bold, brave, gallant, resolute, stout-hearted.
⊟ 1 feminine.

mash v crush, pulp, beat, pound, pulverize, pummel, grind, smash.

mask n disguise, camouflage, façade, front, concealment, cover-up, cover, guise, pretence, semblance, cloak, veil, blind, show, veneer, visor.
➤ v disguise, camouflage, cover, conceal, cloak, veil, hide, obscure, screen, shield.
⊟ expose, uncover.

masquerade n 1 MASQUE, masked ball, costume ball, fancy dress party.
2 DISGUISE, counterfeit, cover-up, cover, deception, front, pose, pretence, guise, cloak.
➤ v disguise, impersonate, pose, pass oneself off, mask, play, pretend, profess, dissimulate.

mass n 1 HEAP, pile, load, accumulation, aggregate, collection, conglomeration, combination, entirety, whole, totality, sum, lot, group, batch, bunch. 2 QUANTITY, multitude, throng, troop, crowd, band, horde, mob. 3 MAJORITY, body, bulk.
4 SIZE, dimension, magnitude, immensity.

5 LUMP, piece, chunk, block, hunk.
➤ *adj* widespread, large-scale, extensive, comprehensive, general, indiscriminate, popular, across-the-board, sweeping, wholesale, blanket.
🔳 limited, small-scale.
➤ *v* collect, gather, assemble, congregate, crowd, rally, cluster, muster, swarm, throng.
🔳 separate.

massacre *n* slaughter, murder, extermination, carnage, butchery, holocaust, blood bath, annihilation, killing.
➤ *v* slaughter, butcher, murder, mow down, wipe out, exterminate, annihilate, kill, decimate.

massage *n* manipulation, kneading, rubbing, rub-down.
➤ *v* manipulate, knead, rub (down).

massive *adj* huge, immense, enormous, vast, colossal, gigantic, big, bulky, monumental, solid, substantial, heavy, large-scale, extensive.
🔳 tiny, small.

master *n* **1** RULER, chief, governor, head, lord, captain, boss (*infml*), employer, commander, controller, director, manager, superintendent, overseer, principal, overlord, owner. **2** EXPERT, genius, virtuoso, past master, maestro, dab hand (*infml*), ace (*infml*), pro (*infml*). **3** TEACHER, tutor, instructor, schoolmaster, guide, guru, preceptor (*fml*).
🔳 **1** servant, underling. **2** amateur. **3** learner, pupil.
➤ *adj* **1** CHIEF, principal, main, leading, foremost, prime, predominant, controlling, great, grand. **2** EXPERT, masterly, skilled, skilful, proficient.
🔳 **1** subordinate. **2** inept.
➤ *v* **1** CONQUER, defeat, subdue, subjugate, vanquish, triumph over, overcome, quell, rule, control. **2** LEARN, grasp, acquire, get the hang of (*infml*), manage.

masterful *adj* **1** ARROGANT, authoritative, domineering, overbearing, high-handed, despotic, dictatorial, autocratic, bossy (*infml*), tyrannical, powerful. **2** EXPERT, masterly, skilful, skilled, dexterous, first-rate, professional.
🔳 **1** humble. **2** inept, unskilful.

masterly *adj* expert, skilled, skilful, dexterous, adept, adroit, first-rate, ace (*infml*), excellent, superb, superior, supreme.
🔳 inept, clumsy.

mastermind *v* devise, think up, contrive, engineer, direct, organize, manage, originate, plan, conceive, design, dream up, frame, hatch, forge, inspire, be behind.
➤ *n* organizer, initiator, manager, planner, creator, director, originator, authority, genius, intellect, engineer, architect, prime mover, virtuoso, brains (*infml*).

masterpiece *n* master-work, magnum opus, pièce de résistance, chef d'oeuvre, jewel.

mastery *n* **1** PROFICIENCY, skill, ability, command, expertise, virtuosity, knowledge, know-how, dexterity, familiarity, grasp. **2** CONTROL, command, domination, supremacy, upper hand, dominion, authority.
🔳 **1** incompetence. **2** subjugation.

match *n* **1** CONTEST, competition, bout, game, test, trial. **2** EQUAL, equivalent, peer, counterpart, fellow, mate, rival, copy, double, replica, look-alike, twin, duplicate. **3** MARRIAGE, alliance, union, partnership, affiliation.
➤ *v* **1** EQUAL, compare, measure up to, rival, compete, oppose, contend, vie, pit against. **2** FIT, go with, accord, agree, suit, correspond, harmonize, tally, co-ordinate, blend, adapt, go together, relate, tone with, accompany. **3** JOIN, marry, unite, mate, link, couple, combine, ally, pair, yoke, team.
🔳 **2** clash. **3** separate.

matching *adj* corresponding, comparable, equivalent, like, identical, co-ordinating, similar, duplicate, same, twin.
🔳 clashing.

matchless *adj* unequalled, peerless, incomparable, unmatched, unparalleled, unsurpassed, unrivalled, inimitable, unique.

mate *n* **1** FRIEND, companion, comrade, pal (*infml*), colleague, partner, fellow-worker, co-worker, associate. **2** SPOUSE, husband, wife. **3** ASSISTANT, helper, subordinate. **4** MATCH, fellow, twin.
➤ *v* **1** COUPLE, pair, breed, copulate. **2** JOIN, match, marry, wed.

material *n* **1** STUFF, substance, body, matter. **2** FABRIC, textile, cloth. **3** INFORMATION, facts, data, evidence, constituents, work, notes.
➤ *adj* **1** PHYSICAL, concrete, tangible, substantial. **2** RELEVANT, significant, important, meaningful, pertinent,

essential, vital, indispensable, serious.
Ea 1 abstract. **2** irrelevant.

materialize v appear, arise, take shape, turn up, happen, occur.
Ea disappear.

maternal adj motherly, motherlike, nurturing, nourishing, loving, caring, kind, protective, vigilant, doting.
Ea paternal.

mathematics

> Mathematical terms include: acute angle, addition, algebra, algorithm, analysis, angle, apex, approximate, arc, area, argument, arithmetic, arithmetic progression, asymmetrical, average, axis, axis of symmetry, bar chart, bar graph, base, bearing, binary, binomial, breadth, calculus, capacity, cardinal number, Cartesian co-ordinates, chance, chord, circumference, coefficient, combination, commutative operation, complement, complementary angle, complex number, concave, concentric circles, congruent, conjugate angles, constant, continuous distribution, converse, convex, co-ordinate, correlation, cosine, covariance, cross section, cube, cube root, curve, decimal, degree, denominator, depth, derivative, determinant, diagonal, diameter, differentiation, directed number, distribution, dividend, division, divisor, edge, equal, equation, equidistant, even number, exponent, exponential, face, factor, factorial, Fibonacci sequence, formula, fraction, function, geometric progression, geometry, gradient, graph, greater than, group, harmonic progression, height, helix, histogram, horizontal, hyperbola, hypotenuse, identity, infinity, integer, integration, irrational number, latitude, length, less than, linear, line, locus, logarithm, longitude, magic square, matrix, maximum, mean, measure, median, minimum, minus, mirror image, mirror symmetry, Möbius strip, mode, modulus, multiple, multiplication, natural logarithm, natural number, negative number, number, numerator, oblique, obtuse angle, odd number, operation, ordinal number, origin, parabola, parallel lines, parallel planes, parameter, percentage, percentile, perimeter, permutation, perpendicular, pi, pie chart, place value, plane figure, plus, point, positive number, prime number, probability, product, proportion, protractor, Pythagoras's theorem, quadrant, quadratic equation, quadrilateral, quartile, quotient, radian, radius, random sample, ratio, rational number, real numbers, reciprocal, recurring decimal, reflection, reflex angle, regression, remainder, right-angle, right-angled triangle, root, rotation, rotational symmetry, sample, scalar segment, secant, sector, set, side, simultaneous equation, sine, speed, spiral, square, square root, standard deviation, straight line, subset, subtractor, supplementary angles, symmetry, tangent, three-dimensional, total, transcendental number, triangulation, trigonometry, unit, universal set, variable, variance, vector, velocity, Venn diagram, vertex, vertical, volume, whole number, width, zero. *see also* **shape**.

matrimonial adj marital, nuptial, marriage, wedding, married, wedded, conjugal.

matter n **1** SUBJECT, issue, topic, question, affair, business, concern, event, episode, incident. **2** IMPORTANCE, significance, consequence, note. **3** TROUBLE, problem, difficulty, worry. **4** SUBSTANCE, stuff, material, body, content.
> v count, be important, make a difference, mean something.

matter-of-fact adj unemotional, prosaic, emotionless, straightforward, sober, unimaginative, flat, deadpan (*infml*).
Ea emotional.

mature adj **1** ADULT, grown-up, grown, full-grown, fully fledged, complete, perfect, perfected, well-thought-out. **2** RIPE, ripened, seasoned, mellow, ready.
Ea 1 childish. **2** immature.
> v grow up, come of age, develop, mellow, ripen, perfect, age, bloom, fall due.

maturity n **1** ADULTHOOD, majority, womanhood, manhood, wisdom, experience. **2** RIPENESS, readiness, mellowness, perfection.
Ea 1 childishness. **2** immaturity.

maudlin adj sentimental, mawkish, emotional, tearful, half-drunk, drunk, fuddled, tipsy, lachrymose (*fml*), gushy (*infml*), schmaltzy (*infml*), mushy (*infml*), sickly (*infml*), slushy (*infml*), soppy (*infml*), weepy (*infml*).
Ea pleasant.

maul v abuse, ill-treat, manhandle, maltreat, molest, paw, beat (up), knock about, rough up, claw, lacerate, batter.

maverick n outsider, rebel, agitator,

nonconformist, individualist, fish out of water (*infml*).

mawkish *adj* sentimental, maudlin, emotional, offensive, nauseous, nauseating, feeble, flat, disgusting, foul, loathsome, soppy (*infml*), gushy (*infml*), schmaltzy (*infml*), mushy (*infml*), sickly (*infml*), slushy (*infml*).
ɛ matter-of-fact, pleasant.

maxim *n* saying, proverb, adage, axiom, aphorism, epigram, motto, byword, precept, rule.

maximum *adj* greatest, highest, largest, biggest, most, utmost, supreme.
ɛ minimum.
➤ *n* most, top (point), utmost, upper limit, peak, pinnacle, summit, height, ceiling, extremity, zenith (*fml*).
ɛ mimimum.

maybe *adv* perhaps, possibly, perchance (*fml*).
ɛ definitely.

mayhem *n* chaos, disorder, confusion, disorganization, tumult, disruption, uproar, riot, bedlam, madhouse, mess, anarchy, lawlessness.

maze *n* labyrinth, network, tangle, web, complex, confusion, puzzle, intricacy.

meadow *n* field, grassland, pasture, lea.

meagre *adj* 1 SCANTY, sparse, inadequate, deficient, skimpy, paltry, negligible, poor. 2 THIN, puny, insubstantial, bony, emaciated, scrawny, slight.
ɛ 1 ample. 2 fat.

meal

Meals include: breakfast, wedding breakfast, elevenses (*infml*), brunch, lunch, luncheon, tea, tea-break, tea-party, tiffin, afternoon tea, cream-tea, high-tea, evening meal, dinner, TV dinner, supper, harvest supper, fork supper, banquet, feast, blow-out (*sl*), barbecue, buffet, spread, picnic, snack, take-away.

---

mean¹ *adj* 1 MISERLY, niggardly, parsimonious (*fml*), selfish, tight (*infml*), tight-fisted (*infml*), stingy (*infml*), penny-pinching (*infml*). 2 UNKIND, unpleasant, nasty, bad-tempered, cruel. 3 LOWLY, base, poor, humble, wretched.
ɛ 1 generous. 2 kind. 3 splendid.

mean² *v* 1 SIGNIFY, represent, denote, stand for, symbolize, suggest, indicate, imply. 2 INTEND, aim, propose, design.

3 CAUSE, give rise to, involve, entail.

mean³ *adj* average, intermediate, middle, halfway, median, normal.
ɛ extreme.
➤ *n* average, middle, mid-point, norm, median, compromise, middle course, middle way, happy medium, golden mean.
ɛ extreme.

meander *v* 1 WIND, zigzag, turn, twist, snake, curve. 2 WANDER, stray, amble, ramble, stroll.

meaning *n* 1 SIGNIFICANCE, sense, import, implication, gist, trend, explanation, interpretation. 2 AIM, intention, purpose, object, idea. 3 VALUE, worth, point.

meaningful *adj* 1 IMPORTANT, significant, relevant, valid, useful, worthwhile, material, purposeful, serious. 2 EXPRESSIVE, speaking, suggestive, warning, pointed.
ɛ 1 unimportant, worthless.

meaningless *adj* 1 SENSELESS, pointless, purposeless, useless, insignificant, aimless, futile, insubstantial, trifling, trivial. 2 EMPTY, hollow, vacuous, vain, worthless, nonsensical, absurd.
ɛ 1 important, meaningful. 2 worthwhile.

meanness *n* mean-spiritedness, miserliness, narrow-mindedness, niggardliness, tight-fistedness (*infml*), close-fistedness, close-handedness, illiberality, parsimony (*fml*), penuriousness (*fml*), stinginess (*infml*).
ɛ generosity, kindness.

means *n* 1 METHOD, mode, way, medium, course, agency, process, instrument, channel, vehicle. 2 RESOURCES, funds, money, income, wealth, riches, substance, wherewithal, fortune, affluence.

meantime, meanwhile *adv* at the same time, for the time being, for now, for the moment, in the meantime, in the meanwhile, in the interim, in the interval, concurrently, simultaneously.

measly *adj* mean, miserable, paltry, meagre, pitiful, scanty, skimpy, petty, poor, puny, trivial, ungenerous, miserly, niggardly, beggarly, contemptible, stingy (*infml*), piddling (*infml*), pathetic (*infml*), mingy (*infml*).
ɛ generous.

measurable *adj* perceptible, significant, quantifiable, noticeable, appreciable, determinable, assessable, computable, gaugeable, fathomable, material,

quantitative, mensurable (*fml*).
🔁 measureless.

measure *n* 1 PORTION, ration, share,
allocation, quota. 2 SIZE, quantity,
magnitude, amount, degree, extent, range,
scope, proportion. 3 RULE, gauge, scale,
standard, criterion, norm, touchstone,
yardstick, test, meter. 4 STEP, course,
action, deed, procedure, method, act, bill,
statute.
➤ *v* quantify, evaluate, assess, weigh,
value, gauge, judge, sound, fathom,
determine, calculate, estimate, plumb,
survey, compute, measure out, measure off.
♦ **measure out** share out, divide,
distribute, proportion, dispense, deal out,
dole out, allot, apportion, hand out, mete
out, parcel out, pour out, issue, assign.
♦ **measure up to** equal, meet, match,
compare with, touch, rival, make the grade.

measured *adj* deliberate, planned,
reasoned, slow, unhurried, steady, studied,
well-thought-out, calculated, careful,
considered, precise.

measurement *n* 1 DIMENSION, size,
extent, amount, magnitude, area, capacity,
height, depth, length, width, weight,
volume. 2 ASSESSMENT, evaluation,
estimation, computation, calculation,
calibration, gauging, judgement,
appraisal, appreciation, survey.

SI (Système International d'Unités) base
units include: ampere, candela, kelvin,
kilogram, metre, mole, second.

SI derivatives and other measurements
include: acre, angstrom, atmosphere, bar,
barrel, becquerel, bushel, cable, calorie,
centimetre, century, chain, coulomb, cubic
centimetre, cubic foot, cubic inch, cubic
metre, cubic yard, day, decade, decibel,
degree, dyne, erg, farad, fathom, fluid ounce,
fresnel, foot, foot-pound, furlong, gallon, gill,
gram, hand, hectare, hertz, horsepower,
hour, hundredweight, inch, joule, kilometre,
knot, league, litre, lumen, micrometre, mile,
millennium, millibar, millilitre, minute, month,
nautical mile, newton, ohm, ounce, pascal,
peak, pint, pound, pound per square inch,
radian, rod, siemens, span, square
centimetre, square foot, square inch, square
kilometre, square metre, square mile, square
yard, steradian, stone, therm, ton, tonne, volt,
watt, week, yard, year.

meat *n* 1 FLESH. 2 (*infml*) FOOD, rations,
provisions, nourishment, sustenance,
subsistence, eats (*infml*).

Kinds of meat include: beef, pork, lamb,
mutton, ham, bacon, gammon, chicken,
turkey, goose, duck, rabbit, hare, venison,
pheasant, grouse, partridge, pigeon, quail;
offal, liver, heart, tongue, kidney, brains,
brawn, pig's knuckle, trotters, oxtail,
sweetbread, tripe; steak, minced beef,
sausage, rissole, faggot, beefburger,
hamburger, black pudding, pâté.

Cuts of meat include: shoulder, collar,
hand, loin, hock, leg, chop, shin, knuckle, rib,
spare-rib, breast, brisket, chine, cutlet, fillet,
rump, scrag, silverside, topside, sirloin, flank,
escalope, neck, saddle.

meaty *adj* 1 FLESHY, hearty, solid, heavy,
brawny, beefy, burly, muscular, strapping,
sturdy, hunky (*infml*). 2 SUBSTANTIAL,
interesting, significant, meaningful,
profound, rich, pithy.

mechanical *adj* automatic, involuntary,
instinctive, routine, habitual, impersonal,
emotionless, cold, matter-of-fact,
unfeeling, lifeless, dead, dull.
🔁 conscious.

mechanism *n* 1 MACHINE, machinery,
engine, appliance, instrument, tool, motor,
works, workings, gadget, device,
apparatus, contrivance, gears,
components. 2 MEANS, method, agency,
process, procedure, system, technique,
medium, structure, operation, functioning,
performance.

meddle *v* interfere, intervene, pry, snoop
(*infml*), intrude, butt in, tamper.

meddlesome *adj* interfering,
meddling, prying, intrusive, intruding,
mischievous.

mediate *v* arbitrate, conciliate, intervene,
referee, umpire, intercede, moderate,
reconcile, negotiate, resolve, settle, step
in.

mediation *n* arbitration, reconciliation,
negotiation, conciliation, intercession,
peacemaking, good offices, intervention,
interposition (*fml*).

mediator *n* arbitrator, referee, umpire,
intermediary, negotiator, go-between,
interceder, judge, moderator, intercessor,
conciliator, peacemaker, Ombudsman.

medical

Medical and surgical equipment
includes: aspirator, audiometer, aural
speculum, auriscope, autoclave, body
scanner, bronchoscope, cannula, catheter,
CAT scanner, clamp, CT (computed
tomography) scanner, curette, defibrillator,
disposable enema pack, ear syringe, ECG
(electrocardiograph),
electroencephalograph, endoscope, first aid
kit, forceps, haemodialysis unit, hypodermic
needle, hypodermic syringe, incubator,
inhaler, instrument table, iron lung, isolator
tent, kidney dish, laparoscope,
laryngoscope, microscope, MRI (magnetic
resonance imaging) scanner, nebulizer,
obstetrical forceps, oesophagoscope,
operating table, ophthalmoscope, oxygen
cylinder, oxygen mask, rectoscope,
respirator, resuscitator, retractor, rhinoscope,
scales, scalpel, sliding-weight scales,
specimen glass, speculum,
sphygmomanometer, sterile donor-pack,
sterilizer, stethoscope, stomach pump,
surgical mask, surgical suture materials,
swabs, syringe, thermometer, tracheostomy
tube, traction apparatus, tweezers,
ultrasound, urethroscope, vaginal speculum,
X-ray unit.

Medical specialists include:
anaesthetist, bacteriologist, cardiologist,
chiropodist, chiropractor, dentist,
dermatologist, dietician, doctor,
embryologist, endocrinologist, forensic
pathologist, gastroenterologist, geriatrician,
gerontologist, gynaecologist, haematologist,
homeopath, immunologist, microbiologist,
neurologist, obstetrician, oncologist,
ophthalmologist, optician (or optometrist),
orthodontist, orthopaedist, orthoptist,
paediatrician, pathologist, pharmacist,
pharmacologist, physiotherapist,
psychiatrist, psychologist, rheumatologist,
toxicologist. *see also* **doctor; nurse**.

Medical terms include: abortion, allergy,
amputation, analgesic, antibiotics, antiseptic,
bandage, barium meal, biopsy, blood bank,
blood count, blood donor, blood group,
blood pressure, blood test, caesarean,
cardiopulmonary resuscitation (CPR), case
history, casualty, cauterization, cervical
smear, check-up, childbirth, circulation,
circumcision, clinic, complication, compress,

consultant, consultation, contraception,
convulsion, cure, diagnosis, dialysis,
dislocate, dissection, doctor, donor,
dressings, enema, examination, gene, health
screening, home visit, hormone replacement
therapy (HRT), hospice, hospital,
immunization, implantation, incubation,
infection, inflammation, injection, injury,
inoculation, intensive care, labour,
miscarriage, mouth-to-mouth, nurse,
ointment, operation, paraplegia, post-
mortem, pregnancy, prescription, prognosis,
prosthesis, psychosomatic, quarantine,
radiotherapy, recovery, rehabilitation, relapse,
remission, respiration, resuscitation, scan,
side effect, sling, smear test, specimen,
splint, sterilization, steroid, surgery, suture,
symptom, syndrome, therapy, tourniquet,
tranquillizer, transfusion, transplant, trauma,
treatment, tumour, ultrasound scanning,
vaccination, vaccine, virus, X-ray. *see also*
therapy.

medicinal *adj* therapeutic, healing,
remedial, curative, restorative, medical.

medicine *n* medication, drug, cure,
remedy, medicament, prescription,
pharmaceutical, panacea.

Types of medicine include: tablet,
capsule, pill, painkiller, lozenge, pastille,
gargle, linctus, tonic, laxative, suppository,
antacid, ointment, arnica, eye drops, ear
drops, nasal spray, inhaler, Ventolin, antibiotic,
penicillin, emetic, gripe-water, paregoric. *see
also* **drug**.

Forms of alternative medicine include:
acupuncture, aromatherapy, chiropractic,
herbal remedies, homeopathy, naturopathy,
osteopathy, reflexology.

medieval *adj* **1** *medieval history*: of the
Middle Ages, of the Dark Ages, historic, old,
archaic. **2** OLD-FASHIONED, obsolete,
primitive, antiquated, archaic, antique,
antediluvian, old-world, outmoded,
unenlightened.

mediocre *adj* ordinary, average, middling,
medium, indifferent, unexceptional,
undistinguished, so-so (*infml*), run-of-the-
mill, commonplace, insignificant, second-
rate, inferior, uninspired.
🔁 exceptional, extraordinary, distinctive.

mediocrity *n* **1** ORDINARINESS,
unimportance, insignificance, poorness,

inferiority, indifference. **2** NONENTITY, nobody.

meditate *v* **1** REFLECT, ponder, ruminate (*fml*), contemplate, muse, brood, think. **2** THINK OVER, consider, deliberate, mull over, study, speculate, scheme, plan, devise, intend.

meditation *n* contemplation, reflection, pondering, musing, thought, ruminating (*infml*), rumination (*infml*), deliberation, brooding, mulling over, speculation, study, reverie, concentration, brown study, cerebration (*fml*), cogitation (*fml*).

medium *adj* average, middle, median, mean, medial, intermediate, middling, midway, standard, fair.
➤ *n* **1** AVERAGE, middle, mid-point, middle ground, compromise, centre, happy medium, golden mean. **2** MEANS, agency, channel, vehicle, instrument, way, mode, form, avenue, organ. **3** PSYCHIC, spiritualist, spiritist, clairvoyant.

medley *n* assortment, mixture, miscellany, pot-pourri, hotchpotch, hodge-podge, collection, jumble.

meek *adj* modest, long-suffering, forbearing, humble, docile, patient, unassuming, unpretentious, resigned, gentle, peaceful, tame, timid, submissive, spiritless.
✲ arrogant, assertive, rebellious.

meet *v* **1** ENCOUNTER, come across, run across, run into, chance on (*fml*), bump into (*infml*). **2** EXPERIENCE, encounter, face, go through, undergo, endure. **3** GATHER, collect, assemble, congregate, convene (*fml*). **4** FULFIL, satisfy, match, answer, measure up to, equal, discharge, perform. **5** JOIN, converge, come together, connect, cross, intersect, touch, abut, unite.
✲ **3** scatter. **5** diverge.

meeting *n* **1** ENCOUNTER, confrontation, rendezvous, engagement, assignation, introduction, tryst (*fml*). **2** ASSEMBLY, gathering, congregation, conference, convention, rally, get-together, forum, conclave, session. **3** CONVERGENCE, confluence, junction, intersection, union.

melancholy *adj* depressed, dejected, downcast, down, down-hearted, gloomy, low, low-spirited, heavy-hearted, sad, unhappy, despondent, dispirited, miserable, mournful, dismal, sorrowful, moody.

✲ cheerful, elated, joyful.
➤ *n* depression, dejection, gloom, despondency, low spirits, blues (*infml*), sadness, unhappiness, sorrow.
✲ elation, joy.

melee *n* **1** BRAWL, rumpus, scuffle, set-to, fight, tussle, ruckus, ruction, broil, affray, fracas, fray, free-for-all, scrum, stramash (*Scot*). **2** MUDDLE, confusion, chaos, disorganization, disorder, mess, mix-up, jumble, clutter, tangle.

mellow *adj* **1** MATURE, ripe, juicy, full-flavoured, sweet, tender, mild. **2** GENIAL, cordial, affable, pleasant, relaxed, placid, serene, tranquil, cheerful, happy, jolly. **3** SMOOTH, melodious, rich, rounded, soft.
✲ **1** unripe. **2** cold. **3** harsh.
➤ *v* mature, ripen, improve, sweeten, soften, temper, season, perfect.

melodious *adj* tuneful, musical, melodic, harmonious, dulcet, sweet-sounding, euphonious (*fml*), silvery.
✲ discordant, grating, harsh.

melodramatic *adj* histrionic, theatrical, overdramatic, exaggerated, overemotional, sensational, hammy (*infml*).

melody *n* tune, music, song, refrain, harmony, theme, air, strain.

melt *v* liquefy, dissolve, thaw, fuse, deliquesce (*fml*).
✲ freeze, solidify.
◆ **melt away** disappear, vanish, fade, evaporate, dissolve, disperse.

member *n* **1** *members of a club*: adherent, associate, subscriber, representative, comrade, fellow. **2** PART, limb, arm, leg, appendage, extremity, organ, element.

membership *n* **1** *membership of a club*: affiliation, adherence, allegiance, participation, enrolment, fellowship. **2** MEMBERS, associates, body, adherents, subscribers, representatives, comrades, fellows, fellowship.

memento *n* souvenir, keepsake, remembrance, reminder, token, memorial, record, relic.

memoirs *n* reminiscences, recollections, autobiography, life story, diary, chronicles, annals, journals, records, confessions, experiences.

memorable *adj* unforgettable, remarkable, significant, impressive, notable, noteworthy, extraordinary, important, outstanding, momentous.

◩ forgettable, trivial, unimportant.

memorandum *n* message, note, reminder, memo (*infml*), memory-jogger (*infml*).

memorial *n* remembrance, monument, souvenir, memento, record, stone, plaque, mausoleum.
➤ *adj* commemorative, celebratory.

memorize *v* learn, learn by heart, commit to memory, remember.
◩ forget.

memory *n* recall, retention, recollection, remembrance, reminiscence, commemoration.
◩ forgetfulness.

menace *v* threaten, frighten, alarm, intimidate, terrorize, loom.
➤ *n* **1** INTIMIDATION, threat, terrorism, warning. **2** DANGER, peril, hazard, jeopardy, risk. **3** NUISANCE, annoyance, pest.

menacing *adj* threatening, intimidating, intimidatory, warning, ominous, alarming, frightening, dangerous, looming, sinister, grim, louring, Damoclean, impending (*fml*), portentous (*fml*), minacious (*fml*), minatory (*fml*).

mend *v* **1** REPAIR, renovate, restore, refit, fix, patch, cobble, darn, heal. **2** RECOVER, get better, improve. **3** REMEDY, correct, rectify, reform, revise.
◩ **1** break. **2** deteriorate. **3** destroy.

menial *adj* low, lowly, humble, base, dull, humdrum, routine, degrading, demeaning, ignominious, unskilled, subservient, servile, slavish.
➤ *n* servant, domestic, labourer, minion, attendant, drudge, slave, underling, skivvy (*infml*), dog's-body (*infml*).

menstruation *n* period, menstrual cycle, monthly flow, courses, flow, menses, menorrhoea, monthlies (*infml*), the usual (*infml*), the curse (*infml*).

mental *adj* **1** INTELLECTUAL, abstract, conceptual, cognitive, cerebral, theoretical, rational. **2** (*infml*) MAD, insane, lunatic, crazy (*infml*), unbalanced, deranged, psychotic, disturbed, loony (*infml*).
◩ **1** physical. **2** sane.

mentality *n* **1** INTELLECT, brains, understanding, faculty, rationality. **2** FRAME OF MIND, character, disposition, personality, psychology, outlook.

mentally *adv* intellectually, in the mind, inwardly, psychologically, rationally, temperamentally, subjectively, emotionally.

mention *v* refer to, speak of, allude to, touch on, name, cite, acknowledge, bring up, report, make known, impart, declare, communicate, broach, divulge, disclose, intimate, point out, reveal, state, hint at, quote.
➤ *n* reference, allusion, citation, observation, recognition, remark, acknowledgement, announcement, notification, tribute, indication.

mentor *n* teacher, tutor, adviser, counsellor, guru, swami, guide, coach, instructor, pedagogue, therapist.

menu *n* bill of fare, tariff, list, card, carte du jour.

mercenary *adj* **1** GREEDY, avaricious, covetous, grasping, acquisitive, materialistic. **2** HIRED, paid, venal.

merchandise *n* goods, commodities, stock, produce, products, wares, cargo, freight, shipment.

merchant *n* trader, dealer, broker, trafficker, wholesaler, retailer, seller, shopkeeper, vendor.

merciful *adj* compassionate, forgiving, forbearing, humane, lenient, sparing, tender-hearted, pitying, gracious, humanitarian, kind, liberal, sympathetic, generous, mild.
◩ hard-hearted, merciless.

merciless *adj* pitiless, relentless, unmerciful, ruthless, hard-hearted, hard, heartless, implacable, inhumane, unforgiving, remorseless, unpitying, unsparing, severe, cruel, callous, inhuman.
◩ compassionate, merciful.

mercurial *adj* volatile, temperamental, unpredictable, unstable, variable, changeable, inconstant, erratic, fickle, impetuous, impulsive, irrepressible, flighty, light-hearted, lively, spirited, sprightly, active, mobile, capricious (*fml*).
◩ saturnine.

mercy *n* **1** COMPASSION, clemency, forgiveness, forbearance, leniency, pity, humanitarianism, kindness, grace. **2** BLESSING, godsend, good luck, relief.
◩ **1** cruelty, harshness.

mere *adj* sheer, plain, simple, bare, utter, pure, absolute, complete, stark, unadulterated, common, paltry, petty.

merge *v* join, unite, combine, converge, amalgamate, blend, coalesce, mix, intermix, mingle, melt into, fuse, meet, meld, incorporate, consolidate.

merger *n* amalgamation, union, fusion, combination, coalition, consolidation, confederation, incorporation.

merit *n* worth, excellence, value, quality, good, goodness, virtue, asset, credit, advantage, strong point, talent, justification, due, claim.
  ea fault.
  ➤ *v* deserve, be worthy of, earn, justify, warrant.

merriment *n* fun, jollity, mirth, hilarity, laughter, conviviality, festivity, amusement, revelry, frolic, liveliness, joviality.
  ea gloom, seriousness.

merry *adj* jolly, light-hearted, mirthful, joyful, happy, convivial, festive, cheerful, glad.
  ea gloomy, melancholy, sober.

mesh *n* net, network, netting, lattice, web, tangle, entanglement, snare, trap.
  ➤ *v* engage, interlock, dovetail, fit, connect, harmonize, co-ordinate, combine, come together.

mesmerize *v* transfix, hypnotize, magnetize, spellbind, hold spellbound, captivate, enthral, fascinate, grip, entrance, stupefy, benumb.

mess *n* 1 CHAOS, untidiness, disorder, disarray, confusion, muddle, jumble, clutter, disorganization, mix-up, shambles (*infml*). 2 DIFFICULTY, trouble, predicament, fix (*infml*).
  ea 1 order, tidiness.
  ◆ **mess about** mess around, fool around, play, play around, play about, muck about (*infml*), interfere, tamper, trifle.
  ◆ **mess up** 1 DISARRANGE, jumble, muddle, tangle, dishevel, disrupt. 2 BOTCH, bungle, spoil, muck up (*infml*).

message *n* 1 COMMUNICATION, bulletin, dispatch, communiqué, report, missive (*fml*), errand, letter, memorandum, note, notice, cable. 2 MEANING, idea, point, theme, moral.

messenger *n* courier, emissary (*fml*), envoy, go-between, herald, runner, carrier, bearer, harbinger, agent, ambassador.

messy *adj* untidy, unkempt, dishevelled, disorganized, chaotic, sloppy, slovenly,

confused, dirty, grubby, muddled, cluttered.
  ea neat, ordered, tidy.

metamorphosis *n* change, alteration, transformation, rebirth, regeneration, transfiguration, conversion, modification, change-over.

metaphor *n* figure of speech, allegory, analogy, symbol, picture, image.

metaphorical *adj* figurative, allegorical, symbolic.

metaphysical *adj* philosophical, theoretical, abstract, unreal, essential, fundamental, basic, subjective, spiritual, supernatural, transcendental, unsubstantial, insubstantial, general, immaterial, speculative, intellectual, ideal, high-flown, intangible, deep, profound, universal, eternal, abstruse (*fml*), esoteric (*fml*), impalpable (*fml*), incorporeal (*fml*), recondite (*fml*).

meteoric *adj* rapid, speedy, swift, sudden, overnight, instantaneous, momentary, brief, spectacular, brilliant, dazzling.

mete out *v* allot, apportion, deal out, dole out, hand out, measure out, share out, ration out, portion, distribute, dispense, divide out, assign, administer.

method *n* 1 WAY, approach, means, course, manner, mode, fashion, process, procedure, route, technique, style, plan, scheme, programme. 2 ORGANIZATION, order, structure, system, pattern, form, planning, regularity, routine.

methodical *adj* systematic, structured, organized, ordered, orderly, tidy, regular, planned, efficient, disciplined, businesslike, deliberate, neat, scrupulous, precise, meticulous, painstaking.
  ea chaotic, irregular, confused.

meticulous *adj* precise, scrupulous, exact, punctilious, fussy, detailed, accurate, thorough, fastidious, painstaking, strict.
  ea careless, slapdash.

métier *n* calling, vocation, line, line of business, business, occupation, profession, sphere, field, forte, trade, pursuit, speciality, specialty, craft.

metropolis *n* capital, city, municipality, megalopolis.

mettle *n* 1 CHARACTER, temperament, disposition. 2 SPIRIT, courage, vigour, nerve (*infml*), boldness, daring, indomitability, pluck, resolve, valour, bravery, fortitude.

microbe *n* micro-organism, bacterium, bacillus, germ, virus, pathogen, bug (*infml*).

microscopic *adj* minute, tiny, minuscule, infinitesimal, indiscernible, imperceptible, negligible.
₤₳ huge, enormous.

middle *adj* central, halfway, mean, median, intermediate, inner, inside, intervening.
➤ *n* centre, halfway point, mid-point, mean, heart, core, midst, inside, bull's eye.
₤₳ extreme, end, edge, beginning, border.

middle-class *adj* conventional, suburban, professional, white-collar, gentrified, bourgeois.

middleman *n* intermediary, go-between, negotiator, entrepreneur, distributor, retailer, broker, fixer.

middling *adj* mediocre, medium, ordinary, moderate, average, fair, unexceptional, unremarkable, run-of-the-mill, indifferent, modest, adequate, passable, tolerable, so-so, OK.

middling *adj* mediocre, medium, ordinary, moderate, average, unexceptional, unremarkable, run-of-the-mill, indifferent, modest, passable, tolerable, so-so (*infml*), OK (*infml*).

midget *n* person of restricted growth, pygmy, dwarf, Tom Thumb, gnome.
₤₳ giant.
➤ *adj* tiny, small, miniature, little, pocket, pocket-sized.
₤₳ giant.

midst *n* middle, centre, mid-point, heart, hub, interior.

midway *adv* halfway, in the middle, at the mid-point, in the centre, equidistant between, betwixt and between.

might *n* power, strength, force, forcefulness, energy, powerfulness, ability, capability, capacity, sway, vigour, stamina, heftiness, muscularity, potency, valour, prowess, efficacy (*fml*), puissance (*fml*), clout (*infml*), muscle (*infml*).

mighty *adj* **1** STRONG, powerful, potent, forceful, vigorous, hefty, robust, tough, stalwart, stout, strapping, muscular, dominant, influential, doughty, grand, hardy, indomitable, lusty, manful. **2** LARGE,

enormous, colossal, huge, immense, vast, massive, gigantic, great, tremendous, towering, titanic, stupendous, monumental, bulky, prodigious.
₤₳ **1** frail, weak. **2** small.

migrant *n* traveller, wanderer, itinerant, emigrant, immigrant, rover, nomad, globe-trotter, drifter, gypsy, tinker, vagrant.

migrate *v* move, resettle, relocate, wander, roam, rove, journey, emigrate, travel, voyage, trek, drift.

migratory *adj* travelling, wandering, peripatetic (*fml*), itinerant, immigrant, roving, nomadic, shifting, transient, globe-trotting, drifting, gypsy, migrant, vagrant.

mild *adj* **1** *mild manners*: gentle, calm, peaceable, placid, tender, soft, good-natured, kind, amiable, lenient, compassionate. **2** *mild weather*: calm, temperate, warm, balmy, clement, fair, pleasant. **3** *mild coffee*: bland, mellow, smooth, subtle, soothing.
₤₳ **1** harsh, fierce. **2** stormy. **3** strong.

milieu *n* environment, location, scene, setting, surroundings, background, locale, medium, arena, element, sphere.

militant *adj* aggressive, belligerent, vigorous, fighting, warring.
₤₳ pacifist, peaceful.
➤ *n* activist, combatant, fighter, struggler, warrior, aggressor, belligerent.

military *adj* martial, armed, soldierly, warlike, service.
➤ *n* army, armed forces, soldiers, forces, services.

Military terms include: about turn, absent without leave (AWOL), action, action stations, adjutant, aide-de-camp (ADC), air cover, air-drop, Airborne Warning and Control System (AWACS), allies, ambush, arm, armed forces, armistice, army, arsenal, artillery, assault course, atomic warfare, attack, attention, barracks, base, battle, battle fatigue, beachhead, billet, bivouac, blockade, bomb, bombardment, brevet, bridgehead, briefing, brigade, bugle call, call up, camouflage, camp, campaign, canteen, carpet-bombing, cease-fire, charge, citation, colours, combat, command, commission, company, conquest, conscript, conscription, corps, counter-attack, court-martial, crossfire, debriefing, decamp, decoration, defeat, defence, demilitarize, demob (*infml*), demotion, depot, desertion, detachment, detail, disarmament, discharge, dispatches, division, draft, drill, duty, encampment, enemy, enlist, ensign, epaulette, evacuation, excursion, expedition, fall out, fatigues, firing line, first post, flank, fleet, flight, flotilla, foe, foray, forced march, friendly fire, front line, fusillade, garrison, guard, incursion, infantry, insignia, inspection, installation, insubordination, intelligence, invasion, kitbag, landing, last post, latrine, leave, left wheel, liaison, lines, logistics, manoeuvres, march, marching orders, march past, married quarters, martinet, minefield, mission, mobilize, munitions, muster, mutiny, national service, navy, Navy, Army and Air Force Institutes (NAAFI), nuclear warfare, observation post, offensive, operational command, operational fleet, operations, orders, ordnance, outpost, padre, parade, parade ground, parley, parole, patrol, pincer movement, platoon, posting, prisoner of war (POW), quartermaster, quarters, quick march, radar, range, rank, ration, rearguard, recce (*infml*), recruit, regiment, reinforcements, requisition, retreat, reveille, rifle range, roll-call, rout, route march, salute, sentry, shell, shell-shock, signal, skirmish, slow march, sniper, sortie, squad, squadron, square-bashing (*sl*), standard, stores, strategy, supplies, surrender, tactics, tank, target, task-force, tattoo, the front, training, trench, trench warfare, troop, truce, unit, vanguard, victory, wing. *see also* **armed services**; **rank¹**; **sailor**; **soldier**.

militate against *v* oppose, counter, counteract, count against, tell against, weigh against, contend, resist.

militia *n* reserve, reservists, Territorial Army, yeomanry, National Guard, minutemen.

milk *v* drain, bleed, tap, extract, draw off, exploit, use, express, press, pump, siphon, squeeze, wring.

milky *adj* white, milk-white, chalky, opaque, clouded, cloudy.

mill *n* 1 FACTORY, plant, works, workshop, foundry. 2 GRINDER, crusher, quern, roller.
➤ *v* grind, pulverize, powder, pound, crush, roll, press, grate.

millstone *n* burden, load, encumbrance, weight, obligation, duty, onus, trouble, affliction, grindstone, quernstone, cross to bear (*infml*).

mime *n* dumb show, pantomime, gesture, mimicry.
➤ *v* gesture, signal, act out, represent, simulate, impersonate, mimic.

mimic *v* imitate, parody, caricature, take off (*infml*), ape, parrot, impersonate, echo, mirror, simulate, look like.
➤ *n* imitator, impersonator, impressionist, caricaturist, copy-cat (*infml*), copy.

mimicry *n* imitation, imitating, impersonation, copying, parody, impression, caricature, take-off (*infml*), burlesque.

mince *v* 1 CHOP, cut, hash, dice, grind, crumble. 2 DIMINISH, suppress, play down, tone down, hold back, moderate, weaken, soften, spare.

mind *n* 1 INTELLIGENCE, intellect, brains, reason, sense, understanding, wits, mentality, thinking, thoughts, grey matter (*infml*), head, genius, concentration, attention, spirit, psyche. 2 MEMORY, remembrance, recollection. 3 OPINION, view, point of view, belief, attitude, judgement, feeling, sentiment.
4 INCLINATION, disposition, tendency, will, wish, intention, desire.
➤ *v* 1 CARE, object, take offence, resent, disapprove, dislike. 2 REGARD, heed, pay attention, pay heed to, note, obey, listen to, comply with, follow, observe, be careful, watch. 3 LOOK AFTER, take care of, watch over, guard, have charge of, keep an eye on (*infml*).
♦ **bear in mind** consider, remember, note.
♦ **make up one's mind** decide, choose, determine, settle, resolve.
♦ **mind out** be careful, take care, look out, watch out, watch, pay attention, beware, be on one's guard, keep one's eyes open.

mindful *adj* aware, conscious, alive (to), alert, attentive, careful, watchful, wary.
🔁 heedless, inattentive.

mindless *adj* 1 THOUGHTLESS, senseless, illogical, irrational, stupid, foolish, gratuitous, negligent. 2 MECHANICAL, automatic, tedious.
🔁 1 thoughtful, intelligent.

mine *n* 1 PIT, colliery, coalfield, excavation, quarry, well, vein, lode, seam, shaft, trench, deposit. 2 SUPPLY, source, stock, store, storehouse, reserve, reservoir, quarry, fund, repository, hoard, treasury, wealth. 3 LAND MINE, explosive, depth charge, bomb.
➤ *v* excavate, dig for, dig up, delve, quarry, extract, unearth, tunnel, remove, undermine.

Parts of a coalmine include: air lock; bord-and-pillar, long-wall, long-wall face, retreat long-wall; bunker, cage, cage-winding system, capping, charging conveyor, coal seam, coal-bearing rock; coal-cutter, jib coal-cutter, plough coal-cutter, scraper chain, pan, shearer loader; fan drift, fault line, gallery, goaf/gob/waste, overburden; pit prop, hydraulic pit prop, powered support; pithead frame, pithead gear; shaft, main shaft, staple shaft, lateral; skip winding system, spoil, sump/sink, tunnelling machine, ventilation shaft, winding engine.

miner *n* coalminer, collier, pitman.

minerals

Minerals include: alabaster, albite, anhydrite, asbestos, aventurine, azurite, bentonite, blacklead, bloodstone, blue john, borax, cairngorm, calamine, calcite, calcspar, cassiterite, chalcedony, chlorite, chrysoberyl, cinnabar, corundum, dolomite, emery, feldspar, fluorite, fluorspar, fool's gold, French chalk, galena, graphite, gypsum, haematite, halite, haüyne, hornblende, hyacinth, idocrase, jacinth, jargoon, jet, kandite, kaolinite, lapis lazuli, lazurite, magnetite, malachite, meerschaum, mica, microcline, montmorillonite, orthoclase, plumbago, pyrites, quartz, rock salt, rutile, saltpetre, sanidine, silica, smithsonite, sodalite, spar, sphalerite, spinel, talc, uralite, uranite, vesuvianite, wurtzite, zircon.

mingle *v* **1** MIX, intermingle, intermix, combine, blend, merge, unite, alloy, coalesce, join, compound. **2** ASSOCIATE, socialize, circulate, hobnob (*infml*), rub shoulders (*infml*).

miniature *adj* tiny, small, scaled-down, minute, diminutive, baby, pocket-sized, pint-size(d) (*infml*), little, mini (*infml*).
▣ giant.

minimal *adj* least, smallest, minimum, slightest, littlest, negligible, minute, token.

minimize *v* **1** REDUCE, decrease, diminish. **2** BELITTLE, make light of, make little of, disparage (*fml*), deprecate, discount, play down, underestimate, underrate.
▣ **1** maximize.

minimum *n* least, lowest point, slightest, bottom.
▣ maximum.

➤ *adj* minimal, least, lowest, slightest, smallest, littlest, tiniest.
▣ maximum.

minion *n* **1** ATTENDANT, follower, underling, lackey, hireling. **2** DEPENDANT, hanger-on, favourite, darling, sycophant, yes-man (*infml*), bootlicker (*infml*).

minister *n* **1** OFFICIAL, office-holder, politician, dignitary, diplomat, ambassador, delegate, envoy, consul, cabinet minister, agent, aide, administrator, executive. **2** CLERGYMAN, churchman, cleric, parson, priest, pastor, vicar, preacher, ecclesiastic (*fml*), divine.
➤ *v* attend, serve, tend, take care of, wait on, cater to, accommodate, nurse.

ministry *n* **1** GOVERNMENT, cabinet, department, office, bureau, administration. **2** THE CHURCH, holy orders, the priesthood.

minor *adj* lesser, secondary, smaller, inferior, subordinate, subsidiary, junior, younger, insignificant, inconsiderable, negligible, petty, trivial, trifling, second-class, unclassified, slight, light.
▣ major, significant, important.

minstrel *n* singer, musician, troubadour, bard, rhymer, joculator, jongleur.

mint *v* **1** COIN, stamp, strike, cast, forge, punch, make, manufacture, produce, construct, devise, fashion. **2** INVENT, make up, coin, fabricate, forge, falsify, fake, trump up, concoct, hatch.
➤ *adj* perfect, brand-new, new, as new, fresh, immaculate, undamaged, unblemished, unused, excellent, first-class.
➤ *n* fortune, wealth, riches, pile (*infml*), packet (*infml*), bomb (*infml*), bundle (*infml*), heap (*infml*), stack (*infml*), million (*infml*).

minuscule *adj* tiny, fine, little, very small, minute, miniature, microscopic, infinitesimal, diminutive, Lilliputian, teeny (*infml*), teeny-weeny (*infml*), itsy-bitsy (*infml*).
▣ gigantic, huge.

minute[1] *n* moment, second, instant, flash, jiffy (*infml*), tick (*infml*).

minute[2] *adj* **1** TINY, infinitesimal, minuscule, microscopic, miniature, inconsiderable, negligible, small. **2** DETAILED, precise, meticulous, painstaking, close, critical, exhaustive.
▣ **1** gigantic, huge. **2** cursory, superficial.

minutes n proceedings, record(s), notes, memorandum, transcript, transactions, details, tapes.

minutiae n details, fine details, finer points, intricacies, complexities, particulars, niceties, subtleties, trifles, trivialities, small print (infml).

miracle n wonder, marvel, prodigy, phenomenon.

miraculous adj wonderful, marvellous, phenomenal, extraordinary, amazing, astounding, astonishing, unbelievable, supernatural, incredible, inexplicable, unaccountable, superhuman.
ᴇ natural, normal.

mirage n illusion, optical illusion, hallucination, fantasy, phantasm.

mirror n 1 GLASS, looking-glass, reflector. 2 REFLECTION, likeness, image, double, copy.
➤ v reflect, echo, imitate, copy, represent, show, depict, mimic.

mirth n merriment, hilarity, gaiety, fun, laughter, jollity, jocularity, amusement, revelry, glee, cheerfulness.
ᴇ gloom, melancholy.

misadventure n bad luck, hard luck, accident, ill-fortune, ill-luck, misfortune, mischance, calamity, catastrophe, tragedy, mishap, disaster, failure, debacle, cataclysm, reverse, setback.

misapprehension n misunderstanding, misconception, misinterpretation, misreading, error, mistake, fallacy, delusion.

misappropriate v steal, embezzle, peculate, pocket, swindle (infml), misspend, misuse, misapply, abuse, pervert.

misbehave v offend, transgress, trespass, get up to mischief, mess about, muck about (infml), play up, act up (infml).

misbehaviour n misconduct, misdemeanour, impropriety, disobedience, naughtiness, insubordination.

miscalculate v misjudge, get wrong, slip up, blunder, boob (infml), miscount, overestimate, underestimate.

miscarriage n failure, breakdown, abortion, mishap, mismanagement, error, disappointment.
ᴇ success.

miscarry v fail, abort, come to nothing,

fall through, misfire, founder, come to grief.
ᴇ succeed.

miscellaneous adj mixed, varied, various, assorted, diverse, diversified, sundry, motley, jumbled, indiscriminate.

miscellany n mixture, variety, assortment, collection, anthology, medley, mixed bag, pot-pourri, hotchpotch, jumble, diversity.

mischief n 1 TROUBLE, harm, evil, damage, injury, disruption. 2 MISBEHAVIOUR, naughtiness, impishness, pranks.

mischievous adj 1 MALICIOUS, evil, spiteful, vicious, wicked, pernicious, destructive, injurious. 2 NAUGHTY, impish, rascally, roguish, playful, teasing.
ᴇ 1 kind. 2 well-behaved, good.

misconception n misapprehension, misunderstanding, misreading, error, fallacy, delusion, the wrong end of the stick (infml).

misconduct n misbehaviour, impropriety, misdemeanour, malpractice, mismanagement, wrong-doing.

misconstrue v misinterpret, misjudge, misread, misunderstand, misconceive, misapprehend, mistranslate, misreckon, mistake, take the wrong way, get hold of the wrong end of the stick (infml).

misdemeanour n wrong-doing, wrong, misdeed, offence, infringement, lapse, fault, error, indiscretion, misbehaviour, misconduct, trespass, peccadillo, transgression (fml).

miser n niggard, skinflint, penny-pincher (infml), Scrooge.
ᴇ spendthrift.

miserable adj 1 UNHAPPY, sad, dejected, despondent, downcast, heartbroken, wretched, distressed, crushed. 2 CHEERLESS, depressing, dreary, impoverished, shabby, gloomy, dismal, forlorn, joyless, squalid. 3 CONTEMPTIBLE, despicable, ignominious, detestable, disgraceful, deplorable, shameful. 4 MEAGRE, paltry, niggardly, worthless, pathetic (infml), pitiful.
ᴇ 1 cheerful, happy. 2 pleasant. 4 generous.

miserly adj mean, niggardly, tight (infml), stingy (infml), sparing, parsimonious (fml), cheese-paring (infml), beggarly, penny-pinching (infml), mingy (infml).
ᴇ generous, spendthrift.

misery n 1 UNHAPPINESS, sadness, suffering, distress, depression, despair, gloom, grief, wretchedness, affliction. 2 PRIVATION, hardship, deprivation, poverty, want, oppression, destitution. 3 (infml) SPOILSPORT, pessimist, killjoy, wet blanket (infml). ⊟ 1 contentment. 2 comfort.

misfire v miscarry, go wrong, abort, fail, fall through, flop (infml), founder, fizzle out, come to grief. ⊟ succeed.

misfit n individualist, nonconformist, eccentric, maverick, drop-out, loner, lone wolf (infml). ⊟ conformist.

misfortune n bad luck, mischance, mishap, ill-luck, setback, reverse, calamity, catastrophe, disaster, blow, accident, tragedy, trouble, hardship, trial, tribulation. ⊟ luck, success.

misgiving n doubt, uncertainty, hesitation, qualm, reservation, apprehension, scruple, suspicion, second thoughts, niggle, anxiety, worry, fear. ⊟ confidence.

misguided adj misled, misconceived, ill-considered, ill-advised, ill-judged, imprudent, rash, misplaced, deluded, foolish, erroneous. ⊟ sensible, wise.

mishap n misfortune, ill-fortune, misadventure, accident, setback, calamity, disaster, adversity.

misinform v mislead, misdirect, misguide, deceive, bluff, hoodwink, lead up the garden path (infml), take for a ride (infml).

misinterpret v misconstrue, misread, misunderstand, mistake, distort, garble.

misjudge v miscalculate, mistake, misinterpret, misconstrue, misunderstand, overestimate, underestimate.

mislay v lose, misplace, miss, lose sight of.

mislead v misinform, misdirect, deceive, delude, lead astray, fool.

misleading adj deceptive, confusing, unreliable, ambiguous, biased, loaded, evasive, tricky (infml). ⊟ unequivocal, authoritative, informative.

mismanage v mishandle, botch, bungle, make a mess of, mess up, misrule, misspend, misjudge, foul up, mar, waste.

misplace v lose, mislay, miss, misapply, misassign, misfile, forget where one has put, lose sight of, lose track of, be unable to find.

misprint n mistake, error, erratum, literal, typo (infml).

misquote v misrepresent, misreport, muddle, misstate, twist, distort, pervert, falsify, garble, misremember.

misrepresent v distort, falsify, slant, pervert, twist, garble, misquote, exaggerate, minimize, misconstrue, misinterpret.

miss¹ v 1 FAIL, miscarry, lose, let slip, let go, omit, overlook, pass over, slip, leave out, mistake, trip, misunderstand, err. 2 AVOID, escape, evade, dodge, forego, skip, bypass, circumvent. 3 PINE FOR, long for, yearn for, regret, grieve for, mourn, sorrow for, want, wish, need, lament. ➤ n failure, error, blunder, mistake, omission, oversight, fault, flop (infml), fiasco.

miss² n girl, schoolgirl, young lady, young woman, teenager, Ms, mademoiselle, damsel, lass, maid, maiden.

misshapen adj deformed, distorted, twisted, malformed, warped, contorted, crooked, crippled, grotesque, ugly, monstrous. ⊟ regular, shapely.

missile n projectile, shot, guided missile, arrow, shaft, dart, rocket, bomb, shell, flying bomb, grenade, torpedo, weapon.

missing adj absent, lost, lacking, gone, mislaid, unaccounted-for, wanting, disappeared, astray, strayed, misplaced. ⊟ found, present.

mission n 1 TASK, undertaking, assignment, operation, campaign, crusade, business, errand. 2 CALLING, duty, purpose, vocation, raison dêtre, aim, charge, office, job, work. 3 COMMISSION, ministry, delegation, deputation, legation, embassy.

missionary n evangelist, campaigner, preacher, proselytizer, apostle, crusader, propagandist, champion, promoter, emissary, envoy, ambassador.

misspent adj wasted, frittered away, squandered, thrown away, idle, idled away, misused, profitless, misapplied, dissipated, unprofitable, prodigal (fml). ⊟ profitable.

mist *n* haze, fog, vapour, smog, cloud, condensation, film, spray, drizzle, dew, steam, veil, dimness.

♦ **mist over** cloud over, fog, dim, blur, steam up, obscure, veil.

🔼 clear.

mistake *n* error, inaccuracy, slip, slip-up, oversight, lapse, blunder, clanger (*infml*), boob (*infml*), gaffe, fault, faux pas, solecism (*fml*), indiscretion, misjudgement, miscalculation, misunderstanding, misprint, misspelling, misreading, mispronunciation, howler (*infml*).

➤ *v* misunderstand, misapprehend, misconstrue, misjudge, misread, miscalculate, confound, confuse, slip up, blunder, err, boob (*infml*).

mistaken *adj* wrong, incorrect, erroneous, inaccurate, inexact, untrue, inappropriate, ill-judged, inauthentic, false, deceived, deluded, misinformed, misled, faulty.

🔼 correct, right.

mistakenly *adv* wrongly, by mistake, erroneously, incorrectly, falsely, inaccurately, inappropriately, misguidedly, unfairly, unjustly, fallaciously (*fml*).

🔼 appropriately, correctly, fairly, justly.

mistreat *v* abuse, ill-treat, ill-use, maltreat, harm, hurt, batter, injure, knock about, molest.

mistress *n* **1** LOVER, live-in lover, kept woman, concubine, courtesan, girlfriend, paramour, woman, lady-love. **2** TEACHER, governess, tutor.

mistrust *n* distrust, doubt, suspicion, wariness, misgiving, reservations, qualm, hesitancy, chariness, caution, uncertainty, scepticism, apprehension.

🔼 trust.

➤ *v* distrust, doubt, suspect, be wary of, beware, have reservations, fear.

🔼 trust.

misty *adj* hazy, foggy, cloudy, blurred, fuzzy, murky, smoky, unclear, dim, indistinct, obscure, opaque, vague, veiled.

🔼 clear.

misunderstand *v* misapprehend, misconstrue, misinterpret, misjudge, mistake, get wrong, miss the point, mishear, get hold of the wrong end of the stick (*infml*).

🔼 understand.

misunderstanding *n* **1** MISTAKE, error,

misapprehension, misconception, misjudgement, misinterpretation, misreading, mix-up. **2** DISAGREEMENT, argument, dispute, conflict, clash, difference, breach, quarrel, discord, rift.

🔼 **1** understanding. **2** agreement.

misuse *n* mistreatment, maltreatment, abuse, harm, ill-treatment, misapplication, misappropriation, waste, perversion, corruption, exploitation.

➤ *v* abuse, misapply, misemploy, ill-use, ill-treat, harm, mistreat, wrong, distort, injure, corrupt, pervert, waste, squander, misappropriate, exploit, dissipate.

mitigating *adj* extenuating, justifying, vindicating, modifying, qualifying.

mix *v* **1** COMBINE, blend, mingle, intermingle, intermix, amalgamate, compound, homogenize, synthesize, merge, join, unite, coalesce, fuse, incorporate, fold in. **2** ASSOCIATE, consort, fraternize, socialize, mingle, join, hobnob (*infml*).

🔼 **1** divide, separate.

➤ *n* mixture, blend, amalgam, assortment, combination, conglomerate, compound, fusion, synthesis, medley, composite, mishmash (*infml*).

♦ **mix up** confuse, bewilder, muddle, perplex, puzzle, confound, mix, jumble, complicate, garble, involve, implicate, disturb, upset, snarl up.

mixed *adj* **1** *mixed race*: combined, hybrid, mingled, crossbred, mongrel, blended, composite, compound, incorporated, united, alloyed, amalgamated, fused. **2** *mixed biscuits*: assorted, varied, miscellaneous, diverse, diversified, motley. **3** *mixed feelings*: ambivalent, equivocal, conflicting, contradicting, uncertain.

mixture *n* mix, blend, combination, amalgamation, amalgam, compound, conglomeration, composite, coalescence, alloy, brew, synthesis, union, fusion, concoction, cross, hybrid, assortment, variety, miscellany, medley, mélange, mixed bag, pot-pourri, jumble, hotchpotch.

moan *n* lament, lamentation, sob, wail, howl, whimper, whine, grumble, complaint, grievance, groan.

➤ *v* **1** LAMENT, wail, sob, weep, howl, groan, whimper, mourn, grieve. **2** (*infml*) COMPLAIN, grumble, whine, whinge (*infml*), gripe (*infml*), carp.

🔼 **1** rejoice.

mob n 1 CROWD, mass, throng, multitude, horde, host, swarm, gathering, group, collection, flock, herd, pack, set, tribe, troop, company, crew, gang. 2 POPULACE, rabble (*infml*), masses, hoi polloi, plebs (*infml*), riff-raff (*infml*).
➤ v crowd, crowd round, surround, swarm round, jostle, overrun, set upon, besiege, descend on, throng, pack, pester, charge.

mobile adj 1 MOVING, movable, portable, peripatetic, travelling, roaming, roving, itinerant, wandering, migrant. 2 FLEXIBLE, agile, active, energetic, nimble. 3 CHANGING, changeable, ever-changing, expressive, lively.
◪ 1 immobile.

mobilize v assemble, marshal, rally, conscript, muster, call up, enlist, activate, galvanize, organize, prepare, ready, summon, animate.

mock v 1 RIDICULE, jeer, make fun of, laugh at, disparage, deride, scoff, sneer, taunt, scorn, tease. 2 IMITATE, simulate, mimic, ape, caricature, satirize.
➤ adj imitation, counterfeit, artificial, sham, simulated, synthetic, false, fake, forged, fraudulent, bogus, phoney (*infml*), pseudo, spurious, feigned, faked, pretended, dummy.

mockery n 1 RIDICULE, jeering, scoffing, scorn, derision, contempt, disdain, disrespect, sarcasm. 2 PARODY, satire, sham, travesty.

mocking adj scornful, derisive, contemptuous, sarcastic, satirical, taunting, scoffing, sardonic, snide (*infml*), insulting, irreverent, impudent, disrespectful, disdainful, cynical.

mode n 1 WAY, style, manner, approach, condition, method, form, plan, practice, procedure, process, technique, system, convention. 2 FASHION, style, custom, trend, vogue, fad, look, craze (*infml*), latest thing (*infml*), rage (*infml*).

model n 1 COPY, replica, representation, facsimile, imitation, mock-up. 2 EXAMPLE, exemplar (*fml*), pattern, standard, ideal, mould, prototype, template. 3 DESIGN, style, type, version, mark. 4 MANNEQUIN, dummy, sitter, subject, poser.
➤ adj exemplary, perfect, typical, ideal.
➤ v 1 MAKE, form, fashion, mould, sculpt, carve, cast, shape, work, create, design, plan. 2 DISPLAY, wear, show off.

moderate adj 1 MEDIOCRE, medium, ordinary, fair, indifferent, average, middle-of-the-road. 2 REASONABLE, restrained, sensible, calm, controlled, cool, mild, well-regulated.
◪ 1 exceptional. 2 immoderate.
➤ v control, regulate, decrease, lessen, soften, restrain, tone down, play down, diminish, ease, curb, calm, check, modulate, repress, subdue, soft-pedal, tame, subside, pacify, mitigate, allay, alleviate, abate, dwindle.

moderately adv somewhat, quite, rather, fairly, slightly, reasonably, passably, to some extent.
◪ extremely.

moderation n 1 DECREASE, reduction. 2 RESTRAINT, self-control, caution, control, composure, sobriety, abstemiousness, temperance, reasonableness.

modern adj current, contemporary, up-to-date, new, fresh, latest, late, novel, present, present-day, recent, up-to-the-minute (*infml*), newfangled (*infml*), advanced, avant-garde, progressive, modernistic, innovative, inventive, state-of-the-art, go-ahead, fashionable, stylish, in vogue, in style, modish, trendy (*infml*).
◪ old-fashioned, old, out of date, antiquated.

modernize v renovate, refurbish, rejuvenate, regenerate, streamline, revamp, renew, update, improve, do up, redesign, reform, remake, remodel, refresh, transform, modify, progress.
◪ regress.

modest adj 1 UNASSUMING, humble, self-effacing, quiet, reserved, retiring, unpretentious, discreet, bashful, shy. 2 MODERATE, ordinary, unexceptional, fair, reasonable, limited, small.
◪ 1 immodest, conceited. 2 exceptional, excessive.

modesty n humility, humbleness, self-effacement, reticence, reserve, quietness, decency, propriety, demureness, shyness, bashfulness, coyness.
◪ immodesty, vanity, conceit.

modicum n little, bit, small amount, little bit, particle, molecule, fragment, grain, scrap, shred, speck, touch, degree, trace, tinge, atom, crumb, dash, drop, pinch, ounce, hint, suggestion, inch, iota, mite, tad (*infml*).

modification n adaptation, adjustment,

alteration, change, revision, variation, improvement, transformation, mutation, refinement, reformation, reorganization, remoulding, reworking, recasting, limitation, moderation, qualification, restriction, tempering, modulation (*fml*).

modify *v* **1** CHANGE, alter, redesign, revise, vary, adapt, adjust, transform, reform, convert, improve, reorganize.
2 MODERATE, reduce, temper, tone down, limit, soften, qualify.

modulate *v* modify, adjust, balance, alter, soften, lower, regulate, vary, harmonize, inflect, tune.

mogul *n* magnate, tycoon, baron, potentate, notable, personage, supremo, big cheese (*infml*), big gun (*infml*), big noise (*infml*), big pot (*infml*), big shot (*infml*), big wheel (*infml*), bigwig (*infml*), Mr Big (*infml*), top dog (*infml*), VIP (*infml*).
ea nobody.

moist *adj* damp, clammy, humid, wet, dewy, rainy, muggy, marshy, drizzly, watery, soggy.
ea dry, arid.

moisten *v* moisturize, dampen, damp, wet, water, lick, irrigate.
ea dry.

moisture *n* water, liquid, wetness, wateriness, damp, dampness, dankness, humidity, vapour, dew, mugginess, condensation, steam, spray.
ea dryness.

molest *v* **1** ANNOY, disturb, bother, harass, irritate, persecute, pester, plague, tease, torment, hound, upset, worry, trouble, badger. **2** ATTACK, accost, assail, hurt, ill-treat, maltreat, mistreat, abuse, harm, injure.

mollify *v* placate, appease, calm, pacify, compose, conciliate, cushion, ease, relax, relieve, lessen, moderate, temper, modify, quell, soften, soothe, lull, quiet, blunt, sweeten, mellow, abate (*fml*), allay (*fml*), mitigate (*fml*), assuage (*fml*), propitiate (*fml*).
ea aggravate, anger.

mollusc

Molluscs include: abalone, conch, cowrie, cuttlefish, clam, cockle, limpet, mussel, nautilus, nudibranch, octopus, oyster, periwinkle, scallop, sea slug, slug, freshwater snail, land snail, marine snail, squid, tusk shell, whelk.

mollycoddle *v* pamper, coddle, indulge, spoil, overprotect, pander to, cosset, spoon-feed (*infml*), mother, pet, baby, ruin.
ea ill-treat, neglect.

moment *n* second, instant, minute, split second, trice, jiffy (*infml*), tick (*infml*).

momentarily *adv* briefly, for a moment, for a short time, for a second, for an instant, fleetingly, temporarily.

momentary *adj* brief, short, short-lived, temporary, transient, transitory, fleeting, ephemeral, hasty, quick, passing.
ea lasting, permanent.

momentous *adj* significant, important, critical, crucial, decisive, weighty, grave, serious, vital, fateful, historic, earth-shaking, epoch-making, eventful, major.
ea insignificant, unimportant, trivial.

momentum *n* impetus, force, energy, impulse, drive, power, thrust, speed, velocity, impact, incentive, stimulus, urge, strength, push.

monarch *n* sovereign, crowned head, ruler, king, queen, emperor, empress, prince, princess, tsar, potentate.

monarchy *n* **1** KINGDOM, empire, principality, realm, domain, dominion.
2 ROYALISM, sovereignty, autocracy, monocracy, absolutism, despotism, tyranny.

monastery *n* friary, priory, abbey, cloister, charterhouse.

monastic *adj* reclusive, withdrawn, secluded, cloistered, austere, ascetic, celibate, contemplative.
ea secular, worldly.

monetary *adj* financial, fiscal, pecuniary (*fml*), budgetary, economic, capital, cash.

money *n* currency, cash, legal tender, banknotes, coin, funds, finances, assets, means, savings, resources, capital, riches, wealth, prosperity, affluence, the necessary (*infml*), readies, megabucks (*sl*), dough, dosh, bread, lolly, spondulicks, brass, loot, gravy, greens (*US*), rhino, shekels, moolah, gelt.

Expressions used when talking about money include: be on the take, bring home the bacon, cash cow, cash in hand, cash on the barrel (head) (*US*), coin it, cost a bomb, cost a packet, cost an arm and a leg, cost the earth, divvy up, easy money, feather one's own nest, get-rich-quick, great oaks out of little acorns grow, have money to burn, I'm not made of money, in pocket, in the money, make a bomb, make a bundle, make a fast buck, make a few bob, make a fortune/a bundle/a killing, make one's pile, making money hand over fist, money for jam/old rope, money is no object, money talks, not cost a bean, not cost a penny, not have a brass razoo, not have two halfpennies to rub together, on easy street, on one's uppers, out of pocket, pay over the odds, pay through the nose for something, pay one's way, poor as a church mouse, quids in, rich as Croesus, rolling in it, scratching, see the colour of someone's money, spend money like it's going out of fashion, spend money like water, stoney broke, throw good money after bad, throw money around, throw money at something, what's the damage?, where there's muck there's brass.

◆ **in the money** rich, wealthy, affluent, prosperous, well-off, well-to-do, rolling in it (*infml*), well-heeled (*infml*), flush (*infml*), loaded (*sl*).
E3 poor.

mongrel *n* cross, crossbreed, hybrid, half-breed.
➤ *adj* crossbred, hybrid, half-breed, bastard, mixed, ill-defined.
E3 pure-bred, pedigree.

monitor *n* **1** SCREEN, display, VDU, recorder, scanner. **2** SUPERVISOR, watchdog, overseer, invigilator, adviser, prefect.
➤ *v* check, watch, keep track of, keep under surveillance, keep an eye on, follow, track, supervise, observe, note, survey, trace, scan, record, plot, detect.

monk *n* brother, religious, friar, frater, prior, abbot, hermit, monastic, mendicant, contemplative, cloisterer, coenobite, beguin, conventual, religieux, religionary, religioner, anchorite, gyrovague.

monkey *n* **1** PRIMATE, simian, ape. **2** (*infml*) SCAMP, imp, urchin, brat, rogue, scallywag (*infml*), rascal.

> Monkeys include: ape, baboon, capuchin, colobus monkey, drill and mandrill, guenon, guereza, howler monkey, langur, leaf monkey, macaque, mangabey, marmoset, night monkey (or douroucouli), proboscis monkey, rhesus monkey, saki, spider monkey, squirrel monkey, tamarin, titi, toque, uakari (or cacajou), woolly monkey.

monolithic *adj* massive, vast, colossal, gigantic, huge, monumental, giant, immovable, immobile, rigid, solid, unmoving, unchanging, inflexible, faceless, undifferentiated, fossilized, hidebound, intractable, unvaried.

monologue *n* speech, soliloquy, lecture, sermon, address, oration, homily, spiel (*infml*).
E3 conversation, dialogue, discussion.

monopolize *v* dominate, take over, appropriate, corner, control, hog (*infml*), engross, occupy, preoccupy, take up, tie up.
E3 share.

monopoly *n* domination, control, corner, exclusive right(s), sole right(s), ascendancy (*fml*).

monotonous *adj* boring, dull, tedious, uninteresting, tiresome, wearisome, unchanging, uneventful, unvaried, uniform, toneless, flat, colourless, repetitive, routine, plodding, humdrum, soul-destroying.
E3 lively, varied, colourful.

monotony *n* tedium, dullness, boredom, sameness, tiresomeness, uneventfulness, flatness, wearisomeness, uniformity, routine, repetitiveness.
E3 liveliness, colour.

monster *n* **1** BEAST, fiend, brute, barbarian, savage, villain, giant, ogre, ogress, troll, mammoth. **2** FREAK, monstrosity, mutant.
➤ *adj* huge, gigantic, giant, colossal, enormous, immense, massive, monstrous, jumbo, mammoth, vast, tremendous.
E3 tiny, minute.

monstrosity *n* **1** EYESORE, blot on the landscape, atrocity, abnormality, enormity, freak, monster, mutant, miscreation, obscenity. **2** DREADFULNESS, frightfulness, hideousness, loathsomeness, horror, hellishness, evil, heinousness (*fml*).

monstrous *adj* **1** WICKED, evil, vicious, cruel, criminal, heinous, outrageous, scandalous, disgraceful, atrocious, abhorrent, dreadful, frightful, horrible, horrifying, terrible. **2** UNNATURAL, inhuman, freakish, grotesque, hideous, deformed, malformed, misshapen. **3** HUGE, enormous, colossal, gigantic, vast, immense, massive, mammoth.

monument *n* memorial, cenotaph, headstone, gravestone, tombstone, shrine, mausoleum, cairn, barrow, cross, marker, obelisk, pillar, statue, relic, remembrance, commemoration, testament, reminder, record, memento, evidence, token.

monumental *adj* 1 IMPRESSIVE, imposing, awe-inspiring, awesome, overwhelming, significant, important, epoch-making, historic, magnificent, majestic, memorable, notable, outstanding, abiding, immortal, lasting, classic. 2 HUGE, immense, enormous, colossal, vast, tremendous, massive, great. 3 COMMEMORATIVE, memorial.
◨ 1 insignificant, unimportant.

mood *n* 1 DISPOSITION, frame of mind, state of mind, temper, humour, spirit, tenor, whim. 2 BAD TEMPER, sulk, the sulks, pique, melancholy, depression, blues (*infml*), doldrums, dumps (*infml*).

moody *adj* changeable, temperamental, unpredictable, capricious, irritable, short-tempered, crabby (*infml*), crotchety, crusty (*infml*), testy, touchy, morose, angry, broody, mopy, sulky, sullen, gloomy, melancholy, miserable, downcast, doleful, glum, impulsive, fickle, flighty.
◨ equable, cheerful.

moon *v* idle, loaf, mooch, languish, pine, mope, brood, daydream, dream, fantasize.

moor¹ *v* fasten, secure, tie up, drop anchor, anchor, berth, dock, make fast, fix, hitch, bind.
◨ loose.

moor² *n* moorland, heath, fell, upland.

moot *v* put forward, propose, suggest, submit, advance, bring up, broach, introduce, pose, discuss, argue, debate, propound (*fml*).
➤ *adj* controversial, problematic, difficult, questionable, vexed, unsettled, unresolved, unresolvable, undecided, undetermined, disputed, disputable, arguable, doubtful, insoluble, knotty, open, open to debate, debatable, crucial, contestable, academic.

mop *n* head of hair, shock, mane, tangle, thatch, mass.
➤ *v* swab, sponge, wipe, clean, wash, absorb, soak.

mope *v* brood, fret, sulk, pine, languish, droop, despair, grieve, idle.

moral *adj* ethical, virtuous, good, right, principled, honourable, decent, upright, upstanding, straight, righteous, high-minded, honest, incorruptible, proper,

blameless, chaste, clean-living, pure, just, noble.
◨ immoral.
➤ *n* lesson, message, teaching, dictum, meaning, maxim, adage, precept, saying, proverb, aphorism, epigram.

morale *n* confidence, spirits, esprit de corps, self-esteem, state of mind, heart, mood.

morality *n* ethics, morals, ideals, principles, standards, virtue, rectitude (*fml*), righteousness, decency, goodness, honesty, integrity, justice, uprightness, propriety, conduct, manners.
◨ immorality.

morals *n* morality, ethics, principles, standards, ideals, integrity, scruples, behaviour, conduct, habits, manners.

morass *n* 1 QUAGMIRE, bog, moss, marsh, marshland, swamp, slough, mire, fen, quag, quicksand. 2 CONFUSION, clutter, chaos, mess, jam, jumble, muddle, mix-up, tangle, can of worms (*infml*).

moratorium *n* delay, postponement, halt, freeze, suspension, stay, standstill, stoppage, respite, ban, embargo.
◨ go-ahead (*infml*), green light (*infml*).

morbid *adj* 1 GHOULISH, ghastly, gruesome, macabre, hideous, horrid, grim. 2 GLOOMY, pessimistic, melancholy, sombre. 3 SICK, unhealthy, unwholesome, insalubrious.

more *adj* further, extra, additional, added, new, fresh, increased, other, supplementary, repeated, alternative, spare.
◨ less.
➤ *adv* further, longer, again, besides, moreover, better.
◨ less.

moreover *adv* furthermore, further, besides, in addition, as well, also, additionally, what is more.

moribund *adj* 1 DYING, failing, fading, expiring, declining, wasting away, senile, in extremis, comatose (*fml*), on one's last legs (*infml*), on the way out (*infml*), with one foot in the grave (*infml*), not long for this world (*infml*). 2 WEAK, feeble, lifeless, declining, wasting away, waning, ebbing, stagnating, stagnant, obsolescent, doomed, dwindling, collapsing, crumbling.
◨ 1 alive, lively, nascent (*fml*). 2 flourishing.

morning *n* daybreak, daylight, dawn,

sunrise, break of day, before noon.

moron n fool, blockhead, fat-head, dolt, dunce, dimwit, simpleton, halfwit, idiot, cretin, imbecile, ignoramus, dupe, stooge, butt, laughing-stock, clown, comic, buffoon, jester, nincompoop (*infml*), ass (*infml*), chump (*infml*), ninny (*infml*), clot (*infml*), dope (*infml*), twit (*infml*), nitwit (*infml*), nit (*infml*), sucker (*infml*), mug (*infml*), twerp (*infml*), birdbrain (*infml*), wally (*sl*), jerk (*infml*), dumbo (*infml*), pillock (*infml*), prat (*infml*), dork (*infml*), geek (*infml*), plonker (*sl*), prick (*sl*), schmuck (*US sl*).

moronic adj foolish, stupid, senseless, silly, absurd, ridiculous, ludicrous, nonsensical, unwise, ill-advised, ill-considered, short-sighted, half-baked, crazy (*infml*), mad, insane, idiotic, hare-brained, half-witted, simple-minded, simple, ignorant, unintelligent, inept, inane, pointless, unreasonable, daft (*infml*), crack-brained (*infml*), gormless (*infml*), dumb (*infml*), dotty (*infml*), potty (*infml*), batty (*infml*), barmy (*infml*), nutty (*infml*), not in one's right mind (*infml*), out of one's mind (*infml*), with a screw missing (*infml*), needing to have one's head examined (*infml*).

morose adj ill-tempered, bad-tempered, moody, sullen, sulky, surly, gloomy, grim, gruff, sour, taciturn, glum, grouchy (*infml*), crabby (*infml*), saturnine.
☒ cheerful, communicative.

morsel n bit, scrap, piece, fragment, crumb, bite, mouthful, nibble, taste, soupçon, titbit, slice, fraction, modicum, grain, atom, part.

mortal adj **1** WORLDLY, earthly, bodily, human, perishable, temporal. **2** FATAL, lethal, deadly. **3** EXTREME, great, severe, intense, grave, awful.
☒ **1** immortal.
➤ n human being, human, individual, person, being, body, creature.
☒ immortal, god.

mortality n **1** HUMANITY, death, impermanence, perishability. **2** FATALITY, death rate.
☒ **1** immortality.

mortification n **1** EMBARRASSMENT, humiliation, confounding, shame, disgrace, dishonour, loss of face, abasement, annoyance, chastening, vexation, chagrin (*fml*), discomfiture (*fml*),

ignominy (*fml*). **2** DISCIPLINE, punishment, asceticism, control, self-control, denial, self-denial, conquering, subjugation (*fml*).

mortified adj humiliated, shamed, ashamed, humbled, embarrassed, crushed.

mortify v **1** HUMILIATE, horrify, shame, put to shame, embarrass, offend, disgrace, dishonour, chastise, chasten, abash, confound, humble, bring low, crush, deflate, affront, annoy, disappoint, discomfit (*fml*), chagrin (*fml*), take down a peg or two (*infml*). **2** DISCIPLINE, restrain, suppress, deny, control, conquer, subdue.

mortuary n morgue, funeral parlour, deadhouse, charnel house.

mostly adv mainly, on the whole, principally, chiefly, generally, usually, largely, for the most part, as a rule.

moth see **butterfly**

moth-eaten adj old, worn, worn-out, old-fashioned, obsolete, outdated, outworn, ragged, tattered, threadbare, dated, ancient, antiquated, archaic, decrepit, dilapidated, decayed, musty, shabby, stale, mouldy, mangy, moribund, seedy.
☒ fresh, new.

mother n **1** PARENT, procreator (*fml*), progenitress (*fml*), dam, mamma, mum (*infml*), mummy (*infml*), matriarch, ancestor, matron, old woman (*infml*). **2** ORIGIN, source.
➤ v **1** BEAR, produce, nurture, raise, rear, nurse, care for, cherish. **2** PAMPER, spoil, baby, indulge, overprotect, fuss over.

motherly adj maternal, caring, comforting, affectionate, kind, loving, protective, warm, tender, gentle, fond.
☒ neglectful, uncaring.

motif n theme, idea, topic, concept, pattern, design, figure, form, logo, shape, device, ornament, decoration.

motion n **1** MOVEMENT, action, mobility, moving, activity, locomotion, travel, transit, passage, passing, progress, change, flow, inclination. **2** GESTURE, gesticulation, signal, sign, wave, nod. **3** PROPOSAL, suggestion, recommendation, proposition.
➤ v signal, gesture, gesticulate, sign, wave, nod, beckon, direct, usher.

motionless adj unmoving, still, stationary, static, immobile, at a standstill, fixed, halted, at rest, resting, standing, paralysed, inanimate, lifeless, frozen, rigid, stagnant.

🔁 active, moving.

motivate *v* prompt, incite, impel, spur, provoke, stimulate, drive, lead, stir, urge, push, propel, persuade, move, inspire, encourage, cause, trigger, induce, kindle, draw, arouse, bring.

🔁 deter, discourage.

motivation *n* reason, incitement, inducement, prompting, spur, stimulus, provocation, drive, push, hunger, desire, wish, urge, impulse, incentive, ambition, inspiration, instigation, momentum, motive, persuasion, interest.

🔁 discouragement, prevention.

motive *n* grounds, cause, reason, purpose, motivation, object, intention, influence, rationale, thinking, incentive, impulse, stimulus, inspiration, incitement, urge, encouragement, design, desire, consideration.

🔁 deterrent, disincentive.

motley *adj* 1 ASSORTED, varied, mixed, miscellaneous, diverse, diversified, multifarious, heterogeneous (*fml*). 2 MULTICOLOURED, variegated, particoloured, colourful, many-hued, pied, piebald, tabby, dappled, brindled, mottled, spotted, striped, streaked.

🔁 1 uniform, homogeneous. 2 monochrome.

motor vehicle

> Parts of a motor vehicle include: ABS (anti-lock braking system), accelerator, airbag, air brake, air-conditioner, air inlet, antidazzle mirror, antiglare switch, anti-roll bar, antitheft device, ashtray, axle, backup light (*US*), battery, bench seat, bezel, bodywork, bonnet, boot, brake drum, brake light, brake pad, brake shoe, bumper, car phone, car radio, catalytic converter, central locking, centre console, chassis, child-safety seat, cigarette-lighter, clock, clutch, courtesy light, crankcase, cruise control, dashboard, differential gear, dimmer, disc brake, door, door-lock, drive shaft, drum brake, electric window, emergency light, engine, exhaust pipe, fender (*US*), filler cap, flasher switch, fog lamp, folding seat, four-wheel drive, fuel gauge, gas tank (*US*), gear, gearbox, gear-lever (or gear-stick), glove compartment, grille, handbrake, hazard warning light, headlight, headrest, heated rear window, heater, hood (*US*), horn, hub-cap, hydraulic brake, hydraulic suspension, ignition, ignition key, indicator, instrument panel, jack, jump lead, kingpin, license plate (*US*), lift gate (*US*), monocoque, number plate, oil gauge, overrider, parcel shelf, parking-light, petrol tank, pneumatic tyre, power brake, prop shaft, quarterlight, rack and pinion, radial-ply tyre, rear light, rear-view mirror, reclining seat, reflector, rev counter (*infml*), reversing light, roof rack, screen-washer bottle, seat belt, shaft, shock absorber, sidelight, side-impact bar, side mirror, silencer, sill, solenoid, spare tyre, speedometer, spoiler, steering-column, steering-wheel, stick shift (*US*), stoplight, sunroof, sun visor, suspension, temperature gauge, towbar, track rod, transmission, trunk (*US*), tyre, vent, wheel, wheel arch, windscreen, windscreen-washer, windscreen-wiper, windshield (*US*), wing, wing mirror. *see also* **car**; **engine**.

mottled *adj* speckled, dappled, blotchy, flecked, piebald, stippled, streaked, tabby, spotted, freckled, variegated.

🔁 monochrome, uniform.

motto *n* saying, slogan, maxim, watchword, catchword, byword, precept, proverb, adage, formula, rule, golden rule, dictum.

mould¹ *n* 1 CAST, form, die, template, pattern, matrix. 2 SHAPE, form, format, pattern, structure, style, type, build, construction, cut, design, kind, model, sort, stamp, arrangement, brand, frame, character, nature, quality, line, make.
➤ *v* 1 FORGE, cast, shape, stamp, make, form, create, design, construct, sculpt, model, work. 2 INFLUENCE, direct, control.

mould² *n* mildew, fungus, mouldiness, mustiness, blight.

mouldy *adj* mildewed, blighted, musty, decaying, corrupt, rotten, fusty, putrid, bad, spoiled, stale.

🔁 fresh, wholesome.

mound *n* 1 HILL, hillock, hummock, rise, knoll, bank, dune, elevation, ridge, embankment, earthwork. 2 HEAP, pile, stack.

mount *v* 1 PRODUCE, put on, set up, prepare, stage, exhibit, display, launch. 2 INCREASE, grow, accumulate, multiply, rise, intensify, soar, swell. 3 CLIMB, ascend, get up, go up, get on, clamber up, scale, get astride.

🔁 2 decrease, descend. 3 descend, dismount, go down.

➤ *n* horse, steed, support, mounting.

mountain *n* **1** HEIGHT, elevation, mount, peak, mound, alp, tor, massif. **2** HEAP, pile, stack, mass, abundance, backlog.

> The highest mountains of the world
> include: *Asia*: Everest (Himalaya-Nepal/ Tibet), K2 (Pakistan/India), Kangchenjunga (Himalaya-Nepal/India), Makalu (Himalaya-Nepal/Tibet), Dhaulagiri (Himalaya-Nepal), Nanga Parbat (Himalaya-India), Annapurna (Himalaya-Nepal); *South America*: Aconcagua (Andes-Argentina); *North America*: McKinley (Alaska Range); *Africa*: Kilimanjaro (Tanzania); *Europe*: Elbruz (Caucasus), Mont Blanc (Alps-France); *Antarctica*: Vinson Massif; *Australasia*: Jaja (New Guinea).

mountaineering

> Mountaineering terms include:
> abseiling, abseil station, adze, adz (*US*), Alpinism, arête, ascender, ascent, avalanche; axe, ax (*US*), ice axe, hammer axe; base camp; belay, belayer, non-belayer, self-belaying; bivouac; bolting, debolting; bouldering, cam, carabiner or karabiner, chalk bag, chalk cliff climbing, chimney, chock, chockstone, cleft, climbing wall, col, cornice, corrie, crag, crampon, crevasse, descender, descent, Dülfer seat, étrier, fissure, glacier, gully; harness, climbing harness, sit harness; hand hold, helmet, helmet lamp, hut, ice climbing, ice ridge, ice screw, ice slope, ice step, Munro; nut, walnut; overhang, pick, piolet, pitch; piton, abseil piton, corkscrew piton, drive-in ice piton, ice piton, ringed piton; prusik knot, prusik loop, rappelling, ridge, rock, rock face, rock spike, rock wall; rope, dynamic rope, kernmantel rope, standing rope, on the rope, unrope; saddle, scree, sérac, Sherpa, shunt; sling, abseil sling, rope sling, sling seat, wrist sling; solo ascent, snow bridge, snow cornice, snow gaiters, snow goggles, spike, sport climbing, spur; stack, sea stack; summit, top out, trad route, traverse, tying in.

mountainous *adj* **1** CRAGGY, rocky, hilly, high, highland, upland, alpine, soaring, steep. **2** HUGE, towering, enormous, immense.
☒ **1** flat. **2** tiny.

mourn *v* grieve, lament, sorrow, bemoan, miss, regret, deplore, weep, wail.
☒ rejoice.

mournful *adj* sorrowful, sad, unhappy, desolate, grief-stricken, heavy-hearted, heartbroken, broken-hearted, cast-down, downcast, miserable, tragic, woeful, melancholy, sombre, depressed, dejected, gloomy, dismal.
☒ joyful.

mourning *n* bereavement, grief, grieving, lamentation, sadness, sorrow, desolation, weeping.
☒ rejoicing.

mouth *n* **1** LIPS, jaws, trap (*infml*), gob (*sl*). **2** OPENING, aperture, orifice, cavity, entrance, gateway, inlet, estuary.
➤ *v* enunciate, articulate, utter, pronounce, whisper, form.

> Parts of the mouth include: cleft palate, gum, hard palate, hare lip, inferior dental arch, isthmus of fauces, labial commissure, lower lip, palatoglossal arch, palatopharyngeal arch, soft palate, superior dental arch, tongue, tonsil, upper lip, uvula. see also **tooth**.

mouthful *n* sample, morsel, spoonful, swallow, taste, bite, nibble, bit, gulp, sip, titbit, drop, forkful, slug, sup, bonne-bouche.

mouthpiece *n* spokesperson, spokesman, spokeswoman, representative, agent, delegate, propagandist, journal, periodical, publication, organ.

movable *adj* mobile, portable, transportable, changeable, alterable, adjustable, flexible, transferable.
☒ fixed, immovable.

move *v* **1** STIR, go, advance, budge, change, proceed, progress, make strides. **2** TRANSPORT, carry, transfer. **3** DEPART, go away, leave, decamp, migrate, remove, move house, relocate. **4** PROMPT, stimulate, urge, impel, drive, propel, motivate, incite, persuade, induce, inspire. **5** AFFECT, touch, agitate, stir, impress, excite.
➤ *n* **1** MOVEMENT, motion, step, manoeuvre, action, device, stratagem. **2** REMOVAL, relocation, migration, transfer.

movement *n* **1** REPOSITIONING, move, moving, relocation, activity, act, action, agitation, stirring, transfer, passage. **2** CHANGE, development, advance, evolution, current, drift, flow, shift, progress, progression, trend, tendency. **3** CAMPAIGN, crusade, drive, group, organization, party, faction, coalition.

moving adj 1 MOBILE, active, in motion.
2 TOUCHING, affecting, poignant,
impressive, emotive, arousing, stirring,
inspiring, inspirational, exciting, thrilling,
persuasive, stimulating.
🔁 1 immobile. 2 unemotional.

mow v cut, trim, crop, clip, shear, scythe.
◆ **mow down** butcher, slaughter,
massacre, shoot down, decimate, cut
down, cut to pieces.

much adv greatly, considerably, a lot,
frequently, often.
➤ adj copious, plentiful, ample,
considerable, a lot, abundant, great,
substantial.
➤ n plenty, a lot, lots (infml), loads (infml),
heaps (infml), lashings (infml).
🔁 little.

muck n dirt, dung, manure, mire, filth,
mud, sewage, slime, gunge (infml), ordure,
scum, sludge.
◆ **muck up** ruin, wreck, spoil, mess up,
make a mess of, botch, bungle, cock up (sl).

mucky adj begrimed, bespattered, dirty,
filthy, grimy, messy, miry, mud-caked,
muddy, oozy, slimy, soiled, sticky.
🔁 clean.

mud n clay, mire, ooze, dirt, sludge, silt.

muddle v 1 DISORGANIZE, disorder, mix
up, mess up, jumble, scramble, tangle.
2 CONFUSE, bewilder, bemuse, perplex.
➤ n chaos, confusion, disorder, mess, mix-
up, jumble, clutter, tangle.

muddled adj confused, chaotic,
disorganized, disordered, jumbled, mixed-
up, tangled, scrambled, disarrayed, messy,
loose, higgledy-piggledy, disorient(at)ed,
perplexed, bewildered, unclear, vague,
woolly, befuddled, stupefied, dazed,
incoherent, infml. at sea.

muddy adj 1 DIRTY, foul, miry, mucky,
marshy, boggy, swampy, quaggy, grimy.
2 CLOUDY, indistinct, obscure, opaque,
murky, hazy, blurred, fuzzy, dull.
🔁 1 clean. 2 clear.

muffle v 1 WRAP, envelop, cloak, swathe,
cover. 2 DEADEN, dull, quieten, silence,
stifle, dampen, muzzle, suppress.
🔁 2 amplify.

mug¹ n cup, beaker, pot, tankard.

mug² v set upon, attack, assault, waylay,
steal from, rob, beat up, jump (on).

muggy adj humid, sticky, stuffy, sultry,

close, clammy, oppressive, sweltering,
moist, damp.
🔁 dry.

mull over v reflect on, ponder,
contemplate, think over, think about,
ruminate, consider, weigh up, chew over,
meditate, study, examine, deliberate.

multiple adj many, numerous, manifold,
various, several, sundry, collective.

multiply v increase, proliferate, expand,
spread, reproduce, propagate, breed,
accumulate, intensify, extend, build up,
augment, boost.
🔁 decrease, lessen.

multitude n crowd, throng, horde, swarm,
mob, mass, herd, congregation, host, lot,
lots, legion, public, people, populace.
🔁 few, scattering.

munch v eat, chew, crunch, masticate
(fml).

mundane adj banal, ordinary, everyday,
commonplace, prosaic, humdrum,
workaday, routine.
🔁 extraordinary.

municipal adj civic, city, town, urban,
borough, community, public.

municipality n city, town, township,
borough, department, district, precinct,
council, local government, burgh,
département.

murder n 1 KILLING, homicide,
manslaughter, slaying, slaughter,
assassination, execution, massacre,
butchery, bloodshed, foul play, patricide
(fml), matricide (fml), infanticide (fml),
fratricide (fml), sororicide (fml), uxoricide
(fml), liquidation (infml). 2 driving in town is
murder: hell, torment, torture, agony,
ordeal, nightmare, misery, wretchedness,
suffering, anguish.
➤ v 1 KILL, slaughter, slay, put to death,
assassinate, butcher, massacre, do in
(infml), bump off (infml), eliminate (infml),
liquidate (infml), knock off (infml), rub out
(infml), wipe out (infml), take out (infml),
waste (infml), blow away (infml). 2 RUIN,
spoil, destroy, botch, mess up, wreck, make
a mess of. 3 DEFEAT EASILY, beat,
overwhelm, rout, annihilate, outplay,
outwit, outsmart, trounce, slaughter
(infml), hammer (infml), clobber (infml),
lick (infml), thrash (infml), wipe the floor
with (infml).

murderer n killer, homicide, slayer,
slaughterer, assassin, butcher, cut-throat.

murderous *adj* 1 HOMICIDAL, brutal, barbarous, bloodthirsty, bloody, cut-throat, killing, lethal, cruel, savage, ferocious, deadly. 2 (*infml*) DIFFICULT, exhausting, strenuous, unpleasant, dangerous.

murky *adj* dark, dismal, gloomy, dull, overcast, misty, foggy, dim, cloudy, obscure, veiled, grey.
Ea bright, clear.

murmur *n* mumble, muttering, whisper, undertone, humming, rumble, drone, grumble.
➤ *v* mutter, mumble, whisper, buzz, hum, rumble, purr, burble.

muscle *n* 1 *strong muscles*: sinew, tendon, ligament. 2 FORCE, brawn, beef, power, forcefulness, strength, stamina, potency, sturdiness, weight, clout (*infml*), might (*fml*).
♦ **muscle in** butt in, push in, shove, strongarm, impose oneself, force one's way in, elbow one's way in, jostle.

muscular *adj* brawny, beefy (*infml*), sinewy, athletic, powerfully built, strapping, hefty, powerful, husky, robust, stalwart, vigorous, strong.
Ea puny, flabby, weak.

muse *v* ponder, think, think over, meditate, mull over, weigh, contemplate, consider, brood, reflect, review, chew, dream, deliberate, speculate, cogitate (*fml*), ruminate.

mushrooms and toadstools

Types of mushroom and toadstool include: *edible*: beefsteak fungus, blewits, boletus, chestnut boletus, button mushroom, cep, champignon, chanterelle, clouded agaric, common morel, cultivated mushroom, dingy agaric, fairy ring, the goat's lip, gypsy mushroom, honey fungus, horn of plenty, horse mushroom, lawyer's wig, man on horseback, march mushroom, oyster mushroom, parasol mushroom, penny bun, saffron milk cap, shaggy parasol, slippery jack, sweetbread mushroom, truffle, trumpet agaric, velvet shank, winter mushroom, wood hedgehog; *inedible/poisonous*: amanita, common ink cap, copper trumpet, death cap, destroying angel, devil's boletus, earth ball, false morel, fly agaric, mower's mushroom, panther cap, purple boletus, satan's mushroom, shaggy milk cap, stinking parasol, sulphur tuft, verdigris agaric, woolly milk cap, yellow-staining mushroom.

music

Types of music include: acid house, ambient, ballet, ballroom, bluegrass, blues, boogie-woogie, chamber, choral, classical, country-and-western, dance, disco, Dixieland, doo-wop, drum and bass, electronic, folk, folk rock, funk, gangsta, garage, gospel, grunge, hardcore, hard rock, heavy metal, hip-hop, honky-tonk, house, incidental, instrumental, jazz, jazz-funk, jazz-pop, jazz-rock, jive, jungle, karaoke, operatic, orchestral, pop, punk rock, ragtime, rap, reggae, rhythm and blues (R & B), rock, rock and roll, sacred, ska, skiffle, soft rock, soul, swing, techno, thrash metal, trance, trip-hop. *see also* **jazz**.

musical *adj* tuneful, melodious, melodic, harmonious, dulcet, sweet-sounding, lyrical.
Ea discordant, unmusical.

Musical instruments include: balalaika, banjo, cello, double-bass, guitar, harp, hurdy-gurdy, lute, lyre, mandolin, sitar, spinet, ukulele, viola, violin, fiddle (*infml*), zither; accordion, concertina, squeeze-box (*infml*), clavichord, harmonium, harpsichord, keyboard, melodeon, organ, Wurlitzer®, piano, grand piano, Pianola®, player-piano, synthesizer, virginals; bagpipes, bassoon, bugle, clarinet, cor anglais, cornet, didgeridoo, euphonium, fife, flugelhorn, flute, French horn, harmonica, horn, kazoo, mouth-organ, oboe, Pan-pipes, piccolo, recorder, saxophone, sousaphone, trombone, trumpet, tuba; castanets, cymbal, glockenspiel, maracas, marimba, tambourine, triangle, tubular bells, xylophone; bass-drum, bongo, kettle-drum, snare-drum, tenor-drum, timpani, tom-tom.

Musical terms include: accelerando, acciaccatura, accidental, accompaniment, acoustic, adagio, ad lib, a due, affettuoso, agitato, al fine, al segno, alla breve, alla cappella, allargando, allegretto, allegro, al segno, alto, amoroso, andante, animato, appoggiatura, arco, arpeggio, arrangement, a tempo, attacca, bar, bar line, double bar line, baritone, bass, beat, bis, breve, buffo, cadence, cantabile, cantilena, chord, chromatic, clef, alto clef, bass clef, tenor clef, treble clef, coda, col canto, con brio, concert, con fuoco, con moto, consonance, contralto, counterpoint, crescendo, crotchet, cross-fingering, cue, da capo, decrescendo, demisemiquaver, descant, diatonic, diminuendo, dissonance, dolce, doloroso, dominant, dotted note, dotted rest, downbeat, drone, duplet, triplet, quadruplet, quintuplet, sextuplet, encore, ensemble, expression, finale, fine, fingerboard, flat, double flat, forte, fortissimo, fret, glissando, grave, harmonics, harmony, hemidemisemiquaver, hold, imitation, improvisation, interval, augmented interval, diminished interval, second interval, third interval, fourth interval, fifth interval, sixth interval, seventh interval, major interval, minor interval, perfect interval, intonation, key, key signature, langsam, larghetto, largo, leading note, ledger line, legato, lento, lyric, maestoso, major, manual, marcato, mediant, medley, melody, metre, mezza voce, mezzo forte, microtone, middle C, minim, minor, moderato, mode, modulation, molto, mordent, movement, mute, natural, non troppo, note, obbligato, octave, orchestra, ostinato, part, pause, pedal point, pentatonic, perdendo, phrase, pianissimo, piano, piece, pitch, pizzicato, presto, quarter tone, quaver, rallentando, recital, refrain, resolution, rest, rhythm, ritenuto, root, scale, score, semibreve, semiquaver, semitone, semplice, sempre, senza, sequence, sforzando, shake, sharp, double sharp, slur, smorzando, solo, soprano, sostenuto, sotto voce, spiritoso, staccato, staff, stave, subdominant, subito, submediant, sul ponticello, supertonic, swell, syncopation, tablature, tacet, tanto, tempo, tenor, tenuto, theme, tie, timbre, time signature, compound time, simple time, two-two time, three-four time, four-four time, six-eight time, tone, tonic sol-fa, transposition, treble, tremolo, triad, trill, double trill, tune, tuning, turn, tutti, upbeat, unison, vibrato, vigoroso, virtuoso, vivace.

musician

Musicians include: instrumentalist, accompanist, performer, player; bugler, busker, cellist, clarinettist, drummer, flautist, fiddler, guitarist, harpist, oboist, organist, pianist, piper, soloist, trombonist, trumpeter, violinist; singer, vocalist, balladeer, diva, prima donna; conductor, maestro; band, orchestra, group, backing group, ensemble, chamber orchestra, choir, duo, duet, trio, quartet, quintet, sextet, octet, nonet.

must *n* necessity, prerequisite, obligation, requirement, stipulation, essential, fundamental, imperative, duty, basic, provision, sine qua non, requisite (*fml*).

muster *v* assemble, convene (*fml*), gather, call together, mobilize, round up, marshal, come together, congregate, collect, group, meet, rally, mass, throng, call up, summon, enrol.

musty *adj* mouldy, mildewy, stale, stuffy, fusty, dank, airless, decayed, smelly.

mutation *n* change, alteration, variation, modification, transformation, deviation, anomaly, evolution.

mute *adj* silent, dumb, voiceless, wordless, speechless, mum (*infml*), unspoken, noiseless, unexpressed, unpronounced.
Ea vocal, talkative.
➤ *v* tone down, subdue, muffle, lower, moderate, dampen, deaden, soften, silence.

mutilate *v* **1** MAIM, injure, dismember, disable, disfigure, lame, mangle, cut to pieces, cut up, butcher. **2** SPOIL, mar, damage, cut, censor.

mutinous *adj* rebellious, insurgent, insubordinate, disobedient, seditious, revolutionary, riotous, subversive, bolshie (*infml*), unruly.
Ea obedient, compliant.

mutiny *n* rebellion, insurrection, revolt, revolution, rising, uprising, insubordination, disobedience, defiance, resistance, riot, strike.
➤ *v* rebel, revolt, rise up, resist, protest, disobey, strike.

mutter *v* **1** MUMBLE, murmur, rumble. **2** COMPLAIN, grumble, grouse (*infml*).

mutual *adj* reciprocal, shared, common, joint, interchangeable, interchanged, exchanged, complementary.

muzzle *v* restrain, stifle, suppress, gag, mute, silence, censor, choke.

myopic *adj* **1** *myopic vision*: short-sighted, near-sighted, purblind, half-blind. **2** *myopic attitudes*: short-sighted, unwise, ill-considered, thoughtless, narrow, narrow-minded, localized, parochial, short-term, imprudent (*fml*), uncircumspect (*fml*).
Ea 2 far-sighted.

myriad *adj* countless, innumerable, limitless, immeasurable, incalculable, untold, boundless, multitudinous (*fml*).
➤ *n* multitude, throng, horde, army, flood,

host, swarm, sea, scores (*infml*), thousands (*infml*), millions (*infml*), zillions (*infml*), mountain (*infml*).

mysterious *adj* enigmatic, cryptic, mystifying, inexplicable, incomprehensible, puzzling, perplexing, obscure, strange, unfathomable, unsearchable, mystical, baffling, curious, hidden, insoluble, secret, weird, secretive, veiled, dark, furtive.
🖛 straightforward, comprehensible.

mystery *n* 1 ENIGMA, puzzle, secret, riddle, conundrum, question.
2 OBSCURITY, secrecy, ambiguity.

mystical *adj* occult, arcane, mystic, esoteric, supernatural, paranormal, transcendental, metaphysical, hidden, mysterious.

mystify *v* puzzle, bewilder, baffle, perplex, confound, confuse.

mystique *n* mystery, secrecy, fascination, glamour, magic, spell, charm, appeal, charisma, awe.

myth *n* legend, fable, fairytale, allegory, parable, saga, story, fiction, tradition, fancy, fantasy, superstition.

mythical *adj* 1 MYTHOLOGICAL, legendary, fabled, fairy-tale. 2 FICTITIOUS, imaginary, made-up, invented, make-believe, nonexistent, unreal, pretended, fanciful.

🖛 1 historical. 2 actual, real.

mythological *adj* legendary, mythical, traditional, mythic, fabled, fairy-tale, fictitious, fabulous (*fml*), folkloric (*fml*).

Mythological creatures and spirits include: abominable snowman (or yeti), afrit, basilisk, bunyip, centaur, Cerberus, Chimera, cockatrice, Cyclops, dragon, dryad, dwarf, Echidna, elf, Erinyes (or Furies), Fafnir, fairy, faun, Frankenstein's monster, genie, Geryon, giant, gnome, goblin, golem, Gorgon, griffin, hamadryad, Harpies, hippocampus, hippogriff, hobgoblin, imp, kelpie, kraken, lamia, leprechaun, Lilith, Loch Ness monster, mermaid, merman, Minotaur, naiad, nereid, nymph, ogre, ogress, orc, oread, Pegasus, phoenix, pixie, roc, salamander, sasquatch, satyr, sea serpent, Siren, Sphinx, sylph, troll, Typhoeus, unicorn, werewolf, wivern.

mythology *n* legend, myths, lore, tradition(s), folklore, folk-tales, tales.

Nn

nab *v* catch, arrest, capture, grab, seize, snatch, apprehend (*fml*), collar (*infml*), nail (*infml*), nick (*sl*), nobble (*infml*).

nadir *n* low point, lowest point, minimum, zero, bottom, depths, all-time low, low-watermark, rock bottom (*infml*).
F3 zenith, peak, acme (*fml*), apex (*fml*).

nag¹ *v* scold, berate, irritate, annoy, pester, badger, plague, torment, harass, henpeck (*infml*), harry, vex, upbraid, goad.

nag² *n* horse, hack, jade, keffel, rip, Rosinante, plug (*infml*).

nagging *adj* **1** *a nagging pain*: continuous, critical, distressing, upsetting, worrying, irritating, niggling, painful, aching, persistent. **2** SCOLDING, shrewish, critical, tormenting, moaning (*infml*), nit-picking (*infml*).

nail *v* fasten, attach, secure, pin, tack, fix, join.
➤ *n* **1** FASTENER, pin, tack, spike, skewer. **2** TALON, claw.

naïve *adj* unsophisticated, ingenuous, innocent, unaffected, artless, guileless, simple, natural, childlike, open, trusting, unsuspecting, gullible, credulous, wide-eyed.
F3 experienced, sophisticated.

naïvety *n* ingenuousness, innocence, inexperience, naturalness, simplicity, openness, frankness, gullibility, credulity.
F3 experience, sophistication.

naked *adj* **1** NUDE, bare, undressed, unclothed, uncovered, stripped, stark-naked, disrobed, denuded, in the altogether (*infml*). **2** OPEN, unadorned, undisguised, unqualified, plain, stark, overt, blatant, exposed.
F3 **1** clothed, covered. **2** concealed.

namby-pamby *adj* sentimental, feeble, spineless, weak, weedy, wet, wishy-washy, mawkish, vapid, maudlin, insipid, colourless, anaemic, pretty-pretty, prim, prissy.

name *n* **1** TITLE, appellation (*fml*), designation, label, term, epithet, handle (*infml*). **2** REPUTATION, character, repute, renown, esteem (*fml*), eminence, fame, honour, distinction, note.

Kinds of name include: full name, first name, given name, Christian name, baptismal name, second name, middle name; surname, family name, last name; maiden name; nickname, sobriquet, agnomen, pet name, term of endearment, diminutive; false name, pseudonym, alias, stage-name, nom-de-plume, assumed name, pen-name; proper name; place name; brand name, trademark; code name.

➤ *v* **1** CALL, christen, baptize, term, title, entitle, dub, label, style. **2** DESIGNATE, nominate, cite, choose, select, specify, classify, commission, appoint.

named *adj* called, known as, by the name of, labelled, termed, titled, entitled, dubbed, styled, baptized, christened, identified, designated, mentioned, chosen, picked, selected, singled out, specified, classified, commissioned, cited, nominated, appointed, dit, denominated (*fml*).
F3 nameless.

nameless *adj* **1** UNNAMED, anonymous, unidentified, unknown, obscure. **2** INEXPRESSIBLE, indescribable, unutterable, unspeakable, unmentionable, unheard-of.
F3 **1** named.

namely *adv* that is, ie, specifically, viz, that is to say.

nap¹ *v* doze, sleep, snooze (*infml*), nod (off), drop off, rest, kip (*infml*).
➤ *n* rest, sleep, siesta, catnap, forty winks (*infml*), kip (*infml*).

nap² *n* down, pile, weave, shag, surface, texture, fibre, grain, fuzz, downiness.

nappy *n* diaper, napkin, towel, serviette.

narcissism *n* self-love, egotism, egomania, egocentricity, self-centredness, self-regard, self-conceit, conceit, vanity.

narcotic *n* drug, opiate, sedative, tranquillizer, painkiller.
➤ *adj* soporific, hypnotic, sedative, analgesic, pain-killing, numbing, dulling, calming, stupefying.

narrate *v* tell, relate, report, recount, describe, unfold, recite, state, detail.

narration *n* account, story, tale, description, explanation, telling, report, statement, history, chronicle, detail, sketch, portrayal, reading, recital, story-telling, voice-over, rehearsal (*fml*), recountal (*fml*).

narrative *n* story, tale, chronicle, account, history, report, detail, statement.

narrator *n* storyteller, chronicler, reporter, raconteur, commentator, writer.

narrow *adj* 1 TIGHT, confined, constricted, cramped, slim, slender, thin, fine, tapering, close. 2 LIMITED, restricted, circumscribed. 3 NARROW-MINDED, biased, bigoted, exclusive, dogmatic.
☒ 1 wide. 2 broad. 3 broad-minded, tolerant.
➤ *v* constrict, limit, tighten, reduce, diminish, simplify.
☒ broaden, widen, increase.

narrowly *adv* 1 BARELY, scarcely, just, only just, by a hair's breadth (*infml*), by a whisker (*infml*). 2 CAREFULLY, closely, strictly, scrutinizingly, precisely, exactly, painstakingly.

narrow-minded *adj* illiberal, biased, bigoted, prejudiced, reactionary, small-minded, conservative, intolerant, insular, petty.
☒ broad-minded.

nastiness *n* 1 UNPLEASANTNESS, repulsiveness, horribleness, disagreeableness, offensiveness, filth, dirtiness, defilement, filthiness, foulness, impurity, pollution, squalor, uncleanliness, unsavouriness. 2 OBSCENITY, indecency, filth, pornography, porn (*infml*), smuttiness (*infml*). 3 MALICE, spitefulness, spite, viciousness, meanness, malevolence (*fml*).

nasty *adj* 1 UNPLEASANT, repellent, repugnant (*fml*), repulsive, objectionable, offensive, disgusting, sickening, horrible, filthy, foul, polluted, obscene. 2 MALICIOUS, mean, spiteful, vicious, malevolent (*fml*).
☒ 1 agreeable, pleasant, decent. 2 benevolent, kind.

nation *n* country, people, race, state, realm, population, community, society.

national *adj* countrywide, civil, domestic, nationwide, state, internal, general, governmental, public, widespread, social.

➤ *n* citizen, native, subject, inhabitant, resident.

nationalism *n* patriotism, allegiance, loyalty, chauvinism, xenophobia, jingoism.

nationality *n* race, nation, ethnic group, birth, tribe, clan.

nationwide *adj* national, countrywide, general, overall, extensive, widespread, comprehensive, state, coast-to-coast.

native *adj* 1 LOCAL, indigenous, domestic, vernacular, home, aboriginal, autochthonous (*fml*), mother, original. 2 INBORN, inherent, innate, inbred, hereditary, inherited, congenital, instinctive, natural, intrinsic, natal.
➤ *n* inhabitant, resident, national, citizen, dweller, aborigine, autochthon (*fml*).
☒ foreigner, outsider, stranger.

natter *v* chat, chatter, gossip, talk, confabulate, blather (*infml*), blether (*infml*), confab (*infml*), gab (*infml*), gabble (*infml*), jabber (*infml*), jaw (*infml*), prattle (*infml*), rabbit (on) (*infml*), chinwag (*infml*), witter (*infml*).
➤ *n* chat, conversation, talk, gossip, prattle, chit-chat, blather (*infml*), blether (*infml*), chinwag (*infml*), confab (*infml*), gab (*infml*), gabble (*infml*), jaw (*infml*).

natural *adj* 1 ORDINARY, normal, common, regular, standard, usual, typical. 2 INNATE, inborn, instinctive, intuitive, inherent, congenital, native, indigenous. 3 GENUINE, pure, authentic, unrefined, unprocessed, unmixed, real. 4 SINCERE, unaffected, genuine, artless, ingenuous, guileless, simple, unsophisticated, open, candid, spontaneous.
☒ 1 unnatural. 2 acquired. 3 artificial. 4 affected, disingenuous.

naturalistic *adj* natural, realistic, true-to-life, representational, lifelike, graphic, real-life, photographic.

naturalize *v* introduce, adopt, incorporate, familiarize, acclimatize, accept, assimilate, accustom, adapt, enfranchise, domesticate, acculturate (*fml*), habituate (*fml*).

naturally *adv* 1 OF COURSE, as a matter of course, simply, obviously, logically, typically, certainly, absolutely. 2 NORMALLY, genuinely, instinctively, spontaneously.

nature *n* 1 ESSENCE, quality, character, features, disposition, attributes, personality, make-up, constitution,

temperament, mood, outlook, temper.
2 KIND, sort, type, description, category,
variety, style, species. **3** UNIVERSE, world,
creation, earth, environment.
4 COUNTRYSIDE, country, landscape,
scenery, natural history.

naughty *adj* **1** BAD, badly behaved,
mischievous, disobedient, wayward,
exasperating, playful, roguish. **2**
INDECENT, obscene, bawdy, risqué, smutty
(*infml*).
F3 **1** good, well-behaved. **2** decent.

nausea *n* **1** VOMITING, sickness, retching,
queasiness, biliousness. **2** DISGUST,
revulsion, loathing, repugnance.

nauseate *v* sicken, disgust, revolt, repel,
offend, turn one's stomach (*infml*).

nautical *adj* naval, marine, maritime, sea-
going, seafaring, sailing, oceanic, boating.

Nautical terms include: afloat, aft, air-sea
rescue, amidships, ballast, beam, bear away,
beat, bow-wave, breeches buoy, broach,
capsize, cargo, cast off, chandler,
circumnavigate, coastguard, compass
bearing, convoy, course, cruise, current,
Davy Jones's locker, dead reckoning,
deadweight, disembark, dock, dockyard,
dry dock, ebb tide, embark, ferry, fleet, float,
flotilla, flotsam, foghorn, fore, foreshore, go
about, gybe, harbour, harbour-bar, harbour
dues, harbour-master, haven, head to wind,
heave to, heavy swell, heel, helm, high tide,
inflatable life-raft, jetsam, jetty, knot, launch,
lay a course, lay up, lee, lee shore, leeward,
life buoy, life-jacket, life-rocket, list, low tide,
make fast, marina, marine, maroon, mayday,
moor, mooring, mutiny, navigation, neap tide,
on board, pitch and toss, plane, put in, put to
sea, quay, reach, reef, refit, ride out, riptide,
roll, row, run, run aground, run before the
wind, salvage, seafaring, sea lane, sea legs,
seamanship, seasick, seaworthy, set sail,
sheet in, shipping, shipping lane, ship's
company, ship water, shipwreck, shipyard,
shore leave, sink, slip anchor, slipway,
stevedore, stowaway, tack, tide, trim, voyage,
wake, wash, watch, wave, weather, weigh
anchor, wharf, wreck. *see also* **sail**.

naval *adj* marine, maritime, nautical, sea,
seagoing, seafaring.

navigable *adj* passable, crossable,
negotiable, open, clear, unblocked,
unobstructed, surmountable, traversable
(*fml*).

navigate *v* steer, drive, direct, pilot, guide,
handle, manoeuvre, cruise, sail, skipper,
voyage, journey, cross, helm, plot, plan.

navigation *n* sailing, steering, cruising,
voyaging, seamanship, helmsmanship.

Navigational aids include: astro-
navigation, bell buoy, channel-marker buoy,
chart, chronometer, conical buoy, Decca®
navigator system, depth gauge, dividers,
echo-sounder, flux-gate compass, Global
Positioning System (GPS), gyrocompass,
lighthouse, lightship, log, loran (long-range
radio navigation), magnetic compass, marker
buoy, nautical table, parallel ruler, pilot, radar,
sectored leading-light, sextant, VHF radio.

navy *n* fleet, ships, flotilla, armada,
warships.

near¹ *adj* **1** NEARBY, close, bordering,
adjacent, adjoining, alongside,
neighbouring. **2** IMMINENT, impending,
forthcoming, coming, approaching.
3 DEAR, familiar, close, related, intimate,
akin.
F3 **1** far. **2** distant. **3** remote.

near² *adv* nearby, close, close by, not far
away, at close quarters, alongside, within
reach, at hand, within close range, a stone's
throw away (*infml*).
➤ *prep* nearby, close to, next to, bordering
on, adjacent to, alongside, in the
neighbourhood of, within reach of,
adjoining (*fml*), contiguous to (*fml*).
➤ *v* approach, get closer to, come nearer/
closer, advance towards, come/move
towards, draw near to, close in on, cling to.
F3 withdraw, keep one's distance.

nearby *adj* near, neighbouring, adjoining,
adjacent, accessible, convenient, handy.
F3 faraway.
➤ *adv* near, within reach, at close quarters,
close at hand, not far away.

nearly *adv* almost, practically, virtually,
closely, approximately, more or less, as
good as, just about, roughly, well-nigh.
F3 completely, totally.

neat *adj* **1** TIDY, orderly, smart, spruce, trim,
clean, spick-and-span (*infml*), shipshape.
2 DEFT, clever, adroit, skilful, expert.
3 UNDILUTED, unmixed, unadulterated,
straight, pure.
F3 **1** untidy. **2** clumsy. **3** diluted.

nebulous *adj* vague, hazy, imprecise,
indefinite, indistinct, cloudy, misty,
obscure, uncertain, unclear, dim,

ambiguous, confused, fuzzy, shapeless, amorphous.

∄ clear.

necessarily *adv* inevitably, incontrovertibly, certainly, compulsorily, by definition, inescapably, of necessity, inexorably, of course, naturally, consequently, automatically, therefore, thus, accordingly, axiomatically, willy-nilly, ineluctably (*fml*), perforce (*fml*).

necessary *adj* needed, required, essential, compulsory, indispensable, vital, imperative, mandatory (*fml*), obligatory, needful, unavoidable, inevitable, inescapable, inexorable, certain.

∄ unnecessary, inessential, unimportant.

necessitate *v* require, involve, entail, call for, demand, oblige, force, constrain, compel.

necessity *n* **1** REQUIREMENT, obligation, prerequisite, essential, fundamental, need, want, compulsion, demand. **2** INDISPENSABILITY, inevitability, needfulness. **3** POVERTY, destitution, hardship.

need *v* miss, lack, want, require, demand, call for, necessitate, have need of, have to, crave.

➤ *n* **1** *a need for caution*: call, demand, obligation, requirement. **2** *the country's needs*: essential, necessity, requisite, prerequisite, desideratum. **3** *a need for equipment*: want, lack, insufficiency, inadequacy, neediness, shortage.

needle *n* **1** *needle and thread*: knitting needle, pin, nib, bodkin, hypodermic needle, stylus. **2** POINTER, indicator, arrow, marker, hand. **3** THORN, prickle, spike, splinter, barb, spine, quill, briar, bristle, bramble, spicule (*fml*).

➤ *v* annoy, irritate, harass, pester, goad, spur, provoke, ruffle, prick, rile, bait, prod, nag, irk, taunt, torment, sting, aggravate (*infml*), nettle (*infml*), niggle (*infml*), wind up (*infml*), cheese off (*infml*), piss off (*sl*).

needless *adj* unnecessary, gratuitous, uncalled-for, unwanted, redundant, superfluous, useless, pointless, purposeless.

∄ necessary, essential.

needy *adj* poor, destitute, impoverished, penniless, disadvantaged, deprived, poverty-stricken, underprivileged.

∄ affluent, wealthy, well-off.

negate *v* **1** NULLIFY (*fml*), annul, cancel, invalidate, undo, countermand (*fml*), abrogate (*fml*), neutralize, quash, retract (*fml*), reverse, revoke (*fml*), rescind, wipe out, void, repeal. **2** DENY, contradict, oppose, disprove, refute, repudiate.

∄ **2** affirm.

negation *n* **1** CANCELLATION, repeal, neutralization, veto, disavowal (*fml*), nullification (*fml*), abrogation (*fml*), countermanding (*fml*). **2** DENIAL, contradiction, rejection, renunciation, disclaimer. **3** OPPOSITE, reverse, contrary, inverse (*fml*), antithesis (*fml*), converse (*fml*).

∄ **2** affirmation.

negative *adj* **1** CONTRADICTORY, contrary, denying, opposing, invalidating, neutralizing, nullifying, annulling. **2** UNCO-OPERATIVE, cynical, pessimistic, unenthusiastic, uninterested, unwilling.

∄ **1** affirmative, positive. **2** constructive, positive.

➤ *n* contradiction, denial, opposite, refusal.

neglect *v* **1** DISREGARD, ignore, leave alone, abandon, pass by, rebuff, scorn, disdain, slight, spurn. **2** FORGET, fail (in), omit, overlook, let slide, shirk, skimp.

∄ **1** cherish, appreciate. **2** remember.

➤ *n* negligence, disregard, carelessness, failure, inattention, indifference, slackness, dereliction of duty, forgetfulness, heedlessness, oversight, slight, disrespect.

∄ care, attention, concern.

neglected *adj* uncared-for, disregarded, abandoned, derelict, overgrown, uncultivated, unmaintained, untended, untilled, unweeded, unhusbanded, underestimated, undervalued, unappreciated.

∄ cherished, treasured.

neglectful *adj* uncaring, careless, inattentive, disregardful, forgetful, thoughtless, unmindful, indifferent, lax, negligent, oblivious, heedless (*fml*), remiss (*fml*), sloppy (*infml*).

∄ attentive, careful.

negligence *n* inattentiveness, carelessness, laxity, neglect, slackness, thoughtlessness, forgetfulness, indifference, omission, oversight, disregard, failure, default.

∄ attentiveness, care, regard.

negligent *adj* neglectful, inattentive, remiss, thoughtless, casual, lax, careless, indifferent, offhand, nonchalant, slack, uncaring, forgetful.
ǝ attentive, careful, scrupulous.

negligible *adj* unimportant, insignificant, small, imperceptible, trifling, trivial, minor, minute.
ǝ significant.

negotiable *adj* **1** DEBATABLE, arguable, questionable, contestable, open to discussion/question, undecided, unsettled. **2** NAVIGABLE, passable, crossable, open, clear, unblocked, unobstructed, surmountable, traversable (*fml*).
ǝ 1 non-negotiable, fixed, definite.

negotiate *v* **1** CONFER, deal, mediate, arbitrate, bargain, arrange, transact, work out, manage, settle, consult, contract. **2** GET ROUND, cross, surmount, traverse, pass.

negotiation *n* mediation, arbitration, debate, discussion, diplomacy, bargaining, transaction.

negotiator *n* arbitrator, go-between, mediator, intermediary, moderator, intercessor, adjudicator, broker, ambassador, diplomat.

neighbourhood *n* district, locality, vicinity, community, locale, environs, confines, surroundings, region, proximity.

neighbouring *adj* adjacent, bordering, near, nearby, adjoining, connecting, next, surrounding.
ǝ distant, remote.

neighbourly *adj* sociable, friendly, amiable, kind, helpful, genial, hospitable, obliging, considerate, companionable.

nerve *n* **1** COURAGE, bravery, mettle, pluck, guts (*infml*), spunk (*infml*), spirit, vigour, intrepidity, daring, fearlessness, firmness, resolution, fortitude, steadfastness, will, determination, endurance, force. **2** (*infml*) AUDACITY, impudence, cheek (*infml*), effrontery, brazenness, boldness, chutzpah (*infml*), impertinence, insolence.
ǝ 1 weakness. **2** timidity.

nerve-racking *adj* harrowing, distressing, trying, stressful, tense, maddening, worrying, difficult, frightening.

nerves *n* nervousness, tension, stress, anxiety, worry, strain, fretfulness.

nervous *adj* highly-strung, excitable, anxious, agitated, nervy (*infml*), on edge, edgy, jumpy (*infml*), jittery (*infml*), tense, fidgety, apprehensive, neurotic, shaky, uneasy, worried, flustered, fearful.
ǝ calm, relaxed.

nest *n* **1** BREEDING-GROUND, den, roost, eyrie, lair. **2** RETREAT, refuge, haunt, hideaway.

nestle *v* snuggle, huddle, cuddle, curl up.

net[1] *n* mesh, web, network, netting, open-work, lattice, lace.
➤ *v* catch, trap, capture, bag, ensnare, entangle, nab (*infml*).

net[2] *adj* nett, clear, after tax, final, lowest.
➤ *v* bring in, clear, earn, make, realize, receive, gain, obtain, accumulate.

network *n* system, organization, arrangement, structure, interconnections, complex, grid, net, maze, mesh, labyrinth, channels, circuitry, convolution, grill, tracks.

neurosis *n* disorder, affliction, abnormality, disturbance, derangement, deviation, obsession, phobia.

neurotic *adj* disturbed, maladjusted, anxious, nervous, overwrought, unstable, unhealthy, deviant, abnormal, compulsive, obsessive.

neuter *v* castrate, emasculate, doctor, geld, spay.

neutral *adj* **1** IMPARTIAL, uncommitted, unbiased, non-aligned, disinterested, unprejudiced, undecided, non-partisan, non-committal, objective, indifferent, dispassionate, even-handed. **2** DULL, nondescript, colourless, drab, expressionless, indistinct.
ǝ 1 biased, partisan. **2** colourful.

neutrality *n* unbiasedness, impartiality, impartialness, detachment, disinterest, disinterestedness, non-alignment, non-intervention, non-involvement.

neutralize *v* counteract, counterbalance, offset, negate, cancel, nullify, invalidate, undo, frustrate.

never *adv* at no time, not ever, not for a moment, under no circumstances, not at all, on no account, not on your life (*infml*), not on your nellie (*infml*), when pigs fly (*infml*), no way (*infml*), not in a month of Sundays (*infml*), not in a million years (*infml*).
ǝ always.

never-ending *adj* everlasting, eternal, non-stop, perpetual, unceasing, uninterrupted, unremitting, interminable, incessant, unbroken, permanent, persistent, unchanging, relentless. 🖪 fleeting, transitory.

nevertheless *adv* nonetheless, notwithstanding (*fml*), still, anyway, even so, yet, however, anyhow, but, regardless.

new *adj* 1 NOVEL, original, fresh, different, unfamiliar, unusual, brand-new, mint, unknown, unused, virgin, newborn. 2 MODERN, contemporary, current, latest, recent, up-to-date, up-to-the-minute (*infml*), topical, trendy (*infml*), ultra-modern, advanced, newfangled (*infml*). 3 CHANGED, altered, modernized, improved, renewed, restored, redesigned. 4 ADDED, additional, extra, more, supplementary. 🖪 1 usual. 2 outdated, out of date. 3 old.

newcomer *n* immigrant, alien, foreigner, incomer, colonist, settler, arrival, outsider, stranger, novice, beginner.

newly *adv* recently, lately, latterly, just, freshly, of late, afresh, anew.

news *n* report, account, information, intelligence, dispatch, communiqué, bulletin, gossip, hearsay, rumour, statement, story, word, tidings, latest, release, scandal, revelation, lowdown (*infml*), exposé, disclosure, gen (*infml*), advice.

newsworthy *adj* reportable, hitting/making the headlines, important, significant, interesting, remarkable, stimulating, notable, noteworthy, arresting, unusual.

next *adj* 1 ADJACENT, adjoining, neighbouring, nearest, closest. 2 FOLLOWING, subsequent, succeeding, ensuing, later. 🖪 2 previous, preceding. ➤ *adv* afterwards, subsequently, later, then.

nibble *n* bite, morsel, taste, titbit, bit, crumb, snack, piece. ➤ *v* bite, eat, peck, pick at, nosh (*sl*), munch, gnaw.

nice *adj* 1 PLEASANT, agreeable, delightful, charming, likable, attractive, good, kind, friendly, well-mannered, polite, respectable. 2 SUBTLE, delicate, fine, fastidious, discriminating, scrupulous, precise, exact, accurate, careful, strict.

🖪 1 nasty, disagreeable, unpleasant. 2 careless.

nicely *adv* satisfactorily, well, agreeably, delightfully, pleasurably, pleasantly, pleasingly, respectably, properly. 🖪 unpleasantly, disagreeably, nastily.

nicety *n* 1 DELICACY, refinement, subtlety, distinction, nuance. 2 PRECISION, accuracy, meticulousness, scrupulousness, minuteness, finesse.

niche *n* 1 RECESS, alcove, hollow, nook, cubby-hole, corner, opening. 2 POSITION, place, vocation, calling, métier, slot.

nick *n* 1 NOTCH, indentation, chip, cut, groove, dent, scar, scratch, mark. 2 (*sl*) PRISON, jail, police station. ➤ *v* 1 NOTCH, cut, dent, indent, chip, score, scratch, scar, mark, damage, snick. 2 (*sl*) STEAL, pilfer, knock off (*infml*), pinch (*infml*).

nickname *n* pet name, sobriquet, epithet, diminutive.

niggardly *adj* 1 MEAN, miserly, close, ungenerous, ungiving, sparing, grudging, hard-fisted, parsimonious (*fml*), stingy (*infml*), tight-fisted (*infml*), cheese-paring (*infml*). 2 MEAGRE, small, miserable, scanty, skimpy, paltry, inadequate, insufficient, measly (*infml*). 🖪 1 generous. 2 bountiful.

niggle *v* 1 BOTHER, worry, trouble, annoy, irritate, upset, bug (*infml*). 2 NAG, criticize, keep on at, pick on, complain, moan (*infml*), carp, quibble, nit-pick (*infml*), hassle (*infml*), henpeck (*infml*).

night *n* night-time, darkness, dark, dead of night. 🖪 day, daytime.

nightfall *n* sunset, dusk, twilight, evening, gloaming. 🖪 dawn, sunrise.

nightmare *n* 1 BAD DREAM, hallucination. 2 ORDEAL, horror, torment, trial.

nil *n* nothing, zero, none, nought, naught, love, duck, zilch (*sl*).

nimble *adj* agile, active, lively, sprightly, spry, smart, quick, brisk, nippy (*infml*), deft, alert, light-footed, prompt, ready, swift, quick-witted. 🖪 clumsy, slow.

nip[1] *v* bite, pinch, squeeze, snip, clip, tweak, catch, grip, nibble.

nip[2] *n* dram, draught, shot, swallow, mouthful, drop, sip, taste, portion.

nit-picking adj quibbling, carping, finicky, fussy, hair-splitting (infml), hypercritical, pedantic, captious, cavilling.

no adv not at all, not really, of course not, absolutely not, most certainly not, no thanks, under no circumstances, no way (infml), nope (infml), not on your life (infml), over my dead body (infml).

nobility n **1** NOBLENESS, dignity, grandeur, illustriousness, stateliness, majesty, magnificence, eminence, excellence, superiority, uprightness, honour, virtue, worthliness. **2** ARISTOCRACY, peerage, nobles, gentry, elite, lords, high society.
☒ **1** baseness. **2** proletariat.

> Titles of the nobility include: aristocrat, baron, baroness, baronet, count, countess, dame, dowager, duchess, duke, earl, grand duke, governor, knight, lady, laird, liege, liege lord, life peer, lord, marchioness, marquess, marquis, noble, nobleman, noblewoman, peer, peeress, ruler, seigneur, squire, thane, viscount, viscountess.

noble n aristocrat, peer, lord, lady, nobleman, noblewoman.
☒ commoner.
➤ adj **1** ARISTOCRATIC, high-born, titled, high-ranking, patrician, blue-blooded (infml). **2** MAGNIFICENT, magnanimous, splendid, stately, generous, dignified, distinguished, eminent, grand, great, honoured, honourable, imposing, impressive, majestic, virtuous, worthy, excellent, elevated, fine, gentle.
☒ **1** low-born. **2** ignoble, base, contemptible.

nobody n no-one, nothing, nonentity, menial, cipher.
☒ somebody.

nod v **1** GESTURE, indicate, sign, signal, salute, acknowledge. **2** AGREE, assent. **3** SLEEP, doze, drowse, nap.
➤ n gesture, indication, sign, signal, salute, greeting, beck, acknowledgement.

noise n sound, din, racket, row, clamour, clash, clatter, commotion, outcry, hubbub, uproar, cry, blare, talk, pandemonium, tumult, babble.
☒ quiet, silence.
➤ v report, rumour, publicize, announce, circulate.

noiseless adj silent, inaudible, soundless, quiet, mute, still, hushed.
☒ loud, noisy.

noisy adj loud, deafening, ear-splitting, clamorous, piercing, vocal, vociferous, tumultuous, boisterous, obstreperous.
☒ quiet, silent, peaceful.

nomad n traveller, wanderer, itinerant, rambler, roamer, rover, migrant.

nomadic adj travelling, itinerant, wandering, roaming, migrant, migratory, drifting, roving, roaming, gypsy, unsettled, vagrant, peregrinating (fml), peripatetic (fml).

nomenclature n naming, classification, vocabulary, terminology, phraseology, taxonomy (fml), codification (fml), locution (fml).

nominal adj **1** TITULAR, supposed, purported, professed, ostensible, so-called, theoretical, self-styled, puppet, symbolic. **2** TOKEN, minimal, trifling, trivial, insignificant, small.
☒ **1** actual, genuine, real.

nominate v propose, choose, select, name, designate, submit, suggest, recommend, put up, present, elect, appoint, assign, commission, elevate, term.

nomination n proposal, choice, selection, submission, suggestion, recommendation, designation, election, appointment.

nominee n candidate, entrant, contestant, appointee, runner, assignee.

nonchalant adj unconcerned, detached, dispassionate, offhand, blasé, indifferent, casual, cool, collected, apathetic, careless, insouciant.
☒ concerned, careful.

non-committal adj guarded, unrevealing, cautious, wary, reserved, ambiguous, discreet, equivocal, evasive, circumspect, careful, neutral, indefinite, politic, tactful, tentative, vague.

nonconformist n dissenter, rebel, individualist, dissident, radical, protester, heretic, iconoclast, eccentric, maverick, secessionist.
☒ conformist.

nondescript adj featureless, indeterminate, undistinctive, undistinguished, unexceptional, ordinary, commonplace, plain, dull, uninspiring, uninteresting, unclassified.
☒ distinctive, remarkable.

none pron no-one, not any, not one, nobody, nil, zero.

nonentity *n* nobody, nothing, menial, cipher, mediocrity, lightweight (*infml*).
🖙 somebody.

nonetheless *adv* nevertheless, still, anyway, even so, yet, however, anyhow, but, regardless, notwithstanding (*fml*).

non-existent *adj* missing, unreal, null, legendary, mythical, fictitious, fictional, fancied, fanciful, hallucinatory, illusory, hypothetical, imaginary, imagined, fantasy, immaterial, insubstantial, chimerical (*fml*), suppositional (*fml*).
🖙 actual, existing, real.

nonplussed *adj* disconcerted, confounded, taken aback, stunned, bewildered, astonished, astounded, dumbfounded, perplexed, stumped, flabbergasted, flummoxed (*infml*), puzzled, baffled, dismayed, embarrassed.

nonsense *n* rubbish, trash, drivel, balderdash, gibberish, gobbledygook, senselessness, stupidity, silliness, foolishness, folly, rot (*infml*), blather, twaddle, ridiculousness, claptrap (*infml*), cobblers (*sl*).
🖙 sense, wisdom.

nonsensical *adj* ridiculous, meaningless, senseless, foolish, inane, irrational, silly, incomprehensible, ludicrous, absurd, fatuous, crazy (*infml*).
🖙 reasonable, sensible, logical.

non-stop *adj* never-ending, uninterrupted, continuous, incessant, constant, endless, interminable, unending, unbroken, round-the-clock, on-going.
🖙 intermittent, occasional.

nook *n* recess, alcove, corner, cranny, niche, cubby-hole, hide-out, retreat, shelter, cavity.

noon *n* midday, twelve o'clock, twelve noon, lunchtime.

norm *n* average, mean, standard, rule, pattern, criterion, model, yardstick, benchmark, measure, reference.

normal *adj* usual, standard, general, common, ordinary, conventional, average, regular, routine, typical, mainstream, natural, accustomed, well-adjusted, straight, rational, reasonable.
🖙 abnormal, irregular, peculiar.

normality *n* usualness, commonness, ordinariness, regularity, routine, conventionality, balance, adjustment, typicality, naturalness, reason, rationality.
🖙 abnormality, irregularity, peculiarity.

normally *adv* ordinarily, usually, as a rule, typically, commonly, characteristically.
🖙 abnormally, exceptionally.

nose *n* **1** *the animal's nose*: bill, neb, proboscis (*fml*), beak (*infml*), boko (*infml*), hooter (*infml*), schnozzle (*infml*), snitch (*infml*), snout (*infml*), snoot (*infml*), conk (*sl*). **2** *a nose for a good story*: sense, flair, feel, perception, instinct.
➤ *v* nudge, inch, edge, ease, push.
♦ **nose around** poke around, search, pry, snoop (*infml*), rubberneck (*infml*), poke one's nose in (*infml*).
♦ **nose out** discover, detect, find out, uncover, reveal, inquire, sniff out (*infml*).

nosedive *v* plummet, dive, drop, plunge, decline, get worse, go down, submerge, swoop.
➤ *n* plummet, dive, drop, plunge, swoop, header, purler.

nosegay *n* bouquet, posy, spray, bunch.

nosey (*infml*) *adj* inquisitive, meddlesome, prying, interfering, snooping (*infml*), curious, eavesdropping.

nostalgia *n* yearning, longing, regretfulness, remembrance, reminiscence, homesickness, pining.

nostalgic *adj* yearning, longing, wistful, emotional, regretful, sentimental, homesick.

notable *adj* noteworthy, remarkable, noticeable, striking, extraordinary, impressive, outstanding, marked, unusual, celebrated, distinguished, famous, eminent, well-known, notorious, renowned, rare.
🖙 ordinary, commonplace, usual.
➤ *n* celebrity, notability, VIP (*infml*), personage, somebody, dignitary, luminary, worthy.
🖙 nobody, nonentity.

notably *adv* markedly, noticeably, particularly, remarkably, strikingly, conspicuously, distinctly, especially, impressively, outstandingly, eminently.

notation *n* symbols, characters, code, signs, alphabet, system, script, noting, record, shorthand.

notch *n* cut, nick, indentation, incision, score, groove, cleft, mark, snip, degree, grade, step.
➤ *v* cut, nick, score, scratch, indent, mark.

note *n* **1** COMMUNICATION, letter, message, memorandum, reminder, memo (*infml*), line, jotting, record. **2** ANNOTATION,

comment, gloss, remark. **3** INDICATION, signal, token, mark, symbol. **4** EMINENCE, distinction, consequence, fame, renown, reputation. **5** HEED, attention, regard, notice, observation.
➤ *v* **1** NOTICE, observe, perceive, heed, detect, mark, remark, mention, see, witness. **2** RECORD, register, write down, enter.

noted *adj* famous, well-known, renowned, notable, celebrated, eminent, prominent, great, acclaimed, illustrious, distinguished, respected, recognized.
◼ obscure, unknown.

notes *n* jottings, record, impressions, report, sketch, outline, synopsis, draft.

noteworthy *adj* remarkable, significant, important, notable, memorable, exceptional, extraordinary, unusual, outstanding.
◼ commonplace, unexceptional, ordinary.

nothing *n* nought, zero, nothingness, zilch (*sl*), nullity, non-existence, emptiness, void, nobody, nonentity.
◼ something.

notice *v* note, remark, perceive, observe, mind, see, discern, distinguish, mark, detect, heed, spot.
◼ ignore, overlook.
➤ *n* **1** NOTIFICATION, announcement, information, declaration, communication, intelligence, news, warning, instruction. **2** ADVERTISEMENT, poster, sign, bill. **3** REVIEW, comment, criticism. **4** ATTENTION, observation, awareness, note, regard, consideration, heed.

noticeable *adj* perceptible, observable, appreciable, unmistakable, conspicuous, evident, manifest, clear, distinct, significant, striking, plain, obvious, measurable.
◼ inconspicuous, unnoticeable.

notification *n* announcement, information, notice, declaration, advice, warning, intelligence, message, publication, statement, communication.

notify *v* inform, tell, advise, announce, declare, warn, acquaint, alert, publish, disclose, reveal.

notion *n* **1** IDEA, thought, concept, conception, belief, impression, view, opinion, understanding, apprehension. **2** INCLINATION, wish, whim, fancy, caprice.

notional *adj* theoretical, abstract, imaginary, hypothetical, illusory,

conceptual, speculative, fanciful, fancied, unfounded, unreal, visionary, thematic, classificatory, ideational (*fml*).
◼ real.

notoriety *n* infamy, disrepute, dishonour, disgrace, scandal.

notorious *adj* infamous, disreputable, scandalous, dishonourable, disgraceful, ignominious, flagrant, well-known.

notwithstanding *adv, prep* nevertheless, nonetheless, although, though, even so, however, yet, despite, in spite of, regardless of.

nought *n* zero, nil, zilch (*sl*), naught, nothing, nothingness.

nourish *v* **1** NURTURE, feed, foster, care for, provide for, sustain, support, tend, nurse, maintain, cherish. **2** STRENGTHEN, encourage, promote, cultivate, stimulate.

nourishment *n* nutrition, food, sustenance, diet.

novel *adj* new, original, fresh, innovative, unfamiliar, unusual, uncommon, different, imaginative, unconventional, strange.
◼ hackneyed, familiar, ordinary.
➤ *n* fiction, story, tale, narrative, romance.

novelty *n* **1** NEWNESS, originality, freshness, innovation, unfamiliarity, uniqueness, difference, strangeness. **2** GIMMICK, gadget, trifle, memento, knick-knack, curiosity, souvenir, trinket, bauble, gimcrack.

novice *n* beginner, tiro, learner, pupil, trainee, probationer, apprentice, neophyte (*fml*), amateur, newcomer.
◼ expert.

now *adv* **1** IMMEDIATELY, at once, directly, instantly, straight away, promptly, next. **2** AT PRESENT, nowadays, these days.

nowadays *adv* at present, today, at the present time, at the moment, at this moment in time, at this time, currently, these days, in this day and age, presently (*US*).

noxious *adj* harmful, poisonous, pernicious, toxic, injurious, unhealthy, deadly, destructive, noisome (*fml*), foul.
◼ innocuous, wholesome.

nuance *n* subtlety, suggestion, shade, hint, suspicion, gradation, distinction, overtone, refinement, touch, trace, tinge, degree, nicety.

nub *n* centre, heart, core, nucleus, kernel, crux, gist, pith, point, essence.

nucleus *n* centre, heart, nub, core, focus, kernel, pivot, basis, crux.

nude *adj* naked, bare, undressed, unclothed, stripped, stark-naked, uncovered, starkers (*infml*), in one's birthday suit (*infml*).
🖝 clothed, dressed.

nudge *v, n* poke, prod, shove, dig, jog, prompt, push, elbow, bump.

nuisance *n* annoyance, inconvenience, bother, irritation, pest, pain (*infml*), drag (*infml*), bore (*infml*), problem, trial, trouble, drawback.

null *adj* void, invalid, ineffectual, useless, vain, worthless, powerless, inoperative.
🖝 valid.

nullify *v* annul, revoke (*fml*), cancel, invalidate, abrogate (*fml*), abolish, negate, rescind (*fml*), quash, repeal, counteract.
🖝 validate.

numb *adj* benumbed, insensible, unfeeling, deadened, insensitive, frozen, immobilized.
🖝 sensitive.
➤ *v* deaden, anaesthetize, freeze, immobilize, paralyse, dull, stun.
🖝 sensitize.

number *n* 1 FIGURE, numeral, digit, integer, unit. 2 TOTAL, sum, aggregate, collection, amount, quantity, several, many, company, crowd, multitude, throng, horde. 3 COPY, issue, edition, impression, volume, printing.
➤ *v* count, calculate, enumerate, reckon, total, add, compute, include.

numberless *adj* innumerable, countless, endless, uncounted, many, unnumbered, unsummed, infinite, untold, myriad, immeasurable, multitudinous (*fml*).

numeral *n* number, figure, digit, integer, unit, character, cipher.

numerous *adj* many, abundant, several, plentiful, copious, profuse, sundry.
🖝 few.

nurse *v* 1 TEND, care for, look after, treat. 2 BREAST-FEED, feed, suckle, nurture, nourish. 3 PRESERVE, sustain, support, cherish, encourage, keep, foster, promote.

Nurses include: charge nurse, children's nurse, dental nurse, district nurse, healthcare assistant, health visitor, home nurse, Iain Rennie nurse, locality manager, Macmillan nurse, matron, midwife, nanny, night nurse, night sister, nursemaid, nursery nurse, nurse tutor, occupational health nurse, psychiatric nurse, Registered General Nurse (RGN), school nurse, sister, staff nurse, State Enrolled Nurse (SEN), State Registered Nurse (SRN), theatre sister, ward sister, wet nurse.

nurture *n* 1 FOOD, nourishment. 2 REARING, upbringing, training, care, cultivation, development, education, discipline.
➤ *v* 1 FEED, nourish, nurse, tend, care for, foster, support, sustain. 2 BRING UP, rear, cultivate, develop, educate, instruct, train, school, discipline.

nut

Varieties of nut include: almond, beech nut, brazil nut, cashew, chestnut, cobnut, coconut, filbert, hazelnut, macadamia, monkey nut, peanut, pecan, pistachio, walnut.

nutrition *n* food, nourishment, sustenance.

nutritious *adj* nourishing, nutritive, wholesome, healthful, health-giving, good, beneficial, strengthening, substantial, invigorating.
🖝 bad, unwholesome.

Oo

oaf *n* lout, boor, dolt, yahoo, barbarian, gawk, island, sanctuary, retreat.

oaf *n* lout, boor, dolt, yahoo, barbarian, gawk, lubber, clod (*infml*), hick (*infml*), hobbledehoy (*infml*), slob (*infml*), yobbo (*infml*), bumpkin (*infml*).

oasis *n* 1 SPRING, watering-hole. 2 REFUGE, haven, island, sanctuary, retreat.

oath *n* 1 vow, pledge, promise, word, affirmation, assurance, word of honour. 2 CURSE, imprecation, swear-word, profanity, expletive, blasphemy.

obedient *adj* compliant, docile, acquiescent, submissive, tractable, yielding, dutiful, law-abiding, deferential, respectful, subservient, observant.
E3 disobedient, rebellious, wilful.

obelisk *n* pillar, column, monument, memorial, needle.

obese *adj* fat, overweight, tubby, stout, big, large, portly, fleshy, round, well-endowed, paunchy, ponderous, plump, podgy, chubby, roly-poly, heavy, bulky, outsize, corpulent (*fml*), rotund (*fml*), gross (*infml*), flabby (*infml*).
E3 skinny, slender, thin.

obesity *n* fatness, overweight, corpulence, stoutness, grossness, plumpness, portliness, bulk.
E3 thinness, slenderness, skinniness.

obey *v* 1 COMPLY (*fml*), submit, surrender, yield, be ruled by, bow to, take orders from, defer (to), give way, follow, observe, abide by, adhere to, conform, heed, keep, mind, respond. 2 CARRY OUT, discharge, execute, act upon, fulfil, perform.
E3 1 disobey.

object¹ *n* 1 THING, entity, article, body. 2 AIM, objective, purpose, goal, target, intention, motive, end, reason, point, design. 3 TARGET, recipient, butt, victim.

object² *v* protest, oppose, demur, take exception, disapprove, refuse, complain, rebut, repudiate.
E3 agree, acquiesce.

objection *n* protest, dissent, disapproval, opposition, demur, complaint, challenge, scruple.
E3 agreement, assent.

objectionable *adj* unacceptable,

unpleasant, offensive, obnoxious, repugnant (*fml*), disagreeable, abhorrent, detestable, deplorable, despicable.
E3 acceptable.

objective *adj* impartial, unbiased, detached, unprejudiced, open-minded, equitable, dispassionate, even-handed, neutral, disinterested, just, fair.
E3 subjective.
➤ *n* object, aim, goal, end, purpose, ambition, mark, target, intention, design.

objectivity *n* impartiality, detachment, disinterest, disinterestedness, equitableness, even-handedness, justness, justice, fairness, open-mindedness, open mind.
E3 subjectivity, bias, prejudice.

obligation *n* duty, responsibility, onus, charge, commitment, liability, requirement, bond, contract, debt, burden, trust.

obligatory *adj* compulsory, mandatory (*fml*), statutory, required, binding, essential, necessary, enforced.
E3 optional.

oblige *v* 1 COMPEL, constrain, coerce, require, make, necessitate, force, bind. 2 HELP, assist, accommodate, do a favour, serve, gratify, please.

obliged *adj* under an obligation, indebted, in debt (to), grateful, thankful, gratified, appreciative, bound, forced, compelled, constrained, duty-bound, honour-bound, required, obligated, under compulsion, beholden (*fml*).

obliging *adj* accommodating, co-operative, helpful, considerate, agreeable, friendly, kind, civil.
E3 unhelpful.

oblique *adj* slanting, sloping, inclined, angled, tilted.

obliterate *v* eradicate, destroy, annihilate, delete, blot out, wipe out, erase.

oblivion *n* obscurity, nothingness, unconsciousness, void, limbo.
E3 awareness.

oblivious *adj* unaware, unconscious,

inattentive, careless, heedless, blind, insensible, negligent.
Ea aware.

obnoxious *adj* unpleasant, disagreeable, disgusting, loathsome, nasty, horrid, odious, repulsive, revolting, repugnant, sickening, nauseating.
Ea pleasant.

obscene *adj* indecent, improper, immoral, impure, filthy, dirty, bawdy, lewd, licentious, pornographic, scurrilous, suggestive, disgusting, foul, shocking, shameless, offensive.
Ea decent, wholesome.

obscenity *n* 1 INDECENCY, immodesty, impurity, impropriety, lewdness, licentiousness, suggestiveness, pornography, dirtiness, filthiness, foulness, grossness, indelicacy, coarseness.
2 ATROCITY, evil, outrage, offence.
3 PROFANITY, expletive, swear-word, four-letter word (*infml*).

obscure *adj* 1 UNKNOWN, unimportant, little-known, unheard-of, undistinguished, nameless, inconspicuous, humble, minor.
2 INCOMPREHENSIBLE, enigmatic, cryptic, recondite, esoteric, arcane, mysterious, deep, abstruse, confusing. 3 INDISTINCT, unclear, indefinite, shadowy, blurred, cloudy, faint, hazy, dim, misty, shady, vague, murky, gloomy, dusky.
Ea 1 famous, renowned. 2 intelligible, straightforward. 3 clear, definite.
➢ *v* conceal, cloud, obfuscate, hide, cover, blur, disguise, mask, overshadow, shadow, shade, cloak, veil, shroud, darken, dim, eclipse, screen, block out.
Ea clarify, illuminate.

obscurity *n* 1 UNIMPORTANCE, insignificance, lowliness, namelessness, inconspicuousness, lack of fame/ recognition, inconspicuousness. 2 INCOMPREHENSIBILITY, impenetrability, unclearness, complexity, intricacy, ambiguity, mystery, confusion, mysticism, abstruseness (*fml*), reconditeness (*fml*).
Ea 1 fame. 2 intelligibility, clarity, lucidity.

obsequious *adj* servile, ingratiating, grovelling, fawning, sycophantic, cringing, deferential, flattering, smarmy (*infml*), unctuous, oily, submissive, subservient, slavish.

observable *adj* noticeable, perceptible, discernible, appreciable, detectable, recognizable, measurable, significant,

visible, apparent, clear, obvious, evident, open, patent, perceivable.

observance *n* 1 ADHERENCE, compliance, observation, performance, obedience, fulfilment, honouring, notice, attention.
2 RITUAL, custom, ceremony, practice, celebration.

observant *adj* attentive, alert, vigilant, watchful, perceptive, eagle-eyed, wide-awake, heedful.
Ea unobservant.

observation *n* 1 ATTENTION, notice, examination, inspection, scrutiny, monitoring, study, watching, consideration, discernment. 2 REMARK, comment, utterance, thought, statement, pronouncement, reflection, opinion, finding, note.

observe *v* 1 WATCH, see, study, notice, contemplate, keep an eye on, perceive.
2 REMARK, comment, say, mention.
3 ABIDE BY, comply with (*fml*), honour, keep, fulfil, celebrate, perform.
Ea 1 miss. 3 break, violate.

observer *n* watcher, spectator, viewer, witness, looker-on, onlooker, eyewitness, commentator, bystander, beholder.

obsess *v* preoccupy, dominate, rule, monopolize, haunt, grip, plague, prey on, possess.

obsession *n* preoccupation, fixation, ideé fixe, ruling passion, compulsion, fetish, hang-up (*infml*), infatuation, mania, enthusiasm.

obsessive *adj* consuming, compulsive, gripping, fixed, haunting, tormenting, maddening.

obsolete *adj* outmoded, disused, out of date, old-fashioned, passé, dated, outworn, old, antiquated, antique, dead, extinct.
Ea modern, current, up-to-date.

obstacle *n* barrier, bar, obstruction, impediment, hurdle, hindrance, check, snag (*infml*), stumbling-block, drawback, difficulty, hitch, catch, stop, interference, interruption.
Ea advantage, help.

obstinacy *n* stubbornness, inflexibility, hard-heartedness, persistence, perseverance, resoluteness, tenacity, wilfulness, wrong-headedness, perversity, firmness, doggedness, relentlessness, mulishness, frowardness (*fml*), intransigence (*fml*), obduracy (*fml*), pertinacity (*fml*), pig-headedness (*infml*).

co-operativeness, flexibility, submissiveness.

obstinate *adj* stubborn, inflexible, immovable, intractable (*fml*), pig-headed (*infml*), unyielding, intransigent (*fml*), persistent, dogged, headstrong, bloody-minded (*sl*), strong-minded, self-willed, steadfast, firm, determined, wilful.
flexible, tractable.

obstruct *v* block, impede, hinder, prevent, check, frustrate, hamper, clog, choke, bar, barricade, stop, stall, retard, restrict, thwart, inhibit, hold up, curb, arrest, slow down, interrupt, interfere with, shut off, cut off, obscure.
assist, further.

obstruction *n* barrier, blockage, bar, barricade, hindrance, impediment, check, stop, stoppage, difficulty.
help.

obstructive *adj* hindering, delaying, blocking, stalling, unhelpful, awkward, difficult, restrictive, inhibiting.
co-operative, helpful.

obtain *v* 1 ACQUIRE, get, gain, come by, attain, procure, secure, earn, achieve. 2 PREVAIL, exist, hold, be in force, be the case, stand, reign, rule, be prevalent.

obtainable *adj* available, at hand, ready, to be had, accessible, achievable, attainable, realizable, on call, procurable (*fml*), on tap (*infml*).
unobtainable, unavailable.

obtrusive *adj* 1 PROMINENT, protruding, noticeable, obvious, blatant, forward. 2 INTRUSIVE, interfering, prying, meddling, nosey (*infml*), pushy (*infml*).
1 unobtrusive.

obtuse *adj* slow, stupid, thick (*infml*), dull, dense, crass, dumb (*infml*), stolid, dull-witted, thick-skinned.
bright, sharp.

obvious *adj* evident, self-evident, manifest, patent, clear, plain, distinct, transparent, undeniable, unmistakable, conspicuous, glaring, apparent, open, unconcealed, visible, noticeable, perceptible, pronounced, recognizable, self-explanatory, straightforward, prominent.
unclear, indistinct, obscure.

obviously *adv* plainly, clearly, evidently, manifestly, undeniably, unmistakably, without doubt, certainly, distinctly, of course.

occasion *n* 1 EVENT, occurrence, incident, time, instance, chance, case, opportunity. 2 REASON, cause, excuse, justification, ground(s). 3 CELEBRATION, function, affair, party.

occasional *adj* periodic, intermittent, irregular, sporadic, infrequent, uncommon, incidental, odd, rare, casual.
frequent, regular, constant.

occasionally *adv* sometimes, on occasion, from time to time, at times, at intervals, now and then, now and again, irregularly, periodically, every so often, once in a while, off and on, infrequently.
frequently, often, always.

occult *adj* mystical, supernatural, magical, esoteric, mysterious, concealed, arcane, recondite, obscure, secret, hidden, veiled.
➤ *n* the supernatural, black arts, mysticism, supernaturalism.

Terms associated with the occult include: amulet, astral projection, astrologer, astrology, bewitch, black cat, black magic, black mass, cabbala, charm, chiromancer, chiromancy, clairvoyance, clairvoyant, conjure, coven, crystal ball, curse, déjà vu, divination, diviner, divining-rod, dream, ectoplasm, evil eye, evil spirit, exorcism, exorcist, extrasensory perception (ESP), familiar, fetish, fortune-teller, garlic, Hallowe'en, hallucination, hoodoo, horoscope, horseshoe, hydromancer, hydromancy, illusion, incantation, jinx, juju, magic, magician, mascot, medium, necromancer, necromancy, obi, omen, oneiromancer, oneiromancy, Ouija board®, palmist, palmistry, paranormal, pentagram, planchette, poltergeist, possession, prediction, premonition, psychic, rabbit's foot, relic, rune, satanic, Satanism, Satanist, séance, second sight, shaman, shamrock, sixth sense, sorcerer, sorcery, spell, spirit, spiritualism, spiritualist, supernatural, superstition, talisman, tarot card, tarot reading, telepathist, telepathy, totem, trance, vision, voodoo, Walpurgis Night, warlock, white magic, witch, witchcraft, witch doctor, witch's broomstick, witch's sabbath.

---

occupancy *n* tenancy, residence, tenure, term, occupation, owner-occupancy, ownership, possession, holding, use, domiciliation (*fml*), habitation (*fml*), inhabitancy (*fml*).

occupant n occupier, holder, inhabitant, resident, householder, tenant, user, lessee, squatter, inmate.

occupation n 1 JOB, profession, work, vocation, employment, trade, post, calling, business, line, pursuit, craft, walk of life, activity. 2 INVASION, seizure, conquest, control, takeover. 3 OCCUPANCY, possession, holding, tenancy, tenure, residence, habitation, use.

occupied adj 1 UNAVAILABLE, in use, taken, busy, full, tenanted. 2 ABSORBED, engrossed, taken up, employed, engaged, preoccupied, immersed, busy, working, tied up, hard at it (infml).
Ea 1 unoccupied, vacant.

occupy v 1 INHABIT, live in, possess, reside in, stay in, take possession of, own.
2 ABSORB, take up, engross, engage, hold, involve, preoccupy, amuse, busy, interest.
3 INVADE, seize, capture, overrun, take over. 4 FILL, take up, use.

occur v happen, come about, take place, transpire, chance, come to pass, materialize, befall, develop, crop up, arise, appear, turn up, obtain, result, exist, be present, be found.

occurrence n 1 INCIDENT, event, happening, affair, circumstance, episode, instance, case, development, action.
2 INCIDENCE, existence, appearance, manifestation.

ocean n main, profound, sea, the deep, briny (infml), the drink (infml).

> The world's oceans and largest seas include: Pacific Ocean, Atlantic Ocean, Indian Ocean, Arctic Ocean, Antarctic (Southern) Ocean, South China Sea, Caribbean Sea, Mediterranean Sea, Bering Sea, Gulf of Mexico, Sea of Okhotsk.

odd adj 1 UNUSUAL, strange, uncommon, peculiar, abnormal, exceptional, curious, atypical, different, queer, bizarre, eccentric, remarkable, unconventional, weird, irregular, extraordinary, outlandish, rare. 2 OCCASIONAL, incidental, irregular, random, casual. 3 UNMATCHED, unpaired, single, spare, surplus, left-over, remaining, sundry, various, miscellaneous.
Ea 1 normal, usual. 2 regular.

oddity n 1 ABNORMALITY, peculiarity, rarity, eccentricity, idiosyncrasy, phenomenon, quirk. 2 CURIOSITY, character, freak, misfit.

oddment n bit, scrap, left-over, fragment, offcut, end, remnant, shred, snippet, patch.

odds n 1 LIKELIHOOD, probability, chances.
2 ADVANTAGE, edge, lead, superiority.

odious adj offensive, loathsome, unpleasant, obnoxious, disgusting, hateful, repulsive, revolting, repugnant, foul, execrable, detestable, abhorrent, horrible, horrid, abominable.
Ea pleasant.

odour n smell, scent, fragrance, aroma, perfume, redolence, stench, stink (infml).

off adj 1 ROTTEN, bad, sour, turned, rancid, mouldy, decomposed. 2 CANCELLED, postponed. 3 AWAY, absent, gone.
4 SUBSTANDARD, below par, disappointing, unsatisfactory, slack.
➤ adv away, elsewhere, out, at a distance, apart, aside.

offbeat adj unorthodox, weird, unconventional, untraditional, abnormal, strange, unusual, bizarre, out of the ordinary, oddball (infml), freaky (infml), kooky (infml), wacky (infml), far-out (sl), way-out (sl).

off-colour adj indisposed, off form, under the weather (infml), unwell, sick, out of sorts (infml), ill, poorly.

offence n 1 MISDEMEANOUR, transgression, violation, wrong, wrong-doing, infringement, crime, misdeed, sin, trespass. 2 AFFRONT, insult, injury.
3 RESENTMENT, indignation, pique, umbrage, outrage, hurt, hard feelings.
♦ take offence resent, be indignant, be angry, be annoyed, be exasperated, be hurt, be offended, be insulted, be upset, be/feel put out, take exception, take personally, take umbrage, be miffed (infml), get huffy (infml), get one's nose out of joint (infml).

offend v 1 HURT, insult, injure, affront, wrong, wound, displease, snub, upset, annoy, outrage. 2 DISGUST, repel, sicken.
3 TRANSGRESS, sin, violate, err.
Ea 1 please.

offender n transgressor, wrong-doer, culprit, criminal, miscreant, guilty party, law-breaker, delinquent.

offensive adj 1 DISAGREEABLE, unpleasant, objectionable, displeasing, disgusting, odious, obnoxious, repellent, repugnant (fml), revolting, loathsome, vile, nauseating, nasty, detestable, abominable.

2 INSOLENT, abusive, rude, insulting, impertinent.

Ea 1 pleasant. **2** polite.

➤ n attack, assault, onslaught, invasion, raid, sortie.

offer v **1** PRESENT, make available, advance, extend, put forward, submit, suggest, hold out, provide, sell. **2** PROFFER, propose, bid, tender. **3** VOLUNTEER, come forward, show willing (*infml*).

➤ n proposal, bid, submission, tender, suggestion, proposition, overture, approach, attempt, presentation.

offering n present, gift, donation, contribution, subscription.

offhand adj casual, unconcerned, uninterested, brusque, abrupt, perfunctory, informal, cavalier, careless.

Ea calculated, planned.

➤ adv impromptu, off the cuff, extempore (*fml*), off the top of one's head, immediately.

office n **1** duty, obligation, charge, commission, occupation, situation, post, employment, function, appointment, business, role, service. **2** WORKPLACE, workroom, bureau.

officer n official, office-holder, public servant, functionary, dignitary, bureaucrat, administrator, representative, executive, agent, appointee.

official adj authorized, authoritative, legitimate, formal, licensed, accredited, certified, approved, authenticated, authentic, bona fide, proper.

Ea unofficial.

➤ n office-bearer, officer, functionary, bureaucrat, executive, representative, agent.

> **Officials include:** agent, ambassador, bailiff, bureaucrat, captain, chairman, chairwoman, chairperson, chancellor, chief, clerk, commander, commissar, commissioner, congressman, congresswoman, consul, coroner, councillor, delegate, diplomat, director, elder, envoy, equerry, Eurocrat, executive, Euro-MP, gauleiter, governor, hakim, inspector, justice of the peace (JP), magistrate, manager, mandarin, marshal, mayor, mayoress, member of parliament, minister, monitor, notary, ombudsman, overseer, prefect, president, principal, proctor, proprietor, public prosecutor, registrar, senator (*US*), sheriff, steward, superintendent, supervisor, usher.

officiate v preside, superintend, conduct, chair, manage, oversee, run.

officious adj obtrusive, dictatorial, intrusive, bossy (*infml*), interfering, meddlesome, over-zealous, self-important, pushy (*infml*), forward, bustling, importunate (*fml*).

offload v unburden, unload, jettison, dump, drop, deposit, get rid of, discharge.

off-putting adj intimidating, daunting, disconcerting, discouraging, disheartening, formidable, unnerving, unsettling, demoralizing, disturbing.

offset v counterbalance, compensate for, cancel out, counteract, make up for, balance out, neutralize.

offshoot n branch, outgrowth, limb, arm, development, spin-off, by-product, appendage.

offspring n child, children, young, issue, progeny (*fml*), brood, heirs, successors, descendants.

Ea parent(s).

often adv frequently, repeatedly, regularly, generally, again and again, time after time, time and again, much.

Ea rarely, seldom, never.

ogle v eye, eye up, leer, make eyes at, look, stare.

ogre n giant, monster, fiend, bogeyman, demon, devil, troll.

oil v grease, lubricate, anoint.

oil rig

> **Parts of an offshore oil rig include:** drilling platform, production platform, jack-up rig, semi-submersible; accommodation module, control room, derrick, drill, rotary drill, emergency flare stack, helicopter deck, hoisting equipment, lifeboats, main deck, materials store, pedestal crane, pig trap, pipe, drilling pipes, pipe rack, power station, production oil and gas separator, test oil and gas separator, pumping station, seawater desalination plant, substructure, valve, whipstock, workshop.

oily adj **1** GREASY, fatty. **2** UNCTUOUS, smooth, obsequious, ingratiating, smarmy (*infml*), glib, flattering.

ointment n salve, balm, cream, lotion, liniment, embrocation.

OK (*infml*) adj acceptable, all right, fine, permitted, in order, fair, satisfactory, reasonable, tolerable, passable, not bad,

good, adequate, convenient, correct, accurate.
➤ *n* authorization, approval, endorsement, go-ahead, permission, green light, consent, agreement.
➤ *v* approve, authorize, pass, give the go-ahead to, give the green light to (*infml*), rubber-stamp, agree to.
➤ *interj* all right, fine, very well, agreed, right, yes.

old *adj* 1 AGED, elderly, advanced in years, grey, senile. 2 ANCIENT, original, primitive, antiquated, mature. 3 LONG-STANDING, long-established, time-honoured, traditional. 4 OBSOLETE, old-fashioned, out of date, worn-out, decayed, decrepit. 5 FORMER, previous, earlier, one-time, ex-.
🖃 1 young. 2 new. 4 modern. 5 current.

old-fashioned *adj* outmoded, out of date, outdated, dated, unfashionable, obsolete, behind the times, antiquated, archaic, passé, obsolescent.
🖃 modern, up-to-date.

omen *n* portent, sign, warning, premonition, foreboding, augury, indication.

ominous *adj* portentous, inauspicious, foreboding, menacing, sinister, fateful, unpromising, threatening.
🖃 auspicious, favourable.

omission *n* exclusion, gap, oversight, failure, lack, neglect, default, avoidance.

omit *v* leave out, exclude, miss out, pass over, overlook, drop, skip, eliminate, forget, neglect, leave undone, fail, disregard, edit out.
🖃 include.

omnipotent *adj* all-powerful, almighty, invincible, supreme, plenipotent (*fml*).
🖃 impotent.

omniscient *adj* all-knowing, all-seeing, all-wise.

once *adv* formerly, previously, in the past, at one time, long ago, in times past, once upon a time, in the old days.
♦ **at once** 1 IMMEDIATELY, instantly, directly, right away, straight away, without delay, now, promptly, forthwith. 2 SIMULTANEOUSLY, together, at the same time.

oncoming *adj* approaching, advancing, upcoming, looming, onrushing, gathering.

one *adj* 1 SINGLE, solitary, lone, individual, only. 2 UNITED, harmonious, like-minded,

whole, entire, complete, equal, identical, alike.

onerous (*fml*) *adj* oppressive, burdensome, demanding, laborious, hard, taxing, difficult, troublesome, exacting, exhausting, heavy, weighty.
🖃 easy, light.

oneself *pron*
♦ **by oneself** 1 ALONE, by oneself, on one's own, lonely, lonesome, deserted, isolated, abandoned, forsaken, forlorn, desolate, unaccompanied, unescorted, unattended, solo. 2 ON ONE'S OWN, independently, unaided, unassisted, without help, without assistance, singly, single-handed, unaccompanied.

one-sided *adj* 1 UNBALANCED, unequal, lopsided. 2 UNFAIR, unjust, prejudiced, biased, partial, partisan. 3 UNILATERAL, independent.
🖃 1 balanced. 2 impartial. 3 bilateral, multilateral.

one-time *adj* former, previous, ex-, late, sometime, erstwhile (*fml*), quondam (*fml*).

ongoing *adj* 1 CONTINUING, continuous, unbroken, uninterrupted, constant. 2 DEVELOPING, evolving, progressing, growing, in progress, unfinished, unfolding.

onlooker *n* bystander, observer, spectator, looker-on, eyewitness, witness, watcher, viewer.

only *adv* just, at most, merely, simply, purely, barely, exclusively, solely.
➤ *adj* sole, single, solitary, lone, unique, exclusive, individual.

onrush *n* surge, rush, push, stream, flood, flow, charge, cascade, career, onset, onslaught, stampede.

onset *n* 1 BEGINNING, start, commencement, inception, outset, outbreak. 2 ASSAULT, attack, onslaught, onrush.
🖃 1 end, finish.

onslaught *n* attack, assault, offensive, charge, bombardment, blitz.

onus *n* burden, responsibility, load, obligation, duty, liability, task.

onward(s) *adv* forward, on, ahead, in front, beyond, forth.
🖃 backward(s).

ooze *v* seep, exude, leak, percolate, escape, dribble, drip, drop, discharge, bleed, secrete, emit, overflow with, filter, drain.

opaque *adj* 1 CLOUDY, clouded, murky, dull, dim, hazy, muddied, muddy, turbid. 2 OBSCURE, unclear, impenetrable, incomprehensible, unintelligible, enigmatic, difficult.
🔼 1 transparent. 2 clear, obvious.

open *adj* 1 UNCLOSED, ajar, gaping, uncovered, unfastened, unlocked, unsealed, yawning, lidless. 2 UNRESTRICTED, free, unobstructed, clear, accessible, exposed, unprotected, unsheltered, vacant, wide, available. 3 OVERT, obvious, plain, evident, manifest, noticeable, flagrant, conspicuous. 4 UNDECIDED, unresolved, unsettled, debatable, problematic, moot. 5 FRANK, candid, honest, guileless, natural, ingenuous, unreserved.
🔼 1 shut. 2 restricted. 3 hidden. 4 decided. 5 reserved.
➤ *v* 1 UNFASTEN, undo, unlock, uncover, unseal, unblock, uncork, clear, expose. 2 EXPLAIN, divulge, disclose, lay bare. 3 EXTEND, spread (out), unfold, separate, split. 4 BEGIN, start, commence, inaugurate, initiate, set in motion, launch.
🔼 1 close, shut. 2 hide. 4 end, finish.

open-air *adj* outdoor, alfresco.
🔼 indoor.

open-handed *adj* generous, free, liberal, large-hearted, lavish, bountiful, unstinting, bounteous (*fml*), munificent (*fml*).
🔼 tight-fisted.

opening *n* 1 APERTURE, breach, gap, orifice, break, chink, crack, fissure, cleft, chasm, hole, split, vent, rupture. 2 START, onset, beginning, inauguration, inception, birth, dawn, launch. 3 OPPORTUNITY, chance, occasion, break (*infml*), place, vacancy.
🔼 2 close, end.
➤ *adj* beginning, commencing, starting, first, inaugural, introductory, initial, early, primary.
🔼 closing.

openly *adv* overtly, frankly, candidly, blatantly, flagrantly, plainly, unashamedly, unreservedly, glaringly, in public, in full view, shamelessly.
🔼 secretly, slyly.

open-minded *adj* unprejudiced, unbiased, broad-minded, broad, impartial, tolerant, liberal, receptive, reasonable, objective, free, catholic, dispassionate,

enlightened, latitudinarian (*fml*).
🔼 bigoted, intolerant, prejudiced, narrow-minded.

operate *v* 1 *it operates on batteries*: function, act, perform, run, work, go. 2 *she can operate that machine*: control, handle, manage, use, utilize, manoeuvre.

operation *n* 1 FUNCTIONING, action, running, motion, movement, performance, working. 2 INFLUENCE, manipulation, handling, management, use, utilization. 3 UNDERTAKING, enterprise, affair, procedure, proceeding, process, business, deal, transaction, effort. 4 CAMPAIGN, action, task, manoeuvre, exercise.

operational *adj* working, in working order, usable, functional, going, viable, workable, ready, prepared, in service.
🔼 out of order.

operative *adj* 1 OPERATIONAL, in operation, in force, functioning, active, effective, efficient, in action, workable, viable, serviceable, functional. 2 KEY, crucial, important, relevant, significant.
🔼 1 inoperative, out of service.

operator *n* 1 OPERATIVE, worker, mechanic, machinist, technician, mover, driver, practitioner. 2 TRADER, contractor, dealer, manager, director, administrator, handler. 3 MANIPULATOR, machinator, punter, manoeuvrer, shyster, speculator, wheeler-dealer (*infml*).

opinion *n* belief, judgement, view, point of view, idea, perception, stance, theory, impression, feeling, sentiment, estimation, assessment, conception, mind, notion, way of thinking, persuasion, attitude.

opinionated *adj* dogmatic, doctrinaire, dictatorial, arrogant, inflexible, obstinate, stubborn, uncompromising, single-minded, prejudiced, biased, bigoted.
🔼 open-minded.

opponent *n* adversary, enemy, antagonist, foe, competitor, contestant, challenger, opposer, opposition, rival, objector, dissident.
🔼 ally.

opportune *adj* suitable, proper, convenient, appropriate, advantageous, apt, fit, seasonable, timely, well-timed, favourable, providential, fitting, fortunate, good, lucky, happy, auspicious (*fml*), felicitous (*fml*), pertinent (*fml*), propitious (*fml*).

◨ unsuitable, inopportune (*fml*).

opportunism *n* exploitation, expediency, pragmatism, realism, taking advantage, unscrupulousness, Machiavellianism, making hay while the sun shines (*infml*).

opportunity *n* chance, opening, break (*infml*), occasion, possibility, hour, moment.

oppose *v* 1 RESIST, withstand, counter, attack, combat, contest, stand up to, take a stand against, take issue with, confront, defy, face, fight, fly in the face of, hinder, obstruct, bar, check, prevent, thwart. 2 COMPARE, contrast, match, offset, counterbalance, play off.
◨ 1 defend, support.

opposed *adj* in opposition, against, hostile, conflicting, opposing, opposite, antagonistic, clashing, contrary, incompatible, anti.
◨ in favour.

opposing *adj* opposite, contrary, differing, at odds, at variance, rival, clashing, conflicting, irreconcilable, incompatible, opposed, contentious, enemy, hostile, antagonistic, fighting, contending, warring, combatant.

opposite *adj* 1 FACING, fronting, corresponding. 2 OPPOSED, antagonistic, conflicting, contrary, hostile, adverse, contradictory, antithetical, irreconcilable, unlike, reverse, inconsistent, different, contrasted, differing.
◨ 2 same.
➢ *n* reverse, converse, contrary, antithesis, contradiction, inverse.
◨ same.

opposition *n* 1 ANTAGONISM, hostility, resistance, obstructiveness, unfriendliness, disapproval. 2 OPPONENT, antagonist, rival, foe, other side.
◨ 1 co-operation, support. 2 ally, supporter.

oppress *v* 1 BURDEN, afflict, lie heavy on, harass, depress, sadden, torment, vex. 2 SUBJUGATE, suppress, subdue, overpower, overwhelm, crush, trample, tyrannize, persecute, maltreat, abuse.

oppressed *adj* tyrannized, burdened, downtrodden, enslaved, subject, crushed, repressed, harassed, abused, maltreated, misused, persecuted, troubled, disadvantaged, underprivileged, subjugated (*fml*).
◨ free.

oppression *n* tyranny, subjugation, subjection, repression, despotism, suppression, injustice, cruelty, brutality, abuse, persecution, maltreatment, harshness, hardship.

oppressive *adj* 1 AIRLESS, stuffy, close, stifling, suffocating, sultry, muggy, heavy. 2 TYRANNICAL, despotic, overbearing, overwhelming, repressive, harsh, unjust, inhuman, cruel, brutal, burdensome, onerous, intolerable.
◨ 1 airy. 2 just, gentle.

oppressor *n* tyrant, bully, taskmaster, slave-driver, despot, dictator, persecutor, tormentor, intimidator, autocrat.

opt *v* choose, pick, decide (on), elect, prefer, select, settle on, single out, go for (*infml*), plump for (*infml*).

optimistic *adj* confident, assured, sanguine, hopeful, positive, cheerful, buoyant, bright, idealistic, expectant.
◨ pessimistic.

optimum *adj* best, ideal, perfect, optimal, superlative, top, choice.
◨ worst.

option *n* choice, alternative, preference, possibility, selection.

optional *adj* voluntary, discretionary, elective, free, unforced.
◨ compulsory.

opulent *adj* 1 RICH, wealthy, prosperous, affluent, well-to-do, well-off, moneyed, well-heeled (*infml*), rolling in it (*infml*). 2 SUMPTUOUS, lavish, luxurious, plush (*infml*), posh (*infml*). 3 ABUNDANT, copious, prolific, plentiful, profuse, superabundant, luxuriant.
◨ 1 poor.

oracle *n* 1 SEER, prophet, sage, soothsayer, wizard, sibyl, high priest, augur. 2 AUTHORITY, adviser, mentor, expert, specialist, guru (*infml*), mastermind (*infml*), pundit (*infml*). 3 PROPHECY, vision, divination, prediction, revelation, answer, augury, prognostication (*fml*).

oral *adj* verbal, spoken, unwritten, vocal.
◨ written.

oration *n* address, speech, lecture, sermon, discourse, harangue, homily, declamation (*fml*), spiel (*infml*).

orator *n* public speaker, speaker, lecturer, rhetorician, demagogue, declaimer, spellbinder, phrasemonger, spieler (*infml*).

orbit *n* 1 CIRCUIT, cycle, circle, course,

path, trajectory, track, revolution, rotation. **2** RANGE, scope, domain, influence, sphere of influence, compass.

➤ *v* revolve, circle, encircle, circumnavigate.

orchestrate *v* arrange, co-ordinate, organize, stage-manage, put together, prepare, present, mastermind, fix, integrate, score, compose.

ordain *v* **1** CONSECRATE, invest, appoint, call, elect, anoint, frock. **2** DECREE, order, require, instruct, rule, set, lay down, fix, dictate, pronounce, will, fate, destine, foreordain (*fml*), predestine (*fml*), predetermine (*fml*), prescribe (*fml*).

ordeal *n* trial, test, tribulation(s), affliction, trouble(s), suffering, anguish, agony, pain, persecution, torture, nightmare.

order *n* **1** COMMAND, directive, decree, injunction, instruction, direction, edict, ordinance, mandate, regulation, rule, precept, law. **2** REQUISITION, request, booking, commission, reservation, application, demand. **3** ARRANGEMENT, organization, grouping, disposition, sequence, categorization, classification, method, pattern, plan, system, array, layout, line-up, structure. **4** PEACE, quiet, calm, tranquillity, harmony, law and order, discipline. **5** ASSOCIATION, society, community, fraternity, brotherhood, sisterhood, lodge, guild, company, organization, denomination, sect, union. **6** CLASS, kind, sort, type, rank, species, hierarchy, family.

▣ **3** confusion, disorder. **4** anarchy.

➤ *v* **1** COMMAND, instruct, direct, bid, decree, require, authorize. **2** REQUEST, reserve, book, apply for, requisition. **3** ARRANGE, organize, dispose, classify, group, marshal, sort out, lay out, manage, control, catalogue.

◆ **in order 1** WORKING, functioning, operative, mended. **2** ORDERED, orderly, organized, tidy, neat, shipshape, arranged, well-organized, systematic, regular, methodical, categorized, classified, in sequence, in alphabetical order. **3** ACCEPTABLE, proper, correct, right, lawful, allowed, permitted, suitable, appropriate, fitting, all right, done, OK (*infml*).

◆ **in order to** with the purpose of, with the intention of, intending to, to, with a view to, so that, with the result that.

◆ **out of order 1** BROKEN, broken down, not working, inoperative. **2** DISORDERED,

disorganized, out of sequence.

3 UNSEEMLY, improper, uncalled-for, incorrect, wrong.

orderly *adj* **1** ORDERED, systematic, neat, tidy, regular, methodical, in order, well-organized, well-regulated. **2** WELL-BEHAVED, controlled, disciplined, law-abiding.

▣ **1** chaotic. **2** disorderly.

ordinarily *adv* as a rule, usually, commonly, normally, in general, generally, familiarly, customarily, habitually, conventionally.

ordinary *adj* common, commonplace, regular, routine, standard, average, everyday, run-of-the-mill, usual, unexceptional, unremarkable, typical, normal, customary, common-or-garden, plain, familiar, habitual, simple, conventional, modest, mediocre, indifferent, pedestrian, prosaic, undistinguished.

▣ extraordinary, unusual.

organ *n* **1** DEVICE, instrument, implement, tool, element, process, structure, unit, member. **2** MEDIUM, agency, forum, vehicle, voice, mouthpiece, publication, newspaper, periodical, journal.

organic *adj* natural, biological, living, animate.

organism *n* **1** LIVING THING, being, creature, entity, body, structure, cell, animal, plant, bacterium. **2** SYSTEM, structure, entity, whole, unity, set-up.

organization *n* **1** ASSOCIATION, institution, society, company, firm, corporation, federation, group, league, club, confederation, consortium.

2 ARRANGEMENT, system, classification, methodology, order, formation, grouping, method, plan, structure, pattern, composition, configuration, design.

organize *v* **1** STRUCTURE, co-ordinate, arrange, order, group, marshal, classify, systematize, tabulate, catalogue.

2 ESTABLISH, found, set up, develop, form, frame, construct, shape, run.

▣ **1** disorganize.

orgy *n* debauch, carousal, revelry, bout, bacchanalia, indulgence, excess, spree.

orient *v* accustom, accommodate, familiarize, acclimatize, adapt, adjust, orientate, align, get one's bearings, habituate (*fml*).

orientation *n* **1** SITUATION, bearings,

location, direction, position, alignment, placement, attitude. **2** INITIATION, training, acclimatization, familiarization, adaptation, adjustment, settling in.

origin *n* **1** SOURCE, spring, fount, foundation, base, cause, derivation, provenance, roots, well-spring. **2** BEGINNING, commencement, start, inauguration, launch, dawning, creation, emergence. **3** ANCESTRY, descent, extraction, heritage, family, lineage, parentage, pedigree, birth, paternity, stock.
F3 2 end, termination.

original *adj* **1** FIRST, early, earliest, initial, primary, archetypal, rudimentary, embryonic, starting, opening, commencing, first-hand. **2** NOVEL, innovative, new, creative, fresh, imaginative, inventive, unconventional, unusual, unique.
F3 1 latest. **2** hackneyed, unoriginal.
➤ *n* prototype, master, paradigm (*fml*), model, pattern, archetype (*fml*), standard, type.

originality *n* inventiveness, creativeness, creativity, imaginativeness, imagination, freshness, boldness, cleverness, creative spirit, daring, innovativeness, innovation, ingenuity, individuality, resourcefulness, newness, novelty, unconventionality, unorthodoxy, singularity, eccentricity.

originally *adv* initially, at first, at the start, at the outset, in the beginning, first, to begin with, in origin, by derivation, by birth.

originate *v* **1** RISE, arise, spring, stem, issue, flow, proceed, derive, come, evolve, emerge, be born. **2** CREATE, invent, inaugurate, introduce, give birth to, develop, discover, establish, begin, commence, start, set up, launch, pioneer, conceive, form, produce, generate.
F3 1 end, terminate.

ornament *n* decoration, adornment, embellishment, garnish, trimming, accessory, frill, trinket, bauble, jewel.
➤ *v* decorate, adorn, embellish, garnish, trim, beautify, brighten, dress up, deck, gild.

ornamental *adj* decorative, embellishing, adorning, attractive, showy.

ornamentation *n* decoration, adornment, embellishment, embroidery, ornateness, elaboration, garniture, frills, fallalery.

ornate *adj* elaborate, ornamented, fancy, decorated, baroque, rococo, florid, flowery, fussy, busy, sumptuous.
F3 plain.

orthodox *adj* conformist, conventional, accepted, official, traditional, usual, well-established, established, received, customary, conservative, recognized, authoritative.
F3 nonconformist, unorthodox.

orthodoxy *n* **1** CONVENTIONALITY, conformity, conformism, correctness, properness, authoritativeness, received wisdom. **2** TRADITIONALISM, soundness, conservatism, devoutness, devotion, trueness, faithfulness, inflexibility, strictness.

oscillate *v* fluctuate, vary, waver, sway, swing, vacillate, move backwards and forwards, move to and fro, vibrate, wigwag, go from one extreme to the other, seesaw (*infml*), yo-yo (*infml*).

ostensible *adj* alleged, apparent, presumed, seeming, supposed, so-called, professed, outward, pretended, superficial.
F3 real.

ostentation *n* showiness, showing off, flamboyance, pretension, pretentiousness, show, flaunting, vaunting, pomp, exhibitionism, boasting, display, flourish, pageantry, parade, trappings, window-dressing, affectation (*fml*), flashiness (*infml*), swank (*infml*), tinsel (*infml*).
F3 unpretentiousness.

ostentatious *adj* showy, flashy, pretentious, vulgar, loud, garish, gaudy, flamboyant, conspicuous, extravagant.
F3 restrained.

ostracize *v* exclude, banish, exile, expel, excommunicate, reject, segregate, send to Coventry, shun, snub, boycott, avoid, cold-shoulder (*infml*), cut.
F3 accept, welcome.

other *adj* **1** DIFFERENT, dissimilar, unlike, separate, distinct, contrasting. **2** MORE, further, extra, additional, supplementary, spare, alternative.

otherwise *adv* **1** UNLESS, if not, or, or else, failing that. **2** DIFFERENTLY, in a different way, along different lines, in other respects.

oust *v* expel, eject, depose, displace, turn out, throw out, overthrow, evict, drive out, unseat, dispossess, disinherit, replace, topple.

🔁 install, settle.

out *adj* **1** AWAY, absent, elsewhere, not at home, gone, outside, abroad. **2** UNCONSCIOUS, knocked out, out cold, comatose (*fml*), insensible (*fml*), KO'd (*infml*). **3** *the book is out*: published, available, obtainable, ready, in print. **4** REVEALED, exposed, known, disclosed, divulged, public, evident, in the open, manifest (*fml*). **5** FORBIDDEN, unacceptable, impossible, excluded, inadmissible, unwelcome, undesirable, inappropriate, unsuitable, disallowed (*fml*). **6** OUT OF DATE, unfashionable, old-fashioned, dated, passé, antiquated, démodé, old hat (*infml*). **7** EXTINGUISHED, finished, expired, dead, not burning, doused, not shining, used up. **8** *the flowers are out*: in bloom, in full bloom, blooming, blossoming, in flower. **9** *out to make money*: determined, bent, insistent, intent, set.

🔁 **1** in, here, at home. **2** conscious. **3** out of print. **4** hidden, concealed. **5** allowed. **6** up-to-date, in (*infml*).

out-and-out *adj* absolute, thorough, total, complete, utter, outright, perfect, downright, inveterate, thoroughgoing, unmitigated, unqualified, uncompromising, arrant (*fml*), consummate (*fml*), dyed-in-the-wool (*infml*).

outbreak *n* eruption, outburst, explosion, flare-up, upsurge, flash, rash, burst, epidemic.

outburst *n* outbreak, eruption, explosion, flare-up, outpouring, burst, fit, gush, surge, storm, spasm, seizure, gale, attack, fit of temper.

outcast *n* castaway, exile, pariah, outsider, untouchable, refugee, reject, persona non grata.

outclass *v* surpass, outshine, beat, excel over, be much better than, outrival, transcend, top, eclipse, outdo, outdistance, outrank, outstrip, overshadow, leave standing, put in the shade.

outcome *n* result, consequence, upshot, conclusion, effect, end result.

outcry *n* protest, complaint, protestation, objection, dissent, indignation, uproar, cry, exclamation, clamour, row, commotion, noise, hue and cry, hullaballoo (*infml*), outburst.

outdated *adj* out of date, old-fashioned, dated, unfashionable, outmoded, behind the times, obsolete, obsolescent, antiquated, archaic.

🔁 fashionable, modern.

outdo *v* surpass, exceed, beat, excel, outstrip, outshine, get the better of, overcome, outclass, outdistance.

outdoor *adj* out-of-door(s), outside, open-air.

🔁 indoor.

outer *adj* **1** EXTERNAL, exterior, outside, outward, surface, superficial, peripheral. **2** OUTLYING, distant, remote, further.

🔁 **1** internal. **2** inner.

outfit *n* **1** CLOTHES, costume, ensemble, get-up (*infml*), togs (*infml*), garb. **2** EQUIPMENT, gear (*infml*), kit, rig, trappings, paraphernalia. **3** (*infml*) ORGANIZATION, firm, business, corporation, company, group, team, unit, set, set-up, crew, gang, squad.

outgoing *adj* **1** SOCIABLE, friendly, unreserved, amiable, warm, approachable, expansive, open, extrovert, cordial, easy-going, communicative, demonstrative, sympathetic. **2** DEPARTING, retiring, former, last, past, ex-.

🔁 **1** reserved. **2** incoming.

outgoings *n* costs, expenditure, outlay, overheads, spending, expenses, disbursement (*fml*).

🔁 income.

outing *n* excursion, expedition, jaunt, pleasure trip, trip, spin, picnic.

outlandish *adj* unconventional, unfamiliar, bizarre, strange, odd, weird, eccentric, alien, exotic, barbarous, foreign, extraordinary.

🔁 familiar, ordinary.

outlandish *adj* unconventional, unfamiliar, unheard-of, unknown, bizarre, strange, odd, unusual, peculiar, weird, eccentric, alien, exotic, curious, quaint, barbarous, grotesque, foreign, extraordinary, preposterous, unreasonable, freaky (*infml*), oddball, wacky, way-out (*infml*), far-out.

🔁 familiar, ordinary.

outlast *v* survive, come through, outlive, outstay, ride, weather.

outlaw *n* bandit, brigand, robber, desperado, highwayman, criminal, marauder, pirate, fugitive.

➤ *v* ban, disallow (*infml*), forbid, prohibit, exclude, embargo, bar, debar, banish, condemn.

✷ allow, legalize.

outlay *n* expenditure, expenses, outgoings, disbursement (*fml*), cost, spending.

✷ income.

outlet *n* 1 EXIT, way out, vent, egress, escape, opening, release, safety valve, channel. 2 RETAILER, shop, store, market.

✷ 1 entry, inlet.

outline *n* 1 SUMMARY, synopsis, précis, bare facts, sketch, thumbnail sketch, abstract. 2 PROFILE, form, contour, silhouette, shape.

➤ *v* sketch, summarize, draft, trace, rough out.

outlook *n* 1 VIEW, viewpoint, point of view, attitude, perspective, frame of mind, angle, slant, standpoint, opinion.

2 EXPECTATIONS, future, forecast, prospect, prognosis.

outlying *adj* distant, remote, far-off, far-away, far-flung, outer, provincial.

✷ inner.

outmoded *adj* out of date, old-fashioned, out of fashion, dated, unfashionable, behind the times, obsolete, obsolescent, superseded, antediluvian (*infml*), antiquated, archaic, passé, démodé, old hat (*infml*), square (*infml*), old-fogeyish (*infml*).

✷ modern, new, fashionable, fresh.

out-of-the-way *adj* remote, isolated, far-flung, far-off, far-away, distant, inaccessible, little-known, obscure, unfrequented.

outpouring *n* flood, deluge, torrent, stream, spate, spurt, flow, outflow, flux, cascade, effusion, emanation, effluence (*fml*).

output *n* production, productivity, product, yield, manufacture, achievement.

outrage *n* 1 ANGER, fury, rage, indignation, shock, affront, horror. 2 ATROCITY, offence, injury, enormity, barbarism, crime, violation, evil, scandal.

➤ *v* anger, infuriate, affront, incense, enrage, madden, disgust, injure, offend, shock, scandalize.

outrageous *adj* 1 ATROCIOUS, abominable, shocking, scandalous, offensive, disgraceful, monstrous, heinous, unspeakable, horrible. 2 EXCESSIVE,

exorbitant, immoderate, unreasonable, extortionate, inordinate, preposterous.

✷ 2 acceptable, reasonable.

outright *adj* total, utter, absolute, complete, downright, out-and-out, unqualified, unconditional, perfect, pure, thorough, direct, definite, categorical, straightforward.

✷ ambiguous, indefinite.

➤ *adv* 1 TOTALLY, absolutely, completely, utterly, thoroughly, openly, without restraint, straightforwardly, positively, directly, explicitly. 2 *killed outright*: instantaneously, at once, there and then, instantly, immediately.

outset *n* start, beginning, opening, inception, commencement, inauguration, kick-off (*infml*).

✷ end, conclusion.

outshine *v* outclass, outstrip, outdo, overshadow, transcend, eclipse, surpass, beat, best, upstage, excel, dwarf, outrank, top, put in the shade, put to shame.

outside *adj* 1 EXTERNAL, exterior, outer, surface, superficial, outward, extraneous, outdoor, outermost, extreme. 2 *an outside chance*: remote, marginal, distant, faint, slight, slim, negligible.

✷ 1 inside.

➤ *n* exterior, façade, front, surface, face, appearance, cover.

✷ inside.

outsider *n* stranger, intruder, alien, non-member, non-resident, foreigner, newcomer, visitor, intruder, interloper, misfit, odd man out.

outskirts *n* suburbs, vicinity, periphery, fringes, borders, boundary, edge, margin.

✷ centre.

outsmart *v* outwit, outperform, outmanoeuvre, best, outthink, beat, get the better of, deceive, trick, dupe, outfox, kid (*infml*), con (*infml*), have on (*infml*), take for a ride (*infml*), pull a fast one on (*infml*).

outspoken *adj* candid, frank, forthright, blunt, unreserved, plain-spoken, direct, explicit.

✷ diplomatic, reserved.

outstanding *adj* 1 EXCELLENT, distinguished, eminent, pre-eminent, celebrated, exceptional, superior, remarkable, prominent, superb, great, notable, impressive, striking, superlative, important, noteworthy, memorable,

special, extraordinary. **2** OWING, unpaid, due, unsettled, unresolved, uncollected, pending, payable, remaining, ongoing, leftover.
Ea 1 ordinary, unexceptional. **2** paid, settled.

outstrip *v* surpass, exceed, better, outdo, beat, top, transcend, outshine, pass, gain on, leave behind, leave standing, outrun, outdistance, overtake, eclipse.

outward *adj* external, exterior, outer, outside, surface, superficial, visible, apparent, observable, evident, supposed, professed, public, obvious, ostensible.
Ea inner, private.

outwardly *adv* apparently, externally, to all appearances, visibly, superficially, supposedly, seemingly, on the surface, at first sight.

outweigh *v* override, prevail over, overcome, take precedence over, cancel out, make up for, compensate for, predominate.

outwit *v* outsmart, outthink, get the better of, trick, better, beat, dupe, cheat, deceive, defraud, swindle.

outworn *adj* outdated, out of date, outmoded, stale, discredited, defunct, old-fashioned, hackneyed, rejected, obsolete, disused, exhausted.
Ea fresh, new.

oval *adj* egg-shaped, elliptical, ovoid, ovate.

ovation *n* applause, acclaim, acclamation, praises, plaudits (*fml*), tribute, clapping, cheering, bravos.
Ea abuse, catcalls.

over *adj* finished, ended, done with, concluded, past, gone, completed, closed, in the past, settled, up, forgotten, accomplished.
➤ *adv* **1** ABOVE, beyond, overhead, on high. **2** EXTRA, remaining, surplus, superfluous, left, unclaimed, unused, unwanted, in excess, in addition.
➤ *prep* **1** ABOVE, on, on top of, upon, in charge of, in command of. **2** EXCEEDING, more than, in excess of.
◆ **over and above** in addition to, on top of, together with, plus, along with, as well as, besides, added to, let alone, not to mention.
◆ **over and over (again)** again and again, repeatedly, frequently, often, continually, endlessly, time and (time) again, ad infinitum, ad nauseam.

overact *v* overplay, exaggerate, overdo, ham (*infml*).
Ea underact, underplay.

overall *adj* total, all-inclusive, all-embracing, comprehensive, inclusive, general, universal, global, broad, blanket, complete, all-over.
Ea narrow, specific.
➤ *adv* in general, on the whole, by and large, broadly, generally speaking.

overbalance *v* lose one's balance, fall over, tip over, topple over, trip, slip, tumble, upset, somersault, lose one's footing, capsize, keel over, overturn, turn turtle.

overbearing *adj* imperious, domineering, arrogant, dictatorial, tyrannical, high-handed, haughty, bossy (*infml*), cavalier, autocratic, oppressive.
Ea meek, unassertive.

overcast *adj* cloudy, grey, dull, dark, sombre, sunless, hazy, lowering.
Ea bright, clear.

overcharge *v* surcharge, short-change, cheat, extort, rip off (*sl*), sting (*sl*), do (*infml*), diddle (*infml*).
Ea undercharge.

overcome *v* conquer, defeat, beat, surmount, triumph over, vanquish, rise above, master, overpower, overwhelm, overthrow, subdue.

overcrowded *adj* congested, packed (out), jam-packed, crammed full, chock-full, overpopulated, overloaded, swarming.
Ea deserted, empty.

overdo *v* exaggerate, go too far, carry to excess, go overboard (*infml*), lay it on thick (*infml*), overindulge, overstate, overact, overplay, overwork.

overdone *adj* **1** OVERCOOKED, burnt, spoiled, dried up, overbaked, charred, burnt to a cinder (*infml*), burnt to a frazzle (*infml*). **2** EXAGGERATED, overstated, overelaborate, undue, unnecessary, overplayed, excessive, immoderate, fulsome, effusive, gushing, inordinate, histrionic, over the top (*infml*).
Ea 1 underdone, raw. **2** underplayed, understated.

overdue *adj* late, behindhand, behind schedule, delayed, owing, unpunctual, slow.
Ea early.

overeat *v* gorge, binge, overindulge,

guzzle, stuff oneself, make a pig of oneself, pig out (*infml*), gormandize.
🔄 abstain, starve.

overflow *v* spill, overrun, run over, pour over, well over, brim over, bubble over, surge, flood, inundate, deluge, shower, submerge, soak, swamp, teem.
➤ *n* overspill, spill, inundation, flood, overabundance, surplus.

overhang *v* jut, project, bulge, protrude, stick out, extend.

overhaul *v* 1 RENOVATE, repair, service, recondition, mend, examine, inspect, check, survey, re-examine, fix.
2 OVERTAKE, pull ahead of, outpace, outstrip, gain on, pass.
➤ *n* reconditioning, repair, renovation, check, service, examination, inspection, going-over (*infml*).

overhead *adv* above, up above, on high, upward.
🔄 below, underfoot.
➤ *adj* elevated, aerial, overhanging, raised.

overheads *n* running costs, outgoings, operating costs, regular costs, expenses, expenditure, burden, oncost, disbursement (*fml*).
🔄 income, profit.

overindulge *v* 1 GORGE, gormandize, gluttonize, guzzle, debauch, eat/drink too much, satiate, sate, binge (*infml*), pig out (*infml*), make a pig of oneself (*infml*), booze (*sl*). 2 PAMPER, mollycoddle, spoil, cosset, pander, pet, spoon-feed (*infml*).
🔄 1 abstain.

overjoyed *adj* delighted, elated, euphoric, ecstatic, in raptures, enraptured, thrilled, jubilant, over the moon (*infml*).
🔄 sad, disappointed.

overload *v* burden, oppress, strain, tax, weigh down, overcharge, encumber.

overlook *v* 1 FRONT ON TO, face, look on to, look over, command a view of. 2 MISS, disregard, ignore, omit, neglect, pass over, let pass, let ride, slight. 3 EXCUSE, forgive, pardon, condone, wink at, turn a blind eye to.
🔄 2 notice. 3 penalize.

overly *adv* too, over, unduly, excessively, exceedingly, immoderately, unreasonably, inordinately.
🔄 inadequately, insufficiently.

overpower *v* overcome, conquer, overwhelm, vanquish, defeat, beat, subdue, overthrow, quell, master, crush, immobilize, floor.

overpowering *adj* overwhelming, powerful, strong, forceful, irresistible, uncontrollable, compelling, extreme, oppressive, suffocating, unbearable, nauseating, sickening.

overrate *v* overestimate, overvalue, overpraise, magnify, blow up, make too much of.
🔄 underrate.

override *v* 1 OUTWEIGH, be more important than, exceed, surpass, be greater than, be superior to, prevail over, overcome. 2 OVERRULE, cancel, annul, set aside, supersede, quash, reverse, disregard, ignore, trample over, abrogate (*fml*), countermand (*fml*), nullify (*fml*), rescind (*fml*), vanquish (*fml*), ride roughshod over (*infml*).

overriding *adj* most important, most significant, principal, first, major, predominant, primary, prime, supreme, compelling, dominant, essential, final, ultimate, overruling, prior, prevailing, ruling, paramount, pivotal, cardinal, determining, number one.
🔄 insignificant, unimportant.

overrule *v* overturn, override, countermand (*fml*), revoke, reject, rescind (*fml*), reverse, invalidate, cancel, vote down.

overrun *v* 1 INVADE, occupy, infest, overwhelm, inundate, run riot, spread over, swamp, swarm over, surge over, ravage, overgrow. 2 EXCEED, overshoot, overstep, overreach.

overseer *n* supervisor, boss (*infml*), chief, foreman, forewoman, manager, superintendent.

overshadow *v* 1 OBSCURE, cloud, darken, dim, spoil, veil. 2 OUTSHINE, eclipse, excel, surpass, dominate, dwarf, put in the shade, rise above, tower above.

oversight *n* 1 LAPSE, omission, fault, error, slip-up, mistake, blunder, carelessness, neglect. 2 SUPERVISION, responsibility, care, charge, control, custody, keeping, administration, management, direction.

overt *adj* open, manifest, plain, evident, observable, obvious, apparent, public, professed, unconcealed.
🔄 covert, secret.

overtake *v* 1 PASS, catch up with, outdistance, outstrip, draw level with, pull ahead of, overhaul. **2** COME UPON, befall, happen, strike, engulf.

overthrow *v* depose, oust, bring down, topple, unseat, displace, dethrone, conquer, vanquish, beat, defeat, crush, overcome, overpower, overturn, overwhelm, subdue, master, abolish, upset. ✺ install, protect, reinstate, restore.
➤ *n* ousting, unseating, defeat, deposition, dethronement, fall, rout, undoing, suppression, downfall, end, humiliation, destruction, ruin.

overtone *n* suggestion, intimation, nuance, hint, undercurrent, insinuation, connotation, association, feeling, implication, sense, flavour.

overture *n* **1** APPROACH, advance, offer, invitation, proposal, proposition, suggestion, signal, move, motion. **2** PRELUDE, opening, introduction, opening move, (opening) gambit.

overturn *v* **1** CAPSIZE, upset, upturn, tip over, topple, overbalance, keel over, knock over, spill. **2** OVERTHROW, repeal, rescind, reverse, annul, abolish, destroy, quash, set aside.

overweight *adj* fat, plump, stout, massive, huge, chunky, obese, ample, hefty, bulky, outsize, podgy, portly, pot-bellied, fleshy, heavy, tubby, chubby, buxom, corpulent (*fml*), flabby (*infml*), gross (*infml*), well-padded (*infml*), well-upholstered (*infml*).
✺ underweight, thin, skinny, emaciated.

overwhelm *v* **1** OVERCOME, overpower, destroy, defeat, crush, rout, devastate. **2** OVERRUN, inundate, snow under, submerge, swamp, engulf. **3** CONFUSE, bowl over, stagger, floor.

overwhelming *adj* **1** OVERPOWERING, powerful, strong, forceful, irresistible, undeniable, irrefutable, uncontrollable, compelling, extreme, oppressive, suffocating, stifling, unbearable, nauseating, sickening. **2** *an overwhelming majority*: great, large, vast, immense, huge.
✺ **1** resistible. **2** insignificant, negligible.

overwork *v* overstrain, overload, exploit, exhaust, overuse, overtax, strain, wear out, oppress, burden, weary.

overwrought *adj* tense, agitated, keyed up, on edge, worked up, wound up, frantic, overcharged, overexcited, excited, beside oneself, uptight (*infml*).
✺ calm.

owe *v* be in debt to, be overdrawn, get into debt, run up debts, be indebted to, be in arrears to, be under an obligation to, be in the red (*infml*), be up to one's ears in debt (*infml*).

owing *adj* unpaid, due, owed, in arrears, outstanding, payable, unsettled, overdue.
♦ **owing to** because of, as a result of, on account of, thanks to.

own *adj* personal, individual, private, particular, idiosyncratic.
➤ *v* possess, have, hold, retain, keep, enjoy.
♦ **own up** admit, confess, come clean (*infml*), tell the truth, acknowledge.

owner *n* possessor, holder, landlord, landlady, proprietor, proprietress, master, mistress, freeholder.

ownership *n* possession, proprietary rights, right of possession, proprietorship, rights, freehold, dominion, title (*fml*).

Pp

pace n **1** step, stride, walk, gait, tread, movement, motion, progress, rate, speed, velocity, celerity, quickness, rapidity, tempo, measure.
➤ v step, stride, walk, march, tramp, pound, patrol, mark out, measure.

pacifist n peace-lover, pacificist, conscientious objector, peacemaker, peace-monger, dove.
🖃 warmonger, hawk.

pacify v appease, conciliate, placate, mollify, calm, compose, soothe, assuage, allay, moderate, soften, lull, still, quiet, silence, quell, crush, put down, tame, subdue.
🖃 anger.

pack n **1** PACKET, box, carton, parcel, package, bundle, burden, load, backpack, rucksack, haversack, knapsack, kitbag. **2** GROUP, company, troop, herd, flock, band, crowd, gang, mob.
➤ v **1** WRAP, parcel, package, bundle, stow, store. **2** FILL, load, charge, cram, stuff, crowd, throng, press, ram, wedge, compact, compress.
♦ **pack in 1** CRAM IN, fill, load, charge, stuff, crowd, throng, mob, jam, press, squeeze, ram, wedge. **2** STOP, end, give up, leave, resign, throw in (infml), jack in (infml), chuck (infml).
♦ **pack up 1** TIDY UP, tidy away, clear up, put things away. **2** STOP, finish, end, give up, throw in (infml), jack in (infml), wrap up (infml), call it a day (infml). **3** BREAK DOWN, stop working, fail, malfunction (fml), seize up (infml), conk out (sl).

package n parcel, pack, packet, box, carton, bale, consignment.
➤ v parcel (up), wrap (up), pack (up), box, batch.

packed adj filled, full, jam-packed, chock-a-block, crammed, crowded, congested.
🖃 empty, deserted.

packet n pack, carton, box, bag, package, parcel, case, container, wrapper, wrapping, packing.

pact n treaty, convention, covenant, bond, alliance, cartel, contract, deal, bargain, compact, agreement, arrangement, understanding.
🖃 disagreement, quarrel.

pad¹ n **1** CUSHION, pillow, wad, buffer, padding, protection. **2** WRITING-PAD, note-pad, jotter, block.
➤ v fill, stuff, wad, pack, wrap, line, cushion, protect.
♦ **pad out** expand, inflate, fill out, augment, amplify, elaborate, flesh out, lengthen, stretch, protract, spin out.

pad² v walk, move, step, run, tread, trudge, tramp, tiptoe, lope.

padding n **1** FILLING, stuffing, wadding, packing, protection. **2** VERBIAGE, verbosity, wordiness, waffle (infml), bombast, hot air.

paddle¹ n oar, scull.
➤ v row, oar, scull, propel, steer.

paddle² v wade, splash, slop, dabble.

pagan n heathen, atheist, unbeliever, infidel, idolater.
🖃 believer.
➤ adj heathen, irreligious, atheistic, godless, infidel, idolatrous.

page¹ n leaf, sheet, folio, side.

page² n page-boy, attendant, messenger, bell-boy, footman, servant.
➤ v call, send for, summon, bid, announce.

pageant n procession, parade, show, display, tableau, scene, play, spectacle, extravaganza.

pageantry n pomp, ceremony, grandeur, magnificence, splendour, glamour, glitter, spectacle, parade, display, show, extravagance, theatricality, drama, melodrama.

pain n **1** HURT, ache, throb, cramp, spasm, twinge, pang, stab, sting, smart, soreness, tenderness, discomfort, distress, suffering, affliction, trouble, anguish, agony, torment, torture. **2** (infml) NUISANCE, bother, bore (infml), annoyance, vexation, burden, headache (infml).
➤ v hurt, afflict, torment, torture, agonize, distress, upset, sadden, grieve.
🖃 please, delight, gratify.

pained adj hurt, injured, wounded, stung,

offended, aggrieved, reproachful, distressed, upset, saddened, grieved. ⊠ pleased, gratified.

painful *adj* 1 SORE, tender, aching, throbbing, smarting, stabbing, agonizing, excruciating. 2 *a painful experience*: unpleasant, disagreeable, distressing, upsetting, saddening, harrowing, traumatic. 3 HARD, difficult, laborious, tedious.
⊠ 1 painless, soothing. 2 pleasant, agreeable. 3 easy.

painfully *adv* distressingly, dreadfully, terribly, excessively, clearly, markedly, alarmingly, pitiably, pitifully, sadly, unfortunately, wretchedly, agonizingly, excruciatingly, woefully, deplorably.

painkiller *n* analgesic, anodyne, anaesthetic, palliative, sedative, drug, remedy.

painless *adj* pain-free, trouble-free, effortless, easy, simple, undemanding. ⊠ painful, difficult.

pains *n* trouble, bother, effort, labour, care, diligence.

painstaking *adj* careful, meticulous, scrupulous, thorough, conscientious, diligent, assiduous, industrious, hard-working, dedicated, devoted, persevering. ⊠ careless, negligent.

paint *n* colour, colouring, pigment, dye, tint, stain.

> Paints include: acrylic paint, colourwash, distemper, eggshell, emulsion, enamel, gloss paint, gouache, glaze, lacquer, masonry paint, matt paint, oil paint, oils, pastel, poster paint, primer, undercoat, varnish, watercolour, whitewash.

➤ *v* 1 COLOUR, dye, tint, stain, lacquer, varnish, glaze, apply, daub, coat, cover, decorate. 2 PORTRAY, depict, describe, recount, picture, represent.

painting *n* oil painting, oil, watercolour, picture, portrait, landscape, still life, miniature, illustration, fresco, mural.

> Painting terms include: abstract, alla prima, aquarelle, aquatint, art gallery, bleeding, bloom; brush, filbert brush, flat brush, round brush, sable brush; brush strokes, canvas, canvas board, capriccio, cartoon, charcoal, chiaroscuro, collage, composition, craquelure, diptych, drawing, easel, encaustic, facture, fête champêtre, fête

galante, figurative, foreshortening, fresco, frieze, frottage, gallery, genre painting, gesso, gouache, grisaille, grotesque, hard edge, icon, illustration, impasto, landscape, mahlstick, miniature, monochrome, montage, mural, oil painting, paint, palette, palette knife, pastels, pastoral, paysage, pencil sketch, pentimento, perspective, picture, pieta, pigment, pochade box, pointillism, portrait, primer, scumble, seascape, secco, sfumato, sgraffito, silhouette, sketch, skyscape, still life, stipple, tempera, thinners, tint, tondo, tone, triptych, trompe l'œil, turpentine, underpainting, vignette, wash, watercolour. *see also* **art**; **picture**.

pair *n* couple, brace, twosome, duo, twins, two of a kind.
➤ *v* match (up), twin, team, mate, marry, wed, splice, join, couple, link, bracket, put together.
⊠ separate, part.

palace *n* castle, château, mansion, stately home, basilica, dome.

palatable *adj* tasty, appetizing, eatable, edible, acceptable, satisfactory, pleasant, agreeable, enjoyable, attractive.
⊠ unpalatable, unacceptable, unpleasant, disagreeable.

palate *n* taste, appreciation, liking, relish, enjoyment, appetite, stomach, heart.

palatial *adj* grand, magnificent, splendid, majestic, regal, stately, grandiose, imposing, luxurious, de luxe, sumptuous, opulent (*fml*), plush (*infml*), spacious.

palaver *n* fuss, bother, fuss about nothing, rigmarole, procedure, carry-on (*infml*), activity, business, bustle, commotion, fluster, song and dance (*infml*), to-do (*infml*), flap (*infml*).

pale *adj* 1 PALLID, livid, ashen, ashy, white, chalky, pasty, pasty-faced, waxen, waxy, wan, sallow, anaemic. 2 *pale blue*: light, pastel, faded, washed-out, bleached, colourless, insipid, vapid, weak, feeble, faint, dim.
⊠ 1 ruddy. 2 dark.
➤ *v* whiten, blanch, bleach, fade, dim.
⊠ colour, blush.

pall[1] *n* shroud, veil, mantle, cloak, cloud, shadow, gloom, damper.

pall[2] *v* tire, weary, jade, sate, satiate, cloy, sicken.

pallid *adj* 1 PALE, pasty, whitish, sallow,

colourless, pasty-faced, ashen, ashy, bloodless, anaemic, wan, waxen, waxy, whey-faced. **2** UNEXCITING, weak, dull, boring, uninteresting, bland, uninspired, tame, sterile, tired, lifeless, insipid, spiritless, vapid.
🔁 **1** vigorous, ruddy, high-complexioned. **2** lively, exciting.

palm n hand, paw (infml), mitt (sl).
➤ v take, grab, snatch, appropriate.
♦ **palm off** foist, impose, fob off, offload, unload, pass off.

palpable adj solid, substantial, material, real, touchable, tangible, visible, apparent, clear, plain, obvious, evident, manifest, conspicuous, blatant, unmistakable.
🔁 impalpable, imperceptible, intangible, elusive.

palpitate v flutter, quiver, tremble, shiver, vibrate, beat, pulsate, pound, thump, throb.

paltry adj meagre, derisory, contemptible, mean, low, miserable, wretched, poor, sorry, small, slight, trifling, inconsiderable, negligible, trivial, minor, petty, unimportant, insignificant, worthless.
🔁 substantial, significant, valuable.

pamper v cosset, coddle, mollycoddle, humour, gratify, indulge, overindulge, spoil, pet, fondle.
🔁 neglect, ill-treat.

pamphlet n leaflet, brochure, booklet, folder, circular, handout, notice.

pan¹ n saucepan, frying-pan, fryer, pot, skillet, casserole, wok, container, vessel, pancheon.
➤ v criticize, censure, flay, find fault with, hammer, knock (infml), pull to pieces (infml), roast (infml), rubbish (infml), slam (infml), slate (infml).
🔁 praise.
♦ **pan out** work out, turn out, result, happen, yield, culminate, come to an end, be exhausted, eventuate (fml).

pan² v sweep, scan, move, turn, follow, track, swing, circle, traverse (fml).

panacea n cure-all, universal remedy, elixir, nostrum, catholicon (fml), diacatholicon (fml), panpharmacon (fml).

panache n flourish, flamboyance, ostentation, style, flair, élan, dash, spirit, enthusiasm, zest, energy, vigour, verve.

pandemonium n chaos, disorder, confusion, commotion, rumpus, turmoil, turbulence, tumult, uproar, din, bedlam,

hubbub, hullaballoo, hue and cry, to-do (infml).
🔁 order, calm, peace.

pander to v humour, indulge, pamper, please, gratify, satisfy, fulfil, provide, cater to.

panel n board, committee, jury, team.

pang n pain, ache, twinge, stab, sting, prick, stitch, gripe, spasm, throe, agony, anguish, discomfort, distress.

panic n agitation, flap (infml), alarm, dismay, consternation, fright, fear, horror, terror, frenzy, hysteria.
🔁 calmness, confidence.
➤ v lose one's nerve, lose one's head, go to pieces, flap (infml), overreact.
🔁 relax.

panic-stricken adj alarmed, frightened, horrified, terrified, petrified, scared stiff, in a cold sweat, panicky, frantic, frenzied, hysterical.
🔁 relaxed, confident.

panorama n view, vista, prospect, scenery, landscape, scene, spectacle, perspective, overview, survey.

panoramic adj scenic, wide, sweeping, extensive, far-reaching, widespread, overall, general, universal.
🔁 narrow, restricted, limited.

pant v puff, blow, gasp, wheeze, breathe, sigh, heave, throb, palpitate.

panting adj **1** PUFFED OUT, breathless, out of breath, gasping, short-winded, winded, puffing, puffed. **2** ANXIOUS, eager, impatient, longing, craving, hankering.

pants n **1** UNDERPANTS, drawers, panties, briefs, knickers (infml), Y-fronts, boxer shorts, trunks, shorts. **2** TROUSERS, slacks, jeans.

pap n **1** MUSH, pulp, purée, soft food, semi-liquid food, goo (infml). **2** RUBBISH, drivel, trash, nonsense, gibberish, rot (infml), claptrap (infml), crap (sl).

paper n **1** NEWSPAPER, daily, broadsheet, tabloid, rag (sl), journal, organ.
2 DOCUMENT, credential, authorization, identification, certificate, deed. **3** a paper on alternative medicine: essay, composition, dissertation, thesis, treatise, article, report.

> Types of paper include: art paper, bank, blotting paper, bond, carbon paper, cartridge paper, crêpe paper, greaseproof paper, graph paper, manila, notepaper, parchment, rice

paper, silver paper, sugar paper, tissue paper, toilet paper, tracing paper, vellum, wallpaper, wrapping paper, writing-paper; card, cardboard, pasteboard; A4, foolscap, quarto, atlas, crown.

parable n fable, allegory, lesson, moral tale, story.

parade n procession, cavalcade, motorcade, march, column, file, train, review, ceremony, spectacle, pageant, show, display, exhibition.
➤ v 1 MARCH, process, file past. 2 SHOW, display, exhibit, show off, vaunt, flaunt, brandish.

paradigm n pattern, model, example, original, ideal, framework, prototype, archetype (fml), exemplar (fml).

paradise n heaven, Utopia, Shangri-La, Elysium, Eden, bliss, delight.
Ea hell, Hades.

paradox n contradiction, inconsistency, incongruity, absurdity, oddity, anomaly, mystery, enigma, riddle, puzzle.

paradoxical adj self-contradictory, contradictory, conflicting, inconsistent, incongruous, absurd, illogical, improbable, impossible, mysterious, enigmatic, puzzling, baffling.

paragon n ideal, exemplar (fml), epitome, quintessence, model, pattern, archetype (fml), prototype, standard, criterion.

paragraph n passage, section, part, portion, subsection, subdivision, clause, item.

parallel adj equidistant, aligned, coextensive, alongside, analogous, equivalent, corresponding, matching, like, similar, resembling.
Ea divergent, different.
➤ n 1 MATCH, equal, twin, duplicate, analogue, equivalent, counterpart.
2 SIMILARITY, resemblance, likeness, correspondence, correlation, equivalence, analogy, comparison.
➤ v match, echo, conform, agree, correspond, correlate, compare, liken.
Ea diverge, differ.

paralyse v cripple, lame, disable, incapacitate, immobilize, anaesthetize, numb, deaden, freeze, transfix, halt, stop.

paralysed adj paralytic, paraplegic, quadriplegic, crippled, lame, disabled, incapacitated, immobilized, numb.
Ea able-bodied.

paralysis n paraplegia, quadriplegia, palsy, numbness, deadness, immobility, halt, standstill, stoppage, shutdown.

paralytic adj 1 CRIPPLED, disabled, paralysed, incapacitated, lame, immobilized, immobile, numb, palsied, quadriplegic, monoplegic, hemiplegic. 2 DRUNK, inebriated, intoxicated, legless (infml), plastered (infml), pie-eyed (infml), stoned (sl), sloshed (sl), smashed (sl), stewed (sl).
Ea 2 (stone-cold) sober.

parameter n variable, guideline, indication, criterion, specification, limitation, restriction, limit, boundary.

paramount adj supreme, highest, topmost, predominant, pre-eminent, prime, principal, main, chief, cardinal, primary, first, foremost.
Ea lowest, last.

paranoid adj suspicious, distrustful, bewildered, confused, afraid, fearful, fazed.

paraphernalia n equipment, gear, tackle, apparatus, accessories, trappings, bits and pieces, odds and ends, belongings, effects, stuff, things, baggage.

paraphrase n rewording, rephrasing, restatement, version, interpretation, rendering, translation.
➤ v reword, rephrase, restate, interpret, render, translate.

parasite n sponger (infml), scrounger (infml), cadger (infml), hanger-on, leech, bloodsucker.

parcel n package, packet, pack, box, carton, bundle.
➤ v package, pack, wrap, bundle, tie up.
♦ **parcel out** divide, carve up, apportion, allocate, allot, share out, distribute, dispense, dole out, deal out, mete out.

parch v dry (up), desiccate, dehydrate, bake, burn, scorch, sear, blister, wither, shrivel.

parched adj 1 ARID, waterless, dry, dried up, dehydrated, scorched, withered, shrivelled. 2 (infml) THIRSTY, gasping (infml).

pardon v forgive, condone, overlook, excuse, vindicate, acquit, absolve, remit, let off, reprieve, free, liberate, release.
Ea punish, discipline.
➤ n forgiveness, mercy, clemency, indulgence, amnesty, excuse, acquittal, absolution, reprieve, release, discharge.

▨ punishment, condemnation.

pardonable *adj* forgivable, excusable, justifiable, warrantable, understandable, allowable, permissible, minor, venial.
▨ inexcusable.

pare *v* peel, skin, shear, clip, trim, crop, cut, dock, lop, prune, cut back, reduce, decrease.

parent *n* father, mother, dam, sire, progenitor, begetter, procreator, guardian.

pariah *n* outcast, outlaw, exile, castaway, leper, undesirable, unperson, untouchable, Ishmael, black sheep (*infml*).

parish *n* district, community, parishioners, church, churchgoers, congregation, flock, fold.

park *n* grounds, woodland, grassland.

Types of park include: amusement park, arboretum, botanical garden, car park, estate, game reserve, industrial park, municipal park, national park, park-and-ride, parking lot, parkland, play area, playground, pleasance, pleasure garden, pleasure ground, recreation ground, reserve, sanctuary, theme park, wildlife park.

➤ *v* put, position, place, deposit, set, leave, stop, plonk (*infml*).

parliament *n* legislature, senate, congress, house, assembly, convocation, council, diet.

Names of parliaments and political assemblies include: House of Representatives, Senate (Australia); Nationalrat, Bundesrat (Austria); Narodno Sobraniye (Bulgaria); House of Commons, Senate (Canada); National People's Congress (China); Folketing (Denmark); People's Assembly (Egypt); Eduskunta (Finland); National Assembly, Senate (France); Bundesrat, Bundestag, Landtag (Germany); Althing (Iceland); Lok Sabha, Rajya Sabha (India); Majlis (Iran); Dáil, Seanad (Ireland); Knesset (Israel); Camera dei Deputati, Senato (Italy); Diet (Japan); Staten-Generaal (Netherlands); House of Representatives (New Zealand); Storting (Norway); Sejm (Poland); Cortes (Portugal); State Duma, Federation Council (Russia); House of Assembly (South Africa); Cortes (Spain); Riksdag (Sweden); Nationalrat, Ständerat, Bundesrat (Switzerland); Porte (Turkey); House of Commons, House of Lords (UK); House of Representatives, Senate (US); National Assembly (Vietnam).

parliamentary *adj* governmental, senatorial, congressional, legislative, law-making.

parochial *adj* insular, provincial, parish-pump, petty, small-minded, narrow-minded, inward-looking, blinkered, limited, restricted, confined.
▨ national, international.

parody *n* caricature, lampoon, burlesque, satire, send-up (*infml*), spoof, skit, mimicry, imitation, take-off (*infml*), travesty, distortion.
➤ *v* caricature, lampoon, burlesque, satirize, send up (*infml*), spoof, mimic, imitate, ape, take off (*infml*).

paroxysm *n* fit, seizure, spasm, convulsion, attack, outbreak, outburst, explosion.

parrot *v* repeat, copy, imitate, mimic, echo, rehearse, reiterate, ape.
➤ *n* mimic, repeater, imitator, copy-cat (*infml*), phraser, ape.

parrot-fashion *adv* by rote, mechanically, mindlessly, unthinkingly, automatically.

parry *v* ward off, fend off, repel, repulse, field, deflect, block, avert, avoid, evade, duck, dodge, sidestep, shun.

parsimonious *adj* mean, niggardly, miserly, tight-fisted (*infml*), stinting, sparing, scrimpy, saving, close, cheese-paring (*infml*), close-fisted, close-handed, frugal, grasping, penurious (*fml*), mingy (*infml*), penny-pinching (*infml*), stingy (*infml*), tight (*infml*).
▨ generous, liberal, open-handed.

parson *n* vicar, rector, priest, minister, pastor, preacher, clergyman, reverend, cleric, churchman.

part *n* **1** COMPONENT, constituent, element, factor, piece, bit, particle, fragment, scrap, segment, fraction, portion, share, section, division, department, branch, sector, district, region, territory. **2** ROLE, character, duty, task, responsibility, office, function, capacity.
▨ **1** whole, totality.
➤ *v* separate, detach, disconnect, sever, split, tear, break, break up, take apart, dismantle, come apart, split up, divide, disunite, part company, disband, disperse, scatter, leave, depart, withdraw, go away.
◆ **part with** relinquish, let go of, give up, yield, surrender, renounce, forgo, abandon, discard, jettison.

partake v take part, share, participate, be involved, engage, enter.
♦ **partake of 1** *partake of food*: consume, eat, drink. **2** *partake of the divine nature*: receive, share, have, show, demonstrate, take, suggest, evoke, evince (*fml*), manifest (*fml*).

partial adj **1** *a partial victory*: incomplete, limited, restricted, imperfect, fragmentary, unfinished. **2** BIASED, prejudiced, partisan, one-sided, discriminatory, unfair, unjust, predisposed, coloured, affected.
◼ **1** complete, total. **2** impartial, disinterested, unbiased, fair.
♦ **partial to** fond of, keen on, crazy about (*infml*), mad about (*infml*).

partiality n liking, fondness, predilection (*fml*), proclivity (*fml*), inclination, preference, predisposition (*fml*).

partially adv incompletely, not fully, fractionally, somewhat, in part, partly.

participant n entrant, contributor, participator, member, party, co-operator, helper, worker.

participate v take part, join in, contribute, engage, be involved, enter, share, partake, co-operate, help, assist.

participation n involvement, sharing, partnership, co-operation, contribution, assistance.

particle n bit, piece, fragment, scrap, shred, sliver, speck, morsel, crumb, iota, whit, jot, tittle, atom, grain, drop.

particular adj **1** *on that particular day*: specific, precise, exact, distinct, special, peculiar. **2** EXCEPTIONAL, remarkable, notable, marked, thorough, unusual, uncommon. **3** FUSSY, discriminating, choosy (*infml*), finicky, fastidious.
◼ **1** general.
➤ n detail, specific, point, feature, item, fact, circumstance.

particularly adv especially, exceptionally, remarkably, notably, extraordinarily, unusually, uncommonly, surprisingly, in particular, specifically, explicitly, distinctly.

parting n **1** DEPARTURE, going, leave-taking, farewell, goodbye, adieu. **2** DIVERGENCE, separation, division, partition, rift, split, rupture, breaking.
◼ **1** meeting. **2** convergence.
➤ adj departing, farewell, last, dying, final, closing, concluding.
◼ first.

partisan n devotee, adherent, follower, disciple, backer, supporter, champion, stalwart, guerrilla, irregular.
➤ adj biased, prejudiced, partial, predisposed, discriminatory, one-sided, factional, sectarian.
◼ impartial.

partition n **1** DIVIDER, barrier, wall, panel, screen, room-divider. **2** DIVISION, break-up, splitting, separation, parting, severance.
➤ v **1** SEPARATE, divide, subdivide, wall off, fence off, screen. **2** SHARE, divide, split up, parcel out.

partly adv somewhat, to some extent, to a certain extent, up to a point, slightly, fractionally, moderately, relatively, in part, partially, incompletely.
◼ completely, totally.

partner n **1** ASSOCIATE, ally, confederate, colleague, co-worker, team-mate, collaborator, co-operator, accomplice, helper, mate, companion, comrade, consort, spouse, husband, wife, sidekick (*infml*), oppo (*infml*). **2** *bring your partner to the party*: spouse, husband, wife, boyfriend, girlfriend, friend, companion, consort, other half (*infml*).

partnership n **1** ALLIANCE, confederation, affiliation, combination, union, syndicate, co-operative, association, society, corporation, company, firm, fellowship, fraternity, brotherhood. **2** COLLABORATION, co-operation, participation, sharing.

party n **1** CELEBRATION, festivity, social, do (*infml*), knees-up (*sl*), rave-up (*sl*), get-together, gathering, reunion, function, reception, at-home, housewarming. **2** *a search party*: team, squad, crew, gang, band, group, company, detachment. **3** *a political party*: faction, side, league, cabal, alliance, association, grouping, combination. **4** PERSON, individual, litigant, plaintiff, defendant.

Types of party include: acid-house party, barbecue, bash (*sl*), beanfeast (*infml*), beano (*infml*), birthday party, bunfight (*infml*), ceilidh, dinner party, disco, discotheque, do (*infml*), flatwarming, garden party, gathering of the clan (*infml*), Hallowe'en party, hen party, hooley, hootenanny (*US infml*), housewarming, orgy, picnic, pyjama party, rave, rave-up (*sl*), social, soirée, stag night, stag party, supper party, tea party, thrash (*infml*), welcoming party.

pass[1] *v* **1** SURPASS, exceed, go beyond, outdo, outstrip, overtake, leave behind. **2** *pass time*: spend, while away, fill, occupy. **3** GO PAST, go by, elapse, lapse, proceed, roll, flow, run, move, go, disappear, vanish. **4** GIVE, hand, transfer, transmit. **5** ENACT, ratify, validate, adopt, authorize, sanction, approve. **6** *pass an exam*: succeed, get through, qualify, graduate.
➤ *n* **1** THROW, kick, move, lunge, swing. **2** PERMIT, passport, identification, ticket, licence, authorization, warrant, permission.
♦ **pass away** die, pass on, expire, decease, give up the ghost.
♦ **pass off 1** FEIGN, counterfeit, fake, palm off. **2** HAPPEN, occur, take place, go off.
♦ **pass out 1** FAINT, lose consciousness, black out, collapse, flake out, keel over (*infml*), drop. **2** GIVE OUT, hand out, dole out, distribute, deal out, share out.
♦ **pass over** disregard, ignore, overlook, miss, omit, leave, neglect.
♦ **pass up** not take advantage of, ignore, miss, refuse, neglect, reject, let slip.

pass[2] *n* col, defile, gorge, ravine, canyon, gap, passage.

passable *adj* **1** SATISFACTORY, acceptable, allowable, tolerable, average, ordinary, unexceptional, moderate, fair, adequate, all right, OK (*infml*), mediocre. **2** CLEAR, unobstructed, unblocked, open, navigable.
🖅 **1** unacceptable, excellent. **2** obstructed, blocked, impassable.

passage *n* **1** PASSAGEWAY, aisle, corridor, hall, hallway, lobby, vestibule, doorway, opening, entrance, exit. **2** THOROUGHFARE, way, route, road, avenue, path, lane, alley. **3** EXTRACT, excerpt, quotation, text, paragraph, section, piece, clause, verse. **4** JOURNEY, voyage, trip, crossing.

passageway *n* passage, corridor, hall, hallway, lobby, entrance, exit, aisle, lane, path, way, track, alley.

passé *adj* outdated, old-fashioned, out of date, dated, obsolete, outmoded, unfashionable, outworn, démodé, antiquated, past its best, old hat (*infml*), out (*infml*).
🖅 fashionable, in (*infml*).

passenger *n* traveller, voyager, commuter, rider, fare, hitch-hiker.

passer-by *n* bystander, witness, looker-on, onlooker, spectator.

passing *adj* ephemeral, transient, short-lived, temporary, momentary, fleeting, brief, short, cursory, hasty, quick, slight, superficial, shallow, casual, incidental.
🖅 lasting, permanent.

passion *n* feeling, emotion, love, adoration, infatuation, fondness, affection, lust, itch, desire, craving, fancy, mania, obsession, craze, eagerness, keenness, avidity, zest, enthusiasm, fanaticism, zeal, ardour, fervour, warmth, heat, fire, spirit, intensity, vehemence, anger, indignation, fury, rage (*infml*), outburst.
🖅 coolness, indifference, self-possession.

passionate *adj* **1** ARDENT, fervent, eager, keen, avid, enthusiastic, fanatical, zealous, warm, hot, fiery, inflamed, aroused, excited, impassioned, intense, strong, fierce, vehement, violent, stormy, tempestuous, wild, frenzied. **2** EMOTIONAL, excitable, hot-headed, impetuous, impulsive, quick-tempered, irritable. **3** LOVING, affectionate, lustful, erotic, sexy, sensual, sultry.
🖅 **1** phlegmatic, laid-back (*infml*). **3** frigid.

passive *adj* receptive, unassertive, submissive, docile, unresisting, non-violent, patient, resigned, long-suffering, indifferent, apathetic, lifeless, inert, inactive, non-participating.
🖅 active, lively, responsive, involved.

password *n* watchword, signal, keyword, open sesame, parole, shibboleth, countersign.

past *adj* **1** OVER, ended, finished, completed, done, over and done with. **2** FORMER, previous, preceding, foregoing, late, recent. **3** ANCIENT, bygone, olden, early, gone, no more, extinct, defunct, forgotten.
🖅 **2** future.
➤ *n* **1** *in the past*: history, former times, olden days, antiquity. **2** LIFE, background, experience, track record.
🖅 **1** future.

pasta

Forms and shapes of pasta include:
agnolotti, anelli, angel's hair, bombolotti, bucatini, cannelloni, capelletti, casarecci, conchiglie, crescioni, ditali, elbow macaroni, farfalline, fedelini, fettuccine, fiochetti, fusilli, gnocchi, lasagne, lasagne verde, linguini, lumache, macaroni, mafalde, manicotti, maruzze, mezzani, noodle, noodle farfel, penne, pennine, ravioli, rigatoni, ruoti,

spaghetti, spaghetti bolognese, stelline, tagliatelle, tortellini, trofie, vermicelli, ziti.

paste n adhesive, glue, gum, mastic, putty, cement.
➤ v stick, glue, gum, cement, fix.

pastel adj delicate, soft, soft-hued, light, pale, subdued, faint.

pastime n hobby, activity, game, sport, recreation, play, fun, amusement, entertainment, diversion, distraction, relaxation.
🗷 work, employment.

pastor n minister, clergyman, priest, rector, vicar, parson, cleric, churchman, canon, prebendary, divine, ecclesiastic.

pastoral adj 1 RURAL, country, rustic, bucolic, agricultural, agrarian, idyllic.
2 ECCLESIASTICAL, clerical, priestly, ministerial.
🗷 1 urban.

pastry

Types of pastry include: American crust pastry, biscuit-crumb pastry, cheese pastry, choux, Danish pastry, filo pastry, flaky pastry, flan pastry, hot-water crust pastry, one-stage pastry, pâte à savarin, pâte brisée, pâte frolle, pâte sablée, pâte sucrée, plain pastry, pork-pie pastry, puff pastry, rich shortcrust pastry, rough-puff pastry, short pastry, shortcrust pastry, suetcrust pastry, sweet pastry.

pasture n grass, grassland, meadow, field, paddock, pasturage, grazing.

pasty adj pale, pallid, wan, anaemic, pasty-faced, sickly, unhealthy.
🗷 ruddy, healthy.

pat v tap, dab, slap, touch, stroke, caress, fondle, pet.
➤ n tap, dab, slap, touch, stroke, caress.
➤ adv precisely, exactly, perfectly, flawlessly, faultlessly, fluently.
🗷 imprecisely, inaccurately, wrongly.
➤ adj glib, fluent, smooth, slick, ready, easy, facile, simplistic.

patch n piece, bit, scrap, spot, area, stretch, tract, plot, lot, parcel.
➤ v mend, repair, fix, cover, reinforce.

patchy adj uneven, irregular, inconsistent, variable, random, fitful, erratic, sketchy, bitty, spotty, blotchy.
🗷 even, uniform, regular, consistent.

patent adj obvious, evident, conspicuous, manifest, clear, transparent, apparent,

visible, palpable, unequivocal, open, overt, blatant, flagrant, glaring.
🗷 hidden, opaque.
➤ n privilege, right, certificate, licence, invention, copyright, registered trademark.

paternal adj fatherly, fatherlike, protective, benevolent, concerned, vigilant.

path n route, course, direction, way, passage, road, avenue, lane, footpath, bridleway, trail, track, walk.

pathetic adj 1 PITIABLE, poor, sorry, lamentable, miserable, sad, distressing, moving, touching, poignant, plaintive, heart-rending, heartbreaking. 2 (infml) CONTEMPTIBLE, derisory, deplorable, useless, worthless, inadequate, meagre, feeble.
🗷 1 cheerful. 2 admirable, excellent, valuable.

pathos n poignancy, misery, sadness, pitiableness, pitifulness, plaintiveness, inadequacy.

patience n calmness, composure, self-control, restraint, tolerance, forbearance, endurance, fortitude, long-suffering, submission, resignation, stoicism, persistence, perseverance, diligence.
🗷 impatience, intolerance, exasperation.

patient adj calm, composed, self-possessed, self-controlled, restrained, even-tempered, mild, lenient, indulgent, understanding, forgiving, tolerant, accommodating, forbearing, long-suffering, uncomplaining, submissive, resigned, philosophical, stoical, persistent, persevering.
🗷 impatient, restless, intolerant, exasperated.
➤ n invalid, sufferer, case, client.

patriot n nationalist, loyalist, chauvinist, flag-waver, jingoist, jingo.

patriotic adj nationalistic, chauvinistic, jingoistic, loyal, flag-waving.

patrol n 1 GUARD, sentry, sentinel, watchman. 2 on patrol: watch, surveillance, policing, protection, defence.
➤ v police, guard, protect, defend, go the rounds, tour, inspect.

patron n 1 BENEFACTOR, philanthropist, sponsor, backer, supporter, sympathizer, advocate, champion, defender, protector, guardian, helper. 2 CUSTOMER, client, frequenter, regular, shopper, buyer, purchaser, subscriber.

Occupations with a patron saint include: Accountants (Matthew), Actors (Genesius; Vitus), Advertisers (Bernardino of Siena), Architects (Thomas, Apostle), Artists (Luke; Angelico), Astronauts (Joseph of Cupertino), Astronomers (Dominic), Athletes (Sebastian), Authors (Francis de Sales), Aviators (Our Lady of Loreto), Bakers (Honoratus), Bankers (Bernardino (Feltre)), Barbers (Cosmas and Damian), Blacksmiths (Eligius), Bookkeepers (Matthew), Book trade (John of God), Brewers (Amand; Wenceslaus), Builders (Barbara; Thomas, Apostle), Butchers (Luke), Carpenters (Joseph), Chemists (Cosmas and Damian), Comedians (Vitus), Cooks (Lawrence; Martha), Dancers (Vitus), Dentists (Apollonia), Doctors (Cosmas and Damian; Luke), Editors (Francis de Sales), Farmers (Isidore), Firemen (Florian), Fishermen (Andrew; Peter), Florists (Dorothy; Thérèse of Lisieux), Gardeners (Adam; Fiacre), Glassworkers (Luke; Lucy), Gravediggers (Joseph of Arimathea), Grocers (Michael), Hotelkeepers (Amand; Julian the Hospitaler), Housewives (Martha), Jewellers (Eligius), Journalists (Francis de Sales), Labourers (James; John Bosco), Lawyers (Ivo; Thomas More), Librarians (Jerome; Catherine of Alexandria), Merchants (Francis of Assisi), Messengers (Gabriel), Metalworkers (Eligius), Midwives (Raymond Nonnatus), Miners (Anne; Barbara), Motorists (Christopher), Musicians (Cecilia; Gregory the Great), Nurses (Camillus de Lellis; John of God), Philosophers (Thomas Aquinas; Catherine of Alexandria), Poets (Cecilia; David), Police (Michael), Postal workers (Gabriel), Priests (Jean-Baptiste Vianney), Printers (John of God), Prisoners (Leonard), Radio workers (Gabriel), Sailors (Christopher; Erasmus; Francis of Paola), Scholars (Thomas Aquinas), Scientists (Albert the Great), Sculptors (Luke; Louis), Secretaries (Genesius), Servants (Martha; Zita), Shoemakers (Crispin; Crispinian), Singers (Cecilia; Gregory), Soldiers (George; Joan of Arc; Martin of Tours; Sebastian), Students (Thomas Aquinas), Surgeons (Luke; Cosmas and Damian), Tailors (Homobonus), Tax collectors (Matthew), Taxi drivers (Fiacre), Teachers (Gregory the Great; John Baptist de la Salle), Theologians (Augustine; Alphonsus Liguori; Thomas Aquinas), Television workers (Gabriel), Undertakers (Dismas; Joseph of Arimathea), Waiters (Martha), Writers (Lucy).

---

patronage n custom, business, trade, sponsorship, backing, support.

patronize v 1 SPONSOR, fund, back, support, maintain, help, assist, promote, foster, encourage. 2 FREQUENT, shop at, buy from, deal with.

patronizing adj condescending, stooping, overbearing, high-handed, haughty, superior, snobbish, supercilious, disdainful.
☒ humble, lowly.

patter v tap, pat, pitter-patter, beat, pelt, scuttle, scurry.
➤ n 1 PATTERING, tapping, pitter-patter, beating. 2 a salesman's patter: chatter, gabble, jabber, line, pitch, spiel (sl), jargon, lingo (infml).

pattern n 1 SYSTEM, method, order, plan. 2 DECORATION, ornamentation, ornament, figure, motif, design, style. 3 MODEL, template, stencil, guide, original, prototype, standard, norm.

patterned adj decorated, ornamented, figured, printed.
☒ plain.

paunch n abdomen, belly, pot-belly, beer-belly, corporation (infml).

pause v halt, stop, cease, discontinue, break off, interrupt, take a break, rest, wait, delay, hesitate.
➤ n halt, stoppage, interruption, break, rest, breather (infml), lull, let-up (infml), respite, gap, interval, interlude, intermission, wait, delay, hesitation.

pave v flag, tile, floor, surface, cover, asphalt, tarmac, concrete.

paw v maul, manhandle, mishandle, molest.
➤ n foot, pad, forefoot, hand.

pawn[1] n dupe, puppet, tool, instrument, toy, plaything.

pawn[2] v deposit, pledge, stake, mortgage, hock (sl), pop (sl).

pay v 1 REMIT, settle, discharge, reward, remunerate, recompense, reimburse, repay, refund, spend, pay out. 2 BENEFIT, profit, pay off, bring in, yield, return. 3 ATONE, make amends, compensate, answer, suffer.
➤ n remuneration, wages, salary, earnings,

income, fee, stipend, honorarium, emoluments, payment, reward, recompense, compensation, reimbursement.

◆ **pay back 1** REPAY, refund, reimburse, recompense, settle, square. **2** RETALIATE, get one's own back, take revenge, get even with, reciprocate, counter-attack.

◆ **pay off 1** DISCHARGE, settle, square, clear. **2** DISMISS, fire, sack (*infml*), lay off. **3** *the preparations paid off*: succeed, work.

◆ **pay out** spend, disburse, hand over, fork out (*infml*), shell out (*infml*), lay out (*infml*).

payable *adj* owed, owing, unpaid, outstanding, in arrears, due, mature.

payment *n* remittance, settlement, discharge, premium, outlay, advance, deposit, instalment, contribution, donation, allowance, reward, remuneration, pay, fee, hire, fare, toll.

peace *n* **1** SILENCE, quiet, hush, stillness, rest, relaxation, tranquillity, calm, calmness, composure, contentment. **2** ARMISTICE, truce, cease-fire, conciliation, concord, harmony, agreement, treaty.
 ◼ **1** noise, disturbance. **2** war, disagreement.

peaceable *adj* pacific, peace-loving, unwarlike, non-violent, conciliatory, friendly, amicable, inoffensive, gentle, placid, easy-going (*infml*), mild.
 ◼ belligerent, aggressive.

peaceful *adj* quiet, still, restful, relaxing, tranquil, serene, calm, placid, unruffled, undisturbed, untroubled, friendly, amicable, peaceable, pacific, gentle.
 ◼ noisy, disturbed, troubled, violent.

peacemaker *n* appeaser, conciliator, mediator, arbitrator, intercessor, peace-monger, pacifist.

peak *n* top, summit, pinnacle, crest, crown, zenith, height, maximum, climax, culmination, apex, tip, point.
 ◼ nadir, trough.
 ➤ *v* climax, culminate, come to a head.

peal *n* chime, carillon, toll, knell, ring, clang, ringing, reverberation, rumble, roar, crash, clap.
 ➤ *v* chime, toll, ring, clang, resonate, reverberate, resound, rumble, roll, roar, crash.

peasant *n* rustic, provincial, yokel, bumpkin, oaf, boor, lout.

peccadillo *n* error, fault, indiscretion, lapse, slip, minor offence, misdeed, misdemeanour, delinquency, infraction (*fml*), boob (*infml*), slip-up (*infml*).

peculiar *adj* **1** *a peculiar sound*: strange, odd, curious, funny, weird, bizarre, extraordinary, unusual, abnormal, exceptional, unconventional, offbeat, eccentric, way-out (*sl*), outlandish, exotic. **2** CHARACTERISTIC, distinctive, specific, particular, special, individual, personal, idiosyncratic, unique, singular.
 ◼ **1** ordinary, normal. **2** general.

peculiarity *n* oddity, bizarreness, abnormality, exception, eccentricity, quirk, mannerism, feature, trait, mark, quality, attribute, characteristic, distinctiveness, particularity, idiosyncrasy.

pedagogue *n* teacher, instructor, educator, master, mistress, educationalist, educationist, schoolmaster, schoolmistress, don, pedant, dogmatist, preceptor.

pedant *n* purist, formalist, literalist, perfectionist, precisionist, precisian, dogmatist, quibbler, casuist, doctrinaire, academic, intellectual, pettifogger, Dryasdust, scholastic, hair-splitter (*infml*), nit-picker (*infml*), egghead (*infml*), highbrow (*infml*).

pedantic *adj* stilted, fussy, particular, precise, exact, punctilious, hair-splitting (*infml*), nit-picking (*infml*), finical, academic, bookish, erudite.
 ◼ imprecise, informal, casual.

pedantry *n* punctiliousness, exactness, meticulousness, cavilling, finicality, quibbling, pomposity, pretentiousness, academicness, intellectualism, bookishness, stuffiness, pedagogism, pedagoguishness, pedantism, hair-splitting (*infml*), nit-picking (*infml*).

peddle *v* sell, vend, flog (*infml*), hawk, tout, push, trade, traffic, market.

pedestal *n* plinth, stand, support, mounting, foot, base, foundation, platform, podium.

pedestrian *n* walker, foot-traveller.
 ➤ *adj* dull, boring, flat, uninspired, banal, mundane, run-of-the-mill, commonplace, ordinary, mediocre, indifferent, prosaic, stodgy, plodding.
 ◼ exciting, imaginative.

pedigree *n* genealogy, family tree, lineage, ancestry, descent, line, family, parentage, derivation, extraction, race, breed, stock, blood.

pedlar *n* seller, hawker, huckster, vendor, walker, street-trader, colporteur, chapman, gutter-man, gutter-merchant, boxwallah, cheap-jack.

peek *v* peep, glance, peer, spy, look, have a gander (*sl*), have a look-see (*infml*).
➤ *n* peep, glance, glimpse, look, blink, dekko (*infml*), look-see (*infml*), shufti (*infml*), gander (*sl*).

peel *v* pare, skin, strip, scale, flake (off).
➤ *n* skin, rind, zest, peeling.

peep[1] *v* look, peek, glimpse, spy, squint, peer, emerge, issue, appear.
➤ *n* look, peek, glimpse, glance, squint.

peep[2] *v* chirp, cheep, chirrup, pipe, tweet, chatter, twitter, warble, squeak.
➤ *n* chirp, cheep, chirrup, pipe, tweet, chatter, twitter, warble, squeak, cry, utterance, sound, noise, word.

peephole *n* spyhole, keyhole, pinhole, hole, opening, aperture, slit, chink, crack, fissure, cleft, crevice.

peer[1] *v* look, gaze, scan, scrutinize, examine, inspect, spy, snoop, peep, squint.

peer[2] *n* 1 ARISTOCRAT, noble, nobleman, lord, duke, marquess, marquis, earl, count, viscount, baron. 2 EQUAL, counterpart, equivalent, match, fellow.

peerage *n* aristocracy, nobility, upper crust.

peeress *n* aristocrat, noble, noblewoman, lady, dame, duchess, marchioness, countess, viscountess, baroness.

peerless *adj* matchless, without equal, unequalled, unexcelled, unmatched, incomparable, beyond compare, unparalleled, unrivalled, unsurpassed, unbeatable, unique, supreme, excellent, paramount, outstanding, superlative, nonpareil (*fml*), second to none (*infml*).

peeved *adj* annoyed, irritated, exasperated, put out, upset, vexed, irked, galled, riled, sore, piqued, nettled, miffed (*infml*), narked (*infml*), having the hump (*infml*), in a huff (*infml*).

peevish *adj* petulant, querulous, fractious, fretful, touchy, irritable, cross, grumpy, ratty (*infml*), crotchety, ill-tempered, crabbed, cantankerous, crusty, snappy, short-tempered, surly, sullen, sulky.
🔁 good-tempered.

peg *v* 1 FASTEN, secure, fix, attach, join,

mark. 2 *peg prices*: control, stabilize, limit, freeze, fix, set.
➤ *n* pin, dowel, hook, knob, marker, post, stake.

pejorative *adj* derogatory, disparaging, belittling, slighting, unflattering, uncomplimentary, unpleasant, bad, negative.
🔁 complimentary.

pelt[1] *v* 1 THROW, hurl, bombard, shower, assail, batter, beat, hit, strike. 2 POUR, teem, rain cats and dogs (*infml*). 3 RUSH, hurry, charge, belt (*infml*), tear, dash, speed, career.

pelt[2] *n* skin, coat, fur, fleece, hide, fell.

pen[1] *n* fountain-pen, ballpoint, Biro®, felt-tip pen.
➤ *v* write, compose, draft, scribble, jot down.

pen[2] *n* enclosure, fold, stall, sty, coop, cage, hutch.
➤ *v* enclose, fence, hedge, hem in, confine, cage, coop, shut up.

penal *adj* punitive, disciplinary, corrective, retaliatory, retributive, vindictive.

penalize *v* punish, discipline, correct, fine, handicap.
🔁 reward.

penalty *n* punishment, retribution, fine, forfeit, handicap, disadvantage.
🔁 reward.

penance *n* atonement, reparation, punishment, penalty, mortification.

penchant *n* fondness, liking, tendency, taste, preference, affinity, bent, inclination, leaning, bias, partiality, weakness, soft spot (*infml*), proneness, disposition (*fml*), predilection (*fml*), predisposition (*fml*), proclivity (*fml*), propensity (*fml*).
🔁 dislike.

pendant *n* medallion, locket, necklace.

pending *adj* impending, in the offing, forthcoming, imminent, undecided, in the balance.
🔁 finished, settled.

penetrate *v* pierce, stab, prick, puncture, probe, sink, bore, enter, infiltrate, permeate, seep, pervade, suffuse.

penetrating *adj* piercing, stinging, biting, incisive, sharp, keen, acute, shrewd, discerning, perceptive, observant, profound, deep, searching, probing.
🔁 blunt.

penitence *n* repentance, contrition,

remorse, regret, shame, self-reproach.

penitent adj repentant, contrite, sorry, apologetic, remorseful, regretful, conscience-stricken, shamefaced, humble.
🔁 unrepentant, hard-hearted, callous.

pennant n flag, banner, ensign, standard, streamer, colours, banderol, gonfalon, jack.

penniless adj poor, poverty-stricken, impoverished, destitute, bankrupt, ruined, bust, broke (infml), stony-broke (sl).
🔁 rich, wealthy, affluent.

pension n annuity, superannuation, allowance, benefit.

pensioner n retired person, old-age pensioner, senior citizen.

pensive adj thoughtful, reflective, contemplative, meditative, ruminative, absorbed, preoccupied, absent-minded, wistful, solemn, serious, sober.
🔁 carefree.

pent-up adj repressed, inhibited, restrained, bottled-up, suppressed, stifled.

people n persons, individuals, humans, human beings, mankind, humanity, folk, public, general public, populace, rank and file (infml), population, inhabitants, citizens, community, society, race, nation.
➤ v populate, inhabit, occupy, settle, colonize.

pep (infml) n energy, vigour, verve, spirit, vitality, liveliness, get-up-and-go (infml), exuberance, high spirits.
♦ **pep up** (infml) invigorate, vitalize, liven up, quicken, stimulate, excite, exhilarate, inspire.
🔁 tone down.

pepper v 1 BOMBARD, attack, assail, pelt, blitz. 2 SPRINKLE, shower, scatter, spatter, bespatter, strew, dot.

perceive v 1 SEE, discern, make out, detect, discover, spot, catch sight of, notice, observe, view, remark, note, distinguish, recognize. 2 SENSE, feel, apprehend, learn, realize, appreciate, be aware of, know, grasp, understand, gather, deduce, conclude.

perceptible adj perceivable, discernible, detectable, appreciable, distinguishable, observable, noticeable, obvious, evident, conspicuous, clear, plain, apparent, visible.
🔁 imperceptible, inconspicuous.

perception n sense, feeling, impression, idea, conception, apprehension (fml), awareness, consciousness, observation, recognition, grasp, understanding, insight, discernment, taste.

perceptive adj discerning, observant, sensitive, responsive, aware, alert, quick, sharp, astute, shrewd.
🔁 unobservant.

perch v land, alight, settle, sit, roost, balance, rest.

percolate v filter, strain, seep, ooze, leak, drip, penetrate, permeate, pervade.

peremptory adj imperious, commanding, dictatorial, autocratic, authoritative, assertive, high-handed, overbearing, domineering, bossy (infml), abrupt, curt, summary, arbitrary.

perennial adj lasting, enduring, everlasting, eternal, immortal, undying, imperishable, unceasing, incessant, never-ending, constant, continual, uninterrupted, perpetual, persistent, unfailing.

perfect adj 1 FAULTLESS, impeccable, flawless, immaculate, spotless, blameless, pure, superb, excellent, matchless, incomparable. 2 EXACT, precise, accurate, right, correct, true. 3 IDEAL, model, exemplary, ultimate, consummate, expert, accomplished, experienced, skilful.
4 perfect strangers: utter, absolute, sheer, complete, entire, total.
🔁 1 imperfect, flawed, blemished.
2 inaccurate, wrong. 3 inexperienced, unskilled.
➤ v fulfil, consummate, complete, finish, polish, refine, elaborate.
🔁 spoil, mar.

perfection n faultlessness, flawlessness, excellence, superiority, ideal, model, paragon, crown, pinnacle, acme, consummation, completion.
🔁 imperfection, flaw.

perfectionist n idealist, purist, pedant, stickler.

perfectly adv 1 UTTERLY, absolutely, quite, thoroughly, completely, entirely, wholly, totally, fully. 2 FAULTLESSLY, flawlessly, impeccably, ideally, exactly, correctly.
🔁 1 partially. 2 imperfectly, badly.

perforate v hole, punch, drill, bore, pierce, prick, stab, puncture, penetrate.

perforation n hole, bore, prick, puncture, dotted line.

perform *v* **1** DO, carry out, execute, discharge, fulfil, satisfy, complete, achieve, accomplish, bring off, pull off, effect, bring about. **2** *perform a play*: stage, put on, present, enact, represent, act, play, appear as. **3** FUNCTION, work, operate, behave, produce.

performance *n* **1** SHOW, act, play, appearance, gig (*sl*), presentation, production, interpretation, rendition, representation, portrayal, acting. **2** ACTION, deed, doing, carrying out, execution, implementation, discharge, fulfilment, completion, achievement, accomplishment. **3** FUNCTIONING, operation, behaviour, conduct.

Types of performance include: act, audition, benefit, box-office hit, bomb (*infml*), charity concert, command performance, concert, début, dress rehearsal, dry run, encore, entertainment, exhibition, farewell performance, first house, first night, flop (*infml*), full house, gala night, gig, last night, last night at the Proms, matinée, one-night stand, opening night, play, pop concert, première, preview, production, read-through, recital, rehearsal, rendition, run-through, second house, sell-out, short run, show, sketch, smash hit (*infml*), sneak preview, theatre, turn. *see also* **theatrical**.

performer *n* actor, actress, player, artiste, entertainer.

perfume *n* scent, fragrance, smell, odour, aroma, bouquet, sweetness, balm, essence, cologne, toilet water, incense.

perfunctory *adj* quick, careless, superficial, cursory, negligent, offhand, slipshod, slovenly, inattentive, hurried, heedless, automatic, mechanical, routine, stereotyped, indifferent, brief, wooden. **Ea** careful, enthusiastic.

perhaps *adv* maybe, possibly, conceivably, feasibly.

peril *n* danger, hazard, risk, jeopardy, uncertainty, insecurity, threat, menace. **Ea** safety, security.

perilous *adj* dangerous, unsafe, hazardous, risky, chancy, precarious, insecure, unsure, vulnerable, exposed, menacing, threatening, dire. **Ea** safe, secure.

perimeter *n* circumference, edge, border, boundary, frontier, limit, bounds, confines, fringe, margin, periphery. **Ea** middle, centre, heart.

period *n* era, epoch, age, generation, date, years, time, term, season, stage, phase, stretch, turn, session, interval, space, span, spell, cycle.

periodic *adj* occasional, infrequent, sporadic, intermittent, recurrent, repeated, regular, periodical, seasonal.

periodical *n* magazine, journal, publication, weekly, monthly, quarterly.

peripheral *adj* **1** MINOR, secondary, incidental, unimportant, irrelevant, unnecessary, marginal, borderline, surface, superficial. **2** OUTLYING, outer, outermost. **Ea** **1** major, crucial. **2** central.

perish *v* rot, decay, decompose, disintegrate, crumble, collapse, fall, die, expire, pass away.

perishable *adj* destructible, biodegradable, decomposable, short-lived. **Ea** imperishable, durable.

perjure oneself *v* lie, commit perjury, bear false witness/testimony, make false statements, give false evidence, forswear oneself (*fml*).

perjury *n* false evidence, false testimony, false witness, false swearing, false oath, false statement, falsification, forswearing (*fml*), mendacity (*fml*).

perk (*infml*) *n* perquisite, fringe benefit, benefit, bonus, dividend, gratuity, tip, extra, plus (*infml*).
♦ **perk up** (*infml*) brighten, cheer up, buck up (*infml*), revive, liven up, pep up (*infml*), rally, recover, improve, look up.

permanence *n* fixedness, stability, imperishability, perpetuity, constancy, endurance, durability. **Ea** impermanence, transience.

permanent *adj* fixed, stable, unchanging, imperishable, indestructible, unfading, eternal, everlasting, lifelong, perpetual, constant, steadfast, perennial, long-lasting, lasting, enduring, durable. **Ea** temporary, ephemeral, fleeting.

permeable *adj* porous, absorbent, absorptive, penetrable. **Ea** impermeable, watertight.

permeate *v* pass through, soak through, filter through, seep through, penetrate, infiltrate, pervade, imbue, saturate, impregnate, fill.

permissible *adj* permitted, allowable, allowed, admissible, all right, acceptable, proper, authorized, sanctioned, lawful, legal, legitimate.
🔁 prohibited, banned, forbidden.

permission *n* consent, assent, agreement, approval, go-ahead, green light (*infml*), authorization, sanction, leave, warrant, permit, licence, dispensation, freedom, liberty.
🔁 prohibition.

permissive *adj* liberal, broad-minded, tolerant, forbearing, lenient, easy-going (*infml*), indulgent, overindulgent, lax, free.
🔁 strict, rigid.

permit *v* allow, let, consent, agree, admit, grant, authorize, sanction, warrant, license.
🔁 prohibit, forbid.
➤ *n* pass, passport, visa, licence, warrant, authorization, sanction, permission.
🔁 prohibition.

permutation *n* alteration, change, shift, transformation, variation, transposition (*fml*), configuration (*fml*), transmutation (*fml*), commutation (*fml*).

pernicious *adj* harmful, damaging, dangerous, destructive, ruinous, detrimental, bad, hurtful, injurious, offensive, malicious, poisonous, venomous, pestilent, toxic, wicked, evil, malignant, fatal, deadly, unhealthy, unwholesome, deleterious (*fml*), maleficent (*fml*), malevolent (*fml*), noisome (*fml*), noxious (*fml*).
🔁 innocuous.

pernickety *adj* fussy, particular, over-particular, over-precise, carping, nice, punctilious, fastidious, fiddly, finical, finicky, exacting, detailed, careful, painstaking, fine, tricky, choosy (*infml*), picky (*infml*), hair-splitting (*infml*), nit-picking (*infml*).

perpendicular *adj* vertical, upright, erect, straight, sheer, plumb.
🔁 horizontal.

perpetrate *v* commit, carry out, execute, do, perform, inflict, wreak.

perpetual *adj* eternal, everlasting, infinite, endless, unending, never-ending, interminable, ceaseless, unceasing, incessant, continuous, uninterrupted, constant, persistent, continual, repeated, recurrent, perennial, permanent, lasting, enduring, abiding, unchanging.

🔁 intermittent, temporary, ephemeral, transient.

perpetuate *v* continue, keep up, maintain, preserve, keep alive, immortalize, commemorate.

perplex *v* puzzle, baffle, mystify, stump (*infml*), confuse, muddle, confound, bewilder, dumbfound.

perplexity *n* **1** PUZZLEMENT, bafflement, bewilderment, confusion, incomprehension, mystification, nonplus. **2** COMPLEXITY, complication, difficulty, intricacy, involvement, dilemma, enigma, mystery, puzzle, paradox, obscurity, labyrinth, obfuscation (*fml*).

persecute *v* hound, pursue, hunt, bother, worry, annoy, pester, harass, molest, abuse, ill-treat, maltreat, oppress, tyrannize, victimize, martyr, distress, afflict, torment, torture, crucify.
🔁 pamper, spoil.

persecution *n* harassment, molestation, abuse, maltreatment, discrimination, oppression, subjugation, suppression, tyranny, punishment, torture, martyrdom.

perseverance *n* persistence, determination, resolution, doggedness, tenacity, diligence, assiduity, dedication, commitment, constancy, steadfastness, stamina, endurance, indefatigability.

persevere *v* continue, carry on, stick at it (*infml*), keep going, soldier on, persist, plug away (*infml*), remain, stand firm, stand fast, hold on, hang on.
🔁 give up, stop, discontinue.

persist *v* remain, linger, last, endure, abide, continue, carry on, keep at it, persevere, insist.
🔁 desist, stop.

persistent *adj* **1** INCESSANT, endless, never-ending, interminable, continuous, unrelenting, relentless, unremitting, constant, steady, continual, repeated, perpetual, lasting, enduring. **2** *persistent effort*: persevering, determined, resolute, dogged, tenacious, stubborn, obstinate, steadfast, zealous, tireless, unflagging, indefatigable.

person *n* individual, being, human being, human, man, woman, body, soul, character, type.

persona *n* image, face, public face, role, part, character, personality, front, façade, mask.

personable *adj* pleasant, pleasing, likable, presentable, nice, agreeable, amiable, affable, attractive, good-looking, handsome, charming, warm, winning, outgoing.
🔁 unpleasant, disagreeable, unattractive.

personal *adj* **1** *give you my personal attention*: individual, special, particular, exclusive, in person. **2** *your personal style*: individual, idiosyncratic, peculiar, characteristic, distinctive, unique, own, subjective. **3** PRIVATE, confidential, intimate, secret. **4** *personal remarks*: offensive, insulting, critical, rude, abusive, hurtful, wounding, disrespectful, upsetting.
🔁 **2** general, universal. **3** public, official.

personality *n* **1** CHARACTER, nature, disposition, temperament, individuality, psyche, traits, make-up, charm, charisma, magnetism. **2** CELEBRITY, notable, personage, public figure, VIP (*infml*), star.

personally *adv* **1** INDIVIDUALLY, in person, specially, particularly, exclusively, solely, alone, independently, subjectively, idiosyncratically, distinctively, characteristically, uniquely, privately, confidentially. **2** *take something personally*: directed against one, as personal criticism, as hurtful comments, insultingly, offensively.

personification *n* essence, embodiment, incarnation, likeness, image, representation, recreation, portrayal, semblance, delineation (*fml*), manifestation (*fml*), quintessence (*fml*).

personify *v* embody, epitomize, typify, exemplify, symbolize, represent, mirror.

personnel *n* staff, workforce, workers, employees, crew, human resources, manpower, people, members.

perspective *n* aspect, angle, slant, attitude, standpoint, viewpoint, point of view, view, vista, scene, prospect, outlook, proportion, relation.

perspiration *n* sweat, secretion, moisture, wetness.

perspire *v* sweat, exude, secrete, swelter, drip.

persuade *v* coax, prevail upon, lean on, cajole, wheedle, inveigle, talk into, induce, bring round, win over, convince, convert, sway, influence, lead on, incite, prompt, urge.
🔁 dissuade, deter, discourage.

persuasion *n* **1** COAXING, cajolery, wheedling, inducement, enticement, pull, power, influence, conviction, conversion. **2** OPINION, school (of thought), party, faction, side, conviction, faith, belief, denomination, sect.

persuasive *adj* convincing, plausible, cogent, sound, valid, influential, forceful, weighty, effective, telling, potent, compelling, moving, touching.
🔁 unconvincing.

pert *adj* impudent, cheeky, presumptuous, impertinent, insolent, bold, brash, gay, forward, fresh, flippant, lively, spirited, brisk, daring, sprightly, jaunty, tossy, perky (*infml*), saucy (*infml*), cocky (*infml*).
🔁 coy, shy.

pertain *v* relate, apply, be appropriate, be part of, be relevant, bear on, have a bearing on, befit, belong, come under, concern, refer, regard, appertain (*fml*).

pertinent *adj* appropriate, suitable, fitting, apt, apposite, relevant, to the point, material, applicable.
🔁 inappropriate, unsuitable, irrelevant.

perturb *v* disturb, bother, trouble, upset, worry, alarm, disconcert, unsettle, discompose (*fml*), ruffle, fluster, agitate, vex.
🔁 reassure, compose.

peruse *v* study, pore over, read, browse, look through, scan, scrutinize, examine, inspect, check.

pervade *v* affect, penetrate, permeate, percolate, charge, fill, imbue, infuse, suffuse, saturate, impregnate.

pervasive *adj* prevalent, common, extensive, widespread, general, universal, inescapable, omnipresent, ubiquitous.

perverse *adj* contrary, wayward, wrong-headed, wilful, headstrong, stubborn, obstinate, unyielding, intransigent (*fml*), disobedient, rebellious, troublesome, unmanageable, ill-tempered, cantankerous, unreasonable, incorrect, improper.
🔁 obliging, co-operative, reasonable.

perversion *n* **1** CORRUPTION, depravity, debauchery, immorality, vice, wickedness, deviance, kinkiness (*infml*), abnormality. **2** TWISTING, distortion, misrepresentation, travesty, misinterpretation, aberration, deviation, misuse, misapplication.

perversity *n* contrariness, waywardness,

wrong-headedness, wilfulness, stubbornness, obstinacy, disobedience, awkwardness, unruliness, rebelliousness, troublesomeness, uncontrollability, unreasonableness, senselessness, contradictoriness, frowardness, gee, intransigence (*fml*), obduracy (*fml*), refractoriness (*fml*).

pervert *v* 1 *pervert the truth*: twist, warp, distort, misrepresent, falsify, garble, misinterpret. 2 CORRUPT, lead astray, deprave, debauch, debase, degrade, abuse, misuse, misapply.
➤ *n* deviant, debauchee, degenerate, weirdo (*infml*).

perverted *adj* twisted, warped, distorted, deviant, kinky (*infml*), unnatural, abnormal, unhealthy, corrupt, depraved, debauched, debased, immoral, evil, wicked.
Ea natural, normal.

pessimistic *adj* negative, cynical, fatalistic, defeatist, resigned, hopeless, despairing, despondent, dejected, downhearted, glum, morose, melancholy, depressed, dismal, gloomy, bleak.
Ea optimistic.

pest *n* nuisance, bother, annoyance, irritation, vexation, trial, curse, scourge, bane, blight, bug.

pester *v* nag, badger, hound, hassle (*infml*), harass, plague, torment, provoke, worry, bother, disturb, annoy, irritate, pick on, get at (*infml*).

pet *n* favourite, darling, idol, treasure, jewel.
➤ *adj* favourite, favoured, preferred, dearest, cherished, special, particular, personal.
➤ *v* stroke, caress, fondle, cuddle, kiss, neck (*sl*), snog (*sl*).

peter out *v* dwindle, taper off, fade, wane, ebb, fail, cease, stop.

petite *adj* dainty, small, slight, little, delicate, bijou, dinky.
Ea big, large.

petition *n* appeal, round robin, application, request, solicitation, plea, entreaty, prayer, supplication, invocation.
➤ *v* appeal, call upon, ask, crave, solicit, bid, urge, press, implore, beg, plead, entreat, beseech, supplicate, pray.

petrified *adj* terrified, terror-stricken, aghast, horrified, horror-stricken, appalled, scared stiff, stunned,

dumbfounded, shocked, speechless, stupefied, transfixed, numb, benumbed, dazed, frozen.

petrify *v* terrify, horrify, appal, paralyse, numb, stun, dumbfound.

petty *adj* 1 MINOR, unimportant, insignificant, trivial, secondary, lesser, small, little, slight, trifling, paltry, inconsiderable, negligible. 2 SMALL-MINDED, mean, ungenerous, grudging, spiteful.
Ea 1 important, significant. 2 generous.

petulant *adj* fretful, peevish, cross, irritable, snappish, bad-tempered, ill-humoured, moody, sullen, sulky, sour, ungracious.

phantom *n* ghost, spectre, spirit, apparition, vision, hallucination, illusion, figment.

Pharisee *n* hypocrite, fraud, pietist, whited sepulchre, dissembler (*fml*), dissimulator (*fml*), phoney (*infml*), humbug (*infml*).

phase *n* stage, step, time, period, spell, season, chapter, position, point, aspect, state, condition.
♦ **phase out** wind down, run down, ease off, taper off, eliminate, dispose of, get rid of, remove, withdraw, close, terminate.

phenomenal *adj* marvellous, sensational, stupendous, amazing, remarkable, extraordinary, exceptional, unusual, unbelievable, incredible.

phenomenon *n* 1 OCCURRENCE, happening, event, incident, episode, fact, appearance, sight. 2 WONDER, marvel, miracle, prodigy, rarity, curiosity, spectacle, sensation.

philanthropic *adj* humanitarian, public-spirited, altruistic, unselfish, benevolent, kind, charitable, alms-giving, generous, liberal, open-handed.
Ea misanthropic.

philanthropist *n* humanitarian, benefactor, patron, sponsor, giver, donor, contributor, altruist.
Ea misanthrope.

philanthropy *n* humanitarianism, public-spiritedness, altruism, unselfishness, benevolence, kind-heartedness, charity, alms-giving, patronage, generosity, liberality, open-handedness.
Ea misanthropy.

philistine *n* lowbrow, ignoramus, barbarian, bourgeois, vulgarian, yahoo, boor (*infml*), lout (*infml*).

➤ *adj* uncultivated, uncultured, uneducated, unrefined, unread, unlettered, ignorant, lowbrow, tasteless, boorish, bourgeois, crass.

philosopher *n* philosophizer, thinker, theorist, theorizer, analyser, scholar, expert, guru, metaphysicist, sage, logician, epistemologist (*fml*), dialectician (*fml*).

philosophical *adj* **1** *a philosophical discussion*: metaphysical, abstract, theoretical, analytical, rational, logical, erudite, learned, wise, thoughtful.
2 RESIGNED, patient, stoical, unruffled, calm, composed.

philosophy *n* metaphysics, rationalism, reason, logic, thought, thinking, wisdom, knowledge, ideology, world-view, doctrine, beliefs, convictions, values, principles, attitude, viewpoint.

Philosophical terms include: absolutism, aesthetics, agnosticism, altruism, antinomianism, a posteriori, a priori, ascetism, atheism, atomism, behaviourism, deduction, deism, deontology, determinism, dialectical materialism, dogmatism, dualism, egoism, empiricism, entailment, Epicureanism, epistemology, ethics, existentialism, fatalism, hedonism, historicism, humanism, idealism, identity, induction, instrumentalism, interactionism, intuition, jurisprudence, libertarianism, logic, logical positivism, materialism, metaphysics, monism, naturalism, nihilism, nominalism, objectivism, ontology, pantheism, phenomenalism, phenomenology, positivism, pragmatism, prescriptivism, rationalism, realism, reductionism, relativism, scepticism, scholasticism, sensationalism, sense data, solipsism, stoicism, structuralism, subjectivism, substance, syllogism, teleology, theism, transcendentalism, utilitarianism.

phlegmatic *adj* placid, stolid, impassive, unemotional, unconcerned, indifferent, matter-of-fact, stoical.
F₃ emotional, passionate.

phobia *n* fear, terror, dread, anxiety, neurosis, obsession, hang-up (*infml*), thing (*infml*), aversion, dislike, hatred, horror, loathing, revulsion, repulsion.
F₃ love, liking.

Phobias (by name of fear) include: zoophobia (*animals*), apiphobia (*bees*), ailurophobia (*cats*), necrophobia (*corpses*), scotophobia (*darkness*), cynophobia (*dogs*), claustrophobia (*enclosed places*), panphobia (*everything*), pyrophobia (*fire*), xenophobia (*foreigners*), phasmophobia (*ghosts*), acrophobia (*high places*), hippophobia (*horses*), entomophobia (*insects*), astraphobia (*lightning*), autophobia (*loneliness*), agoraphobia (*open spaces*), toxiphobia (*poison*), herpetophobia (*reptiles*), ophiophobia (*snakes*), tachophobia (*speed*), arachnophobia (*spiders*), triskaidekaphobia (*thirteen*), brontophobia (*thunder*), hydrophobia (*water*).

phone *v* telephone, ring (up), call (up), dial, contact, get in touch, give a buzz (*infml*), give a tinkle (*infml*).

phonetic alphabet

Communications code words for the letters of the alphabet are: Alpha, Bravo, Charlie, Delta, Echo, Foxtrot, Golf, Hotel, India, Juliet, Kilo, Lima, Mike, November, Oscar, Papa, Quebec, Romeo, Sierra, Tango, Uniform, Victor, Whisky, X-ray, Yankee, Zulu.

phoney (*infml*) *adj* fake, counterfeit, forged, bogus, trick, false, spurious, assumed, affected, put-on, sham, pseudo, imitation.
F₃ real, genuine.

photocopy *v* copy, duplicate, Photostat, Xerox, print, run off.
➤ *n* copy, duplicate, Photostat, Xerox.

photograph *n* photo, snap, snapshot, print, shot, slide, transparency, picture, image, likeness.
➤ *v* snap, take, film, shoot, video, record.

photographic *adj* **1** *photographic equipment*: filmic, graphic, cinematic, pictorial. **2** *photographic memory*: accurate, exact, detailed, faithful, precise, realistic, retentive, vivid, minute, visual, lifelike, natural, naturalistic, representational.

Photographic accessories include: air-shutter release, battery, cable release, camera bag, eye-cup, eyepiece magnifier, film, cartridge film, cassette film, disc film, film pack, filter, colour filter, heat filter, polarizing filter, skylight filter, flashbulb, flashcube, flashgun, flash unit, hot shoe, lens, afocal lens, auxiliary lens, close-up lens, fish-eye lens, macro lens, supplementary lens, telephoto lens, teleconverter, wide-angle lens, zoom lens, lens cap, lens hood, lens shield, light meter, exposure meter, spot meter, diffuser, barn doors, honeycomb diffuser, parabolic reflector, snoot, slide mount, viewfinder, right-angle finder; camcorder battery discharger/charger/tester, cassette adaptor, remote control, tele-cine converter, video editor, video light, video mixer. see also **camera**.

Photographic equipment includes: camera, stand, tripod, flash umbrella, boom arm; developer bath, developing tank, dry mounting press, easel, enlarger, enlarger timer, film-drying cabinet, fixing bath, focus magnifier, light-box, negative carrier, print washer, contact printer, print-drying rack, paper drier, safelight, stop bath, Vertoscope®, viewer; slide viewer, slide projector, film projection screen.

phrase n construction, clause, idiom, expression, saying, utterance, remark.
➤ v word, formulate, frame, couch, present, put, express, say, utter, pronounce.

phraseology n terminology, phrase, phrasing, wording, expression, idiom, language, parlance, speech, writing, style, syntax, diction, argot, cant, patois.

physical adj 1 BODILY, corporeal, fleshly, fleshy, carnal, incarnate, mortal, earthly, unspiritual, somatic (fml). 2 MATERIAL, concrete, solid, substantial, tangible, palpable, visible, real, actual.
ᴇᴀ 1 mental, spiritual. 2 abstract, theoretical.

physician n doctor, medical practitioner, medic (infml), general practitioner, GP, houseman, intern, registrar, consultant, specialist, healer.

physics

Terms used in physics include: absolute zero, acceleration, acoustics, alpha particles, analogue signal, applied physics, Archimedes principle, area, atom, beta particles, Big Bang theory, boiling point, bubble-chamber, capillary action, centre of gravity, centre of mass, centrifugal force, chain reaction, charge, charged particle, circuit, circuit-breaker, couple, critical mass,

cryogenics, density, diffraction, digital, dynamics, efficiency, elasticity, electric current, electric discharge, electricity, electrodynamics, electromagnetic spectrum, electromagnetic waves, electron, energy, engine, entropy, equation, equilibrium, evaporation, field, flash point, force, formula, freezing point, frequency, friction, fundamental constant, gamma ray, gas, gate, grand united theory (GUT), gravity, half-life, heat, heavy water, hydraulics, hydrodynamics, hydrostatics, incandescence, indeterminacy principle, inertia, infrared, interference, ion, kinetic energy, kinetic theory, Kelvin effect, laser (light amplification by stimulated emission of radiation), latent heat, law, laws of motion, laws of reflection, laws of refraction, laws of thermodynamics, lens, lever, light, light emission, light intensity, light source, liquid, longitudinal wave, luminescence, Mach number, magnetic field, magnetism, mass, mechanics, microwaves, mirror, Mohs scale, molecule, moment, momentum, motion, neutron, nuclear, nuclear fission, nuclear fusion, nuclear physics, nucleus, optical centre, optics, oscillation, parallel motion, particle, periodic law, perpetual motion, phonon, photon, photosensitivity, polarity, potential energy, power, pressure, principle, process, proton, quantum chromodynamics (QCD), quantum electrodynamics (QED), quantum mechanics, quantum theory, quark, radiation, radioactive element, radioactivity, radioisotope, radio wave, ratio, reflection, refraction, relativity, resistance, resonance, rule, semiconductor, sensitivity, separation, SI unit, sound, sound wave, specific gravity, specific heat capacity, spectroscopy, spectrum, speed, states of matter, statics, substance, superstring theory, supersymmetry, surface tension, temperature, tension, theory, theory of relativity, thermodynamics, Thomson effect, transverse wave, ultrasound, ultraviolet, uncertainty principle, velocity, visible spectrum, viscosity, volume, wave, wave property, weight, white heat, work, X-ray. see also **atom**; **electricity**.

physique n body, figure, shape, form, build, frame, structure, constitution, make-up.

pick v 1 SELECT, choose, opt for, decide on, settle on, single out. 2 GATHER, collect, pluck, harvest, cull.
➤ n 1 CHOICE, selection, option, decision,

preference. **2** BEST, cream, flower, elite, elect.

♦ **pick on** bully, torment, persecute, nag, get at (*infml*), needle (*infml*), bait.

♦ **pick out** spot, notice, perceive, recognize, distinguish, tell apart, separate, single out, hand-pick, choose, select.

♦ **pick up 1** LIFT, raise, hoist. **2** *I'll pick you up at eight*: call for, fetch, collect. **3** LEARN, master, grasp, gather. **4** IMPROVE, rally, recover, perk up (*infml*). **5** BUY, purchase. **6** OBTAIN, acquire, gain. **7** *pick up an infection*: catch, contract, get.

picket *n* picketer, protester, demonstrator, striker.
➤ *v* protest, demonstrate, boycott, blockade, enclose, surround.

pickle *v* preserve, conserve, souse, marinade, steep, cure, salt.

pick-me-up *n* tonic, boost, refreshment, restorative, fillip, stimulant, stimulus, cordial, shot in the arm (*infml*).

picnic *n* **1** *a picnic lunch*: outing, excursion, outdoor meal, wayzgoose. **2** *minding young children is no picnic*: child's play (*infml*), cinch (*infml*), doddle (*infml*), piece of cake (*infml*), pushover (*infml*), walkover (*infml*).

pictorial *adj* graphic, diagrammatic, schematic, representational, vivid, striking, expressive, illustrated, picturesque, scenic.

picture *n* **1** DESCRIPTION, portrayal, depiction, account, report, story, narrative, tale, semblance, impression, delineation (*fml*), similitude (*fml*). **2** *the picture of health*: embodiment, personification, epitome, essence, archetype (*fml*), exemplar (*fml*), quintessence (*fml*). **3** FILM, motion picture, flick (*old use, infml*). **4** *go to the pictures*: cinema, movies, picture-house, film theatre, entertainment centre, multiplex, picture-palace, flicks (*infml*).

Kinds of picture include: abstract, cameo, canvas, caricature, cartoon, collage, design, doodle, drawing, effigy, engraving, etching, fresco, graffiti, graphics, icon, identikit, illustration, image, kakemono, landscape, likeness, miniature, montage, mosaic, mug shot (*infml*), mural, negative, oil-painting, old master, painting, passport photo, Photofit®, photograph, photogravure, pin-up, plate, portrait, print, representation, reproduction, self-portrait, silhouette, sketch, slide, snap (*infml*), snapshot, still, still life, study, tableau, tapestry, tracing, transfer, transparency, triptych, trompe l'œil, vignette, watercolour.

➤ *v* **1** IMAGINE, envisage, envision, conceive, visualize, see. **2** DEPICT, describe, represent, show, portray, draw, sketch, paint, photograph, illustrate.

picturesque *adj* **1** ATTRACTIVE, beautiful, pretty, charming, quaint, idyllic, scenic. **2** DESCRIPTIVE, graphic, vivid, colourful, striking.
🔁 **1** unattractive. **2** dull.

piebald *adj* black and white, dappled, flecked, mottled, pied, spotted, speckled, variegated, brindle(d), skewbald.

piece *n* **1** FRAGMENT, bit, scrap, morsel, mouthful, bite, lump, chunk, slice, sliver, snippet, shred, offcut, sample, component, constituent, element, part, segment, section, division, fraction, share, portion, quantity. **2** ARTICLE, item, study, work, composition, creation, specimen, example.

pièce de résistance *n* masterpiece, master-work, prize, showpiece, magnum opus, chef-d'oeuvre, jewel.

piecemeal *adv* little by little, intermittently, parcel-wise, partially, at intervals, slowly, bit by bit, by degrees, fitfully, in dribs and drabs (*infml*).
🔁 completely, entirely, wholly.
➤ *adj* fragmentary, intermittent, interrupted, partial, unsystematic, scattered, patchy, sporadic, discrete (*fml*).
🔁 complete, entire, whole, wholesale.

pier *n* **1** JETTY, breakwater, landing-stage, quay, wharf. **2** SUPPORT, upright, pillar, post.

pierce *v* penetrate, enter, stick into, puncture, drill, bore, probe, perforate, punch, prick, stab, lance, bayonet, run through, spear, skewer, spike, impale, transfix.

piercing *adj* **1** *a piercing cry*: shrill, high-pitched, loud, ear-splitting, sharp. **2** PENETRATING, probing, searching. **3** COLD, bitter, raw, biting, keen, fierce, severe, wintry, frosty, freezing. **4** PAINFUL, agonizing, excruciating, stabbing, lacerating.

piety *n* piousness, devoutness, godliness, saintliness, holiness, sanctity, religion, faith, devotion, reverence.
🔁 impiety, irreligion.

pig *n* swine, hog, sow, boar, animal, beast, brute, glutton, gourmand.

pigeonhole *n* compartment, niche, slot, cubby-hole, cubicle, locker, box, place, section, class, category, classification.
➤ *v* compartmentalize, label, classify, sort, file, catalogue, alphabetize, shelve, defer.

pig-headed *adj* stubborn, obstinate, perverse, self-willed, stiff-necked, inflexible, contrary, mulish, stupid, unyielding, wilful, wrong-headed, headstrong, bull-headed, froward (*fml*), intractable (*fml*), intransigent (*fml*).
🖪 flexible, tractable.

pigment *n* colour, hue, tint, dye, stain, paint, colouring, tincture.

pile¹ *n* stack, heap, mound, mountain, mass, accumulation, collection, assortment, hoard, stockpile.
➤ *v* stack, heap, mass, amass, accumulate, build up, gather, assemble, collect, hoard, stockpile, store, load, pack, jam, crush, crowd, flock, flood, stream, rush, charge.

pile² *n* post, column, upright, support, bar, beam, foundation.

pile³ *n* nap, shag, plush, fur, hair, fuzz, down.

pile-up *n* crash, accident, collision, bump, wreck, smash (*infml*), smash-up (*infml*), prang (*infml*).

pilfer *v* steal, pinch (*infml*), nick (*sl*), knock off (*sl*), filch, lift, shoplift, rob, thieve.

pilgrim *n* crusader, traveller, wanderer.

pilgrimage *n* crusade, mission, expedition, journey, trip, tour.

pill *n* tablet, capsule, pellet.

pillage *v* plunder, raid, sack, vandalize, maraud, loot, spoil, ransack, ravage, raze, freeboot, rifle, rob, strip, depredate (*fml*), despoil (*fml*), spoliate (*fml*).
➤ *n* plunder, sack, devastation, marauding, harrying, seizure, spoils, robbery, loot, booty, depredation (*fml*), rapine (*fml*), spoliation (*fml*).

pillar *n* column, shaft, post, mast, pier, upright, pile, support, prop, mainstay, bastion, tower of strength.

pillory *v* ridicule, mock, pour scorn on, laugh at, denounce, lash, hold up to shame, show up, brand, cast a slur on, stigmatize.

pilot *n* **1** FLYER, aviator, airman.
2 NAVIGATOR, steersman, helmsman, coxswain, captain, leader, director, guide.
➤ *v* fly, drive, steer, direct, control, handle, manage, operate, run, conduct, lead, guide, navigate.
➤ *adj* experimental, trial, test, model.

pimple *n* spot, zit (*sl*), blackhead, boil, swelling.

pin *v* tack, nail, fix, affix, attach, join, staple, clip, fasten, secure, hold down, restrain, immobilize.
➤ *n* tack, nail, screw, spike, rivet, bolt, peg, fastener, clip, staple, brooch.
◆ **pin down 1** PINPOINT, identify, determine, specify. **2** FORCE, make, press, pressurize.

pinch *v* **1** SQUEEZE, compress, crush, press, tweak, nip, hurt, grip, grasp. **2** (*infml*) STEAL, nick (*sl*), pilfer, filch, snatch.
➤ *n* **1** SQUEEZE, tweak, nip. **2** DASH, soupçon, taste, bit, speck, jot, mite.
3 EMERGENCY, crisis, predicament, difficulty, hardship, pressure, stress.

pine *v* long, yearn, ache, sigh, grieve, mourn, wish, desire, crave, hanker, hunger, thirst.

pinnacle *n* **1** PEAK, summit, top, cap, crown, crest, apex, vertex, acme, zenith, height, eminence. **2** SPIRE, steeple, turret, pyramid, cone, obelisk, needle.

pinpoint *v* identify, spot, distinguish, locate, place, home in on, zero in on (*infml*), pin down, determine, specify, define.

pioneer *n* colonist, settler, frontiersman, frontierswoman, explorer, developer, pathfinder, trail-blazer, leader, innovator, inventor, discoverer, founder.
➤ *v* invent, discover, originate, create, initiate, instigate, begin, start, launch, institute, found, establish, set up, develop, open up.

pious *adj* **1** DEVOUT, godly, saintly, holy, spiritual, religious, reverent, good, virtuous, righteous, moral.
2 SANCTIMONIOUS, holier-than-thou, self-righteous, goody-goody (*infml*), hypocritical.
🖪 **1** impious, irreligious, irreverent.

pipe *n* tube, hose, piping, tubing, pipeline, line, main, flue, duct, conduit, channel, passage, conveyor.
➤ *v* **1** CHANNEL, funnel, siphon, carry, convey, conduct, transmit, supply, deliver.
2 WHISTLE, chirp, tweet, cheep, peep, twitter, sing, warble, trill, play, sound.

piquant *adj* **1** *piquant sauce*: spicy, tangy, savoury, salty, peppery, pungent, sharp, biting, stinging. **2** LIVELY, spirited, stimulating, provocative, interesting, sparkling.

☒ **1** bland, insipid. **2** dull, banal.

pique n annoyance, irritation, vexation, displeasure, offence, huff (*infml*), resentment, grudge.

piqued adj annoyed, irritated, vexed, riled, angry, displeased, offended, miffed (*infml*), peeved (*infml*), put out, resentful.

pirate n **1** BUCCANEER, brigand, freebooter, filibuster, corsair, marauder, raider, rover, picaroon, sea robber, sea rover, sea wolf, sea rat, water rat, marque. **2** INFRINGER, plagiarist, plagiarizer.
➤ v copy, reproduce illegally, steal, pinch (*infml*), plagiarize, poach, appropriate (*fml*), borrow (*infml*), crib (*infml*), lift (*infml*), nick (*sl*).

pit n mine, coalmine, excavation, trench, ditch, hollow, depression, indentation, dent, hole, cavity, crater, pothole, gulf, chasm, abyss.

pitch v **1** THROW, fling, toss, chuck (*infml*), lob, bowl, hurl, heave, sling, fire, launch, aim, direct. **2** PLUNGE, dive, plummet, drop, fall headlong, tumble, lurch, roll, wallow. **3** *pitch camp*: erect, put up, set up, place, station, settle, plant, fix.
➤ n **1** *cricket pitch*: ground, field, playing-field, arena, stadium. **2** SOUND, tone, timbre, modulation, frequency, level. **3** GRADIENT, incline, slope, tilt, angle, degree, steepness.
◆ **pitch in** join in, co-operate, be involved, participate, help, lend a hand, muck in (*infml*), do one's bit (*infml*).

piteous adj poignant, moving, touching, distressing, heart-rending, plaintive, mournful, sad, sorrowful, woeful, wretched, pitiful, pitiable, pathetic.

pitfall n danger, peril, hazard, trap, snare, stumbling-block, catch, snag, drawback, difficulty.

pith n importance, significance, moment, weight, value, consequence, substance, matter, marrow, meat, gist, essence, crux, nub, heart, core, kernel.

pithy adj succinct, concise, compact, terse, short, brief, pointed, trenchant, forceful, cogent, telling.

☒ wordy, verbose.

pitiful adj **1** CONTEMPTIBLE, despicable, low, mean, vile, shabby, deplorable, lamentable, woeful, inadequate, hopeless,

pathetic (*infml*), insignificant, paltry, worthless. **2** PITEOUS, doleful, mournful, distressing, heart-rending, pathetic, pitiable, sad, miserable, wretched, poor, sorry.

pitiless adj merciless, cold-hearted, unsympathetic, unfeeling, uncaring, hard-hearted, callous, cruel, inhuman, brutal, cold-blooded, ruthless, relentless, unremitting, inexorable, harsh.

☒ merciful, compassionate, kind, gentle.

pittance n modicum, crumb, drop (in the ocean), chicken-feed (*infml*), peanuts (*sl*), trifle.

pitted adj dented, holey, potholed, pockmarked, blemished, scarred, marked, notched, indented, rough.

pity n **1** SYMPATHY, commiseration, regret, understanding, fellow-feeling, compassion, kindness, tenderness, mercy, forbearance. **2** *what a pity!*: shame, misfortune, bad luck.

☒ **1** cruelty, anger, scorn.

➤ v feel sorry for, feel for, sympathize with, commiserate with, grieve for, weep for.

pivot n axis, hinge, axle, spindle, kingpin, linchpin, swivel, hub, focal point, centre, heart.
➤ v **1** SWIVEL, turn, spin, revolve, rotate, swing. **2** DEPEND, rely, hinge, hang, lie.

placard n poster, bill, notice, sign, advertisement.

placate v appease, pacify, conciliate, mollify, calm, assuage, soothe, lull, quiet.

☒ anger, enrage, incense, infuriate.

place n **1** SITE, locale, venue, location, situation, spot, point, position, seat, space, room. **2** CITY, town, village, locality, neighbourhood, district, area, region. **3** BUILDING, property, dwelling, residence, house, flat, apartment, home.
➤ v put, set, plant, fix, position, locate, situate, rest, settle, lay, stand, deposit, leave.
◆ **in place of** instead of, in lieu of, as a replacement for, as a substitute for, as an alternative to.
◆ **out of place** inappropriate, unsuitable, unfitting, unbecoming, unseemly.
◆ **take place** happen, occur, come about.

placid adj calm, composed, unruffled, untroubled, cool, self-possessed, level-headed, imperturbable, mild, gentle, equable, even-tempered, serene, tranquil, still, quiet, peaceful, restful.

excitable, agitated, disturbed.

plagiarism n infringement, copying, reproduction, counterfeiting, piracy, theft, appropriation (fml), borrowing (infml), cribbing (infml), lifting (infml).

plagiarize v crib (infml), copy, reproduce, imitate, counterfeit, pirate, infringe copyright, poach, steal, lift (infml), appropriate (fml), borrow (infml).

plague n 1 PESTILENCE, epidemic, disease, infection, contagion, infestation. 2 NUISANCE, annoyance, curse, scourge, trial, affliction, torment, calamity.
➤ v annoy, vex, bother, disturb, trouble, distress, upset, pester, harass, hound, haunt, bedevil, afflict, torment, torture, persecute.

plain adj 1 plain cookery: ordinary, basic, simple, unpretentious, modest, unadorned, unelaborate, restrained. 2 OBVIOUS, evident, patent, clear, understandable, apparent, visible, unmistakable. 3 FRANK, candid, blunt, outspoken, direct, forthright, straightforward, unambiguous, plain-spoken, open, honest, truthful. 4 UNATTRACTIVE, ugly, unprepossessing, unlovely. 5 plain fabric: unpatterned, unvariegated, uncoloured, self-coloured.
1 fancy, elaborate. 2 unclear, obscure. 3 devious, deceitful. 4 attractive, good-looking. 5 patterned.
➤ n grassland, prairie, steppe, lowland, flat, plateau, tableland.

plaintive adj doleful, mournful, melancholy, wistful, sad, sorrowful, grief-stricken, piteous, heart-rending, high-pitched.

plan n 1 BLUEPRINT, layout, diagram, chart, map, drawing, sketch, representation, design. 2 IDEA, suggestion, proposal, proposition, project, scheme, plot, system, method, procedure, strategy, programme, schedule, scenario.
➤ v 1 PLOT, scheme, design, invent, devise, contrive, formulate, frame, draft, outline, prepare, organize, arrange. 2 AIM, intend, propose, contemplate, envisage, foresee.

plane¹ n 1 FLAT SURFACE, level surface, flat, level. 2 LEVEL, stage, position, class, condition, degree, rank, footing, rung, stratum, echelon.
➤ adj level, smooth, uniform, regular, flat, flush, even, horizontal, planar (fml).

plane² n aeroplane, aircraft, jet, jumbo jet, jumbo, airliner, glider, bomber, fighter, seaplane, swing-wing, VTOL, airplane (US).
➤ v skim, skate, fly, glide, sail, volplane, wing.

planet

Planets within the Earth's solar system (nearest the sun shown first) are: Mercury, Venus, Earth, Mars, Jupiter, Saturn, Uranus, Neptune, Pluto.

plant n 1 garden plants: flower, shrub, herb, bush, vegetable. 2 FACTORY, works, foundry, mill, shop, yard, workshop, machinery, apparatus, equipment, gear.

Plants include: annual, biennial, perennial, herbaceous plant, evergreen, succulent, cultivar, hybrid, house plant, pot plant; flower, herb, shrub, bush, tree, vegetable, grass, vine, weed, cereal, wild flower, air-plant, water-plant, cactus, fern, moss, algae, lichen, fungus; bulb, corm, seedling, sapling, bush, climber. see also **bulbs and corms**; **flower**; **grass**; **leaf**; **poisonous**; **shrub**; **wild flower**.

Parts of a plant include: bark, cambium, cork cambium, cellulose, conducting tissue, cotyledon, monocotyledon, dicotyledon, flower, fruit, leaf, meristem, phellogen, phloem, root, lateral root, root cap, root hair, rootlet, seed, seed leaf, stem, tap root, vascular bundle, vascular tissue, xylem.

➤ v 1 SOW, seed, scatter, implant, put into the ground, bury, transplant. 2 INSERT, put, place, set, position, situate, fix, lodge, embed, root, settle, found, establish. 3 HIDE, put secretly, conceal, bury, disguise, put out of sight, secrete (fml).

plaque n plate, slab, tablet, panel, sign, plaquette, brass, shield, medal, medallion, badge, brooch, cartouche (fml).

plaster n sticking-plaster, dressing, bandage, plaster of Paris, mortar, stucco.
➤ v daub, smear, coat, cover, spread.

plastic adj soft, pliable, flexible, supple, malleable, mouldable, ductile (fml), receptive, impressionable, manageable.
rigid, inflexible.

Types of plastic include: Bakelite®, Biopol®, celluloid®, epoxy resin, Perspex®, phenolic resin, plexiglass, polyester, polyethylene, polymethyl methacrylate,

plate 418 **pleased**

polynorbornene, polypropylene, polystyrene, polythene, polyurethane, PTFE (polytetrafluoroethylene), PVC (polyvinyl chloride), uPVC, silicone, Teflon®, transpolyisoprene, urea formaldehyde, vinyl.

plate n 1 DISH, platter, salver, helping, serving, portion. 2 ILLUSTRATION, picture, print, lithograph.
➤ v coat, cover, overlay, veneer, laminate, electroplate, anodize, galvanize, platinize, gild, silver, tin.

plateau n 1 a grassy plateau: plane, highland, tableland, table, upland, mesa. 2 STABILITY, level, grade, stage.

platform n 1 STAGE, podium, dais, rostrum, stand. 2 POLICY, party line, principles, tenets, manifesto, programme, objectives.

platitude n banality, commonplace, truism, cliché, chestnut.

platonic adj non-physical, spiritual, non-romantic, non-sexual, intellectual, ideal, idealistic, transcendent.
Fa sexual.

plaudits n commendation, approval, praise, acclaim, acclamation, applause, congratulations, hurrahs, accolade, ovation, standing ovation, clapping, approbation (fml), hand (infml), bouquet (infml), pat on the back (infml), rave review (infml), good press (infml).
Fa criticism.

plausible adj credible, believable, reasonable, logical, likely, possible, probable, convincing, persuasive, smooth-talking, glib.
Fa implausible, unlikely, improbable.

play v 1 AMUSE ONESELF, have fun, enjoy oneself, revel, sport, romp, frolic, caper. 2 PARTICIPATE, take part, join in, compete. 3 France played Italy: oppose, vie with, challenge, take on. 4 ACT, perform, portray, represent, impersonate.
Fa 1 work.
➤ n 1 FUN, amusement, entertainment, diversion, recreation, sport, game, hobby, pastime. 2 DRAMA, tragedy, comedy, farce, show, performance. 3 MOVEMENT, action, flexibility, give, leeway, latitude, margin, scope, range, room, space.
Fa 1 work.
♦ **play around with** 1 FIDDLE WITH, toy with, fidget with, meddle with, tamper with, interfere with. 2 DALLY WITH, mess around

with, flirt with, fool with, trifle with, womanize with, philander with.
♦ **play down** minimize, make light of, gloss over, underplay, understate, undervalue, underestimate.
Fa exaggerate.
♦ **play on** exploit, take advantage of, turn to account, profit by, trade on, capitalize on.
♦ **play up** 1 EXAGGERATE, highlight, spotlight, accentuate, emphasize, stress. 2 MISBEHAVE, malfunction, trouble, bother, annoy, hurt.

playboy n philanderer, womanizer, ladies' man, rake, libertine.

player n 1 CONTESTANT, competitor, participant, sportsman, sportswoman. 2 PERFORMER, entertainer, artiste, actor, actress, musician, instrumentalist.

playful adj sportive, frolicsome, lively, spirited, mischievous, roguish, impish, puckish, kittenish, good-natured, jesting, teasing, humorous, tongue-in-cheek.
Fa serious.

plaything n toy, trifle, amusement, game, puppet, trinket, pastime, bauble, gewgaw, gimcrack.

playwright n dramatist, scriptwriter, screenwriter.

plea n 1 APPEAL, petition, request, entreaty, supplication, prayer, invocation. 2 DEFENCE, justification, excuse, explanation, claim.

plead v 1 BEG, implore, beseech, entreat, appeal, petition, ask, request. 2 plead ignorance: assert, maintain, claim, allege.

pleasant adj agreeable, nice, fine, lovely, delightful, charming, likable, amiable, friendly, affable, good-humoured, cheerful, congenial, enjoyable, amusing, pleasing, gratifying, satisfying, acceptable, welcome, refreshing.
Fa unpleasant, nasty, unfriendly.

pleasantry n 1 exchange pleasantries about the weather: friendly remark, polite comment, casual remark. 2 JOKE, jest, banter, badinage, quip, sally, witticism, bon mot.

please v 1 DELIGHT, charm, captivate, entertain, amuse, cheer, gladden, humour, indulge, gratify, satisfy, content, suit. 2 WANT, will, wish, desire, like, prefer, choose, think fit.
Fa 1 displease, annoy, anger, sadden.

pleased adj contented, satisfied, gratified,

glad, happy, delighted, thrilled, euphoric.
Ea displeased, annoyed.

pleasing *adj* gratifying, satisfying,
acceptable, good, pleasant, agreeable,
nice, delightful, charming, attractive,
engaging, winning.
Ea unpleasant, disagreeable.

pleasurable *adj* enjoyable, delightful,
fun, good, lovely, nice, pleasant, gratifying,
welcome, entertaining, amusing, diverting,
agreeable, congenial, groovy (*infml*).
Ea bad, disagreeable.

pleasure *n* amusement, entertainment,
recreation, fun, enjoyment, gratification,
satisfaction, contentment, happiness, joy,
delight, comfort, solace.
Ea sorrow, pain, trouble, displeasure.

pleat *v* tuck, fold, crease, flute, crimp,
gather, pucker.

plebeian *adj* 1 LOWER-CLASS, working-
class, proletarian, low-born, peasant,
mean. 2 COMMON, uncultured, unrefined,
uncultivated, coarse, base, ignoble, low,
non-U (*infml*).
Ea 1 aristocratic, noble, patrician. 2 refined,
sophisticated.

pledge *n* 1 PROMISE, vow, word of honour,
oath, bond, covenant, guarantee, warrant,
assurance, undertaking. 2 DEPOSIT,
security, surety, bail.
➤ *v* promise, vow, swear, contract, engage,
undertake, vouch, guarantee, secure.

plentiful *adj* ample, abundant, profuse,
copious, overflowing, lavish, generous,
liberal, bountiful, fruitful, productive.
Ea scarce, scanty, rare.

plenty *n* abundance, profusion, plethora,
lots (*infml*), loads (*infml*), masses (*infml*),
heaps (*infml*), piles (*infml*), stacks (*infml*),
enough, sufficiency, quantity, mass,
volume, fund, mine, store.
Ea scarcity, lack, want, need.

plethora *n* surfeit, surplus, excess, glut,
overabundance, profusion, overfullness,
superabundance, superfluity (*fml*).

pliable *adj* 1 *pliable pieces of wood*: pliant,
flexible, bendable, supple, lithe, malleable,
elastic, plastic, bendy (*infml*). 2 *a pliable
person*: yielding, adaptable, flexible,
accommodating, manageable, docile,
biddable, persuadable, responsive,
receptive, impressionable, susceptible,
tractable (*fml*), compliant (*fml*).
Ea 1 rigid, inflexible. 2 headstrong.

plight *n* predicament, quandary,

dilemma, extremity, trouble, difficulty,
straits, state, condition, situation,
circumstances, case.

plod *v* 1 TRUDGE, tramp, stump, lumber,
plough through. 2 DRUDGE, labour, toil,
grind, slog, persevere, soldier on.

plot *n* 1 CONSPIRACY, intrigue,
machination, scheme, plan, stratagem.
2 STORY, narrative, subject, theme,
storyline, thread, outline, scenario. 3 *plot
of land*: patch, tract, area, allotment, lot,
parcel.
➤ *v* 1 CONSPIRE, intrigue, machinate,
scheme, hatch, lay, cook up, devise,
contrive, plan, project, design, draft. 2
CHART, map, mark, locate, draw, calculate.

plotter *n* conspirator, intriguer,
machinator, schemer.

plough *v* cultivate, dig, till, work, ridge,
spade, break, turn up, furrow.
◆ **plough into** crash into, drive into,
smash into, run/go into, hit, collide, bump
into.
◆ **plough through** plod through, move
through laboriously, trudge through, wade
through.

ploy *n* manoeuvre, stratagem, tactic,
move, device, contrivance, scheme, game,
trick, artifice, dodge (*infml*), wile, ruse,
subterfuge.

pluck *n* courage, bravery, spirit, mettle,
nerve (*infml*), guts (*infml*), grit, backbone,
fortitude, resolution, determination.
Ea cowardice.
➤ *v* 1 PULL, draw, tug, snatch, pull off,
remove, pick, collect, gather, harvest.
2 *pluck a guitar*: pick, twang, strum.

plucky *adj* brave, courageous, bold,
daring, intrepid, heroic, valiant, spirited.
Ea cowardly, weak, feeble.

plug *n* 1 STOPPER, bung, cork, spigot.
2 (*infml*) ADVERTISEMENT, publicity,
mention, puff.
➤ *v* 1 STOP (UP), bung, cork, block, choke,
close, seal, fill, pack, stuff. 2 (*infml*)
ADVERTISE, publicize, promote, push,
mention.

plumb *adv* 1 VERTICALLY, perpendicularly.
2 PRECISELY, exactly, dead, slap (*infml*),
bang (*infml*).
➤ *v* sound, fathom, measure, gauge,
penetrate, probe, search, explore.

plume *n* feather, crest, pinion, quill, tuft,
aigrette.
◆ **plume oneself on** congratulate oneself,

boast about, pride oneself, preen oneself, exult in, pat oneself on the back (*infml*).

plummet *v* plunge, dive, nosedive, descend, drop, fall, tumble.
ⱻ soar.

plump *adj* fat, obese, dumpy, tubby, stout, round, rotund (*fml*), portly, chubby, podgy, fleshy, full, ample, buxom.
ⱻ thin, skinny.

plump for *v* opt for, choose, select, favour, back, support.

plunder *v* loot, pillage, ravage, devastate, sack, raid, ransack, rifle, steal, rob, strip.
➤ *n* loot, pillage, booty, swag (*sl*), spoils, pickings, ill-gotten gains, prize.

plunge *v* **1** DIVE, jump, nosedive, swoop, dive-bomb, plummet, descend, go down, sink, drop, fall, pitch, tumble, hurtle, career, charge, dash, rush, tear. **2** IMMERSE, submerge, dip.
➤ *n* dive, jump, swoop, descent, drop, fall, tumble, immersion, submersion.

plus *n* advantage, benefit, bonus, good point, asset, credit, gain, extra, surplus, perk (*infml*).
ⱻ disadvantage, drawback, minus (*infml*).
➤ *prep* and, with, together with, as well as, in addition to, over and above, not to mention (*infml*).
ⱻ minus.

plush *adj* luxurious, luxury, lavish, de luxe, palatial, stylish, affluent, sumptuous, costly, rich, opulent (*fml*), ritzy (*infml*), glitzy (*infml*), posh (*infml*), swanky (*infml*), classy (*infml*).

ply *n* layer, fold, thickness, strand, sheet, leaf.

poach *v* steal, pilfer, appropriate, trespass, encroach, infringe.

pocket *n* pouch, bag, envelope, receptacle, compartment, hollow, cavity.
➤ *adj* small, little, mini (*infml*), concise, compact, portable, miniature.
➤ *v* take, appropriate (*fml*), help oneself to, lift (*infml*), pilfer, filch, steal, nick (*sl*), pinch (*infml*), snaffle (*infml*).

pod *n* shell, husk, case, hull.

podgy *adj* fat, chubby, paunchy, plump, fleshy, roly-poly, squat, chunky, dumpy, stout, tubby, stubby, stumpy, corpulent (*fml*), rotund (*fml*).
ⱻ thin, skinny.

podium *n* dais, platform, stage, stand, rostrum.

poem

> Types of poem include: ballad, bucolic, clerihew, couplet, ditty, eclogue, elegy, epic, epigram, epithalamium, epode, epopee, georgic, haiku, idyll, lay, limerick, lipogram, lyric, madrigal, monody, nursery rhyme, ode, palinode, pastoral, prothalamion, rhyme, rondeau, roundelay, song, sonnet, tanka, triolet, verse, verselet, versicle. *see also* **song**.

poet *n* versifier, rhymer, rhymester, lyricist, bard, minstrel.

poetic *adj* poetical, lyrical, moving, artistic, graceful, flowing, metrical, rhythmical, rhyming.
ⱻ prosaic.

poetry *n* verse, lyrics, rhyme, rhyming, versing, poems, poesy, free verse, versification, vers libre.

poignant *adj* moving, touching, affecting, tender, distressing, upsetting, heartbreaking, heart-rending, piteous, pathetic, sad, painful, agonizing.

point *n* **1** FEATURE, attribute, aspect, facet, detail, particular, item, subject, topic. **2** *what's the point?*: use, purpose, motive, reason, object, intention, aim, end, goal, objective. **3** ESSENCE, crux, core, pith, gist, thrust, meaning, drift, burden. **4** PLACE, position, situation, location, site, spot. **5** MOMENT, instant, juncture, stage, time, period. **6** DOT, spot, mark, speck, full stop.
➤ *v* **1** *point a gun*: aim, direct, train, level. **2** INDICATE, signal, show, signify, denote, designate.
♦ **point of view** opinion, view, belief, judgement, attitude, position, standpoint, viewpoint, outlook, perspective, approach, angle, slant.
♦ **point out** show, indicate, draw attention to, point to, reveal, identify, specify, mention, bring up, allude to, remind.

point-blank *adj* direct, forthright, straightforward, plain, explicit, open, unreserved, blunt, frank, candid.
➤ *adv* directly, forthrightly, straightforwardly, plainly, explicitly, openly, bluntly, frankly, candidly.

pointed *adj* sharp, keen, edged, barbed, cutting, incisive, trenchant, biting, penetrating, telling.

pointer *n* **1** ARROW, indicator, needle, hand. **2** TIP, recommendation, suggestion, hint, guide, indication, advice, warning, caution.

pointless adj useless, futile, vain, fruitless, unproductive, unprofitable, worthless, senseless, absurd, meaningless, aimless.
🔁 useful, profitable, meaningful.

poise n calmness, composure, self-possession, presence of mind, coolness, equanimity, aplomb, assurance, dignity, elegance, grace, balance, equilibrium.
➤ v balance, position, hover, hang, suspend.

poised adj 1 DIGNIFIED, graceful, calm, composed, unruffled, collected, self-possessed, cool, self-confident, assured. 2 poised for action: prepared, ready, set, waiting, expectant.

poison n toxin, venom, bane, blight, cancer, malignancy, contagion, contamination, corruption.
➤ v infect, contaminate, pollute, taint, adulterate, corrupt, deprave, pervert, warp.

poisonous adj 1 TOXIC, venomous, lethal, deadly, fatal, mortal. 2 HARMFUL, noxious, pernicious, malicious, vicious, spiteful, virulent, malignant, contaminating, corrupting, cancerous, cankerous.

Poisonous plants include: aconite, amanita, anemone, banewort, belladonna, black nightshade, castor oil plant, common nightshade, cowbane, cuckoo pint, deadly nightshade, digitalis, dwale, foxglove, giant hockweed, helmet flower, hemlock, hemlock water dropwort, jimson-weed, laburnum, lantana, lords-and-ladies, meadow saffron, monkshood, naked boys, naked lady, oleander, poison ivy, stinkweed, stramonium, thorn apple, wake-robin, wild arum, windflower, wolfsbane.

poke v prod, stab, jab, stick, thrust, push, shove, nudge, elbow, dig, butt, hit, punch.
➤ n prod, jab, thrust, shove, nudge, dig, butt, punch.

poky adj confined, cramped, small, tight, tiny, narrow, crowded, incommodious (fml).
🔁 spacious, roomy.

polarity n opposition, oppositeness, contradiction, ambivalence, contrariety, duality, paradox, antithesis (fml), dichotomy (fml).

pole¹ n bar, rod, stick, shaft, spar, upright, post, stake, mast, staff.

pole² n antipode, extremity, extreme, limit.

◆ **poles apart** irreconcilable, worlds apart, incompatible, like chalk and cheese.

polemic n argument, controversy, debate, dispute.
➤ adj argumentative, contentious, controversial, polemical, disputatious (fml).

police n police force, constabulary, the Law (infml), the Bill (sl), the fuzz (sl).
➤ v check, control, regulate, monitor, watch, observe, supervise, oversee, patrol, guard, protect, defend, keep the peace.

policeman, policewoman n officer, constable, PC, cop (sl), copper (infml), bobby (infml).

policy n 1 CODE OF PRACTICE, rules, guidelines, procedure, method, practice, custom, protocol. 2 COURSE OF ACTION, line, course, plan, programme, scheme, stance, position.

polish v 1 SHINE, brighten, smooth, rub, buff, burnish, clean, wax. 2 IMPROVE, enhance, brush up, touch up, finish, perfect, refine, cultivate.
🔁 1 tarnish, dull.
➤ n 1 a tin of polish: wax, varnish. 2 SHINE, gloss, sheen, lustre, brightness, brilliance, sparkle, smoothness, finish, glaze, veneer. 3 REFINEMENT, cultivation, class, breeding, sophistication, finesse, style, elegance, grace, poise.
🔁 2 dullness. 3 clumsiness.
◆ **polish off** 1 EAT UP, consume, devour, put away, bolt, gobble, finish, complete, dispose of, down, stuff, wolf (infml). 2 MURDER, kill, eliminate (infml), bump off (infml), liquidate (infml), rub out (infml).

polished adj 1 SHINING, shiny, glossy, lustrous, gleaming, burnished, smooth, glassy, slippery. 2 FAULTLESS, flawless, impeccable, perfect, outstanding, superlative, masterly, expert, professional, skilful, accomplished, perfected. 3 REFINED, cultivated, genteel, well-bred, polite, sophisticated, urbane, suave, elegant, graceful.
🔁 1 tarnished. 2 inexpert. 3 gauche.

polite adj courteous, well-mannered, respectful, civil, well-bred, refined, cultured, gentlemanly, ladylike, gracious, obliging, thoughtful, considerate, tactful, diplomatic.
🔁 impolite, discourteous, rude.

politic adj wise, prudent, shrewd, sensible, tactful, diplomatic, advisable, advantageous, opportune, expedient, judicious (*fml*), sagacious (*fml*), sage (*fml*). ☞ impolitic.

politician *n* member of parliament, MP, minister, statesman, stateswoman, legislator.

politics *n* public affairs, civics, affairs of state, statecraft, government, diplomacy, statesmanship, political science.

Terms used in politics include: alliance, apartheid, ballot, bill, blockade, cabinet, campaign, civil service, coalition, constitution, council, coup d'etat, detente, election, electoral register, ethnic cleansing, general election, glasnost, go to the country, government, green paper, Hansard, judiciary, left wing, lobby, local government, majority, mandate, manifesto, nationalization, parliament, party, party line, perestroika, prime minister's question time, privatization, propaganda, proportional representation, rainbow coalition, referendum, right wing, sanction, shadow cabinet, sovereignty, state, summit, summit conference, term of office, trade union, veto, vote, welfare state, whip, three-line whip, white paper.

People in politics include: activist, ambassador, Black Rod, capitalist, Communist, commie (*infml*), comrade, Conservative, Democrat, Deputy Speaker, dictator, dissident, dry (*infml*), extremist, Green, high commissioner, independent, lefty (*infml*), Liberal, Liberal Democrat, loyalist, Marxist, Marxist-Leninist, member of parliament, minister, moderate, MP, party chairman, party member, party worker, pinko (*infml*), politician, premier, president, prime minister, radical, red (*infml*), Republican, revolutionary, secretary of state, Social Democrat, Socialist, speaker, Tory, Trotskyite, true-blue, wet (*infml*), Whig.

Political parties include: Alliance, Co-operative, Communist, Conservative and Unionist, Democratic, Democratic Left, Democratic Unionist, Fianna Fáil, Fine Gael, Green, Labour, Liberal, Liberal Democratic, Militant Labour, National Front, Parliamentary, Parliamentary Labour, Plaid Cymru, Progressive Democrats, Republican, Scottish Conservative and Unionist, Scottish Liberal Democratic, Scottish National, Sinn Féin, Social and Liberal Democratic, Social Democratic and Labour, Ulster Democratic

Unionist, Ulster Popular Unionist, Ulster Unionist, Welsh Liberal Democratic. *see also* **government; parliament**.

Political ideologies include: absolutism, anarchism, authoritarianism, Bolshevism, Christian democracy, collectivism, communism, conservatism, democracy, egalitarianism, fascism, federalism, holism, imperialism, individualism, liberalism, Maoism, Marxism, nationalism, Nazism, neocolonialism, neo-fascism, neo-nazism, pluralism, republicanism, social democracy, socialism, syndicalism, Thatcherism, theocracy, totalitarianism, unilateralism, Trotskyism, Whiggism.

poll *n* ballot, vote, voting, plebiscite, referendum, straw-poll, sampling, canvass, opinion poll, survey, census, count, tally.

pollute *v* contaminate, infect, poison, taint, adulterate, debase, corrupt, dirty, foul, soil, defile, sully, stain, mar, spoil.

pollution *n* impurity, contamination, infection, taint, adulteration, corruption, dirtiness, foulness, defilement. ☞ purification, purity, cleanness.

pomp *n* ceremony, ceremonial, ritual, solemnity, formality, ceremoniousness, state, grandeur, splendour, magnificence, pageantry, show, display, parade, ostentation, flourish. ☞ austerity, simplicity.

pompous *adj* self-important, arrogant, grandiose, supercilious, overbearing, imperious, magisterial, bombastic, high-flown, overblown, windy, affected, pretentious, ostentatious. ☞ unassuming, modest, simple, unaffected.

pond *n* pool, puddle, lake, mere, tarn, waterhole, watering-hole.

ponder *v* deliberate, give thought to, reflect, reason, think, contemplate, meditate, consider, brood, examine, analyse, study, ruminate over (*fml*), weigh, muse, puzzle over, mull over, cerebrate (*fml*), cogitate (*fml*), excogitate (*fml*), ratiocinate (*fml*).

pontificate *v* preach, hold forth, lecture, expound, pronounce, sermonize, sound off, harangue, dogmatize, moralize, declaim (*fml*), perorate (*fml*), lay down the law (*infml*).

pony *see* **horse**.

pooh-pooh v dismiss, scorn, make little of, belittle, brush aside, ridicule, disdain, disregard, slight, sneer, sniff at, scoff, spurn, reject, play down, minimize, deride (*fml*), disparage (*fml*), turn up one's nose at (*infml*).
☒ exaggerate, magnify.

pool¹ n puddle, pond, lake, mere, tarn, watering-hole, paddling-pool, swimming-pool.

pool² n **1** FUND, reserve, accumulation, bank, kitty, purse, pot, jackpot.
2 SYNDICATE, cartel, ring, combine, consortium, collective, group, team.
➤ v contribute, chip in (*infml*), combine, amalgamate, merge, share, muck in (*infml*).

poor adj **1** IMPOVERISHED, poverty-stricken, badly off, hard-up, broke (*infml*), stony-broke (*sl*), skint (*sl*), bankrupt, penniless, destitute, miserable, wretched, distressed, straitened, needy, lacking, deficient, insufficient, scanty, skimpy, meagre, sparse, depleted, exhausted.
2 BAD, substandard, unsatisfactory, inferior, mediocre, below par (*infml*), low-grade, second-rate, third-rate, shoddy, imperfect, faulty, weak, feeble, pathetic (*infml*), sorry, worthless, fruitless.
3 UNFORTUNATE, unlucky, luckless, ill-fated, unhappy, miserable, pathetic, pitiable, pitiful.
☒ **1** rich, wealthy, affluent. **2** superior, impressive. **3** fortunate, lucky.

poorly adj ill, sick, unwell, indisposed, ailing, sickly, off-colour, below par (*infml*), out of sorts (*infml*), under the weather (*infml*), seedy, groggy, rotten (*infml*).
☒ well, healthy.

pop v burst, explode, go off, bang, crack, snap.
➤ n bang, crack, snap, burst, explosion.

populace n inhabitants, natives, residents, citizens, occupants, community, society, people, folk, general public, crowd, masses, proletariat, public, mob, multitude(s), common herd, canaille, hoi polloi, plebs (*infml*), punters (*infml*), rabble (*infml*), rank and file (*infml*).
☒ aristocracy, elite, nobility.

popular adj well-liked, favourite, liked, favoured, approved, in demand, sought-after, fashionable, modish, trendy (*infml*), prevailing, current, accepted, conventional, standard, stock, common,

prevalent, widespread, universal, general, household, famous, well-known, celebrated, idolized.
☒ unpopular.

popularity n approval, acceptance, recognition, reputation, favour, vogue, kudos, mass appeal, regard, fame, renown, currency, repute, acclaim, adoration, adulation, glory, worship, idolization, lionization, approbation (*fml*), esteem (*fml*).
☒ unpopularity.

popularize v spread, propagate, universalize, democratize, simplify.

popularly adv commonly, widely, universally, generally, usually, customarily, conventionally, traditionally.

populate v people, occupy, settle, colonize, inhabit, live in, overrun.

population n inhabitants, natives, residents, citizens, occupants, community, society, people, folk.

populous adj crowded, packed, swarming, teeming, crawling, overpopulated.
☒ deserted.

porcelain

> Types of porcelain include: biscuit, bisque, blue and white, bone china, Canton, Capodimonte, chinoiserie, Compagnie des Indes, copper red, eggshell, faïence, famille-rose, famille-verte, First Period Worcester, hard paste, Imari, Kakiemon, Kraak, nankeen, Parian, salt-glazed, soapstone paste, soft paste, Yingqing.

> Famous makes of porcelain include: Arita, Belleek, Bow, Bristol, Caughley, Chantilly, Chelsea, Coalport, Copeland, Derby, Dresden, Limoges, Meissen, Ming, Minton, Nanking, Rockingham, Royal Doulton, Royal Worcester, Satsuma, Sèvres, Vienna, Wedgwood, Worcester.

pore n hole, opening, perforation, aperture, outlet, vent.

pore over v study, study intensely, examine, examine closely, scrutinize, go over, read, scan, contemplate, ponder, dwell on, brood, peruse (*fml*).

pornographic adj obscene, indecent, dirty, filthy, blue, risqué, bawdy, coarse, gross, lewd, erotic, titillating.

pornography n indecency, obscenity,

filth, dirt, smut, erotica, grossness, bawdiness, facetiae, porn (*infml*), porno (*infml*), sexploitation (*infml*), girlie magazines (*infml*).

porous *adj* permeable, pervious, penetrable, absorbent, spongy, honeycombed, pitted.
F3 impermeable, impervious.

port *n* seaport, harbour, jetty, dock, anchorage, harbourage, haven, roads, roadstead, hithe.

portable *adj* movable, transportable, compact, lightweight, manageable, handy, convenient.
F3 fixed, immovable.

porter¹ *n* bearer, carrier, baggage-attendant, baggage-handler.

porter² *n* doorman, commissionaire, door-keeper, gatekeeper, janitor, caretaker, concierge.

portion *n* share, allocation, allotment, parcel, allowance, ration, quota, measure, part, section, division, fraction, percentage, bit, fragment, morsel, piece, segment, slice, serving, helping.

portly *adj* stout, corpulent (*fml*), rotund (*fml*), round, fat, plump, obese, overweight, heavy, large.
F3 slim, thin, slight.

portrait *n* picture, painting, drawing, sketch, caricature, miniature, icon, photograph, likeness, image, representation, vignette, profile, characterization, description, depiction, portrayal.

portray *v* draw, sketch, paint, illustrate, picture, represent, depict, describe, evoke, play, impersonate, characterize, personify.

portrayal *n* representation, characterization, depiction, description, evocation, presentation, performance, interpretation, rendering.

pose *v* 1 MODEL, sit, position. 2 PRETEND, feign, affect, put on an act, masquerade, pass oneself off, impersonate. 3 *pose a question*: set, put forward, submit, present.
➤ *n* 1 POSITION, stance, air, bearing, posture, attitude. 2 PRETENCE, sham, affectation, façade, front, masquerade, role, act.

poser¹ *n* puzzle, riddle, conundrum, brain-teaser, mystery, enigma, problem, vexed question.

poser² *n* poseur, poseuse, posturer, attitudinizer, exhibitionist, show-off, pseud (*infml*), phoney (*infml*).

posh (*infml*) *adj* smart, stylish, fashionable, high-class, upper-class, la-di-da (*sl*), grand, luxurious, lavish, swanky (*infml*), luxury, de luxe, up-market, exclusive, select, classy (*infml*), swish (*infml*).
F3 inferior, cheap.

position *n* 1 PLACE, situation, location, site, spot, point. 2 POSTURE, stance, pose, arrangement, disposition. 3 JOB, post, occupation, employment, office, duty, function, role. 4 RANK, grade, level, status, standing. 5 OPINION, point of view, belief, view, outlook, viewpoint, standpoint, stand.
➤ *v* put, place, set, fix, stand, arrange, dispose, lay out, deploy, station, locate, situate, site.

positive *adj* 1 SURE, certain, convinced, confident, assured. 2 *positive criticism*: helpful, constructive, practical, useful, optimistic, hopeful, promising. 3 DEFINITE, decisive, conclusive, clear, unmistakable, explicit, unequivocal, express, firm, emphatic, categorical, undeniable, irrefutable, indisputable, incontrovertible. 4 ABSOLUTE, utter, sheer, complete, perfect.
F3 1 uncertain. 2 negative. 3 indefinite, vague.

positively *adv* absolutely, definitely, categorically, firmly, finally, decisively, emphatically, expressly, conclusively, certainly, assuredly, surely, unmistakably, unquestionably, incontestably, incontrovertibly, indisputably, unequivocally, undeniably, uncompromisingly.

possess *v* 1 OWN, have, hold, enjoy, be endowed with. 2 SEIZE, take, obtain, acquire, take over, occupy, control, dominate, bewitch, haunt.

possessed *adj* dominated, controlled, mesmerized, enchanted, berserk, bedevilled, bewitched, haunted, cursed, hag-ridden, frenzied, demented, crazed, maddened, raving, consumed, infatuated, obsessed, besotted.

possession *n* ownership, title, tenure, occupation, custody, control, hold, grip.

possessions *n* belongings, property, things, paraphernalia, effects, goods, chattels, movables, assets, estate, wealth, riches.

possessive *adj* selfish, clinging, overprotective, domineering, dominating, jealous, covetous, acquisitive, grasping.
🖛 unselfish, sharing.

possibility *n* likelihood, probability, odds, chance, risk, danger, hope, prospect, potentiality, conceivability, practicability, feasibility.
🖛 impossibility, impracticability.

possible *adj* potential, promising, likely, probable, imaginable, conceivable, practicable, feasible, viable, tenable, workable, achievable, attainable, accomplishable, realizable.
🖛 impossible, unthinkable, impracticable, unattainable.

possibly *adv* perhaps, maybe, hopefully (*infml*), by any means, at all, by any chance.

post[1] *n* pole, stake, picket, pale, pillar, column, shaft, support, baluster, upright, stanchion, strut, leg.
➤ *v* display, stick up, pin up, advertise, publicize, announce, make known, report, publish.

post[2] *n* office, job, employment, position, situation, place, vacancy, appointment, assignment, station, beat.
➤ *v* station, locate, situate, position, place, put, appoint, assign, second, transfer, move, send.

post[3] *n* mail, letters, dispatch, collection, delivery.
➤ *v* mail, send, dispatch, transmit.

poster *n* notice, bill, sign, placard, sticker, advertisement, announcement.

posterity *n* descendants, successors, progeny, issue, offspring, children.

post-mortem *n* autopsy, dissection, necropsy, analysis, examination, review.

postpone *v* put off, defer, put back, hold over, delay, adjourn, suspend, shelve, pigeonhole, freeze, put on ice.
🖛 advance, forward.

postponement *n* adjournment, put-off, deferment, delay, deferral, moratorium, freeze, suspension, stay, respite, prorogation (*fml*).

postscript *n* PS (*infml*), addition, supplement, afterthought, addendum, codicil, appendix, afterword, epilogue.
🖛 introduction, prologue.

postulate *v* theorize, hypothesize, suppose, assume, propose, advance, lay down, stipulate.

posture *n* position, stance, pose, attitude, disposition, bearing, carriage, deportment.

posy *n* bouquet, spray, buttonhole, corsage.

pot *n* receptacle, vessel, teapot, coffee pot, urn, jar, vase, bowl, basin, pan, cauldron, crucible.

potent *adj* powerful, mighty, strong, intoxicating, pungent, effective, impressive, cogent, convincing, persuasive, compelling, forceful, dynamic, vigorous, authoritative, commanding, dominant, influential, overpowering.
🖛 impotent, weak.

potential *adj* possible, likely, probable, prospective, future, aspiring, would-be, promising, budding, embryonic, undeveloped, dormant, latent, hidden, concealed, unrealized.
➤ *n* possibility, ability, capability, capacity, aptitude, talent, powers, resources.

potion *n* mixture, concoction, brew, beverage, drink, draught, dose, medicine, tonic, elixir.

potpourri *n* medley, mixture, jumble, hotchpotch, miscellany, collection.

potter *v* tinker, fiddle, mess about (*infml*), dabble, loiter, fritter.

pottery *n* earthenware, stoneware, terracotta, ceramics, crockery, china, porcelain.

> **Terms used in pottery include:** armorial, art pottery, basalt, blanc-de-chine, bronzing, celadon, ceramic, china clay, cloisonné, crackleware, crazing, creamware, delft, earthenware, enamel, faïence, fairing, figure, firing, flambé, flatback, glaze, grotesque, ground, ironstone, jasper, kiln, lustre, maiolica, majolica, maker's mark, mandarin palette, model, monogram, overglaze, porcelain, sagger, scratch blue, sgraffito, slip, slip-cast, spongeware, Staffordshire, stoneware, terracotta, tin-glazed earthenware, transfer printing, underglaze, Willow pattern. *see also* **porcelain**.

pouch *n* bag, purse, pocket, container, receptacle, sack, wallet, sporran, poke, marsupium (*fml*), sac, reticule (*fml*).

pounce *v* fall on, dive on, swoop, drop,

attack, strike, ambush, spring, jump, leap, snatch, grab.

pound[1] *v* 1 STRIKE, thump, beat, drum, pelt, hammer, batter, bang, bash, smash. 2 PULVERIZE, powder, grind, mash, crush. 3 *his heart was pounding*: throb, pulsate, palpitate, thump, thud.

pound[2] *n* enclosure, compound, corral, yard, pen, fold.

pour *v* 1 *pour a drink*: serve, decant, tip. 2 SPILL, issue, discharge, flow, stream, run, rush, spout, spew, gush, cascade, crowd, throng, swarm.

pout *v* scowl, glower, grimace, pull a face, sulk, mope.
🔁 grin, smile.
➤ *n* scowl, glower, grimace, long face.
🔁 grin, smile.

poverty *n* poorness, impoverishment, insolvency, bankruptcy, pennilessness, penury, destitution, distress, hardship, privation, need, necessity, want, lack, deficiency, shortage, inadequacy, insufficiency, depletion, scarcity, meagreness, paucity, dearth.
🔁 wealth, richness, affluence, plenty.

poverty-stricken *adj* poor, penniless, impoverished, needy, destitute, distressed, bankrupt, beggared, impecunious (*fml*), indigent (*fml*), penurious (*fml*), broke (*infml*), skint (*sl*), stony (*sl*), stony-broke (*sl*), strapped (*infml*), on one's beam-ends (*infml*), on one's uppers (*infml*).
🔁 rich, affluent.

powder *n* dust, grains, pounce, bran, talc, triturate (*fml*), pulvil, pulville.
➤ *v* 1 PULVERIZE, grind, mash, bray, pestle, crush, beat, smash, granulate, comminute (*fml*), triturate (*fml*). 2 SPRINKLE, scatter, cover, dust, strew.

powdery *adj* dusty, sandy, grainy, granular, powdered, pulverized, ground, fine, loose, dry, crumbly, friable, chalky.

power *n* 1 COMMAND, authority, sovereignty, rule, dominion, control, influence. 2 RIGHT, privilege, prerogative, authorization, warrant. 3 POTENCY, strength, intensity, force, vigour, energy. 4 ABILITY, capability, capacity, potential, faculty, competence.
🔁 1 subjection. 3 weakness. 4 inability.

powerful *adj* dominant, prevailing, leading, influential, high-powered, authoritative, commanding, potent, effective, strong, mighty, robust, muscular,

energetic, forceful, telling, impressive, convincing, persuasive, compelling, winning, overwhelming.
🔁 impotent, ineffective, weak.

powerless *adj* impotent, incapable, ineffective, weak, feeble, frail, infirm, incapacitated, disabled, paralysed, helpless, vulnerable, defenceless, unarmed.
🔁 powerful, potent, able.

practicable *adj* possible, feasible, performable, achievable, attainable, viable, workable, practical, realistic.
🔁 impracticable.

practical *adj* 1 REALISTIC, sensible, commonsense, practicable, workable, feasible, down-to-earth, matter-of-fact, pragmatic, hardnosed (*infml*), hard-headed, businesslike, experienced, trained, qualified, skilled, accomplished, proficient, hands on, applied. 2 USEFUL, handy, serviceable, utilitarian, functional, working, everyday, ordinary.
🔁 1 impractical, unskilled, theoretical.

practically *adv* 1 ALMOST, nearly, well-nigh, virtually, pretty well, all but, just about, in principle, in effect, essentially, fundamentally, to all intents and purposes. 2 REALISTICALLY, sensibly, reasonably, rationally, pragmatically.

practice *n* 1 CUSTOM, tradition, convention, usage, habit, routine, way, method, system, procedure, policy. 2 REHEARSAL, run-through, dry run, dummy run, try-out, training, drill, exercise, work-out, study, experience. 3 *in practice*: effect, reality, actuality, action, operation, performance, use, application.
🔁 3 theory, principle.

practise *v* 1 DO, perform, execute, implement, carry out, apply, put into practice, follow, pursue, engage in, undertake. 2 REHEARSE, run through, repeat, drill, exercise, train, study, perfect.

practised *adj* experienced, seasoned, veteran, trained, qualified, accomplished, skilled, versed, knowledgeable, able, proficient, expert, masterly, consummate, finished.
🔁 unpractised, inexperienced, inexpert.

pragmatic *adj* practical, realistic, sensible, matter-of-fact, businesslike, efficient, hard-headed, hardnosed (*infml*), unsentimental.
🔁 unrealistic, idealistic, romantic.

praise n approval, admiration, commendation, congratulation, compliment, flattery, adulation, eulogy, applause, ovation, cheering, acclaim, recognition, testimonial, tribute, accolade, homage, honour, glory, worship, adoration, devotion, thanksgiving.
⊟ criticism, revilement.
➤ v commend, congratulate, admire, compliment, flatter, eulogize, wax lyrical, rave over (infml), extol, promote, applaud, cheer, acclaim, hail, recognize, acknowledge, pay tribute to, honour, laud, glorify, magnify, exalt, worship, adore, bless.
⊟ criticize, revile.

Expressions used when praising someone: can't praise him/her/them highly enough, clever boy/girl!, congratulations!, you deserve a medal, encore!, fair play to you!, give that person a coconut, good for you!, good job! (US), good show!, good work!, nice job! (US), nice one!, sing someone's praises, ten out of ten, way to go! (US), well done!, you beauty!

praiseworthy adj commendable, fine, excellent, admirable, worthy, deserving, honourable, reputable, estimable, sterling.
⊟ blameworthy, dishonourable, ignoble.

prance v 1 LEAP, jump, spring, skip, dance, frisk, frolic, gambol, cavort, caper, bound, romp, vault. 2 SHOW OFF, strut, swagger, stalk, parade, curvet, swank (infml).

prank n trick, practical joke, joke, stunt, caper, frolic, lark, antic, escapade.

prattle v chat, chatter, witter, gabble, rattle, twitter, twaddle, twattle, drivel, gossip, blather, blether, babble (infml), jabber (infml).
➤ n chat, chatter, patter, gossip, talk, jaw, gab, tattle, blather, blether, nonsense, prating, gibberish, foolishness, drivel, hot air (infml), babble (infml).

pray v invoke, call on, supplicate, entreat, implore, plead, beg, beseech, petition, ask, request, crave, solicit.

prayer n collect, litany, devotion, communion, invocation, supplication, entreaty, plea, appeal, petition, request.

preach v address, lecture, harangue, pontificate, sermonize, evangelize, moralize, exhort, urge, advocate.

preacher n minister, clergyman, parson, evangelist, televangelist, missionary, revivalist, sermonizer, moralizer, pulpite(e)r, ranter, homilist, pontificater.

preamble n introduction, lead-in, preliminaries, preparation, prelude, foreword, preface, prologue, overture, exordium (fml), prolegomenon (fml).
⊟ postscript, epilogue.

precarious adj unsafe, dangerous, treacherous, risky, hazardous, chancy, uncertain, unsure, dubious, doubtful, unpredictable, unreliable, unsteady, unstable, shaky, wobbly, insecure, vulnerable.
⊟ safe, certain, stable, secure.

precaution n safeguard, security, protection, insurance, providence, forethought, caution, prudence, foresight, anticipation, preparation, provision.

precautionary adj safety, protective, preventive, provident, cautious, prudent, judicious, preparatory, preliminary.

precede v come before, lead, come first, go before, take precedence, introduce, herald, usher in.
⊟ follow, succeed.

precedence n priority, preference, pride of place, superiority, supremacy, pre-eminence, lead, first place, seniority, rank.

precedent n example, instance, pattern, model, standard, criterion.

preceding adj above, earlier, former, past, previous, prior, precedent, foregoing, antecedent, aforementioned (fml), aforesaid (fml), supra (fml), precursive (fml), anterior (fml).
⊟ following, later.

precept n principle, axiom, command, commandment, charge, direction, directive, ordinance, regulation, guideline, order, injunction, institute, law, instruction, decree, dictum, mandate, rule, statute, convention, canon, maxim, motto, saying, sentence, rubric.

precinct n 1 ZONE, area, district, quarter, sector, division, section. 2 BOUNDARY, limit, bound, confine.

precious adj 1 VALUED, treasured, prized, cherished, beloved, dear, dearest, darling, favourite, loved, revered, adored, idolized. 2 VALUABLE, expensive, costly, high-priced, dear, priceless, inestimable, rare, choice, fine. 3 AFFECTED, overrefined, simulated, contrived, artificial, mannered, pretentious, flowery, twee, chichi.

precipitate v hasten, hurry, speed, accelerate, quicken, expedite, advance, further, bring on, induce, trigger, cause, occasion.

➤ adj sudden, unexpected, abrupt, quick, swift, rapid, brief, hasty, hurried, headlong, breakneck, frantic, violent, impatient, hot-headed, impetuous, impulsive, rash, reckless, heedless, indiscreet.

🖙 cautious, careful.

precipitation

> Types of precipitation include: dew, downpour, drizzle, fog, hail, mist, rain, rainfall, rainstorm, shower, sleet, snow, snowfall, snowflake.

precipitous adj steep, sheer, perpendicular, vertical, high.

🖙 gradual.

précis n summary, abridgement, contraction, abbreviation, condensation, synopsis, abstract, digest, epitome, outline, résumé, sketch, compendium, run-down, table, conspectus (fml), encapsulation.

➤ v summarize, shorten, sum up, outline, abstract, abridge, condense, synopsize, digest, abbreviate, encapsulate, epitomize, contract, compress.

🖙 amplify, expand.

precise adj exact, accurate, right, punctilious, correct, factual, faithful, authentic, literal, word-for-word, express, definite, explicit, unequivocal, unambiguous, clear-cut, distinct, detailed, blow-by-blow, minute, nice, particular, specific, fixed, rigid, strict, careful, meticulous, scrupulous, fastidious.

🖙 imprecise, inexact, ambiguous, careless.

precisely adv exactly, absolutely, just so, accurately, correctly, literally, verbatim, word for word, strictly, minutely, clearly, distinctly.

precision n exactness, accuracy, correctness, faithfulness, explicitness, distinctness, detail, particularity, rigour, care, meticulousness, scrupulousness, neatness.

🖙 imprecision, inaccuracy.

preclude v prevent, exclude, eliminate, rule out, hinder, inhibit, prohibit, restrain, stop, avoid, check, debar, forestall, obviate (fml).

🖙 incur, involve.

precocious adj forward, ahead, advanced, early, premature, mature, developed, gifted, clever, bright, smart, quick, fast.

🖙 backward.

preconceive v presuppose, presume, assume, anticipate, project, imagine, conceive, envisage, expect, visualize, picture.

preconception n presupposition, presumption, assumption, conjecture, anticipation, expectation, prejudgement, bias, prejudice.

precondition n condition, stipulation, requirement, prerequisite, essential, necessity, must.

precursor n antecedent, forerunner, sign, indication, herald, harbinger, messenger, usher, pioneer, trail-blazer.

🖙 follower, successor.

predecessor n ancestor, forefather, forebear, antecedent, forerunner, precursor.

🖙 successor, descendant.

predestination n destiny, fate, lot, doom, predetermination, foreordination.

predetermined adj 1 PREDESTINED, destined, fated, doomed, ordained, foreordained. 2 PREARRANGED, arranged, agreed, fixed, set.

predicament n situation, plight, trouble, mess, fix, spot (infml), quandary, dilemma, impasse, crisis, emergency.

predict v foretell, prophesy, foresee, forecast, prognosticate, project.

predictable adj foreseeable, expected, anticipated, likely, probable, imaginable, foreseen, foregone, certain, sure, reliable, dependable.

🖙 unpredictable, uncertain.

prediction n prophecy, forecast, prognosis, augury, divination, fortune-telling, soothsaying.

predispose v dispose, incline, prompt, induce, make, sway, influence, affect, bias, prejudice.

predominant adj dominant, prevailing, preponderant, chief, main, principal, primary, capital, paramount, supreme, sovereign, ruling, controlling, leading, powerful, potent, prime, important, influential, forceful, strong.

🖙 minor, lesser, weak.

predominate v prevail, dominate,

outnumber, outweigh, override, overrule, overshadow, transcend, tell, reign, rule, obtain (*fml*), preponderate (*fml*).

pre-eminent *adj* supreme, unsurpassed, unrivalled, unequalled, unmatched, matchless, incomparable, inimitable, chief, foremost, leading, eminent, distinguished, renowned, famous, prominent, outstanding, exceptional, excellent, superlative, transcendent, superior.
🔁 inferior, unknown.

pre-empt *v* prevent, forestall, anticipate, assume, acquire, secure, seize, usurp, appropriate (*fml*), arrogate (*fml*).

preen *v* **1** CLEAN, smooth, groom, plume, trim, spruce up, dress up, trick out, doll up, slick, prettify, adorn, beautify, deck, primp, prink, array (*fml*), do up (*infml*), tart up (*infml*). **2** CONGRATULATE, pride, exult, bask, plume, gloat, pique, pat oneself on the back (*infml*).

preface *n* foreword, introduction, preamble, prologue, prelude, preliminaries.
🔁 epilogue, postscript.
➤ *v* precede, prefix, lead up to, introduce, launch, open, begin, start.
🔁 end, finish, complete.

prefer *v* favour, like better, would rather, would sooner, want, wish, desire, choose, select, pick, opt for, go for, plump for, single out, advocate, recommend, back, support, fancy, elect, adopt.
🔁 reject.

preferable *adj* better, superior, nicer, preferred, favoured, chosen, desirable, advantageous, advisable, recommended.
🔁 inferior, undesirable.

preferably *adv* rather, much rather, sooner, much sooner, from choice, for choice, by/for preference, first.

preference *n* **1** FAVOURITE, first choice, choice, pick, selection, option, wish, desire. **2** LIKING, fancy, inclination, predilection, partiality, favouritism, preferential treatment.

preferential *adj* better, superior, favoured, privileged, special, favourable, advantageous.
🔁 equal.

pregnant *adj* **1** *a pregnant woman*: expectant, expecting, with child (*fml*). **2** *a pregnant pause*: meaningful, significant, eloquent, expressive, suggestive, charged, loaded, full.

prehistoric *adj* primitive, primeval, primordial, earliest, early, ancient, archaic, antiquated, old, obsolete, out of date, outmoded, antediluvian (*infml*), out of the ark (*infml*), before the flood (*infml*).
🔁 modern.

prejudice *n* **1** BIAS, partiality, partisanship, discrimination, unfairness, injustice, intolerance, narrow-mindedness, bigotry, chauvinism, racism, sexism. **2** HARM, damage, impairment, hurt, injury, detriment, disadvantage, loss, ruin.
🔁 **1** fairness, tolerance. **2** benefit, advantage.
➤ *v* **1** BIAS, predispose, incline, sway, influence, condition, colour, slant, distort, load, weight. **2** HARM, damage, impair, hinder, undermine, hurt, injure, mar, spoil, ruin, wreck.
🔁 **2** benefit, help, advance.

prejudiced *adj* biased, partial, predisposed, subjective, partisan, one-sided, discriminatory, unfair, unjust, loaded, weighted, intolerant, narrow-minded, bigoted, chauvinist, racist, sexist, jaundiced, distorted, warped, influenced, conditioned.
🔁 impartial, fair, tolerant.

prejudicial *adj* harmful, damaging, hurtful, injurious, detrimental, disadvantageous, unfavourable, inimical.
🔁 beneficial, advantageous.

preliminaries *n* preparation, groundwork, foundations, basics, rudiments, formalities, introduction, preface, prelude, opening, beginning, start.

preliminary *adj* preparatory, prior, advance, exploratory, experimental, trial, test, pilot, early, earliest, first, initial, primary, qualifying, inaugural, introductory, opening.
🔁 final, closing.

prelude *n* overture, introduction, preface, foreword, preamble, prologue, opening, opener, preliminary, preparation, beginning, start, commencement, precursor, curtain raiser.
🔁 finale, epilogue.

premature *adj* early, immature, green, unripe, embryonic, half-formed, incomplete, undeveloped, abortive, hasty, ill-considered, rash, untimely, inopportune, ill-timed.
🔁 late, tardy.

premeditated *adj* planned, intended, intentional, deliberate, wilful, conscious, cold-blooded, calculated, considered, contrived, preplanned, prearranged, predetermined.
🖾 unpremeditated, spontaneous.

premier *n* head of government, prime minister, chief minister, first minister, chancellor, secretary of state.
➤ *adj* principal, leading, highest, top, head, foremost, chief, primary, prime, main, supreme, paramount, pre-eminent, first, cardinal, earliest, original, initial.

première *n* first performance, opening, opening night, first night, début.

premise *n* proposition, statement, assertion, postulate, thesis, argument, basis, supposition, hypothesis, presupposition, assumption.

premises *n* building, property, establishment, office, grounds, estate, site, place.

premium *n* 1 *pay an insurance premium*: regular payment, instalment. 2 *pay a premium rate*: extra sum/charge, surcharging, overcharging, an arm and a leg (*infml*), daylight robbery (*infml*).
♦ **at a premium** scarce, rare, hard to come by, in short supply, in great demand, few and far between, like gold dust (*infml*).
♦ **put a premium on** value greatly, treasure, appreciate, favour, hold dear, attach great/special importance to, regard highly, set great store by.

premonition *n* presentiment, feeling, intuition, hunch, idea, suspicion, foreboding, misgiving, fear, apprehension, anxiety, worry, warning, omen, sign.

preoccupation *n* 1 OBSESSION, fixation, hang-up (*infml*), concern, interest, enthusiasm, hobby-horse. 2 DISTRACTION, absent-mindedness, reverie, obliviousness, oblivion.

preoccupied *adj* 1 OBSESSED, intent, immersed, engrossed, engaged, taken up, wrapped up, involved. 2 DISTRACTED, abstracted, absent-minded, daydreaming, absorbed, faraway, heedless, oblivious, pensive.

preordain *v* destine, prearrange, foreordain, doom, fate, predestine (*fml*), predetermine (*fml*).

preparation *n* 1 READINESS, provision, precaution, safeguard, foundation, groundwork, spadework, basics, rudiments, preliminaries, plans, arrangements. 2 MIXTURE, compound, concoction, potion, medicine, lotion, application.

preparatory *adj* preliminary, introductory, opening, initial, primary, basic, fundamental, rudimentary, elementary.

prepare *v* 1 GET READY, warm up, train, coach, study, make ready, adapt, adjust, plan, organize, arrange, pave the way. 2 *prepare a meal*: make, produce, construct, assemble, concoct, contrive, devise, draft, draw up, compose. 3 PROVIDE, supply, equip, fit out, rig out.
♦ **prepare oneself** brace oneself, steel oneself, gird oneself, fortify oneself.

prepared *adj* ready, waiting, set, fit, inclined, disposed, willing, planned, organized, arranged.
🖾 unprepared, unready.

preponderant *adj* greater, larger, superior, predominant, prevailing, overriding, overruling, controlling, foremost, important, significant.

prepossessing *adj* attractive, charming, good-looking, winning, winsome, appealing, beautiful, likable, lovable, amiable, delightful, fair, handsome, pleasing, striking, captivating, bewitching, enchanting, engaging, inviting, alluring, magnetic, fascinating, fetching, taking.
🖾 unattractive, unprepossessing.

preposterous *adj* incredible, unbelievable, absurd, ridiculous, ludicrous, foolish, crazy, nonsensical, unreasonable, monstrous, shocking, outrageous, intolerable, unthinkable, impossible.
🖾 sensible, reasonable, acceptable.

prerequisite *n* precondition, condition, proviso, qualification, requisite (*fml*), requirement, imperative, necessity, essential, must.
🖾 extra.

prerogative *n* privilege, right, authority, advantage, choice, sanction, exemption, immunity, liberty, due, claim, licence, carte blanche, birthright.

prescribe *v* ordain, decree, dictate, rule, command, order, require, direct, assign, specify, stipulate, lay down, set, appoint, impose, fix, define, limit.

prescription *n* 1 INSTRUCTION, direction,

formula. **2** MEDICINE, drug, preparation, mixture, remedy, treatment.

presence n **1** ATTENDANCE, company, occupancy, residence, existence. **2** AURA, air, demeanour, bearing, carriage, appearance, poise, self-assurance, personality, charisma. **3** NEARNESS, closeness, proximity, vicinity.
₣ **1** absence. **3** remoteness.
♦ **presence of mind** calmness, self-possession, composure, coolness, self-assurance, self-command, level-headedness, alertness, poise, aplomb (*fml*), imperturbability (*fml*), sang-froid (*fml*), cool (*infml*), unflappability (*infml*).
₣ agitation, confusion.

present¹ adj **1** ATTENDING, here, there, near, at hand, to hand, available, ready. **2** *at the present time*: current, contemporary, present-day, immediate, instant, existent, existing.
₣ **1** absent. **2** past, out of date.

present² v **1** SHOW, display, exhibit, demonstrate, mount, stage, put on, introduce, announce. **2** AWARD, confer, bestow, grant, give, donate, hand over, entrust, extend, hold out, offer, tender, submit.

present³ n gift, prezzie (*infml*), offering, donation, grant, endowment, benefaction, bounty, largesse, gratuity, tip, favour.

presentable adj neat, tidy, clean, respectable, decent, proper, suitable, acceptable, satisfactory, tolerable.
₣ unpresentable, untidy, shabby.

presentation n **1** SHOW, performance, production, staging, representation, display, exhibition, demonstration, talk, delivery, appearance, arrangement. **2** AWARD, conferral, bestowal, investiture.

present-day adj current, present, existing, living, contemporary, modern, up-to-date, fashionable.
₣ past, future.

presently adv **1** SOON, shortly, in a minute, before long, by and by. **2** CURRENTLY, at present, now.

preservation n protection, defence, maintenance, keeping, guarding, safeguarding, safekeeping, safety, security, conservation, storage, upkeep, support, retention, upholding, continuation, perpetuation.
₣ destruction, ruin.

preserve v **1** PROTECT, safeguard, guard,

defend, shield, shelter, care for, maintain, uphold, sustain, continue, perpetuate, keep, retain, conserve, save, store.
2 *preserve food*: bottle, tin, can, pickle, salt, cure, dry.
₣ **1** destroy, ruin.
➤ n **1** *home-made preserves*: conserve, jam, marmalade, jelly, pickle. **2** DOMAIN, realm, sphere, area, field, speciality.
3 RESERVATION, sanctuary, game reserve, safari park.

preside v chair, officiate, conduct, direct, manage, administer, control, run, head, lead, govern, rule.

press v **1** CRUSH, squash, squeeze, compress, stuff, cram, crowd, push, depress. **2** *press clothes*: iron, smooth, flatten. **3** HUG, embrace, clasp, squeeze. **4** URGE, plead, petition, campaign, demand, insist on, compel, constrain, force, pressure, pressurize, harass.
➤ n **1** CROWD, throng, multitude, mob, horde, swarm, pack, crush, push.
2 JOURNALISTS, reporters, correspondents, the media, newspapers, papers, Fleet Street, fourth estate.

pressing adj urgent, high-priority, burning, crucial, vital, essential, imperative, serious, important.
₣ unimportant, trivial.

pressure n **1** FORCE, power, load, burden, weight, heaviness, compression, squeezing, stress, strain. **2** DIFFICULTY, problem, demand, constraint, obligation, urgency.

pressurize v force, compel, constrain, oblige, drive, bulldoze, coerce, press, pressure, lean on (*infml*), browbeat, bully.

prestige n status, reputation, standing, stature, eminence, distinction, esteem, regard, importance, authority, influence, fame, renown, kudos, credit, honour.
₣ humbleness, unimportance.

prestigious adj esteemed, respected, reputable, important, influential, great, eminent, prominent, illustrious, renowned, celebrated, exalted, imposing, impressive, up-market.
₣ humble, modest.

presumably adv most likely, very likely, in all likelihood, in all probability, as like as not, doubtless, doubtlessly, no doubt, probably, apparently, seemingly.

presume v **1** ASSUME, take it, think, believe, suppose, surmise, infer,

presuppose, take for granted, count on, rely on, depend on, bank on, trust.
2 *presume to criticize*: dare, make so bold, go so far, venture, undertake.

presumption *n* **1** ASSUMPTION, belief, opinion, hypothesis, presupposition, supposition, surmise, conjecture, guess, likelihood, probability.
2 PRESUMPTUOUSNESS, boldness, audacity, impertinence, cheek (*infml*), nerve (*infml*), impudence, insolence, forwardness, assurance.
≠ **2** humility.

presumptuous *adj* bold, audacious, impertinent, impudent, insolent, over-familiar, forward, pushy, arrogant, over-confident, conceited.
≠ humble, modest.

presuppose *v* assume, presume, suppose, accept, consider, imply, take for granted, posit (*fml*), postulate (*fml*), premise (*fml*).

presupposition *n* assumption, presumption, belief, supposition, theory, preconception, hypothesis (*fml*), premise (*fml*).

pretence *n* show, display, appearance, cover, front, façade, veneer, cloak, veil, mask, guise, sham, feigning, faking, simulation, deception, trickery, wile, ruse, excuse, pretext, bluff, falsehood, deceit, fabrication, invention, make-believe, charade, acting, play-acting, posturing, posing, affectation, pretension, pretentiousness.
≠ honesty, openness.

pretend *v* **1** AFFECT, put on, assume, feign, sham, counterfeit, fake, simulate, bluff, impersonate, pass oneself off, act, play-act, mime, go through the motions. **2** CLAIM, allege, profess, purport. **3** IMAGINE, make believe, suppose.

pretender *n* claimant, aspirant, candidate.

pretension *n* **1** PRETENTIOUSNESS, pomposity, self-importance, airs, conceit, vanity, snobbishness, affectation, pretence, show, showiness, ostentation.
2 CLAIM, profession, demand, aspiration, ambition.
≠ **1** modesty, humility, simplicity.

pretentious *adj* pompous, self-important, conceited, immodest, snobbish, affected, mannered, showy, ostentatious, extravagant, over-the-top, exaggerated, magniloquent, high-sounding, inflated, grandiose, ambitious, overambitious.
≠ modest, humble, simple, straightforward.

pretext *n* excuse, ploy, ruse, cover, cloak, mask, guise, semblance, appearance, pretence, show.

pretty *adj* attractive, good-looking, beautiful, fair, lovely, bonny, cute, winsome, appealing, charming, dainty, graceful, elegant, fine, delicate, nice.
≠ plain, unattractive, ugly.
➤ *adv* fairly, somewhat, rather, quite, reasonably, moderately, tolerably.

prevail *v* **1** PREDOMINATE, preponderate, abound. **2** WIN, triumph, succeed, overcome, overrule, reign, rule.
≠ **2** lose.
◆ **prevail upon** persuade, talk into, prompt, induce, incline, sway, influence, convince, win over.

prevailing *adj* predominant, preponderant, main, principal, dominant, controlling, powerful, compelling, influential, reigning, ruling, current, fashionable, popular, mainstream, accepted, established, set, usual, customary, common, prevalent, widespread.
≠ minor, subordinate.

prevalent *adj* widespread, extensive, rampant, rife, frequent, general, customary, usual, universal, ubiquitous, common, everyday, popular, current, prevailing.
≠ uncommon, rare.

prevaricate *v* hedge, equivocate, quibble, cavil, dodge, evade, shift, shuffle, lie, deceive.

prevent *v* stop, avert, avoid, head off, ward off, stave off, intercept, forestall, anticipate, frustrate, thwart, check, restrain, inhibit, hinder, hamper, impede, obstruct, block, bar.
≠ cause, help, foster, encourage, allow.

prevention *n* avoidance, frustration, check, hindrance, impediment, obstruction, obstacle, bar, elimination, precaution, safeguard, deterrence.
≠ cause, help.

preventive *adj* preventative, anticipatory, pre-emptive, inhibitory, obstructive, precautionary, protective, counteractive, deterrent.
≠ causative.

previous *adj* preceding, foregoing, earlier, prior, past, former, ex-, one-time, sometime, erstwhile.
☒ following, subsequent, later.

previously *adv* formerly, once, earlier, before, beforehand.
☒ later.

prey *n* quarry, victim, game, kill.
♦ prey on **1** HUNT, kill, devour, feed on, live off, exploit. **2** *prey on one's mind*: haunt, trouble, distress, worry, burden, weigh down, oppress.

price *n* value, worth, cost, expense, outlay, expenditure, fee, charge, levy, toll, rate, bill, assessment, valuation, estimate, quotation, figure, amount, sum, payment, reward, penalty, forfeit, sacrifice, consequences.
➢ *v* value, rate, cost, evaluate, assess, estimate.

priceless *adj* **1** INVALUABLE, inestimable, incalculable, expensive, costly, dear, precious, valuable, prized, treasured, irreplaceable. **2** (*infml*) FUNNY, amusing, comic, hilarious, riotous, side-splitting, killing (*infml*), rich (*infml*).
☒ **1** cheap, run-of-the-mill.

pricey *adj* costly, dear, excessive, exorbitant, expensive, extortionate, high-priced, steep (*infml*), over the odds (*infml*), costing an arm and a leg (*infml*).
☒ cheap.

prick *v* pierce, puncture, perforate, punch, jab, stab, sting, bite, prickle, itch, tingle.
➢ *n* puncture, perforation, pinhole, stab, pang, twinge, sting, bite.

prickle *n* thorn, spine, barb, spur, point, spike, needle.
➢ *v* tingle, itch, smart, sting, prick.

prickly *adj* **1** THORNY, brambly, spiny, barbed, spiky, bristly, rough, scratchy. **2** IRRITABLE, edgy, touchy, grumpy, short-tempered.
☒ **1** smooth. **2** relaxed, easy-going (*infml*).

pride *n* **1** CONCEIT, vanity, egotism, bigheadedness, boastfulness, smugness, arrogance, self-importance, presumption, haughtiness, superciliousness, snobbery, pretentiousness. **2** DIGNITY, self-respect, self-esteem, honour. **3** SATISFACTION, gratification, pleasure, delight.
☒ **1** humility, modesty. **2** shame.
♦ **pride oneself on** take satisfaction in, congratulate oneself, flatter oneself, take pride in, revel in, glory in, exult in, vaunt,

crow about, boast about, brag about, pat oneself on the back for (*infml*).
☒ belittle, humble.

priest *n* minister, vicar, padre, father, man of God, man of the cloth, clergyman, churchman.

prig *n* prude, puritan, killjoy, precisian, old maid, Mrs Grundy, goody-goody (*infml*), holy Joe (*infml*), holy Willie (*infml*).

priggish *adj* smug, self-righteous, goody-goody (*infml*), sanctimonious, holier-than-thou, puritanical, prim, prudish, narrow-minded.
☒ broad-minded.

prim *adj* prudish, strait-laced, formal, demure, proper, priggish, prissy, fussy, particular, precise, fastidious.
☒ informed, relaxed, easy-going (*infml*).

primacy *n* supremacy, dominance, paramountcy, pre-eminence, sovereignty, superiority, command, seniority, dominion, leadership, ascendancy (*fml*).
☒ inferiority.

primarily *adv* chiefly, principally, mainly, mostly, basically, fundamentally, especially, particularly, essentially.

primary *adj* **1** FIRST, earliest, original, initial, introductory, beginning, basic, fundamental, essential, radical, rudimentary, elementary, simple. **2** CHIEF, principal, main, dominant, leading, foremost, supreme, cardinal, capital, paramount, greatest, highest, ultimate.
☒ **2** secondary, subsidiary, minor.

prime *adj* best, choice, select, quality, first-class, first-rate, excellent, top, supreme, pre-eminent, superior, senior, leading, ruling, chief, principal, main, predominant, primary.
☒ second-rate, secondary.
➢ *n* height, peak, zenith, heyday, flower, bloom, maturity, perfection.

primeval *adj* earliest, first, original, primordial (*fml*), early, old, ancient, prehistoric, primitive, instinctive.
☒ modern.

primitive *adj* **1** CRUDE, rough, unsophisticated, uncivilized, barbarian, savage. **2** EARLY, elementary, rudimentary, primary, first, original, earliest.
☒ **1** advanced, sophisticated, civilized.

prince *n* lord, ruler, monarch, potentate, sovereign.

princely *adj* 1 SOVEREIGN, imperial, royal, regal, majestic, stately, grand, noble. 2 *princely sum*: generous, liberal, lavish, sumptuous, magnificent, handsome.

principal *adj* main, chief, key, essential, cardinal, primary, first, foremost, leading, dominant, prime, paramount, pre-eminent, supreme, highest.
ﬦ minor, subsidiary, lesser, least.
➤ *n* head, head teacher, headmaster, headmistress, chief, leader, boss (*infml*), director, manager, superintendent.

principally *adv* mainly, mostly, chiefly, primarily, predominantly, above all, particularly, especially.

principle *n* 1 RULE, formula, law, canon, axiom, dictum, precept, maxim, truth, tenet, doctrine, creed, dogma, code, standard, criterion, proposition, fundamental, essential. 2 HONOUR, integrity, rectitude, uprightness, virtue, decency, morality, morals, ethics, standards, scruples, conscience.

principled *adj* upright, virtuous, moral, ethical, high-minded, honourable, conscientious, decent, righteous, just, right-minded, scrupulous.
ﬦ unprincipled.

print *v* mark, stamp, imprint, impress, engrave, copy, reproduce, run off, publish, issue.
➤ *n* 1 LETTERS, characters, lettering, type, typescript, typeface, fount. 2 MARK, impression, fingerprint, footprint. 3 COPY, reproduction, picture, engraving, lithograph, photograph, photo.

Printing methods include: bubble-jet printing, collotype, colour-process printing, copper engraving, die-stamping, duplicating, electrostatic printing, engraving, etching, flexography, gravure, ink-jet printing, intaglio, laser printing, letterpress, lino blocking, litho, lithography, offset lithography, offset printing, photoengraving, rotary press, screen printing, silk-screen printing, stencilling, thermography, twin-etching, xerography.

Printing terms include: anodized plate, author's proof, back margin, backing-up, bad break, base alignment, batter, bi-directional printing, black printer, blanket-to-blanket press, bold face, bromide, camera-ready copy, carding, caret, cast-off, catchword, centre, character set, chase, cliché, cold composition, collograph, colour control bar, colour separation, column inch/centimetre, compose, composing room, composition size, compositor, condensed, copy, cylinder press, dampers, dot-etching, dot gain, drum printer, electrotype, em, en, end even, expanded type, feathering, finishing, first proof, flat-bed press, flong, font, forme, galley, gutter, hard hyphen, hot-metal typesetting, image printing, imposition, impression, indent, initial caps, inking roller, Intertype®, italic, justification, keep standing, kern, kiss impression, large print, leaders, leading, letterset, line printer, Linotype®, literal, logotype, lower-case, machine composition, machine proof, mackle, makeready, manuscript, margin, matrix, misprint, moiré, Monophoto®, Monotype®, mottling, newsprint, non-image area, non-impact printing, offprint, orphan, overprint, Ozalid®, perfecting, phototypesetting, planographic, printing press, progressive proofs, proof, quoin, ragged right/left, registration, relief printing, reprint, roman, run-around, running head, running text, sans serif, see-through, signature, small capitals, soft hyphen, specimen page, spoilage, stereotype, stet, strike-on, strip in, take in, take over, text, thermal printer, tint, trim marks, type, typeface, type scale, typescript, typesetting, type spec, typo, typographer (*US*), upper-case, web-fed, web offset, widow, woodcut, wood engraving, zinco.

prior *adj* earlier, preceding, foregoing, previous, former.
ﬦ later.
♦ **prior to** before, preceding, earlier than.
ﬦ after, following.

priority *n* right of way, precedence, seniority, rank, superiority, pre-eminence, supremacy, the lead, first place, urgency.
ﬦ inferiority.

priory *n* monastery, abbey, cloister, friary, convent, nunnery, religious house, béguinage.

prison *n* jail, nick (*sl*), clink (*sl*), cooler (*sl*), penitentiary, cell, lock-up, cage, dungeon, imprisonment, confinement, detention, custody.

prisoner *n* captive, hostage, convict, jail-bird (*infml*), inmate, internee, detainee.

pristine *adj* 1 IMMACULATE, undefiled, uncorrupted, untouched, virgin, unspoiled, unsullied. 2 ORIGINAL, earliest, first, initial, former, primary,

primitive, primal, primeval (*fml*), primordial (*fml*).
🔃 1 spoiled. 2 developed, later.

privacy *n* secrecy, confidentiality, independence, solitude, isolation, seclusion, concealment, retirement, retreat.

private *adj* 1 CONFIDENTIAL, classified, secret, privileged, unofficial, off the record, hush-hush (*infml*). 2 *your private life/ feelings*: personal, confidential, intimate, innermost, secret, individual. 3 *a private bathroom*: exclusive, particular, own, special, individual, personal. 4 *a private person*: quiet, reserved, withdrawn, independent, solitary, retiring, separate, self-contained. 5 *a private place*: secluded, isolated, hidden, concealed, secret, remote, undisturbed, quiet, out-of-the-way, sequestered (*fml*). 6 *private industries*: independent, commercial, free-enterprise, privatized, non-governmental, denationalized, self-governing, self-determining.
🔃 1 official, public. 5 public. 6 public, state-controlled, state-run, nationalized.
➤ *n* enlisted man, private soldier, Tommy, squaddy, swad, swaddy, Tommy Atkins (*infml*).
♦ **in private** privately, in confidence, secretly, in secret, behind closed doors, in camera.
🔃 publicly, openly.

privilege *n* advantage, benefit, concession, birthright, title, due, right, prerogative, entitlement, freedom, liberty, franchise, licence, sanction, authority, immunity, exemption.
🔃 disadvantage.

privileged *adj* advantaged, favoured, special, sanctioned, authorized, immune, exempt, elite, honoured, ruling, powerful.
🔃 disadvantaged, under-privileged.

privy *n* toilet, lavatory, water closet, WC, public convenience, washroom, cloakroom, latrine, bog (*sl*), loo (*infml*).
♦ **privy to** aware of, cognizant of, informed about, wise to, apprised of (*fml*), in on (*infml*), in the know about (*infml*).
🔃 unaware of.

prize *n* reward, trophy, medal, award, winnings, jackpot, purse, premium, stake(s), honour, accolade.
➤ *adj* best, top, first-class, first-rate, excellent, outstanding, champion,

winning, prize-winning, award-winning.
🔃 second-rate.
➤ *v* treasure, value, appreciate, esteem, revere, cherish, hold dear.
🔃 despise.

probability *n* likelihood, odds, chances, expectation, prospect, chance, possibility.
🔃 improbability.

probable *adj* likely, odds-on, expected, credible, believable, plausible, feasible, possible, apparent, seeming.
🔃 improbable, unlikely.

probably *adv* in all likelihood, in all probability, likely, it looks like the chances are, most likely, as likely as not, doubtless, presumably, possibly, perhaps, maybe, (as) like as not (*infml*), a fair bet (*infml*).
🔃 improbably.

probation *n* apprenticeship, trial period, trial, test.

probe *v* prod, poke, pierce, penetrate, sound, plumb, explore, examine, scrutinize, investigate, go into, look into, search, sift, test.
➤ *n* 1 BORE, drill. 2 INQUIRY, inquest, investigation, exploration, examination, test, scrutiny, study, research.

probity *n* uprightness, righteousness, integrity, honour, honourableness, virtue, morality, worth, honesty, goodness, equity, fairness, justice, truthfulness, trustworthiness, sincerity, rectitude (*fml*).
🔃 improbity (*fml*).

problem *n* 1 TROUBLE, worry, predicament, quandary, dilemma, difficulty, complication, snag (*infml*). 2 QUESTION, poser, puzzle, brain-teaser, conundrum, riddle, enigma.
➤ *adj* difficult, unmanageable, uncontrollable, unruly, delinquent.
🔃 well-behaved, manageable.

problematic *adj* 1 DIFFICULT, fraught with difficulties, troublesome, awkward, hard, puzzling, perplexing, intricate, involved, tricky, thorny, problematical, enigmatic, moot, a can of worms (*infml*), a minefield (*infml*). 2 UNCERTAIN, questionable, debatable, doubtful, dubious
🔃 1 easy, straightforward. 2 certain.

procedure *n* routine, process, method, system, technique, custom, practice, policy, formula, course, scheme, strategy, plan of action, move, step, action, conduct, operation, performance.

proceed *v* 1 *the permission to proceed*:

advance, go ahead, move on, progress, continue, carry on, press on. **2** ORIGINATE, derive, flow, start, stem, spring, arise, issue, result, ensue, follow, come.
☒ **1** stop, retreat.

proceedings *n* **1** MATTERS, affairs, business, dealings, transactions, report, account, minutes, records, archives, annals. **2** EVENTS, happenings, deeds, doings, moves, steps, measures, action, course of action.

proceeds *n* revenue, income, returns, receipts, takings, earnings, gain, profit, yield, produce.
☒ expenditure, outlay.

process *n* **1** PROCEDURE, operation, practice, method, system, technique, means, manner, mode, way, stage, step. **2** COURSE, progression, advance, progress, development, evolution, formation, growth, movement, action, proceeding.
➤ *v* deal with, handle, treat, prepare, refine, transform, convert, change, alter.

procession *n* march, parade, cavalcade, motorcade, cortège, file, column, train, succession, series, sequence, course, run.

proclaim *v* announce, declare, pronounce, affirm, give out, publish, advertise, make known, profess, testify, show, indicate.

proclamation *n* announcement, declaration, pronouncement, affirmation, publication, promulgation (*fml*), notice, notification, manifesto, decree, edict.

procrastinate *v* defer, put off, postpone, delay, retard, stall, temporize, play for time, dally, dilly-dally (*infml*), drag one's feet, prolong, protract.
☒ advance, proceed.

procreate *v* reproduce, produce, father, mother, breed, conceive, generate, propagate, multiply, engender, sire, spawn, beget.

procure *v* acquire, buy, purchase, get, obtain, find, come by, pick up, lay hands on, earn, gain, win, secure, appropriate, requisition.
☒ lose.

prod *v* poke, jab, dig, elbow, nudge, push, shove, goad, spur, urge, egg on (*infml*), prompt, stimulate, motivate.
➤ *n* poke, jab, dig, elbow, nudge, push, shove, prompt, reminder, stimulus, motivation.

prodigious *adj* **1** ENORMOUS, gigantic, huge, massive, vast, immense, colossal, giant, mammoth, immeasurable. **2** EXTRAORDINARY, marvellous, startling, amazing, astounding, staggering, fabulous, fantastic, flabbergasting, striking, impressive, miraculous, wonderful, monumental, inordinate, spectacular, remarkable, stupendous, tremendous, phenomenal, unusual, exceptional, abnormal.
☒ **1** small. **2** commonplace, unremarkable.

prodigy *n* genius, virtuoso, wonder, marvel, miracle, phenomenon, sensation, freak, curiosity, rarity, child genius, wonder child, whizz kid (*infml*).

produce *v* **1** CAUSE, occasion, give rise to, provoke, bring about, result in, effect, create, originate, invent, make, manufacture, fabricate, construct, compose, generate, yield, bear, deliver. **2** ADVANCE, put forward, present, offer, give, supply, provide, furnish, bring out, bring forth, show, exhibit, demonstrate. **3** *produce a play*: direct, stage, mount, put on.
➤ *n* crop, harvest, yield, output, product.

producer *n* director, presenter, impresario, manager, régisseur, manufacturer, maker, farmer, grower.

product *n* **1** COMMODITY, merchandise, goods, end-product, artefact, work, creation, invention, production, output, yield, produce, fruit, return. **2** RESULT, consequence, outcome, issue, upshot, offshoot, spin-off, by-product, legacy.
☒ **2** cause.

production *n* **1** MAKING, manufacture, fabrication, construction, assembly, creation, origination, preparation, formation. **2** *an amateur production*: staging, presentation, direction, management.
☒ **1** consumption.

productive *adj* fruitful, profitable, rewarding, valuable, worthwhile, useful, constructive, creative, inventive, fertile, rich, teeming, busy, energetic, vigorous, efficient, effective.
☒ unproductive, fruitless, useless.

productivity *n* productiveness, yield, output, work rate, efficiency.

profane *adj* secular, temporal, lay, unconsecrated, unhallowed, unsanctified, unholy, irreligious, impious, sacrilegious, blasphemous, ungodly, irreverent, disrespectful, abusive, crude, coarse, foul, filthy, unclean.

🔳 sacred, religious, respectful.

➤ *v* desecrate, pollute, contaminate, defile, debase, pervert, abuse, misuse.

🔳 revere, honour.

profanity *n* 1 SACRILEGE, irreverence, profaneness, impiety, blasphemy, abuse, execration (*fml*), imprecation (*fml*), malediction (*fml*). 2 OBSCENITY, swear-word, swearing, expletive, curse, cursing, four-letter word (*infml*).

🔳 1 politeness, reverence.

profess *v* admit, confess, acknowledge, own, confirm, certify, declare, announce, proclaim, state, assert, affirm, maintain, claim, allege, make out, pretend.

profession *n* 1 CAREER, job, occupation, employment, business, line (of work), trade, vocation, calling, métier, craft, office, position. 2 ADMISSION, confession, acknowledgement, declaration, announcement, statement, testimony, assertion, affirmation, claim.

professional *adj* qualified, licensed, trained, experienced, practised, skilled, expert, masterly, proficient, competent, businesslike, efficient.

🔳 amateur, unprofessional.

➤ *n* expert, authority, specialist, pro (*infml*), master, virtuoso, dab hand (*infml*).

🔳 amateur.

proficiency *n* skill, skilfulness, expertise, mastery, talent, knack, dexterity, finesse, aptitude, ability, competence.

🔳 incompetence.

proficient *adj* able, capable, skilled, qualified, trained, experienced, accomplished, expert, masterly, gifted, talented, clever, skilful, competent, efficient.

🔳 unskilled, incompetent.

profile *n* 1 SIDE VIEW, outline, contour, silhouette, shape, form, figure, sketch, drawing, diagram, chart, graph. 2 BIOGRAPHY, curriculum vitae, thumbnail sketch, vignette, portrait, study, analysis, examination, survey, review.

profit *n* gain, surplus, excess, bottom line, revenue, return, yield, proceeds, receipts, takings, earnings, winnings, interest, advantage, benefit, use, avail, value, worth.

🔳 loss.

➤ *v* gain, make money, pay, serve, avail, benefit.

🔳 lose.

♦ **profit by/from** exploit, take advantage of, use, utilize, turn to advantage, capitalize on, cash in on, reap the benefit of.

profitable *adj* cost-effective, economic, commercial, money-making, lucrative, remunerative, paying, rewarding, successful, fruitful, productive, advantageous, beneficial, useful, valuable, worthwhile.

🔳 unprofitable, loss-making, non-profit-making.

profiteer *n* racketeer, exploiter, extortioner, extortionist.

➤ *v* exploit, extort, racketeer, overcharge, fleece (*infml*), make a fast buck (*infml*), make a quick killing (*infml*).

profound *adj* 1 DEEP, great, intense, extreme, heartfelt, marked, far-reaching, extensive, exhaustive. 2 *a profound remark*: serious, weighty, penetrating, thoughtful, philosophical, wise, learned, erudite, abstruse.

🔳 1 shallow, slight, mild.

profuse *adj* ample, abundant, plentiful, copious, generous, liberal, lavish, rich, luxuriant, excessive, immoderate, extravagant, overabundant, superabundant, overflowing.

🔳 inadequate, sparse.

profusion *n* abundance, plenty, wealth, multitude, plethora, glut, excess, surplus, superfluity, extravagance.

🔳 inadequacy, scarcity.

prognosis *n* diagnosis, expectation, forecast, prediction, outlook, projection, assessment, evaluation, prospect, speculation, surmise, prognostication (*fml*).

programme *n* 1 SCHEDULE, timetable, agenda, calendar, order of events, listing, line-up, plan, scheme, project, syllabus, curriculum. 2 *radio programme*: broadcast, transmission, show, performance, production, presentation.

progress *n* movement, progression, passage, journey, way, advance, headway, step forward, breakthrough, development, evolution, growth, increase, improvement, betterment, promotion.

🔳 recession, deterioration, decline.

➤ *v* proceed, advance, go forward, forge

ahead, make progress, make headway, come on, develop, grow, mature, blossom, improve, better, prosper, increase.
☒ deteriorate, decline.

progression *n* cycle, chain, string, succession, series, sequence, order, course, advance, headway, progress, development.

progressive *adj* 1 MODERN, avant-garde, advanced, forward-looking, enlightened, liberal, radical, revolutionary, reformist, dynamic, enterprising, go-ahead, up-and-coming. 2 ADVANCING, continuing, developing, growing, increasing, intensifying.
☒ 1 regressive.

prohibit *v* forbid, ban, bar, veto, proscribe, outlaw, rule out, preclude, prevent, stop, hinder, hamper, impede, obstruct, restrict.
☒ permit, allow, authorize.

prohibition *n* forbidding, forbiddance, ban, bar, constraint, veto, restriction, obstruction, exclusion, prevention, negation, embargo, injunction, disallowance (*fml*), interdict (*fml*), interdiction (*fml*), proscription (*fml*).
☒ permission.

prohibitive *adj* forbidding, preposterous, excessive, exorbitant, extortionate, impossible, restrictive, restraining, suppressive, repressive, prohibiting, prohibitory, proscriptive (*fml*), sky-high (*infml*), steep (*infml*).
☒ encouraging, reasonable.

project *n* assignment, contract, task, job, work, occupation, activity, enterprise, undertaking, venture, plan, scheme, programme, design, proposal, idea, conception.
➤ *v* 1 PREDICT, forecast, extrapolate, estimate, reckon, calculate. 2 THROW, fling, hurl, launch, propel. 3 PROTRUDE, stick out, bulge, jut out, overhang.

projectile *n* missile, rocket, shell, shot, grenade, bullet, ball, mortar-bomb.

projection *n* 1 PROTUBERANCE, bulge, overhang, ledge, sill, shelf, ridge. 2 PREDICTION, forecast, extrapolation, estimate, reckoning, calculation, computation.

proletariat *n* working class, common people, masses, mob, lower classes, rabble, herd, hoi polloi, canaille, commoners, commonalty, great unwashed

(*infml*), plebs (*infml*), proles (*infml*), riff-raff (*infml*).

proliferate *v* multiply, reproduce, breed, increase, build up, intensify, escalate, mushroom, snowball, spread, expand, flourish, thrive.
☒ dwindle.

prolific *adj* productive, fruitful, fertile, profuse, copious, abundant.
☒ unproductive.

prologue *n* introduction, foreword, preface, preamble, preliminary, prelude, exordium (*fml*), proem (*fml*), prolegomena (*fml*), prooemion (*fml*), prooemium (*fml*).

prolong *v* lengthen, extend, stretch, protract, draw out, spin out, drag out, delay, continue, perpetuate.
☒ shorten.

promenade *n* 1 SEAFRONT, walkway, front, parade, esplanade, prom, boulevard, terrace. 2 WALK, stroll, breather, airing, saunter, turn, walkabout, constitutional (*fml*).
➤ *v* walk, stroll, saunter, strut, swagger, sally forth, parade, perambulate (*fml*), mosey (*infml*).

prominence *n* 1 FAME, celebrity, renown, eminence, distinction, greatness, importance, reputation, name, standing, rank, prestige. 2 BULGE, protuberance, bump, hump, lump, mound, rise, elevation, projection, process, headland, promontory, cliff, crag.
☒ 1 unimportance, insignificance.

prominent *adj* 1 NOTICEABLE, conspicuous, obvious, unmistakable, striking, eye-catching. 2 BULGING, protuberant, projecting, jutting, protruding, obtrusive. 3 *a prominent writer*: famous, well-known, celebrated, renowned, noted, eminent, distinguished, respected, leading, foremost, chief, main, important, popular, outstanding.
☒ 1 inconspicuous. 3 unknown, unimportant, insignificant.

promiscuity *n* looseness, laxity, permissiveness, wantonness, immorality, licentiousness, debauchery, depravity.
☒ chastity, morality.

promiscuous *adj* loose, immoral, licentious, dissolute, casual, random, haphazard, indiscriminate.
☒ chaste, moral.

promise *v* 1 vow, pledge, swear, take an oath, contract, undertake, give one's word,

vouch, warrant, guarantee, assure.
2 AUGUR, presage, indicate, suggest, hint at.

➤ *n* **1** vow, pledge, oath, word of honour, bond, compact, covenant, guarantee, assurance, undertaking, engagement, commitment. **2** POTENTIAL, ability, capability, aptitude, talent.

promising *adj* auspicious (*fml*), propitious, favourable, rosy, bright, encouraging, hopeful, talented, gifted, budding, up-and-coming.
E3 unpromising, inauspicious, discouraging.

promontory *n* cliff, headland, head, foreland, bluff, precipice, point, projection, prominence, ridge, spur, cape, naze, ness, peninsula.

promote *v* **1** ADVERTISE, plug (*infml*), publicize, hype (*sl*), popularize, market, sell, push, recommend, advocate, champion, endorse, sponsor, support, back, help, aid, assist, foster, nurture, further, forward, encourage, boost, stimulate, urge. **2** UPGRADE, advance, move up, raise, elevate, exalt, honour.
E3 **1** disparage, hinder. **2** demote.

promotion *n* **1** ADVANCEMENT, upgrading, rise, preferment, elevation, exaltation. **2** ADVERTISING, plugging (*infml*), publicity, hype (*sl*), campaign, propaganda, marketing, pushing, support, backing, furtherance, development, encouragement, boosting.
E3 **1** demotion. **2** disparagement, obstruction.

prompt[1] *adj* punctual, on time, immediate, instantaneous, instant, direct, quick, swift, rapid, speedy, unhesitating, willing, ready, alert, responsive, timely, early.
E3 slow, hesitant, late.
➤ *adv* promptly, punctually, exactly, on the dot, to the minute, sharp.

prompt[2] *v* cause, give rise to, result in, occasion, produce, instigate, call forth, elicit, provoke, incite, urge, encourage, inspire, move, stimulate, motivate, spur, prod, remind.
E3 deter, dissuade.
➤ *n* reminder, cue, hint, help, jolt, prod, spur, stimulus.

promptly *adv* **1** IMMEDIATELY, instantly, directly, unhesitatingly, quickly, speedily, swiftly, forthwith (*fml*), pronto (*infml*). **2**

PUNCTUALLY, on time, on target, exactly, on the dot, to the minute, sharp, as soon as possible, posthaste, bang on (*infml*), spot on (*infml*), dead on (*infml*), pronto (*infml*), ASAP (*infml*), pdq (*infml*), pretty damn quick (*infml*).

prone *adj* **1** LIKELY, given, inclined, disposed, predisposed, bent, apt, liable, subject, susceptible, vulnerable. **2** *she lay prone*: face down, prostrate, flat, horizontal, full-length, stretched, recumbent.
E3 **1** unlikely, immune. **2** upright, supine.

prong *n* point, spike, projection, spur, tine, tip, fork, grain.

pronounce *v* **1** SAY, utter, speak, express, voice, vocalize, sound, enunciate, articulate, stress. **2** DECLARE, announce, proclaim, decree, judge, affirm, assert.

pronounced *adj* clear, distinct, definite, positive, decided, marked, noticeable, conspicuous, evident, obvious, striking, unmistakable, strong, broad.
E3 faint, vague.

pronouncement *n* declaration, statement, announcement, judgement, notification, proclamation, assertion, decree, edict, manifesto, dictum, promulgation (*fml*).

pronunciation *n* speech, diction, elocution, enunciation, articulation, delivery, accent, stress, inflection, intonation, modulation.

proof *n* evidence, documentation, demonstration, verification, confirmation, corroboration, substantiation.

prop *v* **1** SUPPORT, sustain, uphold, maintain, shore, stay, buttress, bolster, underpin, set. **2** *propped against the wall*: lean, rest, stand.
➤ *n* support, stay, mainstay, strut, buttress, brace, truss.

propaganda *n* advertising, publicity, hype (*sl*), indoctrination, brainwashing, disinformation.

propagate *v* **1** SPREAD, transmit, broadcast, diffuse, disseminate, circulate, publish, promulgate, publicize, promote. **2** INCREASE, multiply, proliferate, generate, produce, breed, beget, spawn, procreate, reproduce.

propel *v* move, drive, impel, force, thrust, push, shove, launch, shoot, send.
E3 stop.

propensity *n* tendency, liability, susceptibility, inclination, leaning, disposition (*fml*), aptness, proneness, bent, bias, readiness, foible, weakness, penchant (*fml*), predisposition (*fml*), proclivity (*fml*).
F3 disinclination.

proper *adj* 1 RIGHT, correct, accurate, exact, precise, true, genuine, real, actual. 2 ACCEPTED, correct, suitable, appropriate, fitting, decent, respectable, polite, formal.
F3 1 wrong. 2 improper, indecent.

property *n* 1 ESTATE, land, real estate, acres, premises, buildings, house(s), wealth, riches, resources, means, capital, assets, holding(s), belongings, possessions, effects, goods, chattels. 2 FEATURE, trait, quality, attribute, characteristic, idiosyncrasy, peculiarity, mark.

prophecy *n* prediction, augury, forecast, prognosis.

prophesy *v* predict, foresee, augur, foretell, forewarn, forecast.

prophet *n* seer, soothsayer, foreteller, forecaster, oracle, clairvoyant, fortune-teller.

proportion *n* 1 PERCENTAGE, fraction, part, division, share, quota, amount. 2 RATIO, relationship, correspondence, symmetry, balance, distribution.
F3 2 disproportion, imbalance.

proportional *adj* proportionate, relative, commensurate, consistent, corresponding, analogous, comparable, equitable, even.
F3 disproportionate.

proportions *n* dimensions, measurements, size, magnitude, volume, capacity.

proposal *n* proposition, suggestion, recommendation, motion, plan, scheme, project, design, programme, manifesto, presentation, bid, offer, tender, terms.

propose *v* 1 SUGGEST, recommend, move (*fml*), advance, put forward, introduce, bring up, table, submit, present, offer, tender. 2 INTEND, mean, aim, purpose, plan, design. 3 NOMINATE, put up.
F3 1 withdraw.

proposition *n* 1 PROPOSAL, suggestion, theory, plan, project, programme, recommendation, scheme, manifesto, motion, tender, theorem (*fml*). 2 TASK, activity, undertaking, venture. 3 *a sexual*

proposition: advance, overture, approach, indecent proposal/suggestion, pass.
➤ *v* accost, solicit, make sexual advances/overtures to, make an indecent proposal to, make a pass at.

propound *v* put forward, suggest, propose, advance, set forth, advocate, contend, lay down, present, submit, move (*fml*), postulate (*fml*).
F3 oppose.

proprietor, proprietress *n* landlord, landlady, title-holder, freeholder, leaseholder, landowner, owner, possessor.

propriety *n* 1 MODESTY, decorum, decency, civility, etiquette, protocol, delicacy, respectability, refinement, rightness, correctness, manners, good manners, politeness, courtesy, breeding, appropriateness, aptness, becomingness, suitableness, fitness, gentlemanliness, ladylikeness, rectitude (*fml*). 2 *observe proprieties*: civility, standard, etiquette, convention, decency, nicety, the done thing (*infml*), p's and q's (*infml*).
F3 1, 2 impropriety.

propulsion *n* drive, driving force, power, pressure, push, thrust, motive force, momentum, impetus, impulse, impulsion.

prosaic *adj* mundane, ordinary, routine, dull, stale, boring, commonplace, humdrum, matter-of-fact, unimaginative, uninspired, uninspiring, monotonous, bland, tame, trite, banal, vacuous, vapid, pedestrian, workaday, flat, dry, hackneyed, everyday.
F3 imaginative, interesting.

proscribe *v* forbid, prohibit, ban, outlaw, bar, banish, condemn, embargo, reject, exclude, boycott, censure, damn, doom, black, blackball, denounce, deport, expel, exile, excommunicate, expatriate, ostracize, interdict (*fml*), disallow (*fml*).
F3 allow, permit.

prosecute *v* accuse, indict, sue, prefer charges, take to court, litigate, summon, put on trial, try.
F3 defend.

prosody

Terms used in prosody include: abstract verse, Alcaic verse, alexandrine, alliteration, amphibrach, amphimacer, Anacreontic verse, anacrusis, analysed rhyme, anapaest, antibacchius, antispast, Archilochian verse, asclepiad, assonance, asynartete, ballade, blank verse, broken rhyme, bouts rimés, caesura, canto, catalexis, choliamb, choree, choriamb, cinquain, couplet, dactyl, decastich, dipody, dispondee, distich, ditrochee, dizain, dochmius, elision, enjambment, envoy, epitrite, epode, eye rhyme, false quantity, feminine caesura, feminine ending, feminine rhyme, foot, free verse, galliambic, glyconic, heptameter, heptapody, heroic couplet, hexameter, hexastich, hypermetrical, iamb, ictus, Ionic, kyrielle, laisse, Leonine rhyme, linked verse, long-measure, macaronic, masculine ending, masculine rhyme, metre, miurus, monometer, monorhyme, paeon, pantoum, pentameter, pentastich, Petrarchan sonnet, Pherecratean, Pindaric, poulters' measure, pyrrhic, Pythian verse, quatorzain, quatrain, reported verses, rhopalic, rhyme royal, rime riche, rime suffisante, rondeau, rondel, rove-over, Sapphic, senarius, septenarius, sonnet, Spencerian stanza, spondee, sprung rhythm, strophe, substituion, synaphea, tetrameter, tetrapody, tetrastich, tribrach, trimeter, triolet, tripody, triseme, trochee, villanelle, virelay.

prospect *n* chance, odds, probability, likelihood, possibility, hope, expectation, anticipation, outlook, future.
🔒 unlikelihood.

prospective *adj* future, -to-be, intended, designate, destined, forthcoming, approaching, coming, imminent, awaited, expected, anticipated, likely, possible, probable, potential, aspiring, would-be.
🔒 current.

prospectus *n* plan, scheme, programme, syllabus, manifesto, outline, synopsis, pamphlet, leaflet, brochure, catalogue, list.

prosper *v* boom, thrive, flourish, flower, bloom, succeed, get on, advance, progress, grow rich.
🔒 fail.

prosperity *n* boom, plenty, affluence, wealth, riches, fortune, well-being, luxury, the good life, success, good fortune.
🔒 adversity, poverty.

prosperous *adj* booming, thriving, flourishing, blooming, successful, fortunate, lucky, rich, wealthy, affluent, well-off, well-to-do.
🔒 unfortunate, poor.

prostitute *n* harlot, call-girl, woman of the streets, rent-boy, woman of the town, woman of ill repute, loose woman, fallen woman, floosie, wench, whore, trollop, street-walker, strumpet, cocotte, courtesan, brass, bawd, fille de joie, fille des rues, drab, grande cocotte, lorette, hooker (*infml*), hustler (*infml*), moll (*infml*), pro (*infml*), tart (*infml*).
➤ *v* cheapen, degrade, debase, demean, devalue, pervert, misapply, misuse, profane.

prostitution *n* harlotry, whoredom, whoring, street-walking, vice, meretriciousness, the game (*infml*), the oldest profession (*infml*).

prostrate *adj* flat, horizontal, prone, fallen, overcome, overwhelmed, crushed, paralysed, powerless, helpless, defenceless.
🔒 triumphant.
➤ *v* lay low, overcome, overwhelm, crush, overthrow, tire, wear out, fatigue, exhaust, drain, ruin.
🔒 strengthen.
◆ **prostrate oneself** bow down, kneel, kowtow, submit, grovel, cringe, abase oneself.

protagonist *n* hero, heroine, lead, principal, leader, prime mover, champion, advocate, supporter, proponent, exponent.

protect *v* safeguard, defend, guard, escort, cover, screen, shield, secure, watch over, look after, care for, support, shelter, harbour, keep, conserve, preserve, save.
🔒 attack, neglect.

protection *n* **1** *protection of the environment*: care, custody, charge, guardianship, safekeeping, conservation, preservation, safety, safeguard. **2** BARRIER, buffer, bulwark, defence, guard, shield, armour, screen, cover, shelter, refuge, security, insurance.
🔒 **1** neglect, attack.

protective *adj* **1** POSSESSIVE, defensive, motherly, maternal, fatherly, paternal, watchful, vigilant, careful. **2** *protective clothing*: waterproof, fireproof, insulating.
🔒 **1** aggressive, threatening.

protégé(e) *n* pupil, student, ward, charge, dependant, discovery, blue-eyed boy (*infml*).
🔒 guardian.

protest *n* objection, disapproval, opposition, dissent, complaint, protestation, outcry, appeal, demonstration.
🔒 acceptance.

➤ *v* **1** OBJECT, take exception, complain, appeal, demonstrate, oppose, disapprove, disagree, argue. **2** *protest one's innocence*: assert, maintain, contend, insist, profess.
𝔼 1 accept.

protester *n* demonstrator, agitator, rebel, dissident, dissenter.

protocol *n* procedure, formalities, convention, custom, etiquette, manners, good form, propriety.

prototype *n* original, model, mock-up, example, standard, type, pattern, precedent, archetype (*fml*), exemplar (*fml*), paradigm (*fml*).

protracted *adj* long, lengthy, prolonged, extended, drawn-out, long-drawn-out, overlong, interminable.
𝔼 brief, shortened.

protrude *v* stick out, poke out, come through, bulge, jut out, project, extend, stand out, obtrude.

protuberance *n* lump, bump, bulge, bulb, knob, outgrowth, swelling, prominence, protrusion, projection, tumour, wart, welt, tuber, tubercle.

proud *adj* **1** CONCEITED, vain, egotistical, bigheaded, boastful, smug, complacent, arrogant, self-important, cocky, presumptuous, haughty, high and mighty, overbearing, supercilious, snooty (*infml*), snobbish, toffee-nosed (*infml*), stuck-up (*infml*). **2** SATISFIED, contented, gratified, pleased, delighted, honoured.
3 DIGNIFIED, noble, honourable, worthy, self-respecting.
𝔼 1 humble, modest, unassuming.
2 ashamed. **3** deferential, ignoble.

prove *v* **1** SHOW, demonstrate, verify, confirm, bear out, bear witness to, document, certify, authenticate, validate, justify, establish, determine, ascertain, try (out), test, check, examine, analyse, attest (*fml*), corroborate (*fml*), substantiate (*fml*). **2** TURN OUT, come about, be the case, transpire (*fml*), eventuate (*fml*), pan out (*infml*).
𝔼 1 disprove, discredit, falsify.

proverb *n* saying, adage, aphorism, maxim, byword, dictum, precept.

proverbial *adj* axiomatic, accepted, conventional, traditional, customary, time-honoured, famous, well-known, legendary, notorious, typical, archetypal.

provide *v* **1** SUPPLY, furnish, stock, equip, outfit, prepare for, cater, serve, present, give, contribute, yield, lend, add, bring. **2** PLAN FOR, allow, make provision, accommodate, arrange for, take precautions. **3** STATE, specify, stipulate, lay down, require.
𝔼 1 take, remove.

providence *n* **1** FATE, destiny, divine intervention, God's will, fortune, luck. **2** PRUDENCE, far-sightedness, foresight, caution, care, thrift.
𝔼 2 improvidence.

provident *adj* prudent, far-sighted, judicious, cautious, careful, thrifty, economical, frugal.
𝔼 improvident.

providential *adj* timely, opportune, convenient, fortunate, lucky, happy, welcome, heaven-sent.
𝔼 untimely.

providing *conj* provided, with the proviso, given, as long as, on condition, on the understanding.

province *n* **1** REGION, area, district, zone, county, shire, department, territory, colony, dependency. **2** RESPONSIBILITY, concern, duty, office, role, function, field, sphere, domain, department, line.

provincial *adj* regional, local, rural, rustic, country, home-grown, small-town, parish-pump, parochial, insular, inward-looking, limited, narrow, narrow-minded, small-minded.
𝔼 national, cosmopolitan, urban, sophisticated.

provision *n* **1** PLAN, arrangement, preparation, measure, precaution. **2** STIPULATION, specification, proviso, condition, term, requirement.

provisional *adj* temporary, interim, transitional, stopgap, makeshift, conditional, tentative.
𝔼 permanent, fixed, definite.

provisions *n* food, foodstuff, groceries, eatables (*infml*), sustenance, rations, supplies, stocks, stores.

proviso *n* condition, term, requirement, stipulation, qualification, reservation, restriction, limitation, provision, clause, rider.

provocation *n* cause, grounds, justification, reason, motive, stimulus, motivation, incitement, instigation, annoyance, aggravation (*infml*), vexation, grievance, offence, insult, affront, injury, taunt, challenge, dare.

provocative *adj* **1** ANNOYING, aggravating (*infml*), galling, outrageous, offensive, insulting, abusive. **2** STIMULATING, exciting, challenging. **3** EROTIC, titillating, arousing, sexy, seductive, alluring, tempting, inviting, tantalizing, teasing, suggestive.
☎ 1 conciliatory.

provoke *v* **1** ANNOY, irritate, rile, aggravate (*infml*), offend, insult, anger, enrage, infuriate, incense, madden, exasperate, tease, taunt. **2** CAUSE, occasion, give rise to, produce, generate, induce, elicit, evoke, excite, inspire, move, stir, prompt, stimulate, motivate, incite, instigate.
☎ 1 please, pacify. **2** result.

prow *n* bow(s), fore, stem, front, head, nose, forepart, cut-water.
☎ stern.

prowess *n* accomplishment, attainment, ability, aptitude, skill, expertise, mastery, command, talent, genius.

prowl *v* creep, hunt, rove, roam, move stealthily, slink, sneak, stalk, lurk, skulk, steal, range, search, scavenge, cruise, patrol, nose, snoop.

proximity *n* closeness, nearness, vicinity, neighbourhood, adjacency, juxtaposition.
☎ remoteness.

proxy *n* agent, factor, deputy, stand-in, substitute, representative, delegate, attorney.

prudence *n* wisdom, judgement, good sense, common sense, care, foresight, forethought, far-sightedness, economy, heedfulness, preparedness, discretion, caution, vigilance, wariness, planning, providence, precaution, policy, canniness, frugality, saving, thrift, husbandry, circumspection (*fml*), judiciousness (*fml*), sagacity (*fml*).
☎ imprudence, rashness.

prudent *adj* wise, sensible, politic, judicious (*fml*), shrewd, discerning, careful, cautious, wary, vigilant, circumspect (*fml*), discreet, provident, far-sighted, thrifty.
☎ imprudent, unwise, careless, rash.

prudish *adj* overmodest, overnice, proper, prim, narrow-minded, squeamish, demure, starchy, strait-laced, stuffy, puritanical, school-marmish, old-maidish, prissy, priggish, ultra-virtuous, Victorian, po-faced (*infml*).
☎ lax, easy-going (*infml*).

pry *v* meddle, interfere, poke one's nose in,

intrude, peep, peer, snoop, nose, ferret, dig, delve.
☎ mind one's own business.

prying *adj* meddlesome, meddling, interfering, intrusive, nosey (*infml*), curious, inquisitive, spying, peering, peery, snooping (*infml*), snoopy (*infml*).
☎ uninquisitive.

psalm *n* hymn, song, poem, prayer, chant, canticle, paean, paraphrase.

pseudonym *n* false name, assumed name, alias, incognito, pen name, nom de plume, stage name.

psyche *n* spirit, soul, mind, self, deepest feelings, heart of hearts, consciousness, personality, awareness, individuality, subconscious, intellect, intelligence, understanding.

psychiatrist *n* analyst, psychoanalyst, therapist, psychotherapist, psychologist, psychoanalyser, headshrinker (*infml*), shrink (*infml*), trick cyclist (*infml*), head doctor (*infml*), person in a white coat (*infml*).

psychic *adj* spiritual, supernatural, occult, mystical, clairvoyant, extra-sensory, telepathic, mental, psychological, intellectual, cognitive.

psychological *adj* mental, cerebral, intellectual, cognitive, emotional, subjective, subconscious, unconscious, psychosomatic, irrational, unreal.
☎ physical, real.

psychology *n* **1** *study psychology*: science of the mind, study of the mind, study of mental processes, science of human/animal behaviour. **2** *the psychology of crowds*: mind, mental characteristics, behavioural characteristics, mental chemistry, make-up, attitudes, habits, motives, mindset, what makes someone tick (*infml*).

psychopath *n* lunatic, mad person, maniac, sociopath, psychotic, psycho (*infml*).

pub *n* public house, inn, tavern, bar, saloon, taproom, lounge, lounge bar, grill, brasserie, counter, table, local (*infml*), hostelry (*infml*), watering-hole (*infml*), boozer (*sl*).

puberty *n* pubescence, adolescence, teens, youth, growing up, maturity.
☎ childhood, immaturity, old age.

public *adj* **1** *public buildings*: state,

national, civil, community, social, collective, communal, common, general, universal, open, unrestricted. **2** KNOWN, well-known, recognized, acknowledged, overt, open, exposed, published.

ⓔ 1 private, personal. **2** secret.

➤ *n* people, nation, country, population, populace, masses, citizens, society, community, voters, electorate, followers, supporters, fans, audience, patrons, clientèle, customers, buyers, consumers.

◆ **public house** pub (*infml*), local (*infml*), bar, saloon, inn, tavern.

publication *n* **1** BOOK, newspaper, magazine, periodical, booklet, leaflet, pamphlet, handbill. **2** ANNOUNCEMENT, declaration, notification, disclosure, release, issue, printing, publishing.

publicity *n* advertising, plug (*infml*), hype (*sl*), promotion, build-up, boost, attention, limelight, splash.

publicize *v* advertise, plug (*infml*), hype (*sl*), promote, push, spotlight, broadcast, make known, blaze.

public-spirited *adj* community-minded, humanitarian, philanthropic, altruistic, charitable, unselfish, generous, conscientious.

ⓔ selfish.

publish *v* **1** ANNOUNCE, declare, communicate, make known, divulge, disclose, reveal, release, publicize, advertise. **2** *publish a book*: produce, print, issue, bring out, distribute, circulate, spread, diffuse.

pucker *v* gather, ruffle, wrinkle, shrivel, crinkle, crumple, crease, furrow, purse, screw up, contract, compress.

pudding *n* dessert, sweet, tart, pie, pastry, afters (*infml*), pud (*infml*).

puerile *adj* childish, babyish, infantile, juvenile, immature, irresponsible, silly, foolish, inane, trivial.

ⓔ mature.

puff *n* **1** BREATH, waft, whiff, draught, flurry, gust, blast. **2** *a puff on a cigarette*: pull, drag.

➤ *v* **1** BREATHE, pant, gasp, gulp, wheeze, blow, waft, inflate, expand, swell. **2** *puff a cigarette*: smoke, pull, drag, draw, suck.

puffy *adj* puffed up, inflated, swollen, bloated, distended, enlarged.

pugnacious *adj* hostile, aggressive, belligerent, contentious, disputatious, argumentative, quarrelsome, hot-tempered.

ⓔ peaceable.

pull *v* **1** TOW, drag, haul, draw, tug, jerk, yank (*infml*). **2** REMOVE, take out, extract, pull out, pluck, uproot, pull up, rip, tear. **3** ATTRACT, draw, lure, allure, entice, tempt, magnetize. **4** DISLOCATE, sprain, wrench, strain.

ⓔ 1 push, press. **3** repel, deter, discourage.

➤ *n* **1** TOW, drag, tug, jerk, yank (*infml*). **2** ATTRACTION, lure, allurement, drawing power, magnetism, influence, weight.

◆ **pull apart** separate, part, dismember, dismantle, take to pieces.

ⓔ join.

◆ **pull down** destroy, demolish, knock down, bulldoze.

ⓔ build, erect, put up.

◆ **pull in 1** STOP, arrive, draw in, pull up, park. **2** ATTRACT, draw, bring in, lure, allure, entice. **3** ARREST, capture, seize, apprehend, detain, take into custody, bust (*infml*), nick (*sl*), collar (*infml*), nab (*infml*), book (*infml*), run in (*infml*). **4** EARN, receive, be paid, make, clear, take home, rake in (*infml*).

1 pull away. **2** repel.

◆ **pull off 1** ACCOMPLISH, achieve, bring off, succeed, manage, carry out. **2** DETACH, remove.

ⓔ 1 fail. **2** attach.

◆ **pull out** retreat, withdraw, leave, depart, quit, move out, evacuate, desert, abandon.

ⓔ join, arrive.

◆ **pull through** recover, rally, recuperate, survive, weather.

◆ **pull together** co-operate, work together, collaborate, team up.

ⓔ fight.

◆ **pull up 1** STOP, halt, park, draw up, pull in, pull over, brake. **2** REPRIMAND, tell off (*infml*), tick off (*infml*), take to task, rebuke, criticize.

pulp *n* flesh, marrow, paste, purée, mash, mush, pap.

➤ *v* crush, squash, pulverize, mash, purée, liquidize.

pulsate *v* pulse, beat, throb, pound, hammer, drum, thud, thump, vibrate, oscillate, quiver.

pulse[1] *n* beat, stroke, rhythm, throb, pulsation, beating, pounding, drumming, vibration, oscillation.

pulse[2] *see* bean.

pulverize v 1 CRUSH, pound, grind, mill, powder. 2 DEFEAT, destroy, demolish, annihilate.

pummel v hit, knock, hammer, beat, batter, pound, punch, strike, thump, bang.

pump v push, drive, force, inject, siphon, draw, drain.
♦ **pump up** blow up, inflate, puff up, fill.

pun n play on words, double entendre, witticism, quip.

punch^1 v hit, strike, pummel, jab, bash, clout, cuff, box, thump, sock (sl), wallop (infml).
➤ n 1 BLOW, jab, bash, clout, thump, wallop (infml). 2 FORCE, impact, effectiveness, drive, vigour, verve, panache.

punch^2 v perforate, pierce, puncture, prick, bore, drill, stamp, cut.

punctilious adj scrupulous, conscientious, meticulous, careful, exact, precise, strict, formal, proper, particular, finicky, fussy.
◪ lax, informal.

punctual adj prompt, on time, on the dot, exact, precise, early, in good time.
◪ unpunctual, late.

punctuality n promptness, promptitude, regularity, readiness, strictness.
◪ unpunctuality.

punctuate v interrupt, sprinkle, break, intersperse, pepper, emphasize, point, accentuate, interject (fml).

punctuation

> Punctuation marks include: apostrophe, asterisk, backslash, brackets, colon, comma, dash, exclamation mark, full stop, hyphen, inverted commas, oblique stroke, parentheses, period, question mark, quotation marks, quotes (infml), semicolon, solidus, speech marks, square brackets, star.

puncture n 1 FLAT TYRE, flat (infml), blow-out. 2 LEAK, hole, perforation, cut, nick.
➤ v prick, pierce, penetrate, perforate, hole, cut, nick, burst, rupture, flatten, deflate.

pundit n authority, expert, master, teacher, maestro, guru, sage, savant, buff (infml).

pungent adj strong, hot, peppery, spicy, aromatic, tangy, piquant, sharp, keen, acute, sour, bitter, acrid, caustic, stinging, biting, cutting, incisive, pointed, piercing, penetrating, sarcastic, scathing.
◪ mild, bland, tasteless.

punish v penalize, discipline, correct, chastise, castigate, scold, beat, flog, lash, cane, spank, fine, imprison.
◪ reward.

punishable adj criminal, convictable, chargeable, unlawful, blameworthy, culpable (fml), indictable (fml).

punishing adj arduous, strenuous, crippling, crushing, burdensome, taxing, grinding, demanding, hard, harsh, severe, cruel, gruelling, fatiguing, tiring, wearying, exhausting, backbreaking.
◪ easy.

punishment n discipline, correction, chastisement, penalty, sentence, deserts, retribution, revenge, short sharp shock (infml).
◪ reward.

> Forms of punishment include:
> banishment, beating, belting, the birch, borstal, the cane, capital punishment, cashiering, chain gang, confinement, confiscation, corporal punishment, defrocking, demotion, deportation, detention, dressing-down, excommunication, execution, exile, expulsion, fine, flaying, flogging, gaol, gating, grounding, hiding (infml), hitting, horsewhipping, house arrest, imprisonment, incarceration, internment, jail, jankers, keelhauling, larruping (infml), lashing, leathering, lines, penal colony, prison, probation, being put away (infml), the rack, rap across the knuckles, scourging, being sent down (infml), being sent to Coventry, sequestration, slapping, the slipper, smacking, spanking, the stocks, suspension, tanning someone's hide (infml), tarring and feathering, thrashing, torturing, transportation, unfrocking, walking the plank, walloping, whipping. see also **execution**.

punitive adj penal, disciplinary, retributive, retaliatory, vindictive, punishing.

punter n 1 GAMBLER, better, backer, wagerer. 2 CUSTOMER, client, consumer, person, individual, fellow, chap, guy (infml), bloke (infml).

puny adj weak, feeble, frail, sickly, undeveloped, underdeveloped, stunted, undersized, diminutive, little, tiny, insignificant.

✷ strong, sturdy, large, important.

pupil n student, scholar, schoolboy, schoolgirl, learner, apprentice, beginner, novice, disciple, protégé(e).

✷ teacher.

puppet n 1 MARIONETTE, finger puppet, glove puppet, doll. 2 *a mere puppet of a government*: tool, instrument, dupe, cat's-paw, pawn, quisling, stooge, gull, figurehead, mouthpiece, creature.

purchase v buy, pay for, invest in (*infml*), procure, acquire, obtain, get, secure, gain, earn, win.

✷ sell.

➤ n acquisition, buy (*infml*), investment, asset, possession, property.

✷ sale.

purchaser n buyer, consumer, shopper, customer, client.

✷ seller, vendor.

pure adj 1 *pure gold*: unadulterated, unalloyed, unmixed, undiluted, neat, solid, simple, natural, real, authentic, genuine, true. 2 STERILE, uncontaminated, unpolluted, germ-free, aseptic, antiseptic, disinfected, sterilized, hygienic, sanitary, clean, immaculate, spotless, clear. 3 SHEER, utter, complete, total, thorough, absolute, perfect, unqualified. 4 CHASTE, virginal, undefiled, unsullied, moral, upright, virtuous, blameless, innocent. 5 *pure mathematics*: theoretical, abstract, conjectural, speculative, academic.

✷ 1 impure, adulterated. 2 contaminated, polluted. 4 immoral. 5 applied.

purely adv 1 UTTERLY, completely, totally, entirely, wholly, thoroughly, absolutely. 2 ONLY, simply, merely, just, solely, exclusively.

purgative n laxative, enema, evacuant, purge, emetic (*fml*), aperient (*fml*), cathartic (*fml*), eccoprotic (*fml*), depurative (*fml*).

➤ adj cleansing, laxative, purging, evacuant, aperient (*fml*), cathartic (*fml*), cathartical (*fml*), eccoprotic (*fml*), abstersive (*fml*), depurative (*fml*).

purge v 1 PURIFY, cleanse, clean out, scour, clear, absolve. 2 OUST, remove, get rid of, eject, expel, root out, eradicate, exterminate, wipe out, kill.

➤ n removal, ejection, expulsion, witch hunt, eradication, extermination.

purify v refine, filter, clarify, clean, cleanse, decontaminate, sanitize, disinfect, sterilize, fumigate, deodorize.

✷ contaminate, pollute, defile.

purist n pedant, literalist, formalist, stickler, quibbler, nit-picker (*infml*).

puritan n pietist, rigorist, disciplinarian, zealot, fanatic, moralist, killjoy, spoilsport, prude.

✷ hedonist, libertarian.

puritanical adj puritan, moralistic, disciplinarian, ascetic, abstemious, austere, severe, stern, strict, strait-laced, prim, proper, prudish, disapproving, stuffy, stiff, rigid, narrow-minded, bigoted, fanatical, zealous.

✷ hedonistic, liberal, indulgent, broad-minded.

purity n 1 CLEARNESS, clarity, cleanness, cleanliness, untaintedness, wholesomeness. 2 SIMPLICITY, authenticity, genuineness, truth. 3 CHASTITY, decency, morality, integrity, rectitude (*fml*), uprightness, virtue, innocence, blamelessness.

✷ 1 impurity. 3 immorality.

purpose n 1 INTENTION, aim, objective, end, goal, target, plan, design, vision, idea, point, object, reason, motive, rationale, principle, result, outcome. 2 DETERMINATION, resolve, resolution, drive, single-mindedness, dedication, devotion, constancy, steadfastness, persistence, tenacity, zeal. 3 USE, function, application, good, advantage, benefit, value.

◆ **on purpose** purposely, deliberately, intentionally, consciously, knowingly, wittingly, wilfully.

✷ accidentally, impulsively, spontaneously.

purposeful adj determined, decided, resolved, resolute, single-minded, constant, steadfast, persistent, persevering, tenacious, strong-willed, positive, firm, deliberate.

✷ purposeless, aimless.

purse n 1 MONEY-BAG, wallet, pouch. 2 MONEY, means, resources, finances, funds, coffers, treasury, exchequer. 3 REWARD, award, prize.

➤ v pucker, wrinkle, draw together, close, tighten, contract, compress.

pursue v 1 *pursue an activity*: perform, engage in, practise, conduct, carry on, continue, keep on, keep up, maintain, persevere in, persist in, hold to, aspire to, aim for, strive for, try for. **2** CHASE, go after, follow, track, trail, shadow, tail, dog, harass, harry, hound, hunt, seek, search for, investigate, inquire into.

pursuit *n* **1** CHASE, hue and cry, tracking, stalking, trail, hunt, quest, search, investigation. **2** ACTIVITY, interest, hobby, pastime, occupation, trade, craft, line, speciality, vocation.

push *v* **1** PROPEL, thrust, ram, shove, jostle, elbow, prod, poke, press, depress, squeeze, squash, drive, force, constrain. **2** PROMOTE, advertise, publicize, boost, encourage, urge, egg on (*infml*), incite, spur, influence, persuade, pressurize, bully.
E3 1 pull. **2** discourage, dissuade.
➤ *n* **1** KNOCK, shove, nudge, jolt, prod, poke, thrust. **2** ENERGY, vigour, vitality, go (*infml*), drive, effort, dynamism, enterprise, initiative, ambition, determination.

♦ **push around** bully, torment, terrorize, intimidate, victimize, pick on.

♦ **push off** go away, depart, leave, move, push along (*infml*), shove off (*infml*), beat it (*infml*), buzz off (*infml*), clear off/out (*infml*), make a move (*infml*), make tracks (*infml*).

pushed *adj* short of, stretched, under pressure, harassed, rushed, hard-pressed, hard-up, hurried, in difficulties, strapped, pinched, pressed, harried.

pushy *adj* assertive, self-assertive, ambitious, forceful, aggressive, over-confident, forward, bold, brash, arrogant, presumptuous, assuming, bossy (*infml*).
E3 unassertive, unassuming.

pussyfoot *v* **1** PREVARICATE, equivocate, hedge, tergiversate (*fml*), mess about (*infml*), beat about the bush (*infml*). **2** CREEP, slink, tiptoe, prowl, pad, steal.

put *v* **1** PLACE, lay, deposit, plonk (*infml*), set, fix, settle, establish, stand, position, dispose, situate, station, post. **2** APPLY, impose, inflict, levy, assign, subject. **3** WORD, phrase, formulate, frame, couch, express, voice, utter, state. **4** *put a suggestion*: submit, present, offer, suggest, propose.

♦ **put across** put over, communicate, convey, express, explain, spell out, bring home to, get through to.

♦ **put aside** put by, set aside, keep, retain, save, reserve, store, stow, stockpile, stash (*infml*), hoard, salt away.

♦ **put away** (*infml*) **1** CONSUME, devour, eat, drink. **2** IMPRISON, jail, lock up, commit, certify.

♦ **put back 1** DELAY, defer, postpone, reschedule. **2** REPLACE, return.
E3 1 bring forward.

♦ **put down 1** WRITE DOWN, transcribe, enter, log, register, record, note. **2** CRUSH, quash, suppress, defeat, quell, silence, snub, slight, squash, deflate, humble, take down a peg, shame, humiliate, mortify. **3** *put down a sick dog*: kill, put to sleep. **4** ASCRIBE, attribute, blame, charge.

♦ **put forward** advance, suggest, recommend, nominate, propose, move (*fml*), table, introduce, present, submit, offer, tender.

♦ **put in** insert, enter, input, submit, install, fit.

♦ **put off 1** DELAY, defer, postpone, reschedule. **2** DETER, dissuade, discourage, dishearten, demoralize, daunt, dismay, intimidate, disconcert, confuse, distract.
E3 2 encourage.

♦ **put on 1** ATTACH, affix, apply, place, add, impose. **2** PRETEND, feign, sham, fake, simulate, affect, assume. **3** STAGE, mount, produce, present, do, perform.

♦ **put out 1** PUBLISH, announce, broadcast, circulate. **2** EXTINGUISH, quench, douse, smother, switch off, turn off. **3** INCONVENIENCE, impose on, bother, disturb, trouble, upset, hurt, offend, annoy, irritate, irk, anger, exasperate.
E3 2 light.

♦ **put through** accomplish, achieve, complete, conclude, finalize, execute, manage, bring off.

♦ **put up 1** ERECT, build, construct, assemble. **2** ACCOMMODATE, house, lodge, shelter. **3** *put up prices*: raise, increase. **4** PAY, invest, give, advance, float, provide, supply, pledge, offer.

♦ **put upon** impose on, exploit, take advantage of, take for granted, take liberties, inconvenience.

♦ **put up to** prompt, incite, encourage, egg on (*infml*), urge, goad.
E3 discourage, dissuade.

♦ **put up with** stand, bear, abide, stomach, endure, suffer, tolerate, allow, accept, stand for, take, take lying down.
E3 object to, reject.

put-down n affront, humiliation, insult, slight, sneer, snub, rebuff, sarcasm, gibe, disparagement (*fml*), slap in the face (*infml*), dig (*infml*).

putrefy v rot, perish, go bad, decay, corrupt, mould, spoil, stink, taint, gangrene, decompose, deteriorate, fester, addle.

putrid adj rotten, decayed, decomposed, mouldy, off, bad, rancid, addled, corrupt, contaminated, tainted, polluted, foul, rank, fetid, stinking.
ᴇᴀ fresh, wholesome.

put-upon adj imposed on, taken advantage of, exploited, used, abused, maltreated, persecuted.

puzzle v 1 BAFFLE, mystify, perplex, confound, stump (*infml*), floor (*infml*), confuse, bewilder, flummox (*infml*).
2 THINK, ponder, meditate, consider, mull over, deliberate, figure, rack one's brains.
➤ n question, poser, brain-teaser, mind-bender, crossword, rebus, anagram, riddle, conundrum, mystery, enigma, paradox.
◆ **puzzle out** solve, work out, figure out, decipher, decode, crack, unravel, untangle, sort out, resolve, clear up.

puzzled adj baffled, mystified, perplexed, confounded, at a loss, beaten, stumped (*infml*), confused, bewildered, nonplussed, lost, at sea, flummoxed (*infml*).
ᴇᴀ clear.

puzzling adj baffling, bewildering, confusing, perplexing, unclear, queer, peculiar, strange, bizarre, mystifying, mysterious, mystical, misleading, unaccountable, unfathomable, impenetrable, inexplicable, intricate, involved, ambiguous, equivocal, mind-bending, mind-boggling, curious, enigmatic, cryptic, tortuous, knotty, Sphynx-like, abstruse (*fml*), labyrinthine (*fml*).

pygmy n person of restricted growth, dwarf, midget, TomThumb, Lilliputian, manikin, thumbling, fingerling, homunculus (*fml*).
ᴇᴀ giant
➤ adj miniature, small, tiny, baby, diminutive, half-pint, undersized, minuscule, minute, pocket, elfin, stunted, dwarf, midget, dwarfish, toy, Lilliputian, wee, pint-size(d) (*infml*).
ᴇᴀ gigantic.

pyromaniac n arsonist, incendiary, fire-raiser, firebug (*infml*).

Qq

quack n charlatan, impostor, fraud, mountebank, pretender, masquerader, humbug, sham, fake, cowboy, swindler, trickster, phoney (*infml*), pseud (*infml*).
➤ *adj* false, bogus, counterfeit, fake, pretended, fraudulent, spurious, supposed, sham, so-called, unqualified, phoney (*infml*).
Ea genuine, real.

quagmire n bog, marsh, quag, fen, swamp, morass, mire, quicksand.

quail v recoil, back away, shy away, shrink, flinch, cringe, cower, tremble, quake, shudder, falter.

quaint *adj* picturesque, charming, twee (*infml*), old-fashioned, antiquated, old-world, olde-worlde (*infml*), unusual, strange, odd, curious, bizarre, fanciful, whimsical.
Ea modern.

quake v shake, tremble, shudder, quiver, shiver, quail, vibrate, wobble, rock, sway, move, convulse, heave.

qualification n **1** CERTIFICATE, diploma, training, skill, competence, ability, capability, capacity, aptitude, suitability, fitness, eligibility. **2** RESTRICTION, limitation, reservation, exception, exemption, condition, caveat, provision, proviso, stipulation, modification.

qualified *adj* **1** CERTIFIED, chartered, licensed, professional, trained, experienced, practised, skilled, accomplished, expert, knowledgeable, skilful, talented, proficient, competent, efficient, able, capable, fit, eligible.
2 *qualified praise*: reserved, guarded, cautious, restricted, limited, bounded, contingent, conditional, provisional, equivocal.
Ea 1 unqualified. **2** unconditional, wholehearted.

qualify v **1** TRAIN, prepare, equip, fit, pass, graduate, certify, empower, entitle, permit, authorize, sanction. **2** MODERATE, reduce, lessen, diminish, temper, soften, weaken, mitigate, ease, adjust, modify, restrain, restrict, limit, delimit, define, classify.
Ea 1 disqualify.

quality n **1** PROPERTY, characteristic, peculiarity, attribute, aspect, feature, trait, mark. **2** *of poor quality*: standard, grade, class, kind, sort, nature, character, calibre, status, rank, value, worth, merit, condition. **3** EXCELLENCE, superiority, pre-eminence, distinction, refinement.

qualm n misgiving, apprehension, fear, anxiety, worry, disquiet, uneasiness, scruple, hesitation, reluctance, uncertainty, doubt.

quandary n dilemma, predicament, impasse, perplexity, bewilderment, confusion, mess, fix, hole (*infml*), problem, difficulty.

quantity n amount, number, sum, total, aggregate, mass, lot, share, portion, quota, allotment, measure, dose, proportion, part, content, capacity, volume, weight, bulk, size, magnitude, expanse, extent, length, breadth.

quarrel n row, argument, slanging match (*infml*), wrangle, squabble, tiff (*infml*), misunderstanding, disagreement, dispute, dissension, controversy, difference, conflict, clash, contention, altercation (*fml*), strife, fight, scrap (*infml*), brawl, feud, vendetta, schism.
Ea agreement, harmony.
➤ v row, argue, bicker, squabble, wrangle, be at loggerheads, fall out, disagree, dispute, dissent, differ, be at variance, clash, contend, fight, scrap, feud.
Ea agree.

quarrelsome *adj* argumentative, disputatious, contentious, belligerent, ill-tempered, irritable.
Ea peaceable, placid.

quarry n prey, victim, object, goal, target, game, kill, prize.

quarter n district, sector, zone, neighbourhood, locality, vicinity, area, region, province, territory, division, section, part, place, spot, point, direction, side.
➤ v station, post, billet, accommodate, put up, lodge, board, house, shelter.

quarters n accommodation, lodgings, billet, digs (*infml*), residence, dwelling, habitation, domicile, rooms, barracks, station, post.

quash v annul, revoke (fml), rescind, overrule, cancel, nullify (fml), void, invalidate, reverse, set aside, squash, crush, quell, suppress, subdue, defeat, overthrow.

E3 confirm, vindicate, reinstate.

quaver v shake, tremble, quake, shudder, quiver, vibrate, pulsate, oscillate, flutter, flicker, trill, warble.

quay n wharf, pier, jetty, dock, harbour.

queasy adj sick, ill, unwell, queer, groggy, green, nauseated, sickened, bilious, squeamish, faint, dizzy, giddy.

queen n 1 monarch, sovereign, ruler, majesty, princess, empress, consort. 2 beauty, belle.

queer adj 1 ODD, mysterious, strange, unusual, uncommon, weird, unnatural, bizarre, eccentric, peculiar, funny, puzzling, curious, remarkable. 2 *I feel queer*: unwell, ill, sick, queasy, light-headed, faint, giddy, dizzy. 3 SUSPECT, suspicious, shifty, dubious, shady (infml). 4 (sl) HOMOSEXUAL, gay, lesbian.

E3 1 ordinary, usual, common. 2 well.

quell v subdue, quash, crush, squash, suppress, put down, overcome, conquer, defeat, overpower, moderate, mitigate, allay, alleviate, soothe, calm, pacify, hush, quiet, silence, stifle, extinguish.

quench v 1 *quench one's thirst*: slake, satisfy, sate, cool. 2 EXTINGUISH, douse, put out, snuff out.

querulous adj peevish, fretful, fractious, cantankerous, cross, irritable, complaining, grumbling, discontented, dissatisfied, critical, carping, captious, fault-finding, fussy.

E3 placid, uncomplaining, contented.

query v ask, inquire, question, challenge, dispute, quarrel with, doubt, suspect, distrust, mistrust, disbelieve.

E3 accept.

➤ n question, inquiry, problem, uncertainty, doubt, suspicion, scepticism, reservation, hesitation.

quest n search, hunt, pursuit, investigation, inquiry, mission, crusade, enterprise, undertaking, venture, journey, voyage, expedition, exploration, adventure.

question v interrogate, quiz, grill, pump,

interview, examine, cross-examine, debrief, ask, inquire, investigate, probe, query, challenge, dispute, doubt, disbelieve.

➤ n 1 QUERY, inquiry, poser, problem, difficulty. 2 ISSUE, matter, subject, topic, point, proposal, proposition, motion, debate, dispute, controversy.

questionable adj debatable, disputable, unsettled, undetermined, unproven, uncertain, arguable, controversial, vexed, doubtful, dubious, suspicious, suspect, shady (infml), fishy (infml), iffy (sl).

E3 unquestionable, indisputable, certain.

questionnaire n quiz, test, survey, opinion poll.

queue n line, tailback, file, crocodile, procession, train, string, succession, series, sequence, order.

quibble v carp, cavil, split hairs (infml), nit-pick (infml), equivocate, prevaricate.
➤ n complaint, objection, criticism, query.

quick adj 1 FAST, swift, rapid, speedy, express, hurried, hasty, cursory, fleeting, brief, prompt, ready, immediate, instant, instantaneous, sudden, brisk, nimble, sprightly, agile. 2 CLEVER, intelligent, quick-witted, smart, sharp, keen, shrewd, astute, discerning, perceptive, responsive, receptive.

E3 1 slow, sluggish, lethargic. 2 unintelligent, dull.

quicken v 1 ACCELERATE, speed, hurry, hasten, precipitate, expedite, dispatch, advance. 2 ANIMATE, enliven, invigorate, energize, galvanize, activate, rouse, arouse, stimulate, excite, inspire, revive, refresh, reinvigorate, reactivate.

E3 1 slow, retard. 2 dull.

quickly adv rapidly, quick, fast, speedily, swiftly, express, briskly, apace, hurriedly, hastily, immediately, instantaneously, readily, soon, abruptly, instantly, promptly, unhesitatingly, cursorily, posthaste, presto, prestissimo, expeditiously (fml), perfunctorily (fml), pronto (infml), lickety-split (infml), at a rate of knots (infml), at the double (infml), before you can say Jack Robinson (infml), by leaps and bounds (infml), hell for leather (infml), like a bat out of hell (infml), like the clappers (infml), like greased lightning (infml).

E3 slowly, tardily (fml).

quick-witted adj intelligent, clever, resourceful, keen, bright, sharp, shrewd, penetrating, acute, perceptive, smart, wide-awake, alert, astute, crafty, ingenious, witty, ready-witted, nimble-witted.

Ea dull, slow, stupid.

quiet *adj* **1** SILENT, noiseless, inaudible, hushed, soft, low. **2** PEACEFUL, still, tranquil, serene, calm, composed, undisturbed, untroubled, placid. **3** SHY, reserved, reticent, uncommunicative, taciturn, unforthcoming, retiring, withdrawn, thoughtful, subdued, meek. **4** *a quiet spot*: isolated, unfrequented, lonely, secluded, private.

Ea 1 noisy, loud. **2** excitable. **3** extrovert.

> Informal ways of telling someone to be quiet include: belt up!, button it!, cut the cackle!, drop dead!, dry up!, enough said!, get knotted!, give it a rest!, give over!, hold your peace!, not another word!, one more word out of you!, pack it in!, pipe down!, put a sock in it!, say no more!, shut up!, shut your face!, shut your gob!, shut your mouth!, wrap up!

➤ *n* quietness, silence, hush, peace, lull, stillness, tranquillity, serenity, calm, rest, repose.

Ea noise, loudness, disturbance, bustle.

quieten *v* **1** SILENCE, hush, mute, soften, lower, diminish, reduce, stifle, muffle, deaden, dull. **2** SUBDUE, pacify, quell, quiet, still, smooth, calm, soothe, compose, sober.

Ea 2 disturb, agitate.

quietly *adv* calmly, noiselessly, inaudibly, mutely, silently, softly, soundlessly, surreptitiously, placidly, tranquilly, peacefully, gently, mildly, meekly, unobtrusively, unostentatiously, undemonstratively, modestly, secretly, privately.

Ea noisily, obtrusively.

quietness *n* calm, quiet, silence, serenity, tranquillity, calmness, hush, peace, placidity, lull, still, stillness, composure, inactivity, inertia, uneventfulness, dullness, quiescence (*fml*), quietude (*fml*), repose (*fml*).

Ea activity, bustle, commotion, disturbance, noise, racket.

quilt *n* bedcover, coverlet, bedspread, counterpane, eiderdown, duvet.

quintessential *adj* essential, ideal, perfect, ultimate, complete, definitive, entire, archetypical (*fml*), consummate (*fml*), prototypical (*fml*).

quip *n* joke, jest, crack, gag (*infml*), witticism, riposte, retort, gibe.

quirk *n* freak, eccentricity, curiosity, oddity, peculiarity, idiosyncrasy, mannerism, habit, trait, foible, whim, caprice, turn, twist.

quit *v* **1** LEAVE, depart, go, exit, decamp, desert, forsake, abandon, renounce, relinquish, surrender, give up, resign, retire, withdraw. **2** *quit smoking*: stop, cease, end, discontinue, desist, drop, give up, pack in (*sl*).

quite *adv* **1** MODERATELY, rather, somewhat, fairly, relatively, comparatively. **2** UTTERLY, absolutely, totally, completely, entirely, wholly, fully, perfectly, exactly, precisely.

quiver *v* shake, tremble, shudder, shiver, quake, quaver, vibrate, palpitate, flutter, flicker, oscillate, wobble.

➤ *n* shake, tremble, shudder, shiver, tremor, vibration, palpitation, flutter, flicker, oscillation, wobble.

quixotic *adj* unrealistic, unworldly, idealistic, impracticable, visionary, extravagant, fanciful, Utopian, fantastical, romantic, starry-eyed, impetuous, impulsive, chivalrous.

Ea hard-headed, practical, realistic.

quiz *n* questionnaire, test, examination, competition.

➤ *v* question, interrogate, grill, pump, examine, cross-examine.

quizzical *adj* questioning, inquiring, curious, amused, humorous, teasing, mocking, satirical, sardonic, sceptical.

quota *n* ration, allowance, allocation, assignment, share, portion, part, slice, cut (*infml*), percentage, proportion.

quotation *n* **1** CITATION, quote (*infml*), extract, excerpt, passage, piece, cutting, reference. **2** ESTIMATE, quote (*infml*), tender, figure, price, cost, charge, rate.

quote *v* cite, refer to, mention, name, reproduce, echo, repeat, recite, recall, recollect.

Rr

rabble *n* crowd, throng, horde, herd, mob, masses, populace, riff-raff (*infml*).

rabble-rouser *n* agitator, troublemaker, incendiary, demagogue, ringleader.

rabid *adj* 1 FANATICAL, ferocious, extreme, burning, ardent, raging, fervent, frantic, unreasoning, intolerant, irrational, furious, obsessive, zealous, overzealous, bigoted, narrow-minded. 2 MAD, hydrophobic, maniacal, wild, berserk, frenzied, crazed, violent, hysterical.

race¹ *n* sprint, steeplechase, marathon, scramble, regatta, competition, contest, contention, rivalry, chase, pursuit, quest.
➤ *v* run, sprint, dash, tear, fly, gallop, speed, career, dart, zoom, rush, hurry, hasten.

> **Types of race and famous races**
> include: cycle race, cyclo-cross, road race, time trial, Milk Race, Tour de France; greyhound race, Greyhound Derby; horserace, Cheltenham Gold Cup, the Classics (Derby, Oaks, One Thousand Guineas, St. Leger, Two Thousand Guineas), Grand National, Kentucky Derby, Melbourne Cup, Prix de l'Arc de Triomphe, steeplechase, trotting race, harness race; motorcycle race, motocross, scramble, speedway, Isle of Man Tourist Trophy (TT); motor-race, Grand Prix, Indianapolis 500, Le Mans, Monte Carlo rally, RAC Rally, stock car race; rowing, regatta, Boat Race; running, cross-country, dash (*US*), hurdles, marathon, London Marathon, relay, sprint, steeplechase, track event; ski race, downhill, slalom; swimming race; walking race, walkathon; yacht race, Admiral's Cup, America's Cup; egg-and-spoon race, pancake race, sack race, wheelbarrow race.

race² *n* nation, people, tribe, clan, house, dynasty, family, kindred, ancestry, line, blood, stock, genus, species, breed.

racecourse *n* racetrack, course, track, circuit, lap, turf, speedway.

racial *adj* national, tribal, ethnic, folk, genealogical, ancestral, inherited, genetic.

racism *n* racialism, xenophobia, chauvinism, jingoism, discrimination, prejudice, bias.

rack *n* shelf, stand, support, structure, frame, framework.

racket *n* 1 NOISE, din, uproar, row, fuss, outcry, clamour, commotion, disturbance, pandemonium, hurly-burly, hubbub. 2 SWINDLE, con (*infml*), fraud, fiddle, deception, trick, dodge, scheme, business, game.

racy *adj* 1 RIBALD, bawdy, risqué, naughty, indecent, indelicate, suggestive. 2 LIVELY, animated, spirited, energetic, dynamic, buoyant, boisterous.

radiance *n* light, luminosity, incandescence, radiation, brightness, brilliance, shine, lustre, gleam, glow, glitter, resplendence, splendour, happiness, joy, pleasure, delight, rapture.

radiant *adj* bright, luminous, shining, gleaming, glowing, beaming, glittering, sparkling, brilliant, resplendent, splendid, glorious, happy, joyful, delighted, ecstatic.
🔁 dull, miserable.

radiate *v* shine, gleam, glow, beam, shed, pour, give off, emit, emanate, diffuse, issue, disseminate, scatter, spread (out), diverge, branch.

radical *adj* 1 BASIC, fundamental, primary, essential, natural, native, innate, intrinsic, deep-seated, profound. 2 *radical changes*: drastic, comprehensive, thorough, sweeping, far-reaching, thoroughgoing, complete, total, entire. 3 FANATICAL, militant, extreme, extremist, revolutionary.
🔁 1 superficial. 3 moderate.
➤ *n* fanatic, militant, extremist, revolutionary, reformer, reformist, fundamentalist.

raffle *n* draw, lottery, sweepstake, sweep, tombola.

rag *n* 1 *an old clothes rag*: cloth, flannel, floorcloth, duster, towel. 2 *dressed in rags*: remnants, shreds, raggedness, tatters, tats, clouts, duddery (*infml*), duds (*infml*).

rage *n* 1 ANGER, wrath, fury, frenzy, tantrum, temper. 2 (*infml*) *all the rage*: craze, fad, thing (*infml*), fashion, vogue,

style, passion, enthusiasm, obsession.
➤ *v* fume, seethe, rant, rave, storm, thunder, explode, rampage.

ragged *adj* 1 *ragged clothes*: frayed, torn, ripped, tattered, worn-out, threadbare, tatty, shabby, scruffy, unkempt, down-at-heel. 2 JAGGED, serrated, indented, notched, rough, uneven, irregular, fragmented, erratic, disorganized.

raging *adj* 1 VIOLENT, wild, stormy, turbulent, tumultuous. 2 ANGRY, furious, enraged, infuriated, irate, fuming, incensed, raving, seething, wrathful, frenzied, mad (*infml*), fulminating (*fml*), furibund (*fml*), ireful (*fml*).

raid *n* attack, onset, onslaught, invasion, inroad, incursion, foray, sortie, strike, blitz, swoop, bust (*sl*), robbery, break-in, hold-up.
➤ *v* loot, pillage, plunder, ransack, rifle, maraud, attack, descend on, invade, storm.

raider *n* attacker, invader, looter, plunderer, ransacker, marauder, robber, thief, brigand, pirate.

rail *v* censure, criticize, attack, abuse, protest, decry, upbraid, vociferate, mock, jeer, revile, ridicule, scoff, arraign (*fml*), castigate (*fml*), denounce (*fml*), fulminate (*fml*), inveigh (*fml*), vituperate (*fml*).

railing *n* fence, paling, barrier, parapet, rail, balustrade.

railway *n* track, line, rails, underground, tube (*infml*), subway, metro.

rain *n* rainfall, precipitation, raindrops, drizzle, shower, cloudburst, downpour, deluge, torrent, storm, thunderstorm, squall.
➤ *v* spit, drizzle, shower, pour, teem, pelt, bucket (*infml*), deluge.

rainbow *n* arc, arch, bow, spectrum, prism, iris.
➤ *adj* rainbow-like, kaleidoscopic, prismatic, variegated, spectral, opalescent, iridescent (*fml*).
🖃 monochrome.

> The colours of the rainbow are: red, orange, yellow, green, blue, indigo, violet.

rainy *adj* wet, damp, showery, drizzly.
🖃 dry.

raise *v* 1 LIFT, elevate, hoist, jack up, erect, build, construct. 2 INCREASE, augment, escalate, magnify, heighten, strengthen, intensify, amplify, boost, enhance.
3 *raise funds*: get, obtain, collect, gather,

assemble, rally, muster, recruit. 4 BRING UP, rear, breed, propagate, grow, cultivate, develop. 5 *raise a subject*: bring up, broach, introduce, present, put forward, moot, suggest.
🖃 1 lower. 2 decrease, reduce. 5 suppress.

rake *v* hoe, scratch, scrape, graze, comb, scour, search, hunt, ransack, gather, collect, amass, accumulate.

rally *v* 1 GATHER, collect, assemble, congregate, convene, muster, summon, round up, unite, marshal, organize, mobilize, reassemble, regroup, reorganize.
2 RECOVER, recuperate, revive, improve, pick up.
➤ *n* 1 GATHERING, assembly, convention, convocation, conference, meeting, jamboree, reunion, march, demonstration.
2 RECOVERY, recuperation, revival, comeback, improvement, resurgence, renewal.

ram *v* 1 HIT, strike, butt, hammer, pound, drum, crash, smash, slam. 2 FORCE, drive, thrust, cram, stuff, pack, crowd, jam, wedge.

ramble *v* 1 WALK, hike, trek, tramp, traipse, stroll, amble, saunter, straggle, wander, roam, rove, meander, wind, zigzag.
2 CHATTER, babble, rabbit (on) (*infml*), witter (on) (*infml*), expatiate, digress, drift.
➤ *n* walk, hike, trek, tramp, stroll, saunter, tour, trip, excursion.

rambler *n* hiker, walker, stroller, rover, roamer, wanderer, wayfarer.

rambling *adj* 1 SPREADING, sprawling, straggling, trailing. 2 CIRCUITOUS, roundabout, digressive, wordy, long-winded, long-drawn-out, disconnected, incoherent.
🖃 2 direct.

ramification *n* branch, offshoot, development, complication, result, consequence, upshot, implication.

ramp *n* slope, incline, gradient, rise.

rampage *v* run wild, run amok, run riot, rush, tear, storm, rage, rant, rave.
➤ *n* rage, fury, frenzy, storm, uproar, violence, destruction.
♦ **on the rampage** wild, amok, berserk, violent, out of control.

rampant *adj* unrestrained, uncontrolled, unbridled, unchecked, wanton, excessive, fierce, violent, raging, wild, riotous, rank, profuse, rife, widespread, prevalent.

rampart *n* earthwork, embankment,

bank, fence, barricade, bastion, bulwark, defence, stronghold, guard, wall, security, parapet, fort, fortification, breastwork, vallum.

ramshackle adj dilapidated, tumbledown, broken-down, crumbling, ruined, derelict, jerry-built, unsafe, rickety, shaky, unsteady, tottering, decrepit.
E3 solid, stable.

rancid adj sour, off, bad, musty, stale, rank, foul, fetid, putrid, rotten.
E3 sweet.

rancour n resentfulness, resentment, spite, hate, hatred, animosity, malice, malignity, ill-feeling, ill-will, hostility, bitterness, enmity, grudge, venom, vindictiveness, spleen, acrimony (fml), animus (fml), antipathy (fml), malevolence (fml).

random adj arbitrary, chance, fortuitous, casual, incidental, haphazard, irregular, unsystematic, unplanned, accidental, aimless, purposeless, indiscriminate, stray.
E3 systematic, deliberate.
♦ **at random** haphazardly, incidentally, fortuitously, arbitrarily, sporadically, irregularly, unsystematically, unmethodically, aimlessly, purposelessly, indiscriminately.

randy adj horny (infml), sexy, raunchy (infml), amorous, aroused, hot, lustful, goatish, lascivious, lecherous, satyric, concupiscent (fml), turned-on (infml).

range n 1 SCOPE, compass, scale, gamut, spectrum, sweep, spread, extent, distance, reach, span, limits, bounds, parameters, area, field, domain, province, sphere, orbit. 2 a range of fittings: variety, diversity, assortment, selection, sort, kind, class, order, series, string, chain.
➤ v 1 EXTEND, stretch, reach, spread, vary, fluctuate. 2 ALIGN, arrange, order, rank, classify, catalogue.

rank¹ n 1 GRADE, degree, class, caste, status, standing, position, station, condition, estate, echelon, level, stratum, tier, classification, sort, type, group, division. 2 ROW, line, range, column, file, series, order, formation.

Ranks in the armed services include: air force: aircraftsman, aircraftswoman, corporal, sergeant, warrant officer, pilot officer, flying officer, flight lieutenant, squadron-leader, wing commander, group-captain, air-commodore, air-vice-marshal, air-marshal, air-chief-marshal, marshal of the Royal Air Force; army: private, lance-corporal, corporal, sergeant, warrant officer, lieutenant, captain, major, lieutenant-colonel, colonel, brigadier, major general, lieutenant-general, general, field marshal; navy: able seaman, rating, petty officer, chief petty officer, sublieutenant, lieutenant, lieutenant-commander, commander, captain, commodore, rear admiral, vice-admiral, admiral, admiral of the fleet. see also **soldier**.

➤ v grade, class, rate, place, position, range, sort, classify, categorize, order, arrange, organize, marshal.

rank² adj 1 UTTER, total, complete, absolute, unmitigated, thorough, sheer, downright, out-and-out, arrant, gross, flagrant, glaring, outrageous. 2 FOUL, repulsive, disgusting, revolting, stinking, putrid, rancid, stale.

rankle v annoy, irritate, rile, nettle, gall, irk, anger.

ransack v search, scour, comb, rummage, rifle, raid, sack, strip, despoil (fml), ravage, loot, plunder, pillage.

ransom n price, money, payment, pay-off, redemption, deliverance, rescue, liberation, release.
➤ v buy off, redeem, deliver, rescue, liberate, free, release.

rant v shout, cry, yell, roar, bellow, declaim, bluster, rave.

rap v 1 KNOCK, hit, strike, tap, thump. 2 (sl) REPROVE, reprimand, criticize, censure.
➤ n 1 KNOCK, blow, tap, thump. 2 (sl) REBUKE, reprimand, censure, blame, punishment.

rape v 1 rape a woman: violate, ravish, assault, assault sexually, abuse, maltreat, defile. 2 rape the land: ravage, sack, ransack, strip, raid, loot, rob, pillage, plunder, devastate, violate, defile, despoil (fml), depredate (fml), spoliate (fml).
➤ n 1 the rape of a young girl: violation, assault, sexual assault, ravishment, abuse, maltreatment, date rape, gang rape. 2 rape of the countryside: ravaging, sacking, ransacking, stripping, raid, looting, plundering, devastation, violation, defilement, rapine (fml), despoliation (fml), depredation (fml), spoliation (fml).

rapid adj swift, speedy, quick, fast, express, lightning, prompt, brisk,

hurried, hasty, precipitate, headlong.
F3 slow, leisurely, sluggish.

rapidly *adv* fast, quickly, speedily, swiftly, hastily, hurriedly, briskly, promptly, expeditiously (*fml*), precipitately (*fml*), lickety-split (*infml*).
F3 slowly.

rapport *n* bond, link, affinity, relationship, empathy, sympathy, understanding, harmony.

rapprochement *n* reconcilement, increased friendliness, agreement, reconciliation, reunion, détente, softening, harmonization.

rapt *adj* engrossed, absorbed, preoccupied, intent, gripped, spellbound, enthralled, captivated, fascinated, entranced, charmed, enchanted, delighted, ravished, enraptured, transported.

rapture *n* delight, happiness, joy, bliss, ecstasy, euphoria, exaltation.

rare *adj* 1 UNCOMMON, unusual, scarce, sparse, sporadic, infrequent. 2 EXQUISITE, superb, excellent, superlative, incomparable, exceptional, remarkable, precious.
F3 1 common, abundant, frequent.

rarefied *adj* exclusive, select, private, esoteric, refined, high, noble, sublime.

rarely *adv* seldom, hardly ever, infrequently, little.
F3 often, frequently.

raring *adj* eager, keen, enthusiastic, ready, willing, impatient, longing, itching, desperate.

rarity *n* 1 CURIOSITY, curio, gem, pearl, treasure, find. 2 UNCOMMONNESS, unusualness, strangeness, scarcity, shortage, sparseness, infrequency.
F3 2 commonness, frequency.

rascal *n* rogue, scoundrel, scamp, scallywag, imp, devil, villain, good-for-nothing, wastrel.

rash[1] *adj* reckless, ill-considered, foolhardy, ill-advised, madcap, hare-brained, hot-headed, headstrong, impulsive, impetuous, hasty, headlong, unguarded, unwary, indiscreet, imprudent, careless, heedless, unthinking.
F3 cautious, wary, careful.

rash[2] *n* eruption, outbreak, epidemic, plague.

rasp *n* grating, scrape, grinding, scratch,

harshness, hoarseness, croak.
➤ *v* grate, scrape, grind, file, sand, scour, abrade, rub.

rate *n* 1 SPEED, velocity, tempo, time, ratio, proportion, relation, degree, grade, rank, rating, standard, basis, measure, scale.
2 CHARGE, fee, hire, toll, tariff, price, cost, value, worth, tax, duty, amount, figure, percentage.
➤ *v* 1 JUDGE, regard, consider, deem (*fml*), count, reckon, figure, estimate, evaluate, assess, weigh, measure, grade, rank, class, classify. 2 ADMIRE, respect, esteem, value, prize. 3 DESERVE, merit.

rather *adv* 1 MODERATELY, relatively, slightly, a bit, somewhat, fairly, quite, pretty, noticeably, significantly, very.
2 PREFERABLY, sooner, instead.

ratify *v* approve, uphold, endorse, sign, legalize, sanction, authorize, establish, affirm, confirm, certify, validate, authenticate.
F3 repudiate, reject.

rating *n* class, rank, degree, status, standing, position, placing, order, grade, mark, evaluation, assessment, classification, category.

ratio *n* percentage, fraction, proportion, relation, relationship, correspondence, correlation.

ration *n* quota, allowance, allocation, allotment, share, portion, helping, part, measure, amount.
➤ *v* apportion, allot, allocate, share, deal out, distribute, dole out, dispense, supply, issue, control, restrict, limit, conserve, save.

rational *adj* logical, reasonable, sound, well-founded, realistic, sensible, clear-headed, judicious (*fml*), wise, sane, normal, balanced, lucid, reasoning, thinking, intelligent, enlightened.
F3 irrational, illogical, insane, crazy.

rationale *n* logic, reasoning, philosophy, principle, basis, grounds, explanation, reason, motive, motivation, theory.

rationalize *v* 1 JUSTIFY, excuse, vindicate, explain, account for. 2 REORGANIZE, streamline.

rations *n* food, provisions, supplies, stores.

rattle *v* clatter, jingle, jangle, clank, shake, vibrate, jolt, jar, bounce, bump.
♦ **rattle off** reel off, list, run through, recite, repeat.

raucous *adj* harsh, rough, hoarse, husky, rasping, grating, jarring, strident, noisy, loud.

ravage *v* destroy, devastate, lay waste, demolish, raze, wreck, ruin, spoil, damage, loot, pillage, plunder, sack, despoil (*fml*).
➤ *n* destruction, devastation, havoc, damage, ruin, desolation, wreckage, pillage, plunder.

rave *v* rage, storm, thunder, roar, rant, ramble, babble, splutter.
➤ *adj* (*infml*) enthusiastic, rapturous, favourable, excellent, wonderful.

ravenous *adj* hungry, starving, starved, famished, greedy, voracious, insatiable.

ravine *n* canyon, gorge, gully, pass.

raving *adj* mad, insane, crazy, hysterical, delirious, wild, frenzied, furious, berserk.

ravish *v* enrapture, delight, overjoy, enchant, charm, captivate, entrance, fascinate, spellbind.

ravishing *adj* delightful, enchanting, charming, lovely, beautiful, gorgeous, stunning, radiant, dazzling, alluring, seductive.

raw *adj* 1 *raw vegetables*: uncooked, fresh. 2 UNPROCESSED, unrefined, untreated, crude, natural. 3 PLAIN, bare, naked, basic, harsh, brutal, realistic. 4 SCRATCHED, grazed, scraped, open, bloody, sore, tender, sensitive. 5 COLD, chilly, bitter, biting, piercing, freezing, bleak. 6 *a raw recruit*: new, green, immature, callow, inexperienced, untrained, unskilled.
🔁 1 cooked, done. 2 processed, refined. 5 warm. 6 experienced, skilled.

ray *n* beam, shaft, flash, gleam, flicker, glimmer, glint, spark, trace, hint, indication.

raze *v* demolish, pull down, tear down, bulldoze, flatten, level, destroy.

re *prep* about, concerning, regarding, with regard to, with reference to.

reach *v* arrive at, get to, attain, achieve, make, amount to, hit, strike, touch, contact, stretch, extend, grasp.
➤ *n* range, scope, compass, distance, spread, extent, stretch, grasp, jurisdiction, command, power, influence.

react *v* respond, retaliate, reciprocate, reply, answer, acknowledge, act, behave.

reaction *n* response, effect, reply, answer, acknowledgement, feedback, counteraction, reflex, recoil, reciprocation, retaliation.

reactionary *adj* conservative, right-wing, rightist, die-hard, counter-revolutionary.
🔁 progressive, revolutionary.
➤ *n* conservative, right-winger, rightist, die-hard, counter-revolutionary.
🔁 progressive, revolutionary.

read *v* 1 STUDY, peruse, pore over, scan, skim, decipher, decode, interpret, construe, understand, comprehend. 2 RECITE, declaim, deliver, speak, utter. 3 *the gauge read zero*: indicate, show, display, register, record.

readable *adj* 1 LEGIBLE, decipherable, intelligible, clear, understandable, comprehensible. 2 INTERESTING, enjoyable, entertaining, gripping, unputdownable (*infml*).
🔁 1 illegible. 2 unreadable.

readily *adv* willingly, unhesitatingly, gladly, eagerly, promptly, quickly, freely, smoothly, easily, effortlessly.
🔁 unwillingly, reluctantly.

readiness *n* willingness, preparedness, skill, preparation, aptitude, fitness, eagerness, keenness, inclination, quickness, rapidity, ease, promptness, facility, availability, handiness, gameness (*infml*).
♦ **in readiness** in preparation, available, prepared, on standby, standing by, on call, on full alert.

reading *n* 1 STUDY, perusal, scrutiny, examination, inspection, interpretation, understanding, rendering, version, rendition, recital. 2 *a reading from the Bible*: passage, lesson.

ready *adj* 1 *ready to go*: prepared, waiting, set, fit, arranged, organized, completed, finished. 2 WILLING, inclined, disposed, happy, game (*infml*), eager, keen. 3 AVAILABLE, to hand, present, near, accessible, convenient, handy. 4 PROMPT, immediate, quick, sharp, astute, perceptive, alert.
🔁 1 unprepared. 2 unwilling, reluctant, disinclined. 3 unavailable, inaccessible. 4 slow.

real *adj* actual, existing, physical, material, substantial, tangible, genuine, authentic, bona fide, official, rightful, legitimate, valid, true, factual, certain, sure, positive, veritable, honest, sincere, heartfelt, unfeigned, unaffected.

◨ unreal, imaginary, false.

realistic *adj* **1** PRACTICAL, down-to-earth, commonsense, sensible, level-headed, clear-sighted, businesslike, hard-headed, pragmatic, matter-of-fact, rational, logical, objective, detached, unsentimental, unromantic. **2** LIFELIKE, faithful, truthful, true, genuine, authentic, natural, real, real-life, graphic, representational.
◨ **1** unrealistic, impractical, irrational, idealistic.

reality *n* truth, fact, certainty, realism, actuality, existence, materiality, tangibility, genuineness, authenticity, validity.

realization *n* **1** UNDERSTANDING, comprehension, grasp, recognition, discernment, perception, acceptance, appreciation, awareness, consciousness, cognizance (*fml*), apprehension (*fml*). **2** ACHIEVEMENT, accomplishment, fulfilment, completion, implementation, performance, consummation (*fml*). **3** EARNING, selling, fetching, making, gain, clearing.

realize *v* **1** UNDERSTAND, comprehend, grasp, catch on, cotton on (*infml*), recognize, accept, appreciate. **2** ACHIEVE, accomplish, fulfil, complete, implement, perform. **3** SELL FOR, fetch, make, earn, produce, net, clear.

really *adv* actually, truly, honestly, sincerely, genuinely, positively, certainly, absolutely, categorically, very, indeed.

realm *n* kingdom, monarchy, principality, empire, country, state, land, territory, area, region, province, domain, sphere, orbit, field, department.

reap *v* **1** HARVEST, cut, crop, gather, mow, garner (*fml*). **2** GAIN, obtain, secure, acquire, get, derive, collect, realize, win.

rear *n* back, stern, end, tail, rump, buttocks, posterior, behind, bottom, backside (*infml*).
◨ front.
➤ *adj* back, hind, hindmost, rearmost, last.
◨ front.
➤ *v* **1** *rear a child*: bring up, raise, breed, grow, cultivate, foster, nurse, nurture, train, educate. **2** RISE, tower, soar, raise, lift.

reason *n* **1** CAUSE, motive, incentive, rationale, explanation, excuse, justification, defence, warrant, ground, basis, case, argument, aim, intention, purpose, object, end, goal. **2** SENSE, logic,

reasoning, rationality, sanity, mind, wit, brain, intellect, understanding, wisdom, judgement, common sense, gumption.
➤ *v* work out, solve, resolve, conclude, deduce, infer, think.
◆ **reason with** urge, persuade, move, remonstrate with, argue with, debate with, discuss with.

reasonable *adj* **1** SENSIBLE, wise, well-advised, sane, intelligent, rational, logical, practical, sound, reasoned, well-thought-out, plausible, credible, possible, viable. **2** *a reasonable price*: acceptable, satisfactory, tolerable, moderate, average, fair, just, modest, inexpensive.
◨ **1** irrational. **2** exorbitant.

reasoned *adj* clear, logical, methodical, organized, rational, sensible, sound, systematic, well-thought-out, judicious (*fml*).
◨ illogical, unsystematic.

reasoning *n* logic, thinking, thought, analysis, interpretation, deduction, supposition, hypothesis, argument, case, proof.

reassure *v* comfort, cheer, encourage, hearten, inspirit, brace, bolster.
◨ alarm.

rebate *n* refund, repayment, reduction, discount, deduction, allowance.

rebel *v* revolt, mutiny, rise up, run riot, dissent, disobey, defy, resist, recoil, shrink.
◨ conform.
➤ *n* revolutionary, insurrectionary, mutineer, dissenter, nonconformist, schismatic, heretic.

rebellion *n* revolt, revolution, rising, uprising, insurrection, insurgence, mutiny, resistance, opposition, defiance, disobedience, insubordination, dissent, heresy.

rebellious *adj* revolutionary, insurrectionary, insurgent, seditious, mutinous, resistant, defiant, disobedient, insubordinate, unruly, disorderly, ungovernable, unmanageable, intractable, obstinate.
◨ obedient, submissive.

rebirth *n* reincarnation, resurrection, renaissance, regeneration, renewal, restoration, revival, revitalization, rejuvenation.

rebound *v* recoil, backfire, return, bounce, ricochet, boomerang.

rebuff *v* spurn, reject, refuse, decline, turn

down, repulse, discourage, snub, slight, cut, cold-shoulder.
> *n* rejection, refusal, repulse, check, discouragement, snub, brush-off (*infml*), slight, put-down, cold shoulder.

rebuke *v* reprove, castigate, chide, scold, tell off (*infml*), admonish, tick off (*infml*), reprimand, upbraid, rate, censure, blame, reproach.
Ea praise, compliment.
> *n* reproach, reproof, reprimand, lecture, dressing-down (*infml*), telling-off (*infml*), ticking-off (*infml*), admonition, censure, blame.
Ea praise, commendation.

rebut *v* refute, quash, defeat, discredit, disprove, invalidate, negate, overturn, give the lie to, confute (*fml*), explode (*infml*).

recalcitrant *adj* disobedient, defiant, uncontrollable, ungovernable, unmanageable, unruly, wayward, wilful, contrary, obstinate, stubborn, unsubmissive, unwilling, unco-operative, contumacious (*fml*), insubordinate (*fml*), intractable (*fml*), refractory (*fml*), renitent (*fml*).
Ea amenable, tractable.

recall *v* remember, recollect, cast one's mind back, evoke, bring back.

recant *v* deny, disown, renounce, repudiate, rescind, apostatize, retract, revoke, withdraw, recall, unsay, abjure (*fml*), abrogate (*fml*), disavow (*fml*), disclaim (*fml*), forswear (*fml*).

recapitulate *v* recap (*infml*), summarize, review, repeat, reiterate, restate, recount.

recede *v* go back, return, retire, withdraw, retreat, ebb, wane, sink, decline, diminish, dwindle, decrease, lessen, shrink, slacken, subside, abate.
Ea advance.

receipt *n* **1** VOUCHER, ticket, slip, counterfoil, stub, acknowledgement. **2** RECEIVING, reception, acceptance, delivery.

receipts *n* takings, income, proceeds, profits, gains, return.

receive *v* **1** TAKE, accept, get, obtain, derive, acquire, pick up, collect, inherit. **2** *receive guests*: admit, let in, greet, welcome, entertain, accommodate. **3** EXPERIENCE, undergo, suffer, sustain, meet with, encounter. **4** REACT TO, respond to, hear, perceive, apprehend.
Ea **1** give, donate.

recent *adj* late, latest, current, present-day, contemporary, modern, up-to-date, new, novel, fresh, young.
Ea old, out of date.

recently *adv* lately, newly, freshly.

receptacle *n* container, vessel, holder.

reception *n* **1** ACCEPTANCE, admission, greeting, recognition, welcome, treatment, response, reaction, acknowledgement, receipt. **2** PARTY, function, do (*infml*), entertainment.

receptive *adj* open-minded, amenable, accommodating, suggestible, susceptible, sensitive, responsive, open, accessible, approachable, friendly, hospitable, welcoming, sympathetic, favourable, interested.
Ea narrow-minded, resistant, unresponsive.

recess *n* **1** BREAK, interval, intermission, rest, respite, holiday, vacation. **2** ALCOVE, niche, nook, corner, bay, cavity, hollow, depression, indentation.

recession *n* slump, depression, downturn, decline.
Ea boom, upturn.

recipe *n* formula, prescription, ingredients, instructions, directions, method, system, procedure, technique.

reciprocal *adj* mutual, joint, shared, give-and-take, complementary, alternating, corresponding, equivalent, interchangeable.

reciprocate *v* respond, reply, requite, return, exchange, swap, trade, match, equal, correspond, interchange, alternate.

recital *n* performance, concert, recitation, reading, narration, account, rendition, interpretation, repetition.

recitation *n* passage, piece, party piece, poem, monologue, narration, story, tale, recital, telling.

recite *v* repeat, tell, narrate, relate, recount, speak, deliver, articulate, declaim, perform, reel off, itemize, enumerate.

reckless *adj* heedless, thoughtless, mindless, careless, negligent, irresponsible, imprudent, ill-advised, indiscreet, rash, hasty, foolhardy, daredevil, wild.
Ea cautious, wary, careful, prudent.

reckon *v* **1** CALCULATE, compute, figure out, work out, add up, total, tally, count, number, enumerate. **2** DEEM, regard, consider, esteem, value, rate, judge, evaluate, assess, estimate, gauge. **3** THINK, believe, imagine, fancy, suppose, surmise, assume, guess, conjecture.

♦ **reckon on** rely on, depend on, bank on, count on, trust in, hope for, expect, anticipate, foresee, plan for, bargain for, figure on, take into account, face.

reckoning n **1** by my reckoning: calculation, computation, estimate. **2** BILL, account, charge, due, score, settlement. **3** JUDGEMENT, retribution, doom.

reclaim v recover, regain, recapture, retrieve, salvage, rescue, redeem, restore, reinstate, regenerate.

recline v rest, repose, lean back, lie, lounge, loll, sprawl, stretch out.

recluse n ascetic, hermit, solitary, loner, monk, eremite, stylite, solitarian, solitaire, anchorite, anchoret, anchoress.

recognition n **1** IDENTIFICATION, detection, discovery, recollection, recall, remembrance, awareness, perception, realization, understanding. **2** CONFESSION, admission, acceptance, acknowledgement, gratitude, appreciation, honour, respect, greeting, salute.

recognize v **1** IDENTIFY, know, remember, recollect, recall, place, see, notice, spot, perceive. **2** CONFESS, own, acknowledge, accept, admit, grant, concede, allow, appreciate, understand, realize.

recoil v move back, jump back, spring back, shy away, flinch, shrink, quail, rebound, react, falter, kick, backfire, boomerang, misfire.
➤ n rebound, reaction, kick, backlash, repercussion.

recollect v recall, remember, cast one's mind back, reminisce.

recollection n recall, remembrance, memory, souvenir, reminiscence, impression.

recommend v advocate, urge, exhort, advise, counsel, suggest, propose, put forward, advance, praise, commend, plug (infml), endorse, approve, vouch for.
☒ disapprove.

recommendation n advice, counsel, suggestion, proposal, advocacy, endorsement, approval, sanction, blessing, praise, commendation, plug (infml), reference, testimonial.
☒ disapproval.

recompense n compensation, indemnification, damages, reparation, restitution, amends, requital, repayment, reward, payment, remuneration, pay, wages.
➤ v compensate, indemnify, remunerate, pay, reward, repay, redress, reimburse, requite, satisfy.

reconcile v reunite, conciliate, pacify, appease, placate, propitiate, accord, harmonize, accommodate, adjust, resolve, settle, square.
☒ estrange, alienate.

reconciliation n reunion, conciliation, pacification, appeasement, propitiation, rapprochement, détente, settlement, agreement, harmony, accommodation, adjustment, compromise.
☒ estrangement, separation.

recondition v renovate, repair, restore, renew, refurbish, overhaul, fix, remodel, revamp.

reconnaissance n exploration, reconnoitring, scouting, survey, expedition, examination, inspection, probe, observation, scrutiny, scan, investigation, search, patrol, recce (sl).

reconnoitre v explore, survey, scan, spy out, recce (sl), inspect, examine, scrutinize, investigate, patrol.

reconsider v think over, rethink, review, revise, re-examine, think twice, modify, reassess, think better of, have second thoughts.

reconstruct v remake, rebuild, reassemble, re-establish, refashion, remodel, reform, reorganize, recreate, restore, renovate, regenerate.

record n **1** REGISTER, log, report, account, minutes, memorandum, note, entry, document, file, dossier, diary, journal, memoir, history, annals, archives, documentation, evidence, testimony, trace. **2** RECORDING, disc, single, CD, compact disc, album, release, LP. **3** break the record: fastest time, best performance, personal best, world record.
4 BACKGROUND, track record, curriculum vitae, career.
➤ v **1** NOTE, enter, inscribe, write down, transcribe, register, log, put down, enrol, report, minute, chronicle, document, keep, preserve. **2** TAPE-RECORD, tape, videotape, video, cut.
♦ **off the record**: unofficial, unofficially,

confidential, confidentially, private, privately, sub rosa (*fml*).

Ea official, officially.

◆ **on record 1** *the wettest April on record*: noted, documented, written down. **2** *to go on record as saying*: officially recorded, publicly known, documented.

recorder *n* **1** REGISTRAR, archivist, annalist, chronicler, diarist, historian, chronologer, secretary, clerk, stenographer, scribe, scorer, score-keeper. **2** TAPE RECORDER, cassette recorder, cassette-player, video recorder, videocassette recorder, video (*infml*).

recording *n* release, performance, record, disc, CD, cassette, tape, video.

> Types of recording include: album, audiotape, cassette, CD, compact disc, digital recording, disc, EP (extended play), 45, gramophone record, long-playing record, LP, magnetic tape, mono recording, record, 78, single, stereo recording, tape, tape-recording, tele-recording, video, videocassette, video disc, videotape, vinyl (*infml*).

recount *v* tell, relate, impart, communicate, report, narrate, describe, depict, portray, detail, repeat, rehearse, recite.

recoup *v* recover, retrieve, regain, get back, make good, repay, refund, reimburse, compensate.

recourse *n* appeal, resort, access, turning to, choice, option, alternative, possibility, remedy, refuge, way out.

recover *v* **1** *recover from illness*: get better, improve, pick up, rally, mend, heal, pull through, get over, recuperate, revive, convalesce, come round. **2** REGAIN, get back, recoup, retrieve, retake, recapture, repossess, reclaim, restore.

Ea **1** worsen. **2** lose, forfeit.

recovery *n* **1** RECUPERATION, convalescence, rehabilitation, mending, healing, improvement, upturn, rally, revival, restoration. **2** RETRIEVAL, salvage, reclamation, repossession, recapture, recouping.

Ea **1** worsening. **2** loss, forfeit.

recreation *n* fun, enjoyment, pleasure, amusement, diversion, distraction, entertainment, hobby, pastime, game, sport, play, leisure, relaxation, refreshment.

recrimination *n* countercharge, accusation, counter-attack, retaliation, reprisal, retort, quarrel, bickering.

recruit *v* enlist, draft, conscript, enrol, sign up, engage, take on, mobilize, raise, gather, obtain, procure.

➤ *n* beginner, novice, initiate, learner, trainee, apprentice, conscript, convert.

rectify *v* correct, put right, right, remedy, cure, repair, fix, mend, improve, amend, adjust, reform.

recuperate *v* recover, get better, improve, pick up, rally, revive, mend, convalesce.

Ea worsen.

recur *v* repeat, persist, return, reappear.

recurrent *adj* recurring, chronic, persistent, repeated, repetitive, regular, periodic, frequent, intermittent.

recycle *v* reuse, reprocess, reclaim, recover, salvage, save.

red *adj* **1** SCARLET, vermilion, cherry, ruby, crimson, maroon, pink, reddish, bloodshot, inflamed. **2** RUDDY, florid, glowing, rosy, flushed, blushing, embarrassed, shamefaced. **3** *red hair*: ginger, carroty, auburn, chestnut, Titian.

redden *v* blush, flush, colour, go red, crimson.

redeem *v* **1** BUY BACK, repurchase, cash (in), exchange, change, trade, ransom, reclaim, regain, repossess, recoup, recover, recuperate, retrieve, salvage. **2** COMPENSATE FOR, make up for, offset, outweigh, atone for, expiate, absolve, acquit, discharge, release, liberate, emancipate, free, deliver, rescue, save.

redemption *n* **1** REPURCHASE, repossession, reclamation, recovery, reparation, retrieval, exchange, reinstatement, trade-in, fulfilment, compensation. **2** ATONEMENT, deliverance, expiation, emancipation, freedom, rescue, salvation, ransom, liberation, release.

redress *v* **1** RIGHT, put right, rectify, remedy, avenge, requite, recompense, make compensation for. **2** ADJUST, amend, correct, balance, regulate.

➤ *n* compensation, recompense, indemnification, remedy, relief, assistance, help, aid, correction, requital, restitution, satisfaction, reparation, payment, justice, atonement.

reduce *v* **1** LESSEN, decrease, contract, shrink, slim, shorten, curtail, trim, cut, slash, discount, rebate, lower, moderate, weaken, diminish, impair. **2** DRIVE, force, degrade, downgrade, demote, humble, humiliate, impoverish, subdue, overpower, master, vanquish.

Ea 1 increase, raise, boost.

reduction *n* decrease, drop, fall, decline, lessening, moderation, weakening, diminution (*fml*), contraction, compression, shrinkage, narrowing, shortening, curtailment, restriction, limitation, cutback, cut, discount, rebate, devaluation, depreciation, deduction, subtraction, loss.

Ea increase, rise, enlargement.

redundancy *n* **1** DISMISSAL, notice, laying-off, discharge, removal, expulsion, marching-orders, papers (*infml*), sacking (*infml*), firing (*infml*), sack (*infml*), push (*infml*), boot (*infml*), elbow (*infml*). **2** SUPERFLUITY, surplus, uselessness, wordiness, excess, repetition, tautology, pleonasm (*fml*), prolixity (*fml*), verbosity (*fml*).

Ea 1 appointment, hiring.

redundant *adj* **1** UNEMPLOYED, out of work, laid off, dismissed. **2** SUPERFLUOUS, surplus, excess, extra, supernumerary, unneeded, unnecessary, unwanted. **3** WORDY, verbose, repetitious, tautological.

Ea 2 necessary, essential. **3** concise.

reek *v* smell, stink, fume, exhale (*fml*), hum (*infml*), pong (*infml*).
➤ *n* smell, odour, stink (*infml*), stench, vapour, fume(s), exhalation (*fml*), effluvium (*fml*), malodour (*fml*), fetor (*fml*), pong (*infml*).

reel *v* stagger, totter, wobble, rock, sway, waver, falter, stumble, lurch, pitch, roll, revolve, gyrate, spin, wheel, twirl, whirl, swirl.

refer *v* **1** SEND, direct, point, guide, pass on, transfer, commit, deliver. **2** *refer to a catalogue*: consult, look up, turn to, resort to. **3** ALLUDE, mention, touch on, speak of, bring up, recommend, cite, quote. **4** APPLY, concern, relate, belong, pertain.

referee *n* umpire, judge, adjudicator, arbitrator, mediator, ref (*infml*).
➤ *v* umpire, judge, adjudicate, arbitrate.

reference *n* **1** ALLUSION, remark, mention, citation, quotation, illustration, instance, note. **2** TESTIMONIAL, recommendation, endorsement, character. **3** RELATION,

regard, respect, connection, bearing.

referendum *n* poll, vote, voting, plebiscite, survey.

refine *v* process, treat, purify, clarify, filter, distil, polish, hone, improve, perfect, elevate, exalt.

refined *adj* civilized, cultured, cultivated, polished, sophisticated, urbane, genteel, gentlemanly, ladylike, well-bred, well-mannered, polite, civil, elegant, fine, delicate, subtle, precise, exact, sensitive, discriminating.

Ea coarse, vulgar, rude.

refinement *n* **1** MODIFICATION, alteration, amendment, improvement. **2** CULTIVATION, sophistication, urbanity, gentility, breeding, style, elegance, taste, discrimination, subtlety, finesse.

Ea 1 deterioration. **2** coarseness, vulgarity.

reflect *v* **1** MIRROR, echo, imitate, reproduce, portray, depict, show, reveal, display, exhibit, manifest, demonstrate, indicate, express, communicate. **2** THINK, ponder, consider, mull (over), deliberate, contemplate, meditate, muse.

reflection *n* **1** IMAGE, likeness, echo, impression, indication, manifestation, observation, view, opinion. **2** THINKING, thought, study, consideration, deliberation, contemplation, meditation, musing.

reflective *adj* thoughtful, contemplative, pondering, deliberative, meditative, pensive, reasoning, absorbed, dreamy, cogitating (*fml*), ruminative.

reform *v* change, amend, improve, ameliorate, better, rectify, correct, mend, repair, rehabilitate, rebuild, reconstruct, remodel, revamp, renovate, restore, regenerate, reconstitute, reorganize, shake up (*infml*), revolutionize, purge.
➤ *n* change, amendment, improvement, rectification, correction, rehabilitation, renovation, reorganization, shake-up (*infml*), purge.

refrain¹ *v* stop, cease, quit, leave off, renounce, desist, abstain, forbear, avoid.

refrain² *n* chorus, response, burden, strain, melody, song, tune.

refresh *v* **1** COOL, freshen, enliven, invigorate, fortify, revive, restore, renew, rejuvenate, revitalize, reinvigorate. **2** *refresh one's memory*: jog, stimulate, prompt, prod.

Ea 1 tire, exhaust.

refreshing *adj* cool, thirst-quenching, bracing, invigorating, energizing, stimulating, inspiring, fresh, new, novel, original.

refreshment *n* sustenance, food, drink, snack, revival, restoration, renewal, reanimation, reinvigoration, revitalization.

refrigerate *v* chill, cool, keep cold, freeze.
Ea heat, warm.

refuge *n* sanctuary, asylum, shelter, protection, security, retreat, hideout, hideaway, resort, harbour, haven.

refugee *n* exile, émigré, displaced person, fugitive, runaway, escapee.

refund *v* repay, reimburse, rebate, return, restore.
➤ *n* repayment, reimbursement, rebate, return.

refurbish *v* renovate, redecorate, re-equip, refit, remodel, revamp, repair, mend, overhaul, restore, recondition, do up (*infml*).

refusal *n* rejection, no, rebuff, repudiation, denial, negation.
Ea acceptance.

refuse¹ *v* reject, turn down, decline, spurn, repudiate, rebuff, repel, deny, withhold.
Ea accept, allow, permit.

refuse² *n* rubbish, waste, trash, garbage, junk, litter.

refute *v* disprove, rebut, confute, give the lie to, discredit, counter, negate.

regain *v* recover, get back, recoup, reclaim, repossess, retake, recapture, retrieve, return to.

regal *adj* majestic, kingly, queenly, princely, imperial, royal, sovereign, stately, magnificent, noble, lordly.

regale *v* amuse, entertain, delight, divert, captivate, fascinate, feast, ply, gratify, serve, refresh.

regard *v* **1** CONSIDER, judge, rate, value, gauge, estimate, think, believe, suppose, imagine, contemplate, weigh up, deem (*fml*), appraise (*fml*). **2** LOOK AT, look upon, see, view, observe, watch, gaze at, scrutinize, eye, behold (*fml*), give the once-over (*infml*). **3** HEED, listen to, observe, follow, note, bear in mind, take notice of, pay attention to, take into account/consideration.
➤ *n* **1** CARE, concern, consideration, attention, notice, heed, respect, deference,

honour, admiration, affection, love, sympathy, approval, esteem (*fml*), approbation (*fml*). **2** *in this regard*: matter, subject, aspect, point, detail, particular. **3** *send her my regards*: best wishes, good wishes, greetings, respects, compliments, salutations.
Ea 1 disregard, contempt.
♦ **with/in regard to** as regards, concerning, with reference to, with respect to, in relation to, in connection with, re, about, as to, on the subject of, apropos.

regarding *prep* with regard to, as regards, concerning, with reference to, re, about, as to.

regardless *adj* disregarding, heedless, unmindful, neglectful, inattentive, unconcerned, indifferent.
Ea heedful, mindful, attentive.
➤ *adv* anyway, nevertheless, nonetheless, despite everything, come what may.

regenerate *v* revive, reinvigorate, reawaken, rekindle, renew, restore, reconstitute, reconstruct, re-establish, renovate, refresh, uplift, change, invigorate, rejuvenate, reproduce, inspirit (*fml*), revivify (*fml*).

regime *n* government, rule, administration, management, leadership, command, control, establishment, system.

regimented *adj* strict, disciplined, controlled, regulated, standardized, ordered, methodical, systematic, organized.
Ea free, lax, disorganized.

region *n* land, terrain, territory, country, province, area, district, zone, sector, neighbourhood, range, scope, expanse, domain, realm, sphere, field, division, section, part, place.

Types of geographical region and community include: antarctic, arctic, area, bailiwick, banana republic, basin, belt, Black Country, borough, built-up area, burgh, capital city, catchment area, city, coast, colony, commune, continent, country, countryside, county, county town, desert, development area, diocese, district, dockland, domain, dominion, duchy, East End, emirate, empire, estate, The Fens, forest, free state, ghetto, ghost town, grassland, green belt, hamlet, health resort, heartland, heath, hemisphere, home-town, hundred, industrial park, inner city, interior, jungle, kibbutz, kingdom, lowlands, manor, market town, marshland, metropolis, The Midlands, mission, municipality, nation, new town, no-man's land, old country, orient, outback, outpost, outskirts, pampas, parish, plain, port, postal district, prairie, principality, protectorate, province, quarter, realm, red-light district, region, republic, reservation, resort, riding, riviera, rural district, satellite town, savannah, scrubland, seaside, settlement, shanty town, shire, spa, state, steppe, subcontinent, suburb, territory, Third World, time zone, town, township, tract, tropics, tundra, urban district, veld, village, wasteland, West Country, West End, wilderness, woodland, zone.

regional *adj* district, local, localized, provincial, sectional, zonal, parochial.
ⅎ national, international, worldwide.

register *n* roll, roster, list, index, catalogue, directory, log, record, chronicle, annals, archives, file, ledger, schedule, diary, almanac.
➤ *v* 1 RECORD, note, log, enter, inscribe, mark, list, catalogue, chronicle, enrol, enlist, sign on, check in. 2 SHOW, reveal, betray, display, exhibit, manifest, express, say, read, indicate.

regret *v* rue, repent, lament, mourn, grieve, deplore.
➤ *n* remorse, contrition, compunction, self-reproach, shame, sorrow, grief, disappointment, bitterness.

regretful *adj* remorseful, rueful, repentant, contrite, penitent, conscience-stricken, ashamed, sorry, apologetic, sad, sorrowful, disappointed.
ⅎ impenitent, unashamed.

regrettable *adj* unfortunate, unlucky, unhappy, sad, disappointing, upsetting, distressing, lamentable, deplorable, shameful, wrong, ill-advised.
ⅎ fortunate, happy.

regular *adj* 1 ROUTINE, habitual, typical, usual, customary, time-honoured, conventional, orthodox, correct, official, standard, normal, ordinary, common, commonplace, everyday. 2 PERIODIC, rhythmic, steady, constant, fixed, set, unvarying, uniform, even, level, smooth, balanced, symmetrical, orderly, systematic, methodical.
ⅎ 1 unusual, unconventional. 2 irregular.

regulate *v* control, direct, guide, govern, rule, administer, manage, handle, conduct,

run, organize, order, arrange, settle, square, monitor, set, adjust, tune, moderate, balance.

regulation *n* rule, statute, law, ordinance, edict, decree, order, commandment, precept, dictate, requirement, procedure.
➤ *adj* standard, official, statutory, prescribed, required, orthodox, accepted, customary, usual, normal.

regurgitate *v* 1 VOMIT, bring up, spew (*infml*), disgorge (*fml*), puke (*infml*), throw up (*infml*). 2 REPEAT, say/tell again, restate, recapitulate, reiterate (*fml*).

rehabilitate *v* restore, renew, reinvigorate, normalize, reform, reinstate, reconstitute, re-establish, renovate, reintegrate, recondition, rebuild, convert, adjust, clear, mend, reconstruct, save, redeem.

rehearsal *n* practice, drill, exercise, dry run, run-through, preparation, reading, recital, narration, account, enumeration, list.

rehearse *v* practise, drill, train, go over, prepare, try out, repeat, recite, recount, relate.

reign *n* rule, sway, monarchy, empire, sovereignty, supremacy, power, command, dominion, control, influence.
➤ *v* rule, govern, command, prevail, predominate, influence.

reimburse *v* refund, repay, return, restore, recompense, compensate, indemnify, remunerate.

rein *n* check, control, curb, restraint, hold, overcheck, restriction, brake, bridle, harness.
➤ *v* check, control, curb, restrain, restrict, limit, hold back, stop, hold, halt, arrest, bridle.

reinforce *v* strengthen, fortify, toughen, harden, stiffen, steel, brace, support, buttress, shore, prop, stay, supplement, augment, increase, emphasize, stress, underline.
ⅎ weaken, undermine.

reinforcements *n* auxiliaries, reserves, back-up, support, help.

reinstate *v* restore, return, replace, recall, reappoint, reinstall, re-establish.

reiterate *v* repeat, recapitulate, resay, restate, retell, emphasize, stress, iterate (*fml*), rehearse, recap (*infml*).

reject *v* refuse, deny, decline, turn down,

veto, disallow, condemn, despise, spurn, rebuff, jilt, exclude, repudiate, repel, renounce, eliminate, scrap, discard, jettison, cast off.

▣ accept, choose, select.
➤ *n* failure, second, discard, cast-off.

rejection *n* refusal, denial, veto, dismissal, rebuff, brush-off, exclusion, repudiation, renunciation, elimination.
▣ acceptance, choice, selection.

rejoice *v* celebrate, revel, delight, glory, exult, triumph.

rejoicing *n* celebration, revelry, merrymaking, festivity, happiness, gladness, joy, delight, elation, jubilation, exultation, triumph.

rejoinder *n* retort, answer, reply, response, quip, repartee, riposte.

rejuvenate *v* revitalize, reinvigorate, reanimate, revive, renew, freshen up, refresh, restore, rekindle, recharge, regenerate.

relapse *v* worsen, deteriorate, degenerate, weaken, sink, fail, lapse, revert, regress, backslide.
➤ *n* worsening, deterioration, setback, recurrence, weakening, lapse, reversion, regression, backsliding.

relate *v* 1 LINK, connect, join, couple, ally, associate, correlate. 2 REFER, apply, concern, pertain, appertain. 3 *relate an anecdote*: tell, recount, narrate, report, describe, recite. 4 IDENTIFY, sympathize, empathize, understand, feel for.

related *adj* kindred, akin, affiliated, allied, associated, connected, linked, interrelated, interconnected, accompanying, concomitant, joint, mutual.
▣ unrelated, unconnected.

relation *n* 1 LINK, connection, bond, relationship, correlation, comparison, similarity, affiliation, interrelation, interconnection, interdependence, regard, reference. 2 RELATIVE, family, kin, kindred.

relations *n* 1 RELATIVES, family, kin, kindred. 2 RELATIONSHIP, terms, rapport, liaison, intercourse, affairs, dealings, interaction, communications, contact, associations, connections.

relationship *n* bond, link, connection, association, liaison, rapport, affinity, closeness, similarity, parallel, correlation, ratio, proportion.

relative *adj* comparative, proportional, proportionate, commensurate, corresponding, respective, appropriate, relevant, applicable, related, connected, interrelated, reciprocal, dependent.
➤ *n* relation, family, kin.

relatively *adv* comparatively, in/by comparison, fairly, quite, rather, somewhat.

relax *v* slacken, loosen, lessen, reduce, diminish, weaken, lower, soften, moderate, abate, remit, relieve, ease, rest, unwind, calm, tranquillize, sedate.
▣ tighten, intensify.

relaxation *n* 1 REST, repose, refreshment, leisure, recreation, fun, amusement, entertainment, enjoyment, pleasure. 2 SLACKENING, lessening, reduction, moderation, abatement (*fml*), let-up (*infml*), détente, easing.
▣ 2 tension, intensification.

relaxed *adj* informal, casual, laid-back (*infml*), easy-going (*infml*), carefree, happy-go-lucky, cool, calm, composed, collected, unhurried, leisurely.
▣ tense, nervous, formal.

relay *n* 1 BROADCAST, transmission, programme, communication, message, dispatch. 2 *work in relays*: shift, turn.
➤ *v* broadcast, transmit, communicate, send, spread, carry, supply.

release *v* loose, unloose, unleash, unfasten, extricate, free, liberate, deliver, emancipate, acquit, absolve, exonerate, excuse, exempt, discharge, issue, publish, circulate, distribute, present, launch, unveil.
▣ imprison, detain, check.
➤ *n* freedom, liberty, liberation, deliverance, emancipation, acquittal, absolution, exoneration, exemption, discharge, issue, publication, announcement, proclamation.
▣ imprisonment, detention.

relegate *v* demote, downgrade, degrade, reduce, consign, entrust, assign, refer, dispatch, delegate, transfer, banish, expatriate, deport, eject, exile, expel.
▣ promote.

relent *v* give in, give way, yield, capitulate, unbend, relax, slacken, soften, weaken.

relentless *adj* unrelenting, unremitting, incessant, persistent, unflagging, ruthless, remorseless, implacable, merciless, pitiless, unforgiving, cruel, harsh, fierce, grim, hard, punishing, uncompromising, inflexible, unyielding, inexorable.

E3 merciful, yielding.

relevant *adj* pertinent, material, significant, germane, related, applicable, apposite, apt, appropriate, suitable, fitting, proper, admissible.

E3 irrelevant, inapplicable, inappropriate, unsuitable.

reliable *adj* unfailing, certain, sure, dependable, responsible, trusty, trustworthy, honest, true, faithful, constant, staunch, solid, safe, sound, stable, predictable, regular.

E3 unreliable, doubtful, untrustworthy.

reliance *n* dependence, trust, faith, belief, credit, confidence, assurance.

relic *n* memento, souvenir, keepsake, token, survival, remains, remnant, scrap, fragment, vestige, trace.

relief *n* reassurance, consolation, comfort, ease, alleviation, cure, remedy, release, deliverance, help, aid, assistance, support, sustenance, refreshment, diversion, relaxation, rest, respite, break, breather (*infml*), remission, let-up (*infml*), abatement (*fml*).

relieve *v* reassure, console, comfort, ease, soothe, alleviate, mitigate, cure, release, deliver, free, unburden, lighten, soften, slacken, relax, calm, help, aid, assist, support, sustain.

E3 aggravate, intensify.

religion

Religions include: Christianity, Church of England (C of E), Church of Scotland, Baptists, Catholicism, Methodism, Protestantism, Presbyterianism, Anglicanism, Congregationalism, Calvinism, evangelicalism, Free Church, Jehovah's Witnesses, Mormonism, Quakerism, Amish; Baha'ism, Buddhism, Confucianism, Hinduism, Islam, Jainism, Judaism, Sikhism, Taoism, Shintoism, Zen, Zoroastrianism, voodoo, druidism. *see also* **scripture**; **worship**.

religious *adj* 1 SACRED, holy, divine, spiritual, devotional, scriptural, theological, doctrinal. 2 *a religious person*: devout, godly, pious, God-fearing, church-going, reverent, righteous.

E3 1 secular. 2 irreligious, ungodly.

Religious officers include: abbess, abbot, archbishop, archdeacon, bishop, canon, cardinal, chancellor, chaplain, clergy, clergyman, clergywoman, curate, deacon, deaconess, dean, elder, father, friar, minister, monk, Monsignor, mother superior, nun, padre, parson, pastor, pope, prelate, priest, prior, proctor, rector, vicar; ayatollah, Dalai Lama, guru, imam, rabbi.

relinquish *v* let go, release, hand over, surrender, yield, cede, give up, resign, renounce, repudiate, waive, forgo, abandon, desert, forsake (*fml*), drop, discard.

E3 keep, retain.

relish *v* like, enjoy, savour, appreciate, revel in.

> *n* 1 SEASONING, condiment, sauce, pickle, spice, piquancy, tang.
2 ENJOYMENT, pleasure, delight, gusto, zest.

reluctant *adj* unwilling, disinclined, indisposed, hesitant, slow, backward, loath, averse (*fml*), unenthusiastic, grudging.

E3 willing, ready, eager.

rely *v* depend, lean, count, bank, reckon, trust, swear by.

remain *v* stay, rest, stand, dwell, abide, last, endure, survive, prevail, persist, continue, linger, wait.

E3 go, leave, depart.

remainder *n* rest, balance, surplus, excess, remnant, remains.

remaining *adj* left, unused, unspent, unfinished, residual, outstanding, surviving, persisting, lingering, lasting, abiding.

remains *n* rest, remainder, residue, dregs, leavings, left-overs, scraps, crumbs, fragments, remnants, oddments, traces, vestiges, relics, body, corpse, carcase, ashes, debris.

remark *v* comment, observe, note, mention, say, state, declare.

> *n* comment, observation, opinion, reflection, mention, utterance, statement, assertion, declaration.

remarkable *adj* striking, impressive, noteworthy, surprising, amazing, strange, odd, unusual, uncommon, extraordinary, phenomenal, exceptional, outstanding, notable, conspicuous, prominent, distinguished.

☰ average, ordinary, commonplace, usual.

remedy *n* cure, antidote, countermeasure, corrective, restorative, medicine, treatment, therapy, relief, solution, answer, panacea.
➤ *v* correct, rectify, put right, redress, counteract, cure, heal, restore, treat, help, relieve, soothe, ease, mitigate, mend, repair, fix, solve.

remember *v* 1 RECALL, recollect, summon up, think back, reminisce, recognize, place. 2 MEMORIZE, learn, retain.
☰ 1 forget.

remembrance *n* 1 MEMORY, recollection, mind, reminder, recall, reminiscence, thought, testimonial, retrospect, nostalgia. 2 COMMEMORATION, memorial, monument, souvenir, memento, token, keepsake, relic, recognition.

remind *v* prompt, nudge, hint, jog one's memory, refresh one's memory, bring to mind, call to mind, call up.

reminder *n* prompt, nudge, hint, suggestion, memorandum, memo, souvenir, memento.

reminiscence *n* memory, remembrance, memoir, anecdote, recollection, recall, retrospection, review, reflection.

reminiscent *adj* suggestive, evocative, nostalgic.

remiss *adj* careless, negligent, neglectful, forgetful, unmindful, heedless, lackadaisical, inattentive, indifferent, lax, slack, slipshod, sloppy, slow, thoughtless, casual, wayward, culpable (*fml*), tardy (*fml*), dilatory (*fml*).
☰ careful, scrupulous.

remission *n* 1 LESSENING, moderation, slackening, relaxation, release, weakening, decrease, reduction, respite, reprieve, ebb, lull, abatement (*fml*), alleviation (*fml*), diminution (*fml*), let-up (*infml*). 2 CANCELLATION, repeal, annulment, suspension, rescinding (*fml*), abrogation (*fml*), revocation (*fml*). 3 PARDON, forgiveness, acquittal, excuse, absolution, exemption, discharge, indulgence, amnesty, exoneration (*fml*).

remit *v* send, transmit, dispatch, post, mail, forward, pay, settle.
➤ *n* brief, orders, instructions, guidelines, terms of reference, scope, authorization, responsibility.

remittance *n* sending, dispatch,

payment, fee, allowance, consideration.

remnant *n* scrap, piece, bit, fragment, end, off cut, left-over, remainder, balance, residue, shred, trace, vestige.

remorse *n* regret, compunction, ruefulness, repentance, penitence, contrition, self-reproach, shame, guilt, bad conscience, sorrow, grief.

remorseful *adj* guilty, regretful, repentant, ashamed, penitent, conscience-stricken, guilt-ridden, sorrowful, sorry, sad, apologetic, rueful, contrite, chastened (*fml*), compunctious (*fml*).
☰ impenitent, remorseless.

remote *adj* 1 DISTANT, far, far-away, far-off, outlying, out-of-the-way, inaccessible, godforsaken, isolated, secluded, lonely. 2 DETACHED, aloof, standoffish, uninvolved, reserved, withdrawn. 3 *a remote possibility*: slight, small, slim, slender, faint, negligible, unlikely, improbable.
☰ 1 close, nearby, accessible. 2 friendly.

removal *n* 1 MOVE, transferral, departure, relocation, uprooting, shift, shifting, transporting, conveyance. 2 WITHDRAWAL, taking away, detachment, extraction, deletion, obliteration, abolition, purging. 3 DISMISSAL, discharge, departure, riddance, ejection, ousting, eviction, expulsion, relegation, disposal, dislodgement (*fml*), firing (*infml*), sacking (*infml*), sack (*infml*), push (*infml*), boot (*infml*), elbow (*infml*).

remove *v* detach, pull off, amputate, cut off, extract, pull out, withdraw, take away, take off, strip, shed, doff, expunge, efface, erase, delete, strike out, get rid of, abolish, purge, eliminate, dismiss, discharge, eject, throw out, oust, depose, displace, dislodge, shift, move, transport, transfer, relocate.

remuneration *n* pay, wages, salary, emolument, stipend, fee, retainer, earnings, income, profit, reward, recompense, payment, remittance, repayment, reimbursement, compensation, indemnity.

renaissance *n* revival, renewal, rebirth, reawakening, awakening, resurrection, rejuvenation, regeneration, re-emergence, restoration, new birth, new dawn, reappearance, resurgence, recrudescence (*fml*), renascence (*fml*).

rend *v* tear, split, break, burst, divide,

separate, rupture, sever, rip, fracture, pierce, shatter, smash, splinter, stab, lacerate, cleave (*fml*).

render *v* **1** *they rendered it harmless*: make, cause to be, leave. **2** GIVE, provide, supply, tender, present, submit, hand over, deliver. **3** TRANSLATE, transcribe, interpret, explain, clarify, represent, perform, play, sing.

rendezvous *n* **1** MEETING, appointment, engagement, assignation, date, tryst (*fml*). **2** MEETING-PLACE, venue, haunt, resort.
➤ *v* meet, come together, gather, collect, assemble, rally, muster, converge, convene (*fml*).

rendition *n* performance, presentation, version, rendering, portrayal, reading, transcription, translation, interpretation, arrangement, construction, delivery, explanation, depiction, execution (*fml*).

renegade *n* deserter, defector, traitor, turncoat, dissident, mutineer, outlaw, rebel, betrayer, apostate, backslider, runaway, tergiversator (*fml*).
F3 adherent, disciple, follower.
➤ *adj* disloyal, rebel, rebellious, recreant, traitorous, unfaithful, apostate, backsliding, dissident, mutinous, outlaw, runaway, perfidious (*fml*).
F3 loyal, faithful.

renege *v* default, repudiate, go back on one's promise, backslide, apostatize, welsh, cross the floor.

renew *v* **1** RENOVATE, modernize, refurbish, refit, recondition, mend, repair, overhaul, remodel, reform, transform, recreate, reconstitute, re-establish, regenerate, revive, resuscitate, refresh, rejuvenate, reinvigorate, revitalize, restore, replace, replenish, restock. **2** REPEAT, restate, reaffirm, extend, prolong, continue, recommence, restart, resume.

renounce *v* abandon, forsake (*fml*), give up, resign, relinquish, surrender, discard, reject, spurn, disown, repudiate, disclaim, deny, recant, abjure.

renovate *v* restore, renew, recondition, repair, overhaul, modernize, refurbish, refit, redecorate, do up (*infml*), remodel, reform, revamp, improve.

renown *n* fame, celebrity, stardom, acclaim, glory, eminence, illustriousness, distinction, note, mark, esteem (*fml*), reputation, honour.
F3 obscurity, anonymity.

renowned *adj* famous, well-known, celebrated, acclaimed, famed, noted, eminent, distinguished, illustrious, notable.
F3 unknown, obscure.

rent *n* rental, lease, hire, payment, fee.
➤ *v* let, sublet, lease, hire, charter.

renunciation *n* abandonment, giving up, relinquishment, surrender, waiving, discarding, rejection, spurning, shunning, disowning, disinheriting, repudiation, denial, forsaking (*fml*), disclaiming (*fml*), abstinence (*fml*), abnegation (*fml*), abdication (*fml*).

repair *v* mend, fix, patch up, overhaul, service, rectify, redress, restore, renovate, renew.
➤ *n* mend, patch, darn, overhaul, service, maintenance, restoration, adjustment, improvement.

reparation *n* amends, redress, requital, restitution, satisfaction, renewal, compensation, recompense, damages, indemnity, atonement, propitiation (*fml*).

repartee *n* banter, badinage, jesting, wit, riposte, retort.

repay *v* refund, reimburse, compensate, recompense, reward, remunerate, pay, settle, square, get even with, retaliate, reciprocate, revenge, avenge.

repeal *v* revoke (*fml*), rescind, abrogate (*fml*), quash, annul, nullify (*fml*), void, invalidate, cancel, countermand (*fml*), reverse, abolish.
F3 enact.

repeat *v* restate, reiterate (*fml*), recapitulate, echo, quote, recite, relate, retell, reproduce, duplicate, renew, rebroadcast, reshow, replay, rerun, redo.
➤ *n* repetition, echo, reproduction, duplicate, rebroadcast, reshowing, replay, rerun.

repeatedly *adv* time after time, time and (time) again, again and again, over and over, frequently, often.

repel *v* **1** DRIVE BACK, repulse, check, hold off, ward off, parry, resist, oppose, fight, refuse, decline, reject, rebuff. **2** DISGUST, revolt, nauseate, sicken, offend.
F3 **1** attract. **2** delight.

repellent *adj* repulsive, revolting, disgusting, nauseating, sickening, offensive, shocking, distasteful, objectionable, off-putting, obnoxious, foul, vile, nasty, loathsome, abominable,

abhorrent, contemptible, despicable, hateful, horrid, unpleasant, disagreeable, repugnant (*fml*).
E3 attractive, pleasant, delightful.

repent *v* regret, rue, sorrow, lament, deplore, atone.

repentance *n* penitence, contrition, remorse, compunction, regret, sorrow, grief, guilt, shame.

repentant *adj* penitent, contrite, sorry, apologetic, remorseful, regretful, rueful, chastened, ashamed.
E3 unrepentant.

repercussion *n* result, consequence, backlash, reverberation, echo, rebound, recoil.

repertoire *n* collection, list, range, repertory, reserve, reservoir, stock, store, supply, repository (*fml*).

repetition *n* restatement, reiteration, recapitulation, echo, return, reappearance, recurrence, duplication, tautology.

repetitive *adj* recurrent, monotonous, tedious, boring, dull, mechanical, unchanging, unvaried.

replace *v* 1 *replace the lid*: put back, return, restore, make good, reinstate, re-establish. 2 SUPERSEDE, succeed, follow, supplant, oust, deputize, substitute.

replacement *n* substitute, stand-in, understudy, fill-in, supply, proxy, surrogate, successor.

replenish *v* refill, restock, reload, recharge, replace, restore, renew, supply, provide, furnish, stock, fill, top up.

replica *n* model, imitation, reproduction, facsimile, copy, duplicate, clone.

replicate *v* repeat, duplicate, copy, mimic, follow, reduplicate, reproduce, recreate, clone, ape.

reply *v* answer, respond, retort, rejoin, react, acknowledge, return, echo, reciprocate, counter, retaliate.
➤ *n* answer, response, retort, rejoinder, riposte, repartee, reaction, comeback, acknowledgement, return, echo, retaliation.

report *n* 1 ACCOUNT, article, piece, item, write-up, record, relation, narrative, description, story, tale, statement, communiqué, bulletin, register, chronicle, minutes, declaration, announcement, communication, information, news, word,

message, note, brief, file, dossier, delineation (*fml*). 2 GOSSIP, hearsay, rumour, talk. 3 REPUTATION, honour, character, standing, stature, opinion, credit, repute, fame, renown, celebrity, distinction, name, esteem (*fml*). 4 EXPLOSION, shot, bang, crack, boom, crash, reverberation, noise.
➤ *v* 1 STATE, announce, declare, proclaim, air, broadcast, relay, publish, circulate, pass on, communicate, notify, tell, recount, relate, narrate, describe, detail, set forth, disclose, divulge, cover, document, chronicle, record, note, delineate (*fml*). 2 COMPLAIN, inform on, tell on (*infml*), shop (*infml*), squeal (*infml*), rat (*infml*), split (*infml*), blow the whistle on (*infml*), grass (*sl*).

reporter *n* journalist, correspondent, columnist, newspaperman, newspaperwoman, hack, newscaster, commentator, announcer.

repository *n* store, storehouse, depository, depot, warehouse, safe, bank, treasury, vault, archive, container, receptacle, magazine.

represent *v* stand for, symbolize, designate, denote, mean, express, evoke, depict, portray, describe, picture, draw, sketch, illustrate, exemplify, typify, epitomize, embody, personify, appear as, act as, enact, perform, show, exhibit, be, amount to, constitute.

representation *n* 1 LIKENESS, image, icon, picture, portrait, illustration, sketch, model, statue, bust, depiction, portrayal, description, account, explanation.
2 PERFORMANCE, production, play, show, spectacle.

representative *n* delegate, deputy, proxy, stand-in, spokesperson, spokesman, spokeswoman, ambassador, commissioner, agent, salesman, saleswoman, rep (*infml*), traveller.
➤ *adj* typical, illustrative, exemplary, archetypal, characteristic, usual, normal, symbolic.
E3 unrepresentative, atypical.

repress *v* inhibit, check, control, curb, restrain, suppress, bottle up, hold back, stifle, smother, muffle, silence, quell, crush, quash, subdue, overpower, overcome, master, subjugate, oppress.

repression *n* inhibition, restraint, suppression, suffocation, gagging, censorship, authoritarianism, despotism, tyranny, oppression, domination, control, constraint, coercion.

repressive adj oppressive, authoritarian, despotic, tyrannical, dictatorial, autocratic, totalitarian, absolute, harsh, severe, tough, coercive.

reprieve v pardon, let off, spare, rescue, redeem, relieve, respite.
➤ n pardon, amnesty, suspension, abeyance, postponement, deferment, remission, respite, relief, let-up (*infml*), abatement (*fml*).

reprimand n rebuke, reproof, reproach, admonition, telling-off (*infml*), ticking-off (*infml*), lecture, talking-to (*infml*), dressing-down (*infml*), censure, blame.
➤ v rebuke, reprove, reproach, admonish, scold, chide, tell off (*infml*), tick off (*infml*), lecture, criticize, slate (*infml*), censure, blame.

reprisal n retaliation, counter-attack, retribution, requital, revenge, vengeance.

reproach v rebuke, reprove, reprimand, upbraid, scold, chide, reprehend, blame, censure, condemn, criticize, disparage, defame.
➤ n rebuke, reproof, reprimand, scolding, blame, censure, condemnation, criticism, disapproval, scorn, contempt, shame, disgrace.

reproachful adj reproving, upbraiding, scolding, censorious, critical, fault-finding, disapproving, scornful.
🆎 complimentary.

reprobate adj immoral, corrupt, depraved, sinful, unprincipled, vile, wicked, bad, shameless, incorrigible, dissolute, degenerate, base, abandoned, hardened, damned, profligate (*fml*).
🆎 upright, virtuous.
➤ n degenerate, miscreant, rake, roué, wrongdoer, criminal, evildoer, sinner, rogue, rascal, scoundrel, scamp, scallywag, villain, vagabond, wretch, mischief-maker, ne'er-do-well, knave, dastard, troublemaker, profligate (*fml*).

reproduce v 1 COPY, transcribe, print, duplicate, mirror, echo, repeat, imitate, emulate, match, simulate, recreate, reconstruct. 2 BREED, spawn, procreate, generate, propagate, multiply.

reproduction n 1 COPY, print, picture, duplicate, facsimile, replica, clone, imitation. 2 BREEDING, procreation,

generation, propagation, multiplication.
🆎 1 original.

reproductive adj procreative, generative, sexual, sex, genital.

reproof n rebuke, reproach, reprimand, admonition, upbraiding, dressing-down (*infml*), scolding, telling-off (*infml*), ticking-off (*infml*), censure, condemnation, criticism.
🆎 praise.

reprove v rebuke, reproach, reprimand, upbraid, scold, chide, tell off (*infml*), reprehend, admonish, censure, condemn, criticize.
🆎 praise.

reptile

> Reptiles include: adder, puff adder, grass snake, tree snake, asp, viper, rattlesnake, sidewinder, anaconda, boa constrictor, cobra, king cobra, mamba, python; lizard, frilled lizard, chameleon, gecko, iguana, skink, slow-worm; turtle, green turtle, hawksbill turtle, terrapin, tortoise, giant tortoise; alligator, crocodile. *see also* **dinosaur**.

repudiate v reject, denounce, deny, renounce, disown, discard, retract, reverse, revoke, cast off, desert, abandon, divorce, abjure (*fml*), disaffirm (*fml*), disavow (*fml*), disclaim (*fml*), disprofess (*fml*), forsake (*fml*), rescind (*fml*), not touch with a barge pole (*infml*), not have anything to do with (*infml*), have nothing to do with (*infml*), turn one's back on (*infml*).
🆎 admit, own.

repugnance n reluctance, distaste, dislike, aversion, hatred, loathing, abhorrence (*fml*), horror, repulsion, revulsion, disgust.
🆎 liking, pleasure, delight.

repulsion n revulsion, disgust, distaste, hatred, aversion, loathing, repugnance (*fml*), abhorrence (*fml*), detestation (*fml*), disrelish (*fml*), repellence (*fml*), repellency (*fml*).
🆎 liking.

repulsive adj repellent, repugnant, revolting, disgusting, nauseating, sickening, offensive, distasteful, objectionable, obnoxious, foul, vile, loathsome, abominable, abhorrent, hateful, horrid, unpleasant, disagreeable, ugly, hideous, forbidding.
🆎 attractive, pleasant, delightful.

reputable *adj* respectable, reliable, dependable, trustworthy, upright, honourable, creditable, worthy, good, excellent, irreproachable.
F3 disreputable, infamous.

reputation *n* honour, character, standing, stature, esteem (*fml*), opinion, credit, repute, fame, renown, celebrity, distinction, name, good name, bad name, infamy, notoriety.

repute *n* reputation, name, standing, stature, renown, fame, good name, celebrity, distinction, esteem (*fml*), estimation (*fml*).
F3 infamy.

reputed *adj* alleged, supposed, said, rumoured, believed, thought, considered, regarded, estimated, reckoned, held, seeming, apparent, ostensible (*fml*).
F3 actual, true.

reputedly *adv* allegedly, apparently, seemingly, supposedly, reputatively, ostensibly (*fml*).
F3 actually.

request *v* ask for, solicit, demand, require, seek, desire, beg, entreat, supplicate, petition, appeal.
➤ *n* appeal, call, demand, requisition, desire, application, solicitation, suit, petition, entreaty, supplication, prayer.

require *v* 1 NEED, want, wish, desire, lack, miss. 2 *you are required to attend*: oblige, force, compel, constrain, make, ask, request, instruct, direct, order, demand, necessitate, take, involve.

required *adj* compulsory, essential, obligatory, recommended, demanded, necessary, stipulated, set, needed, unavoidable, vital, mandatory (*fml*), prescribed (*fml*), requisite (*fml*).
F3 optional, inessential.

requirement *n* need, necessity, essential, must, requisite, prerequisite, demand, stipulation, condition, term, specification, proviso, qualification, provision.

requisite *adj* required, needed, necessary, essential, obligatory, compulsory, set, prescribed (*fml*).

requisition *v* request, put in for, demand, commandeer, appropriate, take, confiscate, seize, occupy.
➤ *n* commandeering, confiscation, seizure, takeover, occupation, order, use, application, summons, request, call, demand, appropriation (*fml*).

rescind *v* cancel, set aside, overturn, quash, reverse, recall, repeal, annul, invalidate, void, negate, abrogate (*fml*), countermand (*fml*), nullify (*fml*), retract (*fml*), revoke (*fml*).
F3 enforce.

rescue *v* save, recover, salvage, deliver, free, liberate, release, redeem, ransom.
F3 capture, imprison.
➤ *n* saving, recovery, salvage, deliverance, liberation, release, redemption, salvation.
F3 capture.

research *n* investigation, inquiry, fact-finding, groundwork, examination, analysis, scrutiny, study, search, probe, exploration, experimentation.
➤ *v* investigate, examine, analyse, scrutinize, study, search, probe, explore, experiment.

resemblance *n* likeness, similarity, sameness, parity, conformity, closeness, affinity, parallel, comparison, analogy, correspondence, image, facsimile.
F3 dissimilarity.

resemble *v* be like, look like, take after, favour, mirror, echo, duplicate, parallel, approach.
F3 differ from.

resent *v* grudge, begrudge, envy, take offence at, take umbrage at, take amiss, object to, grumble at, take exception to, dislike.
F3 accept, like.

resentful *adj* grudging, envious, jealous, bitter, embittered, hurt, wounded, offended, aggrieved, put out, miffed (*infml*), peeved (*infml*), indignant, angry, vindictive.
F3 satisfied, contented.

resentment *n* grudge, envy, jealousy, bitterness, spite, malice, ill-will, ill-feeling, animosity, hurt, umbrage, pique, displeasure, irritation, indignation, vexation, anger, vindictiveness.
F3 contentment, happiness.

reservation *n* 1 DOUBT, scepticism, misgiving, qualm, scruple, hesitation, second thought. 2 PROVISO, stipulation, qualification. 3 RESERVE, preserve, park, sanctuary, homeland, enclave. 4 BOOKING, engagement, appointment.

reserve *v* 1 SET APART, earmark, keep, retain, hold back, save, store, stockpile.

2 *reserve a seat*: book, engage, order, secure.
☒ 1 use up.
➤ *n* **1** STORE, stock, supply, fund, stockpile, cache, hoard, savings. **2** SHYNESS, reticence, secretiveness, coolness, aloofness, modesty, restraint.
3 RESERVATION, preserve, park, sanctuary.
4 REPLACEMENT, substitute, stand-in.
☒ 2 friendliness, openness.

reserved *adj* **1** BOOKED, engaged, taken, spoken for, set aside, earmarked, meant, intended, designated, destined, saved, held, kept, retained. **2** SHY, retiring, reticent, unforthcoming, uncommunicative, secretive, silent, taciturn, unsociable, cool, aloof, standoffish, unapproachable, modest, restrained, cautious.
☒ 1 unreserved, free, available. **2** friendly, open.

reservoir *n* **1** LAKE, pond, pool, loch. **2** TANK, cistern, vat, basin, container, receptacle. **3** STORE, stockpile, stock, supply, source, reserves, accumulation, fund, holder, bank, repository (*fml*), reservatory (*fml*).

reshuffle *n* reorganization, shake-up, upheaval, redistribution, regrouping, rearrangement, realignment, restructuring, revision, change, interchange.
➤ *v* reorganize, restructure, shake up, change, interchange, shift, shuffle, revise, rearrange, regroup, realign, redistribute.

reside *v* live, inhabit, dwell, lodge, stay, sojourn, settle, remain.

residence *n* dwelling, habitation, domicile, abode, seat, place, home, house, lodgings, quarters, hall, manor, mansion, palace, villa, country-house, country-seat.

resident *n* inhabitant, citizen, local, householder, occupier, tenant, lodger, guest.
☒ non-resident.

residual *adj* remaining, left-over, unused, unconsumed, net.

residue *n* remainder, remains, remnant, rest, surplus, excess, extra, overflow, balance, difference, lees, dregs, left-overs.
☒ core.

resign *v* stand down, leave, quit, abdicate, vacate, renounce, relinquish, forgo, waive, surrender, yield, abandon, forsake.
☒ join.

♦ **resign oneself** reconcile oneself, accept, bow, submit, yield, comply, acquiesce.
☒ resist.

resignation *n* **1** STANDING-DOWN, abdication, retirement, departure, notice, renunciation, relinquishment, surrender.
2 ACCEPTANCE, acquiescence, submission, non-resistance, passivity, patience, stoicism, defeatism.
☒ 2 resistance.

resigned *adj* reconciled, philosophical, stoical, patient, unprotesting, unresisting, submissive, defeatist.
☒ resistant.

resilient *adj* **1** *resilient material*: flexible, pliable, supple, plastic, elastic, springy, bouncy. **2** STRONG, tough, hardy, adaptable, buoyant.
☒ 1 rigid, brittle.

resist *v* oppose, defy, confront, fight, combat, weather, withstand, repel, counteract, check, avoid, refuse.
☒ submit, accept.

resistance *n* opposition, defiance, confrontation, fight, fighting, struggle, combat, contention, counteraction, battle, withstanding, repulsion, avoidance, refusal, prevention, thwart, hindrance, obstruction, impedance, impediment, restraint, intransigence (*fml*).
☒ acceptance, submission.

resistant *adj* **1** OPPOSED, antagonistic, defiant, unyielding, intransigent, unwilling. **2** PROOF, impervious, immune, invulnerable, tough, strong.
☒ 1 compliant, yielding.

resolute *adj* determined, resolved, set, fixed, unwavering, staunch, firm, steadfast, relentless, single-minded, persevering, dogged, tenacious, stubborn, obstinate, strong-willed, undaunted, unflinching, bold.
☒ irresolute, weak-willed, half-hearted.

resolution *n* **1** DETERMINATION, resolve, willpower, commitment, dedication, devotion, firmness, steadfastness, persistence, perseverance, doggedness, tenacity, zeal, courage, boldness.
2 DECISION, judgement, finding, declaration, proposition, motion.
☒ 1 half-heartedness, uncertainty, indecision.

resolve *v* decide, make up one's mind, determine, fix, settle, conclude, sort out, work out, solve.

➤ *n* determination, willpower, commitment, dedication, devotion, constancy, firmness, intentness, seriousness, earnestness, steadfastness, persistence, perseverance, doggedness, inflexibility, tenacity, zeal, courage, boldness, sense of purpose.

🔁 indecision.

resort *v* go, visit, frequent, patronize, haunt.

➤ *n* **1** HOLIDAY CENTRE, centre, spot, health resort, spa. **2** RECOURSE, refuge, course (of action), measure, step, alternative, option, chance, possibility, expedient (*fml*).

♦ **resort to** turn to, use, utilize, employ, exercise.

resound *v* resonate, reverberate, echo, re-echo, ring, boom, thunder.

resounding *adj* **1** RESONANT, reverberating, echoing, ringing, sonorous, booming, thunderous, full, rich, vibrant. **2** *a resounding victory*: decisive, conclusive, crushing, thorough.

🔁 **1** faint.

resource *n* **1** SUPPLY, reserve, stockpile, source, expedient, contrivance, device. **2** RESOURCEFULNESS, initiative, ingenuity, inventiveness, talent, ability, capability.

resourceful *adj* ingenious, imaginative, creative, inventive, innovative, original, clever, bright, sharp, quick-witted, able, capable, talented.

resources *n* materials, supplies, reserves, holdings, funds, money, wealth, riches, capital, assets, property, means.

respect *v* **1** ADMIRE, regard, have a good opinion of, think highly of, hold in high regard, set great store by, appreciate, value, praise, honour, approve of, revere, esteem (*fml*), venerate (*fml*). **2** OBEY, observe, heed, follow, adhere to, honour, fulfil, comply with (*fml*). **3** CONSIDER, show consideration for, pay attention to, take into account, show regard for, take cognizance of (*fml*).

🔁 **1** despise, scorn. **2** ignore, disobey.

➤ *n* **1** ADMIRATION, appreciation, recognition, honour, deference, reverence, high opinion, regard, high regard, homage, esteem (*fml*), veneration (*fml*), approbation (*fml*), obeisance (*fml*). **2** CONSIDERATION, attention, attentiveness, notice, regard, heed, thoughtfulness, politeness, courtesy, cognizance (*fml*). **3**

GREETINGS, compliments, regards, salutations, best wishes, good wishes, devoirs (*fml*). **4** *in every respect*: point, aspect, facet, feature, characteristic, particular, detail, sense, matter, way, regard, reference, bearing, relation, connection.

🔁 **1** disrespect.

respectable *adj* **1** HONOURABLE, worthy, respected, dignified, upright, honest, decent, clean-living. **2** ACCEPTABLE, tolerable, passable, adequate, fair, reasonable, appreciable, considerable.

🔁 **1** dishonourable, disreputable. **2** inadequate, paltry.

respectful *adj* deferential, reverential, humble, polite, well-mannered, courteous, civil.

🔁 disrespectful.

respective *adj* corresponding, relevant, various, several, separate, individual, personal, own, particular, special.

respite *n* **1** PAUSE, rest, relief, break, adjournment, intermission, recess, relaxation, interval, interruption, halt, gap, lull, cessation (*fml*), hiatus (*fml*), breather (*infml*), let-up (*infml*). **2** DELAY, reprieve, postponement, deferment, remission, stay, suspension, moratorium, abatement (*fml*).

respond *v* answer, reply, retort, acknowledge, react, return, reciprocate.

response *n* answer, reply, retort, comeback, acknowledgement, reaction, feedback.

🔁 query.

responsibility *n* fault, blame, guilt, culpability, answerability, accountability, duty, obligation, burden, onus, charge, care, trust, authority, power.

responsible *adj* **1** GUILTY, culpable, at fault, to blame, liable, answerable, accountable. **2** DEPENDABLE, reliable, conscientious, trustworthy, honest, sound, steady, sober, mature, sensible, rational. **3** IMPORTANT, authoritative, executive, decision-making.

🔁 **2** irresponsible, unreliable, untrustworthy.

responsive *adj* alert, aware, sensitive, awake, open, sharp, reactive, amenable, receptive, susceptible, sympathetic, perceptive, forthcoming, impressionable, alive, respondent, responsorial (*fml*), on the ball (*infml*), with it (*infml*).

🔁 unresponsive.

rest¹ n **1** LEISURE, relaxation, repose, lie-down, sleep, snooze, nap, siesta, idleness, inactivity, motionlessness, standstill, stillness, tranquillity, calm. **2** BREAK, pause, breathing-space, breather (*infml*), intermission, interlude, interval, recess, holiday, vacation, halt, cessation (*fml*), lull, respite. **3** SUPPORT, prop, stand, base.
Ea 1 action, activity. **2** work.
➤ v **1** PAUSE, halt, stop, cease. **2** RELAX, repose, sit, recline, lounge, laze, lie down, sleep, snooze, doze. **3** DEPEND, rely, hinge, hang, lie. **4** LEAN, prop, support, stand.
Ea 1 continue. **2** work.

rest² n remainder, others, balance, surplus, excess, residue, remains, left-overs, remnants.

restaurant n eating-house, bistro, steakhouse, grill room, dining-room, snack-bar, buffet, cafeteria, café.

restful adj relaxing, soothing, calm, tranquil, serene, peaceful, quiet, undisturbed, relaxed, comfortable, leisurely, unhurried.
Ea tiring, restless.

restitution n amends, reparation, requital, restoration, restoring, return, satisfaction, redress, repayment, damages, compensation, recompense, remuneration, refund, reimbursement, indemnification, indemnity.

restive adj **1** UNRULY, impatient, wayward, wilful, turbulent, uncontrollable, undisciplined, unmanageable, recalcitrant (*fml*), refractory (*fml*). **2** RESTLESS, agitated, fidgety, fidgeting, unsettled, nervous, uneasy, anxious, fretful, tense, edgy, jumpy (*infml*), uptight (*infml*).
Ea 2 calm, relaxed.

restless adj fidgety, unsettled, disturbed, troubled, agitated, nervous, anxious, worried, uneasy, fretful, edgy, jumpy (*fml*), restive, unruly, turbulent, sleepless.
Ea calm, relaxed, comfortable.

restoration n **1** RENOVATION, repair, refurbishing, rebuilding, reconstruction, renewal, rehabilitation. **2** REVIVAL, refreshment, rejuvenation, revitalization, recovery, kiss of life (*infml*). **3** RETURN, replacement, reinstallation, restitution, reinstatement, re-establishment.
Ea 1 damage. **2** weakening. **3** removal.

restore v **1** REPLACE, return, reinstate, rehabilitate, re-establish, reintroduce, re-enforce. **2** *restore a building*: renovate,

renew, rebuild, reconstruct, refurbish, retouch, recondition, repair, mend, fix. **3** REVIVE, refresh, rejuvenate, revitalize, strengthen.
Ea 1 remove. **2** damage. **3** weaken.

restrain v hold back, keep back, suppress, subdue, repress, inhibit, check, curb, bridle, stop, arrest, prevent, bind, tie, chain, fetter, manacle, imprison, jail, confine, restrict, regulate, control, govern.
Ea encourage, liberate.

restrained adj moderate, temperate, mild, subdued, muted, quiet, soft, low-key, unobtrusive, discreet, tasteful, calm, controlled, steady, self-controlled.
Ea unrestrained.

restraint n moderation, inhibition, self-control, self-discipline, hold, grip, check, curb, rein, bridle, suppression, bondage, captivity, confinement, imprisonment, bonds, chains, fetters, straitjacket, restriction, control, constraint, limitation, tie, hindrance, prevention.
Ea liberty.

restrict v limit, bound, demarcate, control, regulate, confine, contain, cramp, constrain, impede, hinder, hamper, handicap, tie, restrain, curtail.
Ea broaden, free.

restriction n limit, bound, confine, limitation, constraint, handicap, check, curb, restraint, ban, embargo, control, regulation, rule, stipulation, condition, proviso.
Ea freedom.

result n effect, consequence, sequel, repercussion, reaction, outcome, upshot, issue, end-product, fruit, score, answer, verdict, judgement, decision, conclusion.
Ea cause.
➤ v follow, ensue, happen, occur, issue, emerge, arise, spring, derive, stem, flow, proceed, develop, end, finish, terminate, culminate.
Ea cause.

resume v restart, recommence, reopen, reconvene, continue, carry on, go on, proceed.
Ea cease.

résumé n summary, précis, synopsis, outline, sketch, breakdown, abstract, digest, recapitulation, review, overview, run-down, epitome.

resumption n restart, recommencement, reopening,

renewal, resurgence, continuation.
▪ cessation.

resurgence n reappearance, re-
emergence, resumption, return, rebirth,
resurrection, revival, renaissance,
renascence (*fml*), recrudescence (*fml*),
revivification (*fml*), risorgimento (*fml*).
▪ decrease.

resurrect v restore, revive, resuscitate,
reactivate, bring back, reintroduce, renew.
▪ kill, bury.

resurrection n restoration, revival,
resuscitation, renaissance, rebirth,
renewal, resurgence, reappearance,
return, comeback.

resuscitate v revive, resurrect, save,
rescue, reanimate, quicken, reinvigorate,
revitalize, restore, renew.

retain v 1 KEEP, hold, reserve, hold back,
save, preserve. 2 *retain information*:
remember, memorize. 3 EMPLOY, engage,
hire, commission.
▪ 1 release. 2 forget. 3 dismiss.

retainer n 1 FEE, retaining fee, deposit,
advance. 2 SERVANT, lackey, footman,
domestic, attendant, supporter, valet,
dependant, vassal, menial.

retaliate v reciprocate, counter-attack, hit
back, strike back, fight back, get one's own
back, get even with, take revenge.

retaliation n reprisal, counter-attack,
revenge, vengeance, retribution.

retard v slow down, delay, hold up,
decelerate, brake, put a/the brake on,
handicap, incapacitate, obstruct, hinder,
impede, check, curb, restrict.
▪ speed up, accelerate.

retch v vomit, heave, reach, disgorge (*fml*),
regurgitate, gag, puke (*infml*), spew (*infml*),
throw up (*infml*).

reticent adj reserved, shy,
uncommunicative, unforthcoming, tight-
lipped, secretive, taciturn, silent, quiet.
▪ communicative, forward, frank.

retinue n entourage, following, followers,
personnel, staff, suite, train, attendants,
escort, cortège, aides, servants.

retire v leave, depart, withdraw, retreat,
recede.
▪ join, enter, advance.

retirement n withdrawal, retreat,
solitude, loneliness, seclusion, privacy,
obscurity.

retiring adj shy, bashful, timid, shrinking,

quiet, reticent, reserved, self-effacing,
unassertive, modest, unassuming,
humble.
▪ bold, forward, assertive.

retort v answer, reply, respond, rejoin,
return, counter, retaliate.
➤ n answer, reply, response, rejoinder,
riposte, repartee, quip.

retract v take back, withdraw, recant,
reverse, revoke, rescind, cancel, repeal,
repudiate, disown, disclaim, deny.
▪ assert, maintain.

retreat v draw back, recoil, shrink, turn
tail (*infml*), withdraw, retire, leave, depart,
quit.
▪ advance.
➤ n 1 WITHDRAWAL, departure,
evacuation, flight. 2 SECLUSION, privacy,
hideaway, den, refuge, asylum, sanctuary,
shelter, haven.
▪ 1 advance, charge.

retrenchment n cutback, cutting back,
cut, economy, reduction, pruning,
curtailment, cost-cutting, run-down,
contraction, shrinkage, tightening one's
belt (*infml*).
▪ increase.

retribution n punishment, reckoning,
justice, satisfaction, retaliation, requital,
reward, reprisal, redress, repayment,
payment, compensation, recompense,
revenge, vengeance, Nemesis, just deserts
(*infml*).

retrieve v fetch, bring back, regain, get
back, recapture, repossess, recoup,
recover, salvage, save, rescue, redeem,
restore, return.
▪ lose.

retrograde adj retrogressive, backward,
reverse, negative, downward, declining,
deteriorating.
▪ progressive.

retrospect n hindsight, afterthought, re-
examination, review, recollection,
remembrance.
▪ prospect.

return v 1 COME BACK, reappear, recur, go
back, backtrack, regress, revert. 2 GIVE
BACK, hand back, send back, deliver, put
back, replace, restore. 3 *return a favour*:
reciprocate, requite, repay, refund,
reimburse, recompense.
▪ 1 leave, depart. 2 take.
➤ n 1 REAPPEARANCE, recurrence,
comeback, home-coming. 2 REPAYMENT,

recompense, replacement, restoration, reinstatement, reciprocation. **3** REVENUE, income, proceeds, takings, yield, gain, profit, reward, advantage, benefit.
🔁 **1** departure, disappearance. **2** removal. **3** payment, expense, loss.

revamp v renovate, recondition, rebuild, reconstruct, repair, restore, revise, refit, refurbish, rehabilitate, overhaul, recast, do up (*infml*).

reveal v expose, uncover, unveil, unmask, show, display, exhibit, manifest, disclose, divulge, betray, leak, tell, impart, communicate, broadcast, publish, announce, proclaim.
🔁 hide, conceal, mask.

revelation n uncovering, unveiling, exposure, unmasking, show, display, exhibition, manifestation, disclosure, confession, admission, betrayed, giveaway, leak, news, information, communication, broadcasting, publication, announcement, proclamation.

revel in v enjoy, relish, savour, delight in, thrive on, bask in, glory in, lap up, indulge in, wallow in, luxuriate in.

reveller n celebrator, party-goer, pleasure-seeker, merrymaker, carouser, roisterer, wassailer, bacchanal.

revelry n celebration, festivity, party, merrymaking, jollity, fun, carousal, debauchery.
🔁 sobriety.

revenge n vengeance, satisfaction, reprisal, retaliation, requital, retribution.
➤ v avenge, repay, retaliate, get one's own back.

revenue n income, return, yield, interest, profit, gain, proceeds, receipts, takings.
🔁 expenditure.

reverberate v echo, re-echo, resound, resonate, ring, boom, vibrate.

reverberation n **1** ECHO, re-echoing, resounding, resonance, ringing, vibration, wave, rebound, recoil, reflection. **2** *reverberations following the resignation*: repercussion, effect, consequence, result, shock wave (*infml*), ripple (*infml*).

revere v respect, esteem, honour, pay homage to, venerate, worship, adore, exalt.
🔁 despise, scorn.

reverence n respect, deference, honour,

homage, admiration, awe, veneration, worship, adoration, devotion.
🔁 contempt, scorn.

reverent adj reverential, respectful, deferential, humble, dutiful, awed, solemn, pious, devout, adoring, loving.
🔁 irreverent, disrespectful.

reverie n daydream, daydreaming, musing, trance, abstraction, absent-mindedness, inattention, preoccupation, brown study, woolgathering.

reversal n negation, cancellation, annulment, nullification (*fml*), countermanding (*fml*), revocation (*fml*), rescinding (*fml*), repeal, reverse, turnabout, turnaround, U-turn, volte-face, upset.
🔁 advancement, progress.

reverse v **1** BACK, retreat, backtrack, undo, negate, cancel, annul, invalidate, countermand, overrule, revoke, rescind, repeal, retract, quash, overthrow.
2 TRANSPOSE, turn round, invert, up-end, overturn, upset, change, alter.
🔁 **1** advance, enforce.
➤ n **1** UNDERSIDE, back, rear, inverse, converse, contrary, opposite, antithesis.
2 MISFORTUNE, mishap, misadventure, adversity, affliction, hardship, trial, blow, disappointment, setback, check, delay, problem, difficulty, failure, defeat.
➤ adj opposite, contrary, converse, inverse, inverted, backward, back, rear.

revert v return, go back, resume, lapse, relapse, regress.

review v **1** CRITICIZE, assess, evaluate, judge, weigh, discuss, examine, inspect, scrutinize, study, survey, recapitulate.
2 *review the situation*: reassess, re-evaluate, re-examine, reconsider, rethink, revise.
➤ n **1** CRITICISM, critique, assessment, evaluation, judgement, report, commentary, examination, scrutiny, analysis, study, survey, recapitulation, reassessment, re-evaluation, re-examination, revision. **2** MAGAZINE, periodical, journal.

reviewer n commentator, critic, judge, observer, connoisseur, arbiter, essayist.

revile v despise, hate, scorn, slander, libel, defame, abuse, smear, reproach, malign, blackguard, denigrate (*fml*), traduce (*fml*), vituperate (*fml*), vilify (*fml*).
🔁 praise.

revise v 1 *revise one's opinion*: change, alter, modify, amend, correct, update, edit, rewrite, reword, recast, revamp, reconsider, re-examine, review. 2 STUDY, learn, swot up (*infml*), cram (*infml*).

revision n 1 CHANGE, amendment, editing, modification, alteration, correction, recast, recasting, re-examination, reconstruction, review, rewriting, rereading, emendation (*fml*). 2 STUDYING, memorizing, homework, learning, updating, swotting (*infml*).

revitalize v revive, renew, restore, refresh, reactivate, reanimate, rejuvenate, resurrect.
ᴇᴀ dampen, suppress.

revival n resuscitation, revitalization, restoration, renewal, renaissance, rebirth, reawakening, resurgence, upsurge.

revive v resuscitate, reanimate, revitalize, restore, renew, refresh, animate, invigorate, quicken, rouse, awaken, recover, rally, reawaken, rekindle, reactivate.
ᴇᴀ weary.

revoke v repeal, rescind, quash, abrogate, annul, nullify, invalidate, negate, cancel, countermand, reverse, retract, withdraw.
ᴇᴀ enforce.

revolt n revolution, rebellion, mutiny, rising, uprising, insurrection, putsch, coup (d'état), secession, defection.
➤ v 1 REBEL, mutiny, rise, riot, resist, dissent, defect. 2 DISGUST, sicken, nauseate, repel, offend, shock, outrage, scandalize.
ᴇᴀ 1 submit. 2 please, delight.

revolting adj disgusting, sickening, nauseating, repulsive, repellent, obnoxious, nasty, horrible, foul, loathsome, abhorrent, distasteful, offensive, shocking, appalling.
ᴇᴀ pleasant, delightful, attractive, palatable.

revolution n 1 REVOLT, rebellion, mutiny, rising, uprising, insurrection, putsch, coup (d'état), reformation, change, transformation, innovation, upheaval, cataclysm. 2 ROTATION, turn, spin, cycle, circuit, round, circle, orbit, gyration.

revolutionary n rebel, mutineer, insurgent, anarchist, revolutionist.
➤ adj 1 REBEL, rebellious, mutinous, insurgent, subversive, seditious, anarchistic. 2 *revolutionary ideas*: new,

innovative, avant-garde, different, drastic, radical, thoroughgoing.
ᴇᴀ 1 conservative.

revolutionize v transform, reform, restructure, cause radical changes in, reorganize, transfigure, turn upside-down.

revolve v rotate, turn, pivot, swivel, spin, wheel, whirl, gyrate, circle, orbit.

revulsion n repugnance, disgust, distaste, dislike, aversion, hatred, loathing, abhorrence, abomination.
ᴇᴀ delight, pleasure, approval.

reward n prize, honour, medal, decoration, bounty, pay-off, bonus, premium, payment, remuneration, recompense, repayment, requital, compensation, gain, profit, return, benefit, merit, desert, retribution.
ᴇᴀ punishment.
➤ v pay, remunerate, recompense, repay, requite, compensate, honour, decorate.
ᴇᴀ punish.

rewarding adj profitable, remunerative, lucrative, productive, fruitful, worthwhile, valuable, advantageous, beneficial, satisfying, gratifying, pleasing, fulfilling, enriching.
ᴇᴀ unrewarding.

rewrite v revise, rework, reword, redraft, recast, correct, edit, emend (*fml*).

rhetoric n eloquence, oratory, grandiloquence, magniloquence, bombast, pomposity, hyperbole, verbosity, wordiness.

Rhetorical devices include: abscission, alliteration, amplification, anacoluthon, anadiplosis, anaphora, anastrophe, anticlimax, antimetabole, antimetathesis, antiphrasis, antithesis, antonomasia, aporia, apostrophe, asyndeton, auxesis, bathos, catachresis, chiasmus, climax, diallage, diegesis, dissimile, double entendre, dramatic irony, dysphemism, ellipsis, enantiosis, enumeration, epanadiplosis, epanalepsis, epanaphora, epanodos, epanorthosis, epigram, epiphonema, epistrophe, epizeuxis, erotema, erotetic, euphemism, figure of speech, hendiadys, hypallage, hyperbole, hypostrophe, hypotyposis, hysteron-proteron, increment, innuendo, irony, litotes, meiosis, metalepsis, metaphor, mixed metaphor, metonymy, onomatopoeia, oxymoron, parabole, paradox, paraleipsis, parenthesis, pathetic fallacy, personification, prolepsis, pun, rhetorical question, simile, syllepsis, symploce, synchoresis, synchrysis, synecdoche, synoeciosis, tautology, transferred epithet, trope, vicious circle, zeugma.

rhetorical *adj* oratorical, grandiloquent, magniloquent, bombastic, declamatory, pompous, high-sounding, grand, high-flown, flowery, florid, flamboyant, showy, pretentious, artificial, insincere.
Ea simple.

rhyme *n* poetry, verse, poem, ode, limerick, jingle, song, ditty.

rhythm *n* beat, pulse, time, tempo, metre, measure, movement, flow, lilt, swing, accent, cadence, pattern.

rhythmic *adj* rhythmical, metric, metrical, pulsating, throbbing, flowing, lilting, periodic, regular, steady.

ribald *adj* rude, obscene, risqué, racy, off-colour, bawdy, earthy, coarse, smutty (*infml*), vulgar, filthy, foul-mouthed, gross, base, scurrilous, low, mean, lewd, disrespectful, licentious (*fml*), indecent, irreverent, satirical, jeering, mocking, derisive, Rabelaisian, blue (*infml*), naughty (*infml*).
Ea polite.

rich *adj* **1** WEALTHY, affluent, moneyed, prosperous, well-to-do, well-off, loaded (*sl*). **2** PLENTIFUL, abundant, copious, profuse, prolific, ample, full. **3** FERTILE, fruitful, productive, lush. **4** *rich food*: creamy, fatty, full-bodied, heavy, full-flavoured, strong, spicy, savoury, tasty, delicious, luscious, juicy, sweet. **5** *rich colours*: deep, intense, vivid, bright, vibrant, warm. **6** EXPENSIVE, precious, valuable, lavish, sumptuous, opulent, luxurious, splendid, gorgeous, fine, elaborate, ornate.
Ea 1 poor, impoverished. **3** barren. **4** plain, bland. **5** dull, soft. **6** plain.

riches *n* wealth, affluence, money, gold, treasure, fortune, assets, property, substance, resources, means.
Ea poverty.

richly *adv* **1** LAVISHLY, splendidly, gorgeously, sumptuously, elegantly, elaborately, expensively, exquisitely, luxuriously, palatially, opulently (*fml*). **2** FULLY, thoroughly, completely, well, strongly, suitably, appropriately, properly.
Ea 1 poorly, scantily.

rickety *adj* unsteady, wobbly, shaky, unstable, insecure, flimsy, jerry-built, decrepit, ramshackle, broken-down, dilapidated, derelict.
Ea stable, strong.

rid *v* free, deliver, relieve, unburden, clear, purge, cleanse, purify.
♦ get rid of throw away, throw out, dispose of, discard, dump, scrap, jettison, abolish, put an end to, eliminate, do away with, chuck (out) (*infml*), ditch (*infml*), junk (*infml*).

riddle[1] *n* enigma, mystery, conundrum, brain-teaser, puzzle, poser, problem.

riddle[2] *v* **1** PERFORATE, pierce, puncture, pepper, fill, permeate, pervade, infest. **2** SIFT, sieve, strain, filter, mar, winnow.

ride *v* sit, move, progress, travel, journey, gallop, trot, pedal, drive, steer, control, handle, manage.
➤ *n* journey, trip, outing, jaunt, spin, drive, lift.

ridicule *n* satire, irony, sarcasm, mockery, jeering, scorn, derision, taunting, teasing, chaff, banter, badinage, laughter.
Ea praise.
➤ *v* satirize, send up (*infml*), caricature, lampoon, burlesque, parody, mock, make fun of, jeer, scoff, deride, sneer, tease, rib (*infml*), humiliate, taunt.
Ea praise.

ridiculous *adj* ludicrous, absurd, nonsensical, silly, foolish, stupid, contemptible, derisory, laughable, farcical, comical, funny, hilarious, outrageous, preposterous, incredible, unbelievable.
Ea sensible.

rife *adj* abundant, rampant, teeming, raging, epidemic, prevalent, widespread, general, common, frequent.
Ea scarce.

rifle[1] *n* gun, airgun, firearm, shotgun, musket, carbine, firelock, flintlock, fusil, bundook.

rifle[2] *v* search, rummage, sack, pillage, plunder, ransack, rob, maraud, loot, strip, burgle, gut, despoil (*fml*).

rift *n* **1** SPLIT, breach, break, fracture, crack, fault, chink, cleft, cranny, crevice, gap, space, opening. **2** DISAGREEMENT, difference, separation, division, schism, alienation.
Ea 2 unity.

rig *n* equipment, kit, outfit, gear, tackle, apparatus, machinery, fittings, fixtures.

♦ **rig out** equip, kit out, outfit, fit (out), supply, furnish, clothe, dress (up).

right *adj* **1** *the right answer*: correct, accurate, exact, precise, true, factual, actual, real. **2** PROPER, fitting, seemly, becoming, appropriate, suitable, fit, admissible, satisfactory, reasonable, desirable, favourable, advantageous. **3** FAIR, just, equitable, lawful, honest, upright, good, virtuous, righteous, moral, ethical, honourable. **4** RIGHT-WING, conservative, Tory.
🆚 **1** wrong, incorrect. **2** improper, unsuitable. **3** unfair, wrong. **4** left-wing.
➤ *adv* **1** CORRECTLY, accurately, exactly, precisely, factually, properly, satisfactorily, well, fairly. **2** *right to the bottom*: straight, directly, completely, utterly.
🆚 **1** wrongly, incorrectly, unfairly.
➤ *n* **1** PRIVILEGE, prerogative, due, claim, business, authority, power. **2** JUSTICE, legality, good, virtue, righteousness, morality, honour, integrity, uprightness.
🆚 **2** wrong.
➤ *v* rectify, correct, put right, fix, repair, redress, vindicate, avenge, settle, straighten, stand up.
♦ **right away** straight away, immediately, at once, now, instantly, directly, forthwith, without delay, promptly.
🆚 later, eventually.

righteous *adj* **1** *a righteous person/ action*: just, good, virtuous, moral, worthy, honourable, upright, fair, ethical, equitable, honest, law-abiding, blameless, irreproachable, incorrupt, guiltless, God-fearing, saintly, pure, sinless. **2** *righteous anger*: justifiable, defensible, excusable, warranted, reasonable, supportable, justified, lawful, legal, legitimate, acceptable, explainable, valid, well-founded, proper.
🆚 **1** unrighteous. **2** unjustifiable.

righteousness *n* goodness, honesty, honour, virtue, uprightness, morality, integrity, justice, blamelessness, faithfulness, equity, ethicalness, purity, holiness, sanctification, dharma (*fml*), probity (*fml*), rectitude (*fml*).
🆚 unrighteousness.

rightful *adj* legitimate, lawful, legal, just, bona fide, true, real, genuine, valid, authorized, correct, proper, suitable, due.
🆚 wrongful, unlawful.

rigid *adj* stiff, inflexible, unbending, cast-iron, hard, firm, set, fixed, unalterable,

invariable, austere, harsh, severe, unrelenting, strict, rigorous, stringent, stern, uncompromising, unyielding.
🆚 flexible, elastic.

rigmarole *n* process, bother, performance, fuss, palaver, nonsense, jargon, gibberish, twaddle, carry-on (*infml*), hassle (*infml*), red tape (*infml*), to-do (*infml*).

rigorous *adj* strict, stringent, rigid, firm, exact, precise, accurate, meticulous, painstaking, scrupulous, conscientious, thorough.
🆚 lax, superficial.

rigour *n* **1** TRIAL, hardship, severity, suffering, ordeal, privation (*fml*). **2** THOROUGHNESS, exactness, meticulousness, accuracy, preciseness, precision, conscientiousness, punctiliousness, inflexibility. **3** STRICTNESS, stringency, rigidity, firmness, toughness, harshness, hardship, hardness, severity, sternness, austerity, intransigence (*fml*).
🆚 **3** leniency, mildness.

rile *v* annoy, irritate, nettle, pique, peeve (*infml*), put out, upset, irk, vex, anger, exasperate.
🆚 calm, soothe.

rim *n* lip, edge, brim, brink, verge, margin, border, circumference.
🆚 centre, middle.

rind *n* peel, skin, husk, crust.

ring[1] *n* **1** CIRCLE, round, loop, hoop, halo, band, girdle, collar, circuit, arena, enclosure. **2** GROUP, cartel, syndicate, association, organization, gang, crew, mob, band, cell, clique, coterie.
➤ *v* surround, encircle, gird, circumscribe, encompass, enclose.

ring[2] *v* **1** CHIME, peal, toll, tinkle, clink, jingle, clang, sound, resound, resonate, reverberate, buzz. **2** TELEPHONE, phone, call, ring up.
➤ *n* **1** CHIME, peal, toll, tinkle, clink, jingle, clang. **2** PHONE CALL, call, buzz (*infml*), tinkle (*infml*).

rinse *v* swill, bathe, wash, clean, cleanse, flush, wet, dip.

riot *n* insurrection, rising, uprising, revolt, rebellion, anarchy, lawlessness, affray, disturbance, turbulence, disorder, confusion, commotion, tumult, turmoil, uproar, row, quarrel, strife.
🆚 order, calm.

➤ *v* revolt, rebel, rise up, run riot, run wild, rampage.

riotous *adj* **1** WILD, violent, uncontrollable, unrestrained, unruly, rebellious, lawless, insurrectionary, insubordinate, disorderly, mutinous, ungovernable, wanton. **2** NOISY, loud, rowdy, tumultuous, boisterous, uproarious.
🖃 **1** orderly, restrained.

rip *v* tear, rend, split, separate, rupture, burst, cut, slit, slash, gash, lacerate, hack.
➤ *n* tear, rent, split, cleavage, rupture, cut, slit, slash, gash, hole.
♦ **rip off** (*sl*) overcharge, swindle, defraud, cheat, diddle (*infml*), do (*infml*), fleece, sting (*sl*), con (*infml*), trick, dupe, exploit.

ripe *adj* **1** RIPENED, mature, mellow, seasoned, grown, developed, complete, finished, perfect. **2** READY, suitable, right, favourable, auspicious, propitious, timely, opportune.
🖃 **2** untimely, inopportune.

ripen *v* develop, mature, mellow, season, age.

rip-off *n* robbery, exploitation, cheat, swindle, theft, fraud, diddle (*infml*), con (*infml*), con trick (*infml*), daylight robbery (*infml*), sting (*sl*).

ripple *n* **1** WAVE, disturbance, eddy, gurgle, lapping, ripplet, undulation, burble, babble, purl, wimple. **2** REPERCUSSION, effect, result, consequence, reverberation, shock wave (*infml*).

rise *v* **1** GO UP, ascend, climb, mount, slope (up), soar, tower, grow, increase, escalate, intensify. **2** STAND UP, get up, arise, jump up, spring up. **3** ADVANCE, progress, improve, prosper. **4** ORIGINATE, spring, flow, issue, emerge, appear.
🖃 **1** fall, descend. **2** sit down. **3** declare.
➤ *n* **1** ASCENT, climb, slope, incline, hill, elevation. **2** INCREASE, increment, upsurge, upturn, advance, progress, improvement, advancement, promotion.
🖃 **1** descent, valley. **2** fall.

risk *n* danger, peril, jeopardy, hazard, chance, possibility, uncertainty, gamble, speculation, venture, adventure.
🖃 safety, certainty.
➤ *v* endanger, imperil, jeopardize, hazard, chance, gamble, venture, dare.

risky *adj* dangerous, unsafe, perilous, hazardous, chancy, uncertain, touch-and-go, dicey (*infml*), tricky, precarious.
🖃 safe.

risqué *adj* indecent, improper, indelicate, suggestive, coarse, crude, earthy, bawdy, racy (*infml*), naughty (*infml*), blue (*infml*).
🖃 decent, proper.

rite *n* ceremony, custom, act, usage, office, form, formality, ceremonial, ordinance, practice, procedure, ritual, service, worship, liturgy, sacrament, observance.

ritual *n* custom, tradition, convention, usage, practice, habit, wont, routine, procedure, ordinance, prescription, form, formality, ceremony, ceremonial, solemnity, rite, sacrament, service, liturgy, observance, act.
➤ *adj* customary, traditional, conventional, habitual, routine, procedural, prescribed, set, formal, ceremonial.
🖃 informal.

rival *n* competitor, contestant, contender, challenger, opponent, adversary, antagonist, match, equal, peer.
🖃 colleague, associate.
➤ *adj* competitive, competing, opposed, opposing, conflicting.
🖃 associate.
➤ *v* compete with, contend with, vie with, oppose, emulate, match, equal.
🖃 co-operate.

rivalry *n* competitiveness, competition, contest, contention, conflict, struggle, strife, opposition, antagonism.
🖃 co-operation.

river *n* waterway, watercourse.

Forms of river or watercourse include:
beck, billabong, bourn, broads, brook, burn, canal, channel, confluence, creek, cut, delta, estuary, firth, frith, inlet, mountain stream, mouth, rill, rillet, rivulet, runnel, source, stream, tributary, wadi, waterway.

The world's longest rivers include: Nile (Africa), Amazon (South America), Yangtze (Asia), Mississippi-Missouri (North America), Yenisey-Angara-Selenga (Asia), Amur-Argun-Kerulen (Asia), Ob-Irtysh (Asia), Plata-Parana-Grande (South America), Yellow (Asia), Congo (Africa).

riveting *adj* fascinating, absorbing, interesting, exciting, gripping, arresting, captivating, engrossing, enthralling, spellbinding, magnetic, hypnotic.
🖃 boring.

road *n* roadway, motorway, bypass, highway, thoroughfare, street, avenue, boulevard, crescent, drive, lane, track, route, course, way, direction.

roam v wander, rove, range, travel, walk, ramble, stroll, amble, prowl, drift, stray. ✄ stay.

roar v, n bellow, yell, shout, cry, bawl, howl, hoot, guffaw, thunder, crash, blare, rumble. ✄ whisper.

rob v steal from, hold up, raid, burgle, loot, pillage, plunder, sack, rifle, ransack, swindle, rip off (*sl*), do (*infml*), cheat, defraud, deprive.

robber n thief, burglar, stealer, hijacker, bandit, swindler, embezzler, fraud, cheat, plunderer, raider, pirate, highwayman, looter, brigand, con man (*infml*), mugger (*infml*).

robbery n theft, stealing, larceny, hold-up, stick-up (*sl*), heist (*sl*), raid, burglary, pillage, plunder, fraud, embezzlement, swindle, rip-off (*sl*).

robe n costume, gown, vestment, habit, bathrobe, dressing-gown, housecoat, peignoir, wrap, wrapper.
➤ v clothe, dress, drape, garb, vest, apparel (*fml*), attire (*fml*).

robot n automaton, machine, android, zombie.

robust adj strong, sturdy, tough, hardy, vigorous, powerful, muscular, athletic, fit, healthy, well.
✄ weak, feeble, unhealthy.

rock¹ n boulder, stone, pebble, crag, outcrop.

> Rocks include: basalt, breccia, chalk, coal, conglomerate, flint, gabbro, gneiss, granite, gravel, lava, limestone, marble, marl, obsidian, ore, porphyry, pumice stone, sandstone, schist, serpentine, shale, slate.

rock² v 1 SWAY, swing, tilt, tip, shake, wobble, roll, pitch, toss, lurch, reel, stagger, totter. 2 *news that rocked the nation*: shock, stun, daze, dumbfound, astound, astonish, surprise, startle.

rocky¹ adj stony, pebbly, craggy, rugged, rough, hard, flinty.
✄ smooth, soft.

rocky² adj unsteady, shaky, wobbly, staggering, tottering, unstable, unreliable, uncertain, weak.
✄ steady, stable, dependable, strong.

rod n bar, shaft, strut, pole, stick, baton, wand, cane, switch, staff, mace, sceptre.

rodent n

> Rodents include: agouti, bandicoot, beaver, black rat, brown rat, cane rat, capybara, cavy, chinchilla, chipmunk, cony, coypu, dormouse, fieldmouse, ferret, gerbil, gopher, grey squirrel, groundhog, guinea pig, hamster, hare, harvest mouse, hedgehog, jerboa, kangaroo rat, lemming, marmot, meerkat, mouse, muskrat, musquash, pika, porcupine, prairie dog, rabbit, rat, red squirrel, sewer-rat, squirrel, vole, water rat, water vole, woodchuck.

rogue n scoundrel, rascal, scamp, villain, miscreant, crook (*infml*), swindler, fraud, cheat, con man (*infml*), reprobate, wastrel, ne'er-do-well.

role n part, character, representation, portrayal, impersonation, function, capacity, task, duty, job, post, position.

roll v 1 ROTATE, revolve, turn, spin, wheel, twirl, whirl, gyrate, move, run, pass. 2 WIND, coil, furl, twist, curl, wrap, envelop, enfold, bind. 3 *the ship rolled*: rock, sway, swing, pitch, toss, lurch, reel, wallow, undulate. 4 PRESS, flatten, smooth, level. 5 RUMBLE, roar, thunder, boom, resound, reverberate.
➤ n 1 ROLLER, cylinder, drum, reel, spool, bobbin, scroll. 2 REGISTER, roster, census, list, inventory, index, catalogue, directory, schedule, record, chronicle, annals. 3 ROTATION, revolution, cycle, turn, spin, wheel, twirl, whirl, gyration, undulation. 4 RUMBLE, roar, thunder, boom, resonance, reverberation.
♦ **roll up** (*infml*) arrive, assemble, gather, congregate, convene.
✄ leave.

rollicking adj lively, noisy, light-hearted, hearty, romping, sprightly, exuberant, frolicsome, jovial, carefree, boisterous, joyous, merry, spirited, sportive, jaunty, cavorting, devil-may-care, roisterous, roisting, frisky, playful, rip-roaring, swashbuckling.
✄ restrained, serious.

romance n 1 LOVE AFFAIR, affair, relationship, liaison, intrigue, passion. 2 LOVE STORY, novel, story, tale, fairytale, legend, idyll, fiction, fantasy. 3 ADVENTURE, excitement, melodrama, mystery, charm, fascination, glamour, sentiment.
➤ v lie, fantasize, exaggerate, overstate.

romantic adj 1 IMAGINARY, fictitious, fanciful, fantastic, legendary, fairy-tale, idyllic, utopian, idealistic, quixotic, visionary, starry-eyed, dreamy, unrealistic, impractical, improbable, wild, extravagant, exciting, fascinating. 2 SENTIMENTAL, loving, amorous, passionate, tender, fond, lovey-dovey (infml), soppy, mushy, sloppy.
Ea 1 real, practical. 2 unromantic, unsentimental.
➤ n sentimentalist, dreamer, visionary, idealist, utopian.
Ea realist.

romp v gambol, frolic, skip, sport, frisk, caper, cavort, revel, rollick, roister.
➤ n caper, frolic, lark, rig, spree.

room n space, volume, capacity, headroom, legroom, elbow-room, scope, range, extent, leeway, latitude, margin, allowance, chance, opportunity.

Types of room include: attic, loft, box-room, bedroom, boudoir, spare room, dressing-room, guest room, nursery, playroom, sitting-room, lounge, front room, living-room, drawing-room, salon, reception room, chamber, lounge-diner, dining-room, study, den (infml), library, kitchen, kitchen-diner, kitchenette, breakfast room, larder, pantry, scullery, bathroom, en suite bathroom, toilet, lavatory, WC, loo (infml), cloakroom, laundry, utility room, porch, hall, landing, conservatory, sun lounge, cellar, basement; classroom, music-room, laboratory, office, sick-room, dormitory, workroom, studio, workshop, storeroom, waiting-room, anteroom, foyer, mezzanine, family room, games room.

roomy adj spacious, capacious, large, sizable, broad, wide, extensive, ample, generous.
Ea cramped, small, tiny.

root¹ n 1 TUBER, rhizome, stem. 2 ORIGIN, source, derivation, cause, starting point, fount, fountainhead, seed, germ, nucleus, heart, core, nub, essence, seat, base, bottom, basis, foundation.
➤ v anchor, moor, fasten, fix, set, stick, implant, embed, entrench, establish, ground, base.
◆ **root out** unearth, dig out, uncover, discover, uproot, eradicate, extirpate, eliminate, exterminate, destroy, abolish, clear away, remove.

root² v dig, delve, burrow, forage, hunt, rummage, ferret, poke, pry, nose.

rooted adj entrenched, established, felt, firm, fixed, deep, deeply, deep-seated, ingrained, confirmed, rigid, radical.
Ea superficial, temporary.

roots n beginning(s), origins, family, heritage, background, birthplace, home.

rope n line, cable, cord, string, strand.
➤ v tie, bind, lash, fasten, hitch, moor, tether.
◆ **rope in** enlist, engage, involve, persuade, inveigle.

ropy adj poor, substandard, deficient, inadequate, inferior, unsatisfactory, rough, unwell, off-colour, below par (infml).
Ea good, well.

roster n rota, schedule, register, roll, list.

rostrum n platform, stage, dais, podium.

rosy adj 1 PINK, reddish, red, rose, rose-coloured, rose-hued, roselike, rose-pink, rose-red, rose-scented, roseate, glowing, fresh, sunny, healthy-looking, blooming, blushing, ruddy, flushed, florid, inflamed, bloodshot, rubicund (fml). 2 PROMISING, cheerful, bright, encouraging, optimistic, hopeful, reassuring, favourable, auspicious (fml).
Ea 2 depressing, sad, unhappy.

rot v decay, decompose, putrefy, fester, perish, corrode, spoil, go bad, go off, degenerate, deteriorate, crumble, disintegrate, taint, corrupt.
➤ n 1 DECAY, decomposition, putrefaction, corrosion, rust, mould. 2 (infml) NONSENSE, rubbish, poppycock (infml), drivel, claptrap (infml).

rotary adj rotating, revolving, turning, spinning, whirling, gyrating.
Ea fixed.

rotate v revolve, turn, spin, gyrate, pivot, swivel, roll.

rotation n revolution, turn, spin, gyration, orbit, cycle, sequence, succession, turning, spinning.

rotten adj 1 DECAYED, decomposed, putrid, addled, bad, off, mouldy, fetid, stinking, rank, foul, rotting, decaying, disintegrating. 2 INFERIOR, bad, poor, inadequate, low-grade, lousy, crummy (sl), ropy (sl), mean, nasty, beastly, dirty, despicable, contemptible, dishonourable, wicked. 3 (infml) ILL, sick, unwell,

poorly, grotty (*sl*), rough (*infml*).
☒ 1 fresh. **2** good. **3** well.

rough *adj* **1** UNEVEN, bumpy, lumpy, rugged, craggy, jagged, irregular, coarse, bristly, scratchy. **2** HARSH, severe, tough, hard, cruel, brutal, drastic, extreme, brusque, curt, sharp. **3** APPROXIMATE, estimated, imprecise, inexact, vague, general, cursory, hasty, incomplete, unfinished, crude, rudimentary. **4** *rough sea*: choppy, agitated, turbulent, stormy, tempestuous, violent, wild. **5** (*infml*) ILL, sick, unwell, poorly, off-colour, rotten (*infml*).
☒ 1 smooth. **2** mild. **3** accurate. **4** calm. **5** well.

round *adj* **1** SPHERICAL, globular, ball-shaped, circular, ring-shaped, disc-shaped, cylindrical, rounded, curved. **2** ROTUND, plump, stout, portly.
➤ *n* **1** CIRCLE, ring, band, disc, sphere, ball, orb. **2** CYCLE, series, sequence, succession, period, bout, session. **3** BEAT, circuit, lap, course, routine.
➤ *v* circle, skirt, flank, bypass.
◆ **round off** finish (off), complete, end, close, conclude, cap, crown.
☒ begin.
◆ **round on** turn on, attack, lay into, abuse.
◆ **round up** herd, marshal, assemble, gather, rally, collect, group.
☒ disperse, scatter.

roundabout *adj* circuitous, tortuous, twisting, winding, indirect, oblique, devious, evasive.
☒ straight, direct.

round-up *n* summary, survey, overview, précis, collation, collection, assembly, gathering, herding, marshalling, muster, rally.
☒ dispersal.

rouse *v* wake (up), awaken, arouse, call, stir, move, start, disturb, agitate, anger, provoke, stimulate, instigate, incite, inflame, excite, galvanize, whip up.
☒ calm.

rousing *adj* stimulating, exciting, inspiring, lively, moving, spirited, stirring, vigorous, exhilarating, brisk, electrifying.
☒ dull, boring, calming.

rout *n* defeat, conquest, overthrow, beating, thrashing, flight, stampede.
☒ win.
➤ *v* defeat, conquer, overthrow, crush,

beat, hammer (*infml*), thrash, lick, put to flight, chase, dispel, scatter.

route *n* course, run, path, road, avenue, way, direction, itinerary, journey, passage, circuit, round, beat.

routine *n* **1** PROCEDURE, way, method, system, order, pattern, formula, practice, usage, custom, habit. **2** *comedy routine*: act, piece, programme, performance.
➤ *adj* customary, habitual, usual, typical, ordinary, run-of-the-mill, normal, standard, conventional, unoriginal, predictable, familiar, everyday, banal, humdrum, dull, boring, monotonous, tedious.
☒ unusual, different, exciting.

row¹ *n* **1** line, tier, bank, rank, range, column, file, queue, string, series, sequence.

row² *n* **1** ARGUMENT, quarrel, dispute, controversy, squabble, tiff, slanging match (*infml*), fight, brawl. **2** NOISE, racket, din, uproar, commotion, disturbance, rumpus, fracas.
☒ 2 calm.
➤ *v* argue, quarrel, wrangle, bicker, squabble, fight, scrap.

rowdy *adj* noisy, loud, rough, boisterous, disorderly, unruly, riotous, wild.
☒ quiet, peaceful.

royal *adj* regal, majestic, kingly, queenly, princely, imperial, monarchical, sovereign, august, grand, stately, magnificent, splendid, superb.

rub *v* **1** STROKE, caress, fondle, pat, massage, scratch, knead, embrocate (*fml*). **2** CLEAN, smooth, polish, buff (up), burnish, shine. **3** SCOUR, scratch, scrape, scrub, wipe, clean, abrade. **4** PUT ON, apply, work in, spread, smear. **5** CHAFE, grate, scrape, pinch.
➤ *n* **1** MASSAGE, stroke, caress, kneading. **2** POLISH, shine, wipe, clean. **3** DIFFICULTY, drawback, hindrance, trouble, impediment, problem, obstacle, hitch, catch, snag (*infml*).
◆ **rub in** emphasize, stress, underline, highlight, make much of, insist on, harp on.
◆ **rub off on** influence, affect, have an effect on, change, alter, transform.
◆ **rub out 1** ERASE, obliterate, efface, cancel, efface (*fml*). **2** (*infml*) KILL, assassinate, murder, put to death, finish off, do away with, do in (*infml*), bump off (*infml*), eliminate (*infml*), liquidate (*infml*).
◆ **rub up the wrong way** annoy, anger, irk,

irritate, get, vex, niggle (*infml*), get to, bug (*infml*), get one's goat (*infml*), get under one's skin (*infml*), needle (*infml*), peeve (*infml*).

🖃 calm.

rubbish *n* 1 REFUSE, garbage, trash, junk, litter, waste, dross, debris, flotsam and jetsam. **2** NONSENSE, drivel, claptrap (*infml*), twaddle, gibberish, gobbledygook, balderdash, poppycock (*infml*), rot (*infml*), cobblers (*sl*).

🖃 **2** sense.

ruddy *adj* red, scarlet, crimson, blushing, flushed, rosy, glowing, healthy, blooming, florid, sunburnt.

🖃 pale.

rude *adj* 1 IMPOLITE, discourteous, disrespectful, impertinent, impudent, cheeky (*infml*), insolent, offensive, insulting, abusive, ill-mannered, ill-bred, uncouth, uncivilized, unrefined, unpolished, uneducated, untutored, uncivil, curt, brusque, abrupt, sharp, short. **2** *a rude joke*: obscene, vulgar, coarse, dirty, naughty (*infml*), gross.

🖃 **1** polite, courteous, civil. **2** clean, decent.

rudimentary *adj* primary, initial, introductory, elementary, basic, fundamental, primitive, undeveloped, embryonic.

🖃 advanced, developed.

rudiments *n* basics, fundamentals, essentials, principles, elements, ABC, beginnings, foundations.

ruffian *n* villain, scoundrel, bully, bully boy, brute, thug, lout, rowdy, rogue, cut-throat, rascal, roughneck, hooligan, bruiser, miscreant (*fml*), hoodlum (*infml*), rough (*infml*), tough (*infml*), yobbo (*infml*), yob (*sl*).

ruffle *v* 1 RUMPLE, dishevel, tangle, tousle, wrinkle, crease, pucker, crumple, ripple, disarrange (*fml*). **2** ANNOY, upset, irritate, anger, put out, vex, irk, exasperate, fluster, rile, nettle, confuse, trouble, discompose (*fml*), perturb (*fml*), aggravate (*infml*), bug (*infml*), hassle (*infml*), rattle (*infml*).

🖃 **1** smooth. **2** pacify.

rugged *adj* 1 ROUGH, bumpy, uneven, irregular, jagged, rocky, craggy, stark. **2** STRONG, robust, hardy, tough, muscular, weather-beaten.

🖃 **1** smooth.

ruin *n* destruction, devastation, wreckage,

havoc, damage, disrepair, decay, disintegration, breakdown, collapse, fall, downfall, failure, defeat, overthrow, ruination, undoing, insolvency, bankruptcy, crash.

🖃 development, reconstruction.

➢ *v* spoil, mar, botch, mess up (*infml*), damage, break, smash, shatter, wreck, destroy, demolish, raze, devastate, overwhelm, overthrow, defeat, crush, impoverish, bankrupt.

🖃 develop, restore.

rule *n* 1 REGULATION, law, statute, ordinance, decree, order, direction, guide, precept, tenet, canon, maxim, axiom, principle, formula, guideline, standard, criterion. **2** REIGN, sovereignty, supremacy, dominion, mastery, power, authority, command, control, influence, regime, government, leadership. **3** CUSTOM, convention, practice, routine, habit, wont.

➢ *v* 1 *rule a country*: reign, govern, command, lead, administer, manage, direct, guide, control, regulate, prevail, dominate. **2** JUDGE, adjudicate, decide, find, determine, resolve, establish, decree, pronounce.

♦ **as a rule** usually, normally, ordinarily, generally.

♦ **rule out** exclude, eliminate, reject, dismiss, preclude, prevent, ban, prohibit, forbid, disallow.

ruler

Titles of rulers include: Aga, begum, caesar, caliph, consul, duce, emir, emperor, empress, Führer, governor, governor-general, head of state, Kaiser, khan, king, maharajah, maharani, mikado, monarch, nawab, nizam, pharaoh, president, prince, princess, queen, rajah, rani, regent, shah, sheikh, shogun, sovereign, sultan, sultana, suzerain, tsar, viceroy.

ruling *n* judgement, adjudication, verdict, decision, finding, resolution, decree, pronouncement.

➢ *adj* reigning, sovereign, supreme, governing, commanding, leading, main, chief, principal, dominant, predominant, controlling.

rummage *v* root (around), search, turn over, poke around, hunt, explore, examine, delve, ransack, forage, rifle.

➢ *n* jumble, junk, tat, bric-à-brac, odds and ends.

rumour n hearsay, gossip, talk, whisper, word, news, report, story, grapevine, bush telegraph.
➤ v say, tell, hint, put about, noise abroad, report, publish, gossip, circulate, whisper, bruit.

rumple v wrinkle, crease, pucker, crumple, ruffle, dishevel, disorder, tousle, crinkle, crush, derange, scrunch.
🖙 smooth.

rumpus n disturbance, noise, uproar, confusion, commotion, disruption, furore, rout, row, tumult, fuss, fracas, brawl, brouhaha, ruction, kerfuffle (infml).
🖙 calm.

run v 1 SPRINT, jog, race, career, tear, dash, hurry, rush, speed, bolt, dart, scoot, scuttle. 2 GO, pass, move, proceed, issue. 3 FUNCTION, work, operate, perform. 4 run a company: head, lead, administer, direct, manage, superintend, supervise, oversee, control, regulate. 5 COMPETE, contend, stand, challenge. 6 LAST, continue, extend, reach, stretch, spread, range. 7 FLOW, stream, pour, gush.
➤ n 1 JOG, gallop, race, sprint, spurt, dash, rush. 2 DRIVE, ride, spin, jaunt, excursion, outing, trip, journey. 3 SEQUENCE, series, string, chain, course.

♦ **run across** meet, encounter, come across, run into, chance upon (fml), bump into (infml).

♦ **run after** chase, pursue, follow, tail.
🖙 flee.

♦ **run away** escape, flee, abscond, bolt, scarper (sl), beat it (infml), run off, make off, clear off (infml).
🖙 stay.

♦ **run down** 1 CRITICIZE, belittle, disparage, denigrate, defame. 2 RUN OVER, knock over, hit, strike. 3 TIRE, weary, exhaust, weaken. 4 run down production: reduce, decrease, drop, cut, trim, curtail.
🖙 1 praise. 4 increase.

♦ **run into** meet, encounter, run across, bump into (infml), hit, strike, collide with.
🖙 miss.

♦ **run off** 1 RUN AWAY, escape, make off, abscond, bolt, decamp, elope, scarper (sl), skedaddle (sl). 2 DUPLICATE, print, produce, xerox®, photostat®.
🖙 1 stay.

♦ **run off with** run away with, make off with, elope with.

♦ **run out** expire, terminate, end, cease, close, finish, dry up, fail.

♦ **run over** 1 HIT, knock down, run down, strike. 2 REPEAT, go over, run through, practise, rehearse, review, survey, reiterate (fml).

♦ **run through** 1 REHEARSE, go through, run over, practise, read, review, survey, examine. 2 SPEND, waste, squander, exhaust, fritter away, dissipate (fml).

runaway n escaper, escapee, fugitive, absconder, deserter, refugee.
➤ adj escaped, fugitive, loose, uncontrolled.

rundown n 1 REDUCTION, decrease, decline, drop, cut. 2 SUMMARY, résumé, synopsis, outline, review, recap, run-through.

run-down adj 1 WEAK, tired, weary, drained, exhausted, fatigued, worn-out, unhealthy, grotty, seedy, peaky, debilitated (fml), enervated (fml). 2 NEGLECTED, dilapidated, uncared-for, tumbledown, ramshackle, broken-down, decrepit, dingy, shabby.
🖙 1 healthy. 2 well-kept.

runner n jogger, sprinter, athlete, competitor, participant, courier, messenger.

running adj successive, consecutive, unbroken, uninterrupted, continuous, constant, perpetual, incessant, unceasing, moving, flowing.
🖙 broken, occasional.
➤ n 1 ADMINISTRATION, direction, management, organization, co-ordination, superintendency, supervision, leadership, charge, control, regulation, functioning, working, operation, performance, conduct. 2 out of the running: contention, contest, competition.

runny adj flowing, fluid, liquid, liquefied, melted, molten, watery, diluted.
🖙 solid.

run-of-the-mill adj ordinary, common, everyday, average, unexceptional, unremarkable, undistinguished, unimpressive, mediocre, middling, no great shakes (infml).
🖙 exceptional.

rupture n split, tear, burst, puncture, break, breach, fracture, crack, separation, division, estrangement, schism, rift, disagreement, quarrel, falling-out, bust-up (infml).
➤ v split, tear, burst, puncture, break, fracture, crack, sever, separate, divide.

rural *adj* country, rustic, pastoral, agricultural, agrarian.

ᴇᴀ urban.

ruse *n* plan, trick, deception, hoax, imposture, stratagem, tactic, manoeuvre, ploy, plot, scheme, wile, subterfuge, artifice, device, blind, sham, dodge (*infml*).

rush *v* hurry, hasten, quicken, accelerate, speed (up), press, push, dispatch, bolt, dart, shoot, fly, tear, career, dash, race, run, sprint, scramble, stampede, charge.
➤ *n* hurry, haste, urgency, speed, swiftness, dash, race, scramble, stampede, charge, flow, surge.

rust *n* corrosion, oxidation.
➤ *v* corrode, decay, rot, oxidize, tarnish, deteriorate, decline.

rustic *adj* **1** PASTORAL, sylvan, bucolic, countrified, country, rural. **2** PLAIN, simple, rough, crude, coarse, rude, clumsy, awkward, artless, unsophisticated, unrefined, uncultured, provincial, uncouth, boorish, oafish.

ᴇᴀ 1 urban. **2** urbane, sophisticated, cultivated, polished.

rustle *v*, *n* crackle, whoosh, swish, whisper.

rusty *adj* **1** CORRODED, rusted, rust-covered, oxidized, tarnished, discoloured, dull. **2** UNPRACTISED, weak, poor, deficient, dated, old-fashioned, outmoded, antiquated, stale, stiff, creaking.

rut *n* **1** DITCH, channel, furrow, groove, gutter, indentation, trough, track, gouge, pothole, wheelmark. **2** ROUTINE, habit, pattern, system, humdrum, grind, daily grind, treadmill, same old round/place, no change of scenery.

ruthless *adj* merciless, pitiless, hard-hearted, hard, heartless, unfeeling, callous, cruel, inhuman, brutal, savage, cut-throat, fierce, ferocious, relentless, unrelenting, inexorable, implacable, harsh, severe.

ᴇᴀ merciful, compassionate.

Ss

sabotage *v* damage, spoil, mar, disrupt, vandalize, wreck, destroy, thwart, scupper, cripple, incapacitate, disable, undermine, weaken.

➤ *n* vandalism, damage, impairment, disruption, wrecking, destruction.

sac *n* bag, pocket, pouch, pod, bladder, capsule, follicle, cyst, saccule, vesicle, bursa (*fml*), vesica (*fml*).

sack¹ (*infml*) *v* dismiss, fire (*infml*), discharge, axe (*infml*), lay off, make redundant.

➤ *n* dismissal, discharge, one's cards, notice, the boot (*infml*), the push (*infml*), the elbow (*infml*), the axe (*infml*), the chop (*infml*).

sack² *v* destroy, raid, plunder, ravage, raze, lay waste, waste, level, devastate, desecrate, demolish, maraud, pillage, rifle, rob, loot, ruin, rape, spoil, strip, depredate (*fml*), despoil (*fml*).

➤ *n* destruction, devastation, ravage, razing, ruin, waste, levelling, looting, plunder, plundering, marauding, desecration, rape, pillage, depredation (*fml*), despoliation (*fml*), rapine (*fml*).

sacred *adj* holy, divine, heavenly, blessed, hallowed, sanctified, consecrated, dedicated, religious, devotional, ecclesiastical, priestly, saintly, godly, venerable, revered, sacrosanct, inviolable.
🖝 temporal, profane.

sacrifice *v* surrender, forfeit, relinquish, let go, abandon, renounce, give up, forgo, offer, slaughter.

➤ *n* offering, immolation, slaughter, destruction, surrender, renunciation, loss.

sacrificial *adj* atoning, votive, oblatory (*fml*), propitiatory (*fml*), expiatory (*fml*), reparative (*fml*), piacular (*fml*).

sacrilege *n* blasphemy, profanity, heresy, desecration, profanation, violation, outrage, irreverence, disrespect, mockery.
🖝 piety, reverence, respect.

sacrosanct *adj* sacred, hallowed, untouchable, inviolable, impregnable, protected, secure.

sad *adj* **1** UNHAPPY, sorrowful, tearful, grief-stricken, heavy-hearted, upset, distressed, miserable, low-spirited, downcast, glum, long-faced, crestfallen, dejected, down-hearted, despondent, melancholy, depressed, low, gloomy, dismal. **2** *sad news*: upsetting, distressing, painful, depressing, touching, poignant, heart-rending, tragic, grievous, lamentable, regrettable, sorry, unfortunate, serious, grave, disastrous.
🖝 **1** happy, cheerful. **2** fortunate, lucky.

Ways of expressing sadness, sorrow or depression: break one's heart, be down in the dumps, feel sorry for oneself, feel low, be in mourning, have a long face, have the weight of the world on one's shoulders, be in the doldrums, get the blues, weep buckets, be cut up, in the depths of despair, cry one's eyes out, cry one's heart out, have a good cry, have a heavy heart, down in the mouth, in low spirits, a tale of woe, my/our deepest sympathy, it's a sad day for …, parting is such sweet sorrow, weep and wail, be/feel choked, have a lump in one's throat, have tears in one's eyes.

---

sadden *v* upset, distress, grieve, depress, dismay, discourage, dishearten.
🖝 cheer, please, gratify, delight.

saddle *v* burden, encumber, lumber, impose, tax, charge, load (*infml*).

sadistic *adj* cruel, inhuman, brutal, savage, vicious, merciless, pitiless, barbarous, bestial, unnatural, perverted.

safe *adj* **1** HARMLESS, innocuous, non-toxic, non-poisonous, uncontaminated. **2** UNHARMED, undamaged, unscathed, uninjured, unhurt, intact, secure, protected, guarded, impregnable, invulnerable, immune. **3** UNADVENTUROUS, cautious, prudent, conservative, sure, proven, tried, tested, sound, dependable, reliable, trustworthy.
🖝 **1** dangerous, harmful. **2** vulnerable, exposed. **3** risky.

➤ *n* cash box, deposit box, safety-deposit box, strongbox, chest, coffer, vault, depository, repository.

safe-conduct *n* authorization, pass,

passport, permit, safeguard, warrant, licence, convoy, laissez-passer.

safeguard *v* protect, preserve, defend, guard, shield, screen, shelter, secure.
🔳 endanger, jeopardize.
➤ *n* protection, defence, shield, security, surety, guarantee, assurance, insurance, cover, precaution.

safekeeping *n* protection, care, custody, keeping, charge, trust, guardianship, surveillance, supervision.

safety *n* protection, refuge, sanctuary, shelter, cover, security, safeguard, immunity, impregnability, safeness, harmlessness, reliability, dependability.
🔳 danger, jeopardy, risk.

sag *v* bend, give, bag, droop, hang, fall, drop, sink, dip, decline, slump, flop, fail, flag, weaken, wilt.
🔳 bulge, rise.

sage *n* wise person, wise man, wise woman, teacher, master, expert, authority, pundit, savant, guru, maharishi, oracle, elder, philosopher, wiseacre, Solomon, mahatma, hakam.
🔳 ignoramus.

sail *v* **1** *sail for France*: embark, set sail, weigh anchor, put to sea, cruise, voyage.
2 CAPTAIN, skipper, pilot, navigate, steer.
3 GLIDE, plane, sweep, float, skim, scud, fly.

> **Types of sail include:** canvas, course, foreroyal, foresail, forestaysail, foretop, fore-topgallant, fore-topsail, gaff sail, gaff-topsail, genoa, headsail, jib, jigger, kite, lateen sail, lugsail, main course, mainsail, maintopsail, mizzen, moonraker, royal, skysail, spanker, spinnaker, spritsail, square sail, staysail, studdingsail, topgallant, topsail, trysail.

sailing

> **Terms used in sailing include:** abaft, across the wind, alongside, astern, backing, bearing, beat, beating, bending on (a sail), blanketing effect, breaking out (the anchor), casting off/letting go, close-hauled, coming about, downwind, fetch, fitting out, fixing a position, going about, gybe, handing (a sail), hard on the wind, heeling (to the wind), in irons/in stays, knockdown (by the wind), laying off (a course), lay up, lee helm, lee-oh!, leeway, lift, points of sailing, port, reaching, beam reach, broad reach, close reach, ready about!, running, running goose-winged, sailing by the lee, sail

trimming, sheeting in a sail, spilling wind, standing on, starboard, stepping/unstepping (the mast), tacking, port tack, starboard tack, steerage way, taking soundings, unbending (a sail), under way, upwind, veer (the anchor cable), weathering, weather helm, windward, yawing. *see also* **knot**.

> **Parts of a sailing boat include:** anchor, CQR anchor, Danford anchor, fisherman's anchor, fluke, ground tackle, hook (*infml*); anti-fouling paint, batten, beam, bilge, bow, bowsprit, bulkhead, buoyancy chamber; cleat, jamming cleat; cockpit, counter, dinghy, doghouse, draught, fender, foredeck, forepeak, guard rail, gudgeon, gymbals, hatch, heads, helm, helmsman, hull, carvel-built, catamaran, clench-built, clinker-built, glass-fibre reinforced plastic (GRP), hard-chined, single-chined, double-chined, multi-chined, mono-hull, multi-hull, moulded hull, trimaran; keel, ballast keel, bilge keels, centreboard, dagger board, fin keel, single-keel, retractable keel, triple keel; mooring, pintle, pulpit, pushpit; reefing, reef cringle, reef points, roller reefing; riding light; rigs, Bermudan rig, catboat rig (*US*), cutter rig, fore-and-aft rig, gaff rig, loose-footed gaff rig, gunter rig, jib-headed rig (*US*), jury rig, ketch rig, lugsail rig, Marconi rig (*US*), performance rig, schooner rig, sloop rig, square rig, Una rig, spritsail rig, yawl rig; rudder, skeg rudder; self-bailer; standing rigging, running rigging; main mast, mizzen mast; boom, main boom, mizzen boom, spinnaker boom; sails, foot, tack, luff, head, leech, clew; batten, batten pocket, cringle; Genoa, jenny (*infml*), headsail, jib, loose-footed sail, mainsail, mainsheet, mizzen sail, set (of the sails), spinnaker, storm jib, storm trysail; halyard, halyard winch, outhaul, painter, rope, sheave, sheet, sheet winch, shock cord; shroud, cap shroud, lower shroud; spring; stay, backstay, forestay; warp; block, fairlead, kicking strap; shackle, stanchion, stern, stern-post, tackle, tender, tiller, transom, trapeze, whisker pole, yard.

> **Types and classes of modern sailing boat include:** sloop, cutter, yawl, ketch, schooner; formula class, one-design class, restricted class; 420, 470, 5-0-5, Cadet, Conway One, Dragon, Enterprise, Finn, Fireball, Firefly, Fisher, Flying Dutchman, Flying Fifteen, Fourteen, Laser, Maxi, Minisail,

Mirror, Moody, Moth, Optimist, Rival, Solo, Tasar, Topper, Tornado, Trapper, Twelve, Wayfarer, Westerley.

sailor *n* seafarer, mariner, seaman.

Types of sailor include: AB, able seaman, bargee, bluejacket, boatman, boatswain, bosun, buccaneer, cabin boy, captain, cox, coxswain, crewman, deck hand, fisherman, galiongee, gob (*US sl*), hearty, helmsman, Jack tar, lascar, leatherneck, limey (*US infml*), marine, master, mate, matelot (*sl*), navigator, oarsman, pilot, pirate, purser, rating, rower, salt, sculler, sea dog, skipper, tar (*infml*), tarry-breeks (*Scot*), water rat, Wren, yachtsman, yachtswoman.

saintly *adj* godly, pious, devout, God-fearing, holy, religious, blessed, angelic, pure, spotless, innocent, blameless, sinless, virtuous, upright, worthy, righteous.
E3 godless, unholy, wicked.

sake *n* benefit, advantage, good, welfare, wellbeing, gain, profit, behalf, interest, account, regard, respect, cause, reason.

salary *n* pay, remuneration, emolument (*fml*), stipend, wages, earnings, income.

sale *n* selling, marketing, vending, disposal, trade, traffic, transaction, deal, auction.

Types of sale include: auction, autumn sale, bargain offer, bazaar, bazumble, boot-sale, bring-and-buy, car-boot sale, charity sale, church bazaar, clearance sale, closing-down sale, cold-call, end-of-line sale, end-of-season sale, exhibition, exposition, fair, fleamarket, forced sale, garage sale, grand opening sale, introductory offer, January sale, jumble sale, mail order, market, mid-season sale, on-promotion, open market, private sale, public sale, pyramid selling, remainder sale, rummage sale, sale of bankrupt stock, sale of the century, sale of work, second-hand sale, special offer, spring sale, stocktaking sale, summer sale, tabletop sale, telesales, trade show, trash and treasure sale, winter sale.

salesperson *n* salesman, saleswoman, sales assistant, shop assistant, shop-boy, shop-girl, shopkeeper, representative, rep (*infml*).

salient *adj* important, significant, chief, main, principal, striking, conspicuous, noticeable, obvious, prominent, outstanding, remarkable.

sallow *adj* yellowish, pale, pallid, wan, pasty, sickly, unhealthy, anaemic, colourless.
E3 rosy, healthy.

salt *n* seasoning, taste, flavour, savour, relish, piquancy.
♦ **salt away** store up, hoard, save, stash (*infml*), stockpile, collect, cache, bank, accumulate, amass, hide.
E3 spend, squander.

salty *adj* salt, salted, saline, briny, brackish, savoury, spicy, piquant, tangy.
E3 fresh, sweet.

salubrious *adj* sanitary, hygienic, health-giving, healthy, wholesome, pleasant.

salutary *adj* good, beneficial, advantageous, profitable, valuable, helpful, useful, practical, timely.

salutation *n* greeting, address, welcome, salute, reverence, respects, homage.

salute *v* greet, acknowledge, recognize, wave, hail, address, nod, bow, honour.
➤ *n* greeting, acknowledgement, recognition, wave, gesture, hail, address, handshake, nod, bow, tribute, reverence.

salvage *v* save, preserve, conserve, rescue, recover, recuperate, retrieve, reclaim, redeem, repair, restore.
E3 waste, abandon.

salvation *n* deliverance, liberation, rescue, saving, preservation, redemption, reclamation.
E3 loss, damnation.

salve *n* ointment, lotion, cream, balm, liniment, embrocation, medication, preparation, application.

same *adj* identical, twin, duplicate, indistinguishable, equal, selfsame, very, alike, like, similar, comparable, equivalent, matching, corresponding, mutual, reciprocal, interchangeable, substitutable, synonymous, consistent, uniform, unvarying, changeless, unchanged.
E3 different, inconsistent, variable, changeable.
♦ **all the same** nevertheless, nonetheless, still, anyway, even so, yet, however, by any means, in any case/event, by some means, anyhow, but, regardless, for all that, notwithstanding (*fml*).

sameness *n* changelessness, invariability, consistency, monotony,

predictability, repetition, tedium, uniformity, standardization, resemblance, similarity, indistinguishability, likeness, identicalness, identity, oneness, duplication, déjà vu.
Ea variety, difference.

sample *n* specimen, example, cross-section, model, pattern, swatch, piece, demonstration, illustration, instance, sign, indication, foretaste.
➤ *v* try, test, taste, sip, inspect, experience.
➤ *adj* representative, specimen, demonstrative, illustrative, dummy, trial, test, pilot.

sanctify *v* hallow, consecrate, bless, anoint, dedicate, cleanse, purify, exalt, canonize.
Ea desecrate, defile.

sanctimonious *adj* self-righteous, holier-than-thou, pious, moralizing, smug, superior, hypocritical, pharisaical.
Ea humble.

sanction *n* 1 AUTHORIZATION, permission, agreement, approval, ratification, confirmation, support, backing, endorsement, licence, authority, approbation (*fml*), accreditation (*fml*), OK (*infml*), go-ahead (*infml*), green light (*infml*), thumbs-up (*infml*). 2 *impose sanctions on a country*: restriction, boycott, embargo, ban, prohibition, penalty, deterrent, punishment, sentence.
➤ *v* authorize, allow, permit, approve, ratify, confirm, support, back, endorse, underwrite, accredit, license, warrant.
Ea veto, forbid, disapprove.

sanctity *n* holiness, sacredness, inviolability, piety, godliness, religiousness, devotion, grace, spirituality, purity, goodness, righteousness.
Ea unholiness, secularity, worldliness, godlessness, impurity.

sanctuary *n* 1 CHURCH, temple, tabernacle, shrine, altar. 2 ASYLUM, refuge, protection, shelter, haven, retreat.

sand *n* beach, shore, strand, sands, grit.

sane *adj* normal, rational, right-minded, all there (*infml*), balanced, stable, sound, sober, level-headed, sensible, judicious, reasonable, moderate.
Ea insane, mad, crazy (*infml*), foolish.

sang-froid *n* composure, self-control, poise, self-possession, indifference, equanimity, assurance, calmness, dispassion, cool-headedness,

nonchalance, coolness, imperturbability, aplomb (*fml*), phlegm (*fml*), nerve (*infml*), cool (*infml*), unflappability (*infml*).
Ea discomposure, excitability, hysteria, panic.

sanguine *adj* 1 CHEERFUL, confident, hopeful, lively, expectant, optimistic, over-confident, over-optimistic, assured, animated, ardent, buoyant, spirited, unabashed, unbowed. 2 RUDDY, rosy, florid, red, pink, fresh-complexioned, fresh, flushed, rubicund (*fml*).
Ea 1 cynical, depressive, gloomy, melancholy, pessimistic. 2 pale, sallow.

sanitary *adj* clean, pure, uncontaminated, unpolluted, aseptic, germ-free, disinfected, hygienic, salubrious, healthy, wholesome.
Ea insanitary, unwholesome.

sanity *n* normality, rationality, reason, sense, common sense, balance of mind, stability, soundness, level-headedness, judiciousness.
Ea insanity, madness.

sap *v* bleed, drain, exhaust, weaken, undermine, deplete, reduce, diminish, impair.
Ea strengthen, build up, increase.
➤ *n* 1 *sap in a plant*: lifeblood, vital fluid, juice, essence, vigour, energy. 2 FOOL, idiot, imbecile, moron, clot (*infml*), twit (*infml*), nit (*infml*), nitwit (*infml*), jerk (*sl*), prat (*sl*), git (*sl*), fink (*sl*).

sarcasm *n* irony, satire, mockery, sneering, derision, scorn, contempt, cynicism, bitterness.

sarcastic *adj* ironical, satirical, mocking, taunting, sneering, derisive, scathing, disparaging, cynical, incisive, cutting, biting, caustic.

sardonic *adj* mocking, jeering, sneering, derisive, scornful, sarcastic, biting, cruel, heartless, malicious, cynical, bitter.

sash *n* belt, girdle, cummerbund, waistband.

Satan *n* the Devil, the Enemy, the Adversary, the Evil One, the Tempter, Beelzebub, Lucifer, Old Nick, Prince of Darkness, Mephistopheles, Belial, Apollyon, Abaddon.

satanic *adj* satanical, diabolical, devilish, demonic, fiendish, hellish, infernal, inhuman, malevolent, wicked, evil, black.
Ea holy, divine, godly, saintly, benevolent.

satellite *n* 1 ORBITING BODY, natural/

artificial satellite, spacecraft, moon, planet, spaceship, sputnik. **2** DEPENDANT, hanger-on, parasite, sycophant, subordinate, follower, attendant, aide, adherent, disciple, minion, lackey, sidekick, retainer, vassal, puppet (*infml*).

satire *n* ridicule, irony, sarcasm, wit, burlesque, skit, send-up (*infml*), spoof (*infml*), take-off (*infml*), parody, caricature, travesty.

satirical *adj* ironical, sarcastic, mocking, irreverent, taunting, derisive, sardonic, incisive, cutting, biting, caustic, cynical, bitter.

satirize *v* ridicule, mock, make fun of, burlesque, lampoon, send up, take off, parody, caricature, criticize, deride.
☒ acclaim, honour.

satisfaction *n* **1** GRATIFICATION, contentment, happiness, pleasure, enjoyment, comfort, ease, well-being, fulfilment, self-satisfaction, pride. **2** SETTLEMENT, compensation, reimbursement, indemnification, damages, reparation, amends, redress, recompense, requital, vindication.
☒ **1** dissatisfaction, displeasure.

satisfactory *adj* acceptable, passable, up to the mark, all right, OK (*infml*), fair, average, competent, adequate, sufficient, suitable, proper.
☒ unsatisfactory, unacceptable, inadequate.

satisfied *adj* **1** HAPPY, contented, pleased, self-satisfied, content, smug. **2** CONVINCED, reassured, persuaded, sure, certain, positive, pacified. **3** FULL, sated, satiated, replete (*fml*).
☒ **1** dissatisfied, disgruntled (*infml*). **2** unconvinced. **3** hungry.

satisfy *v* **1** GRATIFY, indulge, content, please, delight, quench, slake, sate, satiate, surfeit. **2** *satisfy requirements*: meet, fulfil, discharge, settle, answer, fill, suffice, serve, qualify. **3** ASSURE, convince, persuade.
☒ **1** dissatisfy. **2** fail.

satisfying *adj* pleasing, fulfilling, gratifying, cheering, pleasurable, satisfactory, convincing, persuasive, filling, cool, refreshing.
☒ dissatisfying, frustrating, unsatisfactory.

saturate *v* soak, steep, souse, drench, waterlog, impregnate, permeate, imbue, suffuse, fill.

saturated *adj* **1** SOAKED, soaking,

sopping, dripping, soused, steeped, drenched, flooded, wringing, waterlogged, sodden. **2** IMBUED, impregnated, permeated, suffused.

sauce *n* **1** DRESSING, relish, condiment, flavouring, dip, mayonnaise. **2** CHEEKINESS, cheek, impudence, impertinence, presumption, presumptuousness, audacity, freshness, flippancy, pertness, backchat, brazenness, insolence, disrespectfulness, disrespect, irreverence, rudeness, sass, malapertness (*fml*), brass (*infml*), lip (*infml*), nerve (*infml*), sauciness (*infml*), mouth (*infml*).
☒ **2** politeness, respectfulness.

saucy (*infml*) *adj* cheeky (*infml*), impertinent, impudent, insolent, disrespectful, pert, forward, presumptuous, flippant.
☒ polite, respectful.

saunter *v* stroll, amble, mosey (*infml*), mooch (*infml*), wander, ramble (*sl*), meander.
➤ *n* stroll, walk, constitutional, ramble.

savage *adj* wild, untamed, undomesticated, uncivilized, primitive, barbaric, barbarous, fierce, ferocious, vicious, beastly, cruel, inhuman, brutal, sadistic, bloodthirsty, bloody, murderous, pitiless, merciless, ruthless, harsh.
☒ tame, civilized, humane, mild.
➤ *n* brute, beast, barbarian.
➤ *v* attack, bite, claw, tear, maul, mangle.

save *v* **1** ECONOMIZE, cut back, conserve, preserve, keep, retain, hold, reserve, store, lay up, set aside, put by, hoard, stash (*infml*), collect, gather. **2** RESCUE, deliver, liberate, free, salvage, recover, reclaim. **3** PROTECT, guard, screen, shield, safeguard, spare, prevent, hinder.
☒ **1** spend, squander, waste, discard.
➤ *n* economy, thrift, discount, reduction, bargain, cut, conservation, preservation.
☒ expense, waste, loss.

saving *adj* **1** ECONOMICAL, careful, sparing, thrifty, frugal. **2** *a saving grace*: qualifying, compensatory, extenuating, mitigating.
➤ *n* **1** ECONOMY, thrift, discount, reduction, bargain, cut, conservation, preservation. **2** *put your savings in the bank*: capital, investments, nest egg, fund, store, reserves, resources.
☒ **1** expense, loss, waste. **2** expenditure.

saviour *n* **1** RESCUER, deliverer, redeemer,

liberator, emancipator, guardian, protector, defender, champion. **2** *Jesus Christ, the Saviour*: Redeemer, Deliverer, Lamb of God, Mediator, Emmanuel.

🖃 **1** destroyer.

savoir-faire *n* capability, ability, accomplishment, confidence, assurance, discretion, expertise, finesse, poise, diplomacy, tact, urbanity, know-how (*infml*).

🖃 awkwardness, clumsiness, incompetence, inexperience.

savour *n* taste, flavour, smack, smell, tang, piquancy, salt, spice, relish, zest.

➤ *v* relish, enjoy, delight in, revel in, like, appreciate.

🖃 shrink from.

savoury *adj* **1** TASTY, appetizing, delicious, mouthwatering, luscious, palatable. **2** *savoury pancakes*: salty, spicy, aromatic, piquant, tangy.

🖃 **1** unappetizing, tasteless, insipid, **2** sweet.

say *v* **1** EXPRESS, phrase, put, render, utter, voice, articulate, enunciate, pronounce, deliver, speak, orate (*fml*), recite, repeat, read, indicate. **2** ANSWER, reply, respond, rejoin, retort, exclaim, ejaculate, comment, remark, observe, mention, add, drawl, mutter, grunt. **3** TELL, instruct, order, communicate, convey, intimate, report, announce, declare, state, assert, affirm, maintain, claim, allege, rumour, suggest, imply, signify, reveal, disclose, divulge. **4** GUESS, estimate, reckon, judge, imagine, suppose, assume, presume, surmise.

Other words for say include: accuse, acknowledge, add, admit, admonish, advise, affirm, agree, allege, announce, answer, argue, ask, assert, assume, aver (*fml*), avow (*fml*), babble (*infml*), banter, bark, bawl, beg, begin, bellow, blare, blaspheme, blurt, boast, brag, call, chant, chatter, claim, coax, come out with (*infml*), command, comment, communicate, complain, conclude, confide, conjecture (*fml*), continue, contradict, convey, correct, counter, croak, cry, curse, declare, demand, deny, describe, detail, disclose, dispute, divulge, echo, elaborate, elucidate, emphasize, enjoin, estimate, exclaim, expostulate, express, falter, finish, flounder, gasp, greet, groan, growl, grumble, grunt, guess, hint, howl, imagine, implore, imply, indicate, infer, inform, inquire,

insinuate, insist, instruct, interrogate, interrupt, intervene, intimate, jeer, jest, joke, laugh, lecture, lie, maintain, make known, make public, mention, mimic, moan, mock, mouth, mumble, murmur, mutter, nag, observe, offer, orate (*fml*), order, persist, persuade, phrase, pipe, plead, point out, predict, press, presume, proclaim, profess, proffer, prompt, pronounce, propose, protest, put about (*infml*), query, question, quote, rage, rail, rant, read, reassure, rebuke, recite, reckon, recommend, rehearse, reiterate, rejoice, relate, remark, remonstrate, renounce, repeat, reply, report, request, resolve, respond, retaliate, retort, retract, reveal, roar, rumour, scoff, scold, scream, screech, shout, shriek, snap, snarl, speak, specify, speculate, squeak, stammer, state, storm, stutter, submit, suggest, suppose, surmise, swear, sympathize, taunt, tease, tell, testify, thunder, urge, utter, venture, voice, volunteer, vow, whine, whisper, wonder, yell.

saying *n* adage, proverb, dictum, precept, axiom, aphorism, maxim, motto, slogan, phrase, expression, quotation, statement, remark.

scale[1] *n* ratio, proportion, measure, degree, extent, spread, reach, range, scope, compass, spectrum, gamut, sequence, series, progression, order, hierarchy, ranking, ladder, steps, gradation, graduation, calibration, register.

➤ *v* climb, ascend, mount, clamber, scramble, shin up, conquer, surmount.

scale[2] *n* encrustation, deposit, crust, layer, film, lamina, plate, flake, scurf.

scamp *n* rogue, rascal, scallywag, monkey, imp, devil.

scamper *v* scuttle, scurry, scoot, dart, dash, run, sprint, rush, hurry, hasten (*fml*), fly, romp, frolic, gambol.

scan *v* **1** EXAMINE, scrutinize, study, search, survey, sweep, investigate, check. **2** SKIM, glance at, flick through, thumb through.

➤ *n* screening, examination, scrutiny, search, probe, check, investigation, survey, review.

scandal *n* outrage, offence, outcry, uproar, furore, gossip, rumours, smear, dirt, discredit, dishonour, disgrace, shame, embarrassment, ignominy (*fml*).

scandalize *v* shock, horrify, appal, dismay, disgust, repel, revolt, offend, affront, outrage.

scandalous *adj* shocking, appalling, atrocious, abominable, monstrous, unspeakable, outrageous, disgraceful, shameful, disreputable, infamous, improper, unseemly, defamatory, scurrilous, slanderous, libellous, untrue.

scant *adj* little, sparse, limited, little or no, bare, deficient, minimal, hardly any, inadequate, insufficient, exiguous (*fml*), measly (*infml*).
◫ adequate, ample, sufficient.

scanty *adj* deficient, short, inadequate, insufficient, scant, little, limited, restricted, narrow, poor, meagre, insubstantial, thin, skimpy, sparse, bare.
◫ adequate, sufficient, ample, plentiful, substantial.

scapegoat *n* victim, whipping-boy, sucker, fall guy (*infml*), patsy (*US sl*).

scar *n* mark, lesion, wound, injury, blemish, stigma.
➢ *v* mark, disfigure, spoil, damage, brand, stigmatize.

scarce *adj* few, rare, infrequent, uncommon, unusual, sparse, scanty, insufficient, deficient, lacking.
◫ plentiful, common.

scarcely *adv* **1** *I can scarcely hear you*: hardly, barely, only just. **2** *that is scarcely a reason to hit him*: hardly, not, not at all, certainly not, definitely not.

scarcity *n* lack, shortage, dearth, deficiency, insufficiency, paucity, rareness, rarity, infrequency, uncommonness, sparseness, scantiness.
◫ glut, plenty, abundance, sufficiency, enough.

scare *v* frighten, startle, alarm, dismay, daunt, intimidate, unnerve, threaten, menace, terrorize, shock, appal, panic, terrify.
◫ reassure, calm.
➢ *n* fright, start, shock, alarm, panic, hysteria, terror.
◫ reassurance, comfort.

scared *adj* frightened, fearful, nervous, anxious, worried, startled, shaken, panic-stricken, terrified.
◫ confident, reassured.

scaremonger *n* alarmist, pessimist, prophet of doom, doom and gloom merchant, doomwatcher, jitterbug, Cassandra.

scary *adj* frightening, alarming, daunting, intimidating, disturbing, shocking,

horrifying, terrifying, hair-raising, bloodcurdling, spine-chilling, chilling, creepy, eerie, spooky (*infml*).

scathing *adj* sarcastic, scornful, critical, trenchant, cutting, biting, caustic, acid, vitriolic, bitter, harsh, brutal, savage, unsparing.
◫ complimentary.

scatter *v* disperse, dispel, dissipate, disband, disunite, separate, divide, break up, disintegrate, diffuse, broadcast, disseminate, spread, sprinkle, sow, strew, fling, shower.
◫ gather, collect.

scatterbrained *adj* forgetful, absent-minded, empty-headed, feather-brained, scatty (*infml*), careless, inattentive, thoughtless, unreliable, irresponsible, frivolous.
◫ sensible, sober, efficient, careful.

scattering *n* sprinkling, few, handful, smattering.
◫ mass, abundance.

scavenge *v* forage, rummage, rake, search, scrounge.

scenario *n* outline, synopsis, summary, résumé, storyline, plot, scheme, plan, programme, projection, sequence, situation, scene.

scene *n* **1** PLACE, area, spot, locale, site, situation, position, whereabouts, location, locality, environment, milieu, setting, contact, background, backdrop, set, stage. **2** LANDSCAPE, panorama, view, vista, prospect, sight, spectacle, picture, tableau, pageant. **3** EPISODE, incident, part, division, act, clip. **4** *don't make a scene*: fuss, commotion, to-do (*infml*), performance, drama, exhibition, display, show.

scenery *n* landscape, terrain, panorama, view, vista, outlook, scene, background, setting, surroundings, backdrop, set.

scenic *adj* panoramic, picturesque, attractive, pretty, beautiful, grand, striking, impressive, spectacular, breathtaking, awe-inspiring.
◫ dull, dreary.

scent *n* **1** PERFUME, fragrance, aroma, bouquet, smell, odour. **2** *follow the scent*: track, trail.
◫ **1** stink.
➢ *v* smell, sniff (out), nose (out), sense, perceive, detect, discern, recognize.

scented *adj* perfumed, fragrant, sweet-smelling, aromatic.
🔄 malodorous, stinking.

sceptic *n* doubter, unbeliever, disbeliever, agnostic, atheist, rationalist, questioner, scoffer, cynic.
🔄 believer.

sceptical *adj* doubting, doubtful, unconvinced, unbelieving, disbelieving, questioning, distrustful, mistrustful, hesitating, dubious, suspicious, scoffing, cynical, pessimistic.
🔄 convinced, confident, trusting.

scepticism *n* doubt, unbelief, disbelief, agnosticism, atheism, rationalism, distrust, suspicion, cynicism, pessimism.
🔄 belief, faith.

schedule *n* timetable, programme, agenda, diary, calendar, itinerary, plan, scheme, list, inventory, catalogue, table, form.
➤ *v* timetable, time, table, programme, plan, organize, arrange, appoint, assign, book, list.

schematic *adj* diagrammatic, representational, symbolic, illustrative, graphic.

scheme *n* **1** PROGRAMME, schedule, plan, project, idea, proposal, proposition, suggestion, draft, outline, blueprint, schema, diagram, chart, layout, pattern, design, shape, configuration, arrangement. **2** INTRIGUE, plot, conspiracy, device, stratagem, ruse, ploy, shift, manoeuvre, tactic(s), strategy, procedure, system, method.
➤ *v* plot, conspire, connive, collude, intrigue, machinate, manoeuvre, manipulate, pull strings, mastermind, plan, project, contrive, devise, frame, work out.

scheming *adj* crafty, cunning, deceitful, sly, underhand, unscrupulous, wily, devious, artful, calculating, conniving, designing, insidious, tricky, slippery, foxy, Machiavellian, duplicitous (*fml*).
🔄 artless, honest, open, transparent.

schism *n* **1** DIVISION, split, rift, rupture, break, breach, disunion, separation, severance, estrangement, discord. **2** SPLINTER GROUP, faction, sect.

scholar *n* pupil, student, academic, intellectual, egghead (*infml*), authority, expert.
🔄 dunce, ignoramus.

scholarly *adj* learned, erudite, lettered, academic, scholastic, school, intellectual, highbrow, bookish, studious, well-read, knowledgeable, analytical, scientific.
🔄 uneducated, illiterate.

scholarship *n* **1** ERUDITION, learnedness, learning, knowledge, wisdom, education, schooling. **2** *a scholarship to a public school*: grant, award, bursary, endowment, fellowship, exhibition.

school *n* college, academy, institute, institution, seminary, faculty, department, discipline, class, group, pupils, students.
➤ *v* educate, teach, instruct, tutor, coach, train, discipline, drill, verse, prime, prepare, indoctrinate.

schooling *n* education, book-learning, teaching, instruction, tuition, coaching, training, drill, preparation, grounding, guidance, indoctrination.

schoolteacher *n* teacher, instructor, educator, schoolmaster, master, schoolmistress, mistress, schoolmarm, pedagogue.

science *n* technology, discipline, specialization, knowledge, skill, proficiency, technique, art.

Sciences include: acoustics, aerodynamics, aeronautics, agricultural science, anatomy, anthropology, archaeology, astronomy, astrophysics, behavioural science, biochemistry, biology, biophysics, botany, chemistry, chemurgy, climatology, computer science, cybernetics, diagnostics, dietetics, domestic science, dynamics, earth science, ecology, economics, electrodynamics, electronics, engineering, entomology, environmental science, food science, genetics, geochemistry, geographical science, geology, geophysics, graphology, hydraulics, information technology, inorganic chemistry, life science, linguistics, macrobiotics, materials science, mathematics, mechanical engineering, mechanics, medical science, metallurgy, meteorology, microbiology, mineralogy, morphology, natural science, nuclear physics, organic chemistry, ornithology, pathology, pharmacology, physics, physiology, political science, psychology, radiochemistry, robotics, sociology, space technology, telecommunications, thermodynamics, toxicology, ultrasonics, veterinary science, zoology.

scientific *adj* methodical, systematic, controlled, regulated, analytical, mathematical, exact, precise, accurate, scholarly, thorough.

Types of scientific instrument include:
absorptiometer, barostat, cathode ray oscilloscope, centrifuge, chronograph, coherer, collimator, cryostat, decoherer, dephlegmator, dipleidoscope, electromyograph, electrosonde, eudiometer, fluoroscope, Fresnel lens, Geissler tube, heliograph, heliostat, hodoscope, humidistat, hydrophone, hydroscope, hydrostat, hygrograph, hygrostat, iconoscope, image converter, image tube, interferometer, microtome, nephograph, optical character reader, oscillograph, oscilloscope, pantograph, parametric amplifier, phonendoscope, radarscope, radiosonde, rheocord, rheostat, slide-rule, spectroscope, stactometer, stauroscope, strobe, stroboscope, tachistoscope, tachograph, teinoscope, telemeter, telethermoscope, tesla coil, thermostat, thyratron, torsion-balance, transformer, transponder, tunnel diode, vernier, zymoscope. *see also* **laboratory**; **medical**.

scintillating *adj* sparkling, glittering, flashing, bright, shining, brilliant, dazzling, exciting, stimulating, lively, animated, vivacious, ebullient, witty.
🈺 dull.

scoff¹ *v* mock, ridicule, poke fun, taunt, tease, rib (*sl*), jeer, sneer, pooh-pooh, scorn, despise, revile, deride, belittle, disparage, knock (*infml*).
🈺 praise, compliment, flatter.

scoff² *v* eat, consume, devour, put away (*infml*), gobble (*infml*), guzzle (*infml*), wolf (*infml*), bolt, gulp.
🈺 fast, abstain.

scold *v* chide, tell off (*infml*), tick off (*infml*), reprimand, reprove, rebuke, take to task, admonish, upbraid (*fml*), castigate (*fml*), berate (*fml*), reproach, blame, censure, lecture, nag.
🈺 praise, commend.

scolding *n* castigation (*fml*), telling-off (*infml*), ticking-off (*infml*), dressing-down (*infml*), reprimand, reproof, rebuke, lecture, talking-to (*infml*), earful (*infml*).
🈺 praise, commendation.

scoop *n* **1** LADLE, spoon, dipper, bailer, bucket, shovel. **2** EXCLUSIVE, coup, inside

story, revelation, exposé, sensation, latest (*infml*).
➤ *v* gouge, scrape, hollow, empty, dig, excavate, shovel, ladle, spoon, dip, bail.

scope *n* **1** RANGE, compass, field, area, sphere, ambit, terms of reference, confines, reach, extent, span, breadth, coverage. **2** *scope for improvement*: room, space, capacity, elbow-room, latitude, leeway, freedom, liberty, opportunity.

scorch *v* burn, singe, char, blacken, scald, roast, sear, parch, shrivel, wither.

scorching *adj* burning, boiling, baking, roasting, sizzling, blistering, sweltering, torrid, tropical, searing, red-hot.

score *n* **1** RESULT, total, sum, tally, points, marks. **2** SCRATCH, line, groove, mark, nick, notch.
➤ *v* **1** RECORD, register, chalk up, notch up, count, total, make, earn, gain, achieve, attain, win, have the advantage, have the edge, be one up. **2** SCRATCH, scrape, graze, mark, groove, gouge, cut, incise, engrave, indent, nick, slash.

scorn *n* contempt, scornfulness, disdain, sneering, derision, mockery, ridicule, sarcasm, disparagement, disgust.
🈺 admiration, respect.
➤ *v* despise, look down on, disdain, sneer at, scoff at, deride, mock, laugh at, slight, spurn, refuse, reject, dismiss.
🈺 admire, respect.

scornful *adj* contemptuous, disdainful, supercilious, haughty, arrogant, sneering, scoffing, derisive, mocking, jeering, sarcastic, scathing, disparaging, insulting, slighting, dismissive.
🈺 admiring, respectful.

scot-free *adj* clear, unpunished, unrebuked, unreprimanded, unreproached, unharmed, unhurt, unscathed, undamaged, safe, uninjured, without a scratch.

scoundrel *n* rogue, rascal, villain, vagabond, ruffian, ne'er-do-well, good-for-nothing, miscreant (*fml*), scamp, scallywag, cheat, rotter, reprobate, rat (*infml*), swine (*infml*), louse (*sl*), scab (*sl*).

scour¹ *v* scrape, abrade (*fml*), rub, polish, burnish, scrub, clean, wash, cleanse, purge, flush.

scour² *v* search, hunt, comb, drag, ransack, rummage, forage, rake.

scourge *n* **1** AFFLICTION, misfortune, torment, terror, bane, evil, curse, plague, penalty, punishment. **2** WHIP, lash.

▪ **1** blessing, godsend, boon.

➤ *v* **1** AFFLICT, torment, curse, plague, devastate, punish, chastise, discipline. **2** WHIP, flog, beat, lash, cane, flail, thrash.

scout *v* spy out, reconnoitre, explore, investigate, check out, survey, case (*sl*), spy, snoop, search, seek, hunt, probe, look, watch, observe.

➤ *n* spy, reconnoitre, vanguard, outrider, escort, lookout, recruiter, spotter.

scowl *v, n* frown, glower, glare, grimace, pout.

▪ smile, grin, beam.

scrabble *v* clamber, scramble, scrape, scratch, claw, grope, grub, paw, dig, root.

scraggy *adj* scrawny, skinny, thin, lean, lanky, bony, angular, gaunt, undernourished, emaciated, wasted.

▪ plump, sleek.

scramble *v* **1** CLIMB, scale, clamber, crawl, shuffle, scrabble, grope. **2** RUSH, hurry, hasten (*fml*), run, push, jostle, struggle, strive, vie, contend.

➤ *n* rush, hurry, race, dash, hustle, bustle, commotion, confusion, muddle, struggle, free-for-all, mêlée.

scrap¹ *n* bit, piece, fragment, part, fraction, crumb, morsel, bite, mouthful, sliver, shred, snippet, atom, iota, grain, particle, mite, trace, vestige, remnant, leftover, waste, junk.

➤ *v* discard, throw away, jettison, shed, abandon, drop, dump, ditch (*sl*), cancel, axe, demolish, break up, write off.

▪ recover, restore.

scrap² *n* fight, scuffle, brawl, dust-up (*infml*), quarrel, row, argument, squabble, wrangle, dispute, disagreement.

▪ peace, agreement.

➤ *v* fight, brawl, quarrel, argue, fall out, squabble, bicker, wrangle, disagree.

▪ agree.

scrape *v* **1** GRATE, grind, rasp, file, scour, rub, clean, remove, erase, scrabble, claw, abrade (*fml*). **2** SCRATCH, graze, skin, cut, bark, scuff.

➤ *n* **1** GRAZE, scratch, rub, abrasion, scuff, shave. **2** DIFFICULTY, dilemma, predicament, trouble, plight, distress, fix (*infml*), mess (*infml*), pickle (*infml*), tight spot (*infml*), pretty kettle of fish (*infml*).

♦ **scrape by** just manage to live, get by, scrimp, skimp, scarcely have enough to live on.

♦ **scrape through** just pass, only just/barely win, just succeed in, get through by a whisker (*infml*).

♦ **scrape together** get together, round up, pool together, get with difficulty, collect with difficulty, obtain with difficulty, just manage to get.

scrappy *adj* bitty, disjointed, piecemeal, fragmentary, incomplete, sketchy, superficial, slapdash, slipshod.

▪ complete, finished.

scratch *v* claw, gouge, score, mark, cut, incise, etch, engrave, scrape, rub, scuff, graze, gash, lacerate.

➤ *n* mark, line, scrape, scuff, abrasion, graze, gash, laceration.

scrawl *v* scribble, write quickly, pen, jot (down), dash off, doodle.

➤ *n* scribble, squiggle, writing, handwriting, bad/illegible handwriting, scratch, scrabble, cacography (*fml*).

scrawny *adj* scraggy, skinny, thin, lean, lanky, angular, bony, underfed, undernourished, emaciated.

▪ fat, plump.

scream *v, n* shriek, screech, cry, shout, yell, bawl, roar, howl, wail, squeal, yelp.

screech *v, n* squeal, cry, scream, shriek, howl, yell, squawk, yelp.

▪ whisper.

screen *v* **1** *screen a film*: show, present, broadcast. **2** SHIELD, protect, safeguard, defend, guard, cover, mask, veil, cloak, shroud, hide, conceal, shelter, shade. **3** SORT, grade, sift, sieve, filter, process, evaluate, gauge, examine, scan, vet.

▪ **2** uncover, expose.

➤ *n* partition, divider, shield, guard, cover, mask, veil, cloak, shroud, concealment, shelter, shade, awning, canopy, net, mesh.

screw *v* fasten, adjust, tighten, contract, compress, squeeze, extract, extort, force, constrain, pressurize, turn, wind, twist, wring, distort, wrinkle.

♦ **screw up** **1** *screw up one's face*: wrinkle, distort, tighten, knot, crumple, contract, pucker, contort. **2** MESS UP, spoil, botch, bungle, mishandle, mismanage, make a hash of (*infml*), louse up (*sl*), cock up (*sl*).

▪ **2** manage.

scribble *v* write, pen, jot, dash off, scrawl, doodle.

scribe *n* writer, copyist, amanuensis, secretary, clerk.

scrimp *v* skimp, save, economize, cut

back on, limit, reduce, restrict, scrape, curtail, shorten, stint, pinch, tighten one's belt (*infml*), cut one's coat according to one's cloth (*infml*).
🔁 spend.

script *n* **1** *a film script*: text, lines, words, dialogue, screenplay, libretto, book. **2** WRITING, handwriting, hand, longhand, calligraphy, letters, manuscript, copy.

scripture

The sacred writings of religions include: the word of God, the word, Holy Bible, the Gospel, Old Testament, New Testament, Epistle, Torah, Pentateuch, Talmud, Koran, Bhagavad-Gita, Veda, Granth, Zend-Avesta.

scrounge *v* cadge, beg, sponge.

scrounger *n* cadger, sponger, parasite.

scrub *v* **1** *scrub the floor*: rub, brush, clean, wash, cleanse, scour. **2** (*infml*) ABOLISH, cancel, delete, abandon, give up, drop, discontinue.

scruffy *adj* untidy, messy, unkempt, dishevelled, bedraggled, run-down, tattered, shabby, disreputable, worn-out, ragged, seedy, squalid, slovenly.
🔁 tidy, well-dressed.

scruple *n* reluctance, hesitation, doubt, qualm, misgiving, uneasiness, difficulty, perplexity.
➤ *v* hesitate, think twice, hold back, shrink.

scruples *n* standards, principles, morals, ethics.

scrupulous *adj* **1** PAINSTAKING, meticulous, conscientious, careful, rigorous, strict, exact, precise, minute, nice. **2** PRINCIPLED, moral, ethical, honourable, upright.
🔁 **1** superficial, careless, reckless. **2** unscrupulous, unprincipled.

scrutinize *v* examine, inspect, study, scan, analyse, sift, investigate, probe, search, explore.

scrutiny *n* examination, inspection, study, analysis, investigation, inquiry, search, exploration.

scuff *v* scrape, scratch, graze, abrade, rub, brush, drag.

scuffle *v* fight, scrap, tussle, brawl, grapple, struggle, contend, clash.
➤ *n* fight, scrap, tussle, brawl, fray, set-to, rumpus, commotion, disturbance, affray.

sculpt *v* sculpture, carve, chisel, hew, cut, model, mould, cast, form, shape, fashion.

sculpture

Types of sculpture include: bas-relief, bronze, bust, carving, caryatid, cast, effigy, figure, figurine, group, head, herm, high-relief, maquette, marble, moulding, plaster cast, relief, statue, statuette, telamon, waxwork.

scum *n* froth, foam, film, impurities, dross, dregs, rubbish, trash.

scupper *v* **1** *scupper a plan*: foil, wreck, ruin, scuttle, disable, demolish, defeat, destroy, overthrow, overwhelm, put a spanner in the works (*infml*). **2** *scupper a ship*: sink, destroy, submerge, torpedo.
🔁 **1** advance, promote.

scurrilous *adj* rude, vulgar, coarse, foul, obscene, indecent, salacious, offensive, abusive, insulting, disparaging, defamatory, slanderous, libellous, scandalous.
🔁 polite, courteous, complimentary.

scurry *v* dash, rush, hurry, hasten (*fml*), bustle, scramble, scuttle, scamper, scoot, dart, run, sprint, trot, race, fly, skim, scud.

scuttle *v* scurry, hurry, rush, scutter, bustle, scamper, scramble, scud, run, hasten (*fml*).

sea *n* **1** OCEAN, main, deep, briny (*infml*). **2** *a sea of faces*: multitude, abundance, profusion, mass.
➤ *adj* marine, maritime, ocean, oceanic, salt, saltwater, aquatic, seafaring.
🔁 land, air.
◆ **at sea** adrift, lost, confused, bewildered, baffled, puzzled, perplexed, mystified.

seafaring *adj* sea-going, ocean-going, sailing, nautical, naval, marine, maritime.

seal *v* **1** *seal a jar*: close, shut, stop, plug, cork, stopper, waterproof, fasten, secure. **2** SETTLE, conclude, finalize, stamp.
🔁 **1** unseal.
➤ *n* stamp, signet, insignia, imprimatur, authentication, assurance, attestation, confirmation, ratification.
◆ **seal off** block up, close off, shut off, fence off, cut off, segregate, isolate, quarantine.
🔁 open up.

seam *n* **1** JOIN, joint, weld, closure, line. **2** *coal seam*: layer, stratum, vein, lode.

seamy *adj* disreputable, sleazy, sordid,

squalid, unsavoury, rough, dark, low, nasty, unpleasant.

☒ respectable, wholesome, pleasant.

sear _v_ burn, scorch, brown, fry, sizzle, seal, cauterize, brand, parch, shrivel, wither.

search _v_ seek, look, hunt, rummage, rifle, ransack, scour, comb, sift, probe, explore, frisk (_sl_), examine, scrutinize, inspect, check, investigate, inquire, pry.
➤ _n_ hunt, quest, pursuit, rummage, probe, exploration, examination, scrutiny, inspection, investigation, inquiry, research, survey.

searching _adj_ penetrating, piercing, keen, sharp, close, intent, probing, thorough, minute.

☒ vague, superficial.

seaside _n_ coast, shore, beach, sands.

season _n_ period, spell, phase, term, time, span, interval.
➤ _v_ **1** _season food_: flavour, spice, salt. **2** AGE, mature, ripen, harden, toughen, train, prepare, condition, treat, temper.

seasonable _adj_ timely, well-timed, welcome, opportune, convenient, suitable, appropriate, fitting.

☒ unseasonable, inopportune.

seasoned _adj_ mature, experienced, practised, well-versed, veteran, old, hardened, toughened, conditioned, acclimatized, weathered.

☒ inexperienced, novice.

seasoning _n_ flavouring, spice, condiment, salt, pepper, relish, sauce, dressing.

seat _n_ **1** CHAIR, bench, pew, stool, throne. **2** _country seat_: residence, abode, house, mansion. **3** PLACE, site, situation, location, headquarters, centre, heart, hub, axis, source, cause, bottom, base, foundation, footing, ground.
➤ _v_ sit, place, set, locate, install, fit, fix, settle, accommodate, hold, contain, take.

seating _n_ seats, chairs, places, room, accommodation.

secede _v_ separate, split off, withdraw, break away, break, resign, retire, leave, disaffiliate, turn one's back on, apostatize (_fml_), quit (_infml_).

☒ join, unite with.

secession _n_ seceding, split, withdrawal, defection, break, breakaway, disaffiliation, schism, apostasy (_fml_).

☒ amalgamation, unification.

secluded _adj_ private, cloistered, sequestered, shut away, cut off, isolated, lonely, solitary, remote, out-of-the-way, sheltered, hidden, concealed.

☒ public, accessible.

seclusion _n_ privacy, retirement, retreat, isolation, solitude, remoteness, shelter, hiding, concealment.

second¹ _adj_ duplicate, twin, double, repeated, additional, further, extra, supplementary, alternative, other, alternate, next, following, subsequent, succeeding, secondary, subordinate, lower, inferior, lesser, supporting.
➤ _n_ helper, assistant, backer, supporter.
➤ _v_ approve, agree with, endorse, back, support, help, assist, aid, further, advance, forward, promote, encourage.

second² _n_ minute, tick (_infml_), moment, instant, flash, jiffy (_infml_).

secondary _adj_ subsidiary, subordinate, lower, inferior, lesser, minor, unimportant, ancillary, auxiliary, supporting, relief, back-up, reserve, spare, extra, second, alternative, indirect, derived, resulting.

☒ primary, main, major.

second-class _adj_ second-best, second-rate, mediocre, inferior, unimportant, indifferent, uninspiring, undistinguished, uninspired.

☒ valuable.

second-hand _adj_ used, old, worn, hand-me-down, borrowed, derivative, secondary, indirect, vicarious.

☒ new.

second-rate _adj_ inferior, substandard, second-class, second-best, poor, low-grade, shoddy, cheap, tawdry, mediocre, undistinguished, uninspired, uninspiring.

☒ first-rate.

secrecy _n_ privacy, seclusion, confidentiality, confidence, covertness, concealment, disguise, camouflage, furtiveness, surreptitiousness, stealthiness, stealth, mystery.

☒ openness.

secret _adj_ **1** PRIVATE, discreet, covert, hidden, concealed, unseen, shrouded, covered, disguised, camouflaged, undercover, furtive, surreptitious, stealthy, sly, underhand, under-the-counter, hole-and-corner, cloak-and-dagger, clandestine, underground, backstairs, back-door. **2** CLASSIFIED, restricted, confidential, hush-hush (_infml_),

unpublished, undisclosed, unrevealed, unknown. **3** CRYPTIC, mysterious, occult, arcane, recondite, deep. **4** SECRETIVE, close, retired, secluded, out-of-the-way.
☒ **1** public, open. **2** well-known.
➤ *n* **1** CONFIDENTIAL MATTER, confidence, private matter, mystery, enigma, inside story (*infml*). **2** *the secret of eternal youth*: code, key, answer, solution, formula, recipe.
◆ **in secret** confidentially, in confidence, in private, under cover, privately, quietly, surreptitiously, stealthily, unobserved, covertly, furtively, on the quiet, clandestinely (*fml*), in camera (*fml*), privily (*fml*), on the q.t. (*infml*), on the sly (*infml*), behind closed doors (*infml*), hugger-mugger (*infml*).
☒ openly.

secretary *n* personal assistant, PA, typist, stenographer, clerk.

secrete[1] *v* hide, conceal, stash away (*infml*), bury, cover, screen, shroud, veil, disguise, take, appropriate.
☒ uncover, reveal, disclose.

secrete[2] *v* exude, discharge, release, give off, emit, emanate, produce.

secretion *n* exudation, discharge, release, emission.

secretive *adj* tight-lipped, close, cagey (*infml*), uncommunicative, unforthcoming, reticent, reserved, withdrawn, quiet, deep, cryptic, enigmatic.
☒ open, communicative, forthcoming.

secretly *adv* confidentially, in confidence, in private, in secret, under cover, privately, quietly, surreptitiously, stealthily, unobserved, covertly, furtively, on the quiet, clandestinely (*fml*), in camera (*fml*), privily (*fml*), on the q.t. (*infml*), on the sly (*infml*), behind closed doors (*infml*).
☒ openly.

sect *n* denomination, cult, division, subdivision, group, splinter group, faction, camp, wing, party, school.

sectarian *adj* factional, partisan, cliquish, exclusive, narrow, limited, parochial, insular, narrow-minded, bigoted, fanatical, doctrinaire, dogmatic, rigid.
☒ non-sectarian, cosmopolitan, broad-minded.

section *n* division, subdivision, chapter, paragraph, passage, instalment, part, component, fraction, fragment, bit, piece, slice, portion, segment, sector, zone,

district, area, region, department, branch, wing.
☒ whole.

sector *n* zone, district, quarter, area, region, section, division, subdivision, part.
☒ whole.

secular *adj* lay, temporal, worldly, earthly, civil, state, non-religious, profane.
☒ religious.

secure *adj* **1** SAFE, unharmed, undamaged, protected, sheltered, shielded, immune, impregnable, fortified, fast, tight, fastened, locked, fixed, immovable, stable, steady, solid, firm, well-founded, reliable, dependable, steadfast, certain, sure, conclusive, definite. **2** CONFIDENT, assured, reassured.
☒ **1** insecure, vulnerable. **2** uneasy, ill at ease.
➤ *v* **1** OBTAIN, acquire, gain, get. **2** FASTEN, attach, fix, make fast, tie, moor, lash, chain, lock (up), padlock, bolt, batten down, nail, rivet.
☒ **1** lose. **2** unfasten.

security *n* **1** SAFETY, immunity, asylum, sanctuary, refuge, cover, protection, defence, surveillance, safekeeping, preservation, care, custody. **2** *security for a loan*: collateral, surety, pledge, guarantee, warranty, assurance, insurance, precautions, safeguards. **3** CONFIDENCE, conviction, certainty, positiveness.
☒ **1** insecurity.

sedate *adj* staid, dignified, solemn, grave, serious, sober, decorous, proper, seemly, demure, composed, unruffled, serene, tranquil, calm, quiet, cool, collected, imperturbable, unflappable (*infml*), deliberate, slow-moving.
☒ undignified, lively, agitated.

sedative *adj* calming, soothing, anodyne, lenitive, tranquillizing, relaxing, soporific, depressant.
☒ rousing.
➤ *n* tranquillizer, sleeping-pill, narcotic, barbiturate.

sedentary *adj* sitting, seated, desk-bound, inactive, still, stationary, immobile, unmoving.
☒ active.

sediment *n* deposit, residue, grounds, lees, dregs.

sedition *n* agitation, rabble-rousing, subversion, disloyalty, treachery, treason,

insubordination, mutiny, rebellion, revolt.
🠿 calm, loyalty.

seditious *adj* agitating, inciting, rabble-
rousing, subversive, disloyal, traitorous,
mutinous, rebellious, revolutionary,
insubordinate (*fml*), dissident (*fml*),
insurrectionist (*fml*), refractory (*fml*).
🠿 calm, loyal.

seduce *v* entice, lure, allure, attract,
tempt, charm, beguile, ensnare, lead
astray, mislead, deceive, corrupt,
dishonour, ruin.
🠿 repel.

seduction *n* enticement, lure, attraction,
temptation, come-on (*infml*), corruption,
ruin.

seductive *adj* enticing, alluring,
attractive, tempting, tantalizing, inviting,
come-hither (*infml*), flirtatious, sexy
(*infml*), provocative, beguiling,
captivating, bewitching, irresistible.
🠿 unattractive, repulsive.

see *v* 1 PERCEIVE, glimpse, discern, spot,
make out, distinguish, identify, sight,
notice, observe, watch, view, look at, mark,
note. 2 IMAGINE, picture, visualize,
envisage, foresee, anticipate. 3 *I see your
point*: understand, comprehend, grasp,
fathom, follow, realize, recognize,
appreciate, regard, consider, deem.
4 DISCOVER, find out, learn, ascertain,
determine, decide. 5 LEAD, usher,
accompany, escort, court, go out with,
date. 6 VISIT, consult, interview, meet.
◆ **see about** arrange, attend to, deal with,
take care of, look after, organize, manage,
be responsible for, do, fix, repair, sort out.
◆ **see through** 1 *see through a trick*: realize,
understand, fathom, penetrate, not be
deceived by, not be taken in by, get wise to
(*infml*). 2 *see a task through*: stick out,
continue, persist, persevere, not give up,
hang in (*infml*).
◆ **see to** attend to, deal with, take care of,
look after, arrange, organize, manage, do,
fix, repair, sort out.

seed *n* pip, stone, kernel, nucleus, grain,
germ, sperm, ovum, egg, ovule, spawn,
embryo, source, start, beginning.

seedy *adj* 1 SHABBY, scruffy, tatty, mangy,
sleazy, squalid, grotty (*infml*), crummy (*sl*),
run-down, dilapidated, decaying.
2 UNWELL, ill, sick, poorly, ailing, off-
colour.
🠿 2 well.

seek *v* look for, search for, hunt, pursue,
follow, inquire, ask, invite, request, solicit,
petition, entreat, want, desire, aim, aspire,
try, attempt, endeavour, strive.

seem *v* appear, look, feel, sound, pretend
to be.

seeming *adj* apparent, ostensible,
outward, superficial, surface, quasi-,
pseudo, specious.
🠿 real.

seemingly *adv* apparently, superficially,
on the surface, on the face of it, as far as
one can see, outwardly, allegedly,
ostensibly (*fml*).
🠿 really.

seep *v* ooze, leak, exude, well, trickle,
dribble, percolate, permeate, soak.

seepage *n* leak, leakage, dripping,
oozing, exudation, percolation, osmosis
(*fml*).

seethe *v* 1 BOIL, simmer, bubble,
effervesce, fizz, foam, froth, ferment, rise,
swell, surge, teem, swarm. 2 RAGE, fume,
smoulder, storm.

see-through *adj* transparent,
translucent, sheer, filmy, gauzy,
gossamer(y), flimsy.
🠿 opaque.

segment *n* section, division,
compartment, part, bit, piece, slice,
portion, wedge.
🠿 whole.

segregate *v* separate, keep apart, cut off,
isolate, quarantine, set apart, exclude.
🠿 unite, join.

segregation *n* separation, isolation,
quarantine, apartheid, discrimination.
🠿 unification.

seize *v* grab, snatch, grasp, clutch, grip,
hold, take, confiscate, impound,
appropriate (*fml*), commandeer, hijack,
annex, abduct, catch, capture, arrest,
apprehend, nab (*infml*), collar (*infml*).
🠿 let go, release, hand back.

seizure *n* 1 FIT, attack, convulsion,
paroxysm, spasm. 2 TAKING, confiscation,
appropriation, hijack, annexation,
abduction, capture, arrest, apprehension.
🠿 2 release, liberation.

seldom *adv* rarely, infrequently,
occasionally, hardly ever.
🠿 often, usually.

select *v* choose, pick, single out, decide
on, appoint, elect, prefer, opt for.

➢ *adj* selected, choice, top, prime, first-class, first-rate, hand-picked, elite, exclusive, limited, privileged, special, excellent, superior, posh (*infml*).
🆎 second-rate, ordinary, general.

selection *n* choice, pick, option, preference, assortment, variety, range, line-up, miscellany, medley, potpourri, collection, anthology.

selective *adj* particular, choosy (*infml*), careful, discerning, discriminating.
🆎 indiscriminate.

self *n* ego, personality, identity, person.

self-assured *adj* self-confident, confident, assured, sure of oneself, self-collected, self-possessed, overconfident, cocksure, cocky (*infml*).
🆎 humble, unsure.

self-centred *adj* selfish, self-seeking, self-serving, self-interested, egotistic(al), narcissistic, self-absorbed, egocentric.
🆎 altruistic.

self-confident *adj* confident, self-reliant, self-assured, assured, self-possessed, cool (*infml*), fearless.
🆎 unsure, self-conscious.

self-conscious *adj* uncomfortable, ill at ease, awkward, embarrassed, shamefaced, sheepish, shy, bashful, coy, retiring, shrinking, self-effacing, nervous, insecure.
🆎 natural, unaffected, confident.

self-control *n* calmness, composure, cool (*sl*), patience, self-restraint, restraint, self-denial, temperance, self-discipline, self-mastery, willpower.

self-denial *n* moderation, temperance, abstemiousness, asceticism, self-sacrifice, unselfishness, selflessness.
🆎 self-indulgence.

self-esteem *n* ego, self-respect, self-regard, self-assurance, self-confidence, pride, self-pride, dignity, amour-propre.
🆎 inferiority complex.

self-evident *adj* obvious, manifest (*fml*), clear, undeniable, axiomatic, unquestionable, incontrovertible (*fml*), inescapable.

self-government *n* autonomy, independence, home rule, democracy.
🆎 subjection.

self-important *adj* arrogant, pompous, bigheaded (*infml*), conceited, egoistic, vain, proud, overbearing, swaggering,

strutting, self-consequent, swollen-headed (*infml*), cocky (*infml*), pushy (*infml*), bumptious (*infml*).
🆎 humble.

self-indulgent *adj* hedonistic, dissolute, dissipated, profligate, extravagant, intemperate, immoderate.
🆎 abstemious.

selfish *adj* self-interested, self-seeking, self-serving, mean, miserly, mercenary, greedy, covetous, self-centred, egocentric, egotistic(al).
🆎 unselfish, selfless, generous, considerate.

selfless *adj* unselfish, altruistic, self-denying, self-sacrificing, generous, philanthropic.
🆎 selfish, self-centred.

self-possessed *adj* self-assured, self-collected, calm, collected, composed, confident, unruffled, poised, cool (*infml*), unflappable (*infml*), together (*infml*).
🆎 worried.

self-reliant *adj* independent, self-supporting, self-sufficient, self-sustaining.
🆎 dependent.

self-respect *n* pride, dignity, self-esteem, self-assurance, self-confidence.

self-righteous *adj* smug, complacent, superior, goody-goody (*infml*), pious, sanctimonious, holier-than-thou, pietistic, hypocritical, pharisaical.

self-sacrifice *n* self-denial, self-renunciation, selflessness, altruism, unselfishness, generosity.
🆎 selfishness.

self-satisfied *adj* smug, complacent, self-congratulatory, self-righteous.
🆎 humble.

self-seeking *adj* mercenary, self-interested, selfish, self-loving, self-serving, self-endeared, opportunistic, acquisitive, calculating, careerist, fortune-hunting, gold-digging, on the make (*infml*).
🆎 altruistic.

self-styled *adj* self-appointed, professed, so-called, would-be.

self-supporting *adj* self-sufficient, self-financing, independent, self-reliant.
🆎 dependent.

self-willed *adj* stubborn, obstinate, stiff-necked, opinionated, self-opinionative, self-opinionated, headstrong, pig-headed, ungovernable, wilful, bloody-minded,

intractable (*fml*), refractory (*fml*), cussed (*infml*).
F∃ complaisant.

sell *v* barter, exchange, trade, auction, vend, retail, stock, handle, deal in, trade in, traffic in, merchandise, hawk, peddle, push, advertise, promote, market.
F∃ buy.

♦ **sell out 1** *sell out of fruit*: run out of, have none left, be out of stock. **2** BETRAY, fail, double-cross, rat on (*infml*), sell down the river (*infml*), stab in the back (*infml*).

seller *n* vendor, merchant, trader, supplier, stockist.
F∃ buyer, purchaser.

Types of seller include: agent, auctioneer, bagman, barrow-boy, broker, cold caller, colporteur, commercial traveller, costermonger, dealer, demonstrator, door-to-door salesman/saleswoman, estate agent, factor, hawker, huckster, jobber, knight of the road, market trader, merchandiser, milklady, milkman, pedlar, peddler (*US*), rep (*infml*), representative, retailer, sales assistant, sales clerk, sales executive, saleslady, salesman, salesperson, saleswoman, sales staff, shop assistant, shopkeeper, store clerk, storekeeper, street trader, tallyman, telephone salesperson, ticket agent, tout, tradesman, tradeswoman, traveller, wholesaler. *see also* **shop**.

semblance *n* appearance, air, show, pretence, guise, mask, front, façade, veneer, apparition, image, resemblance, likeness, similarity.

seminary *n* college, institute, institution, training-college, academy, school.

send *v* **1** POST, mail, dispatch, consign, remit, forward, convey, deliver.
2 TRANSMIT, broadcast, communicate.
3 PROPEL, drive, move, throw, fling, hurl, launch, fire, shoot, discharge, emit, direct.
♦ **send for** summon, call for, request, order, command.
F∃ dismiss.
♦ **send up** satirize, mock, ridicule, parody, take off, mimic, imitate.

send-off *n* farewell, leave-taking, departure, start, goodbye.
F∃ arrival.

send-up *n* mockery, parody, skit, satire, imitation, mickey-take (*infml*), spoof (*infml*), take-off (*infml*).

senile *adj* old, aged, doddering, decrepit, failing, confused.

senior *adj* older, elder, higher, superior, high-ranking, major, chief.
F∃ junior.

seniority *n* priority, precedence, rank, standing, status, age, superiority, importance.

sensation *n* **1** FEELING, sense, impression, perception, awareness, consciousness, emotion. **2** *the report caused a sensation*: commotion, stir, agitation, excitement, thrill, furore, outrage, scandal.

sensational *adj* **1** EXCITING, thrilling, electrifying, breathtaking, startling, amazing, astounding, staggering, dramatic, spectacular, impressive, exceptional, excellent, wonderful, marvellous, smashing (*infml*).
2 SCANDALOUS, shocking, horrifying, revealing, melodramatic, lurid.
F∃ **1** ordinary, run-of-the-mill.

sense *n* **1** FEELING, sensation, impression, perception, awareness, consciousness, appreciation, faculty. **2** REASON, logic, mind, brain(s), wit(s), wisdom, intelligence, cleverness, understanding, discernment, judgement, intuition. **3** MEANING, significance, definition, interpretation, implication, point, purpose, substance.
F∃ **2** foolishness. **3** nonsense.
➢ *v* feel, suspect, intuit, perceive, detect, notice, observe, realize, appreciate, understand, comprehend, grasp.

senseless *adj* **1** FOOLISH, stupid, unwise, silly, idiotic, mad, crazy (*infml*), daft (*infml*), ridiculous, ludicrous, absurd, meaningless, nonsensical, fatuous, irrational, illogical, unreasonable, pointless, purposeless, futile.
2 UNCONSCIOUS, out, stunned, anaesthetized, deadened, numb, unfeeling.
F∃ **1** sensible, meaningful. **2** conscious.

sensibility *n* **1** *show sensibility*: sensitiveness, sensitivity, susceptibility, discernment, perceptiveness, appreciation, awareness, responsiveness, insight, intuition, delicacy, taste. **2** *offend someone's sensibilities*: feelings, emotions, sentiments, susceptibilities, sensitivities.
F∃ **1** insensibility.

sensible *adj* wise, prudent, judicious, well-advised, shrewd, far-sighted,

intelligent, level-headed, down-to-earth, commonsense, sober, sane, rational, logical, reasonable, realistic, practical, functional, sound.
☒ senseless, foolish, unwise.

sensitive *adj* 1 SUSCEPTIBLE, vulnerable, impressionable, tender, emotional, thin-skinned, temperamental, touchy (*infml*), irritable, sensitized, responsive, aware, perceptive, discerning, appreciative. 2 DELICATE, fine, exact, precise.
☒ 1 insensitive, thick-skinned.
2 imprecise, approximate.

sensitivity *n* 1 SUSCEPTIBILITY, vulnerability, responsiveness, awareness, perceptiveness, receptiveness, reactiveness, discernment, appreciation, sympathy. 2 DELICACY, fineness, fragility, softness.
☒ 1 insensitivity.

sensual *adj* self-indulgent, voluptuous, worldly, physical, animal, carnal, fleshly, bodily, sexual, erotic, sexy, lustful, randy (*infml*), lecherous, lewd, licentious.
☒ ascetic.

sensuous *adj* pleasurable, gratifying, voluptuous, rich, lush, luxurious, sumptuous.
☒ ascetic, plain, simple.

sentence *n* judgement, decision, verdict, condemnation, pronouncement, ruling, decree, order.
➤ *v* judge, pass judgement on, condemn, doom, punish, penalize.

sentiment *n* 1 THOUGHT, idea, feeling, opinion, view, judgement, belief, persuasion, attitude. 2 EMOTION, sensibility, tenderness, soft-heartedness, romanticism, sentimentality, mawkishness.

sentimental *adj* tender, soft-hearted, emotional, gushing, touching, pathetic, tear-jerking, weepy (*infml*), maudlin, mawkish, nostalgic, romantic, lovey-dovey (*infml*), slushy, mushy, sloppy, schmaltzy, soppy, corny (*infml*).
☒ unsentimental, realistic, cynical.

sentimentality *n* tenderness, sentimentalism, emotionalism, romanticism, mawkishness, nostalgia, bathos (*fml*), corniness (*infml*), gush (*infml*), mush (*infml*), pulp (*infml*), schmaltz (*infml*), sloppiness (*infml*), slush (*infml*).

sentry *n* sentinel, guard, picket, watchman, watch, look-out.

separable *adj* divisible, detachable, removable, distinguishable, distinct.
☒ inseparable.

separate *v* divide, sever, part, split (up), divorce, part company, diverge, disconnect, uncouple, disunite, disaffiliate, disentangle, segregate, isolate, cut off, abstract, remove, detach, withdraw, secede.
☒ join, unite, combine.
➤ *adj* single, individual, particular, independent, alone, solitary, segregated, isolated, apart, divorced, divided, disunited, disconnected, disjointed, detached, unattached, unconnected, unrelated, different, disparate (*fml*), distinct, discrete, several, sundry.
☒ together, attached.

separated *adj* separate, split up, divided, disconnected, parted, isolated, disunited, disassociated, apart, segregated.
☒ attached, together.

separately *adv* independently, individually, singly, apart, discriminately, discretely, alone, personally, severally (*fml*).
☒ together.

separation *n* division, severance, parting, leave-taking, farewell, split-up, break-up, divorce, split, rift, gap, divergence, disconnection, disengagement, dissociation, estrangement, segregation, isolation, detachment.
☒ unification.

septic *adj* infected, poisoned, festering, putrefying, putrid.

sequel *n* follow-up, continuation, development, result, consequence, outcome, issue, upshot, pay-off, end, conclusion.

sequence *n* succession, series, run, progression, chain, string, train, line, procession, order, arrangement, course, track, cycle, set.

serene *adj* calm, tranquil, cool, composed, placid, untroubled, undisturbed, still, quiet, peaceful.
☒ troubled, disturbed.

series *n* set, cycle, succession, sequence, run, progression, chain, string, line, train, order, arrangement, course.

serious *adj* 1 IMPORTANT, significant, weighty, momentous, crucial, critical, urgent, pressing, acute, grave, worrying, difficult, dangerous, grim, severe, deep, far-reaching. **2** UNSMILING, long-faced, humourless, solemn, sober, stern, thoughtful, pensive, earnest, sincere. **ES 1** trivial, slight. **2** smiling, facetious, frivolous.

seriously *adv* **1** SOLEMNLY, thoughtfully, earnestly, sincerely, joking apart. **2** ACUTELY, gravely, badly, severely, critically, dangerously, sorely, distressingly, grievously. **ES 1** casually. **2** slightly.

sermon *n* address, discourse, lecture, harangue, homily, talking-to (*infml*).

serrated *adj* toothed, notched, indented, jagged. **ES** smooth.

servant *n* attendant, retainer, hireling, help, helper, assistant, ancillary. **ES** master, mistress.

> People whose occupation is to serve others include: au pair, barmaid, barman, batman, bell-hop (*US*), boots, butler, care assistant, carer, chambermaid, char (*infml*), charlady, chauffeur, chauffeuse, chef, cleaner, coachman, commissionaire, cook, daily (*infml*), dogsbody (*infml*), domestic, domestic help, drudge, equerry, errand boy, factotum, fag, flunkey, footman, governess, groom, henchman, henchperson, henchwoman, home help, house boy, housekeeper, housemaid, kitchen-maid, lackey, lady-in-waiting, lady's maid, maid, manservant, menial, nanny, ostler, page, page-boy, parlour-maid, scullery maid, scullion, seneschal, skivvy (*infml*), slave, steward, stewardess, tweeny (*infml*), valet, waiter, waitress, wet nurse.

serve *v* **1** WAIT ON, attend, minister to, work for, help, aid, assist, benefit, further. **2** *serve a purpose*: fulfil, complete, answer, satisfy, discharge, perform, act, function. **3** DISTRIBUTE, dole out, present, deliver, provide, supply.

service *n* **1** EMPLOYMENT, work, labour, business, duty, function, performance. **2** USE, usefulness, utility, advantage, benefit, help, assistance. **3** SERVICING, maintenance, overhaul, check. **4** *church service*: worship, observance, ceremony, rite. > *v* maintain, overhaul, check, repair, recondition, tune.

serviceable *adj* usable, useful, helpful, profitable, advantageous, beneficial, utilitarian, simple, plain, unadorned, strong, tough, durable, hard-wearing, dependable, efficient, functional, practical, convenient. **ES** unserviceable, unusable.

servile *adj* obsequious (*fml*), sycophantic, toadying, cringing, fawning, grovelling, bootlicking (*infml*), slavish, subservient, subject, submissive, humble, abject, low, mean, base, menial. **ES** assertive, aggressive.

session *n* sitting, hearing, meeting, assembly, conference, discussion, period, time, term, semester, year.

set *v* **1** PUT, place, locate, situate, position, arrange, prepare, lodge, fix, stick, park, deposit. **2** SCHEDULE, appoint, designate, specify, name, prescribe, ordain, assign, allocate, impose, fix, establish, determine, decide, conclude, settle, resolve. **3** ADJUST, regulate, synchronize, co-ordinate. **4** *the sun sets*: go down, sink, dip, subside, disappear, vanish. **5** CONGEAL, thicken, gel, stiffen, solidify, harden, crystallize. **ES 4** rise.
> *n* **1** COLLECTION, batch, series, sequence, kit, outfit, compendium, assortment, class, category, array (*fml*), assemblage (*fml*). **2** *a set of people*: group, band, gang, crowd, circle, clique, faction. **3** *the set of a film*: setting, background, scene, scenery, backdrop, wings, mise-en-scène. **4** *the set of someone's face/body*: expression, turn, look, position, posture, bearing (*fml*).
> *adj* **1** FIXED, established, scheduled, appointed, arranged, prearranged, specified, decided, agreed, settled, firm, strict, rigid, inflexible, ingrained, entrenched, predetermined (*fml*), prescribed (*fml*), ordained (*fml*). **2** REGULAR, routine, usual, customary, everyday, traditional, habitual, standard, stock, stereotyped, conventional. **3** READY, prepared, equipped, arranged, organized, completed, finished, all set. **ES 1** undecided, movable. **2** spontaneous. **3** unprepared.
♦ set about begin, start, embark on, undertake, tackle, attack.
♦ set aside 1 PUT ASIDE, lay aside, keep (back), save, reserve, set apart, separate, select, earmark. **2** ANNUL, abrogate,

cancel, revoke, reverse, overturn, overrule, reject, discard.

◆ **set back** delay, hold up, slow, retard, hinder, impede.

◆ **set off 1** LEAVE, depart, set out, start (out), begin. **2** DETONATE, light, ignite, touch off, trigger off, explode. **3** DISPLAY, show off, enhance, contrast.

◆ **set on** set upon, attack, turn on, go for, fall upon, lay into, beat up (*infml*).

◆ **set out 1** LEAVE, depart, set off, start (out), begin. **2** LAY OUT, arrange, display, exhibit, present, describe, explain.

◆ **set up** raise, elevate, erect, build, construct, assemble, compose, form, create, establish, institute, found, inaugurate, initiate, begin, start, introduce, organize, arrange, prepare.

setback *n* delay, hold-up, problem, snag, hitch, hiccup, reverse, misfortune, upset, disappointment, defeat.

Ea boost, advance, help, advantage.

setting *n* mounting, frame, surroundings, milieu, environment, background, context, perspective, period, position, location, locale, site, scene, scenery.

settle *v* **1** ARRANGE, order, adjust, reconcile, resolve, complete, conclude. **2** SINK, subside, drop, fall, descend, land, alight. **3** CHOOSE, appoint, fix, establish, determine, decide, agree, confirm. **4** COLONIZE, occupy, populate, people, inhabit, live, reside (*fml*). **5** *settle a bill*: pay, clear, discharge.

settlement *n* **1** RESOLUTION, agreement, arrangement, decision, conclusion, termination, satisfaction. **2** PAYMENT, clearance, clearing, discharge. **3** COLONY, outpost, community, kibbutz, camp, encampment, hamlet, village.

settler *n* colonist, colonizer, pioneer, frontiersman, frontierswoman, planter, immigrant, incomer, newcomer, squatter. **Ea** native.

set-to *n* argument, quarrel, conflict, fight, row, squabble, wrangle, disagreement, exchange, fracas, brush, contest, slanging match, altercation (*fml*), argy-bargy (*infml*), barney (*infml*), dust-up (*infml*), scrap (*infml*), spat (*infml*).

set-up *n* system, structure, organization, arrangement, business, conditions, circumstances.

sever *v* cut, cleave, split, rend, part, separate, divide, cut off, amputate, detach,

disconnect, disjoin, disunite, dissociate, estrange, alienate, break off, dissolve, end, terminate.

Ea join, unite, combine, attach.

several *adj* some, many, various, assorted, sundry, diverse, different, distinct, separate, particular, individual.

severe *adj* **1** EXTREME, acute, intense, fierce, violent, strong, forceful, powerful, cruel, pitiless, merciless, relentless, inexorable, harsh, tough, hard, difficult, grim, forbidding, rigorous, stringent, drastic, draconian, tyrannical. **2** STRICT, rigid, unbending, stern, grim, dour, cold, unsympathetic, disapproving, sober, serious, unsmiling, strait-laced. **3** AUSTERE, ascetic, plain, simple, modest, start, spartan, undecorated, unembellished, unadorned, functional. **4** *a severe illness*: serious, grave, critical, acute, dangerous, perilous. **5** HARD, difficult, demanding, rigorous, arduous, burdensome, taxing, exacting, punishing.

Ea 1 mild, kind, compassionate, sympathetic. **2** lenient. **3** decorated, ornate. **4** minor. **5** easy, simple.

severely *adv* **1** EXTREMELY, acutely, intensely, badly, critically, dangerously, gravely. **2** STRICTLY, rigorously, disapprovingly, sternly, hard, harshly, sharply, sorely, grimly, bitterly, coldly, unsympathetically, dourly.

severity *n* **1** EXTREMITY, acuteness, severeness, intensity, strength, forcefulness, fierceness. **2** HARSHNESS, hardness, toughness, sharpness, ungentleness, ruthlessness, pitilessness, mercilessness, grimness, stringency, coldness, sternness, strictness, seriousness, gravity. **3** AUSTERITY, plainness, rigour, asceticism, simplicity, bareness, plainness, spartanism.

Ea 1 mildness. **2** compassion, kindness, leniency.

sew *v* stitch, tack, baste, hem, darn, embroider.

sex *n* **1** GENDER, sexuality. **2** SEXUAL INTERCOURSE, intercourse, sexual relations, copulation, coitus, lovemaking, fornication, reproduction, union, intimacy.

sexual *adj* sex, reproductive, procreative, genital, coital, venereal, carnal, sensual, erotic.

sexuality *n* sexual instincts, sexual urge, sexual orientation, sexual desire, sexiness, sensuality, desire, carnality, eroticism, virility, lust, voluptuousness.

sexy *adj* sensual, voluptuous, nubile, beddable (*infml*), seductive, inviting, flirtatious, arousing, provoking, provocative, titillating, pornographic, erotic, salacious, suggestive.

F∃ sexless.

shabby *adj* **1** RAGGED, tattered, frayed, worn, worn-out, mangy, moth-eaten, scruffy, tatty, disreputable, dilapidated, run-down, seedy, dirty, dingy, poky. **2** *a shabby trick*: contemptible, despicable, rotten, mean, low, cheap, shoddy, shameful, dishonourable.

F∃ 1 smart. **2** honourable, fair.

shack *n* hut, cabin, shanty, hovel, shed, lean-to.

shackle *v* **1** HAMPER, inhibit, impede, encumber, limit, restrict, restrain, secure, thwart, bind, tie, constrain, obstruct, handicap, hamstring. **2** CHAIN, handcuff, bind, restrain, manacle, fetter, trammel, tether.

➣ *n* bond, tether, chain, fetter, iron, handcuff, rope, manacle, trammel, bracelets (*infml*), darbies (*infml*).

shade *n* **1** SHADINESS, shadow, darkness, obscurity, semi-darkness, dimness, gloom, gloominess, twilight, dusk, gloaming. **2** AWNING, canopy, cover, shelter, screen, blind, curtain, shield, visor, umbrella, parasol. **3** COLOUR, hue, tint, tone, tinge. **4** TRACE, dash, hint, suggestion, suspicion, nuance, gradation, degree, amount, variety. **5** GHOST, spectre, phantom, spirit, apparition, semblance.

➣ *v* shield, screen, protect, cover, shroud, veil, hide, conceal, obscure, cloud, dim, darken, shadow, overshadow.

shadow *n* **1** SHADE, darkness, obscurity, semi-darkness, dimness, gloom, twilight, dusk, gloaming, cloud, cover, protection. **2** SILHOUETTE, shape, image, representation. **3** TRACE, hint, suggestion,

suspicion, vestige, remnant.

➣ *v* **1** OVERSHADOW, overhang, shade, shield, screen, obscure, darken. **2** FOLLOW, tail, dog, stalk, trail, watch.

shadowy *adj* dark, gloomy, murky, obscure, dim, faint, indistinct, ill-defined, vague, hazy, nebulous, intangible, unsubstantial, ghostly, spectral, illusory, dreamlike, imaginary, unreal.

shady *adj* **1** SHADED, shadowy, dim, dark, cool, leafy. **2** (*infml*) DUBIOUS, questionable, suspect, suspicious, fishy (*infml*), dishonest, crooked (*infml*), unreliable, untrustworthy, disreputable, unscrupulous, unethical, underhand.

F∃ 1 sunny, sunlit, bright. **2** honest, trustworthy, honourable.

shaft *n* handle, shank, stem, upright, pillar, pole, rod, bar, stick, arrow, dart, beam, ray, duct, passage.

shaggy *adj* hairy, long-haired, hirsute, bushy, woolly, unshorn, dishevelled, unkempt.

F∃ bald, shorn, close-cropped.

shake *v* **1** WAVE, flourish, brandish, wag, waggle, agitate, rattle, joggle, jolt, jerk, twitch, convulse, heave, throb, vibrate, oscillate, fluctuate, waver, wobble, totter, sway, rock, tremble, quiver, quake, shiver, shudder. **2** *the news shook her*: upset, distress, shock, frighten, unnerve, intimidate, disturb, discompose, unsettle, agitate, stir, rouse.

➣ *n* **1** JOLT, rattle, roll, bounce, rocking, jerk, judder, twitch, throbbing, vibration, oscillation. **2** TREMBLING, convulsion, quiver, quake, quaking, shiver, shivering, shudder, shuddering. **3** SHOCK, upset, alarm, disturbance, jolt, unsettling.

♦ shake off get rid of, dislodge, lose, elude, give the slip, leave behind, outdistance, outstrip.

♦ shake up 1 *the accident shook me up*: upset, distress, alarm, shock, unnerve, unsettle, rattle (*infml*). **2** *shake up an organization*: reorganize, rearrange, reshuffle (*infml*).

shake-up (*infml*) *n* reorganization, rearrangement, reshuffle, disturbance, upheaval.

shaky *adj* **1** TREMBLING, quivering, faltering, tentative, uncertain. **2** UNSTABLE, unsteady, insecure, precarious, wobbly, rocky, tottery, rickety, weak. **3** DUBIOUS, questionable, suspect,

unreliable, unsound, unsupported.
☒ 2 firm, strong.

shallow *adj* superficial, surface, skin-deep, slight, flimsy, trivial, frivolous, foolish, idle, empty, meaningless, unscholarly, ignorant, simple.
☒ deep, profound.

sham *n* pretence, fraud, counterfeit, forgery, fake, imitation, simulation, hoax, humbug.
➤ *adj* false, fake, counterfeit, spurious, bogus, phoney (*infml*), pretended, feigned, put-on, simulated, artificial, mock, imitation, synthetic.
☒ genuine, authentic, real.
➤ *v* pretend, feign, affect, put on, simulate, imitate, fake, counterfeit.

shambles *n* mess, chaos, muddle, confusion, disorganization, disorder, havoc, anarchy, bedlam, wreck, disarray (*fml*), madhouse (*infml*), pigsty (*infml*).

shame *n* **1** HUMILIATION, degradation, shamefacedness, remorse, guilt, embarrassment, mortification, compunction (*fml*). **2** DISGRACE, dishonour, discredit, stain, stigma, disrepute, infamy, scandal, ignominy (*fml*), opprobrium (*fml*). **3** *it's a shame*: pity, disappointment, misfortune, unfortunate thing, bad luck.
☒ 1 pride. **2** honour, credit, distinction.
➤ *v* embarrass, mortify, abash, confound, humiliate, ridicule, humble, put to shame, show up, disgrace, dishonour, discredit, debase, degrade, sully, taint, stain.
◆ **put to shame** show up, humiliate, humble, embarrass, mortify, disgrace, upstage, outshine, outclass, outstrip, surpass, eclipse.

shamefaced *adj* ashamed, conscience-stricken, remorseful, contrite, apologetic, sorry, sheepish, red-faced, blushing, embarrassed, mortified, abashed, humiliated, uncomfortable.
☒ unashamed, proud.

shameful *adj* **1** *a shameful waste of money*: disgraceful, outrageous, scandalous, indecent, abominable, atrocious, wicked, mean, low, vile, reprehensible, contemptible, unworthy, ignoble. **2** EMBARRASSING, mortifying, humiliating, ignominious.
☒ 1 honourable, creditable, worthy.

shameless *adj* **1** UNASHAMED, unabashed, unrepentant, impenitent, barefaced, flagrant, blatant, brazen, brash,

audacious, insolent, defiant, hardened, incorrigible. **2** IMMODEST, indecent, improper, unprincipled, wanton, dissolute, corrupt, depraved.
☒ 1 ashamed, shamefaced, contrite. **2** modest.

shape *n* **1** FORM, outline, silhouette, profile, model, mould, pattern, cut, lines, contours, figure, physique, build, frame, format, configuration. **2** APPEARANCE, guise, likeness, semblance. **3** *in good shape*: condition, state, form, health, trim, fettle.

> **Geometrical shapes include:** polygon, circle, semicircle, quadrant, oval, ellipse, crescent, triangle, equilateral triangle, isosceles triangle, scalene triangle, quadrilateral, square, rectangle, oblong, rhombus, diamond, kite, trapezium, parallelogram, pentagon, hexagon, heptagon, octagon, nonagon, decagon; polyhedron, cube, cuboid, prism, pyramid, tetrahedron, pentahedron, octahedron, cylinder, cone, sphere, hemisphere.

➤ *v* form, fashion, model, mould, cast, forge, sculpt, carve, whittle, make, produce, construct, create, devise, frame, plan, prepare, adapt, adjust, regulate, accommodate, modify, remodel.
◆ **shape up** develop, come on, take shape, progress, make progress, move forward, make headway, flourish.

shapeless *adj* formless, amorphous, unformed, nebulous, unstructured, irregular, misshapen, deformed, dumpy.

share *v* divide, split, go halves, partake, participate, share out, distribute, dole out, give out, deal out, apportion, allot, allocate, assign.
➤ *n* portion, ration, quota, allowance, allocation, allotment, lot, part, division, proportion, percentage, cut (*infml*), dividend, due, contribution, whack (*infml*).

shark

> **Types of shark include:** basking, blue, dogfish, fox, ghost, goblin, great white, Greenland, grey reef, hammerhead, leopard, mackerel, mako, man-eating, nurse, porbeagle, requiem, saw, thresher, tiger, whale.

sharp *adj* **1** *a sharp needle*: pointed, keen, edged, knife-edged, razor-sharp, cutting, serrated, jagged, barbed, spiky. **2** CLEAR, clear-cut, well-defined, distinct, marked,

crisp. **3** QUICK-WITTED, alert, shrewd, astute, perceptive, observant, discerning, penetrating, clever, crafty, cunning, artful, sly. **4** SUDDEN, abrupt, violent, fierce, intense, extreme, severe, acute, piercing, stabbing. **5** PUNGENT, piquant, sour, tart, vinegary, bitter, acerbic, acid.
6 TRENCHANT, incisive, cutting, biting, caustic, sarcastic, sardonic, scathing, vitriolic, acrimonious.
Ea 1 blunt. **2** blurred. **3** slow, stupid. **4** gentle. **5** bland. **6** mild.
➤ *adv* punctually, promptly, on the dot, exactly, precisely, abruptly, suddenly, unexpectedly.
Ea approximately, roughly.

sharpen *v* edge, whet, hone, grind, file.
Ea blunt.

shatter *v* break, smash, splinter, shiver, crack, split, burst, explode, blast, crush, demolish, destroy, devastate, wreck, ruin, overturn, upset.

shave *v* cut, trim, barber, shear, crop, fleece, graze, brush, touch, pare, cut, plane, scrape.

sheath *n* **1** SCABBARD, case, sleeve, envelope, shell, casing, covering.
2 CONDOM, rubber (*sl*), French letter (*sl*).

shed[1] *v* cast (off), moult, slough, discard, drop, spill, pour, shower, scatter, diffuse, emit, radiate, shine, throw.

shed[2] *n* outhouse, lean-to, hut, shack.

sheen *n* lustre, gloss, shine, shimmer, brightness, brilliance, shininess, polish, burnish.
Ea dullness, tarnish.

sheepish *adj* ashamed, shamefaced, embarrassed, mortified, chastened, abashed, uncomfortable, self-conscious, silly, foolish.
Ea unabashed, brazen, bold.

sheer *adj* **1** UTTER, complete, total, absolute, thorough, mere, pure, unadulterated, downright, out-and-out, rank, thoroughgoing, unqualified, unmitigated. **2** *a sheer drop*: vertical, perpendicular, precipitous, abrupt, steep. **3** THIN, fine, flimsy, gauzy, gossamer, translucent, transparent, see-through.
Ea 2 gentle, gradual. **3** thick, heavy.

sheet *n* cover, blanket, covering, coating, coat, film, layer, stratum, skin, membrane, lamina, veneer, overlay, plate, leaf, page, folio, piece, panel, slab, pane, expanse, surface.

shelf *n* ledge, mantelpiece, sill, step, bench, counter, bar, bank, sandbank, reef, terrace.

shell *n* covering, hull, husk, pod, rind, crust, case, casing, body, chassis, frame, framework, structure, skeleton.
➤ *v* **1** *shell nuts*: hull, husk, pod. **2** BOMB, bombard, barrage, blitz, attack.

shelter *v* cover, shroud, screen, shade, shadow, protect, safeguard, defend, guard, shield, harbour, hide, accommodate, put up.
Ea expose.
➤ *n* cover, roof, shade, shadow, protection, defence, guard, security, safety, sanctuary, asylum, haven, refuge, retreat, accommodation, lodging.
Ea exposure.

sheltered *adj* covered, shaded, shielded, protected, cosy, snug, warm, quiet, secluded, isolated, retired, withdrawn, reclusive, cloistered, unworldly.
Ea exposed.

shelve *v* postpone, defer, put off, suspend, halt, put aside, pigeonhole, put on ice, mothball.
Ea expedite, implement.

shepherd *n* shepherdess, herdess, shepherdling, herdsman, protector, shepherd boy, herdboy, guardian.
➤ *v* guide, lead, conduct, convoy, escort, usher, steer, marshal, herd.

shield *n* buckler, escutcheon, defence, bulwark, rampart, screen, guard, cover, shelter, protection, safeguard.
➤ *v* defend, guard, protect, safeguard, screen, shade, shadow, cover, shelter.
Ea expose.

shift *v* change, vary, fluctuate, alter, adjust, move, budge, remove, dislodge, displace, relocate, reposition, rearrange, transpose, transfer, switch, swerve, veer.
➤ *n* change, fluctuation, alteration, modification, move, removal, displacement, rearrangement, transposition, transfer, switch.

shifty *adj* untrustworthy, dishonest, deceitful, scheming, contriving, tricky, wily, crafty, cunning, devious, evasive, slippery, furtive, underhand, dubious, shady (*infml*).
Ea dependable, honest, open.

shilly-shally *v* dither, hesitate, vacillate, waver, fluctuate, falter, teeter, seesaw, prevaricate (*fml*), dilly-dally (*infml*), hem and haw (*infml*), mess about (*infml*).

shimmer v glisten, gleam, glimmer, glitter, scintillate, twinkle.
➤ n lustre, gleam, glimmer, glitter, glow.

shin v climb, mount, soar, scramble, ascend, clamber, scale, shoot, swarm.

shine v 1 BEAM, radiate, glow, flash, glare, gleam, glint, glitter, sparkle, twinkle, shimmer, glisten, glimmer. 2 POLISH, burnish, buff, brush, rub. 3 *shine at athletics*: excel, stand out.
➤ n 1 LIGHT, radiance, glow, brightness, glare, gleam, sparkle, shimmer. 2 GLOSS, polish, burnish, sheen, lustre, glaze.

shining adj 1 BRIGHT, radiant, glowing, beaming, flashing, gleaming, glittering, glistening, shimmering, twinkling, sparkling, brilliant, resplendent, splendid, glorious. 2 *a shining example*: conspicuous, outstanding, leading, eminent, celebrated, distinguished, illustrious.
ʀ 1 dark.

shiny adj polished, burnished, sheeny, lustrous, glossy, sleek, bright, gleaming, glistening.
ʀ dull, matt.

ship n vessel, craft, liner, steamer, tanker, trawler, ferry, boat, yacht.

> **Parts of a ship include:** anchor, berth, bilge, boiler room, bollard, bridge, brig, bulkhead, bulwarks, bunk, cabin, capstan, chain locker, chart room, cleat, companion ladder, companionway, crow's nest, davit; deck, after deck, boat deck, flight deck, gun deck, lower deck, main deck, poop deck, promenade deck, quarter deck, top deck; engine room, figurehead, forecastle (fo'c'sle), funnel, galley, gangplank, gangway, gunwale (gunnel), hammock, hatch, hatchway, hawser, head, hold, keel, landing, mast, oar, paddle wheel, pilot house, Plimsoll line, port, porthole, prow, quarter, radio room, rigger, rowlock, rudder, sail, stabilizer, stanchion, starboard, stateroom, stern, superstructure, tiller, transom, wardroom, waterline, wheel, winch. *see also* **boats and ships**; **sail**.

shirk v dodge, evade, avoid, duck (*infml*), shun, slack, skive (*infml*).

shiver v shudder, tremble, quiver, quake, shake, vibrate, palpitate, flutter.
➤ n shudder, quiver, shake, tremor, twitch, start, vibration, flutter.

shock v disgust, revolt, sicken, offend, appal, outrage, scandalize, horrify, astound, stagger, stun, stupefy, numb, paralyse, traumatize, jolt, jar, shake, agitate, unsettle, disquiet, unnerve, confound, dismay.
ʀ delight, please, gratify, reassure.
➤ n fright, start, jolt, impact, collision, surprise, bombshell, thunderbolt, blow, trauma, upset, distress, dismay, consternation, disgust, outrage.
ʀ delight, pleasure, reassurance.

shocking adj appalling, outrageous, scandalous, horrifying, disgraceful, deplorable, intolerable, unbearable, atrocious, abominable, monstrous, unspeakable, detestable, abhorrent, dreadful, awful, terrible, frightful, ghastly, hideous, horrible, disgusting, revolting, repulsive, sickening, nauseating, offensive, distressing.
ʀ acceptable, satisfactory, pleasant, delightful.

shoddy adj inferior, second-rate, cheap, tawdry, tatty, trashy, rubbishy, poor, careless, slipshod, slapdash.
ʀ superior, well-made.

shoe see **footwear**.

shoot v 1 FIRE, discharge, launch, propel, hurl, fling, project. 2 DART, bolt, dash, tear, rush, race, sprint, speed, charge, hurtle. 3 HIT, kill, blast, bombard, gun down, snipe at, pick off.
➤ n sprout, bud, offshoot, branch, twig, sprig, slip, scion.

shop

> **Types of shop include:** bazaar, market, indoor market, mini-market, corner shop, shopping mall, department store, supermarket, superstore, hypermarket, cash-and-carry; butcher, baker, grocer, greengrocer, fishmonger, dairy, delicatessen, health-food shop, farm shop, fish and chip shop, take-away, off-licence, tobacconist, sweet shop, confectioner, tuck shop; bookshop, newsagent, stationer, chemist, pharmacy, tailor, outfitter, dress shop, boutique, milliner, shoe shop, haberdasher, draper, florist, jeweller, toy shop, hardware shop, ironmonger, saddler, radio and TV shop, video shop; launderette, hairdresser, barber, betting shop, bookmaker, bookie (*infml*), pawnbroker, post office.

shore¹ n seashore, beach, sand(s), shingle, strand, waterfront, front, promenade, coast, seaboard, lakeside, bank.

shore² *v* support, hold, prop, stay, underpin, buttress, brace, strengthen, reinforce.

short *adj* **1** BRIEF, cursory, fleeting, momentary, transitory, ephemeral (*fml*), concise, succinct, terse, pithy, compact, compressed, shortened, curtailed, abbreviated, abridged, summarized. **2** BRUSQUE, curt, gruff, snappy, sharp, abrupt, blunt, direct, rude, impolite, discourteous, uncivil. **3** SMALL, little, low, petite, diminutive, squat, dumpy. **4** INADEQUATE, insufficient, deficient, lacking, wanting, low, poor, meagre, scant, sparse.
E3 1 long, lasting. **2** polite. **3** tall. **4** adequate, ample.

shortage *n* inadequacy, insufficiency, deficiency, shortfall, deficit, lack, want, need, scarcity, paucity, poverty, dearth, absence.
E3 sufficiency, abundance, surplus.

shortcoming *n* defect, imperfection, f.. ll, fl..) .l.......l. .l., f.iling, ...l.m..., foible.

shorten *v* cut, trim, prune, crop, dock, curtail, truncate, abbreviate, abridge, reduce, lessen, decrease, diminish, take up.
E3 lengthen, enlarge, amplify.

short-lived *adj* brief, momentary, passing, short, temporary, transient, transitory, fleeting, impermanent, ephemeral (*fml*), evanescent (*fml*), fugacious (*fml*).
E3 abiding, enduring, lasting, long-lived.

shortly *adv* soon, before long, presently, by and by.

short-sighted *adj* **1** MYOPIC, near-sighted. **2** IMPROVIDENT, imprudent, injudicious, unwise, impolitic, ill-advised, careless, hasty, ill-considered.
E3 1 long-sighted, far-sighted.

shot *n* **1** BULLET, missile, projectile, ball, pellet, slug (*infml*), discharge, blast. **2** (*infml*) ATTEMPT, try, effort, endeavour, go (*infml*), bash (*infml*), crack (*infml*), stab (*infml*), guess, turn.

shoulder *v* **1** PUSH, shove, jostle, thrust, press. **2** ACCEPT, assume, take on, bear, carry, sustain.

shout *n*, *v* call, cry, scream, shriek, yell, roar, bellow, bawl, howl, bay, cheer.

shove *v* push, thrust, drive, propel, force, barge, jostle, elbow, shoulder, press, crowd.

shovel *n* spade, scoop, bucket.
➤ *v* dig, scoop, dredge, clear, move, shift, heap.

show *v* **1** REVEAL, expose, uncover, disclose, divulge, present, offer, exhibit, manifest, display, indicate, register, demonstrate, prove, illustrate, exemplify, explain, instruct, teach, clarify, elucidate. **2** *show him out*: lead, guide, conduct, usher, escort, accompany, attend.
E3 1 hide, cover.
➤ *n* **1** OSTENTATION, parade, display, flamboyance, panache, pizzazz (*infml*), showiness, exhibitionism, affectation, pose, pretence, illusion, semblance, façade, impression, appearance, air. **2** DEMONSTRATION, presentation, exhibition, exposition, fair, display, parade, pageant, extravaganza, spectacle, entertainment, performance, production, staging, showing, representation.
◆ **show off** parade, strut, swagger, brag, boast, swank (*infml*), flaunt, brandish, display, exhibit, demonstrate, advertise, set off, enhance.
◆ **show up 1** (*infml*) ARRIVE, come, turn up, appear, materialize (*infml*). **2** HUMILIATE, embarrass, mortify, shame, disgrace, let down. **3** REVEAL, show, expose, unmask, lay bare, highlight, pinpoint.

showdown *n* confrontation, clash, crisis, climax, culmination.

shower *n* rain, stream, torrent, deluge, hail, volley, barrage.
➤ *v* spray, sprinkle, rain, pour, deluge, inundate, overwhelm, load, heap, lavish.

showing *n* display, evidence, impression, representation, record, presentation, performance, exhibition, show, staging, account, statement, appearance, past performance, track record (*infml*).

show-off *n* swaggerer, braggart, boaster, swanker (*infml*), exhibitionist, peacock, poser, poseur, egotist.

showy *adj* flashy, flamboyant, ostentatious, gaudy, garish, loud, tawdry, fancy, ornate, pretentious, pompous, swanky (*infml*), flash (*infml*).
E3 quiet, restrained.

shred *n* ribbon, tatter, rag, scrap, snippet, sliver, bit, piece, fragment, jot, iota, atom, grain, mite, whit, trace.

shrewd *adj* astute, judicious, well-advised, calculated, far-sighted, smart, clever, intelligent, sharp, keen, acute, alert, perceptive, observant, discerning, discriminating, knowing, calculating, cunning, crafty, artful, sly.

ea unwise, obtuse, naïve, unsophisticated.

shriek *v, n* scream, screech, squawk, squeal, cry, shout, yell, wail, howl.

shrill *adj* high, high-pitched, treble, sharp, acute, piercing, penetrating, screaming, screeching, strident, ear-splitting.

ea deep, low, soft, gentle.

shrink *v* 1 CONTRACT, shorten, narrow, decrease, lessen, diminish, dwindle, shrivel, wrinkle, wither. 2 RECOIL, back away, shy away, withdraw, retire, balk, quail, cower, cringe, wince, flinch, shun.

ea 1 expand, stretch. 2 accept, embrace.

shrivel *v* wrinkle, pucker, wither, wilt, shrink, dwindle, parch, dehydrate, desiccate, scorch, sear, burn, frizzle.

shroud *v* wrap, envelop, swathe, cloak, veil, screen, hide, conceal, blanket, cover.

ea uncover, expose.

➤ *n* winding-sheet, pall, mantle, cloak, veil, screen, blanket, covering.

shrub

Shrubs include: azalea, berberis, broom, buddleia, camellia, clematis, cotoneaster, daphne, dogwood, euonymus, firethorn, flowering currant, forsythia, fuchsia, heather, hebe, holly, honeysuckle, hydrangea, ivy, japonica, jasmine, laburnum, laurel, lavender, lilac, magnolia, mallow, mimosa, mock orange, peony, privet, musk rose, rhododendron, rose, spiraea, viburnum, weigela, wistaria, witch hazel. *see also* **flower**; **plant**.

shudder *v* shiver, shake, tremble, quiver, quake, heave, convulse.

➤ *n* shiver, quiver, tremor, spasm, convulsion.

shuffle *v* 1 MIX (UP), intermix, jumble, confuse, disorder, rearrange, reorganize, shift around, switch. 2 *shuffle across the room*: shamble, scuffle, scrape, drag, limp, hobble.

shun *v* avoid, evade, elude, steer clear of, shy away from, spurn, ignore, cold-shoulder, ostracize.

ea accept, embrace.

shut *v* close, slam, seal, fasten, secure, lock, latch, bolt, bar.

ea open.

♦ **shut down** close, stop, cease, terminate, halt, discontinue, suspend, switch off, inactivate.

♦ **shut in** enclose, box in, hem in, fence in, immure, confine, imprison, cage.

♦ **shut off** seclude, isolate, cut off, separate, segregate.

♦ **shut out** 1 EXCLUDE, bar, debar, lock out, ostracize, banish. 2 HIDE, conceal, cover, mask, screen, veil.

♦ **shut up** 1 SILENCE, gag, quiet, hush up, pipe down (*infml*), hold one's tongue, clam up (*infml*). 2 CONFINE, coop up, imprison, incarcerate, jail, intern.

shuttle *v* go to and fro, travel, ply, alternate, commute, shunt, shuttlecock, seesaw.

shy *adj* timid, bashful, reticent, reserved, retiring, diffident, coy, self-conscious, inhibited, modest, self-effacing, shrinking, hesitant, cautious, chary, suspicious, nervous.

ea bold, assertive, confident.

sick *adj* 1 ILL, unwell, indisposed (*fml*), laid up, poorly, ailing, sickly, under the weather, weak, feeble. 2 VOMITING, queasy, bilious, seasick, airsick. 3 *sick of waiting*: bored, fed up (*infml*), tired, weary, disgusted, nauseated.

ea 1 well, healthy.

sicken *v* nauseate, revolt, disgust, repel, put off, turn off (*sl*).

ea delight, attract.

sickening *adj* nauseating, revolting, disgusting, offensive, distasteful, foul, vile, loathsome, repulsive.

ea delightful, pleasing, attractive.

sickly *adj* 1 UNHEALTHY, infirm, delicate, weak, feeble, frail, wan, pallid, ailing, indisposed, sick, bilious, faint, languid. 2 NAUSEATING, revolting, sweet, syrupy, cloying, mawkish.

ea 1 healthy, robust, sturdy, strong.

sickness *n* 1 ILLNESS, disease, malady, ailment, complaint, affliction, ill-health, indisposition, infirmity. 2 VOMITING, nausea, queasiness, biliousness.

ea 1 health.

side *n* 1 EDGE, margin, fringe, periphery, border, boundary, limit, verge, brink, bank, shore, quarter, region, flank, hand, face, facet, surface. 2 STANDPOINT, viewpoint, view, aspect, angle, slant. 3 TEAM, party, faction, camp, cause, interest.

➤ *adj* lateral, flanking, marginal, secondary, subsidiary, subordinate, lesser,

minor, incidental, indirect, oblique.
◆ **side with** agree with, team up with, support, vote for, favour, prefer.

sidelong *adj* indirect, oblique, sideward, sideways, covert.
🄴 direct, overt.

sidestep *v* avoid, dodge, duck, evade, elude, skirt, bypass.
🄴 tackle, deal with.

sidetrack *v* deflect, head off, divert, distract.

sideways *adv* sidewards, edgeways, laterally, obliquely.
➣ *adj* sideward, side, lateral, slanted, oblique, indirect, sidelong.

sidle *v* slink, edge, inch, creep, sneak.

siege *n* blockade, encirclement, besiegement, beleaguerment.

siesta *n* rest, sleep, relaxation, nap, doze, repose (*fml*), catnap (*infml*), forty winks (*infml*), snooze (*infml*).

sieve *v* sift, strain, separate, remove.
➣ *n* colander, strainer, sifter, riddle, screen.

sift *v* 1 SIEVE, strain, filter, riddle, screen, winnow, separate, sort. 2 EXAMINE, scrutinize, investigate, analyse, probe, review.

sigh *v* breathe, exhale, moan, complain, lament, grieve.

sight *n* 1 VISION, eyesight, seeing, observation, perception. 2 VIEW, look, glance, glimpse, range, field of vision, visibility. 3 APPEARANCE, spectacle, show, display, exhibition, scene, eyesore, monstrosity, fright (*infml*).
➣ *v* see, observe, spot, glimpse, perceive, discern, distinguish, make out.

sightseer *n* tourist, visitor, holidaymaker, tripper, excursionist.

sign *n* 1 SYMBOL, token, character, figure, representation, emblem, badge, insignia, logo. 2 INDICATION, mark, signal, gesture, evidence, manifestation, clue, pointer, hint, suggestion, trace. 3 NOTICE, poster, board, placard. 4 PORTENT, omen, forewarning, foreboding.
➣ *v* autograph, initial, endorse, write.
◆ **sign up** enlist, enrol, join (up), volunteer, register, sign on, recruit, take on, hire, engage, employ.

signal *n* sign, indication, mark, gesture, cue, go-ahead, password, light, indicator, beacon, flare, rocket, alarm, alert, warning, tip-off.

➣ *v* wave, gesticulate, gesture, beckon, motion, nod, sign, indicate, communicate.

signature *n* autograph, initials, mark, endorsement, inscription.

significance *n* importance, relevance, consequence, matter, interest, consideration, weight, force, meaning, implication, sense, point, message.
🄴 insignificance, unimportance, pettiness.

significant *adj* 1 IMPORTANT, relevant, consequential, momentous, weighty, serious, noteworthy, critical, vital, marked, considerable, appreciable.
2 MEANINGFUL, symbolic, expressive, suggestive, indicative, symptomatic.
🄴 1 insignificant, unimportant, trivial.
2 meaningless.

signify *v* 1 MEAN, denote, symbolize, represent, stand for, indicate, show, express, convey, transmit, communicate, intimate, imply, suggest. 2 MATTER, count.

silence *n* quiet, quietness, hush, peace, stillness, calm, lull, noiselessness, soundlessness, muteness, dumbness, speechlessness, taciturnity, uncommunicativeness, reticence, reserve.
🄴 noise, sound, din, uproar.
➣ *v* quiet, quieten, hush, mute, deaden, muffle, stifle, gag, muzzle, suppress, subdue, quell, still, dumbfound.

silent *adj* inaudible, noiseless, soundless, quiet, peaceful, still, hushed, muted, mute, dumb, speechless, tongue-tied, taciturn, mum, reticent, reserved, tacit, unspoken, unexpressed, understood, voiceless, wordless.
🄴 noisy, loud, talkative.

silhouette *n* outline, contour, delineation, shape, form, configuration, profile, shadow.

silky *adj* silken, fine, sleek, lustrous, glossy, satiny, smooth, soft, velvety.

silly *adj* foolish, stupid, imprudent, senseless, pointless, idiotic, daft (*infml*), ridiculous, ludicrous, preposterous, absurd, meaningless, irrational, illogical, childish, puerile, immature, irresponsible, scatterbrained.
🄴 wise, sensible, sane, mature, clever, intelligent.

silt *n* sediment, deposit, alluvium, sludge, mud, ooze.
◆ **silt up** block, clog, choke.

similar *adj* like, alike, close, related, akin,

corresponding, equivalent, analogous, comparable, uniform, homogeneous.
☒ dissimilar, different.

similarity n likeness, resemblance, similitude (fml), closeness, relation, correspondence, congruence, equivalence, analogy, comparability, compatibility, agreement, affinity, homogeneity (fml), uniformity.
☒ dissimilarity, difference.

simmer v boil, bubble, seethe, stew, burn, smoulder, fume, rage.
♦ simmer down calm down, cool down, control oneself, collect oneself.

simple adj 1 the answer is simple: easy, elementary, straightforward, uncomplicated, uninvolved, effortless, clear, lucid, plain, understandable, comprehensible, cushy (infml), easy-peasy (infml), a cinch (infml), a doddle (infml), a piece of cake (infml), a pushover (infml), as easy as falling off a log (infml). 2 BASIC, plain, crude, primitive, natural, rough and ready (infml), undecorated, unadorned, unembellished, unsophisticated, ordinary, unpretentious, unfussy, classic, rudimentary, stark, austere, spartan, low-tech (infml), no-frills (infml). 3 the simple truth: plain, basic, straightforward, bald, stark, direct, unambiguous, open, honest, sincere, candid, blunt. 4 UNSOPHISTICATED, natural, innocent, artless, guileless, ingenuous, naïve, green. 5 FOOLISH, stupid, silly, idiotic, half-witted, simple-minded, feeble-minded, slow, backward, retarded.
☒ 1 difficult, hard, complicated, intricate. 2 elaborate, fancy, luxurious. 4 sophisticated, worldly, artful. 5 clever.

simple-minded adj unsophisticated, simple, natural, artless, stupid, foolish, idiot, idiotic, imbecile, moronic, cretinous, brainless, backward, retarded, dim-witted, feeble-minded, addle-brained, dopey (infml), goofy (infml).
☒ bright, clever.

simpleton n idiot, fool, moron, ninny (infml), imbecile, dolt, dullard, dunce, dupe, jackass, flathead (infml), dope (infml), nincompoop (infml), numskull (infml), nitwit (infml), stupid (infml), twerp (infml), clot (infml), twit (infml), greenhorn (infml), soft-head (infml), goose (infml), blockhead (infml), booby (infml).
☒ brain.

simplicity n simpleness, ease, straightforwardness, uncomplicatedness, clarity, purity, plainness, restraint, naturalness, innocence, artlessness, candour, openness, sincerity, directness.
☒ difficulty, complexity, intricacy, sophistication.

simplify v disentangle, untangle, decipher, clarify, paraphrase, abridge, reduce, streamline.
☒ complicate, elaborate.

simplistic adj oversimplified, superficial, shallow, sweeping, facile, simple, naïve.
☒ analytical, detailed.

simply adv 1 MERELY, just, only, solely, purely, utterly, completely, totally, wholly, absolutely, quite, really, undeniably, unquestionably, clearly, plainly, obviously. 2 EASILY, straightforwardly, directly, intelligibly.

simulate v pretend, affect, assume, put on, act, feign, sham, fake, counterfeit, reproduce, duplicate, copy, imitate, mimic, parrot, echo, reflect.

simulated adj pretended, feigned, artificial, assumed, imitation, put-on, sham, fake, mock, make-believe, bogus, spurious, substitute, synthetic, man-made, inauthentic, insincere, phoney (infml), pseudo (infml).
☒ real, genuine.

simultaneous adj synchronous, synchronic, concurrent, contemporaneous, coinciding, parallel.
☒ asynchronous.

sin n wrong, offence, transgression (fml), trespass (fml), misdeed, lapse, fault, error, crime, wrongdoing, sinfulness, wickedness, iniquity, evil, impiety, ungodliness, unrighteousness, guilt.
➤ v offend, transgress (fml), trespass (fml), lapse, err, misbehave, stray, go astray, fall, fall from grace.

sincere adj honest, truthful, candid, frank, open, direct, straightforward, plain-spoken, serious, earnest, heartfelt, wholehearted, real, true, genuine, pure, unadulterated, unmixed, natural, unaffected (fml), artless, guileless, simple.
☒ insincere, hypocritical, affected.

sincerely adv genuinely, honestly, earnestly, in earnest, seriously, really, simply, truly, truthfully, wholeheartedly, unfeignedly, unaffectedly (fml).

sincerity n honour, integrity, probity,

uprightness, honesty, truthfulness, candour, frankness, openness, directness, straightforwardness, seriousness, earnestness, wholeheartedness, genuineness.
F3 **1, 3** insincerity.

sinewy *adj* muscular, brawny, strong, sturdy, robust, vigorous, athletic, wiry, stringy.

sinful *adj* wrong, wrongful, criminal, bad, wicked, iniquitous, erring, fallen, immoral, corrupt, depraved, impious, ungodly, unholy, irreligious, guilty.
F3 sinless, righteous, godly.

sing *v* chant, intone, vocalize, croon, serenade, yodel, trill, warble, chirp, pipe, whistle, hum.

singe *v* scorch, char, blacken, burn, sear.

singer

> Singers include: vocalist, songster, songstress, warbler, balladeer, minstrel, troubadour, opera singer, diva, prima donna, soloist, precentor, choirboy, choirgirl, chorister, chorus, folk-singer, pop star, pop singer, chanteuse, crooner, carol-singer, soprano, coloratura soprano, castrato, tenor, treble, contralto, alto, baritone, bass.

single *adj* **1** ONE, unique, singular, individual, particular, exclusive, sole, only, one and only, by oneself, lone, solitary, isolated, separate, distinct, unshared, undivided, unbroken, simple, one-to-one, person-to-person, man-to-man, woman-to-woman. **2** UNMARRIED, unwed, free, unattached, celibate, on one's own, by oneself, available.
F3 **1** multiple. **2** married.
♦ **single out** choose, select, pick, hand-pick, distinguish, identify, separate, set apart, isolate, highlight, pinpoint.

single-handed *adj, adv* solo, alone, unaccompanied, unaided, unassisted, independent(ly).

single-minded *adj* determined, resolute, dogged, persevering, tireless, unwavering, fixed, unswerving, undeviating, steadfast, dedicated, devoted.

singly *adv* one by one, on their own, one at a time, individually, separately, distinctly, solely, independently.

singular *adj* **1** REMARKABLE, exceptional, unusual, extraordinary, noteworthy,

unique, unparalleled, pre-eminent, outstanding, eminent, conspicuous. **2** PECULIAR, odd, queer, unusual, strange, uncommon, curious, eccentric, atypical.
F3 **1** usual. **2** normal.

sinister *adj* ominous, menacing, threatening, disturbing, disquieting, unlucky, inauspicious, malevolent, evil.
F3 auspicious, harmless, innocent.

sink *v* **1** DESCEND, slip, fall, drop, slump, lower, stoop, succumb, lapse, droop, sag, dip, set, disappear, vanish. **2** DECREASE, lessen, subside, abate, dwindle, diminish, ebb, fade, flag, weaken, fail, decline, worsen, degenerate, degrade, decay, collapse. **3** FOUNDER, dive, plunge, plummet, submerge, immerse, engulf, drown. **4** *sink a well*: bore, drill, penetrate, dig, excavate, lay, conceal.
F3 **1** rise. **2** increase. **3** float.

sinner *n* wrong-doer, miscreant (*fml*), offender, transgressor, trespasser (*fml*) backslider, reprobate, evil-doer, malefactor (*fml*).

sinuous *adj* lithe, slinky, curved, wavy, undulating, tortuous, twisting, winding, meandering, serpentine, coiling.
F3 straight.

sip *v* taste, sample, drink, sup.
➤ *n* taste, drop, spoonful, mouthful.

siren *n* **1** ALARM, tocsin, burglar alarm, car alarm, fire alarm, personal alarm, security alarm. **2** SEDUCTRESS, femme fatale, temptress, vamp, charmer, Lorelei, Circe.

sissy *n* baby, coward, weakling, pansy, softy, mummy's boy, milksop, wimp (*infml*), namby-pamby (*infml*), wet (*infml*).
➤ *adj* unmanly, weak, soft, cowardly, effeminate, feeble, pansy, wimpish (*infml*), namby-pamby (*infml*), wet (*infml*).

sister *n* **1** *brothers and sisters*: sibling, blood-sister, relation, relative. **2** *sisters in the struggle against injustice*: comrade, friend, partner, colleague, associate, fellow, companion. **3** *sisters in a convent*: nun, abbess, prioress, vowess.

sit *v* **1** SETTLE, rest, perch, roost, brood, pose. **2** SEAT, accommodate, hold, contain. **3** MEET, assemble, gather, convene, deliberate.

site *n* location, place, spot, position, situation, station, setting, scene, plot, lot, ground, area.
➤ *v* locate, place, position, situate, station, set, install.

sitting *n* session, period, spell, meeting, assembly, hearing, consultation.

situation *n* 1 SITE, location, position, place, spot, seat, locality, locale, setting, scenario. 2 STATE OF AFFAIRS, case, circumstances, predicament, state, condition, status, rank, station, post, office, job, employment.

sizable *adj* large, substantial, considerable, respectable, goodly, largish, biggish, decent, generous.
🗙 small, tiny.

size *n* magnitude, measurement(s), dimensions, proportions, volume, bulk, mass, height, length, extent, range, scale, amount, greatness, largeness, bigness, vastness, immensity.
♦ **size up** gauge, assess, evaluate, weigh up, measure.

sizzle *v* hiss, crackle, spit, sputter, fry, frizzle.

skeleton *n* bones, frame, structure, framework, bare bones, outline, draft, sketch.

sketch *v* draw, depict, portray, represent, pencil, paint, outline, delineate, draft, rough out, block out.
➤ *n* drawing, vignette, design, plan, diagram, outline, delineation, skeleton, draft.

sketchy *adj* rough, vague, incomplete, unfinished, scrappy, bitty, imperfect, inadequate, insufficient, slight, superficial, cursory, hasty.
🗙 full, complete.

skilful *adj* able, capable, adept, competent, proficient, deft, adroit, handy, expert, masterly, accomplished, skilled, practised, experienced, professional, clever, tactical, cunning.
🗙 inept, clumsy, awkward.

skill *n* skilfulness, ability, aptitude, facility, handiness, talent, knack, art, technique, training, experience, expertise, expertness, mastery, proficiency, competence, accomplishment, cleverness, intelligence.

skilled *adj* trained, schooled, qualified, professional, experienced, practised, accomplished, expert, masterly, proficient, able, skilful.
🗙 unskilled, inexperienced.

skim *v* 1 BRUSH, touch, skate, plane, float, sail, glide, fly. 2 SCAN, look through, skip. 3 CREAM, separate.

skimp *v* economize, scrimp, pinch, cut corners, stint, withhold.
🗙 squander, waste.

skin *n* hide, pelt, membrane, film, coating, surface, outside, peel, rind, husk, casing, crust.
➤ *v* flay, fleece, strip, peel, scrape, graze.

skin-deep *adj* shallow, superficial, surface, external, outward, artificial, empty, meaningless.

skinny *adj* thin, lean, scrawny, scraggy, skeletal, skin-and-bone, emaciated, underfed, undernourished.
🗙 fat, plump.

skip *v* 1 HOP, jump, leap, dance, gambol, frisk, caper, prance. 2 *skip a page*: miss, omit, leave out, cut.

skirmish *n* fight, combat, battle, engagement, encounter, conflict, clash, brush, scrap (*infml*), tussle, set-to, dust-up (*infml*).

skirt *v* circle, circumnavigate, border, edge, flank, bypass, avoid, evade, circumvent.

skit *n* satire, parody, caricature, spoof, take-off, sketch.

skittish *adj* nervous, excitable, fidgety, lively, playful, jumpy, highly-strung, frivolous, fickle, restive (*fml*).

skulk *v* lurk, hide, prowl, sneak, creep, slink.

sky *n* space, atmosphere, air, heavens, blue.

slab *n* piece, block, lump, chunk, hunk, wodge (*infml*), wedge, slice, portion.

slack *adj* 1 LOOSE, limp, sagging, baggy. 2 LAZY, sluggish, slow, quiet, idle, inactive. 3 NEGLECTFUL, negligent, careless, inattentive, remiss, permissive, lax, relaxed, easy-going (*infml*).
🗙 1 tight, taut, stiff, rigid. 2 busy. 3 diligent.
➤ *n* looseness, give, play, room, leeway, excess.
➤ *v* idle, shirk, skive (*infml*), neglect.

slacken off *v* loosen, release, relax, ease, moderate, reduce, lessen, decrease, diminish, abate, slow (down).
🗙 tighten, increase, intensify, quicken.

slacker *n* idler, shirker, skiver (*infml*), dawdler, clock-watcher, good-for-nothing, layabout.

slam *v* 1 BANG, crash, dash, smash, throw, hurl, fling. 2 (*infml*) CRITICIZE, slate (*infml*), pan (*infml*).

slander n defamation, calumny (fml), misrepresentation, libel, scandal, smear, slur, aspersion (fml), backbiting.
➤ v defame, vilify, malign (fml), denigrate, disparage (fml), libel, smear, slur, backbite.
✷ praise, compliment.

slanderous adj defamatory, false, untrue, libellous, damaging, malicious, abusive, insulting.

slang n cant, jargon, argot, patois, patter, cockney, cockney rhyming slang, vulgarism, doublespeak, gobbledygook, colloquialism, informal expressions, lingo (infml), mumbo-jumbo (infml).

slant v 1 TILT, slope, incline, lean, list, skew, angle. 2 DISTORT, twist, warp, bend, weight, bias, colour.
➤ n 1 SLOPE, incline, gradient, ramp, camber, pitch, tilt, angle, diagonal. 2 BIAS, emphasis, attitude, viewpoint.

slanting adj sloping, tilted, oblique, diagonal.

slap n smack, spank, cuff, blow, bang, clap.
➤ v 1 SMACK, spank, hit, strike, cuff, clout (infml), bang, clap. 2 DAUB, plaster, spread, apply.

slapdash adj careless, thoughtless, haphazard, slovenly, disorderly, clumsy, offhand, negligent, messy, slipshod, thrown-together, untidy, hurried, last-minute, hasty, rash, perfunctory, sloppy (infml).
✷ careful, orderly.

slap-up adj excellent, splendid, lavish, elaborate, first-class, first-rate, magnificent, superb, sumptuous, luxurious, princely, superlative.

slash v cut, slit, gash, lacerate, rip, tear, rend.
➤ n cut, incision, slit, gash, laceration, rip, tear, rent.

slate v scold, rebuke, reprimand, berate (fml), censure, blame, criticize, slam (infml).
✷ praise.

slaughter n killing, murder, massacre, extermination, butchery, carnage, blood-bath, bloodshed.
➤ v kill, slay, murder, massacre, exterminate, liquidate, butcher.

slave n servant, drudge, vassal, serf, villein, captive.
➤ v toil, labour, drudge, sweat, grind, slog.

slaver v dribble, drivel, slobber, drool, salivate.

slavery n servitude, bondage, captivity, enslavement, serfdom, thraldom, subjugation.
✷ freedom, liberty.

slavish adj 1 UNORIGINAL, imitative, unimaginative, uninspired, literal, strict. 2 SERVILE, abject, submissive, sycophantic, grovelling, cringing, fawning, menial, low, mean.
✷ 1 original, imaginative. 2 independent, assertive.

sleazy adj disreputable, low, seedy, sordid, squalid, crummy (sl), run-down, tacky (infml).

sleek adj shiny, glossy, lustrous, smooth, silky, well-groomed.
✷ rough, unkempt.

sleep v doze, snooze (infml), slumber, kip (sl), doss (down) (sl), hibernate, drop off, nod off, rest, repose.
➤ n doze, snooze (infml), nap, forty winks (infml), shut-eye (infml), kip (sl), slumber, hibernation, rest, repose, siesta.

sleepless adj unsleeping, awake, wide-awake, alert, vigilant, watchful, wakeful, restless, disturbed, insomniac.

sleepy adj drowsy, somnolent, tired, weary, heavy, slow, sluggish, torpid, lethargic, inactive, quiet, dull, soporific, hypnotic.
✷ awake, alert, wakeful, restless.

slender adj 1 SLIM, thin, lean, slight, svelte, graceful. 2 a slender chance: faint, remote, slight, inconsiderable, tenuous, flimsy, feeble, inadequate, insufficient, meagre, scanty.
✷ 1 fat. 2 appreciable, considerable, ample.

slice n piece, sliver, wafer, rasher, tranche, slab, wedge, segment, section, share, portion, helping, cut (infml), whack (infml).
➤ v carve, cut, chop, divide, segment.

slick adj 1 GLIB, plausible, deft, adroit, dexterous, skilful, professional. 2 SMOOTH, sleek, glossy, shiny, polished.

slide v slip, slither, skid, skate, ski, toboggan, glide, plane, coast, skim.

slight adj 1 MINOR, unimportant, insignificant, negligible, trivial, paltry, modest, small, little, inconsiderable, insubstantial. 2 SLENDER, slim, diminutive, petite, delicate.
✷ 1 major, significant, noticeable, considerable. 2 large, muscular.
➤ v scorn, despise, disdain, disparage,

insult, affront, offend, snub, cut, cold-shoulder, ignore, disregard, neglect.
Ea respect, praise, compliment, flatter.
➤ *n* insult, affront, slur, snub, rebuff, rudeness, discourtesy, disrespect, contempt, disdain, indifference, disregard, neglect.

slightly *adv* rather, quite, a little, a bit, to some degree, to some extent.

slim *adj* 1 SLENDER, thin, lean, svelte, trim. 2 SLIGHT, remote, faint, poor.
Ea 1 fat, chubby. 2 strong, considerable.
➤ *v* lose weight, diet, reduce.

slimy *adj* 1 MUDDY, miry, mucous, viscous, oily, greasy, slippery. 2 SERVILE, obsequious (*fml*), sycophantic, toadying, smarmy (*infml*), oily, unctuous.

sling *v* 1 THROW, hurl, fling, catapult, heave, pitch, lob, toss, chuck (*infml*). 2 HANG, suspend, dangle, swing.

slink *v* sneak, steal, creep, sidle, slip, prowl, skulk.

slinky *adj* close-fitting, figure-hugging, clinging, skin-tight, sleek, sinuous.

slip^1 *v* slide, glide, skate, skid, stumble, trip, fall, slither, slink, sneak, steal, creep.
➤ *n* mistake, error, slip-up (*infml*), bloomer (*infml*), blunder, fault, indiscretion, boob (*infml*), omission, oversight, failure.

slip^2 *n* piece, strip, voucher, chit, coupon, certificate.

slippery *adj* 1 SLIPPY, icy, greasy, glassy, smooth, dangerous, treacherous, perilous. 2 *a slippery character*: dishonest, untrustworthy, false, duplicitous, two-faced, crafty, cunning, devious, evasive, smooth, smarmy.
Ea 1 rough. 2 trustworthy, reliable.

slipshod *adj* careless, slapdash, sloppy (*infml*), slovenly, untidy, negligent, lax, casual.
Ea careful, fastidious, neat, tidy.

slit *v* cut, gash, slash, slice, split, rip, tear.
➤ *n* opening, aperture, vent, cut, incision, gash, slash, split, tear, rent.

slither *v* slide, slip, glide, slink, creep, snake, worm.

sliver *n* flake, shaving, paring, slice, wafer, shred, fragment, chip, splinter, shiver, shard.

slobber *v* dribble, drivel, slaver, drool, salivate.

slog *v* 1 HIT, strike, thump, belt, smite (*fml*), bash (*infml*), slosh (*infml*), slug (*infml*), sock (*infml*), wallop (*infml*). 2 PERSEVERE,

labour, slave, work, plough through, toil, plod, trudge, trek, tramp.
➤ *n* struggle, effort, exertion, grind, labour, hike, trek, trudge, tramp.

slogan *n* jingle, motto, catch-phrase, catchword, watchword, battle-cry, war cry.

slop *v* spill, overflow, slosh, splash, splatter, spatter.

slope *v* slant, lean, tilt, tip, pitch, incline, rise, fall.
➤ *n* incline, gradient, ramp, hill, ascent, descent, slant, tilt, pitch, inclination.

sloping *adj* inclined, inclining, slanting, leaning, oblique, tilting, askew, angled, canting, bevelled.
Ea level.

sloppy *adj* 1 WATERY, wet, liquid, runny, mushy, slushy. 2 *sloppy work*: careless, hit-or-miss, slapdash, slipshod, slovenly, untidy, messy, clumsy, amateurish. 3 SOPPY, sentimental, schmaltzy, slushy, mushy.
Ea 1 solid. 2 careful, exact, precise.

slot *n* hole, opening, aperture, slit, vent, groove, channel, gap, space, time, vacancy, place, spot, position, niche.
➤ *v* insert, fit, place, position, assign, pigeonhole.

slouch *v* stoop, hunch, droop, slump, lounge, loll, shuffle, shamble.

slovenly *adj* sloppy (*infml*), careless, slipshod, untidy, scruffy, slatternly, sluttish.
Ea neat, smart.

slow *adj* 1 LEISURELY, unhurried, lingering, loitering, dawdling, lazy, sluggish, slow-moving, creeping, gradual, deliberate, measured, plodding, delayed, late, unpunctual. 2 STUPID, slow-witted, dim, thick (*infml*). 3 PROLONGED, protracted, long-drawn-out, tedious, boring, dull, uninteresting, uneventful.
Ea 1 quick, fast, swift, rapid, speedy. 2 clever, intelligent. 3 brisk, lively, exciting.
➤ *v* brake, decelerate, delay, hold up, retard, handicap, check, curb, restrict.
Ea speed, accelerate.

slowly *adv* leisurely, at a leisurely pace, slowly but surely, unhurriedly, gradually, little by little, by degrees, steadily, lazily, ploddingly, ponderously, sluggishly, at a snail's pace.
Ea fast, quickly.

sludge *n* mud, ooze, mire, muck, residue, sediment, silt, slime, slush, swill, slop, slag, dregs, gunge (*infml*), gunk (*infml*).

sluggish *adj* lethargic, listless, torpid, heavy, dull, slow, slow-moving, slothful, lazy, idle, inactive, lifeless, unresponsive.
Ea brisk, vigorous, lively, dynamic.

slump *v* **1** COLLAPSE, fall, drop, plunge, plummet, sink, decline, deteriorate, worsen, crash, fail. **2** DROOP, sag, bend, stoop, slouch, loll, lounge, flop.
➤ *n* recession, depression, stagnation, downturn, low, trough, decline, deterioration, worsening, fall, drop, collapse, crash, failure.
Ea boom.

slur *n* smear, slight, insult, disgrace, discredit, reproach, slander, libel, affront, stain, blot, innuendo, insinuation, stigma, aspersion (*fml*), calumny (*fml*).
➤ *v* mumble, speak unclearly, splutter, stumble.

slut *n* loose woman, slattern, sloven, trollop, hussy, drab, prostitute, hooker (*infml*), floosie (*infml*), tart (*sl*), scrubber (*sl*), slag (*sl*).

sly *adj* wily, foxy, crafty, cunning, artful, guileful, clever, canny, shrewd, astute, knowing, subtle, devious, shifty, tricky, furtive, stealthy, surreptitious, underhand, covert, secretive, scheming, conniving, mischievous, roguish.
Ea honest, frank, candid, open.

smack¹ *v* hit, strike, slap, spank, whack (*infml*), thwack (*infml*), clap, box, cuff, pat, tap.
➤ *n* blow, slap, spank, whack (*infml*), thwack (*infml*), box, cuff, pat, tap.
➤ *adv* bang, slap-bang, right, plumb, straight, directly, exactly, precisely.

smack² *n* **1** TASTE, flavour, savour, tang, relish, piquancy, zest. **2** SUGGESTION, hint, trace, impression, intimation, tinge, touch, dash, speck, whiff, nuance.
◆ **smack of** suggest, savour of, hint at, give the impression of, intimate, evoke, bring to mind, remind one of.

small *adj* **1** LITTLE, tiny, minute, minuscule, short, slight, puny, petite, diminutive, pint-size(d) (*infml*), miniature, mini (*infml*), pocket, pocket-sized, young. **2** PETTY, trifling, trivial, unimportant, insignificant, minor, inconsiderable, negligible. **3** INADEQUATE, insufficient, scanty, meagre, paltry, mean, limited.
Ea **1** large, big, huge. **2** great, considerable. **3** ample.

small-minded *adj* petty, mean,

ungenerous, illiberal, intolerant, bigoted, narrow-minded, parochial, insular, rigid, hidebound.
Ea liberal, tolerant, broad-minded.

small-time *adj* unimportant, minor, insignificant, petty, piddling, inconsequential, no-account.
Ea important, major, big-time.

smarmy *adj* smooth, oily, unctuous, servile, obsequious (*fml*), sycophantic, toadying, ingratiating, crawling, fawning.

smart *adj* **1** *smart clothes*: elegant, stylish, chic, fashionable, modish, neat, tidy, spruce, trim, well-groomed. **2** CLEVER, intelligent, bright, sharp, acute, shrewd, astute.
Ea **1** dowdy, unfashionable, untidy, scruffy. **2** stupid, slow.
➤ *v* sting, hurt, prick, burn, tingle, twinge, throb.

smarten *v* neaten, tidy, spruce up, groom, clean, polish, beautify.

smash *v* **1** *smash a window*: break, shatter, shiver, ruin, wreck, demolish, destroy, defeat, crush. **2** CRASH, collide, strike, bang, bash, thump.
➤ *n* accident, crash, collision, pile-up.

smashing *adj* excellent, wonderful, marvellous, superb, terrific (*infml*), tremendous, great, fantastic (*infml*), magnificent, sensational, superlative, stupendous, super, exhilarating, first-class, first-rate, fabulous (*infml*).

smattering *n* bit, modicum, dash, sprinkling, basics, rudiments, elements.

smear *v* **1** DAUB, plaster, spread, cover, coat, rub, smudge, streak. **2** DEFAME, malign (*fml*), vilify, blacken, sully, stain, tarnish.
➤ *n* **1** STREAK, smudge, blot, blotch, splodge, daub. **2** DEFAMATION, slander, libel, mudslinging, muck-raking.

smell *n* odour, whiff, scent, perfume, fragrance, bouquet, aroma, stench, stink, pong (*infml*).
➤ *v* sniff, nose, scent, stink, reek, pong (*infml*).

Ways of describing smells include:
pleasant: aroma, bouquet, fragrance, incense, nose, odour, potpourri, perfume, redolence, scent; *unpleasant*: b.o. (body odour), fetor, funk (*US*), hum, malodour, mephitis, miasma, niff (*sl*), pong (*infml*), pungency, reek, sniff, stench, stink, whiff.

smelly *adj* malodorous, pongy (*infml*), stinking, reeking, foul, bad, off, fetid, putrid, high, strong.

smile *n*, *v* grin, beam, simper, smirk, leer.

smirk *n*, *v* grin, sneer, snigger, leer, simper.

smitten *adj* obsessed, bewitched, beguiled, charmed, attracted, enthusiastic, captivated, infatuated, enamoured, afflicted, plagued, struck, troubled, burdened, beset, bowled over (*infml*).

smoke *n* fumes, exhaust, gas, vapour, mist, fog, smog.
➤ *v* fume, smoulder, cure, dry.

smoky *adj* sooty, black, grey, grimy, murky, cloudy, hazy, foggy.

smooth *adj* **1** LEVEL, plane, even, flat, horizontal, flush. **2** STEADY, unbroken, flowing, regular, uniform, rhythmic, easy, effortless. **3** SHINY, polished, glossy, silky, glassy, calm, undisturbed, serene, tranquil, peaceful. **4** SUAVE, agreeable, smooth-talking, glib, plausible, persuasive, slick, smarmy, unctuous, ingratiating.
☲ **1** rough, lumpy. **2** irregular, erratic, unsteady. **3** rough, choppy.
➤ *v* **1** IRON, press, roll, flatten, level, plane, file, sand, polish. **2** EASE, alleviate, assuage, allay, mitigate, calm, mollify.
☲ **1** roughen, wrinkle, crease.

smother *v* suffocate, asphyxiate, strangle, throttle, choke, stifle, extinguish, snuff, muffle, suppress, repress, hide, conceal, cover, shroud, envelop, wrap.

smoulder *v* burn, smoke, fume, rage, seethe, simmer.

smudge *v* blur, smear, daub, mark, spot, stain, dirty, soil.
➤ *n* blot, stain, spot, blemish, blur, smear, streak.

smug *adj* complacent, self-satisfied, superior, holier-than-thou, self-righteous, priggish, conceited.
☲ humble, modest.

smuggler *n* runner, contrabandist, moonshiner, courier, bootlegger (*infml*), mule (*infml*).

smutty *adj* dirty, crude, coarse, filthy, indecent, improper, indelicate, obscene, pornographic, risqué, racy, bawdy, suggestive, vulgar, gross, lewd, salacious, ribald, prurient (*fml*), blue (*infml*), off-colour (*infml*), raunchy (*infml*), sleazy (*infml*).
☲ clean, decent.

snack *n* refreshment(s), bite, nibble, titbit, elevenses (*infml*).

snag *n* disadvantage, inconvenience, drawback, catch, problem, difficulty, complication, setback, hitch, obstacle, stumbling-block.
➤ *v* catch, rip, tear, hole, ladder.

snap *v* **1** *the twig snapped*: break, crack, split, separate. **2** BITE, nip, bark, growl, snarl, retort, crackle, pop. **3** SNATCH, seize, catch, grasp, grip.
➤ *n* break, crack, bite, nip, flick, fillip, crackle, pop.
➤ *adj* immediate, instant, on-the-spot, abrupt, sudden.
◆ **snap up** grab, grasp, seize, snatch, pounce on, pick up, pluck, nab (*infml*).

snappy *adj* **1** SMART, stylish, chic, fashionable, modish, trendy (*infml*). **2** QUICK, hasty, brisk, lively, energetic. **3** CROSS, irritable, edgy, touchy (*infml*), brusque, quick-tempered, ill-natured, crabbed, testy.
☲ **1** dowdy. **2** slow.

snare *v* trap, ensnare, entrap, catch, net.
➤ *n* trap, wire, net, noose, catch, pitfall.

snarl¹ *v* growl, grumble, complain.

snarl² *v* tangle, knot, ravel, entangle, enmesh, embroil, confuse, muddle, complicate.

snarl-up *n* muddle, tangle, mess, mix-up, jumble, confusion, entanglement, traffic jam, gridlock.

snatch *v* grab, seize, kidnap, take, nab (*sl*), pluck, pull, wrench, wrest, gain, win, clutch, grasp, grip.

sneak *v* **1** CREEP, steal, slip, slink, sidle, skulk, lurk, prowl, smuggle, spirit. **2** TELL TALES, split (*sl*), inform on, grass on (*sl*).
➤ *n* tell-tale, informer, grass (*sl*).

sneaking *adj* private, secret, furtive, surreptitious, hidden, lurking, suppressed, grudging, nagging, niggling, persistent, worrying, uncomfortable, intuitive.

sneer *v* scorn, disdain, look down on, deride, scoff, jeer, mock, ridicule, gibe, laugh, snigger.
➤ *n* scorn, disdain, derision, jeer, mockery, ridicule, gibe, snigger.

snide *adj* derogatory, disparaging, sarcastic, cynical, scornful, sneering, hurtful, unkind, nasty, mean, spiteful, malicious, ill-natured.
☲ complimentary.

sniff *v* breathe, inhale, snuff, snuffle, smell, nose, scent.

snigger *v, n* laugh, giggle, titter, chuckle, sneer.

snip *v* cut, clip, trim, crop, dock, slit, nick, notch.

snippet *n* piece, scrap, cutting, clipping, fragment, particle, shred, snatch, part, portion, segment, section.

snivel *v* cry, weep, bawl, sniff, sniffle, snuffle, sob, blub (*infml*), blubber, whimper, grizzle, moan, whinge (*infml*), whine.

snobbery *n* snobbishness, superciliousness, snootiness (*infml*), airs, loftiness, arrogance, pride, pretension, condescension.

snobbish *adj* supercilious, disdainful, snooty (*infml*), stuck-up (*infml*), toffee-nosed (*infml*), superior, lofty, high and mighty, arrogant, pretentious, affected, condescending, patronizing.

snoop *v* spy, sneak, pry, nose, interfere, meddle.

snooze *v* nap, doze, sleep, kip (*sl*).
➤ *n* nap, catnap (*infml*), forty winks (*infml*), doze, siesta, sleep, kip (*sl*).

snub *v* rebuff, brush off, cut, cold-shoulder, slight, rebuke, put down, squash, humble, shame, humiliate, mortify.
➤ *n* rebuff, brush-off, slight, affront, insult, rebuke, put-down, humiliation.

snug *adj* cosy, warm, comfortable, homely, friendly, intimate, sheltered, secure, tight, close-fitting.

snuggle *v* nestle, nuzzle, curl up, cuddle, embrace, hug.

soak *v* wet, drench, saturate, penetrate, permeate, infuse, bathe, marinate, souse, steep, submerge, immerse.

soaking *adj* soaked, drenched, sodden, waterlogged, saturated, sopping, wringing, dripping, streaming.
🔁 dry.

soar *v* fly, wing, glide, plane, tower, rise, ascend, climb, mount, escalate, rocket.
🔁 fall, plummet.

sob *v* cry, weep, bawl, howl, blubber, snivel.

sober *adj* **1** TEETOTAL, temperate, moderate, abstinent, abstemious. **2** SOLEMN, dignified, serious, staid, steady, sedate, quiet, serene, calm, composed, unruffled, unexcited, cool, dispassionate,

level-headed, practical, realistic, reasonable, rational, clear-headed. **3** *sober dress*: sombre, drab, dull, plain, subdued, restrained.
🔁 **1** drunk, intemperate. **2** frivolous, excited, unrealistic, irrational. **3** flashy, garish.

so-called *adj* alleged, supposed, purported, ostensible, nominal, self-styled, professed, would-be, pretended.

sociable *adj* outgoing, gregarious, friendly, affable, companionable, genial, convivial, cordial, warm, hospitable, neighbourly, approachable, accessible, familiar.
🔁 unsociable, withdrawn, unfriendly, hostile.

social *adj* communal, public, community, common, general, collective, group, organized.
➤ *n* party, do (*infml*), get-together, gathering.

socialize *v* mix, mingle, fraternize, get together, go out, entertain.

society *n* **1** COMMUNITY, population, culture, civilization, nation, people, mankind, humanity. **2** CLUB, circle, group, association, organization, company, corporation, league, union, guild, fellowship, fraternity, brotherhood, sisterhood, sorority. **3** FRIENDSHIP, companionship, camaraderie, fellowship, company. **4** UPPER CLASSES, aristocracy, gentry, nobility, elite.

soft *adj* **1** YIELDING, pliable, flexible, elastic, plastic, malleable, spongy, squashy, pulpy. **2** *soft colours*: pale, light, pastel, delicate, subdued, muted, quiet, low, dim, faint, diffuse, mild, bland, gentle, soothing, sweet, mellow, melodious, dulcet, pleasant. **3** FURRY, downy, velvety, silky, smooth. **4** LENIENT, lax, permissive, indulgent, tolerant, easy-going (*infml*), kind, generous, gentle, merciful, soft-hearted, tender, sensitive, weak, spineless.
🔁 **1** hard. **2** harsh. **3** rough. **4** strict, severe.

soften *v* **1** MODERATE, temper, mitigate, lessen, diminish, abate, alleviate, ease, soothe, palliate, quell, assuage, subdue, mollify, appease, calm, still, relax. **2** MELT, liquefy, dissolve, reduce. **3** CUSHION, pad, muffle, quicken, lower, lighten.

soft-hearted *adj* sympathetic, compassionate, kind, benevolent,

charitable, generous, warm-hearted, tender, sentimental.
🖪 hard-hearted, callous.

soft-pedal *v* moderate, go easy, play down, subdue, tone down.
🖪 highlight, emphasize.

soggy *adj* wet, damp, moist, soaked, drenched, sodden, waterlogged, saturated, sopping, dripping, heavy, boggy, spongy, pulpy.

soil¹ *n* earth, clay, loam, humus, dirt, dust, ground, land, region, country.

soil² *v* dirty, begrime, stain, spot, smudge, smear, foul, muddy, pollute, defile, besmirch, sully, tarnish.

solace *n* comfort, consolation, relief, alleviation, support, cheer, condolence (*fml*), succour (*fml*).

soldier *n* warrior, fighter.

Types of soldier include: cadet, private, sapper, NCO, orderly, officer, gunner, infantryman, trooper, fusilier, rifleman, paratrooper, sentry, guardsman, marine, commando, tommy, dragoon, cavalryman, lancer, hussar, conscript, recruit, regular, Territorial, GI (*US*), mercenary, legionnaire, guerrilla, partisan, centurion; troops; serviceman, servicewoman. *see also* **rank¹**.

◆ **soldier on** continue, persevere, keep on, keep going, remain, hold on, hang on, keep at it (*infml*), stick at it (*infml*), plug away (*infml*).

sole *adj* only, unique, exclusive, individual, single, singular, one, lone, solitary, alone.
🖪 shared, multiple.

solely *adv* exclusively, only, singly, uniquely, merely, completely, entirely, alone, single-handedly.

solemn *adj* 1 *a solemn expression*: serious, grave, sober, sedate, sombre, glum, thoughtful, earnest, awed, reverential. 2 GRAND, stately, majestic, ceremonial, ritual, formal, ceremonious, pompous, dignified, august, venerable, awe-inspiring, impressive, imposing, momentous.
🖪 1 light-hearted. 2 frivolous.

solicit *v* ask, request, seek, crave, beg, beseech, entreat, implore (*fml*), pray, supplicate, sue, petition, canvass, importune.

solicitor *n* lawyer, advocate, attorney, barrister, QC.

solicitous *adj* caring, attentive, considerate, concerned, anxious, worried.

solid *adj* 1 HARD, firm, dense, compact, strong, sturdy, substantial, sound, unshakable. 2 *a solid white line*: unbroken, continuous, uninterrupted. 3 RELIABLE, dependable, trusty, worthy, decent, upright, sensible, level-headed, stable, serious, sober. 4 REAL, genuine, pure, concrete, tangible.
🖪 1 liquid, gaseous, hollow. 2 broken, dotted. 3 unreliable, unstable. 4 unreal.

solidarity *n* unity, agreement, accord, unanimity, consensus, harmony, concord, cohesion, like-mindedness, camaraderie, team spirit, soundness, stability.
🖪 discord, division, schism.

solidify *v* harden, set, jell, congeal, coagulate, clot, cake, crystallize.
🖪 soften, liquefy, dissolve.

solitary *adj* sole, single, lone, alone, lonely, lonesome, friendless, unsociable, reclusive, withdrawn, retired, sequestered, cloistered, secluded, separate, isolated, remote, out-of-the-way, inaccessible, unfrequented, unvisited, untrodden.
🖪 accompanied, gregarious, busy.

solitude *n* aloneness, loneliness, reclusiveness, retirement, privacy, seclusion, isolation, remoteness.
🖪 companionship.

solution *n* 1 ANSWER, result, explanation, resolution, key, remedy. 2 MIXTURE, blend, compound, suspension, emulsion, liquid.

solve *v* work out, figure out, puzzle out, decipher, crack, disentangle, unravel, answer, resolve, settle, clear up, clarify, explain, interpret.

solvent *adj* sound, financially sound, able to pay, creditworthy, out of debt, unindebted, in the black (*infml*).
🖪 insolvent.

sombre *adj* dark, funereal, drab, dull, dim, obscure, shady, shadowy, gloomy, dismal, melancholy, mournful, sad, joyless, sober, serious, grave.
🖪 bright, cheerful, happy.

somebody *n* someone, celebrity, dignitary, name, personage, star, superstar, VIP, notable, luminary, magnate, mogul, heavyweight, nabob, panjandrum, household name (*infml*), bigwig (*infml*), big noise (*infml*), big shot (*infml*), big wheel (*infml*).
🖪 nobody.

someday *adv* sometime, one day, eventually, ultimately.
🔁 never.

somehow *adv* by some means, one way or another, come what may, by fair means or foul (*infml*), by hook or by crook (*infml*), come hell or high water (*infml*).

sometimes *adv* occasionally, now and again, now and then, once in a while, from time to time.
🔁 always, never.

song *n* ballad, madrigal, lullaby, shanty, anthem, hymn, carol, chant, chorus, air, tune, melody, lyric, number, ditty.

> **Types of song include:** air, anthem, aria, ballad, barcarole, bird call, bird song, blues, calypso, cantata, canticle, cantilena, canzone, canzonet, carol, chanson, chansonette, chant, chorus, descant, dirge, ditty, elegy, epinikion, epithalamium, folksong, gospel song, hymn, jingle, love-song, Lied, lilt, lullaby, madrigal, nursery rhyme, ode, plainchant, plainsong, pop song, psalm, recitative, requiem, rock and roll, roundelay, serenade, shanty, spiritual, Negro spiritual, war song, wassail, yodel. *see also* **poem**.

sonorous *adj* resonant, resounding, ringing, rich, rounded, orotund, ororotund, full, full-mouthed, full-voiced, full-throated, loud, sounding, high-flown, high-sounding, grandiloquent (*fml*).

soon *adv* shortly, presently, in a minute, before long, in the near future.

soothe *v* alleviate, relieve, ease, salve, comfort, allay, calm, compose, tranquillize, settle, still, quiet, hush, lull, pacify, appease, mollify, assuage, mitigate, soften.
🔁 aggravate, irritate, annoy, vex.

sophisticated *adj* **1** URBANE, cosmopolitan, worldly, worldly-wise, cultured, cultivated, refined, polished. **2** *sophisticated technology*: advanced, highly-developed, complicated, complex, intricate, elaborate, delicate, subtle.
🔁 **1** unsophisticated, naïve. **2** primitive, simple.

soporific *adj* sleep-inducing, hypnotic, sedative, tranquillizing, sleepy, somnolent.
🔁 stimulating, invigorating.

soppy *adj* sentimental, lovey-dovey (*infml*), weepy (*infml*), sloppy, slushy, mushy, corny (*infml*), mawkish, cloying, soft, silly, daft (*infml*).

sorcery *n* magic, black magic, witchcraft, wizardry, necromancy (*fml*), voodoo, spell, incantation, charm, enchantment.

sordid *adj* dirty, filthy, unclean, foul, vile, squalid, sleazy, seamy, seedy, disreputable, shabby, tawdry, corrupt, degraded, degenerate, debauched, low, base, despicable, shameful, wretched, mean, miserly, niggardly, grasping, mercenary, selfish, self-seeking.
🔁 pure, honourable, upright.

sore *adj* **1** PAINFUL, hurting, aching, smarting, stinging, tender, sensitive, inflamed, red, raw. **2** ANNOYED, irritated, vexed, angry, upset, hurt, wounded, afflicted, aggrieved, resentful.
🔁 **2** pleased, happy.
➤ *n* wound, lesion, swelling, inflammation, boil, abscess, ulcer.

sorrow *n* sadness, unhappiness, grief, mourning, misery, woe, distress, affliction (*fml*), anguish, heartache, heartbreak, misfortune, hardship, trouble, worry, trial, tribulation (*fml*), regret, remorse.
🔁 happiness, joy.

sorrowful *adj* miserable, mournful, sad, unhappy, tearful, sorry, distressing, depressed, dejected, wretched, painful, lamentable, woeful, melancholy, grievous, doleful, heartbroken, heart-rending, piteous, rueful, wae (*Scot*), afflicted (*fml*), disconsolate (*fml*), lugubrious (*fml*), woebegone (*fml*).
🔁 happy, joyful.

sorry *adj* **1** APOLOGETIC, regretful, remorseful, contrite, penitent, repentant, conscience-stricken, guilt-ridden, shamefaced. **2** *in a sorry state*: pathetic, pitiful, poor, wretched, miserable, sad, unhappy, dismal. **3** SYMPATHETIC, compassionate, understanding, pitying, concerned, moved.
🔁 **1** impenitent, unashamed. **2** happy, cheerful. **3** uncaring.

sort *n* kind, type, genre, ilk, family, race, breed, species, genus, variety, order, class, category, group, denomination, style, make, brand, stamp, quality, nature, character, description.
➤ *v* class, group, categorize, distribute, divide, separate, segregate, sift, screen, grade, rank, order, classify, catalogue, arrange, organize, systematize.
◆ **sort out** resolve, clear up, clarify, tidy up, neaten, choose, select.

so-so *adj* average, middling, moderate, indifferent, fair, adequate, ordinary, respectable, neutral, tolerable, unexceptional, undistinguished, passable, fair to middling (*infml*), not bad (*infml*), OK (*infml*), run-of-the-mill (*infml*).

soul *n* 1 SPIRIT, psyche, mind, reason, intellect, character, inner being, essence, life, vital force. 2 INDIVIDUAL, person, man, woman, creature.

soulful *adj* sensitive, emotional, expressive, heartfelt, moving, profound, mournful, meaningful, eloquent.
Ea soulless.

soulless *adj* unfeeling, spiritless, unsympathetic, inhuman, lifeless, cold, callous, cruel, unkind, dead, uninteresting, ignoble, mean, mean-spirited, soul-destroying, mechanical.
Ea soulful.

sound¹ *n* noise, din, report, resonance, reverberation, tone, timbre, tenor, description.
➤ *v* 1 RING, toll, chime, peal, resound, resonate, reverberate, echo.
2 ARTICULATE, enunciate, pronounce, voice, express, utter, say, declare, announce.

> Sounds include: bang, beep, blare, blast, bleep, boom, bubble, buzz, chime, chink, chug, clack, clang, clank, clash, clatter, click, clink, crack, crackle, crash, creak, crunch, cry, drone, echo, explode, fizz, grate, grizzle, groan, gurgle, hiccup, hiss, honk, hoot, hum, jangle, jingle, knock, moan, murmur, patter, peal, ping, pip, plop, pop, rattle, report, reverberate, ring, roar, rumble, rustle, scrape, scream, screech, sigh, sizzle, skirl, slam, slurp, smack, snap, sniff, snore, snort, sob, splash, splutter, squeak, squeal, squelch, swish, tap, throb, thud, thump, thunder, tick, ting, tinkle, toot, twang, wail, whimper, whine, whirr, whistle, whoop, yell.

> Animal sounds include: bark, bay, bellow, bleat, bray, cackle, caw, chirp, chirrup, cluck, coo, croak, crow, gobble, growl, grunt, hiss, hoot, howl, low, mew, miaow, moo, neigh, purr, quack, roar, screech, snarl, squawk, squeak, tweet, twitter, warble, whinny, woof, yap, yelp, yowl.

sound² *adj* 1 FIT, well, healthy, vigorous, robust, sturdy, firm, solid, whole, complete, intact, perfect, unbroken, undamaged,

unimpaired, unhurt, uninjured. 2 VALID, well-founded, reasonable, rational, logical, orthodox, right, true, proven, reliable, trustworthy, secure, substantial, thorough, good.
Ea 1 unfit, ill, shaky. 2 unsound, unreliable, poor.

sound³ *v* measure, plumb, fathom, probe, examine, test, inspect, investigate.
♦ **sound out** ask, canvass, examine, investigate, research, survey, probe, pump, question, suss out (*infml*).

sound⁴ *n* channel, estuary, inlet, passage, strait, firth, fjord, voe.

sour *adj* 1 TART, sharp, acid, pungent, vinegary, bitter, rancid. 2 EMBITTERED, acrimonious, ill-tempered, peevish, crabbed, crusty, disagreeable.
Ea 1 sweet, sugary. 2 good-natured, generous.

source *n* origin, derivation, beginning, start, commencement, cause, root, rise, spring, fountainhead, wellhead, supply, mine, originator, authority, informant.

souvenir *n* memento, reminder, remembrance, keepsake, relic, token.

sovereign *n* ruler, monarch, king, queen, emperor, empress, potentate, chief.
➤ *adj* ruling, royal, imperial, absolute, unlimited, supreme, paramount, predominant, principal, chief, dominant, independent, autonomous.

sovereignty *n* autonomy, independence, supremacy, domination, sway, dominion, kingship, queenship, regality, primacy, raj, ascendancy (*fml*), imperium (*fml*), suzerainty (*fml*).

sow *v* plant, seed, scatter, strew, spread, disseminate, lodge, implant.

space *n* 1 ROOM, place, seat, accommodation, capacity, volume, extent, expansion, scope, range, play, elbow-room, leeway, margin. 2 BLANK, omission, gap, opening, lacuna, interval, intermission, chasm.

spacious *adj* roomy, capacious, ample, big, large, sizable, broad, wide, huge, vast, extensive, open, uncrowded.
Ea small, narrow, cramped, confined.

span *n* spread, stretch, reach, range, scope, compass, extent, length, distance, duration, term, period, spell.
➤ *v* arch, vault, bridge, link, cross, traverse, extend, cover.

spank *v* smack, slap, wallop (*infml*), whack (*infml*), thrash, slipper, cane.

spar *v* argue, dispute, contest, fall out, contend, wrangle, squabble, bicker, wrestle, box, skirmish, scrap (*infml*), spat (*infml*), tiff (*infml*).

spare *adj* reserve, emergency, extra, additional, leftover, remaining, unused, over, surplus, superfluous, supernumerary, unwanted, free, unoccupied.
E3 necessary, vital, used.
➤ *v* **1** PARDON, let off, reprieve, release, free. **2** GRANT, allow, afford, part with.

sparing *adj* economical, thrifty, careful, prudent, frugal, meagre, miserly.
E3 unsparing, liberal, lavish.

spark *n* flash, flare, gleam, glint, flicker, hint, trace, vestige, scrap, atom, jot.
➤ *v* kindle, set off, trigger, start, cause, occasion, prompt, provoke, stimulate, stir, excite, inspire.

sparkle *v* **1** TWINKLE, glitter, scintillate, flash, gleam, glint, glisten, shimmer, coruscate, shine, beam. **2** EFFERVESCE, fizz, bubble.
➤ *n* twinkle, glitter, flash, gleam, glint, flicker, spark, radiance, brilliance, dazzle, spirit, vitality, life, animation.

sparse *adj* scarce, scanty, meagre, scattered, infrequent, sporadic.
E3 plentiful, thick, dense.

spartan *adj* austere, harsh, severe, rigorous, strict, disciplined, ascetic, abstemious, temperate, frugal, plain, simple, bleak, joyless.
E3 luxurious, self-indulgent.

spasm *n* burst, eruption, outburst, frenzy, fit, convulsion, seizure, attack, contraction, jerk, twitch, tic.

spasmodic *adj* sporadic, occasional, intermittent, erratic, irregular, fitful, jerky.
E3 continuous, uninterrupted.

spate *n* flood, deluge, torrent, rush, outpouring, flow.

spatter *v* splatter, splash, splodge, spray, sprinkle, shower, speckle, scatter, daub, bedaub, bestrew, besprinkle, bespatter, dirty, soil.

speak *v* talk, converse (*fml*), say, state, declare, express, utter, voice, articulate, enunciate, pronounce, tell, communicate, address, lecture, harangue, hold forth, declaim, argue, discuss.
♦ **speak for** speak on behalf of, represent,

act for, stand for, act as spokesperson for.
♦ **speak out/up** say publicly, speak openly, defend, support, protest, stand up and be counted (*infml*).

speaker *n* lecturer, orator (*fml*), spokesperson, spokesman, spokeswoman.

spearhead *v* lead, head, initiate, launch, front, pioneer.
➤ *n* vanguard, front line, leading position, pioneer, trailblazer, leader, guide, overseer, van (*infml*), cutting edge (*infml*).

special *adj* **1** *a special occasion*: important, significant, momentous, major, noteworthy, distinguished, memorable, remarkable, extraordinary, exceptional.
2 DIFFERENT, distinctive, characteristic, peculiar, singular, individual, unique, exclusive, select, choice, particular, specific, unusual, precise, detailed.
E3 1 normal, ordinary, usual. **2** general, common.

specialist *n* consultant, authority, expert, master, professional, connoisseur.

speciality *n* strength, forte, talent, field, specialty, pièce de résistance.

species *n* class, kind, breed, sort, type, category, variety, genus, group, collection, description.

specific *adj* precise, exact, fixed, limited, particular, special, definite, unequivocal, clear-cut, explicit, express, unambiguous.
E3 vague, approximate.

specification *n* requirement, condition, qualification, description, listing, item, particular, detail.

specify *v* stipulate, spell out, define, particularize, detail, itemize, enumerate, list, mention, cite, name, designate, indicate, describe, delineate.

specimen *n* sample, example, instance, illustration, model, pattern, paradigm, exemplar, representative, copy, exhibit.

speck *n* mark, fleck, dot, speckle, shred, grain, particle, bit, blot, defect, blemish, fault, flaw, stain, spot, atom, mite, iota, jot, trace, whit, tittle.

speckled *adj* spotted, spotty, flecked, dotted, dappled, mottled, sprinkled, stippled, brinded, brindle(d), fleckered, freckled.

spectacle *n* show, performance, display, exhibition, parade, pageant, extravaganza, scene, sight, curiosity, wonder, marvel, phenomenon.

spectacles

Types of spectacle include: bifocals, diving mask, eyeglass, goggles, half-glasses, lorgnette, monocle, pince-nez, Polaroid® glasses, quizzing glass, reading glasses, safety glasses, shooting glasses, sports spex, sunglasses, trifocals, varifocals.

spectacular *adj* grand, splendid, magnificent, sensational, impressive, striking, stunning, staggering, amazing, remarkable, dramatic, daring, breathtaking, dazzling, eye-catching, colourful.
Ea unimpressive, ordinary.

spectator *n* watcher, viewer, onlooker, looker-on, bystander, passer-by, witness, eyewitness, observer.
Ea player, participant.

spectre *n* ghost, phantom, spirit, wraith, apparition, vision, presence.

speculate *v* 1 GUESS, wonder, contemplate, meditate, muse, reflect, consider, deliberate, theorize, suppose, conjecture (*fml*), surmise (*fml*), hypothesize (*fml*), cogitate (*fml*). 2 GAMBLE, risk, hazard, venture.

speculative *adj* conjectural, hypothetical, theoretical, notional, abstract, academic, tentative, risky, hazardous, uncertain, unpredictable.

speech *n* 1 DICTION, articulation, enunciation, elocution, delivery, utterance, voice, language, tongue, parlance, dialect, jargon. 2 *make a speech*: oration (*fml*), address, discourse, talk, lecture, harangue, spiel (*sl*), conversation, dialogue, monologue, soliloquy.

speechless *adj* dumbfounded, thunderstruck, amazed, aghast, tongue-tied, inarticulate, mute, dumb, silent, mum.
Ea talkative.

speed *n* velocity, rate, pace, tempo, quickness, swiftness, rapidity, celerity (*fml*), alacrity, haste, hurry, dispatch, rush, acceleration.
Ea slowness, delay.
➤ *v* race, tear, belt (*infml*), zoom, career, bowl along, sprint, gallop, hurry, rush, hasten (*fml*), accelerate, quicken, put one's foot down (*infml*), step on it (*infml*).
Ea slow, delay.
◆ **speed up** 1 ACCELERATE, quicken, speed, drive faster, go faster, pick up/gather speed, gain momentum, open up (*infml*),

put one's foot down (*infml*), step on it/the gas/the juice (*infml*), put on a spurt (*infml*). 2 *speed up a process*: hurry, step up, stimulate, facilitate, advance, further, promote, spur on, forward, hasten (*fml*), expedite (*fml*), precipitate (*fml*).

speedy *adj* fast, quick, swift, rapid, nimble, express, prompt, immediate, hurried, hasty, precipitate, cursory.
Ea slow, leisurely.

spell[1] *v* signal, suggest, mean, indicate, imply, promise, signify, herald, augur (*fml*), portend (*fml*), presage (*fml*).
◆ **spell out** explain, clarify, make clear, elucidate, emphasize, detail, stipulate, specify.

spell[2] *n* period, time, bout, session, term, season, interval, stretch, patch, turn, stint.

spell[3] *n* charm, incantation, magic, sorcery, witchery, bewitchment, enchantment, fascination, glamour.

spellbound *adj* transfixed, hypnotized, mesmerized, fascinated, enthralled, gripped, entranced, captivated, bewitched, enchanted, charmed.

spend *v* 1 *spend money*: disburse, pay out, fork out (*infml*), shell out (*infml*), invest, lay out, splash out (*infml*), waste, squander, fritter, expend, consume, use up, exhaust. 2 PASS, fill, occupy, use, employ, apply, devote.
Ea 1 save, hoard.

spendthrift *n* squanderer, prodigal, profligate, wastrel.
Ea miser.
➤ *adj* improvident, extravagant, prodigal, wasteful.

spent *adj* 1 USED (UP), finished, expended, exhausted, consumed, gone. 2 TIRED OUT, exhausted, weary, wearied, drained, weakened, debilitated (*fml*), effete (*fml*), worn out, fagged (out) (*infml*), burnt out (*infml*), all in (*infml*), bushed (*infml*), dead beat (*infml*), dog-tired (*infml*), done in (*infml*), jiggered (*infml*), knackered (*infml*), shattered (*infml*), whacked (*infml*), zonked (*infml*).

sphere *n* 1 BALL, globe, orb, round. 2 DOMAIN, realm, province, department, territory, field, range, scope, compass, rank, function, capacity.

spherical *adj* round, rotund, ball-shaped, globe-shaped.

spice *n* 1 FLAVOURING, seasoning, piquancy, relish, savour, tang. 2

EXCITEMENT, life, colour, zest, gusto, kick (*infml*), pep (*infml*), zap (*infml*), zip (*infml*).
➤ *v* liven (up), enliven, vitalize, put life into, rouse, invigorate, animate, energize, brighten, stir (up), buck up (*infml*), pep up (*infml*), perk up (*infml*), hot up (*infml*).

spicy *adj* 1 PIQUANT, hot, pungent, tangy, seasoned, aromatic, fragrant. 2 RACY, risqué, ribald, suggestive, indelicate, improper, indecorous, unseemly, scandalous, sensational.
◼ 1 bland, insipid. 2 decent.

spike *n* point, prong, tine, spine, barb, nail, stake.
➤ *v* impale, stick, spear, skewer, spit.

spill *v* overturn, upset, slop, overflow, disgorge, pour, tip, discharge, shed, scatter.

spin *v* turn, revolve, rotate, twist, gyrate, twirl, pirouette, wheel, whirl, swirl, reel.
➤ *n* 1 TURN, revolution, twist, gyration, twirl, pirouette, whirl, swirl. 2 COMMOTION, agitation, panic, flap (*infml*), state (*infml*), tizzy (*infml*). 3 DRIVE, ride, run.
◆ **spin out** prolong, protract, extend, lengthen, amplify, pad out.

spindle *n* axis, pivot, pin, rod, axle.

spine *n* 1 BACKBONE, spinal column, vertebral column, vertebrae. 2 THORN, barb, prickle, bristle, quill.

spineless *adj* weak, feeble, irresolute, ineffective, cowardly, faint-hearted, lily-livered, yellow (*sl*), soft, wet (*infml*), submissive, weak-kneed.
◼ strong, brave.

spiral *adj* winding, coiled, corkscrew, helical, whorled, scrolled, circular.
➤ *n* coil, helix, corkscrew, screw, whorl, convolution.

spire *n* steeple, pinnacle, peak, summit, top, tip, point, spike.

spirit *n* 1 SOUL, psyche, mind, breath, life. 2 GHOST, spectre, phantom, apparition, angel, demon, fairy, sprite. 3 LIVELINESS, vivacity, animation, sparkle, vigour, energy, zest, fire, ardour, motivation, enthusiasm, zeal, enterprise, resolution, willpower, courage, backbone, mettle. 4 *the spirit of the law*: meaning, sense, substance, essence, gist, tenor, character, quality. 5 MOOD, humour, temper, disposition, temperament, feeling, morale, attitude, outlook.

spirited *adj* lively, vivacious, animated, sparkling, high-spirited, vigorous, energetic, active, ardent, zealous, bold,

courageous, mettlesome, plucky.
◼ spiritless, lethargic, cowardly.

spirits *n* 1 LIQUOR, alcohol, strong drink, strong liquor, moonshine, fire-water (*infml*), hooch (*infml*), the hard stuff (*infml*). 2 FEELINGS, emotions, mood, temperament, temper, attitude, humour.

spiritual *adj* unworldly, incorporeal, immaterial, otherwordly, heavenly, divine, holy, sacred, religious, ecclesiastical.
◼ physical, material.

spit *v* expectorate, eject, discharge, splutter, hiss.
➤ *n* spittle, saliva, slaver, drool, dribble, sputum, phlegm, expectoration.

spite *n* spitefulness, malice, venom, gall, bitterness, rancour, animosity, ill feeling, grudge, malevolence, malignity, ill nature, hate, hatred.
◼ goodwill, compassion, affection.
➤ *v* annoy, irritate, irk, vex, provoke, gall, hurt, injure, offend, put out.

spiteful *adj* malicious, venomous, catty, bitchy, snide, barbed, cruel, vindictive, vengeful, malevolent, malignant, ill-natured, ill-disposed, nasty.
◼ charitable, affectionate.

splash *v* 1 BATHE, wallow, paddle, wade, dabble, plunge, wet, wash, shower, spray, squirt, sprinkle, spatter, splatter, splodge, spread, daub, plaster, slop, slosh, plop, surge, break, dash, strike, buffet, smack. 2 PUBLICIZE, flaunt, blazon, trumpet.
➤ *n* 1 SPOT, patch, splatter, splodge, burst, touch, dash. 2 PUBLICITY, display, ostentation, effect, impact, stir, excitement, sensation.
◆ **splash out** invest in, lash out, spend, splurge, be extravagant, push the boat out (*infml*).

splendid *adj* brilliant, dazzling, glittering, lustrous, bright, radiant, glowing, glorious, magnificent, gorgeous, resplendent, sumptuous, luxurious, lavish, rich, fine, grand, stately, imposing, impressive, great, outstanding, remarkable, exceptional, sublime, supreme, superb, excellent, first-class, wonderful, marvellous, admirable.
◼ drab, ordinary, run-of-the-mill.

splendour *n* brightness, radiance, brilliance, dazzle, lustre, glory, resplendence, magnificence, richness, grandeur, majesty, solemnity, pomp, ceremony, display, show, spectacle.
◼ drabness, squalor.

splice v join, unite, wed, marry, bind, tie, plait, braid, interweave, interlace, intertwine, entwine, mesh, knit, graft.

splinter n sliver, shiver, chip, shard, fragment, flake, shaving, paring.
➤ v split, fracture, smash, shatter, shiver, fragment, disintegrate.

split v divide, separate, partition, part, disunite, disband, open, gape, fork, diverge, break, splinter, shiver, snap, crack, burst, rupture, tear, rend, rip, slit, slash, cleave, halve, slice up, share, distribute, parcel out.
➤ n **1** DIVISION, separation, partition, break, breach, gap, cleft, crevice, crack, fissure, rupture, tear, rent, rip, rift, slit, slash. **2** SCHISM, disunion, dissension, discord, difference, divergence, break-up.
➤ adj divided, cleft, cloven, bisected, dual, twofold, broken, fractured, cracked, ruptured.
♦ **split up** part, part company, disband, break up, separate, divorce.

spoil v **1** MAR, upset, wreck, ruin, destroy, damage, impair, harm, hurt, injure, deface, disfigure, blemish. **2** spoil a child: indulge, pamper, cosset, coddle, mollycoddle, baby, spoon-feed. **3** DETERIORATE, go bad, go off, sour, turn, curdle, decay, decompose.

spoils n plunder, loot, booty, haul, swag (sl), pickings, gain, acquisitions, prizes, winnings.

spoken adj verbal, oral, voiced, said, stated, told, uttered, phonetic, expressed, declared, unwritten, viva voce.
🔳 unspoken, unexpressed, written.

spokesman, spokeswoman n spokesperson, representative, delegate, agent, voice, negotiator, arbitrator, intermediary, mediator, go-between, broker, mouthpiece, propagandist.

sponge v **1** WIPE, mop, clean, wash. **2** CADGE, scrounge.

sponger n cadger, scrounger, parasite, hanger-on.

spongy adj soft, cushioned, yielding, elastic, springy, porous, absorbent, light.

sponsor n patron, supporter, backer, angel (infml), promoter, underwriter, guarantor, surety.
➤ v finance, fund, bankroll, subsidize, patronize, back, promote, underwrite, guarantee.

spontaneous adj natural, unforced, untaught, instinctive, impulsive, unpremeditated, free, willing, unhesitating, voluntary, unprompted, impromptu, extempore.
🔳 forced, studied, planned, deliberate.

spontaneously adv voluntarily, willingly, freely, impromptu, extempore, impulsively, on impulse, unplanned, unprompted, instinctively, of one's own accord, on the spur of the moment, off the cuff (infml), off the top of one's head (infml).

spoof n joke, hoax, game, travesty, trick, prank, fake, deception, caricature, bluff, burlesque, parody, mockery, satire, lampoon, send-up (infml), take-off (infml), con (infml), leg-pull (infml).

sporadic adj occasional, intermittent, infrequent, isolated, spasmodic, erratic, irregular, uneven, random, scattered.
🔳 frequent, regular.

sport n **1** GAME, exercise, activity, pastime, amusement, entertainment, diversion, recreation, play. **2** FUN, mirth, humour, joking, jesting, banter, teasing, mockery, ridicule.

Sports include: badminton, fives, lacrosse, squash, table-tennis, ping-pong (infml), tennis; American football, baseball, basketball, billiards, boules, bowls, cricket, croquet, football, golf, handball, hockey, netball, pétanque, pitch and putt, polo, pool, putting, rounders, Rugby, snooker, soccer, tenpin bowling, volleyball; athletics, cross-country, decathlon, discus, high-jump, hurdling, javelin, long-jump, marathon, pentathlon, pole vault, running, shot put, triple-jump; angling, canoeing, diving, fishing, rowing, sailing, skin-diving, surfing, swimming, synchronized swimming, water polo, water-skiing, windsurfing, yachting; bobsleigh, curling, ice-hockey, ice-skating, skiing, speed skating, tobogganing (luging); aerobics, fencing, gymnastics, jogging, keep-fit, roller-skating, trampolining; archery, darts, quoits; boxing, judo, jujitsu, karate, tae kwon do, wrestling; climbing, mountaineering, rock-climbing, walking, orienteering, pot-holing; cycle racing, drag-racing, go-karting, motor racing, speedway racing, stock-car racing, greyhound-racing, horse-racing, show-jumping, trotting, hunting, shooting, clay-pigeon shooting; gliding, sky-diving.

Types of sports equipment include: ball, basketball, boule, bowl, jack, wood, football, netball, rugby ball, tenpin bowling ball, volleyball; fishing-rod, fly rod, spinning rod, fishing-line, paternoster, reel, fly reel, hook, gaff, gang-hook, jig, trace, lure, bait, fly, float, net, keep-net, priest, disgorger; bow, arrow, crossbow, bolt; badminton racket, shuttlecock, net; baseball bat, baseball, mitt, catcher's glove; boxing glove, gum shield, punch-bag, punch-ball; cricket bat, cricket ball, wicket, stump, bail, nets; épée, foil, sabre, face-guard, mask; discus, hammer, javelin, shot; golf club, golf ball, tee, golfing glove; asymmetrical bars, horizontal bar, isometric bar, parallel-bars, beam, balance-beam, mat, pommel horse, vaulting horse, rings, rope, springboard, trampoline; hockey stick, hockey ball, ice-hockey stick, puck, hockey skate; curling stone; ice-skate, roller-skate, rollerblade, roller boot, speed skate, skateboard; ski, ski stick, snow board, toboggan; snooker ball, billiard ball, cue ball, table, cue, rest, bridge, rack, chalk; squash racket, squash ball; table-tennis bat, table-tennis ball, net; tennis racket, tennis ball, net, racket press; oar, aqualung, snorkel, water-ski, sailboard, surfboard. see also **golf club**.

➤ *v* wear, display, exhibit, show off.

sporting *adj* sportsmanlike, gentlemanly, decent, considerate, fair.
🔁 unsporting, ungentlemanly, unfair.

sporty *adj* 1 ATHLETIC, fit, energetic, outdoor. 2 STYLISH, trendy (*infml*), jaunty, natty (*infml*), snazzy (*infml*), showy, loud, flashy, casual, informal.

spot *n* 1 DOT, speckle, fleck, mark, speck, blotch, blot, smudge, daub, splash, stain, discoloration, blemish, flaw, pimple. 2 PLACE, point, position, situation, location, site, scene, locality. 3 (*infml*) PLIGHT, predicament, quandary, difficulty, trouble, mess.
➤ *v* see, notice, observe, detect, discern, identify, recognize.

spotless *adj* immaculate, clean, white, gleaming, spick and span, unmarked, unstained, unblemished, unsullied, pure, chaste, virgin, untouched, innocent, blameless, faultless, irreproachable.
🔁 dirty, impure.

spotlight *v* emphasize, stress, accentuate, focus on, highlight, underline, illuminate, feature, point up, draw attention to, give prominence to, throw into relief.
🔁 tone down, play down.
➤ *n* attention, public attention, public eye, fame, emphasis, notoriety, interest, limelight (*infml*).

spotted *adj* dotted, speckled, flecked, mottled, dappled, pied.

spotty *adj* pimply, pimpled, blotchy, spotted.

spouse *n* husband, wife, partner, mate, better half (*infml*).

spout *v* jet, spurt, squirt, spray, shoot, gush, stream, surge, erupt, emit, discharge.
➤ *n* jet, fountain, geyser, gargoyle, outlet, nozzle, rose, spray.

sprawl *v* spread, straggle, trail, ramble, flop, slump, slouch, loll, lounge, recline, repose.

spray[1] *v* shower, spatter, sprinkle, scatter, diffuse, wet, drench.
➤ *n* 1 MOISTURE, drizzle, mist, foam, froth. 2 AEROSOL, atomizer, sprinkler.

spray[2] *n* sprig, branch, corsage, posy, bouquet, garland, wreath.

spread *v* 1 STRETCH, extend, sprawl, broaden, widen, dilate, expand, swell, mushroom, proliferate, escalate, open, unroll, unfurl, unfold, fan out, cover, lay out, arrange. 2 SCATTER, strew, diffuse, radiate, disseminate, broadcast, transmit, communicate, promulgate, propagate, publicize, advertise, publish, circulate, distribute.
🔁 1 close, fold. 2 suppress.
➤ *n* 1 STRETCH, reach, span, extent, expanse, sweep, compass. 2 *the spread of disease*: advance, development, expansion, increase, proliferation, escalation, diffusion, dissemination, dispersion.

spree *n* bout, fling, binge, splurge, orgy, revel.

sprightly *adj* agile, nimble, spry, active, energetic, lively, spirited, vivacious, hearty, brisk, jaunty, cheerful, blithe, airy.
🔁 doddering, inactive, lifeless.

spring[1] *v* 1 JUMP, leap, vault, bound, hop, bounce, rebound, recoil. 2 ORIGINATE, derive, come, stem, arise, start, proceed, issue, emerge, emanate, appear, sprout, grow, develop.
➤ *n* 1 JUMP, leap, vault, bound, bounce. 2 SPRINGINESS, resilience, give, flexibility, elasticity, buoyancy.

spring² *n* source, origin, beginning, cause, root, fountainhead, wellhead, wellspring, well, geyser, spa.

springy *adj* bouncy, resilient, flexible, elastic, stretchy, rubbery, spongy, buoyant.
ⓔ hard, stiff.

sprinkle *v* shower, spray, spatter, scatter, strew, dot, pepper, dust, powder.

sprint *v* run, race, dash, tear, belt (*infml*), dart, shoot.

sprout *v* shoot, bud, germinate, grow, develop, come up, spring up.

spruce *adj* smart, elegant, neat, trim, dapper, well-dressed, well-turned-out, well-groomed, sleek.
ⓔ scruffy, untidy.
◆ **spruce up** neaten, tidy, smarten up, groom.

spry *adj* sprightly, quick, alert, agile, energetic, brisk, ready, nimble, active, supple, nippy (*infml*), peppy (*infml*).
ⓔ doddering, inactive, lethargic.

spur *v* goad, prod, poke, prick, stimulate, prompt, incite, drive, propel, impel, urge, encourage, motivate.
ⓔ curb, discourage.
➤ *n* incentive, encouragement, inducement, motive, stimulus, incitement, impetus, fillip.
ⓔ curb, disincentive.

spurious *adj* false, fake, counterfeit, forged, bogus, phoney (*infml*), mock, sham, feigned, pretended, simulated, imitation, artificial.
ⓔ genuine, authentic, real.

spurn *v* reject, turn down, scorn, despise, disdain, rebuff, repulse, slight, snub, cold-shoulder, ignore, disregard.
ⓔ accept, embrace.

spurt *v* gush, squirt, jet, shoot, burst, erupt, surge.
➤ *n* burst, rush, surge, spate, fit, access.

spy *n* secret agent, undercover agent, double agent, mole (*infml*), fifth columnist, scout, snooper.
➤ *v* spot, glimpse, notice, observe, discover.

squabble *v* bicker, wrangle, quarrel, row, argue, dispute, clash, brawl, scrap (*infml*), fight.

squad *n* crew, team, gang, band, group, company, brigade, troop, force, outfit.

squalid *adj* dirty, filthy, unclean, foul, disgusting, repulsive, sordid, seedy, dingy, untidy, slovenly, unkempt, broken-down, run-down, neglected, uncared-for, low, mean, nasty.
ⓔ clean, pleasant, attractive.

squalor *n* squalidness, dirtiness, dirt, filthiness, filth, foulness, uncleanness, grime, griminess, grubbiness, muckiness, dinginess, decay, neglect, meanness, wretchedness, sleaziness (*infml*).

squander *v* waste, misspend, misuse, lavish, blow (*sl*), fritter away, throw away, dissipate, scatter, spend, expend, consume.

square *v* settle, reconcile, tally, agree, accord, harmonize, correspond, match, balance, straighten, level, align, adjust, regulate, adapt, tailor, fit, suit.
➤ *adj* **1** QUADRILATERAL, rectangular, right-angled, perpendicular, straight, true, even, level. **2** FAIR, equitable, just, ethical, honourable, honest, genuine, above-board, on the level (*infml*).

squash *v* **1** CRUSH, flatten, press, squeeze, compress, crowd, trample, stamp, pound, pulp, smash, distort. **2** SUPPRESS, silence, quell, quash, annihilate, put down, snub, humiliate.
ⓔ **1** stretch, expand.

squat *adj* short, stocky, thickset, dumpy, chunky, stubby.
ⓔ slim, lanky.
➤ *v* crouch, stoop, bend, sit.

squawk *v, n* screech, shriek, cry, croak, cackle, crow, hoot.

squeak *v, n* squeal, whine, creak, peep, cheep.

squeal *v, n* cry, shout, yell, yelp, wail, scream, screech, shriek, squawk.

squeamish *adj* queasy, nauseated, sick, delicate, fastidious, particular, prudish.

squeeze *v* **1** PRESS, squash, crush, pinch, nip, compress, grip, clasp, clutch, hug, embrace, enfold, cuddle. **2** *squeeze into a corner*: cram, stuff, pack, crowd, wedge, jam, force, ram, push, thrust, shove, jostle. **3** WRING, wrest, extort, milk, bleed, force, lean on (*infml*).
➤ *n* **1** PRESS, squash, crush, crowd, congestion, jam. **2** HUG, embrace, hold, grasp, clasp.

squint *adj* crooked, indirect, oblique, off-centre, aslant, askew, awry, cock-eyed, strabismic (*fml*), skew-whiff (*infml*).
ⓔ straight.

squirm v wriggle, twist, writhe, squiggle, move, shift, wiggle, fidget, agonize, flounder.

squirt v spray, spurt, jet, shoot, spout, gush, ejaculate, discharge, emit, eject, expel.
➣ n spray, spurt, jet.

stab v pierce, puncture, cut, wound, injure, gore, knife, spear, stick, jab, thrust.
➣ n **1** ACHE, pang, twinge, prick, puncture, cut, incision, gash, wound, jab. **2** (infml) TRY, attempt, endeavour, bash (infml).

stability n steadiness, firmness, soundness, constancy, steadfastness, strength, sturdiness, solidity, durability, permanence.
◾ instability, unsteadiness, insecurity, weakness.

stable adj steady, firm, secure, fast, sound, sure, constant, steadfast, reliable, established, well-founded, deep-rooted, strong, sturdy, durable, lasting, enduring, abiding, permanent, unchangeable, unalterable, invariable, immutable, fixed, static, balanced.
◾ unstable, wobbly, shaky, weak.

stack n heap, pile, mound, mass, load, accumulation, hoard, stockpile.
➣ v heap, pile, load, amass, accumulate, assemble, gather, save, hoard, stockpile.

staff n **1** member of staff: personnel, workforce, employees, workers, crew, team, teachers, officers. **2** STICK, cane, rod, baton, wand, pole, prop.

stage n point, juncture, step, phase, period, division, lap, leg, length, level, floor.
➣ v mount, put on, present, produce, give, do, perform, arrange, organize, stage-manage, orchestrate, engineer.

stagger v **1** LURCH, totter, teeter, wobble, sway, rock, reel, falter, hesitate, waver.
2 SURPRISE, amaze, astound, astonish, stun, stupefy, dumbfound, flabbergast (infml), shake, shock, confound, overwhelm.

stagnant adj still, motionless, standing, brackish, stale, sluggish, torpid, lethargic.
◾ fresh, moving.

stagnate v vegetate, idle, languish, decline, deteriorate, degenerate, decay, rot, rust.

staid adj sedate, calm, composed, sober, demure, solemn, serious, grave, quiet, steady.

jaunty, debonair, frivolous, adventurous.

stain v **1** MARK, spot, blemish, blot, smudge, discolour, dirty, soil, taint, contaminate, sully, tarnish, blacken, disgrace. **2** DYE, tint, tinge, colour, paint, varnish.
➣ n mark, spot, blemish, blot, smudge, discoloration, smear, slur, disgrace, shame, dishonour.

stake¹ n post, pole, standard, picket, pale, paling, spike, stick.

stake² n bet, wager, pledge, interest, concern, involvement, share, investment, claim.
➣ v gamble, bet, wager, pledge, risk, chance, hazard, venture.

stale adj **1** stale bread: dry, hard, old, musty, fusty, flat, insipid, tasteless. **2** OVERUSED, hackneyed, clichéed, stereotyped, jaded, worn-out, unoriginal, trite, banal, commonplace.
◾ **1** fresh. **2** original.

stalemate n draw, tie, deadlock, impasse, standstill, halt.
◾ progress.

stalk¹ v track, trail, hunt, follow, pursue, shadow, tail, haunt.

stalk² n stem, twig, branch, trunk.

stall v temporize, play for time, delay, hedge, equivocate, obstruct, stonewall, drag one's feet (infml).

stalwart adj strong, sturdy, robust, rugged, stout, strapping, muscular, athletic, vigorous, valiant, daring, intrepid, indomitable, determined, resolute, staunch, steadfast, reliable, dependable.
◾ weak, feeble, timid.

stamina n energy, vigour, strength, power, force, grit, resilience, resistance, endurance, indefatigability, staying power.
◾ weakness.

stammer v stutter, stumble, falter, hesitate, splutter.

stamp v **1** TRAMPLE, crush, beat, pound. **2** IMPRINT, impress, print, inscribe, engrave, emboss, mark, brand, label, categorize, identify, characterize.
➣ n print, imprint, impression, seal, signature, authorization, mark, hallmark, attestation, brand, cast, mould, cut, form, fashion, sort, kind, type, breed, character, description.
◆ **stamp out** eradicate, suppress, crush,

quell, quash, put down, scotch, destroy, eliminate, end, extinguish, quench, kill, extirpate (*fml*).

stampede *n* charge, rush, dash, sprint, flight, rout.
➤ *v* charge, rush, dash, tear, run, sprint, gallop, shoot, fly, flee, scatter.

stance *n* posture, deportment, carriage, bearing, position, standpoint, viewpoint, angle, point of view, attitude.

stand *v* **1** PUT, place, set, erect, up-end, position, station. **2** *I can't stand it*: bear, tolerate, abide, endure, suffer, experience, undergo, withstand, weather. **3** RISE, get up, stand up.
➤ *n* base, pedestal, support, frame, rack, table, stage, platform, place, stall, booth.
◆ **stand by** support, back, champion, defend, stick up for, uphold, adhere to, hold to, stick by.
🔁 let down.
◆ **stand down** step down, resign, abdicate, quit, give up, retire, withdraw.
🔁 join.
◆ **stand for** represent, symbolize, mean, signify, denote, indicate.
◆ **stand in for** deputize for, cover for, understudy, replace, substitute for.
◆ **stand out** show, catch the eye, stick out, jut out, project.
◆ **stand up for** defend, stick up for, side with, fight for, support, protect, champion, uphold.
🔁 attack.
◆ **stand up to** defy, oppose, resist, withstand, endure, face, confront, brave.
🔁 give in to.

standard *n* **1** NORM, average, type, model, pattern, example, sample, guideline, benchmark, touchstone, yardstick, rule, measure, gauge, level, criterion, requirement, specification, grade, quality. **2** FLAG, ensign, pennant, pennon, colours, banner.
➤ *adj* normal, average, typical, stock, classic, basic, staple, usual, customary, popular, prevailing, regular, approved, accepted, recognized, official, orthodox, set, established, definitive.
🔁 abnormal, unusual, irregular.

standardize *v* normalize, equalize, homogenize, stereotype, mass-produce.
🔁 differentiate.

standards *n* principles, ideals, morals, ethics.

stand-in *n* deputy, representative, delegate, proxy, substitute, surrogate, second, second-in-command, understudy, locum.

standing *n* **1** REPUTATION, status, rank, position, seniority, eminence, station, repute, experience, footing. **2** DURATION, existence, continuance.
➤ *adj* **1** UPRIGHT, erect, perpendicular, vertical, upended, on one's feet. **2** PERMANENT, perpetual, lasting, fixed, regular, repeated.
🔁 **1** horizontal, lying. **2** temporary.

stand-off *n* deadlock, impasse, standstill, halt, blockade.

standoffish *adj* aloof, remote, distant, unapproachable, unsociable, uncommunicative, reserved, cold.
🔁 friendly.

standpoint *n* position, station, vantagepoint, stance, viewpoint, angle, point of view.

standstill *n* stop, halt, pause, lull, rest, stoppage, jam, log-jam, hold-up, impasse, deadlock, stalemate.
🔁 advance, progress.

staple *adj* basic, fundamental, primary, key, main, chief, major, principal, essential, necessary, standard.
🔁 minor.

star *n* **1** HEAVENLY BODY, sun, celestial body, sphere, orb. **2** CELEBRITY, personage, luminary, idol, lead, leading man, leading lady, superstar, principal, household name (*infml*), big name (*infml*), bigwig (*infml*), big shot (*infml*), leading light (*infml*).
➤ *adj* brilliant, well-known, famous, leading, illustrious, celebrated, prominent, talented, principal, major, pre-eminent, paramount.
🔁 minor.

> **Types of star include:** nova, supernova, pulsar, quasar, falling-star, shooting-star, meteor, comet, Halley's comet, red giant, supergiant, white dwarf, red dwarf, brown dwarf, neutron star, Pole Star, Polaris, North Star. *see also* **constellation**.

starchy *adj* formal, stiff, prim, punctilious, ceremonious, conventional, stuffy, strait-laced.
🔁 informal.

stare *v* gaze, look, watch, gape, gawp, gawk, goggle, glare.
➤ *n* gaze, look, glare.

stark adj 1 *stark landscape*: bare, barren, bleak, bald, plain, simple, austere, harsh, severe, grim, dreary, gloomy, depressing. 2 UTTER, unmitigated, total, consummate, absolute, sheer, downright, out-and-out, flagrant, arrant.

start v 1 BEGIN, commence, originate, initiate, introduce, pioneer, create, found, establish, set up, institute, inaugurate, launch, open, kick off (infml), instigate, activate, trigger, set off, set out, leave, depart, appear, arise, issue. 2 JUMP, jerk, twitch, flinch, recoil.
■ 1 stop, finish, end.
➤ n 1 BEGINNING, commencement, outset, inception, dawn, birth, break, outburst, onset, origin, initiation, introduction, foundation, inauguration, launch, opening, kick-off (infml). 2 JUMP, jerk, twitch, spasm, convulsion, fit.
■ 1 stop, finish, end.

startle v surprise, amaze, astonish, astound, shock, scare, frighten, alarm, agitate, upset, disturb.
■ calm.

startling adj surprising, astonishing, astounding, extraordinary, shocking, staggering, unexpected, sudden, dramatic, alarming, unforeseen, electrifying.
■ boring, calming, ordinary.

starvation n hunger, undernourishment, malnutrition, famine.
■ plenty, excess.

starve v hunger, fast, diet, deprive, refuse, deny, die, perish.
■ feed, gorge.

starving adj hungry, underfed, undernourished, ravenous, famished.

stash v store, hide, conceal, hoard, closet, lay up, save up, stockpile, stow, cache, secrete (fml), salt away (infml).
■ bring out, uncover.
➤ n hoard, store, collection, accumulation, mass, heap, pile, fund, reservoir, reserve, stockpile, cache.

state v say, declare, announce, report, communicate, assert, aver, affirm, specify, present, express, put, formulate, articulate, voice.
➤ n 1 CONDITION, shape, situation, position, circumstances, case. 2 NATION, country, land, territory, kingdom, republic, government. 3 (infml) PANIC, flap (infml), tizzy (infml), bother, plight, predicament. 4 POMP, ceremony, dignity, majesty,

grandeur, glory, splendour, display.
➤ adj national, governmental, public, official, formal, ceremonial, pompous, stately.

stately adj grand, imposing, impressive, elegant, majestic, regal, royal, imperial, noble, august, lofty, pompous, dignified, measured, deliberate, solemn, ceremonious.
■ informal, unimpressive.

statement n account, report, bulletin, communiqué, announcement, declaration, assertion, proclamation, communication, utterance, testimony, affirmation.

statesman, stateswoman n politician, leader, elder statesman, diplomat, GOM, grand old man (infml).

static adj stationary, motionless, immobile, unmoving, still, inert, resting, fixed, constant, changeless, unvarying, stable.
■ dynamic, mobile, varying.

station n place, location, position, post, headquarters, base, depot.
➤ v locate, set, establish, install, garrison, post, send, appoint, assign.

stationary adj motionless, immobile, unmoving, still, static, inert, standing, resting, parked, moored, fixed.
■ mobile, moving, active.

stationery

Items of stationery include: account book, address book, adhesive tape, blotter, bulldog clip, calendar, carbon paper, card index, cartridge ribbon, cash book, clipboard, computer disk, copying paper, correcting paper, correction fluid, correction ribbon, desk-diary, diary, divider, document folder, document wallet, drawing pin, dry-transfer lettering, elastic band, envelope, brown manila envelope, reply-paid envelope, self-seal envelope, window envelope, eraser, expanding file, file, file tab, filing tray, Filofax®, flip chart, floppy disk, folder, graph paper, headed notepaper, index card, ink, Jiffy bag®, label, lever arch file, marker, memo pad, notepaper, paper clip, paper fastener, paper knife, pen, pencil, pencil-sharpener, personal organizer, pin, pocket calculator, pocket folder, Post-it note®, printer label, printer paper, printer ribbon, reinforcement ring, ring binder, rubber, rubber band, rubber stamp, ruler, scissors, Sellotape®, shorthand notebook, spiral notebook, stamp pad, staple, suspension file, tape dispenser, Tipp-Ex®, toner, treasury tag, typewriter ribbon, wall chart, writing paper. *see also* **paper**.

statue *n* figure, head, bust, effigy, idol, statuette, carving, bronze.

stature *n* **1** HEIGHT, tallness, elevation, attitude, loftiness, size. **2** IMPORTANCE, reputation, standing, prominence, prestige, fame, renown, eminence, rank, consequence, weight.
☒ 2 unimportance.

status *n* rank, grade, degree, level, class, station, standing, position, state, condition, prestige, eminence, distinction, importance, consequence, weight.
☒ unimportance, insignificance.

statute *n* law, rule, regulation, act, decree, ordinance, edict, enactment.

staunch *adj* loyal, faithful, hearty, strong, stout, firm, sound, sure, true, trusty, reliable, dependable, steadfast.
☒ unfaithful, weak, unreliable.

stave off *v* fend off, ward off, avoid, avert, deflect, repel, repulse, turn aside, parry, foil, keep back, keep at bay.
☒ cause, encourage.

stay¹ *v* **1** REMAIN, last, continue, endure, linger, persist, keep, stay put, abide (*infml*), tarry (*fml*). **2** *stay in a hotel*: live, settle, stop, board, lodge, put up, rest, halt, pause, wait, visit, be accommodated at, take a room at, reside (*fml*), dwell (*fml*), sojourn (*fml*). **3** *stay judgement*: suspend, halt, postpone, put off, delay, defer, adjourn, reprieve, prorogue (*fml*). **4** *stay your anger*: control, restrain, arrest, check, curb, stop, halt, prevent, hinder, block, obstruct.
➤ *n* **1** VISIT, holiday, vacation, stopover, sojourn (*fml*). **2** *a stay of execution*: suspension, postponement, deferment, delay, reprieve, remission (*fml*).

stay² *n* prop, brace, buttress, reinforcement, stanchion, support, shoring.

steadfast *adj* firm, fixed, resolute, stable, steady, intent, single-minded, loyal, faithful, stout-hearted, sturdy, dedicated, constant, dependable, staunch, reliable, established, persevering, unswerving, unwavering, unfaltering, implacable, unflinching.
☒ unreliable, wavering, weak.

steady *adj* stable, balanced, poised, fixed,

immovable, firm, poised, settled, still, calm, imperturbable, equable, even, uniform, consistent, unvarying, unchanging, constant, persistent, unremitting, incessant, uninterrupted, unbroken, regular, rhythmic, steadfast, unwavering.
☒ unsteady, unstable, variable, wavering.
➤ *v* balance, stabilize, fix, secure, brace, support.

steal *v* **1** *steal a car*: thieve, pilfer, filch (*infml*), pinch (*infml*), nick (*sl*), take, appropriate (*fml*), snatch, swipe (*infml*), shoplift, poach, embezzle, lift (*infml*), plagiarize. **2** CREEP, tiptoe, slip, slink, sneak.
☒ 1 return, give back.

stealth *n* stealthiness, furtiveness, surreptitiousness, covertness, secrecy, slyness, sneakiness, unobtrusiveness.

stealthy *adj* surreptitious, clandestine, covert, secret, unobtrusive, secretive, quiet, furtive, sly, cunning, sneaky, underhand.
☒ open.

steam *n* vapour, mist, haze, condensation, moisture, dampness.

steep¹ *adj* **1** *a steep slope*: sheer, precipitous, headlong, abrupt, sudden, sharp. **2** (*infml*) EXCESSIVE, extreme, stiff, unreasonable, high, exorbitant, extortionate, overpriced.
☒ 1 gentle, gradual. **2** moderate, low.

steep² *v* saturate, seethe, soak, damp, moisten, souse, submerge, suffuse, drench, fill, imbrue, imbue, immerse, infuse, permeate, pervade, marinate, pickle, brine, macerate.

steer *v* pilot, guide, direct, control, govern, conduct.

stem¹ *n* stalk, shoot, stock, branch, trunk.

stem² *v* stop, halt, arrest, stanch, staunch, block, dam, check, curb, restrain, contain, resist, oppose.
☒ encourage.

stench *n* stink, reek, pong (*infml*), smell, odour.

step *n* **1** PACE, stride, footstep, tread, footprint, print, trace, track. **2** MOVE, act, action, deed, measure, procedure, process, proceeding, progression, movement, stage, phase, degree. **3** RUNG, stair, level, rank, point.
➤ *v* pace, stride, tread, stamp, walk, move.

♦ **step down** stand down, resign, abdicate, quit, leave, retire, withdraw.
F3 join.

♦ **step in** intervene, mediate, arbitrate, intercede, interfere, interrupt, intrude, involve oneself in.

♦ **step up** increase, raise, augment, boost, build up, intensify, escalate, accelerate, speed up.
F3 decrease.

stereotype n formula, convention, mould, pattern, model.
➢ v categorize, pigeonhole, typecast, standardize, formalize, conventionalize, mass-produce.
F3 differentiate.

sterile adj 1 GERM-FREE, aseptic, sterilized, disinfected, antiseptic, uncontaminated. 2 INFERTILE, barren, arid, bare, unproductive, fruitless, pointless, useless, abortive.
F3 1 septic. 2 fertile, fruitful.

sterilize v disinfect, fumigate, purify, clean, cleanse.
F3 contaminate, infect.

sterling adj excellent, great, superlative, first-class, genuine, real, sound, standard, authentic, true, pure, worthy.
F3 false, poor.

stern¹ adj strict, severe, authoritarian, rigid, inflexible, unyielding, hard, tough, rigorous, stringent, harsh, cruel, unsparing, relentless, unrelenting, grim, forbidding, stark, austere.
F3 kind, gentle, mild, lenient.

stern² n rear, back, tail, tail end, poop.
F3 bow.

stew v boil, simmer, braise, casserole.

stick¹ v 1 THRUST, poke, stab, jab, pierce, penetrate, puncture, spear, transfix. 2 GLUE, gum, paste, cement, bond, fuse, weld, solder, adhere, cling, hold. 3 ATTACH, affix, fasten, secure, fix, pin, join, bind. 4 PUT, place, position, set, install, deposit, drop.

♦ **stick at** persevere, plug away (infml), persist, continue.
F3 give up.

♦ **stick by** stand by, support, back, champion, defend, stand up for, stick up for, uphold, side with, adhere to, hold to.
F3 let down.

♦ **stick out** protrude, jut out, project, extend.

♦ **stick up for** stand up for, speak up for,

defend, champion, support, uphold.
F3 attack.

stick² n branch, twig, wand, baton, staff, sceptre, cane, birch, rod, pole, stake.

stickler n fanatic, maniac, perfectionist, pedant, purist, precisionist, fusspot, nut (infml).

sticky adj 1 ADHESIVE, gummed, tacky, gluey, gummy, viscous, glutinous (fml), gooey (infml). 2 (infml) a sticky situation: difficult, tricky, awkward, unpleasant, awkward, embarrassing, delicate. 3 HUMID, clammy, muggy, close, oppressive, sultry.
F3 1 dry. 2 easy. 3 fresh, cool.

stiff adj 1 RIGID, inflexible, unbending, unyielding, hard, solid, hardened, solidified, firm, tight, taut, tense. 2 FORMAL, ceremonious, pompous, standoffish, cold, prim, priggish, austere, strict, severe, harsh. 3 DIFFICULT, hard, tough, arduous, laborious, awkward, exacting, rigorous.
F3 1 flexible. 2 informal. 3 easy.

stiffen v harden, solidify, tighten, tense, brace, reinforce, starch, thicken, congeal, coagulate, jell, set.

stiff-necked adj proud, stubborn, obstinate, arrogant, haughty, uncompromising, opinionated, contumacious (fml).
F3 humble, flexible.

stifle v smother, suffocate, asphyxiate, strangle, choke, extinguish, muffle, dampen, deaden, silence, hush, suppress, quell, check, curb, restrain, repress.
F3 encourage.

stigma n brand, mark, stain, blot, spot, blemish, disgrace, shame, dishonour.
F3 credit, honour.

still adj stationary, motionless, lifeless, stagnant, smooth, undisturbed, unruffled, calm, tranquil, serene, restful, peaceful, hushed, quiet, silent, noiseless.
F3 active, disturbed, agitated, noisy.
➢ v calm, soothe, allay, tranquillize, subdue, restrain, hush, quieten, silence, pacify, settle, smooth.
F3 agitate, stir up.
➢ adv yet, even so, nevertheless, nonetheless, notwithstanding (fml), however.

stilted adj artificial, unnatural, stiff, wooden, forced, constrained.
F3 fluent, flowing.

stimulant *n* tonic, restorative, reviver, pick-me-up (*infml*), pep pill (*infml*).

stimulate *v* rouse, arouse, animate, quicken, fire, inflame, inspire, motivate, encourage, induce, urge, impel, spur, prompt, goad, provoke, incite, instigate, trigger off.
€ discourage, hinder, prevent.

stimulus *n* incentive, encouragement, inducement, spur, goad, provocation, incitement.
€ discouragement.

sting *v* **1** *bees sting*: bite, prick, hurt, injure, wound. **2** SMART, tingle, burn, pain.
➤ *n* bite, nip, prick, smart, tingle.

stingy *adj* mean, miserly, niggardly, tight-fisted (*infml*), parsimonious, penny-pinching.
€ generous, liberal.

stink *v* smell, reek, pong (*infml*), hum (*sl*).
➤ *n* smell, odour, stench, pong (*infml*), niff (*sl*).

stint *n* spell, stretch, period, time, shift, turn, bit, share, quota.

stipulate *v* specify, lay down, require, demand, insist on.

stipulation *n* specification, requirement, demand, condition, proviso.

stir *v* **1** MOVE, budge, touch, affect, inspire, excite, thrill, disturb, agitate, shake, tremble, quiver, flutter, rustle. **2** MIX, blend, beat.
➤ *n* activity, movement, bustle, flurry, commotion, ado, fuss, to-do (*infml*), uproar, tumult, disturbance, disorder, agitation, excitement, ferment.
€ calm.
◆ **stir up** rouse, arouse, awaken, animate, quicken, kindle, fire, inflame, stimulate, spur, prompt, provoke, incite, instigate, agitate.
€ calm, discourage.

stirring *adj* rousing, exciting, spirited, inspiring, stimulating, moving, animating, thrilling, exhilarating, heady, emotive, dramatic, lively, impassioned, intoxicating.
€ calming, uninspiring.

stitch *v* sew, tack, darn, mend, repair, seam, embroider, hem.

stock *n* **1** GOODS, merchandise, wares, commodities, capital, assets, inventory, repertoire, range, variety, assortment, source, supply, fund, reservoir, store, reserve, stockpile, hoard. **2** PARENTAGE,

ancestry, descent, extraction, family, line, lineage, pedigree, race, breed, species, blood. **3** LIVESTOCK, animals, cattle, horses, sheep, herds, flocks.
➤ *adj* standard, basic, regular, routine, ordinary, run-of-the-mill, usual, customary, traditional, conventional, set, stereotyped, hackneyed, overused, banal, trite.
€ original, unusual.
➤ *v* keep, carry, sell, trade in, deal in, handle, supply, provide.
◆ **stock up** gather, accumulate, amass, lay in, provision, fill, replenish, store (up), save, hoard, pile up.

stocky *adj* sturdy, solid, thickset, chunky, short, squat, dumpy, stubby.
€ tall, skinny.

stodgy *adj* **1** *stodgy food*: solid, heavy, indigestible, filling, starchy, substantial. **2** STUFFY, unimaginative, uninspired, unexciting, unenterprising, solemn, heavy, boring, dull, tedious, staid, formal, leaden, laboured, turgid, spiritless, fuddy-duddy (*infml*).
€ exciting, informal, light.

stoical *adj* patient, long-suffering, uncomplaining, resigned, philosophical, indifferent, impassive, unemotional, phlegmatic, dispassionate, cool, calm, imperturbable.
€ excitable, anxious.

stoicism *n* patience, long-suffering, resignation, indifference, dispassion, unexcitability, impassivity, calmness, acceptance, forbearance, imperturbability, stolidity, fatalism, fortitude (*fml*).
€ anxiety, depression, fury.

stolid *adj* slow, heavy, dull, bovine, wooden, blockish, lumpish, impassive, phlegmatic, unemotional.
€ lively, interested.

stomach *n* tummy (*infml*), gut, inside(s), belly, abdomen, paunch, pot.
➤ *v* tolerate, bear, stand, abide, endure, suffer, submit to, take.

stony *adj* **1** BLANK, expressionless, hard, cold, frigid, icy, indifferent, unfeeling, heartless, callous, merciless, pitiless, inexorable, hostile. **2** *stony beach*: pebbly, shingly, rocky.
€ **1** warm, soft-hearted, friendly.

stooge *n* puppet, pawn, lackey, henchman, dupe, foil, butt, cat's paw (*infml*), fall guy (*infml*).

stoop *v* **1** HUNCH, bow, bend, incline, lean,

duck, squat, crouch, kneel. **2** *stoop to blackmail*: descend, sink, lower oneself, resort, go so far as, condescend, deign.

stop *v* **1** HALT, cease, end, finish, conclude, terminate, discontinue, suspend, interrupt, pause, quit, refrain, desist, pack in (*sl*).
2 PREVENT, bar, frustrate, thwart, intercept, hinder, impede, check, restrain.
3 SEAL, close, plug, block, obstruct, arrest, stem, stanch.
Ea 1 start, continue.
➤ *n* **1** STATION, terminus, destination.
2 REST, break, pause, stage. **3** HALT, standstill, stoppage, cessation, end, finish, conclusion, termination, discontinuation.
Ea 3 start, beginning, continuation.

stopgap *n* improvisation, makeshift, substitute, temporary substitute, expedient, resort, shift.
➤ *adj* improvised, makeshift, provisional, temporary, emergency, impromptu, rough-and-ready (*infml*).
Ea finished, permanent.

stoppage *n* stop, halt, standstill, arrest, blockage, obstruction, check, hindrance, interruption, shutdown, closure, strike, walk-out, sit-in.
Ea start, continuation.

stopper *n* cork, bung, plug.

store *v* save, keep, put aside, lay by, reserve, stock, lay in, deposit, lay down, lay up, accumulate, hoard, salt away (*infml*), stockpile, stash (*infml*).
Ea use.
➤ *n* **1** STOCK, supply, provision, fund, reserve, mine, reservoir, hoard, cache, stockpile, heap, load, accumulation, amassment, deposit, quantity, abundance, plenty, lot. **2** SHOP, retail outlet, supermarket, hypermarket, chain store, department store, corner shop. **3** STOREROOM, storehouse, warehouse, repository, depository, larder, buttery.
Ea 1 scarcity.
♦ **set/lay store by** value, think highly of, consider highly, admire, hold in high regard, esteem (*fml*).

storey *n* floor, level, stage, tier, flight, deck.

storm *n* **1** TEMPEST, thunderstorm, squall, blizzard, gale, hurricane, whirlwind, tornado, cyclone. **2** OUTBURST, uproar, furore, outcry, row, rumpus, commotion, tumult, disturbance, turmoil, stir, agitation, rage, outbreak, attack, assault.
Ea 2 calm.

Kinds of storm include: blizzard, buran, cloudburst, cyclone, downpour, dust-devil, dust-storm, electrical storm, gale, haboob, hailstorm, hurricane, monsoon, rainstorm, sand storm, snow storm, squall, tempest, thunderstorm, tornado, typhoon, whirlwind. *see also* **wind**.

➤ *v* charge, rush, attack, assault, assail, roar, thunder, rage, rant, rave, fume.

stormy *adj* tempestuous, squally, rough, choppy, turbulent, wild, raging, windy, gusty, blustery, foul.
Ea calm.

story *n* **1** TALE, fairy-tale, fable, myth, legend, novel, romance, fiction, yarn (*infml*), anecdote, episode, plot, narrative, history, chronicle, record, account, relation, recital, report, article, feature. **2** LIE, falsehood, untruth.

Types of story include: adventure story, bedtime story, blockbuster (*infml*), children's story, comedy, black comedy, crime story, detective story, fable, fairy-tale, fantasy, folk tale, ghost story, historical novel, horror story, legend, love story, Mills & Boon®, mystery, myth, parable, romance, saga, science fiction, sci-fi (*infml*), short story, spiel, spine-chiller, spy story, supernatural tale, tall story, thriller, western, whodunit (*infml*), yarn (*infml*).

stout *adj* **1** FAT, plump, fleshy, portly, corpulent, overweight, heavy, bulky, big, brawny, beefy, hulking, burly, muscular, athletic. **2** *stout packaging*: strong, tough, durable, thick, sturdy, robust, hardy, vigorous. **3** BRAVE, courageous, valiant, plucky, fearless, bold, intrepid, dauntless, resolute, stalwart.
Ea 1 thin, lean, slim. **2** weak. **3** cowardly, timid.

stow *v* put away, store, load, pack, cram, stuff, stash (*infml*).
Ea unload.

straight *adj* **1** *a straight line*: level, even, flat, horizontal, upright, vertical, aligned, direct, undeviating, unswerving, true, right. **2** TIDY, neat, orderly, shipshape, organized. **3** HONOURABLE, honest, law-abiding, respectable, upright, trustworthy, reliable, straightforward, fair, just. **4** FRANK, candid, blunt, forthright, direct. **5** *straight whisky*: undiluted, neat, unadulterated, unmixed.

☙ 1 bent, crooked. **2** untidy. **3** dishonest. **4** evasive. **5** diluted.

➤ *adv* directly, point-blank, honestly, frankly, candidly.

◆ **straight away** at once, immediately, instantly, right away, directly, now, there and then.

☙ later, eventually.

straighten *v* unbend, align, tidy, neaten, order, arrange.

☙ bend, twist.

◆ **straighten out** clear up, sort out, settle, resolve, correct, rectify, disentangle, regularize.

☙ confuse, muddle.

straightforward *adj* **1** EASY, simple, uncomplicated, clear, elementary. **2** HONEST, truthful, sincere, genuine, open, frank, candid, direct, forthright.

☙ **1** complicated. **2** evasive, devious.

strain¹ *v* **1** PULL, wrench, twist, sprain, tear, stretch, extend, tighten, tauten. **2** SIEVE, sift, screen, separate, filter, purify, drain, wring, squeeze, compress, express. **3** WEAKEN, tire, tax, overtax, overwork, labour, try, endeavour, struggle, strive, exert, force, drive.

➤ *n* stress, anxiety, burden, pressure, tension, tautness, pull, sprain, wrench, injury, exertion, effort, struggle, force.

☙ relaxation.

strain² *n* **1** STOCK, ancestry, descent, extraction, family, lineage, pedigree, blood, variety, type. **2** TRAIT, streak, vein, tendency, trace, suggestion, suspicion.

strained *adj* forced, constrained, laboured, false, artificial, unnatural, stiff, tense, unrelaxed, uneasy, uncomfortable, awkward, embarrassed, self-conscious.

☙ natural, relaxed.

strait *n* **1** *the Straits of Gibraltar*: sound, narrows, inlet, channel, kyle. **2** *in desperate straits*: crisis, difficulty, emergency, hardship, predicament, plight, perplexity, distress, dilemma, embarrassment, extremity, poverty, hole (*infml*), mess (*infml*), fix (*infml*), pickle (*infml*).

strait-laced *adj* prudish, stuffy, starchy, prim, proper, strict, narrow, narrow-minded, puritanical, moralistic.

☙ broad-minded.

strand *n* fibre, filament, wire, thread, string, piece, length.

stranded *adj* marooned, high and dry, abandoned, forsaken, in the lurch, helpless, aground, grounded, beached, shipwrecked, wrecked.

strange *adj* **1** ODD, peculiar, funny (*infml*), curious, queer, weird, bizarre, eccentric, abnormal, irregular, uncommon, unusual, exceptional, remarkable, extraordinary, mystifying, perplexing, unexplained. **2** NEW, novel, untried, unknown, unheard-of, unfamiliar, unacquainted, foreign, alien, exotic.

☙ **1** ordinary, common. **2** well-known, familiar.

stranger *n* newcomer, visitor, guest, non-member, outsider, foreigner, alien.

☙ local, native.

strangle *v* throttle, choke, asphyxiate, suffocate, stifle, smother, suppress, gag, repress, inhibit.

strap *n* thong, tie, band, belt, leash.

➤ *v* **1** BEAT, lash, whip, flog, belt. **2** FASTEN, secure, tie, bind.

strapping *adj* brawny, strong, sturdy, well-built, beefy, big, burly, hefty, robust, hulking, husky, hunky (*infml*).

☙ puny.

stratagem *n* plan, scheme, plot, intrigue, ruse, ploy, trick, dodge (*infml*), manoeuvre, device, artifice, wile, subterfuge.

strategic *adj* important, key, critical, decisive, crucial, vital, tactical, planned, calculated, deliberate, politic, diplomatic.

☙ unimportant.

strategy *n* tactics, planning, policy, approach, procedure, plan, programme, design, scheme.

stratum *n* **1** LEVEL, grade, class, rank, table, tier, category, bracket, caste, station, group, region. **2** LAYER, seam, vein, lode, bed, stratification.

stray *v* wander (off), get lost, err, ramble, roam, rove, range, meander, straggle, drift, diverge, deviate, digress.

➤ *adj* **1** LOST, abandoned, homeless, wandering, roaming. **2** RANDOM, chance, accidental, freak, odd, erratic.

streak *n* line, stroke, smear, band, stripe, strip, layer, vein, trace, dash, touch, element, strain.

➤ *v* **1** BAND, stripe, fleck, striate, smear, daub. **2** SPEED, tear, hurtle, sprint, gallop, fly, dart, flash, whistle, zoom, whizz, sweep.

stream *n* **1** RIVER, creek, brook, beck, burn, rivulet, tributary. **2** CURRENT, drift, flow, run, gush, flood, deluge, cascade, torrent.

➤ *v* issue, well, surge, run, flow, course, pour, spout, gush, flood, cascade.

streamer *n* ribbon, banner, pennant, pennon, flag, ensign, standard.

streamlined *adj* aerodynamic, smooth, sleek, graceful, efficient, well-run, smooth-running, rationalized, time-saving, organized, slick.

🔁 clumsy, inefficient.

strength *n* 1 POWER, force, energy, vigour, brawn, muscle, sinew, stoutness, toughness, stamina, fitness, health, vigour, clout (*infml*). 2 TOUGHNESS, resilience, robustness, sturdiness, impregnability, durability, solidity, solidness, resistance, firmness, soundness, hardiness. 3 DETERMINATION, resolution, forcefulness, firmness, assertiveness, persistence, spirit, bravery, courage, fortitude (*fml*), guts (*infml*). 4 INTENSITY, depth, vividness, graphicness, sharpness, keenness, pungency, passion, fervency, ardour, vehemence. 5 FORCEFULNESS, effectiveness, power, force, potency, persuasiveness, weight, validity, soundness, urgency, cogency (*fml*). 6 STRONG POINT, talent, gift, aptitude, advantage, asset, bent, forte, specialty, speciality, métier, thing (*infml*).

🔁 1 weakness, frailty. 2 weakness. 3 weakness, feebleness. 4 mildness, blandness, faintness. 5 weakness, ineffectiveness. 6 weakness.

◆ **on the strength of** because of, because of the influence of, on account of, based on, on the basis of, by virtue of (*fml*).

strengthen *v* reinforce, brace, steel, fortify, buttress, bolster, support, toughen, harden, stiffen, consolidate, substantiate, corroborate, confirm, encourage, hearten, refresh, restore, invigorate, nourish, increase, heighten, intensify.

🔁 weaken, undermine.

strenuous *adj* 1 *strenuous work*: hard, tough, demanding, gruelling, taxing, laborious, uphill, arduous, tiring, exhausting. 2 ACTIVE, energetic, vigorous, eager, earnest, determined, resolute, spirited, tireless, indefatigable.

🔁 1 easy, effortless.

stress *n* 1 PRESSURE, strain, tension, worry, anxiety, weight, burden, trauma, hassle (*infml*). 2 EMPHASIS, accent, accentuation,

beat, force, weight, importance, significance.

🔁 1 relaxation.

➤ *v* emphasize, accentuate, highlight, underline, underscore, repeat.

🔁 understate, downplay.

stretch *n* 1 EXPANSE, spread, sweep, reach, extent, distance, space, area, tract. 2 PERIOD, time, term, spell, stint, run.

➤ *v* pull, tighten, tauten, strain, tax, extend, lengthen, elongate, expand, spread, unfold, unroll, inflate, swell, reach.

🔁 compress.

◆ **stretch out** extend, relax, hold out, put out, lie down, reach.

🔁 draw back.

stricken *adj* affected, afflicted, hit, struck, injured, wounded, smitten.

🔁 unaffected.

strict *adj* 1 *a strict teacher*: stern, authoritarian, no-nonsense, firm, rigid, inflexible, stringent, rigorous, harsh, severe, austere. 2 EXACT, precise, accurate, literal, faithful, true, absolute, utter, total, complete, thoroughgoing, meticulous, scrupulous, particular, religious.

🔁 1 easy-going (*infml*), flexible. 2 loose.

strident *adj* loud, clamorous, vociferous, harsh, raucous, grating, rasping, shrill, screeching, unmusical, discordant, clashing, jarring, jangling.

🔁 quiet, soft.

strife *n* conflict, discord, dissension, controversy, animosity, friction, rivalry, contention, quarrel, row, wrangling, struggle, fighting, combat, battle, warfare.

🔁 peace.

strike *n* 1 INDUSTRIAL ACTION, work-to-rule, go-slow, stoppage, sit-in, walk-out, mutiny, revolt. 2 HIT, blow, stroke, raid, attack.

➤ *v* 1 STOP WORK, down tools, work to rule, walk out, protest, mutiny, revolt. 2 HIT, knock, collide with, slap, smack, cuff, clout (*infml*), thump, wallop (*infml*), beat, pound, hammer, buffet, raid, attack, afflict. 3 IMPRESS, affect, touch, register. 4 FIND, discover, unearth, uncover, encounter, reach.

◆ **strike out** cross out, delete, strike through, cancel, strike off, remove.

🔁 add.

striking *adj* noticeable, conspicuous, salient, outstanding, remarkable, extraordinary, memorable, impressive, dazzling, arresting, astonishing, stunning (*infml*).

F3 unimpressive.

string *n* **1** *a piece of string*: twine, cord, rope, yarn, cable, line, strand, fibre. **2** SERIES, succession, sequence, chain, line, row, column, file, queue, procession, stream, train. **3** *with no strings attached*: qualifications, conditions, limitations, restrictions, stipulations, provisos, obligations, requirements, catches, prerequisites (*fml*).

➣ *v* thread, link, connect, fasten, tie up, sling, hang, suspend, festoon, loop.

◆ **string along** deceive, fool, bluff, dupe, play (someone) false, hoax, humbug, play fast and loose with (*infml*), put one over on (*infml*), take for a ride (*infml*).

◆ **string out** space out, spread out, stretch out, straggle, fan out, disperse, extend, lengthen, wander, protract (*fml*).

F3 gather, shorten.

◆ **string up** hang, kill, lynch, send to the gallows/scaffold/gibbet, top (*infml*).

stringent *adj* binding, strict, severe, rigorous, tough, rigid, inflexible, tight.

F3 lax, flexible.

strip[1] *v* peel, skin, flay, denude, divest, deprive, undress, disrobe, unclothe, uncover, expose, lay bare, bare, empty, clear, gut, ransack, pillage, plunder, loot.

F3 dress, clothe, cover.

strip[2] *n* ribbon, thong, strap, belt, sash, band, stripe, lath, slat, piece, bit, slip, shred.

stripe *n* band, line, bar, chevron, flash, streak, fleck, strip, belt.

striped *adj* banded, barred, streaky, stripy, variegated, striated, vittate (*fml*).

strive *v* try, attempt, endeavour, struggle, strain, work, toil, labour, fight, contend, compete.

stroke *n* **1** CARESS, pat, rub. **2** BLOW, hit, knock, swipe. **3** SWEEP, flourish, movement, action, move, line.

➣ *v* caress, fondle, pet, touch, pat, rub, massage.

stroll *v* saunter, amble, dawdle, ramble, wander.

➣ *n* saunter, amble, walk, constitutional, turn, ramble.

strong *adj* **1** TOUGH, resilient, durable, hard-wearing, heavy-duty, robust, sturdy, firm, sound, lusty, strapping, stout, burly,

well-built, beefy (*infml*), brawny (*infml*), muscular, sinewy, athletic, fit, healthy, hardy, powerful, mighty, potent. **2** INTENSE, deep, vivid, fierce, violent, vehement, keen, eager, zealous, fervent, ardent, dedicated, staunch, stalwart, determined, resolute, tenacious, strong-minded, strong-willed, self-assertive. **3** HIGHLY-FLAVOURED, piquant, hot, spicy, highly-seasoned, sharp, pungent, undiluted, concentrated. **4** *strong argument*: convincing, persuasive, cogent, effective, telling, forceful, weighty, compelling, urgent.

F3 **1** weak, feeble. **2** indecisive. **3** mild, bland. **4** unconvincing.

stronghold *n* citadel, bastion, fort, fortress, castle, keep, refuge.

structure *n* construction, erection, building, edifice, fabric, framework, form, shape, design, configuration, conformation, make-up, formation, arrangement, organization, set-up.

➣ *v* construct, assemble, build, form, shape, design, arrange, organize.

struggle *v* strive, work, toil, labour, strain, agonize, fight, battle, wrestle, grapple, contend, compete, vie.

F3 yield, give in.

➣ *n* difficulty, problem, effort, exertion, pains, agony, work, labour, toil, clash, conflict, strife, fight, battle, skirmish, encounter, combat, hostilities, contest.

F3 ease, submission, co-operation.

strut *v* parade, prance, stalk, swagger, peacock, swank (*infml*).

stub *n* end, stump, remnant, fag-end (*infml*), dog-end (*infml*), butt, counterfoil.

stubborn *adj* obstinate, stiff-necked, mulish, pig-headed, obdurate (*fml*), intransigent (*fml*), rigid, inflexible, unbending, unyielding, dogged, persistent, tenacious, headstrong, self-willed, wilful, refractory (*fml*), difficult, unmanageable.

F3 compliant, flexible, yielding.

stuck *adj* **1** FAST, jammed, firm, fixed, fastened, joined, glued, cemented. **2** BEATEN, stumped (*infml*), baffled.

F3 **1** loose.

stuck-up (*infml*) *adj* snobbish, toffee-nosed (*infml*), supercilious, snooty (*infml*), haughty, high and mighty, condescending, proud, arrogant, conceited, bigheaded (*infml*).

F3 humble, modest.

studded *adj* dotted, flecked, set, spotted, speckled, sprinkled, ornamented, spangled, scattered.

student *n* undergraduate, postgraduate, scholar, schoolboy, schoolgirl, pupil, disciple, learner, trainee, apprentice.

studied *adj* deliberate, conscious, wilful, intentional, premeditated, planned, calculated, contrived, forced, unnatural, over-elaborate.
ⓔ unplanned, impulsive, natural.

studio *n* workshop, workroom.

studious *adj* scholarly, academic, intellectual, bookish, serious, thoughtful, reflective, diligent, hard-working, industrious, assiduous, careful, attentive, earnest, eager.
ⓔ lazy, idle, negligent.

study *v* read, learn, revise, cram, swot (*infml*), mug up (*infml*), read up, research, investigate, analyse, survey, scan, examine, scrutinize, peruse, pore over, contemplate, meditate, ponder, consider, deliberate.
➤ *n* **1** READING, homework, preparation, learning, revision, cramming, swotting (*infml*), research, investigation, inquiry, analysis, examination, scrutiny, inspection, contemplation, consideration, attention. **2** REPORT, essay, thesis, paper, monograph, survey, review, critique. **3** OFFICE, den (*infml*).

Subjects of study include: accountancy, agriculture, anatomy, anthropology, archaeology, architecture, art, astrology, astronomy, biology, botany, building studies, business studies, calligraphy, chemistry, CDT (craft, design and technology), civil engineering, the Classics, commerce, computer studies, cosmology, craft, dance, design, domestic science, drama, dressmaking, driving, ecology, economics, education, electronics, engineering, environmental studies, ethnology, eugenics, fashion, fitness, food technology, forensics, genetics, geography, geology, heraldry, history, home economics, horticulture, information technology (IT), journalism, languages, law, leisure studies, lexicography, linguistics, literature, logistics, management studies, marketing, mathematics, mechanics, media studies, medicine, metallurgy, metaphysics, meteorology, music, mythology, natural history, oceanography, ornithology, pathology, penology, personal and social education (PSE); personal, health and social education (PHSE), pharmacology, philosophy, photography, physics, physiology, politics, pottery, psychology, religious studies, science, shorthand, social sciences, sociology, sport, statistics, surveying, technology, theology, typewriting, visual arts, word processing, writing, zoology.

stuff *v* **1** PACK, stow, load, fill, cram, crowd, force, push, shove, ram, wedge, jam, squeeze, compress. **2** GORGE, gormandize, overindulge, guzzle (*infml*), gobble (*infml*), sate, satiate.
ⓔ **1** unload, empty. **2** nibble.
➤ *n* **1** MATERIAL, fabric, matter, substance, essence. **2** (*infml*) BELONGINGS, possessions, things, objects, articles, goods, luggage, paraphernalia, gear (*infml*), clobber (*infml*), kit, tackle, equipment, materials.

stuffing *n* padding, wadding, quilting, filling, force-meat.

stuffy *adj* **1** *a stuffy room*: musty, stale, airless, unventilated, suffocating, stifling, oppressive, heavy, close, muggy, sultry. **2** STAID, strait-laced, prim, conventional, old-fashioned, pompous, dull, dreary, uninteresting, stodgy.
ⓔ **1** airy, well-ventilated. **2** informal, modern, lively.

stumble *v* **1** TRIP, slip, fall, lurch, reel, stagger, flounder, blunder. **2** STAMMER, stutter, hesitate, falter.
◆ **stumble on** come across, chance upon, happen upon, find, discover, encounter.

stumbling-block *n* obstacle, hurdle, barrier, bar, obstruction, hindrance, impediment, difficulty, snag.

stump *n* end, remnant, trunk, stub.
➤ *v* (*infml*) defeat, outwit, confound, perplex, puzzle, baffle, mystify, confuse, bewilder, flummox (*infml*), bamboozle (*infml*), dumbfound.
ⓔ assist.
◆ **stump up** (*infml*) pay, hand over, fork out (*infml*), shell out (*infml*), donate, contribute, cough up (*infml*).
ⓔ receive.

stun *v* amaze, astonish, astound, stagger, shock, daze, stupefy, dumbfound, flabbergast (*infml*), overcome, confound, confuse, bewilder.

stunning (*infml*) *adj* beautiful, lovely,

gorgeous, ravishing, dazzling, brilliant, striking, impressive, spectacular, remarkable, wonderful, marvellous, great, sensational.
Ea ugly, awful.

stunt¹ *n* feat, exploit, act, deed, enterprise, trick, turn, performance.

stunt² *v* stop, arrest, check, restrict, slow, retard, hinder, impede, dwarf.
Ea promote, encourage.

stupefy *v* daze, stun, numb, dumbfound, shock, stagger, amaze, astound.

stupendous *adj* huge, enormous, gigantic, colossal, vast, prodigious, phenomenal, tremendous, breathtaking, overwhelming, staggering, stunning (*infml*), amazing, astounding, fabulous (*infml*), fantastic (*infml*), superb, wonderful, marvellous.
Ea ordinary, unimpressive.

stupid *adj* 1 SILLY, foolish, irresponsible, ill-advised, indiscreet, foolhardy, rash, senseless, mad, lunatic, brainless, half-witted, idiotic, imbecilic, moronic, feeble-minded, simple-minded, slow, dim, dull, dense, thick (*infml*), dumb, dopey (*infml*), crass, inane, puerile, mindless, futile, pointless, meaningless, nonsensical, absurd, ludicrous, ridiculous, laughable. 2 DAZED, groggy, stupefied, stunned, sluggish, semiconscious.
Ea 1 sensible, wise, clever, intelligent. 2 alert.

stupor *n* daze, stupefaction, torpor, lethargy, inertia, trance, coma, numbness, insensibility, unconsciousness.
Ea alertness, consciousness.

sturdy *adj* strong, robust, durable, well-made, stout, substantial, solid, well-built, powerful, muscular, athletic, hardy, vigorous, flourishing, hearty, staunch, stalwart, steadfast, firm, resolute, determined.
Ea weak, flimsy, puny.

stutter *v* stammer, hesitate, falter, stumble, mumble.

style *n* 1 APPEARANCE, cut, design, pattern, shape, form, sort, type, kind, genre, variety, category. 2 ELEGANCE, smartness, chic, flair, panache, stylishness, taste, polish, refinement, sophistication, urbanity, fashion, vogue, trend, mode, dressiness, flamboyance, affluence, luxury, grandeur. 3 *style of working*: technique, approach, method, manner, mode, fashion, way,

custom. 4 WORDING, phrasing, expression, tone, tenor.
Ea 2 inelegance, tastelessness.
➤ *v* 1 DESIGN, cut, tailor, fashion, shape, adapt. 2 DESIGNATE, term, name, call, address, title, dub, label.

stylish *adj* chic, fashionable, à la mode, modish, in vogue, voguish, trendy (*infml*), snappy, natty (*infml*), snazzy (*infml*), dressy, smart, elegant, classy (*infml*), polished, refined, sophisticated, urbane.
Ea old-fashioned, shabby.

suave *adj* polite, courteous, charming, agreeable, affable, soft-spoken, smooth, unctuous, sophisticated, urbane, worldly.
Ea rude, unsophisticated.

subconscious *adj* subliminal, unconscious, intuitive, inner, innermost, hidden, latent, repressed, suppressed.
Ea conscious.

subdue *v* overcome, quell, suppress, repress, overpower, crush, defeat, conquer, vanquish (*fml*), overrun, subject, subjugate (*fml*), humble, break, tame, master, discipline, control, check, moderate, reduce, soften, quieten, damp, mellow.
Ea arouse, awaken.

subdued *adj* 1 SAD, downcast, dejected, crestfallen, quiet, serious, grave, solemn. 2 QUIET, muted, hushed, soft, dim, shaded, sombre, sober, restrained, unobtrusive, low-key, subtle.
Ea 1 lively, excited. 2 striking, obtrusive.

subject *n* 1 TOPIC, theme, matter, issue, question, point, case, affair, business, discipline, field. 2 NATIONAL, citizen, participant, client, patient, victim.
Ea 2 monarch, ruler, master.
➤ *adj* 1 LIABLE, disposed, prone, susceptible, vulnerable, open, exposed. 2 SUBJUGATED, captive, bound, obedient, answerable, subordinate, inferior, subservient, submissive. 3 DEPENDENT, contingent, conditional.
Ea 1 vulnerable. 2 free, superior. 3 unconditional.
➤ *v* expose, lay open, submit, subjugate, subdue.

subjection *n* subjugation, defeat, captivity, bondage, chains, shackles, slavery, enslavement, oppression, domination, mastery.

subjective *adj* biased, prejudiced, personal, individual, idiosyncratic, emotional, intuitive, instinctive.

☒ objective, unbiased, impartial.

sublimate *v* channel, divert, transfer, redirect, turn, exalt, elevate, heighten, purify, refine, transmute (*fml*).

☒ let out.

sublime *adj* exalted, elevated, high, lofty, noble, majestic, great, grand, imposing, magnificent, glorious, transcendent, spiritual.

☒ lowly, base.

submerge *v* submerse, immerse, plunge, duck, dip, sink, drown, engulf, overwhelm, swamp, flood, inundate, deluge.

☒ surface.

submerged *adj* submersed, immersed, underwater, sunk, sunken, drowned, swamped, inundated, hidden, concealed, unseen.

submission *n* **1** SURRENDER, capitulation, resignation, acquiescence, assent, compliance, obedience, deference, submissiveness, meekness, passivity. **2** PRESENTATION, offering, contribution, entry, suggestion, proposal.

☒ **1** intransigence, intractability.

submissive *adj* yielding, unresisting, resigned, patient, uncomplaining, accommodating, biddable, obedient, deferential, ingratiating, subservient, humble, meek, docile, subdued, passive.

☒ intransigent, intractable.

submit *v* **1** YIELD, give in, surrender, capitulate, knuckle under, bow, bend, stoop, succumb, agree, comply. **2** PRESENT, tender, offer, put forward, suggest, propose, table, state, claim, argue.

☒ **1** resist. **2** withdraw.

subordinate *adj* secondary, auxiliary, ancillary, subsidiary, dependent, inferior, lower, junior, minor, lesser.

☒ superior, senior.

➤ *n* inferior, junior, assistant, attendant, second, aide, dependant, underling (*infml*).

☒ superior, boss.

subordination *n* inferiority, subjection, submission, dependence, servitude, subservience.

☒ superiority.

subscribe *v* **1** *subscribe to a theory*: support, endorse, back, advocate, approve, agree. **2** GIVE, donate, contribute.

subscription *n* membership fee, dues, payment, donation, contribution, offering, gift.

subsequent *adj* following, later, future, next, succeeding, consequent, resulting, ensuing.

☒ previous, earlier.

subsequently *adv* later, after, afterwards, consequently.

☒ previously.

subside *v* sink, collapse, settle, descend, fall, drop, lower, decrease, lessen, diminish, dwindle, decline, wane, ebb, recede, moderate, abate, die down, quieten, slacken, ease.

☒ rise, increase.

subsidence *n* decline, decrease, descent, settlement, sinking, slackening, lessening, ebb, de-escalation, settling, abatement (*fml*), detumescence (*fml*), diminution (*fml*).

☒ increase.

subsidiary *adj* auxiliary, supplementary, additional, ancillary, assistant, supporting, contributory, secondary, subordinate, lesser, minor.

☒ primary, chief, major.

➤ *n* branch, offshoot, division, section, part.

subsidize *v* support, back, underwrite, sponsor, finance, fund, aid, promote.

subsidy *n* grant, allowance, assistance, help, aid, contribution, sponsorship, finance, support, backing.

subsistence *n* living, survival, existence, livelihood, maintenance, support, keep, sustenance, nourishment, food, provisions, rations.

substance *n* **1** MATTER, material, stuff, fabric, essence, pith, entity, body, solidity, concreteness, reality, actuality, ground, foundation. **2** SUBJECT, subject-matter, theme, gist, meaning, significance, force.

substandard *adj* second-rate, inferior, imperfect, damaged, shoddy, poor, inadequate, unacceptable.

☒ first-rate, superior, perfect.

substantial *adj* large, big, sizable, ample, generous, great, considerable, significant, important, worthwhile, massive, bulky, hefty, well-built, stout, sturdy, strong, sound, durable.

☒ small, insignificant, weak.

substantially *adv* **1** SIGNIFICANTLY, largely, considerably, to a great extent. **2**

ESSENTIALLY, fundamentally, mainly, in the main, materially, to all intents and purposes.
F₃ 1 slightly.

substantiate v prove, verify, confirm, support, corroborate (fml), authenticate, validate.
F₃ disprove, refute.

substitute v **1** CHANGE, exchange, swap, switch, interchange, replace. **2** STAND IN, fill in (infml), cover, deputize, understudy, relieve.
➤ n reserve, stand-by, temp (infml), supply, locum, understudy, stand-in, replacement, relief, surrogate, proxy, agent, deputy, makeshift, stopgap.
➤ adj reserve, temporary, acting, surrogate, proxy, replacement, alternative.

substitution n change, exchange, replacement, interchange, swap, swapping, switch, switching.

subterfuge n trick, stratagem, scheme, ploy, ruse, dodge (infml), manoeuvre, machination, deviousness, evasion, deception, artifice, pretence, excuse.
F₃ openness, honesty.

subtle adj **1** DELICATE, understated, implied, indirect, slight, tenuous, faint, mild, fine, nice, refined, sophisticated, deep, profound. **2** ARTFUL, cunning, crafty, sly, devious, shrewd, astute.
F₃ 1 blatant, obvious. **2** artless, open.

subtlety n **1** DELICACY, nicety, nuance, refinement, finesse, faintness, indistinctness, indefiniteness, muteness, sophistication. **2** ARTFULNESS, cunning, wiliness, guile, deviousness, craftiness, cleverness, discernment, astuteness, skill, discrimination, intricacy, slyness, acuteness, acumen, sagacity (fml).

subtract v deduct, take away, remove, withdraw, debit, detract, diminish.
F₃ add.

suburbs n suburbia, commuter belt, residential area, outskirts.
F₃ centre, heart.

subversive adj seditious, treasonous, treacherous, traitorous, inflammatory, incendiary, disruptive, riotous, weakening, undermining, destructive.
F₃ loyal.
➤ n seditionist, terrorist, freedom fighter, dissident, traitor, quisling, fifth columnist.

subvert v undermine, destroy, ruin, pervert, corrupt, confound, deprave, demoralize, contaminate, poison, overturn, upset, disrupt, invalidate, wreck, demolish, debase, raze, sabotage, vitiate (fml).
F₃ boost, uphold.

succeed v **1** TRIUMPH, make it, get on, thrive, flourish, prosper, make good, manage, work. **2** winter succeeds autumn: follow, replace, result, ensue.
F₃ 1 fail. **2** precede.

succeeding adj following, next, subsequent, ensuing, coming, to come, later, successive.
F₃ previous, earlier.

success n **1** TRIUMPH, victory, luck, fortune, prosperity, fame, eminence, happiness. **2** CELEBRITY, star, somebody, winner, bestseller, hit, sensation.
F₃ 1 failure, disaster.

successful adj **1** VICTORIOUS, winning, lucky, fortunate, prosperous, wealthy, thriving, flourishing, booming, moneymaking, lucrative, profitable, rewarding, satisfying, fruitful, productive. **2** a successful writer: famous, well-known, popular, leading, bestselling, top, unbeaten.
F₃ 1 unsuccessful, unprofitable, fruitless. **2** unknown.

succession n sequence, series, order, progression, run, chain, string, cycle, continuation, flow, course, line, train, procession.

successive adj consecutive, sequential, following, succeeding.

succinct adj short, brief, terse, pithy, concise, compact, condensed, summary.
F₃ long, lengthy, wordy, verbose.

succulent adj fleshy, juicy, moist, luscious, mouthwatering, lush, rich, mellow.
F₃ dry.

succumb v give way, yield, give in, submit, knuckle under, surrender, capitulate, collapse, fall.
F₃ overcome, master.

suck v draw in, imbibe, absorb, soak up, extract, drain.

sudden adj unexpected, unforeseen, surprising, startling, abrupt, sharp, quick, swift, rapid, prompt, hurried, hasty, rash, impetuous, impulsive, snap (infml).
F₃ expected, predictable, gradual, slow.

suddenly adv unexpectedly, all of a

sudden, quickly, sharply, abruptly, immediately, instantaneously, without warning, out of the blue (*infml*), from out of nowhere (*infml*).

sue *v* prosecute, charge, indict, summon, solicit, appeal.

suffer *v* **1** HURT, ache, agonize, grieve, sorrow. **2** BEAR, support, tolerate, endure, sustain, experience, undergo, go through, feel.

suffering *n* pain, discomfort, agony, anguish, affliction (*fml*), distress, misery, hardship, ordeal, torment, torture.
☒ ease, comfort.

suffice *v* do, satisfy, be sufficient, be adequate, answer, measure up, serve, content, fit/fill the bill (*infml*).

sufficient *adj* enough, adequate, satisfactory, effective.
☒ insufficient, inadequate.

suffocate *v* asphyxiate, smother, stifle, choke, strangle, throttle.

suffrage *n* franchise, right to vote, right of representation, enfranchisement (*fml*).

suffuse *v* spread, imbue, infuse, permeate, pervade, steep, transfuse, cover, flood, mantle, bathe, colour, redden.

sugar

> **Kinds of sugar include:** beet sugar, brown sugar, cane sugar, caster sugar, crystallized sugar, demerara, dextrose, fructose, glucose, golden syrup, granulated sugar, icing sugar, invert sugar, jaggery, lactose, maltose, maple syrup, molasses, powdered sugar, refined sugar, sucrose, sugar loaf, sugar lump, sweets, candy (*US*), sugar candy (*US*), syrup, treacle, unrefined sugar.

> **Artificial sweeteners include:** acesulfame K, aspartame, Canderel®, cyclamate, Hermesetas®, NutraSweet®, saccharin, sorbitol, Sweetex®. *see also* **sweets**.

suggest *v* **1** PROPOSE, put forward, advocate, recommend, advise, counsel. **2** IMPLY, insinuate, hint, intimate, evoke, indicate.

suggestion *n* **1** PROPOSAL, proposition, motion, recommendation, idea, plan. **2** IMPLICATION, insinuation, innuendo, hint, intimation, suspicion, trace, indication.

suggestive *adj* **1** EVOCATIVE, reminiscent, expressive, meaning, indicative. **2** *a suggestive remark*: indecent, immodest, improper, indelicate, off-colour (*infml*), risqué, bawdy, dirty, smutty, provocative.
☒ **1** inexpressive. **2** decent, clean.

suit *v* **1** SATISFY, gratify, please, answer, match, tally, agree, correspond, harmonize. **2** FIT, befit, become, tailor, adapt, adjust, accommodate, modify.
☒ **1** displease, clash.
➢ *n* outfit, costume, dress, clothing.

suitable *adj* appropriate, fitting, convenient, opportune, suited, due, apt, apposite, relevant, applicable, fit, adequate, satisfactory, acceptable, befitting, becoming, seemly, proper, right.
☒ unsuitable, inappropriate.

suite *n* **1** APARTMENT, rooms, set of rooms, household. **2** SET, series, collection, sequence, train, furniture. **3** ATTENDANTS, retinue, entourage, escort, followers, retainers, servants.

suitor *n* admirer, boyfriend, lover, young man, wooer, beau, follower, pretendant (*fml*).

sulk *v* mope, brood, pout.

sulky *adj* brooding, moody, morose, resentful, grudging, disgruntled, put out, cross, bad-tempered, sullen, aloof, unsociable.
☒ cheerful, good-tempered, sociable.

sullen *adj* **1** SULKY, moody, morose, glum, gloomy, silent, surly, sour, perverse, obstinate, stubborn. **2** DARK, gloomy, sombre, dismal, cheerless, dull, leaden, heavy.
☒ **1** cheerful, happy. **2** fine, clear.

sully *v* dirty, soil, defile, pollute, contaminate, taint, spoil, mar, spot, blemish, besmirch, stain, tarnish, disgrace, dishonour.
☒ cleanse, honour.

sultry *adj* hot, sweltering, stifling, stuffy, oppressive, close, humid, muggy, sticky.
☒ cool, cold.

sum *n* total, sum total, aggregate (*fml*), whole, entirety, number, quantity, amount, tally, reckoning, score, result.
◆ **sum up** summarize, review, recapitulate, conclude, close.

summarize *v* outline, précis, condense, abridge, abbreviate, shorten, sum up, encapsulate, review.
☒ expand (on).

summary n synopsis, résumé, outline, abstract, précis, condensation, digest, compendium, abridgement, summing-up, review, recapitulation.
➤ adj short, succinct, brief, cursory, hasty, prompt, direct, unceremonious, arbitrary.
🔁 lengthy, careful.

summit n top, peak, pinnacle, apex, point, crown, head, zenith, acme, culmination, height.
🔁 bottom, foot, nadir.

summon v call, send for, invite, bid, beckon, gather, assemble, convene, rally, muster, mobilize, rouse, arouse.
🔁 dismiss.

sumptuous adj luxurious, plush, lavish, extravagant, opulent, rich, costly, expensive, dear, splendid, magnificent, gorgeous, superb, grand.
🔁 plain, poor.

sunbathe v sun, bask, tan, brown, bake.

sunburnt adj brown, tanned, bronzed, weather-beaten, burnt, red, blistered, peeling.
🔁 pale.

sundry adj various, diverse, miscellaneous, assorted, varied, different, several, some, a few.

sunken adj submerged, buried, recessed, lower, depressed, concave, hollow, haggard, drawn.

sunny adj 1 FINE, cloudless, clear, summery, sunshiny, sunlit, bright, brilliant. 2 CHEERFUL, happy, joyful, smiling, beaming, radiant, light-hearted, buoyant, optimistic, pleasant.
🔁 1 sunless, dull. 2 gloomy.

sunrise n dawn, crack of dawn, daybreak, daylight.

sunset n sundown, dusk, twilight, gloaming, evening, nightfall.

super adj great (infml), excellent, superb, wonderful, outstanding, marvellous, magnificent, glorious, incomparable, peerless, matchless, sensational, smashing (infml), terrific (infml), top-notch (infml), neat (infml), ace (infml).
🔁 poor, lousy (infml).

superb adj excellent, first-rate, first-class, superior, choice, fine, exquisite, gorgeous, magnificent, splendid, grand, wonderful, marvellous, admirable, impressive, breathtaking.
🔁 bad, poor, inferior.

supercilious adj arrogant, condescending, patronizing, overbearing, scornful, lofty, lordly, imperious, insolent, proud, disdainful, haughty, contemptuous, vainglorious (fml), snooty (infml), snotty (infml), stuck-up (infml), toffee-nosed (infml), uppish (infml), uppity (infml), hoity-toity (infml), jumped up (infml), too big for one's boots (infml).
🔁 humble, self-effacing.

superficial adj surface, external, exterior, outward, apparent, seeming, cosmetic, skin-deep, shallow, slight, trivial, lightweight, frivolous, casual, cursory, sketchy, hasty, hurried, passing.
🔁 internal, deep, thorough.

superfluous adj extra, spare, excess, surplus, remaining, redundant, supernumerary, unnecessary, needless, unwanted, uncalled-for, excessive.
🔁 necessary, needed, wanted.

superhuman adj great, immense, supernatural, herculean, heroic, stupendous, divine, paranormal, phenomenal.
🔁 average, ordinary.

superintend v supervise, oversee, overlook, inspect, run, manage, administer, direct, control, handle.

superior adj 1 EXCELLENT, first-class, first-rate, top-notch (infml), top-flight (infml), high-class, exclusive, choice, select, fine, de luxe, admirable, distinguished, exceptional, unrivalled, par excellence. 2 BETTER, preferred, greater, higher, senior. 3 HAUGHTY, lordly, pretentious, snobbish, snooty (infml), supercilious, disdainful, condescending, patronizing, stuck-up (infml), toffee-nosed (infml).
🔁 1 inferior, average. 2 worse, lower. 3 humble.
➤ n senior, elder, better, boss, chief, principal, director, manager, foreman, supervisor.
🔁 inferior, junior, assistant.

superiority n advantage, lead, edge, supremacy, ascendancy, pre-eminence, predominance.
🔁 inferiority.

superlative adj best, greatest, highest, supreme, transcendent, unbeatable, unrivalled, unparalleled, matchless, peerless, unsurpassed, unbeaten, consummate, excellent, outstanding.
🔁 poor, average.

supernatural *adj* paranormal, unnatural, abnormal, metaphysical, spiritual, psychic, mystic, occult, hidden, mysterious, miraculous, magical, phantom, ghostly.
➤ natural, normal.

supersede *v* succeed, replace, supplant, usurp, oust, displace, remove.

superstition *n* myth, old wives' tale, fallacy, delusion, illusion.

superstitious *adj* mythical, false, fallacious, irrational, groundless, delusive, illusory.
➤ rational, logical.

supervise *v* oversee, watch over, look after, superintend, run, manage, administer, direct, conduct, preside over, control, handle.

supervision *n* surveillance, care, charge, superintendence, oversight, running, management, administration, direction, control, guidance, instruction.

supervisor *n* overseer, inspector, superintendent, boss, chief, director, administrator, manager, foreman, forewoman.

supervisory *adj* administrative, managerial, executive, overseeing, superintendent, directorial (*fml*).

supplant *v* replace, supersede, usurp, oust, displace, remove, overthrow, topple, unseat.

supple *adj* flexible, bending, pliant, pliable, plastic, lithe, graceful, loose-limbed, double-jointed, elastic.
➤ stiff, rigid, inflexible.

supplement *n* addition, extra, insert, pull-out, addendum, appendix, codicil, postscript, sequel.
➤ *v* add to, augment (*fml*), boost, reinforce, fill up, top up, complement, extend, eke out.
➤ deplete, use up.

supplementary *adj* additional, extra, auxiliary, secondary, complementary, accompanying.

supplication *n* request, appeal, entreaty, petition, plea, pleading, prayer, orison, suit, invocation (*fml*), imploration (*fml*), solicitation (*fml*), rogation (*fml*).

supplies *n* stores, provisions, food, equipment, materials, necessities.

supply *v* provide, furnish, equip, outfit, stock, fill, replenish, give, donate, grant, endow, contribute, yield, produce, sell.
➤ take, receive.
➤ *n* source, amount, quantity, stock, fund, reservoir, store, reserve, stockpile, hoard, cache.
➤ lack.

support *v* 1 BACK, second, defend, champion, advocate, promote, foster, help, aid, assist, rally round, finance, fund, subsidize, underwrite. 2 HOLD UP, bear, carry, sustain, brace, reinforce, strengthen, prop, buttress, bolster. 3 MAINTAIN, keep, provide for, feed, nourish. 4 *support a statement*: endorse, confirm, verify, authenticate, corroborate, substantiate, document.
➤ 1 oppose. 3 live off. 4 contradict.
➤ *n* 1 BACKING, allegiance, loyalty, defence, protection, patronage, sponsorship, approval, encouragement, comfort, relief, help, aid, assistance.
2 PROP, stay, post, pillar, brace, crutch, foundation, underpinning.
➤ 1 opposition, hostility.

supporter *n* fan, follower, adherent, advocate, champion, defender, seconder, patron, sponsor, helper, ally, friend.
➤ opponent.

supportive *adj* helpful, caring, attentive, sympathetic, understanding, comforting, reassuring, encouraging.
➤ discouraging.

suppose *v* assume, presume, expect, infer, conclude, guess, conjecture, surmise, believe, think, consider, judge, imagine, conceive, fancy, pretend, postulate, hypothesize.
➤ know.

supposed *adj* alleged, reported, rumoured, assumed, presumed, reputed, putative, imagined, hypothetical.
➤ known, certain.
◆ **supposed to** meant to, intended to, expected to, required to, obliged to.

supposition *n* assumption, presumption, guess, conjecture, speculation, theory, hypothesis, idea, notion.
➤ knowledge.

suppress *v* crush, stamp out, quash, quell, subdue, stop, silence, censor, stifle, smother, strangle, conceal, withhold, hold back, contain, restrain, check, repress, inhibit.
➤ encourage, incite.

suppression n crushing, quashing, quelling, elimination, prohibition, censorship, check, inhibition, dissolution, cover-up, smothering, termination, extinction, clampdown (*infml*), crackdown (*infml*).
🗲 encouragement, incitement.

supremacy n dominance, domination, dominion, mastery, lordship, rule, power, control, predominance, primacy, sovereignty, sway, pre-eminence, ascendancy (*fml*), hegemony (*fml*), paramountcy (*fml*).

supreme adj best, greatest, highest, top, crowning, culminating, first, leading, foremost, chief, principal, head, sovereign, pre-eminent, predominant, prevailing, world-beating, unsurpassed, second-to-none, incomparable, matchless, consummate, transcendent, superlative, prime, ultimate, extreme, final.
🗲 lowly, poor.

sure adj 1 CERTAIN, convinced, assured, confident, decided, positive, definite, unmistakable, clear, accurate, precise, unquestionable, indisputable, undoubted, undeniable, irrevocable, inevitable, bound. 2 SAFE, secure, fast, solid, firm, steady, stable, guaranteed, reliable, dependable, trustworthy, steadfast, unwavering, unerring, unfailing, infallible, effective.
🗲 1 unsure, uncertain, doubtful. 2 unsafe, insecure.

surely adv certainly, without doubt, doubtlessly, undoubtedly, unquestionably, indubitably (*fml*), definitely, assuredly, firmly, confidently, inevitably, inexorably.

surety n guarantee, indemnity, pledge, security, safety, warrant, warranty, certainty, bail, insurance, mortgagor, sponsor, bond, deposit, guarantor, hostage, bondsman.

surface n outside, exterior, façade, veneer, covering, skin, top, side, face, plane.
🗲 inside, interior.
➤ v rise, arise, come up, emerge, appear, materialise, come to light.
🗲 sink, disappear, vanish.

surfeit n surplus, superfluity, excess, glut, satiety, superabundance, overindulgence, plethora (*fml*), bellyful (*infml*).
🗲 lack.
➤ v fill, overfill, overfeed, stuff, cram, glut, gorge, satiate.

surge n 1 RUSH, gush, stream, sweep, pouring, flow, wave(s), billow, breaker, roller, swell, eddy, efflux (*fml*). 2 INCREASE, upswing, upsurge, rise, escalation, intensification.
➤ v 1 RUSH, gush, stream, sweep, pour, flow, break, swell, swirl, eddy, heave, roll, seethe. 2 INCREASE, rise, escalate.

surly adj gruff, brusque, churlish, ungracious, bad-tempered, cross, crabbed, grouchy, crusty, sullen, sulky, morose.
🗲 friendly, polite.

surmount v overcome, get over, conquer, master, triumph over, prevail over, surpass, exceed, vanquish (*fml*).

surpass v beat, outdo, exceed, outstrip, better, excel, transcend, outshine, eclipse.

surpassing adj exceptional, incomparable, outstanding, matchless, unrivalled, unsurpassed, rare, inimitable, extraordinary, supreme, phenomenal, transcendent.
🗲 poor.

surplus n excess, residue, remainder, balance, superfluity, glut, surfeit.
🗲 lack, shortage.
➤ adj excess, superfluous, redundant, extra, spare, remaining, unused.

surprise v startle, amaze, astonish, astound, stagger, flabbergast (*infml*), bewilder, confuse, nonplus, disconcert, dismay.
➤ n amazement, astonishment, incredulity, wonder, bewilderment, dismay, shock, start, bombshell, revelation.
🗲 composure.

Expressions of surprise include: bless my soul!, blow me down!, by Jove!, come off it!, did you ever!, fancy that!, for goodness' sake!, for heaven's sake!, good heavens!, Gordon Bennett!, great Scott!, heavens above!, holy smoke!, how about that, then!, I ask you!, I don't know!, I'll be blessed!, I'll be damned!, imagine that!, in heaven's name!, just a moment!, my eye!, my foot!, my goodness!, my word!, no kidding!, of all the ...!, oh mother!, oh my!, stone me!, that'll be the day!, that's news to me!, the (very) idea!, to think!, well, did you ever!, well, I'll be blowed!, well, I never!, wonders will never cease!, would you believe it!, you don't say!, you're joking!, you're kidding!

surprised *adj* startled, amazed, astonished, astounded, staggered, flabbergasted (*infml*), thunderstruck, dumbfounded, speechless, shocked, nonplussed.
🔁 unsurprised, composed.

surprising *adj* amazing, astonishing, astounding, staggering, stunning, incredible, extraordinary, remarkable, startling, unexpected, unforeseen.
🔁 unsurprising, expected.

surrender *v* capitulate, submit, resign, concede, yield, give in, cede, give up, quit, relinquish, abandon, renounce, forgo, waive.
➤ *n* capitulation, resignation, submission, yielding, relinquishment (*fml*), renunciation (*fml*).

surreptitious *adj* furtive, stealthy, sly, covert, veiled, hidden, secret, clandestine, underhand, unauthorized.
🔁 open, obvious.

surrogate *n* substitute, replacement, representative, stand-in, deputy, proxy.

surround *v* encircle, ring, girdle, encompass, envelop, encase, enclose, hem in, besiege.

surrounding *adj* encircling, bordering, adjacent, adjoining, neighbouring, nearby.

surroundings *n* neighbourhood, vicinity, locality, setting, environment, background, milieu, ambience.

surveillance *n* watch, observation, inspection, superintendence, supervision, vigilance, stewardship, guardianship, monitoring, scrutiny, check, care, charge, control, direction, regulation.

survey *v* view, contemplate, observe, supervise, scan, scrutinize, examine, inspect, study, research, review, consider, estimate, evaluate, assess, measure, plot, plan, map, chart, reconnoitre.
➤ *n* review, overview, scrutiny, examination, inspection, study, pull, appraisal, assessment, measurement.

survive *v* outlive, outlast, endure, last, stay, remain, live, exist, withstand, weather.
🔁 succumb, die.

susceptible *adj* liable, prone, inclined, disposed, given, subject, receptive, responsive, impressionable, suggestible, weak, vulnerable, open, sensitive, tender.
🔁 resistant, immune.

suspect *v* 1 DOUBT, distrust, mistrust, call into question. 2 *I suspect you're right*: believe, fancy, feel, guess, conjecture, speculate, surmise, suppose, consider, conclude, infer.
➤ *adj* suspicious, doubtful, dubious, questionable, debatable, unreliable, iffy (*sl*), dodgy (*infml*), fishy (*infml*).
🔁 acceptable, reliable.

suspend *v* 1 HANG, dangle, swing. 2 ADJOURN, interrupt, discontinue, cease, delay, defer, postpone, put off, shelve. 3 EXPEL, dismiss, exclude, debar.
🔁 2 continue. 3 restore, reinstate.

suspense *n* uncertainty, insecurity, anxiety, tension, apprehension, anticipation, expectation, expectancy, excitement.
🔁 certainty, knowledge.

suspension *n* adjournment, interruption, break, intermission, respite, remission, stay, moratorium, delay, deferral, postponement, abeyance.
🔁 continuation.

suspicion *n* 1 DOUBT, scepticism, distrust, mistrust, wariness, caution, misgiving, apprehension. 2 TRACE, hint, suggestion, soupçon, touch, tinge, shade, glimmer, shadow. 3 IDEA, notion, hunch.
🔁 1 trust.

suspicious *adj* 1 DOUBTFUL, sceptical, unbelieving, suspecting, distrustful, mistrustful, wary, chary, apprehensive, uneasy. 2 DUBIOUS, questionable, suspect, irregular, shifty, shady (*infml*), dodgy (*infml*), fishy (*infml*).
🔁 1 trustful, confident. 2 trustworthy, innocent.

sustain *v* 1 NOURISH, provide for, nurture, foster, help, aid, assist, comfort, relieve, support, uphold, endorse, bear, carry. 2 MAINTAIN, keep going, keep up, continue, prolong, hold.

sustained *adj* prolonged, protracted, long-drawn-out, steady, continuous, constant, perpetual, unremitting.
🔁 broken, interrupted, intermittent, spasmodic.

sustenance *n* nourishment, food, provisions, fare, maintenance, subsistence, livelihood.

svelte *adj* slender, slim, lithe, elegant, graceful, lissom, willowy, sylphlike, shapely, sophisticated, urbane, polished.
🔁 bulky, ungainly.

swagger *v* bluster, boast, crow, brag, swank (*infml*), parade, strut.
➤ *n* bluster, show, ostentation, arrogance.

swallow *v* 1 CONSUME, devour, eat, gobble up, guzzle (*infml*), drink, quaff, knock back (*infml*), gulp, down (*infml*). 2 ENGULF, enfold, envelop, swallow up, absorb, assimilate, accept, believe.

swamp *n* bog, marsh, fen, slough, quagmire, quicksand, mire, mud.
➤ *v* flood, inundate, deluge, engulf, submerge, sink, drench, saturate, waterlog, overload, overwhelm, besiege, beset.

swap, swop *v* exchange, transpose, switch, interchange, barter, trade, traffic.

swarm *n* crowd, throng, mob, mass, multitude, myriad, host, army, horde, herd, flock, drove, shoal.
➤ *v* 1 flock, flood, stream, mass, congregate, crowd, throng. 2 *swarming with tourists*: teem, crawl, bristle, abound.

swarthy *adj* dark, dark-skinned, dark-complexioned, dusky, black, brown, tanned.
🗲 fair, pale.

swashbuckling *adj* daring, courageous, adventurous, bold, spirited, swaggering, exciting, gallant, flamboyant, dare-devil, dashing, robust.
🗲 tame, unadventurous, unexciting.

swathe *v* wrap, bandage, bind, wind, cloak, envelop, drape, enshroud, enwrap, fold, shroud, swaddle, lap, sheathe, furl.
🗲 unwind, unwrap.

sway *v* 1 ROCK, roll, lurch, swing, wave, oscillate, fluctuate, bend, incline, lean, divert, veer, swerve. 2 INFLUENCE, affect, persuade, induce, convince, convert, overrule, dominate, govern.

swear *v* 1 vow, promise, pledge, avow, attest (*infml*), asseverate (*infml*), testify, affirm, assert, declare, insist. 2 CURSE, blaspheme.

swearing *n* bad language, foul language, cursing, profanity, expletives, blasphemy, imprecations (*fml*), maledictions (*fml*), cussing (*infml*), effing and blinding (*infml*).

swear-word *n* expletive, four-letter word, curse, oath, imprecation, obscenity, profanity, swearing, bad language.

sweat *n* 1 PERSPIRATION, moisture, stickiness. 2 ANXIETY, worry, agitation, panic. 3 TOIL, labour, drudgery, chore.
➤ *v* perspire, swelter, exude (*fml*).

sweaty *adj* damp, moist, clammy, sticky, sweating, perspiring.
🗲 dry, cool.

sweep *v* 1 *sweep the floor*: brush, dust, clean, clear, remove. 2 PASS, sail, fly, glide, scud, skim, glance, whisk, tear, hurtle.
➤ *n* arc, curve, bend, swing, stroke, movement, gesture, compass, scope, range, extent, span, stretch, expanse, vista.

sweeping *adj* general, global, all-inclusive, all-embracing, blanket, across-the-board, broad, wide-ranging, extensive, far-reaching, comprehensive, thoroughgoing, radical, wholesale, indiscriminate, oversimplified, simplistic.
🗲 specific, narrow.

sweet *adj* 1 SUGARY, syrupy, sweetened, honeyed, saccharine, luscious, delicious. 2 PLEASANT, delightful, lovely, attractive, beautiful, pretty, winsome, cute, appealing, lovable, charming, agreeable, amiable, affectionate, tender, kind, treasured, precious, dear, darling. 3 FRESH, clean, wholesome, pure, clear, perfumed, fragrant, aromatic, balmy. 4 *sweet music*: melodious, tuneful, harmonious, euphonious, musical, dulcet, soft, mellow.
🗲 1 savoury, salty, sour, bitter.
2 unpleasant, nasty, ugly. 3 foul.
4 discordant.
➤ *n* dessert, pudding, afters (*infml*).

sweets

> Sweets include: barley sugar, bull's eye, butterscotch, caramel, chewing-gum, chocolate, fondant, fruit pastille, fudge, gobstopper, gumdrop, humbug, jelly, jelly bean, liquorice, liquorice allsort, lollipop, Mars®, marshmallow, marzipan, nougat, peppermint, praline, rock, Edinburgh rock, toffee, toffee apple, truffle, Turkish delight.

sweeten *v* sugar, honey, mellow, soften, soothe, appease, temper, cushion.
🗲 sour, embitter.

sweetheart *n* darling, dear, boyfriend, girlfriend, love, lover, truelove, suitor, valentine, admirer, beloved, betrothed, follower, inamorata, inamorato, Romeo, flame (*infml*), steady (*infml*), sweetie (*infml*).

swell *v* expand, dilate, inflate, blow up, puff up, bloat, distend, fatten, bulge, balloon, billow, surge, rise, mount, increase, enlarge, extend, grow, augment, heighten, intensify.

☒ shrink, contract, decrease, dwindle.

➤ *n* billow, wave, undulation, surge, rise, increase, enlargement.

swelling *n* lump, tumour, bump, bruise, blister, boil, inflammation, bulge, protuberance, puffiness, distension, enlargement.

sweltering *adj* hot, tropical, baking, scorching, stifling, suffocating, airless, oppressive, sultry, steamy, sticky, humid.

☒ cold, cool, fresh, breezy, airy.

swerve *v* turn, bend, incline, veer, swing, shift, deviate, stray, wander, diverge, deflect, sheer.

swift *adj* fast, quick, rapid, speedy, express, flying, hurried, hasty, short, brief, sudden, prompt, ready, agile, nimble, nippy (*infml*).

☒ slow, sluggish, unhurried.

swiftly *adv* quickly, posthaste, fast, rapidly, speedily, express, hurriedly, instantly, promptly, at full tilt, expeditiously (*fml*), double-quick (*infml*), hotfoot (*infml*).

☒ slowly, tardily (*fml*).

swill *v* drink, swallow, swig, quaff, gulp, guzzle, drain, consume, imbibe (*fml*), knock back (*infml*), toss off (*infml*).

➤ *n* **1** DRINK, gulp, swallow, swig. **2** WASTE, slops, hogwash, pigswill, scourings, refuse.

◆ **swill out** wash out, wash down, rinse, clean, cleanse, drench, flush, sluice.

swim *v* bathe, take a dip, tread water, float, bob, snorkel.

The main swimming strokes include:
backstroke, breaststroke, butterfly, crawl, doggy-paddle, sidestroke.

swimsuit *n* swimming costume, bathing-costume, bathing-suit, bikini, trunks.

swindle *v* cheat, defraud, diddle, do (*infml*), overcharge, fleece, rip off (*sl*), trick, deceive, dupe, con (*infml*), bamboozle (*infml*).

➤ *n* fraud, fiddle, racket, sharp practice, double-dealing, trickery, deception, con (*infml*), rip-off (*sl*).

swindler *n* cheat, fraud, impostor, con man (*infml*), trickster, shark, rogue, rascal.

swing *v* hang, suspend, dangle, wave, brandish, sway, rock, oscillate, vibrate, fluctuate, vary, veer, swerve, turn, whirl, twirl, spin, rotate.

➤ *n* sway, rock, oscillation, vibration,

fluctuation, variation, change, shift, movement, motion, rhythm.

swingeing *adj* harsh, severe, stringent, drastic, punishing, devastating, excessive, extortionate, oppressive, heavy.

☒ mild.

swinging *adj* lively, exciting, dynamic, fashionable, contemporary, modern, up-to-date, up-to-the-minute, stylish, jet-setting (*infml*), trendy (*infml*), with it (*infml*), hip (*sl*).

☒ old-fashioned, fuddy-duddy.

swipe *v* **1** HIT, strike, lunge, lash out, slap, whack (*infml*), wallop (*infml*), sock (*sl*). **2** (*infml*) STEAL, pilfer, lift, pinch (*infml*).

➤ *n* stroke, blow, slap, smack, clout, whack (*infml*), wallop (*infml*).

swirl *v* churn, agitate, spin, twirl, whirl, wheel, eddy, twist, curl.

switch *v* change, exchange, swap, trade, interchange, transpose, substitute, replace, shift, rearrange, turn, veer, deviate, divert, deflect.

➤ *n* change, alteration, shift, exchange, swap, interchange, substitution, replacement.

swivel *v* pivot, spin, rotate, revolve, turn, twirl, pirouette, gyrate, wheel.

swollen *adj* bloated, distended, inflated, tumid, puffed up, puffy, inflamed, enlarged, bulbous, bulging.

☒ shrunken, shrivelled.

swoop *v* dive, plunge, drop, fall, descend, stoop, pounce, lunge, rush.

➤ *n* dive, plunge, drop, descent, pounce, lunge, rush, attack, onslaught.

swop *see* swap.

sword *n* blade, foil, rapier, sabre, scimitar.

swot (*infml*) *v* study, work, learn, memorize, revise, cram, mug up (*infml*), bone up (*sl*).

sycophant *n* cringer, fawner, flatterer, groveller, backscratcher, slave, parasite, hanger-on, toady, toad-eater, truckler, bootlicker (*infml*), sponger (*infml*), yes-man (*infml*).

sycophantic *adj* cringing, fawning, flattering, grovelling, servile, slavish, ingratiating, parasitical, backscratching, slimy, toad-eating, toadying, time-serving, unctuous, truckling, obsequious (*fml*), bootlicking (*infml*), smarmy (*infml*).

syllabus *n* curriculum, course, programme, schedule, plan.

symbol *n* sign, token, representation, mark, emblem, badge, logo, character, ideograph, figure, image.

Symbols include: badge, brand, cipher, coat of arms, crest, emblem, hieroglyph, icon, ideogram, insignia, logo, logogram, monogram, motif, pictograph, swastika, token, totem, trademark; ampersand, asterisk, caret, dagger, double-dagger, obelus.

symbolic *adj* symbolical, representative, emblematic, token, figurative, metaphorical, allegorical, meaningful, significant.

symbolize *v* represent, stand for, denote, mean, signify, typify, exemplify, epitomize, personify.

symmetrical *adj* balanced, even, regular, parallel, corresponding, proportional.
⊟ asymmetrical, irregular.

symmetry *n* balance, evenness, regularity, parallelism, correspondence, proportion, harmony, agreement.
⊟ asymmetry, irregularity.

sympathetic *adj* understanding, appreciative, supportive, comforting, consoling, commiserating, pitying, interested, concerned, solicitous, caring, compassionate, tender, kind, warm-hearted, well-disposed, affectionate, agreeable, friendly, congenial, like-minded, compatible.
⊟ unsympathetic, indifferent, callous, antipathetic.

sympathize *v* understand, comfort, commiserate, pity, feel for, empathize, identify with, respond to.
⊟ ignore, disregard.

sympathizer *n* supporter, friend in need, condoler, admirer, backer, adherent, well-wisher, fan, fellow-traveller, partisan.
⊟ enemy, opponent, adversary.

sympathy *n* 1 UNDERSTANDING, comfort, consolation, condolences, commiseration, pity, compassion, tenderness, kindness, warmth, thoughtfulness, empathy, fellow-feeling, affinity, rapport. 2 AGREEMENT, accord, correspondence, harmony.

⊟ 1 indifference, insensitivity, callousness.
2 disagreement.

symptom *n* sign, indication, evidence, manifestation, expression, feature, characteristic, mark, token, warning.

symptomatic *adj* indicative, typical, characteristic, associated, suggestive.

synonymous *adj* interchangeable, substitutable, the same, identical, similar, comparable, tantamount, equivalent, corresponding.
⊟ antonymous, opposite.

synopsis *n* outline, abstract, summary, résumé, précis, condensation, digest, abridgement, review, recapitulation.

synthesis *n* amalgamation, combination, compound, fusion, integration, union, welding, blend, alloy, amalgam, coalescence, composite, pastiche, unification (*fml*).

synthesize *v* unite, combine, amalgamate, integrate, merge, blend, compound, alloy, fuse, weld, coalesce, unify.
⊟ separate, analyse, resolve.

synthetic *adj* manufactured, man-made, simulated, artificial, ersatz, imitation, fake, bogus, mock, sham, pseudo (*infml*).
⊟ genuine, real, natural.

system *n* 1 METHOD, mode, technique, procedure, process, routine, practice, usage, rule. 2 ORGANIZATION, structure, set-up, systematization, co-ordination, orderliness, methodology, logic, classification, arrangement, order, plan, scheme.

systematic *adj* methodical, logical, ordered, well-ordered, planned, well-planned, organized, well-organized, structured, systematized, standardized, orderly, businesslike, efficient.
⊟ unsystematic, arbitrary, disorderly, inefficient.

systematize *v* arrange, order, structure, plan, organize, rationalize, methodize, standardize, schematize, regulate, regiment, classify, tabulate, make uniform, dispose (*fml*).

Tt

tab *n* flap, tag, marker, label, sticker, ticket.

table *n* **1** BOARD, slab, counter, worktop, desk, bench, stand. **2** DIAGRAM, chart, graph, timetable, schedule, programme, list, inventory, catalogue, index, register, record.
➢ *v* propose, suggest, submit, put forward.

tableau *n* representation, picture, portrayal, scene, spectacle, vignette, diorama.

taboo *adj* forbidden, prohibited, banned, proscribed, unacceptable, unmentionable, unthinkable.
🖙 permitted, acceptable.
➢ *n* ban, interdiction, prohibition, restriction, anathema, curse.

tabulate *v* order, arrange, arrange in columns, chart, classify, list, sort, systematize, table, catalogue, categorize, range, index, codify, tabularize.

tacit *adj* unspoken, unexpressed, unvoiced, silent, understood, implicit, implied, inferred.
🖙 express, explicit.

taciturn *adj* silent, quiet, uncommunicative, unforthcoming, reticent, reserved, withdrawn, aloof, distant, cold.
🖙 talkative, communicative, forthcoming.

tack *n* **1** NAIL, pin, drawing-pin, staple. **2** COURSE, path, bearing, heading, direction, line, approach, method, way, technique, procedure, plan, tactic, attack.
➢ *v* add, append, attach, affix, fasten, fix, nail, pin, staple, stitch, baste.

tackle *n* **1** *a rugby tackle*: attack, challenge, interception, intervention, block. **2** EQUIPMENT, tools, implements, apparatus, rig, outfit, gear, trappings, paraphernalia.
➢ *v* **1** BEGIN, embark on, set about, try, attempt, undertake, take on, challenge, confront, encounter, face up to, grapple with, deal with, attend to, handle, grab, seize, grasp. **2** INTERCEPT, block, halt, stop.
🖙 **1** avoid, sidestep.

tacky[1] *adj* sticky, adhesive, gluey, gummy, gooey (*infml*).

tacky[2] *adj* **1** SHABBY, scruffy, tatty, threadbare, shoddy, dingy, tattered, ragged, untidy, messy, sloppy, grotty (*infml*). **2** TASTELESS, vulgar, tawdry, flashy, gaudy, kitschy, naff (*infml*).

tact *n* tactfulness, diplomacy, discretion, prudence, delicacy, sensitivity, perception, discernment, judgement, understanding, thoughtfulness, consideration, skill, adroitness, finesse.
🖙 tactlessness, indiscretion.

tactful *adj* diplomatic, discreet, politic, judicious, prudent, careful, delicate, subtle, sensitive, perceptive, discerning, understanding, thoughtful, considerate, polite, skilful, adroit.
🖙 tactless, indiscreet, thoughtless, rude.

tactic *n* approach, course, way, means, method, procedure, plan, stratagem, scheme, ruse, ploy, subterfuge, trick, device, shift, move, manoeuvre.

tactical *adj* strategic, planned, calculated, artful, cunning, shrewd, skilful, clever, smart, prudent, politic, judicious.

tactician *n* strategist, orchestrator, planner, politician, diplomat, director, campaigner, co-ordinator, mastermind, brain (*infml*).

tactics *n* strategy, campaign, plan, policy, approach, line of attack, moves, manoeuvres.

tactless *adj* undiplomatic, indiscreet, indelicate, inappropriate, impolitic, imprudent, careless, clumsy, blundering, insensitive, unfeeling, hurtful, unkind, thoughtless, inconsiderate, rude, impolite, discourteous.
🖙 tactful, diplomatic, discreet.

tag *n* label, sticker, tab, ticket, mark, identification, note, slip, docket.
➢ *v* **1** LABEL, mark, identify, designate, term, call, name, christen, nickname, style, dub. **2** ADD, append, annex, adjoin, affix, fasten.
◆ **tag along** follow, shadow, tail, trail, accompany.

tail *n* end, extremity, rear, rear end, rump, behind (*infml*), posterior (*infml*), appendage.

➤ *v* follow, pursue, shadow, dog, stalk, track, trail.

◆ **tail off** decrease, decline, drop, fall away, fade, wane, dwindle, taper off, peter out, die (out).

🔁 increase, grow.

tailor *n* outfitter, dressmaker.

➤ *v* fit, suit, cut, trim, style, fashion, shape, mould, alter, modify, adapt, adjust, accommodate.

tailor-made *adj* made-to-measure, custom-built, ideal, perfect, right, suited, fitted.

🔁 unsuitable.

taint *v* contaminate, infect, pollute, adulterate, corrupt, deprave, stain, blemish, blot, smear, tarnish, blacken, dirty, soil, muddy, defile, sully, harm, damage, blight, spoil, ruin, shame, disgrace, dishonour.

➤ *n* contamination, infection, pollution, corruption, stain, blemish, fault, flaw, defect, spot, blot, smear, stigma, shame, disgrace, dishonour.

take *v* **1** SEIZE, grab, snatch, clutch, grasp, hold, get hold of, grip, catch, capture, get, obtain, acquire, secure, gain, receive, win, derive, adopt, assume, pick, choose, select, decide on, settle on, accept, receive, procure (*fml*). **2** REMOVE, eliminate, take away, subtract, deduct, steal, seize, kidnap, abduct, carry off, confiscate, purloin (*fml*), appropriate (*fml*), filch (*infml*), nick (*sl*), pinch (*infml*), lift (*infml*), have one's fingers in the till (*infml*). **3** *take me home* convey, carry, bring, fetch, deliver, drive, transport, ferry, accompany, escort, show, lead, guide, conduct, usher, shepherd, bear (*fml*), whisk (*infml*). **4** BEAR, tolerate, put up with, stand, stomach, abide, endure, suffer, undergo, experience, withstand. **5** NEED, necessitate, require, demand, call for, use (up), last. **6** CAPTURE, win, seize, conquer, occupy, vanquish (*fml*). **7** *take pleasure in something*: derive, obtain, draw, gain, receive, attain, secure, achieve, be given, come by, get, procure (*fml*). **8** *take the blame/responsibility*: accept, bear, be responsible for, admit, acknowledge, undertake. **9** CONSIDER, believe, assume, presume, suppose, note, remember, examine, bear in mind. **10** UNDERSTAND, comprehend, grasp, gather, apprehend,

follow, fathom (out), cotton on (*infml*), twig (*infml*). **11** *take the news badly*: react to, accept, respond to, cope with, deal with, handle. **12** *take him for a fool*: believe, think, consider, regard, look upon, view, reckon, suppose, hold, deem (*fml*). **13** *the hall takes 400 people*: hold, contain, accommodate, seat, have a capacity of, have room for, have space for. **14** *take a measurement*: find out, discover, measure, establish, determine, ascertain. **15** BUY, purchase, rent, hire, lease, pay for, book, receive. **16** *take a subject at university*: study, learn, pursue, be taught, research, read, major in. **17** *take the new road*: use, travel along, drive along, go along, follow. **18** *take food/drink*: consume, swallow, eat, drink, devour, imbibe (*fml*), tuck in (*infml*), guzzle (*infml*), scoff (*infml*). **19** *Will the drug take?*: succeed, work, produce results, be effective, be efficacious (*fml*).

🔁 **1** leave, refuse. **2** replace, put back. **6** lose. **15** sell. **19** fail.

◆ **take aback** surprise, astonish, astound, stagger, stun, startle, disconcert, bewilder, dismay, upset.

◆ **take apart** take to pieces, dismantle, disassemble, analyse.

◆ **take back** reclaim, repossess, withdraw, retract, recant, repudiate, deny, eat one's words.

◆ **take down 1** DISMANTLE, disassemble, demolish, raze, level, lower. **2** NOTE, record, write down, put down, set down, transcribe.

◆ **take in 1** ABSORB, assimilate, digest, realize, appreciate, understand, comprehend, grasp, admit, receive, shelter, accommodate, contain, include, comprise, incorporate, embrace, encompass, cover. **2** DECEIVE, fool, dupe, con (*infml*), mislead, trick, hoodwink, bamboozle (*infml*), cheat, swindle.

◆ **take off 1** REMOVE, doff, divest, shed, discard, drop. **2** LEAVE, depart, go, decamp, disappear. **3** IMITATE, mimic, parody, caricature, satirize, mock, send up.

◆ **take on 1** ACCEPT, assume, acquire, undertake, tackle, face, contend with, fight, oppose. **2** *take on staff*: employ, hire, enlist, recruit, engage, retain.

◆ **take over** gain control of, take charge of, become responsible for, assume responsibility for, buy out.

◆ **take up 1** OCCUPY, fill, engage, engross, absorb, monopolize, use up. **2** *take up a hobby*: start, begin, embark on, pursue, carry on, continue. **3** RAISE, lift. **4** ACCEPT, adopt, assume.

take-off *n* **1** DEPARTURE, flight, flying, lift-off, ascent, climbing. **2** (*infml*) IMITATION, mimicry, impersonation, parody, caricature, travesty, spoof (*infml*), send-up (*infml*).

takeover *n* merger, amalgamation, combination, incorporation, coup.

takings *n* receipts, gate, proceeds, profits, gain, returns, revenue, yield, income, earnings, pickings.

tale *n* story, yarn (*infml*), anecdote, spiel (*sl*), narrative, account, report, rumour, tall story, old wives' tale, superstition, fable, myth, legend, saga, lie, fib, falsehood, untruth, fabrication.

talent *n* gift, endowment, genius, flair, feel, knack, bent, aptitude, faculty, skill, ability, capacity, power, strength, forte.
ⓔ inability, weakness.

talented *adj* gifted, brilliant, well-endowed, versatile, accomplished, able, capable, proficient, adept, adroit, deft, clever, skilful.
ⓔ inept.

talisman *n* amulet, charm, fetish, mascot, totem, symbol, idol, ju-ju, phylactery, periapt, abraxas.

talk *v* **1** SPEAK, say, utter, articulate, voice, communicate, express, have a conversation/discussion, converse (*fml*), confer (*fml*), orate (*fml*), natter (*infml*), jabber (*infml*), babble (*infml*), prattle (*infml*), chinwag (*infml*), jaw (*infml*). **2** NEGOTIATE, discuss, bargain, haggle, work out an agreement. **3** GOSSIP, spread rumours, chat, chatter, natter (*infml*). **4** *talk to the police*: tell, confess, give (secret) information to, inform on, tell tales (*infml*), squeal (*infml*), blab (*infml*), spill the beans (*infml*), let the cat out of the bag (*infml*), give the game away (*infml*), grass (*sl*).
➤ *n* **1** CONVERSATION, dialogue, discussion, conference, meeting, consultation, negotiation, chat, chatter, natter (*infml*), gossip, hearsay, rumour, tittle-tattle. **2** *give a talk*: lecture, seminar, symposium, speech, address, discourse, sermon, spiel (*sl*). **3** LANGUAGE, dialect, slang, jargon, speech, utterance, words.
♦ **talk down to** patronize, speak condescendingly towards, look down on, despise.
♦ **talk into** encourage, coax, sway,

persuade, convince, bring round, win over.
ⓔ dissuade.
♦ **talk out of** discourage, deter, put off, dissuade.
ⓔ persuade, convince.

talkative *adj* garrulous, voluble, vocal, communicative, forthcoming, unreserved, expansive, chatty, gossipy, verbose, wordy, loquacious.
ⓔ taciturn, quiet, reserved.

talker *n* speaker, conversationalist, raconteur, communicator, public speaker, lecturer, speech-maker, orator (*fml*), chatterbox (*infml*).

talking-to (*infml*) *n* lecture, dressing-down (*infml*), telling-off (*infml*), ticking-off (*infml*), scolding, reprimand, rebuke, reproof, reproach, criticism.
ⓔ praise, commendation.

tall *adj* high, lofty, elevated, soaring, towering, big, great, giant, gigantic.
ⓔ short, low, small.

tally *v* **1** AGREE, concur, tie in, square, accord, harmonize, coincide, correspond, match, conform, suit, fit. **2** ADD (UP), total, count, reckon, figure.
ⓔ **1** disagree, differ.
➤ *n* record, count, total, score, reckoning, account.

tame *adj* **1** *a tame rabbit*: domesticated, broken in, trained, disciplined, manageable, tractable, amenable, gentle, docile, meek, submissive, unresisting, obedient, biddable. **2** DULL, boring, tedious, uninteresting, humdrum, flat, bland, insipid, weak, feeble, uninspired, unadventurous, unenterprising, lifeless, spiritless.
ⓔ **1** wild, unmanageable, rebellious.
2 exciting.
➤ *v* domesticate, house-train, break in, train, discipline, master, subjugate, conquer, bridle, curb, repress, suppress, quell, subdue, temper, soften, mellow, calm, pacify, humble.

tamper *v* interfere, meddle, mess (*infml*), tinker, fiddle, fix, rig, manipulate, juggle, alter, damage.

tang *n* sharpness, bite, piquancy, pungency, taste, flavour, savour, smack, smell, aroma, scent, whiff, tinge, touch, trace, hint, suggestion, overtone.

tangible *adj* touchable, tactile, palpable, solid, concrete, material, substantial, physical, real, actual, perceptible, discernible, evident, manifest, definite, positive.

ɛꟻ intangible, abstract, unreal.

tangle n knot, snarl-up, twist, coil, convolution, mesh, web, maze, labyrinth, mess, muddle, jumble, mix-up, confusion, entanglement, embroilment, complication.
➢ v entangle, knot, snarl, ravel, twist, coil, interweave, interlace, intertwine, catch, ensnare, entrap, enmesh, embroil, implicate, involve, muddle, confuse.

ɛꟻ disentangle.

tangled adj knotty, snarled, matted, tousled, dishevelled, messy, muddled, jumbled, confused, twisted, convoluted, tortuous, involved, complicated, complex, intricate.

tangy adj sharp, biting, acid, tart, spicy, piquant, pungent, strong, fresh.

ɛꟻ tasteless, insipid.

tank n container, reservoir, cistern, aquarium, vat, basin.

tantalize v tease, taunt, torment, torture, provoke, lead on, titillate, tempt, entice, bait, balk, frustrate, thwart.

ɛꟻ gratify, satisfy, fulfil.

tantamount adj as good as, equivalent, commensurate, equal, synonymous, the same as.

tantrum n temper, rage, fury, storm, outburst, fit, scene, paddy (infml).

tap¹ v hit, strike, knock, rap, beat, drum, pat, touch.
➢ n knock, rap, beat, pat, touch.

tap² n 1 STOPCOCK, valve, faucet, spigot, spout. 2 STOPPER, plug, bung.
➢ v use, utilize, exploit, mine, quarry, siphon, bleed, milk, drain.

tape n band, strip, binding, ribbon, video, cassette.
➢ v record, video, bind, secure, stick, seal.

taper v narrow, attenuate, thin, slim, decrease, reduce, lessen, dwindle, fade, wane, peter out, tail off, die away.

ɛꟻ widen, flare, swell, increase.
➢ n spill, candle, wick.

tardy adj slow, slack, sluggish, late, unpunctual, overdue, delayed, dawdling, loitering, behindhand, backward, last-minute, eleventh-hour, belated (fml), dilatory (fml), procrastinating (fml), retarded (fml).

ɛꟻ prompt, punctual.

target n aim, object, end, purpose, intention, ambition, goal, destination, objective, butt, mark, victim, prey, quarry.

tariff n price list, schedule, charges, rate, toll, tax, levy, customs, excise, duty.

tarnish v discolour, corrode, rust, dull, dim, darken, blacken, sully, taint, stain, blemish, spot, blot, mar, spoil.

ɛꟻ polish, brighten.

tart¹ n 1 cherry tart: pie, flan, pastry, tartlet, patty, quiche, strudel. 2 (sl) PROSTITUTE, call girl, loose woman, fallen woman, slut, strumpet, street-walker, broad, whore, harlot, scarlet woman, trollop, drab, fille de joie, floosie (infml), hooker (infml), scrubber (sl), tramp (sl).
◆ **tart up** smarten (up), renovate, decorate, redecorate, embellish, doll up (infml).

tart² adj sharp, acid, sour, bitter, vinegary, tangy, piquant, pungent, biting, cutting, trenchant, incisive, caustic, astringent, acerbic, scathing, sardonic.

ɛꟻ bland, sweet.

task n job, chore, duty, charge, imposition, assignment, exercise, mission, errand, undertaking, enterprise, business, occupation, activity, employment, work, labour, toil, burden.

taste n 1 FLAVOUR, savour, relish, smack, tang. 2 SAMPLE, bit, piece, morsel, titbit, bite, nibble, mouthful, sip, drop, dash, soupçon. 3 a taste for adventure: liking, fondness, partiality, preference, inclination, leaning, desire, appetite. 4 DISCRIMINATION, discernment, judgement, perception, appreciation, sensitivity, refinement, polish, culture, cultivation, breeding, decorum, finesse, style, elegance, tastefulness.

ɛꟻ 1 blandness. 3 distaste. 4 tastelessness.
➢ v savour, relish, sample, nibble, sip, try, test, differentiate, distinguish, discern, perceive, experience, undergo, feel, encounter, meet, know.

Ways of describing taste include: acid, acrid, appetizing, bitter, bittersweet, citrus, creamy, delicious, flavoursome, fruity, hot, meaty, moreish, peppery, piquant, pungent, sapid, salty, savoury, scrumptious (infml), sharp, sour, spicy, sugary, sweet, tangy, tart, tasty, yummy (infml).

tasteful adj refined, polished, cultured, cultivated, elegant, smart, stylish, aesthetic, artistic, harmonious, beautiful,

exquisite, delicate, graceful, restrained, well-judged, judicious, correct, fastidious, discriminating.
🔁 tasteless, garish, tawdry.

tasteless *adj* **1** FLAVOURLESS, insipid, bland, mild, weak, watery, flat, stale, dull, boring, uninteresting, vapid. **2** INELEGANT, graceless, unseemly, improper, indiscreet, crass, rude, crude, vulgar, kitsch, naff (*sl*), cheap, tawdry, flashy, gaudy, garish, loud.
🔁 **1** tasty. **2** tasteful, elegant.

tasty *adj* luscious, palatable, appetizing, mouthwatering, delicious, flavoursome, succulent, scrumptious (*infml*), yummy (*infml*), tangy, piquant, savoury, sweet.
🔁 tasteless, insipid.

tattered *adj* ragged, frayed, threadbare, ripped, torn, tatty, shabby, scruffy.
🔁 smart, neat.

tatters *n* rags, shreds, ribbons, pieces.

taunt *v* tease, torment, provoke, bait, goad, jeer, mock, ridicule, gibe, rib (*sl*), deride, sneer, insult, revile, reproach.
➤ *n* jeer, catcall, gibe, dig, sneer, insult, reproach, taunting, teasing, provocation, ridicule, sarcasm, derision, censure.

taut *adj* tight, stretched, contracted, strained, tense, unrelaxed, stiff, rigid.
🔁 slack, loose, relaxed.

tautological *adj* repetitive, superfluous, redundant, pleonastic, verbose, wordy.
🔁 succinct, economical.

tautology *n* repetition, duplication, superfluity, redundancy, pleonasm.

tawdry *adj* cheap, vulgar, tasteless, fancy, showy, flashy, gaudy, garish, tinselly, glittering.
🔁 fine, tasteful.

tax *n* levy, charge, rate, tariff, customs, contribution, imposition, burden, load.

Taxes include: airport tax, capital gains tax, capital transfer tax, community charge, corporation tax, council tax, customs, death duty, estate duty, excise, income tax, inheritance tax, PAYE, poll tax, property tax, rates, surtax, tithe, toll, value added tax (VAT).

➤ *v* levy, charge, demand, exact, assess, impose, burden, load, strain, stretch, try, tire, weary, exhaust, drain, sap, weaken.

taxing *adj* burdensome, exacting, demanding, exhausting, punishing, stressful, heavy, tough, hard, tiring, trying, onerous, draining, wearing, wearying, wearisome, enervating (*fml*).
🔁 easy, gentle, mild.

teach *v* instruct, train, coach, tutor, lecture, drill, ground, verse, discipline, school, educate, enlighten, edify, inform, impart, inculcate, advise, counsel, guide, direct, show, demonstrate.
🔁 learn.

teacher *n* schoolteacher, educator, guide.
🔁 pupil.

Kinds of teacher include: adviser, coach, college lecturer, counsellor, crammer, dean, demonstrator, deputy head, doctor, don, duenna, fellow, form teacher, governess, guru, head of department, head of year, headmaster, headmistress, headteacher, housemaster, housemistress, instructor, lecturer, maharishi, master, mentor, middle school teacher, mistress, nursery school teacher, pastoral head, pedagogue, pedant, preceptor, preceptress, primary school teacher, principal, private tutor, professor, pundit, reception teacher, schoolma'am, schoolmaster, schoolmistress, schoolteacher, secondary school teacher, senior lecturer, student teacher, subject co-ordinator, supply teacher, trainer, tutor, university lecturer, upper school teacher.

teaching *n* **1** INSTRUCTION, tuition, education, pedagogy. **2** DOGMA, doctrine, tenet, precept, principle.

Methods of teaching include: apprenticeship, briefing, coaching, computer-aided learning, correspondence course, counselling, demonstration, distance learning, drilling, familiarization, grounding, guidance, hands-on training, home-learning, indoctrination, induction training, in-service training, instruction, job training, lecturing, lesson, master-class, on-the-job training, practical, preaching, private tuition, role play, rote learning, schooling, seminar, shadowing, special tuition, theory, training, tuition, tutelage, tutorial, vocational training, work experience.

team *n* side, line-up, squad, shift, crew, gang, band, group, company, stable.
◆ **team up** join, unite, couple, combine, band together, co-operate, collaborate, work together.

teamwork *n* collaboration, co-operation, co-ordination, joint effort, team spirit,

fellowship, esprit de corps, harmony.
🖅 disharmony, disunity.

tear *v* **1** RIP, rend, divide, rupture, sever, shred, scratch, claw, gash, lacerate, mutilate, mangle. **2** PULL, snatch, grab, seize, wrest. **3** *tear down the street*: dash, rush, hurry, speed, race, run, sprint, fly, shoot, dart, bolt, belt (*infml*), career, charge.
➤ *n* rip, rent, slit, hole, split, rupture, scratch, gash, laceration.

tearful *adj* crying, weeping, sobbing, whimpering, blubbering, sad, sorrowful, upset, distressed, emotional, weepy (*infml*).
🖅 happy, smiling, laughing.

tears *n* crying, weeping, sobbing, wailing, whimpering, blubbering, sorrow, distress.

tease *v* taunt, provoke, bait, annoy, irritate, aggravate (*infml*), needle (*infml*), badger, worry, pester, plague, torment, tantalize, mock, ridicule, gibe, banter, rag (*sl*), rib (*sl*).

technical *adj* mechanical, scientific, technological, electronic, computerized, specialized, expert, professional.

technique *n* method, system, procedure, manner, fashion, style, mode, way, means, approach, course, performance, execution, delivery, artistry, craftsmanship, skill, facility, proficiency, expertise, know-how (*infml*), art, craft, knack, touch.

tedious *adj* boring, monotonous, uninteresting, unexciting, dull, dreary, drab, banal, humdrum, tiresome, wearisome, tiring, laborious, long-winded, long-drawn-out.
🖅 lively, interesting, exciting.

tedium *n* boredom, tediousness, monotony, dullness, dreariness, lifelessness, drabness, banality, sameness, routine, prosiness, ennui, vapidity.
🖅 excitement, interest.

teem *v* swarm, bristle, crawl, burst, proliferate, abound, increase, multiply, overflow, produce, bear, brim, pullulate (*fml*).
🖅 lack, want.

teeming *adj* swarming, crawling, alive, bristling, seething, full, packed, brimming, overflowing, bursting, replete, abundant, fruitful, thick.
🖅 lacking, sparse, rare.

teenage *adj* teenaged, adolescent, young, youthful, juvenile, immature.

teenager *n* adolescent, youth, boy, girl, minor, juvenile.

teeter *v* sway, rock, roll, reel, stagger, totter, shake, tremble, waver, wobble, balance, lurch, pitch, pivot, seesaw.

teetotal *adj* temperate, abstinent, abstemious, sober, on the wagon (*sl*).

teetotaller *n* non-drinker, abstainer, nephalist, Rechabite, water-drinker.

telegram *n* Telemessage®, cable, telex, fax, telegraph, wire (*infml*).

telegraph *n* cable, teleprinter, telex, telegram, radiotelegraph, wire (*infml*).
➤ *v* send, transmit, signal, cable, telex, wire (*infml*).

telepathy *n* mind-reading, thought transference, sixth sense, ESP, clairvoyance.

telephone *n* phone, handset, receiver, blower (*infml*).

> **Types of telephone include:**
> Ansaphone®, answering machine, caller display phone, cardphone, carphone, cashphone, cellphone, cellular phone, corded phone, cordless phone, fax, fax-phone, hazardous area phone, Minicom®, mobile phone, pager, payphone, push-button telephone, system phone, textphone, 3-G phone, tone-dialling phone, Touchtone®, Uniphone®, videophone, WAP phone, weather-resistant phone.

➤ *v* phone, ring (up), call (up), dial, buzz (*infml*), contact, get in touch.

telescope *v* contract, shrink, compress, condense, abridge, squash, crush, shorten, curtail, truncate, abbreviate, reduce, cut, trim.

television *n* TV, receiver, set, telly (*infml*), the box (*infml*), goggle-box (*infml*), idiot box (*infml*), small screen.

> **Parts of a television set include:** aerial, aerial socket, amplifier, cathode-ray tube, chrominance signal extractor, colour decoder module, deflector coil, electron gun, horizontal synchronizing module, intermediate frequency amplifier module, loudspeaker, luminance signal amplifier, phosphor dots, picture tube, remote control, scanning current generator, screen, set-top box, shadow mask, sound demodulator, stand-by switch, synchronizing pulse separator, tuner.

tell *v* 1 INFORM, notify, let know, acquaint, impart, communicate, speak, utter, say, state, confess, divulge, disclose, reveal. 2 *tell a story*: narrate, recount, relate, report, announce, describe, portray, mention. 3 ORDER, command, direct, instruct, authorize. 4 DIFFERENTIATE, distinguish, discriminate, discern, recognize, identify, discover, see, understand, comprehend.

◆ **tell off** (*infml*) scold, chide, tick off (*infml*), upbraid (*fml*), reprimand, rebuke, reprove, lecture, berate, dress down (*infml*), reproach, censure.

telling *adj* revealing, significant, impressive, marked, effective, powerful, convincing, persuasive, impressive, cogent (*fml*).

telling-off *n* scolding, chiding, rebuke, reprimand, reproach, reproof, lecture, row, castigation (*fml*), upbraiding (*fml*), dressing-down (*infml*), ticking-off (*infml*), bawling-out (*infml*).

tell-tale *adj* revealing, meaningful, revelatory, noticeable, perceptible, unmistakable, give-away (*infml*).
➤ *n* informer, secret agent, sneak, spy, clype (*Scot*), squealer (*infml*), snake in the grass (*infml*), snitch (*infml*), snitcher (*infml*), grass (*sl*).

temerity *n* impudence, impertinence, cheek (*infml*), gall, nerve (*infml*), audacity, boldness, daring, rashness, recklessness, impulsiveness.
☒ caution, prudence.

temper *n* 1 MOOD, humour, nature, temperament, character, disposition, constitution. 2 ANGER, rage, fury, passion, tantrum, paddy (*infml*), annoyance, irritability, ill-humour. 3 CALM, composure, self-control, cool (*sl*).
☒ 2 calmness, self-control. 3 anger, rage.
➤ *v* 1 MODERATE, lessen, reduce, calm, soothe, allay, assuage, palliate, mitigate, modify, soften. 2 HARDEN, toughen, strengthen.

temperament *n* nature, character, personality, disposition, tendency, bent, constitution, make-up, soul, spirit, mood, humour, temper, state of mind, attitude, outlook.

temperamental *adj* 1 MOODY, emotional, neurotic, highly-strung, sensitive, touchy (*infml*), irritable, impatient, passionate, fiery, excitable, explosive, volatile, mercurial, capricious, unpredictable, unreliable. 2 NATURAL, inborn, innate, inherent, constitutional, ingrained.
☒ 1 calm, level-headed, steady.

temperance *n* teetotalism, prohibition, abstinence, abstemiousness, sobriety, continence, moderation, restraint, self-restraint, self-control, self-discipline, self-denial.
☒ intemperance, excess.

temperate *adj* 1 *temperate climate*: mild, clement, balmy, fair, equable, balanced, stable, gentle, pleasant, agreeable. 2 TEETOTAL, abstinent, abstemious, sober, continent, moderate, restrained, controlled, even-tempered, calm, composed, reasonable, sensible.
☒ 2 intemperate, extreme, excessive.

tempest *n* 1 STORM, gale, squall, tornado, typhoon, hurricane, cyclone. 2 FURORE, upheaval, uproar, ferment, disturbance, commotion, tumult.

tempestuous *adj* stormy, windy, gusty, blustery, squally, turbulent, tumultuous, rough, wild, violent, furious, raging, heated, passionate, intense.
☒ calm.

temple *n* shrine, sanctuary, church, tabernacle, mosque, pagoda.

tempo *n* time, rhythm, metre, beat, pulse, speed, velocity, rate, pace.

temporal *adj* secular, profane, worldly, earthly, terrestrial, material, carnal, fleshly, mortal.
☒ spiritual.

temporary *adj* impermanent, provisional, interim, makeshift, stopgap, temporal, transient, transitory, passing, ephemeral, evanescent, fleeting, brief, short-lived, momentary.
☒ permanent, everlasting.

tempt *v* entice, coax, persuade, woo, bait, lure, allure, attract, draw, seduce, invite, tantalize, provoke, incite.
☒ discourage, dissuade, repel.

temptation *n* enticement, inducement, coaxing, persuasion, bait, lure, allure, appeal, attraction, draw, pull, seduction, invitation.

tempting *adj* attractive, inviting, alluring, tantalizing, enticing, appetizing, mouthwatering, seductive.
☒ unattractive, uninviting.

tenable *adj* credible, defensible, justifiable, reasonable, rational, sound, arguable, believable, defendable, plausible, viable, feasible.
🗲 untenable, indefensible, unjustifiable.

tenacious *adj* 1 DETERMINED, persistent, dogged, firm, single-minded, adamant, resolute, purposeful, steadfast, relentless, unyielding, unshakeable, unswerving, obstinate, stubborn, intransigent (*fml*), obdurate (*fml*). 2 ADHESIVE, cohesive, sticky, clinging, secure, firm, tight, fast.
🗲 1 loose, slack, weak.

tenancy *n* occupancy, possession, renting, residence, tenure, holding, lease, leasehold, occupation, incumbency.

tenant *n* renter, lessee, leaseholder, occupier, occupant, resident, inhabitant.

tend¹ *v* incline, lean, bend, bear, head, aim, lead, go, move, gravitate.

tend² *v* look after, care for, cultivate, keep, maintain, manage, handle, guard, protect, watch, mind, nurture, nurse, minister to, serve, attend.
🗲 neglect, ignore.

tendency *n* trend, drift, movement, course, direction, bearing, heading, bias, partiality, predisposition, propensity, readiness, liability, susceptibility, proneness, inclination, leaning, bent, disposition.

tender¹ *adj* 1 KIND, gentle, caring, humane, considerate, compassionate, sympathetic, warm, fond, affectionate, loving, amorous, romantic, sentimental, emotional, sensitive, tender-hearted, soft-hearted. 2 YOUNG, youthful, immature, green, raw, new, inexperienced, impressionable, vulnerable. 3 SOFT, succulent, fleshy, dainty, delicate, fragile, frail, weak, feeble. 4 SORE, painful, aching, smarting, bruised, inflamed, raw.
🗲 1 hard-hearted, callous. 2 mature. 3 tough, hard.

tender² *v* offer, proffer, extend, give, present, submit, propose, suggest, advance, volunteer.
➤ *n* 1 *legal tender*: currency, money. 2 OFFER, bid, estimate, quotation, proposal, proposition, suggestion, submission.

tenet *n* principle, belief, precept, presumption, conviction, opinion, teaching, rule, thesis, view, doctrine, dogma, maxim, creed, credo, canon, article of faith.

tenor *n* meaning, tendency, theme, trend, essence, substance, gist, aim, point, direction, drift, purpose, sense, spirit, intent, course, path, way, burden, purport (*fml*).

tense *adj* 1 TIGHT, taut, stretched, strained, stiff, rigid. 2 NERVOUS, anxious, worried, jittery, uneasy, apprehensive, edgy, fidgety, restless, jumpy, overwrought, keyed up. 3 STRESSFUL, exciting, worrying, fraught.
🗲 1 loose, slack. 2 calm, relaxed.
➤ *v* tighten, contract, brace, stretch, strain.
🗲 loosen, relax.

tension *n* 1 TIGHTNESS, tautness, stiffness, strain, stress, pressure. 2 NERVOUSNESS, anxiety, worry, uneasiness, apprehension, edginess, restlessness, suspense.
🗲 1 looseness. 2 calm(ness), relaxation.

tent *n* tepee, wigwam, marquee, big top.

tentative *adj* experimental, exploratory, speculative, hesitant, faltering, cautious, unsure, uncertain, doubtful, undecided, provisional, indefinite, unconfirmed.
🗲 definite, decisive, conclusive, final.

tenuous *adj* thin, slim, slender, fine, slight, insubstantial, flimsy, fragile, delicate, weak, shaky, doubtful, dubious, questionable.
🗲 strong, substantial.

tenure *n* possession, proprietorship, residence, tenancy, term, time, holding, occupancy, occupation, incumbency, habitation (*fml*).

tepid *adj* lukewarm, cool, half-hearted, unenthusiastic, apathetic.
🗲 cold, hot, passionate.

term *n* 1 WORD, name, designation, appellation, title, epithet, phrase, expression. 2 TIME, period, course, duration, spell, span, stretch, interval, space, semester, session, season.
➤ *v* call, name, dub, style, designate, label, tag, title, entitle.

terminal *adj* 1 LAST, final, concluding, ultimate, extreme, utmost. 2 FATAL, deadly, lethal, mortal, incurable.
🗲 1 initial.

terminate *v* finish, complete, conclude, cease, end, stop, close, discontinue, wind up, cut off, abort, lapse, expire.
🗲 begin, start, initiate.

terminology *n* language, jargon, phraseology, vocabulary, words, terms, nomenclature.

terminus *n* end, close, termination, extremity, limit, boundary, destination, goal, target, depot, station, garage, terminal.

terms *n* **1** *on good terms*: relations, relationship, footing, standing, position. **2** CONDITIONS, specifications, stipulations, provisos, provisions, qualifications, particulars. **3** RATES, charges, fees, prices, tariff.

terrain *n* land, ground, territory, country, countryside, landscape, topography.

terrestrial *adj* earthly, worldly, global, mundane.
 cosmic, heavenly.

terrible *adj* bad, awful, frightful, dreadful, shocking, appalling, outrageous, disgusting, revolting, repulsive, offensive, abhorrent, hateful, horrid, horrible, unpleasant, obnoxious, foul, vile, hideous, gruesome, horrific, harrowing, distressing, grave, serious, severe, extreme, desperate.
 excellent, wonderful, superb.

terribly (*infml*) *adv* very, much, greatly, extremely, exceedingly, awfully, frightfully, decidedly, seriously.

terrific (*infml*) *adj* **1** EXCELLENT, wonderful, marvellous, super, smashing (*infml*), outstanding, brilliant (*infml*), magnificent, superb, fabulous (*infml*), fantastic (*infml*), sensational, amazing, stupendous, breathtaking. **2** HUGE, enormous, gigantic, tremendous, great, intense, extreme, excessive.
 1 awful, terrible, appalling.

terrified *adj* frightened, petrified, scared, scared stiff, panic-stricken, intimidated, horrified, horror-struck, dismayed, appalled, alarmed, awed, scared out of one's wits (*infml*), scared to death (*infml*), having kittens (*infml*), in a blue funk (*infml*).

terrify *v* petrify, horrify, appal, shock, terrorize, intimidate, frighten, scare, alarm, dismay.

territory *n* country, land, state, dependency, province, domain, preserve, jurisdiction, sector, region, area, district, zone, tract, terrain.

terror *n* fear, panic, dread, trepidation, horror, shock, fright, alarm, dismay, consternation, terrorism, intimidation.

terrorize *v* threaten, menace, intimidate, oppress, coerce, bully, browbeat, frighten, scare, alarm, terrify, petrify, horrify, shock.

terse *adj* short, brief, succinct, concise, compact, condensed, epigrammatic, pithy, incisive, snappy, curt, brusque, abrupt, laconic.
 long-winded, verbose.

test *v* try, experiment, examine, assess, evaluate, check, investigate, analyse, screen, prove, verify.
 n trial, try-out, experiment, examination, assessment, evaluation, check, investigation, analysis, proof, probation, ordeal.

testament *n* testimony, witness, demonstration, proof, evidence, exemplification, tribute, will, earnest, attestation (*fml*).

testify *v* give evidence, depose (*fml*), state, declare, assert, swear, avow, attest (*fml*), vouch, certify, corroborate, affirm, show, bear witness.

testimonial *n* reference, character, credential, certificate, recommendation, endorsement, commendation, tribute.

testimony *n* evidence, statement, affidavit (*fml*), submission, deposition, declaration, profession, attestation, affirmation, support, proof, verification, confirmation, witness, demonstration, manifestation, indication.

tetchy *adj* irritable, irascible, peevish, bad-tempered, crusty, grumpy, short-tempered, snappish, touchy (*infml*), crotchety (*infml*), shirty (*infml*), ratty (*infml*).

tether *n* chain, rope, cord, line, lead, leash, bond, fetter, shackle, restraint, fastening.
 v tie, fasten, secure, restrain, chain, rope, leash, bind, lash, fetter, shackle, manacle.

text *n* words, wording, content, matter, body, subject, topic, theme, reading, passage, paragraph, sentence, book, textbook, source.

texture *n* consistency, feel, surface, grain, weave, tissue, fabric, structure, composition, constitution, character, quality.

thank *v* say thank you, be grateful, appreciate, acknowledge, recognize, credit.

thankful *adj* grateful, appreciative, obliged, indebted, pleased, contented, relieved.
 ungrateful, unappreciative.

thankless *adj* unrecognized, unappreciated, unrequited, unrewarding, unprofitable, fruitless.
🔁 rewarding, worthwhile.

thanks *n* gratitude, gratefulness, appreciation, acknowledgement, recognition, credit, thanksgiving, thank-offering.

> Expressions used when thanking someone include: how can I ever thank you?, how kind of you!, I can't thank you enough, I'm so/very grateful, many thanks, bless you, much obliged, please accept my grateful/sincere thanks, cheers, ta, thanks a lot, thanks be (to …), thanks for that, that's very good of you, that's very kind of you, you're too kind, you shouldn't have.

♦ **thanks to** because of, owing to, due to, on account of, as a result of, through.

thaw *v* melt, defrost, defreeze, de-ice, soften, liquefy, dissolve, warm, heat up.
🔁 freeze.

theatre *n* **1** *go to the theatre*: auditorium, hall, playhouse, amphitheatre, lyceum, odeon, opera house. **2** DRAMA, the stage, dramatics, theatrics, show business, Thespian art (*fml*), the boards (*infml*), the footlights (*infml*), rep (*infml*).

> Parts of a theatre include: apron, auditorium, backstage, balcony, border, box, bridge, catwalk, circle, coulisse, cut drop, cyclorama, decor, downstage, flat, flies, forestage, fourth wall, gallery, the gods (*infml*), green room, grid, leg drop, lights, floats, floods, footlights, spots, loge, loggia, logum, mezzanine, open stage, opposite prompt, orchestra pit, picture-frame stage, pit, prompt side, proscenium, proscenium arch, revolving stage, rostrum, safety curtain, scruto, set, stage, stalls, tormentor, trapdoor, upper circle, upstage, wings.

theatrical *adj* **1** DRAMATIC, thespian. **2** MELODRAMATIC, histrionic, mannered, affected, artificial, pompous, ostentatious, showy, extravagant, exaggerated, overdone.

> Theatrical forms include: ballet, burlesque, cabaret, circus, comedy, black comedy, comedy of humours, comedy of manners, comedy of menace, commedia dell'arte, duologue, farce, fringe theatre, Grand Guignol, kabuki, Kensington gore, Kitchen-Sink, legitimate drama, masque, melodrama, mime, miracle play, monologue, morality play, mummery, music hall, musical, musical comedy, mystery play, Noh, opera, operetta, pageant, pantomime, play, Punch and Judy, puppet theatre, revue, street theatre, tableau, theatre-in-the-round, Theatre of the Absurd, Theatre of Cruelty, tragedy. *see also* **performance**.

theft *n* robbery, thieving, stealing, pilfering, larceny, shop-lifting, kleptomania, fraud, embezzlement.

theme *n* subject, topic, thread, motif, keynote, idea, gist, essence, burden, argument, thesis, dissertation, composition, essay, text, matter.

theological *adj* religious, divine, doctrinal, ecclesiastical, scriptural.

theorem *n* formula, principle, rule, statement, deduction, proposition, hypothesis.

theoretical *adj* hypothetical, conjectural, speculative, abstract, academic, doctrinaire, pure, ideal.
🔁 practical, applied, concrete.

theorize *v* hypothesize, suppose, guess, conjecture, speculate, postulate, propound, formulate.

theory *n* hypothesis, supposition, assumption, presumption, surmise, guess, conjecture, speculation, idea, notion, abstraction, philosophy, thesis, plan, proposal, scheme, system.
🔁 certainty, practice.

therapeutic *adj* remedial, curative, healing, restorative, tonic, medicinal, corrective, good, beneficial.
🔁 harmful, detrimental.

therapy *n* treatment, remedy, cure, healing, tonic.

> Types of therapy include: acupressure, acupuncture, Alexander technique, aromatherapy, art therapy, aversion therapy, beauty therapy, behaviour therapy, biofeedback, chemotherapy, chiropractic, cognitive therapy, confrontation therapy, drama therapy, electro-convulsive therapy, electrotherapy, faith healing, family therapy, Gestalt therapy, group therapy, heat treatment, herbalism, homeopathy, hormone-replacement therapy, horticulture therapy, hydrotherapy, hypnotherapy, irradiation, moxibustion, music therapy,

naturopathy, occupational therapy, osteopathy, phototherapy, physiotherapy, play therapy, primal therapy, psychotherapy, radiotherapy, reflexology, regression therapy, reminiscence therapy, Rolfing, sex therapy, shiatsu, speech therapy, ultrasound, zone therapy.

therefore *adv* so, then, consequently, as a result.

thesaurus *n* dictionary, lexicon, wordbook, vocabulary, synonymy, encyclopedia, storehouse, repository, treasury.

thesis *n* 1 *doctoral thesis*: dissertation, essay, composition, treatise, paper, monograph. 2 SUBJECT, topic, theme, idea, opinion, view, theory, hypothesis, proposal, proposition, premise, statement, argument, contention.

thick *adj* 1 WIDE, broad, fat, heavy, solid, dense, impenetrable, close, compact, concentrated, condensed, viscous, coagulated, clotted. 2 FULL, packed, crowded, chock-a-block, swarming, teeming, bristling, brimming, bursting, numerous, abundant. 3 (*infml*) STUPID, foolish, slow, dull, dim-witted, brainless, simple.
Ea 1 thin, slim, slender, slight. 2 sparse. 3 clever, brainy (*infml*).

thicken *v* condense, stiffen, congeal, coagulate, clot, cake, gel, jell, set.
Ea thin.

thicket *n* wood, copse, coppice, grove, spinney.

thickness *n* 1 WIDTH, breadth, diameter, density, viscosity, bulk, body. 2 LAYER, stratum, ply, sheet, coat.
Ea 1 thinness.

thickset *adj* stocky, heavy, heavily built, well-built, sturdy, powerful, strong, muscular, burly, solid, bulky, squabby, squat, dense, beefy (*infml*), brawny (*infml*), hefty.
Ea lanky.

thick-skinned *adj* insensitive, unfeeling, callous, tough, hardened, hard-boiled.
Ea thin-skinned, sensitive.

thief *n* robber, bandit, mugger, pickpocket, shop-lifter, burglar, house-breaker, plunderer, poacher, stealer, pilferer, filcher, kleptomaniac, swindler, embezzler.

thin *adj* 1 LEAN, slim, slender, narrow,

attenuated, slight, skinny, bony, skeletal, scraggy, scrawny, lanky, gaunt, spare, underweight, undernourished, emaciated. 2 *thin fabric*: fine, delicate, light, flimsy, filmy, gossamer, sheer, see-through, transparent, translucent. 3 SPARSE, scarce, scattered, scant, meagre, poor, inadequate, deficient, scanty, skimpy. 4 WEAK, feeble, runny, watery, diluted.
Ea 1 fat, broad. 2 thick, dense, solid. 3 plentiful, abundant. 4 strong.
➤ *v* 1 NARROW, attenuate, diminish, reduce, trim, weed out. 2 WEAKEN, dilute, water down, rarefy, refine.

thing *n* 1 ARTICLE, object, entity, creature, body, substance, item, detail, particular, feature, factor, element, point, fact, concept, thought. 2 DEVICE, contrivance, gadget, tool, implement, instrument, apparatus, machine, mechanism. 3 ACT, deed, feat, action, task, responsibility, problem. 4 CIRCUMSTANCE, eventuality, happening, occurrence, event, incident, phenomenon, affair, proceeding. 5 (*infml*) OBSESSION, preoccupation, fixation, fetish, phobia, hang-up (*infml*).

things *n* belongings, possessions, effects, paraphernalia, stuff (*infml*), goods, luggage, baggage, equipment, gear (*infml*), clobber (*infml*), odds and ends, bits and pieces.

think *v* 1 BELIEVE, hold, consider, regard, esteem, deem, judge, estimate, reckon, calculate, determine, conclude, reason. 2 CONCEIVE, imagine, suppose, presume, surmise, expect, foresee, envisage, anticipate.
♦ **think over** reflect upon, consider, weigh up, contemplate, meditate, ponder, chew over (*infml*), ruminate, mull over.
♦ **think up** devise, contrive, dream up, imagine, conceive, visualize, invent, design, create, concoct.

thinker *n* philosopher, theorist, ideologist, brain, intellect, mastermind.

thinking *n* reasoning, philosophy, thoughts, conclusions, theory, idea, opinion, view, outlook, position, judgement, assessment.
➤ *adj* reasoning, rational, intellectual, intelligent, cultured, sophisticated, philosophical, analytical, reflective, contemplative, thoughtful.

thin-skinned *adj* sensitive, easily upset, snappish, soft, susceptible, tender,

vulnerable, hypersensitive, irritable, touchy (*infml*).
F3 thick-skinned, unfeeling, callous.

third-rate *adj* low-grade, poor, bad, inferior, mediocre, indifferent, shoddy, cheap and nasty.
F3 first-rate.

thirst *n* **1** THIRSTINESS, dryness, drought. **2** DESIRE, longing, yearning, hankering, craving, hunger, appetite, lust, passion, eagerness, keenness.

thirsty *adj* **1** DRY, parched (*infml*), gasping (*infml*), dehydrated, arid. **2** *thirsty for knowledge*: desirous, longing, yearning, hankering, craving, hungry, burning, itching, dying, eager, avid, greedy.

thorn *n* spike, point, barb, prickle, spine, bristle, needle.

thorny *adj* **1** SPIKY, pointed, sharp, barbed, prickly, spiny, bristly, acanthous (*fml*), spinous (*fml*), spinose (*fml*). **2** *a thorny problem*: difficult, troublesome, irksome, vexed, worrying, trying, upsetting, problematic, knotty, complex, intricate, tough, awkward, delicate, tricky, ticklish, convoluted (*fml*).

thorough *adj* full, complete, total, entire, utter, absolute, perfect, pure, sheer, unqualified, unmitigated, out-and-out, downright, sweeping, all-embracing, comprehensive, all-inclusive, exhaustive, thoroughgoing, intensive, in-depth, conscientious, efficient, painstaking, scrupulous, meticulous, careful.
F3 partial, superficial, careless.

thoroughbred *adj* pedigree, pedigreed, pure-blood, pure-blooded, full-blooded, blooded.
F3 cross-bred, hybrid, mixed, mongrel.

thoroughly *adv* **1** CAREFULLY, painstakingly, meticulously, scrupulously, intensively, conscientiously, assiduously, efficiently, comprehensively, sweepingly, exhaustively, root and branch, inside out. **2** FULLY, perfectly, completely, absolutely, downright, entirely, quite, totally, utterly, every inch (*infml*), with a fine-tooth comb (*infml*).
F3 **1** carelessly, haphazardly. **2** partially.

though *conj* although, even if, notwithstanding, while, allowing, granted.
➤ *adv* however, nevertheless, nonetheless, yet, still, even so, all the same, for all that.

thought *n* **1** THINKING, attention, heed,

regard, consideration, study, scrutiny, introspection, meditation, contemplation, cogitation, reflection, deliberation. **2** IDEA, notion, concept, conception, belief, conviction, opinion, view, judgement, assessment, conclusion, plan, design, intention, purpose, aim, hope, dream, expectation, anticipation.
3 THOUGHTFULNESS, consideration, kindness, care, concern, compassion, sympathy, gesture, touch.

thoughtful *adj* **1** PENSIVE, wistful, dreamy, abstracted, reflective, contemplative, introspective, thinking, absorbed, studious, serious, solemn.
2 CONSIDERATE, kind, unselfish, helpful, caring, attentive, heedful, mindful, careful, prudent, cautious, wary.
F3 **2** thoughtless, insensitive, selfish.

thoughtless *adj* **1** INCONSIDERATE, unthinking, insensitive, unfeeling, tactless, undiplomatic, unkind, selfish, uncaring. **2** absent-minded, inattentive, heedless, mindless, foolish, stupid, silly, rash, reckless, ill-considered, imprudent, careless, negligent, remiss.
F3 **1** thoughtful, considerate. **2** careful.

thrash *v* **1** PUNISH, beat, whip, lash, flog, scourge, cane, belt (*infml*), spank, clobber (*infml*), wallop (*infml*), lay into. **2** DEFEAT, beat, trounce, hammer (*infml*), slaughter (*infml*), crush, overwhelm, rout. **3** THRESH, flail, toss, jerk.
♦ **thrash out** discuss, debate, negotiate, settle, resolve.

thrashing *n* **1** PUNISHMENT, flogging, lashing, caning, hiding, beating, tanning, whipping, leathering, pasting, chastisement (*fml*), belting (*infml*). **2** DEFEAT, drubbing, beating, rout, crushing, trouncing, lamming, hammering (*infml*), clobbering (*infml*), licking (*infml*).

thread *n* **1** COTTON, yarn, strand, fibre, filament, string, line. **2** COURSE, direction, drift, tenor, theme, motif, plot, storyline.

threadbare *adj* **1** *threadbare clothes*: worn, frayed, ragged, moth-eaten, scruffy, shabby. **2** HACKNEYED, overused, old, stale, tired, trite, commonplace, stock, stereotyped.
F3 **1** new. **2** fresh.

threat *n* menace, warning, omen, portent, presage, foreboding, danger, risk, hazard, peril.

threaten *v* menace, intimidate,

browbeat, pressurize, bully, terrorize, warn, portend, presage, forebode, foreshadow, endanger, jeopardize, imperil.

threatening *adj* menacing, intimidatory, warning, cautionary, ominous, inauspicious, sinister, grim, looming, impending.

threshold *n* doorstep, sill, doorway, door, entrance, brink, verge, starting-point, dawn, beginning, start, outset, opening.

thrift *n* economy, husbandry, saving, conservation, frugality, prudence, carefulness.
 extravagance, waste.

thrifty *adj* economical, saving, frugal, sparing, prudent, careful.
 extravagant, profligate, prodigal, wasteful.

thrill *n* excitement, adventure, pleasure, stimulation, charge, kick, buzz (*sl*), sensation, glow, tingle, throb, shudder, quiver, tremor.
 ➤ *v* excite, electrify, galvanize, exhilarate, rouse, arouse, move, stir, stimulate, flush, glow, tingle, throb, shudder, tremble, quiver, shake.
 bore.

thrilling *adj* exciting, stimulating, stirring, rousing, riveting, sensational, exhilarating, gripping, electrifying, rip-roaring, heart-stirring, soul-stirring, shaking, shuddering, shivering, trembling, vibrating, quaking, hair-raising (*infml*).

thrive *v* flourish, prosper, boom, grow, increase, advance, develop, bloom, blossom, gain, profit, succeed.
 languish, stagnate, fail, die.

thriving *adj* prosperous, successful, blossoming, booming, developing, flourishing, growing, healthy, wealthy, affluent, well, comfortable, blooming, burgeoning (*fml*).
 ailing, failing, languishing, stagnating, dying.

throb *v* pulse, pulsate, beat, palpitate, vibrate, pound, thump.
 ➤ *n* pulse, pulsation, beat, palpitation, vibration, pounding, thumping.

throe *n* convulsion, fit, pain, pang, paroxysm, seizure, spasm, stab, suffering, distress, agony, anguish, torture, travail (*fml*).

throng *n* crowd, mass, mob, multitude, pack, press, crush, jam, swarm, flock,

congregation, herd, bevy, horde, host, assemblage (*fml*).
 ➤ *v* flock, fill, crowd, cram, converge, herd, press, swarm, pack, bunch, congregate, jam, mill around (*infml*).

throttle *v* strangle, choke, asphyxiate, suffocate, smother, stifle, gag, silence, suppress, inhibit.

through *prep* **1** BETWEEN, by, via, by way of, by means of, using. **2** *all through the night*: throughout, during, in. **3** BECAUSE OF, as a result of, thanks to.
 ➤ *adj* **1** FINISHED, ended, completed, done. **2** *through train*: direct, express, non-stop.

throughout *adv* everywhere, in every part, extensively, widely, completely, from beginning to end, ubiquitously (*fml*).
 ➤ *prep* **1** DURING, during/in the whole of, all through, in the course of, for the duration of. **2** IN ALL PARTS, in every part of, all over, all round, everywhere.

throw *v* **1** HURL, heave, lob, pitch, chuck (*infml*), sling, cast, fling, toss, launch, propel, send. **2** *throw light*: shed, cast, project, direct. **3** BRING DOWN, floor, upset, overturn, dislodge, unseat, unsaddle, unhorse. **4** (*infml*) PERPLEX, baffle, confound, confuse, disconcert, astonish, dumbfound.
 ➤ *n* heave, lob, pitch, sling, fling, toss, cast.
 ◆ **throw away 1** DISCARD, jettison, dump, ditch (*sl*), scrap, dispose of, throw out. **2** WASTE, squander, fritter away, blow (*infml*).
 1 keep, preserve, salvage, rescue.
 ◆ **throw off** shed, cast off, drop, abandon, shake off, get rid of, elude.
 ◆ **throw out 1** EVICT, turn out, expel, turf out (*infml*), eject, emit, radiate, give off. **2** REJECT, discard, dismiss, turn down, jettison, dump, ditch (*sl*), throw away, scrap.
 ◆ **throw up 1** (*infml*) VOMIT, spew, regurgitate, disgorge, retch, heave. **2** GIVE UP, abandon, renounce, relinquish, resign, quit, leave.

throwaway *adj* **1** *throwaway comments*: careless, casual, offhand, passing, unemphatic, undramatic. **2** *a throwaway product*: disposable, cheap, expendable, non-returnable, biodegradable.

thrust *v* push, shove, butt, ram, jam, wedge, stick, poke, prod, jab, lunge, pierce, stab, plunge, press, force, impel, drive, propel.

➤ *n* push, shove, poke, prod, lunge, stab, drive, impetus, momentum.

thud *n, v* thump, clump, knock, clunk, smack, wallop (*infml*), crash, bang, thunder.

thug *n* ruffian, tough, robber, bandit, mugger, killer, murderer, assassin, gangster, hooligan.

thump *n* knock, blow, punch, clout (*infml*), box, cuff, smack, whack (*infml*), wallop (*infml*), crash, bang, thud, beat, throb.
➤ *v* hit, strike, knock, punch, clout (*infml*), box, cuff, smack, thrash, whack (*infml*), wallop (*infml*), crash, bang, thud, batter, pound, hammer, beat, throb.

thunder *n* boom, reverberation, crash, bang, crack, clap, peal, rumble, roll, roar, blast, explosion.
➤ *v* boom, resound, reverberate, crash, bang, crack, clap, peal, rumble, roll, roar, blast.

thunderous *adj* booming, resounding, reverberating, roaring, loud, noisy, deafening, ear-splitting.

thunderstruck *adj* stunned, shocked, staggered, amazed, astonished, astounded, dazed, dumbfounded, open-mouthed, paralysed, aghast, agape, petrified, flabbergasted (*infml*), floored (*infml*), flummoxed (*infml*), nonplussed (*infml*), bowled over (*infml*), knocked for six (*infml*).

thus *adv* so, hence, therefore, consequently, then, accordingly, like this, in this way, as follows.

thwack *v* beat, bash, hit, flog, smack, thump, slap, buffet, cuff, clout (*infml*), wallop (*infml*), whack (*infml*).
➤ *n* blow, bash, slap, thump, smack, cuff, buffet, wallop (*infml*), whack (*infml*).

thwart *v* frustrate, foil, stymie, defeat, hinder, impede, obstruct, block, check, baffle, stop, prevent, oppose.
🖙 help, assist, aid.

tick *n* 1 CLICK, tap, stroke, tick-tock. 2 (*infml*) *wait a tick*: moment, instant, flash, jiffy (*infml*), second, minute.
➤ *v* 1 MARK, indicate, choose, select. 2 CLICK, tap, beat.
♦ **tick off** 1 *tick off items on a list*: put a tick against, mark, indicate, check (off) (*US*). 2 SCOLD, chide, reprimand, rebuke, reproach, reprove, upbraid (*fml*), tell off (*infml*), give someone a dressing-down

(*infml*), haul over the coals (*infml*), tear off a strip (*infml*).
🖙 2 praise, compliment.

ticket *n* pass, card, certificate, token, voucher, coupon, docket, slip, label, tag, sticker.

tickle *v* excite, thrill, delight, please, gratify, amuse, entertain, divert.

ticklish *adj* sensitive, touchy, delicate, thorny, awkward, agape, difficult, tricky, critical, risky, hazardous, dodgy (*infml*).
🖙 easy, simple.

tide *n* current, ebb, flow, stream, flux, movement, course, direction, drift, trend, tendency.
♦ **tide over** help (through), help out, assist, aid, see through, keep going.

tidy *adj* 1 NEAT, orderly, methodical, systematic, organized, clean, spick-and-span, shipshape, smart, spruce, trim, well-kept, ordered, uncluttered. 2 (*infml*) *a tidy sum*: large, substantial, sizable, considerable, good, generous, ample.
🖙 1 untidy, messy, disorganized. 2 small, insignificant.
➤ *v* neaten, straighten, order, arrange, clean, smarten, spruce up, groom.

tie *v* knot, fasten, secure, moor, tether, attach, join, connect, link, unite, rope, lash, strap, bind, restrain, restrict, confine, limit, hamper, hinder.
➤ *n* 1 KNOT, fastening, joint, connection, link, liaison, relationship, bond, affiliation, obligation, commitment, duty, restraint, restriction, limitation, hindrance. 2 DRAW, dead heat, stalemate, deadlock.
♦ **tie down** restrain, constrain, restrict, confine, limit, hamper, hinder.
♦ **tie up** 1 MOOR, tether, attach, secure, rope, lash, bind, truss, wrap up, restrain. 2 CONCLUDE, terminate, wind up, settle. 3 OCCUPY, engage, engross.

tie-in *n* connection, relationship, link, relation, co-ordination, association, liaison, tie-up, affiliation, hook-up (*infml*).

tier *n* floor, storey, level, stage, stratum, layer, belt, zone, band, echelon, rank, row, line.

tight *adj* 1 TAUT, stretched, tense, rigid, stiff, firm, fixed, fast, secure, close, cramped, constricted, compact, snug, close-fitting. 2 SEALED, hermetic, -proof, impervious, airtight, watertight. 3 (*infml*) MEAN, stingy, miserly, niggardly, parsimonious, tight-fisted (*infml*). 4 *tight*

security: strict, severe, stringent, rigorous.
Ea 1 loose, slack. **2** open. **3** generous.
4 lax.

tighten *v* tauten, stretch, tense, stiffen, fix, fasten, secure, narrow, close, cramp, constrict, crush, squeeze.
Ea loosen, relax.

tight-fisted (*infml*) *adj* mean, stingy, miserly, mingy (*infml*), niggardly, penny-pinching, sparing, parsimonious, tight (*infml*), grasping.
Ea generous, charitable.

till¹ *prep* until, up to, to, up to the time of, all through, through (*US*).

till² *v* cultivate, work, plough, dig, farm.

tilt *v* slope, incline, slant, pitch, list, tip, lean.
➤ *n* slope, incline, angle, inclination, slant, pitch, list.

timber *n* wood, trees, forest, beam, lath, plank, board, log.

timbre *n* quality, voice quality, tone, tonality, resonance, ring, colour.

time *n* **1** SPELL, stretch, period, term, season, session, span, duration, interval, space, while. **2** TEMPO, beat, rhythm, metre, measure. **3** MOMENT, point, juncture, stage, instance, occasion, date, day, hour. **4** AGE, era, epoch, life, lifetime, generation, heyday, peak.

> Periods of time include: eternity, eon, era, age, generation, epoch, millennium, chiliad, century, lifetime, decade, decennium, quinquennium, year, light-year, yesteryear, quarter, month, fortnight, week, midweek, weekend, long weekend, day, today, tonight, yesterday, tomorrow, morrow, weekday, hour, minute, second, moment, instant, millisecond, microsecond, nanosecond; dawn, sunrise, sun-up, the early hours, wee small hours (*infml*), morning, morn, a.m., daytime, midday, noon, high noon, p.m., afternoon, tea-time, evening, twilight, dusk, sunset, nightfall, bedtime, night, night-time; season, spring, summer, midsummer, autumn, fall (*US*), winter.

➤ *v* clock, measure, meter, regulate, control, set, schedule, timetable.
♦ **all the time** continually, constantly, perpetually, incessantly, interminably, always, forever.
Ea never.
♦ **at times** sometimes, on occasions, from time to time, now and again, now and

then, off and on, every so often.
♦ **in time** not too late, early enough, punctually, on time.
♦ **time after time** repeatedly, frequently, often, recurrently, many times, on many occasions, time and (time) again, again and again, over and over again.

time-honoured *adj* age-old, traditional, long-established, usual, accustomed, conventional, customary, established, fixed, old, ancient, historic, venerable.

timeless *adj* ageless, immortal, everlasting, eternal, endless, permanent, changeless, unchanging.

timely *adj* well-timed, seasonable, suitable, appropriate, convenient, opportune, propitious, prompt, punctual.
Ea ill-timed, unsuitable, inappropriate.

timetable *n* schedule, programme, agenda, calendar, diary, rota, roster, list, listing, curriculum.

timid *adj* shy, bashful, modest, shrinking, retiring, nervous, apprehensive, afraid, timorous, fearful, cowardly, faint-hearted, spineless, irresolute.
Ea brave, bold, audacious.

tinge *n* tint, dye, colour, shade, touch, trace, suggestion, hint, smack, flavour, pinch, drop, dash, bit, sprinkling, smattering.
➤ *v* tint, dye, stain, colour, shade, suffuse, imbue.

tingle *v* sting, prickle, tickle, itch, thrill, throb, quiver, vibrate.
➤ *n* stinging, prickling, pins and needles, tickle, tickling, itch, itching, thrill, throb, quiver, shiver, gooseflesh, goose-pimples.

tinker *v* fiddle, play, toy, trifle, potter, dabble, meddle, tamper.

tint *n* dye, stain, rinse, wash, colour, hue, shade, tincture, tinge, tone, cast, streak, trace, touch.
➤ *v* dye, colour, tinge, streak, stain, taint, affect.

tiny *adj* minute, microscopic, infinitesimal, teeny (*infml*), small, little, slight, negligible, insignificant, diminutive, petite, dwarfish, pint-size(d) (*infml*), pocket, miniature, mini (*infml*).
Ea huge, enormous, immense.

tip¹ *n* end, extremity, point, nib, apex, peak, pinnacle, summit, acme, top, cap, crown, head.
➤ *v* cap, crown, top, surmount.

tip² v lean, incline, slant, list, tilt, topple over, capsize, upset, overturn, spill, pour out, empty, unload, dump.
➤ n dump, rubbish-heap, refuse-heap.

tip³ n 1 CLUE, pointer, hint, suggestion, advice, warning, tip-off, information, inside information, forecast. 2 GRATUITY, gift, perquisite.
➤ v 1 ADVISE, suggest, warn, caution, forewarn, tip-off (infml), inform, tell. 2 *tip the driver*: reward, remunerate.

tip-off n hint, pointer, clue, suggestion, warning, information, inside information.

tirade n harangue, diatribe, denunciation, abuse, lecture, outburst, rant, fulmination (fml), invective (fml).

tire v weary, fatigue, wear out, exhaust, drain, enervate.
🖾 enliven, invigorate, refresh.

tired adj 1 WEARY, drowsy, sleepy, flagging, fatigued, worn out, exhausted, dog-tired (infml), drained, jaded, fagged (sl), bushed (infml), whacked (infml), shattered (infml), beat (infml), deadbeat (infml), all in (infml), knackered (infml). 2 *tired of waiting*: fed up (infml), bored, sick.
🖾 1 lively, energetic, rested, refreshed.

tireless adj untiring, unwearied, unflagging, indefatigable, energetic, vigorous, diligent, industrious, resolute, determined.
🖾 tired, lazy.

tiresome adj troublesome, trying, annoying, irritating, exasperating, wearisome, dull, boring, tedious, monotonous, uninteresting, tiring, fatiguing, laborious.
🖾 interesting, stimulating, easy.

tiring adj wearying, fatiguing, exhausting, draining, demanding, exacting, taxing, arduous, strenuous, laborious.

tissue n substance, matter, material, fabric, stuff, gauze, web, mesh, network, structure, texture.

titbit n morsel, scrap, appetizer, snack, delicacy, dainty, treat.

titillate v stimulate, arouse, turn on (sl), excite, thrill, tickle, provoke, tease, tantalize, intrigue, interest.

title n 1 NAME, appellation, denomination, term, designation, label, epithet, nickname, pseudonym, rank, status, office, position. 2 HEADING, headline, caption, legend, inscription. 3 RIGHT,

prerogative, privilege, claim, entitlement, ownership, deeds.
➤ v entitle, name, call, dub, style, term, designate, label.

titter v laugh, chortle, chuckle, giggle, snigger, mock.

tittle-tattle n gossip, rumour, hearsay, chatter, cackle, prattle, chitchat (infml), babble (infml), blather (infml), blether (infml), jaw (infml), natter (infml), twaddle (infml), ya(c)k (infml), yackety-yak (infml).
➤ v gossip, chat, chatter, cackle, prattle, chitchat (infml), tell tales (infml), witter (infml), babble (infml), blather (infml), blether (infml), jaw (infml), natter (infml), ya(c)k (infml), yackety-yak (infml).

titular adj honorary, formal, official, so-called, nominal, token.

toadstool see **mushrooms and toadstools.**

toast v grill, brown, roast, heat, warm.
➤ n drink, pledge, tribute, salute, compliment, health.

Toasts include: all the best!, auf Ihre Gesundheit, à votre santé, bottoms up!, cheers!, down the hatch!, good health!, good luck!, happy landings!, here's how!, here's looking at you!, here's mud in your eye!, here's to ...!, here's to you!, prosit!, skoal!, slàinte!, to absent friends!, your health!

tobacco

Forms of tobacco include: baccy (infml), cheroot, chewing tobacco; cigar, Havana cigar; cigarette, cork-tipped cigarette, filter-tip cigarette, king-size cigarette, menthol cigarette, Russian cigarette; ciggie (infml), coffin nail (sl), fag (infml); cigarette end, cigarette butt, dog-end (sl), fag end (sl); cigarillo, corona, high-tar, low-tar, panatella, plug, snuff, flake tobacco, pipe tobacco, shag tobacco, Turkish tobacco, Virginia tobacco, the weed (infml).

Tobacco accessories include: ashtray, cigar box, cigar case, cigar cutter, cigar-holder, cigarette box, cigarette case, cigarette-holder, cigarette lighter, gas lighter, petrol lighter, cigarette machine, cigarette paper, cigarette roller, humidor, match, matchbook, box of matches, match striker, pipe, chibouk, church-warden, clay pipe, hookah, meerschaum, narghile, peace pipe

(pipe of peace), tobacco pipe, pipe-cleaner, pipe-rack, pipe-rest, smoker's companion, snuffbox, tobacco-pouch, vesta.

to-do n commotion, fuss, furore, bother, disturbance, flurry, stir, tumult, turmoil, uproar, unrest, excitement, bustle, agitation, rumpus, ruction, quarrel, performance (*infml*), brouhaha (*infml*), flap (*infml*), hoo-ha (*infml*), stew (*infml*).

together adv jointly, in concert, side by side, shoulder to shoulder, in unison, as one, simultaneously, at the same time, all at once, collectively, en masse, closely, continuously, consecutively, successively, in succession, in a row, hand in hand.
Ea separately, individually, alone.

toil n labour, hard work, donkey-work, drudgery, sweat, graft (*infml*), industry, application, effort, exertion, elbow grease (*infml*).
➤ v labour, work, slave, drudge, sweat, grind, slog, graft (*infml*), plug away (*infml*), persevere, strive, struggle.

toilet n lavatory, WC, loo (*infml*), bog (*sl*), bathroom, cloakroom, washroom, rest room, public convenience, Ladies (*infml*), Gents (*infml*), urinal, convenience, powder room.

token n 1 SYMBOL, emblem, representation, mark, sign, indication, manifestation, demonstration, expression, evidence, proof, clue, warning, reminder, memorial, memento, souvenir, keepsake. 2 *gift token*: voucher, coupon, counter, disc.
➤ adj symbolic, emblematic, nominal, minimal, perfunctory, superficial, cosmetic, hollow, insincere.

tolerable adj bearable, endurable, sufferable, acceptable, passable, adequate, reasonable, fair, average, all right, OK (*infml*), not bad (*infml*), mediocre, indifferent, so-so (*infml*), unexceptional, ordinary, run-of-the-mill (*infml*).
Ea intolerable, unbearable, insufferable.

tolerance n 1 TOLERATION, patience, forbearance, open-mindedness, broad-mindedness, magnanimity, sympathy, understanding, lenity, indulgence, permissiveness. 2 VARIATION, fluctuation, play, allowance, clearance. 3 RESISTANCE, resilience, toughness, endurance, stamina.
Ea 1 intolerance, prejudice, bigotry, narrow-mindedness.

tolerant adj patient, forbearing, long-suffering, open-minded, fair, unprejudiced, broad-minded, liberal, charitable, kind-hearted, sympathetic, understanding, forgiving, lenient, indulgent, easy-going (*infml*), permissive, lax, soft.
Ea intolerant, biased, prejudiced, bigoted, unsympathetic.

tolerate v endure, suffer, put up with, bear, stand, abide, stomach, swallow, take, receive, accept, admit, allow, permit, condone, countenance, indulge.

toll¹ v ring, peal, chime, knell, sound, strike, announce, call.

toll² n charge, fee, payment, levy, tax, duty, tariff, rate, cost, penalty, demand, loss.

tomb n grave, burial-place, vault, crypt, sepulchre, catacomb, mausoleum, cenotaph.

tone n 1 *tone of voice*: note, timbre, pitch, volume, intonation, modulation, inflection, accent, stress, emphasis, force, strength. 2 TINT, tinge, colour, hue, shade, cast, tonality. 3 AIR, manner, attitude, mood, spirit, humour, temper, character, quality, feel, style, effect, vein, tenor, drift.
➤ v match, co-ordinate, blend, harmonize.
◆ **tone down** moderate, temper, subdue, restrain, soften, dim, dampen, play down, reduce, alleviate, assuage, mitigate.
◆ **tone up** shape up, touch up, trim, tune up, sharpen up, limber up, freshen, invigorate, brighten.

tongue n language, speech, discourse, talk, utterance, articulation, parlance, vernacular, idiom, dialect, patois.

tongue-tied adj speechless, dumbstruck, inarticulate, silent, mute, dumb, voiceless.
Ea talkative, garrulous, voluble.

tonic n cordial, pick-me-up (*infml*), restorative, refresher, bracer, stimulant, shot in the arm (*infml*), boost, fillip.

too adv 1 ALSO, as well, in addition, besides, moreover, likewise. 2 EXCESSIVELY, inordinately, unduly, over, overly, unreasonably, ridiculously, extremely, very.

tool n 1 IMPLEMENT, instrument, utensil, gadget, device, contrivance, contraption, apparatus, appliance, machine, means, vehicle, medium, agency, agent, intermediary. 2 PUPPET, pawn, dupe, stooge, minion, hireling.

Types of tool include: axe, bolster, caulking-iron, crowbar, hod, jackhammer, jointer, mattock, pick, pick-axe, plumb-line, sledgehammer; chaser, clamp, dividers, dolly, drill, hacksaw, jack, pincers, pliers, protractor, punch, rule, sander, scriber, snips, socket-wrench, soldering-iron, spraygun, tommy bar, vice, wrench; auger, awl, bevel, brace and bit, bradawl, chisel, file, fretsaw, hammer, handsaw, jack-plane, jig-saw, level, mallet, plane, rasp, saw, screwdriver, set-square, spirit level, tenon-saw, T-square; billhook, chainsaw, chopper, dibber, fork, grass-rake, hay fork, hoe, pitchfork, plough, pruning-knife, pruning-shears, rake, scythe, secateurs, shears, shovel, sickle, spade, thresher, trowel; needle, scissors, pinking-shears, bodkin, crochet hook, forceps, scalpel, tweezers, tongs, cleaver, steel, gimlet, mace, mortar, pestle, paper-cutter, paper-knife, stapler, pocket-knife, penknife.

tooth *n* cog, denticle, denticulation, dentil, fang, incisor, jag, masticator, molar, prong, tush, tusk.

Types of tooth include: baby tooth, back tooth, bicuspid, bucktooth, canine, carnassial, dog-tooth, eye tooth, fang, first tooth, gold tooth, grinder, incisor, central incisor, lateral incisor, milk tooth, molar, first molar, second molar, third molar, premolar, first premolar, second premolar, snaggletooth, tush, tusk, wisdom tooth; false teeth, false teeth, bridge, cap, crown, denture, dentures, plate.

top *n* **1** HEAD, tip, vertex, apex, crest, crown, peak, pinnacle, summit, acme, zenith, culmination, height. **2** LID, cap, cover, cork, stopper.
ɛ **1** bottom, base, nadir.
➤ *adj* highest, topmost, upmost, uppermost, upper, superior, head, chief, leading, first, foremost, principal, sovereign, ruling, pre-eminent, dominant, prime, paramount, greatest, maximum, best, finest, supreme, crowning, culminating.
ɛ bottom, lowest, inferior.
➤ *v* **1** TIP, cap, crown, cover, finish (off), decorate, garnish. **2** BEAT, exceed, outstrip, better, excel, best, surpass, eclipse, outshine, outdo, surmount, transcend. **3** HEAD, lead, rule, command.
◆ **top up** refill, recharge, reload, add to, supplement, increase, boost, replenish (*fml*), augment (*fml*).

topic *n* subject, theme, issue, question, matter, point, thesis, text.

topical *adj* current, contemporary, up-to-date, up-to-the-minute, recent, newsworthy, relevant, popular, familiar.

topple *v* totter, overbalance, tumble, fall, collapse, upset, overturn, capsize, overthrow, oust.

topsy-turvy *adj* confused, in confusion, jumbled, chaotic, inside out, upside down, disorganized, disarranged, disorderly, in disorder, untidy, mixed-up, messy.
ɛ ordered, tidy.

torment *v* tease, provoke, annoy, vex, trouble, worry, harass, hound, pester, bother, bedevil, plague, afflict, distress, harrow, pain, torture, persecute.
➤ *n* provocation, annoyance, vexation, bane, scourge, trouble, bother, nuisance, harassment, worry, anguish, distress, misery, affliction, suffering, pain, agony, ordeal, torture, persecution.

torn *adj* **1** CUT, ragged, ripped, slit, split, rent, lacerated. **2** DIVIDED, uncertain, undecided, unsure, irresolute, vacillating, wavering, dithering.

tornado *n* storm, cyclone, gale, hurricane, whirlwind, typhoon, monsoon, tempest, squall, twister (*infml*).

torrent *n* stream, volley, outburst, gush, rush, flood, spate, deluge, cascade, downpour.
ɛ trickle.

torrid *adj* **1** HOT, blazing, sweltering, blistering, boiling, sizzling, scorching, tropical, stifling, arid, parched, scorched, waterless, desert. **2** PASSIONATE, erotic, red-hot, sexy, amorous, steamy (*infml*).

tortuous *adj* twisting, winding, meandering, serpentine, zigzag, circuitous, roundabout, indirect, convoluted, complicated, involved.
ɛ straight, straightforward.

torture *v* pain, agonize, excruciate, crucify, rack, martyr, persecute, torment, afflict, distress.
➤ *n* pain, agony, suffering, affliction, distress, misery, anguish, torment, martyrdom, persecution.

toss *v* **1** FLIP, cast, fling, throw, chuck (*infml*), sling, hurl, lob. **2** ROLL, heave, pitch, lurch, jolt, shake, agitate, rock, thrash, squirm, wriggle.
➤ *n* flip, cast, fling, throw, pitch.

tot *n* **1** TODDLER, child, infant, mite, baby, bairn (*Scot*). **2** DRAM, measure, nip, shot, slug, finger.

total *n* sum, whole, entirety, totality, all, lot, mass, aggregate (*fml*), amount.
➤ *adj* full, complete, entire, whole, integral, all-out, utter, absolute, unconditional, unqualified, outright, undisputed, perfect, consummate, thoroughgoing, sheer, downright, thorough.
◪ partial, limited, restricted.
➤ *v* add (up), sum (up), tot (up), count (up), reckon, amount to, come to, reach.

totalitarian *adj* authoritarian, one-party, despotic, dictatorial, oppressive, tyrannous, monolithic, undemocratic, omnipotent (*fml*).
◪ democratic.

totality *n* total, sum, whole, wholeness, entirety, entireness, everything, fullness, completeness, all, cosmos, universe, aggregate (*fml*), pleroma (*fml*).

totally *adv* completely, fully, wholly, entirely, perfectly, utterly, quite, thoroughly, wholeheartedly, absolutely, unconditionally, comprehensively, undividedly, undisputedly, consummately (*fml*).
◪ partially.

totter *v* stagger, reel, lurch, stumble, falter, waver, teeter, sway, rock, shake, quiver, tremble.

touch *n* **1** FEEL, texture, brush, stroke, caress, pat, tap, contact. **2** *a touch of garlic*: trace, spot, dash, pinch, soupçon, suspicion, hint, suggestion, speck, jot, tinge, smack. **3** SKILL, art, knack, flair, style, method, manner, technique, approach.
➤ *v* **1** FEEL, handle, finger, brush, graze, stroke, caress, fondle, pat, tap, hit, strike, contact, meet, abut, adjoin, border.
2 MOVE, stir, upset, disturb, impress, inspire, influence, affect, concern, regard.
3 REACH, attain, equal, match, rival, better.
◆ **touch off** spark off, trigger (off), begin, cause, set off, initiate, provoke, foment, fire, ignite, inflame, light, arouse, actuate (*fml*).
◆ **touch on** mention, broach, speak of, remark on, refer to, allude to, cover, deal with.
◆ **touch up** renovate, improve, brush up,
retouch, revamp, enhance, finish off, round off, patch up, perfect, polish up.

touched *adj* **1** MOVED, stirred, affected, disturbed, impressed. **2** MAD, crazy (*infml*), deranged, disturbed, eccentric, dotty (*infml*), daft (*infml*), barmy (*infml*).

touching *adj* moving, stirring, affecting, poignant, pitiable, pitiful, pathetic, sad, emotional, tender.

touchy *adj* irritable, irascible, quick-tempered, bad-tempered, grumpy, grouchy, crabbed, cross, peevish, captious, edgy, over-sensitive.
◪ calm, imperturbable.

tough *adj* **1** STRONG, durable, resilient, resistant, hardy, sturdy, solid, rigid, stiff, inflexible, hard, leathery. **2** *tough criminal*: rough, violent, vicious, callous, hardened, obstinate. **3** HARSH, severe, strict, stern, firm, resolute, determined, tenacious.
4 ARDUOUS, laborious, exacting, hard, difficult, puzzling, perplexing, baffling, knotty, thorny, troublesome.
◪ **1** fragile, delicate, weak, tender. **2** gentle, soft. **3** gentle. **4** easy, simple.
➤ *n* brute, thug, bully, ruffian, hooligan, lout, yob (*sl*).

tour *n* circuit, round, visit, expedition, journey, trip, outing, excursion, drive, ride, course.
➤ *v* visit, go round, sightsee, explore, travel, journey, drive, ride.

tourist *n* holidaymaker, visitor, sightseer, tripper, excursionist, traveller, voyager, globetrotter.

tournament *n* championship, series, competition, contest, match, event, meeting.

tousled *adj* dishevelled, ruffled, messed up, disordered, disarranged, tangled, rumpled, tumbled.

tout *v* **1** SELL, hawk, peddle, trade. **2** ADVERTISE, promote, market, solicit, petition, ask, appeal, seek, plug (*infml*), hype (*infml*), push (*infml*).

tow *v* pull, tug, draw, trail, drag, lug, haul, transport.

towards *prep* **1** TO, approaching, nearing, close to, nearly, almost. **2** *his feelings towards her*: regarding, with regard to, with respect to, concerning, about, for.

tower *n* steeple, spire, belfry, turret, fortification, bastion, citadel, fort, fortress, castle, keep.

➤ *v* rise, rear, ascend, mount, soar, loom, overlook, dominate, surpass, transcend, exceed, top.

Types of tower and famous towers include: barbican, bastille, bastion, belfry, bell tower, belvedere, campanile, castle, church tower, citadel, column, demi-bastion, donjon, Eiffel Tower, fort, fortification, fortress, gate-tower, high-rise building, hill-fort, keep, lookout tower, martello tower, minar, minaret, mirador, pagoda, peel-tower, scaffold tower, skyscraper, smock mill, spire, steeple, tower block, tower mill, Tower of London, Tower of Pisa, turret, watchtower, water tower.

---

towering *adj* soaring, tall, high, lofty, elevated, monumental, colossal, gigantic, great, magnificent, imposing, impressive, sublime, supreme, surpassing, overpowering, extreme, inordinate.
⊟ small, tiny, minor, trivial.

town *n* borough, village, municipality, burgh, market town, county town, new town, city, suburbs, outskirts, conurbation, metropolis, urban district, settlement, township, pueblo.
⊟ country.

toxic *adj* poisonous, harmful, noxious, unhealthy, dangerous, deadly, lethal.
⊟ harmless, safe.

toy *n* plaything, knick-knack, trinket, trifle, bauble.

Kinds of toy include: Action Man®, activity centre, aeroplane, baby-bouncer, baby-walker, ball, balloon; bicycle, bike (*infml*), mountain bike; blackboard and easel, boxing-gloves, building-block, building-brick, catapult, climbing-frame, computer game, crayon; doll, Barbie doll®, kewpie doll, rag-doll, Sindy doll®, Tiny-Tears doll®, doll's buggy, doll's cot, doll's house, doll's pram; drum set, electronic game, executive toy, farm, fivestones, football, fort, Frisbee®, game, garage, glove puppet, go-kart, golliwog, guitar, gun, cap-gun, pop-gun, gyroscope, hobby-horse, hula-hoop, jack-in-the-box, jigsaw puzzle, kaleidoscope, kite, box-kite, Lego®, marble, Matchbox®, Meccano®, model car, model kit, model railway, modelling clay, musical box, ocarina, paddling-pool, paints, pantograph, pedal-car, peashooter, Plasticene®, Play-Doh®, playhouse, pogo stick, Power Rangers®, puzzle, rattle, rocker, rocking-horse, Rubik's Cube®, sandpit, Scalextric®, scooter, seesaw, sewing machine, shape-sorter, skateboard, skipping-rope, slide, soft-toy, spacehopper, Space Invaders®, spinning top, Subbuteo®, swing, swingball, teaset, teddy-bear, toy soldier, train set, trampoline, tricycle, trike (*infml*), Turtles®, typewriter; video game, Game Boy®, Dreamcast®, Nintendo®, Sega®, Super Mario®; walkie-talkie (*infml*), water pistol, Wendy house, yo-yo. *see also* **game**.

---

trace *n* trail, track, spoor, footprint, footmark, mark, token, sign, indication, evidence, record, relic, remains, remnant, vestige, shadow, hint, suggestion, suspicion, soupçon, dash, drop, spot, bit, jot, touch, tinge, smack.
➤ *v* **1** COPY, draw, sketch, outline, delineate, depict, mark, record, map, chart. **2** FIND, discover, detect, unearth, track (down), trail, stalk, hunt, seek, follow, pursue, shadow.

track *n* footstep, footprint, footmark, scent, spoor, trail, wake, mark, trace, slot, groove, rail, path, way, route, orbit, line, course, drift, sequence.
➤ *v* stalk, trail, hunt, trace, follow, pursue, chase, dog, tail, shadow.
♦ **track down** find, discover, trace, hunt down, run to earth, sniff out, ferret out, dig up, unearth, expose, catch, capture.

tract *n* stretch, extent, expanse, plot, lot, territory, area, region, zone, district, quarter.

trade *n* **1** COMMERCE, traffic, business, dealing, buying, selling, shopkeeping, barter, exchange, transactions, custom. **2** OCCUPATION, job, business, profession, calling, craft, skill.
➤ *v* traffic, peddle, do business, deal, transact, buy, sell, barter, exchange, swap, switch, bargain.

trademark *n* brand, label, name, sign, symbol, logo, insignia, crest, emblem, badge, hallmark.

trader *n* merchant, tradesman, broker, dealer, buyer, seller, vendor, supplier, wholesaler, retailer, shopkeeper, trafficker, peddler.

tradesman, tradeswoman *n*
1 SHOPKEEPER, retailer, buyer, seller, merchant, dealer, vendor. **2** ARTISAN, craftsman, craftswoman, worker, mechanic, journeyman.

tradition n convention, custom, usage, way, habit, routine, ritual, institution, folklore.

traditional adj conventional, customary, habitual, usual, accustomed, established, fixed, long-established, time-honoured, old, historic, folk, oral, unwritten.
ɛ unconventional, innovative, new, modern, contemporary.

traffic n **1** VEHICLES, shipping, transport, transportation, freight, passengers. **2** TRADE, commerce, business, dealing, trafficking, barter, exchange. **3** COMMUNICATION, dealings, relations.
➤ v peddle, buy, sell, trade, do business, deal, bargain, barter, exchange.

tragedy n adversity, misfortune, unhappiness, affliction, blow, calamity, disaster, catastrophe.

tragic adj sad, sorrowful, miserable, unhappy, unfortunate, unlucky, ill-fated, pitiable, pathetic, heartbreaking, shocking, appalling, dreadful, awful, dire, calamitous, disastrous, catastrophic, deadly, fatal.
ɛ happy, comic, successful.

trail v **1** DRAG, pull, tow, droop, dangle, extend, stream, straggle, dawdle, lag, loiter, linger. **2** TRACK, stalk, hunt, follow, pursue, chase, shadow, tail.
➤ n track, footprints, footmarks, scent, trace, path, footpath, road, route, way.

train v **1** TEACH, instruct, coach, tutor, educate, improve, school, discipline, prepare, drill, exercise, work out, practise, rehearse. **2** POINT, direct, aim, level.
➤ n **1** *train of events*: sequence, succession, series, progression, order, string, chain, line, file, procession, convoy, cortège, caravan. **2** RETINUE, entourage, attendants, court, household, staff, followers, following.

trainer n teacher, instructor, coach, tutor, handler.

training n teaching, instruction, coaching, tuition, education, schooling, discipline, preparation, grounding, drill, exercise, working-out, practice, learning, apprenticeship.

traipse v trudge, tramp, plod, slouch, trail.
➤ n trudge, trek, slog, plod, tramp.

trait n feature, attribute, quality, characteristic, idiosyncrasy, peculiarity, quirk.

traitor n betrayer, informer, deceiver, double-crosser, turncoat, renegade, deserter, defector, quisling, collaborator.
ɛ loyalist, supporter, defender.

trajectory n line, orbit, path, route, flight, flight path, course, track, trail.

tramp v walk, march, tread, stamp, stomp, stump, plod, trudge, traipse, trail, trek, hike, ramble, roam, rove.
➤ n vagrant, vagabond, hobo, down-and-out, dosser (sl).

trample v tread, stamp, crush, squash, flatten.

trance n dream, reverie, daze, stupor, unconsciousness, spell, ecstasy, rapture.

tranquil adj calm, composed, cool, imperturbable, unexcited, placid, sedate, relaxed, laid-back (infml), serene, peaceful, restful, still, undisturbed, untroubled, quiet, hushed, silent.
ɛ agitated, disturbed, troubled, noisy.

tranquillize v calm, quiet, pacify, relax, sedate, soothe, quell, lull, compose, narcotize (fml).
ɛ disturb, agitate, upset.

tranquillizer n sedative, opiate, narcotic, barbiturate.

transact v carry out, conduct, do, perform, settle, handle, manage, carry on, accomplish, negotiate, conclude, dispatch, discharge, enact, execute, prosecute (fml).

transaction n deal, bargain, agreement, arrangement, negotiation, business, affair, matter, proceeding, enterprise, undertaking, deed, action, execution, discharge.

transcend v surpass, excel, outshine, eclipse, outdo, outstrip, beat, surmount, exceed, overstep.

transcribe v write out, copy, reproduce, rewrite, transliterate, translate, render, take down, note, record.

transcript n transcription, copy, reproduction, duplicate, transliteration, translation, version, note, record, manuscript.

transfer v change, transpose, move, shift, remove, relocate, transplant, transport, carry, convey, transmit, consign, grant, hand over.
➤ n change, changeover, transposition, move, shift, removal, relocation, displacement, transmission, handover, transference.

transfix v **1** FASCINATE, spellbind,

mesmerize, hypnotize, paralyse. **2** IMPALE, spear, skewer, spike, stick.

transform *v* change, alter, adapt, convert, remodel, reconstruct, transfigure, revolutionize.
☒ preserve, maintain.

transformation *n* change, alteration, mutation, conversion, metamorphosis, transfiguration, revolution.
☒ preservation, conservation.

transfuse *v* transfer, imbue, pervade, instil, permeate, suffuse.

transient *adj* transitory, passing, flying, fleeting, brief, short, momentary, ephemeral, short-lived, temporary, short-term.
☒ lasting, permanent.

transit *n* passage, journey, travel, movement, transfer, transportation, conveyance, carriage, haulage, shipment.

transition *n* passage, passing, progress, progression, development, evolution, flux, change, alteration, conversion, transformation, shift.

transitional *adj* provisional, temporary, passing, intermediate, developmental, changing, fluid, unsettled.
☒ initial, final.

transitory *adj* transient, passing, flying, fleeting, brief, short, momentary, short-lived, temporary, short-term, impermanent, ephemeral.
☒ lasting, permanent.

translate *v* interpret, render, paraphrase, simplify, decode, decipher, transliterate, transcribe, change, alter, convert, transform, improve.

translation *n* rendering, version, interpretation, gloss, crib, rewording, rephrasing, paraphrase, simplification, transliteration, transcription, change, alteration, conversion, transformation.

translator *n* linguist, polyglot, paraphraser, interpreter, glosser.

transmission *n* **1** BROADCASTING, diffusion, spread, communication, conveyance, carriage, transport, shipment, sending, dispatch, relaying, transfer. **2** *a live transmission*: broadcast, programme, show, signal.
☒ **1** reception.

transmit *v* communicate, impart, convey, carry, bear, transport, send, dispatch, forward, relay, transfer, broadcast, radio,

disseminate, network, diffuse, spread.
☒ receive.

transparency *n* slide, photograph, picture.

transparent *adj* **1** *transparent plastic*: clear, see-through, translucent, sheer. **2** PLAIN, distinct, clear, lucid, explicit, unambiguous, unequivocal, apparent, visible, obvious, evident, manifest, patent, undisguised, open, candid, straightforward.
☒ **1** opaque. **2** unclear, ambiguous.

transpire *v* **1** BECOME KNOWN, turn out, come to light, come out, be disclosed, become apparent, appear, prove. **2** HAPPEN, occur, take place, ensue, arise, come about, come to pass, befall (*fml*).

transplant *v* move, shift, displace, remove, uproot, transfer, relocate, resettle, repot.
☒ leave.

transport *v* convey, carry, bear, take, fetch, bring, move, shift, transfer, ship, haul, remove, deport.
➤ *n* conveyance, carriage, transfer, transportation, shipment, shipping, haulage, removal.

transpose *v* swap, exchange, switch, interchange, transfer, shift, rearrange, reorder, change, alter, move, substitute.

transverse *adj* cross, crosswise, transversal, diagonal, oblique.

trap *n* snare, net, noose, springe, gin, booby-trap, pitfall, danger, hazard, ambush, trick, wile, ruse, stratagem, device, trickery, artifice, deception.
➤ *v* snare, net, entrap, ensnare, enmesh, catch, take, ambush, corner, trick, deceive, dupe.

trapped *adj* caught, beguiled, cornered, ensnared, ambushed, snared, stuck, netted, surrounded, tricked, deceived, duped, inveigled (*fml*).
☒ free.

trappings *n* ornaments, accompaniments, clothes, adornments, dress, decorations, fripperies, equipment, paraphernalia, fixtures, fittings, furnishings, housings, finery, livery, gear, trimmings, accoutrements (*fml*), panoply (*fml*), raiment (*fml*), things (*infml*).

trash *n* rubbish, garbage, refuse, junk, waste, litter, sweepings, offscouring(s), scum, dregs.

trauma *n* injury, wound, hurt, damage, pain, suffering, anguish, agony, torture, ordeal, shock, jolt, upset, disturbance, upheaval, strain, stress.
🔁 healing.

traumatic *adj* painful, hurtful, injurious, wounding, shocking, upsetting, distressing, disturbing, unpleasant, frightening, stressful.
🔁 healing, relaxing.

travel *v* journey, voyage, go, wend, move, proceed, progress, wander, ramble, roam, rove, tour, cross, traverse.
🔁 stay, remain.
➤ *n* travelling, touring, tourism, globetrotting.

Methods of travel include: fly, aviate, pilot, shuttle, sail, cruise, punt, paddle, row, steam, ride, cycle, bike (*infml*), freewheel, drive, motor, bus, walk, hike, march, ramble, trek, orienteer, hitch-hike, commute.

Forms of travel include: flight, cruise, sail, voyage, ride, drive, march, walk, hike, ramble, excursion, holiday, jaunt, outing, tour, trip, visit, expedition, safari, trek, circumnavigation, exploration, journey, migration, mission, pilgrimage.

traveller *n* **1** TOURIST, explorer, voyager, globetrotter, holidaymaker, tripper (*infml*), excursionist, passenger, commuter, wanderer, rambler, hiker, wayfarer, migrant, nomad, gypsy, itinerant, tinker, vagrant. **2** SALESMAN, saleswoman, representative, rep (*infml*), agent.

travelling *adj* touring, wandering, roaming, roving, wayfaring, migrant, migratory, nomadic, itinerant, peripatetic, mobile, moving, vagrant, homeless.
🔁 fixed.

travels *n* voyage, expedition, passage, journey, trip, excursion, tour, wanderings.

travesty *n* mockery, parody, take-off, send-up (*infml*), farce, caricature, distortion, sham, apology.

treacherous *adj* **1** TRAITOROUS, disloyal, unfaithful, faithless, unreliable, untrustworthy, false, untrue, deceitful, double-crossing. **2** *treacherous roads*: dangerous, hazardous, risky, perilous, precarious, icy, slippery.
🔁 **1** loyal, faithful, dependable. **2** safe, stable.

treachery *n* treason, betrayal, disloyalty, infidelity, falseness, duplicity, double-dealing.
🔁 loyalty, dependability.

tread *v* walk, step, pace, stride, march, tramp, trudge, plod, stamp, trample, walk on, press, crush, squash.
➤ *n* walk, footfall, footstep, step, pace, stride.

treason *n* treachery, perfidy, disloyalty, duplicity, subversion, sedition, mutiny, rebellion.
🔁 loyalty.

treasonable *adj* traitorous, perfidious, disloyal, false, subversive, seditious, mutinous.
🔁 loyal.

treasure *n* fortune, wealth, riches, money, cash, gold, jewels, hoard, cache.
➤ *v* prize, value, esteem (*fml*), revere, worship, love, adore, idolize, cherish, preserve, guard.
🔁 disparage, belittle.

treasury *n* bank, exchequer, repository, resources, revenues, finances, capital, money, funds, assets, coffers, cache, hoard, vault, store, storehouse, thesaurus, corpus.

treat *n* indulgence, gratification, pleasure, delight, enjoyment, fun, entertainment, excursion, outing, party, celebration, feast, banquet, gift, surprise, thrill.
➤ *v* **1** DEAL WITH, manage, handle, use, regard, consider, discuss, cover. **2** TEND, nurse, minister to, attend to, care for, heal, cure. **3** PAY FOR, buy, stand, give, provide, entertain, regale, feast.

treatise *n* essay, dissertation, thesis, monograph, paper, pamphlet, tract, study, exposition.

treatment *n* **1** HEALING, cure, remedy, medication, therapy, surgery, care, nursing. **2** MANAGEMENT, handling, use, usage, conduct, discussion, coverage.

treaty *n* pact, convention, agreement, covenant, compact, negotiation, contract, bond, alliance.

tree *n* bush, shrub, evergreen, conifer.

Trees include: acacia, acer, alder, almond, apple, ash, aspen, balsa, bay, beech, birch, blackthorn, blue gum, box, cedar, cherry, chestnut, coconut palm, cottonwood, cypress, date palm, dogwood, Dutch elm, ebony, elder, elm, eucalyptus, fig, fir, gum, hawthorn, hazel, hickory, hornbeam, horse chestnut, Japanese maple, larch, laurel, lime, linden, mahogany, maple, monkey puzzle, mountain ash, oak, palm, pear, pine, plane, plum, poplar, prunus, pussy willow, redwood, rowan, rubber tree, sandalwood, sapele, sequoia, silver birch, silver maple, spruce, sycamore, teak, walnut, weeping willow, whitebeam, willow, witch hazel, yew, yucca; bonsai, conifer, deciduous, evergreen, fruit, hardwood, ornamental, palm, softwood.

trek *n* hike, walk, march, tramp, journey, expedition, safari.
➤ *v* hike, walk, march, tramp, trudge, plod, journey, rove, roam.

tremble *v* shake, vibrate, quake, shiver, shudder, quiver, wobble, rock.
➤ *n* shake, vibration, quake, shiver, shudder, quiver, tremor, wobble.
🖪 steadiness.

tremendous *adj* wonderful, marvellous, stupendous, sensational, spectacular, extraordinary, amazing, incredible, terrific (*infml*), impressive, huge, immense, vast, colossal, gigantic, towering, formidable.
🖪 ordinary, unimpressive.

tremor *n* shake, quiver, tremble, shiver, quake, quaver, wobble, vibration, agitation, thrill, shock, earthquake.
🖪 steadiness.

trench *n* ditch, channel, excavation, trough, waterway, earthwork, furrow, gutter, pit, cut, drain, rill, sap, entrenchment, fosse.

trenchant *adj* 1 INCISIVE, pungent, caustic, biting, scathing, acerbic, penetrating, acute, astute, sharp, clear, perceptive, effective, clear-cut, mordant (*fml*), perspicacious (*fml*). 2 FORTHRIGHT, vigorous, forceful, emphatic, blunt, terse, unequivocal, no-nonsense (*infml*).
🖪 woolly.

trend *n* course, flow, drift, tendency, inclination, leaning, craze, rage (*infml*), fashion, vogue, mode, style, look.

trendy *adj* fashionable, latest, modish, stylish, up to the minute, voguish, all the rage (*infml*), natty (*infml*), hip (*infml*), cool (*infml*), funky (*infml*), in (*infml*), groovy (*infml*), with it (*infml*).
🖪 unfashionable.

trepidation *n* fear, apprehension, alarm, dread, anxiety, worry, unease, qualms,

disquiet, misgivings, dismay, uneasiness, excitement, emotion, trembling, nervousness, shaking, agitation, quivering, tremor, palpitation, fright, consternation (*fml*), perturbation (*fml*), butterflies (*infml*), cold sweat (*infml*), jitters (*infml*), nerves (*infml*).
🖪 calm.

trespass *v* invade, intrude, encroach, poach, infringe, violate, offend, wrong.
🖪 obey, keep to.
➤ *n* invasion, intrusion, encroachment, poaching, infringement, violation, contravention, offence, misdemeanour.

trespasser *n* intruder, poacher, offender, criminal.

trial *n* 1 LITIGATION, lawsuit, hearing, inquiry, tribunal. 2 EXPERIMENT, test, examination, check, dry run, dummy run, practice, rehearsal, audition, contest. 3 AFFLICTION (*fml*), suffering, grief, misery, distress, adversity, hardship, ordeal, trouble, nuisance, vexation, tribulation (*fml*).
🖪 3 relief, happiness.
➤ *adj* experimental, test, pilot, exploratory, provisional, probationary.

triangle

Types of triangle include: acute-angled, congruent, equilateral, isosceles, obtuse-angled, right-angled, scalene, similar.

tribe *n* race, nation, people, clan, family, house, dynasty, blood, stock, group, caste, class, division, branch.

tribulation *n* suffering, grief, pain, sorrow, vexation, ordeal, misery, unhappiness, misfortune, wretchedness, worry, care, woe, burden, blow, distress, heartache, trial, reverse, adversity, hardship, trouble, curse, affliction (*fml*), travail (*fml*).
🖪 happiness, rest.

tribunal *n* court, committee, hearing, examination, inquisition, trial, bar, bench.

tribute *n* 1 PRAISE, commendation, compliment, accolade, homage, respect, honour, credit, acknowledgement, recognition, gratitude. 2 PAYMENT, levy, charge, tax, duty, gift, offering, contribution.

trick *n* fraud, swindle, deception, deceit, artifice, illusion, hoax, practical joke, joke, leg-pull (*infml*), prank, antic, caper, frolic, feat, stunt, ruse, wile, dodge (*infml*),

subterfuge, trap, device, knack, technique, secret.
➤ *adj* false, mock, artificial, imitation, ersatz, fake, forged, counterfeit, feigned, sham, bogus.
🔁 real, genuine.
➤ *v* deceive, delude, dupe, fool, hoodwink, beguile, mislead, bluff, hoax, pull someone's leg (*infml*), cheat, swindle, diddle, defraud, con (*infml*), trap, outwit.

trickery *n* deception, illusion, sleight-of-hand, pretence, artifice, guile, deceit, dishonesty, cheating, swindling, fraud, imposture, double-dealing, monkey business, funny business (*sl*), chicanery, skulduggery, hocus-pocus.
🔁 straightforwardness, honesty.

trickle *v* dribble, run, leak, seep, ooze, exude, drip, drop, filter, percolate.
🔁 stream, gush.
➤ *n* dribble, drip, drop, leak, seepage.
🔁 stream, gush.

tricky *adj* 1 *a tricky problem*: difficult, awkward, problematic, complicated, knotty, thorny, delicate, ticklish. 2 CRAFTY, artful, cunning, sly, wily, foxy, subtle, devious, slippery, scheming, deceitful.
🔁 1 easy, simple. 2 honest.

trifle *n* 1 LITTLE, bit, spot, drop, dash, touch, trace. 2 TOY, plaything, trinket, bauble, knick-knack, triviality, nothing.
➤ *v* toy, play, sport, flirt, dally, dabble, fiddle, meddle, fool.

trifling *adj* small, paltry, slight, negligible, inconsiderable, unimportant, insignificant, minor, trivial, petty, silly, frivolous, idle, empty, worthless.
🔁 important, significant, serious.

trigger *v* cause, start, initiate, activate, set off, spark off, provoke, prompt, elicit, generate, produce.
➤ *n* lever, catch, switch, spur, stimulus.

trim *adj* 1 NEAT, tidy, orderly, shipshape, spick-and-span, spruce, smart, dapper. 2 SLIM, slender, streamlined, compact.
🔁 1 untidy, scruffy.
➤ *v* 1 CUT, clip, crop, dock, prune, pare, shave. 2 DECORATE, ornament, embellish, garnish, dress, array, adjust, arrange, order, neaten, tidy.
➤ *n* condition, state, order, form, shape, fitness, health.

trimmings *n* 1 GARNISH, decorations, ornaments, frills, extras, accessories. 2 CUTTINGS, clippings, parings, ends.

trinket *n* bauble, jewel, ornament, knick-knack.

trio *n* threesome, triad, triumvirate, trinity, triplet, trilogy.

trip *n* outing, excursion, tour, jaunt, ride, drive, spin, journey, voyage, expedition, foray.
➤ *v* stumble, slip, fall, tumble, stagger, totter, blunder.

triple *adj* treble, triplicate, threefold, three-ply, three-way.
➤ *v* treble, triplicate.

trite *adj* banal, commonplace, ordinary, run-of-the-mill, stale, tired, worn, threadbare, unoriginal, hackneyed, overused, stock, stereotyped, clichéd, corny (*infml*).
🔁 original, new, fresh.

triumph *n* 1 WIN, victory, conquest, walk-over, success, achievement, accomplishment, feat, coup, masterstroke, hit, sensation. 2 EXULTATION, jubilation, rejoicing, celebration, elation, joy, happiness.
🔁 1 failure.
➤ *v* win, succeed, prosper, conquer, vanquish, overcome, overwhelm, prevail, dominate, celebrate, rejoice, glory, gloat.
🔁 lose, fail.

triumphant *adj* winning, victorious, conquering, successful, exultant, jubilant, rejoicing, celebratory, glorious, elated, joyful, proud, boastful, gloating, swaggering.
🔁 defeated, humble.

trivia *n* details, trifles, trivialities, irrelevancies, minutiae, pap (*infml*).
🔁 essentials.

trivial *adj* unimportant, insignificant, inconsequential, incidental, minor, petty, paltry, trifling, small, little, inconsiderable, negligible, worthless, meaningless, frivolous, banal, trite, commonplace, everyday.
🔁 important, significant, profound.

triviality *n* unimportance, insignificance, pettiness, smallness, worthlessness, meaninglessness, frivolity, trifle, detail, technicality.
🔁 importance, essential.

trivialize *v* minimize, play down, underestimate, underplay, undervalue, devalue, belittle, depreciate, scoff at.
🔁 exalt.

troop *n* contingent, squadron, unit,

division, company, squad, team, crew, gang, band, bunch, group, body, pack, herd, flock, horde, crowd, throng, multitude.
➤ *v* go, march, parade, stream, flock, swarm, throng.

troops *n* army, military, soldiers, servicemen, servicewomen.

trophy *n* cup, prize, award, souvenir, memento.

tropical *adj* hot, torrid, sultry, sweltering, stifling, steamy, humid.
ಶ arctic, cold, cool, temperate.

trot *v* jog, run, scamper, scuttle, scurry.
➤ *n* jog, canter, run.
◆ **trot out** bring out, bring up, drag up, relate, repeat, bring forward, exhibit, reiterate, adduce (*fml*), recite (*fml*), rehearse (*fml*).

trouble *n* **1** PROBLEM, difficulty, struggle, annoyance, irritation, bother, nuisance, inconvenience, misfortune, adversity, trial, tribulation (*fml*), pain, suffering, affliction (*fml*), distress, grief, woe, heartache, concern, uneasiness, worry, anxiety, agitation. **2** UNREST, strife, tumult, commotion, disturbance, disorder, upheaval. **3** *back trouble*: disorder, complaint, ailment, illness, disease, disability, defect. **4** EFFORT, exertion, pains, care, attention, thought.
ಶ 1 relief, calm. **2** order. **3** health.
➤ *v* annoy, vex, harass, torment, bother, inconvenience, disturb, upset, distress, sadden, pain, afflict (*fml*), burden, worry, agitate, disconcert, perplex.
ಶ reassure, help.

troublemaker *n* agitator, rabble-rouser, incendiary, instigator, ringleader, stirrer, mischief-maker.
ಶ peacemaker.

troublesome *adj* **1** ANNOYING, irritating, vexatious, irksome, bothersome, inconvenient, difficult, hard, tricky, thorny, taxing, demanding, laborious, tiresome, wearisome. **2** UNRULY, rowdy, turbulent, trying, unco-operative, insubordinate, rebellious.
ಶ 1 easy, simple. **2** helpful.

trough *n* gutter, conduit, trench, ditch, gully, channel, groove, furrow, hollow, depression.

trounce *v* defeat, rout, beat, thrash, overwhelm, paste (*infml*), punish, best, crush, wallop (*infml*), wipe the floor with (*infml*), slaughter (*infml*), hammer (*infml*),

clobber (*infml*), lick (*infml*), drub (*infml*).

troupe *n* company, group, set, band, cast, troop.

trousers *n* pants, slacks, jeans, denims, Levis®, flannels, bags (*infml*), dungarees, breeches, shorts.

truancy *n* absence, absenteeism, shirking, skiving (*infml*).
ಶ attendance.

truant *n* absentee, deserter, runaway, idler, shirker, skiver (*infml*), dodger.
➤ *adj* absent, missing, runaway.

truce *n* cease-fire, peace, armistice, cessation, moratorium, suspension, stay, respite, let-up (*infml*), lull, rest, break, interval, intermission.
ಶ war, hostilities.

truck *n* lorry, van, wagon, trailer, float, cart, barrow.

truculent *adj* aggressive, belligerent, defiant, disobedient, quarrelsome, antagonistic, contentious, hostile, violent, savage, combative, fierce, argumentative, rude, bad-tempered, ill-tempered, sullen, cross, obstreperous, discourteous, disrespectful, bellicose (*fml*), pugnacious (*fml*).
ಶ co-operative, good-natured.

trudge *v* tramp, plod, clump, stump, lumber, traipse, slog, labour, trek, hike, walk, march.
➤ *n* tramp, traipse, slog, haul, trek, hike, walk, march.

true *adj* **1** REAL, genuine, authentic, actual, veritable, exact, precise, accurate, correct, right, factual, truthful, veracious, sincere, honest, legitimate, valid, rightful, proper. **2** FAITHFUL, loyal, constant, steadfast, staunch, firm, trustworthy, trusty, honourable, dedicated, devoted.
ಶ 1 false, wrong, incorrect, inaccurate. **2** unfaithful, faithless.

truism *n* truth, platitude, commonplace, cliché.

truly *adv* very, greatly, extremely, really, genuinely, sincerely, honestly, truthfully, undeniably, indubitably, indeed, in fact, in reality, exactly, precisely, correctly, rightly, properly.
ಶ slightly, falsely, incorrectly.

trumped-up *adj* false, fabricated, fake, faked, falsified, invented, made-up, untrue, cooked-up, concocted, contrived, spurious, phoney (*infml*).

trumpet *n* bugle, horn, clarion, blare, blast, roar, bellow, cry, call.
➤ *v* blare, blast, roar, bellow, shout, proclaim, announce, broadcast, advertise.

truncate *v* shorten, abbreviate, curtail, cut, lop, dock, prune, pare, clip, trim, crop.
⊟ lengthen, extend.

truncheon *n* baton, club, cudgel, cosh, stick, staff, shillelagh, knobkerrie.

trunk *n* **1** CASE, suitcase, chest, coffer, box, crate. **2** TORSO, body, frame, shaft, stock, stem, stalk.

truss *v* tie, strap, bind, pinion, fasten, secure, bundle, pack.
⊟ untie, loosen.
➤ *n* binding, bandage, support, brace, prop, stay, shore, strut, joist.

trust *n* **1** FAITH, belief, credence, credit, hope, expectation, reliance, confidence, assurance, conviction, certainty. **2** CARE, charge, custody, safekeeping, guardianship, protection, responsibility, duty.
⊟ 1 distrust, mistrust, scepticism, doubt.
➤ *v* **1** BELIEVE, imagine, assume, presume, suppose, surmise, hope, expect, rely on, depend on, count on, bank on, swear by. **2** ENTRUST, commit, consign, confide, give, assign, delegate.
⊟ 1 distrust, mistrust, doubt, disbelieve.

trusting *adj* trustful, credulous, gullible, naïve, innocent, unquestioning, unsuspecting, unguarded, unwary.
⊟ distrustful, suspicious, cautious.

trustworthy *adj* honest, upright, honourable, principled, dependable, reliable, steadfast, true, responsible, sensible.
⊟ untrustworthy, dishonest, unreliable, irresponsible.

trusty *adj* faithful, dependable, reliable, responsible, strong, supportive, firm, honest, loyal, staunch, trustworthy, true, solid, straightforward, steady, upright.
⊟ unreliable.

truth *n* **1** TRUTHFULNESS, veracity, candour, frankness, honesty, sincerity, genuineness, authenticity, realism, exactness, precision, accuracy, validity, legitimacy, honour, integrity, uprightness, faithfulness, fidelity, loyalty, constancy. **2** *tell the truth*: facts, reality, actuality, fact, axiom, maxim, principle, truism.

⊟ 1 deceit, dishonesty, falseness. **2** lie, falsehood.

truthful *adj* veracious, frank, candid, straight, honest, sincere, true, veritable, exact, precise, accurate, correct, realistic, faithful, trustworthy, reliable.
⊟ untruthful, deceitful, false, untrue.

try *v* **1** ATTEMPT, endeavour, venture, undertake, seek, strive. **2** HEAR, judge. **3** EXPERIMENT, test, sample, taste, inspect, examine, investigate, evaluate, appraise.
➤ *n* **1** ATTEMPT, endeavour, effort, go (*infml*), bash (*infml*), crack (*infml*), shot (*infml*), stab (*infml*). **2** EXPERIMENT, test, trial, ample, taste.
◆ **try out** test, evaluate, try on, check out, inspect, sample, taste, appraise (*fml*).

trying *adj* annoying, irritating, aggravating (*infml*), vexatious, exasperating, troublesome, tiresome, wearisome, difficult, hard, tough, arduous, taxing, demanding, testing.
⊟ easy.

tub *n* bath, basin, vat, tun, butt, cask, barrel, keg.

tube *n* hose, pipe, cylinder, duct, conduit, spout, channel.

tuck *v* **1** INSERT, push, thrust, stuff, cram. **2** FOLD, pleat, gather, crease.
➤ *n* fold, pleat, gather, pucker, crease.
◆ **tuck in/into** eat, eat up, gorge, devour, dine, feast, gobble (*infml*), scoff (*infml*), wolf down (*infml*).
◆ **tuck in/up** put to bed, make comfortable, make snug, cover up, wrap up, fold in/under.

tuft *n* crest, beard, tassel, knot, clump, cluster, bunch.

tug *v* pull, draw, tow, haul, drag, lug, heave, wrench, jerk, pluck.
➤ *n* pull, tow, haul, heave, wrench, jerk, pluck.

tuition *n* teaching, instruction, coaching, training, lessons, schooling, education.

tumble *v* fall, stumble, trip, topple, overthrow, drop, flop, collapse, plummet, pitch, roll, toss.
➤ *n* fall, stumble, trip, drop, plunge, roll, toss.

tumbledown *adj* broken-down, ramshackle, rickety, dilapidated, unstable, unsteady, shaky, unsafe, ruinous, ruined, crumbling, crumbly, disintegrating, decrepit, tottering.
⊟ well-kept.

tumour n cancer, growth, lump, swelling, carcinoma (fml), melanoma (fml), lymphoma (fml), myeloma (fml), sarcoma (fml), neoplasm (fml).

tumult n commotion, turmoil, disturbance, upheaval, stir, agitation, unrest, disorder, chaos, pandemonium, noise, clamour, din, racket, hubbub, hullabaloo, row, rumpus, uproar, riot, fracas, brawl, affray, strife.
Fa peace, calm, composure.

tumultuous adj turbulent, stormy, raging, fierce, violent, wild, hectic, boisterous, rowdy, noisy, disorderly, unruly, riotous, restless, agitated, troubled, disturbed, excited.
Fa calm, peaceful, quiet.

tune n melody, theme, motif, song, air, strain.
➤ v pitch, harmonize, set, regulate, adjust, adapt, temper, attune, synchronize.

tuneful adj melodious, melodic, catchy, musical, euphonious, harmonious, pleasant, mellow, sonorous.
Fa tuneless, discordant.

tunnel n passage, passageway, gallery, subway, underpass, burrow, hole, mine, shaft, chimney.
➤ v burrow, dig, excavate, mine, bore, penetrate, undermine, sap.

turbulent adj rough, choppy, stormy, blustery, tempestuous, raging, furious, violent, wild, tumultuous, unbridled, boisterous, rowdy, disorderly, unruly, undisciplined, obstreperous, rebellious, mutinous, riotous, agitated, unsettled, unstable, confused, disordered.
Fa calm, composed.

turf n grass, clod, sod, divot, sward, green, lawn, glebe.

turf out v discharge, dismiss, eject, turn out, throw out, evict, banish, fling out, expel, oust, dispossess (fml), kick out (infml), chuck out (infml), elbow (infml), fire (infml), sack (infml), give the elbow to (infml).

turmoil n confusion, disorder, tumult, commotion, disturbance, trouble, disquiet, agitation, turbulence, stir, ferment, flurry, bustle, chaos, pandemonium, bedlam, noise, din, hubbub, row, uproar.
Fa calm, peace, quiet.

turn v 1 REVOLVE, circle, spin, twirl, whirl, twist, gyrate, pivot, hinge, swivel, rotate, roll, move, shift, invert, reverse, bend, veer, swerve, divert. 2 MAKE, transform, change, alter, modify, convert, adapt, adjust, fit, mould, shape, form, fashion, remodel. 3 turn cold: go, become, grow. 4 RESORT, have recourse, apply, appeal. 5 SOUR, curdle, spoil, go off, go bad.
➤ n 1 REVOLUTION, cycle, round, circle, rotation, spin, twirl, twist, gyration, bend, curve, loop, reversal. 2 CHANGE, alteration, shift, deviation. 3 it's your turn: go, chance, opportunity, occasion, stint, period, spell. 4 ACT, performance, performer.

♦ **turn away** reject, avert, deflect, deviate, depart.
Fa accept, receive.

♦ **turn down 1** turn down an offer: reject, decline, refuse, spurn, rebuff, repudiate. 2 LOWER, lessen, quieten, soften, mute, muffle.
Fa 1 accept. 2 turn up.

♦ **turn in 1** GO TO BED, retire. 2 HAND OVER, give up, surrender, deliver, hand in, tender, submit, return, give back.
Fa 1 get up. 2 keep.

♦ **turn off 1** BRANCH OFF, leave, quit, depart from, deviate, divert. 2 SWITCH OFF, turn out, stop, shut down, unplug, disconnect. 3 (sl) REPEL, sicken, nauseate, disgust, offend, displease, disenchant, alienate, bore, discourage, put off.
Fa 1 join. 2 turn on. 3 turn on (sl).

♦ **turn on 1** SWITCH ON, start (up), activate, connect. 2 (sl) AROUSE, stimulate, excite, thrill, please, attract. 3 HINGE ON, depend on, rest on. 4 ATTACK, round on, fall on.
Fa 1 turn off. 2 turn off (sl).

♦ **turn out 1** HAPPEN, come about, transpire, ensue, result, end up, become, develop, emerge. 2 SWITCH OFF, turn off, unplug, disconnect. 3 APPEAR, present, dress, clothe. 4 PRODUCE, make, manufacture, fabricate, assemble. 5 EVICT, throw out, expel, deport, banish, dismiss, discharge, drum out, kick out (infml), sack (infml). 6 turn out the attic: empty, clear, clean out.
Fa 2 turn on. 5 admit. 6 fill.

♦ **turn over 1** THINK OVER, think about, mull over, ponder, deliberate, reflect on, contemplate, consider, examine. 2 HAND OVER, surrender, deliver, transfer. 3 OVERTURN, upset, upend, invert, capsize, keel over.

♦ **turn up 1** ATTEND, come, arrive, appear, show up (infml). 2 AMPLIFY, intensify, raise, increase. 3 DISCOVER, find, unearth,

dig up, expose, disclose, reveal, show.
🠒 **1** stay away. **2** turn down.

turning n turn-off, junction, crossroads, fork, bend, curve, turn.

turning-point n crossroads, watershed, crux, crisis.

turnout n **1** ATTENDANCE, audience, gate, crowd, assembly, congregation.
2 APPEARANCE, outfit, dress, clothes.

turnover n income, profits, productivity, business, production, output, yield, volume, outturn, change, movement, flow, replacement.

tussle v struggle, battle, wrestle, compete, vie, fight, contend, grapple, scrap, brawl, scuffle, scramble.
🠒 n struggle, battle, conflict, contest, scramble, fight, brawl, bout, fracas, fray, mêlée, punch-up, scrap (infml), scuffle, scrum, set-to, competition, contention, scrimmage, dust-up (infml).

tutor n teacher, instructor, coach, educator, lecturer, supervisor, guide, mentor, guru, guardian.
🠒 v teach, instruct, train, drill, coach, educate, school, lecture, supervise, direct, guide.

tutorial n class, lesson, seminar, teach-in.
🠒 adj coaching, didactic, educative, educatory, guiding, instructional, teaching.

tweak v, n twist, pinch, squeeze, nip, pull, tug, jerk, twitch.

twee (infml) adj sweet, cute, pretty, dainty, quaint, sentimental, affected, precious.

twiddle v turn, twirl, swivel, twist, wiggle, adjust, fiddle, finger.

twig[1] n branch, sprig, spray, shoot, offshoot, stick, wattle, whip, withe, withy, ramulus (fml).

twig[2] v understand, see, get, comprehend, grasp, fathom, rumble, catch on (infml), cotton on (infml), tumble to (infml).

twilight n dusk, half-light, gloaming, gloom, dimness, sunset, evening.

twin n double, look-alike, likeness, duplicate, clone, match, counterpart, corollary, fellow, mate.
🠒 adj identical, matching, corresponding, symmetrical, parallel, matched, paired, double, dual, duplicate, twofold.
🠒 v match, pair, couple, link, join.

twine n string, cord, thread, yarn.
🠒 v wind, coil, spiral, loop, curl, bend, twist, wreathe, wrap, surround, encircle, entwine, plait, braid, knit, weave.

twinge n pain, pang, throb, spasm, throe, stab, stitch, pinch, prick.

twinkle v sparkle, glitter, shimmer, glisten, glimmer, flicker, wink, flash, glint, gleam, shine.
🠒 n sparkle, scintillation, glitter, shimmer, glisten, glimmer, flicker, wink, flash, glint, gleam, light.

twirl v spin, whirl, pirouette, wheel, rotate, revolve, swivel, pivot, turn, twist, gyrate, wind, coil.
🠒 n spin, whirl, pirouette, rotation, revolution, turn, twist, gyration, convlution, spiral, coil.

twist v **1** TURN, screw, wring, spin, swivel, wind, zigzag, bend, coil, spiral, curl, wreathe, twine, entwine, intertwine, weave, entangle, wriggle, squirm, writhe. **2** twist one's ankle: wrench, rick, sprain, strain. **3** CHANGE, alter, garble, misquote, misrepresent, distort, contort, warp, pervert.
🠒 n **1** TURN, screw, spin, roll, bend, curve, arc, curl, loop, zigzag, coil, spiral, convolution, squiggle, tangle. **2** CHANGE, variation, break. **3** PERVERSION, distortion, contortion. **4** SURPRISE, quirk, oddity, peculiarity.

twisted adj warped, perverted, deviant, unnatural.
🠒 straight.

twitch v jerk, jump, start, blink, tremble, shake, pull, tug, tweak, snatch, pluck.
🠒 n spasm, convulsion, tic, tremor, jerk, jump, start.

twitter v chirp, chirrup, tweet, cheep, sing, warble, whistle, chatter.

two-faced adj hypocritical, insincere, false, lying, deceitful, treacherous, double-dealing, devious, untrustworthy.
🠒 honest, candid, frank.

tycoon n industrialist, entrepreneur, captain of industry, magnate, mogul, baron, supremo, capitalist, financier.

type n **1** SORT, kind, form, genre, variety, strain, species, breed, group, class, category, subdivision, classification, description, designation, stamp, mark, order, standard. **2** ARCHETYPE, embodiment, prototype, original, model, pattern, specimen, example. **3** PRINT, printing, characters, letters, lettering, face, fount, font.

typhoon *n* whirlwind, cyclone, tornado, twister (*infml*), hurricane, tempest, storm, squall.

typical *adj* standard, normal, usual, average, conventional, orthodox, stock, model, representative, illustrative, indicative, characteristic, distinctive.
☞ atypical, unusual.

typify *v* embody, epitomize, encapsulate, personify, characterize, exemplify, symbolize, represent, illustrate.

tyrannical *adj* dictatorial, despotic, autocratic, absolute, arbitrary, authoritarian, domineering, overbearing, high-handed, imperious, magisterial, ruthless, harsh, severe, oppressive, overpowering, unjust, unreasonable.
☞ liberal, tolerant.

tyrannize *v* oppress, crush, intimidate, terrorize, coerce, repress, suppress, dictate, domineer, enslave, browbeat, bully, lord it over, subjugate (*fml*).

tyranny *n* dictatorship, despotism, autocracy, absolutism, authoritarianism, imperiousness, ruthlessness, harshness, severity, oppression, injustice.
☞ democracy, freedom.

tyrant *n* dictator, despot, autocrat, absolutist, authoritarian, bully, oppressor, slave-driver, taskmaster.

Uu

ubiquitous *adj* omnipresent, ever-present, everywhere, universal, global, pervasive, common, frequent.
≠ rare, scarce.

ugly *adj* 1 UNATTRACTIVE, unsightly, plain, unprepossessing, ill-favoured, hideous, monstrous, misshapen, deformed.
2 UNPLEASANT, disagreeable, nasty, horrid, objectionable, offensive, disgusting, revolting, repulsive, vile, frightful, terrible.
≠ 1 attractive, beautiful, handsome, pretty. 2 pleasant.

ulcer *n* sore, open sore, fester, abscess, boil, canker, ulceration, noma (*fml*).

ulterior *adj* secondary, hidden, concealed, undisclosed, unexpressed, covert, secret, private, personal, selfish.
≠ overt.

ultimate *adj* final, last, closing, concluding, eventual, terminal, furthest, remotest, extreme, utmost, greatest, highest, supreme, superlative, perfect, radical, fundamental, primary.

ultimately *adv* finally, eventually, at last, in the end, after all.

umbrella *n* 1 *put up your umbrella*: parasol, sunshade, brolly (*infml*), gamp (*infml*). 2 PROTECTION, cover, agency, patronage, aegis (*fml*).

umpire *n* referee, linesman, judge, adjudicator, arbiter, arbitrator, mediator, moderator.
➤ *v* referee, judge, adjudicate, arbitrate, mediate, moderate, control.

umpteen (*infml*) *adj* a good many, numerous, plenty, millions, countless, innumerable.
≠ few.

unabashed *adj* unashamed, unembarrassed, brazen, blatant, bold, confident, undaunted, unconcerned, undismayed.
≠ abashed, sheepish.

unable *adj* incapable, powerless, impotent, unequipped, unqualified, unfit, incompetent, inadequate.
≠ able, capable.

unacceptable *adj* intolerable, inadmissible, unsatisfactory, undesirable, unwelcome, objectionable, offensive, unpleasant.
≠ acceptable, satisfactory.

unaccompanied *adj* alone, unescorted, unattended, lone, solo, single-handed.
≠ accompanied.

unaccountable *adj* inexplicable, unexplainable, unfathomable, impenetrable, incomprehensible, baffling, puzzling, mysterious, astonishing, extraordinary, strange, odd, peculiar, singular, unusual, uncommon, unheard-of.
≠ explicable, explainable.

unaccustomed *adj* 1 *unaccustomed to such luxury*: unused, unacquainted, unfamiliar, unpractised, inexperienced.
2 STRANGE, unusual, uncommon, different, new, unexpected, surprising, uncharacteristic, unprecedented.
≠ 1 accustomed, familiar. 2 customary.

unaffected *adj* 1 UNMOVED, unconcerned, indifferent, impervious, untouched, unchanged, unaltered. 2 UNSOPHISTICATED, artless, naïve, ingenuous, unspoilt, plain, simple, straightforward, unpretentious, unassuming, sincere, honest, genuine.
≠ 1 moved, influenced. 2 affected, pretentious, insincere.

unalterable *adj* unchangeable, invariable, unchanging, immutable, final, inflexible, unyielding, rigid, fixed, permanent.
≠ alterable, flexible.

unanimity *n* consensus, unity, concord, agreement, concurrence, accord, like-mindedness, harmony, unison, concert.
≠ disagreement, disunity.

unanimous *adj* united, concerted, joint, common, as one, in agreement, in accord, harmonious.
≠ disunited, divided.

unapproachable *adj* inaccessible, remote, distant, aloof, standoffish, withdrawn, reserved, unsociable, unfriendly, forbidding.
≠ approachable, friendly.

unarmed *adj* defenceless, unprotected, exposed, open, vulnerable, weak, helpless.
E3 armed, protected.

unashamed *adj* shameless, unabashed, impenitent, unrepentant, unconcealed, undisguised, open, blatant.

unasked *adj* uninvited, unbidden, unrequested, unsought, unsolicited, unwanted, voluntary, spontaneous.
E3 invited, wanted.

unassailable *adj* invulnerable, secure, impregnable, invincible.

unassuming *adj* unassertive, self-effacing, retiring, modest, humble, meek, unobtrusive, unpretentious, simple, restrained.
E3 presumptuous, assertive, pretentious.

unattached *adj* unmarried, single, free, available, footloose, fancy-free, independent, unaffiliated.
E3 engaged, committed.

unattended *adj* ignored, disregarded, unguarded, unwatched, unsupervised, unaccompanied, unescorted, alone.
E3 attended, escorted.

unauthorized *adj* unofficial, unlawful, illegal, illicit, illegitimate, irregular, unsanctioned.
E3 authorized, legal.

unavoidable *adj* inevitable, inescapable, inexorable, certain, sure, fated, destined, obligatory, compulsory, mandatory, necessary.
E3 avoidable.

unaware *adj* oblivious, unconscious, ignorant, uninformed, unknowing, unsuspecting, unmindful, heedless, blind, deaf.
E3 aware, conscious.

unawares *adv* off guard, by surprise, accidentally, inadvertently, mistakenly, suddenly, unexpectedly, aback, abruptly, unintentionally, unconsciously, unknowingly, unprepared, unthinkingly, unwittingly, insidiously, on the hop (*infml*).

unbalanced *adj* 1 INSANE, mad, crazy (*infml*), lunatic, deranged, disturbed, demented, irrational, unsound. 2 *an unbalanced report*: biased, prejudiced, one-sided, partisan, unfair, unjust, unequal, uneven, asymmetrical, lopsided, unsteady, unstable.
E3 1 sane. 2 unbiased.

unbearable *adj* intolerable,

unacceptable, insupportable, insufferable, unendurable, excruciating.
E3 bearable, acceptable.

unbeatable *adj* invincible, unconquerable, unstoppable, unsurpassable, matchless, supreme, excellent.

unbecoming *adj* unseemly, improper, unsuitable, inappropriate, unbefitting, ungentlemanly, unladylike, unattractive, unsightly.
E3 suitable, attractive.

unbelief *n* atheism, agnosticism, scepticism, doubt, incredulity, disbelief.
E3 belief, faith.

unbelievable *adj* incredible, inconceivable, unthinkable, unimaginable, astonishing, staggering, extraordinary, impossible, improbable, unlikely, implausible, unconvincing, far-fetched, preposterous.
E3 believable, credible.

unborn *adj* embryonic, expected, awaited, coming, future.

unbounded *adj* boundless, limitless, unlimited, unrestricted, unrestrained, unchecked, unbridled, infinite, endless, immeasurable, vast.
E3 limited, restrained.

unbreakable *adj* indestructible, shatterproof, toughened, resistant, proof, durable, strong, tough, rugged, solid.
E3 breakable, fragile.

unbridled *adj* immoderate, excessive, uncontrolled, unrestrained, unchecked.

unbroken *adj* 1 INTACT, whole, entire, complete, solid, undivided.
2 UNINTERRUPTED, continuous, endless, ceaseless, incessant (*fml*), unceasing, constant, perpetual, progressive, successive. 3 *unbroken record*: unbeaten, unsurpassed, unequalled, unmatched.
E3 1 broken. 2 intermittent, fitful.

unburden *v* confess, admit, reveal, tell, lay bare, divulge, offload, disclose, confide, uncover, let out, pour out, bare, tell all (*infml*).
E3 hide, conceal, suppress.

uncalled-for *adj* gratuitous, unprovoked, unjustified, unwarranted, undeserved, unnecessary, needless.
E3 timely.

uncanny *adj* weird, strange, queer, bizarre, mysterious, unaccountable, incredible, remarkable, extraordinary, fantastic, unnatural, unearthly, supernatural, eerie, creepy, spooky (*infml*).

uncaring *adj* unconcerned, unmoved, unsympathetic, inconsiderate, unfeeling, cold, callous, indifferent, uninterested.
F3 caring, concerned.

unceasing *adj* ceaseless, incessant (*fml*), unending, endless, never-ending, non-stop, continuous, unbroken, constant, perpetual, continual, persistent, relentless, unrelenting, unremitting.
F3 intermittent, spasmodic.

uncertain *adj* 1 UNSURE, unconvinced, doubtful, dubious, undecided, ambivalent, hesitant, wavering, vacillating.
2 INCONSTANT, changeable, variable, erratic, irregular, shaky, unsteady, unreliable. 3 UNPREDICTABLE, unforeseeable, undetermined, unsettled, unresolved, unconfirmed, indefinite, vague, insecure, risky, iffy (*sl*).
F3 1 certain, sure. 2 steady. 3 predictable.

uncertainty *n* doubt, scepticism, irresolution, dilemma, hesitation, misgiving, confusion, bewilderment, perplexity, puzzlement, unreliability, unpredictability, insecurity.
F3 certainty.

unchanging *adj* unvarying, changeless, steady, steadfast, constant, perpetual, lasting, enduring, abiding, eternal, permanent.
F3 changing, changeable.

uncharitable *adj* unkind, cruel, hard-hearted, callous, unfeeling, insensitive, unsympathetic, unfriendly, mean, ungenerous.
F3 kind, sensitive, charitable, generous.

uncharted *adj* unexplored, undiscovered, unplumbed, foreign, alien, strange, unfamiliar, new, virgin.
F3 familiar.

uncivilized *adj* primitive, barbaric, savage, wild, untamed, uncultured, unsophisticated, unenlightened, uneducated, illiterate, uncouth, antisocial.
F3 civilized, cultured.

unclean *adj* dirty, soiled, filthy, foul, polluted, contaminated, tainted, impure, unhygienic, unwholesome, corrupt, defiled, sullied.
F3 clean, hygienic.

unclear *adj* indistinct, hazy, dim, obscure, vague, indefinite, ambiguous, equivocal,

uncertain, unsure, doubtful, dubious.
F3 clear, evident.

uncomfortable *adj* 1 CRAMPED, hard, cold, ill-fitting, irritating, painful, disagreeable. 2 AWKWARD, embarrassed, self-conscious, uneasy, troubled, worried, disturbed, distressed, disquieted, conscience-stricken.
F3 1 comfortable. 2 relaxed.

uncommon *adj* rare, scarce, infrequent, unusual, abnormal, atypical, unfamiliar, strange, odd, curious, bizarre, extraordinary, remarkable, notable, outstanding, exceptional, distinctive, special.
F3 common, usual, normal.

uncommunicative *adj* silent, taciturn, tight-lipped, close, secretive, unforthcoming, unresponsive, curt, brief, reticent, reserved, shy, retiring, withdrawn, unsociable.
F3 communicative, forthcoming.

uncompromising *adj* unyielding, unbending, inflexible, unaccommodating, rigid, firm, strict, tough, hard-line, inexorable, intransigent, stubborn, obstinate, die-hard.
F3 flexible.

unconcealed *adj* open, patent, obvious, evident, manifest, blatant, conspicuous, noticeable, visible, apparent.
F3 hidden, secret.

unconcerned *adj* indifferent, apathetic, uninterested, nonchalant, carefree, relaxed, complacent, cool, composed, untroubled, unworried, unruffled, unmoved, uncaring, unsympathetic, callous, aloof, remote, distant, detached, dispassionate, uninvolved, oblivious.
F3 concerned, worried, interested.

unconditional *adj* unqualified, unreserved, unrestricted, unlimited, absolute, utter, full, total, complete, entire, wholehearted, thoroughgoing, downright, outright, positive, categorical, unequivocal.
F3 conditional, qualified, limited.

unconnected *adj* 1 IRRELEVANT, unrelated, unattached, detached, separate, independent. 2 DISCONNECTED, incoherent, irrational, illogical.
F3 1 connected, relevant.

unconscionable *adj* unprincipled, amoral, outrageous, unethical, unjustifiable, unscrupulous, unreasonable, unwarrantable, unpardonable, preposterous, criminal, exorbitant, extreme, extravagant, excessive, immoderate, inordinate.

unconscious *adj* **1** STUNNED, knocked out, out, out cold, out for the count, concussed, comatose, senseless, insensible. **2** UNAWARE, oblivious, blind, deaf, heedless, unmindful, ignorant. **3** *an unconscious reaction*: involuntary, automatic, reflex, instinctive, impulsive, innate, subconscious, subliminal, repressed, suppressed, latent, unwitting, inadvertent, accidental, unintentional.
≠ **1** conscious. **2** aware. **3** intentional.

uncontrollable *adj* ungovernable, unmanageable, unruly, wild, mad, furious, violent, strong, irrepressible.
≠ controllable, manageable.

uncontrolled *adj* unrestrained, unbridled, unchecked, rampant, wild, unruly, undisciplined.
≠ controlled, restrained.

unconventional *adj* unorthodox, alternative, different, offbeat, eccentric, idiosyncratic, individual, original, odd, unusual, irregular, abnormal, bizarre, way-out (*sl*).
≠ conventional, orthodox.

unconvincing *adj* implausible, unlikely, improbable, questionable, doubtful, dubious, suspect, weak, feeble, flimsy, lame.
≠ convincing, plausible.

unco-ordinated *adj* clumsy, awkward, ungainly, ungraceful, inept, disjointed.
≠ graceful.

uncouth *adj* coarse, crude, vulgar, rude, ill-mannered, unseemly, improper, clumsy, awkward, gauche, graceless, unrefined, uncultivated, uncultured, uncivilized, rough.
≠ polite, refined, urbane.

uncover *v* unveil, unmask, unwrap, strip, bare, open, expose, reveal, show, disclose, divulge, leak, unearth, exhume, discover, detect.
≠ cover, conceal, suppress.

uncritical *adj* undiscerning, undiscriminating, unselective, unquestioning, credulous, accepting, trusting, gullible, naïve.
≠ discerning, discriminating, sceptical.

unctuous *adj* **1** INSINCERE, fawning, ingratiating, smooth, suave, sycophantic,

gushing, slick, plausible, glib, sanctimonious, obsequious (*fml*), servile, pietistic, smarmy (*infml*). **2** GREASY, oily, creamy.

uncultivated *adj* fallow, wild, rough, natural.
≠ cultivated.

uncultured *adj* unsophisticated, unrefined, uncultivated, uncivilized, rough, uncouth, boorish, rustic, coarse, crude, ill-bred.
≠ cultured, sophisticated.

undaunted *adj* undeterred, undiscouraged, undismayed, unbowed, resolute, steadfast, brave, courageous, fearless, bold, intrepid, dauntless, indomitable.
≠ discouraged, timorous.

undecided *adj* uncertain, unsure, in two minds, ambivalent, doubtful, hesitant, wavering, irresolute, uncommitted, indefinite, vague, dubious, debatable, moot, unsettled, open.
≠ decided, certain, definite.

undemonstrative *adj* aloof, distant, remote, withdrawn, reserved, reticent, uncommunicative, stiff, formal, cool, cold, unemotional, restrained, impassive, phlegmatic.
≠ demonstrative, communicative.

undeniable *adj* irrefutable (*fml*), unquestionable, incontrovertible (*fml*), sure, certain, undoubted, proven, clear, obvious, patent, evident, manifest (*fml*), unmistakable.
≠ questionable.

under *prep* below, underneath, beneath, lower than, less than, inferior to, subordinate to.
≠ over, above.
♦ **under way** moving, in motion, going, in operation, started, begun, in progress, afoot.

underclothes *n* underwear, underclothing, undergarments, underlinen, frillies (*infml*), lingerie, smalls (*infml*), undies (*infml*), unmentionables (*infml*).

undercover *adj* secret, hush-hush (*infml*), private, confidential, spy, intelligence, underground, clandestine, surreptitious, furtive, covert, hidden, concealed.
≠ open, unconcealed.

undercurrent *n* undertone, overtone,

hint, suggestion, tinge, flavour, aura, atmosphere, feeling, sense, movement, tendency, trend, drift.

undercut v 1 UNDERPRICE, undersell, undercharge, underbid, undermine. 2 EXCAVATE, hollow out, mine, gouge out, scoop out.

underestimate v underrate, undervalue, misjudge, miscalculate, minimize, belittle, disparage, dismiss.
🔁 overestimate, exaggerate.

undergo v experience, suffer, sustain, submit to, bear, stand, endure, weather, withstand.

underground adj 1 an underground passage: subterranean, buried, sunken, covered, hidden, concealed. 2 SECRET, covert, undercover, revolutionary, subversive, radical, experimental, avant-garde, alternative, unorthodox, unofficial.

undergrowth n brush, scrub, vegetation, ground cover, bracken, bushes, brambles, briars.

underhand adj unscrupulous, unethical, immoral, improper, sly, crafty, sneaky, stealthy, surreptitious, furtive, clandestine, devious, dishonest, deceitful, deceptive, fraudulent, crooked (infml), shady (infml).
🔁 honest, open, above board.

underline v mark, underscore, stress, emphasize, accentuate, italicize, highlight, point up.
🔁 play down, soft-pedal.

underling n minion, subordinate, inferior, lackey, menial, nonentity, flunkey, hireling, servant, slave, nobody.
🔁 boss (infml), leader, master.

underlying adj basic, fundamental, essential, primary, elementary, root, intrinsic, latent, hidden, lurking, veiled.

undermine v mine, tunnel, excavate, erode, wear away, weaken, sap, sabotage, subvert, vitiate (fml), mar, impair.
🔁 strengthen, fortify.

underprivileged adj disadvantaged, deprived, poor, needy, impoverished, destitute, oppressed.
🔁 privileged, fortunate, affluent.

underrate v underestimate, undervalue, belittle, disparage, depreciate, dismiss.
🔁 overrate, exaggerate.

undersized adj small, tiny, minute, miniature, pygmy, dwarf, stunted,

underdeveloped, underweight, puny.
🔁 oversized, big, overweight.

understand v 1 I don't understand: grasp, comprehend, take in, follow, get (infml), cotton on (infml), fathom, penetrate, make out, discern, perceive, see, realize, recognize, appreciate, accept.
2 SYMPATHIZE, empathize, commiserate.
3 BELIEVE, think, know, hear, learn, gather, assume, presume, suppose, conclude.
🔁 1 misunderstand.

understanding n 1 GRASP, comprehension, knowledge, wisdom, intelligence, intellect, sense, judgement, discernment, insight, appreciation, awareness, impression, perception, belief, idea, notion, opinion, interpretation.
2 AGREEMENT, arrangement, pact, accord, harmony. 3 SYMPATHY, empathy.
➤ adj sympathetic, compassionate, kind, considerate, sensitive, tender, loving, patient, tolerant, forbearing, forgiving.
🔁 unsympathetic, insensitive, impatient, intolerant.

understate v underplay, play down, soft-pedal, minimize, make light of, belittle, dismiss.
🔁 exaggerate.

understood adj accepted, assumed, presumed, implied, implicit, inferred, tacit, unstated, unspoken, unwritten.

understudy n stand-in, double, substitute, replacement, reserve, deputy.

undertake v 1 PLEDGE, promise, guarantee, agree, contract, covenant.
2 BEGIN, commence, embark on, tackle, try, attempt, endeavour, take on, accept, assume.

undertaker n funeral director, funeral furnisher, mortician (US).

undertaking n 1 ENTERPRISE, venture, business, affair, task, project, operation, attempt, endeavour, effort. 2 PLEDGE, commitment, promise, vow, word, assurance.

undertone n hint, suggestion, whisper, murmur, trace, tinge, touch, flavour, feeling, atmosphere, undercurrent.

undervalue v underrate, underestimate, misjudge, minimize, depreciate, disparage, dismiss.
🔁 overrate, exaggerate.

underwater adj subaquatic, undersea, submarine, submerged, sunken.

underwear n underclothes, undergarments, lingerie, undies (*infml*), smalls (*infml*).

underweight adj thin, undersized, underfed, undernourished, half-starved.
Ea overweight.

underworld n 1 CRIMINAL WORLD, organized crime, gangland, the mob (*sl*). 2 NETHER WORLD, infernal regions, Hades, hell, the inferno.

underwrite v endorse, authorize, sanction, approve, back, guarantee, insure, sponsor, fund, finance, subsidize, subscribe, sign, initial, countersign.

undesirable adj unwanted, unwelcome, unacceptable, unsuitable, unpleasant, disagreeable, distasteful, repugnant (*fml*), offensive, objectionable, obnoxious.
Ea desirable, pleasant.

undeveloped adj 1 *undeveloped nations*: developing, underdeveloped, less advanced,Third-World. 2 UNFORMED, embryonic, potential, latent, immature, stunted, dwarfed, inchoate (*fml*), primordial (*fml*).
Ea 1 advanced, industrialized. 2 developed, mature.

undignified adj inelegant, ungainly, clumsy, foolish, unseemly, improper, unsuitable, inappropriate.
Ea dignified, elegant.

undisguised adj unconcealed, open, overt, explicit, frank, genuine, apparent, patent, obvious, evident, manifest, blatant, naked, unadorned, stark, utter, outright, thoroughgoing.
Ea secret, concealed, hidden.

undisputed adj uncontested, unchallenged, unquestioned, undoubted, indisputable, incontrovertible, undeniable, irrefutable, accepted, acknowledged, recognized, sure, certain, conclusive.
Ea debatable, uncertain.

undistinguished adj unexceptional, unremarkable, unimpressive, ordinary, run-of-the-mill, everyday, banal, indifferent, mediocre, inferior.
Ea distinguished, exceptional.

undivided adj solid, unbroken, intact, whole, entire, full, complete, combined, united, unanimous, concentrated, exclusive, wholehearted.

undo v 1 UNFASTEN, untie, unbuckle, unbutton, unzip, unlock, unwrap, unwind, open, loose, loosen, separate. 2 ANNUL,

nullify, invalidate, cancel, offset, neutralize, reverse, overturn, upset, quash, defeat, undermine, subvert, mar, spoil, ruin, wreck, shatter, destroy.
Ea 1 fasten, do up.

undoing n downfall, ruin, ruination, collapse, destruction, defeat, overthrow, reversal, weakness, shame, disgrace.

undone adj 1 UNACCOMPLISHED, unfulfilled, unfinished, uncompleted, incomplete, outstanding, left, omitted, neglected, forgotten. 2 UNFASTENED, untied, unlaced, unbuttoned, unlocked, open, loose.
Ea 1 done, accomplished, complete. 2 fastened.

undoubted adj unchallenged, undisputed, acknowledged, unquestionable, indisputable, incontrovertible, undesirable, indubitable (*fml*), sure, certain, definite, obvious, patent.

undoubtedly adv certainly, definitely, doubtless, without doubt, no doubt, beyond doubt, surely, of course, undeniably, unquestionably, unmistakably, assuredly, indubitably (*fml*).

undreamed-of adj undreamt, inconceivable, unheard-of, unhoped-for, unimagined, unexpected, incredible, unforeseen, unsuspected, amazing, astonishing, miraculous.

undress v strip, peel off (*infml*), disrobe, take off, divest, remove, shed.

undressed adj unclothed, disrobed, stripped, naked, stark naked, nude.
Ea clothed.

undue adj unnecessary, needless, uncalled-for, unwarranted, undeserved, unreasonable, disproportionate, excessive, immoderate, inordinate, extreme, extravagant, improper.
Ea reasonable, moderate, proper.

undulate v rise and fall, swell, roll, surge, wave, ripple, billow, heave.

unduly adv too, over, excessively, immoderately, inordinately, disproportionately, unreasonably, unjustifiably, unnecessarily.
Ea moderately, reasonably.

undying adj eternal, deathless, lasting, perpetual, everlasting, immortal, infinite, continuing, constant, perennial, permanent, unending, unfading, indestructible, inextinguishable,

imperishable, undiminished, abiding (*fml*), sempiternal (*fml*).
☒ impermanent, inconstant.

unearth *v* dig up, exhume, disinter, excavate, uncover, expose, reveal, find, discover, detect.
☒ bury.

unearthly *adj* **1** SUPERNATURAL, ghostly, eerie, uncanny, weird, strange, spine-chilling. **2** *at this unearthly hour*: unreasonable, outrageous, ungodly.
☒ **2** reasonable.

uneasy *adj* uncomfortable, anxious, worried, apprehensive, tense, strained, nervous, agitated, shaky, jittery, edgy, upset, troubled, disturbed, unsettled, restless, impatient, unsure, insecure.
☒ calm, composed.

uneconomic *adj* unprofitable, uncommercial, loss-making, non-profit-making.
☒ economic, profitable, profit-making, remunerative.

uneducated *adj* unschooled, untaught, unread, ignorant, illiterate, uncultivated, uncultured, philistine, benighted.
☒ educated.

unemotional *adj* cool, cold, unfeeling, impassive, indifferent, apathetic, unresponsive, undemonstrative, unexcitable, phlegmatic, objective, dispassionate.
☒ emotional, excitable.

unemployed *adj* jobless, out of work, laid off, redundant, unwaged, on the dole (*infml*), idle, unoccupied.
☒ employed, occupied.

unending *adj* endless, never-ending, unceasing, ceaseless, incessant, interminable, constant, continual, perpetual, everlasting, eternal, undying.
☒ transient, intermittent.

unenviable *adj* undesirable, unpleasant, disagreeable, uncongenial, uncomfortable, thankless, difficult.
☒ enviable, desirable.

unequal *adj* different, varying, dissimilar, unlike, unmatched, uneven, unbalanced, disproportionate, asymmetrical, irregular, unfair, unjust, biased, discriminatory.
☒ equal.

unequivocal *adj* unambiguous, explicit, clear, plain, evident, distinct, unmistakable, express, direct, straight, definite, positive, categorical,

incontrovertible (*fml*), absolute, unqualified, unreserved.
☒ ambiguous, vague, qualified.

unerring *adj* unfailing, perfect, impeccable, infallible, faultless, exact, certain, sure, accurate, uncanny, dead (*infml*).
☒ fallible.

unethical *adj* unprofessional, immoral, improper, wrong, unscrupulous, unprincipled, dishonourable, disreputable, illegal, illicit, dishonest, underhand, shady (*infml*).
☒ ethical.

uneven *adj* **1** *uneven ground*: rough, bumpy. **2** ODD, unequal, inequitable, unfair, unbalanced, one-sided, asymmetrical, lopsided, crooked. **3** IRREGULAR, intermittent, spasmodic, fitful, jerky, unsteady, variable, changeable, fluctuating, erratic, inconsistent, patchy.
☒ **1** flat, level. **2** even, equal. **3** regular.

uneventful *adj* uninteresting, unexciting, quiet, unvaried, boring, monotonous, tedious, dull, routine, humdrum, ordinary, commonplace, unremarkable, unexceptional, unmemorable.
☒ eventful, memorable.

unexceptional *adj* unremarkable, unmemorable, typical, average, normal, usual, ordinary, indifferent, mediocre, unimpressive.
☒ exceptional, impressive.

unexpected *adj* unforeseen, unanticipated, unpredictable, chance, accidental, fortuitous (*fml*), sudden, abrupt, surprising, startling, amazing, astonishing, unusual.
☒ expected, predictable.

unfailing *adj* constant, certain, dependable, reliable, sure, steady, true, steadfast, faithful, loyal, staunch, undying, unfading, inexhaustible, infallible.
☒ fickle, impermanent, transient.

unfair *adj* unjust, inequitable, partial, biased, prejudiced, bigoted, discriminatory, unbalanced, one-sided, partisan, arbitrary, undeserved, unmerited, unwarranted, uncalled-for, unethical, unscrupulous, unprincipled, wrongful, dishonest.
☒ fair, just, unbiased, deserved.

unfaithful *adj* disloyal, treacherous, false, untrue, deceitful, dishonest,

untrustworthy, unreliable, fickle, inconstant, adulterous, two-timing, duplicitous, double-dealing, faithless, unbelieving, godless.
ᴇᴢ faithful, loyal, reliable.

unfamiliar *adj* strange, unusual, uncommon, curious, alien, foreign, uncharted, unexplored, unknown, different, new, novel, unaccustomed, unacquainted, inexperienced, unpractised, unskilled, unversed.
ᴇᴢ familiar, customary, conversant.

unfashionable *adj* outmoded, dated, out of date, out, passé, old-fashioned, antiquated, obsolete.
ᴇᴢ fashionable.

unfasten *v* undo, untie, loosen, unlock, open, uncouple, disconnect, separate, detach.
ᴇᴢ fasten.

unfathomable *adj* inexplicable, incomprehensible, impenetrable, baffling, fathomless, immeasurable, unknowable, mysterious, deep, profound, hidden, bottomless, unplumbed, unsounded, inscrutable, indecipherable, abstruse (*fml*), esoteric (*fml*).
ᴇᴢ comprehensible, explicable, penetrable

unfavourable *adj* inauspicious, unpromising, ominous, threatening, discouraging, inopportune (*fml*), untimely, unseasonable, ill-suited, unfortunate, unlucky, disadvantageous, bad, poor, adverse, contrary, negative, hostile, unfriendly, uncomplimentary.
ᴇᴢ favourable, auspicious, promising.

unfeeling *adj* insensitive, cold, hard, stony, callous, heartless, hard-hearted, cruel, inhuman, pitiless, uncaring, unsympathetic, apathetic.
ᴇᴢ sensitive, sympathetic.

unfinished *adj* incomplete, uncompleted, half-done, sketchy, rough, crude, imperfect, lacking, wanting, deficient, undone, unaccomplished, unfulfilled.
ᴇᴢ finished, perfect.

unfit *adj* 1 UNSUITABLE, inappropriate, unsuited, ill-equipped, unqualified, ineligible, untrained, unprepared, unequal, incapable, incompetent, inadequate, ineffective, useless. 2 UNHEALTHY, out of condition, flabby, feeble, decrepit.
ᴇᴢ 1 fit, suitable, competent. 2 healthy.

unflappable *adj* calm, collected, composed, level-headed, unworried, unexcitable, unruffled, equable, cool, impassive, self-possessed, phlegmatic, imperturbable (*fml*).
ᴇᴢ excitable, nervous, temperamental, panicky (*infml*).

unfold *v* 1 DEVELOP, evolve. 2 REVEAL, disclose, show, present, describe, explain, clarify, elaborate. 3 *unfold a map*: open, spread, flatten, straighten, stretch out, undo, unfurl, unroll, uncoil, unwrap, uncover.
ᴇᴢ 2 withhold, suppress. 3 fold, wrap.

unforeseen *adj* unpredicted, unexpected, unanticipated, surprising, startling, sudden, unavoidable.
ᴇᴢ expected, predictable.

unforgettable *adj* memorable, momentous, historic, noteworthy, notable, impressive, remarkable, exceptional, extraordinary.
ᴇᴢ unmemorable, unexceptional.

unforgivable *adj* unpardonable, inexcusable, unjustifiable, indefensible, reprehensible, shameful, disgraceful, deplorable.
ᴇᴢ forgivable, venial.

unfortunate *adj* 1 UNLUCKY, luckless, hapless, unsuccessful, poor, wretched, unhappy, doomed, ill-fated, hopeless, calamitous, disastrous, ruinous.
2 REGRETTABLE, lamentable, deplorable, adverse, unfavourable, unsuitable, inappropriate, inopportune, untimely, ill-timed.
ᴇᴢ 1 fortunate, happy. 2 favourable, appropriate.

unfounded *adj* baseless, groundless, unsupported, unsubstantiated, unproven, unjustified, idle, false, spurious, trumped-up, fabricated.
ᴇᴢ substantiated, justified.

unfriendly *adj* unsociable, standoffish, aloof, distant, unapproachable, inhospitable, uncongenial, unneighbourly, unwelcoming, cold, chilly, hostile, aggressive, quarrelsome, inimical, antagonistic, ill-disposed, disagreeable, surly, sour.
ᴇᴢ friendly, amiable, agreeable.

ungainly *adj* clumsy, awkward, gauche, inelegant, gawky, unco-ordinated, lumbering, unwieldy.
ᴇᴢ graceful, elegant.

ungodly adj 1 UNREASONABLE, outrageous, intolerable, unearthly, unsocial. 2 IMPIOUS, irreligious, godless, blasphemous, profane, immoral, corrupt, depraved, sinful, wicked.

ungrateful adj unthankful, unappreciative, ill-mannered, ungracious, selfish, heedless.
Ea grateful, thankful.

unguarded adj 1 in an unguarded moment: unwary, careless, incautious, imprudent, impolitic, indiscreet, undiplomatic, thoughtless, unthinking, heedless, foolish, foolhardy, rash, ill-considered. 2 UNDEFENDED, unprotected, exposed, vulnerable, defenceless.
Ea 1 guarded, cautious. 2 defended, protected.

unhappily adv unfortunately, regrettably, unluckily, sadly, alas, sad to say, sad to relate, worse luck (infml).
Ea fortunately.

unhappy adj 1 SAD, sorrowful, miserable, melancholy, depressed, dispirited, despondent, dejected, downcast, crestfallen, long-faced, gloomy. 2 UNFORTUNATE, unlucky, ill-fated, unsuitable, inappropriate, inapt, ill-chosen, tactless, awkward, clumsy.
Ea 1 happy. 2 fortunate, suitable.

unharmed adj undamaged, unhurt, uninjured, unscathed, whole, intact, safe, sound.
Ea harmed, damaged.

unhealthy adj 1 UNWELL, sick, ill, poorly, ailing, sickly, infirm, invalid, weak, feeble, frail, unsound. 2 UNWHOLESOME, insanitary, unhygienic, harmful, detrimental, morbid, unnatural.
Ea 1 healthy, fit. 2 wholesome, hygienic, natural.

unheard-of adj 1 UNTHINKABLE, inconceivable, unimaginable, undreamed-of, unprecedented, unacceptable, offensive, shocking, outrageous, preposterous. 2 UNKNOWN, unfamiliar, new, unusual, obscure.
Ea 1 normal, acceptable. 2 famous.

unheeded adj ignored, disregarded, disobeyed, unnoticed, unobserved, unremarked, overlooked, neglected, forgotten.
Ea noted, observed.

unhesitating adj immediate, instant, instantaneous, prompt, ready, automatic,

spontaneous, unquestioning, unwavering, unfaltering, wholehearted, implicit.
Ea hesitant, tentative.

unhinge v unbalance, unnerve, unsettle, upset, confuse, distract, disorder, drive mad, madden, craze, derange.

unholy adj 1 IMPIOUS, irreligious, sinful, iniquitous, immoral, corrupt, depraved, wicked, evil. 2 (infml) an unholy mess: unreasonable, shocking, outrageous, ungodly, unearthly.
Ea 1 holy, pious, godly. 2 reasonable.

unhurried adj slow, leisurely, deliberate, easy, relaxed, calm, easy-going (infml), laid-back (sl).
Ea hurried, hasty, rushed.

unidentified adj unknown, unrecognized, unmarked, unnamed, nameless, anonymous, incognito, unfamiliar, strange, mysterious.
Ea identified, known, named.

unification n union, uniting, merger, alliance, amalgamation, combination, federation, fusion, incorporation, coalescence, coalition, confederation, enosis (fml).
Ea separation, split, division.

uniform n outfit, costume, livery, insignia, regalia, robes, dress, suit.
➤ adj same, identical, like, alike, similar, homogeneous, consistent, regular, equal, smooth, even, flat, monotonous, unvarying, unchanging, constant, unbroken.
Ea different, varied, changing.

uniformity n sameness, constancy, invariability, regularity, similarity, evenness, flatness, monotony, drabness, dullness, tedium, monogeneity (fml), homomorphism (fml), similitude (fml).
Ea difference, dissimilarity, variation.

unify v unite, join, bind, combine, integrate, merge, amalgamate, consolidate, coalesce, fuse, weld.
Ea separate, divide, split.

unimaginable adj inconceivable, mind-boggling (infml), unbelievable, incredible, impossible, fantastic, undreamed-of, unthinkable, unheard-of.

unimaginative adj uninspired, unoriginal, predictable, hackneyed, banal, ordinary, dull, boring, routine, matter-of-fact, dry, barren, lifeless, unexciting, tame.
Ea imaginative, creative, original.

unimportant adj insignificant,

inconsequential, irrelevant, immaterial, minor, trivial, trifling, petty, slight, negligible, worthless.
☞ important, significant, relevant, vital.

unimpressive *adj* unspectacular, undistinguished, unexceptional, unremarkable, uninteresting, dull, average, commonplace, indifferent, mediocre.
☞ impressive, memorable, notable.

uninhabited *adj* unoccupied, vacant, empty, deserted, abandoned, unpeopled, unpopulated.

uninhibited *adj* unconstrained, unreserved, unselfconscious, liberated, free, unrestricted, uncontrolled, unrestrained, abandoned, natural, spontaneous, frank, candid, open, relaxed, informal.
☞ inhibited, repressed, constrained, restrained.

unintelligible *adj* incomprehensible, incoherent, inarticulate, double Dutch (*infml*), garbled, scrambled, jumbled, muddled, indecipherable, illegible.
☞ intelligible, comprehensible, clear.

unintentional *adj* unintended, accidental, fortuitous, inadvertent, unplanned, unpremeditated, involuntary, unconscious, unwitting.
☞ intentional, deliberate.

uninterested *adj* indifferent, unconcerned, uninvolved, bored, listless, apathetic, unenthusiastic, blasé, impassive, unresponsive.
☞ interested, concerned, enthusiastic, responsive.

uninteresting *adj* boring, tedious, monotonous, humdrum, dull, drab, dreary, dry, flat, tame, uneventful, unexciting, uninspiring, unimpressive.
☞ interesting, exciting.

uninterrupted *adj* unbroken, continuous, non-stop, unending, constant, continual, steady, sustained, undisturbed, peaceful.
☞ broken, intermittent.

uninvited *adj* unasked, unsought, unsolicited, unwanted, unwelcome.
☞ invited.

union *n* alliance, coalition, league, association, federation, confederation, confederacy, merger, combination, amalgamation, blend, mixture, synthesis, fusion, unification, unity.

☞ separation, alienation, estrangement.

unique *adj* single, one-off, sole, only, lone, solitary, unmatched, matchless, peerless, unequalled, unparalleled, unrivalled, incomparable, inimitable.
☞ common.

unison *n* concert, co-operation, unanimity, unity.

unit *n* item, part, element, constituent, piece, component, module, section, segment, portion, entity, whole, one, system, assembly.

unite *v* join, link, couple, marry, ally, co-operate, band, associate, federate, confederate, combine, pool, amalgamate, merge, blend, unify, consolidate, coalesce, fuse.
☞ separate, sever.

united *adj* allied, affiliated, corporate, unified, combined, pooled, collective, concerted, one, unanimous, agreed, in agreement, in accord, like-minded.
☞ disunited.

unity *n* agreement, accord, concord, harmony, peace, consensus, unanimity, solidarity, integrity, oneness, wholeness, union, unification.
☞ disunity, disagreement, discord, strife.

universal *adj* worldwide, global, all-embracing, all-inclusive, general, common, across-the-board, total, whole, entire, all-round, unlimited.

universally *adv* always, everywhere, uniformly, invariably, ubiquitously (*fml*).

universe *n* cosmos, world, nature, creation, firmament, heavens, macrocosm (*fml*).

unjustifiable *adj* indefensible, inexcusable, unforgivable, unreasonable, unwarranted, immoderate, excessive, unacceptable, outrageous.
☞ justifiable, acceptable.

unkempt *adj* dishevelled, tousled, rumpled, uncombed, ungroomed, untidy, messy, scruffy, shabby, slovenly.
☞ well-groomed, tidy.

unkind *adj* cruel, inhuman, inhumane, callous, hard-hearted, unfeeling, insensitive, thoughtless, inconsiderate, uncharitable, nasty, malicious, spiteful, mean, malevolent, unfriendly, uncaring, unsympathetic.
☞ kind, considerate.

unknown *adj* unfamiliar, unheard-of,

strange, alien, foreign, mysterious, dark, obscure, hidden, concealed, undisclosed, secret, untold, new, uncharted, unexplored, undiscovered, unidentified, unnamed, nameless, anonymous, incognito.
ᴇᴀ known, familiar.

unlawful *adj* illegal, criminal, illicit, illegitimate, unconstitutional, outlawed, banned, prohibited, forbidden, unauthorized.
ᴇᴀ lawful, legal.

unleash *v* loose, let loose, free, release, unloose, untie, untether.
ᴇᴀ restrain.

unlike *adj* dissimilar, different, distinct, opposite, opposed, incompatible, contrasted, ill-matched, unrelated, unequal, divergent, diverse, disparate (*fml*).
ᴇᴀ similar, related
➤ *prep* dissimilar to, different from, in contrast to, as opposed to, as against.
ᴇᴀ like.

unlikely *adj* 1 IMPROBABLE, implausible, far-fetched, unconvincing, unbelievable, incredible, unimaginable, unexpected, doubtful, dubious, questionable, suspect, suspicious. 2 SLIGHT, faint, remote, distant.
ᴇᴀ 1 likely, plausible.

unlimited *adj* limitless, unrestricted, unbounded, boundless, infinite, endless, countless, incalculable, immeasurable, vast, immense, extensive, great, indefinite, absolute, unconditional, unqualified, all-encompassing, total, complete, full, unconstrained, unhampered.
ᴇᴀ limited.

unload *v* unpack, empty, discharge, dump, offload, unburden, relieve.
ᴇᴀ load.

unlock *v* unbolt, unlatch, unfasten, undo, open, free, release.
ᴇᴀ lock, fasten.

unlooked-for *adj* unexpected, unforeseen, unanticipated, unpredicted, unhoped-for, unthought-of, undreamed-of, surprising, surprise, fortunate, chance, lucky, fortuitous (*fml*).
ᴇᴀ expected, predictable

unloved *adj* unpopular, disliked, hated, detested, unwanted, rejected, spurned, loveless, uncared-for, neglected.
ᴇᴀ loved.

unlucky *adj* unfortunate, luckless, unhappy, miserable, wretched, ill-fated, ill-starred, jinxed, doomed, cursed, unfavourable, inauspicious, ominous, unsuccessful, disastrous.
ᴇᴀ lucky.

unmanageable *adj* 1 UNWIELDY, bulky, cumbersome, awkward, inconvenient, unhandy. 2 UNCONTROLLABLE, wild, unruly, disorderly, difficult.
ᴇᴀ 1 manageable. 2 controllable.

unmarried *adj* single, unwed, celibate, unattached, available.
ᴇᴀ married.

unmask *v* unveil, uncloak, uncover, bare, expose, reveal, show, disclose, discover, detect.
ᴇᴀ mask, conceal.

unmentionable *adj* unspeakable, unutterable, taboo, immodest, indecent, shocking, scandalous, shameful, disgraceful, abominable.

unmistakable *adj* clear, plain, distinct, pronounced, obvious, evident, manifest (*fml*), patent, glaring, explicit, unambiguous, unequivocal, positive, definite, sure, certain, unquestionable, indisputable, undeniable.
ᴇᴀ unclear, ambiguous.

unmitigated *adj* utter, absolute, complete, pure, rank, perfect, outright, downright, out-and-out, thorough, thoroughgoing, sheer, relentless, persistent, intense, unqualified, unalleviated, unrelieved, unbroken, unrelenting, unredeemed, unmodified, undiminished, harsh, grim, arrant (*fml*), consummate (*fml*), unabated (*fml*), unremitting (*fml*).

unmoved *adj* unaffected, untouched, unshaken, dry-eyed, unfeeling, cold, dispassionate, indifferent, impassive, unresponsive, unimpressed, firm, adamant, inflexible, unbending, undeviating, unwavering, steady, unchanged, resolute, resolved, determined.
ᴇᴀ moved, affected, shaken.

unnatural *adj* 1 ABNORMAL, anomalous, freakish, irregular, unusual, strange, odd, peculiar, queer, bizarre, extraordinary, uncanny, supernatural, inhuman, perverted. 2 AFFECTED, feigned, artificial, false, insincere, unspontaneous, contrived, laboured, stilted, forced,

strained, self-conscious, stiff.
≊ 1 natural, normal. **2** sincere, fluent.

unnecessary *adj* unneeded, needless, uncalled-for, unwanted, non-essential, dispensable, expendable, superfluous, redundant, tautological.
≊ necessary, essential, indispensable.

unnerve *v* daunt, intimidate, frighten, scare, discourage, demoralize, dismay, disconcert, upset, worry, shake, rattle (*infml*), confound, fluster.
≊ nerve, brace, steel.

unnoticed *adj* unobserved, unremarked, unseen, unrecognized, undiscovered, overlooked, ignored, disregarded, neglected, unheeded.
≊ noticed, noted.

unobtrusive *adj* inconspicuous, unnoticeable, unassertive, self-effacing, humble, modest, unostentatious, unpretentious, restrained, low-key, subdued, quiet, retiring.
≊ obtrusive, ostentatious.

unoccupied *adj* uninhabited, vacant, empty, free, idle, inactive, workless, jobless, unemployed.
≊ occupied, busy.

unofficial *adj* unauthorized, illegal, informal, off-the-record, personal, private, confidential, undeclared, unconfirmed.
≊ official.

unorthodox *adj* unconventional, nonconformist, heterodox, alternative, fringe, irregular, abnormal, unusual.
≊ orthodox, conventional.

unpaid *adj* **1** *unpaid bills*: outstanding, overdue, unsettled, owing, due, payable. **2** *unpaid work*: voluntary, honorary, unsalaried, unwaged, unremunerative, free.
≊ 1 paid.

unpalatable *adj* **1** UNAPPETIZING, distasteful, insipid, bitter, uneatable, inedible. **2** UNPLEASANT, disagreeable, unattractive, offensive, repugnant (*fml*).
≊ 1 palatable. **2** pleasant.

unparalleled *adj* unequalled, unmatched, matchless, peerless, incomparable, unrivalled, unsurpassed, supreme, superlative, rare, exceptional, unprecedented.

unpleasant *adj* disagreeable, ill-natured, nasty, objectionable, offensive, distasteful, unpalatable, unattractive, repulsive, bad, troublesome.

≊ pleasant, agreeable, nice.

unpopular *adj* disliked, hated, detested, unloved, unsought-after, unfashionable, undesirable, unwelcome, unwanted, rejected, shunned, avoided, neglected.
≊ popular, fashionable.

unprecedented *adj* new, original, revolutionary, unknown, unheard-of, exceptional, remarkable, extraordinary, abnormal, unusual, freakish, unparalleled, unrivalled.
≊ usual.

unpredictable *adj* unforeseeable, unexpected, changeable, variable, inconstant, unreliable, fickle, unstable, erratic, random, chance.
≊ predictable, foreseeable, constant.

unprepared *adj* unready, surprised, unsuspecting, ill-equipped, unfinished, incomplete, half-baked, unplanned, unrehearsed, spontaneous, improvised, ad-lib, off-the-cuff.
≊ prepared, ready.

unpretentious *adj* unaffected, natural, plain, simple, unobtrusive, honest, straightforward, humble, modest, unassuming, unostentatious.
≊ pretentious.

unproductive *adj* infertile, sterile, barren, dry, arid, unfruitful, fruitless, futile, vain, idle, useless, ineffective, unprofitable, unremunerative, unrewarding.
≊ productive, fertile.

unprofessional *adj* amateurish, inexpert, unskilled, sloppy, incompetent, inefficient, casual, negligent, lax, unethical, unprincipled, improper, unseemly, unacceptable, inadmissible.
≊ professional, skilful.

unprotected *adj* unguarded, unattended, undefended, unfortified, unarmed, unshielded, unsheltered, uncovered, exposed, open, naked, vulnerable, defenceless, helpless.
≊ protected, safe, immune.

unqualified *adj* **1** UNTRAINED, inexperienced, amateur, ineligible, unfit, incompetent, incapable, unprepared, ill-equipped. **2** ABSOLUTE, categorical, utter, total, complete, thorough, consummate (*fml*), downright, unmitigated, unreserved, wholehearted, outright, unconditional, unrestricted.
≊ 1 qualified, professional. **2** conditional, tentative.

unquestionable adj unequivocal, beyond question, incontestable, faultless, flawless, indisputable, obvious, patent, clear, conclusive, definite, absolute, sure, certain, self-evident, unchallenged, undeniable, unmistakable, incontrovertible (fml), indubitable (fml), irrefutable (fml), manifest (fml).
ɛ dubious, questionable.

unravel v unwind, undo, untangle, disentangle, free, extricate, separate, resolve, sort out, solve, work out, figure out, puzzle out, penetrate, interpret, explain.
ɛ tangle, complicate.

unreadable adj unintelligible, too difficult to read, incomprehensible, incoherent, inarticulate, garbled, scrambled, muddled, jumbled, indecipherable, illegible, impenetrable, unfathomable, puzzling, mysterious, obscure, complicated, complex, involved, double Dutch (infml).
ɛ intelligible, comprehensible, clear.

unreal adj false, artificial, synthetic, mock, fake, sham, imaginary, visionary, fanciful, make-believe, pretend (infml), fictitious, made-up, fairy-tale, legendary, mythical, fantastic, illusory, immaterial, insubstantial, hypothetical.
ɛ real, genuine.

unrealistic adj impractical, idealistic, romantic, quixotic, impracticable, unworkable, unreasonable, impossible.
ɛ realistic, pragmatic.

unreasonable adj 1 UNFAIR, unjust, biased, unjustifiable, unjustified, unwarranted, undue, uncalled-for.
2 IRRATIONAL, illogical, inconsistent, arbitrary, absurd, nonsensical, far-fetched, preposterous, mad, senseless, silly, foolish, stupid, headstrong, opinionated, perverse.
3 unreasonable prices: excessive, immoderate, extravagant, exorbitant, extortionate.
ɛ 1 reasonable, fair. 2 rational, sensible. 3 moderate.

unrecognizable adj unidentifiable, disguised, incognito, changed, altered.

unrefined adj raw, untreated, unprocessed, unfinished, unpolished, crude, coarse, vulgar, unsophisticated, uncultivated, uncultured.
ɛ refined, finished.

unrelated adj unconnected, unassociated, irrelevant, extraneous, different, dissimilar, unlike, disparate (fml), distinct, separate, independent.
ɛ related, similar.

unrelenting adj relentless, unremitting, uncompromising, inexorable, incessant (fml), unceasing, ceaseless, endless, unbroken, continuous, constant, continual, perpetual, steady, unabated (fml), remorseless, unmerciful, merciless, pitiless, unsparing.
ɛ spasmodic, intermittent.

unreliable adj unsound, fallible, deceptive, false, mistaken, erroneous, inaccurate, unconvincing, implausible, uncertain, undependable, untrustworthy, unstable, fickle, irresponsible.
ɛ reliable, dependable, trustworthy.

unremitting adj unrelenting, unceasing, ceaseless, remorseless, relentless, tireless, constant, continual, continuous, perpetual, unbroken, incessant (fml), unabated (fml).
ɛ spasmodic, intermittent.

unrepentant adj impenitent, unapologetic, unabashed, unashamed, shameless, incorrigible, confirmed, hardened, obdurate.
ɛ repentant, penitent, ashamed.

unrest n protest, rebellion, turmoil, agitation, restlessness, dissatisfaction, dissension, disaffection, worry.
ɛ peace, calm.

unrestricted adj unlimited, unbounded, unopposed, unhindered, unimpeded, unobstructed, clear, free, open, public, unconditional, absolute.
ɛ restricted, limited.

unripe adj unripened, green, immature, undeveloped, unready.
ɛ ripe, mature.

unrivalled adj unequalled, unparalleled, unmatched, matchless, peerless, incomparable, inimitable, unsurpassed, supreme, superlative.

unruffled adj undisturbed, untroubled, imperturbable, collected, composed, cool, calm, tranquil, serene, peaceful, smooth, level, even.
ɛ troubled, anxious.

unruly adj uncontrollable, ungovernable, unmanageable, intractable, disorderly, wild, rowdy, riotous, rebellious, mutinous, lawless, insubordinate, obstreperous, disobedient, wayward, wilful, headstrong.
ɛ manageable, orderly.

unsafe *adj* dangerous, perilous, risky, hazardous, treacherous, unreliable, uncertain, unsound, unstable, precarious, insecure, vulnerable, exposed.
◨ safe, secure.

unsatisfactory *adj* unacceptable, imperfect, defective, faulty, inferior, poor, weak, inadequate, insufficient, deficient, unsuitable, displeasing, dissatisfying, unsatisfying, frustrating, disappointing, leaving much to be desired.
◨ satisfactory, pleasing.

unsavoury *adj* distasteful, disagreeable, unpleasant, disgusting, nauseating, revolting, sickening, nasty, undesirable, repulsive, objectionable, obnoxious, offensive, repellent, unattractive, sordid, squalid, unpalatable, unappetizing, repugnant (*fml*).
◨ palatable, pleasant.

unscathed *adj* unhurt, uninjured, unharmed, undamaged, untouched, whole, intact, safe, sound.
◨ hurt, injured.

unscrupulous *adj* unprincipled, ruthless, shameless, dishonourable, dishonest, crooked (*infml*), corrupt, immoral, unethical, improper.
◨ scrupulous, ethical, proper.

unseasonable *adj* inappropriate, ill-timed, unsuitable, untimely, mistimed, inopportune (*fml*), intempestive (*fml*), malapropos (*fml*).
◨ timely.

unseat *v* remove, depose, dethrone, dismount, displace, dismiss, discharge, oust, throw, overthrow, topple, unhorse, unsaddle, dishorse.

unseemly *adj* improper, indelicate, indecorous (*fml*), unbecoming, undignified, unrefined, disreputable, discreditable, undue, inappropriate, unsuitable.
◨ seemly, decorous.

unseen *adj* unnoticed, unobserved, undetected, invisible, hidden, concealed, veiled, obscure.
◨ visible.

unselfish *adj* selfless, altruistic, self-denying, self-sacrificing, disinterested, noble, magnanimous, generous, liberal, charitable, philanthropic, public-spirited, humanitarian, kind.
◨ selfish.

unsentimental *adj* realistic, practical, pragmatic, hard-headed, tough, unromantic, level-headed.
◨ sentimental, idealistic.

unsettle *v* disturb, upset, trouble, bother, discompose, ruffle, fluster, unbalance, shake, agitate, rattle (*infml*), disconcert, confuse, throw.

unsettled *adj* **1** DISTURBED, upset, troubled, agitated, anxious, uneasy, tense, edgy, flustered, shaken, unnerved, disoriented, confused. **2** UNRESOLVED, undetermined, undecided, open, uncertain, doubtful. **3** *unsettled weather*: changeable, variable, unpredictable, inconstant, unstable, insecure, unsteady, shaky. **4** UNPAID, outstanding, owing, payable, overdue.
◨ **1** composed. **2** certain. **3** settled. **4** paid.

unshakable *adj* firm, well-founded, fixed, stable, immovable, unassailable, unwavering, constant, steadfast, staunch, sure, resolute, determined.
◨ insecure.

unsightly *adj* ugly, unattractive, unprepossessing, hideous, repulsive, repugnant (*fml*), off-putting, unpleasant, disagreeable.
◨ attractive.

unskilled *adj* untrained, unqualified, inexperienced, unpractised, inexpert, unprofessional, amateurish, incompetent.
◨ skilled.

unsociable *adj* unfriendly, aloof, distant, standoffish, withdrawn, introverted, reclusive, retiring, reserved, taciturn, unforthcoming, uncommunicative, cold, chilly, uncongenial, unneighbourly, inhospitable, hostile.
◨ sociable, friendly.

unsolicited *adj* unrequested, unsought, uninvited, unasked, unwanted, unwelcome, uncalled-for, gratuitous, voluntary, spontaneous.
◨ requested, invited.

unsophisticated *adj* artless, guileless, innocent, ingenuous, naïve, inexperienced, unworldly, childlike, natural, unaffected, unpretentious, unrefined, plain, simple, straightforward, uncomplicated, uninvolved.
◨ sophisticated, worldly, complex.

unsound *adj* **1** *unsound reasoning*: faulty, flawed, defective, ill-founded, fallacious, false, erroneous, invalid, illogical. **2** UNHEALTHY, unwell, ill, diseased, weak,

frail, unbalanced, deranged, unhinged.
3 UNSTABLE, unsteady, wobbly, shaky,
insecure, unsafe.
🔁 **1** sound. **2** well. **3** stable.

unspeakable *adj* unutterable,
inexpressible, indescribable, awful,
dreadful, frightful, terrible, horrible,
shocking, appalling, monstrous,
inconceivable, unbelievable.

unspoilt *adj* preserved, unchanged,
untouched, natural, unaffected,
unsophisticated, unharmed, undamaged,
unimpaired, unblemished, perfect.
🔁 spoilt, affected.

unspoken *adj* unstated, undeclared,
unuttered, unexpressed, unsaid, voiceless,
wordless, silent, tacit, implicit, implied,
inferred, understood, assumed.
🔁 stated, explicit.

unstable *adj* **1** CHANGEABLE, variable,
fluctuating, vacillating, wavering, fitful,
erratic, inconsistent, volatile, capricious,
inconstant, unpredictable, unreliable,
untrustworthy. **2** UNSTEADY, wobbly, shaky,
rickety, insecure, unsafe, risky, precarious,
tottering, unbalanced.
🔁 **1** stable. **2** steady.

unsteady *adj* unstable, wobbly, shaky,
rickety, insecure, unsafe, treacherous,
precarious, tottering, unreliable,
inconstant, irregular, flickering.
🔁 steady, firm.

unsuccessful *adj* failed, abortive, vain,
futile, useless, ineffective, unavailing,
fruitless, unproductive, sterile, luckless,
unlucky, unfortunate, losing, beaten,
defeated, frustrated, thwarted.
🔁 successful, effective, fortunate, winning.

unsuitable *adj* inappropriate, inapt,
unsuited, unfit, unacceptable, improper,
unseemly, unbecoming, incompatible,
incongruous.
🔁 suitable, appropriate.

unsung *adj* unhonoured, unpraised,
unacknowledged, unrecognized,
overlooked, disregarded, neglected,
forgotten, unknown, obscure.
🔁 honoured, famous, renowned.

unsure *adj* uncertain, doubtful, dubious,
suspicious, sceptical, unconvinced,
unpersuaded, undecided, hesitant,
tentative.
🔁 sure, certain, confident.

unsurpassed *adj* surpassing, supreme,
transcendent, unbeaten, unexcelled,
unequalled, unparalleled, unrivalled,
incomparable, matchless, superlative,
exceptional.

unsuspecting *adj* unwary, unaware,
unconscious, trusting, trustful,
unsuspicious, credulous, gullible,
ingenuous, naïve, innocent.
🔁 suspicious, knowing.

unswerving *adj* unflagging, unwavering,
unfaltering, untiring, undeviating, staunch,
steadfast, dedicated, devoted, steady, sure,
true, firm, constant, fixed, immovable,
resolute, single-minded, direct.
🔁 irresolute, tentative.

unsympathetic *adj* unpitying,
unconcerned, unmoved, unresponsive,
indifferent, insensitive, unfeeling, cold,
heartless, soulless, hard-hearted, callous,
cruel, inhuman, unkind, hard, stony,
hostile, antagonistic.
🔁 sympathetic, compassionate.

untangle *v* disentangle, extricate,
unravel, undo, resolve, solve.
🔁 tangle, complicate.

untenable *adj* indefensible,
unreasonable, unmaintainable, unsound,
unjustifiable, inexcusable, insupportable,
unsustainable, flawed, illogical, fallacious,
rocky, shaky.
🔁 tenable, sound.

unthinkable *adj* inconceivable,
unimaginable, unheard-of, unbelievable,
incredible, impossible, improbable,
unlikely, implausible, unreasonable,
illogical, absurd, preposterous,
outrageous, shocking.

unthinking *adj* thoughtless,
inconsiderate, insensitive, tactless,
indiscreet, rude, heedless, careless,
negligent, rash, impulsive, instinctive,
unconscious, automatic, mechanical.
🔁 considerate, conscious.

untidy *adj* messy, cluttered, disorderly,
muddled, jumbled, unsystematic, chaotic,
topsy-turvy, scruffy, dishevelled, unkempt,
slovenly, sloppy, slipshod.
🔁 tidy, neat.

untie *v* undo, unfasten, unknot, unbind,
free, release, loose, loosen.
🔁 tie, fasten.

untimely *adj* early, premature,
unseasonable, ill-timed, inopportune
(*fml*), inconvenient, awkward, unsuitable,
inappropriate, unfortunate, inauspicious.
🔁 timely, opportune.

untiring *adj* unflagging, tireless, indefatigable, dogged, persevering, persistent, tenacious, determined, resolute, devoted, dedicated, constant, incessant, unremitting, steady, staunch, unfailing.
☒ inconstant, wavering.

untold *adj* uncounted, unnumbered, unreckoned, incalculable, innumerable, uncountable, countless, infinite, measureless, boundless, inexhaustible, undreamed-of, unimaginable.

untouched *adj* unharmed, undamaged, unimpaired, unhurt, uninjured, unscathed, safe, intact, unchanged, unaltered, unaffected.
☒ damaged, affected.

untoward *adj* unfortunate, troublesome, inconvenient, annoying, adverse, unfavourable, unexpected, unsuitable, unfitting, untimely, vexatious, irritating, worrying, awkward, disastrous, improper, contrary, unlucky, inappropriate, inauspicious, ominous, ill-timed, indecorous (*fml*), inopportune (*fml*), unbecoming (*fml*), unpropitious (*fml*), unseemly (*fml*).
☒ suitable, auspicious.

untrained *adj* unskilled, untaught, unschooled, uneducated, inexperienced, unqualified, amateur, unprofessional, inexpert.
☒ trained, expert.

untried *adj* untested, unproved, experimental, exploratory, new, novel, innovative, innovatory.
☒ tried, tested, proven.

untrue *adj* **1** FALSE, fallacious, deceptive, misleading, wrong, incorrect, inaccurate, mistaken, erroneous. **2** UNFAITHFUL, disloyal, untrustworthy, dishonest, deceitful, untruthful.
☒ **1** true, correct. **2** faithful, honest.

untrustworthy *adj* dishonest, deceitful, untruthful, disloyal, unfaithful, faithless, treacherous, false, untrue, capricious, fickle, fly-by-night, unreliable, untrusty.
☒ trustworthy, reliable.

untruth *n* lie, fib, whopper (*infml*), story, tale, fiction, invention, fabrication, falsehood, lying, untruthfulness, deceit, perjury.
☒ truth.

untruthful *adj* lying, deceitful, dishonest, crooked (*infml*), hypocritical,

two-faced, insincere, false, untrue.
☒ truthful, honest.

unused *adj* leftover, remaining, surplus, extra, spare, available, new, fresh, blank, clean, untouched, unexploited, unemployed, idle.
☒ used.

unusual *adj* uncommon, rare, unfamiliar, strange, odd, curious, queer, bizarre, unconventional, irregular, abnormal, extraordinary, remarkable, exceptional, different, surprising, unexpected.
☒ usual, normal, ordinary.

unutterable *adj* unspeakable, indescribable, unimaginable, extreme, overwhelming, ineffable.

unveil *v* uncover, expose, bare, reveal, disclose, divulge, discover.
☒ cover, hide.

unwanted *adj* undesired, unsolicited, uninvited, unwelcome, outcast, rejected, unrequired, unneeded, unnecessary, surplus, extra, superfluous, redundant.
☒ wanted, needed, necessary.

unwarranted *adj* unjustified, undeserved, unprovoked, uncalled-for, groundless, unreasonable, unjust, wrong.
☒ warranted, justifiable, deserved.

unwary *adj* unguarded, incautious, careless, imprudent, indiscreet, thoughtless, unthinking, heedless, reckless, rash, hasty.
☒ wary, cautious.

unwelcome *adj* **1** UNWANTED, undesirable, unpopular, uninvited, excluded, rejected. **2** *unwelcome news*: unpleasant, disagreeable, upsetting, worrying, distasteful, unpalatable, unacceptable.
☒ **1** welcome, desirable. **2** pleasant.

unwell *adj* ill, sick, poorly, indisposed, off-colour, ailing, sickly, unhealthy.
☒ well, healthy.

unwieldy *adj* unmanageable, inconvenient, awkward, clumsy, ungainly, bulky, massive, hefty, weighty, ponderous, cumbersome.
☒ handy, dainty.

unwilling *adj* reluctant, disinclined, indisposed, resistant, opposed, averse, loath, slow, unenthusiastic, grudging.
☒ willing, enthusiastic.

unwind *v* **1** UNROLL, unreel, unwrap, undo, uncoil, untwist, unravel,

disentangle. **2** (*infml*) RELAX, wind down, calm down.
⇄ **1** wind, roll.

unwitting *adj* unaware, unknowing, unsuspecting, unthinking, unconscious, involuntary, accidental, chance, inadvertent, unintentional, unintended, unplanned.
⇄ knowing, conscious, deliberate.

unworldly *adj* spiritual, transcendental, metaphysical, otherworldly, visionary, idealistic, impractical, unsophisticated, inexperienced, innocent, naïve.
⇄ worldly, materialistic, sophisticated.

unworthy *adj* undeserving, inferior, ineligible, unsuitable, inappropriate, unfitting, unbecoming, unseemly, improper, unprofessional, shameful, disgraceful, dishonourable, discreditable, ignoble, base, contemptible, despicable.
⇄ worthy, commendable.

unwritten *adj* verbal, oral, word-of-mouth, unrecorded, tacit, implicit, understood, accepted, recognized, traditional, customary, conventional.
⇄ written, recorded.

up-and-coming *adj* promising, ambitious, eager, assertive, enterprising, go-getting (*infml*), pushing (*infml*).

upbeat *adj* positive, buoyant, hopeful, optimistic, encouraging, favourable, promising, forward-looking, bright, cheerful, heartening, cheery, rosy, bullish (*infml*).
⇄ downbeat, gloomy.

upbraid *v* reprimand, admonish, rebuke, reprove, reproach, scold, chide, castigate (*fml*), berate, criticize, censure.
⇄ praise, commend.

upbringing *n* bringing-up, raising, rearing, breeding, parenting, care, nurture, cultivation, education, training, instruction, teaching.

update *v* modernize, revise, amend, correct, renew, renovate, revamp.

upgrade *v* promote, advance, elevate, raise, improve, enhance.
⇄ downgrade, demote.

upheaval *n* disruption, disturbance, upset, chaos, confusion, disorder, turmoil, shake-up (*infml*), revolution, overthrow.

uphill *adj* hard, difficult, arduous, tough, taxing, strenuous, laborious, tiring, wearisome, exhausting, gruelling, punishing.
⇄ easy.

uphold *v* support, maintain, hold to, stand by, defend, champion, advocate, promote, back, endorse, sustain, fortify, strengthen, justify, vindicate (*fml*).
⇄ abandon, reject.

upkeep *n* maintenance, preservation, conservation, care, running, repair, support, sustenance, subsistence, keep.
⇄ neglect.

uplift *v* improve, better, boost, upgrade, advance, enlighten, exalt, inspire, elate, lift, elevate, raise, hoist, heave, refine, cultivate, edify, civilize, ameliorate (*fml*).

upper *adj* higher, loftier, superior, senior, top, topmost, uppermost, high, elevated, exalted, eminent, important.
⇄ lower, inferior, junior.

upper-class *adj* aristocratic, noble, well-bred, well-born, high-born, high-class, patrician, blue-blooded, exclusive, elite, swanky (*infml*), top-drawer (*infml*).
⇄ humble, working-class.

uppermost *adj* highest, loftiest, top, topmost, greatest, supreme, first, primary, foremost, leading, principal, main, chief, dominant, predominant, paramount, pre-eminent.
⇄ lowest.

upright *adj* **1** VERTICAL, perpendicular, erect, straight. **2** RIGHTEOUS, good, virtuous, upstanding, noble, honourable, ethical, principled, incorruptible, honest, trustworthy.
⇄ **1** horizontal, flat. **2** dishonest.

uprising *n* rebellion, revolt, mutiny, rising, insurgence, insurrection, revolution.

uproar *n* noise, din, racket, hubbub, hullabaloo, pandemonium, tumult, turmoil, turbulence, commotion, confusion, disorder, clamour, outcry, furore, riot, rumpus.

uproot *v* pull up, rip up, root out, weed out, remove, displace, eradicate, destroy, wipe out.

upset *v* **1** DISTRESS, grieve, dismay, trouble, worry, agitate, disturb, bother, fluster, ruffle, discompose, shake, unnerve, disconcert, confuse, disorganize. **2** TIP, spill, overturn, capsize, topple, overthrow, destabilize, unsteady.
➢ *n* **1** TROUBLE, worry, agitation, disturbance, bother, disruption, upheaval,

shake-up (*infml*), reverse, surprise, shock.
2 *stomach upset*: disorder, complaint, bug
(*infml*), illness, sickness.

➤ *adj* distressed, grieved, hurt, annoyed,
dismayed, troubled, worried, agitated,
disturbed, bothered, shaken,
disconcerted, confused.

upshot *n* result, consequence, outcome,
issue, end, conclusion, finish, culmination.

upside down *adj* inverted, upturned,
wrong way up, upset, overturned,
disordered, muddled, jumbled, confused,
topsy-turvy, chaotic.

upstanding *adj* upright, honest,
honourable, strong, true, trustworthy,
ethical, moral, principled, incorruptible,
erect, good, virtuous, firm, four-square.
EA untrustworthy.

upstart *n* social climber, arriviste,
parvenu, parvenue, nouveau riche,
nobody.

up-to-date *adj* current, contemporary,
modern, fashionable, trendy (*infml*), latest,
recent, new.
EA out-of-date, old-fashioned.

upturn *n* revival, recovery, upsurge,
upswing, rise, increase, boost,
improvement.
EA downturn, drop.

urban *adj* town, city, inner-city,
metropolitan, municipal, civic, built-up.
EA country, rural.

urbane *adj* cultivated, suave,
sophisticated, refined, polished, mannerly,
civilized, courteous, cultured, debonair,
well-bred, well-mannered, civil, elegant,
smooth.
EA gauche, uncouth.

urchin *n* brat, guttersnipe, ragamuffin,
waif, gamin, street Arab, kid.

urge *v* advise, counsel, recommend,
advocate, encourage, exhort, implore, beg,
beseech, entreat, plead, press, constrain,
compel, force, push, drive, impel, goad,
spur, hasten, induce, incite, instigate.
EA discourage, dissuade, deter, hinder.
➤ *n* desire, wish, inclination, fancy,
longing, yearning, itch, impulse,
compulsion, impetus, drive, eagerness.
EA disinclination.

urgency *n* hurry, haste, pressure, stress,
importance, seriousness, gravity,
imperativeness, need, necessity.

urgent *adj* immediate, instant,

top-priority, important, critical, crucial,
imperative, exigent, pressing, compelling,
persuasive, earnest, eager, insistent,
persistent.
EA unimportant.

usable *adj* working, operational,
serviceable, functional, practical,
exploitable, available, current, valid.
EA unusable, useless.

usage *n* **1** TREATMENT, handling,
management, control, running, operation,
employment, application, use. **2**
TRADITION, custom, practice, habit,
convention, etiquette, rule, regulation,
form, routine, procedure, method.

use *v* utilize, employ, exercise, practise,
operate, work, apply, wield, handle, treat,
manipulate, exploit, enjoy, consume,
exhaust, expend, spend.
➤ *n* utility, usefulness, value, worth, profit,
advantage, benefit, good, avail, help,
service, point, object, end, purpose,
reason, cause, occasion, need, necessity,
usage, application, employment,
operation, exercise.
◆ **used to** accustomed to, adjusted to, in
the habit of, familiar with, acclimatized to,
given to, prone to, habituated to (*fml*),
inured to (*fml*), wont to (*fml*), at home with
(*infml*), no stranger to (*infml*).
◆ **use up** finish, exhaust, drain, sap,
deplete, consume, devour, absorb, waste,
squander, fritter.

used *adj* second-hand, cast-off, hand-me-
down, nearly new, worn, dog-eared, soiled.
EA unused, new, fresh.

useful *adj* handy, convenient, all-purpose,
practical, effective, productive, fruitful,
profitable, valuable, worthwhile,
advantageous, beneficial, helpful.
EA useless, ineffective, worthless.

useless *adj* futile, fruitless, unproductive,
vain, idle, unavailing, hopeless, pointless,
worthless, unusable, broken-down,
clapped-out (*sl*), unworkable, impractical,
ineffective, inefficient, incompetent, weak.
EA useful, helpful, effective.

usher *n* usherette, doorkeeper, attendant,
escort, guide.
➤ *v* escort, accompany, conduct, lead,
direct, guide, show, pilot, steer.
◆ **usher in** herald, inaugurate, initiate,
introduce, launch, precede, announce,
ring in, pave the way for.

usual *adj* normal, typical, stock, standard,

regular, routine, habitual, customary, conventional, accepted, recognized, accustomed, familiar, common, everyday, general, ordinary, unexceptional, expected, predictable.
Ea unusual, strange, rare.

usually *adv* normally, generally, as a rule, ordinarily, typically, traditionally, regularly, commonly, by and large, on the whole, mainly, chiefly, mostly.
Ea exceptionally.

usurp *v* take over, assume, arrogate, seize, take, annex, appropriate (*fml*), commandeer, steal.

utensil *n* tool, implement, instrument, device, contrivance, gadget, apparatus, appliance.

utility *n* usefulness, use, value, profit, advantage, benefit, avail, service, convenience, practicality, efficacy, efficiency, fitness, serviceableness.

utilize *v* use, employ, make use of, put to use, resort to, take advantage of, turn to account, exploit, adapt.

utmost *adj* 1 *with the utmost care*: extreme, maximum, greatest, highest, supreme, paramount. **2** FARTHEST, furthermost, remotest, outermost, ultimate, final, last.

➤ *n* best, hardest, most, maximum.

Utopia *n* paradise, Eden, Garden of Eden, bliss, Elysium, heaven, heaven on earth, Shangri-la, seventh heaven (*infml*).

Utopian *adj* ideal, idealistic, illusory, imaginary, perfect, visionary, wishful, fanciful, fantastic, airy, dream, romantic, unworkable, impractical, Elysian, chimerical (*fml*).

utter¹ *adj* absolute, complete, total, entire, thoroughgoing, out-and-out, downright, sheer, stark, arrant (*fml*), unmitigated, unqualified, perfect, consummate (*fml*).

utter² *v* speak, say, voice, vocalize, verbalize, express, articulate, enunciate, sound, pronounce, deliver, state, declare, announce, proclaim, tell, reveal, divulge.

utterance *n* statement, remark, comment, expression, articulation, delivery, speech, declaration, announcement, proclamation, pronouncement.

utterly *adv* absolutely, completely, totally, fully, entirely, wholly, thoroughly, downright, perfectly.

U-turn *n* about-turn, volte-face, reversal, backtrack.

Vu

vacancy *n* opportunity, opening, position, post, job, place, room, situation.

vacant *adj* 1 EMPTY, unoccupied, unfilled, free, available, void, not in use, unused, uninhabited. 2 BLANK, expressionless, vacuous, inane, inattentive, absent, absent-minded, unthinking, dreamy.
☒ 1 occupied, engaged.

vacate *v* leave, depart, evacuate, abandon, withdraw, quit.

vacillate *v* waver, hesitate, fluctuate, shilly-shally, sway, oscillate, keep changing one's mind, haver, temporize, tergiversate (*fml*).

vacillating *adj* wavering, hesitant, irresolute, uncertain, unresolved, shilly-shallying, shuffling, oscillating.
☒ resolute, unhesitating.

vacuum *n* emptiness, void, nothingness, vacuity, space, chasm, gap.

vagabond *n* vagrant, tramp, wanderer, wayfarer, down-and-out, hobo, rascal, beggar, rover, runabout, itinerant, migrant, outcast, nomad, bum (*sl*).

vagary *n* caprice, fancy, notion, prank, quirk, whim, whimsy, humour, crotchet.

vague *adj* 1 ILL-DEFINED, blurred, indistinct, hazy, dim, shadowy, misty, fuzzy, nebulous, obscure. 2 INDEFINITE, imprecise, unclear, uncertain, undefined, undetermined, unspecific, generalized, inexact, ambiguous, evasive, loose, woolly.
☒ 1 clear. 2 definite.

vain *adj* 1 *a vain attempt*: useless, worthless, futile, abortive, fruitless, pointless, unproductive, unprofitable, unavailing, hollow, groundless, empty, trivial, unimportant. 2 CONCEITED, proud, self-satisfied, arrogant, self-important, egotistical, bigheaded (*infml*), swollen-headed (*infml*), stuck-up (*infml*), affected, pretentious, ostentatious, swaggering.
☒ 1 fruitful, successful. 2 modest, self-effacing.

◆ **in vain** to no avail, unsuccessfully, uselessly, fruitlessly, vainly, ineffectually (*fml*).
☒ successfully.

valiant *adj* brave, courageous, gallant, fearless, intrepid, bold, dauntless, heroic, plucky, indomitable, staunch.
☒ cowardly, fearful.

valid *adj* 1 LOGICAL, well-founded, well-grounded, sound, good, cogent, convincing, telling, conclusive, reliable, substantial, weighty, powerful, just. 2 OFFICIAL, legal, lawful, legitimate, authentic, bona fide, genuine, binding, proper.
☒ 1 false, weak. 2 unofficial, invalid.

validate *v* confirm, authenticate, endorse, legalize, authorize, substantiate, underwrite, ratify, certify, attest (*fml*), corroborate (*fml*).

validity *n* soundness, legality, lawfulness, legitimacy, foundation, grounds, justifiability, strength, power, force, weight, substance, logic, point, authority, cogency (*fml*).
☒ invalidity.

valley *n* dale, vale, dell, glen, hollow, cwm, depression, gulch.

valour *n* boldness, courage, bravery, heroism, intrepidity, lion-heartedness, fearlessness, mettle, spirit, gallantry, hardiness, doughtiness, fortitude (*fml*).
☒ cowardice, weakness.

valuable *adj* 1 *valuable necklace*: precious, prized, valued, costly, expensive, dear, high-priced, treasured, cherished, estimable. 2 *valuable suggestions*: helpful, worthwhile, useful, beneficial, invaluable, constructive, fruitful, profitable, important, serviceable, worthy, handy.
☒ 1 worthless. 2 useless.

value *n* 1 COST, price, rate, worth. 2 WORTH, use, usefulness, utility, merit, importance, desirability, benefit, advantage, significance, good, profit.
➤ *v* 1 PRIZE, appreciate, treasure, esteem, hold dear, respect, cherish. 2 EVALUATE, assess, estimate, price, appraise, survey, rate.
☒ 1 disregard, neglect. 2 undervalue.

valued *adj* highly regarded, cherished, treasured, prized, respected, dear, loved, beloved, esteemed (*fml*).

vanguard n forefront, most advanced part, front, front line, firing line, spearhead, lead, fore, leading/foremost position.

vanish v disappear, fade, dissolve, evaporate, disperse, melt, die out, depart, exit, fizzle out, peter out.
🖝 appear, materialize.

vanity n 1 CONCEIT, conceitedness, pride, arrogance, self-conceit, self-love, self-satisfaction, narcissism, egotism, pretension, ostentation, affectation, airs, bigheadedness (infml), swollen-headedness (infml). 2 WORTHLESSNESS, uselessness, emptiness, futility, pointlessness, unreality, hollowness, fruitlessness, triviality.
🖝 1 modesty, worth.

vapour n steam, mist, fog, smoke, breath, fumes, haze, damp, dampness, exhalation.

variable adj changeable, inconstant, varying, shifting, mutable, unpredictable, fluctuating, fitful, unstable, unsteady, wavering, vacillating, temperamental, fickle, flexible.
🖝 fixed, invariable, stable.

variance n 1 VARIATION, difference, discrepancy, divergence, inconsistency, disagreement. 2 DISAGREEMENT, disharmony, conflict, discord, division, dissent, dissension, quarrelling, strife.
🖝 1 agreement. 2 harmony.

variant n alternative, variation, modification, development, deviant, rogue.
➤ adj alternative, different, divergent, modified, derived, deviant, exceptional.
🖝 normal, standard, usual.

variation n diversity, variety, deviation, discrepancy, diversification, alteration, change, difference, departure, modification, modulation, inflection, novelty, innovation.
🖝 monotony, uniformity.

varied adj assorted, diverse, different, miscellaneous, mixed, various, sundry, heterogeneous (fml), wide-ranging.
🖝 standardized, uniform.

variegated adj multicoloured, many-coloured, parti-coloured, varicoloured, speckled, mottled, dappled, pied, streaked, motley.
🖝 monochrome, plain.

variety n 1 ASSORTMENT, miscellany, mixture, collection, medley, potpourri, range. 2 DIFFERENCE, diversity,

dissimilarity, discrepancy, variation, multiplicity. 3 SORT, kind, class, category, species, type, breed, brand, make, strain.
🖝 2 uniformity, similitude (fml).

various adj different, differing, diverse, varied, varying, assorted, miscellaneous, heterogeneous (fml), distinct, diversified, mixed, many, several.

varnish n lacquer, glaze, resin, polish, gloss, coating.

vary v 1 CHANGE, alter, modify, modulate, diversify, reorder, transform, alternate, inflect, permutate. 2 DIVERGE, differ, disagree, depart, fluctuate.

vast adj huge, immense, massive, gigantic, enormous, great, colossal, extensive, tremendous, sweeping, unlimited, fathomless, immeasurable, never-ending, monumental, monstrous, far-flung.

vault¹ v leap, spring, bound, clear, jump, hurdle, leap-frog.

vault² n 1 CELLAR, crypt, strongroom, repository, cavern, depository, wine-cellar, tomb, mausoleum. 2 ARCH, roof, span.

vaunt (fml) v boast, brag, exult in, flaunt, show off, parade, trumpet, crow.
🖝 belittle, minimize.

veer v swerve, swing, change, shift, diverge, deviate, wheel, turn, sheer, tack.

vegetable

Vegetables include: artichoke, aubergine, bean, beetroot, broad bean, broccoli, Brussels sprout, butter bean, cabbage, calabrese, capsicum, carrot, cauliflower, celeriac, celery, chicory, courgette, cress, cucumber, eggplant (US), endive, fennel, French bean, garlic, kale, leek, lentil, lettuce, mangetout, marrow, mushroom, okra, onion, parsnip, pea, pepper, petit pois, potato, spud (infml), pumpkin, radish, runner bean, shallot, soya bean, spinach, spring onion, swede, sweetcorn, sweet potato, turnip, watercress, yam, zucchini (US).

Vegetable dishes include: aubergine roll, baba ganoush, bhaji, onion bhaji, bubble and squeak, cauliflower cheese, champ, chilada, colcannon, coleslaw, couscous, crudités, dal, dolma, duchesse potatoes, fasolia, felafel, fondue, gado-gado, gnocchi, guacamole, gumbo, hummus, imam bayildi, latke, macaroni cheese, macedoine, mushy peas, nut cutlet, paella, pakora, pease pudding, peperonata, pilau, pissaladière, polenta, raita, ratatouille, risotto, rösti, salad, caesar salad, green salad, warm salad, mixed salad, salade niçoise, Waldorf salad, winter salad, sauerkraut, stovies, stuffed marrow, stuffed mushroom, succotash, tabbouleh, tahina, tsatsiki, vegetable chilli, vegetable curry, vegetable soup, vegetarian goulash, vichyssoise.

vegetate *v* stagnate, degenerate, deteriorate, rusticate, go to seed, idle, rust, languish.

vehement *adj* impassioned, passionate, ardent, fervent, intense, forceful, emphatic, heated, strong, powerful, urgent, enthusiastic, animated, eager, earnest, forcible, fierce, violent, zealous.
Ⓔ apathetic, indifferent.

vehicle *n* 1 CONVEYANCE, transport. 2 MEANS, agency, channel, medium, mechanism, organ.

Vehicles include: plane, boat, ship, car, taxi, hackney-carriage, bicycle, bike (*infml*), cycle, tandem, tricycle, boneshaker (*infml*), penny-farthing, motor-cyclemotor-bike, scooter, bus, omnibus, minibus, double-decker (*infml*), coach, charabanc, caravan, caravanette, camper, train, Pullman, sleeper, wagon-lit, tube, tram, monorail, maglev, trolleybus; van, Transit®, lorry, truck, juggernaut, pantechnicon, trailer, tractor, fork-lift truck, steam-roller, tank, wagon; bobsleigh, sled, sledge, sleigh, toboggan, troika; barouche, brougham, dog-cart, dray, four-in-hand, gig, hansom, landau, phaeton, post-chaise, stagecoach, sulky, surrey, trap; rickshaw, sedan-chair, litter. *see also* **aircraft**; **boats and ships**; **car**.

veil *v* screen, cloak, cover, mask, shadow, shield, obscure, conceal, hide, disguise, shade.
Ⓔ expose, uncover.
➤ *n* cover, cloak, curtain, mask, screen, disguise, film, blind, shade, shroud.

vein *n* 1 STREAK, stripe, stratum, seam, lode, blood vessel. 2 MOOD, tendency, bent, strain, temper, tenor, tone, frame of mind, mode, style.

Veins and arteries include: aorta, axillary, brachial, carotid, femoral, frontal, gastric, hepatic, iliac, jugular, portal, pulmonary, radial, renal, saphena, subclavian, superior, temporal, tibial.

velocity *n* speed, rate, quickness, rapidity, pace, impetus, swiftness, celerity (*fml*).

vendetta *n* feud, blood-feud, enmity, rivalry, quarrel, bad blood, bitterness.

veneer *n* front, façade, appearance, coating, surface, show, mask, gloss, pretence, guise, finish.

venerable *adj* respected, revered, esteemed, honoured, venerated, dignified, grave, wise, august, aged, worshipped.

venerate *v* revere, respect, honour, esteem, worship, hallow (*fml*), adore.
Ⓔ despise, anathematize.

vengeance *n* retribution, revenge, retaliation, reprisal, requital, tit for tat.
Ⓔ forgiveness.
♦ **with a vengeance 1** FORCEFULLY, violently, vigorously, powerfully, energetically, furiously, flat out (*infml*), like crazy (*infml*). **2** TO A GREAT DEGREE, greatly, to a great extent, fully, to the full, to the utmost, with no holds barred (*infml*).

venom *n* 1 POISON, toxin. 2 RANCOUR, ill-will, malice, malevolence, spite, bitterness, acrimony, hate, virulence.

venomous *adj* 1 POISONOUS, toxic, virulent, harmful, noxious. 2 MALICIOUS, spiteful, vicious, vindictive, baleful, hostile, malignant, rancorous, baneful.
Ⓔ 1 harmless.

vent *n* opening, hole, aperture, outlet, passage, orifice, duct.
➤ *v* air, express, voice, utter, release, discharge, emit.

ventilate *v* 1 *ventilate a room*: air, aerate, freshen. 2 *ventilate one's feelings*: air, broadcast, debate, discuss.

venture *v* 1 DARE, advance, make bold, put forward, presume, suggest, volunteer. 2 RISK, hazard, endanger, imperil, jeopardize, speculate, wager, stake.
➤ *n* risk, chance, hazard, speculation, gamble, undertaking, project, adventure, endeavour, enterprise, operation, fling.

veracity *n* truthfulness, truth, trustworthiness, integrity, honesty, frankness, precision, accuracy, candour, credibility, exactitude, probity (*fml*), rectitude (*fml*).
Ⓔ untruthfulness.

verbal *adj* spoken, oral, verbatim, unwritten, word-of-mouth.

verbatim *adv* word for word, exactly, literally, to the letter, precisely.

verbose *adj* long-winded, wordy, prolix, loquacious (*fml*), diffuse, circumlocutory. ☒ succinct, brief.

verdict *n* decision, judgement, conclusion, finding, adjudication, assessment, opinion, sentence.

verge *n* border, edge, margin, limit, rim, brim, brink, boundary, threshold, extreme, edging.
♦ **verge on** approach, border on, come close to, near.

verify *v* confirm, corroborate, substantiate, authenticate, bear out, prove, support, validate, testify, attest. ☒ invalidate, discredit.

vernacular *adj* indigenous, local, native, popular, vulgar, informal, colloquial, common.
➤ *n* language, speech, tongue, parlance, dialect, idiom, jargon.

versatile *adj* adaptable, flexible, all-round, multipurpose, multifaceted, adjustable, many-sided, general-purpose, functional, resourceful, handy, variable. ☒ inflexible.

verse *n* poetry, rhyme, stanza, metre, doggerel, jingle.

versed *adj* skilled, proficient, practised, experienced, familiar, acquainted, learned, knowledgeable, conversant, seasoned, qualified, competent, accomplished.

version *n* 1 RENDERING, reading, interpretation, account, translation, paraphrase, adaptation, portrayal. 2 TYPE, kind, variant, form, model, style, design.

vertical *adj* upright, perpendicular, upstanding, erect, on end. ☒ horizontal.

vertigo *n* dizziness, giddiness, light-headedness.

verve *n* vitality, vivacity, animation, energy, dash, élan, liveliness, sparkle, vigour, enthusiasm, gusto, life, relish, spirit, force. ☒ apathy, lethargy.

very *adv* extremely, greatly, highly, deeply, truly, terribly (*infml*), remarkably, excessively, exceeding(ly), acutely, particularly, really, absolutely, noticeably, unusually. ☒ slightly, scarcely.
➤ *adj* actual, real, same, selfsame, identical, true, genuine, simple, utter, sheer, pure, perfect, plain, mere, bare, exact, appropriate.

vessel *n* 1 SHIP, boat, craft, barque. 2 CONTAINER, bowl, receptacle, holder, jar, pot, pitcher, jug.

vest *v* give, endow, supply, grant, empower, authorize, sanction, bestow (*fml*), confer (*fml*).

vestibule *n* foyer, hall, entrance, entrance hall, entranceway, lobby, porch, anteroom, portico.

vestige *n* trace, suspicion, indication, sign, hint, evidence, whiff, inkling, glimmer, token, scrap, remains, remainder, remnant, residue.

vet *v* investigate, examine, check, scrutinize, scan, inspect, survey, review, appraise, audit.

veteran *n* master, past master, old hand, old stager, old-timer, pro (*infml*), war-horse. ☒ novice, recruit.
➤ *adj* experienced, practised, seasoned, long-serving, expert, adept, proficient, old. ☒ inexperienced.

veto *v* reject, turn down, forbid, disallow, ban, prohibit, rule out, block. ☒ approve, sanction.
➤ *n* rejection, ban, embargo, prohibition, thumbs down (*infml*). ☒ approval, assent.

vex *v* irritate, annoy, provoke, pester, trouble, upset, worry, bother, put out (*infml*), harass, hassle (*infml*), aggravate (*infml*), needle (*infml*), disturb, distress, agitate, exasperate, torment, fret. ☒ calm, soothe.

vexed *adj* 1 IRRITATED, annoyed, provoked, upset, troubled, worried, nettled, put out, exasperated, bothered, confused, perplexed, aggravated (*infml*), harassed, hassled (*infml*), ruffled, riled, disturbed, distressed, displeased, agitated. 2 *a vexed question*: difficult, controversial, contested, disputed.

viable *adj* feasible, practicable, possible, workable, usable, operable, achievable, sustainable. ☒ impossible, unworkable.

vibrant *adj* 1 ANIMATED, vivacious, vivid, bright, brilliant, colourful, lively, responsive, sparkling, spirited, sensitive. 2 THRILLING, dynamic, electrifying, electric.

vibrate *v* quiver, pulsate, shudder, shiver, resonate, reverberate, throb, oscillate, tremble, undulate, sway, swing, shake.

vicarious *adj* indirect, second-hand, substituted, surrogate, delegated, deputed, acting, commissioned.

vice *n* 1 EVIL, evil-doing, depravity, immorality, wickedness, sin, corruption, iniquity (*fml*), profligacy (*fml*), degeneracy. 2 FAULT, failing, defect, shortcoming, weakness, imperfection, blemish, bad habit, besetting sin.
F3 1 virtue, morality.

vice versa *adv* reciprocally, oppositely, contrariwise, the other way round, inversely.

vicinity *n* neighbourhood, area, locality, district, precincts, environs, proximity.

vicious *adj* 1 WICKED, bad, wrong, immoral, depraved, unprincipled, diabolical, corrupt, debased, perverted, profligate (*fml*), vile, heinous.
2 MALICIOUS, spiteful, vindictive, virulent, cruel, mean, nasty, slanderous, venomous, defamatory. 3 SAVAGE, wild, violent, barbarous, brutal, dangerous.
F3 1 virtuous. 2 kind.

victim *n* sufferer, casualty, prey, scapegoat, martyr, sacrifice, fatality.
F3 offender, attacker.

victimize *v* 1 OPPRESS, persecute, discriminate against, pick on, prey on, bully, exploit. 2 CHEAT, deceive, defraud, swindle (*infml*), dupe, hoodwink, fool.

victorious *adj* conquering, champion, triumphant, winning, unbeaten, successful, prize-winning, top, first.
F3 defeated, unsuccessful.

victory *n* conquest, win, triumph, success, superiority, mastery, vanquishment, subjugation, overcoming.
F3 defeat, loss.

vie *v* strive, compete, contend, struggle, contest, fight, rival.

view *n* 1 OPINION, attitude, belief, judgement, estimation, feeling, sentiment, impression, notion. 2 SIGHT, scene, vision, vista, outlook, prospect, perspective, panorama, landscape. 3 SURVEY, inspection, examination, observation, scrutiny, scan. 4 GLIMPSE, look, sight, perception.
➤ *v* 1 CONSIDER, regard, contemplate, judge, think about, speculate. 2 OBSERVE, watch, see, examine, inspect, look at,

scan, survey, witness, perceive.

viewer *n* spectator, watcher, observer, onlooker.

viewpoint *n* attitude, position, perspective, slant, standpoint, stance, opinion, angle, feeling.

vigilant *adj* watchful, alert, attentive, observant, on one's guard, on the lookout, cautious, wide-awake, sleepless, unsleeping.
F3 careless.

vigorous *adj* energetic, active, lively, healthy, strong, strenuous, robust, lusty, sound, vital, brisk, dynamic, forceful, forcible, powerful, stout, spirited, full-blooded, effective, efficient, enterprising, flourishing, intense.
F3 weak, feeble.

vigour *n* energy, vitality, liveliness, health, robustness, stamina, strength, resilience, soundness, spirit, verve, gusto, activity, animation, power, potency, force, forcefulness, might, dash, dynamism.
F3 weakness.

vile *adj* 1 *a vile sinner*: base, contemptible, debased, depraved, degenerate, bad, wicked, wretched, worthless, sinful, miserable, mean, evil, impure, corrupt, despicable, disgraceful, degrading, vicious, appalling. 2 *a vile meal*: disgusting, foul, nauseating, sickening, repulsive, repugnant (*fml*), revolting, noxious, offensive, nasty, loathsome, horrid.
F3 1 pure, worthy. 2 pleasant, lovely.

vilify *v* criticize, revile, denigrate, denounce, slander, defame, stigmatize, abuse, smear, debase, malign (*fml*), disparage (*fml*), asperse (*fml*), berate (*fml*), calumniate (*fml*), decry (*fml*), traduce (*fml*), vilipend (*fml*), vituperate (*fml*), badmouth (*infml*), slate (*infml*), slam (*infml*).
F3 praise, compliment, adore, eulogize, glorify.

village *n* hamlet, community, settlement, town, one-horse town (*infml*).

villain *n* evil-doer, miscreant (*fml*), scoundrel, rogue, malefactor (*fml*), criminal, reprobate, rascal.

villainous *adj* wicked, bad, criminal, evil, sinful, vicious, notorious, cruel, inhuman, vile, depraved, disgraceful, terrible.
F3 good.

vindicate (*fml*) *v* 1 CLEAR, acquit, excuse, exonerate, absolve, rehabilitate. 2 JUSTIFY, uphold, support, maintain, defend, establish, advocate, assert, verify.

vindictive *adj* spiteful, unforgiving, implacable, vengeful, relentless, unrelenting, revengeful, resentful, punitive, venomous, malevolent, malicious.

Fa forgiving.

vintage *n* year, period, era, epoch, generation, origin, harvest, crop.
➤ *adj* choice, best, fine, prime, select, superior, rare, mature, old, ripe, classic, venerable, veteran.

violate *v* 1 CONTRAVENE, disobey, disregard, transgress, break, flout, infringe. 2 OUTRAGE, debauch, defile, rape, ravish, dishonour, desecrate, profane, invade.

Fa 1 observe.

violence *n* 1 FORCE, strength, power, vehemence, might, intensity, ferocity, fierceness, severity, tumult, turbulence, wildness. 2 BRUTALITY, destructiveness, cruelty, bloodshed, murderousness, savagery, passion, fighting, frenzy, fury, hostilities.

violent *adj* 1 INTENSE, strong, severe, sharp, acute, extreme, harmful, destructive, devastating, injurious, powerful, painful, agonizing, forceful, forcible, harsh, ruinous, rough, vehement, tumultuous, turbulent. 2 CRUEL, brutal, aggressive, bloodthirsty, impetuous, hot-headed, headstrong, murderous, savage, wild, vicious, unrestrained, uncontrollable, ungovernable, passionate, furious, intemperate, maddened, outrageous, riotous, fiery.

Fa 1 calm, moderate. 2 peaceful, gentle.

VIP *n* celebrity, luminary, magnate, somebody, notable, personage, dignitary, star, headliner, lion, bigwig (*infml*), big name (*infml*), big noise (*infml*), big shot (*infml*), big cheese (*infml*), heavyweight (*infml*).

Fa nobody, nonentity.

virgin *n* girl, maiden, celibate, vestal.
➤ *adj* virginal, chaste, intact, immaculate, maidenly, pure, modest, new, fresh, spotless, stainless, undefiled, untouched, unsullied.

virginal *adj* pure, spotless, virgin, untouched, undefiled, uncorrupted, undisturbed, stainless, white, snowy, vestal, immaculate, chaste, fresh,

celibate, maidenly, pristine (*fml*).

virginity *n* purity, chastity, chasteness, maidenhood, virtue.

virile *adj* man-like, masculine, male, manly, macho (*infml*), robust, vigorous, potent, lusty, red-blooded, forceful, strong, rugged.

Fa effeminate, impotent.

virtual *adj* effective, essential, practical, implied, implicit, potential.

virtually *adv* practically, in effect, almost, nearly, as good as, in essence.

virtue *n* 1 GOODNESS, morality, rectitude, uprightness, worthiness, righteousness, probity (*fml*), integrity, honour, incorruptibility, justice, high-mindedness, excellence. 2 QUALITY, worth, merit, advantage, asset, credit, strength.

Fa 1 vice.

virtuoso *n* expert, master, maestro, prodigy, genius.

virtuous *adj* good, moral, righteous, upright, worthy, honourable, irreproachable, incorruptible, exemplary, unimpeachable, high-principled, blameless, clean-living, excellent, innocent.

Fa immoral, vicious.

virulent *adj* 1 POISONOUS, toxic, venomous, deadly, lethal, malignant, injurious, pernicious, intense. 2 HOSTILE, resentful, spiteful, acrimonious, bitter, vicious, vindictive, malevolent, malicious.

Fa 1 harmless.

viscous *adj* sticky, adhesive, gluey, thick, clammy, mucous, tacky, syrupy, treacly, gummy, tenacious, gelatinous (*fml*), glutinous (*fml*), mucilaginous (*fml*), gooey (*infml*).

Fa runny, thin, watery.

visible *adj* perceptible, discernible, detectable, apparent, noticeable, observable, distinguishable, discoverable, evident, unconcealed, undisguised, unmistakable, conspicuous, clear, obvious, manifest, open, palpable, plain, patent.

Fa invisible, indiscernible, hidden.

vision *n* 1 APPARITION, hallucination, illusion, delusion, mirage, phantom, ghost, chimera, spectre, wraith. 2 IDEA, ideal, conception, insight, view, picture, image, fantasy, dream, daydream. 3 SIGHT, seeing, eyesight, perception, discernment, far-sightedness, foresight, penetration.

visionary *adj* idealistic, impractical, romantic, dreamy, unrealistic, utopian, unreal, fanciful, prophetic, speculative, unworkable, illusory, imaginary.
➤ *n* idealist, romantic, dreamer, daydreamer, fantasist, prophet, mystic, seer, utopian, rainbow-chaser, theorist.
Ea pragmatist.

visit *v* call on, call in, stay with, stay at, drop in on (*infml*), stop by (*infml*), look in, look up, pop in (*infml*), see.
➤ *n* call, stay, stop, excursion, sojourn (*fml*).

visitor *n* caller, guest, company, tourist, holidaymaker.

vista *n* view, prospect, panorama, perspective, outlook, scene.

visual *adj* visible, observable, discernible, perceptible, optical, ocular (*fml*), optic (*fml*), specular (*fml*).

visualize *v* picture, envisage, imagine, conceive.

vital *adj* **1** CRITICAL, crucial, important, imperative, key, significant, basic, fundamental, essential, necessary, requisite, indispensable, urgent, life-or-death, decisive, forceful. **2** LIVING, alive, lively, life-giving, invigorating, spirited, vivacious, vibrant, vigorous, dynamic, animated, energetic, quickening (*fml*).
Ea 1 inessential, peripheral. **2** dead.

vitality *n* life, liveliness, animation, vigour, energy, vivacity, spirit, sparkle, exuberance, go (*infml*), strength, stamina.

vitamin

> Vitamins include: aneurin (thiamine), ascorbic acid, bioflavonoid/citrin, biotin, calciferol, cholecalciferol, cyanocobalamin, ergocalciferol, folic acid, linoleic acid, linolenic acid, menadione, nicotinic acid (niacin), pantothenic acid, phylloquinone, pteroic acid, pyridoxine (adermin), retinol, riboflavin, tocopherol.

vitriolic *adj* bitter, abusive, virulent, vicious, venomous, malicious, caustic, biting, sardonic, scathing, destructive.

vivacious *adj* lively, animated, spirited, high-spirited, effervescent, ebullient, cheerful, sparkling, bubbly, light-hearted.

vivid *adj* **1** BRIGHT, colourful, intense, strong, rich, vibrant, brilliant, glowing, dazzling, vigorous, expressive, dramatic, flamboyant, animated, lively, lifelike,
spirited. **2** MEMORABLE, powerful, graphic, clear, distinct, striking, sharp, realistic.
Ea 1 colourless, dull. **2** vague.

vocabulary *n* language, words, glossary, lexicon, dictionary, word-book, thesaurus, idiom.

vocal *adj* **1** SPOKEN, said, oral, uttered, voiced. **2** ARTICULATE, eloquent, expressive, noisy, clamorous, shrill, strident, outspoken, frank, forthright, plain-spoken.
Ea 1 unspoken. **2** inarticulate.

vocation *n* calling, pursuit, career, métier, mission, profession, trade, employment, work, role, post, job, business, office.

vociferous *adj* noisy, vocal, clamorous, loud, obstreperous, strident, vehement, thundering, shouting.
Ea quiet.

vogue *n* fashion, mode, style, craze, popularity, trend, prevalence, acceptance, custom, fad (*infml*), the latest (*infml*), the rage (*infml*), the thing (*infml*).

voice *n* **1** SPEECH, utterance, articulation, language, words, sound, tone, intonation, inflection, expression, mouthpiece, medium, instrument, organ. **2** SAY, vote, opinion, view, decision, option, will.
➤ *v* express, say, utter, air, articulate, speak of, verbalize, assert, convey, disclose, divulge, declare, enunciate.

void *adj* **1** EMPTY, emptied, free, unfilled, unoccupied, vacant, clear, bare, blank, drained. **2** ANNULLED, inoperative, invalid, cancelled, ineffective, futile, useless, vain, worthless.
Ea 1 full. **2** valid.
➤ *n* emptiness, vacuity, vacuum, chasm, blank, blankness, space, lack, want, cavity, gap, hollow, opening.

volatile *adj* changeable, inconstant, unstable, variable, erratic, temperamental, unsteady, unsettled, fickle, mercurial, unpredictable, capricious, restless, giddy, flighty, up and down (*infml*), lively.
Ea constant, steady.

volcano

> The world's active volcanoes include: Mayon (Philippines); Hudson (Chile); Kilauea (Hawaii); Pinatubo, Mt (Philippines); Vulcano (Italy); St Helens, Mt (USA); Etna (Italy); Ruapehu (New Zealand); Stromboli (Italy); Klyuchevskoy

(Russia); Mauna Loa (Hawaii); Nyamuragira (Congo, DR); Hekla (Iceland); Krakatoa (Sumatra); Taal (Philippines); Vesuvius (Italy).

volition *n* will, free will, choice, choosing, determination, option, election, preference, discretion, purpose, resolution.

volley *n* barrage, bombardment, hail, shower, burst, blast, discharge, explosion.

voluble *adj* fluent, glib, articulate, loquacious (*fml*), talkative, forthcoming, garrulous.

volume *n* 1 BULK, size, capacity, dimensions, amount, mass, quantity, aggregate, amplitude, body. 2 BOOK, tome, publication.

voluminous *adj* roomy, capacious, ample, spacious, billowing, vast, bulky, huge, large.

voluntarily *adv* willingly, freely, intentionally, consciously, deliberately, purposely, spontaneously, of one's own free will, by choice, on one's own initiative, of one's own accord.
☒ involuntarily, unwillingly.

voluntary *adj* 1 FREE, gratuitous, optional, spontaneous, unforced, willing, unpaid, honorary. 2 CONSCIOUS, deliberate, purposeful, intended, intentional, wilful.
☒ 1 compulsory. 2 involuntary.

volunteer *v* offer, propose, put forward, present, suggest, step forward, advance.

voluptuous *adj* 1 SENSUAL, licentious, luxurious. 2 EROTIC, shapely, sexy (*infml*), seductive, provocative, enticing.

vomit *v* be sick, bring up, heave, retch, throw up (*infml*), puke (*infml*).

voracious *adj* insatiable, greedy, hungry, gluttonous, acquisitive, avid, devouring, ravenous, ravening, uncontrolled, unquenchable, edacious (*fml*), omnivorous (*fml*), prodigious (*fml*), rapacious (*fml*).

vortex *n* whirlpool, maelstrom, eddy, whirlwind, whirl.

vote *n* ballot, poll, election, franchise, referendum.
➤ *v* elect, ballot, choose, opt, plump for, declare, return.

voucher *n* coupon, token, ticket, document, paper.

vouch for *v* guarantee, support, back, endorse, confirm, certify, affirm, assert, attest to, speak for, swear to, uphold.

vow *v* promise, pledge, swear, dedicate, devote, profess, consecrate, affirm.
➤ *n* promise, oath, pledge.

voyage *n* journey, trip, passage, expedition, crossing.

vulgar *adj* 1 TASTELESS, flashy, gaudy, tawdry, cheap and nasty (*infml*). 2 UNREFINED, uncouth, coarse, common, crude, ill-bred, impolite, indecorous. 3 INDECENT, suggestive, risqué, rude, indelicate. 4 ORDINARY, general, popular, vernacular.
☒ 1 tasteful. 2 correct. 3 decent.

vulgarity *n* 1 CRUDENESS, indecency, crudity, dirtiness, rudeness, suggestiveness, ribaldry, coarseness. 2 TASTELESSNESS, tawdriness, gaudiness, showiness, ostentation, garishness.
☒ 1 decency, politeness. 2 tastefulness.

vulnerable *adj* unprotected, exposed, defenceless, susceptible, weak, sensitive, wide open.
☒ protected, strong.

Ww

wad _n_ chunk, plug, roll, ball, wodge (_infml_), lump, hunk, mass, block.

waddle _v_ toddle, totter, wobble, sway, rock, shuffle.

wade _v_ cross, ford, loll, lie, wallow, roll, welter, lurch, flounder, splash, traverse (_fml_).
♦ **wade in** pitch in, launch in, tear in, set to, get stuck in, wade through, trawl through, plough through.

waffle _v_ jabber, prattle, blather, rabbit on (_infml_), witter on (_infml_).
➤ _n_ blather, prattle, wordiness, padding, nonsense, gobbledygook (_infml_), hot air (_infml_).

waft _v_ drift, float, blow, transport, transmit.
➤ _n_ breath, puff, draught, current, breeze, scent, whiff.

wag _v_ shake, waggle, wave, sway, swing, bob, nod, wiggle, oscillate, flutter, vibrate, quiver, rock.

wage _n_ pay, fee, earnings, salary, wage-packet, payment, stipend, remuneration, emolument (_fml_), allowance, reward, hire, compensation, recompense.
➤ _v_ carry on, conduct, engage in, undertake, practise, pursue.

waggle _v_ wiggle, wobble, shake, jiggle, wave, oscillate, wag, bobble, flutter.

waif _n_ orphan, stray, foundling.

wail _v_ moan, cry, howl, lament, weep, complain, yowl (_infml_).
➤ _n_ moan, cry, howl, lament, complaint, weeping.

wait _v_ delay, linger, hold back, hesitate, pause, hang around, hang fire, remain, rest, stay.
🖃 proceed, go ahead.

➤ _n_ hold-up, hesitation, delay, interval, pause, halt.

♦ **wait on** serve, attend to, minister to, look after, take care of, tend, work for.

waiter, waitress _n_ server, attendant, steward, stewardess, host, hostess, butler.

waive _v_ renounce, relinquish, forgo, resign, surrender, yield.

waiver _n_ disclaimer, postponement, resignation, surrender, abandonment, abdication (_fml_), deferral (_fml_), relinquishment (_fml_), remission (_fml_), renunciation (_fml_).

wake¹ _v_ **1** RISE, get up, arise, waken, awake, awaken, rouse, stir, come to, bring round. **2** STIMULATE, stir, activate, arouse, animate, excite, fire, galvanize, prod, goad, whet, egg on (_infml_). **3** ALERT, notify, warn, signal, make/become aware of, make/become conscious of.
🖃 **1** sleep.
➤ _n_ funeral, death-watch, vigil, watch.

wake² _n_ trail, track, path, aftermath, backwash, wash, rear, train, waves.

walk _v_ accompany, escort, guide, lead, conduct, usher, shepherd.

➤ _n_ **1** _he has an odd walk_: carriage, gait, step, pace, stride. **2** _go for a walk_: stroll, amble, ramble, saunter, march, hike, tramp, promenade, trek, traipse, trudge, trail. **3** _a tree-lined walk_: footpath, path, walkway, avenue, pathway, promenade, alley, esplanade, lane, drive, track, pavement, sidewalk. **4** BEAT, round, rounds, circuit, way, path, route, trail.
♦ **walk off/away with** go off with, make off with, run off with, steal, pocket, pinch

(*infml*), nick (*sl*), lift (*infml*), purloin (*fml*).

♦ **walk out** go on strike, strike, stop work, down tools, protest, mutiny, revolt, take industrial action.

♦ **walk out on** abandon, desert, forsake (*fml*), run out on (*infml*), jilt, dump (*infml*), leave in the lurch (*infml*), leave high and dry (*infml*).

walker *n* pedestrian, rambler, hiker.

walk-out *n* strike, stoppage, industrial action, protest, rebellion, revolt.

walk-over *n* pushover (*infml*), doddle (*infml*), child's play, piece of cake (*infml*), cinch (*infml*).

wall

> Types of wall and famous walls include: abutment, bailey, barricade, barrier, block, breeze-block wall, brick wall, bulkhead, bulwark, buttress, cavity wall, curtain wall, dam, dike, divider, embankment, enclosure wall, fence, flying buttress, fortification, garden wall, Great Wall of China, Hadrian's Wall, hedge, inner wall, load-bearing wall, mural, obstacle, outer bailey, paling, palisade, parapet, partition, party wall, rampart, retaining wall, screen, sea-wall, shield wall, stockade, stud partition, wall of death.

wallet *n* pouch, purse, folder, holder, case, notecase, pochette, bill-fold (*US*).

wallow *v* 1 *wallow in mud*: loll, lie, roll, wade, welter, lurch, flounder, splash. 2 *wallow in nostalgia*: indulge, luxuriate, relish, revel, bask, enjoy, glory, delight.

wand *n* rod, baton, staff, stick, sprig, mace, sceptre, twig.

wander *v* 1 ROAM, rove, ramble, meander, saunter, stroll, prowl, drift, range, stray, straggle. 2 DIGRESS, diverge, deviate, depart, go astray, swerve, veer, err. 3 RAMBLE, rave, babble, gibber, talk nonsense.

➢ *n* excursion, ramble, stroll, saunter, meander, prowl, cruise.

wanderer *n* itinerant, traveller, voyager, drifter, rover, rambler, stroller, stray, straggler, ranger, nomad, gypsy, vagrant, vagabond, rolling stone (*infml*).

wane *v* diminish, decrease, decline, weaken, subside, fade, dwindle, ebb, lessen, abate, sink, drop, taper off, dim, droop, contract, shrink, fail, wither.
🄴 increase, wax.

wangle (*infml*) *v* manipulate, arrange, contrive, engineer, fix, scheme, manoeuvre, work, pull off, manage, fiddle (*infml*).

want *v* 1 DESIRE, wish, crave, covet, fancy, long for, pine for, yearn for, hunger for, thirst for. 2 NEED, require, demand, lack, miss, call for.

➢ *n* 1 DESIRE, demand, longing, requirement, wish, need, appetite. 2 LACK, dearth, insufficiency, deficiency, shortage, inadequacy. 3 POVERTY, privation, destitution.

wanting *adj* 1 ABSENT, missing, lacking, short, insufficient. 2 INADEQUATE, imperfect, faulty, defective, substandard, poor, deficient, unsatisfactory.
🄴 1 sufficient. 2 adequate.

wanton *adj* malicious, immoral, shameless, arbitrary, unprovoked, unjustifiable, unrestrained, rash, reckless, wild.

war *n* warfare, hostilities, fighting, battle, combat, conflict, strife, struggle, bloodshed, contest, contention, enmity.
🄴 peace, cease-fire.

> Types of war include: ambush, armed conflict, assault, attack, battle, biological warfare, blitz, blitzkrieg, bombardment, chemical warfare, civil war, Cod wars, cold war, counter-attack, engagement, germ warfare, guerrilla warfare, holy war, hot war, invasion, jihad, jungle warfare, limited war, manoeuvres, nuclear war, Opium Wars, private war, resistance, skirmish, state of siege, struggle, total war, trade war, war of attrition, war of nerves, world war.

> Famous wars include: American Civil War (Second American Revolution), American Revolution (War of Independence), Boer War, Crimean War, Crusades, English Civil War, Falklands War, Franco-Prussian War, Gulf War, Hundred Years War, Indian Wars, Iran-Iraq War, Korean War, Mexican War, Napoleonic War, Peasants' War, Russo-Finnish War (Winter War), Russo-Japanese War, Russo-Turkish Wars, Seven Years War, Six-Day War, Spanish-American War, Spanish-American Wars of Independence, Spanish Civil War, Suez Crisis, Thirty Years War, Vietnam War, War of 1812, War of the Pacific, Wars of the Roses, World War I (the Great War), World War II.

➤ *v* wage war, fight, take up arms, battle, clash, combat, strive, skirmish, struggle, contest, contend.

◆ **war cry** rallying-cry, battle cry, war-song, slogan, watchword.

warble *v* sing, chirrup, chirp, twitter, quaver, yodel, trill.

➤ *n* song, cry, call, chirp, chirrup, quaver, trill, twitter.

ward *n* 1 ROOM, apartment, unit. 2 DIVISION, area, district, quarter, precinct, zone. 3 CHARGE, dependant, protégé(e), minor.

◆ **ward off** avert, fend off, deflect, parry, repel, stave off, thwart, beat off, forestall, evade, turn away, block, avoid.

warden *n* keeper, custodian, guardian, warder, caretaker, curator, ranger, steward, watchman, superintendent, administrator, janitor.

warder *n* jailer, keeper, prison officer, guard, wardress, custodian.

wardrobe *n* 1 CUPBOARD, closet. 2 CLOTHES, outfit, attire.

warehouse *n* store, storehouse, depot, depository, repository, stockroom, entrepot.

wares *n* goods, merchandise, commodities, stock, products, produce, stuff.

warfare *n* war, fighting, hostilities, battle, arms, combat, strife, struggle, passage of arms, contest, conflict, contention, discord, blows.

 peace.

warily *adv* cautiously, carefully, guardedly, watchfully, vigilantly, hesitantly, apprehensively, gingerly, cagily, charily, suspiciously, uneasily, distrustfully, circumspectly (*fml*).

 heedlessly, recklessly, thoughtlessly, unwarily.

wariness *n* caution, care, watchfulness, vigilance, suspicion, distrust.

warlike *adj* belligerent, aggressive, bellicose, pugnacious, combative, bloodthirsty, war-mongering, militaristic, hostile, antagonistic, unfriendly.

 friendly, peaceable.

warlock *n* witch, wizard, sorcerer, enchanter, conjurer, magician, demon, necromancer (*fml*).

warm *adj* 1 HEATED, tepid, lukewarm. 2 ARDENT, passionate, fervent, vehement,

earnest, zealous. 3 *warm colours*: rich, intense, mellow, cheerful. 4 FRIENDLY, amiable, cordial, affable, kindly, genial, hearty, hospitable, sympathetic, affectionate, tender. 5 FINE, sunny, balmy, temperate, close.

 1 cool. 2 indifferent. 3 cold. 4 unfriendly. 5 cool.

➤ *v* 1 HEAT (UP), reheat, melt, thaw. 2 ANIMATE, interest, please, delight, stimulate, stir, rouse, excite.

 1 cool.

warmth *n* 1 WARMNESS, heat. 2 FRIENDLINESS, affection, cordiality, tenderness. 3 ARDOUR, enthusiasm, passion, fervour, zeal, eagerness.

 1 coldness. 2 unfriendliness. 3 indifference.

warn *v* caution, alert, admonish, advise, notify, counsel, put on one's guard, inform, tip off (*infml*).

warning *n* 1 CAUTION, alert, admonition, advice, notification, notice, advance notice, counsel, hint, lesson, alarm, threat, tip-off (*infml*). 2 OMEN, augury, premonition, presage, sign, signal, portent.

warp *v* twist, bend, contort, deform, distort, kink, misshape, pervert, corrupt, deviate.

 straighten.

➤ *n* twist, bend, contortion, deformation, distortion, bias, kink, irregularity, turn, bent, defect, deviation, quirk, perversion.

warrant *n* authorization, authority, sanction, permit, permission, licence, guarantee, warranty, security, pledge, commission, voucher.

➤ *v* 1 GUARANTEE, pledge, certify, assure, declare, affirm, vouch for, answer for, underwrite, uphold, endorse. 2 AUTHORIZE, entitle, empower, sanction, permit, allow, license, justify, excuse, approve, call for, commission, necessitate, require.

warranty *n* guarantee, contract, certificate, bond, authorization, assurance, pledge, justification, covenant (*fml*).

warrior *n* fighter, soldier, fighting man, combatant, champion, warhorse, wardog.

wary *adj* cautious, guarded, careful, chary, on one's guard, on the lookout, prudent, distrustful, suspicious, heedful, attentive, alert, watchful, vigilant, wide-awake.

◨ unwary, careless, heedless.

wash *v* **1** CLEAN, cleanse, launder, scrub, swab down, rinse, swill. **2** BATHE, bath, shower, douche, shampoo.

➤ *n* **1** CLEANING, cleansing, bath, bathe, laundry, laundering, scrub, shower, shampoo, washing, rinse. **2** FLOW, sweep, wave, swell.

washed-out *adj* pale, pallid, blanched, bleached, faded, wan, colourless, drained, drawn, exhausted, tired out, fatigued, worn out, weary, spent, flat, lacklustre, haggard, all in (*infml*), dead on one's feet (*infml*), dog-tired (*infml*), knackered (*infml*).

washout (*infml*) *n* failure, disaster, disappointment, fiasco, flop (*infml*), debacle.

◨ success, triumph.

waste *v* **1** SQUANDER, misspend, misuse, fritter away, dissipate, lavish, spend, throw away, blow (*infml*). **2** CONSUME, erode, exhaust, drain, destroy, spoil.

◨ **1** economize. **2** preserve.

➤ *n* **1** SQUANDERING, dissipation, prodigality, wastefulness, extravagance, loss. **2** MISAPPLICATION, misuse, abuse, neglect. **3** RUBBISH, refuse, trash, garbage, leftovers, debris, dregs, effluent, litter, scrap, slops, offscouring(s), dross.

➤ *adj* **1** USELESS, worthless, unwanted, unused, left-over, superfluous, supernumerary, extra. **2** BARREN, desolate, empty, uninhabited, bare, devastated, uncultivated, unprofitable, wild, dismal, dreary.

wasted *adj* **1** UNNECESSARY, needless, useless. **2** EMACIATED, withered, shrivelled, shrunken, gaunt, washed-out, spent.

◨ **1** necessary. **2** robust.

wasteful *adj* extravagant, spendthrift, prodigal, profligate, uneconomical, thriftless, unthrifty, ruinous, lavish, improvident.

◨ economical, thrifty.

wasteland *n* wilderness, desert, barrenness, waste, wild(s), void.

watch *v* **1** OBSERVE, see, look at, regard, note, notice, mark, stare at, peer at, gaze at, view. **2** GUARD, look after, keep an eye on, mind, protect, superintend, take care of, keep. **3** PAY ATTENTION, be careful, take heed, look out.

➤ *n* **1** TIMEPIECE, wristwatch, clock, chronometer. **2** VIGILANCE, watchfulness,

vigil, observation, surveillance, notice, lookout, attention, heed, alertness, inspection, supervision.

◆ **watch out** notice, be vigilant, look out, keep one's eyes open.

◆ **watch over** guard, protect, stand guard over, keep an eye on, look after, mind, shield, defend, shelter, preserve.

watchdog *n* **1** GUARD DOG, house-dog. **2** MONITOR, inspector, scrutineer, vigilante, ombudsman, guardian, custodian, protector.

watcher *n* spectator, observer, onlooker, looker-on, viewer, lookout, spy, witness.

watchful *adj* vigilant, attentive, heedful, observant, alert, guarded, on one's guard, wide-awake, suspicious, wary, chary, cautious.

◨ unobservant, inattentive.

watchman *n* guard, security guard, caretaker, custodian.

watchword *n* catch-phrase, slogan, catchword, maxim, password, motto, rallying-cry, battle-cry, signal, byword, buzz word, magic word, shibboleth.

water *n* rain, sea, ocean, lake, river, stream.

➤ *v* wet, moisten, dampen, soak, spray, sprinkle, irrigate, drench, flood, hose.

◨ dry out, parch.

◆ **water down** dilute, thin, water, weaken, adulterate, mix, tone down, soften, qualify.

waterfall *n* fall, cascade, chute, cataract, torrent.

watertight *adj* **1** WATERPROOF, sound, hermetic. **2** IMPREGNABLE, unassailable, airtight, flawless, foolproof, firm, incontrovertible.

◨ **1** leaky.

watery *adj* **1** LIQUID, fluid, moist, wet, damp. **2** WEAK, watered-down, diluted, insipid, tasteless, thin, runny, soggy, flavourless, washy, wishy-washy (*infml*).

◨ **1** dry.

wave *v* **1** BECKON, gesture, gesticulate, indicate, sign, signal, direct. **2** BRANDISH, flourish, flap, flutter, shake, sway, swing, waft, quiver, ripple.

➤ *n* **1** BREAKER, roller, billow, ripple, tidal wave, wavelet, undulation, white horse (*infml*). **2** SURGE, sweep, swell, upsurge, ground swell, current, drift, movement, rush, tendency, trend, stream, flood, outbreak, rash.

waver *v* **1** VACILLATE, falter, hesitate,

dither, fluctuate, vary, seesaw.
2 OSCILLATE, shake, sway, wobble, tremble, totter, rock.
🖛 **1** decide.

wavy *adj* undulating, rippled, curly, curvy, ridged, sinuous, winding, zigzag.

wax *v* grow, increase, rise, swell, develop, enlarge, expand, magnify, mount, fill out, become.
🖛 decrease, wane.

way *n* **1** METHOD, approach, manner, technique, procedure, means, mode, system, fashion. **2** CUSTOM, practice, habit, usage, characteristic, idiosyncrasy, trait, style, conduct, nature. **3** DIRECTION, course, route, path, road, channel, access, avenue, track, passage, highway, street, thoroughfare, lane.
♦ **by the way** incidentally, in passing.
♦ **give way 1** COLLAPSE, break, fall in, sink, disintegrate, subside, cave in. **2** GIVE IN, yield, surrender, capitulate, submit, concede.

waylay *v* lie in wait for, ambush, attack, accost, set upon, surprise, catch, hold up, intercept, seize, buttonhole.

wayward *adj* wilful, capricious, perverse, contrary, changeable, fickle, unpredictable, stubborn, self-willed, unmanageable, headstrong, obstinate, disobedient, rebellious, insubordinate, intractable (*fml*), unruly, incorrigible.
🖛 tractable, good-natured.

weak *adj* **1** FEEBLE, frail, infirm, unhealthy, sickly, delicate, debilitated, exhausted, fragile, flimsy. **2** VULNERABLE, unprotected, unguarded, defenceless, exposed. **3** POWERLESS, impotent, spineless, cowardly, indecisive, ineffectual, irresolute, poor, lacking, lame, inadequate, defective, deficient, inconclusive, unconvincing, untenable. **4** FAINT, slight, low, soft, muffled, dull, imperceptible. **5** INSIPID, tasteless, watery, thin, diluted, runny.
🖛 **1** strong. **2** secure. **3** powerful. **4** strong. **5** strong.

weaken *v* **1** ENFEEBLE, exhaust, debilitate, sap, undermine, dilute, diminish, lower, lessen, reduce, moderate, mitigate, temper, soften (up), thin, water down. **2** TIRE, flag, fail, give way, droop, fade, abate, ease up, dwindle.
🖛 **1** strengthen.

weakling *n* coward, underling, underdog,

mouse, wimp (*infml*), wet (*infml*), wally (*infml*), weed (*infml*), drip (*infml*), doormat (*infml*), sissy (*infml*).
🖛 hero, stalwart.

weakness *n* **1** FEEBLENESS, debility, infirmity, impotence, frailty, powerlessness, vulnerability. **2** FAULT, failing, flaw, shortcoming, blemish, defect, deficiency, foible. **3** LIKING, inclination, fondness, penchant, passion, soft spot (*infml*).
🖛 **1** strength. **2** strength. **3** dislike.

wealth *n* **1** MONEY, cash, riches, assets, affluence, prosperity, funds, mammon, fortune, capital, opulence, means, substance, resources, goods, possessions, property, estate. **2** ABUNDANCE, plenty, bounty, fullness, profusion, store.
🖛 **1** poverty.

wealthy *adj* rich, prosperous, affluent, well-off, moneyed, opulent, comfortable, well-heeled, well-to-do, flush (*infml*), loaded (*sl*), rolling in it (*infml*).
🖛 poor, impoverished.

weapon

Weapons include: gun, airgun, pistol, revolver, automatic, Colt®, Luger®, magnum, Mauser, six-gun, six-shooter, rifle, air rifle, Winchester® rifle, carbine, shotgun, blunderbuss, musket, elephant gun, machine-gun, kalashnikov, submachine-gun, Uzi, tommy-gun, sten gun, Bren gun, cannon, field gun, gatling-gun, howitzer, mortar, turret-gun; knife, bowie knife, flick-knife, stiletto, dagger, dirk, poniard, sword, épée, foil, rapier, sabre, scimitar, bayonet, broadsword, claymore, lance, spear, pike, machete; bomb, atom bomb, H-bomb, cluster-bomb, depth-charge, incendiary bomb, Mills bomb, mine, land-mine, napalm bomb, time-bomb; bow and arrow, longbow, crossbow, blowpipe, catapult, boomerang, sling, harpoon, bolas, rocket, bazooka, ballistic missile, Cruise missile, Exocet®, Scud (*infml*), torpedo, hand grenade, flame-thrower; battleaxe, pole-axe, halberd, tomahawk, cosh, cudgel, knuckleduster, shillelagh, truncheon; gas, CS gas, mustard gas, tear-gas.

wear *v* **1** DRESS IN, have on, put on, don, sport, carry, bear, display, show.
2 DETERIORATE, erode, corrode, consume, fray, rub, abrade, waste, grind.
➢ *n* **1** CLOTHES, clothing, dress, garments,

outfit, costume, attire. **2** DETERIORATION, erosion, corrosion, wear and tear, friction, abrasion.

♦ **wear down** reduce, rub away, corrode, abrade, erode, grind down, chip away at, consume, undermine, diminish, lessen, overcome, macerate (*fml*).

♦ **wear off** decrease, abate, dwindle, diminish, subside, wane, weaken, fade, lessen, ebb, peter out, disappear.
F3 increase.

♦ **wear out 1** EXHAUST, fatigue, tire (out), enervate, sap. **2** DETERIORATE, wear through, erode, impair, consume, fray.

wearing *adj* exhausting, fatiguing, tiresome, tiring, wearisome, trying, taxing, oppressive, irksome, exasperating.
F3 refreshing.

weary *adj* tired, exhausted, fatigued, sleepy, worn out, drained, drowsy, jaded, all in (*infml*), done in (*infml*), fagged out (*sl*), knackered (*infml*), dead beat (*infml*), dog-tired (*infml*), whacked (*infml*).
F3 refreshed.

wearying *adj* tiring, fatiguing, exhausting, wearisome, wearing, taxing, trying.
F3 refreshing.

weather *n* climate, conditions, temperature.

| Types of weather include: breeze, wind, squall, gale, hurricane, tornado, typhoon, monsoon, cyclone, whirlwind, chinook, mistral, cloud, mist, dew, fog, smog, rain, drizzle, shower, deluge, downpour, rainbow, sunshine, heatwave, haze, drought, storm, tempest, thunder, lightning, frost, hoar frost, hail, sleet, snow, snowstorm, ice, black ice, thaw, slush. |

➤ *v* **1** ENDURE, survive, live through, come through, ride out, rise above, stick out, withstand, surmount, stand, brave, overcome, resist, pull through, suffer.
2 EXPOSE, toughen, season, harden.
F3 1 succumb.

♦ **under the weather** ill, sick, poorly, queer, ailing, off-colour, the worse for wear, seedy, groggy, below par, squeamish, nauseous, hung over, out of sorts, indisposed (*fml*).

weave *v* **1** INTERLACE, lace, plait, braid, intertwine, spin, knit, entwine, intercross, fuse, merge, unite. **2** CREATE, compose, construct, contrive, put together, fabricate.

3 WIND, twist, zigzag, criss-cross.

web *n* network, net, netting, lattice, mesh, webbing, interlacing, weft, snare, tangle, trap.

wedding *n* marriage, matrimony, nuptials (*fml*), wedlock, bridal (*fml*).
F3 divorce.

wedge *n* lump, block, chunk, wodge, chock.
➤ *v* jam, cram, pack, ram, squeeze, stuff, push, lodge, block, thrust, crowd, force.

weed out *v* get rid of, remove, root out, eradicate, eliminate, purge, extirpate (*fml*).
F3 add, fix, infiltrate.

weedy (*infml*) *adj* thin, skinny, puny, scrawny, undersized, weak, feeble, frail, weak-kneed, insipid, wet (*infml*), wimpish (*infml*).
F3 strong.

weep *v* cry, sob, moan, lament, wail, mourn, grieve, bawl, blubber, snivel, whimper, blub (*infml*).
F3 rejoice.

weigh *v* **1** BEAR DOWN, oppress. **2** CONSIDER, contemplate, evaluate, meditate on, mull over, ponder, think over, examine, reflect on, deliberate.

♦ **weigh down** oppress, overload, load, burden, bear down, weigh upon, press down, get down (*infml*), depress, afflict (*fml*), trouble, worry.
F3 lighten, hearten.

♦ **weigh up** assess, examine, size up, balance, consider, contemplate, deliberate, mull over, ponder, think over, discuss, chew over (*infml*).

weight *n* **1** HEAVINESS, gravity, burden, load, pressure, mass, force, ballast, tonnage, poundage. **2** IMPORTANCE, significance, substance, consequence, impact, moment, influence, value, authority, clout (*infml*), power, preponderance, consideration.
F3 1 lightness.
➤ *v* **1** LOAD, weigh down, oppress, handicap. **2** BIAS, unbalance, slant, prejudice.

weighty *adj* **1** HEAVY, burdensome, substantial, bulky. **2** IMPORTANT, significant, consequential, crucial, critical, momentous, serious, grave, solemn.
3 DEMANDING, difficult, exacting, taxing.
F3 1 light. **2** unimportant.

weird *adj* strange, uncanny, bizarre, eerie, creepy, supernatural, unnatural, ghostly, freakish, mysterious, queer, grotesque, spooky (*infml*), far-out (*infml*), way-out (*infml*).

Ea normal, usual.

welcome *adj* acceptable, desirable, pleasing, pleasant, agreeable, gratifying, appreciated, delightful, refreshing.

Ea unwelcome.

➢ *n* reception, greeting, salutation (*infml*), acceptance, hospitality, red carpet (*infml*).

➢ *v* greet, hail, receive, salute, meet, accept, approve of, embrace.

Ea reject, snub.

weld *v* fuse, unite, bond, join, solder, bind, connect, seal, link, cement.

Ea separate.

welfare *n* well-being, health, prosperity, happiness, benefit, good, advantage, interest, profit, success.

well¹ *n* spring, well-spring, fountain, fount, source, reservoir, pool, well-head.

> **Types of well include:** artesian well, borehole, draw-well, gas well, geyser, gusher, hot spring, inkwell, lift-shaft, mineral spring, oil-well, pump-well, stairwell, thermal spring, waterhole, wishing-well.

➢ *v* flow, spring, surge, gush, stream, brim over, jet, spout, spurt, swell, pour, flood, ooze, run, trickle, rise, seep.

well² *adv* rightly, correctly, properly, skilfully, ably, expertly, successfully, adequately, sufficiently, suitably, easily, satisfactorily, thoroughly, greatly, fully, considerably, completely, agreeably, pleasantly, happily, kindly, favourably, splendidly, substantially, comfortably, readily, carefully, clearly, highly, deeply, justly.

Ea badly, inadequately, incompetently, wrongly.

➢ *adj* 1 HEALTHY, in good health, fit, able-bodied, sound, robust, strong, thriving, flourishing. 2 SATISFACTORY, right, all right, good, pleasing, proper, agreeable, fine, lucky, fortunate.

Ea 1 ill. 2 bad.

well-balanced *adj* 1 RATIONAL, reasonable, level-headed, well-adjusted, stable, sensible, sane, sound, sober, together (*sl*). 2 SYMMETRICAL, even, harmonious.

Ea 1 unbalanced. 2 asymmetrical.

well-being *n* welfare, happiness, comfort, good.

well-bred *adj* well-mannered, polite, well-brought-up, mannerly, courteous, civil, refined, cultivated, cultured, genteel.

Ea ill-bred.

well-dressed *adj* smart, well-groomed, elegant, fashionable, chic, stylish, neat, trim, spruce, tidy.

Ea badly dressed, scruffy.

well-known *adj* famous, renowned, celebrated, famed, eminent, notable, noted, illustrious, familiar.

Ea unknown.

well-off *adj* rich, wealthy, affluent, prosperous, well-to-do, moneyed, thriving, successful, comfortable, fortunate.

Ea poor, badly-off.

well-thought-of *adj* respected, highly regarded, esteemed, admired, honoured, revered.

Ea despised.

well-worn *adj* timeworn, stale, tired, trite, overused, unoriginal, hackneyed, commonplace, stereotyped, threadbare, corny (*infml*).

Ea original.

welter *n* mess, confusion, jumble, muddle, tangle, web, hotchpotch, mish-mash (*infml*).

wet *adj* 1 DAMP, moist, soaked, soaking, sodden, saturated, soggy, sopping, watery, waterlogged, drenched, dripping, spongy, dank, clammy. 2 RAINING, rainy, showery, teeming, pouring, drizzling, humid. 3 (*infml*) WEAK, feeble, weedy (*infml*), wimpish (*infml*), spineless, soft, ineffectual, namby-pamby, irresolute, timorous.

Ea 1 dry. 2 dry. 3 strong.

➢ *n* wetness, moisture, damp, dampness, liquid, water, clamminess, condensation, humidity, rain, drizzle.

Ea dryness.

➢ *v* moisten, damp, dampen, soak, saturate, drench, steep, water, irrigate, spray, splash, sprinkle, imbue, dip.

Ea dry.

whack *v* hit, strike, smack, thrash, slap, beat, bash (*infml*), bang, cuff, thump, box, buffet, rap, wallop (*infml*), belt (*infml*), clobber (*infml*), clout (*infml*), sock (*infml*).

➢ *n* smack, slap, blow, hit, rap, stroke, thump, cuff, box, bang, clout (*infml*), bash (*infml*), wallop (*infml*).

wharf *n* dock, quay, quayside, jetty, landing-stage, dockyard, marina, pier.

wheedle *v* cajole, coax, persuade, inveigle, charm, flatter, entice, court, draw. 🔁 force.

wheel *n* turn, revolution, circle, rotation, gyration, pivot, roll, spin, twirl, whirl.

> Types of wheel include: balance-wheel, big wheel, buff-wheel, cartwheel, castor, Catherine wheel, charka, cogwheel, crown-wheel, drive-wheel, escape wheel, Ferris wheel, flywheel, gearwheel, idle wheel, mill wheel, paddle wheel, potter's wheel, prayer wheel, ratchet-wheel, roulette wheel, spinning-jenny, spinning-wheel, sprocket, spur gear, steering-wheel, wagon wheel, water-wheel, wheel of fortune, worm wheel.

➤ *v* turn, rotate, circle, gyrate, orbit, spin, twirl, whirl, swing, roll, revolve, swivel.
♦ **at the wheel 1** DRIVING, steering, behind the wheel, in the driver's seat, turning. **2** IN CHARGE, at the helm, in control, in command, responsible, directing, heading up (*infml*).

wheeze *v* pant, gasp, cough, hiss, rasp, whistle.

whereabouts *n* location, position, place, situation, site, vicinity.

wherewithal *n* means, resources, supplies, money, cash, funds, capital, necessary, readies (*infml*).

whet *v* **1** SHARPEN, hone, file, grind. **2** STIMULATE, stir, rouse, arouse, provoke, kindle, quicken, incite, awaken, increase. 🔁 **1** blunt. **2** dampen.

whiff *n* breath, puff, hint, trace, blast, draught, odour, smell, aroma, sniff, scent, reek, stink, stench.

whim *n* fancy, caprice, notion, quirk, freak, humour, conceit, fad, vagary, urge.

whimper *v* cry, sob, weep, snivel, whine, grizzle, mewl, moan, whinge (*infml*).
➤ *n* sob, snivel, whine, moan.

whimsical *adj* fanciful, capricious, playful, impulsive, eccentric, funny, droll, curious, queer, unusual, weird, odd, peculiar, quaint, dotty (*infml*).

whine *n* **1** CRY, sob, whimper, moan, wail. **2** COMPLAINT, grumble, grouse, gripe (*infml*), grouch (*infml*).
➤ *v* **1** CRY, sob, whimper, grizzle, moan, wail. **2** COMPLAIN, carp, grumble, whinge (*infml*), gripe (*infml*), grouch (*infml*).

whip *v* **1** BEAT, flog, lash, flagellate, scourge, birch, cane, strap, thrash, punish, chastise, discipline, castigate (*fml*). **2** PULL, jerk, snatch, whisk, dash, dart, rush, tear, flit, flash, fly. **3** GOAD, drive, spur, push, urge, stir, rouse, agitate, incite, provoke, instigate.
➤ *n* lash, scourge, switch, birch, cane, horsewhip, riding-crop, cat-o'-nine-tails.
♦ **whip up** stir up, work up, agitate, excite, arouse, incite, inflame, kindle, instigate, provoke, foment, psych up (*infml*).

whirl *v* swirl, spin, turn, twist, twirl, pivot, pirouette, swivel, wheel, rotate, revolve, reel, roll, gyrate, circle.
➤ *n* **1** SPIN, twirl, twist, gyration, revolution, pirouette, swirl, turn, wheel, rotation, circle, reel, roll. **2** CONFUSION, daze, flurry, commotion, agitation, bustle, hubbub, hurly-burly, giddiness, tumult, uproar.

whirlwind *n* tornado, cyclone, vortex.
➤ *adj* hasty, impulsive, quick, rapid, speedy, swift, lightning, headlong, impetuous, rash. 🔁 deliberate, slow.

whisk *v* **1** WHIP, beat. **2** DART, dash, rush, hurry, speed, hasten, race. **3** BRUSH, sweep, flick, wipe, twitch.

whisper *v* **1** MURMUR, mutter, mumble, breathe, hiss, rustle, sigh. **2** HINT, intimate, insinuate, gossip, divulge.
🔁 **1** shout.
➤ *n* **1** MURMUR, undertone, sigh, hiss, rustle. **2** HINT, suggestion, suspicion, breath, whiff, rumour, report, innuendo, insinuation, trace, tinge, soupçon, buzz.

white *adj* **1** PALE, pallid, wan, ashen, colourless, anaemic, pasty. **2** LIGHT, snowy, milky, creamy, ivory, hoary, silver, grey. **3** PURE, immaculate, spotless, stainless, undefiled.
🔁 **1** ruddy. **2** dark. **3** defiled.

whiten *v* bleach, blanch, whitewash, pale, fade.
🔁 blacken, darken.

whitewash *n* cover-up, concealment, deception, camouflage.
🔁 exposure.
➤ *v* **1** COVER UP, conceal, hide, make light of, suppress, gloss over, camouflage. **2** THRASH, beat, crush, drub (*infml*), best, clobber (*infml*), hammer (*infml*), lick (*infml*), paste (*infml*), trounce (*infml*).
🔁 **1** expose.

whittle *v* **1** CARVE, cut, scrape, shave, trim, pare, hew, shape. **2** ERODE, eat away, wear away, diminish, consume, reduce, undermine.

whole *adj* 1 COMPLETE, entire, integral, full, total, unabridged, uncut, undivided, unedited. 2 INTACT, unharmed, undamaged, unbroken, inviolate, perfect, in one piece, mint, unhurt. 3 WELL, healthy, fit, sound, strong.
☒ 1 partial. 2 damaged. 3 ill.
➢ *n* total, aggregate, sum total, entirety, all, fullness, totality, ensemble, entity, unit, lot, piece, everything.
☒ part.
◆ **on the whole** generally, mostly, in general, generally speaking, as a rule, for the most part, all in all, all things considered, by and large.

wholehearted *adj* unreserved, unstinting, unqualified, passionate, enthusiastic, earnest, committed, dedicated, devoted, heartfelt, emphatic, warm, sincere, unfeigned, genuine, complete, true, real, zealous.
☒ half-hearted.

wholesale *adj* comprehensive, far-reaching, extensive, sweeping, wide-ranging, mass, broad, outright, total, massive, indiscriminate.
☒ partial.

wholesome *adj* 1 *wholesome food*: healthy, hygienic, salubrious, sanitary, nutritious, nourishing, beneficial, salutary, invigorating, bracing. 2 *wholesome entertainment*: moral, decent, clean, proper, improving, edifying, uplifting, pure, virtuous, righteous, honourable, respectable.
☒ 1 unhealthy. 2 unwholesome.

wholly *adv* completely, entirely, fully, purely, absolutely, totally, utterly, comprehensively, altogether, perfectly, thoroughly, all, exclusively, only.
☒ partly.

whoop *v, n* shout, cry, yell, cheer, scream, shriek, roar, hoop, hoot, hurrah, holler (*infml*).

wicked *adj* 1 EVIL, sinful, immoral, depraved, corrupt, vicious, unprincipled, iniquitous, heinous, debased, abominable, ungodly, unrighteous, shameful. 2 BAD, unpleasant, harmful, offensive, vile, worthless, difficult, dreadful, distressing, awful, atrocious, severe, intense, nasty, injurious, troublesome, terrible, foul, fierce. 3 NAUGHTY, mischievous, roguish.

☒ 1 good, upright. 2 harmless.

wickedness *n* evil, depravity, corruption, fiendishness, immorality, shamefulness, sin, vice.

wide *adj* 1 BROAD, roomy, spacious, vast, immense. 2 DILATED, expanded, full. 3 EXTENSIVE, wide-ranging, comprehensive, far-reaching, general. 4 LOOSE, baggy. 5 OFF-TARGET, distant, remote.
☒ 1 narrow. 3 restricted. 5 near.
➢ *adv* 1 ASTRAY, off course, off target, off the mark. 2 FULLY, completely, all the way.
☒ 1 on target.

widen *v* distend, dilate, expand, extend, spread, stretch, enlarge, broaden.
☒ narrow.

widespread *adj* extensive, prevalent, rife, general, sweeping, universal, wholesale, far-reaching, unlimited, broad, common, pervasive, far-flung.
☒ limited.

width *n* breadth, diameter, wideness, compass, thickness, span, scope, range, measure, girth, beam, amplitude, extent, reach.

wield *v* 1 *wield a weapon*: brandish, flourish, swing, wave, handle, ply, manage, manipulate. 2 *wield power*: have, hold, possess, employ, exert, exercise, use, utilize, maintain, command.

wife *n* partner, spouse, mate, better half, bride.

wiggle *v, n* jiggle, shake, jerk, wriggle, wag, waggle, twist, squirm, twitch, writhe.

wild *adj* 1 UNTAMED, undomesticated, feral, savage, barbarous, primitive, uncivilized, natural, ferocious, fierce. 2 UNCULTIVATED, desolate, waste, uninhabited. 3 UNRESTRAINED, unruly, unmanageable, violent, turbulent, rowdy, lawless, disorderly, riotous, boisterous. 4 STORMY, tempestuous, rough, blustery, choppy. 5 UNTIDY, unkempt, messy, dishevelled, tousled. 6 RECKLESS, rash, imprudent, foolish, foolhardy, impracticable, irrational, outrageous, preposterous, wayward, extravagant. 7 MAD, crazy (*infml*), frenzied, distraught, demented.
☒ 1 civilized, tame. 2 cultivated. 3 restrained. 4 calm. 5 tidy. 6 sensible. 7 sane.

wilderness *n* desert, wasteland, waste, wilds, jungle.

wild flower

Wild flowers include: Aaron's rod, ale hoof, bird's foot trefoil, birth-wort, bistort, black-eyed susan, bladder campion, bluebell, broomrape, butter-and-eggs, buttercup, campion, celandine, clary, clustered bellflower, clover, columbine, comfrey, common evening-primrose, common mallow, common toadflax, cowslip, crane's bill, crowfoot, cuckoo flower, daisy, edelweiss, field cow-wheat, foxglove, goatsbeard, goldcup, goldenrod, great mullein, harebell, heartsease, heather, horsetail, lady's slipper, lady's smock, lungwort, marguerite, masterwort, moneywort, multiflora rose, New England aster, oxeye daisy, oxslip, pennyroyal, poppy, primrose, ragged robin, rock rose, rough-fruited cinquefoil, self-heal, shepherd's club, solomon's seal, stiff-haired sunflower, stonecrop, teasel, toadflax, violet, water lily, white campion, wild chicory, wild endive, wild gladiolus, wild iris, wild orchid, wild pansy, wood anemone, yarrow, yellow rocket.

wiles *n* trick, stratagem, ruse, ploy, device, contrivance, guile, manoeuvre, subterfuge, cunning, dodge (*infml*), deceit, cheating, trickery, fraud, craftiness, chicanery.
🔁 guilelessness.

wilful *adj* **1** DELIBERATE, conscious, intentional, voluntary, premeditated. **2** SELF-WILLED, obstinate, stubborn, pig-headed, obdurate (*fml*), intransigent (*fml*), inflexible, perverse, wayward, contrary.
🔁 **1** unintentional. **2** good-natured.

will *n* **1** VOLITION, choice, option, preference, decision, discretion. **2** WISH, desire, inclination, feeling, fancy, disposition, mind. **3** PURPOSE, resolve, resolution, determination, willpower, aim, intention, command.
➤ *v* **1** WANT, desire, choose, compel, command, decree, order, ordain. **2** BEQUEATH, leave, hand down, pass on, transfer, confer, dispose of.

willing *adj* disposed, inclined, agreeable, compliant, ready, prepared, consenting, content, amenable, biddable, pleased, well-disposed, favourable, happy, eager, enthusiastic.
🔁 unwilling, disinclined, reluctant.

willingly *adv* readily, unhesitatingly, eagerly, freely, happily, cheerfully, by choice, voluntarily, gladly, nothing loth.
🔁 unwillingly.

willingness *n* readiness, inclination, will, wish, consent, desire, favour, enthusiasm, agreeableness, agreement, disposition, volition, complaisance (*fml*), compliance (*fml*).
🔁 unwillingness.

willpower *n* determination, resolution, resolve, single-mindedness, commitment, will, self-control, self-discipline, self-mastery, self-command, persistence, doggedness, drive, grit (*infml*).

wilt *v* droop, sag, wither, shrivel, flop, flag, dwindle, weaken, diminish, fail, fade, languish, ebb, sink, wane.
🔁 perk up.

wily *adj* shrewd, cunning, scheming, artful, crafty, foxy, intriguing, tricky, underhand, shifty, deceitful, deceptive, astute, sly, guileful, designing, crooked (*infml*), fly (*infml*).
🔁 guileless.

win *v* **1** BE VICTORIOUS, triumph, succeed, prevail, overcome, conquer, come first, carry off, finish first. **2** GAIN, acquire, achieve, attain, accomplish, receive, procure, secure, obtain, get, earn, catch, net.
🔁 **1** fail, lose.
➤ *n* victory, triumph, conquest, success, mastery.
🔁 defeat.
♦ **win over** persuade, prevail upon, convince, influence, convert, sway, talk round, charm, allure, attract.

wince *v* start, jump, draw back, recoil, flinch, jerk, shrink, cringe, blench, cower, quail.
➤ *n* start, cringe, flinch, jerk.

wind[1] *n* air, breeze, draught, gust, puff, breath, air-current, blast, current, bluster, gale, hurricane, tornado, cyclone.

Types of wind include: anticyclone, austral wind, berg wind, bise, bora, Cape doctor, chinook, cyclone, doctor, east wind, El Niño, etesian, Favonian wind, föhn, gregale, harmattan, helm wind, khamsin, levant, libeccio, meltemi, mistral, monsoon, north wind, nor'wester, pampero, prevailing wind, samiel, simoom, sirocco, snoweater, southerly, southerly buster, trade wind, tramontana, westerly, wet chinook, williwaw, willy-willy, zephyr, zonda. *see also* **storm**.

wind² *v* coil, twist, turn, curl, curve, bend, loop, spiral, zigzag, twine, encircle, furl, deviate, meander, ramble, wreathe, roll, reel.

◆ **wind down 1** SLOW (DOWN), slacken off, lessen, reduce, subside, diminish, dwindle, decline. **2** RELAX, unwind, quieten down, ease up, calm down.

🔁 **1** increase.

◆ **wind up 1** CLOSE (DOWN), end, conclude, terminate, finalize, finish, liquidate. **2** END UP, finish up, find oneself, settle. **3** (*infml*) ANNOY, irritate, disconcert, fool, trick, kid (*infml*).

🔁 **1** begin.

windfall *n* bonanza, godsend, jackpot, treasure-trove, stroke of luck, find.

winding *adj* curving, turning, twisting, bending, crooked, tortuous, indirect, roundabout, spiral, circuitous, meandering, serpentine, sinuous (*fml*), sinuate(d) (*fml*), flexuose (*fml*), flexuous (*fml*), anfractuous (*fml*), convoluted (*fml*).

🔁 straight.

window *n* pane, light, opening, skylight, rose-window, casement, oriel, dormer.

windy *adj* breezy, blowy, blustery, squally, windswept, stormy, tempestuous, gusty.

🔁 calm.

wine

Types of wine include: alcohol-free, dry, brut, sec, demi-sec, sweet, sparkling, table wine, house wine; red wine, house red (*infml*), white wine, house white (*infml*), rosé, blush wine, fortified wine, mulled wine, tonic wine, vintage wine, plonk (*infml*); sherry, dry sherry, fino, medium sherry, amontillado, sweet sherry, oloroso; port, ruby, tawny, white port, vintage port.

Varieties of wine include: Alsace, Asti, Auslese, Beaujolais, Beaujolais Nouveau, Beaune, Bordeaux, Burgundy, cabernet sauvignon, Chablis, Chambertin, champagne, Chardonnay, Chianti, claret, Côtes du Rhône, Dão, Douro, Frascati, Graves, hock, Lambrusco, Liebfräumilch, Mâcon, Madeira, Malaga, Marsala, Mateus Rosé, Médoc, Merlot, moselle, Muscadet, muscatel, Niersteiner, retsina, Riesling, Rioja, Sauterne, Sekt, Soave, Spätlese, Tarragona, Valpolicella, vinho verde.

Sizes of wine-bottles include: magnum, flagon, jeroboam, methuselah, rehoboam, salmanazar, balthazar, nebuchadnezzar.

wing *n* **1** SECTION, branch, arm, faction, group, grouping, flank, circle, coterie, set, segment, side. **2** ANNEXE, adjunct, extension, attachment, side.
➤ *v* fly, glide, flit, hurry, move, travel, pass, speed, race, soar, zoom, hasten (*fml*).

wink *v* blink, flutter, glimmer, glint, twinkle, gleam, sparkle, flicker, flash.
➤ *n* **1** BLINK, flutter, sparkle, twinkle, glimmering, gleam, glint. **2** INSTANT, second, split second, flash.

◆ **wink at** ignore, disregard, overlook, neglect, pass over, condone, take no notice of, turn a blind eye to (*infml*).

winkle *v* extract, extricate, draw out, worm, force, prise, flush.

winner *n* champion, victor, prizewinner, medallist, title-holder, world-beater, conqueror.

🔁 loser.

winning *adj* **1** CONQUERING, triumphant, unbeaten, undefeated, victorious, successful. **2** WINSOME, charming, attractive, captivating, engaging, fetching, enchanting, endearing, delightful, amiable, alluring, lovely, pleasing, sweet.

🔁 **1** losing. **2** unappealing.

winnow *v* sift, separate, screen, divide, cull, select, part, fan.

wintry *adj* cold, chilly, bleak, cheerless, desolate, dismal, harsh, snowy, frosty, freezing, frozen, icy.

wipe *v* **1** RUB, clean, dry, dust, brush, mop, swab, sponge, clear. **2** REMOVE, erase, take away, take off.

◆ **wipe out** eradicate, obliterate, destroy, massacre, exterminate, annihilate, erase, expunge, raze, abolish, blot out, efface.

wiry *adj* muscular, sinewy, lean, tough, strong.

🔁 puny.

wisdom *n* discernment, penetration, sagacity, reason, sense, astuteness, comprehension, enlightenment, judgement, judiciousness, understanding, knowledge, learning, intelligence, erudition, foresight, prudence.

🔁 folly, stupidity.

wise *adj* **1** DISCERNING, sagacious, perceptive, rational, informed, well-informed, understanding, erudite,

enlightened, knowing, intelligent, clever, aware, experienced. **2** WELL-ADVISED, judicious, prudent, reasonable, sensible, sound, long-sighted, shrewd.
Ea 1 foolish, stupid. **2** ill-advised.

wisecrack *n* quip, joke, jest, funny, witticism, gag, barb, gibe, pun, in-joke, one-liner (*infml*).

wish *v* **1** DESIRE, want, yearn, long, hanker, covet, crave, aspire, hope, hunger, thirst, prefer, need. **2** ASK, bid, require, order, instruct, direct, command.
➤ *n* **1** DESIRE, want, hankering, aspiration, inclination, hunger, thirst, liking, preference, yearning, urge, whim, hope. **2** REQUEST, bidding, order, command, will.

wisp *n* shred, strand, thread, twist, piece, lock.

wispy *adj* thin, straggly, frail, fine, attenuated, insubstantial, light, flimsy, fragile, delicate, ethereal, gossamer, faint.
Ea substantial.

wistful *adj* **1** THOUGHTFUL, pensive, musing, reflective, wishful, contemplative, dreamy, dreaming, meditative.
2 MELANCHOLY, sad, forlorn, disconsolate, longing, mournful.

wit *n* **1** HUMOUR, repartee, facetiousness, drollery, banter, jocularity, levity.
2 INTELLIGENCE, cleverness, brains, sense, reason, common sense, wisdom, understanding, judgement, insight, intellect. **3** HUMORIST, comedian, comic, satirist, joker, wag.
Ea 1 seriousness. **2** stupidity.

witch *n* sorceress, enchantress, occultist, magician, hag.

witchcraft *n* sorcery, magic, wizardry, occultism, the occult, the black art, black magic, enchantment, necromancy (*fml*), voodoo, spell, incantation, divination, conjuration.

withdraw *v* **1** RECOIL, shrink back, draw back, pull back. **2** RECANT, disclaim, take back, revoke, rescind, retract, cancel, abjure, recall, take away. **3** DEPART, go (away), absent oneself, retire, remove, leave, back out, fall back, drop out, retreat, secede. **4** DRAW OUT, extract, pull out.

withdrawal *n* **1** REPUDIATION, recantation, disclaimer, disavowal, revocation, recall, secession, abjuration.
2 DEPARTURE, exit, exodus, retirement, retreat. **3** EXTRACTION, removal.

withdrawn *adj* **1** RESERVED, unsociable,

shy, introvert, quiet, retiring, aloof, detached, shrinking, uncommunicative, unforthcoming, taciturn, silent. **2** REMOTE, isolated, distant, secluded, out-of-the-way, private, hidden, solitary.
Ea 1 extrovert, outgoing.

wither *v* shrink, shrivel, dry, wilt, droop, decay, disintegrate, wane, perish, fade, languish, decline, waste.
Ea flourish, thrive.

withering *adj* **1** DESTRUCTIVE, deadly, death-dealing, devastating. **2** SCORNFUL, contemptuous, scathing, snubbing, humiliating, mortifying, wounding.
Ea 2 encouraging, supportive.

withhold *v* keep back, retain, hold back, suppress, restrain, repress, control, check, reserve, deduct, refuse, hide, conceal.
Ea give, accord.

withstand *v* resist, oppose, stand fast, stand one's ground, stand, stand up to, confront, brave, face, cope with, take on, thwart, defy, hold one's ground, hold out, last out, hold off, endure, bear, tolerate, put up with, survive, weather.
Ea give in, yield.

witness *n* **1** TESTIFIER, attestant, deponent (*fml*). **2** ONLOOKER, eyewitness, looker-on, observer, spectator, viewer, watcher, bystander.
➤ *v* **1** SEE, observe, notice, note, view, watch, look on, mark, perceive. **2** TESTIFY, attest (*fml*), bear witness, depose (*fml*), confirm, bear out, corroborate. **3** ENDORSE, sign, countersign.

witticism *n* quip, riposte, pun, repartee, pleasantry, bon mot, wisecrack, epigram, one-liner (*infml*).

witty *adj* humorous, amusing, comic, sharp-witted, droll, whimsical, original, brilliant, clever, ingenious, lively, sparkling, funny, facetious, fanciful, jocular.
Ea dull, unamusing.

wizard *n* **1** SORCERER, magician, warlock, enchanter, necromancer (*fml*), occultist, witch, conjurer. **2** (*infml*) EXPERT, adept, virtuoso, ace, master, maestro, prodigy, genius, star (*infml*), whiz (*infml*), hotshot (*infml*).

wizened *adj* shrivelled, shrunken, dried up, withered, wrinkled, gnarled, thin, worn, lined.

wobble *v* shake, oscillate, tremble, quake, sway, teeter, totter, rock, seesaw, vibrate, waver, dodder, fluctuate, hesitate,

dither, vacillate, shilly-shally.
➤ *n* shake, unsteadiness, tremble.

wobbly *adj* unstable, shaky, rickety, unsteady, wonky (*infml*), teetering, tottering, doddering, doddery, uneven, unbalanced, unsafe.
🖪 stable, steady.

woe *n* misery, adversity, distress, sadness, sorrow, unhappiness, wretchedness, grief, melancholy, misfortune, suffering, hardship, trouble, pain, agony, anguish, gloom, curse, trial, depression, dejection, burden, disaster, calamity, heartache, heartbreak, tears, affliction (*fml*), tribulation (*fml*).
🖪 joy.

wolf down *v* put away (*infml*), pack away (*infml*), gobble (*infml*), gulp, devour, cram, bolt, stuff, gorge, scoff.
🖪 nibble.

woman *n* female, lady, girl, matriarch, maiden, maid.

womanizer *n* philanderer, seducer, wolf, lady-killer, ladies' man, lecher, Casanova, Don Juan, Romeo.

womanly *adj* feminine, female, ladylike, womanish.

wonder *n* 1 MARVEL, phenomenon, miracle, prodigy, sight, spectacle, rarity, curiosity. 2 AWE, amazement, astonishment, admiration, wonderment, fascination, surprise, bewilderment.

> The seven wonders of the world
> are: Pyramids of Egypt, Hanging Gardens of Babylon, Statue of Zeus at Olympia, Temple of Artemis at Ephesus, Mausoleum of Halicarnassus, Colossus of Rhodes, Pharos of Alexandria.

➤ *v* 1 MEDITATE, speculate, ponder, ask oneself, question, conjecture (*fml*), puzzle, enquire, query, doubt, think.
2 MARVEL, gape, be amazed, be surprised.

wonderful *adj* 1 MARVELLOUS, magnificent, oustanding, excellent, superb, admirable, delightful, phenomenal, sensational, stupendous, tremendous, super (*infml*), terrific (*infml*), brilliant (*infml*), great (*infml*), fabulous (*infml*), fantastic (*infml*). 2 AMAZING, astonishing, astounding, startling, surprising, extraordinary, incredible, remarkable, staggering, strange.
🖪 1 appalling, dreadful. 2 ordinary.

wont *adj* inclined, used, accustomed, given, habituated (*fml*).
➤ *n* habit, custom, routine, practice, rule, use, way.

woo *v* 1 (*fml*) *woo a lover*: court, chase, pursue. 2 *woo custom*: encourage, cultivate, attract, look for, seek.

wood *n* 1 TIMBER, lumber, planks. 2 FOREST, woodland, trees, plantation, thicket, grove, coppice, copse, spinney.

> Types of wood include: timber, lumber (*US*), hardwood, softwood, heartwood, sapwood, seasoned wood, green wood, bitterwood, brushwood, cordwood, firewood, kindling, matchwood, plywood, pulpwood, whitewood, chipboard, hardboard, wood veneer; afrormosia, ash, balsa, beech, cedar, cherry, chestnut, cottonwood, deal, ebony, elm, mahogany, African mahogany, maple, oak, pine, redwood, rosewood, sandalwood, sapele, satinwood, teak, walnut, willow. *see also* tree.

wooded *adj* forested, timbered, woody, tree-covered, sylvan (*fml*).

wooden *adj* 1 TIMBER, woody. 2 EMOTIONLESS, expressionless, awkward, clumsy, stilted, lifeless, spiritless, unemotional, stiff, rigid, leaden, deadpan, blank, empty, slow.
🖪 2 lively.

wool *n* fleece, down, yarn.

woolly *adj* 1 WOOLLEN, fleecy, woolly-haired, downy, shaggy, fuzzy, frizzy.
2 UNCLEAR, ill-defined, hazy, blurred, confused, muddled, vague, indefinite, nebulous.
🖪 2 clear, distinct.
➤ *n* jumper, sweater, jersey, pullover, cardigan.

word *n* 1 NAME, term, expression, designation, utterance, vocable (*fml*). 2 CONVERSATION, chat, talk, discussion, consultation. 3 INFORMATION, news, report, communication, notice, message, bulletin, communiqué, statement, dispatch, declaration, comment, assertion, account, remark, advice, warning.
4 PROMISE, pledge, oath, assurance, vow, guarantee. 5 COMMAND, order, decree, commandment, go-ahead (*infml*), green light (*infml*).
➤ *v* phrase, express, couch, put, say, explain, write.

wording n words, choice of words, language, phrasing, expression, phraseology, terminology, style, diction, wordage, verbiage.

words n 1 ARGUMENT, dispute, quarrel, disagreement, altercation, bickering, row, squabble. 2 LYRICS, libretto, text, book.

wordy adj verbose, long-winded, loquacious (fml), garrulous, prolix, rambling, diffuse, discursive.
☒ concise.

work n 1 OCCUPATION, job, employment, profession, trade, business, career, calling, vocation, line, métier, livelihood, craft, skill. 2 TASK, assignment, undertaking, job, chore, responsibility, duty, commission. 3 TOIL, labour, drudgery, effort, exertion, industry, slog (infml), graft (infml), elbow grease (infml). 4 CREATION, production, achievement, composition, opus.
☒ 1 play, rest, hobby.
➤ v 1 BE EMPLOYED, have a job, earn one's living. 2 LABOUR, toil, drudge, slave. 3 FUNCTION, go, operate, perform, run, handle, manage, use, control. 4 BRING ABOUT, accomplish, achieve, create, cause, pull off (infml). 5 CULTIVATE, farm, dig, till. 6 MANIPULATE, knead, mould, shape, form, fashion, make, process.
☒ 1 be unemployed. 2 play, rest. 3 fail.
♦ **work out** 1 SOLVE, resolve, calculate, figure out, puzzle out, sort out, understand, clear up. 2 DEVELOP, evolve, go well, succeed, prosper, turn out, pan out (infml). 3 PLAN, devise, arrange, contrive, invent, construct, put together. 4 ADD UP TO, amount to, total, come out.
♦ **work up** incite, stir up, rouse, arouse, animate, excite, move, stimulate, inflame, spur, instigate, agitate, generate.

workable adj practicable, feasible, possible, practical, realistic, viable, doable.
☒ unworkable.

worker n employee, labourer, working man, working woman, artisan, craftsman, tradesman, hand, operative, wage-earner, breadwinner, proletarian.

workforce n workers, employees, personnel, labour force, staff, labour, work-people, shop-floor.

working n functioning, operation, running, routine, manner, method, action.
➤ adj 1 FUNCTIONING, operational, going, running, operative. 2 EMPLOYED, active.
☒ 1 inoperative. 2 idle.

workmanship n skill, craft, craftsmanship, expertise, art, handicraft, handiwork, technique, execution, manufacture, work, finish.

works n 1 FACTORY, plant, workshop, mill, foundry, shop. 2 ACTIONS, acts, doings. 3 PRODUCTIONS, output, oeuvre, writings, books. 4 MACHINERY, mechanism, workings, action, movement, parts, installations.

workshop n 1 WORKS, workroom, atelier, studio, factory, plant, mill, shop. 2 STUDY GROUP, seminar, symposium, discussion group, class.

world n 1 EARTH, globe, planet, star, universe, cosmos, creation, nature. 2 EVERYBODY, everyone, people, human race, humankind, humanity. 3 SPHERE, realm, field, area, domain, division, system, society, province, kingdom. 4 TIMES, epoch, era, period, age, days, life.

worldly adj 1 TEMPORAL, earthly, mundane, terrestrial, physical, secular, unspiritual, profane. 2 WORLDLY-WISE, sophisticated, urbane, cosmopolitan, experienced, knowing, streetwise (infml). 3 MATERIALISTIC, selfish, ambitious, grasping, greedy, covetous, avaricious.
☒ 1 spiritual, eternal. 2 unsophisticated.

worldwide adj international, global, general, universal, catholic, mondial (fml), ubiquitous (fml).
☒ local.

worn adj 1 SHABBY, threadbare, worn out, tatty, tattered, frayed, ragged. 2 EXHAUSTED, tired, weary, spent, fatigued, careworn, drawn, haggard, jaded.
☒ 1 new, unused. 2 fresh.
♦ **worn out** 1 SHABBY, threadbare, useless, used, tatty, tattered, on its last legs, ragged, moth-eaten, frayed, decrepit. 2 TIRED OUT, exhausted, weary, done in (infml), all in (infml), dog-tired (infml), knackered (infml).
☒ 1 new, unused. 2 fresh.

worried adj anxious, troubled, uneasy, ill at ease, apprehensive, concerned, bothered, upset, fearful, afraid, frightened, on edge, overwrought, tense, strained, nervous, disturbed, distraught, distracted, fretful, distressed, agonized, perturbed, dismayed.
☒ calm, unworried, unconcerned.

worry v 1 BE ANXIOUS, be troubled, be distressed, agonize, fret. 2 IRRITATE,

plague, pester, torment, upset, unsettle, annoy, bother, disturb, vex, tease, nag, harass, harry, perturb, hassle (*infml*).
3 ATTACK, go for, savage.
⊟ **1** be unconcerned. **2** comfort.
➢ *n* **1** PROBLEM, trouble, responsibility, burden, concern, care, trial, annoyance, irritation, vexation. **2** ANXIETY, apprehension, unease, misgiving, fear, disturbance, agitation, torment, misery, perplexity.
⊟ **2** comfort, reassurance.

worsen *v* **1** EXACERBATE, aggravate, intensify, heighten. **2** GET WORSE, weaken, deteriorate, degenerate, decline, sink, go downhill (*infml*).
⊟ improve.

worship *v* venerate, revere, reverence, adore, exalt, glorify, honour, praise, idolize, adulate, love, respect, pray to, deify.
⊟ despise, hate.
➢ *n* veneration, reverence, adoration, devotion(s), homage, honour, glory, glorification, exaltation, praise, prayer(s), respect, regard, love, adulation, deification, idolatry.

> Places of worship include: abbey, bethel, cathedral, chantry, church, fane, kirk, masjid, meeting-house, minster, mosque, pagoda, shrine, shul, synagogue, tabernacle, temple, wat. *see also* **religion**.

worst *v* beat, defeat, get the better of, overcome, overpower, overthrow, conquer, crush, master, subdue, drub (*infml*), whitewash, best, subjugate (*fml*), vanquish (*fml*).

worth *n* worthiness, merit, value, benefit, advantage, importance, significance, use, usefulness, utility, quality, good, virtue, excellence, credit, desert(s), cost, rate, price, help, assistance, avail.
⊟ worthlessness.

worthless *adj* **1** VALUELESS, useless, pointless, meaningless, futile, unavailing, unimportant, insignificant, trivial, unusable, cheap, poor, rubbishy, trashy, trifling, paltry. **2** CONTEMPTIBLE, despicable, good-for-nothing, vile.
⊟ **1** valuable. **2** worthy.

worthwhile *adj* profitable, useful, valuable, worthy, good, helpful, beneficial, constructive, gainful, justifiable, productive.
⊟ worthless.

worthy *adj* praiseworthy, laudable, creditable, commendable, valuable, worthwhile, admirable, fit, deserving, appropriate, respectable, reputable, good, honest, honourable, excellent, decent, upright, righteous.
⊟ unworthy, disreputable.

would-be *adj* aspiring, budding, striving, endeavouring, ambitious, enterprising, keen, eager, hopeful, optimistic, wishful, longing.

wound *n* **1** INJURY, trauma, hurt, cut, gash, lesion, laceration, scar. **2** HURT, distress, trauma, torment, heartbreak, harm, damage, anguish, grief, shock.
➢ *v* **1** DAMAGE, harm, hurt, injure, hit, cut, gash, lacerate, slash, pierce. **2** DISTRESS, offend, insult, pain, mortify, upset, slight, grieve.

wrangle *n* argument, quarrel, dispute, controversy, squabble, tiff (*infml*), row, bickering, disagreement, clash, altercation (*fml*), contest, slanging match (*infml*), set-to (*infml*).
⊟ agreement.
➢ *v* argue, quarrel, disagree, dispute, bicker, altercate, contend, fall out (*infml*), row, squabble, scrap (*infml*), fight, spar.
⊟ agree.

wrap *v* envelop, fold, enclose, cover, pack, shroud, wind, surround, package, muffle, cocoon, cloak, roll up, bind, bundle up, immerse.
⊟ unwrap.
◆ wrap up **1** WRAP, pack up, package, parcel. **2** (*infml*) CONCLUDE, finish off, end, bring to a close, terminate, wind up, complete, round off.

wrapper *n* wrapping, packaging, envelope, cover, jacket, dust jacket, sheath, sleeve, paper.

wrath *n* anger, bitterness, rage, fury, exasperation, indignation, irritation, annoyance, temper, resentment, passion, displeasure, spleen, choler, ire (*fml*).
⊟ calm, pleasure.

wreak *v* inflict, exercise, create, cause, bring about, perpetrate, vent, unleash, express, execute, carry out, bestow.

wreath *n* garland, coronet, chaplet, festoon, crown, band, ring.

wreathe *v* encircle, surround, enfold, entwine, twine, twist, wind, coil, wrap, envelop, crown, adorn, shroud, enwrap, festoon, intertwine, interweave.

wreck v destroy, ruin, demolish, devastate, shatter, smash, break, spoil, play havoc with, ravage, write off.
  F3 conserve, repair.
  ➤ n ruin, destruction, devastation, mess, demolition, ruination, write-off, disaster, loss, disruption.

wreckage n debris, remains, rubble, ruin, fragments, flotsam, pieces.

wrench v yank, wrest, jerk, pull, tug, force, sprain, strain, rick, tear, twist, wring, rip, distort.

wrest v seize, force, extract, pull, take, win, wring, wrench, twist, strain.

wrestle v struggle, strive, fight, scuffle, grapple, tussle, combat, contend, contest, vie, battle.

wretch n scoundrel, rogue, villain, good-for-nothing, ruffian, rascal, vagabond, miscreant (fml), outcast.

wretched adj 1 ATROCIOUS, awful, deplorable, appalling. 2 UNHAPPY, sad, miserable, melancholy, depressed, dejected, disconsolate, downcast, forlorn, gloomy, doleful, distressed, broken-hearted, crestfallen. 3 PATHETIC, pitiable, pitiful, unfortunate, sorry, hopeless, poor. 4 CONTEMPTIBLE, despicable, vile, worthless, shameful, inferior, low, mean, paltry.
  F3 1 excellent. 2 happy. 3 enviable. 4 worthy.

wriggle v squirm, writhe, wiggle, worm, twist, snake, slink, crawl, edge, sidle, manoeuvre, squiggle, dodge, extricate, zigzag, waggle, turn.
  ➤ n wiggle, twist, squirm, jiggle, jerk, turn, twitch.

wring v 1 SQUEEZE, twist, wrench, wrest, extract, mangle, screw. 2 EXACT, extort, coerce, force. 3 DISTRESS, pain, hurt, rack, rend, pierce, torture, wound, stab, tear.

wrinkle n furrow, crease, corrugation, line, fold, gather, pucker, crumple.
  ➤ v crease, corrugate, furrow, fold, crinkle, crumple, shrivel, gather, pucker.

writ n court order, summons, decree, subpoena.

write v pen, inscribe, record, jot down, set down, take down, transcribe, scribble, scrawl, correspond, communicate, draft, draw up, copy, compose, create.
  ◆ **write off** 1 DELETE, cancel, cross out, disregard. 2 WRECK, destroy, crash, smash up.

writer n author, scribe, wordsmith, novelist, dramatist, essayist, playwright, columnist, diarist, hack, penpusher, scribbler, secretary, copyist, clerk.

> **Writers include:** annalist, author, autobiographer, bard, biographer, calligraphist, chronicler, clerk, columnist, composer, contributor, copyist, copywriter, correspondent, court reporter, diarist, dramatist, editor, essayist, fabler, fiction writer, ghost writer, hack, historian, journalist, leader-writer, lexicographer, librettist, lyricist, novelist, pen-friend, penman, pen-pal, penpusher (infml), penwoman, playwright, poet, poet laureate, reporter, rhymer, satirist, scribbler, scribe, scriptwriter, short-story writer, sonneteer, stenographer, storyteller (infml).

writhe v squirm, wriggle, thresh, thrash, twist, wiggle, toss and turn, coil, contort, struggle.

writing n 1 HANDWRITING, calligraphy, script, penmanship, scrawl, scribble, hand, print. 2 DOCUMENT, letter, book, composition, letters, literature, work, publication.

> **Types of writing instrument include:** pen, ballpoint, Biro®, calligraphy pen, cartridge pen, dip pen, eraser pen, felt-tip pen, fountain pen; marker pen, rollerball pen; writing brush, pencil, chinagraph pencil, coloured pencil, crayon, ink pencil, lead pencil, propelling pencil, board marker, laundry marker, permanent marker, highlighter; cane pen, quill, reed, Roman metal pen, steel pen, stylus; brailler, typewriter, word-processor. see also **alphabets and writing systems**.

wrong adj 1 INACCURATE, incorrect, mistaken, erroneous, false, fallacious, in error, imprecise. 2 INAPPROPRIATE, unsuitable, unseemly, improper, indecorous, unconventional, unfitting, incongruous, inapt. 3 UNJUST, unethical, unfair, unlawful, immoral, illegal, illicit, dishonest, criminal, crooked (infml), reprehensible, blameworthy, guilty, to blame, bad, wicked, sinful, iniquitous, evil. 4 DEFECTIVE, faulty, out of order, amiss, awry.
  F3 1 correct, right. 2 suitable, right. 3 good, moral.
  ➤ adv amiss, astray, awry, inaccurately,

incorrectly, wrongly, mistakenly, faultily, badly, erroneously, improperly.
Ea right.

➤ *n* sin, misdeed, offence, crime, immorality, sinfulness, transgression, wickedness, wrongdoing, trespass (*fml*), injury, grievance, abuse, injustice, iniquity, inequity, infringement, unfairness, error.
Ea right.

➤ *v* abuse, ill-treat, mistreat, maltreat, injure, ill-use, hurt, harm, discredit, dishonour, misrepresent, malign, oppress, cheat.

◆ **in the wrong** at fault, guilty, to blame.

wrongdoer *n* offender, law-breaker, transgressor, criminal, delinquent, felon, miscreant, evil-doer, sinner, trespasser, culprit.

wrongful *adj* immoral, improper, unfair, unethical, unjust, unlawful, illegal, illegitimate, illicit, dishonest, criminal, blameworthy, dishonourable, wrong, reprehensible, wicked, evil.
Ea rightful.

wrongly *adv* incorrectly, mistakenly, by mistake, in error, erroneously.

wry *adj* **1** *wry humour*: ironic, sardonic, dry, sarcastic, mocking, droll. **2** TWISTED, distorted, deformed, contorted, warped, uneven, crooked.
Ea **2** straight.

Yy

yank *v*, *n* jerk, tug, pull, wrench, snatch, haul, heave.

yap *v* **1** BARK, yelp. **2** (*infml*) CHATTER, jabber, babble, prattle, yatter, jaw (*infml*).

yardstick *n* measure, gauge, criterion, standard, benchmark, touchstone, comparison.

yarn *n* **1** THREAD, fibre, strand. **2** STORY, tale, anecdote, fable, fabrication, tall story, cock-and-bull story (*infml*).

yawning *adj* gaping, wide, wide-open, huge, vast, cavernous.

yearly *adj* annual, per year, per annum, perennial.
➤ *adv* annually, every year, once a year, perennially.

yearn for *v* long for, pine for, desire, want, wish for, crave, covet, hunger for, hanker for, ache for, languish for, itch for.

yell *v* shout, scream, bellow, roar, bawl, shriek, squeal, howl, holler (*infml*), screech, squall, yelp, yowl, whoop.
🔁 whisper.
➤ *n* shout, scream, cry, roar, bellow, shriek, howl, screech, squall, whoop.
🔁 whisper.

yelp *v* yap, bark, squeal, cry, yell, yowl, bay.
➤ *n* yap, bark, yip, squeal, cry, yell, yowl.

yes *adv* right, quite, absolutely, certainly, agreed, of course, affirmative, yeah (*infml*), yep (*infml*).
🔁 no.

yes-man *n* sycophant, crawler, toady, lackey, minion, bootlicker (*infml*), arse-licker (*sl*).

yet *adv* **1** UP TILL NOW, until now, up to this time, up till then, by now, by then, now, already, as yet, thus far (*fml*), hitherto (*fml*), heretofore (*fml*). **2** IN ADDITION, still, even, too, also, furthermore, besides, moreover, into the bargain (*infml*).

➤ *conj* but, however, nevertheless, nonetheless, anyway, even so, all/just the same, for all that, notwithstanding (*fml*).

yield *v* **1** SURRENDER, renounce, abandon, abdicate, cede, part with, relinquish. **2** GIVE WAY, capitulate, concede, submit, succumb, give (in), admit defeat, bow, cave in, knuckle under, resign oneself, go along with, permit, allow, acquiesce, accede, agree, comply, consent. **3** PRODUCE, bear, supply, provide, generate, bring in, bring forth, furnish, return, earn, pay.
🔁 **1** hold. **2** resist, withstand.
➤ *n* return, product, earnings, harvest, crop, produce, output, profit, revenue, takings, proceeds, income.

yoke *n* **1** HARNESS, bond, link. **2** BURDEN, bondage, enslavement, slavery, oppression, subjugation, servility.
➤ *v* couple, link, join, tie, harness, hitch, bracket, connect, unite.

young *adj* **1** YOUTHFUL, juvenile, baby, infant, junior, adolescent. **2** IMMATURE, early, new, recent, green, growing, fledgling, unfledged, inexperienced.
🔁 **1** adult, old. **2** mature, old.
➤ *n* offspring, babies, issue, litter, progeny, brood, children, family.

youngster *n* child, boy, girl, toddler, youth, teenager, kid (*infml*).

youth *n* **1** ADOLESCENT, youngster, juvenile, teenager, kid (*infml*), boy, young man. **2** YOUNG PEOPLE, the young, younger generation. **3** ADOLESCENCE, childhood, immaturity, boyhood, girlhood.
🔁 **3** adulthood.

youthful *adj* young, boyish, girlish, childish, immature, juvenile, inexperienced, fresh, active, lively, well-preserved.
🔁 aged.

Zz

zany (*infml*) *adj* comical, funny, amusing, eccentric, odd, absurd, droll, crazy (*infml*), clownish, loony (*infml*), wacky (*infml*), ridiculous.
☒ serious.

zeal *n* ardour, fervour, passion, warmth, fire, enthusiasm, devotion, spirit, keenness, zest, eagerness, earnestness, dedication, fanaticism, gusto, verve.
☒ apathy, indifference.

zealot *n* fanatic, extremist, bigot, militant, partisan.

zealous *adj* ardent, fervent, impassioned, passionate, devoted, burning, enthusiastic, intense, fanatical, militant, keen, eager, earnest, spirited.
☒ apathetic, indifferent.

zenith *n* summit, peak, height, pinnacle, apex, high point, top, optimum, climax, culmination, acme, meridian, vertex.
☒ nadir.

zero *n* nothing, nought, nil, nadir, bottom, cipher, zilch (*infml*), duck, love.

zest *n* **1** GUSTO, appetite, enthusiasm, enjoyment, keenness, zeal, exuberance, interest. **2** FLAVOUR, taste, relish, savour, spice, tang, piquancy.
☒ **1** apathy.

zigzag *v* meander, snake, wind, twist, curve.

➤ *adj* meandering, crooked, serpentine, sinuous, twisting, winding.
☒ straight.

zip *n* energy, verve, vitality, life, liveliness, enthusiasm, drive, sparkle, spirit, vigour, zest, gusto, élan, go (*infml*), get-up-and-go (*infml*), oomph (*infml*), pizzazz (*infml*), pep (*infml*), punch (*infml*), zing (*infml*).
☒ listlessness.

➤ *v* fly, dash, tear, rush, race, hurry, speed, shoot, flash, scoot, zoom, whiz (*infml*), whoosh (*infml*).

zodiac

> The signs of the zodiac (with their symbols) are: Aries (Ram), Taurus (Bull), Gemini (Twins), Cancer (Crab), Leo (Lion), Virgo (Virgin), Libra (Balance), Scorpio (Scorpion), Sagittarius (Archer), Capricorn (Goat), Aquarius (Water-bearer), Pisces (Fishes).

zone *n* region, area, district, territory, section, sector, belt, sphere, tract, stratum.

zoo *n* zoological gardens, safari park, wildlife park, animal park, aquarium, aviary, menagerie.

zoom *v* race, rush, tear, dash, speed, fly, hurtle, streak, flash, shoot, whirl, dive, buzz, zip.

Index of Special Lists

Lists of related words can be found in the thesaurus under the following entries:

Index of Special Lists